POLICE AND PROTEST
IN ENGLAND AND IRELAND
1780–1850

HEIGHT OF IMPUDENCE.

Irishman to John Bull: "Spare a Thrifle, yer Honour, for a Poor Irish Lad to buy a bit of
———— a blunderbuss with." (*Punch*, 1846)

Police and Protest
in England and Ireland
1780–1850

STANLEY H. PALMER

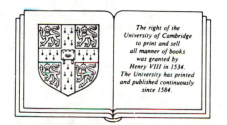

The right of the
University of Cambridge
to print and sell
all manner of books
was granted by
Henry VIII in 1534.
The University has printed
and published continuously
since 1584.

CAMBRIDGE UNIVERSITY PRESS

CAMBRIDGE

NEW YORK   PORT CHESTER   MELBOURNE   SYDNEY

Published by the Press Syndicate of the University of Cambridge
The Pitt Building, Trumpington Street, Cambridge CB2 1RP
40 West 20th Street, New York, NY 10011, USA
10 Stamford Road, Oakleigh, Melbourne 3166, Australia

First published 1988
Reprinted 1990

Printed in the United States of America

Library of Congress Cataloging-in-Publication Data
Palmer, Stanley H.
Police and protest in England and Ireland, 1780 – 1850.
Bibliography: p.
Includes index.
1. Police – England – History. 2. Police – Ireland –
History. 3. Social movements – England – History.
4. Social movements – Ireland – History. I. Title.
HV8196.A2P36 1988 363.2'2'0941 87–6318

British Library Cataloguing in Publication Data
Palmer, Stanley H.
Police and protest in England and Ireland,
1780 – 1850.
1. Police – England – History – 18th
century 2. Police – England –
History – 19th century 3. Police –
Ireland – History – 18th century
4. Police – Ireland – History –
19th century
I. Title
363.2'0942 HV8196.A2

ISBN 0 521 30216 1 hardback

The author is grateful to the Woodrow Wilson International Center for Scholars, Smithsonian Institution, Washington, D.C., where in 1981 he spent a pleasant and stimulating fellowship leave in the researching and writing of a part of this book.

For BETTIE,
and VANESSA, DAVID, SONIA, INGRID

Every policeman knows that though governments may change, the police remains.

– Leon Trotsky, *What Next?*, 1932

Contents

CONTENTS

CONTENTS

Tables

Maps

Illustrations and graphs

Preface

This book seeks to right an imbalance and recognize a contribution. The imbalance is the result of two decades of scholarship on English popular protest; the contribution, that of Ireland to British police history. Thanks to pioneering work in the 1960s by Eric Hobsbawm, George Rudé, and Edward Palmer Thompson, work that has been ably continued by succeeding generations of graduate students, historians have made a quantum leap in our knowledge of the motivations and aims, composition and tactics, of crowds and protesters in Georgian and early Victorian England. By contrast, we still know little about the *other* side of the confrontation, the forces of order. The result has been an emerging, indeed a growing imbalance in our knowledge about crowds and the authorities.

Scholars beg the question when they tack onto their work a chapter (usually late in the book) on "Repression," or add afterthoughts on punishment or police and military action. Just as protest was changing in the critical period 1780–1850, so too was the *mentalité* of the elite, the ruling classes, or whatever else we choose to call the people in charge of making or administering the laws of the land. Is it not time to reassert the importance of power in history and the role of individual and collective decision making?[1] One need not be a Whig to insist that the classic protest era was also an era of major reform or rethinking on the part of society's rulers, as may be seen by the stream of legislation, parliamentary committees, and royal commissions. I have become convinced that it is necessary to investigate seriously not only the *challenges* to authority – crowds, rioters, demonstrations (in a word, protest) – but also the *responses* by the authorities. Study of both sides – governed and governors, protest and repression – will balance the question and in the process perhaps help to clarify it.

In the early stages of research for this book, my eyes were only on England. For me this was a natural development. In college I had written a senior thesis on the Factory Act of 1833. In graduate school at Harvard, I continued to study the Industrial Revolution and nineteenth-century English social and economic history. (My mentor, Professor David Landes, was sufficiently persuasive that I subsequently produced a book on the sources of English economic statistics.[2]) It was in the process of peeking at the other side of the protest coin – reading about the forces of order in early-nine-teenth-century England, and in particular the new police – that I realized that to *understand* developments I would have to widen my focus. In this fashion I, personally, discovered Ireland. I had never studied Irish history. In college and graduate school, I had had courses on British history, but by "British" was of course meant "English." Ireland was mentioned only occasionally, usually because it represented an intrusive crisis: One felt that that island's history existed only for its nuisance value. (Scotland, too, was seldom dis-cussed after 1603 or 1707 at the latest; and poor Wales was abandoned early on, apparently never making it out of the Middle Ages.) Nowadays things have changed. On both sides of the Atlantic a new generation of scholars (led by Oliver MacDonagh, who teaches in Australia) is beginning to integrate Irish into English history. In short, the history of the British Isles is no longer so anglocentric as it was twenty years ago.

My own work in Irish history began as a result of reading histories of the English police. There, in stray sentences and footnotes, tantalizing if transient references were made to earlier police developments in Ireland. One day I came across a sentence that transformed my thinking and sowed the seeds of the present work. In *Justice and Police*, a series of lectures published in 1885, F. W. Maitland wrote that "a full history of the new police would probably lay its first scene in Ireland, and begin with the Dublin Police Act passed by the Irish Parliament in 1786."[3] Had the British police been born not in London in 1829 but in Dublin a half-century earlier? Who had ever heard of this Dublin police? Who indeed had ever bothered to look across the Irish Sea in an attempt to understand developments in England? It is sometimes said that Irish history cannot be understood without knowing the history of England, but that English history can be readily understood without knowing much about Ireland. I wonder.

A century has elapsed since Maitland made his statement. Indeed now, unnoticed, we are at the bicentennial of the birth of modern police in the British Isles. If scholars (mostly Englishmen) have over the years persistently ignored the Irish developments, I have become the more convinced that Maitland was right. The story of British police and protest was, in fact, a tale of two countries. Having been trained as an English historian, I was sur-prised to discover, in the course of my research, that the Westminster Parliament had devoted great amounts of time to Irish affairs. As I worked, I began to enter the minds of the authorities in Dublin Castle and Whitehall. It dawned on me that Pitt, Wellington and Peel, Russell, Melbourne, and Palmerston were all well aware that their responsibility for containing the challenges from below embraced Ireland as well as England: They could no more ignore the restive Irish peasantry than they could the radical English working class. Today's events only testify to the *continued* ties between the two islands and the common concerns of their Governments. Northern Ireland maintains its stormy existence even as Ulster Protestants challenge an English Tory Government and argue that "the British are incapable of understanding Ulster problems."[4] Against widespread Ulster protests, in

November 1985 England's Prime Minister Thatcher concluded with "our closest neighbour," the Irish Republic, an historic Anglo-Irish Agreement whose first agenda item was improved arrangements for intergovernmental policing.*

The present historical work does not argue for any sustained interconnectedness between the protest movements in Ireland and England from 1780 to 1850. By and large, the movements were separate and unrelated. Nevertheless, for certain key periods – the 1790s, the early 1830s, and the 1840s – the materials for such a provocative study do exist. My emphasis, rather, is on the pattern of developments in police as triggered by conditions in each country. David Bayley has suggested that early-eighteenth-century French police reforms stimulated emulative police innovations in absolutist Prussia, Austria, and Russia; but he notes that all of this change on the Continent "seems only to have blighted" police reform in England.[5] The new Irish police, I think, had something of the same effect. If Ireland from the 1780s on was the testing ground for English ministers' ideas on police, the experiments there did make it more difficult for Pitt and Peel to sell the radical concept to an English Parliament and public. The forbidding character of the Irish police – armed, military in nature, and controlled by the central govern-

---

* "Agreement between the Government of the United Kingdom of Great Britain and Northern Ireland and the Government of the Republic of Ireland, 15 November 1985 (with Joint Communiqué)," Hillsborough Castle, Northern Ireland, Command Paper 9657, HMSO, £1.85. The Agreement established an Intergovernmental Conference, which is to meet on "a regular and frequent" basis; Ulster's grievance is that there is no provision for the province's (majority Protestant) representation at Conference proceedings.

Article 9 of the Agreement regularizes communications between the Chief Constable of the Royal Ulster Constabulary and the Commissioner of the *Gárda Síochána*, each of course still responsible, respectively, to the United Kingdom's Secretary of State for Northern Ireland and to the Republic's Minister for Justice. At the inaugural meeting of the Anglo-Irish Intergovernmental Conference, on 11 December 1985, discussion centered on ways to achieve "security cooperation"; in attendance with the politicians were the heads of the RUC and the *Gárda*.

Although it cannot be denied that there has long been a need for more regular communication on police matters between the governments in London and Dublin, there is a grim irony in the timing of the Agreement. Over the period 1969–85 most of the killings in Ulster, and virtually all of the 226 RUC and RUC reservists killed, were at the hands of IRA republicans. But in 1985–6 the RUC, identified now with Prime Minister Thatcher's leftward, pro-Republic shift, came under heavy attack by some Ulster Unionists; in the spring of 1986 ultra-Loyalists not only targeted RUC men for assassination but also bombed, burned, or machine-gunned policemen's homes in more than a dozen towns. The Agreement itself has produced much disquiet and a mood of ugliness throughout Ulster. On the anniversary of the signing, in November 1986, a crowd in excess of 100,000 Protestants assembled in protest in front of Belfast City Hall. Some in the crowd looted stores and fought running battles with the police, who were armed with bullet-proof vests, riot shields, and plastic bullets.

Author's acknowledgments to British Information Services (BIS), 845 Third Avenue, New York, N.Y. 10022. Since late 1985, I have received from them a steady flow of press releases and policy statements on current British–Irish relations; in a phone call to New York I was told that more than 1,000 persons, mainly academics, are on their American mailing list. "Our closest neighbour": quotation from a speech of Home Secretary Douglas Hurd, in Swindon, Wilts., 22 March 1986, BIS Policy Statement 11/86, "Anglo-Irish Agreement: Unionist Opposition," 31 March 1986, p. 2.

ment – had to be transformed and tamed before it could be brought to England.

As much as anything else, this book is about "the values *actually held* by those who lived"[6] in Ireland and England in 1780–1850. It is difficult for us today to appreciate the importance then of the simple word "liberty." One encounters it time and again in correspondence, speeches, newspapers, and handbills. In the era before universal suffrage, legalized trade unions, and the myriad other lobbies and interest groups that are a familiar part of our world, the phrase "rights of the people" had a vague but powerful resonance. In the English-speaking world the antithesis of "liberty" was "police." In the words of a New York citizen in 1812, "Perfection and power of police ... can only accompany despotism, and is the hateful attribute of tyrants." Englishmen, and also Irishmen, felt the same way. As Patrick Pringle (1955) has stated without exaggeration, "The eighteenth-century Briton regarded the French gendarmerie as his descendants were to regard the Nazi Gestapo and the Soviet Security Police."[7]

It is important at the outset to emphasize this point, for it will be a central theme in my book. "Protest" in my title, *Police and Protest*, I have taken to mean not only public disorder but also the opposition to the new police idea. "It is *easy for later generations* to be scornful of these timid men who thought that freedom and an effective police system were incompatible," Jenifer Hart (1951) has written, "but we must remember that they had heard much of the excesses of the police of the *Ancien Régime* in France and had lived through Napoleonic times and the reign of Fouché." We look back now and praise the famous reformers – Fielding, Colquhoun, Peel – but I believe the perceptive Mr. Pringle was correct in stating that "few of us [today] can honestly claim that if we had lived then, we should have supported the reforming minority." Indeed, we ought perhaps to be grateful for the police opponents' shortsightedness, selfishness, and stubbornness – be glad that they were jealous of their "liberty" and traditional rights – for "if they had not made police reform so difficult we should have a harsher police today."[8] These authors, Pringle and Hart, writing in the 1950s, made uncommonly shrewd observations about the formative period of the English police. But characteristic of *their* time, they neglected to make any reference to England's police in Ireland or the opposition there to that new development.

I must confess that my own opinions have changed with time. Many of the conclusions in this book differ from those in my doctoral dissertation (Harvard, 1973). As a younger man, no doubt influenced by recent historiography, I adhered to the Thompsonian view that England in 1790–1840 was never far from revolutionary outbreak; I argued in the dissertation that it was largely Englishmen's reverence for traditional institutions and fear of government tyranny that delayed the creation and softened the nature of the new English police institutions. Ireland, similarly turbulent, was made the pioneer in implementing the new police because of English prejudice against the "subhuman" Irish and English disregard for any notions of Irish rights and liberties. I do not now deny the importance of these values and attitudes. But in the present work, I do argue that other explanatory factors were even more significant. These were notably, in Ireland, the extraordinary incidence of (agrarian) crime and protest, the widespread lack of respect for the law, the authorities' alarmism after 1798 and their anxiety about a recurrence of risings, and the comparative weakness of local institutions of government. It was because of the greater *need* in Ireland for a new and strengthened civil power that Ireland received first the new police. The harsh nature of Irish society generated harsh forms of social protest, which in turn, coupled with weak and timorous local authorities, required the creation of a police harsh by English standards.

Police history, when broadly conceived, can tell us much about social history.[9] If the older police histories suffered from being detached institutional studies, the most recent have emphasized that policing be studied in context, that is, in the milieu of political, social, and economic history.[10] Charles Tilly has remarked that the nature of a society's collective violence speaks volumes about that society.[11] Equally, we may say that the nature and duties of policemen, "the most conspicuous representatives of the political and social order,"[12] educate us about a society's structure, dynamics, and needs. In this sense, the adage is true that a society gets the police it deserves. A police *force* is, of course, only one force for the maintenance of political and social order, and is sometimes simply a coercive force of last resort. In sum, it is also true that "we shall not fully appreciate the nature of the political and social transformation [in a society] ... until we know more about the sources of order in ... society."[13]

The different paths of police development in England and Ireland do reveal basic truths about each society. The one, immediately to the west of the British mainland, was wracked by agrarian unrest and political mass movements; it was a fragile settler society ruled by the firm hand of Dublin and London. The other was a mature, wealthy modern society characterized by a basic stability and orderliness that was evident in its rooted, centuries-old local and central governing institutions. For all of its inequities of wealth, status, and power, England, unlike Ireland, remained an essentially harmonious society throughout a period (1780–1850) that saw many upheavals on the Continent. The English lower orders scarcely ever used serious violence against persons (homicide), never mounted continuous campaigns in defiance of the law (as did the Irish secret societies), and never staged anything that approximated an Irish rising or revolution. One is struck in fact by English society's remarkable ability to restrain or police itself; both sides, crowds and authorities, set limits to protest and repression. The comparative tameness of English protest combined with the viability of existing institutions to produce in England police that were pale imitations of the semimilitary forces established earlier in Ireland.

Professor Lawrence Stone has noted "the revival of narrative" in recent historical writing. He divides historians, somewhat arbitrarily, into four groups: "old narrative historians," primarily political and biographical; the cliometricians, "statistical junkies"; "hard-nosed social historians," the analysts of "impersonal structures"; and historians of *mentalité* who "chas[e] ideals, values, mind-sets, and patterns."[14] Despite the forty-odd tables that burden this book, I am not the second or third type of historian; I guess I am a mix of the first and fourth. I think history is most effectively conveyed when told as a story with a purpose. Narrative and style should convey analysis. Precision is of course important, but I prefer and most readers appreciate a text that renders "31.8 percent" as simply "one-third."

In this book, I present the material "in a chronologically sequential order" and shape "the content into a single coherent story, albeit with sub-plots."[15] The text took shape in my mind as a procession of light and shadow, alternating between England and Ireland, for this presentation reflects the actual process of the growth of police in the two countries. The resulting work, although it treats both, has emphasized the Irish case, not only because little is known of developments in Ireland but also because, before about 1840, Ireland was the theater for innovations in police in the British Isles. My story spans a long period. It is a grand drama that in Ireland begins with Henry Grattan and the Volunteers and ends with Smith O'Brien and the Irish Famine; in England it opens with Lord George Gordon and the "No Popery" riots and closes on Kennington Common with Feargus O'Connor, the Irish leader of Chartist workingmen. This history of police and protest stretches the length of the British Isles, from Tipperary to Lancashire, from Kent to Cork. My aim, in part, is for scholars and general readers alike to realize that important events were happening close in time in both England and Ireland, to visualize those shifting scenes, and to sense the relationships and ramifications. We historians in particular need to end our artificial compartmentalization of the history of these two countries. We must cross the Irish Sea, not merely to unearth buried parts of the Irish past but also to restore Ireland to its important place in British history.

Nowadays it is a rash or foolish historian who seeks to paint on such a broad canvas. Ours is an age of microcosm, of scholarly studies that are often local in context and social and economic in subject. My work, by contrast, is national and political as well as social. Toward the close of the twentieth century, when historiography is much more intensely "factually knowledgeable" and also considerably less innocent than it was in the nineteenth, I believe it is time for historians to return to the large questions that have frequently gone unasked, or been avoided, in an age of specialization and local studies. The present work is thus necessarily one of synthesis as much as of archival spadework, and I am greatly indebted to a number of scholars upon whose work I have relied. My book could not have been written without their articles and books. For any errors, oversights, or misinterpretations I have made in reading their work I apologize, but I am of course still accountable.

On the Irish side, where the good secondary literature tends to be thin and recent, I have found particularly helpful for "protest" the work of Thomas Bartlett, Michael Beames, Marianne Elliott, Denis Gwynn, Joseph

Lee, Lawrence McCaffrey, Kevin Nowlan, Patrick O'Donoghue, James Reynolds, Paul Roberts, and above all James S. Donnelly, Jr. Professor Donnelly, a prolific scholar now at work on a major study of Irish agrarian societies, has been a constant source of advice and help. He has saved me from numerous errors; those that remain are mine alone. For their work on the Irish police, I am indebted to Séamus Breathnach, Conor Brady, Gregory Fulham, Tadgh O Ceallaigh, and especially Kevin Boyle and Galen Broeker. In particular, correspondence and conversation with Professor Boyle have helped me to elucidate late-eighteenth-century developments.

Much more work has, of course, been published on English protest and public order. My debts are correspondingly greater. In particular, I must acknowledge the work on protest by Asa Briggs, Craig Calhoun, F. O. Darvall, Nicholas Edsall, James Epstein, John Foster, David Goodway, Joseph Hamburger, Francis Hearn, E. J. Hobsbawm (with thanks for his stimulating Birkbeck seminar on modern British social history), David Jones, David Large, Donald Read, D. J. Rowe, George Rudé, John Stevenson, Malcolm Thomis, Edward and Dorothy Thompson, and Henry Weisser. For their scholarship on public order I owe much to A. P. Donajgrodski, Tony Hayter, F. C. Mather, and David Philips. Of the many studies on the English police, those I have found the most helpful are by Victor Bailey, Douglas Browne, Anthony Brundage, Belton Cobb, T. A. Critchley, Clive Emsley, Jenifer Hart, W. J. Lowe, Eric Midwinter, Wilbur Miller, Patrick Pringle, Charles Reith, Donald Rumbelow, Philip John Stead, Carolyn Steedman, Robert Storch, and J. J. Tobias. For his massive study of police and criminal law I am especially indebted to Sir Leon Radzinowicz; and for his masterly biography of Sir Robert Peel, to Norman Gash.

In the course of archival research in England, I have also acquired a large number of obligations. In London, I wish to thank the staffs of the Public Record Office (PRO) and the British Library. At the PRO I am particularly grateful for the help of Commander Godfrey and Mr. C. J. Kiching; at the British Library, special thanks must go to Lena Braganza of the Newspaper Library (Colindale) and the staffs at the North Room and the Manuscripts Room. At the National Register of Archives, Chancery Lane, I was on more than one occasion provided tea and helpful advice. I am also grateful to the personnel at the Institute of Historical Research and at the D. M. S. Watson Library, University College, University of London.

Elsewhere in England, I must thank for their help and many kindnesses the archivists at the Devonshire Record Office, Exeter; the Staffordshire Record Office, Stafford; the Surrey Record Office, Kingston-on-Thames; the Department of Paleography and Diplomatic, University of Durham; and the Brotherton Library, University of Leeds, in particular Mrs. R. S. Mortimer. My thanks also to the authorities at the Mulgrave Castle Archives, Whitby, Yorkshire, and the Castle Howard Archives, especially Mr. Simon Howard and archivist Eeyan Hartley, at Castle Howard, Yorkshire.

Given the relative paucity of published work on Irish police and protest, I have spent much time in Irish archives. I am delighted to acknowledge the assistance in Belfast of the staff of the Public Record Office of Northern Ireland; and in Dublin, of the staffs of the Royal Irish Academy, the Public Record Office (Four Courts), and the National Library of Ireland. At the National Library the custodians of Manuscripts and Maps and Mr. D. Ó Luanaigh, Keeper of Printed Books, have been especially helpful. Most of my researches in Dublin took place *in* Dublin Castle, home now to the Irish State Paper Office. It was an eerie feeling to conduct historical research on police and protest inside the former nerve center of the English Government in Ireland. For making the research also pleasant and productive I wish to thank the retired Keeper, Mr. Brendan MacGiolla Choille; and also his assistant, Marion Fitzpatrick, and the late paperkeeper, Denis McDonald, who brought the yellowed dusty documents to the wide-eyed American.

Back on my side of the Atlantic I am obliged to the staffs of a number of great libraries: Widener Library, Pusey Library, and the Fogg Art Museum at Harvard; Sterling Library at Yale; Firestone Library at Princeton; and the Library of Congress, Washington, D.C. At Harvard I benefited from the guidance and useful criticisms of Professor David S. Landes and from the expertise of Mr. Duncan Dwinell, who coached me in computer programming. It is with pleasant memories that I acknowledge the fellowship leave awarded me by the Woodrow Wilson International Center for Scholars. For eight months in 1981, in Washington, I was able to work uninterruptedly on this project. My work there was facilitated by the help of student interns Roberta Rose and Dan Lewis, the support of Director Jim Billington and his staff, the helpful comments from other Fellows, and in general the scholarly seductiveness of the Center. In the years after my fellowship I have come to owe much to a friend and former colleague, Professor Charles Royster, who at a critical juncture gave some very good advice; and above all to my editor, Frank Smith, for his support, regular correspondence, and, not least, his patience with my prolixity.

At my home university, the University of Texas at Arlington, I must thank a number of people for their constant helpfulness. I am especially grateful for the generous summer research and writing funding provided over the years thanks to the support of Graduate Dean Bob Perkins. The staff at Inter-Library Loan have gotten to know me too well: For their patience and their jokes about yet another request for microcards of the British *Parliamentary Papers*, I wish to thank Mary Price, Lila Hedrick, Brenda Robinson, and Ann Szeto. For computer assistance I am indebted to Mel Pierce, Charles Kennedy, and, above all, my colleague John Kushma. The book's maps and illustrations have been produced by UT–Arlington's Media Services Center, where special thanks must go to Eleanor Forfang, Yafit Avizemal, and Joseph Patrick Francis ("Joe") Doherty.

An army of typists has labored at various stages of this project. To each person I am grateful. In New Haven, Glena Ames; at the Wilson Center, Eloise Doane, Ann Smith, and Pat Sheridan. Most recently, at UT–Arlington, a succession of typists – Sarah Brannon, Kay Brown, Suzie Connolly, June McGee, Elizabeth Rhea, and, above them all, Olga Esskandanian – has worked uncomplainingly to meet the apparently endless demands of the author to produce final copy. I must also thank my colleagues for their encouragement and for their respect for a closed door to the chairman's office. My gratitude, too, goes to June McGee, History Department senior secretary, whose efficiency and good humor have helped me immeasurably.

My final debts are more personal and private. Over the years, both of my parents have been positive and constant in their encouragement of this work. Above all, I wish to thank my family. The book is dedicated to my wife Bettie and to our children. I am indebted to all five of them for reminding me that there are things in life besides Chartists and Whiteboys and Bobbies and Peelers.

THE COUNTIES OF ENGLAND AND IRELAND

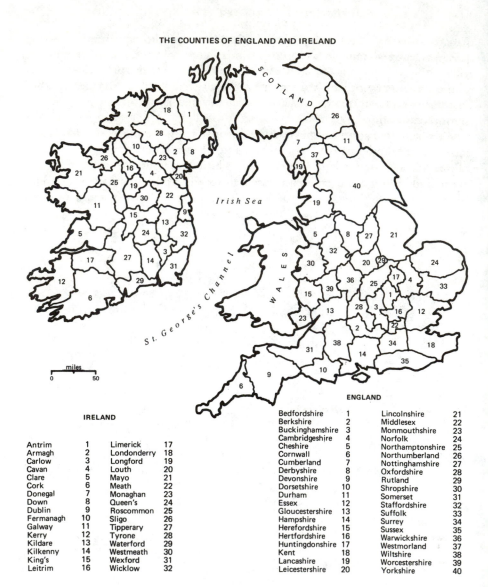

IRELAND			
Antrim	1	Limerick	17
Armagh	2	Londonderry	18
Carlow	3	Longford	19
Cavan	4	Louth	20
Clare	5	Mayo	21
Cork	6	Meath	22
Donegal	7	Monaghan	23
Down	8	Queen's	24
Dublin	9	Roscommon	25
Fermanagh	10	Sligo	26
Galway	11	Tipperary	27
Kerry	12	Tyrone	28
Kildare	13	Waterford	29
Kilkenny	14	Westmeath	30
King's	15	Wexford	31
Leitrim	16	Wicklow	32

ENGLAND			
Bedfordshire	1	Lincolnshire	21
Berkshire	2	Middlesex	22
Buckinghamshire	3	Monmouthshire	23
Cambridgeshire	4	Norfolk	24
Cheshire	5	Northamptonshire	25
Cornwall	6	Northumberland	26
Cumberland	7	Nottinghamshire	27
Derbyshire	8	Oxfordshire	28
Devonshire	9	Rutland	29
Dorsetshire	10	Shropshire	30
Durham	11	Somerset	31
Essex	12	Staffordshire	32
Gloucestershire	13	Suffolk	33
Hampshire	14	Surrey	34
Herefordshire	15	Sussex	35
Hertfordshire	16	Warwickshire	36
Huntingdonshire	17	Westmorland	37
Kent	18	Wiltshire	38
Lancashire	19	Worcestershire	39
Leicestershire	20	Yorkshire	40

CHAPTER I

Introduction

The calm, patient, undisturbed attitude of the London constable
sometimes under circumstances of the most ... provoking nature,
has become proverbial.... [T]he force enjoys a splendidly deserved
reputation for courtesy ... and consideration in its dealings with the
public. Indeed, a London "Bobby" is more or less a favorite with the
people. He is liked, respected, and generally admired.... This public
attitude of support ... is the product of many years of unstrained
relationship between police and people. It is due to the fact that the public
generally is in full accord not only with the methods of their constables,
but with the laws which the constables are called upon to enforce.
> – Raymond Fosdick, American police historian,
> *European Police Systems*, 1915

The people of Ireland ought not to fraternise ... with the forces which
are the main instruments in keeping them in subjection.... Their history
[that of the Royal Irish Constabulary] is a continuity of brutal treason
against their own people. From their very foundation they have been ...
the great obstacle to every movement for social as well as national liberty.
> – Eamon de Valera, President of Sinn Fein, 1919

The people in this area are warned that ... they should avoid absolutely
all communications ... with the members of the RIC.... Let no Irish
man or woman with any sense of principle or honour be seen speaking to
or in any way tolerating the existence of a peeler either in public or in
private.
> – Sinn Fein proclamation, posted throughout Ireland, 1919

We consider it is almost an impossibility to carry out our function as a
civil police force under the present circumstances. The strain on the force
is so great, by the daily assassination of our comrades ... and by the
boycotting and threats arraigned against us ..., that the agony of a long
suffering force cannot be much further prolonged.... We consider the
best thing to be done is to wind up the force.
> – Petition from the County Galway police to Dublin Castle, 1920,
> [Two years later, exactly a century after its creation, the RIC was
> disbanded; it has continued in Northern Ireland as the Royal Ulster
> Constabulary (RUC).]

This is not police work. This is war.
> – RUC Constable Peter Mercer. Belfast, 1979

Ireland, John Bull's "oldest and most restless dominion,"[1] continues to present the major challenge to public order in the British Isles. Today's headlines in Northern Ireland have deep historical roots; indeed, in few places does history maintain a more intrusive, insistent reality than in Ireland. Of the various parts – England, Wales, Scotland, Ireland – that make up the British Isles, only Ireland over the past two centuries has produced violent political revolution, once in 1798 and again in 1916–22. Most recently, some four decades after Southern Ireland's declaration of national independence, collective violence has been concentrated in Ulster, England's remaining outpost on the western island. Even to an American, inured to the violence of his own society, the statistics of a decade of violence in Northern Ireland are difficult to comprehend. Specifically, the balance sheet for 1969–82 reads:

> 2,268 persons killed[2]
> 491 military
> 187 police
> 1,590 civilians
> 25,120 persons injured
> 29,035 shooting incidents
> 7,533 explosions
> 4,250 malicious fires
> 9,871 armed robberies

The persistent violence and random terror, inflicted by means of the most modern scientific techniques, have claimed lives in cars, pubs, restaurants, and shops, in homes, at bus stops and at places of work. The brutalities have (through 1982) included 153 tarrings and featherings and 1,006 knee-cappings.[3] The violence touches the families of Protestants and Catholics alike; it targets workingmen and clergymen, members of Parliament and security forces; it has even reached into the royal family, with the murder of Earl Mountbatten in August 1979.

The situation in Ulster has nearly driven the forces of order to the breaking point. In a part of the world where outside Ulster homicide is rare, the army and police during the years 1969–82 arrested and the courts charged 1,770 persons with murder or attempted murder.[4] During the same period, authorities seized 9,035 firearms, defused 3,467 bombs, confiscated 1.1 million rounds of ammunition and 83 tons of explosives, and conducted 326,270 house searches. To those affected by the violence, the courts have over the decade 1969–79 awarded £46 million in personal injury compensation and £276 million in property damage compensation. In an attempt to control the violence in Northern Ireland – an area the size of Connecticut, with a population of only 1.5 million – Her Majesty's Government has flooded the province with some 7,000 police and 12,000 soldiers.[5] In 1830 the Crown was able to hold all of Ireland, which then had a population of 7.5 million, with 25,000 troops and a newly created constabulary of 7,000 men. In Northern Ireland in the 1980s, the security forces, concentrated in only one of the island's four provinces, are, relative to the population, *three times as great* as they were 150 years ago, with scarcely more successful results.

To the South, in the Republic of Ireland, home to 3 million people, the police force is comparatively small. The 11,000-men *Gárda Síochána* is centrally controlled, a legacy from the days of British rule, but since independence the force has been unarmed. Until recently the Republic has been spared the variety of collective violence prevalent in the North. Over the period 1922–68 only twenty-six *Gardaí* were killed in the line of duty, most of them in shootings in the early years of the state.[6] Much of the present political violence is related to the troubles in the North and occurs in the border counties of Cavan, Monaghan, and Donegal (where, for example, Lord Mountbatten, at Mullaghmore, had a summer home). In one incident in August 1979, on the same day as Mountbatten's murder, eighteen soldiers were killed at Warrenpoint, County Down, by a detonation *from across the Border* in County Louth.[7] Though less terrorized than Belfast, Dublin, as the capital of the southern state, has on occasion fallen victim to the violence. In December 1972, two persons were killed and eighty injured in bombings as the *Dáil* debated tougher legislation against the Irish Republican Army (IRA); in May 1974, twenty-two Dubliners were killed in a wave of car bombings. British institutions in the Irish capital have also been targets of violence. Following "Bloody Sunday" (February 1972) in Londonderry, where the British army killed thirteen demonstrators, a mob in Dublin burned down the British Embassy. In 1976 the IRA assassinated the British ambassador to Dublin, Christopher Ewart-Biggs. In July 1981, protesting Prime Minister Margaret Thatcher's intransigence in dealing with IRA hunger strikers in Ulster (six had already starved themselves to death, and the final toll at the end of August would reach ten), a Dublin crowd of 15,000, armed with bricks and iron bars, attacked 1,000 *Gardaí* guarding the British Embassy. "I thought we were going to be murdered," said one constable. Police Superintendent Tom Brennan noted: "I am twenty-five years in the job, and I have never seen anything like it. . . . I do not know how we managed to hold them." Seventy in the crowd were injured but no one was killed, and the building escaped a second burning as the police baton charged the rioters across gardens and through hedges.[8]

In England ordinary, daily crime is more prevalent than in Eire, and it has neither the political nor the personally violent character of crime in Northern Ireland. Visiting Americans marvel that in densely populated (50 million) England the 120,000 police go about unarmed. Indeed, as late as 1981, only 4,000 of the 23,000 London police had ever had training in the use of firearms. The absence of violence in English society is reflected in the fact that over the past fifty years only fifteen policemen in London have been killed in the line of duty; only two since 1975, one in a drugstore stabbing and the other in an Irish terrorist bombing. Modern England has developed a "relatively mild, unoppressive system of police," T. A. Critchley, the English police historian, wrote in 1972. It is the case of "a tolerant, mature society well matched by a tolerant police force."[9]

Significantly, however, Critchley also expressed some fears about whether the "traditional" English police system could withstand the challenges of the late twentieth century.[10] One hundred fifty years ago the Government laid the foundations of the present system in response to a perceived threat from below: the radicalized lower classes. Nowadays, in postindustrial, post-imperial England, the challenges are more diffuse: the cultural alienation of English youth of whatever class; the resumption of the kind of Irish terrorism that a century ago (1884) led to the creation of a separate antiterrorist unit, the Special Irish Branch, ancestor of today's Special Branch; the wave of immigration of nonwhites – blacks and Asians – from the old imperial lands to a country hitherto all white and largely Anglo-Saxon; and finally, a general public perception of growing violence and lawlessness in society, ranging from industrial disputes (e.g., the particularly nasty Yorkshire coal strike in 1984) to sports rowdiness (the "outrage" at Brussels in May 1985, which left thirty-six Italians dead after a brawl with drunken Liverpool soccer "fans"). All of these developments are underscored by criminal statistics that show sizable increases in offenses involving personal violence.[11]

These recent trends came together, quite visibly, in July 1981 in a prolonged spasm of urban rioting of a severity not seen in England for a century and a half. The poorer districts of more than two dozen cities – principally London and Liverpool but also many of the decaying northern and Midlands industrial towns – disintegrated into scenes of burning, looting, and attacks on the police on a scale that led some observers to make comparisons with America's urban riots of the 1960s. Begun by blacks and Asians mired in unemployment and angry over alleged discrimination and police harassment, the disorders came to attract lower-class white youths in an unlikely alliance against the police. Against the rioters' assaults with bricks, concrete blocks, and Molotov cocktails, the police, armed with plastic shields, responded with their traditional baton charges and, for the first time in English police history, the use of tear gas. The fortnight of violence took an enormous toll in property destruction (several million pounds sterling in Liverpool alone); more than 1,000 persons were arrested and a few thousand were reported injured, including 300 policemen.[12] But in one respect, the disorders remained characteristically English: Almost miraculously, only one person was killed.[13]

These events were sobering to thoughtful observers. Such disorders were known to occur in Northern Ireland or the United States, but few Englishmen had thought them possible on English soil. "To Think This Is England!" ran one newspaper headline. A *New York Times* correspondent caught the spirit of outrage and surprise in reporting that the extent of the outbreaks and "the fury of the mobs attacking the police came as a shock to many middle-class Britons and to foreigners who cherish the image of the kindly Bobby." The aftermath, he continued, was sure to bring "anguished re-evaluations of the British police and how they operate in this traditionally calm and civilized society."[14] Toward the end of the 1981 riots, Prime Minister Thatcher's Government went so far as to authorize police in future disturbances to employ most un-English weapons of force – plastic or rubber bullets, water cannon, even armored vehicles. And William Whitelaw, who before becoming Home Secretary had served a stint (1972–3) as political peacekeeper in Ireland (an officeholding pattern dating to the early nineteenth century), dispatched top English police officials to Belfast for instruction in riot control from experts in the Royal Ulster Constabulary.[15]

More recently, in localized outbreaks of violence in October 1985, in a West Indian section of north London, the rioting turned savage. Now the crowds used machetes and shotguns. The unrest, reported the police, was the first in modern times in which rioters used guns and a police officer was killed. The appearance of guns is only part of a larger problem, the general rise in gun-related crimes. It is an urban problem that centers particularly on London: Armed robberies in England and Wales have increased fourfold in only a decade, 1972–81, and three of every four such crimes in 1981 occurred in the capital. This recent rapid escalation in violence has led to some historically surprising developments. In 1983, in response to the surge in crimes involving firearms, the Manchester police placed armed police mobile units on the city's streets for the first time in English history. In the 1985 riots the London police carried, but did not use, plastic bullets and tear gas. In the aftermath Mrs. Thatcher's Government introduced controversial legislation to strengthen the police, and some police officials have called for the creation of small, separate, permanently armed police corps. London Police Commissioner Sir Kenneth Newman, who prior to his appointment had headed the Royal Ulster Constabulary in 1976–82, announced in a carefully worded statement that against future crowd violence he could not rule out police use of guns, "should I believe it a practical option."[16]

Although it is true, as London Police Commissioner Sir David McNee remarked in 1981, that "the fabric of our policing philosophy" is under greater stress than at any other time in this century,[17] it bears repeating that England remains a society essentially calm and civilized. Homicide is still rare, and rioting is still respectful of human life. In England death by criminal violence comes seldom at the hands of the "old" or "new" English, but rather through the "outrage" of IRA bombings: in Birmingham nineteen persons killed in November 1974, and in London ten soldiers blown up in July 1982 and six persons killed in December 1983.[18] In confronting the question of reshaping the forces of order, it must be stressed that in England the Government, the police, and the people remain highly sensitive, as they have been since 1829, to the consequences of establishing an armed force to police society.

Whatever changes are made in the English police, it remains certain that they will only reflect changing conditions in society. How assimilable are the nonwhite new English, and how deep are the racial attitudes of native Englishmen? What effect will England's political and economic decline have on social behavior? For how long will Irish terrorism plague the island? Will crimes of violence and the use of firearms continue to increase? In balancing the demands for order with the imperatives of liberty, Englishmen in the

1980s, and 1990s will be facing questions that were of deep concern to earlier generations of Englishmen. A correspondent for the *New York Times*, covering the 1981 riots, noted perceptively that

although the problems are worse now than they have been in some time, the London police force is no stranger to controversy. Sir Robert Peel, the Home Secretary who created the force in 1829 and whose name was the source for the word bobbies, had a very difficult time overcoming opposition from Englishmen who considered the very idea an abridgment of cherished liberties. For example, a parliamentary committee rejected Peel's proposal in 1822 saying: "It is difficult to reconcile an effective system of police with that perfect freedom of action and exemption from interference which are the great privileges and blessings of society in this country. The forfeiture or curtailment of such advantages would be too great a sacrifice."[19]

I. The British police and the historians

Today the police are so integral a part of society that it is extraordinarily hard to imagine a time when they were not there. The policeman is the most visible representative of the state; for most people he is its most commonly encountered authority figure. Criminals fear him; drunks, vagrants, and motorists watch for him; children are in awe of him; and even law-abiding adults respect the power of the man in uniform. The policeman is also the lynchpin of our criminal justice system. "Prosecutors and judges do not and cannot catch criminals," Lawrence Friedman has written. Trial and conviction must wait on apprehension. "The police are the hinge on which the whole system turns."[20]

The modern British system of policing originated in the period 1780–1850. In 1780 in the British Isles, police forces as we know them today – large, well-trained, coordinated bodies of men – did not exist; by 1850 they were widespread, and public order was becoming the responsibility no longer of the army, but of the police. Frederic Maitland, writing in 1885, observed:

It may seem to us a matter of course that there is a large body of policemen, highly organized on a military plan, paid to maintain order, detect crime, and arrest offenders. But all this is very new; it has come into existence during the last sixty years; indeed, down to 1856 there was no law for the whole of England requiring that there should be paid policemen.... We have been living very fast.[21]

A curious matter of neglect

Given the contemporary importance of the police and the curiosity of its comparatively recent origins, it is surprising that the subject has drawn the attention of only a handful of scholars. Historians are more inclined to trace the rise and fall of political parties or empires than to investigate an institution that when once established, exists in perpetuity and grows by its own momentum. Perhaps the police, like any other bureaucracy, is one of those historical items that by its very permanence and ordinariness appears colorless by contrast to more evanescent or apparently more changing phenomena. I myself was one of those who had long taken the police for granted, ignoring the obvious truth that they, like everything else, were "products of distinct historical circumstances." My own end of innocence was part of a generational awakening. Wilbur Miller, writing in 1975, has noted that "until American society seemed to be falling apart in the mid 1960s, social historians on this side of the Atlantic gave only a passing nod to the cop on the beat."[22]

The scholarly neglect of the police may also be explained by political or philosophic inclinations. The English historian F. C. Mather, writing in 1959, observed that the historian is "a natural Whig. His sympathies are with peoples against governments, with political reformers against conservatives."[23] Although this is an arguable point, the fact remains that since 1959 in the field of modern British social history – thanks to the pioneering work of Hobsbawm, Rudé, and Thompson and of generations of their students – far more work has been done on working-class politics and culture, on protest, crowds, and riots, than on the Government's response to popular challenges, the agencies of public order, or the minds of the authorities (the obverse of the "consciousness" of the working class). The nature of academe can also influence the shape of the debate. Antipolice bias on campus, every bit as insidious as antiblack or anti-Irish sentiment among social groups off campus, can restrict or prohibit proper investigation of the subject. As a graduate student at Harvard in the early 1970s, I can recall being hooted down as a "fascist" because I was about to give a lecture on police history.

Until quite recently, histories of the English police were popular works or, if scholarly, were steeped in Tory bias. The former, which date to the 1920s and even earlier, tend to be chatty and interesting in an anecdotal way; in its origins, the police is rather complacently seen as a home-grown institution descended from the Saxon "tithingmen."[24] More scholarly are the now somewhat aging standard histories of the English police. These are factually useful, but they rob the police of their context within political and social history. Policemen emerge as heroes warding off revolution and performing miracles in bringing order out of chaos. One must not, however, fault the solid works of Melville Lee, Reith, Moylan, Hart, and, most recently, Critchley for being something their authors did not intend them to be. These institutional histories laid the necessary foundation for subsequent studies of police, politics, and society.[25]

Police origins: benevolence or repression?

Victor Bailey has observed that modern explanations for the emergence of the English police may be divided into two schools. The *consensual* historians – Reith, Browne, Radzinowicz, Critchley, Tobias, and Miller – argue that the new police represented a rational attempt to impose impartial order and inject much-needed efficiency into the country's civil institutions. Acting above class, Peel and Edwin Chadwick and the Benthamites were "farsighted reformers acting with a benign regard for the public interest." The more recent *conflict* historians – Hart, Mather, Silver, Foster, and Philips – see the origins of police as a class-based "reassertion of state power in the face of a new and threatening conjuncture," the working-class radicalism of the 1830s and 1840s. Class conflict, not social consensus, provided the spur to the creation of the new police.[26]

Bailey's distinctions are useful, if not wholly accurate. The police reformers, as interpreted by the so-called consensual historians, were in fact hoping to build a consensus for effective police reform; they were not, as Bailey says, unaware of the extent of the resistance within the ruling elite to the new ideas of police. It is more correct to argue that the reformers were contemptuous of critics of the new police idea; they tended to dismiss opponents as stupid, shortsighted, or self-interested. Bailey's consensual historians may more aptly be termed "enlightened statists" who sought to impose unpopular ideas for the public good. Nor were the statists unaware of the working-class disorders that triggered the debates on the police; rather, if social conflict was the spur to action, enlightened statism, they believed, was the solution. The conflict historians, on the other hand, have tended to ignore or downplay the resistance within the elite to the establishment of a powerful police; hence, they view the propertied class as more unified than it was. So, too, the conflict historians tend to overstate the extent of the threat from below. They are thus hard put to explain the slow, almost grudging development of the police outside of London and the relative tameness of the creature itself.[27]

My own interpretation falls somewhere between the enlightened statist and conflict schools. Chadwick, Peel, and the other police proponents were, I believe, seeking to establish a new principle of governance – law enforcement above local or petty interests – but they were also inevitably enmeshed in the values of their own class. They were revolutionaries in both their impatience with local civic "rights and liberties" and their disrespect for the traditional value systems of working-class culture. Over both they wanted to ride roughshod. These enlightened statists were roused to action by the assertion of working-class claims to inclusion within the process of governance, as articulated most broadly in the demand for universal suffrage. This convergence of the state's imposition of norms of social order (police) with the workers' assertions of their rights (protest) has led a recent scholar, Robert Storch, to see the new police as "missionaries" bringing alien values of work and discipline to a reluctant proletariat. This interpretation I believe to be sound in that it catches the interaction of conflicting value systems, although it somewhat narrowly spotlights only one aspect of the new police power.[28]

Crime or crowds?

Most intriguingly, Storch and the enlightened statist and conflict historians *all* see the origins of the new police institution as essentially unrelated to questions of ordinary daily crime. So overwhelmingly have scholars concentrated on the suppression of popular disorders as the primum mobile that only recently, in reaction, have a few argued the case for crime prevention and detection as the spur to creation. These *crime* scholars disagree over the police's effectiveness in repressing crime. For the provincial police, Tobias and Jones judge the forces to be rather successful, whereas Midwinter concludes (for Lancashire until 1860) that they were on the whole disappointing; for London, Miller argues that the new police succeeded largely by working out an accommodation with community values on criminal matters.[29] Significantly, virtually all authorities agree that the early police emphasis was on preventive maintenance of order, whether by patrolling or baton charging. The great majority of arrests were of drunks, vagrants, and disorderly characters, not serious criminals. Emphasis on the detection of crime did not emerge until the second half of the century, after the period of collective disorders, and even after 1870 detective departments were kept small and constables' training in police science lagged behind that available on the Continent.[30] In explaining police origins, I would argue that if in the formative period 1829–56 the authorities' dominant motivation had been to apprehend felons and prevent serious crime, the new police forces would have developed rather differently; we would expect to see, early on, efficient detective units and constables schooled in crime detection rather than drilled in military-style patrolling. Finally, it is noteworthy that among the crime historians only Tobias insists on the repression of indictable crime as the stimulus to the creation of the police. The other scholars at least allow for the control of popular protest as one of the main reasons for the establishment of the police in England.[31]

The present work argues that, in its origins and early years, the new police were more embroiled in politics and protest than in fighting crime. Over the period 1815–48, for government ministers and magistrates, the recurrent concerns, preserved in the archival sources, are riots and demonstrations, workingmen's crowds, and radical politics. Ordinary criminality was of course a concern, as it always had been, but the frightening post-Waterloo development was the new stridency of the laboring classes. What E. P. Thompson has rather generously called "the making of the English working class" served as the trigger to substantive police reform. Lawrence Friedman, in contrasting the early development of the police in England and America, has noted that in England the new police were charged with "protecting the social structure"; thus, the institution "always had as a function control of unruly mobs, and in particular, the suppression of working class demonstrations."[32] This aboriginal concern with protest has led to some surprising emphases in the secondary literature on the police. T. A. Critchley, in his classic *History of Police in England and Wales* (1967; 2d ed., 1972), has virtually nothing to say about nineteenth-century crime,[33] and his 1970 study, *The Conquest of Violence: Order and Liberty in Britain*, is even more explicitly devoted to police, protest, and public disorder. Sir Leon Radzinowicz's misnamed opus, *A History of English Criminal Law and Its Administration from 1750* (4 vols., 1948–68), is another classic work that traces in detail the themes of police and protest but looks only fleetingly at crime and criminal law.[34] For F. C. Mather, who ignores the challenges of daily crime, "The

New Police" (chapter 4) in the boroughs and counties reflected the need for *Public Order in the Age of the Chartists* (1959). Jenifer Hart, in an important article (1955), dismisses the notion of rising crime as the trigger to borough police reform and sees Chartism, not crime, as the stimulus to creation of the county police.[35] More recent scholars – Donald Rumbelow, John Foster, David Philips – continue to press the case for social control, not repression of crime.[36]

The conflict historians, in my view, have the better of the argument in explaining the origins of the police. The institution represents the authorities' response to the new challenge from below – political radicalism and protest. Problems associated with crime, large towns, and the lower orders were not new to early-nineteenth-century England; they had been around for some time. Why, then, did police reform not occur in 1780, 1800, or 1810? Why the wait until the 1830s and 1840s? I find myself in agreement with George Rudé that "it appears [that] the decisive factor that tipped the balance in favour of the 'proposers' [of the new police] was the alarm caused by the new wave of civil commotion starting about 1829."[37]

The principal British police historians appear to endorse such an interpretation. Radzinowicz notes that in the first half-dozen years of its existence, "the most urgent challenge" facing the London police of 1829 was "the keeping of the peace rather than the growth of crime.... On its success in curbing disorder by non-military means the Metropolitan Police would stand or fall."[38] The early 1830s, agrees Critchley, was the force's "testing time." What he calls "the growth of subversive activities" and disturbances associated with parliamentary reform provided "endless opportunities for the police to perfect techniques of crowd control and practice the newly acquired art of baton charges."[39] In the provinces, too, Critchley argues that it was the "confluence of political currents – above all, the new tide of radicalism" – that lay behind the creation of the county police. In the summer of 1839, a "nervous" Whig Government "resolved to provide police to quell the popular riots its liberal policies had done much to encourage.... The success of the Metropolitan Police and the desire to suppress crime were undoubtedly relevant factors; but politics rather than [Benthamite or Whig] policies provided the sharper and more immediate spurs to action."[40] Radzinowicz offers a similar explanation. He argues that "there can be no doubt that the need to control disorder during these years [1838–42] was even more influential than the rise in ordinary crime in bringing the authorities to terms with the idea of professional police throughout the country."[41]

These conclusions take on a greater importance since they mesh with the findings of recent scholars of comparative police history. In his analysis of the emergence of police systems in England, France, Prussia, and Italy from the late seventeenth to the mid-nineteenth century, David Bayley concludes that the origins of the new police "cannot be accounted for" by the traditional explanations of urbanization, population growth, industrialization, or even the increasing incidence of crime. "The development of today's systems can be accounted for in terms of a transformation of political power, prolonged violent popular resistance to government, and the creation of new law and order tasks as well as the erosion of social bases upon which community authority relations were established."[42] Endorsing Bayley's study, Charles Tilly sees changes in the organization of the police as a result of challenges to the existing distribution of power in society; or, more precisely, the new police, whatever its characteristics, represents "the national elite's responses to the perceived threats of new groups making bids for power from outside the political system."[43] Ted Robert Gurr, in his cross-cultural analysis of the new police in four major cities, shifts the focus beyond Europe. Gurr argues that the evidence from mid-nineteenth-century London, Stockholm, Sydney, and Calcutta suggests that "crises of public order ... catalyzed the implementation of police reforms that had long been sought by forward-thinking officials and ... by some members of the middle classes." For "the political elite," a principal concern was "increased security against collective behavior by the lower classes."[44]

II. Police in Europe and America in the lifetime of Robert Peel, 1788–1850

The police forces of Great Britain were formed only in the nineteenth century. . . . Rowan and Mayne, first Commissioners of our \
Metropolitan Police, . . . were members of a community which had grown up without strong policing; France's powerful police-system was ancient long before they were born.
– P. J. Stead, *The Police of Paris* (1957)

If the origins of the modern police may be explained as a response more to pressing political and social challenges than to long-standing problems of daily criminality, it becomes necessary to study the police in a political context. Each society generates systems of civil control that reflect that society's most basic beliefs, values, and needs. To varying degrees, the imperatives of freedom or control, liberty or order, determine the nature of a society's policing. Historical developments in a nation's police thus serve as a sensitive if inexact barometer of social changes and of challenges to those in political authority. To understand the new police that emerged in England and Ireland in Robert Peel's lifetime, we need to re-create the world of the police as it was known to Peel and his contemporaries. The police was not an institution familiar to Englishmen; in their minds, a strong police was associated with societies on the Continent, above all with France, the state that created the first powerful police system in the Western world.

France

The *maréchaussée*, France's rural police, was established as far back as 1544. Originally intended to police the king's soldiers, the force, following reforms in 1720, evolved into a powerful weapon against civil crime. In the mid-eighteenth century the *maréchaussée* numbered 3,000 men, veteran soldiers, uniformed and heavily armed (hence their common name, *gens d'armes*). Controlled by and responsible only to the central government (the king) in Paris, the force was divided into thirty companies, one to each *généralité*, the French administrative territory equivalent to an English county. Each provincial company – headed by a *prévôt général*, a kind of inspector of police – was divided into twenty brigades with an average of five men each, composed of a sergeant (*exempt*) and four constables (*archers*). The intricate chain of command included *lieutenants*, or subinspectors, between the ranks of *exempt* and *prévôt*; and five men chosen from among the thirty *prévôts* and rotated annually to serve as inspectors-general of this centralized national rural police.[45]

The French countryside, unlike the English, was dotted with small police stations, none more than a half-day's march from another. From these 600 stations patrols circulated regularly, making contact and exchanging information with other police at the borders of their jurisdiction. In a country twice as large as England and with a population of about 20 million at midcentury, 3,000 police could not, of course, be omnipresent – "it is not pretended that they are actually so," noted an English traveler in the 1760s – but the patrolling "has, however, its effect, in striking a terror, by its being known, that they frequently do it at stated times, on private notice to each other: especially they are out at all times when any public disorders may be suspected." Sir William Mildmay, the English visitor, reported that the *maréchaussée* attended at fairs, escorted troops and political governors, and protected revenue collectors and (for "a certain price fixed at so much per mile") even travelers "apprehensive of danger." This military body functioned as an embryonic preventive police force "engaged," in Mildmay's words, "in a kind of perpetual war . . . against such of the native subjects as disturb the peace, and violate the laws of their country; and who as such must be deemed common enemies to all society."[46] Many Frenchmen apparently agreed with the English baronet, for when the Revolution came, the new government decided to keep the force intact, changing its name to the *Gendarmerie nationale* (1791) and increasing its ranks to 11,000 men. Even in the Revolution's most radical phase, no attempt was made to dismantle the force; indeed, under Napoleon it became a model to be exported to other European countries.[47] By the mid-nineteenth century the *Gendarmerie* grew to 25,000 men, and it functions today with a force of 70,000.[48]

The police of Paris, another royal creation, dates to the *commissaires* established by Philip IV in the early fourteenth century. Its modern form may be traced to the late seventeenth and early eighteenth centuries.[49] By an edict of 1667, Louis XIV established a single police commissioner, the *Lieutenant de Police*; in 1708, forty (later forty-eight) *inspecteurs* were added. Beginning in 1698, police stations were introduced, and by the 1720s there were stations every half mile. The police patrol force grew from 600 men early in the century to 1,100 by the 1780s.[50] Unlike the police established later in the British Isles, the Paris police had functions that were comprehensive.

Lighting, garbage collection, fire protection, inspection of buildings, and supervision of market trading and regulation of the food supply were among the myriad police duties.[51] The force's highly specialized bureaucracy was intimidating to Englishmen. In 1788, only a third of the city's 3,100 police were in the blue-uniformed, armed *garde*, the main semimilitary patrol force (there were, in addition, five lesser patrol units); the majority of Paris's policemen were assigned, to use the terminology of Alan Williams, to investigation and intelligence, services, inspection, justice, and administration and communication.[52]

It was these nonpatrol functions that especially alarmed Englishmen. The extent of the spy system has been exaggerated, concludes Williams, but nevertheless he notes that one in every ten policemen worked in "investigation and intelligence." Twenty police inspectors were specifically assigned to the supervision of 340 persons, men and women, who served as regularly paid spies known as *sous-inspecteurs* (subinspectors) or, more popularly, *mouches* or *mouchards*.[53] There were, according to Williams, perhaps 500 other persons who were not on the regular payroll but who were paid as "observers" or informers.[54] Another function that raised eyebrows among Englishmen was police censorship of books, newspapers, pamphlets, and the theater; a total of 178 policemen, 6 percent of the city force, performed this duty on the eve of the Revolution.[55] Unlike older studies, Professor Williams's recent analysis of the eighteenth-century Paris police emphasizes the force's comprehensiveness and efficiency of function and the positive direction of its policies. This slighting of the darker side of police activities would have astounded most contemporary Englishmen.

The Paris police emerged from the French Revolution largely intact, renamed the Ministry of the General Police of the Republic (1796–1818).[56] Its most famous police minister was Joseph Fouché (1799–1810, 1814–15), who perfected a political police, saying he had little time for "whores, thieves, and streetlamps."[57] Neglect of such ordinary matters of policing led to the establishment in 1800 of the modern Prefecture of the Police of Paris; this constituted, in effect, the restoration of the pre-1789 Lieutenancy of Police. The Prefecture revived the old functions of market policing, city services, and public health, as well as military patrolling, surveillance, and censorship. In 1812 emerged the modern *Sûreté*, the criminal investigation department, led by the infamous Vidocq, an ex-criminal who used his underworld contacts as police agents.[58] The patrol function was given new emphasis in 1829 by Prefect Louis Debelleyme who, six months before the new London police took to the streets, created a civil force of 100 *sergents de ville* to assist the traditional military patrol, the *garde*, now grown to 1,500 men. Debelleyme's small force, with its tall cocked hats and blue uniforms (but also sabers for night patrol), was roughly similar in appearance to Peel's London police. Under Prefect Gabriel Delessert (1835–48) the civil police grew to 600 and the *garde* to 3,000 men.[59]

Significantly, in the revolutions of 1830 and 1848, both the army and the police, officers and men, showed little inclination to defend the government;

in Philip Stead's words, they "laid down their arms and made themselves scarce." In March 1848 the revolutionary government attempted to "form a police force on the lines of the one established in London since 1829 – a uniformed civil force, patrolling the city by beats." This force was never recruited. In the conservative aftermath, President Louis Napoleon in April 1849 brought back the *sergents de ville* and established a 2,500-man *Garde républicaine*. "Political policing was rapidly resumed. Ministries spied zestfully on the public."[60]

Following his *coup d'état* and yet another rising in Paris in December 1851, Napoleon declared the empire reestablished.[61] Baron Haussmann presided over the rebuilding of Paris, which included the widening of streets and the opening of plazas to stymie any further barricaded street risings. Napoleon, who had served as a special constable in London in 1848 and thus had observed the Metropolitan Police in action against the Chartists, now established in Paris in 1854 a uniformed, 3,000-man civil police force. The force grew to 4,700 by 1859 and to 5,700 by 1867. These *sergents de ville*, aided by 100 detective *inspecteurs de police* at the *Sûreté*, replaced the old military *garde*. The men went on beat patrol in blue frock coats, with hats and collar numerals (the latter "thought to have been due to the Emperor himself who borrowed the device from the Metropolitan Police"), but unlike their London counterparts, they were armed with long swords.[62] A contemporary, M. du Camp, noted that some "people have often suggested giving them the English policeman's truncheon" as a simple emblem of authority; but du Camp was insistent that "the mere sight of a sword" produced a more dramatic effect in deterring criminals. The newspaper *La Patrie* (12 October 1854) observed: "If the London constable has above all a civilian character, it is because he meets the requirements of a population distinguished by its methodical habits. In France, essentially a military country, the municipal policeman must also take his character from the national spirit."[63] Louis Napoleon's police would disappear with his Empire in 1870, only to reappear as *gardiens de la paix*, 7,000 strong, in 1871.[64] The name stuck, and today 20,000 *gardiens*, armed with small automatic pistols, patrol the streets of the French capital.[65]

Central and southern Europe

Because modern police institutions on the Continent evolved as part of the growth of the nation-state, the police were most developed in the premier state, France. We know considerably less about the police in those parts of Europe where modern states were later in developing.[66] Prussia, small but highly centralized, stands out as the exception among the various autonomous, ruler-controlled German principalities in existence before Germany's unification (under Prussia) in 1870. Italy, after 1815 and before its national unification in the 1860s, remained "a geographical expression," being composed of nine states, the strongest Piedmont (Turin), and all effectively under Austrian control. The Austrian Empire, which in 1815 annexed the

Italian states of Lombardy (Milan) and Venetia, was a congeries of federated territories and disparate nationalities united under the repressive rule of the Hapsburg Crown, the army, and the bureaucracy.

For such nations, France, under both Louis XIV and Napoleon, served as the model for police reforms. French innovations, notes David Bayley, had "a pronounced demonstration effect" on absolutist states in Europe. The Paris police system (1667) inspired Peter the Great, Frederick II, and Maria Theresa to create police commissioners for St. Petersburg (1718), Berlin (1742), and Vienna (1751). Apparently little emphasis was given to developing large uniformed forces, but as in the pioneer city, Paris, police functions ranged far beyond simple crime prevention and control resided firmly with the state.[67] Authority was thus imposed from above, not generated from municipal authorities below; continental police were "ruler-appointed," to borrow Charles Reith's phrase, whereas in England policing evolved from the common law tradition.[68]

The dissemination of liberal democratic and nationalist ideas to the absolutist continental states led their rulers to restructure the eighteenth-century police system. Stunned by the fury of the mobs in Berlin during the abortive 1848 revolution (300 persons killed, including 40 military men), Prussian authorities responded by establishing Berlin's first uniformed police, the *Schutzmannshaft*, a 1,400-man royal state police. Its prototype, according to Frank Thomason, was the London police of 1829, but the men were armed and regulations required that recruits be "capable of fighting."[69] Secondly, in Italy, the 1848 revolution led the reformed Piedmontese government to issue a constitution and to establish a uniformed, military, highly disciplined National Guard. In 1852 the Guard was placed under the Ministry of the Interior and renamed the *Guardie di Pubblica Sicurezza* (public security guard); from 1870 on, these centrally controlled police for the larger towns were established throughout Italy; today they work with locally based *Vigili Urbani*, forces established in many cities in the later nineteenth century.[70] Finally, Vienna was also rocked by unrest in 1848. The city's 1,100-man *Militärpolizeiwache*, the aging military guard established in Austria's larger towns in 1775, was overwhelmed and had to be reinforced by police imported from Italy. Vienna emerged from 1848 without major reform of its patrol force, although the secret police, which dated to 1713, was completely reorganized after the uprising. It was not until 1869, in a period of constitutionalist reforms, that the government established in Vienna the *Sicherheitswache* (civil security guard), a uniformed, 1,300-man armed police on the Berlin model.[71]

If police reforms in Paris and Berlin and in the cities of northern Italy were a result of the risings of 1848, the establishment of national military police forces on the Continent may be attributed to the French wars of 1792–1815. A gendarmerie, by the *ancien régime* appellation of *maréchaussée*, was introduced in Belgium following the French annexation of 1795, and it was not until after the Belgian revolution of 1830 that the patriots renamed the force the "gendarmerie." In tiny Luxembourg, the modern gendarmerie dates from the French occupation of 1798.[72] It is well known that Napoleon, in expanding the French Empire, fostered nationalism and nation building in the defeated states; he is less recognized for his key role in producing new police institutions in those states in 1810–15. Bonaparte established *marachausses* (to use the Dutch word) in the Low Countries in 1810–11; the French innovations broke the Dutch tradition of local policing and, notes James Cramer, "left a lasting mark on the Dutch law-enforcement system" by instilling irresistible principles of centralization.[73] In Prussia in 1812, shortly after Napoleon's ill-fated invasion of Russia, the government established a gendarmerie on the French model; the force endured but its control from Berlin would be challenged by the Junkers, great local magnates, until 1872.[74] In Austria, too, during the last years of the Napoleonic wars, the government established a state-directed gendarmerie on the French and recent Prussian model.[75] In Piedmont, Italy, in 1814, after the defeat of Napoleon, the restored absolutist monarchy created the *Carabinieri*, a state police drawing its recruits from the cream of the army; this Piedmont force, in turn, became the prototype and namesake for Italy's national police after the peninsula's unification.[76] Newly independent Greece established a gendarmerie in 1833. Modern police forces in Spain also date from the early nineteenth century; the *Carbineros* (1829) and the *Guardie Civil* (1844) merged in 1940 to form the present-day *Guardia Civil*. Created by politically illiberal governments, the original forces owed much to both the French and Piedmontese examples[77] (see Table 1.1).

In sum, building on French precedent and tightening up governmental controls in the age of political reaction after Napoleon's downfall, many European states put in place efficient military-style police forces. Whether in town or country, in or out of uniform, control of these police rested firmly with the Crown or state authorities, not with elected municipal bodies or local landowners. Throughout central and southern Europe, nation building and police seemed to go hand in hand with repression of liberalism and radicalism.

Russia

Obscurantist imperial Russia was famous, since the sixteenth century, for having the most secretive police system. P. S. Squire has traced the complex activities of these groups – from the Oprichnina, the Prikaz for Secret Affairs, and the Secret Chancellery to modern police institutions.[78] As a result of wartime exigencies and on the advice of Napoleon's minister, Fouché, Czar Alexander I (1801–25) established a number of police boards and departments – among them the wryly titled Committee for Public Safety (1807) and the Ministry of Police (1811–19) – which conducted widespread spying on foreigners and Russians alike and caused considerable anxieties among government bureaucrats themselves. The Minister of Internal Affairs dubbed the police the "Ministry of Espionage" and charged that the police and their agents "have not been confining themselves to gathering news and

Table 1.1. *The establishment of modern police in Europe and the United States to 1860*

Urban Police		District or national police
	1544,	France (*maréchaussée*)
	1720	[reformed]
Paris 1667		
Police Commissioners		
St. Petersburg 1718		
Berlin 1742		
Vienna 1751		
Dublin 1786ᵃ		
	1787ᵇ	*Ireland (partial: disturbed counties)*
	1790	France (*Gendarmerie*)
	1795	Belgium
	1810	Holland
	1812	Austria; Prussia
	1814ᶜ	*Ireland (partial: disturbed counties)*
	1814	Piedmont, Italy
	1822	*Ireland (all counties: compulsory)*
	1826	Russia
London 1829		
	1833	Greece
English boroughs *1835*		
(incorporated towns)		
	1836	*Ireland [reformed]*
Dublin [reformed] *1837*		
	1839	*England (partial: optional in counties)*
	1844	Spain
New York 1845		
Berlin 1848		
Turin, Italy 1852		
Paris [reformed] 1854		
Boston, Chicago, 1855		
Philadelphia		
	1856	*England (all counties: compulsory)*

Italicized print: See Table 1.2 for details of police development in England and Ireland.
ᵃThis centralized police was abolished in 1795, revived in 1799, and reformed in 1808.
ᵇExperiment lapsed c. 1800.
ᶜThis force was abolished in 1836.

making it possible for the government to anticipate crimes; they have been seeking to incite crimes and suspicions."[79]

In the immediate aftermath of the abortive Decembrist revolt (1825), the new czar, Nicholas I, established the powerful Third Department, a comprehensive police ministry divided into four sections and devoted largely to surveillance.[80] A gendarmerie, again based on the French model, may be dated to 1815, but it was Nicholas who must be credited with establishing (1826) the famous Corps of Gendarmes (the French name was retained) as the executive arm of his new Third Department. The 4,000-man police force, dressed in sky-blue uniform, with silver epaulettes, helmet, white gloves, and sword, reflected the force's military recruiting ground, the cavalry wing of the army. Apart from continuing the surveillance of foreigners and Russians, the gendarmes were active in keeping order at fairs and markets and in apprehending thieves and smugglers, as well as suppressing illegal meetings and incipient revolts. Poland, after its subjugation in 1832, became a gendarme district, and other districts were established as the Russian Empire expanded south and west to the Black Sea and east over the Caucasus Mountains. The expansion of the Third Department and its development as the eyes and ears of the emperor, who took a daily personal interest in his creation, made the Russian police an awesome force for political and social oppression. "The Russian," wrote an English traveler in the 1840s,

is not only subject to this terrible *surveillance* within the pale of the empire, but when he travels abroad it follows him like his shadow. In the drawing-rooms of London and Paris, he dreads that the eye of the secret police may be upon him. Foreigners, in their own country, laugh at his terrors, but experience has taught him too painfully how truly they are grounded. The secret police has rendered itself all eyes; its very spies are spied upon.[81]

In the years after our period of study, in the reign of Alexander II (1855–81), a reformer who freed the serfs and set up local government boards, the police's spy system was lightened, a development that may have contributed to Alexander's own murder in a terrorist bombing. His son, Alexander III, and Nicholas II reinvigorated the system of espionage in the Ochrana, as the police was now called.[82] The legacy of a highly centralized, secretive, political police would be passed on to and perfected by the new regime after the Russian Revolution of 1917. The names would change – from Ochrana to Cheka, GPU, NKVD, and KGB – but the functions would remain essentially the same.[83]

Such, then, in brief, were the major police systems on the Continent of Europe in the lifetime of Robert Peel. The word "police," as we shall see, was French, and Englishmen living from the period of the Gordon Riots to that of the Great Exhibition tended to associate the concept with things French or, most darkly, Russian. The *idea* of a police force was often equated with the absence of basic civil liberties. Whether it was autocracy of czarist Russia, or the France of the Bourbon or Orleanist era where political power was successively royal, aristocratic, and bourgeois, Englishmen reacted to state police practices of espionage and censorship with outraged cries of "despotism" and "tyranny." For many Englishmen, the mere fact of central control was sufficient to trigger the utterance of these epithets. The para-military state constabularies, not only in France, Germany, and Russia but also in Austria, Spain, Italy, and even in liberal Holland and Belgium, served the negative function for Englishmen of models that were to be avoided, not emulated.

INTRODUCTION

United States of America

If Englishmen prided themselves on being different – having no police until
1829 and after that date, with the exception of London, having no state-
directed police – Americans carried the English attitudes to the extreme. In
the eighteenth and early nineteenth centuries, Americans, most of whose
ancestral roots lay in England or the British Isles, were very conscious of
living in a newer and freer part of the world. Not for them the corruption,
bureaucracy, and state omnipotence of Old Europe or the aristocracy and
royalty of Britain. Englishmen might talk of their "liberties," but the American social experiment in the New World was founded on the idea of liberty.
Its corollary, order, has always struggled to gain a respectable footing in the
Republic. Moreover, the early Americans left their land of inheritance,
England, *before* the new ideas of police had taken root; "police" to Americans
from the colonial to the Jacksonian period conjured up images of village
constables, beadles, and watchmen. The American Revolution, the struggle
for independence from central control by distant England, only reinforced
Americans views on the proper locus of power over police.[84] Even today
notions of local control and of accountability of the police to the citizenry
remain very strong; the nation's domestic investigative police, the Federal
Bureau of Investigation (est. 1908, originally to deal with labor troubles),[85]
and its overseas secret police, the Central Intelligence Agency (1947), are
relatively recent creations still regarded with suspicion by many Americans.
America's 36,000 local people forces – in numbers a strong contrast to the 43
separate forces in England today – have historically been fragmented and
isolated from each other in a manner reminiscent of eighteenth-century
England.[86] America will most likely never develop a single centralized police
system. But today's computer revolution, which enables the country's highly
particularized police departments to communicate with each other instan-
taneously, may mean that at least a nationally coordinated system can be
established in the future.

America's police have been shaped by English cultural norms and conditioned by American circumstances. There was, as in England, the same long
resistance to the notion of powerful professional police, and for the same
reasons; in like fashion, the success and rather rapid English acceptance of the
London police experiment of 1829 caused some Americans to press for police
reform in imitation of England. Secondly, once established, the new police
resembled the English model in being purely civil forces, that is, without
swords or firearms. It was only in response to conditions in America's cities
– among them the massive immigration, rise in violent crime, and criminals' use of handguns – that American policemen abandoned their English
inheritance and began to carry and use firearms.[87] On the touchy subject of
uniforms, the Americans were even more resistant than the English. Most of
the new police wore only badges as a sign of their authority, and even this
practice sometimes met with strong opposition. Uniforms were chided as
"undemocratic" and "un-American," rejected as "an imitation of royalty" or

"King's livery"; America's new policemen were not uniformed until several years after the creation of the new forces.[88] Finally, the nature of the American political system meant that the new police would be accountable to the elected local or state authorities. In England such elective control existed only in the incorporated towns; the English county police were responsible to unelected county magistrates (until 1888) and to the central government in the person of the Home Secretary. The new London police was entirely in the control of His Majesty's Government. But in post-1776 America, in the absence of a legitimate tradition of Crown or central authority and of unpaid gentlemanly Justices of the Peace, the controversy over control of the new police occurred amid the hurly-burly of democratic politics; control *had* to oscillate between city or state elective authorities. Thus, nowhere was the embrace of police and politics tighter than in America.

As in England, the first professional police forces in America were established in the cities. Apart from the Texas Rangers (est. 1835), an early frontier border patrol,[89] the first statewide police was established in Massachusetts in 1865. Charged with enforcing liquor prohibition laws, this rural force numbered 130 men, a handful in each county. But the experiment was expensive, unpopular, and (some thought) unconstitutional, and ten years later this controversial police force was reorganized into a small state detective squad.[90] Not until 1905, in response to violent riots in the coal fields, did Pennsylvania establish a state constabulary, a mounted and uniformed force known in its early years for a propensity to clubbing and shooting.[91] New York and California (Highway Patrol) did not create state police forces until 1917 and 1929, respectively; like many of the other smaller twentieth-century state police forces, these were established to deal not only with crime and industrial unrest but, above all, with the problems generated by the appearance of the automobile.[92] The men's uniforms reflected the public's significant change in attitude toward police: The state troopers, with their guns, military belts, tailored (and oft-striped) trousers, and "battledress style of jacket,"[93] would have shocked early-nineteenth-century Americans.

Modern police forces in America's older cities date from the middle decades of the last century. New York established a police department in 1845; New Orleans and Cincinnati in 1852; Boston, Philadelphia, and Chicago in 1855; Baltimore and Newark in 1857; and Providence in 1864. The new police were founded during "a period of sustained urban rioting" that produced perhaps "the greatest urban violence that America has ever experienced." One scholar states flatly that America's "modern urban police system was created in reaction to the riots of the 1830s, 1840s, and 1850s."[94]

During these years, thirty-five major riots occurred in just the four cities of Baltimore, Philadelphia, New York, and Boston; there were labor riots, election riots, antiabolitionist and antiblack riots, and anti-Catholic and anti-Irish riots.[95] The heating up of the slavery question and the large influx of German Catholic and especially Irish Catholic immigrants generated great social fears among many native-born white Protestants in America's seaboard cities. In Philadelphia, for example, of twelve major riots between 1828 and

1849, only three were not related to the black and Irish issues. The greatest nativist-versus-Irish disorders, erupting intermittently over three months in the summer of 1844, were repressed by militia at the cost of fourteen lives.[96] Four years later, following the example set in Boston and New York, Philadelphia established a day police force of 34 men to supplement a night-watch of 120 men; "another race riot" – against blacks in 1849 – "helped convince many waverers," and from 1855 on the city had its first single day-and-night police force operating over a greatly enlarged jurisdiction.[97] The original policemen were, by law, all native-born Americans.[98]

Let us look briefly but in some detail at the new developments in policing in two of the best-studied cities, Boston and New York. For two centuries Boston's policing was conducted by a handful of amateur part-time constables and watchmen; as late as 1832 the city of 65,000 got by with about fifty of these early patrolmen.[99] Following a series of riots in 1834–7, including a culminating fracas in June 1837 between nativists and Irish immigrants,[100] the Boston city council recommended the creation of a police force that might "imitate, as far as may be, the system of London"; nevertheless, from "inertia" and "the fear of expense" the 100-man watch was retained and only 9 new policemen were appointed.[101] Both police bodies grew slowly in size as Boston was transformed in 1846–51 by the large influx of wretched Irish fleeing the Potato Famine. In 1847 alone, 37,000 Irish arrived in the city of 115,000 inhabitants; by 1855, two-fifths of Boston's population of 170,000 was Irish-born. Boston, complained city authorities, was being made "the Botany Bay of Britain," "the moral cess pool of the civilized world."[102] It was in 1854, as a result of a series of antislavery and nativist–Irish riots and the liquor and social problems attendant on the large Irish immigration, that the city acted to merge its police constables and night-watch by creating the 200-man "Boston Police Department."[103]

The city-controlled force, on the streets the next year, continued to evolve somewhat haphazardly as it grew in size (to 375 men by 1865). Uniforms were still regarded as "despotic," and dress was not standardized until 1859. From the beginning, constables' carrying of firearms was also done on an individual basis; most of the men had them after the Civil War, and the official arming in 1884 was intended to regulate the men's resort to arms.[104] As the city, and its politics and police force, became increasingly Irish, a nativist movement developed that restored (1878) Yankee control of the police and culminated in 1885 in the transfer of control over the force to the largely rural Republican legislature. The battle, historian Roger Lane tells us, was led by the (Protestant) Law and Order League and the Society for the Suppression of Vice, and the 1885 bill passed amid "appeals to fear and bigotry on the floor, and ... no masking of ethnic and political jealousies in the corridors." Control did not revert to city authorities until 1962. In the interim, Boston's police developed a reputation for professionalism and increasing Irishness.[105]

The history of the police was broadly similar in the larger city, New York. According to historian James Richardson, in the early eighteenth century four night watchmen "constituted the entire nocturnal police of the city" of 10,000. The "Negro Conspiracy" of 1741 led New York authorities to create a militia guard and subsequently a twelve-man paid nightwatch. Various small and apparently tolerably effective systems existed in the second half of the century, including wartime arrangements (1776–83) that saw a British military patrol system countered by a civilian eighty-man watch established by patriotic New Yorkers. Until about 1820, New York appears to have been relatively free of crime and disorder; 100 watchmen patrolled each night in 1825 in the city of 125,000.[106]

New Yorkers' adherence to what were traditional English modes of policing reflected strong feelings against professional police. A pamphleteer of 1812 worried about "the difficulties of establishing such a system in a country so proud of its freedom from arbitrary government as the United States." A number of factors, however, argued the case for police reform. Beginning in the 1820s, contemporaries commented on a rising rate of theft and homicide. There was a wave of disorders in 1834, including one riot between newly arrived Irish and blacks that lasted for three days and required 3,000 militiamen to suppress. The great fire of 1835, the most destructive since 1776, produced widespread looting and intervention by the militia. City authorities reacted by increasing the nightwatch patrol to 250 men. A proposal by the city mayor in 1836 to reorganize the police led to this protest by the city council:

Though it may become necessary, at some future period, to adopt a system of police similar to that of London ...; yet they [sic] believe the present system, with some alterations, may be made amply sufficient for this city, for many years to come. The nature of our institutions are [sic] such that more reliance may be placed upon the people for aid, in case of any emergency, than in despotic governments.

Antipolice attitudes were part of the Anglo-American transatlantic political culture; the difference was that whereas in London such sentiments issued from working-class protests in the streets, in democratic New York they took the form of official resolutions from city council chambers. In the years after 1836 many police reform proposals were submitted to city authorities, only to be rejected; aldermen objected to a "standing army," civil or military, and to such "surveillance as is exercised by the police of London and Paris."[107]

Finally, on the very eve of the Irish immigrant invasion, in 1845, a compromise plan was agreed upon for the city of 400,000. The aldermen and mayor would appoint and control a civil "Day and Night Police" of 800 men headed by a "chief of police."[108] A constable's tenure was to be for only one year. There was no standardized arming, either with club or with gun. Not until 1856 were the police issued a blue-coated uniform that, Richardson says, "the men objected to ... as an innovation of English origin and an infringement on their rights as freeborn American citizens." This first New York police force suffered from corruption, petty political control, and ineffectiveness against crime that was both rising and more violent. In 1853 constables' tenure was made permanent (that is, depending on good behavior), the men were officially armed with two-foot "batons" (note the use of the English term for billyclubs), and control of the force was transferred to three police commissioners (the mayor and two high-ranking city authorities).[109] The police, nevertheless, remained mired in politics. New York, like Boston, was swamped with Irish fleeing the Famine in their homeland; from 1847 to 1854, 850,000 Irish exiles – an average of more than 100,000 a year and 163,000 in 1851 – arrived virtually penniless at the port of New York. By 1855, more than half of the city's population of 630,000 was foreign born.[110] Political controversies raged over the involvement of the new police in the immigrant and liquor issues. Nativist groups charged the city's Democratic mayor, Fernando Wood, with lax enforcement of licensing and sabbatarian laws and with filling the police with Irish Catholics. In fact, in 1855, 143 of 246 appointments were of Irishmen, and more than one-fourth of the men on the force in that year had been born in Ireland.[111]

The xenophobic crisis climaxed in 1857 with the passage of a law that transferred control of New York City's police to the Protestant, Republican state governor in Albany. The act, which (in the words of a contemporary supporter) was "modelled after the world renowned police act of London," placed the governor in the role of England's Home Secretary: He was to appoint five police commissioners (not to include the mayor), with whom he would determine police policies, and all costs were to be borne by city taxpayers. But Mayor Wood refused to recognize the legality of the new "Metropolitan Police," and for three months in 1857 the city suffered the dubious distinction of having two rival police forces. One force would rescue prisoners taken by the other, and there were even affrays between the two law enforcement groups. In one riot 500 municipal police, assisted by what one observer described as a "miscellaneous assortment of suckers, soaplocks, Irishmen and plug uglies officiating in a guerrilla capacity," were thrashing a smaller band of Metropolitans until the arrival of state militiamen turned the battle in favor of the state police. The crisis ended and the municipal force was disbanded only when Mayor Wood submitted to a court ruling in July that upheld the 1857 police act.[112]

New York's police remained Albany controlled until 1870 when, in the aftermath of statewide Democratic victories at the polls, control of the police was restored to the city, where it has remained ever since. The era of state control, 1857–70, appears to have had little effect on police behavior or crime prevention. The force, increasingly Irish,[113] earned a reputation for toughness and professionalism in quelling the largely Irish–black Draft Riots of 1863.[114] During and after the Civil War the rate of crime, especially violent crime, skyrocketed. Newspapers were filled with commentaries on police brutality.[115] Policemen now routinely carried firearms; the standardized arming with .32s in 1895 would represent an attempt to regulate this practice. In the 1860s the increasing costs for the police irritated city taxpayers who financed a force that was beyond their control. A final reason for the return of the police to city control was the constitutional argument; in

Richardson's words, "the centralization of power which state control represented was alien to the American tradition."[116]

III. The police in political and regional contexts

To understand the new police in the British Isles, we must not only make the contemporary comparison with other police in Europe and America but also examine the police as one of many modern institutions of state governance in the British Isles. If Englishmen, like Americans, were opposed to continental concepts of gendarmerie, it was in great measure because they were generally critical of authoritarian and highly centralized systems of government, of which state police were simply one part. In England in the early nineteenth century, government centralization increased, though at a slow pace. In the police the centralist advance was similarly restrained: Of the various new police forces, only the one in London was government controlled. But the new ideas of centralization, although blocked at home, did find an outlet in a less happy land. Ireland proved to be the experiment station where the English Government could readily implement projects of centralization, including one in police.

The growth of central government in England and Ireland

"Centralization. No. Never with my consent. Not English." Mr. Podsnap in Charles Dickens's novel, *Our Mutual Friend* (1865), spoke for most Englishmen. The very idea conjured up images of French bureaucracy, French despotism. The functions of the state in England at the turn of the nineteenth century reflected these attitudes. The central government "did nothing to secure the public safety, provided no schools, made no roads, gave no relief to the poor. With the solitary exception of the postal service, the State performed no function of immediate benefit to the taxpayer. In the eyes of the public the State appeared only as the power that enlisted men and levied taxes."[117] But as cities grew and industries boomed in the early nineteenth century, state interference came slowly, grudgingly, to England. Its progress, encouraged by reform-minded Benthamites and Evangelicals, was nevertheless impeded by a constantly changing chorus of local interests. Factory owners and economists opposed regulation of working hours, the poor resisted implementation of the New Poor Law, Non-Conformists opposed a system of national education, town authorities obstructed public health reform, and a variety of local interests delayed the establishment of urban and rural police forces. Such centralization as did occur was the result of "a helter-skelter series of statutes and agencies, unrelated and uncoordinated"; it did not reflect any commitment by successive governments to general interventionist principles. England developed a state bureaucracy, "as it had won the Empire, piecemeal and in almost absence of mind."[118]

The nineteenth-century growth of the English central government has been the subject of much historical debate.[119] It now seems clear that traditional explanations of an ideological conflict between "individualism" and "collectivism" are, in H. J. Perkin's words, "a false antithesis." The progress of laissez-faire and of selective state intervention in fact went hand in hand; growth of centralization was pragmatic and tentative, and where Benthamite ideas seemed inappropriate or were found not to work, they were abandoned.[120] The government-controlled London police (1829) was not replicated in the counties and provincial cities. The ambitious New Poor Law (1834), after it provoked widespread resistance, was altered to outdoor relief; and a national public health ministry, instituted in 1848, was repealed ten years later. A series of acts did establish important precedents of state intervention in a number of areas – the new textile factories (1833) and the mines (1842), education (1833, 1839), poor relief, prisons (1835), and the railways (1840). What is most significant, however, is not the chronology but the small scale of this new state intervention.

The Factory Act of 1833 regulated the labor only of children and young persons, adult men and women being left outside the state's protection, and only four government inspectors were appointed to enforce the act's provisions in some 5,000 factories. The 2,000 mines in England were, until 1854, placed under a single inspector, whose powers were limited. The state grants to education were small (£20,000, increased to £30,000 in 1839) and payable to private educational societies; only two government inspectors were appointed (1839) to monitor the schools. The New Poor Law centralized and rationalized relief, but its basic aim was to lower rates and push as many people as possible into the free labor market. The act did not establish a large government bureaucracy, and in any case "contemporary suspicion and dislike of centralization set limits to the scale of a central government machine."[121] The Prison Act created a few inspectors but left administration in the hands of local bodies;[122] similarly, the Railways Act only conferred on the Board of Trade certain powers of regulation and inspection over the private railway companies. Although all of this interventionist legislation in the period 1830–50 does mark the beginning of modern British collectivism, and although in many areas Irish and continental precedents did serve as subjects for discussion, the characteristic feature of the slowly evolving Victorian state was the continuing tension between individualism (laissez-faire) and interventionism (centralization).[123]

By contrast, in early-nineteenth-century Ireland, the growth of central government proceeded steadily, even relentlessly. The island, to quote W. L. Burn, served as a kind of "social laboratory ... where the most conventional of Englishmen were willing to experiment on lines which they were not prepared to contemplate or tolerate at home."[124] Ireland indeed seemed a natural place for nationwide, government-controlled experiments or improvisations: The country was wretchedly poor and the tax base weak, local government was ineffective because Protestants were scarce and the bulk of the population was hostile, and the need to court public opinion was felt to be slight.

To strengthen its grip on Ireland, the English Government between 1786 and 1838 inaugurated a number of centralized schemes in the areas of public order, welfare, planning, and education.[125] Crown-controlled police and prison inspectors were installed as early as the 1780s, and militia and Yeomanry were created in the next decade. By the 1840s, Irish police reform, in the view of one scholar, represented "perhaps the most striking success" of the British policies of centralization. "In public health, Ireland was *formally* more advanced than Britain during most of the nineteenth century."[126] From 1805 on, hospitals and infirmaries were nationally organized and in part state funded; by 1840, there were 600 public health clinics or dispensaries. In 1817, Chief Secretary Robert Peel established a national system of state lunatic asylums; not until 1845 did England begin to provide state care for the insane.[127] Perhaps because of the magnitude of the task, the Government delayed making a state commitment to poor relief until 1838, when a national system patterned on the English New Poor Law of 1834 was adopted for Ireland. Although the punitive terms of eligibility, the assumption of an existing free labor market, and the total reliance on local funding were distinctly unsuited to Irish circumstances, the nature of government in Ireland "ensured that the establishment of workhouses there was achieved with a speed and ease quite unlike the painful, patchy, and contested English undertakings."[128] Moreover, unlike the English, the Irish Poor Law soon branched out into peripheral areas like pharmacy and technical education.

National and economic development in Ireland was also largely the work of the central government. In 1817 (Peel again) a central loan fund was established for public works – roads, bridges, public buildings, fisheries, mines, even resettlement projects. Fourteen years later the Board of Works emerged as a separate department; administered by a central inspectorate of engineers, this state bureaucracy soon found itself setting wage rates as well as coordinating a wide variety of public projects.[129] To economic planning was added educational standardization. In 1831 a state-supported system of elementary schooling was established; a national Board of Education purchased buildings and equipment; appointed, trained, and paid teachers; and prescribed books and course work. Education inspectors monitored the workings of the system, which soon broadened into extensive schemes of vocational and agricultural training. Whatever the Government's motivations (and weaning Irish children from clerical or radical influences was certainly prominent), the gains in literacy (in English) were remarkable and the state's commitment to mass education in Ireland went unmatched by any similar state intervention on behalf of the children of the English poor.[130]

In sum, as Oliver MacDonagh has noted, "in contrast to the British, Irish government was remarkable for the extent to which centralization, uniformity, inspection, and professionalism spread throughout the system before 1850." The mirror image of this triumph of "rationality, autocracy, and expert rule" was the collapse of local government and local initiative in early-nineteenth-century Ireland. County grand juries became mere tax-gathering bodies, and local magistrates were pushed aside before the advance of officials responsible to Dublin and London. Nowhere was this centralist trend seen more strikingly than in the Municipal Reform Act of 1840. Whereas local government reform in England involved rectifying abuses and broadening the local electorate, problems in local government in Ireland were "solved" by abolishing fifty of the sixty old oligarchic corporations and raising voting qualifications in the few remaining local government bodies. Given the dearth of Protestants and of people of substance, the alternative – the advance of Irish Catholic democracy – was unthinkable.[131]

The contrast of thoroughgoing centralization in Ireland with the much more limited growth of central government in England reveals the important truth that government in the one society functioned by monolithic control from above and, in the other, by much finer gradations of authority throughout society. The question of governance and social control in England was more complex. In Ireland the state imposed its will on the people. In England state interventionist legislation reflected pressures from a variety of social groups, including the Benthamites and utilitarians, who sought to rationalize society, and the high-minded, duty-conscious Evangelicals, who, following "the call to seriousness," sought to improve society. The achievement of mid-Victorian orderliness or (to use W. L. Burn's happy word) "equipoise" was produced not by police forces and government decrees but by what Francis Hearn has called "the incorporation of the nineteenth-century English working class." The lower classes – whether they were Methodists, Chartists, or members of trade unions, benefit societies, and political clubs – came to accept the wide-spreading ethic of work, respectability, and orderliness. The English workers' slow "incorporation" of the new industrial society's dominant values would not only shape the nature of their political protest and collective violence but also, thanks to their own self-policing, would moderate the character of the new police institutions created to control them.[132] It was different in Ireland. There public order was essentially the business of government police and troops; the achievement of relative social tranquility by the 1850s would be due neither to their successes nor to any evolving popular consensus for orderliness, but rather to the devastating effects of the Great Famine of 1846–51.

Police in England and Ireland

If the new police must be seen within the larger framework of government centralization, the institution also needs to be examined in its regional context. In the period 1780–1850 the new police were established not only in England but also in English-ruled Ireland; indeed, they were planted first in Ireland. Yet historians of the English police have continued to write from an inward-looking, unconsciously nationalist perspective. Charles Reith and Douglas Browne are wrong to characterize Peel's London police of 1829 as a "unique" creation. The new English police of the 1830s and 1840s was not a home-grown institution, the highest stage of Saxon policing; rather, as Patrick Pringle has noted, it *was* a foreign import, an unarmed gendarmerie.[133] The reluctance of modern English police historians to cross the

Irish Sea would have surprised Robert Peel, who made the crossing many times. The Irish connection was clearer to some Victorian Englishmen. Fourteen years after Peel's death, a civil servant, in preparing the Irish judicial statistics for 1863, noted that

the dates at which the Irish police force originated and was formed into a complete system are remarkable, ... as contrasting with the corresponding dates in England. The Irish county police, commencing in 1787, was completely organized on its present basis in 1836; the English county police did not commence till 1839, and was not extended to all the counties in England and Wales till 1856.

Two decades later, the great English constitutional historian Frederic William Maitland observed that "a full history of the new police would probably lay its first scene in Ireland, and begin with the Dublin Police Act passed by the Irish Parliament in 1786."[134]

In the years since Maitland's injunction in 1885, the Irish dimension of British police history has been noted in passing by scholars but, apart from a brief general essay,[135] no comparative study has been undertaken. A number of historians, among them Critchley, Gash, and Radzinowicz, have acknowledged that an abortive London police bill of 1785 became the Dublin Police Act of 1786.[136] But David Ascoli's offhand remark (made as late as 1979) that "history here provides a curious footnote" is typical of English historians' persistent refusal to investigate this early Irish police. We have made little headway since the time of Melville Lee, who, writing in 1901, sixteen years after Maitland's insight, was content to dismiss the 1786 Dublin police experiment with the laconic comment that "on the principle of applying the remedy to any limb except the diseased one, Dublin was quickly provided with what London lacked."[137]

Other scholars have discovered the existence of the 1787 Irish county police, which the American historian Raymond Fosdick (1915) described as "the oldest police force in Great Britain."[138] Still others have given this honor to Peel's Irish police of 1814. "It may perhaps be said," wrote Sir Charles Jeffries in his book *The Colonial Police* (1952), "that modern police history begins not in Britain itself, but in Ireland" with Peel's Peace Preservation Police. G. A. Minto, suggesting a direct link between Peel's police of 1814 and 1829, argued in 1965 that young Peel "in a manner of speaking, tried it [the new idea of police] on the dog. The dog was Ireland." As early as 1934, E. H. Glover noted that Peel's "sojourn in Ireland was timely, although the seed of his apprenticeship was yet to bear fruit in England.... He grasped the practicality of such a similar Police Force in England and stored it in his mind for future action."[139] In 1961, Norman Gash, in his biography of Peel, traced the young Englishman's police ideas during his career as Irish Chief Secretary and later as English Home Secretary. Most recently, in 1979, Oliver MacDonagh pointed to the importance of Peel's Irish apprenticeship. The London police of 1829 "resembled closely the Irish peace preservation corps ... in scale, structure, and purpose.... The London reform was probably much more a product of Irish experience than of police theorists such as Patrick Colquhoun or penal philosophers such as Bentham."[140]

It is perhaps significant that the first serious study of the Irish contributions to British police history has been done by Irishmen not trained as professional historians. One is a lawyer with experience in Northern Irish civil rights cases; the other, a former policeman in the *Gárda Síochána*. Kevin Boyle, now a professor of law at University College, Galway, has argued, in three articles on "Police in Ireland Before the Union" (*Irish Jurist*, 1972–3), that Dublin and the Irish counties were subject to novel experiments in policing decades before London and the rest of England received the new police. The other writer, Séamus Breathnach, the former *Gárda* member, has written a short history of *The Irish Police from Earliest Times to the Present Day* (Dublin: Anvil Books, 1974), a book that deserves wider circulation than it has enjoyed. Breathnach devotes about forty pages to the Irish police before 1850 and appears to enjoy "questioning the myth which British writers have misleadingly propagated, namely, that the 'peelers' of 1829 were the first professional police force in the world."[141]

Given the fact that Ireland was the theater for police innovations in the British Isles, the paucity of writing on the Irish police is remarkable, if not surprising. Until fairly recently, English historians have been prone to believe that little of significance ever came out of Ireland or to dismiss the island as a separate, semicolonial, unrelated case study. Irishmen themselves have long had to contend with the English-based cultural stereotype of Irish inferiority. Is it surprising that they have shown little interest in writing about a police that was not theirs? The Royal Irish Constabulary (RIC) did develop a strong service function in the second half of the nineteenth century, but unlike the English police it never completely shed its original role as an imposer of force on the people. The constabulary was a constant reminder that Ireland appeared to be governable only by military force. On the one hand, Irish policemen were torn between their sense of professional duty and their feelings as Irishmen. On the other, the Irish people daily confronted the forces that (in de Valera's words) were "the main instruments in keeping them in subjection"; hence any inquiry into the origins and nature of the institution was bound to trigger painful discussions about colonizer and colonized. The dearth of *Irish* writing on the police may be seen as part of the legacy of colonialism that has bedeviled so much of Irish history. The nature of the Irish psychological straitjacket, suggests Breathnach, may be "best understood by trying to imagine a Northern Catholic attempting to write an impartial and non-incriminating history of the RUC."[142]

Thus, whereas London has attracted numerous, often admiring, and mostly English police historians, Dublin, the second most populous city in the British Isles in 1800, is still without its police historian.[143] The rural police, the force later (1867) called the Royal Irish Constabulary, has produced memoirs by some of its officers,[144] but until recently its history was available only in a valuable if unscholarly little volume by Robert Curtis published in 1869.[145] It was not until a century later that two scholars, one

American and the other Irish, began to rescue the Irish police from its long era of neglect. Galen Broeker (1961) and Tadhg O Ceallaigh (1966) produced scholarly articles on the first Peelers, 1814–21;[146] Breathnach (1974) contributed what, to the knowledge of this writer, is the only comprehensive history of the Irish police; and the late Professor Broeker, who taught at the University of Tennessee–Knoxville, published (1970) his study of *Rural Disorder and Police Reform in Ireland, 1812–36.*[147]

Broeker's scholarly monograph fills an important gap in our knowledge of a key quarter-century of Irish police development. It is the only detailed study we have of this period.[148] The book nevertheless suffers from some serious shortcomings. In the first place, Broeker restricted himself almost exclusively to English records, principally those housed around London. (Besides the printed *Hansard* and *Parliamentary Papers*, he relied heavily on the HO 100 series at the Public Record Office, on the Peel Papers at the British Library, and on the Goulburn Papers at the Surrey Record Office.) He ignored newspapers, important English provincial holdings, and all of the archives in Dublin. Moreover, Broeker also was apparently unaware of important police innovations dating to the 1780s; 1814 represents in fact a midpoint, not the beginning, of modern Irish police history. Finally, and in the opinion of this writer, most importantly, Broeker may be criticized for not studying the Irish police in context. The reader gets no notion of the police as an experiment in England's "social laboratory." Because we are told nothing about contemporaneous police developments in the metropolitan country, England,[149] we do not appreciate the novelty of the Irish innovations, nor can we understand the strong resistance in Ireland to the new police ideas. We also miss any sense of the scale of the challenge of public disorder in Ireland compared to that in England. In short, Broeker's account is just as limited as the standard English police histories. The stories are straightforward enough, but not as complete or revealing as when they are studied in context and comparison.

The present work seeks to trace the origins and early developments in the modern police in England and Ireland from 1780 to 1850. These two countries were administered by a common Government and together presented the major challenges to public order in the British Isles. In the course of this seventy-year period, both countries, beginning with an antiquated, ineffective civil power, produced police forces that in structure and function have served as the basis for today's system of police.

Before the reader begins to trek through the chapters that follow, it may be useful to offer a brief overview of the institutional changes in the police (see Table 1.2). Most scholars agree that the first shock to the old system of policing was the Gordon Riots in London in 1780. In the aftermath, the Government proposed a bill (1785) to create a single police force for the metropolis. This bill was defeated in Parliament amid cries of "French despotism." The next year, a copy of the rejected London bill was imposed on Dubliners against their protests of English despotism; in 1787, a national rural police was proposed for all of Ireland, but in fact was established in only four of the most disturbed counties. Both experiments proved to be short-lived as the acts were repealed or fell into disuse in the 1790s. During the war years, 1792–1815, there was a general lull in police reform in the British Isles. Salaried magistrates were installed in a half dozen new London police courts (1792), but no supporting police force was created. In Ireland it was only in Dublin that the police was again reformed, in 1799 and 1808, along the lines of the centralizing act of 1786.

Intensive police reforms came in the period 1814–40. Changes came first in Ireland, where the twenty-five-year-old Chief Secretary, Robert Peel, devised in 1814 the Peace Preservation Police. Controlled from Dublin Castle, the seat of English government in Ireland, this paramilitary force was despatched to the most disturbed parts of the country. These "Peelers" were a highly controversial body: Many Irishmen, Protestant and Catholic, objected to their unconstitutionality and expense. (A similar police measure, proposed in England in 1812 to deal with the Luddites, had been rejected as too innovative and too dangerous to liberty.) In 1822 Peel's successor, Henry Goulburn, created a national rural police, or "constabulary," the men being stationed in every Irish county. The force replaced, or in some cases supplemented, Peel's riot police, which by this date had become entrenched in half of the counties of Ireland. Finally, in 1836, under the guidance of Castle Under-Secretary Thomas Drummond, the Peelers, now shrunk in numbers, were merged with the large reformed county police to produce a single nationwide force, the Irish constabulary. The next year, Dublin's police received its final reform. By 1840, then, the whole of Ireland was policed by two modern, highly centralized, and efficient police forces.

By contrast, police reform came slowly and fitfully to England. Until the 1830s, only London was the focus for debates over police reform. A wearisome series of parliamentary committees invariably concluded that the establishment of a uniform police force for the capital was not worth the destruction of personal liberties that such reform entailed. "Half a century slipped by" after Pitt's abortive 1785 bill "before the necessary change began in England."[150] At length, in 1829, Peel, now Home Secretary, persuaded Parliament to accept his proposal of a single government-controlled police force for London; the new Metropolitan Police, a gendarmerie without the arms, represented a tamer, anglicized version of the police he had established earlier in Ireland. The working-class radicalism of the next decade produced a spate of police reforms in England. Many incorporated boroughs instituted in 1835 "new," though hardly efficient, locally controlled police forces; the counties were given the option in 1839 of setting up forces, and some did so; and briefly, in 1839–42, to meet the threat of Chartism, the Whig Government created centrally controlled police forces in three of the most disturbed northern cities. The county police, though locally controlled, remained controversial, and many counties refused to establish forces. Only in 1856, well after the era of serious popular unrest (1815–48), was an act passed that required all the counties of England to adopt county-controlled police forces.

Such, then, in brief chronology, was the pattern of implementation of the

Table 1.2. *The establishment of police forces in England and Ireland, 1750–1856*

| England | | | | Ireland | |
Description of force	Location	Year	Location	Description of force	
Bow Street Police Office. Magistrate and four thief takers. C/D/N	London	1750			
Short-lived, eight-man Bow Street Horse Patrol. C/S?/N	London	1763–4			
Small Bow Street Foot Patrol. Initial size unknown, seventy men by 1797. C/S/N	London	1773	Counties	Tiny, scattered baronial police. L/D/N	
		1778	Dublin	Citywide force, constables and watch, totaling 425 men. L/D/N	
		1786	Dublin	450-man new police. C/F/U	
		1787	Counties	Originally in disturbed Cork, Kerry, Kilkenny, Tipperary; from 1795, in eleven counties. Lapses, c. 1800. C/F/U (motley)	
Seven Police Offices. Twenty-one magistrates and forty-two constables. C/D/N	London	1792	Counties	Small forces in fifteen counties other than those policed by the 1787 act. L/F/N	
		1795	Dublin	Local force restored, 1786 police abolished. L/D/U	
		1799	Dublin	Centralized police replaces 1795 force. Fifty peace officers and 500 watchmen. C/F & S/U	
Thames River Police. Three magistrates and a 60-man patrol. C/S/N	London	1800			
Bow Street [Mounted] Horse Patrol reestablished. Fifty men ("Redbreasts"). C/F & S/U	London	1805			

Year	Place	Description
1808	Dublin	Consolidation of 1799 police and addition of Horse Patrol (50 men) and Foot Patrol (100). *C/F & S/U*
1814	Counties	Peel's Peace Preservation Force. Initially in Tipperary; by 1822, 2,300 Peelers in 16 disturbed counties. *C/F & S/U (motley)*
1821	London	"Dismounted" Horse Patrol [foot patrol]. Ninety men. *C/F & S/U*
1822	Counties	Irish constabulary. *Compulsory* in all counties. Mostly replaces, or in a few counties supplements, the Peelers. Initially 4,800 men; 7,500 by 1836. *C, L/F & S/U*
1829	London	Peel's 3,200-man Metropolitan Police. Bow Street Patrols and Thames Police abolished, 1839. *C/D/U*
1835	Boroughs	Police forces begin to replace constables and watch in incorporated towns. *L/D/U*
1836	Counties	Constabulary reformed and Peelers (1814 force) abolished. Force grows to 12,000 men by 1850. *C/F & S/U*
1837	Dublin	1,100-man police replaces force established in 1808. *C/D/U*
1839	Counties	*Optional* police forces; adopted in fifteen whole counties by 1842 (a total of 1,900 men) and in nineteen by 1856 (3,300 men). *L/D/U*
1839–42	Manchester Birmingham Bolton	Temporary government-controlled police. *C/D/U*
1856	Counties	*Compulsory* forces in all counties. *L, C/D/U*

Note: London: The metropolis, *not* the City of London.

Key:
- C Central (i.e., government) control
- D Disarmed: staff, or truncheon, only
- F Armed with firearms
- L Local control
- N No uniform
- S Armed with short sword or cutlass
- U Uniformed

new police in England and Ireland. In the pages that follow, the author seeks to answer a number of questions related to this study of comparative police development. How did the nature of crime differ in the two countries? In what ways did the character of protest – in incidence, use of personal violence, and the "mind" of the crowd – differ in the two countries? What was the difference in the "threat of revolution" in the two countries?

Why were the new police established first in Ireland and only later, hesitantly, in England? Why was rural Ireland by 1850 five times more heavily policed, relative to population, than the counties of England? Given Englishmen's reluctance to establish the controversial new institution, what other forces of order – militia and Yeomanry, special constables, and the army – did they rely on to keep the peace? What lessons lie in this English resort to traditional alternatives to the police? In comparing the two emerging police systems, why was the Irish police from 1786 on always highly centralized, whereas the English police, with the exception of the London force, was kept firmly under local control? Why was the Irish police heavily armed, and how could the English forces get by with being uniformly *disarmed*, the men carrying only truncheons? Why, above all, was it that "two entirely different police systems should be developed for a supposedly 'united' kingdom"?[151]

Two societies

Historically, collective violence has flowed regularly out of the central processes of Western countries. . . . [T]he character of collective violence at a given time is one of the best signs we have of what is going on in a country's political life. The nature of violence and the nature of the society are intimately related.

— Charles Tilly, 1969

The people of London, though haughty and ungovernable, are in themselves good-natured and humane: this holds even amongst those of the lowest rank. . . .

— P. J. Grosley, a French visitor to England, 1765

I really know not what to say about Ireland.

— Lord Melbourne, 1832

England and Ireland constitute the two principal parts of what J. G. A. Pocock has called "the Atlantic archipelago." Their peoples and politics have not developed in hermetic isolation, but rather have "interacted so as to modify the conditions of one another's existence." Although some Englishmen may be skeptical of this concept, virtually no Irishmen doubt that their history has been largely determined by the larger island, since "the effective determinants of power lay in England." Over the centuries, in law, language, economy, and politics, Ireland was made over, remarkably thoroughly, in the image of England. When this secular anglicization failed to tame Ireland, as the events of the 1790s proved, England responded by incorporating it within a "united kingdom" of Britain and Ireland. In the course of the nineteenth century, this solution only heightened the tension and interaction in the Anglo-Irish relationship.[1]

From the 1760s on, the increasing centripetal force in Irish politics may be seen in the growth of English administration at Dublin Castle, which eroded the powers of the Irish colonial elite. The Union of 1800 turned the country into a political dependency of Westminster, and early-nineteenth-century Ireland became a training ground for ambitious young English politicians. Of the six different men who rose to be Prime Minister of England from 1828 to 1852, four had served previously as Chief Secretary in Ireland. The list was distinguished: Wellington (1807–9), Peel (1812–18), Melbourne (1827–8), and Derby (1830–3). Peel's and Melbourne's road to the top also took them through the English office of Home Secretary. If popular unrest and public order arguably formed the dominant political question of the first half of the century, Ireland was the most appropriate place within the archipelago to search for solutions. Conversely, with the decline in importance of these issues after 1850, Ireland became less useful as a place for political apprenticeship. Excepting Lord Derby (who served again, 1858–9, 1866–8), no Prime Minister in the second half of the century had cut his political teeth in Ireland. Not a single one before Balfour in 1902 had had an apprenticeship as Irish Chief Secretary, nor had the greatest – Gladstone, Disraeli, Salisbury – even served as Home Secretary.[2]

I. England and Ireland: a study in contrasts

Economy and society

At no time in the past two centuries has the contrast between "the Siamese twins," England and Ireland, been greater than it was in the years 1780–1850. Ireland's proximity to the metropolitan mainland made it virtually inseparable from England; yet the attached "twins" exhibited very different personality characteristics. In the eighteenth century both societies, English and Irish, were governed by a landed aristocracy, and the great mass of the people were unrepresented in the modern electoral sense. But there the similarities ended. English society was marked by hierarchy, deference, and racial homogeneity; there existed, in Trevelyan's words, "a national solidarity and unity . . . which bound Englishmen of all classes together." Irish society was divided along fault lines of race, religion, and culture. Politics reflected the social realities. In England the victors of 1688, the landed aristocracy, had since the Tudor period matured into a stable and self-confident ruling elite; and the Glorious Revolution represented the triumph of Protestantism, Parliament, and the people's liberties. But in Ireland the mirror of 1688 reflected a reverse image: defeat of the people. Roman Catholicism, the religion of four-fifths of the population, was proscribed. Confiscations took more of the natives' land: Catholic ownership fell by 1720 to 10 percent of the total, down from 60 percent in 1640. And whereas the English lower classes were guaranteed poor relief, all Irish Catholics were subjected to penal laws that abridged their basic civil and political rights.[3]

In Ireland the Protestant victory of 1688 led to the uneasy governance by a minority settler elite defensive about the land acquisitions upon which their political power rested. Like the English, the Irish Parliament, with its English-modeled borough and county seats, was not directly representative of the people; but beyond this the Irish Parliament was also grotesquely unrepresentative of the social and economic realities, the basic needs and beliefs, of rural Catholic Ireland. In Ireland the political situation was complicated by the fact that, as Catholic was subservient to Protestant by the penal laws, so Dublin's Protestant Parliament, by Poynings' Law and "the

Sixth of George I," was subservient to the mother Parliament in London. The Anglo-Irish patriotism that developed in mid-century was marked by this dilemma: It articulated its demands to London for a free federal parliament within the archipelago even as it relied on England to safeguard its political control from the native majority below.[4]

If from the late eighteenth century on Ireland and England were increasingly interlinked in politics and administration, they were societies sharply diverging in economic development and material well-being. Both countries doubled their populations between 1780 and 1840, England growing from 7 to 15 million and Ireland from 4 to 8 million. The English demographic revolution was linked to an explosive economic productivity that led statistically minded contemporaries to celebrate the *Progress of the Nation*; by contrast, in Ireland a swelling population pressing hard against the sole national resource, the land, exacerbated economic crisis and social unrest.[5]

England, the metropolitan mainland, was in 1780 a wealthy society becoming rapidly wealthier. On the solid foundation of an improving agriculture its businessmen were building the world's leading urban industrial nation. English agriculture, mostly tillage and thoroughly capitalist, was based on enclosed, consolidated holdings of large size: By 1850 a third of the cultivated acreage was in farms of 300 or more acres. The contrast to Ireland was extreme. In England at mid-century four-fifths of the land in use was worked in units (farms and holdings) of 100 or more acres, but in Ireland by 1845 two-thirds of the land lay in units of less than 15 acres.[6] Whereas the Irish population was dispersed across the countryside, a large and increasing share of the English population was concentrated in towns. In 1780, one in five Englishmen lived in towns with a population of 5,000 or more; by 1850, the ratio was one in two. In 1840, when England had seventy-one towns of 10,000 people, twenty-three of them above 50,000, Ireland had only eighteen towns of over 10,000, and thirteen of these were *below* 20,000. At mid-century a third of the English population lived in towns of over 20,000 people; in Ireland less than a tenth of the population lived in settlements half that size.[7]

England's increasing urbanization was linked to its industrialization. Blessed with a rich historical legacy of capital and labor skills, a developed internal market, and high domestic and overseas demand, England in 1780–1850 eagerly implemented new technologies to create what scholars call the classic stage of the Industrial Revolution. The new cotton and iron industries, as well as the older ones in woolens and coal, raced along in high gear to unprecedented levels of production. In the seventy years after 1780, cotton textile output jumped in value from £4 to £46 million; iron output (1820–50) trebled in value to £35 million. In a variety of industries, including these key growth sectors, Ireland was left far behind. English-imposed laws in the late seventeenth and early eighteenth centuries had killed nascent Irish industries – woolens, glass, brewing – since they competed with manufacturers on the British mainland. Only the linen industry, concentrated in Ulster, was allowed to develop. From 1780 on, nature made its contribution, for Ireland was deficient in coal and iron ore, the sinews of the Industrial Revolution.

The economic statistics dramatically record the enormous and ever-widening gap. In 1825 English pig iron output was 600,000 tons produced at 370 furnaces; Irish output, 3,000 tons from 2 furnaces. In 1835 England had 2,555 cotton mills employing 300,000 persons; Ireland, 80 mills employing 10,000.[8]

It is important to understand that Ireland functioned not as an "isolated ... isle, encased in pre-industrial time," but rather as "an annex to the 'workshop of the world.'" In 1720, 44 percent of all Irish exports had gone to Britain; by 1800, this had increased to 85 percent. From the late eighteenth century on, and rapidly after Waterloo, Ireland was a deindustrializing country meeting, with its tillage and pasturage products, the needs of urban industrial Britain. Over the period 1760–1815 the increasing commercialization of Irish agriculture led to a great expansion of grain crops in response to surging British demand; in just two decades, 1778–98, grain exports to Britain quadrupled in value. This tillage revolution of 1760–1815 doubled prices and quadrupled rents, encouraged land subdivision, and produced high employment. But in the postwar years of crisis, 1815–20, prices collapsed and continued to fall until mid-century. Grain exports continued to expand – fourfold in 1815–40 – even though after Waterloo tillage was no longer so profitable and the great bulk of Britain's grain imports now came from Europe. The rising British demand for Irish meat, the economic efficiency of pasturage versus tillage, and the lower transport costs of the steamship age encouraged Irish farmers to make the transition to a pastoral economy. Live cattle exports to the British mainland tripled from 1820 to 1840. On the eve of the Potato Famine, 55 percent of the land in use was in grassland and meadow as against 26 percent in cereal cultivation.[9]

These exogenous economic trends had serious social consequences for an Irish peasantry that was growing in numbers, tied to the land, and bereft of the safety valves (available in England) of towns, industries, and (until 1838) even a Poor Law. The social impact was differentiated. Before 1815, rising prices benefited landlords and tenants holding land on a long lease but tended to hurt laborers and short-term tenants, the cottiers and small farmers. Moreover, tillage land, though it brought employment, was also subject to a clerical tax (tithe), and the burden was heavy because pasturage land was tithe exempt until 1823. Tithe became a national burden after this date, and the post-Waterloo deflation of agricultural prices generated widespread protests because the economic crisis incorporated social groups, the middle and large farmers, who themselves now experienced hard times. This rural crisis in an age of demographic expansion was made worse by the "economic desirability" of switching to acre-intensive pasturage. Not only did livestock require much space for grazing; by requiring less supervision than crops, they also seriously lowered employment opportunities for laborers. Extension of pasturage also reduced the amount of land available for the potato, the people's subsistence crop and a root used to restore soil for tillage. By 1845, only 17 percent of the land in use was given over to potatoes.[10]

But achievement of this post-Waterloo economic rationality, a pastoral economy along the lines of agricultural consolidation, was "not merely difficult but impossible" precisely because of the population explosion and land subdivision resulting from the tillage expansion of 1760–1815. Where were the evicted, economically excess population to go? What were they to do? With no economic alternatives the people clung to their bit of land, "literally for life," and improving landlords and agents had to fear for theirs. The success of the popular resistance was remarkable. Pasturage expanded but not so much as tillage; potato patches proliferated into glens and bogs and up mountainsides as "the rising human tide of people seeped in everywhere." The economic rationalists were held at bay. "Nothing characterized the Irish peasantry in that twilight of the old economy more than the desperate and often violent tenacity with which they clung to their small farms."[11] On the eve of the Famine in overwhelmingly agrarian Ireland, two-thirds of the farming population were the poorest, potato-dependent people, the landless laborers and virtually landless cottiers; one in five persons was "economically surplus," having zero marginal productivity. Yet, had pasturage made even further inroads into the economy, the proportion of paupers would have been higher. Only the Great Famine, by winnowing the population, unblocked the economy, allowing it to take what since Waterloo has been its natural course, pastoral farming.[12]

It is one of the great ironies of the social and economic context of protest that the one nation – wealthy and increasingly urban and industrial – had a state system of relief for its poor, whereas the other – agrarian, impoverished, and desperately in need of such a system – had none. England's poor laws had originated in the sixteenth century as a means of controlling the beggary and lawlessness produced by the extension of sheep pasturage and consequent displacement of the rural poor at a time when the relief agencies of the Catholic church had been dismantled. By the eighteenth century, the English poor laws, locally rated and administered, constituted an institutional guarantee of subsistence to the state's poorest citizens. For the propertied, those taxed, the poor laws continued to be "an insurance against unrest"; for the recipients, the "right of parish relief" was perhaps the most tangible of their rights as freeborn Englishmen. The poor man received "no alms, but his legal dues," proclaimed William Cobbett, son of an agricultural laborer. "The poor man in England is as secure from beggary as the king upon his throne."[13] From 1795 to 1834, under the Speenhamland system, relief even functioned as a wage supplement – that is, a kind of locally prescribed minimum wage guarantee – at the expense of farmers' profits and landlords' rents. In England as a whole over the period 1785–1830, poor relief expenditures (up 242 percent, to £6.8 million) more than kept up with population increases (up 72 percent).[14] By contrast, in Ireland, whose population rose by 92 percent over these same years, there was *no* system of poor laws. The country was too poor to be able to afford one; British taxpayers were unwilling to subsidize one; and British politicians considered a centralized system of poor relief throughout the archipelago to be out of the question. When finally instituted in 1838, Irish poor relief proved unworkable, since it was largely copied from the English locally rated system.

Paddy and the free-born Englishman

Two such contrasting societies generated very different images about their citizens. Protest, repression, and the development of new police institutions occurred within this framework of differing perceptions, of oneself and of others. An Englishman's *liberty* was his classless birthright; "freedom," notes E. P. Thompson, "was the coinage of patrician, demagogue, and radical alike." The eighteenth-century "moral consensus" was sealed by the Bill of Rights (1689), but it rested on the widely shared belief that the Old Saxon Constitution, established by Alfred and overturned by the Norman French, had been restored in 1688. The "Norman Yoke" theory was challenged from the 1790s on by cosmopolitan French ideas of the rights of man; yet the nativist tradition of the rights of Englishmen displayed (in Thompson's words) "an astonishing vitality." Indeed, to the present day, a notable feature of the modern English working-class movement has been its nonespousal of internationalism.[15]

Englishmen, "this happy breed of men," had long seen their land – "this little world, this precious stone set in the silver sea" – as separate, different from Europe. For centuries before 1789, Englishmen associated "foreigners" with the absolutism and Catholicism of the Continent. Liberty consisted of "being English": Englishmen believed that their society since Tudor and Stuart times had – in politics, law, the reformed religion, and many other ways – evolved beyond the standards on the Continent.[16] Key catchwords, repeated by plebeian mobs, were in fact tokens of the Englishman's birthright. "If we are English men," urged an anonymous scribbler in the midst of riots in London in 1736, "let us show we have English spirits and not tamely submit to the yoak [*sic*] just ready to be fastened about our necks.... Let them see that wooden shoes are not so easy to be worn as they imagine." The Englishman's contempt for foreign shackles – immortalized in the triplet "brass money, wooden shoes, and popery" – functioned in a negative, emotive fashion to define his own liberties. The glorious year 1688 was hymned as one of nativist liberty expelling foreign Catholic tyranny: James II, who threatened to use "Irish papists" to destroy England's Protestant constitution, was unseated as William arrived on a "Protestant wind." A song that was composed in 1740 and became a national anthem, "Rule, Britannia!" made the same point in its insistent refrain: "Britons never, never, never shall be slaves."[17]

The French Revolution introduced Englishmen to pan-European ideas about the "rights of man." What is remarkable is the hardiness of the nativist strain in English radicalism. The highest compliment that John Baxter, a leader in the London Corresponding Society, could pay the English Jacobins was to call them "Saxons" (fighting the "Norman" ruling class). William Cobbett opposed

any wild theories about liberty.... We want *nothing new*. We have great constitutional laws and principles, to which we are immovably attached.... I want to see no *innovation* in England. All I wish and all I strive for is *The Constitution of England*, undefiled by corruption.

In the same period, that of the Napoleonic wars, a contributor to the *Edinburgh Review* summed it up for most Englishmen: "[All] civilized Governments may be divided into free and arbitrary: or, more accurately, into the Government of England, and the other European Governments."[18]

After Waterloo the new Paineite ideas in speeches and pamphlets assaulted the nativist English tradition but did not displace it; rather, they overlay the older tradition. Factory workers were likened to "white slaves" and were reminded that their oppression was "such as no negroes were ever subjected to." A radical handbill of 1830 challenged the people to follow the French and Belgians in revolutionary example by chiding them, "You are not Englishmen" if you don't. The demands of the "Swing" rioters that same year were for "the customary rights of the rural poor as freeborn Englishmen." In concluding his classic account of the development of a "collective self-consciousness" among early-nineteenth-century English workingmen, E. P. Thompson argues for internationalism and industrial syndicalism as twin legacies of the period. More to the point, he notes also that the workers suffered and protested as "articulate, free-born Englishmen." Even as they were denied the vote, and on occasion ridden down or imprisoned, they knew that they had rights, "they knew that they were born free"[19] (Figure 2.1).

The nativist notion of English liberty provided every Englishman with a positive sense of identity and heritage. In 1812 Edward Wakefield, noting the contrast to Ireland, boasted of the "proud example" of England, where the lower orders were given their "due weight" in society. "Every man, however low his station, is aware of his own importance, ... and to this may be ascribed ... the prosperity of the country, and the comparative tranquillity which it enjoys."[20] In the English collective consciousness, the strain of antiabsolutism and xenophobia helped not only to define English liberty but also to alleviate class conflict in the post–Waterloo period of radicalism. By the same token, the English national and race pride inhibited within the British archipelago any developing relationship between English radicalism and Irish popular movements. Mutual hostility, not class solidarity, would characterize relations between the English and Irish lower classes.

"The Irish character," pronounced Frederick Engels in 1845, "is comfortable only in the dirt." The Irishman he ranked "but little above the savage."[21] This opinion by the foreign friend of the English working class was shared by Englishmen of all classes. The English image of Paddy – rustic, rude, filthy, credulous, "beastly ... cruell and blodie" – had a history dating to the eleventh century.[22] The age-old glaring contrast in economic development and political and social organization, coupled with Ireland's proximity, predisposed Englishmen to make the comparison to their own island. In England, the people saw only the poorest Irish, the seasonal laborers traversing the countryside and the proletarians whom Engels encountered in Lancashire's towns. On visits to Ireland, Englishmen used to a diet of beef and white bread and to the visual "tidiness" of large wheat fields and towns of substantial buildings with glass windows were appalled by the number of windowless

NOT SO *VERY* UNREASONABLE!!! EH?

John. "My Mistress says she hopes you won't call a Meeting of her Creditors; but if you will leave your Bill in the usual way, it shall be properly attended to."

Figure 2.1 English Chartists petition for universal suffrage. (*Punch*, 1848)

mud cabins, by the shoeless, stockingless "beings who seem to form a different race from the rest of mankind," and by the pigs, livestock, and potato gardens of pastoral Ireland.[23]

To the legacy of a premodern economy, society, and religion was added in the seventeenth and early eighteenth centuries political conquest, land confiscation, and penal laws that (in Edmund Burke's words) degraded the Catholic Irish into "a race of savages." Shortly after these laws were relaxed and the native Irish began to be perceived as less threatening and more civilized

THE IRISH FRANKENSTEIN.

Figure 2.2 Daniel O'Connell conjures up the Irish movement for
Repeal of the Union. (*Punch*, 1843)

(c. 1750–90), demographic pressures and, after Waterloo, economic crisis
worked to turn Paddy into a dangerous, desperate person. Sectarian savagery
in the 1790s, the Rebellion of 1798, and ensuing endemic agrarian "outrages
that would appear to come from a nation of savages" appeared to confirm
the image as a true reflection of social realities.[24] The convergence of the
deterioration in Paddy's living standards and collective behavior with
England's increased responsibilities for governing the island after the Union

of the two kingdoms meant that the negative image of Paddy intruded increasingly on the consciousness of Englishmen (Figure 2.2).

The Irish stereotype remained human, if savage; Paddy was not yet portrayed as subhuman and simian. The turbulent Irishman might be compared to North American "savages" or described as "white negroes." "If niggers were not niggers, Irishmen would be niggers" was a remark made on the floor of the House of Commons in 1847. But the transformation of Paddy into ape-man began only in the latter 1840s, during the Famine horrors, and was not complete until the 1860s, when Darwin's theories were gaining popularity and the Fenians' bombs were exploding in England's towns.[25] There is a certain irony, or perhaps a cultural lag, in the fact that the image of the simianized Celt developed essentially *after* the Famine at a time when conditions in the Irish countryside were less congested, impoverished, violent, and crime-ridden – in short, less brutalized – than they had been in the first half of the century.

Much less is known, by the nature of the historical record, about the Irish peasant's self-image. But whatever his governors thought, Pat did not regard himself as savage or simian. He did live with the burden of an image purveyed by Englishmen and assented to by many Anglo-Irish; and as the post-Waterloo criminal statistics show, his behavior, by English standards, *was* frequently "brassy, cunning, and brutalized." Yet, as the word "cunning" suggests, Paddy was not without intelligence. If his overlords characterized the native Irish as "barbarians, idolaters, and outlaws," Pat responded by seeing them as "foreigners, heretics, and [land] robbers." England had its nativist mythology of the "Norman yoke"; Ireland, its belief in "Saxon oppression." Secondly, even the exogenous image carried occasional inconsistencies. Just as Englishmen generalized about Ireland from the wretchedness of Connaught and were surprised to find rich farming districts, so English visitors were surprised to notice positive traits in Paddy. Arthur Young (1780) found the common Irish "infinitely more cheerful and lively" than the English lower orders; Edward Wakefield (1812) judged them "more quick of comprehension" than the "boorishly stupid ... labourers in England." Significantly, such comments became rarer after Waterloo as living standards deteriorated, but after the Famine many observers were astounded by the relative success of many immigrant Irish in the United States.[26]

Given Pat's environment in the late eighteenth and early nineteenth centuries, it is remarkable that he behaved as well as he did. Whiteboy punishments could certainly be savage, but Whiteboy codes of behavior were strict, rule-bound, and consistent; they were marked by their own logic, pragmatism, and what Joseph Lee has aptly called "relentless realism." The diet of the lower Irish was below English standards and worsening after Waterloo, yet it was not so monotonous or primitive as the stereotype stated.[27] Literacy was an urban phenomenon, and Ireland was rural. In 1840, two-thirds of the adult male population of England was literate; in Ireland, roughly half. Of the Irish agrarian criminals transported in 1826–53, half were literate; indeed, the percentage of literacy was rising slightly.[28] These Irish were far more literate than England's Captain Swing exiles (34 percent) but much less literate than the urban Chartists (70 percent).[29] Other recent, if more tentative, findings suggest that Paddy could and did respond in rational ways to changes in his economic environment. High emigration provided an outlet; about 1.2 million people went to North America between 1780 and 1845. But those left behind, who formed a rising share of the population, tended to be the very poor, the smallest farmers, cottiers, and laborers. Ireland's population continued to grow, but the *rate* of growth slackened after 1821 and fell dramatically after 1831. After Waterloo, national marriage and birth rates declined; more people married later in life or never married. If many Irish were thus not behaving in a "headstrong, feckless" fashion, the problem nevertheless remained that an increasing population pressed ever harder on available land.[30] The trend to deferred marriages and fewer children suggests that after Waterloo the island's population, thanks to the marital and baby boom of about 1780–1820, was composed of increasing numbers of young men reaching maturity who were restless, rootless, semiliterate, and single – in short, prime recruiting material for Whiteboyism in an environment of economic deterioration.

II. Crime and protest

> For the last seventy years Ireland has been the scene of constantly recurring disturbances.... [I]n a large part of Ireland there is ... less security of persons and property than in any other part of Europe, except perhaps the wildest districts of Calabria or Greece.... [Some] reasoners conceive that there is an innate and indelible tendency in the Irish to disturbance and outrage; that Ireland has been cut off by nature from the rest of the civilized world, and been foredoomed to a state of endless disorder....
> – George Cornewall Lewis, *On Local Disturbances in Ireland* (1836)

England and Ireland generated very different kinds of social disorder. Early-nineteenth-century crime figures – national totals of committals are available from 1805 – indicate that, relative to population, Ireland was roughly twice as "crime-ridden" as England. These statistics understate the Irish reality because of the difficulty there in apprehending and prosecuting offenders. Crime in the two countries was different not only in volume but also in character. First, English crime was individual, committed by a person for personal gain; Irish crime was collective, committed by a group for group interests. In other words, offenses in England were more of the nature we would call "crime"; in Ireland, crime often took the form of protest. Second, English crime was characterized by little violence against persons; in Ireland, "outrages," or attacks on people and animals, were far more common. Third, by its collective nature, crime in Ireland tended to have the support of the community to a degree that was unheard of in England.

In England larceny and theft were by far the most common offenses. Perhaps the most dramatic example of that typically English crime, theft, was the incident in 1753 when George II, walking one evening in Kensington

Palace gardens, was accosted by an individual and stripped of his watch, money, and shoe buckles. In England the vast majority of the 200 capital statutes in 1800 were for property crimes. By contrast, in Ireland, individual and property crime was far less common. "It is well known," reported a Dublin newspaper in 1786, "that fewer robberies are committed in the country parts of Ireland, than in those of any other country in Europe." This paper even argued, in a burst of patriotic hyperbole, that "more are committed in England in a week, than in this country in two years." Crime statistics, first arranged by general categories in the 1830s, show that "crimes against property without violence" accounted for four-fifths of all English indictable offenses but only one-third of the Irish totals. The nature of Irish crime – group attacks against the agrarian system – is caught in the outraged objection of a military officer in 1823 that "a set of cowardly Ruffians should fancy that they could legislate for Landlords."[31]

English crime was also marked by a low incidence of personal violence. Homicide rates were low, and had been since the early eighteenth century and even earlier.[32] In early-nineteenth-century England, annual committals for murder were half as numerous as in Ireland, and England not only had twice the population of Ireland but benefited from better crime reporting and prosecution. The Irish constabulary in the decade before the Famine reported almost 1,900 homicides, an average of 170 killings a year. Like Irish crime in general, Irish murders were not individually motivated but rather, in the words of a Tipperary magistrate, formed part of "a System of Terror established by the Insurgents and Assassins of this cursed Region."[33]

The incidence of what came to be known as "Irish" violence ebbed and flowed, but the evidence suggests that it increased in the sectarian 1790s, intensified under economic and demographic pressures after 1815, and eased only after the Famine. Although the early statistics are sketchy, we may agree with Thomas Bartlett's assertion that an era of apparently low violence, at least by later Irish standards, came to an end in the early 1790s. Homicide in Ireland in the first half of the nineteenth century was in fact concentrated in certain regions, and its incidence was probably exaggerated by the retelling of the grisly details. Of one victim (in Waterford, 1814), for example, it was reported that his "Hands and Arms were cut off and not found with the Body and but a very small part of the Head." In an "inhuman murder" in Westmeath in 1824, the victim's skull was "smashed into small pieces with a large stone, and his brains scattered about the field." In Roscommon in 1820, the assailants actually impaled their victim: They "forced a sharp wooden instrument into the rectum, and a considerable way up through the body."[34]

The punitive nature of Irish violence could be seen in those survivors who were maimed or disfigured. Ears were cropped, eyes gouged, and tongues ripped out. One night in Tipperary in 1828 a man was set upon "by a party of nine men who cut off his thumbs, chopped his arms, and cut off his knee-cap with swords and a scythe." "Carding," the shredding of the victim's back by the stroking of a wool card (a small iron-spiked board), was extremely painful; "diamond carding," with the strokes administered

diagonally in the shape of a diamond, was particularly barbarous. Psychological tortures were also employed: Women were raped "in order to wreak
vengeance on their husbands or fathers," who were forced to watch the
outrage.[35]

The violence touched animals as well – dogs and horses, but especially
pasture livestock, sheep and cattle. Ears and tails were cut off; cows' teats
were hacked off and their legs "houghed" (tendons severed). "Sheep are
likewise shorn and mangled in a barbarous manner, not for the sake of the
wool, but in order to spoil the sheep." A police report from Clare in 1825
described how ten cows had had iron instruments "forced . . . into their
Bodies by the posterior"; twenty-one other "poor brutes" had their tails cut
off, including "part of their backbone," and "some" had their eyes "scooped
out." Significantly, the poor man's pig was never abused.[36]

Such examples could be multiplied. The point, for our comparative study,
is that these forms of collective violence hardly ever occurred in England;[37]
and although their sensational character may have given rise to exaggerated
notions of their frequency in Ireland, such protest incidents were nevertheless
distinctively Irish, not English. Even more importantly, in the minds of
many, violence itself came to be associated with Irishness; in the trenchant
words of one mid-Victorian Englishman, "Roman Catholic and midnight
assassin are synonymous terms." A second and, in English eyes, equally
damning point is that Irish collective crime against persons or property,
whether lethal or nonlethal, drew widespread community support. Again
and again, Irish authorities trying to track down criminals encountered only
the peasantry's sullen, silent consent to the crimes; indeed, daytime assassinations occurred with some frequency before loudly approving crowds. In
England the "hue and cry" brought either public pursuit or cooperation with
constables in crime fighting; in Ireland, aiding the authorities was called
"informing" and informers lived in peril of popular retribution. An Irish
magistrate, testifying before a parliamentary committee in 1852, used these
words to describe the contrast between the two countries: "There is that sort
of feeling in Ireland against the law; it is exactly contrary to the feeling which
prevails in England, [where] every man is in favour of the law, and aids it in
almost every way. It appears that in Ireland crime is generally, somehow or
other, the crime of the community, whereas in England it is the crime of an
individual."[38]

It is not really possible to quantify the incidence of social protest in England
and Ireland. Most scholarly attempts to do so rely on the criminal statistics;
but much protest did not involve actually breaking the law, and when it did,
many rioters escaped arrest and indictment. Second, to incorporate protest
with crime misses the point that riot in England had a certain historical
legitimacy, whereas protest in Ireland operated in search of it. Third, a
quantified definition of social unrest overlooks the importance and role of
attitudes, preconceptions, and expectations of both the protesters and the
authorities.

These admonitions aside, the crime statistics do provide us with the dimensions of *indictable* social protest. Having tabulated selected social protest offenses,[39] George Rudé found that in the ten most disturbed English counties in 1834–53, a disturbed period, only 3 to 6 percent of all committals concerned protest, compared to 9 to 25 percent of all committals in the seven most disturbed Irish counties in 1845–60, a period that after 1851 was quiet compared to the years before and during the Famine.[40] My own calculations of annual public order (Class 6) offenses from 1835 to 1850, as a proportion of all committals, yield figures ranging from 3 to 5 percent for England and 21 to 29 percent for Ireland. In addition, offenses against the person with violence, in Ireland largely a protest crime, accounted for 26 to 32 percent of the annual total committals in the pre-Famine years 1835–45 (falling to 14 to 22 percent during the Famine years); by contrast, over the period 1835–50 in England, this offense category consistently accounted for only 8 or 9 percent of the annual totals.[41] These statistics serve to support the contemporary opinion that Ireland was a much more disorderly and violent country than England.

Scholars have divided popular protest into various classifications. Charles Tilly has described "collective violence" as existing in three stages: (1) *primitive*: small-scale, localized, personally oriented, and apolitical; (2) *reactionary*: still localized, only implicitly political, with highly specific goals and "backward-looking" concerns for lost rights or past grievances; and (3) *modern*: heavily politicized, based on abstract ideas about "rights," and "forward looking" in the sense that these "new" rights are due the people.[42] George Rudé, on the other hand, creates a twofold classification: "preindustrial" protest and "industrial" protest. The former he defines as direct-action rioting characterized by spontaneity yet careful selection of targets, no continuous acknowledged leadership, and (as with Tilly) highly specific and backward-looking crowd aims. By contrast, Rudé's industrial protest, like Tilly's modern collective violence, is characterized by marches, petitions, rallies, and demonstrations; is forward looking in its demands for the right to strike and to vote; and is essentially an urban phenomenon.[43]

Tilly's and Rudé's classifications are generally useful, but they do not adequately meet the needs of the Irish case. Ireland's agrarian criminals, like England's food rioters, were preindustrial or reactionary. But faction fighting at Irish fairs, which falls under the rubric of primitive protest in Tilly's system, was in fact sometimes class based and ideated. And "party fights," which for Tilly are "mutual attacks of hostile religious groups" and thus primitive violence, were in fact marked, especially from the 1790s on, by a political consciousness. More importantly, Rudé's equation of the term "industrial" with modern protest bars us from talking about those forms of Irish rural protest that were both modern and preindustrial.[44] Indeed, in his discussion of Ireland, Rudé leaves out of his classification system the United Irish, Emancipation, Tithe, and Repeal movements. In the following discussion, then, I propose simply to divide popular protest by the terms "premodern" and "modern."

Premodern collective violence

In Ireland this type of disorder assumed a number of forms. Family *feuds* were endemic to the peasant society, which had little respect for English law and little trust in law courts.[45] To a people reared on the Gaelic warrior legends,[46] *faction fighting* at fairs was something entered into with gusto. The flying fists, sticks, and cudgels produced bloodshed, even fatalities, but the fighting was ritualized: Strangers were usually safe, and the authorities intervened only when the violence spilled outside the original combatant groups.[47] The "donnybrooks" (a word derived from Donnybrook Fair outside Dublin[48]) were not always innocent affairs, for a recent scholar has found strong elements of class conflict in early-nineteenth-century Tipperary fair fights.[49] Nor were the *party fights* always senseless sectarian head bashings. These Protestant–Catholic brawls required two sizable factions and hence were concentrated in south Ulster. Recent scholarship has discovered a political complexion to these disorders. The Protestant Peep o'Day Boys and Catholic Defenders of the 1780 matured, respectively, into Orangemen (institutionalized as the Orange Order, 1795), who benefited from middle- and upper-class approval, and United Irishmen, who established French republican connections.[50] Party, like faction, fighting was apparently a fluid phenomenon with more modern features than has hitherto been believed.

The most extensive and persistent premodern Irish collective violence in the seventy years after 1780 was a product of the system of landholding. The disorders were concentrated in central, southern, and to some extent western Ireland, where an expanding population of small farmers and cottiers vied fiercely for the privilege of land occupancy, however small the plot. Competition was intense because there was no custom of tenant security or compensation for improvements, as in Ulster, and, until just before the Famine, no last resort of even token poor relief. Unlike English protest movements, which are clearly separable in time and place, it often seems that the Irish agrarian disturbances "can scarcely be told apart and pass almost imperceptibly from one to the other."[51] In fact, the disorders were discrete and highly localized, and they varied in their intensity and particular litany of demands from district to district. The names, too, changed: the Whiteboys (1761–2, 1769–75), Rightboys (1785–7), and Rockites (1821–4) of Munster, and the Thrashers (1806–7) and Terry Alts (1831–2) of Connaught, to name only the most prominent.[52] Yet there were common features to the various movements that led contemporaries to describe·them simply by the generic term "Whiteboyism." This term originated with the Munster movement of the 1760s when protesters donned white shirts, smocks, or other garb.[53] Chief among the recurring concerns of the various Whiteboy movements was the occupation of the land: to hold on to it or to get it back. Whiteboys fought eviction, rent collection or increases, competitive bidding ("land jobbing"), and turnover in tenancies. A second concern was the extension of pasturage, which removed scarce land from tillage and exacerbated unemployment by reducing the need for human labor. Further, because pasture land until 1823 was not subject to tithe, the tithe burden fell heavily on small farmers in grazing districts. The battle was deftly characterized by an English MP in the 1840s as "a contest between men and women, and bullocks and sheep, for the possession of the soil."[54] Third, and of special importance in economic hard times, were those obligations beyond rent payment: tithes paid to the Anglican church and Catholic priests' dues, the customary fees charged peasant parishioners.

Whiteboy unrest was most prevalent in south central Ireland, in an area between prosperous East Leinster and the impoverished western seaboard. Historian Louis Cullen's observation that serious sustained unrest was "notably absent from the poorest regions" seems to endorse the remark by a Dublin Castle official in 1828 that "the finest soil is to be found where Barbarism most prevails."[55] Whiteboyism posed the greatest problems in developing, increasingly market-oriented areas where the middle poor – peasant tenants on five- to fifteen-acre holdings – were pressed by larger, pasturage-oriented, profit-minded farmers and harassed by the prospect of sinking, through eviction, into the poorest landless class.[56] In parts of Munster, and above all in Tipperary, it was not so much poverty as land use and commercialization in an age of demographic expansion that drove a defensive peasantry to violent protest. Whiteboyism flourished in "exuberantly fertile" Tipperary, a county of small farms where dairy cattle, sheep, and grain vied with pigs, potatoes, and oats for the use of the rich soil. It is risky and, in the present state of scholarship, premature to generalize about the "typical" Whiteboy, but he seems to have been poor, though not the poorest of the poor, and also essentially conservative. He opposed the rich – the large farmer, the grazier, the improving landlord – and those who, by bidding up the land, collaborated with them. He saw himself as the victim or potential victim of economic progress (enclosure, commercialized rents).[57] In this self-perception the Irish Whiteboy was somewhat akin to the English Luddite, Swing rioter, and Lancashire handloom weaver who protested against the progress of the new technology and industrialism.

Premodern English collective violence differed in a number of ways from its Irish counterpart. Family disagreements were settled through the entrenched institutions of law courts. English fairs could be boisterous, but fighting, like the typically English crime of pickpocketing, was an affair between individuals.[58] Party fights and faction fights did not exist. If Irish premodern disorders revolved around land, clan, and religion, English disturbances occurred in both town and country and targeted a variety of issues.[59] Protest against military service took the form of riots against militia balloting (1757, 1796) and impressment (1794).[60] Disturbances could be motivated by strong feelings of plebeian patriotism and of a "true-born Englishman's" Protestantism: Witness the anti-Methodist riots of 1740–60,[61] the Jewish naturalization riots of 1753,[62] the anti-Catholic riots of 1715, 1736, 1763, and 1780, and the Church-and-King riots of 1790–2.[63]

Other premodern disorders were a product of the vigorously capitalist system in which Englishmen lived. In England the question of use and occupancy of the land was no longer a bone of contention: The English peasantry had long ago lost the soil to the great magnates and their secure large tenant farmers. The eighteenth-century English countryside was orderly, gentrified, businesslike: The land enclosure movement, at its height in 1793–1815, in taking common and waste land from the rural poor, produced surprisingly few ripples of protest.[64] Rural riots concerned laborers' wages, food prices, and taxes. By far the most numerous disorders, indeed the classic riots of the eighteenth century, were the food riots that swirled around the villages, river ports, and market towns of southern and central England. Poor harvests produced high prices that triggered bread riots; in the worst years – 1766, 1795, 1800–1 – the disturbances became widespread. Two-thirds of the 275 disorders discovered by Rudé in the period 1735–1800 were bread riots; more recently, John Stevenson has counted 175 bread riots in 1792–1818 alone.[65]

With the post-1815 drop in agricultural prices and the economy's shift to capital intensiveness, the character of premodern collective violence changed in England. The classic food riot era came to an end, and protests in both town and country targeted the new technology that seemed to threaten workingmen's jobs. The Luddites (1811–17) attacked the stocking-frame knitting machines and Captain Swing's farm laborers the threshing machines.[66] From the 1830s on, industrial workers came to accept the terms of the modern economic order in seeking the regulation, not abolition, of the new machinery and in limiting their demands to wages and unions. Rural workers were slower to modernize: Arson in the countryside continued intermittently until the 1860s, and farm laborers began to unionize only in the following decade.[67]

It is important to note the similarities in English and Irish premodern collective violence. First, the aims of both groups were essentially preventive. The Whiteboys were "defensive and specific," the English food rioters "remedial rather than rebellious."[68] The groups obstructed economic change that they perceived to be not in their best interests: hence in Ireland, the peasant opposition to agricultural improvement and extension of pasturage; and in England, the food rioters' resistance to a distributive urban market infrastructure and the machine breakers' battle against technological innovation. Second, both groups operated within the framework of the traditional capitalist system. Whiteboys sought not to abolish tenancies or to cancel rents but to give security to tenure and fair value to rents. England's bread rioters opposed outrageous profit-taking in periods of dearth and demanded a "just price" within the terms of the old "moral economy." The followers of King Ludd and Captain Swing fought to preserve the old capitalist system from the onslaught of the new industrial one. Third, both groups claimed to represent popular values, indeed to act for the common good. The Irish Whiteboys termed themselves "regulators," and their social superiors objected to them as "legislators." In the same way, English rioters sought to assert moral laws over the state's economic laws. Both groups, Irish and English, emulated the state in harassing people who broke the laws. Protesters warned the malefactor by issuing "threatening" notices, usually written in pseudo-legal jargon; if these "legal" notices were disregarded, punishment ensued. Both movements were guided by strong codes of behavior. In England bread was to be regulated in price, not pilfered for private gain; machinery was destroyed but the mill was rarely burned to the ground. In Ireland, a house or mail coach raided for arms was not plundered as well; cattle were maimed, not stolen; even rape was a collective assault on a man's wife or daughter, not the individual lustful enjoyment of a woman. In sum, both groups saw themselves as law enforcers, not law breakers. They were "administrators of a law of opinion, generally prevalent among the class to which they belong." A contemporary, George Cornewall Lewis, drew the comparison to English workers' organizations when he described the Whiteboys as "a vast trades' union for the protection of the Irish peasantry."[69]

For all the similarities, it was the differences between the two groups that most struck contemporaries. First, there was the contrast between the legitimacy of English protest and (in the eyes of Ireland's rulers) the illegitimacy of Irish protest. Premodern English collective violence was an officially sanctioned feature of eighteenth-century society. Elie Halévy has noted that "the right to riot ... was an integral part of the national traditions," which included free speech, petitioning, and public assembly. To a laboring class without the ballot, rioting was a means of expressing opinions and "a way of demanding redress."[70] Protest in Ireland enjoyed no such tolerance. Whiteboyism was so pervasive and popularly accepted that the Government could not afford to recognize Whiteboy legitimacy without surrendering control of large sections of the countryside. It is significant that the Whiteboys themselves – who adopted names like "Captain Right" and signed notices "The Commons of Rathkeale" – had no doubts about their own legitimacy.

Second, England's pre-1815 tradition of riot was defined by the unwritten rules of paternalism and deference. Rioting, which "had a close connection with routine, peaceful political life," was essentially bargaining between the rioters and authorities.[71] Each side was eager for a quick and mutually satisfactory settlement. In Ireland it was different: There was no deference, no paternalism. "An Englishman," wrote a traveler in 1830,

cannot fail to remark the different behaviour of the two countries in one particular. We never were saluted with a bow or a curtsey from any of them, from the beginning to the end of our journey; *conduct quite unnatural*, and only to be accounted for by the relation in which they stand to the native gentry.

Whiteboyism was a product not only of the class but also of the ethnic and religious chasms in the Irish countryside. The corollary to Arthur Young's observation on Irish gentry brutality – "knocking down is spoken of in the country in a manner that makes an Englishman stare" – was the cold, calculating "outrage" perpetrated by the Whiteboy.[72]

A third, and key, difference lay in the kind and degree of violence employed by the crowds. English rioters abstained from serious personal violence; wheat factors or mill owners might be jostled or assaulted, but were hardly ever killed. English rioting, like English crime, produced very low homicide statistics. In England, talk of "Bread or Blood" was rhetorical; in Ireland, the bloodshed was quite real. The murders and personal assaults – beatings, rapings, cuttings, stonings, and shootings – were often selective and judicially administered, but the scale of this personal violence, especially from the early 1790s on, shocked Ireland's English governors because they came from a society far more respectful of human life. The Whiteboys, of course, attacked property as well, raiding houses, stealing arms, spading up fields, and leveling hedges, but even the assaults against animate property – cattle, sheep, and horses – were marked by their grisly nature. Property damage was characteristic of English rioting. Overturned flour carts, slit wheat sacks, broken windows, arson of hay ricks, and mangled machinery form the scenario of English premodern collective violence. If English disorders were "far more muted and restrained" than Irish ones,[73] it must be noted that when property damage did go beyond acceptable limits – as in the 1766 food riots, the Gordon Riots, and the Swing and Reform disorders – the authorities moved quickly against the crowds. But in England, repression was as temporary as the outbursts were exceptional. Ireland, on the other hand, seemed to suffer from a nearly permanent state of disorder requiring more severe state controls.

A final difference lay in the movements' degrees of success. Networks of Whiteboy government, though highly localized, crisscrossed southern and central Ireland. "Committees" (note the parliamentary term) arranged outrages; members were sworn to secrecy; "strangers" executed Whiteboy orders both to prevent detection and to ensure anonymity and also impartiality of punishment; and the neighboring peasantry was sympathetic or intimidated. The result was a remarkable record of success. One Member chided his colleagues in the Irish Parliament in 1787 that they "thought they governed the country; but a new power had risen in the land, who laughed at their edicts.... This royal Will-o'-the-Wisp, whom no man could catch, made laws infinitely more effectual, or better enforced, than those of parliament." In 1834 the Irish Lord Lieutenant, Marquess Wellesley, informed Prime Minister Melbourne: "The combination established surpasses the law in vigour, promptitude, and efficacy ... [so that] it is more safe to violate the law than to obey it." So pervasive could Whiteboy control be that an Anglo-Irish nobleman said in the House of Lords in 1846 that "he believed the absence of outrage could only be attributed to the combined law-breakers having it all their own way."[74] By contrast, the English countryside was never subdued to the rule of the lower orders. Even in the Luddite and Swing periods, when concessions in wages and poor relief were granted and technological innovation was briefly delayed, popular victories were temporary and control quickly reverted to the gentry and Government.[75] The final irony, however, was that if the English premodern rioters lost their battles, the country itself, once past the "Hungry Forties," prospered under the new urban and industrial system. In Ireland, the Whiteboys were so successful that they were broken only by the horrors of the Famine, which, ironically, by their obstruction of land consolidation and improvement, they had to some extent unwittingly helped to bring on.

Modern collective violence

The character and frequency of premodern collective violence in Ireland were sufficient to call forth new forces of order, the police. In England the crowds' restraint in demands and tactics was matched by the authorities' refrainment from introducing new, unconstitutional, and extraordinary forces of order. In Ireland, modern collective violence was a secondary, if occasionally critical, inducement to add to the arsenal of armed authority. In England, the emergence of modern collective violence in 1815–50 would be the critical factor in getting the Government and the propertied to consider seriously the introduction of modern police forces.

In England the new type of collective violence was aimed at new political rights (universal manhood suffrage) and economic rights (the right to strike and to unionize) spawned by the new industrial system. In Ireland democratic demands focused on increased political rights for the majority population (O'Connell's movement for Catholic Emancipation); the demand for economic rights, in the absence of industrialization, was seen in the almost nationwide boycott (1830–3) against payment of tithe. In Ireland there was a third modern issue: nationalism, the struggle for Irish self-rule.

Modern protest was of critical importance in England because the new emphasis on group rights tore into the old social compact of paternalism and deference. A view of society as organically whole and composed of complementary constituent groups or "orders" gave way to one of it as a collection of competing interests, or, in the new language, "classes."[76] Thus, for example, industrial workers confronted the new captains of industry, who in turn challenged landlords over the Corn Laws; or again, in the period 1815–32, the lower and middle classes demanded of the aristocracy concessions on the suffrage question. In Ireland the new ideas of class were perhaps less unsettling. That country had never developed the notion of a social compact; nevertheless, the new sense of class rights became important simply because the small farmers, the poor, and the Catholics formed such a large majority of the population. In England the new definition of society as a collection of interest groups had the effect of transforming the idea of a "moral economy" into class-based talk of "moral force." The nonprivileged now claimed a preponderance of right or morality: England's benevolent eighteenth-century ruling elite became Cobbett's "Old Corruption." The concept of bargaining within the old moral economy was replaced by the idea of struggle. Rioters were no longer bonded to JPs and troops in a mutual relationship but were now competing mass against mass, crowd *against* authorities. The jittery new relationship is seen most graphically at Peterloo in 1819.

The tactics of modern collective violence have been described by the terms "moral force" and "physical force." Over the period 1815–50, in both England and Ireland, moral force predominated. It commonly took the forms of petitioning, public processions, and mass meetings. Rioters evolved into "demonstrators" and machine breakers into "workers" organized or "incorporated" within the new economic system, whose benefits they now sought through better wages and trade organizations. Old words carried new definitions. Working-class political "unions" appeared after 1815, and "trade union" and "demonstration" took on their modern meaning in the 1830s. It is not surprising that physical force failed to materialize in England beyond the level of intimidating speeches; violence in the disturbances of the old moral economy had been restrained and governed by the rules of the social compact.[77] The situation was, again, different in Ireland. It was not difficult for a country with a tradition of premodern violent protest to turn to the modern protest of physical force. But the lesson of Irish revolutionary force in the late 1790s – leading as it did to the death of 30,000 rebels but of only 1,600 troops – was well learned by early-nineteenth-century Irishmen. They returned to the safer guerrilla tactics of the Whiteboys and the moral force arguments of O'Connell.[78] In England after Waterloo, protesters came to learn what Irishmen had long known: that the forces of order were controlled by the ruling classes for their own interests. Since riot in the post–moral economy period now produced repression, demonstrators learned to abstain from violence altogether. Indeed, violence in the new political climate tended to come from the authorities, since they felt threatened by the workingmen who, in fact, were challenging the right of the authorities to determine the rules of governing.

In England, modern collective violence appeared in the 1760s with the agitation by John Wilkes and his followers for parliamentary reform. The movement was restricted to London and, as Rudé concedes, was built on "as yet a fragile and unstable base."[79] The agitation revived briefly in 1778–80 in London, and appeared in Yorkshire and some other counties before collapsing in the wake of the Gordon Riots.[80] The outbreak of the French Revolution revived London radicalism, at least until 1794, but the response in the provincial towns was very modest, and in general the years in which England was at war with France, 1792–1815, may be described as a peculiar combination of working-class patriotism and government repression of the country's handful of republicans.[81]

The scenario was different in Ireland. There the first powerful challenge to British political rule came during the years of the American Revolution. Anglo-Irish gentlemen, middle-class Presbyterians, and even some Catholics took the large step of organizing into companies of armed Volunteers, some 80,000 men being under arms by 1782. In imitation of the Americans, Irish quasi-parliamentary groups from across the kingdom met in "conventions," and Irish merchants boycotted English goods. A nervous Government in London conceded Irish free trade and parliamentary autonomy.[82] In the 1790s, as the Irish agitation deepened, the Government repealed most of the remaining Catholic disabilities and granted Catholics the county franchise on the same terms as Protestants. But still the United Irishmen proliferated and cemented ties with domestic agrarian groups and French republicans. Threatened wartime conscription led to heavily politicized antimilitia riots, which the Government bloodily suppressed. In 1796, only the weather prevented French ships from landing in Ireland. The next year, the Government instituted a countrywide policy of terrorization and repression under the infamous General Lake. In 1798 came the United Irish Rebellion, its leaders seeking Irish independence and the creation of a cosmopolitan francophile republic. Amid scenes of savage fighting beyond the comprehension of Englishmen, the rebellion was crushed and, by the subsequent Act of Union, the country's legislative independence forfeited. There would be subsequent whimpers of rebellion in 1803 and more than a generation later, in 1848, but 1798 represents in fact the last serious rising for self-rule until the early twentieth century.[83]

Modern collective violence became tamer but pervasive in Ireland, and pervasive for the first time in England, after the close of the French wars. In England demands for universal suffrage revived in London but now came also, indeed more pressingly, from the urban industrial Midlands and the North. Popular petitioning, processions, and public meetings reached a climax at Peterloo and were followed by a wave of industrial strikes that led Parliament to legalize the right to unionize (1824). The middle classes won the vote (1832) and the radicalized working classes demanded it in the ensuing Chartist period, 1836–48[84] (see Figure 2.1). In post-Rebellion Ireland, Daniel O'Connell mobilized the peasantry in his campaign for Catholic Emancipation (1826–9). Just as Feargus O'Connor, the Irish leader of English Chartists, exhorted his followers to refrain from violence, so he told the Irish peasantry to give no support to "driftless acts of outrage." In the so-called Tithe War of 1830–3 they showed themselves capable of conducting a highly successful campaign of passive resistance to payment of the tithe. In O'Connell's final movement, that for the Repeal of the Union with England (1843), literally millions of Irishmen attended "monster meetings" and confounded the authorities by their quiet, disciplined, sober behavior[85] (see Figure 2.2).

III. Calling out the troops: the military "in aid of the civil power"

> Successive governments have apparently exhausted every means in their power to suppress the evil, but without success.... The country has been covered with military and police ... Australia has been crowded with transported convicts, and all to no purpose.... [T]here are persons who altogether despair of establishing permanent tranquillity in Ireland, and who think it is an exception to all the ordinary rules of government.
> – George Cornewall Lewis, *On Local Disturbances in Ireland* (1836)

Repression was, of course, the other side of the protest coin. In this period, by far the most frequently employed punishment for serious crimes was "transportation," a state-paid one-way trip to Australia. Between 1787 and 1868 162,000 persons were loaded on convict ships bound from the British Isles to the antipodes.[86] This figure is equal to the population of Dublin in 1790 or of Manchester in 1820. Almost all of those transported had committed ordinary, nonprotest crimes; only about 3,500 were protest offenders. George Rudé has calculated (Table 2.1) that of all protesters transported from the two islands, two-thirds left from Ireland,[87] a country that accounted for only a third of the islands' combined populations. One of every 8 Irishmen transported went because of a protest crime compared to 1 of every 100 persons leaving from Britain. Three-fourths of the Irish protesters transported had been convicted of agrarian offenses; in England two-fifths of all protesters transported were exiled for their participation in a single movement, Captain Swing's in 1830. Thanks to the rebellions of 1798 and 1803, Ireland also predominated in political protest offenses, the 329 transported rebels outnumbering Britain's political total of 171.[88] The high figures for arson and poaching in Britain – amounting to one-fourth of the total – acknowledge not only the protest- but also the property-oriented character of these offenses on the British mainland.

Such, then, were the dimensions of punishment for the most serious protest crimes in Britain and Ireland. But what were the means at hand, the forces available for repression? Effective police forces existed in disturbed districts in Ireland only from 1814 on and in all of the counties from 1822 on. In England the new police were not in existence in the provincial towns until 1835, at the earliest, and they were not in any county until 1839 and not in all counties until 1856. With the old police "almost perversely ineffective"[89] in the late eighteenth century and (in England) well into the nineteenth, the authorities were often forced to rely on the laws of riot, the local magistrates, and the military.

The Riot Act

In England, common and statute law defined and proscribed affrays, routs, armed and unlawful assembly, tumultuous petitioning, and riots.[90] Enforcement against both misdemeanor and felonious riots was selective in a country famous for its liberty and its tolerance of public assembly and plebeian riot.

In the early eighteenth century, the victors of 1688, the Whig oligarchs, harried by Jacobite opposition to the new Hanoverian succession, passed the Riot Act (1714), which in effect restored to the statute book stern Tudor laws against riot.[91] The Riot Act provided that twelve or more persons "unlawfully, riotously, and tumultuously assembled together" were liable to arrest, conviction, and execution as felons. The statute introduced a proclamation that was required to be read, in full, word for word, to the rioters:

Our Sovereign Lord the King chargeth and commandeth all Persons, being assembled, immediately to disperse themselves, and peaceably to depart to their Habitations, or to their lawful Business, upon the pains contained in the Act made in the first Year of King *George*, for preventing Tumults and riotous Assemblies.

GOD save the King

Table 2.1. *Protesters transported to Australia, 1788–1868*

From Britain	Number	Percent	From Ireland	Number	Percent
Political Radicals, 1790s[a]	21	1.8	Pre-1798 agrarian criminals	160	7.1
Luddites, 1812–17	42	3.5	1798 and 1803 rebels	329	14.6
Pentridge rebels, 1817	14	1.2	Agrarian criminals		
Cato St. conspirators, 1820	5	0.4	1814–25	589	26.2
Captain Swing rioters, 1830	483	40.4	1827–40	604	26.9
Bristol rioters, 1831	26	2.2	1840–53	339	15.1
Chartists				1,532	68.1
1839	11	0.9	1848 rebels	12	0.5
1842	75	6.3	Fenians, 1868	62	2.8
1848	16	1.3	Marginal protesters		
	102	8.5	Arsonists	117	5.2
Marginal protesters			Cattle maimers and houghers	35	1.6
Arsonists	218	18.2		152	6.8
Poachers	75	6.3	Other	2	0.1
Cattle maimers	20	1.7	TOTAL	2,249	100.0
	313	26.1			
Other[b]	191	16.0			
TOTAL	1,197	100.1			

Of the British total, only twenty-five are identifiably Scots; twelve, Welsh. Of the British and Irish total, only 120 are women.

[a] Includes six Scots Jacobins.
[b] Divided among thirteen categories, led by "riots," fifty-two; "machine breakers," twenty-two; etc.

Source: Rudé, *Protest,* pp. 8–10. Percentages calculated are my own.

The Riot Act also introduced a new provision for a *one-hour hiatus* before the act went into effect.[92] This curious concept permitting rioters "peaceably to depart" would open the door to much confusion over the legal responsibilities of magistrates, soldiers, and private citizens in the suppression of riots.[93]

Henry Fielding tells us (1749) that many Englishmen resented the new law as "unconstitutional, unprecedented, ... an oppressive innovation, and dangerous to the liberty of the subject."[94] In fact, the 1714 act proved to be the opposite of oppressive. First, it acted mostly as a deterrent to disorder; in the Jacobite crisis of 1714–15, there was never any Whig talk of setting up an "oppressive" police force to apprehend those who broke the new riot law. Second, Fielding could find only two prosecutions under the act in its thirty-four-year history. In subsequent eighteenth-century cases, prosecution of rioters was blocked or convictions even overturned when it was proven that a phrase, or even a word, was omitted during the reading of the proclamation, or indeed that the reading was not audible to the crowd.[95] Third, the act operated, in the words of Chief Justice Mansfield in 1780, as "a step *in terrorem* of gentleness; the reading of the proclamation operates as a notice." As T. A. Critchley has noted, the one-hour "'cooling off' period" worked in "a characteristically British way": It warned the crowd of imminent danger and allowed the innocent plenty of time to go home or, in the act's words, "to their lawful Business." That the Government felt it could permit sixty minutes to elapse before moving in the soldiers tells us much about the legitimacy of riot and the behavior of "mobs" in eighteenth-century England. Far from legalizing bloody repression, the Riot Act established a ritualized procedure of crowd control that in effect afforded constitutional protection to English rioters.[96]

The Riot Act was not extended to Ireland until 1787 (see Chapter 3, Section III). In 1715, as again in 1745, Catholic Ireland, groaning under the penal laws, showed no interest in aiding Stuart pretenders to the English throne. By not intervening in England's politics, Ireland surely escaped a fresh round of repression. But ironically, Ireland also escaped the protections of the new Riot Act. In Ireland after 1715, there was in law no formal reading of the proclamation, no warning to the innocent to stand clear, no one-hour hiatus before repression. If riot law went unamended, a lengthening string of statutes in Ireland prescribed the death penalty for Whiteboy offenses. Provisions in the Irish Riot Act of 1787 would add more agrarian crimes to the capital code.[97]

Magistrates, military, and mobs

"It is so purely English, perhaps the most distinctively English part of all our governmental organization," Maitland wrote of the English local magistracy. The office granted great discretionary powers to the JPs in the towns and across the countryside of England. These "rulers of the county," as the Webbs called them, took no orders from London, nor did the Government seek to issue any.[98] Recent research has challenged the traditional view of the eighteenth century English JP as a boor or tyrant, drunk or womanizer. Most magistrates belonged to the lesser gentry, a level below the county elite, and were men of some competence as well as property, education, and philanthropy.[99]

With the shiring of the Irish counties had come the English system of local magistrates, but the nature of Irish society and demography dictated that the Irish JPs in education, property, and status were poor, "contemptible" cousins to the English. Magistrates had to be Protestant, and throughout rural Ireland there were never enough Protestants, let alone ones of substance. In modern England the work of the magistracy could be intimidating due to the legal complexities and paperwork: There was "heaped upon them such an infinite variety of business, that few care to understand, and fewer understand, the office."[100] In Ireland, the work tended to be intimidating because active JPs found themselves targets for popular retribution. Lord Norbury could colorfully describe Tipperary JPs (in 1811) as "driven from their public affairs in terror and dismay, with a volley of shots fired at them in the noon day."[101]

In about the year 1800 there were some 4,000 commissioned magistrates in each country. In England perhaps only a fifth of the JPs, or 800 men, were both legally competent and active on a regular basis.[102] The Irish rolls were especially padded. Dublin Castle officials discovered in 1815 that of 4,175 commissioned JPs, in fact only half, or 1,952 men, were alive (!), living in Ireland, and serving as magistrates. Of these perhaps about 400 were reliable, useful magistrates.[103] These 1,200 active JPs in the two countries were very unevenly distributed. In England the JPs were concentrated in the rural south, away from the burgeoning mining and industrial areas of the Midlands and North. The situation was the same in Ireland, where most of them lived in the anglicized and commercialized areas of east Ulster, Leinster, and east Munster. Extensive and populous districts in both countries were thinly policed. This highly uneven distribution of unpaid amateur local magistrates was the price paid by a system that resisted central and even rational control.

Eighteenth-century magistrates had, in theory, several kinds of physical force, or bodies of men, available for use against crowds. They had the authority by ancient statutes to raise the "power of the county" (*posse comitatus*) against any sudden commotions; in practice, the posse was a "loyal" mob of respectable farmers and gentry posed against a plebeian one.[104] But there were problems: Mobilization was only occasional, had to be specially arranged, and presupposed an individual's assent to service. In Ireland, the posse was also hampered by the paucity of loyalists and men of property; and even those so inclined served under the threat of physical harm from the generally hostile peasantry.[105]

There were similar constraints on the use of the militia. In theory, the English militia, commanded by gentlemen of property and filled with freeborn Englishmen, was the soundest constitutional force for repression. In practice, as J. R. Western has noted, "the arming of the manhood of the nation at large by a regime which was fairly liberal and yet not democratic was bound to be a delicate operation." Government attempts to embody the English militia at the outset of the Seven Years War triggered widespread riots against compulsory service. In Ireland in 1793, a similar attempt to raise a militia that included Catholics produced large-scale resistance and much bloodshed. In either case, the part-time militiamen had local ties and interests that could shape, even determine, the outcome of riotous protest. After a wartime experiment in 1811–15 with the interchange of English and Irish militias, the Government disbanded the militias rather than use them as peacekeeping forces in peacetime. Some of the reasons were discussed by the author of an 1833 law article on "The Suppression of Riots":

The people should learn to regard the executors of the law as *altogether distinct from the law itself*, to consider their actions as *altogether mechanical* and *independent of the merits and demerits of the law*, and in terms of riot to regard them as solely endeavoring to re-establish order, without any reference to the cause from which the disturbance arose. How this notion can gain ground, if ... militia, or any persons principally interested in the causes of disturbance, are themselves to repress it, we are at a loss to conceive.[106]

Throughout the eighteenth century, Englishmen lived with an uncomfortable paradox: A standing army was constitutionally odious yet seemingly necessary. "Our laws," wrote Blackstone in 1768, "know no such state as that of a perpetual standing soldier, bred up to no other profession than that of war." Standing armies were "temporary excrescences bred out of the distemper of the state." Blackstone, like his contemporaries, was reacting to both the abuses of military power of the later Stuart period and the growth of huge peacetime armies on the Continent. In England the army had grown from 2,000 in 1670 to 30,000 under James II. This military buildup and the use of soldiers as "an armed police acting under the direct orders of the Crown" came to a crashing halt in 1688 when Englishmen, in the words of the mid-Victorian military historian Charles Clode, "did – what any Free People would do ..., namely, they got rid both of the Dynasty and the Army."[107] The Glorious Revolution brought the army under the control of Parliament, and its peacetime force was kept at 17,000 men. By contrast, in mid-eighteenth-century France, where (according to Blackstone) "the main principle of their constitution ... is that of governing by fear," the army's peacetime strength was about 150,000 men. Austria maintained an army of 100,000, and tiny Prussia 80,000.[108]

Constitutional niceties were not fussed over in Ireland. "I presume," noted Robert Peel in 1817, that "there has always been a Standing Army in Ireland from the Reign of Henry the 2d." The Norman invasion was followed by Tudor military subjugation; "the first Legislative notice" of the army in Ireland was a statute of Henry VII concerning the provisioning of his troops "in time of hostility." A military presence was necessary for several reasons: to suppress a succession of Irish rebellions from the 1570s to the 1690s; to protect England's western island from becoming a strategic base for unfriendly powers, notably Catholic Spain and France; and to act as a peacetime police force. From the 1760s on, the army served as the chief suppressor of agrarian crime. Magistrates and troops "conducted innumerable sweeps through the countryside" against the Whiteboys of 1761–5 and would do so again, repeatedly, in subsequent agitations. "If it were not for the army," General Cunningham told Parliament in 1785, "that House would have been long ago tarred and feathered; and the Kilkenny whiteboys would have ravaged the whole country."[109] If England had an army of 17,000, Ireland, only half as populous, required one of 12,000, raised after 1769 to 15,000. A higher proportion of soldiers on the English establishment, perhaps one-third as compared to one-fifth in Ireland, were on service abroad.[110]

English constitutionalism required that soldiers be quartered among the population. In Blackstone's words, there must be "no separate camp, no barracks, no *inland* fortresses." After 1688, the first barrack was not erected until 1722, and then it was at Berwick-on-Tweed, a coastal town on the Scottish border. From the 1740s on, more were built, but again at coastal, predominantly southern coastal sites. Even this development was viewed with alarm. During the Seven Years War, for example, Lord Bath remarked that a proposal to build coastal forts "twenty years ago would have ruined any Minister." Until the 1790s, when the French wars began to convince the nation of the importance of security as well as liberty, most Englishmen would have agreed with a contemporary's comment in 1722. "It would be a vast Ease to the inhabitants in most great Towns if they had them everywhere," said Mr. Mackay of the barracks at Berwick, but "*English* liberty will never consent to what will seem a nest for a Standing Army."[111]

Ireland, on the other hand, was a heavily barracked country. The army, reported the *Dublin Evening Post*, was "a distinct body dwelling apart.... The military should be suffered to incorporate with the people by being diffused amongst them in private quarters as in England."[112] Dublin's Phoenix Park barracks, which could accommodate 3,000 troops, were "superior to any thing of the kind in London, or in England," indeed were "esteemed the first in Europe."[113] By 1792, there were throughout Ireland thirty-one permanent barracks, many of them in the interior, compared to the twenty-six largely coastal ones in England. Temporary barracks and military posts proliferated in Ireland. An official report of 1760 listed seventy-eight barracks of all kinds maintained by the Government; an English traveler in the late 1770s reported "barracks being built all over the island"; by 1815 the number of military "stations" was estimated at 400.[114] Army detachments moved from post to post along lightly traveled, "beautiful roads without break or hindrance," the hedges and trees cut well back to lessen opportunities for ambush. English travelers commented on the "magnificence" of Irish highways, in contrast to the narrow, poorly maintained roads of England.[115]

The military policing of crowds

In both England and Ireland, magistrates and military officers had only very general guidelines for dealing with rioters. Legal rulings were developed and applied more frequently in England, but it bears stating that law in eighteenth-century Ireland was essentially English law applied to Ireland. The Irish Whiteboy acts enumerated a large number of protest crimes as capital, but not until the first Insurrection Act (1796) did peculiarly Irish repressive legislation appear.[116] This bellweather statute, signaling the end of the moral economy in Ireland, foreshadowed the strongly coercive legislation of the nineteenth century.

At first blush, one is tempted to assume that Paddy was the object of more brutal policing than was the freeborn Englishman. One can cite the English and Anglo-Irish settlers' attitudes toward the native Irish, which found an outlet in the broad discretionary powers inherent in riot suppression (including the absence, until 1787, of the warning proclamation and the one-hour hiatus). But in fact, at least before the 1790s, official repression was relatively restrained. This was so for perhaps two reasons. First, because the magistracy was weak and the peasantry uncooperative, the military had to develop self-protective policies of restraint. Nocturnal patrol parties, often unaccompanied by magistrates, were kept well manned. A few key rules were followed: Keep the troops concentrated; never leave a soldier alone or a detachment isolated; avoid narrow defiles, bogland, or other likely places of ambush. There was even a certain tolerance for disorders: In each of the three great peasant outbursts between 1760 and 1790 the Government waited for several months before flooding the disturbed areas with soldiers.[117]

A second reason for the light repression may be that, until the 1790s, Irish protesters acted with "forebearance and circumspection." The peasantry staged very few pitched battles; they usually fled at the arrival of troops, who conducted arrests, not shooting sprees. Most of the deaths came when tiny military parties, overwhelmed by huge crowds seeking to rescue prisoners, opened fire in desperation and fear.[118] Irish protest did include torture and murder, but the incidence of such violence was low, as was the lethal repression, compared to the post-1790 period.[119] Thirty-five Rightboys were killed in all clashes in 1785–8, a figure not disproportionate to the thirteen rioters killed in the equally large-scale but chronologically much shorter English bread riots of August–November 1766.[120] This circumspect Irish collective violence came to an end in the heated 1790s, when both sides exchanged shots and a dozen or more persons were killed in a single incident. The 1793 militia riots claimed 250 lives, and at the end of the decade General Lake's brutalities and the Rebellion escalated the violence to unprecedented levels.

Fuller documentation exists for the civil–military relationship in the home country. The military in England was to be used only when "the strength of the civil power was not sufficient," a phrase that, although occurring with formulaic regularity, does assure the hegemony of civil over military authority

Magistrates, military officers, and private soldiers, as public servants and as private citizens, were liable before the law for the consequences of their actions. Early-eighteenth-century Governments were cautious in authorizing the use of soldiers in aid of the civil power. After 1688, the first recorded instance was not until 1717 in a case involving revenue collection. A legal ruling of 1721, necessitated by rioting at Taunton, authorized military aid in civil commotions but required JPs and, above all, military officers first to obtain a warrant from the Secretary at War, who was to consult with the Secretary of State. This policy was apparently followed regularly until about 1770, in part to ward off parliamentary objections that "the army was acting *ultra vires* or eroding the liberties of the state." Over this half-century the wording of the warrant underwent slight modifications, but the essential idea of not using force "unless it shall be found absolutely necessary" or "unless the Civil Magistrates shall find it necessary" remained unchanged.[121]

It was not until the widespread English food and militia riots of 1757 that the Government's system first broke down. In response to the crisis, the War Office deployed 5,200 soldiers from some twenty regiments. That summer London for the first time gave officers carte blanche in answering magistrates' call for troops: No longer was it necessary to obtain prior authorization from the War Office. Nevertheless, despite the extent of the disorders, no troops were furnished on mere anticipation of riot and the number of violent clashes was not large.[122] In 1766 an even larger wave of bread disturbances, the century's greatest before 1795, swept through sixty-eight towns in twenty counties, principally in the southwest. The Secretary at War William Wildman, Viscount Barrington, again permitted magistrates to employ troops without London's prior approval. The War Office despatched Lieutenant-Colonel Warde, commanding parts of four regiments, to establish a military headquarters in the west. The troops made over 200 arrests and, toward the end of the crisis, in a most uncharacteristic statement, a harassed Barrington suggested that magistrates deal roughly with any mob rescue attempts, "and the more roughly it is done the better.... Some bloody heads would be a real kindness to humanity." The riots produced thirteen crowd deaths, eight of them in a single, "stubbornly contested fight" at Kidderminster.[123] Generally, however, the troops were on orders to avoid confrontations. Overall, in Tony Hayter's opinion, "the clashes and bloodshed in and out of the West Country seem proportionately light for such a widespread, prolonged, and bitter outbreak." The disturbances of 1766 did reconfirm local magistrates' power to call in troops at their own discretion. They did so at their own legal peril, of course, as the Wilkes Riots (1768) would make clear, but their right to do so was established.[124]

Operating without modern riot control handbooks and with no training in crowd psychology, the eighteenth-century authority figure had to be guided by his own common sense and legal and moral judgment. At precisely what point was the magistrate to call out the troops or allow the use of firearms? When the crowd appeared threatening? When stones or brickbats were hurled? When property damage began, or when it became extensive? If the JP was too slow to repel force with force, he might be indicted for neglect of duty; if he acted impulsively, he was liable for use of excessive force.

The two most famous cases before the Gordon Riots – those of John Porteous, captain of the Edinburgh City Guard, and of Samuel Gillam, a London magistrate – illustrate the legal principles involved. In 1737, Porteous ordered soldiers to fire on a disorderly mob protesting the controversial hanging of a notorious smuggler. Seventeen persons were killed and wounded. A jury convicted Porteous of murder and sentenced him to death; Porteous appealed but, before his case was heard, the Edinburgh mob dragged him from jail and lynched him.[125] A generation later, in London, Samuel Gillam was one of many magistrates who tried to keep order during the turbulent Wilkesite years, 1763–8. Two weeks of almost continuous riots came to a head on 10 May 1768 when a huge crowd gathered in St. George's Fields to escort the radical MP, John Wilkes, from prison to Parliament. Under extreme provocation, magistrate Gillam finally ordered the troops to fire. Six fell dead, another fifteen wounded. A jury indicted Gillam and one soldier for murder; each was acquitted.[126] Porteous and Gillam had both authorized use of the ultimate weapon, lethal force against rioters: One man paid with his life, the other was indicted for murder. In the Gordon Riots of 1780 the Mayor of the City of London would learn that the other extreme of behavior, negligence in taking action against mobs, could also place a man at legal peril.

Military officers and common soldiers faced a kind of double jeopardy: They were responsible to civil as well as military law. "The soldier," commented a legal authority in 1833, might be "condemned before the court of his regiment, although his only crime was a refusal to obey his officer and fire upon a mob, when that act would have rendered him, in the eyes of a common jury, liable to conviction for murder." Maj.-Gen. Sir Charles Napier, who would be responsible for policing the Chartists in 1839–41, stated the dilemma in a famous and colorful passage:

Such a principle dissolves the army at once; it reduces the soldier to a choice between the hanging awarded him by the local [civil] law for obeying his officer, and the shooting awarded him by the military law for disobeying his officer!!! In such law there is neither sense nor justice and (being one of those unlucky redcoated gents thus agreeably placed between shooting and hanging) I beg to enter my protest against this choice of deaths.[127]

Napier's understandable frustration was the price to be paid for keeping troops answerable to the civil law affecting all Englishmen. If crowds were expected to operate within certain social and legal parameters of protest, so magistrates and soldiers, aware of their own legal responsibilities and liabilities, had to curb any tendency either to ignore or to bloody a crowd.

Military behavior and tactics

Bloodshed resulting from the confrontation of military with mob was rare. Those incidents that have splashed their way into history books were atypical; they have distorted our picture of the realities of crowd control. In fact, fatalities came only when the military assumed what Tony Hayter has called the "unlimited offensive" role.[128]

A look at two incidents from England in the 1760s – a little-known militia riot at Hexham and the celebrated Wilkes affair in London – reveals how blood could be spilled when the harassed authorities turned, after other tactics had failed, to the tactic of last resort. At Hexham in 1761, the crowd, which was trying to get the militia ballot lists from magistrates, was apparently strengthened by earlier victories at two nearby towns where the JPs had been "terrorised" into surrendering their ballot lists. The Hexham crowd was large – 8,000 persons – and "made no secret of their murderous intentions." The regimental commander filed this report: "No words would pacify them. The Riot Act was read *several times*, all to no purpose. The mob came to the very points of the bayonets endeavouring to break in upon our men, who bore the greatest insults for *over two hours*. At last they were commanded to fire." Twenty-one rioters fell dead. Two soldiers were killed: Ensign Hart, "shot ... in the confusion by our own men," and an unnamed private, shot by the mob. Hart and three privates were later discovered to have been struck by pistol balls from the mob. Excepting the Gordon Riots, the affair at Hexham was the bloodiest in eighteenth-century England.[129]

The Wilkes Riots of 1768 are well known; less so the scenario culminating in bloodshed. During most of the disorders the Government kept the troops off the streets. Parading of soldiers was avoided; citizen requests that cavalry be quartered in nearby inns were denied as provocative to the crowds. Few JPs, in fact, called for military assistance. Against a background of recurrent disorder in the metropolis since March, the stage was set for the bloodshed of 10 May.[130] About noon, after an hour of stone throwing by a large crowd at St. George's Fields outside Wilkes's prison, magistrate Daniel Ponton read the Riot Act proclamation for the first time. Shortly afterward, four soldiers from the 3d Infantry, an unpopular and predominantly Scottish regiment, broke ranks to chase "a young man whose behavior they thought particularly insulting." The chase, a long and heated one, ended with an innocent man being shot and killed. At 1 o'clock, another JP, Samuel Gillam, informed the crowd outside King's Bench Prison that the Riot Act's one-hour waiting period had expired. The people protested as Gillam read the proclamation again. Between 2 and 3 o'clock, Gillam reappeared to tell the crowd, now swollen to 40,000 persons, that the Riot Act had twice been read and "that they were every soul liable to be taken up." The crowd responded with volleys of stones against the hated Scots soldiers. "For God's sake, good people, go away," exhorted Gillam. "If I see any more stones thrown I will order the guards to fire." At this point a stone struck Gillam with such force that he reeled backward. He then told the officer to order his men to fire. Even now Gillam stated his fear for casualties, but the commanding officer assured him, "You may depend upon it, there is no mischief done, because we always fire in the air." The firing resulted in six persons killed and fifteen wounded, the casualties coming at a distance from the line of firing. Government and people were both shaken by the brief, bloody incident, some three hours after the Riot Act had first been read. But for a time the crowds thinned and rioting diminished in the metropolis.[131]

The authorities' trump card, "unlimited" military violence, was seldom played. "On the whole," concludes Hayter of the army's role, "few lives were lost when it is remembered how widespread rioting" was in eighteenth-century England.[132] Restraint on the part of crowds was matched by that of the Government, the magistrates, and the military. Cavalrymen armed with sabers, 14-inch pistols, and 27-inch short carbines, and infantry soldiers with muskets effective to 300 feet and accurate to half that distance, seldom used them and, even more rarely, with lethal effect.[133] The military was certainly placed in a difficult situation. Called out on riot duty, the men were in fact schooled only in drill maneuvers for warfare on foreign soil. By force of circumstances, sometimes without a supportive magistracy and always in the absence of police forces, the eighteenth-century army had to act as a domestic police. To do so effectively, it had to develop self-disciplined, discretionary crowd control tactics that Hayter has described by the terms "control," "defensive," and "limited offensive."[134]

A crowd was frequently overawed simply by the arrival or the parading of troops; sometimes the rumor of soldiers coming was sufficient to scatter a crowd. Chase and arrest, another *control* tactic, seldom eventuated in bloodshed. Officers' speeches, like magistrate Gillam's at St. George's Fields, sometimes placated a crowd. A newspaper editor during the Wilkes disorders commented "how easy it is to appease the rage of a tumultuous mob by giving them good words." One officer told a throng that "he should be sorry to fight against his countrymen"; another gentlemanly commander "pathetically exhorted them not to put either his humanity or his duty to so severe a trial as to oblige him to proceed to extremities." Some officers arranged meetings with representatives from the crowd. For others, the disincentive to violence was the very honor of arms: It would be disdainful to sully military glory by bloodying a mob. Among the private soldiers there was, equally, little predisposition to bully a crowd. The eighteenth-century soldier – drawn from the lowest classes, serving on long enlistment (reduced to eleven years only in 1847), and subject to flogging for petty offenses[135] – was in a sense of the crowd, not against it. As one guardsman announced during the Wilkes Riots, "We are all ready to fire on our enemies the French and Spaniards but never will on our own countrymen." It is perhaps significant that the soldiers who fired the lethal volleys in London on 10 May 1768 were Scotsmen who had endured for hours the taunts of the English crowd.[136]

When a crowd developed into a riot, the military usually responded by shifting to *defensive* tactics. The men would guard buildings or property, or stand their ground against the mob. Against showers of insults and stones, sometimes for fairly long periods, officers would counsel the men to stand firm, even to be contemptuous of the crowd. If no JPs were present, officers often felt legally constrained not to act on their own; on the occasions when a magistrate was present, the magistrate sometimes hesitated to employ the soldiers, who thus continued to bear the crowd's taunts or violence. By definition, this difficult stage was a temporary one, and if the crowd did not withdraw or, as sometimes happened, the military did not depart in some disgust, the confrontation usually moved to the next stage.[137]

The *limited offensive* was the most commonly used tactic for dispersing crowds in eighteenth-century England. The soldiers moved against rioters but sought to inflict minimal casualties. The tactic could assume many forms. Infantry would advance or cavalry wade into the throng. If weapons were authorized, the men were most often told to use only the flat side of their swords, or the stock of their muskets as truncheons. Saber cutting was only infrequently resorted to, hence the outrage over the Yeomanry's behavior at Peterloo (1819). If the use of firearms was authorized, the soldiers might take aim but not actually fire; or, if ordered to fire, the men usually fired high, individual soldiers doing so from either compassion or contempt for the crowd. Given the number of occasions over the century when troops fired on rioters and the very low rate of crowd deaths, we must conclude that high firing was a prevalent practice. Certainly, as we have seen, there were times when firing, high or low, was lethal; but even then, we must note, never in London, not even during the Gordon Riots, did the authorities move to the next stage of using heavy artillery or cannon against crowds, as was done in Paris in 1795 and again in 1871.[138]

In conclusion, the military was routinely employed "in aid of the civil power." This constitutional, if somewhat empty, phrase referred to the magistrate or two who might be on the spot and to the parish constables and watchmen in the neighborhood. By default, the soldiers in time of crisis had to function as a surrogate civil power. For a number of reasons, they made a poor police. The men were rarely on site, but instead had to march to a disturbance. Before the era of railroads, a military unit was fortunate in fair weather to advance 15 miles a day; in 1768 one regiment on the march took six days, including one rest day, to travel the 70 miles from Exeter to Bristol. Communications from magistrates in large towns to the Secretary of State in London went faster – the Bath-to-London coach took twenty-nine hours in 1765 – but news from villages and remote districts took far longer, and it could be several days before a reply from London was received.[139] Once on the spot, troops had to wait on the magistracy before they could be employed. Officers and men lacked training in crowd control. The soldiers' accoutrements proved to be little help: The bulky weapons impeded movement and were useful only as a final resort. Use of the flats of sabers and of high firing was simply an acknowledgment of the inutility of the military's weaponry. Moreover, cavalry, although highly suitable for pursuit in the countryside, were much less effective in the crowded streets of a town; and if infantry were slightly better for urban chases, the heavily burdened foot soldiers lost many races across open fields. Standing above all was the stark fact that officer and common soldier alike disliked riot duty. "There was no profit or glory in it, but rather a good chance of being insulted in the press, attacked in Parliament or pursued in a court of law for his actions."[140]

IV. Police

The word itself was strange to Englishmen. A French visitor to London about 1720 remarked on the disorder in the streets, "and asking about the Police, but finding none that understood the Term, he cried out Good Lord! how can one expect Order among these People, who have no such Word as Police in their Language." Englishmen boasted of this gap in their vocabulary. The French word *police*, sniffed Lord Chesterfield in 1756, "we have been obliged to adopt, not having, as they say, the thing." In 1763, in a letter to the *Public Advertizer*, "Tom Tipsey," a true-born Briton if ever there was one, reported that

the Word *Police* has made many bold Attempts to get a Footing ... but as neither the Word nor the Thing itself are [sic] much understood in London, I fancy it will require a considerable Time to bring it into Fashion; ... from an Aversion to the French, ... English Prejudices will not soon be reconciled to it.

Jonas Hanway in 1780 stated the case perhaps most succinctly: "The nature of our constitution will not admit of a *police*."[141]

When Englishmen did use the word, they were referring to the general regulation or government, the morals or economy, of a city or country. The French word derived from the Greek *polis*, the root base of the words "politics," "polity," and "policy." Frenchmen used the word as a subject noun, as in *la police de Paris*, or as an object, as in *faire la police*, "to keep order"; and as a transitive verb, *policer*, meaning to bring order to, organize, or civilize (a place). In England, Adam Smith noted in 1763, the imported French word "properly signified the policy of civil government, but *now* means the regulation of the inferior parts of government, viz.: cleanliness, security [the modern definition], and cheapness or plenty [i.e., the police of grain]." William Blackstone in 1765 detected the same trend toward a narrower definition. Beginning in the 1770s, the word appears in a number of English pamphlets in reference to the maintenance of order and the prevention of crime. Hanway wrote on *The Defects of Police* (1775) in London; his tract was reprinted in 1780 as *The Citizen's Monitor: Shewing the necessity of a Salutary Police*. Sir William Blizard offered *Desultory Reflections on Police* (1785). And J. Aikin, in his guide to *Manchester* (1795), could report that "the police of the town is managed by two constables."[142]

From this point, it was only a short step to the modern English definition of "police" as a body of men. Apparently the first such usage was by John Fielding in 1758 in his pamphlet, *An Account of the Origins and Effects of a Police Set on Foot by His Grace the Duke of Newcastle in the Year 1753*. The author of a tract written in 1774 against a proposal to reform the London magistracy also used the word in its new sense; the writer, who signed himself "A Friend to Justice and the English Constitution," was strongly opposed to the creation of any "officers of police, or by whatever other new-fangled name they may be called."[143] The new usage was slow to catch on. The term itself appears rarely in the London police bill of 1785 and the Dublin police act of 1786, though in both the French-derived phrase "Commissioners of Police" makes it first appearance. The first popular usage of "police" as a term referring to a body of men came in Dublin in 1786, though the men themselves retained the official titles of "constable" and "watchman." Peel's Irish police of 1814, the "Peelers," was legally titled the "Peace Preservation Force," and the "policemen" were officially constables and subconstables. Similarly, in regard to the Irish constabulary of 1822, as a witness told a parliamentary committee, "the term police, as applied to the constables, is, in fact, a popular word, which I believe is not in the Acts of Parliament."[144] In England the earliest statutory use of the word to refer to a body of men is the Thames River Police of 1800. In Peel's Metropolitan Police Act of 1829 the men were still called "constables," not "policemen." Edwin Chadwick, writing in 1830, used the word in its new and its old sense:

Before considering the formation of a general municipal police on the model of the new police it may be as well to ascertain how much has really been accomplished by the new police establishment in the Metropolis. . . . By the substitution of a body of stout active men, men who are well clothed and lodged and so well paid as to be well fed . . ., by placing this body under one central management, with gradations of rank so as to preserve discipline, and give the means of combined and systematic exertion, a considerable improvement has already been made in the police of the Metropolis.[145]

The concept of the police as a force of men was still sufficiently novel that throughout the 1830s Peel's creation was known simply as "the New Police."

In the same fashion, the word "constable" took on new meaning. Originally in England a Norman term for a high-ranking military position, the term later was used to signify the civil officer of a parish or hundred. Its modern definition, as a member of a large, uniformed civil force, may be traced to the police of Dublin and four Irish counties in 1786–7. Members of all subsequently established forces in Ireland and England were known as "constables"; indeed, the Irish rural police had the novel rank of "subconstable."[146] Unlike "constable," a constitutional word of long usage in England, the word "constabulary" had a distinctly foreign, threatening ring to it. In its meaning of a large civil force of men to keep the peace, the word entered the language only as late as 1822 and then through England's backdoor, Ireland. The term appeared in the parliamentary debates on the Irish constables' bill of that year; Peel attributed the word to the Irish Chief Secretary, Charles Grant, and noted that "the Irish Papers" were quick to seize on the phrase "Constabulary Act" because of its despotic connotations.[147] The word made its first official appearance in England with Chadwick's *Constabulary Report* of 1839. Here, too, English radicals seized on the word as a term of opprobrium, and when Whig ministers framed the legislation creating the new optional county police they wisely avoided using the word "constabulary," selecting instead the less threatening name "County" or "Rural Police."[148]

Explaining the historic hostility to police

In their opposition to the idea of police, Englishmen constantly cited their historic liberties and, by contrast, deplored French despotism and centralization. English liberty was as continuously commented on by foreign visitors as it was boasted about by Englishmen. "Even the populace," noted a Frenchman in 1725, "will give you to understand that there is no country where such perfect freedom may be enjoyed as in England." In 1787 a German visitor observed that "the great difference" between people in England and the rest of Europe "proceeds entirely from the liberty which they enjoy.... No nation can boast of having for so long a period of time possessed so many social and political blessings." In 1789, after the fall of the Bastille, a citizen group in Dijon wrote to thank English well wishers by noting the centenary of England's Glorious Revolution: "In securing their own happiness, Englishmen have prepared the way for that of the Universe."[149]

In their discussions of police and liberty it was natural for Englishmen to make the comparison to France. France was the most populous and hegemonic state in Europe. It was Albion's neighbor and historic enemy. And it was the pioneer, or model, of the police state. What was behind Englishmen's equation of police with despotism in *French* society? That France was a Catholic country was certainly not a happy fact in English eyes: The clergy were a privileged order within the state, and Protestantism had been outlawed (1685) in the same decade that Englishmen had wrested their liberties from the Catholic James II. Second, there were the contrasts in government. English government, "essentially local, both in feeling and in organization," was the work of gentlemen amateurs; French government was centralized and staffed largely by professionals and bureaucrats. In the thirty provinces of France, salaried royal officials, the *intendants*, responsible only to Versailles, discharged a wide variety of functions. By contrast, in the 15,000 parishes and 40 counties of England, a host of locally appointed private individuals performed myriad separate duties; justices of the peace were reprimanded for seeking advice too frequently from London.[150]

But the differences went beyond the contrast of government in France being the work of "specialized executive officers" and in England of "unspecialized civic ... laymen."[151] These authority figures symbolized the different nature of political legitimacy in the two countries. In France all authority still resided with the King; in England, law making and enforcement originated with the people. The English Parliament, since the Glorious Revolution of 1688, served as the custodian of the nation's liberties. Though decidedly unrepresentative of the population, Parliament was elected, met annually, debated national issues, and passed all laws. Representative government was far less developed in France. Some provincial estates and *parlements* (law courts) continued to meet, but the last national *parlement* had met as far back as 1615. The nature of the law was different, too. English law was "common" to the nation; French law made distinctions for persons in the different social orders. Likewise, national taxation in England required parliamentary approval and was shared among the classes, certainly more so than in France, where the burden fell disproportionately on the unprivileged classes. For a number of reasons, France's political system found little favor not only with the average free-born Englishman but also with the rulers of eighteenth-century England, the nobility and gentlemen of broad acres. In France the monarchy controlled the people, and, even more to the point, Versailles had tamed the aristocracy.

When the English workingman, tradesman, or gentleman associated "police" with France and equated policing with executive tyranny, what he objected to was not simply that the Paris police or *maréchaussée* did sinister things but also that they did what the central government told them to do. The police was a part of state paternalism in France. As Alan Williams has recently reminded us, policing in *ancien régime* France had positive as well as negative functions: the regulation of health, welfare, and the marketplace, as well as spying and censorship. The problem, for Englishmen, was that in heavily policed France the two seemed to go hand in hand, the good with the bad. Good order existed in France, but at the price of liberty; in England, a certain disorderliness appeared to be inherent in the condition of liberty. Was it impossible to have order *and* liberty? Visiting Frenchmen noted that Englishmen believed they had to make the choice. The Abbé le Blanc reported in 1737 that the English said they "had rather be robb'd ... by wretches of desperate fortune than by ministers." In 1814, the Duc de Lévis, when asking Englishmen why they had no force like the *maréchaussée*, invariably encountered the reply: "Such an institution is incompatible with liberty." Yet another French visitor, in 1811, found this English attitude so pervasive that he noted in some disgust: "All I can say is that the glory of having no police at all, seems easier to acquire than the glory of developing a good one."[152]

Most Englishmen dismissed out of hand the desirability of establishing a powerful police in their own country. Even the great police reformers, Henry and John Fielding and Patrick Colquhoun, steered clear of recommending the creation of a large, salaried, professional police force. One of the few eighteenth-century Englishmen to see any good in such an institution was Sir William Mildmay. In his book, *The Police of France* (1763), Mildmay marveled at the efficiency of the Paris foot and horse police, who by "the quickness of their circulation" deter criminals and "effectually suppress" rioters. Yet, for all its praise of the French police, Mildmay's work is most interesting for its theme of the tension between liberty and authority. He found that "the inhabitants of Paris are protected, day and night, by a guard of armed and disciplined watchmen," yet felt compelled to add, "if being so watched may be called a protection." He reported that police were stationed in Paris theaters, yet had to admit that "such a guard ... in the pit of any of our theatres in London, would be apt to create, rather than silence, a noise and disturbance." Throughout his book, Mildmay reminded his English readers that his "principal view in making these enquiries" was to determine whether any aspects of the French system could be applied "to reform the abuses complained of in London." His answer was essentially that it was not possible. The French police was too military, too much a creature of executive government. Mildmay came away with the conviction that, for all their merits as a preventive police, "the *maréchaussée* ... and the watch-guard at Paris ... cannot as such be imitated by our administration, under a free and civil constitution of government."[153]

English suspicions about the police were a product not only of foreign observation but also of their own history. Memories of the seventeenth-century standing armies of Oliver Cromwell and the later Stuart kings made eighteenth-century Englishmen wary of the whole notion of armed, paid servants of the Crown. In particular, most remembered was that Cromwell had fashioned his New Model Army into a domestic police. Financed by a tax on royalists' estates, this "novel and arbitrary" scheme of 1655–7 represented the Puritans' attempt to implement their revolutionary program against widespread resistance. Only a few years after his conquest of Ireland, Cromwell divided England into twelve military districts (two being the City of London, and Westminster and Middlesex) and placed each under the control of a "Major-General."[154] Cromwell's 6,200-man cavalry police busied itself with politics and morals, as well as crime prevention. The police nabbed vagrants, highwaymen, and footpads; collected taxes and initiated a nationwide registration of householders; supervised poor relief; monitored alehouses and suppressed gaming establishments; and generally encouraged the promotion of "godliness and virtue." This evangelical constabulary banned a wide array of popular pleasures: bear baitings and cockfights, horse racing and prize fighting, dancing, drunkenness, swearing, singing, and theater going. (Cromwell's dour bid to "improve" lower-class manners was to find a distant echo in the "missionary" duties of the new police in the 1840s.) But the effort to secure the postmonarchical new order by enforcing the gospel of virtue failed due to its own heavy-handedness. Early in 1657 Cromwell's own Parliament voted the police experiment out of existence. The ephemeral Cromwellian innovation did, however, produce an important legacy: "memories of oppression which had not been forgotten in Peel's day."[155] Cromwell's police, followed as it was by the standing armies of the later Stuart kings, had taught eighteenth-century Englishmen to value liberty over authority, freedom over control. Standing armies and police became national bugbears.

Police in eighteenth-century England and Ireland

The police of the towns, villages, and countryside of England was in the hands of the high constables and parish constables. Appointment to these offices, established respectively in the reigns of Edward I and Edward III, lay with "an infinitely complex and confused network" of courts leet, liberties, and parish vestries; and also, since 1662, with any two county magistrates. Service was for a year, renewable, and not well paid. By the mid-eighteenth century the high constable, responsible for the hundred (several parishes), had become mostly an inspector (of roads, buildings) and rate collector.[156] To the petty constables of the parish and township fell the task of keeping the local community orderly and honest. Constables were to appoint watchmen as "regulated by the custom of the place," to keep "watch and ward ... in order to apprehend rioters, and robbers," and to issue the hue and cry to rouse the townspeople against criminals. Among a constable's myriad routine duties was to settle quarrels, control drunkenness, arrest sabbath breakers, break up affrays and unlawful assemblies, nab vagrants, assist with relief of the poor, and enforce wage, market, and trade regulations.[157]

The quality of the men and their work is now a matter of some debate. Traditional accounts have dismissed the constables and watchmen as bumbling characters like Shakespeare's Dogberry and Verges – inept or corrupt men, "at best illiterate fools."[158] Recent scholars, looking beyond "upper-class complaints and playwrights' jibes," paint a more favorable picture.[159] Parish constables were from the lower orders but were not paupers; many were sober, hard-working, often literate, even honest. The system appears to have worked better than was previously believed; where it broke down, as evidenced by the rise of Improvement Act commissions,[160] was in the larger towns and the fast-growing northern industrial cities at the end of the century. The chief merit of this highly localized system was that it operated through "bonds of kinship, friendship, and neighborliness." Constables preferred to admonish or counsel rather than arrest and prosecute. Law enforcement was highly individualistic and discretionary, not bureaucratic and rigid. Constables had to be responsive to the values of the "moral communities," of which they were a part, and the needs of the law, which they were charged to enforce.[161]

This ancient system, which "slumbered on" in the rural districts and was not dramatically changed in the towns,[162] was characterized by an ongoing tension between local and Crown imperatives. But in this boisterous, self-policed society the tension often resulted in accommodation. It could hardly have been otherwise because the state or "yeoman elite" had no exogenous power, no force of men recruited from outside the parish, to enforce the law in the parishes. The constables were probably most effective in the area of moral, misdemeanor policing; restricted in number and jurisdiction, they were less useful in cases involving serious crimes or large-scale public disturbances. From the Government's perspective, the problem in the old parish system was not so much the men as the system itself, with its popular base, separate local jurisdictions, and want of sufficient numbers of law enforcement officers.

Conquest and colonization resulted in the introduction of English laws and institutions to Ireland. Common and statute law was applied as far as possible; the Statute of Winchester (1285) was legally extended to Ireland as early as 1308. By the close of the Tudor period, most of the island had been shired, that is, divided into counties, and each county divided into baronies (analogous to the English hundreds) and the baronies into parishes. Fourteenth- and fifteenth-century statutes provided for "wardens of the peace," the later justices of the peace, in every barony and for constables in every town and parish.[163] The intent was to create, as in England, a "self-policed society,"[164] complete with hue and cry and collective fines for lawless parishes, baronies, or even counties.[165]

Local policing was performed by high and petty constables. The baronial High Constable, since 1733 appointed by the county grand jury, served a one-year nonrenewable term, and as in England performed largely administrative duties, principally the collection of the county cess.[166] For centuries, the petty constables in the parishes were named by the feudal courts leet and sheriffs' tourns. By the early eighteenth century, many of these appointments were made irregularly or neglected entirely; and of those appointed, apparently some were Catholics. Two acts sought to redress these problems. One of 1715 barred "papists" from serving and made all appointments subject to appraisal by the county grand juries. A subsequent act of 1749, analogous to the English act of 1662, authorized justices of the peace to make constable appointments as needed.[167] The JPs already had the power to appoint the parish nightwatch, an institution that in rural Ireland never developed an importance comparable to that of town-dotted England.[168] Irish policing at mid-century was thus marked by two trends: one, a sustained effort at Protestantization; and two, transfer of control of the high and petty constables from locally prominent individuals and ancient feudal institutions to county authorities, the grand juries and JPs.

A third trend was toward the enlargement of police jurisdiction. The scarcity of Protestants, the exclusion of Catholics, and the persistence of those animosities peculiar to Irish society prevented the imported English system of "neighborly" self-policing from working well in parishes in Ireland. Moreover, some parish business was hard to conduct because, unlike England, civil and ecclesiastical parishes in Ireland were not coterminous and some boundaries spilled over into the next county. For these reasons, in 1773, a small police experiment was initiated at the next highest jurisdictional level, the barony. The *county* grand jury was to appoint four "subconstables" to assist the head constable in every barony or half-barony; in 1783, the number of baronial subconstables was raised to eight. The men had to be Protestants, in conformity with the act 2 Anne, c. 6, and were paid £2 p.a. from a special police tax levied by new tax collectors and their deputies. The police were to assist magistrates and the existing parish constables in executing warrants, collecting revenues, and preserving the peace at assizes, elections, and "at all times in such county."[169]

This new "corps of conservators of the Peace, . . . peculiar to Ireland," was not, however, widely adopted. Full implementation in the island's 316 baronies would have raised 2,500 constables; instead there were in the 1780s only about 600 of these new policemen. The forces were "useless" in all but three or four counties, Tipperary, with sixty-six men, having the largest force. Though these baronial police forces remained largely on the drawing board, it must be said that Ireland was conceptually already forging ahead of England in cutting the local ties of police. The county-appointed Irish baronial police represented a somewhat more centralized notion of policing than the English parish-based system. "If the spirit of their Institution had been kept up to," wrote a Dublin Castle administrator in 1786, it "might have rendered a revisal of the Police Laws of this Kingdom at this time unnecessary."[170] As it was, the obscure, largely unimplemented acts of 1773 and 1783 marked the faint beginnings of the baronial police that would be established in 1787 and 1792.[171]

London

In 1780 a sprawling metropolis of more than 800,000 inhabitants, London was the largest city in Europe. Whereas Paris (pop. 600,000) was administratively unified and *bien policé*, London was a loosely administered agglomeration of small, independent political jurisdictions. In highly localized London the parish was the basic unit of government. There were some 200 parishes. Most of the parish vestries were "open," that is, run by the body of ratepayers; about one in four were "close" or "select," governed by a smaller group of men, usually the "principal inhabitants." Parish authorities were charged with the duties of street paving, lighting, and cleaning; relieving the poor; and maintaining the watch and keeping the peace. In many parishes, whether they were governed by the "rowdy direct democracy of the open vestries" (as, for example, in St. Pancras) or the "self-perpetuating exclusiveness of the select vestries" (St. George's, Hanover Square), the burden of work or the vestry's negligence had led ratepayers to obtain local acts of Parliament to provide necessary city services. Hundreds of such acts regulated metropolitan neighborhoods. In the parish of Lambeth, for example, private acts had established nine local "trusts" for lighting alone; in St. Pancras, eighteen paving trusts existed within the four-square-mile parish. By 1800, some fifty trusts maintained the turnpikes throughout the metropolis. This same multiplicity of jurisdiction was also evident in the policing of the metropolis.[172]

At the end of the eighteenth century, the metropolis contained between 3,000 to 4,000 constables and watchmen, about 1,000 of whom were petty tradesmen who served as constables, beadles, and marshals and who together formed a conglomerate daytime police force. The remainder were the night watchmen. Colquhoun in 1797 concluded that the watch of the metropolis, exclusive of the City of London, was "under the direction of no less than above seventy different trusts; regulated by perhaps double the number of local acts ... under which the *directors, guardians, governors, trustees,* or *vestries* ... are authorised to act, each attending to their own particular Ward,

Parish, Hamlet, Liberty, or Precinct." A tiny precinct or liberty had its own watch, whereas a large parish like St. Pancras had no fewer than eighteen different watch trusts. Many of the watchmen, poorly paid and encumbered with staff, rattle, and lantern, were not as aged or infirm as was traditionally credited. But for both constables and watchmen, the extreme fragmentation inherent in the system made impossible any coordination of forces or even the exchange of information.[173]

Roughly two of every five Londoners in 1780 lived in the City of Westminster or the City of London. In Westminster, the oligarchic Court of Burgesses (est. 1585), appointed by the Dean and Chapter of Westminster, had slowly been losing its powers over the police. The eighty constables were still appointed by the burgesses, but the men were increasingly being directed, fined, or removed by the City's justices of the peace. From 1735 on, the watch forces steadily came under the control of the vestries. An act of 1774 sought to regulate the Westminster watches by establishing detailed regulations and duties and by setting wages and force levels. But the act was not widely implemented or enforced, and authority over the 200 watchmen continued to be dispersed among the vestries, trustees, directors, or governors of the twelve parish watches.[174]

In the tiny City of London the police were densely concentrated. In 1780, the 150,000 inhabitants living within the City's one-square-mile jurisdiction were served by more than 1,000 constables, beadles, watchmen, and patrols. The men were comparatively well paid and generally able-bodied. But the efficiency of these men was impaired by the extreme decentralization of authority. The City Corporation maintained only a small force of twenty-three day and sixteen night patrolmen officered by six marshalsmen. All of the other men, 400 constables and 800 night watchmen, were controlled by the 26 wards formed from the City's 169 precincts. Each of the twenty-six ward common councils maintained day and night police operating within its tiny separate jurisdiction. From the 1760s on, attempts by the City Corporation, the central authority, to control these several forces came to naught.[175]

The City's policing, the *reductio ad absurdum* of the argument for local control, had a distinctly political dimension. Unlike aristocratically governed Westminster, the City of London was "a resident ratepayers' democracy," a little Switzerland of 15,000 freeman electors. The City Common Council and the ward governments were filled with men of "the lower middle class." The City Corporation, the largest legally constituted deliberative assembly outside of Parliament, was highly accountable to the people. Freeman ratepayers elected for life 26 citizens to the Board of Aldermen and annually elected the 200 humbler members of the Common Council. Historically, City politics revolved around national, not merely local, issues. The vestries and the Corporation, since Charles II's reign, had established themselves as fiercely independent of the Crown. Jealousy of their local privileges went hand in hand with their self-perceived role as custodian of the nation's liberties. City representatives regularly petitioned Parliament on the great issues of the day. For the Corporation that acted as the nation's "sounding-board of political

Radicalism," police was but one issue in politics. From the late eighteenth century on, the City democracy resisted government reform of their police on two grounds: as an extension of "executive government" and growth of "the influence of the Crown," which trampled on historic local liberties; and as a call for reform from a Parliament that itself resisted reform.[176] Not until the 1830s, the era of political reform, would the City overhaul its police; and even then, so strong was City opinion and tradition that the new City police remained steadfastly separate from Home Secretary Peel's police for the rest of the metropolis.[177]

If responsibility for the policing of London was diffused and highly localized, it was also true that the first efforts to establish a central police authority originated with concerned private individuals, not the Government. Thomas de Veil (b. 1684–d. 1746), an ex-army officer and JP for Westminster and Middlesex, was the first magistrate to assume the burden of watching over the entire metropolis. In 1729 de Veil set up his office near present-day Leicester Square; in 1738 he moved it to a house in Bow Street, Covent Garden.[178] Shortly after de Veil's death, Henry Fielding (1748–54) and then John Fielding (1754–80) filled the post of magistrate at the Bow Street Police Office. The Fieldings, Henry the novelist and his half-brother John, the blind "beak" of Bow Street, are celebrated in English history as founders of the modern London police.[179] They were in fact lonely heroes combatting crime with little help from the myriad vestry watches and little funding from an indifferent Government. They were without the support of anything resembling a modern police force. Nor did they seek one. In his pamphlet of 1750, written in response to a wave of robberies and three days of riots in the Strand, Henry Fielding railed against "the wild notions of liberty" that had condemned the civil power to "its present lethargic state," but, like most Englishmen, he also condemned "those pernicious schemes [of police] which are destructive of true liberty."[180]

Although the Fieldings never pressed the idea of a single large police force for the metropolis, they did institute three minor reforms at Bow Street. In 1750 Henry Fielding hired his first official policemen, *four* plainclothes "thief takers" – "runners," as they were called by the 1780s – and *two* "horsemen." Three years later, the Government contributed its first annual funding, the paltry sum of £600, which was cut to £400 in 1757. This tiny band of men, in existence until 1839, would be involved in a number of colorful exploits, but their impact on crime in a city the size of London was necessarily negligible. These few men, by their very nature, "more nearly resembled a . . . private detective agency than a branch of a modern police force."[181] A second reform was the short-lived experiment with a Horse Patrol, also woefully understaffed. In 1763, the same year that Mildmay published his book on the police of France, John Fielding instituted a government-financed *eight-man* "horse-patrol" to watch the highways leading into London. But twelve months later, after spending £1,014, Fielding was forced in October 1764 to abandon his project when the Government chose to cut off funding.[182]

About the third Bow Street reform – a small night foot patrol – we know even less. Scholars give a variety of dates, from 1755 to 1782, for the patrol's founding. According to Patrick Pringle, Fielding was running a number of temporary night patrols as early as 1755–9. Leon Radzinowicz cites a private foot patrol of unpaid parish constables organized by Fielding, apparently in the 1760s; in 1773 that Government began to provide a small annual subsidy of £120.[183] The force certainly could not have been large, and the patrols probably operated only intermittently. Seven years later, during the Gordon Riots, there is no mention in any contemporary records of a Bow Street foot patrol. The force seems to have been put on a regular basis after the riots; extant government records, beginning in 1782, indicate that the Bow Street patrol was paid £300 every six weeks (if in continuous service, this would be an annual cost of £2,600). The nightly patrol was not large. By 1797, when we have the first indication of its size, the Foot Patrol totaled only sixty-eight constables. The men were paid 2s., 6d. a night, and were armed with cutlasses and divided into thirteen patrol parties to monitor the streets and outlying highways of the metropolis.[184]

To sum up, the steps taken by the Government to create a police force in late-eighteenth-century London were timid and tentative. In 1780 Bow Street had six detectives and a small, loosely organized, irregularly patrolling foot patrol. A brief experiment with a horse patrol had lapsed seventeen years earlier. John Fielding was a pioneer of modern police ideas who was uncomfortable with the concept of a professional police force. He was in many ways a traditionalist. Fearful of encroachments on the individual liberties of Englishmen, Fielding saw as the best solution to crime and disorder the injection of some central control but not its bureaucratic institutionalization in the form of a police force; he looked, above all, to the rejuvenation of the existing parochial system and the encouragement of community self-policing. In June 1780, ill and in retirement, the fifty-nine-year-old Fielding must have heard with horror the news of the collapse of the traditional system and the burning of his beloved Bow Street Office in the maelstrom of the Gordon Riots. Three months later, in early September, he was dead.

A half-century would go by before the establishment of a large uniformed police force for the metropolis. The inspiration for Peel's 1829 police would be not the thief takers and patrols of Bow Street but the constabulary that Peel had helped to establish in Ireland.

Dublin

Georgian Dublin was "the second city of the British Empire" and the seventh largest in Europe. The town of 65,000 inhabitants at the turn of the century had become a city of 150,000 by 1780. Dublin was the third largest city in the British Isles after the two other capitals, London and Edinburgh; Dublin in 1780 was more than twice the size of Birmingham, Manchester, or Liverpool. The importance of the Irish capital did not rest on industry, finance, or even commerce, but rather on its position as the center of government and society in the island. Dublin's image as a city of privilege and poverty was grounded in part on its lack of productive wealth. Dublin struck Arthur Young as being founded on the rape of the countryside. An English visitor in 1807 thought the "magnificence" of the public buildings "disproportioned to the appearance of the city in other respects." Other travelers recorded similar impressions. The unrelieved rows of "low and beggarly cabins" on the outskirts "discredit the avenues, in all directions, to this great city." The lower-class districts gave evidence of "more mud, rags, and wretchedness than London can exhibit in its most miserable quarters."[185]

Dublin's population was three-fourths Catholic, but the city's government was entrusted to the exclusively Protestant Dublin Corporation. Like its parent body in London, the Corporation consisted of the Lord Mayor, Board of Aldermen, and Common Council. The Mayor was elected annually from among the aldermen. The twenty-four Aldermen, who also served as city magistrates, were elected to life terms from among a group known as "sheriffs' peers." These wealthy men, the sheriffs' peers, had to meet two requirements: past service of an annual term as one of the city's two sheriffs and a high (£2,000) net worth in property. Since 1672, Dublin Castle had restricted the independence of the Corporation by having a veto power over persons elected to the important office of sheriff.[186]

The influence of England and of property extended to the Common Council, where roughly a third of the representation (some forty-six seats) was held in perpetuity by the sheriffs' peers. However, in the 144-man Common Council, the large majority of seats were elective – two sheriffs being elected annually (and presiding over the Council) and ninety-six guild representatives elected every three years by the guilds or companies. A third (thirty-one) of the guilds' seats went to the city's merchants. The remaining two-thirds (sixty-five seats) were reserved for the skilled Protestant democracy, artisans and craftsmen from the city's two dozen guilds. Overall, these sixty-five men – tailors and shoemakers, goldsmiths, brewers, and butchers[187] – were outnumbered in the Common Council by the combined total of seventy-nine men who were sheriffs (two), sheriffs' peers (forty-six), and merchant guildsmen (thirty-one). But if representation in the Dublin Corporation excluded Catholics and favored propertied Protestants, it also offered a political voice to the Protestant artisanal class in a city still economically traditional and uninvolved in the Industrial Revolution. Although the Mayor and Aldermen were often "in subservience to the Castle," the Common Council – with its large majority of members from the guilds and almost half from the Protestant artisanal democracy – was often the scene of free and acrimonious debates.[188]

The policing of Dublin was long the duty of the city's churchwardens. But in 1715 the Corporation had taken over control of the nightwatch and in 1721 had required each of the city's twenty-one parishes to elect fifteen persons, reduced to nine in 1723, to serve as watch "directors," who were to employ and pay the watchmen. The parish vestry was also required to nominate "a suitable number" of "fit and able, ... good and sufficient housekeepers," whom the Lord Mayor then appointed as constables to oversee the watchmen. Like the watch, the constables had to be Protestants; an act of 1729 restated this point, an indication perhaps that the parish forces were not without Catholics. Constables received a salary of £10 p.a. in 1765 when the watch rate was doubled to sixpence in the pound.[189]

In 1778, the Dublin Corporation moved to centralize the watch system by grouping the city's parishes into six wards. Each of the new wards was placed under the superintendence of a "president" or "guardian," chosen by the Lord Mayor and Aldermen from among the Board of Aldermen. The ward president appointed as his deputy a person in the Common Council who resided in that ward. The deputy was a person of means, for the requirement was a net worth of £800 in real or personal estate. At another level, in the parishes comprising each ward, the Protestant "freemen" – a status conferred by a £1 annual payment – elected from six to twelve persons to form a new ward watch board. These six boards appointed the city's constables and watchmen. These men numbered in 1780 about two dozen constables and 368 watchmen in summer and 463 in winter. A watchman received £3 for summer work and £4 for winter work. The total cost of the force was £4,667, about three-quarters of this sum going for wages. The 1778 act empowered all constables and watchmen to "seize, arrest, and detain all robbers, thieves, rioters, drunken and disorderly persons, and other offenders against the peace, whom they shall find within ... their respective wards, *or shall pursue from thence into any other ward.*" The men, as well as the magistrates and aldermen, were also permitted to enter all public houses, licensed or unlicensed, at any hour of the day or night to seize suspected criminals or "idle and disorderly persons."[190]

In sum, it may be said that the police of Dublin, like that of metropolitan London, continued to be divided among day and night forces, the number of night watchmen greatly predominating. In each capital the police were understaffed and fairly ineffective. Indeed, the 400 watchmen in sprawling Dublin, a city of the same population as the City of London, were scattered much more thinly than the 800 watchmen in the one-square-mile City. Yet in organization and control, Dublin was ahead of the various parts of the English metropolis, including the City of London. Whereas the City was policed over twenty-six different wards, Dublin, though larger in area, was policed over six. Moreover, although the City of London Corporation had been unsuccessful in controlling the wards' police, the Dublin Corporation had recently created and in part controlled the wards. To be sure, the six wards maintained separate forces and the parish vestries, in electing the six ward watch boards, indirectly had a say in the appointment of ward constables and watchmen. Nevertheless, in Dublin in 1780, the recent trend toward more centralized control was unmistakable. On balance, however, the police of both Dublin and London remained inefficient and, through the parishes, wards, and Corporations, were still locally controlled. Like Londoners, Dubliners, albeit Protestant Dubliners, still managed the police of their city.

More broadly, we may describe the patterns of civil authority in England and Ireland in 1780 as being roughly similar. Numerous locally controlled, small groups of constables and watchmen attempted to keep the peace. But over the next seventy years, revolutionary changes would destroy systems of peacekeeping that for centuries had remained relatively unchanged. A visitor to the two countries in 1850 would find constables and watch vanished, and in their places policemen. He would be struck by the fact that the new structures of social control, established in England and Ireland over this comparatively short period of time, were as different from each other as they had hitherto been similar. He would probably have underestimated the durability of this new institution, which has served as the foundation for present-day systems of police.

CHAPTER 3

A new idea: the controversy over police

A full history of the new police would probably lay its first scene in Ireland, and begin with the Dublin Police Act passed by the Irish Parliament in 1786.

– Frederic Maitland, *Justice and Police* (1885)

He has made Judges dependent on his Will alone, for the tenure of their offices, and the amount and payment of their salaries. He has erected a multitude of New Offices, and sent hither Swarms of Officers to harass our People, ... to subject us to a jurisdiction foreign to our constitution, and unacknowledged by our laws. For Quartering large bodies of armed troops among us.... For taking away our Charters, abolishing our most valuable Laws, and altering fundamentally the Forms of our Governments.... In every stage of these Oppressions We have petitioned for Redress in the most humble terms: Our repeated Petitions have been answered only by repeated injury....

– American Declaration of Independence, 1776

England in 1780 was a country of contrasts. The wealthiest country in Europe was pockmarked by poverty in London, the growing towns, and the countryside. England, the most urban of nations, was still overwhelmingly rural. Blessed with the most liberal political constitution in Europe, the great mass of the English people, including some of great prosperity, were disenfranchised. A land that boasted of its tradition of common law and trial by jury had capital codes for nearly 200 crimes, though fewer offenders now went to the gibbet than in Daniel Defoe's day. Violent crime was rare; property crimes predominated. The majesty of the law, private prosecutions, and neighborly policing formed the core of the criminal justice system: Nowhere in the country was there anything resembling a modern police force.[1]

In the British archipelago in 1780, the domestic political situation was three-sided: England, America, and Ireland. Wilkism, which ten years ago had "hag-ridden" His Majesty's ministers, was now quiescent but, perhaps more ominously, many gentlemen of property were calling for some administrative and parliamentary reform. The young William Pitt was swept along, and Edmund Burke, the Irish Protestant in English politics, submitted five reform bills. The high point of the movement came in April 1780 when

Parliament passed a resolution that "the influence of the Crown has increased, is increasing, and ought to be diminished." Such challenges to the King and his ministers stemmed largely from concern for recent events in America and Ireland. The American Revolution, which had dragged on for five years, was increasingly disheartening – first the humiliation at Saratoga (October 1777), then the Americans' treaty with France (March 1778) and the breakdown in peace talks (October), and now the fears of a French invasion. In June 1779, the King had gloomily predicted to his ministers: If we lose America, the West Indies will go and then Ireland.[2]

The third problem in 1780 was an old one: Ireland. The restive Protestants there, catching some of the enthusiasm of the Americans, were demanding greater economic and political freedom for themselves. A Patriot Party had emerged, led by Henry Grattan, the George Washington of Anglo-Irish Ireland. England was faced with an economic boycott and blackmail by 80,000 armed and uniformed "Volunteers," Irish Protestants who talked at once of protecting their island from a French invasion and of gaining constitutional concessions from England. To the English Government, it seemed that the American war might acquire an Irish front. Rather than face this nightmare, Lord North, in early 1780, abolished a number of restrictions on Ireland's trade with England and the Empire. In addition, discriminatory laws against Irish Presbyterians were repealed; the same would not be done for English Dissenters until forty-eight years later.[3]

I. Failure of police reform in London

If the nation seemed to be besieged emotionally in June 1780, certainly no one expected the explosion about to rock the metropolis. The background seemed harmless enough. Lord North's Government had granted certain rights to Catholics in recently acquired French Canada (Quebec Act, 1774); four years later, to meet manpower requirements for the army – the King had been advised that 80,000 more soldiers were needed to subdue America – Parliament relaxed certain penal laws against English Catholics.[4] Presbyterian Scots in 1779 thwarted the extension of any relief to the Highlanders; the following year, to win repeal of the English act of 1778, a Protestant Association was organized in England by George Gordon, a "half-mad fanatic" and younger son of the Duke of Gordon. The group collected, one way or another, some 120,000 signatures, and on 2 June, led by their hero, a crowd of 50,000 collected in St. George's Fields to submit "the largest petition ever presented to a British House of Parliament."[5] What was about to happen resulted from frustration (with the American war), anger (about concessions already made to Catholic Canada and Ireland), resentment (what of the petitions of decent English Protestant workingmen?), and patriotism (the long tradition of anti-Catholicism in a nation now at war with Catholic France and Spain). One recent scholar has argued that the disorders were actually in the Radical tradition – "a groping desire to settle accounts with the rich ... to achieve some rough kind of social justice" – but the evidence indicates that the riots were more fundamentally of an anti-Catholic nature by mobs "ready for pillage."[6] The disorders were fueled not by radical demands but by the need for a scapegoat for England's current problems.

The Gordon Riots and their aftermath

The demonstrators in St. George's Fields on 2 June 1780 jostled arriving Members of Parliament and, after the Commons refused to receive their petition, they laid siege to the building. As the honorable MPs slipped quietly away at nightfall, the disorders began. They would not be brought under control for ten days. First to be destroyed were the Sardinian and Bavarian embassies, then Catholic houses and chapels. "There was nothing but Roman Catholics in it," one woman rioter later explained, "they were Irish ... and the house must come down." The houses of notorious "Catholic lovers" – men like Sir George Savile, who had sponsored the 1778 bill, and the Lord Chief Justice, William Murray, 1st Earl of Mansfield – were targeted and destroyed, as were those of magistrates like Sir John Fielding who dared to stand up to the crowds. If "No Popery!" was the resounding cry through the streets, soon everything associated with the Government was the target. The Bow Street Police Office was plundered and its records burned, the Old Bailey courthouse invaded, and the half-dozen prisons in the metropolis smashed open and put to the torch. The crowd violence was highly selective until the evening of 7 June, when Langdale's whiskey distillery, with 350 tons of spirits on the Catholic-owned premises, was invaded and drunk dry. From this point on, the disorders ceased being political, or even Protestant, and for the next five days in an apocalyptic orgy of violence "the submerged nine-tenths of London were out for what they could get."[7] When order finally replaced chaos, the statistics read as follows: more than 700 dead; 450 arrested, of whom 160 were indicted and 25 hanged; and property damage, based on claims submitted, assessed at about £100,000.[8]

In the words of two Dublin newspapers, London's Gordon Riots left a "lasting stain," "eternal disgrace on ... their nation. Let the barbarism with which the English have upbraided the Irish be now retorted on themselves." The stain was the more dishonorable because the rioters were *not* a "lawless rabble" or "persecuting protestants, French enemies, anti-ministerialists, thieves, and Americans."[9] A recent scholar has confirmed the contemporary view that it was not, at least not at the outset, the slum dweller or criminal but "the English tradesman [who] quits his business to burn his neighbour's house." Of those arrested, the great majority were free-born English Protestant journeymen and apprentices, shopkeepers, and craftsmen. Put another way, "Most of Wilkes's poorer followers were in the front ranks of the rioters."[10] This finding is hardly surprising, for London workingmen had a long and proud tradition of faction fights against the papists, the most famous of which occurred in 1736, when the rallying cry was "Down with the Irish."[11]

85

But it was the "remissness of the English ministry, and London magistrates, in not checking the disorder" that brought further dishonor to the nation.[12] The problem was, of course, exacerbated by the absence of a proper civil force to guard the metropolis; "should a regular and vigilant police be established," prophesied *London's Public Advertiser* on 14 June, "nothing of the kind can happen in the future." In Westminster on the night of 2 June, a group of six constables had to face a crowd of 14,000; wisely, they did nothing. That same night, at the burning of the Sardinian Embassy, a few constables who tried to arrest a ringleader were lucky to escape with their lives. The men returned with 100 soldiers and took 13 prisoners, but for his trouble a mob of 5,000 subsequently destroyed the high constable's house. Even when the constables numbered as many as 100, as at Newgate Prison on the 6th, they were still ineffective, being absorbed by the crowd and beaten up.[13] Paucity of police was not the only problem. One constable announced that he would not "protect any such Popish rascals." Moreover, the Government was apparently reluctant to direct parties of constables, since they were "not always the most orderly set of men." Most fitting perhaps is the story, the bizarre image, of an old night watchman, in all serenity and oblivious to the swirl around him, calling the hour of the night at a spot where one of the fiercest conflagrations was raging.[14]

This serious state of civil incompetence was relieved by the pouring of soldiers into the metropolis, 6,000 by 4 June, rising to 12,000 a week later. One thousand troops guarded the Bank of England and the recently founded British Museum (1753); the 12th Foot Guards alone were scattered over forty-four posts. The military required magistrates to direct them. Troops were requested for Leicester Fields and Clare Market, but no one could find a JP; for this reason, too, Lord Mansfield's house burned as 300 soldiers watched. Or, as at the destruction of the Bow Street Police Office, a magistrate would be present but refuse to read the Riot Act. In the aftermath, the Lord Mayor of London, Barkley Kennett, a Wilkite of strong anti-Catholic sentiments, would be convicted of criminal negligence and fined £1,000. The situation was ably summarized by a government official:

The Civil Magistracy, having called for the Troops, was not ready to attend them; in another instance, the Troops having been called out, were left to the fury of the populace; and in two other instances, after the Troops had marched to the places appointed for them, several of the Magistrates refused to act.... Such a conduct as this tends even to encourage Riots, and to bring matters to the last fatal extremity.[15]

After almost two weeks the disorders ended, a combination of the rioters' exhaustion and the authorities' repression. The latter took three forms. First, there were the traditional civil methods – printed handbills; calls to employers to discharge workers wearing Blue Cockades; a £50 reward for prosecuting rioters; a ban on street celebrations over the news of the British victory at Charleston in America (12 May). Citizen groups – organized first on 7 June by the proprietor of the Globe Tavern, Fleet Street, and his "Moderate Men" – formed private associations to patrol their neighborhoods. Soon, all across the metropolis, shopkeepers, lawyers, noblemen, and parish authorities formed similar groups as more formal organizations – the City of London Association, the Westminster Military Society – came to the fore. Although these quasi-legal bodies of armed men created constitutional problems and infringed on the military's jurisdiction, the troops were grateful for the assistance and the difficulties were good-humoredly resolved.[16]

The second reason for the return to order was the change of heart by local authorities after three of the prisons were burned on 7 June. A government observer noted that "many who were active in spiriting up the Mob to commit devastation, now have changed sides." It was none other than Alderman John Wilkes, JP, who commanded the soldiers guarding the Bank of England to fire on the mob, killing and wounding hundreds; on another occasion, Wilkes took prisoner a man who had helped to burn down Lord Mansfield's house – the printer of Wilkes's *North Briton*![17]

The third and probably the most important reason was the decision taken by the King, meeting in Privy Council on 7 June, to permit the military to act *without* the direction of magistrates. Long betrayed by the civil power, the surly troops, who had had to endure stones and brickbats, jeers and ridicule, now stood for no nonsense from the mobs. On the 8th, the military hanged one man on the spot in Cheapside and two in Southwark; that evening, in a wild affray on Fleet Bridge, a party of Horse Guards hacked unrestrainedly at a charging mob, leaving twenty dead and thirty-five wounded. Many similar incidents would follow, but the back of the disorders was now broken.[18] Nevertheless, troop levels in the city would not return to normal until the end of July, and military law was lifted only two months later. Guards lingered at the city's prisons until March 1781, and at the Bank of England and Buckingham "House" the military protection begun in 1780 has continued to the present day.[19]

What were the lessons of the Gordon Riots? One was that mobs were not always controllable: They could in fact become dangerous.[20] A second, quite different lesson, to which the riots contributed a small part, was the need for the Government to have an official versed only in domestic affairs. The two Secretaries of State each handled foreign and domestic business; from March 1782 on, a division was made between the two. In the long term, this decision to have a single "Home Secretary" would have a great impact on the policing of England.[21] A third lesson was a traditional and well-known one. Where there was no strong civil power, there had to be, in times of crisis, military force. Indeed, a general condition of disorderliness occasionally deteriorated into unacceptably high levels of disorder, necessitating the intervention of troops. Creation of a strong regular police would break this pattern by preventing that deterioration, which had traditionally required military aid. But so long as an efficient police remained a concept abhorrent to free-born Englishmen, the daily disorderliness of freedom and the emergency interposition of troops would continue. "Your true Englishman," remarked Dr. Charles Burney after the riots, "is never so happy as under a bad government."[22]

This dilemma was complicated by the fact that Englishmen considered unconstitutional not only police but the very institution that had saved the metropolis from destruction. "What!" exclaimed a gentleman perambulating the city. "Do we live in Turkey? Are the free people to be *dragooned* out of their independence?" Members of both Lords and Commons bemoaned the reliance on a standing army. The Duke of Richmond objected that the rows of soldiers everywhere signified that England was "as completely a military country as any in Europe," a sentiment repeated by Edmund Burke. Charles James Fox claimed that he would rather "be governed by a mob than a standing army," a view from which Lord Mansfield, who had had the experience, dissented.[23]

Traditional solutions were found to be more comfortable than radical reforms. Some writers wanted to strengthen and clarify the Riot Act. Others thought that "the only Safe Means of Defending a free People" was a strengthening of the militia. A Wilkite City of London alderman offered *A Plan for Rendering the Militia of London Useful and Respectable, and for Raising an Effective and Well-Regulated Watch, Without Subjecting the Citizens to additional Taxes or the Interposition of Parliament* (1782). The proposal, by coordinating these two forces, would in effect establish a kind of police force, but for this reason it was never implemented, since "the experiment" was judged "dangerous, even though the mercenaries should be ... under the control of *themselves*, and in their own pay."[24] The suggestions most frequently offered were for private associations of men of property, "gentlemen and tradesmen," who would assist the existing local authorities in times of emergency. After the Gordon Riots, the response of the Government was similarly tentative and traditional. It was argued that the riots, no doubt never to be repeated, were exceptional; the existing constable and watch system was generally functional. Why, therefore, adopt a strange new institution, a police, that might create worse evils? For five years the Government's only action was to toy with the idea of impressing the idle and disorderly into the army and to enact a law making these sorts of people, when caught with arms, subject to an old vagrancy act.[25]

In the face of overwhelming opposition and against all the accepted norms of their own time, a few individuals suggested that no less was needed than that the police of London "be entirely new modelled." Even as the Gordon Riots began, the Earl of Shelburne noted that the civil power of the city would remain ineffectual until it was properly coordinated, strengthened, and staffed. To protect liberty and ensure the popularity of the forces, he opposed any government control, offering instead a locally controlled system of "elective" police magistrates and constables for the City, Westminster, Southwark, and the other areas of the metropolis. Unfortunately, and irredeemably, Shelburne hurt his case by making a comparison of the London with the Paris police.

Let them examine its good, and not be blind to its evil. They would find its construction excellent, its use and direction abominable. The police of France was wise to the last degree in its institution but .... perverted in its use ... into an *espionage*, a word, which he thanked God, would not *yet* admit of an English interpretation.

By conjuring up the French bogeyman, Shelburne ensured that his plan would not be taken seriously in an English Parliament.[26]

The debate resumed in March 1781 when Richard Sheridan, the young politician-playwright, offered a motion in the Commons that the imposition of military force on 7 June 1780 afforded "a strong presumption" of the inadequacy of the Westminster police. Significantly, he began by asking the Members to "understand what he meant by the term police; it was not an expression of our law *or of our language*, but was perfectly understood." Carefully avoiding any references to France, he, like Shelburne, urged a reform that would not involve the Crown or "purchase internal protection at the expence of slavery." But Sheridan found no supporters; the Government, speaking through the Solicitor General, judged the police "adequate to every common purpose," and Sir George Savile, whose house the mob had destroyed for his sponsorship of the Catholic Relief Act, feared any reform to be "a disguise" for "that constant object of terror to every man who valued constitutional liberty, a standing army." Sheridan's motion, which did not even call for the creation of a new police force, was soundly defeated by a vote of 171–94.[27] The subject would remain closed for the next four years, even though for eight months in 1782–3 the Earl of Shelburne, as Prime Minister, had the opportunity to pursue his idea of police.

The London and Westminster police bill of 1785

In January 1784 the elevation to the prime ministership of the twenty-five-year-old William Pitt, son of the Earl of Chatham, the political mastermind (1757–61) of the successful first war in North America, brought forward for the first time new, bold, and innovative ideas. In matters of policing, Pitt's ministry would produce far-reaching results, though not so much in England as in Ireland.

Pitt intended his reforms of the civil power to begin in London. The Government paid attorney John Reeves £300 to draft a police bill, and in June 1785 the Solicitor-General introduced the bill to create a single, full-time, paid, professional police for the entire metropolis. Crime was rising, argued Sir Archibald Macdonald, and the preventive checks of harsh punishments had proved ineffective. The Government was tired of the traditional resort to military arms in times of crisis. Macdonald "knew of no way of rendering the aid of the military unnecessary, but by strengthening the hands of the civil power.... To keep the bayonet out of employ, the power of a civil officer must be rendered efficacious." To do this, the Government proposed to create a police "District of the Metropolis," which would be composed of nine "Divisions." Each division would have a force of horse and foot constables, superintended by a Chief Constable who would be responsible to the district's High Constable, himself responsible to three "Commissioners of Police" appointed by the Government. The commissioners were to have all the powers of JPs, as well as new police powers. They were to appoint all policemen, who would be "furnished with proper Arms and Accoutrements," and only they could fine or fire the men. In addition, a salaried magistrate, appointed and removable by the commissioners, would preside over each divisional office. Besides their regular judicial duties, these magistrates were expected, in times of riot or "unlawful Assembly," to "attend in Person, together with a sufficient Number of Constables ... at such Time and Place" as the commissioners should direct.[28]

The bill did not propose to abolish the existing groups of constables and watchmen in the many parishes, vestries, and wards of the metropolis or to terminate any magistrate's commission of the peace, but it clearly sought to usurp their functions and powers. The new Commissioners were, in theory, to have control over the various local forces through powers of inspection, of manpower removals and appointments, and of direct command of any constable or watchman whose "Aid and Assistance ... they shall think necessary and proper." The new police would be given special powers of search, seizure, and social control that went far beyond the rights of ordinary JPs. With a Commissioner's warrant, any building could be entered, if not opened on demand. Within the City of London local authorities would have to endorse the warrant, and in any nocturnal searches throughout the metropolis a parish constable had to accompany the new police; these were the only concessions to local privileges in the whole bill. No local acquiescence was necessary for searches of beer and spirits houses, which the police might enter at all hours and without a warrant. The police were to superintend a complex system of licensing and record keeping, with compulsory fees and fines on publicans, pawnbrokers, and a variety of other tradesmen. The police were to enforce a revised vagrancy code, which had been expanded only two years earlier. Now "notorious" thieves and "Night Walkers," "all Persons in the Day Time loitering about" unable to give "a good Account of Themselves," and "friendless and deserted Boys" would qualify as vagrants subject to arrest by the new police.[29]

The Government's police proposal of 1785 would, in sum, revolutionize law and life in London. A centrally controlled, numerous, and altogether new body of men would not only override the preexisting localized forms of police but would alter the old patterns of justice, affect a variety of businesses and trades both reputable and disreputable, and create broad new powers of search, seizure, and social control.

The controversial bill agitated Londoners in the last week of June 1785, exactly five years after the Gordon Riots. In Parliament no one supported the bill except Sir James Johnstone, and he spoke for only a few minutes, noted that London had fewer murders than Paris, and raised the bogey of France. The many opponents, who objected to the lateness of the session and the emptiness of the Commons, thought that the Government should not act "rashly and hastily to adopt a new system merely because it was such," especially at an annual cost of £20,000. The powers of the government-controlled police were too sweeping and usurped too many local prerogatives; moreover, the precedent of salaried magistrates constituted a threat to all who held the commissions of magistracy throughout the country. The system, in short, was altogether too similar to that of the Paris police. The reply of the Solicitor-General was hardly reassuring: If the commissioners in Paris were "like his proposed commissioners," said Macdonald, "there could be no objection to them."[30]

The Government's mismanagement of the bill, not only in impatiently pressing it at the end of the parliamentary session but also in ignoring the City of London's authorities, traditional rivals of the Crown, contributed to "the alarm which," admitted its author, "it at first naturally excites." The Home Secretary had sent a copy "a fortnight late" to the Lord Mayor, indeed a copy "containing some of the exceptionable parts which we had purged"; the result was that the City aldermen, hastily glancing through the bill, went into Parliament with an attitude of "unanimous" and "furious" opposition. There they noticed the absence of many government ministers, a fact that further strengthened their opposition. The Prime Minister was present but woefully unprepared; in his too brief remarks, Pitt admitted that he was only "slightly" acquainted with the bill's provisions. Reeves, who had drafted the bill, complained to the Home Secretary that the police of London was "a subject that has been more agitated and is better understood than most subjects of executive government, particularly since 1780.... My Lord, if this plan is lost, it is lost for want of the common exertions of Government in the House of Commons."[31]

While the Government stumbled, opposition throughout the metropolis mounted. The City of London petitioned against the bill, and a large meeting of Middlesex magistrates unanimously denounced it. The public press, though generally in favor of some police reform, was opposed to this particular proposal. The *Morning Chronicle* discerned "many and great evils"; the *Daily Universal Register* judged it "radically bad" and reported receiving letters of protest "from innumerable correspondents." The showdown in Parliament came on 29 June. One of the many to speak was City Alderman James Townsend, who was described as "perfectly frantic." In a long and impassioned speech, he claimed to favor police reform as much as any man but was unalterably opposed to this plan to replace a tried system of local controls and liberties with a system of executive tyranny "altogether new and arbitrary in the extreme." The bill did nothing less, thundered Townsend, than abolish "the forms established by the wisdom of our ancestors, and goes to the entire subversion of the chartered rights of the greatest city in the world." The Government, embarrassed by its blundering and reeling before the onslaught of public opinion, decided to withdraw the controversial bill – "on account of an informality in the drawing it up," the Home Secretary sheepishly explained to the Lord Mayor. The Government promised to submit a new bill, but "without containing the alarm" of the present measure. Seven years would elapse before Parliament was presented with this redrafted police bill, and it would be a pale imitation indeed of the proposal of 1785.[32]

In London the attempt had failed, but an experiment was about to begin across the Irish Sea.[33] In Ireland a powerful government-directed police was not only politically more necessary, but there the traditions of civil and parliamentary liberty and the powers of local vested interests were more fragile. The Dublin *Freeman's Journal* predicted that "the police bill, recently produced in England, should prove a model for a similar act ... in this country."[34] Indeed, Pitt's Government, after learning a lesson from its rebuff in Westminster, would work with great determination to establish a strong police in the Irish capital.

II. Success in Ireland: the Dublin Police Act of 1786

Tumult and unrest

Ireland in the 1780s was in a turbulent and aggressive mood. As Londoners set their capital ablaze for "No Popery" in the summer of 1780, and as the Americans humiliated Cornwallis and won their independence at Yorktown in the fall of the next year, Irishmen of varying classes and religions were extorting concessions from England. The Protestant nation in arms, the Volunteers, numbering 80,000 by 1780, won free trade in 1780 and a measure of legislative autonomy in 1782. Some went on to demand a substantial reform of Parliament, but only a few wanted to consider the question of Catholic political rights and économic grievances. To the prevailing excitement was added, beginning in 1785, a threat from below of volcanic proportions. For three years a peasant protest movement swept across eleven counties in the southern half of the country. Its principal aim was a reduction in the payment of tithes, and the county magistrates, deficient in police and troops, were so supine, outnumbered, and in some cases sympathetic that the protesters were temporarily successful in achieving a redress of grievances. In short, the two Irelands, overclass and underclass, mounted in the 1780s strong and successful challenges to the English authorities.[35]

In quick succession, Dublin Castle responded with legislation to prevent further challenges. Despite pressures from the Rightboys and Volunteers, neither the tithe nor the Irish House of Commons was reformed. The Government adopted instead a number of coercive measures: an abortive militia bill; a Riot Act modeled on the English statute of 1714; acts to reform criminal procedures, the county magistracy, and quarter sessions; and two police acts, one for the capital, the other for the counties. The new police were thus only one part of the government crackdown of the later 1780s.

Why was the police of Dublin reformed in 1786? The city had not been rocked by gigantic disorders, as London had in 1780. There was no series of heinous murders, which in London in 1811–12 would trigger a parliamentary investigation of the police. There was no alarming crime wave, an argument that would be made in debates preceding the creation of the

London police in 1829. Dublin was plagued by traditional disorders: food riots over the price of bread or the export of bacon; riots by vagrants rounded up for a term in the House of Industry; and affrays between the King's soldiers and the city's inhabitants.[36]

But more timely and crucial were the political excitement and violence of the Volunteer era. After the Dungannon Congress had exorted the political revolution of 1782, thousands of Volunteers held peaceable meetings in Dublin, demanding further reforms. One at the Rotunda in November 1783 constituted virtually an alternate parliament; the next year a "National Congress" (the movement borrowing the American term) was suppressed by the Attorney-General, John Fitzgibbon. Such meetings could easily spill over into violence. In November 1779, a crowd of Volunteers had broken the windows in the Harcourt Place residence of the then Attorney-General, John Scott, and marched to the Parliament in College Green, where they flourished cutlasses and demanded free trade. In April 1784 a similar assemblage invaded Parliament, occupied the Speaker's chair, and from the august seat demanded political reform.[37]

The violence could be more savage. "Tarring and feathering committees" targeted unpopular figures for the American practice of stripping, smearing with pitch tar, and covering with goose down. The uniquely Irish custom of "houghing" – the cutting of leg tendons, usually of cattle – was inflicted by one mob on some unfortunate soldiers in broad daylight in Dublin in March 1784.[38] Relations between Dubliners and the 2,500 soldiers in the capital had never been cordial. There were too many incidents like one in 1778 when five soldiers had raped a woman in Fishamble Street, two of the men alternately standing guard to keep back the gathering angry crowd; or another in 1784 when a drunken officer had fondled a publican's wife, setting off two weeks of tarring and feathering and houghing.[39]

It was in reporting these disturbances to Prime Minister Pitt that the Irish Chief Secretary, Thomas Orde, insisted that "some regular and decisive amendment must be made in the Police, for it is impossible yet to foresee, that a new Mob may not in an instant renew the disturbances." Dublin Castle's correspondence of August 1784 reveals a city "under the dominion and tyranny of the mob."[40] The problem was not only the poor record of the soldiery – "the most earnest exertions are made to provoke them into rashness ... how difficult it is to restrain the resentment which the soldiers feel at this Conduct towards them" – but also the impossibility of effective local policing and of getting information, even from those who would lose everything "if any revolution should take place." Earlier that year, in April, when Parliament was briefly under siege, the Commons had censured the Lord Mayor for his inactivity and demanded that he improve the city police. As for the Volunteers, they either "countenance[d] these outrages" or refused to assist the civil power when requested. In sum, the maintenance of public order seemed, for very different reasons, to be as elusive in Dublin as it had been in London at the time of the Gordon Riots.[41]

Political principals

Irish Chief Secretary Thomas Orde was thirty-five years old when he began service under the thirty-year-old Lord Lieutenant, Charles Manners, 4th Duke of Rutland. Rutland was Orde's opposite: a convivial young nobleman who had been elected at age twenty to the English House of Commons (where he voted with Burke and Fox and supported the Americans) and who had inherited the family title and estates at age twenty-five. Thomas Orde had none of Rutland's advantages of birth. Like Robert Peel, a future Irish Chief Secretary, he was from the propertied but untitled ranks of English society. But he had none of Peel's brilliance or political skills; in Sir Jonah Barrington's assessment, Orde was a hard-working, "cautious, slow man, tolerably well informed, but not at all talented." He was also, throughout his chief secretaryship, in such chronic poor health as to disrupt his business habits. Prior to his Irish appointment, Orde had been an Under-Secretary of State and secretary to the Treasury. In 1794, as a result of his marriage, he would inherit great estates and become Orde-Powlett, and in 1797 be created Baron Bolton.[42]

Although the young Rutland would die in October 1787 from a fever contracted on a tour of the countryside and Orde would never hold another important political post, two men did rise to prominence in the early 1780s who would dominate Irish politics for two decades. The son of a Catholic who had converted and become a Dublin lawyer and a wealthy Limerick landowner, John Fitzgibbon followed his father into a legal career that included riding the Munster circuit. In 1780 the thirty-one-year-old lawyer entered Parliament in the Patriot camp, but the growing militancy of the Volunteer movement disturbed him. Fitzgibbon would later remark: "If Ireland seeks to quarrel with Great Britain, she is a besotted nation. Great Britain is not easily aroused, nor easily appeased. Ireland is easily roused, and easily put down." Fitzgibbon's conservative instincts, brilliant political mind, and the rapid and forceful speeches delivered by this small, slight man with the "awful," riveting gaze, soon recommended him to the Government. Appointed Attorney-General in 1783, he now supported English supremacy on all questions and became on all popular measures the villain whom the Whig Patriots loved to hate. Fitzgibbon's political and social advancement would be rapid. He was made Lord Chancellor (1789) and served as an indispensable Dublin Castle administrator throughout the 1790s; he was created an Irish viscount (1793) and earl (1795), and finally an English viscount (1799). John Fitzgibbon, Earl of Clare, was an intensely controversial man. For many, his political views and his accumulation of offices and honors made him an object of hatred; at his death in 1802, aged fifty-three, a crowd following the funeral procession shouted curses, "and dead cats were flung upon his coffin." To others, Fitzgibbon's brilliance outshone his caustic, imperious personality. Lord Lieutenant Cornwallis, though he often differed with him, called Fitzgibbon "the most right-headed politician in this country." The death of Fitzgibbon's grandson, fighting for England in the

Figure 3.1 The great adversaries in the Irish police debates: John Fitzgibbon (*left*), later Earl of Clare, mantled in the robes of state; and Henry Grattan, shown in Volunteer uniform. (Maxwell, *History of the Irish Rebellion*; Grattan, *Memoirs*)

charge of the Light Brigade at Balaclava, would bring the family lineage to an end.[43] (See Figure 3.1.)

Henry Grattan, the Whig gadfly who pestered Dublin Castle for the better part of two decades, the principal political foe of his former friend and schoolmate Fitzgibbon, was the leader of the Patriot parliamentary party. Son of the Recorder and later MP for the City of Dublin, Grattan trained for the law in London and in 1775, at age twenty-nine, entered the Irish House of Commons. His maiden speech a Dublin newspaper heralded as "the spontaneous flow of natural eloquence." Grattan soon established himself as a friend of the Americans and a proponent of various reform measures in his own country. In the next few years, the right of Catholics to take long land leases, the granting of free trade and habeas corpus, and the repeal of Poynings' Law were all pressed and won by this Patriot leader. Other causes would be lost (parliamentary reform and redress of tithe) or deferred (Catholic enfranchisement), but not for any want of eloquence or persistence on Grattan's part. Liberal Protestants called him "the father of our country" and raised for him the stupendous sum of £100,000, half of which he accepted, buying estates in Queen's County and Wicklow.[44] (Figure 3.1.)

Grattan was short and unimpressive in appearance. But when he spoke – his long arms perpetually gesticulating, his body swaying, his air abstracted – all of his mannerisms dissolved before the intense animation and enthusiasm of his speeches. Grattan had no skill in sarcasm or wit, like Fitzgibbon, but he was a master of the extended philosophical argument and the political aphorism. His speeches combined poetic beauty with clear, constitutional lessons: No other parliamentarian of his day could match his ability to instruct or inspire his fellow Members in patriotism. His role was as the conscience of the Commons, virtually his entire career being spent in opposition. Grattan was a reformer but no democrat; he "saw the Irish gentry as the natural leaders of their country." He was a nationalist who never advocated Irish separation from Great Britain; his faith was in "the sober blessings of the British constitution."[45] From 1794 on, Grattan would grow increasingly critical of Dublin Castle authorities for what he considered their brutal mismanagement of government before the Rebellion. A firm believer in conciliation, he withdrew from politics in 1797 rather than participate in further repression. During the bloody summer of 1798, Grattan was in self-imposed exile in England; he never recovered from the Rebellion, suffering a steady physical decline until his death in London in 1820, at age seventy-three. To the end he never forgave his childhood friend, John Fitzgibbon, for, as Grattan saw it, destroying first the liberty, then the sovereign independence, of Ireland. Writing of the Rebellion, Grattan noted in 1817, "The question men should have asked was not, 'Why was Mr. Sheares upon the gallows?' but 'Why was not Lord Clare along with him?'"[46]

An Irish militia?

Dublin's troubled summer of 1784 produced, the following spring, the Government's first measure of coercion, the Irish militia bill. The way to do away with the Volunteers, that extragovernmental armed body of men, was to supplant them with a conscripted government-controlled militia. Theoretically, the idea was sound; no one doubted the constitutionality of the English militia. More to the point, the Volunteers of 1785 were not those of 1778 or 1780. "Gentlemen and original volunteers I hold to be synonymous," remarked the clever Fitzgibbon, flattering the Whig Patriots, but the Volunteers were now "the dregs of the people." Significantly, Fitzgibbon's arch-opponent, the Patriot leader, Henry Grattan, now described them as "a cankered part of the dregs of the people." The Government and the Whig opposition thus found themselves for once in agreement: The Commons voted to appropriate £20,000 for a militia. But here the scheme ended, for reasons that are unclear. Orde's shortcomings as an administrator are only part of the explanation. The Volunteer movement by 1785 appeared to be ebbing as a political force; to push the militia bill might only reintensify popular protest. It was felt, moreover, that the militia must be a Protestant one. As such, a militia would be a financial burden on Anglo-Irish property owners and suffer serious problems of staffing in heavily Catholic, disturbed counties.[47]

After a year in office, Thomas Orde had fallen into disfavor with the English Prime Minister. Blamed for the collapse of the militia plan, he was also accused of allowing the Irish Parliament to subvert Pitt's "Commercial

Propositions" for improved trade between Ireland and England. This latest reverse, in August 1785, was in fact the doing of jealous English manufacturers and the Whig opposition in London, who made the bill unacceptable to Irish interests.[48] Nevertheless, the furious Pitt summoned his Irish Chief Secretary to London for a stern lecture on governance. Orde returned to his Irish post no doubt conscious that any future failure would result in a permanent recall. In November 1785 Orde, now in poor health, wrote Pitt that his principal concerns for the new parliamentary session would be a revived militia bill, a bill against "voluntary assemblings of the people in arms and array ... with the direct view of *suppressing the Volunteers*," and a "Police Bill, chiefly for the regulation of the Capital." The militia bill would be soon dropped and the riot bill deferred to the 1787 session, but the police bill would become law.[49]

The Dublin Police Act of 1786

The police of Dublin remained ineffective despite a reform in 1778 whereby the city's seventeen parishes and 150,000 inhabitants had been reorganized into six wards (Map 3.1). Though the act provided for vestry appointment of the constables and night watch, it injected a dose of centralization by giving the City Corporation the appointment of two officers in each ward. The daytime police still numbered about two dozen, but the number of watchmen had been increased from 315 men to about 400.[50] Now, in 1786, Orde planned to carry the centralization to its final stage, transferring entire control of the police to Dublin Castle. There were numerous precedents for his plan. Since 1780, the Castle, by acts of Parliament, had usurped many of the City's functions of "police" in the comprehensive eighteenth-century understanding of the term. Regulating the port and harbor of Dublin, superintending the city's lighting, water, and sewage needs, and presiding over the paving, widening, and building of its streets were now the responsibility, not of the City Corporation, but of commissioners appointed and paid by the Government. Dublin householders continued to be assessed for these municipal services but, protest as they might, they no longer controlled them. Similar improvement commissioners independent of town corporations developed in English cities from the mid-eighteenth century on, but in that country they were locally accountable as well as rated.[51]

In Dublin, therefore, given the legislative precedents and the tumults of the 1780s, centralized police reform was in one sense simply a logical next step. Moreover, the anxious Chief Secretary, under the scrutiny of Pitt and Rutland, knew he had to proceed at once. "His Majesty's Ministers" had informed the Lord Lieutenant in January 1786 "that a police is much wanted in the Capital of Ireland, not much more than in that of Great Britain, and they hope that as the [Irish] Capital is so much smaller, the Plan will in the proportion be more easy to accomplish."[52]

But if Dublin was to have an entirely new police, what form should it take? Orde had before him three models of urban police. The model least

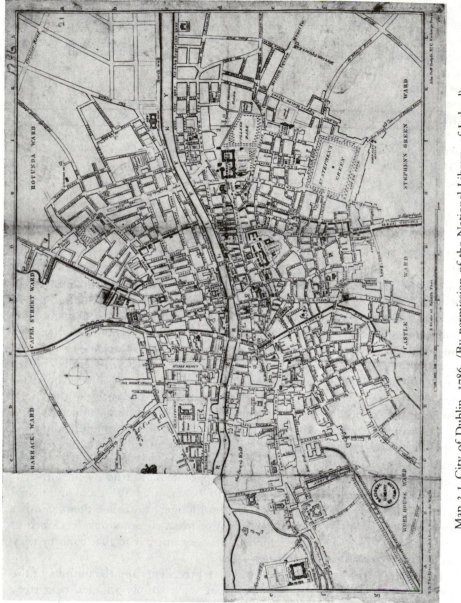

Map 3.1 City of Dublin. 1786. (By permission of the National Library of Ireland)

likely of emulation was that of London: A centralized force at Bow Street of three magistrates and four thief takers would be absurdly insufficient. A second model was the Edinburgh town guard, which consisted of 100 men divided into three companies and "armed and clothed like regular Soldiers." They were said to be "disciplined and [to] fire as well as any regulars"; on one occasion, they quelled a mutiny of 200 soldiers in which several police-men and troops were killed.[53]

The third model – the police of Paris – was the most efficient and controversial. This remarkable proposal originated with Sackville Hamilton. Under-Secretary in the Civil Department since 1780, Hamilton was a man of enormous power, secrecy, and talents. Because of the high turnover in the higher offices of Lord Lieutenant and Chief Secretary, the civil, like the military, under-secretaryship was a critically important post. And Orde's ill health made Hamilton's responsibilities all the greater.[54] It was Hamilton and his predecessor, Thomas Waite, who in a sense governed Ireland from 1747 to 1796: "between them they built the idea of the 'Castle' as the executive centre of English government in Ireland." Thomas Pelham, Chief Secretary in 1783–4, observed that "without Hamilton I think no man in his senses would remain in Ireland an hour." Lord Lieutenant Earl Fitzwilliam would remove him in 1795 for being too powerful and too conservative; upon Fitzwilliam's removal, Hamilton was restored for a year until his successor could be trained.[55]

Hamilton's long memorandum on the police of Paris relied heavily on Sir William Mildmay's book, *The Police of France* (1763), though he did not cite it. Mildmay's hopes for London were now suggested by Hamilton for Dublin. The Paris police, the Under-Secretary remarked with some envy, was efficient, centrally controlled by a Lieutenant of Police and forty-eight commissioners ("some what like our justices of the peace"), and staffed with 800 constables, of whom 200 were mounted (*Guet à cheval*). Though five times larger than Dublin, Paris with only twice as many police was by far the better policed city, and at an annual cost of £18,000 was relatively less expensive than the £4,000 "wasted" yearly on the Dublin watch.[56]

On 20 March 1786, Thomas Orde, in such poor health as to label himself "an invalid," introduced the Government's "Bill for the better Execution of the Law within the City of Dublin, and certain parts adjacent thereto." The bill was at once moderate and revolutionary. It did not propose for Dublin the military guard of Edinburgh or the gendarmerie of Paris, but it did call for the abolition of local policing throughout the metropolis and the substi-tution of a centrally controlled body of men within a single jurisdiction. Enactment of this copy of Pitt's scheme of the previous year for London would make the Dublin police a unique institution in the British Isles.[57]

Orde's bill proposed to abolish the watchman-magistrate system, re-organize the parishes and wards into a metropolitan police district of four divisions, and place the policing of the city in the hands of three com-missioners, two assistants and one chief. The commissioners would recruit as "ministerial officers of the peace" 1 High Constable, 4 Chief Constables, 40 petty constables, and some 400 watchmen (368 in summer, 463 in winter). In addition, the Lord Lieutenant would appoint a paid, full-time magistrate for each division to dispense justice from his public office. The new Dublin policemen were to be young, Protestant, and in good health; they would be salaried and prohibited from other employment. The force would be recognizable by its uniform and arms, to consist of bayonets and muskets. The Castle and the commissioners would, in William Lecky's words, have "almost absolute power."[58]

The 1786 Dublin bill differed in some ways from the 1785 London proposal. First, the Dublin commissioners and magistrates would be picked from the ranks of the city magistracy; the London bill had contained no such concession to local interests. The result in Dublin would be the comparative absence of opposition from the City Corporation.[59] Second, the London bill had stated that the new police could not enter the City without authorized permission; with the Dublin police officials appointed from the ranks of the city magistracy, no such clause was necessary.[60] Third, whereas the London bill had prohibited the commissioners from being aldermen or Members of Parliament, the Dublin bill specified that a commissioner could be an alderman and serve as a Member of Parliament.[61] Fourth, whereas the London bill's financing provision centered on fines, forfeitures, and penalties levied by the magistrates, the Dublin bill established a citywide police tax and fees on a variety of trades to pay for the police.[62]

The Dublin police bill of 1786 moved quickly through a Parliament that the Castle effectively controlled. Parliamentary proponents of the bill – led by the acerbic Attorney-General Fitzgibbon – argued that the new police would be able to function unhampered by the multiple jurisdictions of parishes, Liberties, and wards. Nothing could be more constitutional than to lessen the reliance on the army; at present "there is not the smallest thing that can be done ... without a military guard." Fitzgibbon welcomed the argument that the police would be used against the Volunteers. Had not that group changed radically in recent years? Would any man deny that "there is scarce a drunken weaver in the Liberty that has not arms concealed? ... If any argument was wanting to prove the necessity of the bill, it is the frequency of ... tumultuous assemblies ... [and] aggregate meetings." Other Members agreed that much "mischief" could have been avoided, had there been a strong police a few years ago.[63]

From its introduction, opposition to the Dublin police bill was intense. In the week that the bill passed through the Commons, eighteen Members spoke in favor of and nineteen against it. But in voting, the outcome was never in doubt. The opposition at its height could command only forty-six votes and lost ballot counts by ratios of three or four to one. The Government was nevertheless prepared for virulent protests and timed the introduction of its police bill to coincide with many Members' attendance at county Quarter Sessions, "where," Orde noted dryly, "they are much more wanted than in the House of Commons." Half a dozen Members objected to so serious a bill coming before "so thin a House": two speakers protested receiving copies of the bill only an hour before the debate. Apparently, some Members did leave their spring assizes to hurry back to Dublin: A parliamentary motion of 20 March to delay consideration of the bill lost by a vote of 68–19, whereas a similar motion two days later was defeated by 139–37. Clearly, in the meantime, the Government had also marshaled its supporters.[64]

The bill could not be delayed, and therefore the opposition unleashed one week of impassioned and occasionally wild rhetoric against the measure. Orde's proposal triggered a political debate in which the issues soon became those of Dublin Castle against the Irish people, English-paid hirelings against Irish patriots – in a word, tyranny against freedom. In this highly charged atmosphere, the Patriot Party showed considerable impatience with the Castle's arguments that the real issues were police efficiency versus inefficiency, a strengthened civil power versus mob rule.[65]

The opposition objected to the measure for a number of reasons. First, it was incompatible with Anglo-Irish, that is, English, law; the proposal was strange, "foreign." One member "imagined himself transported to the regions of Indostan.... The city of Dublin would be in a more oppressive situation ... than the city of Delhi." The bill was "calculated for the meridian of the most absolute monarchy," and certainly not "for a country that had the least pretensions to freedom." Another speaker observed sarcastically that "if we admit that to prevent abuses we are to part with our free constitution, we may as well adopt at once the police of Paris, which is the best police in the world."[66]

The police bill, in Grattan's judgment, was "the most obnoxious and alarming that ever, perhaps, arrested the attention of an Irish senate." The opposition warned that not only would the city's liberties be destroyed, but the "counties would experience a similar fate, if a proper spirit was not exerted in the beginning of danger." The bill would establish a new half-civil, half-military standing army, unregulated by Parliament or the City Corporation, responsible only to the Crown. This "armed patronage" of the Government would add to the bloated pension list and create a new salaried bureaucracy paid for by the people but unaccountable to them. As the power of the Crown multiplied, the city's independence would wither and the Lord Mayor, sheriffs, and aldermen would become "mementoes," "cyphers." It would, in short, establish a "new Constitution for the city of Dublin." For these reasons, the policemen themselves would be unpopular, "a banditti in whom the people can have no faith" and with whom they would therefore not cooperate.[67]

For the assembled Anglo-Irish gentlemen, it was bad enough that the police bill was "foreign" and "unconstitutional." What appeared outrageous was that the Government should seek to impose on Dubliners a police that had been judged unacceptable for Londoners. The 1785 London bill had been "so reprobated, not only by the whole kingdom, but also by the whole House of Commons" that the Government "was glad to withdraw it."[68] Objections were raised to the "difference of sentiment" that the Government showed for the two cities, despite the common knowledge that London "suffered more than perhaps any metropolis ever did by riots."[69] "What are our riots compared to those of London?" asked Henry Grattan. "Nothing, and yet we hear of no police bill there of such a nature as this before the House." Grattan could hardly contain himself when he thought of

the contempt which you are advised to entertain for the city of Dublin – This is the argument – the Commons of England paid attention to the petition of London because the body was respectable, and the Commons of Ireland would pay no attention to the petition of Dublin because her citizens are despicable.[70]

Protest against the police bill was as loud and emotional among Dubliners as it was on the floor of the Commons. The *Dublin Evening Post* and *Saunders's News-letter* denounced this bill "smuggled on the nation." The riots of 1784 were described as "assemblages of half-famished artisans [who had] tarred and feathered a few obnoxious individuals.... They committed neither bloodshed nor secured to themselves plunder." After the fearsome Gordon Riots in London, had not "things [there] returned to their former channels without any innovation, without any alteration of her police"? Indeed, the failure of reform in London appeared to ensure that "a new-modelled Police was an improvement left for an experiment to Irish enterprize, and for adoption, to Irish passiveness!"[71]

The first half of this prediction would prove correct, the latter half mistaken. A crowd of 3,000 City freeholders, "the most numerous that ever was known," met at the Royal Exchange; County Dublin freeholders assembled at the Court House in Kilmainham to petition Parliament to withdraw the police bill; the public galleries in the Commons overflowed with spectators. But Parliament refused to consider the petitions. After opposition protests that "the rejection of the petitions of the people has become the fashion," even though the petitioners were men "of the first rank and consequence," Attorney-General Fitzgibbon delivered a stinging speech against the petitions and promised, "I shall not be quite so gentle if the offence be repeated."[72]

Opposition oratory was stirring, but clearly the votes, the power, lay with the Government. Toward the end, the opposition became dispirited and the debate lackluster; the bill, introduced on 20 March, passed in the Common on the 28th, without even a division.[73] Over in England, a London newspaper, the *Morning Herald*, on the 29th was already too late when it predicted that the Dublin bill "will be warmly opposed, both in and out of Parliament. It has already caused an alarm similar to that raised by the Police bill introduced into our House of Commons last Session."

Thomas Orde was exultant. After the bungled militia and commercial proposals of the previous parliamentary session, the sickly Chief Secretary at last had good news for William Pitt. "We have made a successful foundation at least to a scheme of Effectual Police in this Capital. We thought it right to begin with moderation, but We have established the principle, and obtained ... an influence in the Magistracy of the City." On 5 April the Irish House of Peers approved the police bill by 35–8, with the minority penning a dissent that concentrated on the issues of unconstitutionality and Crown patronage; the Duke of Leinster added that "such a law would never [have] been listened to in England."[74]

Even after the bill was sent to London for certain approval, the protests continued in Dublin. The same bill that "was rejected with horror in Britain ... must become law in Ireland!" moaned the *Dublin Evening Post*. From mid-April to early May, this newspaper ran a series of articles purporting to prove that crime levels were lower in Ireland than in England. Against a background of lingering protest, the police bill received the royal assent on 8 May. Beginning 30 September, the new police would patrol Dublin's streets: The city, in one important respect, would no longer belong to Dubliners. The *Post* caught the essence of the change:

What strange revolutions occur in a short space of time! ... But a short time since, a Reform in Parliament was the general cry – it was afloat and in all conversations; even Parliament itself seemed to admit there was need for some reform, [but] then ... they found it was the *People* wanted reform ..., and therefore instead of a reform in Parliament, we have been presented a *reform* in the *police*.[75]

Police: principles and parties

Since police was clearly a political issue in late-eighteenth-century Ireland, the nature of the parliamentary opposition bears closer examination. The absence of division lists specifying names of aye and nay voters during the 1786 debates renders impossible quantitative analysis of voting patterns. But we do have the names of the eighteen Members who spoke in favor of and the nineteen Members who opposed Orde's police bill; correlation of these names with those of speakers, or with division lists when available, on other issues enables us to offer some tentative conclusions. First, in analyzing each speaker's constituency, we find that the proponents and opponents represented both counties and boroughs. A Member's type of seat, whether county or borough, is not a predictable variable. Support for Orde's bill was not restricted to Castle "placemen" or to MPs sitting for "rotten boroughs," just as opposition to the police bill did not come exclusively from representatives of the counties' Protestant electorate.[76] Whatever their constituency, Members' political affiliations are clear: Whigs opposed and Tories (supporters of Pitt's Government) favored the police bill. Of the nineteen opponents, thirteen became members of the Whig Club in 1789; only one of the eighteen proponents became a member.[77]

Because police was a party question, we find significant differences between the views of proponents and opponents on other issues. Proponents tended to *oppose* repeal of Poynings's Law in 1780, parliamentary reform in 1783, free trade and the Volunteers in 1785 (by supporting the Government's diluted Commercial Propositions and the militia bill), and Pension List reform in 1786; conversely, those speaking against the police legislation tended to *support* these "patriot" and reform measures. After 1786, the same voting patterns emerged, although not so sharply, on the questions of a rural police and an Irish riot act, with the Tories favoring and the Whigs opposing these measures; and on tithe reform and some concessions to Catholics, with

Whigs generally in favor and Tories opposed. The lesson appears to be that those who supported an armed, government-controlled police opposed a number of reform or conciliatory measures, whereas those who fought *against* such a police also fought *for* a variety of reforms in Irish society.[78] It is in this broad political context that we must interpret Orde's remark that Grattan during the police debates "thought fit to risk the tryal [sic] of his ascendancy in matters of Popular apprehension" by opposing "the extension of the influence of Government, and the armed force which," Orde added sarcastically, "might make all our wicked designs irresistible."[79]

The constitutional revolution of 1782 had consolidated a strong minority party within a Parliament still effectively controlled by London through Dublin Castle. In this autonomous law-making body, now checked only by the royal veto power, issues gained a new importance to Protestant Irishmen. Police was one of those issues. The new Dublin force was hotly debated not only because it would be the first government-controlled police in the British Isles, and not merely because this force was one resisted successfully by Londoners and the English Parliament – though these alone were powerful reasons – but also because the philosophy behind this type of police was anathema to Whig political principles. These fundamental beliefs emphasized liberty over authority, the rights of the people against the prerogatives of the Crown, local accountability in place of centralization, and governance by the "natural" rulers of society instead of salaried, government-appointed bureaucrats.

These sets of assumptions were common to Whigs in both England and Ireland. In England, Whig "liberty" meant a Parliament untrammeled by the Crown and free of the worst abuses of corruption and patronage. The Irish Whigs were similar to their English cousins by reason of geographical proximity, the class system, and a shared British culture. English and Irish Whigs opposed what Grattan called "armed patronage" because they believed that power should emanate from "representative bodies," representative, that is to say, of land, wealth, and education.[80] To English and Irish Whigs, liberty certainly did not mean democracy. Inclusion of the English proletariat, rural and urban, and of the rural Irish Catholic proletariat in the political system would entail its destruction. The fact that in Ireland the underclass was different in race and religion, language and customs, from the ruling class, Tory and Whig, only rigidified the class system in that country, making it unrecognizable to an Englishman.

III. Extending the innovation: the Irish County Police Act of 1787

The political, national, and Protestant challenge of 1778–84, centered in Dublin and the North, was only the first of two challenges to public order in Ireland in the 1780s. More frightening, in the long term, was the rural Catholic threat, social and economic in nature. The Rightboy movement of 1785–8, which followed earlier agrarian eruptions in 1761–5 and 1769–76, swept across Munster and western Leinster in what was, geographically speaking, the broadest challenge to established law before the tumultuous 1790s.[81]

Armed bodies of men, chiefly cottiers and laborers but also some farmers, numbering in the hundreds and sometimes thousands (7,000 on one occasion in Kerry in August 1786), converted entire districts to the rule of their law. Spawned by the shift from pasturage to tillage as a result of Foster's Corn Law of 1784 (tilled, unlike grazing, land being titheable), the protest movement succeeded in halving tithe income and even lowering priests' dues for religious services. The Rightboys (for so they called themselves) issued threatening notices, swore entire baronies under their oaths, requisitioned horses, raided successfully for firearms, destroyed crops, and maimed livestock. The movement produced widespread threats and "carefully staged rituals" of violence against persons, but killings were surprisingly rare; the Rightboys murdered only a half-dozen persons, whereas thirty-five of their own fell before the soldiers' muskets. In its extent and tactics, the uprising was impressive and remarkably successful. In the words of one observer in March 1786, "All law ceases but what the Rightboys like."[82]

Though many of the gentry organized private armed associations, local efforts were hampered by a widespread antipathy to the tithe system even among the respectable classes, and also by the threat of Rightboy reprisals, the "criminal state of torpidity" among the magistrates, and the magnitude of a revolt that "simply outran the capacity of ordinary institutions for the maintenance of public order." In the late summer of 1786, the Government was forced to send 2,000 troops into Munster, where Major-General Lord Luttrell mixed coercion with conciliation to establish a bloodless, if temporary, repression.[83] Renewal of the disturbances in the winter of 1786–7 led the Government to abandon its policy of conciliation. Still, compared to the threat, the crackdown was relatively mild. Fewer than 100 Rightboys were convicted at assizes in 1786–8; fewer than two dozen were sentenced to death, of whom a dozen were executed and 1 transported. Difficulties in prosecution and low levels of Rightboy personal violence explain in part this judicial leniency, but the Government also realized that the disorders constituted neither "concerted Insurrection" nor "Popish plots," but stemmed rather from "some real grievance, at bottom."[84]

In the aftermath, opposition from the Anglican establishment frustrated Pitt's wish for tithe reform and even won a Compensation Act whereby the recently lowered rates, now said to have been agreed to under duress, were nullified and the old valuations restored. In 1787 the Government turned to a series of reforms in law enforcement. An act was passed that created special officers to collect "forfeited recognizances" from plaintiffs, defendants, or witnesses who, having posted "sureties," failed to show up for court sessions. Second, the Government proposed a bill to extend the English Riot Act of 1714 to Ireland. A strong law against tumultuous meetings, Chief Secretary Orde explained to Pitt, would mean that "we need not put such force into the plan which is to follow" for a strengthened county police.[85]

The Irish Riot Act of 1787

Like the English Riot Act, the proposed Irish one would make unlawful assembly by a dozen or more persons a felony punishable by death without benefit of clergy. It would carry into Irish law the theoretical one-hour cooling-off period after reading of the proclamation, during which time the insurgents were presumably to disperse; if the reading was obstructed (a capital offense), the magistrates were to proceed at once to use force against the crowd. The Irish riot bill also transformed a host of agrarian crimes from misdemeanors into felonies. Tumultuous assembling and the administering of oaths were, prior to 1787, misdemeanors punishable by whipping, imprisonment, or fines. Misdemeanants sought and magistrates had had to accept bail on "recognizances," which were often forfeited and whose collection was virtually impossible.[86]

The new felony offenses of 1787 carried stiff penalties. Administering illegal oaths was punishable by transportation for life; taking an oath *without compulsion*, by transportation for seven years. The harshest punishment was reserved for anyone who tried, by either threat or infliction of personal violence or property destruction, to induce persons to enter into "any unlawful combination," to deter them from giving evidence, or to prevent the collection of rates or taxes. Such offenders "shall suffer death," with the body to be delivered to the county surgeon "to be by him publickly dissected." Virtually all Rightboy activities were now punishable with death: seizing of arms and ammunition, horses, and "money or goods"; writing, posting, or circulating any threatening "notice, letter or message"; and destroying "any building used for religious worship" or obstructing any clergyman, Catholic or Protestant, from "celebrating divine service." The only misdemeanor in the statute was the defrauding of *Anglican* clergymen of their dues and tithes, now made punishable by fine, imprisonment, or corporal punishment; no such protection was extended to Catholic priests, who had been favorite Rightboy targets.[87]

The Government appeared to believe that the Catholic priests could police their flocks, despite the fact that many of the Rightboys had rioted over priests' dues. The riot bill thus contained a controversial clause whereby any illegal meeting or oath taking in a Catholic chapel would result in the razing of the building and the selling of its contents. If a second chapel were built in the same parish within three years, it too would be pulled down. This proposal was the inversion of a clause in the English Riot Act that made it a capital felony for rioters to demolish any church or chapel belonging to Dissenters; the Irish bill would *legalize* similar destruction by the authorities.[88]

On balance, however, the Irish riot bill was a traditional and not unexpected response to rural social protest. It sought to enlarge the code of capital offenses, seeing this as a deterrent to crime; its purpose was more punitive than preventive. The bill would apply English law to Ireland, with the harsh clauses necessitated by the special character of rural protest in Ireland.

What was essentially Attorney-General Fitzgibbon's bill, introduced in late January 1787, provoked strong debate. Opponents charged that the bill unduly extended the influence of the Crown.[89] Virtually all criticism of the Government was to be judged "riotous." There was no provision for abuses of power by magistrates. The bill applied stern English law to a country that had few countervailing statutes of liberty. It was a proclamation of religious civil war, a multiplication of "capital offenses ... to a degree that makes human nature shudder." And it was directed at Irishmen who had merely sought redress of grievances (the tithe), not the overthrow of the monarchy, as in England in 1714.[90]

The debates did produce some victories for the bill's opponents. Although they lost in attempts to insert penalties for overzealous magistrates and to make the act local in application (to four Munster counties), the opposition did succeed in limiting the duration of the act (to three years) and in removing the severe "chapel" clause. Grattan noted that he "had heard of transgressors being dragged from the sanctuary, but never heard of the sanctuary being demolished."[91] On its second reading, on 19 February, the bill passed by a vote of 192–30; and on its the third reading, without a division. The bill passed so easily not only because the Government controlled the Commons but because ministers had made some concessions. Moreover, the bill applied English law to Ireland; it employed the traditional civil power, the county magistrates; and it would be most frequently invoked against the Catholic peasantry. Passage in the Lords was swift, with only a handful of liberal Whigs penning a dissent. The Duke of Leinster and three Earls, Charlemont, Mountgarret, and Desart, observed that "no coercive law ... can obviate or remove the effects while the cause remains unexplored."[92] On 25 March the bill became law; it would be renewed triennially until it was made permanent in 1800. Like the Insurrection Act of a decade later, the Irish Riot Act would in the early nineteenth century be a frequently employed weapon in the Government's continuing war against agrarian crime in Ireland.[93]

Rural police and magistracy: a wealth of proposals

The Chief Secretary and the Attorney-General now turned to their final two projects: reform of the magistracy and the county police. In January, Orde had observed to Pitt that "the forbearance of Persons employed under government to use force in the reduction of the tumults furnishes now an irresistible argument for the necessity of a settled police, of sufficient power not only to suppress but to keep in subjection the lawless spirits of the country." Such a police would require the increase of Castle influence, even Castle control. This would, of course, produce a chorus of protest from the Whigs. During the debates one opponent claimed to see Orde's project as "part of a general scheme of enslavement ..., first by getting into their power the metropolis of the Kingdom," next by a riot act, and finally by a proposed government-controlled rural police. It appeared that "administration wanted to pave the way to a union" of the two countries. To many observers, the Union of 1801 would be the product not simply of the nightmarish Rebellion of 1798 but of long-term Government plans, of which police "reform" was but a part.[94]

The Government's intended reform of the county magistracy was controversial for two reasons. In the eighteenth century, county magistrates, independent gentlemen of property and social standing, functioned not only as judges but as officers of police, with the baronial constables their rank and file. Moreover, the Castle now proposed that magistrates be "assisted" by Crown lawyers, and that they should only execute the law while a new set of constables and officers enforced it.

The Government proposed to place in every county a system of local magistrates, rotated in office, meeting in more frequent sessions, and assisted by a salaried Crown officer. It was these "assistant barristers," thirty-two in number, that were the heart of the controversial proposal.[95] The ablest critic of the plan was a thirty-six-year-old County Wicklow landowner and former Volunteer, Lord Carysfort, who argued that despite "its apparent utility," it would be "a most unpopular and dangerous measure." In a memorandum dated 31 January, Carysfort proposed instead a rotating system using only local magistrates who would receive a salary plus a fee each time they held a session. "Men of rank when they see the Magistracy upon a respectable footing, and its authority constantly & visibly operating, will be more ready to engage in it, & will discern their own personal Consequence immediately & essentially connected with it." Carysfort anticipated the Castle's objections to his scheme. He realized that "England would not gain a single additional Friend." A strong and independent local magistracy could block the extension of "the Influence of *English* Government in this Country," perhaps even encourage notions of Irish independence. Carysfort's own incisive analysis thus helped to kill his plan. Two weeks later, Orde cautioned the English Government not to "throw too much weight ... into the hands of the Aristocracy in this Country, however well attached the present Chiefs of them are to His Majesty's Administration."[96]

If a reformed magistracy was to execute the law, a strong police was necessary to enforce it. As early as January 1786, in his opening remarks to Parliament, the Lord Lieutenant had suggested a rural police to suppress the Rightboy movement. During the Dublin police debates, several speakers demanded a "universal" police for the country.[97] In April 1786, even before the Dublin police bill had reached the Lords, Orde submitted a hastily assembled bill "for rendering subconstables more useful": Sixteen government-appointed but locally paid constables would be placed in baronies judged by county magistrates to be in a state of disturbance. But their expense, control, and aims were questioned by enough Members – among them Lord Luttrell, the military commander, who would in the coming summer be sent to quell the Munster insurgents – that the Government withdrew its proposal the same day that it introduced it.[98]

"The design of the Ministry in the last session," noted the Earl of Charlemont, the military head of the Volunteers, "was to extend the Police Bill all over Ireland. This they were made to relinquish and found themselves compelled to be content with establishing it in Dublin.... The danger to liberty [there] is trifling compared to an extension of this *maréchaussée* through the country." The Dublin press diagnosed police reform as "the reigning influenza at present" and correctly predicted that a rural police bill would "undoubtedly be introduced" in the coming parliamentary session, "with the Munster disturbances the sanction for it."[99]

Dublin Castle formulated its plans amid great secrecy. As late as 19 February 1787, in answer to a question from Thomas Conolly about whether it was "the intention of Government to establish a general police," the Attorney-General professed his ignorance, for (so he said) "he never heard of such a measure but through the medium of a newspaper."[100] Indeed, newspapers suggested and correspondents to the Castle volunteered myriad proposals for reform of the civil power. One newspaper recommended a revived *posse comitatus* under the County Sheriff, only to complain that most Sheriffs were examples of "neglect and indolence" – in short, the problem, not the solution. Sir Richard Musgrave, Sheriff of County Waterford, was one of the exceptions; in September 1786, he had personally whipped a Rightboy when no one, "not even his own constables," would do it. Musgrave, who would later join the Whig Club and author a history of the 1798 Rebellion, proposed a reformed baronial police, county controlled but with proper arms, "a musket or a Bayonet." Many agreed with Lord Hillsborough – the Ulster nobleman and English politician who had been Secretary of State during the Gordon Riots – that the present laws need only be "duly executed": Frequent court sessions, rewards for active sheriffs, a tax on disturbed areas, and refurbishing of the existing system of constables were the answer.[101]

The most carefully reasoned argument for retention of local control was submitted by Lord Carysfort. "In order to maintain a regular Police," he wrote Orde in January 1787,

a constant and uniform support is necessary which can be had from the principal inhabitants alone. The occasional interference of the superior government may quell an insurrection and repress a temporary violence, but will contribute nothing towards establishing habitual obedience to law, and will infallibly produce this bad effect at least, the confirming [of] the Indolence and Inaction of the gentry.

A government-controlled police would not only alienate the resident gentry but also anger the lower orders, who "would renew the clamours which have in a great measure subsided." Control of the police should be transferred from county grand juries to the magistrates in each barony. They should appoint high and petty constables "without distinction of religion," for it was "an obvious good policy" to appoint Catholics. "It is a mark set upon them, and consequently a pledge for their good behaviour, and the least invidious as well as most effectual mode of making them personally responsible for the Peace." The office of constable needed to be upgraded with character and literacy requirements, for "if the constables are taught to consider themselves as (what they really are) the principal Persons, & Governors in their respective Districts, the People will be ambitious of the Office, as well as diligent in its Execution." Carysfort's noble aims paralleled his hopes for the magistracy, but they were blocked by the same problem: Strong local government was not in the best long-term interests of the English Government in Ireland. But in one major respect – the inclusion of Catholics – Carysfort's ideas would come to fruition in the Irish police of the early nineteenth century.[102]

More attractive to Dublin Castle than proposals favoring some local initiative were those that stressed the need for strong central control. Isaac Espinasse, former High Sheriff of County Dublin, proposed quartering throughout Munster seventy-two companies of infantry and light cavalry in barracks 15 miles apart, each company to be commanded by a salaried magistrate, at a total expense of £18,000, to be paid by county grand juries. More practical and constitutional was the innovative suggestion of Sir John Blacquière. Son of a Languedoc Huguenot *émigré*, with predictable views on the Catholic question, Blacquière had been a colonel in the dragoons, secretary in the English Embassy at Versailles (1771–2), and Irish Chief Secretary (1772–6). Blacquière urged the establishment of a government-controlled police in every county (otherwise "you invite the rest into rebellion"), but he cautioned Orde to find "other names, by the blessing of God" than a "general police or *maréchaussée*." The annual cost of this system of 130 magistrates and 3,500 constables Blacquière calculated to be £18,600, which could be met by using the funds appropriated but not yet spent for the militia.[103] Blacquière's proposal was remarkably similar to Orde's initial plan for a rural police. In its boldness it went beyond Orde's final proposal in 1787, and beyond Robert Peel's notions of police in 1814 as a temporary force used in disturbances. Blacquière's ideas foreshadowed the county constabulary of 1822 and, in its emphasis on total central control and financing, anticipated the national constabulary of 1836. But in the context of the 1780s, his ideas were radical and unrealistic. Perhaps it was Sir John's French background that enabled him to think in such un-British terms.

Yet another proposal that Orde considered was the study originally commissioned for the Dublin police bill, Sackville Hamilton's "Sketch of the Police of France." This memorandum argued the merits of the *maréchaussée*, the national rural police of 3,000 men divided into thirty companies, "one for each *Généralité* or County as it may be called." Across each district the police were quartered not "half a days journey from each other," in parties often as small as four privates and one lieutenant. Communication between districts was excellent, and the whole was "a great System of Intelligence and quick Pursuit." The police assisted the military, escorted revenue officers, apprehended poachers, vagrants, and "Idle fellows ... with Guns," and when taking "any criminal or rioter" had the power of "handcuffing and binding." In short, concluded Hamilton, "they are everything that our Subconstables were intended to be if corruption and Stupidity had not frustrated the good intent of their Institution."[104]

Faced with this extraordinary variety of proposals, Chief Secretary Orde and Attorney-General Fizgibbon worked together toward their goal of "a greater uniformity and a sort of universal System" of police. In its early stages, the Castle plan proposed to have each county governed by three Police Commissioners, who would appoint a High Constable for each police district and a Chief Constable with "a little body of petty constables" for each barony. The force was to be strictly Protestant, and where the demographic facts made this extremely difficult, the army should be concentrated. The county grand jury and magistrates would be barred from making any county appointments, since "it would be a job." To assist the county Police Commissioners, there was to be a new board of four magistrates, three of them being county justices serving on a rotating basis, the fourth a barrister selected by the Lord Lieutenant to act as chairman at quarter sessions. Financing the force would be unpopular if done by an addition to the county rate or by a special police tax, so income would have to come from the militia allocation, or general revenues, or a tax on disturbed baronies. The Police Commissioners were to have full power to direct "the whole Body or Parts of it generally as they please," and the policemen, who would be armed, were expected to patrol, obtain information, suppress tumults, and search for "the Arms of the Popish peasantry." The police was not intended to replace the army – "to which the Protestants of Ireland owe the little security they have for their Lives & Property."[105]

The Irish County Police Act of 1787

Such were Orde's hopes, early in 1787, for a general police throughout Ireland. "This Project," he believed, "or some very like it, if it can be carried into execution, would make a very happy change in the country of Ireland." By March, however, when the Government introduced its police bill, substantial modifications had been made in the Castle's project. Reasons of political expediency and expense no doubt dictated these changes. Orde's bill, as presented by Fitzgibbon, did not propose a nationwide police; indeed, there was no mention of Police Commissioners. The bill did not propose permanence, but would be in effect for only three years. "A good mode of experiment," it was asserted, would be to install the police only in disturbed baronies, "particularly not in the North if possible." Such baronies, when proclaimed by the Lord Lieutenant, would form a police "district." Each baronial police force would be commanded by a Chief Constable appointed by the Government, but the subconstables would be appointed by the county grand jury. These subconstables, no more than sixteen to a barony, would replace all existing baronial subconstables. Together the Chief Constable and the subconstables, all Protestants, would form "ministerial officers of the peace," on horse and foot, and be "provided with proper arms and accoutrements."[106]

In the absence of Police Commissioners, the police force would be directed by "new commissioners of the peace." The Government would examine the existing rolls of the magistracy, weed out the superannuated, inactive, or incompetent, and issue new commissions of the peace for which a property qualification would no longer be required. Sessions of the peace would be increased to eight a year in every county, and "a certain number of" county magistrates would serve at sessions on a rotating basis. These justices would be joined by a "counsel learned in the law," who would be their "constant assistant." Every county, disturbed or not, would receive this assistant barrister, a lawyer of six years' service who would be salaried and appointed by the Lord Lieutenant and forbidden to be a Member of Parliament. In addition to interpreting and executing the law at sessions, these magistrates would certify the good conduct of the subconstables, who might be dismissed by the assize judge. Financing of the force was to be divided between central and local authorities: the Chief Constable (£150 p.a.) and assistant barrister (£300) to be paid by the Government; the subconstables (£12), by the baronies as assessed at the county grand jury presentment.[107]

It is clear, as Fitzgibbon said in introducing the bill in the Commons, that the Government had "endeavoured to avoid innovation as much as possible."[108] Payment, control, and employment of the force were mixed, and at times would even be muddled, between central and local authorities. But the Attorney-General's reassuring remarks could not hide the truth that a strong police was itself an innovation. The concept of the police of 1787 – a *force* of men active in disturbed districts – was precisely the same as that of Peel's Peace Preservation Police of 1814. The dual control by local and central authorities anticipated the power relations behind the county constabulary of 1822. And the assistant barristers, men of talent and ambition, if not property (itself a radical idea), foreshadowed the Castle's "Stipendiary Magistrates" of the early nineteenth century.

The parliamentary scenario of the county police bill was reminiscent of that of the Dublin bill of the previous year. Fitzgibbon introduced the measure late in the session, on 30 March, to a Commons only one-third full; many Members were absent at assizes, and those present, in the unflattering and rhetorical words of one opponent, were "aide-de-camps, searchers, gaugers, placemen of all descriptions, and pensioners." Opposition attempts to defer consideration of the bill were defeated. The bill passed in the Commons ten days after its introduction, and with no changes whatsoever. On 13 April, two freeholders' petitions against the bill – one from County Mayo, the other from Belfast – were received after its passage in the Commons; they were referred to the Lords, where they were rejected.[109]

Though the Government proposed a much weaker police than it probably desired, the bill did draw some familiar criticism. The Castle's willingness to compromise and work with the county magistrates and grand juries at once blunted any widespread opposition and made some speakers appear to be overreacting in their criticism of the bill. During the debates Henry Grattan was remarkably silent; most of the vehemence came from Thomas Conolly, a personal enemy of Fitzgibbon, and from a number of Members from Ulster.[110] Nine of the thirteen speakers in opposition sat for Ulster constituencies. This preponderance of Ulster, the center of the original Volunteer movement and of political radicalism in late-eighteenth-century Ireland, had also been evident during the debates on the Riot Act, when many of Grattan's Whigs had supported the Government, whereas "the Presbyterian party" spoke in opposition. It is instructive to note that only two of the thirteen speakers against the rural police *lived* in Munster or Connaught.[111]

Opposition to the county police bill was not as intense or protracted as it had been the previous year over the Dublin one, but it was emotional and bitter. Thomas Conolly, MP for County Derry, thundered that the proposed "armed Maréchaussée ... [was] designed to crush to atoms every vestige of the Constitution." William Todd Jones, MP for the Belfast township of Lisburne, a Reformer and Volunteer captain, asserted that had the bill been introduced "in a British parliament, the matter of it would have hazarded an impeachment; but this kingdom is broken to the yoke."[112] Others described the proposal as "the most exceptionable [bill] ... ever seen" or opposed it simply as "a police bill, in the present acceptation of the word police; that is, to disguise an army of soldiers under the name of constables."[113]

Attempts to alter the provisions in the bill were easily defeated. The opposition described the Chief Constables and assistant barristers as salaried hirelings of state despotism who would usurp the functions of local gentlemen of standing. A motion, proposed by Grattan, opposing the abolition of an income requirement for magistrates was defeated by 111–41; an attempt to have the Chief Constables named by the county grand juries was defeated without a division.[114]

Having failed to alter the substance of the bill, the opposition now tried to restrict it territorially. A bid to saddle only Munster with the new police was defeated without a division. Grattan announced that he would not oppose the clause permitting the Government to divide a county into police districts if their number was no more than six. Government draft proposals had referred to "not more than 3 or 4 districts in any county." Orde now assured Grattan that "the highest average number" in any county would not be four; Fitzgibbon was certain that there would not be six. The clause was accepted without a division. When in July the Castle created the new districts, Kerry and Kilkenny were given five districts; Tipperary, seven; and Cork, ten.[115]

One objection that the Whig opposition did *not* make is significant: Not a single speaker quarreled with the Government's requirement that all of the policemen in a district must be Protestants.[116]

Government had offered a police bill laden with compromises regarding control and financing. When the opposition persisted in its protests against this second police bill in as many years, Government officials became increasingly impatient. Toward the end of the debate on 5 April the dam burst. In a brief speech, Secretary of State John Hely-Hutchinson brusquely observed that the Government possessed "the power of the sword," which included the police as well as the army. The Attorney-General took another tack. He called on those who spoke of "an innovation in the constitution to ... support their assertion with something like reason or argument." The bill, claimed Fitzgibbon, merely implemented "the old constitution of England" by creating in Ireland the Saxon-descended hundred and tithing constables incorporated in the English statute of 1285. "He defied them to come forward and argue the point – he set their whole stock of sagacity at defiance."[117]

Who would reply? Only two Members took up the challenge. John O'Neill, of an ancient Ulster family and Member for County Antrim, delivered a long, rambling, and emotional speech with a memorable peroration. "I advise administration," he bristled, "not to pursue the same system in parliament with the gentlemen of this country, as Great Britain has pursued with America. She first despised her weakness – she then roused her to fight, and in the end TAUGHT HER TO CONQUER." Thomas Conolly's reply was shorter but more to the point. He asked to be "forgiven for talking constitutional nonsense through anxiety to serve his country," but in England he knew of no government stipendiaries who intimidated local magistrates and quarter sessions or of any "high constables ... named and paid by Government.... [He] challenged him to confute this assertion." Referring to Fitzgibbon's denial of 19 February of any knowledge of a police bill (see page 109), Conolly said "he never thought, after what had passed from the right honourable gentleman upon a former session, he should ever see the riot act, for which he was then induced to vote, executed by paid justices." Fitzgibbon did not reply or speak again. The bill passed its Second Reading in the Commons by a vote of 110–29. It had its Third Reading with no division on 9 April, and sailed through the Lords on 21 May.[118]

Opinion in the public press paralleled the lines of argument in Parliament. The *Freeman's Journal* and the *Volunteer Evening Post* favored the rural police on the grounds of need (agrarian turmoil and "negligent" local magistrates) and efficiency (a strong police was superior to "ten times the number" of soldiers). Because of the compromise nature of the bill and the enervating debates of the previous year, opposition newspapers, like Grattan's parliamentary Whigs, were generally restrained in comment.[119]

But the radical *Hibernian Journal* did unload a rhetorical fusillade. The new police, a product of the "specious politicks of one ambitious lawyer" (Fitzgibbon), were woven from an "anti-constitutional fabric." They were the descendants not only of the French *maréchaussée* but even of the *Latrunculatores*, the police of ancient Rome, "despised by the Legions, abhorred by the Citizens, and cherished by abandoned Ministers." In a burst of hyperbole of amusing exactitude the *Journal* announced the new police would consist of "3573 Lawyers and constables" at an annual cost of "£64,960," and "it may be increased by Government *ad libitum*." The newspaper was accurate in its prediction for the future of Anglo-Irish Ireland:

Beware, my fellow citizens, of the accommodating principles which can combine an appearance of giving energy to the laws, with the reality of conveying an armed patronage to the Crown!.... Gentlemen of real property and conscious honour, disgusted by the petulant arrogance of professional self-sufficiency [the Castle magistrates], ... will retire from such versatile associates, and content themselves with the simple observance of those laws they once thought it their duty to enforce.... The political horizon lowers.[120]

The *Journal*'s estimates of police numbers and cost, outrageous exaggerations at the time, would underrepresent police realities in Ireland less than forty years later.

IV. Overview

It is easy today to wonder what all the fuss was about: 40 police by day and 400 by night in a city of 150,000 and perhaps 400 police in only four of the thirty-two Irish counties. The fuss, of course, was not over numbers but rather over the constitutional novelty of police controlled by the Government and the use of Ireland as a laboratory to test a thing rejected earlier in England.

The police angered both Catholics and many Protestants. The aggrieved Catholic peasantry would probably have willingly agreed to the exchange of local Protestant control for the perhaps less partial influence of the Castle had it not been for the increased efficiency expected from the new forces; in any case, they were upset that reform had been made in the police rather than in the land and tithe system. Many Protestants, on the other hand, now felt alienated from the English authorities upon whom they relied for their very lives and property. Within a decade they would be glad for order at any cost, but in the late 1780s they were concerned with what they perceived to be a threat to their own powers of self-government.

The question arises of whether the Protestants had had the power of police taken from them, or had forfeited that power. For Dublin, on balance, the former appears to be true; hence the greater vehemence of the opposition. For the countryside, the case is more complex. First, in the 1787 act, the Government took pains to share power with local Protestant authorities. Second, it is true that during the Rightboy disorders many magistrates, gentry, and constables had been inactive, whether from supineness, sympathy, or intimidation. To be sure, local authorities in England had also been guilty of neglect or misbehavior during disturbances. But, third, the special circumstances in Ireland argued more insistently for a new system of civil order than did English circumstances. In Ireland the religious, social, and economic cleavage between classes was so great and the size of the resident rural ruling class so small that it was impossible to police the countryside using special constables, private associations of property owners, and appeals to morality.

Related to these considerations was a fourth Irish problem: the absence of a unified nation-state. In England, from the time of Alfred the Great until

1688, powerful monarchs had, intermittently but surely, fashioned a powerful nation-state and a long tradition of common and statute law. Indeed, the Stuart and Cromwellian excesses had produced an emotional reaction: the eighteenth-century worship of local rights to the frustration of police reformers in England. But Ireland was only in the process of becoming a nation, thanks in large part to the legislative enactments of its English rulers. This slowly emerging, and still Protestant, nation spawned among the Presbyterians and Anglo-Irish strong nationalist sentiments. This nationalism was, in part, antipolice because the new police was viewed as an *English* experiment and because, paradoxically, it was part of the Castle policy of centralization. Irish Protestants feared that police reform would strengthen England's control of the island at a time when these patriots were zealous to increase their own political rights and powers.

What most of the Protestant nationalists left out of their political equation – just as they excluded them from the police – were the Catholic masses. Many Irish Whigs who could make fine speeches about "English liberties" forgot that they lived in Ireland: They were not so much hypocrites as one-eyed patriots who agreed with the strong views of Fitzgibbon more than they cared to admit. Even for those who championed the Catholics' cause, there were hidden problems. "The Irish Protestant could never be free," Grattan had asserted, "till the Irish Catholic had ceased to be a slave." But once the bondsmen were emancipated, men like Grattan no doubt believed that they would still be the natural rulers of society, that Anglo-Irish Ireland would somehow prevail.[121]

In the 1780s the Irish Whigs opposed a government-controlled police because they identified the rights of a drunken, even papist, Dublin weaver with those of a Wilkite London artisan. In either case, the Irish Whigs believed that if the Crown abused this man's rights, it also destroyed the liberties and historic powers of the natural rulers of society – themselves. But events in Ireland, and in France, in the 1790s would teach Protestant Ireland that English values might not always be applicable to their country – at least not an Ireland in which the privileged Protestant position could be kept intact. By the end of that decade, most of these erstwhile champions of liberty would realize that survival meant suppression of both that United Irish weaver's rights *and* their own local liberties. In Ireland the powers of the state – in the form of Dublin Castle, the British army, and in time even the new idea of police – would wax from the imperatives of necessity. From the 1790s on, and especially after Waterloo, the rising democratic demands in England would reintroduce the idea of police but would also demonstrate the strength of that nation's traditional liberties and local institutions.

CHAPTER 4

The Irish police experiment

The Police of Dublin ... was allowed to take place under circumstances of enormous misrepresentation.... The very working of the act [of 1786] implied that the metropolis was in a state of insurrection, or the most barbarous incivilization.... Everyone knows that there was no circumstance to justify this formidable array – but the parasites of the Court called it STRONG GOVERNMENT, and maintained that Ireland had particular occasion for it. Lord Fitzwilliam's friends will establish strong government of a different nature – Government, strong in the affections and goodwill of the people.

– *Dublin Evening Post*, 30 September 1794

What was called the Middlesex Justices Bill of 1792 was a copy in faint colours of the Dublin measure.

– F. W. Maitland, 1885

Historians have traditionally cited a series of police reforms in London and the writings of Patrick Colquhoun, police reformer, as the significant developments in British police history during the period of the French wars.[1] In fact, passage of the Irish police acts meant that the governments in London and Dublin committed themselves to trying out the new police idea in Ireland. Prime Minister William Pitt had been chastened by his defeat on the 1785 London police bill; he dared not propose the Dublin act of 1786 as a prototype for London. Were he to try, observed the *Dublin Evening Post*, "the ambitious youth would soon be hurled from power by the united voice of the people." Nor could he even flirt with the idea of an armed police. In Westminster and London, asked an Irish Whig, "do you see a watchman armed as a soldier, with a firelock and bayonet? His only appointments are a lantern, a rattle, and a handstaff." Police reform in London would have to consist of "a few improved and spirited modifications of the laws at present in force without any promulgation of novel principles."[2]

I. Police in London: traditionalism and tepid change

In that spirit, Bow Street in April 1790 had established in tiny city foot patrol to supplement the metropolis' few dozen highway foot patrols.[3] In the spring of 1792, Pitt's Government gave its support to the passage of the

Middlesex Justices Act, which created seven Police Offices, with three salaried magistrates and six constables attached to each office. In the brief debates in a thinly attended House, the Whigs, led by Charles James Fox, Richard Brinsley Sheridan, and Lord North, objected to this "dangerous innovation in principle," specifically the increase in Crown patronage and intrusion on the powers of local magistrates. Despite the fact that the new magistrates could not vote or sit in Parliament, Lord North warned of "excessive and unrestrained powers [such] as were vested in the two consuls of Rome formerly." Those in favor of the bill pointed to the volume of crime in the metropolis, and chided the opposition for considering the bill "too much in the abstract" and not weighing "the measure as opposed to the mischief." The bill passed without a division.[4]

The Middlesex Justices Act revolutionized the magistracy system in metropolitan London. Before, there had been the three government magistrates at Bow Street, with their few thief takers and small patrols; from 1792 on, there were some eight police offices complete with twenty-four magistrates and forty-eight constables or thief takers and the patrols. Both the magistrates (£400 p.a.) and constables (£30 p.a.) were well paid. The new system cost £12,300 a year in salaries alone. But the act of 1792 was in fact a half-measure: It created no body of men to enforce the law. It is "absurd in the extreme," complained the *Public Advertiser*, to reform the magistracy while leaving the apprehension of ruffians to "superannuated and decrepid [*sic*] watchmen armed with their lanthorns [lanterns], staffs, and rattles." Patrick Colquhoun, one of the new police magistrates, complained that "the Act of 1792 ... did no more than establish a purer Magistracy.... There has been no establishment of Police at all." A recent scholar has restated Colquhoun's conclusions. For a city with a population of 1 million, writes Norman Gash, a force of forty-eight constables at eight police offices was clearly "too small and decentralized to have any perceptible effect on the state of the metropolis."[5]

In police history, Patrick Colquhoun is remembered as the author of *A Treatise on the Police of the Metropolis* (1795), a monumental study that went through seven editions by 1806 and was translated into French in 1807. The work established him as the father of police science in England.[6] A Scottish businessman and former mayor of Glasgow who had moved to London in 1789, Colquhoun believed that a body of men was necessary in order to prevent crime and apprehend criminals. In his book he called for the creation in London of a "Central Board of Police" composed of five "Commissioners" appointed by the Home Secretary. This Board should appoint a "High Constable" for each police "Division" and under him some "Parochial Chief Constables" to direct the parish constables chosen locally from among the ratepayers. Colquhoun thus proposed to retain but improve the systems of local policing by bringing them under central control. Colquhoun's new police would apprehend vagrants as well as criminals, enforce licensing, keep criminal statistics, establish an intelligence network, publish a police gazette of known offenders, and at all times be in contact with the Government's Stipendiary Magistrates.

Behind these revolutionary recommendations lie several curiosities. These were the very principles of Pitt's police bill of 1785, yet not once does Colquhoun mention that proposal. Nor does he refer to the police developments in Dublin from 1786 on. Also, Colquhoun is curiously silent on the structure and details of his police for the capital; this statistically conscious man goes no further than to say that a body of men was necessary for an effective police. In his book of 400, and later more than 600, pages, he devotes but 6 pages to a discussion of this body of men.[7] Clearly, a police force was for Colquhoun only a part of what he called "the General Police Machine" – a grand system of morality, police science, criminology, and jurisprudence. In neglecting to explore the details of a professional police force, this pioneer in policing remained, in some ways, very much a man of his times.

II. The new police in Dublin

Substantive police reform in the 1790s came not in London but in the Irish capital. The authors of a history of Dublin, writing in 1818, said of the implementation of the new Dublin police that "no political event perhaps which occurred in Dublin exclusive of the rebellion and the union excited more agitation among the citizens." Another city historian, writing in 1821, reported that "the memorable Police Act, passed in 1786 ... for ten years was a source of the most vexatious disquietude to the city of Dublin." Henry Grattan, speaking in 1793, was less restrained:

If ever a city entertained a deep rooted and cordial hatred of any measure, if ever a city entertained an odium capable of being ascertained by numerical calculation, the city of Dublin entertained such an hatred for this institution. No measure, no expence, no enormity of administration had ever excited discontent so strong or so general as this abominable establishment.

The Attorney-General protested in 1791 that "the name *police* was invented to make them odious.... They were called by the offensive name, police, and the mob was set at them, to prevent, as far as might be, their efficiency." In Ireland police continued to be a subject tied to the politics of the period.[8]

A force of men

The new Dublin police, which began patrolling on 30 September 1786, was outfitted with green uniforms faced with blue for the constables and khaki faced with white for the watchmen. In November 1787 the drab uniform for the watch was replaced by "a more respectable" blue faced with crimson.[9] Each constable and watchman was armed with a musket, bayonet, and nine rounds of ball cartridge.[10] The initial force comprised 40 horse police (the petty constables) and 400 watchmen. This cavalry police was expensive and unpopular (even the horses were outfitted, with hempen brogans over the hoof, "in imitation of ... the *Guet* at Paris"); the force was reduced to twenty men in 1788 and eliminated two years later.[11] As early as November 1786 the commissioners requested that the foot police, the watch, be increased to 600 men, but they had to settle for 500 in 1788. These policemen were called the "watch," but as early as 1788 the distinction between day constables and night watchmen was disappearing. The 100 additional police authorized in 1788 were to be "watchmen by day"; in the debates of that year the watchmen were described as being "on duty day and night"; indeed, they even "go on particular occasions to any part of the kingdom." The men must have served long shifts, for the Police Commissioners, in seeking additional men in 1787, had observed that "the exertions and hard Duty ... have quite exhausted and worn ... down [the men].... They cannot hold out under a continuance of the same fatigue."[12]

Whereas the old watch was "principally composed of discharged or invalid soldiers ... [with] miserable pay," men who "cried the hour and accompanied the citizen very often ... from stand to stand," the new police were "younger ruffians." Recruits had to give securities for clothing and arms – £10 for watchmen and £20 for constables. This was difficult for watchmen, whose annual pay, at one shilling a day, amounted to £18 a year and even for constables, who annually earned £30, cut to £20 in 1788.[13] Police pay was, nevertheless, still clearly superior to that of an agricultural laborer, who, if he worked 280 days a year, earned about £6. The policemen, "the horse, [police] in particular," were "vastly more respectable than, from the salary could have been expected." Despite police advertisements for able-bodied, intelligent young men, there is some evidence that the commissioners had to draw on the Blue-coat Hospital at Oxmantown and the Royal Hospital at Kilmainham (discharged and invalided soldiers). Despite the *Post*'s claim that "since the formation" of the force 150 of the watchmen were Kilmainham outpensioners, and despite possible recruitment problems due to the unpopularity of the police, the average age of the men was almost certainly lower than that of the old watch.[14]

Problems with unserviceable arms, absenteeism, and discipline led to the creation in 1788 of eight "inspectors of the watch" to drill, review, and fine the men. The reform was not altogether successful, for deficiencies in accoutrements and discipline continued to be a problem. Maintenance of authorized force strength (440 in 1786, 520 in 1788, and 500 from 1790 on) was also difficult. Of the 100 extra day constables authorized in 1788, 95 were hired but only 60 remained in April 1789. An amending act of 1788 empowered the Lord Lieutenant to *reduce* the number of constables and watch "so often as he ... shall think fit." An unsubstantiated *Post* report of October 1790 put the watch at 250 men, some 150 having allegedly been transferred to a new Kilmainham Invalid Corps; this critic of the police claimed that it was "always too small, always inadequate to the protection of the citizens." A parliamentary speaker in 1791 stated that no more than 300 men were constantly on duty. In 1792 the watch establishment of 100 men in one of the four divisions had only 42 effective men. An official police return of February 1795 listed only 303 watchmen, some 200 below the authorized force level. In sum, an estimate based on scattered evidence would have the initial force of 440 effective men decline to about 300 a decade later.[15]

Controlling leisure and licensing, crime and crowds

The duties of this police force that patrolled the streets of the capital for a decade (1786–95) were onerous and varied. The men were charged with repressing crime and immorality, suppressing popular amusements and disturbances, and licensing trades and regulating traffic. The police functioned as agents against public immorality: Prostitutes were hustled off the streets; beggars were periodically rounded up and taken to the House of Industry; "idle vagabonds" were prevented from assembling in public places on the Sabbath; traditional locations for fairs and markets, "too often the source of Riot and Disorder," were proscribed; and May Day festivities were discouraged. Police repression was not limited to the lower classes; on one occasion, "three bucks of the first fashion" who amused themselves "for several hours" breaking street lights around St. Stephen's Green were arrested, jailed, and fined 20 guineas.[16]

Perhaps the most controversial duties of the new police were regulating liquor establishments, licensing workmen's trades, and controlling the city's traffic. The 1786 act stated that "every journeyman, apprentice, servant, or labourer who shall be found ... drinking, tipling, or gaming at unseasonable [and unspecified] hours" was to be "taken into custody" and the owner of the public house fined £10. This new law, aimed at lower-class imbibers, had clear political overtones because pubs were centers for radicalism and union activities. Enforcement inevitably led to trouble; the most serious incident occurred in April 1789 when some journeymen tailors, resisting arrest in a tavern, killed a constable, seriously wounded three others, and had one of their own killed.[17]

Another means of social control was licensing. Since the cost of the police establishment was defrayed not only from a house tax but from licensing revenues, the police commissioners were vigilant in enforcement. From 1786 on, all retailers in beer and liquor, metals, pawnbroking, car hire, stables, and secondhand goods had to register with the police and pay a 1-shilling licensing fee, on penalty of £5 fine (£10 for liquor dealers); the licensing fee was increased in one fiscal year, 1788–9, to 10 shillings for liquor sellers, £2 for hawkers of plants, printed materials, and old clothes, and £10 for pawnbrokers! The police also, from 1787 on, required butchers and workers in produce markets to be licensed and to wear badges.[18] These regulations helped the police to monitor stolen goods, but many citizens cited other purposes: government spying, erosion of individual economic liberties, raising of police revenues, and tax burdens on petty businessmen and their employees. The licensing requirements often led to bizarre situations. In one incident of nonpayment, the police seized law books at the venerable Four Courts over the objections of an irate and flustered Mr. Serjeant Toler. There was also the case of police distraint of goods at an old–clothes shop; a group of butchers' apprentices intervened and, in a wild affray, with clothes flying everywhere, the assailants rescued the shopkeeper's apparel as the police retreated.[19]

Controlling the vehicular traffic within seven miles of the city center was another task that fell to the police. Carmen, coal carriers, sedan chairmen, and other drivers of business or hired transport were issued badges and might be arrested for speeding, obstructing thoroughfares, driving recklessly, or other misbehavior. For many citizens this was a popular aspect of police work: one newspaper was pleased that the "incorrigible" drivers were now subject to a control for which we have "so long and so repeatedly called." Traffic matters apparently occupied "a great part of the time of the Police Commissioners." At a special police court, citizens were permitted to lodge complaints against drivers; in a single day in November 1789 the commissioners processed 130 citizen complaints. For their part, the harassed hackney sedan chairmen could also complain, as they did in a petition against the police presented to Parliament in 1788.[20]

If the city was undoubtedly more thoroughly regulated, was crime now more effectively controlled? In the first months of police patrolling in 1786, there was general agreement that crime had diminished. An earlier critic, *Saunders's News-letter*, pronounced the force "of the utmost utility to this city"; indeed, in a single night in October, the police made more than 100 arrests.[21] Footpads and highwaymen, child thieves and house robbers, counterfeiters and gamblers all felt the effects of the new police vigilance. Prisoners transported from jail to the courthouse were now escorted, not by the military, but by a police guard. By December, one newspaper admitted that

it is but justice to declare, that the public have benefitted by the police establishment, and however high the general prejudice has risen against the institution, candour must subscribe so far as to allow that the citizens have experienced a degree of quiet from nocturnal broils long unknown to the metropolis.[22]

In fact, it was reported that the police had chased many of the criminals beyond the Circular Road, the limit of police jurisdiction, into the neighboring County of Dublin. For this reason, Justice Graham in February 1787 proposed the creation of a five-man horse patrol for the city's outskirts.[23] Then, in April and May, the city was hit with a wave of robberies and housebreakings: The immunity to crime proved to have been "but of short duration." One newspaper theorized that the criminals have returned because "the police is not quite so dangerous, as they, at first, apprehended." From September to November 1787 another wave of crime, highlighted by the murder of two servants in the Bishop of Dublin's Palace, inundated the city as newspapers called for a strengthened police. One hundred constables were added to the force in 1788.[24]

Other crime waves – especially in June 1789, May–June 1792, and January–February 1795 – would hit the city, to be followed by periodic bursts of police vigilance. In the period 1786–95 the Dublin police certainly had its moments of brilliance. On one occasion a party was dispatched to Baltinglass, County Wicklow, where they arrested some counterfeiters; the police solved a number of robberies and even arrested a London embezzler who had fled to Dublin.[25] In one zealous nocturnal incident, the police stopped a man with a bulky sack over his back. When it was discovered to contain a body, the protesting man and his sack were taken to a police station. It turned out that the culprit was a student at Trinity College and the corpse was "a subject for dissection." The embarrassed officers discharged the student.[26]

The question remains as to whether police vigilance was able to reduce the level of criminality in the metropolis. In the absence of extant judicial statistics, we must rely on the qualitative judgments of newspapers and politicians.[27] Speaking in 1789, Attorney-General Fitzgibbon claimed that the police had dealt "a fatal blow to the mobocracy in Dublin." The propolice Freeman's Journal argued in 1792 that the city had been spared a recurrence of the "enormities" of 1784. Any increase in daily criminality, it noted, should not be the excuse for the "death warrant of the Police" but "tended rather to establish its necessity, than to prove its inutility." In other words, the incidence of crime required that an already "efficient Police" be strengthened. Yet four years later, after the disbanding of the government police, the same newspaper argued that until 1795 "this city was one of the most peaceable in Europe ... which [fact] was allowed by foreigners who had witnessed its protection and tranquillity."[28]

There is little argument that crime flourished before 1786 and after 1795, but what of crime rates in the interim? The Attorney-General, speaking in 1789 and again in 1791, observed that the statistics of criminal offenses and convictions showed a decline since 1786, and concluded that the police were thus *preventing* crime.[29] But it is more likely, based on newspaper reports of crime, that the figures indicate that the police were not *apprehending* criminals. Contemporary newspapers record the widespread use of knives, cutlasses, pistols, and "blunderbusses" in robberies and housebreakings, though the reported incidence of murder is rare.[30] The *Hibernian Journal* complained in April 1787 that robbers "plunder, cut, maim and knock down the passenger ... in the most public parts of town." It is "notorious," reported the *Dublin Evening Post* in November 1790, that persons and property are not secure. Henry Grattan stated in March 1791 that crime was widespread. These observations come, of course, from two newspapers and a politician opposed to the police institution. But the dispassionate *Saunders's News-letter* in January 1795 could bemoan "the frequency of robberies ... by armed banditti," several of them committed, significantly, "almost at the watch-house doors." Even more important was a statement by the propolice *Freeman's Journal*, which in 1792 was contemptuous of critics who wanted the policeman

to be deprived of his musket and bayonet, as it was *unconstitutional* to use instruments of death, against miscreants who demand the citizen's property at the mouth of a pistol or the point of a knife! And the cause of *liberty* required nothing less, than that he should be arrayed like a child with his *rattle* and be distinguished by his *cry* – in order by his vociferations and his lights, to warn the freebooter of his approach![31]

If the police, with notable exceptions, seemed unequal to the challenge of crime in the metropolis, they also proved to be unsuccessful in handling riots and affrays. Despite an early claim that "the civil power [is] now found abundantly sufficient to awe the most licentious into obedience," the record indicates that they had only three notable successes: containing a riot in January 1787 at Marshalsea Prison (shooting dead one prisoner), breaking up a theater riot in December 1793, and dispersing in June 1794 youthful stone throwers who had besieged a watchhouse (the police injuring one with musket fire).[32] On the other hand, the police were unable to disperse a Sabbath crowd of 2,000 in Merrion Square in March 1787, unable to control two nights of rioting in December 1787 on the arrival of a new Lord Lieutenant, and unable to control another two nights of disturbance outside the House of Commons in February 1789. A police attempt to quell some May Day disorders in 1789 resulted only in their being rescued by the military. In May 1790 troops had to intervene to end a five-hour riot at Ormond Bridge and the Quays, the police having stayed away; in election riots that same month, besieged watchmen had to be rescued by the military. In January 1791 the police were useless in disorders outside the townhouse of the Speaker of the House of Commons. In June 1793 the police were overpowered during grain riots in which a mob carried off fifty sacks of flour from unprotected carmen.[33]

Expensive ruffianism

The Dublin police were finding it difficult to contain both criminals and crowds. Perhaps their frustration helps to account for their growing reputation for misbehavior. A correspondent for the *Hibernian Journal* granted that there were "many respectable characters" in the police, but he also knew by experience that there were "some scabby sheep" as well. How did the Police Commissioners deal with their scabby sheep? They could fine them up to 40 shillings (one-seventh of their annual wage), send them to jail for up to thirty days, and even subject them to the humiliation of being marched through the streets with their coats on backward. In the first two weeks of operation three men were "turncoated" and discharged, and subsequently many policemen were punished with varying severity for several malpractices.[34] Controlling the men appears to have become a problem. A newspaper favorable to the police, the *Freeman's Journal*, complained that "turning a policeman's coat and confining him in gaol for a few days" were tepid punishments; one of the police commissioners, who advocated corporal punishment, admitted that "our powers are insufficient for enforcing ... strict discipline amongst our men." The Government responded in 1788 by creating eight inspectors of the watch to monitor the men. In addition, policemen were now required to give their names, in writing within one hour, to anyone arrested and to state the crime he was charged with. Tavern keepers were to be fined for serving watchmen on duty.[35]

Apart from the policemen's illegal imbibing, other examples of misbehavior were numerous enough to make the men unpopular. The correspondent who talked of scabby sheep in the force had, with his wife and child, been assaulted on the sidewalk by two of the horse police, "a bastard son of Mars, a ruffian horseman" and his fellow "centaur." In another incident, a watchman, whom Sheriff Williams had accidentally jostled in the press of a crowd, turned surly and knocked the sheriff down "with the butt end of his musket – *Quis custodiet custodes ipsos*? [Who will protect us from our protectors?]"[36] A Mr. Fleming, "a respectable house-keeper in Church Street," reported being attacked by a police officer; Fleming prosecuted Chief Constable Godfrey, who was sentenced to six months' imprisonment. On another occasion, one night when a not so respectable woman ("the half-naked wretch") was being dragged through Eustace Street by a party of police, "Counsellor E—n—lds, ... shocked at the barbarity of the proceeding," tried to intervene on her behalf. He was "instantly struck in the face and knocked down four times" by one of the police. Later when the man's friend, "a Mr. B-s—q--t," and another "gentleman" tried to intervene, they were "surrounded and attacked by a reinforcement of the police," and Mr. B., "seeing his life in danger, was necessitated to draw his sword."[37]

"Ruffians" is the recurring word used to describe the policemen. The former watch, observed the *Dublin Morning Post*, "was not young enough to indulge the licentiousness of the younger ruffians who compose the police"; seven weeks later the same newspaper, which announced that it was not against "a proper System of Police," was complaining of "the Ruffians who form the Police." Police brutality could, of course, easily become a partisan question. Critics of the force could gleefully itemize or exaggerate stories; indeed, the *Freeman's Journal* in October 1786 upbraided the *Hibernian Journal*, "the Cap-of-Liberty Journal," for allegedly inflating accounts of police misconduct. Yet even the *Freeman's Journal* first mentioned receiving "several unauthenticated complaints of misconduct of the Police Guard," then reported watchmen breaking open doors with too much enthusiasm and too little reason, and at length editorialized that many policemen were acting out of the control of the commissioners.[38]

Part of the problem was the quasi-military nature of the Dublin policemen. A loaded musket, remarked one observer, made them "very soon forget that they were peace officers." Reviewing and drilling like soldiers, calling themselves "captains," they "get the military insolence without military discipline." Behaving with "flippancy and insolence," they "seemed to consider themselves entirely as servants of the Crown, not of the people."[39] Citizens' requests for police aid were frequently treated with contempt. A shop owner seeking police protection was rebuffed with insults. A merchant who reported a warehouse robbery was "treated with rudeness and desired to go to the devil." A householder who reported that a mob was breaking his windows was informed that the police sergeant was asleep and not to be awakened. "If one of the Journeymen Tyrants is called upon or even spoke to," complained one newspaper, "nothing is answered but surly insolence – and it is well if the person who speaks to them is not seized and confined in a watch house."[40]

Police misbehavior showed itself in a variety of misdeeds, even crimes. There was a celebrated case of illegal detention that caused a stir in Parliament; an elderly woman, the wife of an Englishman who had come to Ireland to establish a manufacturing trade, had been seized without warrant and held without charges for twenty-two hours. The police were charged by the *Freeman's Journal* with "the crying evil" of "villainous connivance" with prostitutes and criminals.[41] It was "rare" to find watchmen at their posts after midnight. Intoxication while on duty appears to have been an offense early on punished severely by the commissioners; newspaper accounts like the one of a drunken watchman assaulting passersby were rare.[42] More serious were cases of police pilferage. Two watchmen, in the act of robbing the house of a blind man, were stopped by the neighbors; when more police arrived, the men threatened the angry crowd with bayonets. During a fire at a merchant's shop, a group of police were seen stealing liquor, which onlookers made them put down. At another fire, a watchman protecting a gentleman's house from looters was afterward discovered to have on him portable booty consisting of framed pictures and handkerchiefs! There was even, for a while, the bizarre scenario of several successful robberies by a gang of seven thieves, one of whom "wore a police uniform."[43]

In addition to its other sins, the Dublin police force was expensive. Police costs for the pre-1786 watch system had averaged less than £5,000 annually. In 1787 and 1788 police protection cost £20,000 a year; £18,000 annually in 1789–92 and £17,000 in 1793–4. The expense of the new, compared with the old, police was thus enormous. In its first two and a half years, the police cost £51,000, whereas over a similar period, the watch would have cost £11,500. The parish watch system was admitted to have been ineffective, but many agreed with Grattan that before 1786 "the citizens were robbed on cheaper terms than the inhabitants [who] ... now pay enormously for dragooning the city."[44] Revenues for the new police came from three sources. A police tax, assessed on the yearly rental value of all houses and tenements, accounted for about half or £10,000 of the revenues. The old watch rate of 1 shilling in the pound (5 percent valuation) was changed to a police rate of 1s. 6d., initially on all properties, but amended in 1788 to only those over £5 in value, the 1-shilling rate being restored to properties below this valuation. Income from a city tax on carriages and coaches produced about £5,000 a year. The remainder of police revenues came from licensing fees.[45]

How these revenues were expended was what disturbed many citizens. Parliamentary committees of inquiry into the police accounts revealed exorbitant charges for questionable items. Just under half – £9,500 – of the annual expenditures went for the salaries of constables and watchmen. Some £3,500 was spent annually on salaries for thirty-six men ranging from Commissioners to secretaries and "third clerks"; in the accounts this sum was given *in addition* to the £20,000 annual expense of the force. Over a two-and-a-half-year period, £4,000 had been spent for the rental and restoration of, and for furniture in, various police buildings. In the same period, costs for the horses, forage, saddles, and accoutrements of the forty-man horse police came to £4,600 and stationers' bills, to £3,316. In one year, unspecified "tradesmen's bills" totaled £1,658. "An excessive charge," some £750, was spent annually on coals and candles (heat and light), 180 of the 436 tons of coal being not used but embezzled. Then there were the charges, in Grattan's words, that were "enormous and their quality ridiculous": mirrors, £138; Wilton carpets, £99; gilt-edged writing paper, £150; "sundry necessaries" for the jail, £321; and "incidents" (unspecified items), £591.[46]

As these fiscal details became public knowledge, the Government decided not to try to cover them up. In the 1788 session, when an opposition motion to revive debate was defeated by 56–49, Chief Secretary Alleyne Fitzherbert immediately moved to reopen the discussion; nevertheless, a subsequent Whig resolution condemning the fiscal irregularities was lost by 100–41. The next year, after long and lively debate, the Commons rejected the findings of its own committee on the police accounts by 132–78, even though the police commissioners themselves had concluded that much in the 1787 accounts was irregular and extravagant. As John Philpot Curran, MP, wryly noted, the House's acquittal of the police was "not unlike the verdict of a Welsh jury that said to the judge, 'My lord, we find the man that stole the mare, not guilty.'"[47]

In sum, the police establishment had become, in the words of the Commons' investigating committee, one of "unnecessary patronage, waste, and dissipation," or in the inspired rhetoric of the *Dublin Evening Post*, "a system of profusion, defalcation, and peculation." Despite the Government's defense of the police throughout the controversy, some changes were made, not least for "the decency of appearances."[48] Dublin Castle dismissed the head Police Accountant, reduced the number of clerks, awarded all contracts "to the most reasonable bidder invited by public advertisement," regularized the accounts, cut stationery expenses, eliminated the horse police altogether, and reduced costs overall by "one-third" – even as the number of police had been increased by one-fourth. The Chancellor of the Exchequer claimed that the expenses of the force for 1789 were £13,000; at the time this figure was accepted as accurate, but Grattan would later demonstrate that official police returns for 1789 put the cost at £18,000.[49] The issue of expense continued to generate controversy. In 1791 a member of the Whig opposition, Major John Doyle, performed detailed computations, of admittedly dissimilar police authorities, that purported to prove that Dubliners paid

compared with your former establishment [the old watch], ... more than twice the sum for little more than half the protection; that compared with *Westminster*, your parish pays ... more per annum for less than half the protection; that compared with [the City] of *London* your parishes pay ... more than *seven times the sum* paid by those in London.

Doyle's calculations might be disputed (though no Member rose to do so), but his conclusion reflected the feelings of most Dubliners: "Good God, Sir, is not this oppression?"[50]

We have seen, in short, how an understrength and yet expensive police was hard put not only to repress crime but also to curtail popular amusements, curb immorality, quell disturbances, and enforce controversial licensing and traffic regulations. The armed, quasi-military policeman, even if a respectable character, was a member of an exceedingly unpopular institution; and there were in the force enough scabby sheep, whose behavior was criminal, brutal, or simply insolent, to keep alive strong public feelings against the police.

Growing protest against the new police

The articulated opposition to the Dublin police came from two quite different parts of the Protestant community: the householders and tradesmen, on the one hand, and the Whig politicians on the other. For the former, redress through petitioning was the resort. In February 1788, 7,000 householders from every parish called for the restoration of a locally controlled "constitutional guard ... at half the expense of the present police establishment." Parliament rejected their petition, as it did a second one in April 1789. In January 1791 eleven petitions from city freeholders and the guilds of merchants, chandlers, smiths, and weavers protesting the "insufficient, burdensome, and dangerous and unconstitutional" institution were presented and rejected. The next year, petitions from sixteen of the city's twenty parishes met a similar fate.[51] The Government complained of the "Repetition of the Old Charges, without anything either new or important"; the Attorney-General objected to "the overstrained language of Party" in the petitions, which he "would not pay regard to ... merely from their number." Grattan, by 1792, had to admit that the protests were listened to "with a very dull ear." The city now seemed to "acquiesce with a torpid indifference." Not until early 1795 would more petitions, from eight parishes, be presented to Parliament.[52]

For the Whig politicians, opposition to the police was a part of their opposition to British control of Irish politics. "The adoption of a police ... [had been] merely and obnoxiously experimental," and its "continuation ... must be allowed a shameful national disgrace." Ireland should not "servilely acquiesce with every prescription of Britain."[53] The *fin-de-siècle* Anglo-Irish patriots demanded not only repeal of the Dublin Police Act but also the exclusion of pensioners, placemen, and revenue officers from Parliament, a reduction of Crown influence, and adjustments of tithe grievances. This Whig campaign of "grand principle," pressed by the "patriotic Whig Club" established in 1789, was the consolidation of a program in its formative stages during the police debates of 1786–7.[54]

For the Whigs until the early 1790s, the threat to liberty in Ireland and the challenge to their own political power came from outside, from Britain. The propertied, aristocratic, "natural" rulers of the Irish nation had not, as in England, been allowed to be masters in their own country. This situation created feelings of resentment that were repeatedly articulated by the Anglo-Irish during the police debates of 1789–91. Mr. Arthur Browne, quoting Swift, protested that the English "seem to think of us as one of their petty colonies.... It is the misfortune of this country to take all the insults which England would spurn at." Another MP, Charles Francis Sheridan – brother of the London playwright-MP, Richard Brinsley Sheridan – objected to "this French imitation of the police, unknown in London, and reprobated and rejected as to Westminster." Henry Grattan was livid that "the abomination of London was made the police of Dublin." "A scavenger would have found it in the streets of London," Grattan observed on another occasion, but "the groaping [sic] hands of the Irish ministry picked it up, and made it the law of the land." Major Doyle was more restrained: "The citizen of London is respected and cherished by the Minister; the citizen of Dublin oppressed and scoffed at by his shadow [the Chief Secretary]." Mr. Kearney noted, more abstractly, that "the preservation of the independency of the capital of either kingdom is essentially necessary to the preservation of the liberty of the entire kingdom."[55]

Despite the brilliance of Whig rhetoric, year after year, against the police, the protests were in vain. Whig-supported petitions were rejected. Whig resolutions condemning the police failed by 140–94 in 1790 and by 135–87 the next year. Grattan might storm against the Castle's "puerile obstinacy and stubborn stupidity," but to no effect.[56] There were, however, local victories. The police was an important issue in city politics. A celebrated example was the election of the Lord Mayor in April 1790. The Board of Aldermen, whose ranks furnished the three Police Commissioners and four divisional justices, were opposed by the Common Council, which was dominated by the city's organized trades. The councilmen three times rejected the Board's nominee, Alderman William James, a Police Commissioner, for the mayoralty, and, "instructed by their respective guilds to vote against every police Alderman," they rejected seven other Board nominees before finding an acceptable one. The entire affair, crowed the Dublin Evening Post, was "a death blow to the police influence in the city." Two years later, the Board again tried to nominate Alderman James and again he was rejected – as was their second nominee, Alderman Moncrieffe, also a Police Commissioner. The much-abused James retired from city politics in 1794 but continued to serve as Police Commissioner until the dissolution of the force in August 1795.[57]

In the aftermath of the mayoral controversy of 1790, city elections were held for representatives to Parliament. With the police again a central issue, Protestant electors in the freeman borough returned two Whigs, Lord Henry Fitzgerald and Henry Grattan, by majorities of two to one. A huge triumphal procession, "beyond conception numerous," carried the victors, dressed in the uniform of the Whig Club, to the hustings. Liberty Boys sported patriotic sprigs of laurel, and each of the city's guilds carried a banner. "Light to the

Cause of Independence" read the chandlers' cloth, "and Obscurity to the Police Establishment." In the early evening of 12 May the disorders began. Whig supporters placed candles in their street windows, in the traditional manner of celebration, and mobs cried "Light, Light," outside darkened houses. Scores of windows were broken, the chief targets being houses of police aldermen. When a mob attacked a police watch house, the besieged watchmen fired, killing two young men and wounding several others. The military had to be called out to restore order in the city's streets.[58]

If the police continued to be a political question, the transformation in national politics profoundly altered perspectives on the police. In the 1780s "liberty" and "the people" had been understood to refer to the Protestant community; from 1791 on, with the activities of the Catholic Committee and the United Irishmen, those terms were being used by groups that included Catholics, who in Dublin constituted three of every four inhabitants. Whig demands had been for the restoration of police powers to the (Protestant) citizenry, for the "recovery of [the] chartered rights" of the City Corporation; now new spokesmen for previously unrepresented groups demanded rights for themselves.[59]

When Dublin Castle extended a broad range of new rights and powers to His Majesty's Catholic subjects in 1792–3, many Protestants opposed their implementation. In Dublin the trade guilds refused to admit Catholic members, and the Common Council of the City Corporation refused Catholics the vote and membership in the Council. In 1792 the Corporation arranged a triumphal procession to the Castle, where they presented a resolution demanding retention of the Protestant ascendancy "which their forefathers won with their swords, and which is therefore their birthright." What was happening, quickly in the early 1790s, was that the "Dublin common council and the guilds from being the focal points for city liberalism were becoming strongholds of protestant conservatism." Indeed, until 1835 the City Corporation would remain an exclusively Protestant body.[60]

A similar transformation was occurring in national politics. The Whigs were being outflanked on their left by Catholic radicals and Northern Presbyterian republicans; the Whigs, said Wolfe Tone, "dread the people as much as the Castle does." The Whig Club, established in June 1789 and composed of liberal Protestant patricians, endorsed what were really only "measures of secondary reform" – the elimination of pensioners, placemen, and police. Individuals like Grattan did press the Catholic claims, but the Whig Club did not demand Catholic enfranchisement. Even in their abortive parliamentary reform bill of 1794, the Whigs proposed neither to purify the boroughs nor to enlarge the electorate.[61]

Like the City Corporation, the Irish Whigs, once an engine for liberal reform, were by the mid-1790s increasingly on the defensive. Their patriotism was backward-looking; the constitution they idealized was the Anglo-Irish one of 1688 and 1782. In short, the new cross-sectarian forces of republicanism were challenging the Whigs' unspoken assumption that the natural rulers of the nation were the aristocratic Anglo-Irish. In the 1780s the

Whigs had judged the threat to Irish liberty to come from outside, from Britain; to the Whigs in the 1790s it became increasingly clear that the threat to liberty, to Anglo-Irish freedom, had shifted location – it now came from within Ireland.

It is crucial to understand this rapid political change in order to understand the developments in the police. In their opposition to the Dublin police of 1786, the Whigs cannot be accused of being simply negative and rhetorical. As early as April 1789, Grattan had offered an alternative plan of police. The force would be disarmed and locally controlled. Each parish (some to be united) would have its own constables and watchmen, commanded by a Chief Constable chosen by the Lord Mayor. Each parish force would be regulated by a city alderman and an elected committee of parish ratepayers; overall superintendence of the various parish forces would lie with the City Corporation. Police power would thus rest with the citizens, not the Government. Grattan recognized the hopelessness of his bill's passing, for it was not until two years later, in March 1791, that he introduced the bill in Parliament. Its main features were parish watch forces totaling 700 men in winter and 500 in summer; retention of the 40 constables; 2 police offices, one on each side of the River Liffey; and a total cost of £9,000. After long debate, Grattan's proposal was defeated by 135–87.[62]

When the Whig bill was revived two years later, in June 1793, the political climate had changed drastically. To the new challenge of Catholic radicalism was added the grim catalogue of recent events in Jacobin France: the execution of Louis XVI (21 January), the declaration of war against England (1 February), the creation of the Committee of Public Safety (6 April), the arrest of the Girondists (2 June), and the onset of the Reign of Terror. Significantly, in the Irish police debates of 24 June, hardly anyone objected to Grattan's own cost estimate for the proposed parish forces totaling 550 men; at £14,000, the budget cut current police expenditures by only one-fifth. Of more concern to parliamentary members in a session that gave the franchise to Catholics ("a precedent fatal to all legitimate authority," moaned Fitzgibbon) was the issue of control of the police.[63] Petitions against the Castle's police were now seen as coming not from the people but from "petty factions" using "clandestine means." Parish control of the watchmen would be "highly dangerous" because it would "suffer the democracy to acquire an excessive preponderance" in the city; the House was reminded of "the present state of Paris resulting from the same cause." It was charged that the civil power would be "under the direction of persons who were now outlaws"; if the democracy controlled the police, which man would "step forward and crush the growing sedition?" In the current temper, it was only groups of men "under the title of the United Irishmen ..., and these only ... [who] execrate your [current] police." In these times, the Government should "never let its power for a moment be diminished." Was this a time "to wrest the control of armed men from the executive power, and vest it in a democracy, by popular election?"[64]

The fears of the bill's foes might be real enough, but their foundations were weak. Dublin's city politics was still firmly Protestant. Grattan "laughed at" the charge that his bill "went to establish a democracy in the city"; it was a "shallow artifice" contrived by the Castle.

> Much as democracy was now reprobated ... as it existed in France, yet our respect for corporations and corporate rights should be preserved. ... What! Should it be said that a city is governed by democracy, if the executive power have not the government of it?

Grattan argued, rather, that the long history of executive rule in Ireland had thrown "the state into a kind of popular fever" that might ultimately produce a democracy.[65] One Member, referring to James Napper Tandy, had claimed that Grattan's police would be directed by "outlaws." But Tandy's case may in fact be used to refute the charge. An ironmonger's son who became "the most indefatigable of the agitators in Ireland," Tandy had been a parliamentary reformer in the 1780s and in 1790 had become a member of the City's Common Council and the Whig Club. In the latter year, he chaired a freeholders' meeting calling for repeal of the 1786 Police Act, and in the electoral procession for Grattan and Fitzgerald he had been seen, "in all the surliness of republicanism, grinning most ghastly smiles," directing the cheers of the crowd. In 1791 he joined the new United Irish movement; the next year he was arrested, tried, and found not guilty. In 1793, fearing a second prosecution, he resigned his Common Council seat and fled to America. At a time when the City Corporation was pledging its loyalty to the Crown and a Protestant state, Napper Tandy's views hardly typified those of Dublin's local politicians.[66]

Grattan's 1793 bill had been easily defeated by 86–30, but for a number of reasons some reform in the police was seen as necessary. One was the force itself; as Grattan observed, "the history of the police is its strongest condemnation." Another was the Government's promise of some relief. The Lord Lieutenant in January 1793 had pledged to improve the police; indeed, the Whigs were upset by the Government's lack of support for Grattan's bill. A third reason was Pitt's wartime coalition ministry, formed in July 1794, which allied Whigs and Tories in a common cause. The Irish Whigs were firm supporters of the struggle against republican France; surely, amid the swirl of far greater events, some redress of the Whigs' chief local grievance, the Dublin police, would occur. By the end of 1794 some modification of the present police seemed certain.[67]

The new Lord Lieutenant, the Whig Earl Fitzwilliam, pledged himself to two causes: full Catholic Emancipation and repeal of the Dublin Police Act. Fitzwilliam arrived in Ireland in January 1795; six weeks later he was out of office. Political inexperience and unfamiliarity with Irish politics, idealism overladen with righteous moralizing, his advanced political views on the Catholic question, and his rash dismissals of high Tory officeholders all explain his quick recall.[68] Grattan, with Fitzwilliam's approval, had introduced his Dublin police bill on 17 February. The press was ecstatic. The *Hibernian Journal* argued that "in no instance can the good intentions of

Government be better elucidated than their breaking down that monstrous, burdensome, and ineffectual institution, the Police." The premature *Morning Post* announced the "REPEAL OF [THE] DUBLIN POLICE LAW." A week later, Fitzwilliam was informed he was no longer Lord Lieutenant.[69]

The arrival of the new viceroy, Earl Camden, triggered riots in Dublin. For two nights, mobs "armed with blunderbusses, muskets, pistols, [and] long knives" swirled through the streets, attacked the head police office, stormed Fitzgibbon's house and even stoned his person (a £500 reward was issued), and engaged in an orgy of window breaking throughout the metropolis. "The miserable shadow of the police that remain [being] insufficient to protect themselves," the military took to the streets, killing two men before order was restored.[70] Throughout April the police demonstrated their total inability to function. A crowd of protesting carmen and coal porters put to flight a party of police; a mob rescued two prisoners from their police escort; robberies occurred on the very doors of the police offices; and on the eve of Grattan's presentation of the Catholic emancipation bill, the Government placed a military guard in the police watch houses. In the aftermath of Fitzwilliam's recall, the outcome of the vote on 4 May on the Catholic bill was never in doubt. Despite the bill's rejection by a vote of 155–84, the streets of Dublin remained quiet.[71]

In Lecky's opinion, this defeat was the last constitutional hope for the majority of the people in Ireland. The rejection of further Catholic relief and of parliamentary and tithe reform paved the way for the Rebellion in 1798. To add insult to injury, the Government rewarded the unpopular Lord Chancellor, John Fitzgibbon, with an earldom; two years later, his longtime political foe, Grattan, would walk out of a Parliament in which his usefulness had long since ended.[72]

In May 1795, one week after the defeat of the Catholic emancipation bill, the Government introduced its bill to return the police to the citizens of Dublin. Lord Lieutenant Camden's proposal met little opposition; in the Lords, which gave its approval on 21 May, only Fitzgibbon, now the Earl of Clare, criticized the Government for abandoning the police principles of 1786. His stance is understandable, since for a decade he had been the chief advocate for the unpopular force. But Fitzgibbon need not have worried: Local control had far different implications in 1795 than it would have had in 1786 or 1790. Camden sought to accommodate "the wishes of the respectable persons in this country"; the force would be controlled by "men of respectability in point of knowledge and character." What more reliable body could be found than the Corporation of the City of Dublin? As recently as March, those Protestant gentlemen had petitioned the King not to abandon his Loyal subjects and "the first Protestant Corporation in Ireland"; on 4 May Grattan had claimed that "with the single exception of the Corporation of Dublin," no petitions had been submitted against Catholic emancipation.[73]

The Dublin Police Act of 1795: restoration of local control

The reform of the Dublin police was a part of the growing Protestant reaction against the rising tide of radicalism. In a period when political reforms were blocked and men like Fitzgibbon rewarded, when habeas corpus would be suspended and an Insurrection Act enacted within the year, it made sense to the Government to restore the police of the capital to local Protestant control.[74] The 1795 act can be seen as a long-delayed sop to Dublin's Protestants. In any case, the record of the Dublin police seemed to indicate that a Dublin Castle-controlled force had not been a success. The Government could take comfort in the knowledge that in the event of any serious trouble in the capital, the military could be ordered onto the streets.

The Police Act of 1795, modeled after Grattan's proposals of 1787, 1791, and 1793, repealed the 1786 act and provided for a locally directed, unarmed "Civic Guard." The Dublin "police district" comprised two "divisions," north and south of the Liffey. The whole was overseen by a single "Superintendant Magistrate," and each division was headed by a "divisional justice." These three men, who could not sit in Parliament, were nominated by the Lord Mayor and aldermen and elected by the Common Council, subject to the Lord Lieutenant's approval. The Superintendent Magistrate was to appoint for each division twenty-five petty constables and, with the Lord Lieutenant's approval, a Chief Constable for each division and a High Constable for the police district. This Corporation-controlled force of fifty men and their officers would coexist with the separate night watches furnished by the parishes. Church wardens and parish directors in each of the twenty parishes would appoint 2 constables and 2 subconstables (aged thirty to fifty) and a number of watchmen (aged twenty to fifty), "as shall be alloted to each parish," the total in the city to be at least 500.[75]

The pay of the new force was comparable to that of the previous police. The Superintendent Magistrate and the divisional justices were salaried at £600 and £300, respectively; the parish constables received £35 a year and the subconstables £25. The watchmen, at £18, earned as much as the "watchmen" in the police of 1786–95; the pre-1786 watchmen had earned £7. The act listed no salary for the Corporation-appointed petty constables, but presumably they received at least £25.[76] All expenses of the Corporation police were to be paid from a special government fund, with the parish forces to be funded by a watch rate slightly lower than the previous police tax.[77] Nonpayment of the watch tax could lead to distraint of goods. The powers of the previous Police Commissioners were transferred to the Lord Mayor. Licensing requirements for a variety of trades, traffic regulations, and penalties for after-hours drinking were all continued.[78] The Corporation constables were to be uniformed, but the clothing of the parish watch was each to have "a distinct variation"; one parish rejected the Lord Lieutenant's offer of 140 unused suits of police clothing.[79] The new watch was not issued firearms, but instead equipment of "a more constitutional degree of power": lanterns, watch poles, and rattles ("clappers"), these last to be used to call the hour of the night and summon aid. The watchman was now judged to be "formidable to the rioter and the robber, without being dangerous to the peaceable citizen."[80]

The 1795 Police Act did not constitute a return to pre-1786 patterns of policing. It represented, instead, a somewhat awkward compromise between the constitutionality of the pre-1786 watch and the potential efficiency, or centralization, of the police of 1786–95. Within a single police district the City Corporation controlled 50 constables and the parishes some 576 constables and watchmen. If control was local, it was not hopelessly fragmented. The Lord Mayor reviewed the parish forces four times a year. All instances of misconduct or complaint, whether brought by citizens against a watchman or by a watchman "against any superior," were to be dealt with by the Mayor. Although the parishes were to hire the watchmen and provide clothing and equipment,

yet the whole watch of the metropolis are to be considered but as one body for the protection and defence of each and every part thereof, without distinction of parish or any boundary, and the said parish constables, sub-constables, and watchmen, shall in all things lawful, pay entire obedience to the lord mayor....

Thus, even in the decentralization of power (from Castle to Corporation to parishes) that the statute represented, the intended aim continued to be "one body for the protection" of the city.[81] Keeping alive this simple concept, the police of Dublin remained far in advance of the police of its sister capital, the metropolis of London.

The immediate effects of the new force, which replaced the police in September 1795, were reminiscent of those of a decade earlier. Robbers, rioters, and prostitutes appeared to be controlled; citizens even assisted watchmen in apprehensions. "On the whole," one newspaper pronounced after a fortnight, "we do not remember to have seen a better appointed civic protection."[82] But the police, constitutional though it might be, was soon beset with problems. The chief one was financial. The Government advanced £3,200 to get the watch started and a year later had to issue £5,000 to the city authorities; even so, the force was run on a tight budget. Various debts from the previous police, totaling £18,000 over "a Period of Nine Years," became unforeseen expenses. Collection of the watch rate in the various parishes was sporadic. Enforcement of licensing was lax; hence, revenues declined.[83]

Problems developed in administering the new force. Some parish directors of the watch were negligent in communicating with divisional police justices, and others became embroiled with churchwardens in disputes over local control. Directors, constables, and watchmen fell into practices of illegal fee taking, and watchmen on duty came to accept drinks from publicans. Daytime policing suffered, with only fifty Corporation constables on the streets. The watch, which had been on duty day and night in 1786–95, was now restricted to being "nightly centinels." The practice of patrolling was also abandoned. The parish watchmen were now, as before 1786, posted at watch stands, some 250 of which were scattered across the city. The men were to go no further than "twenty Paces" from their stand, be relieved every two hours, and serve at a different stand on each shift.[84]

Within a year, an amending act was passed to deal with these problems. The 1796 act abolished fee taking, allowed the head police offices £50 for office renovation (a paltry sum compared to previous police expenditures), awarded churchwardens equal powers with watch directors in the parishes, required constables and watchmen to take an oath of office and provided for fines on publicans serving on-duty watchmen, prohibited beer and liquor retailers from serving as parish directors, levied fines on ineffectual parish directors, attempted to regularize tax collection and awarded the Lord Mayor the power to dismiss parish collectors, and restated the licensing requirements. The amending act also effected administrative changes. Three small parishes were consolidated into a single parish district, and one large parish was given more directors and police.[85]

The most important change in 1796 was the attempt to coordinate and centralize control of the parish forces through the creation of a "standing committee." Composed of a salaried secretary, the Lord Mayor, and one churchwarden or watch director for each parish, the committee was empowered to conduct business with a quorum of only five present, including the Mayor. The provision that decisions could be made with representatives from twelve parishes absent indicates both the indifference of parish authorities to local policing and the extent of the problem that this section of the act addressed. The standing committee was to make all rules and orders; levy fines and punishments; provide clothing, equipment, coals and candles; and draw any bills on the City Treasury in order "to render the said watch an effectual guard."[86]

III. The threat of revolution

Policing the Irish countryside

Compared to the history of the Dublin police, the story of the implementation of the new rural police is considerably clouded. We do know that in July 1787 Dublin Castle ambitiously drew up plans for new rural police in Clare, Galway, Limerick, Mayo, Queen's County, Waterford, Cork, Kerry, Kilkenny, and Tipperary. But after encountering widespread opposition over "pecuniary distress," constitutionality, and the paucity of Protestants, government officials decided to place forces in only the last four counties.[87] Even there the protests were loud. In Cork the Sheriff banned a protest meeting by freeholders and forced the county grand jury, swelled by 600 onlookers, to accept the new police measure. In Tipperary, too, there was strong opposition from gentlemen full of "Jealousies, ... affectation of Popularity, and real Selfishness or political resentments." In Kerry, the Government imposed the police after the county grand jury had voted to reject the measure. One opponent averred that "nothing has occurred within my memory that has caused a greater alarm among the gentlemen of property" than this expense of £960 for eighty subconstables, which would lead to "the total ruin and distress of our lower orders." Moreover, it was alleged, "the insidious Sub Constables" would doubtless stir the embers of Rightboyism "in order to increase their own perquisites."[88]

It is difficult to trace the development of these baronial forces of almost 500 Chief Constables and subconstables, spread across five districts in Kerry and Kilkenny, seven in Tipperary, and ten in Cork. As Kevin Boyle has written, "Only limited information is available . . . on what use was made of the various measures and what impact they might have had on the country-side."[89] The Government abandoned plans to revise the county magistracy rolls; instead, from November 1787 on, assistant barristers attended special sessions of the peace eight times a year in twenty-one towns in the four counties. In at least one barony, Iffa and Offa East, Tipperary, the police began service with a colorful uniform – blue jacket, crimson lapels, white waistcoat, and a felt hat topped with a black feather. In their first months of operation, the forces were moderately effective; in Tipperary and Cork we read that the police apprehended "notorious" Rightboys and in Kilkenny a murderer who had eluded the military.[90]

The effectiveness of the police can be gauged by the brief debates at the time of the renewal of the police act in 1790. The Whig opposition argued that "its cause has ceased to exist"; the police were an "unnecessary expence" and an "injury to the independence of the counties." But the Member for Kerry argued that his county was now "as well policed as Middlesex" (a dubious honor); indeed, the grand jury had petitioned for renewal. The Member for Kilkenny claimed that the police had proved to be effective "against whiteboyism and turbulence." In Tipperary "100 active men had been substituted in the place of 80 constables who were a public charge without a public benefit." An amendment that aimed to remove executive fiat by requiring county authorities to petition for the police was defeated by a vote of 107–66; a similar motion in the Lords was also lost. The act was renewed, unchanged, by 30 Geo. 3, c.35. The debates generally revealed the admitted potential of the police for preserving the peace but also the continued opposition on the grounds of expense and constitutionality. Many Members did not want the institution for their neighborhoods – it "hung over the other twenty-eight counties like a scourge" – and many more wanted more local control.[91]

Two years later, at a time when Catholics were winning concessions from a Government alarmed by developments in France, the Whig opposition scored a victory for local control. The 1792 "Act for regulating the office of Constable" reaffirmed (see pages 75–6) the right of county grand juries to appoint and dismiss eight constables for each barony. But this totally locally controlled police had several shortcomings. In an age of Catholic concilia-tion, only Protestants could serve; the men wore no uniform; arms and accoutrements were budgeted at £2 and could not be replaced for twelve years; policing was only a part-time job because the constables, at £4 a year, were paid only a third of the salary of the 1787 Peace Preservation sub-

RURAL POLICE REFORM 1787–1795

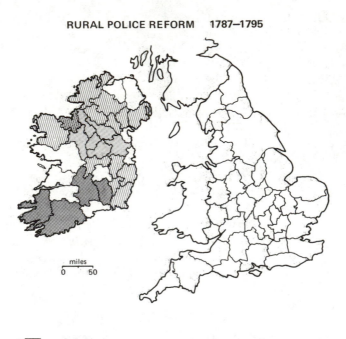

Counties subject to the Irish Peace Preservation Act of 1787

Counties voting **not** to adopt the Irish Constables Act of 1792 (all other counties adopted this act in principle)

Counties subject to the Irish Peace Preservation Act of 1795

Map 4.1

constables. The small salary meant that the constables would often "execute warrants according to the wealth of the criminal." The small rank and file were handicapped by an absence of officers: There is no mention of Chief Constables or Stipendiary Magistrates.[92]

The 1792 act did not repeal the Police Act of 1787; rather, it was intended to create local forces in counties not affected by the 1787 act. But even this purpose went unfulfilled. Thirteen counties petitioned to be excluded from the 1792 act; most parts of Leinster and Ulster were totally unaffected. (Map 4.1.) For the counties receiving police, "there are no records showing the numbers actually appointed in 1792."[93] It is difficult to understand the objections – "dragooned by an army of corruption," "an intolerable . . . burthen and expence" – to this tame, parsimonious statute in which Castle influence was totally absent.[94] Despite the patchiness of their implementation, these baronial constables, the "Barnies" (from old Barny McKeown, the most celebrated one), would constitute the principal rural police in Ireland when Robert Peel arrived as Chief Secretary in 1812. Generally speaking, they were completely ineffectual. Because of their constitutional fear of the police, opposition to the expense, and stubbornness in excluding Catholics, the Anglo-Irish were slow to create strong civil forces of order. In

138

the event, the 1790s, a decade of mounting unrest, was a difficult time to implant effective local government in Ireland.

Rising Catholic militancy led the Government to try the new police solution one final time before the Rebellion. The Defenders were Catholic insurgents who moved beyond agrarian demands to notions of political rights and French aid. In 1792–3, throughout much of south Ulster and the east midlands, Defenders engaged in arms raids, drilling, and skirmishes that produced a few hundred deaths.[95] In the summer of 1795, following Lord Lieutenant Fitzwilliam's removal, there was a massive resurgence of Defenderism, now strongly tinctured with French republicanism. Lord Lieutenant Camden turned to Orde's 1787 Peace Preservation Act, which had been renewed again in 1793. In July 1795, Camden proclaimed thirty-four police districts in Cavan, Leitrim, Longford, Meath, Roscommon, Sligo, and Westmeath.[96] The effectiveness of these new police forces was limited, however, because the 600 men were scattered in small parties across the seven counties. Opposition to their expense – constitutionality was becoming an expendable issue – led some grand juries to appoint less than the full number of subconstables. An amending act of 1796 met this objection by reducing a subconstable's salary to £6 p.a. but authorized the Government to fill any vacancies left by county authorities.[97] But the new police continued to be hamstrung by their small size and functioned effectively only in conjunction with the military. In one Cork barony, for example, Chief Constable John Holmes was able to rout a party of "banditti" because he had with him not only three subconstables but also an army corporal and six privates. Virtually all of the 1,200 Crown prisoners held in preventive custody of January 1798 had been seized by the military.[98]

Newspapers tell us little about the daily activities of these policemen in eleven Irish counties; had the men been really serviceable, we would probably know more. Yet the Peace Preservation Police were useful enough for the act of 1787 to be routinely renewed until 1815. Thomas Orde's rural police constituted a beginning, but from his blueprint no permanent edifice was erected. A generation later, a young architect named Robert Peel would build his own monument from plans conceived by that early draftsman, Thomas Orde.

In broad terms, the minor eddies in police development in Ireland in the 1790s can be explained by two facts: England from 1793 on was preoccupied with the French wars and had little inclination to indulge in domestic experiments in police; second, the unrest in Ireland was moving beyond the control of any police force. In 1793, resurrecting Orde's proposal of 1785, the Government pressed in Parliament a militia bill that "passed speedily and with little discussion." The act created a 16,000-man militia to be recruited from among Catholics as well as Protestants.[99] The balloted conscription of the peasantry for military service at home and, many suspected, abroad triggered huge antimilitia riots in the summer of 1793. Disturbances flared in all but four counties and were repressed by regular troops who found themselves in pitched battles with the insurgents. Altogether, about 250 persons were killed in the disorders. The Militia Act went into effect, and Irishmen were soon sent abroad for service.[100]

The new militia was part of growing government coercion in Ireland. The year 1793 also saw the passage of an act requiring the licensing of all firearms and a Convention Act prohibiting so-called representative assemblies of the people. In 1795 a number of events – the continuing war against France, Fitzwilliam's removal, economic distress in the west, the "Armagh Outrages" (the expulsion of Catholics from that county), the failure of a Catholic relief bill – drove the Defender and United Irish movements together and urged on a fresh round of repression.[101] In 1796 the Government passed the first Insurrection Act, banning all meetings, setting a nightly curfew, and giving JPs broad powers of search, seizure, and detention; the statute would be used frequently in the early nineteenth century.[102] Also that year, habeas corpus was suspended and a second new peacekeeping force, the Protestant Yeomanry, was established.[103] All of this occurred *before* the arrival, in December, of General Lazare Hoche's 15,000-man invasion force off the southwest coast of Ireland. Revolutionary France's unsuccessful bid to land an army in Bantry Bay swelled loyalist enrollment in the Irish Yeomanry (24,000 men by March 1797, 40,000 by June 1798) and led the Government to dispatch General Gerard Lake to disarm French sympathizers in Ulster, stronghold of the United Irish movement.[104]

As Ireland lurched toward catastrophe, the new police played scarcely any part in the repression. It was the magistrates, militia, Yeomanry, and regular troops, armed with emergency powers, who policed rural Ireland on the eve of the Rebellion.[105] In Dublin, where the unarmed police had since 1795 been under local control, the Government relied on its own agents to keep the peace. The city police was rarely mentioned in the feverish press accounts of the spring and summer of 1798;[106] it was "the two Majors," William Swan and Henry Sirr, military officers working for Dublin Castle, who nabbed United Irish leaders in the capital.[107] Due to "the pressure of the times," the streets of Dublin were patrolled by the military and some 800 Yeomanry, divided into parties of 15 men for duty "in diverse parts of the metropolis."[108]

The 1790s in England

The mounting violence and repression in Ireland found no match in England. If events in Ireland were escalating beyond the control of civil authorities, in England the threat of revolution could be contained without dragooning the country. The greatest disturbances in the early 1790s were in fact reactionary. Church-and-King mobs targeted political reformers, francophiles, liberal intellectuals, Dissenters, and manufacturers. The biggest riots occurred in Birmingham (1791) and Manchester (1792), but crowds also rampaged through a number of towns and villages; property destruction in Birmingham totaled £30,000, one-third the value of the losses in the gigantic Gordon Riots.[109] Local magistrates and even soldiers were smilingly supine; government officials saw no reason to intervene.[110] In Birmingham, a city of 50,000 with a "police" force of 5 men, 12 persons were brought to trial (4 were later convicted) from among crowds as large as 2,000.[111] Since they constituted no apparent threat to the established order, the Church-and-King riots provided no pretext for reform of the civil power.

The most widespread disorders in the war years, 1793–1815, were food riots. Closed Continental sources of wheat and the demands for bread in English towns and cities resulted in serious local food shortages and resulting high prices throughout the country. Three years after the outbreak of the French wars, wheat prices had nearly doubled and by 1800 had almost tripled; for the last fifteen years of the war, they remained at extremely high levels. As a result, food riots swept across England's southern wheat belt with an intensity experienced only once before (1766) in that century. The most frenzied period, 1795–6, "the English *crise des subsistances*," produced seventy-four disturbances, and the years 1800–1 triggered fifty. In their extent the riots were alarming, but their nature remained traditional. Food riots were classic, ritualized affairs that had long been accepted by the authorities as legitimate means of protest by the English poor. The crowds' aims were local retention of grain and lowered prices; personal violence was rare, and damage to property (sacks of flour, carts) was extremely selective.[112] In terms of numbers, the food rioters offered the best potential for revolutionary mobs in England – but only in numbers. The disturbances were spontaneous and highly localized, deficient in permanent leadership, and "on the whole showed little political involvement or motivation." The sophisticated followers of Tom Paine "neither obtained nor sought" the aid of these traditional protesters. According to John Stevenson, there is "no evidence to suggest that the disturbances of 1795–96 denoted a crisis of revolutionary proportions."[113]

There was one force active in the 1790s that did threaten English society: the ideas of *la grande révolution* across the Channel. The London-based Wilkism of two decades earlier seemed tame by contrast to the "French ideas" of liberty and equality that now infected many workingmen not only in the capital but also in provincial towns like Sheffield, Nottingham, Norwich, Manchester, and Birmingham. In France the killing of Louis XVI, the execution or exile of the aristocracy, and the establishment of a Jacobin republic produced panic among the English propertied classes, who came to equate revolutionary ideas in England with violent revolutionism itself. From 1793, with the war begun, traditional English rights of petitioning and pamphleteering became branded as conspiracy and treason. Workingmen's conventions were described as alternative Parliaments; demands for universal suffrage as the subversion of English government; naval mutinies over pay and conditions as French conspiracies. The prodigious popularity of Thomas Paine's *The Rights of Man* (200,000 copies sold in three years), the immense size of reform demonstrations in London (crowds of 50,000–100,000), and the mobbing of the King's carriage in October 1795 did nothing to lessen the anxieties.[114]

Against a background of ferocious inflation in bread prices and widespread food rioting, fears of an international Jacobin conspiracy, and the pressures of conducting a war in Europe, the panic among the English governing classes is understandable. But if the English radicals' aims were revolutionary, headed by the demand for universal suffrage, their tactics were nonviolent. Thomas Hardy, leader of the most popular of the Paineite groups, the London Corresponding Society (LCS), was acquitted of treason in 1794 because the Crown could produce absolutely no evidence against him. The radicals' groups were localized, few in number (the LCS had 5,000 subscription members), and their leaders, even had they wanted revolution, were totally unschooled in that tradition.[115]

The Government's repressive legislation in England must be seen as "pre-emptive, based on fears of what might occur rather than what was actually happening." By contrast, repression in Ireland was in response to widespread domestic unrest and an actual French invasion attempt. The fears in England were genuine enough. From 1794 to 1799, a series of acts cracked down on the radical threat. Habeas corpus was suspended, and seditious libel made treasonable and illegal oaths punishable by transportation. Newspapers were restricted; meetings had to be licensed by magistrates; and illegal societies and trade unions were suppressed. But in England there was no Insurrection Act and no General Lake to scourge the country.[116]

IV. 1798, 1803, and their aftermath

The Great Irish Rebellion of 1798 was short and bloody. It claimed more lives in four months than the guillotine did in France during the Reign of Terror in 1793–4.[117] Conceived by the United Irishmen as a war for independence from England, the struggle quickly degenerated into a civil war of peculiar savagery. It is thought that more deaths resulted from atrocities, by both sides, than from pitched battles. The Irish horrors made the English Gordon Riots of 1780 pale by comparison. The total loss of life in the Irish Rebellion was about 30,000 persons. "Suffering loyalists" submitted claims for property losses totaling £1.02 million. In the aftermath, the Government executed 81 persons for treason and transported more than 700. As an anticlimax, the punitive Act of Union of 1800 abolished Ireland's Parliament and annexed the country to Great Britain.[118]

"The Irish '98" triggered no emulative rising in England. The republican group, the "United Englishmen," dominated by the Irish in Britain, drew little following among English workers. London's republicans were disorganized, and the LCS was unswervingly constitutionalist. "Determined government repression and increasing popular loyalism" provided the backdrop to England's nonrevolution in 1798. "That the conspiracy was one ... of Irish rather than domestic growth, only served to further justify government policy for the protection of the majority."[119] When a revolutionary threat in London was finally found in November 1802 – the Despard conspiracy – it was again linked to the United Irishmen. But the execution of

Col. Edward Despard and six others at Newgate in February 1803 was an isolated incident. Once again "the United Irishmen had miscalculated on the revolutionary content of English protest."[120]

In Ireland, five years after the Great Rebellion, there was a second attempt at a rising. Led by twenty-five-year-old Robert Emmet, younger son of the physician to the Lord Lieutenant at Dublin Castle, the affair was restricted to Dublin and lasted for one day, 23 July 1803. Skirmishes in Thomas Street killed five soldiers and forty rebels; near Chapelizod the 62d Regiment lost eight men "but amply avenged themselves in the slaughter of near a hundred rebels." In James Street, Chief Justice Lord Kilwarden and his nephew were dragged from their carriage and "butchered in the open day ... by a party of villains, headed by well-dressed barbarians." Emmet had counted on aid from Wicklow and Kildare, but in 1803 the Irish peasants stayed in their cabins. Emmet was arrested by Major Henry Sirr and in October the former Trinity College student and sixteen other rebels went to the gallows. "Emmet's Rising" had been easily suppressed. But it left an important legacy. In the years ahead, the Government and loyalists would always refer to the twin threats, "the '98 and '03," as if the pop-gun bang after the explosion proved that Ireland was always on the verge of insurrection.[121]

The police of London: more minor reforms

The police in Patrick Colquhoun's London was little changed since the Gordon Riots. Composed of 152 parishes spread over some 200 square miles, the metropolis contained perhaps 2,500 night watchmen and almost 900 day constables. These men were tied to a bewildering array of petty local authorities. Westminster and the tiny City of London had their own forces, but in the former the 300 watchmen were "virtually uncontrolled" and in the latter the 300 constables and 800 watchmen were divided among and controlled by the twenty-six independent City wards. To problems of control and coordination were added those of uneven distribution of the local forces. One in three Londoners lived in Westminster or the City, jurisdictions that contained half of the constables and watchmen in the metropolis. Half of London's population lived in twenty-nine outlying parishes that were rapidly growing in population and increasingly underpoliced. Most importantly, more than nine-tenths of the "policemen" in the metropolis were administered by the parishes and wards. This total absence of system, in Colquhoun's understated assessment, "prevented the full operation of a proper system of vigilance and energy."[122]

In the preceding half-century, the Government had taken only a few hesitant steps to inject some centralization into this tangle of local interests, privileges, and liberties. In the 1750s the Fieldings had established the Bow Street police, complete with four thief takers and two horsemen. An experiment with a horse patrol had been short-lived (1763–4). A sixty-man foot patrol, also administered from Bow Street, had proved more enduring. From 1792 on there were forty-two constables at the new Seven Police Offices, but they did not function as a patrol. In sum, at the turn of the century, there were in a city approaching 1 million population some 100 policemen controlled by the Government and divided into three different forces.

Colquhoun's hopes for a metropolitan police were sparked when Prime Minister Pitt in 1797 authorized a parliamentary committee to inquire into the state of the police and convict establishments. Without fanfare the committee called only three but very key witnesses: John Reeves (author of the 1785 bill and treasurer of the Seven Police Offices), Jeremy Bentham, and Colquhoun. The committee clearly appeared to be prejudiced in favor of thorough changes. Its report, issued in June 1798 while the Rebellion was raging in Ireland, recommended the establishment of a "Central Board of Police." Two police offices would be created in the City of London (three magistrates, nominated by the City, at each office), with an unspecified number of constables; these forces would act in conjunction with the Seven Police Offices and Bow Street. Financed by the income from licenses, fees, and penalties, the Board would require throughout the metropolis the licensing of hackney coaches, hawkers, and pedlars, and would keep a register of all trades, lodging houses, and aliens.[123]

A year later, in June 1799, it appeared that the Government was ready to bring in a metropolitan police bill. A jubilant Patrick Colquhoun rushed into print a tract arguing his *General View of the National Police System* (1799). But here the matter abruptly ended. A leading researcher has concluded that we have "no clue to the reasons why the reforms were so suddenly abandoned." Colquhoun, who should have been informed as a common courtesy, never knew why. Many years later, when testifying before a parliamentary committee, he was asked why the 1799 proposal was abandoned. "I do not know," he replied. "I have never heard any reason assigned." Undoubtedly, the outcry from vested interests and the City played a part. To one critic, the proposed police represented "a new Engine of Power and Authority so enormous and extensive as to threaten a species of despotism and inquisition hitherto without a parallel in this country."[124] Against such opposition, the Government, preoccupied with wartime demands and armed with a variety of traditional repressive measures, was apparently reluctant to press forward with controversial innovations in the police.

Significantly, "the first preventive police unit in the country" was a creation not of the Government but of businessmen concerned about property losses in the Port of London. In June 1798, as the Government issued its report recommending a "Central Board of Police," a group of West India merchants instituted a private police force to protect their portion of the city's dockyards. The brainchild of Patrick Colquhoun and a certain Captain John Harriott, the Marine Police Establishment won government approval largely because the West India gentlemen contributed four-fifths of its financing.

The revolutionary aspect of this Marine Police was its force of men. The office staff had ten men, and the actual "Marine Police, or Preventive Department," eight officers and fifty-three river constables. The patrolling force of some sixty men, without a uniform but armed with cutlasses, seems to have had an immediate impact. According to Colquhoun, pilferage at the patrolled docks declined dramatically and government revenue collection substantially increased. The effectiveness of this police of private enterprise stimulated other merchants to press the Government to establish a general river police. An eager Jeremy Bentham and the persistent Colquhoun drafted a bill. Overcoming opposition from the City of London, which feared jurisdictional encroachments, and following the abandonment of its own scheme for a citywide Central Board of Police, the Government presented in July 1800 its bill for establishing a Thames River Police. The proposal passed quickly through Parliament.[125]

The act of 1800 converted the Marine Police into the Thames River Police. With headquarters at Wapping, the force consisted of three magistrates (at £400 p.a.), officers known as "surveyors" (not to exceed thirty), and constables. Apparently, there were initially about a dozen surveyors; by 1827, the number would grow to twenty-two. In 1811 there were five land constables and forty-three river constables; by 1827, seven and sixty-four, respectively. Each surveyor acted as captain for a group of usually three constables. The Thames River Police, recruiting men no older than thirty-five, was the first government police force to use its constables in essentially patrol functions, maritime though they might be. The men were issued cutlasses but wore no uniform, and the dozen police boats were not marked with identification.[126]

The force steadily gained in power and reputation. Among the "very general and extensive" powers of the three magistrates was the right to control and dismiss parish watchmen within their jurisdiction, and one of the duties of the land constables was to inspect nightly the watch houses along the river. Government expenditures for the force rose slowly, from £5,000 in 1800 to £8,000 by 1817. But the force's jurisdiction was constantly growing: originally from Limehouse to Greenwich, but by 1828 encompassing the thirteen miles of river from Vauxhall to Woolwich. In its sense of territoriality, the Thames Police Office was quite different from the more local Seven Police Offices; the jurisdiction of the Thames Police rivaled that of Bow Street in its citywide claims. But whereas Bow Street had six detectives, the River Police in 1810 had fifty constables. The existence of so large a coordinated force of young men made the Thames Police Office popular with the other police offices. When in need of a supporting force of constables, they would frequently request a loan of ten to thirty men from the Thames Office. For example, in a period of only two months in 1810, parties of police were dispatched on thirteen occasions to eight different police offices; upon the release of Sir Francis Burdett from the Tower of London in June 1810, thirty Thames constables were sent to assist in crowd control at Piccadilly. What had begun as a force to prevent thefts along the river, the Government was learning, could be used for quite different purposes on land.[127]

Government-controlled patrolling policemen were a recent innovation in the sprawling English metropolis. At the turn of the century, the Bow Street Foot Patrol numbered no more than sixty-eight constables, and only since 1790 had they patrolled the city's streets *as well as* the main roads leading out of the metropolis. Operating in parties of four or five men under a captain, eight parties patrolled the highways and five parties watched the principal avenues of the city's center. The men wore no uniform on the theory that wearing one would identify them to the criminals, and yet each patrolman in the party carried a truncheon and a cutlass, and the captain sported a pair of pistols, a carbine, and a cutlass, so that they hardly functioned in mufti. The men patrolled from dusk until midnight; they were free to work at other jobs in the daytime. The Foot Patrol constituted the beginnings of a police force for the metropolis, for its jurisdiction was citywide, but with some seventy constables split into a dozen or so patrol groups across a city the size of London, its effectiveness was necessarily negligible.[128]

In 1805, Sir Richard Ford, chief magistrate at Bow Street, persuaded the Government to reestablish the Horse Patrol. Ford deployed his men so that each patrolled, singly, from dusk to midnight, along the highways from a point four miles from the city center outward to a point some twenty miles from London. The Horse Patrol was colorful and developed a high esprit de corps. The men shared a common background of cavalry service and the pay was good, 28 shillings a week. This Horse Patrol of 1805 was the first civil force in the metropolis to wear a uniform. And resplendent it was: scarlet waistcoat with blue trousers, blue greatcoat, white leather gloves, high boots with spurs, and tall black leather hat. The waistcoat gave the men their nickname, "Redbreasts." Each patrolman was issued a pair of pistols, a truncheon, and a pair of handcuffs worn inside his greatcoat, and a saber, worn outside.[129]

The chief problems of this force were its size and jurisdictional restrictions. There were only 52 men and two inspectors. The activities of the force were limited by its perceived functions. Charged to watch and protect travelers on the highways, the horse patrolman was instructed not to investigate crimes on side streets or even suspicious circumstances or persons on the highway itself. Nevertheless, even with these limitations, Bow Street was able to report after one year that its preventive patrol "had answered every expectation." Unfortunately, the Government was not impressed. In 1806 the number of men was reduced to 40, and the annual funding of £8,000 was cut to £6,000. For a decade, as the city's population continued to increase, the Horse Patrol struggled against overwhelming odds, 40 men in the midst of 1 million. When in 1816 the force was enlarged to sixty-two men, those odds were scarcely improved.[130] The idea of the police as a preventive body of law enforcers was still very much dormant, despite the gallant tiny experiment with the Bow Street Horse Patrol.

Patrick Colquhoun did not live to see the creation of a single police force for London. He served as a police magistrate until 1818 and testified before a series of parliamentary committees that refused to recommend any thoroughgoing reform of London's police. Ignored by the Government and the public, Colquhoun drifted into other interests. His final book on the police, *A Treatise on the Commerce and Police of the River Thames*, appeared in 1800, the year that the Government passed him over to appoint Sir Richard Ford as head magistrate at Bow Street. For the rest of his life, Colquhoun devoted his intellectual energies to economics, publishing in 1814 his statistical *Treatise on the Wealth, Power, and Resources of the British Empire*. When he died in 1820 at age seventy-five, Colquhoun was remembered as a retired metropolitan police magistrate who had produced an important work on political economy and had held eccentric opinions about the need for a new police system in London.[131]

England's moral police

The continued absence of a single system of police for the metropolis was interpreted by most Londoners as a sign of the civility of English society. Reformers prided themselves on advocating the improvement, not the abolition, of the myriad parish forces; bizarre proposals to arm watchmen with sticks 3 yards long with "an iron talon or hook" at the tip, or to furnish every householder with an alarm bell or tocsin, stemmed simply from the hallowed tradition of citizen self-policing. One writer in 1805 articulated the prevalent public opinion when he challenged Colquhoun's conclusion that the metropolis required radical police reform. Sir Richard Phillips argued that "the slight restraints of the police and the general good order [in the city] ... *mutually illustrate each other*." "A few old men and a few magistrates and police officers" somehow managed to keep the peace. Metropolitan tranquility, he deduced, "is not to be explained on *systems of police*," but is the product of "a happy union of moral causes, the chief of which is the ancient freedom of all ranks in England." Sir Richard shuddered to think what Patrick Colquhoun "would make of London, by planting his bodies of police officers at pleasure and erecting his central board of police in the heart of this metropolis."[132]

The wartime lull in projects for English police reform has been described by Leon Radzinowicz as "a diversion into moral regeneration."[133] In the age of the French Revolution, the lower orders were to be taught the virtues of "labour, sobriety, frugality, and religion." Patriotism was stimulated by the belief that virtue itself was the hallmark of the *English* nation; certainly "no one will attribute a virtuous feeling, of *any* kind, to the present Government of France."[134] Thus, whereas social (and political) deviance in Dublin had to be controlled by a professional police force, in England private citizens and organized groups acted as "a missionary police" to maintain order. It was in this old-fashioned definition of the word that a national conference of magistrates in 1790 called for "the general Reform of the Police" of the country. Apart from the Methodists who labored in similar vineyards, two principal organizations – the Society for Giving Effect to His Majesty's Proclamation against Vice and Immorality (est. 1787) and the Society for the Suppression of Vice and the Encouragement of Religion and Virtue (1801) – monitored the behavior of the English lower classes. The societies merged in 1802 to strengthen their assault against profanation of the Sabbath; blasphemous and seditious publications; drunkenness and vagrancy; Jacobinism; gambling; cruelty to animals; trade unionism; and prostitution, dancing, and promiscuous public sea bathing.[135]

England's moral police – its citizen self-policing – was embodied not only in such societies and in the myriad small forces controlled by local governing authorities but, even more significantly, in the numerous peacekeeping associations sponsored by private individuals and groups. As late as 1828, private police units, averaging some two to five men in size, functioned in forty-five parishes in London. Throughout England as late as 1839, "upward of 500" private associations existed specifically for the prosecution of felons.[136] Most important in times of disturbance were the special constables. "One of the most peculiarly English ways of dealing with an emergency ..., [t]hey kept reappearing on the scene with remarkable regularity," so much so that "their enlistment became a matter of routine whenever the peace was seriously threatened." In the spring of 1804, for example, the Bow Street Police Office alone swore in 504 "specials" to meet the threat of a French invasion.[137]

Special constables were first recognized by statute in 1662, but in spirit and practice they can be traced to the *posse comitatus* of medieval times. Specials were recruited largely from the propertied classes, but they could also include "our poor inhabitants"; the only rule, for one London parish committee, was "to avoid Irishmen, except of very good character." The initiative for mobilization was usually local, but in emergencies "the enlistment of special constables assumed the character of an organized mobilization" directed from the Home Office. In the first decade of the nineteenth century, the grandest display of special constables came in April 1810 when the Radical MP, Sir Francis Burdett, was committed to the Tower of London. To control the crowds of his supporters, magistrates at the Seven Police Offices enrolled some 140 specials; City of London authorities raised 900 specials who were aided by Volunteer corps and a number of private associations. The citizens remained on duty for ten days, and except for a brief clash between the soldiers and the people at Piccadilly, the anticipated disturbances failed to develop.[138] Throughout the early nineteenth century, successive Governments would rely on the physical and psychological support generated by this small army of the well affected. This resource of a mobilized citizenry is one reason why, in England, modern police forces were slow to emerge.

The police of Dublin: a return to Castle control

Ireland after 1798 was an occupied province of Britain; Dublin, the garrisoned headquarters of a conquered colony. Gone from the city were the gentlemen of society and the brilliant patriot politicians; in their place were the bland bureaucrats of the Castle. Before the Union, Dublin's lower classes had reviled some men but idolized others; now they showed only "the bitterest hatred" for all of their betters. The new mood could be seen everywhere in the former Irish capital. The Irish Parliament became the Bank of Ireland; the Duke of Leinster's mansion now accommodated the Dublin Society; Lord Powerscourt's became the Stamp Office; and various other town houses became military barracks. Sackville Street after 1808 was dominated by the statue of an English hero, Admiral Lord Nelson. Perhaps most fittingly, Dublin Castle was refurbished. Included in the work was the building of the Lord Lieutenant's private Gothic chapel, with superb stained glass and ninety heads of sculptured Tullamore marble, completed in 1808– 14 at a cost of £42,000.[139]

If in 1799 the proposed Union of Ireland with Great Britain was the dominant political issue in the city, the authorities in Dublin Castle had also to be concerned with the continuing threat of rebellion. In February the Government believed "from authentic information" that a landing of French troops was imminent; the next month there were reports of an "influx of Rebels from various Parts who use the Capital as a hiding Place." At this time, the policing of Dublin was almost entirely in the hands of the army and Yeomanry.[140] The city's locally controlled police had proved useless during the Rebellion. The Lord Mayor himself admitted that "at the present important Period" the police force was "highly dangerous and inimical to the Peace and good Government of this City." Even apart from political considerations, the force was in financial trouble. By late 1798, Dublin's police had built up "a continually accumulating" debt of more than £8,000, "for payment of which no provision whatever exists."[141] Watchmen went unpaid and watch houses had to be closed, the morale of the 72 constables and 544 watchmen was "degraded," and a "general Spirit of disobedience and insubordination has pervaded the whole system." Repeated petitions to the Government for financial assistance had met with no response, and so "an Institution, which might have reflected honor on the Police of the Metropolis, and afforded secure protection to the Inhabitants, has ... become the disgrace, not the Safe Guard of the Capital."[142]

With the collapse of the city police, Dublin Castle moved in May 1799 to take over, once again, the policing of the capital. There were whimpers of protest. A city meeting objected to "the interference of the Executive power" in appointing "any" policemen, and some members of the City Corporation complained of lost liberties. But in the current political climate, with the Union question and the loss of national sovereignty the center of controversy, police reform was necessarily a minor issue. The act of 1799 created a single Superintendent Magistrate, salaried (£600 p.a.) and appointed by the Lord Lieutenant; the Magistrate, Col. William Alexander, in turn, appointed one High Constable, four Chief Constables, 48 petty constables or "peace officers," and all of the watch constables and watchmen (32 and 450 for summer, 38 and 600 for winter). Most of the men had served in "the late Establishment." The city was divided into four police divisions, and over each presided a government-appointed "divisional justice" (£300 p.a.). The peace officers were to be paid £40 a year; the watch constables, £30; and the watchmen, "armed and accoutred as the ... Magistrate shall direct," at 1s.,

1d. per night (£20 p.a.). In salaries alone, the projected annual cost of the force was £15,800.[143]

The new police began patrolling the city streets at the end of June. They were apparently initially effective. The catalogue of police activity is familiar: prostitutes cleared from the streets, hackney coaches strictly inspected, and robbers apprehended as far as five miles from the city center. The chief problems were administrative. The Superintendent Magistrate claimed to be overworked. Three professional magistrates were not sufficient for a city of 180,000; the other city magistrates were fee-collecting businessmen or "trading justices."[144] Regular payment of the watch continued to be a problem. In turn, the quality of the men who were hired and who stayed on as watchmen led critics to charge them with "supineness" and "imbecility." The entire force was "ineffectual ... [and at an] enormous expense."[145]

Six years later, the Irish Government prepared a bill that would revise the Dublin Police Act of 1799. For reasons that are unclear, the Castle did not bring forward its bill for almost two years.[146] This delay ended with the arrival of a new Chief Secretary in 1807. The thirty-eight-year-old younger son of an Irish earl, Sir Arthur Wellesley had already gained a military reputation in India. For two years, from the spring of 1807 to the spring of 1809, Wellesley, who described himself as "the *willing horse*," reluctantly held the office of Irish Chief Secretary. His soldier's heart was not in the job, and he was glad to get away for military service – in Copenhagen in the summer of 1807 and in Spain the following summer. In April 1809 Wellesley would gladly resign his Irish post in order to lead an invasion force to Portugal and Spain. He would win glory for England and fame for himself – successively, Viscount, Earl, and finally Duke of Wellington – in the Peninsular campaign (1809–13) and at Waterloo (1815).[147] (See Figure 4.1.)

Perhaps the major accomplishment of Wellesley's service on "the old Irish treadmill" was his reform of the Dublin police.[148] The reasons behind the reform were political: Fear of rebellion, not the control of daily crime, motivated Castle authorities. Wellesley was worried that with the growing European war, Ireland would be stripped of its troops; the countryside would require reinforcements from Dublin, leaving the capital vulnerable.

There is no doubt ... that in such a case there are persons ready to take possession of that city. ... Let any man look at Emmett's account of his plans and his operations, and contemplate the temper of the people of Dublin ... and he will see clearly that we depend much more upon their discretion than upon anything else. ... An accident in Dublin might have the most serious consequences throughout this country.

Wellesley and the Lord Lieutenant, the Duke of Richmond, were also prodded by the former Irish Chief Secretary, who had drafted the now dust-covered 1805 police bill. "[Y]ou know," Charles Long reminded the Lord Lieutenant in August 1807,

how little the Police of Dublin ever did towards the detection of Treason or Sedition. ... I cannot help suggesting to you upon this occasion that it might be very desirable to increase the Castle Police. ... A new Dublin Police Bill ... would I am

Figure 4.1 Sir Arthur Wellesley, age forty-three, in civilian dress, 1812. (Watercolor by J. Bauzit, by permission of the Victoria and Albert Museum)

sure tend most materially to suppress disturbance in the Capital, and as the Capital has always been the focus of Rebellion it would also conduce much to keep things quiet in every other part of the Island.[149]

The Dublin Police Act of 1808

The Castle's proposal was finally ready in the spring of 1808. The bill proposed to enlarge the "Police District of Dublin Metropolis" from 12 to 200 square miles by increasing police jurisdiction from two to eight miles from Dublin Castle. The four police divisions would be increased to six. In place of the existing Superintendent Magistrate and two "divisional justices," there would be eighteen divisional justices, one of them to be the "Chief Magistrate of Police." As in London from 1792 on, there would be three magistrates at each police office and a head magistrate corresponding to the Bow Street magistrate. Twelve of the eighteen Dublin justices were to be appointed by the Lord Lieutenant; the remaining six would be named by the City Corporation, subject to the approval of the Lord Lieutenant. The Chief Magistrate of Police had to be a city alderman. Every divisional justice would have jurisdictional powers not only in his division but throughout the police district. No justice could practice law or vote for a Member of Parliament. The Lord Lieutenant was entrusted with the power of removal from office.

The number of day constables at the police offices was to be increased only slightly. The four existing "Chief Peace Officers" would become six "Chief Constables," one at each divisional office. The six "Office Constables" would be increased to eighteen, or three at each office. The number of "peace officers" (petty constables) was unchanged, but these forty-eight men were now divided as follows: four to be attached to each of the five police offices, with the remaining twenty-eight to be concentrated at the head or "Castle" divisional office (Table 4.1).

Yet another indication of the strength of the Castle office – presided over by the Chief Magistrate of Police and two divisional justices, who formed in effect a commissioner and two assistant commissioners of police – was that the entire force of watchmen would be appointed by these Castle magistrates. The number of watch constables and watchmen was unchanged from existing levels (32 and 450 in summer, 38 and 600 in winter, respectively). The men were to continue to be armed with "lanterns, poles, bayonets, carbines, blunderbusses, [and] Swords." The existing dozen watch houses were to be maintained, and the concept of the watch stand was continued; watchmen were not to be posted to the same stand on successive nights. The concept of a patrol, experimented with in 1786–95, was revived in the 1808 bill. The Castle divisional justices were to "employ a sufficient Number of fit and able Men, not exceeding One Hundred, to act as Patroling Constables in all Parts of the said District by Night and by Day," and also to employ not more than 100 "Horse Patroling Constables ... in all Parts of the said District by Night or by Day."[150] Finally, the cost of the police was to be nearly doubled. The existing police in 1808 cost £21,100 a year; Castle

Table 4.1. *Government police in Dublin, 1786–1808*

	1786	1799	1808
Police Magistrates	4	3	18
Police Commissioners	3	—	—
POLICE FORCE			
High Constables	1	1	—
Chief Constables	4	4	6
Office Constables	—	6	18
Day Constables	40[b]	48	48
Watch Constables	—	35	35
Night watch[a]	415	525	525
Foot Patrol	—	—	100
Horse Patrol	—[b]	—	50
Total	460	619	782

[a]Average of summer and winter force levels.
[b]Functioned as the Horse Patrol, 1786–8.

authorities estimated that the new police would cost £36,300; the actual first-year expenses would come to £37,700. Future costs could be expected from the novel idea of a pension for any policeman, from watchman to justice, after twenty-five years of service or any permanently disabling injury.[151]

Wellesley's detailed and lengthy proposal – the final parliamentary act would contain 128 sections and run to thirty-seven printed pages – was in fact a revised version of the police of Pitt, Orde, and Fitzgibbon. The 1786 force of 450 men was now to be nearly doubled in size; the 3 Commissioners of Police were now three commissioners at the Castle Police Office *plus* 15 other magistrates scattered throughout the city. There would be a Foot Patrol and a Horse Patrol, perhaps 200 men altogether; London, a city five times larger in population, had Bow Street patrols of 120 men. Unlike London, Dublin would be "united in One District" entirely under the control of the Government. The proposal not only reasserted the principles of 1786 but anticipated, if not in a single inseparable body of men, at least in the concept of central control within only one jurisdiction, the police reforms in London in 1829.

On 23 March 1808, in the Imperial Parliament in London, the hero of Assaye and Copenhagen, who for the past six months had labored on the Irish treadmill, proposed his bill to reform the Dublin police. Chief Secretary Wellesley argued that "notwithstanding the authority of the police already established," crime and all manner of "evil had long been increasing, indeed ever since the rebellion in Dublin in 1803." City magistrates were "entirely independent of Government" and the watch had become ineffectual. The only reason Dublin had been kept quiet, he noted, somewhat contradictorily, was that 7,000 soldiers, stationed in forty guard houses, patrolled from one to the other throughout the night. Both Members for Dublin opposed the bill. Robert Shaw, a Dublin banker and city magistrate, who eight years earlier had voted against the Union, now in the London House of Commons upbraided Wellesley for consulting neither him "till the present moment" nor the Dublin Corporation, "inasmuch as it was an infringement of their charter." The other Member wryly noted that a new Dublin police, "under the direction of Government", had been tried in 1786, "and it had failed." The speaker was the now aged, and disillusioned, Henry Grattan.[152]

The fate of the Dublin police was totally in the hands of "English gentlemen who legislate for Ireland." In this prerailway age, news from London was already four days old when it reached Dublin; any protest from Ireland would thus reach London at least a week after the subject was initially raised. Progovernment papers in the former Irish capital naturally endorsed the measure. The *Correspondent* claimed to see no irregular extension of the powers of executive government; there was "no common resemblance in principle" to the 1786 bill, which had admittedly been "a gross violation of the Chartered Rights of the Corporation." But opposition papers, although approving the idea of an enlarged police district, were critical of the central control and expense. "It is inconceivable what an agitation has pervaded the public mind in consequence of ... the new Police Bill," reported the *Hibernian Journal*:

The most moderate and best affected to our King and happy Constitution feel very sensibly at the idea of ... Divisional Justices, invested with the most extensive powers, and dependent on the will of every Chief Governor.... It requires no Oedipus to divine how much the interest of the people who pay them will be attended to.[153]

The Castle's police proposal was heatedly debated by the City of Dublin Corporation. At a meeting on 8 April, proponents laid bare their fears of recurrent rebellion; opponents spoke "with considerable energy" against patronage and venality, infringement of corporate rights, and dangers to liberty. The Chief Magistrate of Police was "likened to Bonaparte" and the bill itself to the infamous statute of 1786, which had been repealed "because the citizens of Dublin could not bear it." The meeting voted by "a great majority" to reject the bill and to appoint an investigating committee of ten aldermen and twenty common councilmen. On 14 April an equally boisterous Corporation meeting voted to limit the cost of any new police to £19,000 and to require that all police magistrates be elected by the Corporation. A week later the Corporation committee issued its report, which found the bill "exceptionable" in its patronage, expense, and constitutionality. In the ensuing discussion in the Common Council, Mr. Macauley asked,

Was it likely the City of London would entertain such a proposition? Dare a minister propose it? Would it for a moment be entertained in Guildhall? It would not. And shall it be said that we are less tenacious of our Chartered rights?

Council members subsequently voted, by 68–1, that it was "the undoubted right of the City of Dublin to appoint their own magistrates." But the Board of Aldermen, from whose ranks one-third of the new justices, including the

Chief Magistrate, were to be selected, rejected the Common Council's resolution, arguing that the new police would be a boon to the city.[154]

The political stakes were raised on 29 April as passions mounted in a final Council meeting on the police question. "We are yet a free corporation, unbought, unpensioned, and unplaced by Government. Our charter," declaimed Mr. Patterson, "is still unviolated; but how long in this age of innovation it will remain so, will shortly be determined." Councilman Willis then threw the room into an uproar by making a motion for the repeal of the Union with Great Britain. The ensuing speeches showed that those favoring the new police also favored the Union. The views of police opponents varied. Some, like Councilmen Willis and Patterson, also opposed the Union. Others, like Mr. Macauley, deplored the corruption that had bought it but firmly believed that after the Rebellion of 1798 Ireland's only choice was to "unite with England or become a province of France." At length, by a vote of 49–32, the Common Council declared itself against the Union with Britain. Mr. Semple then "moved a string of resolutions against the Police Bill," which were "unanimously" carried. It may be observed that with disaffection creeping even into Protestant bastions like the City of Dublin Corporation, it is hardly surprising that Dublin Castle should seek to seize control of the city's magistracy and police.[155]

Three hundred miles away, in June, Sir Arthur Wellesley's bill moved inexorably through the English Parliament. It was late in the session and few Irish, or English, members were in attendance. Opponents of the bill reported the Dublin Corporation's opposition to the proposed measure. They repeated, in one newspaper's words, "the usual grounds" of objection and asserted that crime was less of a problem in Dublin than in London. (Perusal of Dublin newspapers from March to May 1808 turns up three *reported* incidents of crime.)[156] But Denis Browne, who as a former member of the Irish Parliament had supported the 1786 police, now asked "whether or not the great and atrocious evils of the rebellion of 1798, and of 1803, did not proceed from concealed traitors in that corrupt focus of mischief, the City of Dublin?" Seeing his old adversary, the sixty-two-year-old Member for Dublin must have recalled the earlier heroic debates in another Parliament that many had described as "his." Now, in 1808, Henry Grattan pointed to "the absurdity of addressing the enormities" of the Rebellion as a "pretext" for this new police. Had the proposed police existed in 1798, "it would not have averted the evil."[157] In the debates over the 1808 bill, opposition motions to dilute the radicalism of the proposed police reform were all easily defeated. The radius of jurisdiction was kept at 8 miles, not lowered to 4; the eighteen justices were not reduced to twelve; the six police divisions were not cut to four. The bill passed without a division, was duly approved in the Lords, and received the royal assent on 30 June.[158]

The authorities in Dublin moved quickly to assemble the new police. The Corporation elected its six police magistrates on 23 July. The remaining twelve – half to be barristers and half from the Corporation – were appointed by the Government. Dublin Castle named Alderman Joseph Pemberton as

Chief Magistrate. With little help from the Castle, Pemberton hired the watchmen, patrols, and clerks, selected buildings, and arranged compensation for discharged policemen. Nine of the 48 peace officers were dismissed and 108 of the 453 watchmen were judged "too old" for the police; at the higher levels, 12 men, ranging from clerks and chief peace officers to the former Superintendent Magistrate, were not reappointed but were paid compensation totaling £4,079. Pemberton had strong opinions on pay: The watchmen should be paid not 7 shillings, 7 pence, but "half a Guinea" (10 shillings, 6 pence) per week; the Foot Patrol, the full 14 shillings authorized by act of Parliament; and the Horse Patrol, not the authorized 28 shillings but only "one Guinea" a week.[159]

The act of Parliament had not specified officers for the patrols, so Pemberton arranged for the peace officers at the Castle Police office to head them. The Foot Patrol, which was kept at the maximum of 100 men, was responsible "for everything within the Circular Road" (the previous police jurisdiction). Within each police division, the men were responsible to the Chief Constable and were divided into groups of twelve and subdivided further into parties of four or more. The Horse Patrol, also administered directly from the Castle Police Office, was expensive (mostly due to lodging and forage for the animals), so the actual number of men in the patrol was only half the authorized force strength. These fifty horsemen patrolled from dusk to dawn in groups of four and were expected to make their rounds "twice in the course of the night," a total distance of sixteen to twenty miles. Upon reaching an outlying village, the patrol party was to have a certificate signed by any military guard stationed "near the extreme point of the Patrole"; this would be a guarantee that the patrol had actually been completed.[160]

The Dublin police of 1808 was a remarkable creation (Table 4.2). It was not a single unit of men, like the London force of 1829, but the police were all accountable to a single authority and acted within a single jurisdiction. In these respects, the police force of Dublin was modernized two decades earlier than that of London; indeed, if we cite the experiment of 1786–95, more than four decades earlier.

Secondly, the jurisdiction of the 1808 Dublin police was far greater than that of the 1829 London force. The Irish force, in a city of 180,000, acted within a jurisdictional radius of 8 miles (201 square miles); the English force, in a city of 1,450,000, would police a radius of 12 miles (452 square miles).[161] That is, a city with only 12 percent of the population of London had a police jurisdiction 45 percent as large. The greater reach of the Dublin force made it potentially more effective in crime detection; it also required the development of exurban, or suburban, skills of policing.

Thirdly, in terms of the size of its force, Dublin was more heavily policed than London in 1808 or even after 1829. Adjusted for population, there were in 1808 almost four times more government police magistrates, and eighteen times more centrally controlled policemen, in Dublin than in London. If we choose a representative force level for the London police after 1829 – for

Table 4.2. *Government police in Dublin and London in 1808 and 1831*

	Dublin 1808	London 1808	London 1831
Population	178,000	959,000	1,474,000
Police			
Constables	72[a]	122[b]	2,937
Nightwatch	525[a]	—	—
Foot Patrol	100	68	—
Horse Patrol	50	40	—
Total	747	230	2,937
Proportion of police to population	1:238	1:4,170	1:502
Police magistrates	18	27	—
Proportion of magistrates to population	1:9,889	1:35,519	—
Total expense of government police	£37,717	£38,181[c]	£206,689[d]
Proportion of expense to population	£1:5 persons	£1:25	£1:7

[a]Excludes thirty-five watch constables.
[b]Six at Bow Street, fifty-six at the Seven Police Offices, and sixty at the Thames Police Office (including surveyors).
[c]Bow Street, £7,900; Seven Police Offices, £18,281; Horse Patrol, £6,000; Thames Police, £5,000; and Foot Patrol, £1,000.
[d]Expense in 1832.

example, the year 1831[162] – we find that Dublin in 1808 was relatively twice as heavily policed as the English capital. These comparisons are of bodies of men controlled by the Government. The numbers hold firm for nighttime policing, for the largest Dublin component was the night watch. If we exclude this group, and the nightly foot and horse patrols in both cities, *daytime* Dublin remains numerically better (by three times) policed than London in 1808 and somewhat less well policed (by one-third) than London after 1829.

Fourthly, in the important matter of expense, the Dublin force was again ahead of the police in London. In Dublin £1 was spent for every five inhabitants, a proportion five times greater than for government-controlled police in London in 1808 and proportionally even ahead of the expenditures for the police of 1829. The bulk of the Dublin expense fell on the Government, for only one-third to two-fifths of the cost was paid from local taxes. The force was simply too expensive to be entirely locally subsidized.[163]

In sum, to speak only on the basis of these figures, it can be said that the centralized Dublin police of 1808 was, relative to population, superior to the equivalent London forces in terms of jurisdictional area, number of magistrates and policemen, and expense. In these respects, it can be claimed that this Dublin police, and not Peel's force of 1829, was the first modern police force in the British Isles.

The performance of the new police drew generally favorable reviews. Only the radical *Dublin Evening Post* continued to be critical; other newspapers spoke of the "extraordinary celerity" and "great exertions" of the policemen. At the November sessions of the King's Bench Court, Lord Justice Day "in a manner peculiarly energetic" complimented the new establishment. The streets were quiet, "nightwalkers" (prostitutes) controlled, and patronage of public houses at unlawful hours curtailed. The Castle Police Office regulated the licensing of publicans and hotel keepers, pawnbrokers, certain types of tradesmen, and hawkers of all merchandise.[164] In the years after 1808, visitors remarked on the efficiency of Dublin's police. In 1818 the men were described as "extremely active and effective" and the city as "remarkably secure and peaceable at all hours." Three years later, a writer commented: "Such is the present system of Police in the Irish capital, which has already been found so efficacious, that there is not, perhaps, a great city in Europe where fewer outrages are committed." A police report for 1822 describes a fairly orderly city – no murders, few burglaries and highway robberies, little prostitution – in which petty larcenies and street begging were the main problems.[165] Throughout the period 1810–30, the police of Dublin regularly committed to city jails a number of persons equal to about one-sixth of all committals in Ireland. For a city that accounted for only one-thirtieth of Ireland's total population, and with a countryside that was in constant turmoil, this was a remarkable feat of policing.[166]

The force was effective because of the quality of its men. The seventy-two Chief Constables and peace officers were in attendance day and night, awaiting the magistrates' commands. In 1818 the 26 watch constables and 493 watchmen were described as "in general stout, young, and able-bodied men," many with previous military service. Indeed, from 1815 on, a preference was given to discharged militia men "whose spirit and good conduct have been certified."[167]

The Horse Patrol did not prosper, probably for reasons of expense. Though 100 men were originally authorized, no more than 50 ever took to the highways. By 1820 the number had dropped to thirty; in 1824 it stood at thirty-eight and in 1834 at twenty-nine. But the Foot Patrol, selected from among the strongest watchmen, did thrive. The Circular Road, the original limit of the patrol's jurisdiction, was increasingly becoming an artificial barrier. As early as February 1810 the Foot Patrol added sixty men, assisted by twelve members of the Horse Patrol to serve specifically beyond the Circular Road. In 1817 this "country" patrol was increased to 70 Foot plus 20 Horse Patrol, and in 1824 to 112 men assisted by 38 Horse Patrol. The number of "police houses" in outlying villages increased from the original six to nine (1817), sixteen (1824), and twenty-one (1834). The Foot Patrol within the Circular Road rose from the original 100 men to 121 by 1824. Overall, the Foot Patrol had increased from the original authorization of 100 men to 160 (1810), 170 (1817), and 233 (1824). The police was clearly becoming more a patrolling force.[168]

In terms of the number of Horse and Foot Patrols, the greatest growth was reached by the mid-1820s. The establishment in 1824 of an efficient County Dublin police apparently permitted reductions in the city force; by 1834 the

Horse Patrol had declined to 29 men, the Foot Patrol in the city center to 100, and the Foot country patrol beyond the Circular Road to only 69.[169]

The growth of the force through the mid-1820s – about 850 men in 1824 and the same number a decade later – meant rising expenditures. In 1822 salaries and the watch's weekly pay continued to account for three-fifths of the costs; stationery and the publication *Hue and Cry* alone amounted to £2,283. In the twelve years since 1810, total annual expeditures rose by one-fifth to £52,000; from this peak in 1822, costs declined to £40,000–42,000 a year in the decade 1826–36.[170] Administrative reforms improved the force's efficiency. In 1810 the six divisions were redistricted to create more equal workloads, and in 1824 the number of divisions and police offices was reduced to four and the number of magistrates to twelve (the Government still appointing two-thirds of them).[171] In 1824 the jurisdiction of the Dublin police was again enlarged. The magistrates and thirty-two constables and peace officers of the Castle Police Office were given authority to act not only throughout the entire metropolis but also, in cases of "Treason or Felony," in County Dublin and even in Kildare, Wicklow, and Meath. Also in 1824, all the constables in outlying County Dublin were placed under one of the Dublin police magistrates, who acted as their Superintendent. The power of appointment of constables, whenever vacancies might exist, was transferred from county magistrates to the Castle; this meant that over time, Dublin Castle came increasingly to control the rank and file in the County Dublin police. By the terms of the County Constabulary Act of 1822, the Government already had control of the Chief Constables in County Dublin, as throughout Ireland.[172]

Given the political climate of the decade after 1798, it is not surprising that Dublin Castle conducted this remarkable experiment with the police of Dublin. But with the receding of the revolutionary threat and in the absence of crime of any sizable dimensions, the affairs of the former Irish capital became comparatively humdrum. No doubt, if Dublin had not descended to the status of a third-rate provincial British town, the police experiment of 1786–1808 would have had a lasting importance; it would certainly be better known. But in the early nineteenth century, Dublin's importance faded before the rising threat of terror in the rural districts.[173]

V. Postscript: military solutions to peacekeeping in wartime

The police experiment in the British Isles during the war years was limited to Ireland and essentially to Dublin. In the absence of police forces, and with the growth in military institutions brought on by the war in Europe, the authorities had at their disposal an unprecedented amount of physical force. Most of the men were raised for shipment to the Continent but, given the great increase in numbers, those remaining at home still formed a larger peacekeeping force than in the prewar years. The wartime military buildup would leave an important legacy of military peacekeeping after 1815.

The growth in the military had a number of important features. Throughout the eighteenth century, the size of the standing army in the British archipelago had changed little. The war brought rapid changes. In a decade and a half, the effective strength of the army in Britain increased nearly fourfold and in Ireland threefold:

	Britain	Ireland
1793	17,000	10,000
1798	40,000	24,000
1808	60,000	30,000

The war produced a boom in barrack building: Of the 96 *permanent* barracks in England and the 109 in Ireland built between 1660 and 1847, fully one-half were erected in the years 1792–1815. The coastal sites of these barracks built in England, and to a lesser degree in Ireland, indicate that the wartime building boom was meant to thwart a French invasion.[174] But in England the new trend away from lodging the men in private quarters or public houses reflected the Government's desire to keep the soldiers away from the influences of alcohol and radical politics.[175] Barracks continued to be more numerous in Ireland – the country, relative to its population, was twice as barracked as England – and they were located farther inland than in England, where they were still clustered on the east and south coasts. The army in Ireland was far more devoted to internal peacekeeping; in 1811 there were 1,304 scattered military "*Detachments* for the assistance of the Police." By the end of the war, the great majority of inland English counties still had no permanent barracks; in Ireland only five of the thirty-two counties did *not* have one.[176]

The pressures of war spawned new military institutions: in Ireland a militia and in both countries a Yeomanry. The size of the English militia, in existence before 1793, trebled in three years to 95,000 men by 1796, and it stayed at 50,000–80,000 until the end of the war. The Irish militia swelled. In 1795–7 there were often more militiamen than regular troops in Ireland. The Rebellion of 1798 was suppressed by an admixture of the new forces: 28,000 troops, 20,000 Irish Yeomanry, 23,000 largely Catholic Irish militia, and 12,000 English militia. The Irish Yeomanry, Protestant and concentrated in Ulster, was a home force that in 1798 won a reputation for savage peacekeeping. The Yeomanry trebled its original size to 60,000 men by the time of Emmet's Rising, and for the remainder of the war numbered about 30,000. In England the Yeomanry, established in 1794, totaled 11,000 men by 1798 and held steady at about 25,000 after 1803.[177]

The militia served not only as "a recruiting ground for the Standing Army" but as a backup peacekeeping force.[178] When, for example, army levels in Ireland rose (29,000 in February 1805) and fell (16,000 in December 1805) due to the changing demands for soldiers on the Continent, the 19,000-man Irish militia was counted on to pick up the slack.[179] The system was given a twist by the Militia Act of 1811, which legalized the interchange of militias between Britain and Ireland. Up to a fourth of the British and a third of the Irish militia could be sent to the sister country. In 1811–15 militias from thirty-two of the forty English counties and from sixteen of the thirty-two Irish counties were exchanged. The registers show the greater importance of having British militia in Ireland than Irish militia in England. The Irish forces were exported not from the North but from Catholic Munster and Connaught, their places being taken by bemused militiamen from Kent or Cornwall; although the practice bolstered British forces in Ireland, it risked trouble at home for free-born Englishmen resented this influx of armed Irish papists. The impact of these exchanges was more strongly felt in Ireland, where a mosaic of military forces kept the peace; in December 1813, of a military total of 36,000 men, 14,000 were regular troops; 11,000, Irish militia; and 11,000, British militia. The militia solution to problems of public order ended with the return of peace in 1815. The militias were disembodied; new solutions would have to be found.[180]

One institution, born in wartime, did survive the end of the war in Europe. This was the Yeomanry, the cavalry branch of the Volunteer movement. Composed of county gentlemen and town merchants, the English Yeomanry was to serve as a defense force in case of invasion; in the meantime, they saw service in the suppression of domestic disturbances. The Yeomanry was frequently called out against food rioters; after the war, with a force of about 20,000, the institution would continue to be used against crowds.[181] In both countries the Yeomanry were class based, but in Ireland the force was also distinguished from the people by race and religion. Exclusively Protestant, the Irish Yeomanry had come into existence in part to counterbalance the predominantly Catholic militia. The Yeomanry was strongest in Ulster, where its origins were tied to the growth of Orange Lodges. Its members pledged "to support and defend the King and Constitution, to preserve the peace of the country, and to discourage and resist all endeavours to excite sedition and rebellion."[182] "The country was delivered up to the will of the Protestant Yeomanry," complained Lord Cloncurry in 1806. The Yeomen were "taught that they were a garrison entrusted with the keeping of Ireland for England; and that the foes ... were their fellow countrymen." Edward Wakefield, an Englishman visiting Ireland in 1812, found the Yeomanry intoxicated with a sense of their own "pre-eminence," an attitude that "cause them ignorantly to conceive that they are authorized to domineer over the majority." Because many Yeomen were so extreme in their politics and prejudices, Dublin Castle was reluctant to send them south, since they tended to stimulate, not stifle unrest. A report to the Castle by a Meath JP in 1812 is representative:

[The Yeomanry] very cooly and deliberately fired at ... the unfortunate Irish [as if they] were to be treated like Bengal Tigers. The Violence of party rages at present too high in this Country. A Yeoman officer in raising his Corp very lately in this neighbourhood declared he wou'd raise a Corp of true Blues to keep down the croppies. Such expressions tend to disunite and Confuse the Country; it clearly appears to me that the yeoman [*sic*] are of Very little use in this country & in General were the original Causes of all the disorders of our Neighbourhood.[183]

The militarization, if we may so call it, of English and Irish society from 1793 to 1815 reflected the demands of the French wars. The important point is that, in wartime, both the challenge abroad and the radical threat at home were met by the Government's unprecedented accumulation of physical force; equally importantly, in England with its antimilitary constitutionalist traditions, the war justified the rise of these military institutions, making them appear both necessary and respectable. With the defeat of Napoleon the national militias were disbanded, but both countries were left with a peace-time legacy of large Yeomanry and military forces and a widespread barrack system. The postwar army strength in England was double and in Ireland triple the pre-1793 levels. The end of the war on the Continent would open the door to repressed domestic radicalism in England and widespread agrarian turbulence in Ireland. For the authorities, the military establishment evolved in 1793–1815 would prove most useful after Waterloo. In England, there would be a final round of barrack building. A fifth of the permanent barracks erected in 1660–1847 were built after 1815, and for the first time the majority of the new barracks were inland ones, virtually all of them in the disturbed North.[184] In peacetime Ireland, the greater challenges to public order would lead the Government to press ahead with innovations in police on a greater scale than those already established in Dublin and in parts of the countryside during the war years.

CHAPTER 5

England under Sidmouth: traditional
responses to modern disorders

This was not BUONAPARTE;
'tis said Mankind now sin without his aid.
    – Thomas Brown, *The Field of Peterloo* (1819)

What can be stable with these enormous cities? One insurrection in
London and all is lost.
    – Lord Liverpool, from the windows of Whitehall

The decade 1812–1821 was perhaps the most convulsive in English history since the mid-seventeenth century. It was a time of the highest food prices ever recorded and then, after 1815, of high unemployment and economic depression. The nation was pressed to win the seemingly endless war against Napoleon and then to cope with the tens of thousands of demobilized and discontented former soldiers. The decade began with horrific mass murders in London, the assassination of a Prime Minister, and the deployment of the largest army in the nation's history against protesting workingmen in central and northern England. It ended with an abortive plot to assassinate the entire Cabinet, a murderous legal dispersal of a peaceful meeting in Manchester, and a spate of laws that greatly restricted Englishmen's liberties. The capital and countryside were traumatized by a series of major disorders and an unprecedented popular commitment to political radicalism. In retrospect, it is remarkable that in the face of all of these challenges, the local police institutions in London and provincial England survived virtually unchanged.

The man in charge of the policing of England in this decade was fifty-five years old when in June 1812 he was named Home Secretary. The son of a physician, Henry Addington, created Viscount Sidmouth in 1805, had abandoned a career in law for one in politics. He had served as a popular Speaker of the House of Commons (1789–1800) and as an ineffectual Prime Minister (1801–4), in which post more than one Member of Parliament referred to him as "the fool." Sidmouth's politics were Old Tory and Church of England. Doting on his local Yeomanry Corps and describing himself as belonging to "the port-wine faction," he opposed Catholic emancipation, parliamentary reform, and anything in the interests of workingmen. In talents, Sidmouth was decidedly mediocre; in personality,

163

he was grave and industrious, dull and pompous, qualities that became more pronounced after the death of his wife in 1811. Sidmouth never traveled to Europe, nor indeed to any part of England north of Oxfordshire; what he knew of the French Revolution he read in Burke or in the newspapers. As Home Secretary in 1812–21, the aging Sidmouth would be at once alarmist and unimaginative. Confronted by widespread disorders, he was too traditional to consider the remedy of fundamental reform of the local police system.[1]

I. Challenges in London

Murders most foul, more abortive police reform

On the eve of Sidmouth's appointment, London was still recovering from an "almost unheard of" wave of murders. In May 1812 John Bellingham, a deranged office seeker, had assassinated Prime Minister Spencer Perceval as he walked through the lobby of the House of Commons. Though the crime was not ideologically motivated, the lauding of Bellingham by some lower-class radicals gave the savage deed alarming political implications.[2] Earlier, in December 1811, the city had been rocked by the serial killings of seven people, from an infant in his crib to a seventy-year-old pub proprietor, in the Ratcliffe Highway in Wapping in the East End of London. That the murder weapons were a carpenter's maul and a ripping chisel imparted to the slayings an "un-English" dimension of savagery.[3] At this time, capital convictions for murder in London and Middlesex were averaging *one* a year; in 1810 only fifteen persons were convicted of murder in all of England and Wales.[4] The public assumed that foreigners were responsible for the Ratcliffe outrages: First Portuguese sailors and then the Irish community in London were hounded by the citizenry.[5] Officers from Bow Street and the Shadwell Police Office eventually arrested a suspect, an English sailor named John Williams, who hanged himself in his jail cell. No further murders ensued.

In the aftermath of the killings, London's parishes placed more watchmen on duty. A number of letter writers suggested reforms: The watch should be composed of young men who were adequately armed and on patrol, not asleep in their watch stands. After an inconclusive debate in Parliament, a select committee recommended only that the Police Offices establish greater contact with parish authorities. The Government responded in May 1812 by drafting a nightly watch bill that proposed some central control over the numerous parish forces. Appointments to and control of the watch would remain in local hands through new twelve-man committees in each of some four dozen new divisions. The divisions would be grouped into eight districts, each district to come under the supervision of one of the Police Offices. In each district, a new officer attached to each of the Nine Police Offices would communicate with the twelve-man parish committees. The Police Magistrates would have the power to fire ineffectual parish watchmen. Finally, a new officer attached to Bow Street would oversee watch reports submitted from all over the metropolis.[6]

The Government's bill, which sought essentially to improve the coordination of existing local forces, drew widespread opposition. Most of the city's parishes petitioned against it. During the brief debates in the Commons in July, Samuel Romilly, the advocate of criminal law reform, and Henry Brougham, the Whig reformer, were among those who not only objected to the infringement of local liberties but even questioned the constitutionality of the Police Offices founded in 1792. Public opinion resurrected the bogey of the French police, to which this timid police bill of 1812 was incongruously compared. A pamphleteer argued that any system other than the parish night watches was

a system of tyranny ... of spies and informers, ... [a] despotism, which is to be hoped will not light on English ground.... The police of *France*, say some, is admirable. Then go to France and enjoy it, be the reply of every free-born *Briton*!

Another writer repeated the argument:

They have an admirable police at Paris, but they pay for it dear enough. I had rather half a dozen people's throats should be cut in Ratcliffe Highway every three or four years than be subject to domiciliary visits, spies, and all the rest of Fouché's contrivances.

The Government abandoned its bill amid an outcry reminiscent of that against Pitt's police proposals of 1785. France's police system, whether Bourbon or Napoleonic, continued to frustrate any reform efforts in England.[7]

In the aftermath of the police reform controversy, the Government did quietly accomplish some minor reforms in the police establishments under its control. The appointment of the forty-two constables at the Seven Police offices established in 1792 had always rested with the police magistrates. From July 1812 on, however, the Government directly assumed and frequently exercised this right, and after 1813 employed the power of dismissal as well. Second, the number of constables at each office, raised to eight in 1802, was augmented in 1811 to twelve. The age of the constables was a problem still not addressed; at the Whitechapel Office, for example, the ages ranged from thirty-six to sixty-eight, with two men in their sixties and three in their forties.[8]

Home Office control over the other forces was also increased. In 1811 the men in the Foot Patrol were officially empowered to act as constables (giving them a police as well as a patrol function); in 1813 the control of and appointments to the Horse Patrol were transferred from Bow Street to the Home Office itself. By such tentative steps, the Government was slowly gaining ever greater power over its own various creations in the metropolis.[9] In 1815 Home Secretary Sidmouth had at his disposal some 250 police constables in five separate forces: 84 men at the Seven Police Offices, 68 in the Foot Patrol, 60 at the Thames River Office, 40 in the Horse Patrol, and a mere 6 at Bow Street.

The concept of such a body of men assembled for special occasions looked better on paper than in reality. By the time the men had been divided and subdivided into detachments, their efficiency was reduced; the lines of command, below the senior Bow Street magistrate, were far from clear; and in any case, there were hardly enough men for a metropolis of more than a million inhabitants. With all of these problems, however, the Government had developed certain methods of dealing with *potential* civil disorders. Between 1812 and 1820 at least eighteen official processions through the streets of the metropolis – half of them involving the Prince Regent's opening and closing sessions of Parliament – did not lead to riots by the increasingly radicalized London populace.[10]

Although the public peace continued to be kept largely at the discretion of the populace, it may also have been partly attributable to allocations of police at key points along the route. Bow Street and the Home Office, in order "to preserve the Public Tranquillity," had the power to call out magistrates and constables from the Seven Police Offices and the Thames River Police.[11] For example, during the procession of the Prince Regent from Carlton House to the Guildhall in the City of London on 21 June 1814, a total of 178 government constables were deployed along the routes as far as Temple Bar, the entrance to the City and the limit of their jurisdiction. From Piccadilly and St. James's Square, through Charing Cross, and eastward along the Strand, twenty-one groups of police – Foot Patrol, Horse Patrol, and constables from the Thames River and Seven Police Offices – were deployed every one-sixth of a mile in parties of eight to ten men each. On this occasion order was maintained, and only groans and hisses were aimed at the Prince Regent.[12]

Riots and conspiracies: From the corn bill to Cato Street, 1815–20

The first of the major disturbances in London in the decade 1812–21 were the Corn Bill Riots, which lasted for almost a week in March 1815. Great agitation developed against the Government's corn bill, a protectionist measure that favored British and Irish agricultural interests but that, by keeping bread prices high, angered consumers. Mass meetings against the bill were held around the country, and forty-two petitions reached Parliament demanding a stop to the bill. A Manchester petition bore 52,000 signatures; one in London was signed by 41,000 persons. More menacingly, the Home Office received a spate of letters wishing protectionists "all a good Bellingham" and eulogizing Bonaparte, who a few days earlier had escaped from Elba. MPs arriving at Parliament on 6 March were jostled by the large crowd that urged them to consider "the sufferings of the poor during a long war" and vowed "not to be offered up to the interests of the Irish."[13]

Home Secretary Sidmouth and the magistrates from the Police Offices bungled their preparations for crowd control. On 6 March one magistrate, Sir Robert Baker, left his fifty constables *inside* Parliament while he went to the Horse Guards for troops; another police magistrate brought thirty constables to Old Palace Yard but then left for another part of town. The

High Bailiff of Westminster showed up with forty of his eighty constables. When the military arrived at 3 P.M., they found only 80 of 180 constables outside, the rest remaining in the lobby. This left the soldiers to bear the insults and pressures from the crowd, which carried one arriving MP "a hundred yards" and knocked another about "like a shuttlecock." The panicky Life Guards overreacted and charged the crowd. Using *"drawn Sabres,"* protested Lord Hinrich to Sidmouth, the soldiers began "cutting and hacking His Majesty's loyal subjects among the number of which I take leave to rank myself!!" The inadequacy and misallocation of police, and the resort to troops, were premonitions of the days ahead.[14]

The police, both old and new (1792), proved helpless. In Spitalfields a crowd attacked a parish watchman, "taking his Rattle"; in Stoke Newington a constable yelled at a well-to-do householder, "all persons who were not against the Corn Bill ought to be hung up – we want more Bellinghams to settle the business." For the government-controlled constables, the problems were not age or politics so much as numbers and coordination.[15] Communications between police magistrates and military officers were strained or nonexistent; officers on the spot refused or granted aid as they thought best; detachments protected one spot only after abandoning another. Some Police Offices were more active than others, but with twelve constables on duty at Bow Street and forty-nine men on the streets from the other Police Offices, ultimate reliance had to be on the troops. The nature of the mob, "a skirmishing set [which moves] so suddenly and speedily that it is exceedingly difficult to come up with them," required what was totally lacking, a large mobile force of police.[16]

For four days, 7–10 March, the metropolis had to be governed by the traditional emergency measures: special constables and troops. Each Police Office swore in a number of specials, and each parish was directed to do the same. The issue was delicate, for most Londoners favored cheap bread; nevertheless, with pay at 7 shillings a night, several localities produced patrols totaling several hundred men, many of whom, with government authorization, were issued pistols. The mobilization of special constables, in Robert Peel's judgment, "has done more to secure us from tumult than any other demonstration of power."[17]

But Irish Chief Secretary Peel, writing a few days later to the Lord Lieutenant in Dublin, was probably more correct when he concluded that the crowds in the metropolis had been controlled "solely" by the presence of the military. Home Secretary Sidmouth assembled various Yeomanry corps and stationed 1,300 infantry and cavalry at dozens of key locations, including large parties at the British Museum, the Bank of England, and Newgate Prison. For five days, nine military parties constantly patrolled the streets, from Whitechapel west to Knightsbridge and from Whitehall north as far as Russell Square. Reserve forces, each totaling from 300 to 600 men, were kept at the Tower, the Horse Guards, Portman Square, Knightsbridge, St. James's Park, and Regent's Park. The Home Office granted thirty-seven of forty-eight personal requests for detachments of soldiers to protect the houses of protectionist MPs; despite these precautions, a score of substantial houses were damaged by the crowds.[18]

The destruction wrought by these roving bands of urban bread rioters in 1815 was mild indeed compared to that produced during the Gordon Riots of 1780,[19] but the objections raised in the aftermath of the disorders were remarkably similar. It was a disgrace that the metropolis had to be occupied by a military force. The police had not been "properly mustered and judiciously directed"; everyone knew that constables should be "young, healthy, and vigorous, instead of decayed and decrepit men." Particularly "defective" was the absence of any "provision for an extraordinary number of constables in case of riots." The entire system demanded "a very rigorous inquiry": The Government should "pay attention to the subject."[20]

In the immediate aftermath, two gentlemen took the trouble to write the Home Office with suggestions. J. P. Hipkins, a military officer living in Uxbridge, proposed "regulations wanted for the police of London." Hipkins urged Sidmouth to create nothing less than a centrally controlled, uniformed, and armed police, partly mounted and operating day and night. The force should have its headquarters near the Horse Guards and Whitehall, and should be directed by an Inspector General and two or three Deputy Inspectors. His plan included the separation of police and judicial functions, for "it is inconsistent, they should remove from the Bench of Justice to Quel [sic] a Riot." Hipkins's proposal was remarkably similar to Peel's police plan of 1829.[21]

The second scheme for Sidmouth's consideration was submitted by J. T. Barber Beaumont, a Middlesex magistrate. He noted that the military were ineffective because they "feel themselves degraded" to arrest "a woman, or a boy, or even an unarmed man"; crowd control duty was "derogatory to the profession of arms." Moreover, military detachments were too cumbersome to pursue rioters "into holes and corners" of courts and alleys. Beaumont proposed the creation of police parties made up of "skirmishers," a reserve, and a guard. The skirmishers would seize the mob leaders, the reserve would then move in to assist, and both would retreat to the guard, the largest group, which would escort the entire party to jail. Beaumont hoped that his "hints" might "generate a methodical efficient and improved application of the civil power in case of riot."[22] Sidmouth proved indifferent to Beaumont's ideas, but he instructed an under-secretary to "thank him for his suggestion."[23]

The end of the European war (June 1815) brought severe domestic unemployment and a revival of political radicalism in London. The new radicalism was many-headed, but all factions agreed at least on the need for parliamentary reform and wider suffrage. The movement at this time was led by two men. The best-known Radical writer was William Cobbett, whose "twopenny trash" pamphlets excoriated the corrupt political system; his *Address to Journeymen and Labourers* sold 44,000 copies by 1816 and 200,000 by 1818. No publication since Tom Paine's *The Rights of Man* had had such a circulation. The principal postwar popular orator was Henry Hunt, a wealthy Radical gentleman farmer who in 1816 was beginning his sixteen-year career as the preeminent spokesman at the mass meetings of the lower classes.[24] The London radicals, formed into "Hampden Clubs," whose most extreme leaders were Dr. James Watson and his son, James, and Arthur Thistlewood, called a national convention for January 1817. To whip up enthusiasm, it was decided to call a series of outdoor meetings. The first, on 15 November 1816, drew "an enormous gathering," the largest political meeting in the metropolis since 1795. Its organizers vowed to reconvene on 2 December.[25]

Thus was the scene set for the second confrontation of the Government with the London crowds.[26] Home Secretary Sidmouth was disdainful of "these self-appointed meetings for the public discussion of alleged grievances"; for him, the "material point" was to "preserve regularity ... in the midst of alarm and confusion." Sidmouth spent all of Sunday, 1 December, at the Home Office coordinating arrangements. Special constables were held in readiness at each Police Office. A dozen of the Horse Patrol were placed around Spa Fields, the site of the meeting. The adjacent Artillery Ground was fortified by 120 infantrymen. Two cavalry troops were quartered at the nearby stables of the Light Horse Volunteers, nearly a hundred of whom were also called out. At the Hyde Park and Portman Square barracks, two infantry regiments were put on the alert. Other traditional tactics were invoked. Householders were instructed to prevent their servants, apprentices and "children" from going to Spa Fields from "idle curiosity" or any other reason. City authorities arrested strangers and detained 106 "foreign and black sailors."[27]

The crowd that gathered on 2 December was even larger than the one two weeks earlier. Henry Hunt had not yet arrived when, just after noon, a small peripheral group, led by Watson's son, who had been drinking, made their own speeches, replete with references to the French Revolution of 1789. Young James Watson, carrying a tricolor, then steered his small following away from Spa Fields southward toward the City of London. Off Fleet Street the ransacking of gunsmiths shops began; small handguns were preferred, with Brander & Potts's alone losing seventy pairs of pocket pistols. Most looting was confined to the Minories in the eastern part of the City. The nearby Whitechapel and Worship Street Police Offices reported their areas quiet all day.[28] The riots, which lasted through the evening, were geographically confined and only one person, a shopkeeper in Skinner Street, was killed. In one incident in Cateaton Street, young Watson shot a customer by accident. "'You have shot me,' Mr. Platt said, 'and I was no enemy of yours.' 'Then I am sorry for it,' apologized the revolutionary." It should be stressed that the vast majority of the crowd at Spa Fields stayed to hear Hunt's oration and then dispersed peacefully.[29]

From a police point of view, the problem with the Spa Fields Riots was that the small bands of rioters darted too quickly to be caught.[30] Police magistrate Nathaniel Conant later complained that they slipped away without being seen, thus frustrating his plan of action involving a signal to

Colonel Herries at the nearby stables. Similarly, rioters managed to get past City of London police stationed at points between the Fields and the Mansion House. On one occasion, a half-dozen City constables and Alderman Sir James Shaw came by accident upon a part of the crowd near the Royal Exchange; with the aid of a convenient gate, they "locked up" a portion of the mob. Other rioters moved south down Bishopsgate Street and into the Minories. It was here that the diminished crowd broke open gunsmiths' shops and controlled the area until they "voluntarily departed." A magistrate from Essex, who tried in vain to call out soldiers from the Tower of London, reported later that for several hours he "never saw a single constable."[31]

E. P. Thompson has described the Spa Fields Riots as "not a simple drunken outbreak, nor a carefully-planned provocation, nor yet a definite attempt to simulate the fall of the Bastille, but they partook in some degree of all three." However we characterize them, the effects of these minor street riots were far-reaching. The hotheads were immediately discredited. Young Watson, who had escaped arrest due to a constable's negligence, subsequently fled to America. His father, who claimed to have stayed to hear Hunt, was tried for treason in June 1817 but acquitted by a London jury.[32] As in the late 1790s, it was the ideology, not the revolutionary action, of postwar radicalism that triggered repression. The Spa Fields Riots were fairly minor disturbances out of all proportion to the subsequent coercive legislation. The mobbing and breaking of the windowpane of the Prince Regent's carriage during his procession to open Parliament in January 1817 was reminiscent of the perceived threat to George III when his carriage had been mobbed in 1795. A House of Lords committee in 1817 claimed to have discovered a conspiracy in the metropolis to overthrow the Government "by means of a general insurrection." Parliament subsequently suspended habeas corpus and banned all meetings of more than fifty persons without prior notice to the magistrates. Suppression of public demonstrations of radicalism only drove a few of its adherents into secret plots and violence.[33]

The Cato Street Conspiracy of February 1820 was the only attempt at a coup d'etat in the capital in the early nineteenth century.[34] Arthur Thistlewood, the young Watson, and other veterans of the Spa Fields Riots, encouraged by the government spy George Edwards, devised a fantastic scheme to assassinate the entire British Cabinet at a dinner party. For two months Sidmouth was kept informed of their intentions; indeed, he arranged the hoax of advertising a false dinner on the 23rd at the Earl of Harrowby's in order to ensnare the conspirators. The bizarre affair ended when the Bow Street police raided the conclave in a cow barn in Cato Street, off the Edgware Road. Five leaders were subsequently hanged and five other men transported.[35]

The conspiracy, in great measure orchestrated by Edwards the Spy, shocked public opinion and appeared to justify the Government's latest bout of repression. At their trial, the conspirators declared that they had been driven by the Government's legislative repression since 1817, most recently by the harsh Six Acts passed after the suppression of the peaceful protest at

Manchester (1819). The conspirators' strategy was far from thought-out and drew no support from other radical groups in the metropolis. The Cato Street Conspiracy was a highly atypical form of English radical protest. Nevertheless, the "plot" was disconcerting. Such fantastic schemes *appeared* to lay the capital under siege.[36]

Sidmouth's police reforms

It is remarkable how, in this turbulent decade, the police of the metropolis resisted any basic reform. In the space of three years, Parliament issued four reports on the subject. A select committee in 1816 published a mass of information but made no recommendations. Two reports of 1817 explored aspects of policing – chiefly licensing, vagrancy, mendicity, and prostitution – but did not advocate any reorganization of the various local and government forces in the metropolis. The virtual absence of discussion on the floor of the Commons reflected the general indifference to the subject of police. The report of 1818 was the first to criticize the very lack of a police system. It suggested that parish constables be young and salaried and that coordination of the various forces be improved. But the idea of a single police force for the metropolis the committee rejected as "odious and repulsive.... The very proposal would be rejected with abhorrence." Thirty-three years after Pitt's proposal of 1785, it was still argued that the best police rested, "above all, in the moral habits and opinions of the people." Indeed, Englishmen appeared to glory in the inefficiency of formal police structures in London. "The more ... the system ... was inquired into," reported a Member of the House of Commons, "the more it would be found to be defective and rotten. But the most surprising consideration of all was ... [that] a machine so defective in itself could have been so long kept together."[37]

Although opposed to any thoroughgoing reform, the Government continued to institute some minor changes.[38] In 1818 Sidmouth appointed a separate inspector to head the Bow Street Foot Patrol, thus bringing this force more within Home Office control. Minimum height (5 feet 5 inches) and maximum age (thirty-five) requirements for recruits were standardized and a preference given to men with military service. The force continued to be armed with truncheons and cutlasses, but still served without a uniform and only at night. Changes were made in the nightly Horse Patrol as well. In 1816 its annual budget was restored to £8,000, the figure authorized in 1805, and the number of patrolmen was increased from 40 to 62, and in 1821 to 72.[39]

Home Secretary Sidmouth instituted perhaps his greatest police reform in April 1821 with the creation of the "Dismounted Horse Patrol." This quaintly named force in effect substituted for the Foot Patrol that, three months earlier, had been withdrawn to the city center. Composed of ninety patrolmen, eight Subinspectors, and four Inspectors, divided into four divisions, the dismounted Horse Patrol nightly patrolled the highways up to five miles from London, with the mounted Horse Patrol responsible for a jurisdiction from five to twenty miles from the city center. Horse Patrol recruits were required to serve first in the dismounted branch, from which they might be promoted to the mounted branch. The dismounted force was apparently quite effective, apprehending some 350 persons in its first nine months of existence. The combined Horse Patrol, dismounted and mounted, was annually funded at £16,000 and formed "the strongest single professional force in the metropolis before Peel's new police came into being." Both branches would see service in a new wave of street disturbances.[40]

The Queen Caroline affair, 1820–1

The death of George III brought to the throne the Prince of Pleasure, the obese, dandified Prince Regent, now George IV. His person symbolized to London's radicals the corruption of Liverpool's unreformed Tory Government. George's wife, Caroline of Brunswick, had left him in 1814. Though she herself was hardly a paragon of virtue, Caroline, living abroad in Italy, became the darling of London's reformers and radicals. With the death of her father-in-law, George III, Caroline returned to England to claim her title by marriage, Queen of England.[41]

Caroline's reception on landing at Dover in June 1820 was tumultuous. She dismissed her military guard, saying that "it was the people and not the soldiers she wanted." Throngs of well wishers lined her triumphal procession to the capital. "If this be a specimen of what is to be expected on her arrival in London," prophesied one observer, "I fear the consequences." For two nights, 6–7 June, Londoners went wild with celebration. Crowds assailed the townhouses of Lord Eldon, the Duke of Wellington, and other "obnoxious individuals"; rioters broke all of the windowpanes in Home Secretary Sidmouth's residence. The situation was potentially serious, for the Whigs sided with the Queen and the City of London adored her. When her procession had passed the King's residence at Carlton House, even his soldiers had saluted her.[42]

The turmoil continued for a week. Stories spread of the mutiny of three battalions of the Life Guards; anonymous letters threatened the firing of barracks in the heart of London. Outside the Portman Square barracks, prostitutes urged the soldiers to go over to the Queen; "Damn your eyes," said one, "if you present arms you shall not come to Bed to me." At the Charing Cross barracks on the evening of 15 June, a large crowd urged the soldiers to come over to them. A magistrate and a small band of constables read the Riot Act, but the crowd overwhelmed the police party. Order was restored when a troop of the 2d Life Guards, led by Lord Sidmouth himself, who had left a dinner party near Piccadilly, dispersed the rioters "with considerable force."[43]

Two months later, at the parliamentary divorce proceedings instituted by George IV, the authorities prepared for large-scale disorders. "An extraordinary number" of special constables was enrolled from the city's parishes. Between Carlton House and Parliament, the Government posted more than a

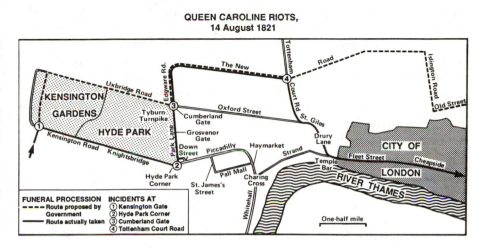

Map 5.1

hundred constables at five stations a quarter of a mile apart, and large parties of soldiers waited in readiness at Westminster Bridge, the Horse Guards, and Carlton House. But the King's procession to Parliament on 17 August proved to be uneventful. The House of Lords approved the King's divorce bill, but the Cabinet, faced with a hostile Commons, chose to drop the matter. In January 1821 a distraught Caroline renounced her royal claims and accepted an annuity of £50,000; the people's favorite passed from the camp of the "oppressed" to that of the pensioners. Caroline died seven months later at age fifty-three.[44] To the London mob, their Queen appeared to be the victim not of peritonitis but of the corruption and privilege of her husband's Government. The funeral procession on 14 August 1821 to return Caroline's body to her native Germany would be the last opportunity for London radicals to demonstrate on behalf of their deceased favorite.

How to get the Queen's funeral cortège safely through London? A waterborne procession of state barges down the Thames was rejected because three of the eight bridges in the metropolis were within the radical City of London. Moreover, the 10,000 merchant seamen in the metropolis had been among the petitioners for the Queen.[45] The secret land route that the Government selected (Map 5.1) purposely passed north of the City of London. Nowhere in the metropolis was pro-Caroline sentiment more concentrated than in the City. The night before the scheduled procession, the Common Council voted unanimously to meet the cortège and conduct it through the City; in taverns and at public meetings, committees elected "the people's constables ... to marshall and arrange the procession."[46] The Government's decision to avoid the City thus only exacerbated discontent: The choice of the route for the cortège would become the paramount issue during the disorders.

The chief police officer in London, Sir Robert Baker, senior magistrate at

Bow Street, had been in his post for only a year. He had worked for the Government to suppress discontent in 1811–12 in the Midlands. Since 1812 he had been a metropolitan police magistrate; in 1815 he had headed parties of troops against corn bill rioters. In the early hours of 14 August 1821, Baker stationed groups of twenty men each from the Foot and Horse Patrols at key points. "A considerable portion of patrole constables" and "several" Office constables, "dressed as mutes and pages ... in readiness in case of riot," were assigned places in the funeral procession. Across the metropolis five military regiments were put on the alert. Troop levels in the Home Counties swelled by one-third to 9,400 men; nearly half of the soldiers in Britain (22,600) were positioned around London.[47] Of all of the traditional machinery of public order, only one part, the system of special constables, was noticeably absent from the streets of the agitated metropolis.

Daybreak arrived wet and drizzly. Dirt streets became muddy pools. The elaborate hearse, drawn by eight horses, moved away from Caroline's residence, Brandenburg House, at 8 A.M. The first test of the procession came in Kensington. A crowd had shut the gates to Kensington Gardens, through which the hearse was to have gone, and chanted, "The City, the City ... the City or death!" At this point a member of the procession, Maj.-Gen. Sir Robert Wilson, MP for Southwark, allegedly was heard to offer 5 shillings and drinks to anyone who would oppose the route through Kensington Gardens.[48] On orders from Prime Minister Liverpool, the route was changed: The procession was now to go eastward to Knightsbridge, then north up the eastern edge of Hyde Park. Sir Robert Baker, who headed the cortège, was about to comply with the new instructions when he became involved in a heated argument with Capt. Richard Montagu Oakes of the 1st Life Guards. "I feared," Oakes later told the Government, "that ... yielding this point would encourage the Mob, step by step, and with increased boldness, to attempt forcing the procession from the prescribed Route." Baker at length overruled Captain Oakes, and the cortège proceeded eastward toward Hyde Park Corner. Oakes's suggestion that he go ahead with some soldiers to Tyburn Gate "to remove any obstacles" was also overruled by the Bow Street magistrate.[49] The crowd had won its first victory: The procession was turned eastward in the direction of the City.

Skirting the southern edge of Hyde Park, the procession arrived at Hyde Park Corner to discover the gates closed and Park Lane barricaded. Oakes now entreated Baker to open the gates at any cost, but Baker again overruled him, out of "fear ... and the presence of the mob." The procession waited in the drizzle, while on Baker's order Oakes in vain requested reinforcements from the Horse Guards. Baker and Oakes then had their final quarrel, which ended when Oakes, defying orders, broke through the barricaded gates at Hyde Park Corner and headed for Oxford Street. The cortège now slipped through the opening, with Baker, by turning up Down Street, rejoining the procession in Park Lane. At Hyde Park Corner the Government emerged victorious, for the eastward drift toward the City had been checked. But a bad precedent was set: squabbling among those in authority as a military

Figure 5.1 Queen Caroline Riots: the military fires on the crowd at Cumberland Gate. (Contemporary satirical print, by permission of the British Museum)

captain, the Bow Street magistrate, and the procession had gone off in three different directions.[50]

Baker and the procession were halfway between Grosvenor and Cumberland gates when pistol shots, lasting for some two minutes, were heard from the direction of Cumberland Gate. The area (the site of present-day Marble Arch) had been heavily barricaded by the people, and persons with "constables' staves in their hands" persisted in shutting the gate. A military detachment of thirteen Life Guards under Sub-Lt. Charles Gore was assaulted for thirty minutes by stones and cries of "You bloody murdering rascals.... Piccadilly butchers" (a reference to the Life Guards' killing of a man during the Burdett Riots in 1810).[51] Gore's party was finally joined by the remainder of the Life Guards under Captain Oakes. Ten minutes later, under continuous stoning, and with still no magistrate present and the front of the funeral procession approaching Cumberland Gate, Oakes had all of his men draw their pistols. The men later denied that before firing they "painted their faces" with mud; Oakes later told the Government that they "mostly fired in the air rather to intimidate than to hurt."[52] The soldiers killed two in the crowd and wounded many others. The troops took heavy casualties: thirty-seven of seventy-five Life Guards and eight horses were wounded. These figures, the Government would later conclude, were "evidence of [the soldiers'] humanity and forebearance and convincing proof that they did not resort to these weapons until all other means had failed." Though thirty to forty shots were fired over a period of two minutes, the Government claimed that "only two shots ... were fired in a horizontal direction at the people"[53] (Figure 5.1).

Among those watching the affair at Cumberland Gate from his official place in the funeral procession was Maj.–Gen. Sir Robert Wilson, a veteran of the Egyptian and Peninsular campaigns and of the Irish Rebellion of 1798.[54] The forty-three-year-old Wilson watched as the Life Guards fired into a crowd of unarmed if disorderly Englishmen. The man who earlier had allegedly been involved in the obstruction at Kensington Gardens now intervened to prevent further bloodshed. Wilson rode up to Captain Oakes and publicly rebuked him for firing without the orders of a magistrate. Wilson then reprimanded several soldiers; when one of them, Private Thomas Waite, objected that he was only performing his duty, Wilson bellowed, "You damned rascal, I have a good mind to knock you off your horse." William White, police magistrate at the Queen Square Police Office, then arrived on the scene and ordered Captain Oakes to withdraw his men for the day. Some in the crowd now tried to pull the hearse down Oxford Street, eastward toward the City, but their attempts failed.[55] The military had won the battle of Cumberland Gate.

The procession headed north up Edgware Road, eventually turning east into the New Road. The fourth and decisive obstruction to the Government's planned route came at the corner of the New Road and Tottenham Court Road. Here a "Blockade of all sorts of carriages locked together across the Road" made the eastward route impassable. Reports circulated that to the north, up Tottenham Court Road (an alternative route acceptable to the Government), more barricades, and "even trenches . . . cut across the Road," awaited the procession. Lt.–Col. Clement Hill informed Baker that it would be impossible to proceed north. White wanted to wait for the Foot Guards expected shortly from the Strand, but Baker overruled him because "their presence [would] create fresh irritation." The crowd meanwhile "kept tormenting" Baker to let the procession "go through the City." The Bow Street magistrate then made his fateful decision: "I suppose I must take it all upon myself," he told White, who replied, "Indeed you must." Baker would later inform the Government that "had I determined otherwise than I did at Tottenham Court Road, a succession of sanguinary conflicts must have been sustained, and a delay would have occurred," the procession having already "been out 7 hours . . . in extreme bad weather, which would have rendered it impracticable to convey the Corpse beyond the Suburbs of the Metropolis before dark."[56]

The Bow Street magistrate turned the procession southward. Down Tottenham Court Road, through Drury Lane, then finally to Temple Bar, and through its open gates, traveled the deceased Queen and her wet caravan. Against all the wishes of the Government, they were now in that bastion of radicalism, the City of London. The City and the people had won.

Aftermath of "Carol-loo"

Even as the cortège left London for the Channel and Germany, Sir Robert Baker and Sir Robert Wilson knew that their problems were only beginning. Baker had been unable to keep the procession out of the City of London. A series of problems had come to a head in Tottenham Court Road, where, to quote Under-Secretary Henry Hobhouse, Baker's "*Courage failed him. He determined to give the point up!*" Hobhouse summed up the Government's feelings: "I dread the moral Effect of this day. The Mob glory in having carried their object by force, and in having beaten the Military. Neither of these is the Fact, but the public Impression is the same." A few weeks later, in September 1821, Baker was forced to resign as Bow Street magistrate.[57] He was succeeded by police magistrate Richard Birnie, who had denounced Baker and argued that Sir Robert Wilson should "not remain long one of His Majesty's Major Generals." The sixty-one-year-old Birnie was knighted at the time of his appointment and held his Bow Street post until his death in 1832.[58] Others were rewarded or punished. A month after the riots, Captain Oakes was promoted to the rank of major in the Life Guards and in 1823 promoted to lieutenant-colonel and retired on half-pay. Only four days after the Caroline Riots, Sidmouth informed Liverpool that Sir Robert Wilson "must be dismissed from the Army." The matter was "a Crisis, at which the Authority and Reputation of the Government will be strengthened and raised, or irrevocably lost." In September 1821 Wilson was dismissed. He continued as MP for Southwark (until 1831) and on the accession of William IV in 1830 was reinstated in the army with a promotion to lieutenant-general.[59]

The Queen Caroline Riots of 1820–1 had enormous symbolic importance. Of all of the popular agitations in this disturbed decade, they constituted the single undeniable victory for "the people." Retrospectively, the year 1821 represents something of a watershed: Government ministers, like it or not, were coming to believe that some redress of popular grievances was necessary. One of the casualties of "Carol-loo" was the Home Secretary himself; four months after the riots, the sixty-four-year-old Sidmouth, worn out by a decade of disorder, resigned his office.[60] Sidmouth's successor was Robert Peel, a man half his age. Peel had recently completed a successful term as Chief Secretary in Ireland, where he had established a new rural police, "the Peelers." During the Caroline Riots the new Home Secretary had noted with disgust the ineffectuality of the police and the traditional resort to the military. The disorders, like the earlier corn bill and Spa Fields disturbances, demonstrated the total inability of the existing civil power to deal with crowds. In 1822 Peel chaired a parliamentary committee, the sixth in eleven years, to investigate the state of the London police. The committee recommended continuance of the existing parish system and the creation of a government-controlled daytime police patrol. Further than this the committee members would not go. Their report concluded in a famous passage that

it is difficult to reconcile an effective system of police with that perfect freedom of action and exemption from interference, which are the great privileges and blessings of society in this country.... The forfeiture or curtailment of such advantages would be too great a sacrifice for improvements in police ..., however desirable in themselves if abstractedly considered.[61]

A disappointed Peel pledged on the floor of the Commons that during his Home Secretaryship he would seek to establish "a vigorous, preventive police, consistent with the free principles of our free constitution." In the meantime he had to be content with a small daytime contingent of the Bow Street Foot Patrol, created in August 1822, to police the main thoroughfares in the heart of the city. Peel did insist that these men wear a uniform (blue coats and trousers with red waistcoats); he knew, however, that twenty-four men and three inspectors were a ludicrous addition to the miscellaneous daytime police in a city of 1.5 million.[62] What the metropolis really needed was a single, government-directed force of men that in structure and control was not dissimilar to his Irish Peelers and to the newly forming county constabulary in that country.

II. Disturbances in the English provinces

Luddism, 1811–12

At a time when the recently created Earl of Wellington was still embattled in Spain and Napoleon was caught up in his Russian misadventure, parts of central and northern England erupted in persistent warfare between the disaffected and the authorities. Originating in Nottinghamshire and eastern Derbyshire at the end of 1811, and spreading the next year to Yorkshire, southern Lancashire, and adjacent Cheshire, the disorders were of sufficient magnitude to constitute a theater of war operations within England.[63] At first the Government sent in 2,000 troops, the largest number (in Home Secretary Richard Ryder's words) that "had ever been found necessary in any period of our history to be employed in the quelling of a local disturbance." At the end, the disturbed districts were filled with 12,000 troops, an army as large as the one Wellington had in the Peninsula.[64]

These "Luddite"[65] disorders were produced by an economic crisis characterized by high food prices, reduced wages, and rising unemployment due to the collapse of overseas markets. The Luddites' destruction of machinery was neither novel nor inherently antitechnological, but rather represented working-class anger over the failure of collective bargaining and petitioning on minimum wage and trade union questions. What was new was the intensity of the violence; the merging of food riots, industrial radicalism, and revolutionary rhetoric; and, after the degeneration into arms raids and property thefts, the widespread panic among the propertied classes. The Luddites' concerns were local and their grievances economic. Their interest in political reform was marginal, and there is little evidence of any coordination across counties or of any plan for national revolution. The number of actual Luddites was probably fairly small, and the number of incidents in 1811–12 totaled a few dozen in Yorkshire and Lancashire and about a hundred in the Midlands.[66]

What was alarming about Luddism was its organization, secrecy, and solidarity. The lower-class movement was "frightening because of its efficiency and ... the systematic use of organised and controlled violence for the achievement of its aims." Bodies of men, strangers numbering anywhere from 20 to 300, sometimes armed and disguised by blackened faces, traveled at night through isolated country districts. Equally alarming was the selective destruction of machinery and property; the calling of the roll of the men and their answering by number, not name; the pistol shot signifying departure; the orderly retreat in strict military fashion; and finally, the dispersal of the group in many different directions.[67]

Classical Luddism in fact represented an English version of Irish terrorism. The comparison was noted by Sir Francis Wood in a letter to Earl Fitz-william, Lord Lieutenant of Yorkshire (as he had been formerly of Ireland): "The Similarity of our Present State to that of Ireland strikes every one who witnessed the Transactions of 1797 and 1798 in that Country." In their secrecy and swearing of the inhabitants, nocturnal marches, arms, threat-ening letters and notices, tight organization and code of behavior, use of strangers, and local and economic aims, the Luddites were indeed similar to the Whiteboys of Ireland. But in one area – the avoidance of personal violence – the movement was peculiarly English. The Luddites destroyed property valued at more than £100,000, but they hardly ever harmed people; these terrorists killed only two carefully chosen persons.[68]

The absence of avowedly political aims or revolutionary plans hardly reassured the propertied classes in the disturbed areas. The degeneration of pure Luddism as early as January 1812 into arms raids, housebreaking and robbery, and the unrelated assassination of Prime Minister Perceval in London in May only intensified class fears. Correspondents flooded the Home Office with discoveries of "a deep laid system," of villages where everyone was "a most determined and revolutionary Jacobin." Wild esti-mates placed 8,000 Luddites and other revolutionaries at Sheffield and an equal number at Leeds; it was alleged that "40,000 Heroes are ready to break out" in a rising in Yorkshire.[69] The Luddites never did live up to their revolutionary billing, but the evolution of a climate of fear throughout the Midlands and the North is undoubted. A few observers like General Thomas Maitland argued that the local authorities were "frightening themselves by their inefficiency and incompetence"; in May 1812 he wrote the Home Office that the Manchester magistrates "seem .... to have rather overthought the whole of this Subject," though he added that this was "very natural under these circumstances." What was unquestionably disturbing was the scale of property destruction, the impunity with which laws were broken, and the secrecy and organization of the Luddite system.[70] Perhaps most alarming of all was the indication that certain sections of the working class had made the transition from Church-and-King deference and ritualized food rioting to a radicalism premised on working-class independence and self-sufficiency.

The establishments of police that had to confront these disorders were pitiful. In the rural districts, parish forces were either nonexistent or tiny and staffed with aged incompetents. The situation was little better in the towns. Leicester (pop. 23,000) had six constables; Oldham (pop. 29,000), two

"Methodistical, Jacobinical" constables. Manchester, "the greatest village in England" (pop. 116,000), was governed by its redoubtable Deputy Constable Joseph Nadin, but his force totaled only fifteen beadles and streetkeepers and seventy night watchmen. Nottingham (pop. 34,000), perhaps "the most efficiently governed of the disturbed towns," had six constables; "it was necessary on the very first occasion of riot, in March 1811, as always thereafter, to call on the regular military garrison" to restore order.[71]

In the towns, the traditional resort to special constables was somewhat successful. Nottingham in December 1811 had 600 specials on nightly street patrols; in April 1812 Salford, a township adjacent to Manchester, was able to raise 1,500 special constables (one-tenth of the adult male population). Bolton recruited as many as 400, and many other towns enrolled lesser numbers of specials.[72] The problem was that the institution could not function where it was most needed. Special constables were an urban and middle-class phenomenon; the vast majority of the disorders were in the countryside. Here there was no large middle class, and the lower orders, whether from sympathy with or fear of the insurgents, were either reluctant to serve or unreliable as a volunteer police force. In the war against Luddism, special constables were of decidedly marginal importance.

Because of the inefficiency of local police institutions in the Luddite areas, the Government on two occasions sent to Nottingham two London police magistrates and a small band of constables. The reports from Nathaniel Conant and Robert Baker, on loan from the Marlborough Street and Hatton Garden Police Offices, would be among the most perceptive and impartial available to the Government. Town authorities welcomed the arrival of these professionals; indeed, as late as July 1815, requests poured into the Home Office for more policemen. But the Government was reluctant to establish a pattern of London loans, so no police were sent after the original grant to Nottingham in 1811–12.[73]

The local authorities were generally ineffective against the disorders. The county magistrates displayed petty jealousies, demanded selfish protection of their own properties, and proved unable to establish any coordinated system of repression. Many were paralyzed by fear, others by incompetence. Still others were alarmist to the point of being psychopathic. Nottinghamshire magistrates in general performed the most creditable service, but those in Lancashire were "more dangerous in their excessive zeal than the Yorkshire officials in their apathy." On the whole, one recent scholar has concluded, the "local officers of the law constituted one of the most serious obstacles to its proper enforcement."[74] For all of their inefficiency, JPs with massive military support rounded up large numbers of Luddites. About 200 persons were indicted; two-fifths were acquitted or discharged without trial, but some three dozen were hanged and a like number transported.[75]

In the absence of a strong civil power, the Government resorted to the military to crush Luddism. Yeomanry corps were called out, but the troops were small (about fifty men each) and scattered. The county militias – at a time when many English regiments were in Ireland – were more effective.

Because it was felt that the use of local forces would be "putting arms in the hands of the most powerfully disaffected," militia regiments from Berkshire, Cumberland, South Lincoln, Devon, and Buckinghamshire were sent to Nottinghamshire in the spring of 1812. Not only did the 3,000 militia in Yorkshire, the 3,000 in the Midlands, and the 1,000 in Lancashire prove to be "absolutely trustworthy," they formed a major part of the Government's spy service.[76] Adjutants of militia were often in charge of local espionage and its financial accounts, and the units supplied many undercover agents. Perhaps the most famous was Capt. Francis Raynes of the Stirlingshire (Scot.) militia. His detachment was active in Lancashire and then Yorkshire, "fixed nowhere ... constantly moving about ... [with] Orders ... not to remain two days in the same place, and always to move in the night perfectly at his own discretion." Throughout 1812 he busied himself in "consorting with the disaffected," swearing in constables, and recruiting spies. For his services, the Government paid Raynes £200 in 1813, then refused his requests for other government service. In frustration Raynes published in 1817 *An Appeal to the Public*, which, in its disclosures, was highly embarrassing to the Government.[77]

The more public response of the authorities to the challenges of Luddism frequently fitted a general pattern. In the first stage, local magistrates used such local constables and military as were available. They often found themselves swamped, beaten by their own inferior numbers, lack of coordination, and fear of acting resolutely. In the second stage, local authorities would request the Home Office to send military reinforcements and sometimes London police officers. At this stage, the Government almost invariably denied initial requests and exhorted local authorities to take stronger local action; sometimes small troop reinforcements would be supplied to encourage local activity. Stage three, massive military inflow and usurpation of civil powers, occurred only after the total collapse of stage one. But, in practice, it was stunning how quickly and frequently the model progressed to stage three, the national and military solution. Indeed, F. O. Darvall has concluded that, given the "wholly inadequate" size of the local civil forces, their limited funds and the already burdened county rates, and the magistrates' manifold weaknesses, it was "inevitable" that the Government would be "forced ... to intervene directly" and the local authorities "content in the end to see the watch become wholly military."[78]

It was for these reasons that the largest domestic military force in the history of England up to that time invaded the Midlands and North of England. When the Nottingham disorders began, sixty cavalry were lodged in the local barracks; similar numbers were stationed in Manchester and York at the onset of the disorders there. The militia and regulars sent to the Midlands rose to 2,000 men by December 1811, doubling to 4,000 two months later. The coming and going of troops gave "an appearance of a state of war."[79] In May 1812, an even larger force of 5,500 infantry and 1,400 cavalry were moved into Lancashire and 1,800 troops into Yorkshire. By the summer, in the area between Leicester and York, towns only 100 miles apart, the Government had assembled a total force of 12,000 men. This was a larger army than Wellesley had taken to Portugal in 1808. It was also six times larger than the force of men that His Majesty's Government, only three months earlier, had admitted was the largest ever to be deployed against its own citizens.[80]

One can hardly appreciate the bewilderment, burden, and resentment that the military commanders felt in this unprecedented situation. The ineffectuality of the local institutions of order put the responsibility for policing squarely on the army. A half-dozen generals were assigned entire districts: General Dyott and then General Hawker in the Midlands; General Grey in Yorkshire; and General Maitland in Lancashire, where he was assisted by Major-General Dixon at Liverpool and Major-General Acland at Manchester. From June 1812 on, the entire Luddite command was put on the shoulders of Lt.-Gen. Sir Thomas Maitland.[81] The initial and natural policy of these military leaders, who were used to battlefield tactics, was to concentrate the troops in large bodies. It was thought best to avoid "minute detachments"; do not "fritter them away in small or unnecessary Parties," Maitland instructed Major Hawkins at Manchester. A policy of dispersion would make the men vulnerable to attack or subjects to "be tampered with ... [by] the immense Population of these villages." In addition, a policy of too easy and numerous loans of soldiers would only "give that degree of security, as to induce the Inhabitants themselves to relax in their exertions" to keep the peace.[82]

This policy, which arose from the military's objection to being used as a civil police force, was from the beginning almost impossible to enforce. The geographical nature of the Luddite challenge and the endless importunities for protection led the army to be separated into police parties across large sections of the five counties. At Huddersfield (pop. 9,671) in Yorkshire, 1,000 soldiers were quartered in the town's 33 public houses, where they were daily exposed to intoxication, indiscipline, and political tampering. The innumerable detachments, in motion "as much as possible," were put on nightly, ever-changing routes of patrol. In the more remote districts there was "much inconvenience" not only from the hostility of the local people but from the difficulties of provisioning the soldiers. Problems arose because civil magistrates could not make arrests without troops and seldom communicated effectively with them, even as the military questioned its ability to act without magistrates.[83] Meanwhile, the requests for soldiers were continuous: Magistrates, High Constables, mill owners, and other property owners all clamored for protection. "Were I to give way to all such applications," Maitland wryly noted, "the whole of the British army would not be sufficient for the calls that would instantly be made upon me." To the military the source of their problems was clear enough. Writing from Stockport, Lt.-Col. George Nelthorpe stormed that "the entire inadequacy of the efforts of the civil power [is] I believe ... the rendezvous of everything which is bad."[84]

To meet the Luddite challenge the English Parliament enacted two public order statutes in February 1812. One was a strong act of punishment, the other a mild measure for prevention. The Framebreaking Act made destruction of machinery a capital offense; the Nottingham Peace Act, known generally as the Watch and Ward Act, sought to strengthen local institutions of police.[85] The latter act provided that "in places where disturbances prevail, or are apprehended," local magistrates should appoint constables to serve as a ward by day and a watch by night. Selections were to be made from a list of all male householders aged seventeen to fifty who paid £20 in yearly rents; failure of a man or his substitute to serve was to result in a stiff fine; and all expenses were to be charged to the local poor rates. The cost and control of the forces were thus kept in local hands. The act proposed to encourage local authorities to establish the kinds of police that should already have been in existence. "Stimulate them in enforcing the Watch and Ward Act," was the Home Office advice to the military. It was an order cheerfully carried out. As General Maitland informed the Mayor of Leicester, "I necessarily presume the Watch and Ward Bill must be carried into complete effect, ... [for] without this no Military Aid can be effective."[86]

The results were disappointing. Nottingham, the best policed town during the disturbances, had increased its night watch from twelve in March to thirty-six in December 1811. But Nottingham never implemented the new Watch and Ward Act, and the town watch disbanded in the summer of 1813. Watch and ward systems were set up in Macclesfield, Stockport, and Oldham, but by 1813 they, too, were dissolved. In Yorkshire, small systems of watch and ward were established at Halifax and Huddersfield, "so far as local conditions allowed," but only after a direct order from Lord Lieutenant Fitzwilliam.[87] In most of the instances where constables were sworn in under the act, "they do not patrole or think it necessary," or "fight shy of their duty and are not to be trusted." In September 1812 Captain Raynes, on a tour of the West Riding, computed that of seventeen villages visited, only two had ever instituted watch and ward; the Vice-Lieutenant of the Riding counted ninety-eight townships that had never established the system.[88] The reasons for the continued futility of the civil power were not far to seek. In a time of economic distress local authorities were opposed to further burdens on the poor rates, which financed watch and ward. For this reason many villages petitioned against implementation of the act. Moreover, in rural areas it was difficult to find enough persons who were reliable. Those who were often proved reluctant to serve; "with many people," reported Raynes, "it is fear [that] causes their backwardness." Magistrates themselves were not inclined to earn a dangerous notoriety. Finally, many sections of the local population sympathized with the aims, if not always the tactics, of the Luddites.[89] For all of these reasons, 12,000 of the King's soldiers continued to perform police duties in the broad area between Leicester and York.

By 1813 the Luddite challenge had been overcome. Economic conditions improved: Food prices began to decline and trade to improve. The spy network and military patrols operated as a continuing deterrent. Many of the movement's leaders had been seized. The Luddite remnant turned to political organizations to resume petitioning to Parliament, and to trade unions to settle wage negotiations.[90] In the Midlands there would be a brief recurrence of disorder for a few months in 1813, 1814, and 1816.[91] In retrospect, the Luddism of 1811–12 may be described as the greatest physical threat to property and social order during Home Secretary Sidmouth's tenure of office. But the movement was not political, national, or revolutionary. After 1812 popular radicalism would become increasingly politicized, vociferous, and widespread.

A threat of revolution?

The postwar years were undeniably turbulent and distressed, with high unemployment as an industrial economy geared to two decades of wartime demand suddenly went flat. The country was swept by waves of disorders. In the summer of 1816 bread and wage riots spread across agricultural East Anglia. Maj.-Gen. Sir John Byng was sent in with some troops; a special commission sentenced twenty-four men to death, of whom five were executed, nine transported, and the remainder imprisoned. There were also intermittent disorders throughout the Midlands, including the final gasp of Luddism.[92] In late 1816 London was disturbed by the Spa Fields Riots. Early the next year Parliament rejected the Hampden Clubs' national petition, signed by half a million persons demanding annual parliaments, manhood suffrage, and the secret ballot. In this swirl of events, responding to reports from zealous spies and alarmist magistrates, Sidmouth and the Cabinet interpreted the widespread protest as insurrection. In February 1817 Parliament suspended habeas corpus and banned public meetings.[93]

Some workers responded to this repression by staging three famous events – "the March of the Blanketeers," "the Huddersfield Rising," and "the Pentridge Rising" – glamorized titles for what were in fact minor protests. In Manchester, 12,000 people assembled in March 1817 at St. Peter's Fields. They proposed to march to London, blankets on their backs, there to demand parliamentary reform. But troops and special constables persuaded most of the crowd to go home even before the procession had left the city; on the trek south, people left, rather than joined, the march, and the lone survivor to reach Nottingham was arrested when he entered the town. The abortive March of the Blanketeers permitted the Government to be generous: All of those who had been arrested along the way were subsequently discharged without trial.[94]

There were two risings in 1817. The first occurred on 8 June at Huddersfield, Yorkshire. A few hundred men scattered at the approach of a Yeomanry troop and "one or two constables"; the leaders escaped, and the few men arrested and charged (with burglary) were subsequently acquitted.[95] The more well-known Pentridge Rising occurred the next day. Here the conspirators had a vague plan to coordinate "100,000 men" from the Midlands, Lancashire, and Yorkshire in a march on London in order to take over the Government. Probably no more than 200 men in east Derbyshire and west Nottinghamshire were actively involved. Through W. J. Richards ("Oliver the Spy"), the Government was kept informed of virtually every movement; in historian Malcolm Thomis's words, "a harmless enemy was about to deliver itself into their hands." When a party of 20 men from the 15th Hussars rode out from Nottingham to investigate the doings at Pentridge, they came upon some 50 men and (after what magistrate Lancelot Rolleston described as "a most successful chase") arrested twenty-eight of them and seized 17 small arms and 45 pikes. The soldiers killed no one; the rebels, by accident, killed a farm servant. Government repression, "a matter of political decision and not of legal necessity," was savage: Of 45 men subsequently indicted 3 leaders were hanged and 30 followers sentenced to transportation.[96] The Pentridge Rising was repressed by the Government's reliance on spies, the hangman, and Botany Bay. The antics of the spy Oliver undoubtedly set back the hopes for any serious police reform in England. Ironically, if efficient police forces had existed, prevaricators and *provocateurs* like Oliver would have been less needed.

Peterloo, 1819

The post-Waterloo radicalized English working class had shown a marked disinclination for violent political revolution. In January 1818 the Government lifted the suspension of habeas corpus, and in July public meetings again became legal. The radicals – that is, workingmen who wanted the vote and repeal of the Corn Laws – eagerly grasped their new legal weapon, the outdoor, peaceable mass meeting. Unlike rioting and property destruction, "the constitutionalist reform demonstration" did not invite military repression; and unlike petitioning Parliament, it did not imply self-abasement before a body of social superiors. So long as the meeting remained peaceable, it was thoroughly legal. Yet the unspoken threat of power generated by a crowd numbering in the tens of thousands was unmistakable.[97] Above all, the monster meeting was a morality play in which the people sought to prove that they were not "a disorderly and ragged rabble" but were in fact deserving of the vote. The meetings were clearly disconcerting to the authorities. A Crown law adviser believed that "it was not in human nature" for such throngs to meet and disperse quietly; even the temperate and sympathetic General Byng felt that "the peaceable demeanour of so many thousand unemployed men is not natural."[98]

In the North of England the earliest of the open-air meetings were held at Manchester and Blackburn in October 1816 and at Oldham in January 1817. By 1819, the new radical technique blossomed as crowds numbering in the thousands met at Ashton, Blackburn, Leeds, Macclesfield, Ripponden, Rochdale, and Stockport. In July of that year a meeting in London drew 10,000 persons, and a crowd of 60,000 in Birmingham "elected" a "legislatorial attorney" to represent them in Parliament. The next month, a meeting was scheduled for Manchester, with Henry Hunt to speak before a crowd expected to be the largest in the city's history.[99]

The forces of order in Manchester consisted of the police, magistrates, special constables, and Yeomanry. The police were headed by a borough-reeve and two constables, both honorific posts, and a deputy constable who had "the actual superintendence of the police." Since his appointment sixteen years ago, fifty-four-year-old Joseph Nadin had directed a day and night watch of some seventy men, built a strong network of spies and informers, and established himself as the most fearsome policeman in northern England. Still, Nadin's force was inadequate for the city of 160,000; by contrast, Dublin, a city of comparable size, had a police force of 850.[100] The Manchester magistracy was in even worse shape. As late as 1808, not a single magistrate resided in the city. Only two unpaid JPs made themselves responsible for city business, but one was chronically ill and the other wanted to resign because of overwork.[101] Since 1813, Manchester had had one paid "stipendiary magistrate," a position created after riots in the city the previous year.[102] This man was the able but alarmist James Norris, a forty-five-year-old barrister who had held the office only since March 1818.[103] On paper Manchester's special constables looked impressive. Divided into sixteen districts, each led by a "conductor," the force totaled 4,000 men. But they had proved useless in the Exchange Riots of April 1812. General Byng complained of "a total want of Organisation or System among them ... a terrible Blank in Efficiency.... Their very numbers ... [are] a source of weakness rather than of strength."[104] The Yeomanry in Lancashire were much reduced since the war. The largest corps was at Liverpool; the one at Bolton had disbanded in 1816. The fifty-man Manchester and Salford Corps of Yeomanry Cavalry was founded only in June 1817.[105] Its members were not all wealthy manufacturers or merchants. There were more publicans and butchers than cotton masters; the roster included cheesemongers, tobacconists, sadlers, and dyers, as well as attorneys and iron merchants. Their social diversity was less important, however, than a shared conviction against popular agitation and universal suffrage.[106]

Such, then, were the forces of order in Manchester that prepared for the great meeting at St. Peter's Fields on 16 August 1819. The meeting was to be one of a series of peaceable monster meetings that had been held in England over the past eight months. In Manchester itself, on numerous occasions, the magistrates had effectively handled large demonstrations. In October and November 1816, meetings attracting 10,000 persons had ended quietly. In March 1817 Nadin's men, assisted by troops and special constables, had arrested three dozen radicals without bloodshed in dispersing a crowd of 12,000 at the Blanket Meeting in St. Peter's Fields. As recently as 18 January and 21 June 1819, large meetings at the Fields had passed off quietly. There seemed little reason to *expect* bloodshed on 16 August 1819.[107] If the "massacre" that day was premeditated, it was also produced by panic.[108] Throughout 1819 the local authorities at Manchester had worked themselves into a state of general alarm. Their correspondence shows that they consistently and continuously misread protest for revolution. In March, Norris, the stipendiary magistrate, informed the Home Office that "a general insurrection is now seriously meditated"; by June he believed that the people were "ripe for any purpose.... I fear it is now too late." In early July, seventy of the city's principal inhabitants formed a Committee in Aid of the Civil Power. The group coordinated the town constables, Yeomanry, and special constables, monitored the radicals' activities, and wrote innumerable letters to London. They predicted that the Gordon Riots were about to be reenacted in Manchester, that "some alarming insurrection is in contemplation." They even asked the Government to issue them 1,000 small arms from military stores.[109]

General Byng, the commanding officer in the Northern District, reported that he had "no fear of any disturbances." Henry Hunt, the radical leader, did fear that spies and other "sanguinary agents" might try to induce disorder in order to justify swift repression. To forestall coercion, he announced that there would be no electing of "legislatorial attorneys," as had been done at Birmingham. As early as 17 July the Home Office informed the Manchester authorities that any dispersing of the projected gathering would be illegal unless a mock parliamentary representative was elected or violence erupted. Alarm-filled letters continued to arrive from Manchester. On 4 August the Government went a step further. Its orders were phrased with unmistakable clarity.

Lord Sidmouth desires me to say that reflexion convinces him the more strongly of the inexpediency of attempting forcibly to prevent the [projected] meeting [on 16 August].... But *even if they utter sedition or proceed to the election of a representative*, Lord S. is of the opinion that *it will be the wisest course to abstain from any endeavour to disperse the mob, unless they should proceed to acts of felony or riot*. We have the strongest reason to believe that Hunt means to preside and to deprecate disorder. I ought to have mentioned that the opinion which I have expressed for Lord S. is supported by that of the highest law authorities.

Magistrate Norris's final letter (15 August) grudgingly conceded that the meeting would be permitted. "I hope the peace may be preserved," he opined, "but under all circumstances, it is scarcely possible to expect it."[110]

Beginning in the late morning of 16 August 1819, men, women, and children streamed into St. Peter's Fields, all dressed in their Sunday best.[111] Bands played and banners flapped in the bright day. The various groups, political, industrial, and religious, arrived in smart marching formation, led by men wearing white hats. The signs and banners demanded full suffrage, tax reform, and repeal of the Corn Laws. Probably a third of the crowd were "strangers," weavers from the industrial villages and towns surrounding Manchester.[112] "The meeting was the largest I ever saw," a witness at Hunt's trial observed later. So dense was the crowd that "in all parts their hats seemed to touch"; at least 60,000 persons were in attendance that day.[113] Most impressive, perhaps, were the discipline and orderliness of this vast assemblage.[114]

At 11 A.M. the magistrates assembled at their command post at the eastern edge of St. Peter's Fields. From it a double line of 300 special constables was formed, leading to the speaker's platform at the center of the Fields. In the side streets, away from the crowds, waited an impressive military assemblage: the Manchester Yeomanry, the Cheshire Yeomanry, and 250 soldiers from the 31st Infantry, 160 from the 88th Infantry, 300 cavalry from the 15th Hussars, and two pieces of light artillery. At 1:20 P.M., Henry Hunt entered the Fields and waded through the cheering crowd to the hustings.[115] He had scarcely begun to speak before the trouble began. At 1:30, Deputy Constable Nadin sent a note to the Manchester Yeomanry directing their immediate presence. Why the city's magistrates made the decision to call on the 50-man Yeomanry when they had 300 special constables and nearly 1,000 troops on the spot remains unclear. It is clear that, against the Government's express instructions, they were determined to disperse the meeting.[116]

The Manchester Yeomanry arrived at St. Peter's Fields at 1:40 P.M. For a moment they halted, then suddenly charged into the dense mass of surprised, peaceable demonstrators. Perhaps these fifty men now simply panicked; they must have realized the impossibility of dispersing such a throng. But instead of pulling back, they waded in deeper and began "striking with their sabres as if they were insane." Almost immediately the tiny corps was engulfed by the crowd. Minutes later the 15th Hussars (the regiment that had snuffed out the Pentridge Rising) rode up to rescue the trapped Yeomanry. "English Soldiers, ever brave! Seiz'd *Yeomen's* swords that they might save."[117] All of the violence occurred in the next fifteen minutes. Certainly the horses, pressed on all sides, must have panicked and their riders been frustrated by the humiliation of immobility. But as the defenseless crowd scattered, the furious, and now freed, Yeomen rode up and down the fields, hacking away at the fleeing demonstrators and yelling, "Damn you, I'll reform you!" and "You'll come again, will you?"[118] Sidmouth later admitted that not a single death was the work of the regular soldiers; Hunt himself praised the "coolness and comparative moderation" of the troops.[119] It was days later before the true horror of the Yeomanry's behavior was revealed: 11 in the crowd killed and 560 wounded.[120] The radicals quickly dubbed the one-sided battle "Peterloo" (Figure 5.2).

This, then, was the "revolution" dreaded by the Manchester magistrates: Defenseless families ridden down by a troop of uncontrolled cavalry.[121] Peterloo was a turning point in post-Waterloo politics because it demonstrated that the threat to community values could come not only from the Thistlewoods and Watsons but also from dangerous alarmists in positions of authority. The incident, writes E. P. Thompson, "outraged every belief and prejudice of the 'free-born Englishman' – the right of free speech, the desire for 'fair play,' the taboo against attacking the defenseless."[122] The Government, which had privately counseled the Manchester magistrates against violence, now lost a marvelous opportunity to win itself some popular affection. Liverpool, Sidmouth, and the Prince Regent himself applauded the Yeomanry's "heroics." Crown law advisers assured everyone of the legality of the Manchester atrocities. The infamous, repressive Six Acts were rushed through Parliament. Henry Hunt and three others were tried and convicted of unlawful and seditious assembly. Earl Fitzwilliam, Lord Lieutenant of

Figure 5.2 Peterloo: "Manchester Heroes." The Yeomanry, a part-time quasi-military local force, attempts to break up the meeting at St. Peter's Fields, 16 August 1819. (Contemporary satirical print, by permission of the British Museum)

Yorkshire, protested the day's events and was removed from his post for insubordination, as he had been recalled a quarter-century earlier from his Lieutenancy in Ireland.[123] Stipendiary Magistrate Norris was kept on over General Byng's pleas that he be forced to resign. In 1822, at a trial brought by a Middleton hatter named Redford, Captain H. H. Birley and three other Yeomen were exonerated of any wrongdoing at Peterloo.[124]

In the immediate post-Peterloo period, as the working classes licked their wounds, the Government poured regular troops into the "rebellious" North (Table 5.1). By December 1819, 11,000 troops, a third of the army in Britain, were stationed in the Northern District; this figure was double the number there at the time of Peterloo.[125] The Yeomanry were not only not punished, they were strengthened. Nationwide force levels rose from 18,000 in 1816 to 31,000 in the post-Peterloo year, 1820. In Lancashire itself in 1817 there had been only three corps totaling 276 men; in 1820, there were seven corps comprising 678 men. Sidmouth justified the increase by saying, "The Disease is far beyond the reach of Special Constables."[126]

III. Overview

The control of crowds in the corn bill, Spa Fields, and Caroline disturbances, and in the Luddite, Blanketeer, Pentridge, and Peterloo affairs, was delegated

Table 5.1. *Army force levels in the Northern District and in England and Wales,*
1812–20

Year	Northern District	England and Wales	Percent in North
1812	2,520	104,000[a]	2%
1816	2,100	30,000	7
1818	3,260	28,500	11
1819			
Jan.–Mar.	4,700	28,000	17
Apr.–June	4,700	24,600	19
July–Sept.	4,800	24,600	20
Oct.–Dec.	8,050[b]	27,800	29
1820			
Jan.–Mar.	9,250	32,200	30
Apr.–June	9,050	30,400	31
Jul.–Sept.	7,950	30,800	26
Oct.–Dec.	7,800	31,400	25

Note: For 1819–20, three-month averages of force levels on the first of each month; for earlier
years, average of force levels in April, August, and December.
[a] Wartime: includes militia.
[b] Peaks at 10,780 in December 1819; 31 percent of the army was in the Northern District.

to the military. Infantry and cavalry soldiers did not relish these assigned
duties; after 1816 they no longer had militia to help them and, after August
1819, in a sense, they no longer had the Yeomanry either. Yeomanry corps
would still be called out over the next thirty years, but the images of Peterloo
remained alive in the minds of both crowds and authorities. The affair at
Manchester so tainted the Yeomanry as to hinder its usefulness for peacekeeping purposes.[127] With the militia gone and the Yeomanry questionable,
the army would have to shoulder an increasing share of the burden of
peacekeeping.

For some citizens however, one of the lessons of all these disturbances was
that the creation of a new institution of the civil power was necessary.
Throughout his term of office, Home Secretary Sidmouth received
numerous suggestions for reforming the country's police. In 1812 Dr.
Samuel Meyrick proposed "a plan of systematized [government] police ...
without endangering the liberties of the people." All of England should be
divided into police districts. On a permanent map of the country there
should be fixed notations about military posts, roads, population, grain
movements, and marching times between each police post. On an overlay
map the Home Office could track disturbances and make other "pencilled
remarks of temporary comment." In his reply, Sidmouth noted that the plan
was "worth attentive consideration." In 1814 Mr. J. Hardy from Surrey
proposed a military police to replace the night watches "in every part of the
United Kingdom"; the force would be funded by both the old watch rates
and Treasury grants, and would be available "in case of Insurrections of any

kind." In 1816 a Mr. Allsopp, writing in response to disturbances in the Midlands, informed the Government that "a permanent police establishment with regular police is the only solution." Later that year, Sidmouth, in a letter to the Lord Lieutenant of Ireland, described the Insurrection and Peace Preservation acts as "two powerful instruments ... which Parliament has placed in your hands," but apparently he never considered such measures for England. In 1819, in the aftermath of Peterloo, two correspondents separately came up with the idea of establishing a special movable riot police recruited from among the numerous army pensioners. Finally, in 1820, the Duke of Wellington suggested that the militia be revived and reorganized into a police force for use during disturbances. "What is to become of us," Wellington asked, "if we have not some force in Reserve upon which we can rely?"[128]

Why did Sidmouth and the Government not act on any of these proposals? For London there were at least parliamentary inquiries into the state of the police. But a decade of unrest in the provinces sparked no discussion of police in the House of Commons, led to no investigating committees, and produced no police bills. Historian F. O. Darvall has described this lack of interest as "rather astonishing." Luddism, he notes, produced "not any suggestion ... of anything more far-reaching than a slight modernization of the old system of Watch and Ward."[129] In part, the absence of reform can be explained by the nature of the Home Secretary: An unimaginative Tory traditionalist, Sidmouth was not the person to press for radical reform of cherished local institutions of the civil power. Second, it must be stressed that in the national mind, "police" was still associated with espionage[130] and "French despotism"; the fears surrounding the institution still prevailed over the perceived need for such an outlandish measure. The police experiment in Ireland – in Dublin dating to 1786 and, most recently, since 1808, and in the rural districts since 1814 (see Chapter 6) – reinforced Englishmen's fears about the curtailment of their traditional liberties. Third, the army, heavily burdened as it was, had shown itself able to contain the disorders. The King's soldiers had repressed riots in London and a series of provincial "risings," intervened heroically at Peterloo, and been outmaneuvered but not physically beaten by the Queen Caroline crowds.

A final reason for the continuing absence of police reform in England is that, by contrast to Ireland, the existing system of justice – parish constables, JPs, juries, and assizes and sessions – worked well enough so that, for many, there seemed no pressing need for overhaul of the system. The country was not dysfunctional in the basic way that Ireland was. In England disturbances were periodic, not continuous. The "risings" of 1817 and the Cato Street Conspiracy attracted minimal popular support. Similarly, the use of violence against persons was neither common nor popularly legitimated. Prime Minister Perceval's assassination by a deranged office seeker had not triggered any further political murders. Murder itself was a rare and unacceptable outrage: Witness the national horror over the Ratcliffe Highway killings and the Peterloo massacre.[131] In the major disturbances in this decade, rioters in London produced a total of one fatality and those in the provinces a total of three (two by the Luddites, one by the Pentridge "rebels"). The record of those in authority was far bloodier: two killed in the Caroline riots, thirteen during the Luddite period, and eleven at Peterloo.

The Government's continued reliance on the military as its principal agent against protest did present problems. The army was a heavy-handed instrument to use against peaceable demonstrators and a cumbersome one against fast-moving rioters. And thousands of soldiers – mere numbers – were ineffective without proper authorities to guide and coordinate their use. There were limits to the value of sending 1,600 troops and four howitzers to Carlisle and Newcastle to subdue these northern towns, as the Government did after Peterloo; for their part, the radicals could respond by massing their followers, as they did in September 1819, when a crowd of 300,000 turned out to cheer Henry Hunt's triumphal entry into London.[132] Such mutual overawing produced stalemate and continued unrest. What the Government needed was a more flexible, less regimented body of men that did not have to depend for direction on outsiders, the traditional JPs, but rather on leaders who somehow combined the functions of magistrate and military. The solution – as a young Lancashire factory owner's son fresh from Oxford was learning in Ireland – lay in the creation of revolutionary new civil authorities placed midway between the crowds and the army.

CHAPTER 6

Ireland under Peel and Grant: innovations in police

We deprecate riotous mobs ... but we see no reason why such evils should not be met in Ireland by the same means which are uniformly resorted to in England, or why any extraordinary measure should be adopted towards the one country which has never even been proposed with regard to the other.... As to riotous mobs, we surely have had enough, and more than enough, of that evil in England. But yet, upon the disgraceful riots of 1780, and the still more disgraceful outrages at Birmingham [1791], the established energy of the Law was found sufficient to answer the ends of Justice.... Nay, what was done upon the more recent and alarming outrages in the North of England, which were known to be the result of a systematic conspiracy? ... Yet it was never proposed to put the Counties in which this Conspiracy raged, out of the pale of the Constitution.... What a contrast to Mr. Peele's Law with respect to Ireland! Can any just Englishman reflect upon such a contrast without regret and disapprobation, and are not the feelings of an Irishman excusable if he review it with indignation?
– London *Morning Chronicle*, 25 September 1814

Robert Peel was only twenty-four years old when he arrived in Ireland in September 1812 as Chief Secretary. The eldest son of a Lancashire cotton manufacturer, Peel was already a "coming man" in Tory political circles. Only four years earlier he had graduated with highest honors from Christ Church, Oxford. In 1809 he entered Parliament as a Member for Cashel, County Tipperary – the town to which, five years later, he would first despatch his new police. In 1810, Peel was named Under-Secretary for War and the Colonies, and in this post he "acquired all the necessary habits of official business." It was in Lord Liverpool's Cabinet reshuffling of 1812, which saw Sidmouth named to the Home Office and Henry Goulburn to War and Colonies, that Peel was promoted to the Irish post.[1]

The handsome young man was brilliant yet likeable, quick-witted and quietly self-confident. Peel was heir to a baronetcy, but his love of work betrayed his middle-class origins. At Harrow and Oxford he had not been smitten with the vices of the English aristocracy. His political career would mark him as a pragmatic administrator, a man who, in Norman Gash's words, "preferred facts to phrases." Like all Chief Secretaries, Peel arrived in Ireland "educated in total ignorance of Irish affairs." Critics charged him

Figure 6.1 Irish Chief Secretary Peel, age twenty-three, in 1812. (Painting by William Owen, R. A., by permission of the 3d Earl Peel)

with an "overweaning collegiate self-sufficiency," but in fact Peel quickly demonstrated a great capacity to learn[2] (Figure 6.1). Peel came to appreciate that an uneducated, impoverished, "enormous and overgrown" population "must be vicious." The social and economic system under which the mass of people lived made it not in "their interest to be industrious." "The great obstacle [is] the want of manufacture," wrote the industrialist's son, "or any employment except agricultural." Unfortunately, young Peel concluded that the numerous necessary reforms would have to be the work of "wiser men than I am." During the six years he was in office, Robert Peel sponsored no legislation to remedy what he understood to be the fundamentally economic causes of Irish crime. In 1818 he opposed a bill to reform tithe assessment and even a parliamentary proposal to inquire into the problem of massive unemployment throughout the island.[3]

If Peel understood the roots of Irish lawlessness, he never was able to accept its violence. He would admit that the poor showed "great honesty . . . and great fidelity towards each other." Yet, in concluding one account of a grisly incident, he wrote: "You can have no idea of the moral depravation of the lower orders." The murder of an entire family prompted this sarcastic outburst to his friend, John Wilson Croker: "You must give me a specimen – one specimen – of the humanity of the poor, suffering, oppressed natives of this country." After a year in Ireland, Peel was wondering how he could continue to live in a place given over to continuous outrages without its irreparably warping his own character. "A letter from England is a treasure to me."[4]

Peel's years in Ireland were made bearable by the strong friendships he made at Dublin Castle. The Lord Lieutenant who replaced the Duke of Richmond in August 1813 was Earl Whitworth, a sixty-one-year-old career diplomat. After an unspectacular military career, Whitworth had served for fourteen years in the English Embassy at St. Petersburg. For the last decade he had lived in "comparative insignificance" in London. In his Irish post, Whitworth took "substantial comfort and consolation" in his friendship with Peel. On political issues the two men almost invariably agreed, and the elder statesman usually deferred to Peel in matters of business.[5] The third man in the Castle triumvirate was forty-five-year-old William Gregory, Civil Under-Secretary since October 1812. Gregory would hold this critically important post until 1830. The younger son of a Galway landowner who had amassed a fortune in India, Gregory had been educated at Harrow (Peel's school) and at Trinity College, Cambridge, and had read law at the Inner Temple in London. In Ireland he had held a series of minor administrative posts and served briefly (1798–1800) in the Irish Parliament. His marriage to the Earl of Clancarty's daughter provided social legitimacy to his political role as intermediary between the Anglo-Irish gentry and the higher Castle authorities; it also reinforced his "stiff Protestant outlook." Peel got on well with Gregory, for not only was he "a perfect gentleman" and an "excellent man of business," but his political views and wry sense of humor appealed to the young Chief Secretary.[6]

I. Peel's Peace Preservation Police, 1814–18

Old problems, old remedies

Robert Peel made one of his first tasks the review of the forces of order available to Dublin Castle. These consisted principally of the militia, Yeomanry, and army. The militia he found heavily Catholic in rank and file, tainted with Orangeism in many of its officer staffs, and in some corps fiscally corrupt. Moreover, he realized that "exchanging . . . our Irish Regiments for honest John Bulls" – 12,000 of whom were in Ireland in 1813 – was a practice that could not outlive the war.[7] That other peacekeeping force, the Yeomanry, was well armed. Over the last decade from the Ordnance stores had flowed the following armament: 8,160 pistols, 10,419 swords, 11,848 carbines, and 92,275 muskets. The all too frequent and unfortunate result was that the Yeomen were "the terror" of the countryside.[8] They committed robberies in Wicklow and Kilkenny, led foot riots in Down and Orange processions in Londonderry and Armagh, and clashed in sectarian brawls with Catholics. In an affray at Shercock, County Cavan, in May 1814, Yeomen had killed thirteen "papists" and injured scores of others; this little-known incident was more lethal than Peterloo.[9] There were even frequent clashes with British militia and regulars; "the Yeomanry in this Country," Col. W. H. Beckwith wryly remarked, "do not attach disloyalty to illegal distillation."[10] Dublin Castle in 1812–13 went so far as to discuss the replacement of the Yeomanry by a new force, a "local militia"; failing this, the commander-in-chief of the army in Ireland wanted the establishment of a "Yeomanry Court of Inquiry." For political reasons, both ideas were abandoned. "Do not hint it to a Soul on Earth that I ever alluded to the Subject" of Yeomanry abolition, Peel enjoined the Earl of Desart. The most that the Castle decided to do was to freeze the numbers and expenses of the establishment.[11]

By default, then, peacekeeping in Ireland devolved upon the regular army. "Scarcely a village is entered," observed an English visitor, "without a detachment being obtruded on the traveller." The system of troop dispersal, complained General Sir George Hewett, "had prevailed almost from time immemorial ... [against] the remonstrance of every successive Commander of the Forces." As in England, the police duties were unpopular with the men; for this reason, when it could get them, the Government preferred English or Scottish to Irish regiments.[12] The military demonstrated its discontent in many ways. Military headquarters frequently rejected troop requests; and overworked officers on the spot were known to disobey magistrates' orders, to march their men away from duty they judged to be unnecessary or unworthy, and to perform their patrols indifferently. Angry magistrates would then respond like one JP from Limerick: "Had I any military aid, no exertion of mine should be wanting, but without it, it is impossible to do anything."[13] The military's problems were compounded in 1812–13 by the drain of troops out of the country both to reinforce Wellesley in Spain and to repress the Luddites in England. Peel's correspondence reveals a rare emotionalism in his pleas for the English Government to stop tapping the Irish reservoir: Force levels in Ireland of only 7,000 infantry, he repeatedly warned, invited an uprising. The Chief Secretary once actually demanded that the Horse Guards countermand its order for troop shipments; the Lord Lieutenant argued that the London Government "cannot want them in England, and to us they would be Peace & Tranquillity."[14] The demands of disorders in both countries were thus placing an enormous strain on the traditional military system.

A further problem was that the criminal justice system was not working well. Peel, the young Oxford scholar looking over the criminal records for 1805–12, would have noted that only 22 percent of those committed for all crimes were convicted; this compared with a 60 percent conviction rate in England. For riot and riotous assembly in 1805–14 the regional differences were striking: Ulster had a 74 percent conviction rate; Leinster and Munster, 51 and 53 percent, respectively; and Connaught, only 37 percent. In 1812–13 certain counties – Cork, Limerick, Tipperary – had disastrous conviction rates of 23, 26, and 32 percent, respectively. Homicides were frequently reported in the newspapers, but only twelve persons a year were executed for murder in the period 1805–10.[15]

The "outrages" – to use the English term for Irish crime – that the young Peel was now discovering were seemingly innumerable. They stemmed from grievances over rents, tithes, wages, taxes, and priests' dues. There were faction fights at village fairs; sectarian feuds between Protestants and Catholics in Ulster; ongoing violence among the tenantry; Whiteboy raids for arms on mail coaches and farmers' houses; and the recurrent threat of political rebellion.[16] To an Englishman, the shocking common thread in the lawlessness was the use of brutal personal violence. "Scarce a Fair passes without Murder ... or Mutilation." Rape was sometimes used by the Whiteboys to punish their victims' loved ones. In one incident, four men in succession raped a farmer's daughter; another case involving two farmers' wives Under-Secretary Gregory described as "as frightful an account as the annals of Irish violence can produce."[17] In 1813 the Castle was informed of the murder of a wealthy farmer in Waterford who had "incurred the hatred and detestation of every person.... His Death meets the approbation of this whole County." Peel was shocked to learn of the attempted assassination, in broad daylight before hundreds of approving spectators, of a Westmeath farmer who had defended his house from Whiteboys.[18] In disturbances in Westmeath and King's County, farmers were "carded," tortured by the stroking of a woolcomber's iron-spiked "card" along the victim's skin. In Westmeath a man named James Connell was murdered for daring to prosecute at the recent assizes. Lord Castlemaine reported to the Castle:

Such Butchery I never beheld.... Caesar had not more wounds. His Wife was also shot thro' both her eyes but still has life in her.... I am scarcely able to write [the handwriting is a scrawl] – with the Bloody Corps [*sic*] before me as it is.... He was stabbed and battered with stones as flat as a board.[19]

Two organized agrarian movements had agitated parts of the country in recent years. In the province of Connaught and in parts of the counties of Longford and Cavan in 1806–8, the "Thrashers" had sought to regulate church tithes and priests' dues by issuing warning notices and staging nightly house visits by armed and disguised men. More recently, the activities of the "Caravats" and "Shanavests" had disturbed Munster. Originating in Tipperary in 1806 and spreading to Waterford, Kilkenny, Limerick, and Cork, these groups were active in eleven counties by 1811. Spawned by the wartime inflation in land prices, the "proletarian" Caravats – mostly laborers and small farmers given to wearing colorful neckerchiefs or "cravats" – sought to stop land ejectments, regulate rents, and raise wages. In response, the larger farmers, many of them with United Irish backgrounds, formed a defensive organization called the Shanavests ("Old Waistcoats"). The aggressors, the nocturnal "Caravat-whiteboys" operated as armed, mounted parties of men who issued threatening notices, administered beatings, and raided houses for arms. By day, each side attended fairs where they staged fierce battles. Twenty were killed in the mayhem at May Fair at Golden, County Tipperary, in 1807; altogether, according to a recent scholar, several hundred persons died in these faction fights in Munster in 1806–11. To repress the large-scale violence, the Irish Government had sent in Yeomanry officers, troops "more [numerous] ... than in 1798," and special police magistrates led by Richard Willcocks. A special commission in 1811 secured convictions against thirty-seven men, twenty of whom were sentenced to be executed and the rest to be transported, flogged, or imprisoned. The Caravat–Shanavest outburst had demonstrated to Dublin Castle the powerlessness of local authorities to contain the disorders, especially at their core in south central Tipperary. It was to this area, in 1814, that Willcocks, the Castle's ablest agent, would return with a new force of government police.[20]

To traditional outrages were added, in the summer of 1813, the fears of another attempted rising. For more than a decade, alarmism among local magistrates had become a normal state of mind. Peel complained that "no part of my official duty [is] more irksome than ... discovering the real truth of [these] representations." Reports to Dublin Castle claimed that French arms had been landed on the coast of Mayo; counties as different as Roscommon and Antrim were ready to rise; men in Tipperary were taking United Irishmen's oaths, "as they did in 1798"; meetings in Kerry and Cork denounced the Government and the war against Napoleon. In Kildare, army officers reported rumors that 100,000 arms were hidden for a joint Irish and English rising once the French had landed. In Westmeath, magistrates stated that meetings were openly declaring support for the French. By the end of the year, expectations for a January 1814 invasion were reported in Limerick, Clare, Kerry, and Cork.[21]

A fresh approach: establishing a strong police

The invasion existed only in some men's minds and in others' hopes, but the situation in Ireland clearly dismayed the young Peel. The bulk of the population was hostile, crime went unpunished, the militia appeared unreliable, the Yeomanry was troublesome, and the army was irritable and overworked. The civil power outside Dublin seemed nonexistent: The baronial police were inactive, and the Peace Preservation Police of 1787 now functioned only in parts of Meath and Cork. The Castle received a great number of complaints from magistrates bemoaning the absence of any constables to carry out the law. Moreover, reported Lt.-Gen. Thomas Meyrick, "The Civil Power alone is not adequate, or competent, to repress any disturbances."[22] Magistrates were apathetic or afraid to act. Two exceptions, men whose names recur in Dublin Castle's correspondence in 1812–13, were the

County Roscommon Sheriff, Edward Mills, and the Earl of Desart in County Kilkenny. These men formed defense associations, offered rewards, guaranteed secrecy to informers, swore the peasantry to loyalty, organized patrols using troop detachments, and, most importantly, were personally active. Mills once reported searching for a Whiteboy by saying, somewhat improbably, "I tracked him by his Blood near Three Miles today." In vain did Peel instruct the magistrates in Tipperary in January 1814 to follow Desart's example; in May, Gregory complained to Peel, "There must be some dreadful apathy or panic amongst the Gentry, not to make some effort. I wish they would all imitate Lord Desart."[23]

A number of observers were aware of the need for police reform. Only this "measure," noted a Limerick magistrate in October 1812, was "the most likely to restore tranquillity." In the same year Edward Wakefield published his acclaimed *Account of Ireland, Statistical and Political*; had the scholarly Chief Secretary, only recently arrived in Ireland, read this work, he might have noticed this sentence: "What Ireland requires, and must soon have, as experience will soon show, is an enlarged and energetic system of police, extending to the whole kingdom." In May 1813, Thomas English, a Westmeath magistrate, sent Peel a detailed analysis of the state of the rural police. Ten days later, Peel wrote Gregory that he was convinced that "the whole system [of police] seems to require revision."[24] It was too late to act in the present parliamentary session, but Peel did see to the arming of existing local constables.[25] In September the Earl of Desart proposed that the police should be placed "more immediately" under the Government's control; Peel's reply indicated that he would "care very little for any Odium that may attach to any increase of the powers of the Government which I believe to be necessary." In November a Westmeath magistrate named Sterne Tighe suggested the creation of a police that was remarkably similar to Peel's proposals of the next year: a government magistrate and perhaps twenty constables in a district designated as disturbed with a "Tax upon the Landholders ... [to] operate as a Stimulus to exertions to prevent such a charge." Three months later, Peel himself stated these terms as the essence of his police proposal. The Chief Magistrate would be "a stranger put over" the district. The constables should be well salaried at £80 p.a. As to the police tax, "I should wish to put the magistracy to shame," to make them pay "the expense of their own disgrace by paying the men who performed their duty."[26]

Peel's plans were now hurried by events. In the spring of 1814 the great war in Europe was at last winding down. "The horrors of peace" would be disastrous for Ireland. With Napoleon exiled to Elba on 4 May, the Government began to consider military demobilization. The army in Ireland would be cut from 43,000 to 28,000, despite the Lord Lieutenant's protests that "a Peace Establishment may do in England, *but here we are not at peace*." Whitworth hoped that "the war in America will give us at least a legal pretext for delaying" militia disbandment. But the London Government replied that it would begin on 3 June.[27] At just this moment, some magistrates in Kildare inundated the Castle with reports of an uprising planned to coincide with the disbanding of the county militias. The rebels, it was alleged, aimed to "break the connexion with England," murder Protestants, and establish a "New System for Liberty and Equality." Military officers in Leinster and Dublin Castle authorities were skeptical of these "false and groundless" reports, but they remained wary, for, in Gregory's words, "I remembered Emmett and the Castle caught napping."[28] The rising proved to be only the product of the magistrates' wild imaginations. The surviving records suggest that the Kildare magistrates may have used the "conspiracy" to argue for restoration of the Insurrection Act, which had lapsed in 1810. Chief Secretary Peel seized the crisis presented to him as yet another justification for reform of the Irish police.[29]

It is a serious mistake to say, as the late Galen Broeker has said, that "there was little original in Peel's proposal" for police reform. In 1814 the rural areas in England and Ireland had no police forces worthy of the name. The only relevant police precedent was the unsuccessful Irish experiment of 1787, a development that Broeker does not mention. Broeker says in passing that the Dublin police of 1808 was a model, but in which ways he does not make clear, and that "it is also probable that the chief secretary had some knowledge of recent developments in France"; for both assertions, he offers no evidence. Broeker is also misleading when he states that "stipendiary magistrates and specialized police forces had been used in England for some time."[30] Broeker, and Tadgh O Ceallaigh, are on the mark when they say that the Castle had already sent special magistrates into disturbed counties to work with the military and local magistrates there. But in his claim that Peel sought "to sanction a measure which had already been adopted, rather than introducing a new system," O Ceallaigh misses the point that the police as a *body of men* was an entirely new concept.[31] Further, from O Ceallaigh's own evidence, it is difficult to understand his statement that Peel's new police "tried to be cheap, it tried to avoid the stigma of central control, and it tried to spare both the pride and the pocket of the local gentlemen." Peel himself rightly feared that the gentry would find his ideas "unpalatable"; he was "afraid there will be some objection made to the Bill – it completely supersedes the ordinary magistracy in a proclaimed district.... The constables shall not attend any other magistrate without the express orders of the Chief Magistrate." Probably because of his fears, Peel chose, in June 1814, to give his measure the modest title "A Bill to provide for the better Execution of the Laws in Ireland."[32]

Peel's revolutionary proposal would create salaried, Castle-controlled police forces as needed in disturbed districts in Ireland. Following a request from local magistrates, the Lord Lieutenant could proclaim any county, barony, or half-barony to be in "a state of disturbance"; appoint a Stipendiary Magistrate (£700 p.a.) and a clerk (£150 p.a.), a Chief Constable (£150 p.a.), and a force of constables (£50 p.a.) "not exceeding fifty in the whole"; and send this "extraordinary Establishment of Police" into the area. All local magistrates were to obey this Stipendiary Magistrate (subsequently called Chief or Superintending Magistrate), who was to make weekly reports to the

Castle. All costs were to be paid by ratepayers in the disturbed area by means of grand jury presentments. The police could be withdrawn only on the Lord Lieutenant's announcement of the restoration of "Peace and Good Order."[33]

Dublin Castle's first task was to win over the English Cabinet to the proposed police. Liverpool, Sidmouth, and Castlereagh, an Anglo-Irishman, showed initial opposition. The Prime Minister was reminded that the bill applied to Ireland, not England. Castlereagh was chastised that "he ought to know his Country men, and that they cannot be governed by the ordinary means." Home Secretary Sidmouth was given a lecture. "Your Lordship knows well," said Lord Lieutenant Whitworth,

and I have already been long enough in the Country to convince myself, that it is not to be governed as England is, the Character and Spirit of the governed are completely different.... The great object is not to lose sight of the Distinction to be made between England and this part of His Majesty's Dominions.... There never was a Country in which such an Establishment was more wanted.... Extreme virulence of ... spirit, operating on Character, blind and infuriated as that of the French, to whom in all respects the lower orders of this country bear a striking resemblance, must convince the most common observer that good order is only to be maintained by the same means in both Countries. This Government must in fact be considered as a Military Government; and to be effectual, must be made a very strong one, aided by all the means which an active and vigilant Police can afford.[34]

All three ministers were won over; Sidmouth in particular would give the bill his strong support in the House of Lords.

Two weeks before the police bill's introduction in the Commons, Peel proposed two critical changes. He would give the Lord Lieutenant the right to proclaim a district even without a request from local magistrates. Second, he would give his police extraordinary powers by incorporating in the bill clauses from the defunct Insurrection Act. But the Cabinet, especially Lord Castlereagh, balked at this last suggestion. Irish Attorney-General William Saurin deftly persuaded Peel to abandon his proposal. Pass the police bill, he advised, then try for the Insurrection Act.[35] What was happening, almost unnoticed, was that Dublin Castle was coming to view Peel's extraordinary police proposal as "for everyday use ... for ordinary disturbances, for the every-day state of Ireland," and the Insurrection Act only for "great occasions."[36]

Peel introduced his bill in the House of Commons on 23 June. His presentation, dispassionate, researched, and balanced, was masterful, worthy of a man who had won a "double first" at Oxford. Peel spoke of the Irish land system, of Whiteboys and carding, of the terrorization of witnesses and the "romantic feeling" against giving information, of calm, deliberate murders, of political troubles like the "Kildare conspiracy," of faction fights at fairs, and of the problems of ineffectual local police, unreliable militia, contentious Yeomanry, and a reduced regular army. He did not mean to disparage the magistracy, but with notable exceptions like Lord Desart, they were simply swamped by the demands made upon them. The solution, as he saw it, was the new kind of police that he now proposed. Peel concluded his speech by remarking, "In this country the appointment of stipendiary magistrates was not necessary and therefore would be improper; but in Ireland the state of the country was so different, that the measure appeared to him indispensable for the public safety."[37] The excellence of the presentation produced the desired effect: Of seven subsequent speakers, only one opposed the bill, and he spoke in a rambling, inarticulate manner.[38] The next day, in letters to Dublin, a relieved Peel almost gloated like a schoolboy:

I think it went off most favourably.... No objection was made to the principle of the measure, or to the permanence of its operation.... [The incident of carding] appeared to produce a due effect upon the minds of English country gentlemen, tho' I fear it will not encourage them to settle with their families in Ireland.[39]

Subsequent readings proceeded smoothly and the bill passed easily. That the bill applied to another country, the parliamentary session was nearly ended, and many Irish Members were absent all help to explain the lack of opposition to the extraordinary measure.[40]

Flushed with easy victory and aware that Parliament would not reconvene until November, Peel pushed ahead to try to secure a new Insurrection Act. He tamely called it "A Bill to Provide for the preserving and restoring of Peace in ... Ireland"; it was this bill's title that would give his new police their common name, the Peace Preservation Police. In his parliamentary speech in early July, to sway his English audience, Peel traced the history of Irish agrarian disorders since the 1760s, giving disproportionate emphasis to the practice of carding. Only a few Whigs, whom Peel dismissed as "a host of enlightened and philosophic Scotch lawyers," spoke against the measure, which passed easily.[41] The twenty-six-year-old Chief Secretary was delighted by the success of his first forays into lawmaking. In the space of three weeks, against little opposition, he had secured the restoration of an old weapon and the creation of an altogether new one in the Government's battle against "outrages" in Ireland.

The reaction to the lawmaking in London was muted in the Dublin newspapers, most being content to report without comment the parliamentary proceedings.[42] Only the *Dublin Evening Post* objected to "Mr. Peel's Penal Laws." In the provincial press the *Cork Mercantile Chronicle*, that "seditious and disaffected paper,"[43] raised strong objections to Peel's police. Was the new institution not a superficial palliative when what was needed was purification of the magistracy and agrarian reforms? Would the local magistracy help or fight the new Castle-directed magistrates? The old charge was revived that such a police would be a "source of coercion and patronage" for the Government. The lack of opposition in London in 1814 was contrasted to the heroic debates of the late-eighteenth-century Irish Whigs whose "eloquence threw a stream of glory on our sinking efforts, and when our sun went down made it set in a wave of gold – all, all is gone."[44]

Of more immediate concern, could local ratepayers in disturbed districts afford to pay for the new police? Many throughout the country were "horror struck at the idea of additional taxes." It was feared that the new police, once sent to an area, would acquire a certain permanence. The *Dublin Evening Post* noted that they would "thrive in a storm and starve in a calm." The *Cork Mercantile Chronicle* explained that the new police magistrates, whose large salaries hung in the balance, "will be naturally anxious that the causes of their appointment should continue, namely the disturbances; and they will therefore probably represent places as disturbed for the sake of their own gain as long as they can." Peel's bill, the paper concluded, would better be renamed "A Bill for the Preservation of Disturbances in Ireland."[45]

Perhaps the most poignant objection was that "Bills for restricting the Liberties of Irishmen proceed in the course of mere routine business" in the English Parliament. An extraordinary police and a coercion act, "if applied to England, would set the whole country in an uproar." Why reserve this new coercion only for Ireland when "the amiable and civilized" English Luddites commit crimes that "in Ireland we would designate ... as open Rebellion"?[46]

The first Peelers

Throughout the summer of 1814, applications for the post of Chief Magistrate poured into Dublin Castle. As early as 29 June, Gregory termed them "innumerable" and observed that every applicant reported his area as the most disturbed. "Without the salary," the Under-Secretary dryly added, "the Country might have slept in peace, or been burnt to cinders." The applications – totaling more than 200 by September – came mostly from county magistrates and army, militia, and Yeomanry officers. Peel cast a skeptical eye on this horde of patronage seekers. He envisioned "a responsible and impartial and scientific Magistrate," a man with no local interests, connections, or experience.[47]

To fill the rank and file, Peel stated his preference for "disbanded Sergeants and veteran soldiers." Castle authorities looked favorably on men from the militia, for, among other reasons, they could "keep up a kind of watch over the disbanded Militia." This force was heavily Catholic, and early on Peel decided that Catholics should be accepted into the police. Finally, there is evidence that many of the new constables were drawn from the Dublin police, which itself recruited from the militia.[48] Arms, including light carbines fixed with bayonets, were furnished to the new police from central stores in Dublin. The force was not issued a standard uniform. The early outfits were colorful and military in appearance; one magistrate hoped that the variegated colors would "frighten the people into obedience and fear of the law."[49]

The new police was first tried in Tipperary. The winter and spring of 1813–14 had seen a resurgence of outrages in the historically disturbed county. A zealous magistrate, Richard Long, was murdered in July 1814; and when Isaac Fawcett, Jr. – a man who had "provoked death by incessantly taunting the unfortunate mother of an out-law whom he had shot last

THE PROCLAIMING OF MIDDLETHIRD, COUNTY TIPPERARY
6 September 1814

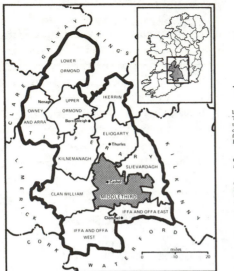

By the Lord Lieutenant and Council of *Ireland*,

A PROCLAMATION.

WHITWORTH.

WHEREAS by an Act of Parliament passed in the last Session, entitled " An " Act for the better Execution of the Law in *Ireland*, by appointing " Superintending Magistrates and additional Constables in Counties, in " certain Cases," it is amongst other Things enacted, that it shall be lawful for the Lord Lieutenant, or other Chief Governor or Governors of *Ireland* for the Time being, by the Advice of the Privy Council of *Ireland*, to declare by Proclamation, that any County, County of a City, or County of a Town in *Ireland*, or any Barony or Baronies, or Half Barony or Half Baronies, in any County at large, to be therein specified, is or are in a State of Disturbance, and requires or require an extraordinary Establishment of Police.

AND whereas it has sufficiently appeared to Us, that the Barony of *Middlethird*, in the County of *Tipperary*, is in a State of Disturbance, and requires an extraordinary Establishment of Police.

NOW We, the Lord Lieutenant, by and with the Advice of His Majesty's Privy Council, by Virtue of the said Act, and the Powers thereby vested in Us, do by this our Proclamation, declare, that the said Barony of *Middlethird*, in the County of *Tipperary*, in this Part of the United Kingdom called *Ireland*, is in a State of Disturbance and requires an extraordinary Establishment of Police.

Given at the Council Chamber in *Dublin*, the 6th Day of *September* 1814.

Westmeath. Erne. Frankfort. Norbury. W. Downes. Wm. M'Mahon. Robert Peel. G. Hewett. Wm. Saurin.

GOD save the KING.

DUBLIN Printed by GEORGE GRIERSON and JOHN BOWE POWER, Printers to the King's Most Excellent Majesty. 1814.

Map 6.1

winter" – was murdered in August, the stage was set for the new experiment in police.[50] Magistrate William Baker called a meeting to petition for the new police act. Dublin Castle sent down its top special agents, Richard Willcocks and Hugh Eccles, to seek the JPs' consent to the proclamation of seven of the county's eleven baronies. The meeting on 1 September lasted for three hours amid much opposition to the new police. Baker was accused of being "busy writing letters to the Castle, full of all manner of stories." Speakers feared that the police tax would be placed "in those Baronies in which their Properties were situated." Magistrate Baker, a resident of Clanwilliam, narrowly carried a motion that the barony of Middlethird, the largest in the county, should receive the new police. A motion that no other baronies should soon be proclaimed was narrowly defeated by a vote of 14–13.[51]

On 6 September Dublin Castle duly proclaimed Middlethird to be in a state of disturbance requiring the Peace Preservation Police (Map 6.1). Into Cashel rode Chief Magistrate Willcocks and "a portion of the Dublin police ... drilled to the smooth flags of Dublin streets," twenty-one constables who were all former cavalry sergeants. A native of Palmerston, County Dublin, Willcocks had served as a Dublin police magistrate. In 1803 "he obtained the first information of Emmett's designs" and personally committed to jail thirty-five of the rebels. In the same year he founded a Yeomanry corps in County Dublin, which he commanded until 1809. Beginning in 1807, Willcocks served the Castle as a special magistrate sent into disturbed areas, and by 1814 he had worked in eight counties. Most recently, he had been in Westmeath and Limerick and, since the spring of 1814, in

Waterford and Kilkenny, where, in August, he wrote Gregory that he awaited "your further Commands."[52] Willcocks's reports show him to have been, as a man, sensitive to the lot of the peasantry and the economic causes of outrage; and, as a policeman, sensitive to the difference between rumor and fact. Whitworth thought Willcocks "a sensible man, and not led astray by fancy or apprehension." Peel, appropriately, valued him for his love of the facts, unlike another Stipendiary Magistrate who "unfortunately . . . thinks himself rather a fine writer." Even those who opposed the new police liked Willcocks. The Whig Lord Donoughmore, a strong critic, thought that the Castle could not have chosen a better man; the *Dublin Evening Post* declared him "a meritorious and excellent Magistrate."[53]

The Middlethird into which Richard Willcocks rode in September 1814 was suspiciously quiet. After six weeks of duty the Chief Magistrate could write, "No outrage has occurred since my arrival here." The extant records indicate that he did not file the first of his weekly reports to the Castle until 30 October. To police the barony of 150 square miles, Willcocks had only twenty-one constables; not until February 1815 would the force be supplemented with sixteen "dismounted" constables.[54] With "not the slightest support" from local magistrates, the handful of "Peelers" (as the force had come to be called) set about their work. They patrolled day and night along constantly changing routes; appeared at fairs to try to prevent faction fights; roamed the countryside, "disguised" in search of individuals; and investigated some mail robberies and the murder on 23 December of a tithe proctor, William Ryan.[55]

Ryan's murder shattered four months of relative tranquility and raised fears that the police would be retained in the barony. It is doubtful that the lull in crime was caused by some two dozen policemen scattered among a hostile population. By February 1815, Willcocks's police had arrested three men for the murders of Long and Ryan but only eleven men for other crimes. The Clonmel assizes of the spring and summer of 1815 produced twelve capital convictions, but the murder indictments all resulted in acquittals. Taxpayers grumbled that these results were not worth an annual baronial charge of £4,776. For his part, Willcocks argued in April 1815 that he needed more policemen "scattered through each Barony [and] in every village."[56]

In the fall and winter of 1814 intense opposition developed to Peel's small police experiment. In Middlethird, meetings attended by "some of the most loyal, respectable, and wealthy gentlemen of the county" denounced the institution and accused letter writers to the Castle of being "the *only* disturbers of our county." One Middlethird magistrate, in an open letter to Peel that was printed in the *Post*, fumed against "this angry Boy" and charged that the new police "may be sport to you, but it is death to us." The Chief Secretary helped to fan the fires by dismissing his critics as "evil and designing men."[57] In November, for the first time, protests were voiced in Parliament. Using the occasion of a minor amending bill proposed by Peel, a small group of English and Irish Whigs objected to the unconstitutionality and expense of Willcocks's force, bemoaned the misrepresentations of Irish crime in England, and demanded an inquiry into the social and economic state of Ireland. In the Lords, the Irish peer, the Earl of Donoughmore – the new Grattan, the *Post* called him – was virulent in his hostility to the Castle's police. The Peelers, created with little controversy in July, were becoming intensely controversial by year's end.[58]

Newspapers previously supportive of the police began to criticize "the Blister," as Peel's act was called. "No measure," declared the *Freeman's Journal*, "has set clamour and invective in more activity than this Bill." This pro-Government paper now denounced the absence of prior public inquiry, the Castle's willingness to believe "the worst authorities" in Tipperary, and the resort to a remedy that was only "a plaster for the surface of a wound." Ireland needed tithe reform, purification of the local magistracy, and wholesale improvements in agriculture, commerce, and education. "Has Mr. Peele made any effort at curing one of them?"[59]

More traditional critics continued the assault. The *Post* ran a series of eight long articles on Peel's police. The force would be "as everlasting as it is burdensome.... There was a time when the immense patronage created by this Bill would have excited a constitutional jealousy." The paper objected to a police despatched to a district by Castle fiat or as a result of letters from "scribbling, whispering, pimping, place-hunting, *proclaiming* Gentry." Among its criticisms the *Post* revived a familiar argument. If the new police was in fact workable and desirable, why not establish it in England as well?

A capital offence in Lancashire and in Middlethird is the same in principle.... Why, then, should the ... Judge of Assize be deemed sufficient in the one case and an unconstitutional Magistracy be preferred to keep the peace in a small district of the other? Why not generalize the principle? If the Magistracy Act be good for the Peace of Ireland, surely it ought to prove equally beneficial to that of England.... We really wish to be candid.... Why not apply it to the Framebreakers of Bolton – to the murderers of Nottingham? Their *atrocities* are, at least, equal in point of guilt to the Irish Peasant – why should there, then, be a different *regime* for each?[60]

Dublin Castle chose to ignore all of the criticisms. In April 1815 the Irish Attorney-General wrote Peel that he was "still very confident" that the police "will prove useful and ... with a little management ... will cease to be unpopular." In May, eleven Tipperary magistrates asked the Government to apply the Insurrection Act; the Castle responded by sending fifty Peelers into the baronies of Kilnemanagh and Eliogarty. To the north, at Roscrea, a meeting of twenty-seven gentlemen "alive to the danger of taxation" petitioned the Castle not to include the baronies of Ikerrin and Upper Ormond in the proclamation. After some discussion, the Government decided to confer the chief magistracy of Kilnemanagh and Eliogarty on Edward Wilson. Like Willcocks, Wilson had served in the Dublin police. He had been an officer in that force since 1788, had made "several" arrests of "leaders" in Emmet's Rising in 1803, and had retired in 1808 on an annual pension of £280. Since 1811 he had been active as a Castle magistrate-extraordinary in Roscommon, Westmeath, Waterford, and, most recently, Queen's County.

Now, in May 1815, he arrived in Tipperary and for the first time had a supporting body of police. Unlike Willcocks's force in Middlethird, Wilson's fifty men were all foot constables.[61]

At this time, in the spring of 1815, Peel tried a small experiment of sending his unpopular police into other counties. The Castle repeatedly countered magistrates' demands for the Insurrection Act with "offers" of "the Police Bill." So opposed were Westmeath magistrates to Peel's police that an imaginative group of them at a meeting on 9 April petitioned, unsuccessfully, for the Watch and Ward Act "passed in England at the time of the Luddites." Three weeks later, the Castle decided to send in some Peelers unsolicited by the Westmeath magistrates and *at government expense*. The tiny force was headed by Major John Wills, a veteran of the Dublin police (1797–1812) who had previously served the Castle as a special magistrate in Connaught and parts of Leinster, including Westmeath.[62] Although "very zealous and active," Wills was less highly regarded by Castle authorities than Wilson or Willcocks. "I fear," Gregory wrote Peel, that "he is too garrulous to be useful.... He is too communicative of his information." Peel later rejected him as Superintending Magistrate for Clare on Gregory's advice that Wills "has no discretion; he would be guided by any Gentleman who he thought of consequence." Wills's personality may have been one reason why the Peeler policing of Westmeath was short-lived; in July Wills showed up in County Longford and in September in Cork.[63] Similar tentative Peeler policing was begun in Limerick and Clare in mid-May. Of these experiments we know even less except that they were definitely tried. They lapsed not only for reasons of expense and unpopularity but because, as Gregory confessed to Peel, "We shall be much puzzled to find Proper Officers for all."[64]

By September 1815, at the end of the first year of its existence, the Peace Preservation Police existed in only three baronies of one county and totaled only eighty-seven men. This small force was unpopular and expensive; it was also ineffective against the upsurge of crime that began in Tipperary in the spring of 1815. By September, Whitworth and Sidmouth had decided that the police experiment was a failure. With the remaining true believer, Peel, on the Continent ready to fight a duel at Ostend with the rising Catholic agitator Daniel O'Connell, with whom he had quarreled that summer, the Lord Lieutenant was left on his own in Dublin to manage the worsening crisis. The police in London arrested O'Connell and the duel never took place, but the incident had serious repercussions in Ireland. During Peel's six-week absence, Whitworth gave in to reports from Tipperary of "smothered Rebellion ... approaching a general Blow up" and on 25 September placed seven baronies in that county under the Insurrection Act. Within two months, all of Limerick, King's County, and Westmeath were proclaimed as "insurrectionary." On his return, Peel objected strongly and insisted that his police be worked hard during the crisis. Aided by the mandatory night curfew and arms searches permitted by the Insurrection Act, the tiny police, with the support of military detachments, intensified their preventive patrolling and apprehension of suspects. Willcocks and

Wilson continued to receive little help from local magistrates. A single event, however, changed everything.[65]

On 27 November 1815, magistrate William Baker was murdered. His death was a daytime ritual execution on the road to his home. The spectacle was witnessed by hundreds of peasants who emitted a "savage yell of triumph" and then quickly dispersed. The murdered magistrate had been instrumental in bringing the new police into Tipperary the previous year. A retired barrister and a captain in the local Yeomanry, Baker had been one of the most zealous local magistrates; one of his murderers later confessed that the Whiteboy "committees" had finally decided to kill him for "his being too forward a Justice." It was on his way home from Cashel, where he had successfully prosecuted some firearms possession cases, that Baker was set upon by the peasantry and murdered.[66]

Lord Lieutenant Whitworth and Home Secretary Sidmouth correctly interpreted the outrage as an attempt to crush the energy of the magistrates. The Government immediately announced rewards totaling £5,000 for the first five convictions of Baker's killers. Two weeks after the murder seventy-five terrified magistrates crammed into the courthouse at Cashel to demand that the Government impose the new police in Clanwilliam barony. The Castle had "with management ... previously taken care to insure unanimity," but under the circumstances this was probably unnecessary. All of the former opponents, led by Lord Donoughmore, now called for more police protection. The meeting adjourned quickly, so that the magistrates, "all attended ... by armed servants or dragoons," could get home before nightfall.[67]

Clanwilliam was given to Willcocks's charge. He was authorized to enroll an additional thirteen constables, bringing his force to thirty mounted and twenty dismounted men. Willcocks selected his men from the 14th Light Dragoons, just landed in Waterford, two troops of which were disbanded in Clonmel. They were, explained the Chief Magistrate, "the description of Men best suited to the Police Service here, being strangers in this Country, and in strict discipline." Willcocks's police were active in apprehending a number of suspected criminals, including Michael Stack, who was charged with murder of the tithe proctor Ryan in December 1814. Many local magistrates were by early 1816 having a change of attitude toward the Peelers: They now thanked Willcocks for "the very material Service" performed by the "Small Number of Constables at present under his Command."[68]

If the new police were becoming more appreciated by local JPs, they suffered from deep and continuing noncooperation from the peasantry. In the winter of 1815–16 special Insurrection Act courts tried and convicted persons seized by the authorities (see Table 6.1). Many of those taken up had been simply out at night in defiance of the curfew; few of these persons held in detention were subsequently prosecuted. Tipperary did have the highest indictment figures and one of the highest conviction rates. But it is impossible to say whether the figures simply reflect the highly disturbed state of the county or represent the effectiveness of the Tipperary Peelers

Table 6.1. *Offenses against the public peace in disturbed Irish counties, 1813–16*

| | County Assizes | | | | | | | | | Special Commissions, 1815–16 | | Special Sessions under the Insurrection Act 1815–16 | |
| | 1813 | | 1814 | | 1815 | | 1816 | | | | | | |
	I	II	I	II	I	II	I	II	I	II	I	II
King's County	5	40.0%	8	62.5	7	57.1	5	80.0	—		9	22.2
Limerick	37	51.4	63	52.4	96	49.0	17	17.6	25	60.0	78	16.7
Tipperary	23	13.0	31	16.1	40	25.0	37	10.8	58	43.1	178	25.8
Westmeath	13	46.1	31	45.2	23	47.8	9	11.1	—		63	11.1

Notes: Returns are only for "criminal acts connected with the Disturbance of the Public Peace," namely, murder and attempted murder, appearing in arms at night, attacking houses, burglary [*sic*], robbing arms, felony under Whiteboy acts, riot, administering oaths, and issuing threatening notices. Special sessions met from September 1815 to February 1816; special commissions, November 1815 to February 1816. Limerick figures are for the City as well as the County of Limerick.

Key: I   Number of persons indicted and tried.

  II   *Percentage conviction rate.*

compared to the efforts of JPs in the non–Peeler counties. We are told that at the special sessions at Clonmel, Willcocks was "as usual most active, intelligent, and useful." At the Tipperary special sessions, thirteen men were sentenced to be executed and fourteen to be transported. The record at the Tipperary Assizes was worse. The conviction rate of 25 percent was about half of the rate in Limerick and Westmeath, counties that had had few Peelers and then only briefly compared to the ongoing police experiment in Tipperary. Intimidation of witnesses and popular sympathy with those charged with crimes were factors largely beyond police control but the low number of indictments (forty) at the Tipperary Assizes was a matter for concern. In sum, the record in 1815 of the new police's ability to bring crime to the indictment stage in the courts was mixed and hardly persuasive.[69]

Beyond Tipperary: extending the experiment

Mulling over the problem of public order in Ireland, Robert Peel believed with increasing conviction that the solution was an effective government-controlled police. Halfheartedly, he turned to the reform of other institutions. In the summer of 1815 he steered through Parliament an act to amend "the old 32d of Geo. 3," the 1792 baronial police act. Peel's act raised a constable's annual salary from £4 to £10 and required county grand juries to pay for the men's firearms and to guarantee a retirement allowance to constables of long service. If necessary, the expense would be paid by the Government from its own monies in the Consolidated Fund, the loan being subsequently repayable by the county grand jury. Peel thus established two precedents – police pensions and use of "the Consols" – that would be of great significance in the future of the police in Ireland.[70]

Peel avoided the herculean task of purifying the local magistracy. A government investigation of November 1815 concluded that of the 4,100 magistrates on the rolls, only 1,900 were still active and regularly resident in Ireland. Attorney-General Saurin informed Peel that magistracy reform "seems to have been in contemplation in 1787 and a provision made in the police act of that year – but the measure was not pursued." As Orde had earlier, so Peel in 1816 stopped short of the purgation of the magistracy because it "would be very wounding to the feelings of many loyal and good men." He also abandoned an idea to transfer the appointment of county Sheriffs from county Members of Parliament to assize judges. Peel was coming to believe that traditional institutions should not be reformed but bypassed.[71]

With the end of the war in Europe, military levels would necessarily be greatly reduced. After Waterloo the 13,000 British militiamen in Ireland would be gone and the Irish militia disbanded. Maj.-Gen. Sir George Hewett, commander-in-chief of the army in Ireland, wanted to abolish the Irish Yeomanry, but Peel and the London Cabinet prevailed. The Yeomanry establishment was halved to 20,000 "effectives," the staff cut from 77 men to 14, and funding slashed for 1817 to one-twenty-sixth of the sum allocated ten years earlier. "They can beat off a Carding party as well in an old red coat as a new one," quipped Peel, who added more seriously, "The attempt to new clothe them may lead to their final abolition." Peel continued to be vexed by the behavior of the Yeomanry. A bloody brawl at Roscrea in March 1816 between five Yeomen and the townspeople resulted in the death of one Catholic laborer. "For God's sake," moaned Peel, "there is enough bad blood in Tipperary without those blockheads aggravating it."[72]

Most serious of all was what was happening to the regular army in Ireland. The postwar English Government was committed to two policies: maintaining an occupying army of 30,000 in France (1815–18) and overall military reductions and fiscal retrenchment. Each year fewer troops were authorized for Ireland: 45,000 (including militia) in 1814, 30,000 in 1815, 25,000 in 1816, and 22,000 projected for 1817. In only six years (1814–19) Irish force levels would decline by three-fifths and army expenditures by two-fifths. Dublin Castle authorities resisted the reductions but were helpless before the paring knife of the London Cabinet and Parliament.[73] These trends produced considerable hand wringing but also serious long-term thinking. Magistrates requesting troops were told to develop "some adequate system of Police." Writing to the military authorities in London, Peel stated that

a good mounted Police is of more service to us ... than the Military.... I should feel much more uneasy at its reduction to 22,000 men [for 1817] if we had not the power which a late Act has given us of appointing a Superintending Magistrate and a Mounted Police in a disturbed District. I hope by some modification of that Act to be enabled to extend these Police Establishments more generally throughout Ireland.

Toward the end of his tenure in office, in a letter of February 1818 to his new Lord Lieutenant, Earl Talbot, Peel summed up his past policies: "Of course the substitute for Troops must be found in the Peace Preservation Bill."[74]

By early 1816, Peel's police had become entrenched only in four baronies in Tipperary. During that year, Dublin Castle would place the force temporarily in Cavan and Louth and permanently in Clare. "Just the thing for the county of Cavan," Peel exulted to Lord Lieutenant Whitworth, as he transferred Major Wills and seventy men from Tipperary to Cavan in March 1816. Exactly one year later, the force would be removed. Also in March 1816, after a request from eighteen local magistrates, Peel sent 100 police into four baronies in County Louth. The Louth police were headed by two superintending magistrates. The first appointment was a good one: Thomas D'Arcy, County Longford Brigade-Major of Yeomanry, now began a successful public career that would see him named Inspector-General of Constabulary for Ulster in 1824.[75] The second appointment was a disaster. Samuel Pendleton was a coarse and garrulous man who had seen his brother-in-law, a clergyman, butchered in the 1798 Rebellion. In Louth, Pendleton soon made "himself unpopular with all parties" by making "Cases from any materials" and too zealously jailing peasants "when in fact the poor Creatures ought to be set at large." By April 1817 Peel was moaning, "I wish he would resign his situation," and Whitworth exclaimed, "Would to God we could recall Willcox from Tipperary and send him to Louth in the room of this horrible fellow!" Peel noted philosophically: "The credit and character of the Peace Preservation Bill depends so much upon the instruments who are entrusted with the execution of it.... The mischief done by a [Police] Magistrate who conducts himself improperly is far more extensive than the District within which he acts." In Willcocks, Wilson, Wills, and D'Arcy, the Castle had been singularly fortunate; with Pendleton, "we made a bad choice."[76]

The reception accorded the Peelers in Louth was hardly cordial. In the summer and fall of 1816, local magistrates and landowners petitioned for removal of the force from certain parishes or baronies. Then, as in Tipperary in 1815, one incident changed everything. A farmer named Edward Lynch had made the mistake of prosecuting three men for raiding his house for firearms; on the testimony of Lynch and his son-in-law, the men were convicted and hanged. Whiteboy retribution came at Reaghstown, Ardee barony, on the evening of 30 October 1816. Arriving by boat across Dundalk Bay and overland on fifteen horses each with double riders, strangers surrounded the Lynch homestead and burned it to the ground. Everyone inside – Lynch and his daughter and son-in-law, two children, and three maids – all perished in the flames. In the aftermath, Lynch's neighbors raised £1,500 for a fund to obtain information and to prosecute the murderers. All thirty-one county magistrates met at Dundalk on 9 November to demand not only continuation of the Peeler police but also the introduction of the Insurrection Act. In early 1817 the Government placed the entire county under the Insurrection Act.[77]

In spring 1816 the western part of County Clare was swept by a wave of cattle houghings, sheep killings, and arms raids on farmhouses by men "assembling in considerable numbers with Arms dressed in white uniforms or shirts over their cloaths." Local magistrates asked for troops and the Insurrection Act, since police would be "Expensive without being Efficient." Then, in May 1816, in response to a request by twenty JPs for "Mr. Peel's Act," the Castle despatched Major George Warburton and fifty police to Clare's three westernmost baronies.[78] Dublin's first choice, Major William Stewart of the Donegal militia, had declined the post; but Warburton, though he subsequently requested reassignment to Leinster, would perform valuable services for the Government in the west. Described by Peel as "very intelligent ... [and] active," the thirty-nine-year-old Warburton had been a magistrate and a brigade major of Yeomanry in King's County. It was his knowledge of Gaelic that must have assured his selection for western Clare.[79]

The arrival of Major Warburton and his Peelers stimulated the Clare magistrates to activity. They reported having sworn some 300 peasants to loyalty oaths and enlisted Catholic priests to help calm the disturbed districts. "The great dread of an heavy tax," one correspondent wrote the Castle, "has more than any other cause induced the country people to ... [return to] tranquillity." By July Warburton had collected 138 sworn statements against a number of Whiteboys, but he was able to arrest only fourteen persons.

At the summer assizes, the cases against twelve of them were dismissed for want of evidence and the two others resulted in acquittals. Whiteboy law prevailed; Warburton noted that the few individuals who dared to testify were "even attacked and insulted in the Court House." The district was quiet but "at this time of general distress" many wondered whether the police were worth the total tax of £5,635.[80]

By 1817, the police experiment had been tried in parts of six counties (Map 6.2). Chief Secretary Peel was generally pleased with his Peelers, but with the means of payment for the force he was not happy. Those areas requiring police were often places that, burdened with poverty and numerous small-holders, were least able to support the expense. In March 1817, therefore, Peel steered through Parliament an amending act that allowed the Government, using the Consolidated Fund, to pay up to two-thirds of police costs. Local contributions were to be assessed relative to the ability to pay. Thus, Tipperary taxpayers in 1818 paid two-thirds of the total bill, whereas in distressed south and west Clare they contributed one-half of the costs and after July 1819, only one-third. When, however, the *entire* county of Clare was proclaimed in March 1820, the local assessment was fixed at half of the total police expense. From about 1820 on, it became the general practice throughout Ireland for the proclaimed district and the Government to divide the cost equally.[81]

The changed financing led to smoother innovation. In his remaining sixteen months in office, Peel established the police in four more counties. In March 1817 two baronies in King's County were proclaimed. In June 1817 Bunratty in east Clare was placed under Warburton's superintendence, and neighboring Tulla was spared only after pleas from local magistrates there. In July the Castle proclaimed Ennishowen, County Donegal, a barony notorious for illicit distillation; Major D'Arcy and twenty constables, twelve of them mounted, were transferred there from County Louth. For the next two years, D'Arcy devoted much of his time to searching for illicit stills. The police presence produced widespread protests, so that D'Arcy was forced to pull back from his war on the traffic in untaxed whiskey. The last area proclaimed in Peel's chief secretaryship was in County Dublin itself. In February 1818 the Government sent twenty police into the county's two northernmost baronies, a "lawless" area where "the middling farmers were afraid to prosecute."[82]

The Castle's inclination to use Peelers was growing but not unrestrained. In June 1817, after serious consideration, it was decided not to inject the new police into four baronies in Meath. Similarly, in February 1818 the Government resisted temptation in Sligo, Roscommon, and Limerick, believing that in the absence of serious disorders it would be provocative to proclaim parts of those counties. Occasionally, the Peelers were even removed after a period of service. The twenty constables sent into King's County in March 1817 were taken out in April 1818. As Peel dryly remarked, "We must not make the Peelers unpopular by maintaining them against the declared and unequivocal sense of the County in which they act."[83]

Undoubtedly the most controversial Castle decision in 1817 was to proclaim seven baronies in Kildare, a county with many "*very liberal*" Whig gentry and noblemen, including Lord Cloncurry and the Duke of Leinster. Lord Lieutenant Whitworth had been eager "for some time past" to send in police, since "it is highly unreasonable that we should go on feeding them with Military." When on 25 March Whitworth placed the Kildare baronies under Peel's police act, Leinster was furious that the Lord Lieutenant had not consulted him. At a dinner party a few days later, Leinster upbraided Attorney-General Saurin "in the presence of all the assembled Footmen," who reportedly enjoyed the argument. Whitworth described the incident in a letter to Peel in London. "We owe him nothing," the Lord Lieutenant wrote of the greatest nobleman in the country,

We are under no necessity of consulting him, and certainly he has no right to expect Courtesy. When we proclaimed the county of Tipperary, we held no communication with Lord Donoughmore or even with [Lord] Rosse, Governor [of Tipperary], who are friendly to our measures. The same may be said in every instance, and particularly now as to the King's County of which two Baronies are proclaimed with those of Kildare, without any Communication with the Marquis of Drogheda or Lord Rosse, both of whom are Privy Councillors. In short the Duke of Leinster has put himself so much in the wrong, that one is almost inclined to pity him.[84]

Dublin Castle transferred Major Wills and fifty mounted constables from Cavan to Kildare. The Peelers' arrival produced renewed local exertions and a chorus of protests. Many of the larger farmers organized voluntary patrols and by June they were enrolling special constables, "their chief motive" being the desire of "getting Rid of the Police." Wills found the latter practice "extremely hazardous," for many of those enrolled were not "possessed of sufficient property" and some were rumored to have "connections with the lower orders and the Marauders who disturb the Country."[85]

Landowners and magistrates petitioned against the police, to have them removed from or not extended to their baronies. To one complaint that the police tax "added to our already numerous taxes [and] ... will drive many Landholders to despair and utter ruin," Gregory coldly instructed a Castle clerk to "send [a] similar answer as has been given to similar representations." In October, a petition signed by 128 "Magistrates, Gentlemen, and Principal Landholders" argued that their barony had been quiet "for a considerable time back" and should be freed from the police tax. A county meeting produced a memorial signed by the Duke of Leinster and "a large majority" of the most important landowners. Dublin Castle believed that much of the opposition was "under party influence" and orchestrated by Leinster; Wills wrote that the organizer of the county meeting, Lt.-Col. John Bagot, "much seeks popularity ... [and] came there *Prejudiced* against the Police Establishment *on Constitutional Grounds*."[86] But the complaints were not just politically inspired. In proclaimed Carbery, taxpayers objected to paying for a police based *outside* their barony: The Peelers patrolled from Wills's headquarters at Rathangan, nine miles distant, and from a post in neighboring King's County. By far, most of the complaints cited the financial hardship. John Aylmer wrote Wills that he had

a strong feeling of the utility of your Corps ... yet the expense is so enormous that the amount cannot be raised.... Half [of] our Tenants [are] without a four-footed Beast, or Crops in the Ground. How then in the name of God are they to pay near £700 in Barony Police Tax, and a similar Sum for county Charges – the thing is as unjust as it is Physically impossible.[87]

Despite the widespread opposition to its expense, some correspondents judged the new police to be necessary. The existing baronial constables constituted "but a *Mockery* of civil support." Removal of the Peelers will make "[us] feel .... forsaken. Through despondence, [we will] relapse back into Chaos." One writer thought that Wills's force deserved "the highest praise," pronouncing the new tranquility "astonishing.... Ten policemen are more feared by the worst class than one hundred soldiers." In fact, the crop failures and severe rural distress in 1817 were primarily responsible for the temporary tranquility. In 1818 there was a renewal of outrages including raids on farmhouses for arms, one rape and three murders, the beating of an old man and his wife, the houghing of cattle, sheep, and goats, the firing of homes and hayricks, and the stabbing to death of a horse with a pitchfork. Amid building opposition to the Peelers, who reported but seemed unable to prevent these crimes, Dublin Castle decided to withdraw the forces from Kildare in August and November 1818.[88]

The longest continuously policed part of the country was Tipperary. Willcocks continued to serve in Middlethird and Wilson in Kilnemanagh and Eliogarty. Wills was responsible for Clanwilliam until he was sent to County Cavan; his successor in Clanwilliam in 1816–17 was Daniel O'Donoghue, an army major who had been stationed at Limerick since 1808. In September 1817, Clanwilliam was united with Middlethird and placed under Willcocks's command. In the years after 1815, the 150 constables in these baronies formed a belt around the center of the county, with areas north and south remaining unpoliced. The Chief Magistrates' most frequent lament was their lack of sufficient manpower. Patrols had to include soldiers, for the constables "could not, *Individually*, without the Assistance of those Military Detachments, act with any effect." Whenever troop were withdrawn from outlying stations, the one or two constables assigned to these remote posts had to be called in as well. With all of their handicaps, the police stayed active. During one week in 1816, when the police reported no outrages, we find Wilson's men not only conducting nightly patrols and (under the Insurrection Act) searching houses for arms but also apprehending four men for a house robbery and seven men for assaults.[89] Perhaps the police's most spectacular achievement was the arrest of five of the murderers of Tipperary magistrate William Baker. For this crime, one man was transported and four were hanged in April and August 1816. In May 1818 the Insurrection Act was lifted from Tipperary, but the Peelers stayed on in the county that served as the showcase for the Government's new police. Tipperary taxpayers paid the highest Peeler police taxes in Ireland: £15,000 in 1816, a similar amount in 1817, and £9,000 in 1818.[90]

Peel's legacy

The extension of the Peelers into parts of ten counties in 1814–18 reflected young Peel's confidence in the police as the type of force best calculated to keep the lid on Irish disorders. Local objections he continued to discount, and, in his zeal to argue the case for the new police, he downplayed the role of hunger and epidemic disease in restoring peace to disturbed districts. "Compare the present state of Tipperary and Clare," Peel wrote the Earl of Farnham in January 1817, "with the state in which they were before the Police Establishments were placed in them – I am sure that the sum ... which has been paid is a trifling return for the tranquillity and personal security which those who pay it have enjoyed."[91]

Peel and others viewed the Peace Preservation Police as an opening wedge, a first step toward the establishment of a general police for Ireland. By the spring of 1817, the Peelers had become such a fixture in the disturbed districts that news of Peel's amending bill before that session of Parliament was at first widely misinterpreted as establishing a regular police throughout the country. The Earl of Desart asked that Peel give him and the other Irish Members "the fullest opportunities" to discuss the "measure regarding our general and permanent police in contemplation." To letter writers, Dublin Castle had not only to deny the rumors about but even to reject requests for positions in the allegedly newly forming constabulary. The idea did, in fact, occur to Peel. As he recalled in April 1822,

I frequently considered the possibility of introducing a general system of Police.... I was more inclined to the establishment of a Body of Gendarmerie (to be called by some less startling name) who should act under the control of Superintendents constantly varying their stations and reporting to the Lord Lieutenant the mode in which the subordinate officers were employed by the magistrates.[92]

Perhaps it was Peel's experience with the costliness and unpopularity of the Peelers that dissuaded him from attempting to introduce a countrywide continental-style police that, had it been, like the Peelers, totally government controlled, would have unleashed storms of protest. Perhaps, too, he realized that establishing by increments strong forces in the most disturbed areas would prepare the country to accept, in future, the concept of a national police.

By the summer of 1818, Robert Peel, now only thirty years old, had served as Chief Secretary for six years. No one since 1737 had stayed in this difficult post for so long.[93] It is clear from his correspondence that he was eager to return to England. In August, he set sail from Belfast for a long holiday in the Scottish Highlands, where he remarked on the hospitality and kindness of the local people. Like Arthur Wellesley, who had departed nine years before him, Robert Peel would never again set foot in Ireland.[94] Though he had sponsored no remedial legislation, the rising young English politician had had the good fortune of arriving in Ireland when it was disturbed and of leaving it tranquil. Peel's successors would not be so fortunate.

II. Charles Grant and the proliferation of Peelers, 1818–21

The forty-year-old new Lord Lieutenant, the 2d Earl Talbot, had succeeded Whitworth in October 1817. "A stout, jovial man, looking like a jolly good-humoured [Staffordshire] farmer," Talbot was a well-intentioned man who courted popularity and possessed only mediocre administrative abilities. His political views, which included opposition to all Catholic claims, were in line with those of the previous Administration and of Home Secretary Sidmouth. With his own Chief Secretary, however, he differed.[95] Charles Grant, Jr., was not Prime Minister Liverpool's first choice to be Peel's successor. William Huskisson and Henry Goulburn had both declined the ordeal of service in Ireland. In August 1818, a third offer was made and accepted. Charles Grant was born in India into an East India Company family that returned to England when the boy was twelve years old. His Evangelical father, who disapproved of the English public schools, had his son privately tutored before sending him to Magdalene College, Cambridge (1795–1804), where he distinguished himself in Latin and poetry. Grant trained for the bar (1807) but never practiced, and pursued an indifferent literary career until 1811, when he was elected an MP for a Scottish borough (Inverness). His maiden speech in the Commons was a brilliant defense of Lord Castlereagh's bill of July 1812 to suppress the Luddite disturbances.[96]

Charles Grant was forty years old when he was named Irish Chief Secretary. In the Liverpool Administration he was an anomaly: a political liberal of Whiggish persuasion (his closest friends were Huskisson and Brougham) who favored Catholic Emancipation, suffrage reform, and some vaguely articulated milder form of government for Ireland. The "amiable and benevolent" Grant, "possessed of genius and sensibility," was well informed about the condition of the Irish peasantry; his memorandum of 1820 is the best contemporary work on the subject before Sir George Cornewall Lewis's book published in 1836. Grant's feelings were so strong that Under-Secretary Gregory would complain about the Chief Secretary's "uncalled for and unfounded Encomiums on the Catholic Priest-hood" and his "fatal Error" of trying to govern Ireland in the belief that "Protestant Tyranny and Catholic Slavery are the Causes of Disturbance in this Country."[97]

To the difficulties of steering a liberal Whig course between Anglo-Irish Tories and Catholic peasants were added Grant's personality flaws. The chief of these were his irregular business habits and his seeming inability to take decisive action. In his three years in office, Grant tried to suppress Orangeism, and he had plans for a nonsectarian scheme of national education and purification of the local magistracy. None of these did he accomplish. His friend Lord Cloncurry noted that Grant's "inactivity . . . counteracted his wise and benevolent intentions towards this unfortunate country." Gregory believed that Grant "made many Enemies amongst the Gentry of Ireland" simply because of his extreme tardiness in answering correspondence and his failure to keep appointments. In the last year of his secretaryship, faced with widespread violence in the countryside, Grant continued to vacillate and procrastinate. Home Secretary Sidmouth, in disgust, came to rely almost entirely on Talbot to manage affairs in Ireland. Charles Grant's inept, liberal secretaryship only enhanced the reputation of an able, conservative administrator like Robert Peel and convinced many persons of the truth of Peel's dictum that Ireland required "an honest, despotic Government."[98]

Renewed unrest and a resort to the new civil power

Chief Secretary Grant continued his predecessor's policy of substituting police for troops. "The peace preservation bill," he wrote Sidmouth in December 1818, "is a much more efficient guardian of public tranquillity than a numerous army." Against the opposition of Talbot, Sidmouth, and army leaders in Ireland and Britain, Grant pressed for substantial force level reductions and, after a bitter fight lasting for six months, settled for 17,500 military for 1820 and 17,000 for 1821. Irish troop levels, at 19,000 in 1819, were at their lowest level in two decades, and with 9,000 soldiers tied up in England's Northern District, the London Government had none to spare. In this context, with a resurgence of agrarian agitation in the fall of 1819, the Castle authorities would feel compelled to resort to the Peace Preservation Police.[99]

It was at first feared that Irish turbulence would link up with English radicalism. Rumors circulated that Arthur Thistlewood had arrived in Ireland. Rural districts were said to be in correspondence with England. In Tipperary, Willcocks's seizure from "a miserable looking creature" at Thurles Fair of 300 copies of a handbill about Peterloo and "The Grand Procession of Mr. Hunt into London Surrounded by Half a Million of People," did nothing to allay these fears. But the link with English radicalism never developed. Gregory noted that "the national hatred of England is much too strong." Grant, a sympathetic observer, stated that the issues in the Queen Caroline affair, "which seems to have shaken England to the centre," were of little concern to the Irish peasantry. What did alarm Dublin Castle was the eruption of "Ribbonism" in the west in 1819–20. From its stronghold in south and west Ulster, the movement had spread to Roscommon in 1816 and now resurfaced throughout Connaught. The politically sophisticated Catholic Ribbonmen added to the customary rent and tithe demands a crusade for the extirpation of Protestant heresy. This millenarianism would become widespread in the Rockite movement of 1821–4. This new dimension to social protest did not overshadow the basic fact that the agitations of both 1819–20 and 1821–4 concerned age-old land grievances.[100]

The Castle's reaction to the revival of disorders followed the guidelines laid down by Robert Peel. Chief Secretary Grant refused requests for troops and the Insurrection Act and instead sent in the Peelers. In November 1819 the Castle proclaimed the entire county of Roscommon. Major Wills, who had last served in Kildare, marched in with 3 Chief Constables and 130 constables. In other counties opposition to the police continued. In King's County and in Limerick, magistrates petitioned against the idea of bringing in Peelers. In Tipperary in December, local magistrates felt "hurt" at the reinstatement "without a public meeting" of Chief Magistrate Wilson, who, together with thirty mounted police, had been removed in June as an economy measure and a gesture of Castle good will. There was widespread local feeling that "the Police Tax ... operates against the punctual payment of ... Rents"; indeed, with the demands of "rent, tithes, and taxes," payment of Peelers was "not only very precarious but almost impossible." Wilson nevertheless returned and the Tipperary police remained at 130 men.[101]

In Galway, Dublin Castle was faced with an unprecedented problem. Magistrates in four baronies adjacent to Roscommon requested Peelers in mid-December 1819. For the first time, the Castle was caught empty-handed: It maintained no reserve force and had no men to loan. A month elapsed before Chief Magistrate Pendleton, that "horrible fellow" last in Louth, could be sent from Dublin with sixty constables. The murder of a local magistrate, Edward Browne, led to a raucous meeting on 3 February at Loughrea, where, by a narrow vote (25–22), the Government was asked to proclaim nine additional baronies. This time the Castle was not caught napping. Major D'Arcy, who since 1817 had been chasing illicit distillers in Donegal, and a large force of 140 constables were despatched immediately.[102] By March 1820, only the four western baronies in Galway remained unproclaimed; the rest of the county boasted an unheard-of number of police, 262 dismounted and 28 mounted constables.

The Peeler army in Galway did generate some protests. There is evidence that "in order to lighten the expence upon the [four] disturbed" baronies proclaimed in December, many magistrates had voted to proclaim the additional nine in February.[103] The minority of twenty-two magistrates at the Loughrea meeting filed a protest with the Government for inflicting police on nine "confessedly tranquil" baronies. The Galway police were not cheap: Grand jury presentments for 1820–1 would total £19,000. Meetings at Athenry on 17 February and at Loughrea on 2 March censured the Castle for not reviving the Insurrection Act. But the magistrates had no reason to question Dublin's generosity with troops. Military forces in Connaught rose from 2,500 in December 1819 to 5,900 by April 1820, and as late as September 4,700 soldiers remained in the province. Galway alone contained 3,700 troops in April and 2,000 as late as September. In addition, the Government shipped into Galway a battalion of army pensioners.[104]

Outrages "too numerous to specify" persisted throughout the winter and spring of 1820. "Unusual Audacity ... almost universally prevails," reported Chief Magistrate Pendleton. "It is my firm belief," affirmed the High Sheriff in early February, "that the County of Galway was never (even in 1798) in so alarming a state as at this moment." By the end of the month, an army officer feared that the situation was "now only a shade removed from open rebellion." Pendleton and the local magistrates criticized the military for keeping the soldiers in large regional cantonments instead of dividing the men into small patrolling parties. In February the Government issued commissions of the peace to military captains and police constables, and permitted constables to lead detached military parties.[105]

The overwhelming pressure of troops and police in Galway brought "no change in the attitude of the people." The military often slept in the fields, for when they did "forcefully" quarter themselves in a village, "the wretches ... [were] often murdered for collaboration within a few days." Local people boycotted the Peelers, and provisions had to be brought in under military escort from Ballinasloe. Even at Pendleton's headquarters on Sir Ross Mahon's estate, "despite long habits of intimacy," the Chief Magistrate had to procure everything "by actual force." The country people alternately shunned or "hiss[ed] and revile[d]" anyone in uniform, but the soldiers they at least "feared and respected," feelings that "strongly contrasted" with the "dreadful enmity" displayed toward the Peelers.[106]

The 300 police, divided into scores of mixed civil-military parties, regularly patrolled "upwards of twenty miles" a night. There is "no regular time for sleeping," reported Pendleton; "each [Peeler] gets rest as he can, on whatever bed is unoccupied." By mid-March two constables had died "from the effects of Fatigue." The patrols and outstations came under frequent attack: A police barracks on one occasion was stormed by a mob of nearly 3,000 persons; in one patrolling party, twelve men were severely injured and one constable was killed by a mob numbering in the hundreds.[107] Despite the continuous harassment and hostility, the police under the ferocious leadership of Pendleton helped to produce at the Spring Assizes twenty-eight felony convictions (including seven capital sentences and four life transportations) plus thirty-nine misdemeanor convictions for Whiteboy offenses. In part from exhaustion, but also because of his abrasive relations with military officers and local magistrates and his overzealousness in prosecution, Chief Magistrate Pendleton resigned his post with the subsidence of the disorders in April 1820.[108]

The success of the Peelers in Galway resulted largely from their coordinated use with troops totaling nearly 4,000 men. In addition to activating 1,000 military pensioners, Dublin Castle in March 1820 placed 1,200 Yeomanry on duty in Ulster in order to free regular soldiers for Connaught. In April the Government toyed with the idea of reviving the militia, defunct since 1816. But the cost of clothing and one month's training would come to £73,000. Gregory judged the idea "hazardous" to the Government and "most objectionable" to the people. These feelings were reiterated by General David Baird, who argued for embodiment only if the Irish militia were to be transferred to England! By June, the idea was abandoned.[109]

Another measure considered by Castle authorities in the spring of 1820

GROWTH OF THE PEACE PRESERVATION POLICE 1814-1822

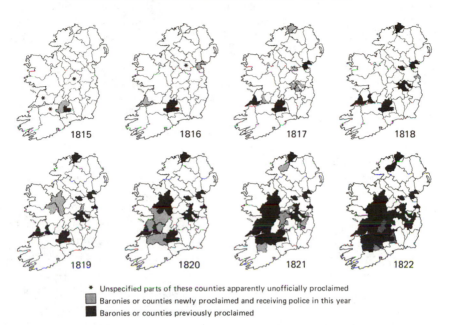

* Unspecified parts of these counties apparently unofficially proclaimed

Baronies or counties newly proclaimed and receiving police in this year

Baronies or counties previously proclaimed

Map 6.2

was whether to revive the Insurrection Act, which had lapsed in 1818. Gregory and Talbot thought it indispensable, but Grant demurred. He hesitated to propose such an extreme measure before the English Parliament, although this same assembly had only four months earlier passed Sidmouth's savage Six Acts to suppress English protest. Grant argued that the police and troops had been able to quell the Galway discontents without the Insurrection Act. Moreover, he believed, like Peel before him, that many local magistrates demanded the act as an easy and certainly cheaper substitute for the Peace Preservation Police. So long as Grant was Chief Secretary, the Insurrection Act lay dormant. But in February 1822, six weeks after his departure, the statute would be reenacted.[110]

In 1820 and 1821, Charles Grant responded to the growing crisis in Ireland by planting Peel's new police in thirteen counties (Map 6.2). As early as November 1819, "immense" numbers of "Strangers" were reported to be moving from Galway into Clare. Magistrates in Clare demanded the Insurrection Act. All agreed that "the common Barony Constables [were] a most inefficient Body," but the JPs were divided over whether to call in the Peelers. The southern half of *Clare* had been policed by Major Warburton since 1817; in March 1820 Dublin Castle proclaimed the remaining five baronies in the county. Warburton's force was increased to 150 and eventually to 200 men, with each constable authorized to act as a surrogate magistrate in command of a military party.[111]

With the disturbances continuing to spread south, the entire county of *Limerick* was proclaimed on 15 April, six weeks after all of Clare was opened to the police. The chief magistracy of Limerick was conferred on Richard Going, a Tipperary militia major whom Willcocks had known since 1815 and who had joined the Peelers as a chief constable in 1819. Going was given a force of 250 men and military support that included outposts "almost every five miles." In the space of two months (18 February–15 April), three entire western counties had been placed under the new police. Eighteen months would elapse before the southwest would receive its final injection of Peelers; in November 1821, two northern *Cork* baronies, adjacent to Limerick, received a fifty-man detachment under Major Samson Carter.[112]

Elsewhere in the island, in one pocket after another, the Government put its new police. In August 1820 and January 1821, Peeler establishments were placed in four baronies in *Westmeath* despite five memorials signed by a total of 242 persons who looked "with Grief" on the expensive police, which "in [our] great distress ... we are utterly unable to bear." Many outrages, they claimed, were committed by "strangers and persons not resident in ... this County"; the police tax would not "in the slightest degree ... punish the guilty." Under-Secretary Gregory apparently recognized the truth of this statement because he authorized Major O'Donoghue's men to enter King's County and Kildare, even though these counties were unproclaimed. West-meath taxpayers were thus paying for police protection for neighboring counties. In January and May 1821, this situation was rectified when most of King's County and parts of Kildare were officially proclaimed. The month of May produced a rash of Peeler proclamations: 8 May, one barony in *Carlow*; 18 May, one barony in *Kilkenny* and another in *Queen's County*; and 30 May, one barony in *Wicklow*, one in *Dublin*, four in *Kildare*, and eight in *King's County*.[113]

The police in Kildare were as controversial in 1821 as they had been in 1817–18. A memorial signed by twenty-eight persons, including Lord Cloncurry and two of the Ponsonbys, the great Whig family, protested that South Salt had been declared disturbed by persons not holding property in the barony; local residents were "unjustly stygmatized and subjected to an expense which they are little able to bear and which they do not at all deserve." Another barony escaped the police act after seventy-four of the "principal inhabitants and landholders" petitioned the Lord Lieutenant not to proclaim it. Police Magistrate James Tandy and his 182 constables were given jurisdiction not only in the four Kildare baronies but also in three in Carlow, Wicklow, and Dublin.[114] In King's County the 165 policemen led by Major Thomas Powell met a less tumultuous reception. Powell, whom Talbot called "a very sensible man, ... cautious in delivering an opinion," was a Welshman (the first Chief Magistrate who was not an Irishman) and a career army officer and Peninsular War veteran. Eighteen months later Powell would be named the first Inspector-General of Constabulary for Leinster.[115]

"From riot to . . . rebellion," and Grant's recall

Charles Grant's handling of the disturbances, relying as it did on extensive use of the Peace Preservation Police, managed to anger the Anglo-Irish gentry and officials in London and Dublin. He further alienated them by his neglect of daily office work, his intransigence against the use of the Insurrection Act, and his views on the Irish question. In May 1820, when Sidmouth demanded that Grant inform him about what he was doing to repress the disorders in Connaught, Grant instead sent the Home Secretary a long memorandum on the historical causes of Irish disturbances. The document was insightful but, at the moment, out of place and was interpreted by the Government as a sign of Grant's "leaning" to the Catholics.[116] What Saurin, Gregory, and Talbot, and also Liverpool and Sidmouth, could not or would not appreciate was that police and military reports confirmed the Chief Secretary's analysis. Warburton and Willcocks reported that the disturbances originated from the poor being "tyrannically treated; [they] naturally view the Laws with contempt." Warburton concluded that "from the deep distress of the country" the opposition to the Peelers "is not surprising." Major-General Lord Aylmer, the military commander in the southwest, believed that economic distress fueled the disorders and that the police tax only "increase[d] the evil by imposing an additional burthen on the county."[117]

By the fall of 1821, parts of the west of Ireland seemed to be approaching a crisis. Warburton reported from Limerick that some 4,000 potential rebels had sequestered 4 light cannon, 400 pikes, and 3,000 stand of arms. "I am not an Alarmist," wrote the experienced Willcocks, but "I never before had so bad an opinion of the disposition of the People." In distant London, Sidmouth was becoming alarmed by reports of this "rapid Progress from Riot to Insurrection, and from Insurrection to Rebellion." The crisis was magnified by an unprecedented event: the murder of a Peeler Chief Magistrate.[118] Since April 1820, Richard Going had headed the 250-man police in Limerick. Going was an Orangeman. To make matters worse, he had encouraged the founding of Orange Lodges within his force. Going's police were widely believed to be brutal as well as politically partisan; a rumor circulated that Going's men had buried alive a captured Whiteboy. One Whiteboy missive summed up peasant sentiment in Limerick: Richard Going was "the greatest Tyrant that ever stepped in shoe leather."[119] On 13 October 1821, near Rathkeale in a district where "there was more wretchedness . . . than in any other part of the county," Going, traveling alone, was set upon by a small party of men who battered him to death and took his pistols, leaving a watch and £200 found later on his body. News of Going's murder produced "exultation . . . in the Streets" of Rathkeale.[120] The Government responded to the murder by announcing rewards totaling £2,000. Major William Stewart, Chief Magistrate in Westmeath, was sent in as Going's successor, but within three weeks he was relieved by Richard Willcocks. "Certainly no man is more calculated to establish security and tranquillity," noted Lord Lieutenant Talbot. Willcocks confirmed that Going's force was riddled with

Orangeism and "in a state of inconceivable inefficiency and disorganization." He set about "re-casting" the Limerick police, which, he reported, was deservedly unpopular with not only the peasantry but many local magistrates and gentry, who resented paying (£11,424 in 1820–1) for the mismanaged force.[121]

In the mounting crisis of late 1821, the country's most seasoned police magistrates, Warburton and Willcocks, called for new arms and gunpowder acts and the revival of the Insurrection Act. Troops in Dublin were placed on an emergency alert. Almost 5,000 military pensioners were mobilized as reinforcements for the regular soldiers. Against Grant's strong protests, the Government placed forty-four Yeomanry corps, some 3,000 men, on permanent duty in Ulster to free additional army units for service in the disturbed districts. The army, formerly scattered in detachments, was now concentrated at depots and in the principal towns. Sidmouth, alive to the danger of having only 14,500 troops in Ireland, informed Talbot that reinforcements would be sent at once. "Some Risque must be incurred in England for the purpose of putting down an Actual, and most formidable Danger in Ireland; and I am convinced that this can only be done by an overwhelming Military Force, instantly assembled and instantly deployed.... Any Delay, compromise, or concession will be fatal." Scheduled embarkations of Irish regiments were canceled, and four regiments in England were despatched to Ireland. All of this coordination was done by the military commanders, Talbot, Sidmouth, and Gregory, as Grant, ignored by all, withdrew into inactivity and petulance.[122]

As the military buildup in Ireland crested in late 1821, Lord Liverpool moved to restructure his Government. Home Secretary Sidmouth, weary and eager to step down, had begun his term of office amid English Luddism, and now contemplated a retirement marred by the recent Queen Caroline Riots and a threatened Rebellion in Ireland. Robert Peel, who had proven an able administrator in that troubled island, was ready for the Home Office: He succeeded Sidmouth in January 1822. Lord Lieutenant Talbot, on a private visit to London, had requested that Grant be replaced. Instead, the Prime Minister decided in December 1821 "to make a clean sweep" of the Irish administration. On receiving the news of his recall, Grant was nonplussed. But Talbot, who sensed he was being sacrificed, was furious, claiming that he had been "dismissed ... like a drunken Butler at a moment's notice."[123] The new administration in Ireland would consist of the Duke of Wellington's elder brother, the Marquess Wellesley, and Peel's close friend, Henry Goulburn. This arrangement would produce strong ties between London and Dublin over the next six years.

III. Police and protest

Within eight years, starting with twenty men under Willcocks in Middle-third, the Irish Peace Preservation Police grew by 1822 to 2,300 men patrolling half of the counties of Ireland (Table 6.2). Most of this growth

Table 6.2. *Growth of the Irish Peace Preservation Police, 1814–29*

Date	Counties	Magistrates	Chief Constables	Constables and subconstables		Total
				Horse	Foot	
Sept. 1814	1	1	1	21	0	23
Dec. 1815	1	3	3	21	66	93[a]
Dec. 1817	7	7	11	214	147	379
Sept. 1820	13	10	20	250	865	1,145
Feb. 1822	16	13	38	324	1,340	1,715
Oct. 1822	16	15	53	414	1,859	2,341
June 1825	3[b]	4	5	61	420	490
Mar. 1828	2[c]	4	4	11	319	338
Dec. 1829	1[d]	2	2	2	105	111

Totals exclude office clerks and paymasters.
[a] Excludes an unknown number of small temporary parties of Peelers in Westmeath, Limerick, and Clare, spring and summer 1815.
[b] Tipperary, Cork, County and City of Limerick.
[c] Tipperary, County and City of Limerick.
[d] County and City of Limerick.

came during Grant's chief secretaryship; when Peel left Ireland in 1818, there were only about 400 Peelers active in seven counties. At its height, the force was spread very unevenly across Ireland. Virtually absent from Ulster, the police were concentrated in north Munster, east Connaught, and, to a lesser extent, in west Leinster (Map 6.3).

Profiling the Peelers

Of the social characteristics of this 2,300-man police we unfortunately know little. Some of the Chief Magistrates – Willcocks, Wilson, and Wills, veterans of the Dublin police – had "long been acting under the Government in capacities similar to that in which they are now placed." Warburton, D'Arcy, and O'Donoghue had, as brigade majors, held high positions in the Yeomanry. Powell and Pendleton had been career military men. The paramilitary nature of the police naturally led to appointments of men with military backgrounds, but Peel emphasized that military officers would not necessarily make the best magistrates. Personality was important: A man had to perform well in the "delicate and embarrassing Situations" in which he would "often [be] placed." The one rigid rule, applied without exception, was that a Peeler magistrate could never serve in his native county.[124]

The police constables were mostly men who were serving, or had served, in infantry or cavalry regiments of the army. A preference was given to noncommissioned officers, sergeants or corporals. Thomas D'Arcy stated in

DISTRIBUTION OF THE PEACE PRESERVATION POLICE
IN 1821

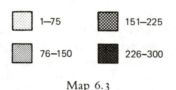

Number of Constables in each County

▨	1–75	▨	151–225
▨	76–150	■	226–300

Map 6.3

1818 that all of his mounted police had served in the dragoons. A second source was the demobilized militia staff, though it never provided the number of police that Peel in 1816 intended.[125] A third recruiting pool was the Dublin police, itself composed of army veterans. The evidence here is patchy, but we know that members of the Dublin police comprised Willcocks's original Middlethird force and that 95 of Powell's 130 Peelers in King's County in 1821 were raised by Major Henry Sirr at the Head Police Office in Dublin.[126] No complete register of the 2,300 Peelers is extant. Our only quantitative source is a police pension register (H.O. 184/1), which lists only sixty-six constables recruited in the period 1816–21 (see Appendix V). Two-fifths of these recruits joined at the recommendation of military officers.

The findings from this small register must be treated with great caution. Half of these sixty-six recruits came from Leinster, with 16 percent from King's County alone. The predominance of this county may reflect the influence of Warburton, who resided there. The register confirms that the rule prohibiting a man's serving in his native county was widely enforced. The only exception I have found was in King's County in 1821, where 19 of 130 policemen were natives; significantly, Major Powell took pains to point out that these men "have conducted themselves respectable and conformable [sic] to my intentions." Apparently a few Englishmen served in this early Irish police. Although the police pension register lists no native Englishmen among the sixty-six names, we know that Willcocks recruited thirteen disbanded British soldiers in Tipperary in 1816 and Powell reported that among the thirty-five men he hired in King's County in 1821 were an unspecified number of "Englishmen who have served in the army."[127]

In the absence of other evidence, we must rely on the police pension register, specifically on an analysis of the sixty-six men joining in 1816–22. Only 16 percent of these men gave their religion as Catholic. This low figure is not surprising and strengthens the validity of the register as a source worthy of analysis because we know that the police over time recruited increasing numbers of Catholics. The information yielded on age, height, and marital status is also what we would expect. In the early years of the police, there were neither strict age or height requirements nor restrictions against marriage. According to the register, the constables joining in 1816–22 were more often married and more varied in height and age than any group recruited after 1822. Only 14 percent were bachelors (by comparison, 54 percent of the recruits in 1837–40 never married); and fully 26 percent were 5 feet 7 inches or shorter (compared to 1 percent in 1837–40). In age at joining, the men of 1816–22 ranged widely from eighteen to over thirty. Nineteen percent joining in 1816–22 were over twenty-eight years old, compared to only 1 percent of those hired in 1837–40; 62 percent of the recruits in 1816–22 were age nineteen to twenty-four, compared to 87 percent in 1837–40.[128] The early Peelers were a more varied force than the constabulary of later years, when strict requirements produced a more homogeneous force.

The police were uniformed but the clothing, different in each force, varied from drab to colorful. In Tipperary in 1817, the horse constables wore "grey Overalls" and "blue Jackets," and the foot constables "grey Trowsers" and "grey Coats." In Queen's County in 1821, Major Joseph Nicolson's fifty cavalry police, "on splendid horses," were a colorful if "motley force," with cloaks of different colors and brass helmets and plumes. In Cavan, Kildare, King's County, and Louth, the fashions were similarly varied. In March 1817, one year after the police were placed in Clare, Warburton complained to Gregory that his dismounted men should be given a uniform, like his cavalry constables; it would help enforce discipline and keep the police "as distinct as possible from the peasantry."[129]

Information on pay, promotion, and punishment is also sketchy. Initially, a constable's annual salary was excellent (£50); indeed, it was so high that the Government later reduced it to £40 (1820) and then £35 (1822). There were occasional stoppages from weekly pay for clothing; in Limerick in 1820, when these amounted to one-fifth of the base pay, the married police constables petitioned Chief Secretary Grant against extortions that "drove [them] to destruction." In one case, there were even charges of "horrid Peculations and Corruptions" by a Chief Magistrate in matters of pay, lodging, and foraging.[130]

In matters of promotion, the Government pursued a policy of merit. We have no data apart from the small police register of sixty-six men, but indications are that men moved back and forth between the ranks of constable and subconstable, depending on seniority and behavior. The position of Chief Constable was attainable but rarely available. On the death of his Chief Constable in 1818, Magistrate Edward Wilson in Tipperary took "the liberty of suggesting and I trust you will see the propriety of appointing the most deserving" of his constables to the vacancy. The Lord Lieutenant replied that he "entirely approves" and asked Wilson to send him the man's name. Nepotism was also an occasional factor. Wilson once asked permission to appoint his son as police clerk "in order to fit him for a higher situation hereafter"; Warburton's brother-in-law, George Drought, was named the Chief Magistrate in the Limerick City police; Willcocks's son, John, became a Chief Constable.[131]

The evidence for punishment of wayward Peelers is, again, incomplete. Much, no doubt, depended on the character of the Chief Magistrate; Pendleton and Going set a different example for their men than did Warburton or Willcocks. These latter two officers noted the importance of curbing any "awkward and undisciplined conduct" in the men, for when the police in the popular mind are "once held cheap, it is almost impossible to obtain any ascendancy over the people." Police misbehavior took many forms. One Tipperary subconstable absconded with his salary and all of his police clothing; Dublin police magistrates issued a warrant for his arrest. Drunkenness was the most common offense. A first offense usually led to suspension, a second to dismissal. In Tipperary in 1819, when two constables sent to fetch the force's weekly pay got drunk on the way back, Willcocks suspended one and dismissed the other, who had been drunk before. In King's County in 1821, Powell replaced "several worthless characters," victims of drink, with men "whose characters have borne the strictest investigation."[132]

More serious offenses could also be sternly punished. Much depended on the man who was Chief Magistrate. In July 1816, Major Wills discovered that *twelve* of his subconstables were celebrating a Protestant holiday by wearing Orange lilies and drinking with soldiers and local Protestants in a pub in Tipperary town. He marched there at once and on the spot fined each constable 5 shillings, equivalent to two days' pay. The next morning, he berated them at police parade, made "an example of" Subconstable John Curran before the other men and then dismissed him, and informed all involved that he would lay their conduct before the Government. In another incident in Tipperary in 1817, a subconstable killed a peasant at a fair. Chief Magistrate Wilson reported that John Maguire "did not get provocation sufficient or was in that danger, that warranted him in shooting a Man." Moreover, this was Maguire's second breach of the firing regulations in the past four months. Wilson recommended to Peel that Maguire be dismissed from the police even if, at his trial, the jury should acquit him.[133]

Criticisms of the Peace Preservation Police

Ireland was a poor country. Since the Union, it had contributed to the British Exchequer only two-seventeenths of the total revenues in the United Kingdom.[134] The Peace Preservation Police in its first eight years of existence cost Irish taxpayers almost exactly £200,000. Having to raise such a sum in the poorer parts of the country opened the new police to intense criticisms about not only its cost but also its constitutionality and effectiveness.

The leading critic was Valentine Lawless, 2d Baron Cloncurry (1773–1853), who had objected to the introduction of the police in Kildare in 1817. Cloncurry's father, Sir Nicholas Lawless, a wealthy merchant and banker, had chaired the parliamentary committee that investigated abuses in the Dublin police in 1788. Valentine Lawless's boyhood heroes were Grattan and Fitzwilliam. After he became a United Irishman, his father shipped him for his own safety to London to study law. Here he kept up his United Irish contacts, and was arrested and held in the Tower for six weeks in 1798 and for nearly two years in 1799–1801. In 1805 he returned to Ireland, heir to the family estate at Lyons, County Kildare. He became a quiet, improving landlord and "a sedate, Loyal subject, and one of the best and most impartial Magistrates of Ireland."[135]

In his *Letter to the Duke of Leinster on the Police and Present State of Ireland*, published in Dublin in 1822, Lord Cloncurry charged that "innovation has always been the bane of Ireland." Like the Union, the Whiteboy statutes and "Mr. Peel's" police were "innovations to degrade and oppress the people, whilst hardly one Act has been thought of ... to better their situations, civilize, or instruct them." Cloncurry objected to the unconstitutionality of the Peace Preservation Police. In words reminiscent of Grattan's a generation earlier, Cloncurry argued that "a stipendiary police ... [would] startle an English Senate, being altogether contrary to the general tenor of the English constitution and to the best feelings of Britons."[136] He opposed the Peeler idea as entirely misconceived, since it treated Irishmen differently from other inhabitants of the British Isles. Districts were proclaimed without notice or consultation, and the total centralization of control encouraged local laxity, even hostility, to Dublin Castle. The unfortunate result was to push even the law-abiding to protest the measures of the Government. Cloncurry's analysis in 1822 was reminiscent of Lord Carysfort's in 1787 (see pp. 108, 109–10).

Peel's police also encouraged patronage and permanence. The Chief Magistrate, observed Cloncurry, holds his government position "only so long as the district continues to be disturbed!! I would not like to speak ill of any man, but if I was to lose £1,000 p.a., by certifying the good sense or moderation even of the Chancellor, I would hesitate to do it." Peel had believed that "the disposition to exaggerate danger ... [was] tolerably well counterbalanced by the apprehension" of the expense levied on a proclaimed district.[137] But in fact, local magistrates frequently had little say concerning

Table 6.3. *County grand jury presentments for the Peace Preservation Police,
1817–21*

County	Total	No. of years presented	Average annual presentment
Tipperary	£47,287	5	£9,450
Clare	25,953	5	5,200
Galway	19,095	2	9,500
Louth	13,858	3	4,620
Limerick	11,424	2	5,720
Roscommon	7,537	2	3,760
Kildare	4,537	3	1,510
Meath	2,586	2	1,290
King's County	2,301	1	2,301
Dublin	1,700	4	425
Westmeath	1,344	1	1,344
Wicklow	370	1	370
	£137,992[a]	2.6[b]	£3,790[c]

[a]Twelve-county total, 1817–21.
[b]Average number of years presented per county.
[c]Average per county.

the introduction or removal of police. Moreover, the Peeler magistrates'
weekly police reports routinely recorded no outrages, even for months at a
time, yet the forces remained in place. The removal of police from baronies
in Cavan, Louth, Kildare, and King's County were the exceptions to the rule
of permanence.

In post-Rebellion Ireland, many Anglo-Irish local magistrates accepted the
fact that English law could not always be applied to their country. Objections based on constitutionality had lost much of their luster since Grattan's
heyday. But the costliness of the Peelers was felt by all taxpayers. In 1817–
21, a period of fast falling farm prices and rents, taxpayers in twelve Irish
counties paid £138,000 for the new police (Table 6.3). These figures,
published by the British Parliament in 1824, do not give costs in Tipperary,
Louth, and Clare before 1817 and omit all expenses in Donegal (for two
baronies, 1817–21, and 1821), Cavan (one barony, 1817), Kilkenny (one
barony, 1821), and Cork (one barony, 1821). In addition, local taxes for
Peelers in thirteen counties in 1822 totaled £47,500.[138] Thus, local assessments for police from September 1814 until October 1822, when the county
constabulary replaced most Peeler forces, totaled almost exactly £200,000.
Total costs, including the share drawn from the Consolidated Fund, were
around £400,000. Analysis of the parliamentary return of 1817–21 reveals
that Tipperary, with the oldest establishment, accounted for over one-third

of the local taxation, but Galway, a poorer and more recently proclaimed county, was paying more annually by 1820–1 than was Tipperary. Limerick and Clare were the third and fourth most heavily taxed areas, paying over £5,000 a year. Districts requiring the government police, Lord Cloncurry noted, were often those least able to bear additional taxation. A policeman dressed in "a whole coat" provided a simple but glaring contrast to the tattered garb of many of the peasantry. "The spruce Policeman or his more spruce Commandant" was easily resented by distressed laborers and small farmers.[139]

If the force was expensive, even burdensome in times of "deep distress," was it worth the cost? The police presence may have been most effective as a preventive force "whilst everything continued tranquil," or when the district was only moderately disturbed. In periods of widespread unrest, Col. Thomas Sorell remarked, "it was immediately discovered that the Police could not shew themselves without the Military." This was the case in Limerick, where, concluded Sorell, "the inefficiency of this Force for keeping the Country quiet, has been I think clearly demonstrated ... [although] they already have 200 men."[140] The Peelers' ineffectiveness was due, in part, to numbers. Limerick's 250 policemen were responsible for a county of 1,037 square miles. More to the point, by the time the Peelers were divided and posted to remote stations, a detachment would be fortunate to include more than a half dozen men. The problem of numbers was compounded by the hostility shown to the men. Isolated and surrounded by a populace eager "to do for the Police ... once [they] get the Soldiers out of the way," the typical Peeler outpost was extremely vulnerable. This was dramatically demonstrated in January 1822, when "at least one thousand Whiteboys" attacked and burned a thatched-roof police barrack near Churchtown, Cork; of the seventeen Peelers inside, three perished and eight were seriously wounded.[141] Equally unsettling was the speed with which the peasantry put other police stations to the torch as soon as the police evacuated them.[142]

What was the Peelers' impact on crime? For the period 1813–21 there exist no easily accessed national totals of the number of persons committed to trial at assizes and quarter sessions in Ireland. From the national totals submitted to the English Parliament, we do know that the figures jumped from 3,500–4,300 in 1805–12 to 14,600–16,300 in 1822–6. This apparent near quadrupling from 1813 to 1821 was accompanied by a rise in the conviction rate from 22 percent in 1805–12 to about 50 percent in 1822–6. G. R. Porter, an English statistician writing in 1843, stated that the great increase in the figures from 1812 to 1822 was the result of "either a fearful increase of crime, or a much more vigilant police." The postwar period was one of economic deflation, rising crime, and rural distress; there was no reform of the system of local constables and magistrates. Although these officials and private individuals may have stepped up prosecutions, it was probably the rising tide of crime, not police vigilance, that produced the swollen number of committals.[143]

The effect of the Peelers on the committal totals and the conviction rates was necessarily marginal. Numbering only 400 men by late 1817 and 2,300 by the end of 1822, the new police were scattered throughout those parts of

Table 6.4. *Prosecutions and convictions at Irish County Assizes, 1816–22*

Dates and districts proclaimed under the Peace Preservation Act	County	1816		1817		1818		1819		1820		1821		1822	
		I	II	I	II	I	II	I	II	I	II	I	II	I	II
Four baronies, 1814–15; one barony, Dec. 1821; five baronies, Apr. 1822	Tipperary	221	23.1%	209	31.1	195	34.9	220	35.9	119	50.4	234	52.1	243	34.6
Four baronies, 1816–17; whole county, Mar. 1820	Clare	187	19.8	220	16.4	203	18.2	164	29.3	144	31.9	158	32.3	311	23.5
Seven baronies, Mar. 1817; revoked Aug., Nov. 1818. Four baronies, May 1821	Kildare	99	38.4	154	50.6	96	42.7	175	42.9	130	46.9	103	54.4	80	40.0
Thirteen baronies, Dec. 1819–Feb. 1820	Galway	153	21.6	182	25.9	217	19.4	220	37.7	399	40.1	316	30.7	307	24.1
Whole county, Apr. 1820	Limerick	186	26.3	157	29.9	178	23.6	196	20.9	184	25.0	131	29.8	259	45.2
Three baronies, Nov. 1821–Jan. 1822; one barony, Dec. 1822	Cork	456	24.8	274	25.5	304	28.3	259	29.0	223	36.8	264	31.8	327	35.5
Never proclaimed	Kerry	132	22.7	252	19.0	377	23.3	378	20.4	493	7.3	442	26.9	471	28.7
Never proclaimed	Longford	199	26.7	140	27.1	171	22.2	164	17.7	117	15.4	174	31.0	271	36.9
Never proclaimed	Mayo	149	47.7	232	33.2	226	36.3	254	46.1	227	35.7	287	40.1	443	29.3

Key: I Numbers of persons indicted and tried.
II *Percentage conviction rate.*

Ireland high in popular unrest. The Peelers were primarily flying squads sent in to deal with civil disturbances, not crime. The bulk of ordinary crime and the highest conviction rates, which buoyed up the national average, were in the city of Dublin and in Ulster. The Peelers were not expected to deal with larceny, burglary, and robbery, nor was it their duty to initiate prosecutions or secure convictions. Nevertheless, where they existed, the new police were supposed to encourage the law–abiding, protect and serve as witnesses, and begin to learn how to gather evidence and present it in court. The Peelers were, of course, handicapped because they had been sent into districts where the problem was precisely that of widespread hostility to the law.

The most serious offenses, whether ordinary or agrarian crimes, were tried at assizes rather than quarter sessions. Table 6.4 shows that the Peelers had, in fact, little influence on prosecutions and convictions. In Clare their introduction had no appreciable effect on either. In Galway the number of persons brought to trial in 1820, a very disturbed year, was nearly double the figure for the previous year, but the conviction rate changed little and even declined in 1821–2. In Limerick committals to trial in 1820–2 fell, then rose, compared to the prepolice years; conviction rates rose in 1820–2, but in two of these years the rates only equaled the rates in 1816–17. In none of these heavily Peeler counties did the coming of the new police result in a dramatic rise in committals or a downturn in committals indicative of a deterrent function. The Peelers came late to Cork, and then only to three eastern baronies; similarly, their influence in Cloncurry's Kildare proved minimal. The counties of Kerry, Longford, and Mayo never experienced the new police: although the first two had low conviction rates in certain years, and Mayo surprisingly high rates, the broad trends in these non-Peeler counties were not noticeably different from those in the counties with the new police. What stands out in Table 6.4 is not the difference between counties policed or not policed by the Peelers but rather the trend since 1816, building in the disturbed years 1820–2, of a general rise in prosecutions and convictions at these county assizes.

The police served longest in County Tipperary. But for six years after their introduction in the period September 1814–December 1815, the Peelers acted in only four baronies; not until December 1821 and April 1822 were six additional baronies proclaimed. The number of persons prosecuted yearly at assizes held fairly steady in 1816–21, but the conviction rate rose from 23 to 52 percent (dropping to 35 percent in 1822). But with two-thirds of the county's baronies without the new police until 1821–2, it could not have been Willcocks and Wilson and their men who were primarily responsible for the rise in the county conviction rate. This trend at the assizes holds true even when we compare the county totals for two disturbed periods, 1813–14 (245 persons tried, of whom 33.1 percent were convicted) and 1821–2 (477 tried, 43.2 percent convicted).[144] If we look further, at quarter sessions in County Tipperary, we note that the rise in the number of persons tried and the conviction rates at Cashel (Willcocks's headquarters) and Thurles (Wilson's) follow the trends for the county as a whole:

	County Tipperary		Cashel & Thurles	
	Tried	Convicted	Tried	Convicted
1816–18	3,273	14.3%	1,475	12.0%
1820–2	3,628	25.9	1,531	26.9

Again, what stands out is not the difference between Peeler and non-Peeler districts in the successful prosecution of crime but rather the low conviction rates throughout Tipperary in 1816–18, a quiet period of disease and dearth (the 9 percent conviction rate at Thurles in 1817 and at Cashel in 1818 may reflect a merciful unwillingness to convict), and the much higher conviction rates throughout the county in 1820–2, a period of disturbance when the authorities pressed hard to get convictions.[145]

Realistic alternatives?

Those, like Lord Cloncurry, who criticized Robert Peel's new institution as unconstitutional and expensive and who questioned its effectiveness, had decided opinions on the kind of police that should exist in Ireland. They opposed a centrally controlled force run by Dublin Castle and favored instead a reformed local police administered by local gentlemen of property and standing.

The first reform, suggested Cloncurry in his pamphlet of 1822, should be purification of the magistracy. County grand juries should furnish assize judges with the names of all active resident landowners whose annual income was at least £500. The list would include both Catholic and Protestant gentlemen but *not* Anglican clergymen or Catholic priests; no newly certified magistrate should be younger than twenty-five or older than fifty years. All magistrates would serve a seven-year term that might be extended upon the Castle's review of their service.

To assist the magistrates and upon their recommendation, the county grand jury would appoint baronial constables, Catholic as well as Protestant, and would be responsible for any suspensions or dismissals. Each constable would receive an annual salary of £20 and a pension after twenty years' service. Every county should hold assizes six times a year and maintain an adequate jail or house of correction. For minor crimes, punishment should be slight but certain, with "dreadful" retribution reserved for serious offenses.[146]

To make the local policing system work, "Governors of Counties" should be established as significant offices having "the same power as Lords Lieutenant in England." County magistrates were to be in frequent correspondence with each other and, as needed, with magistrates in other counties; they would be required to report frequently to the County Governor and discouraged from corresponding directly with Dublin Castle. This closing of the pipeline to the Castle was meant to increase the responsibility and activity of Ireland's local magistrates.

No person, not in [on] the secret, can imagine the love our inferior Magistrates have for the Castle-yard.... Nothing tends so much to keep away English capital and to encrease the number of Absentees, as the lies told of the country by those who fatten on its misery and degradation.

In the event of actual disorders, County Governors, like England's county Lords Lieutenant, should have "control of all civil power." After calling a meeting of "the principal Landholders" in the county, they would be empowered "if necessary" to send the militia staff into the disturbed districts. They might also direct the local constables and raise volunteers for nightly patrols; those refusing to serve were to find substitutes or be fined. The army might be employed after due consultation with the County Governor.[147]

Had Home Secretary Peel read Lord Cloncurry's pamphlet, he would have dismissed it as the work not so much of an aging radical as of a misguided liberal who suffered from unrealistic perceptions of the viability of local government in Ireland. To Peel, British standards simply did not fit Irish realities. The differences between the two men were great. Robert Peel represented English interests in Ireland; Cloncurry, the interests of an enlightened section of the Anglo-Irish gentry. The confrontation was not new: A similar divergence of views had occurred a generation earlier between Lord Carysfort and Thomas Orde. Since 1787, the most important new ingredient in the debate over local or central control was itself the principal event of recent Irish history: the Rebellion of 1798. To English officials, the clear lesson was the need for strong central control; to many of the jittery Anglo-Irish, who had defeated the Rebellion but "lost" the Union, the twin threat was violence from below and seizure from above of historic Anglo-Irish liberties. First, the Protestant Parliament had been taken; would the magistracy and police be next? The final factor shaping the differences between Peel and Cloncurry was generational. In 1822, Peel was thirty-four years old; Cloncurry, forty-nine. Peel was born in 1788, the year that Cloncurry's father chaired the committee investigating corruption in the new Dublin police. Peel was ten when the Irish Rebellion erupted; he left home for Harrow the year the Union Act passed. In 1798, Cloncurry was twenty-five, involved, and arrested; he was held for two years in the Tower of London while Peel studied at public school. In sum, whereas Cloncurry had grown into manhood in the last decade of Grattan's Anglo-Irish Ireland, Peel as a young man knew only post-1798 Ireland when it was a conquered province of the United Kingdom.

As Irish Chief Secretary, Peel, then only twenty-six, had created the police that quickly came to bear his name. From the introduction of the Peelers into Tipperary in 1814 until the publication of Cloncurry's pamphlet in 1822, these Castle-controlled policemen had been planted in parts of half of the counties in Ireland. Many people questioned their effectiveness, constitutionality, and cost; many others argued that the Irish magistracy and local authorities were beset by challenges unknown in England. By 1822, all admitted the need for substantial Irish police reform. But what shape would the reform take under a new Dublin Castle administration and a new English Home Secretary, Robert Peel? Would Irish local interests rally to win concessions, as in 1787, or succumb finally to a Castle-directed gendarmerie in every county of Ireland?

CHAPTER 7

The making of the Irish constabulary

Q. Do you approve of those constables being dressed like soldiers ...?
A. Indeed, I think there should be some distinctive mark, but the more they were reduced to the level of the people ..., I think the more grateful would it be to the people, and the more would it bring about a deference to the law among the people themselves; the more civil the constables may be considered to be, the sooner would the people come to that general feeling of respect for the laws, that I think very necessary for Ireland and which distinguishes England.
　　　　　　　　　　　　　– Rev. John Keily, Roman Catholic clergyman,
　　　　　　　　　　　　　　　　　　Mitchelstown, County Cork, 1825

The situation of a police man is an extremely valuable one to the Irish peasant ... and he would not lightly forfeit it.
　　　　　　　　　　　　　　　　　　– Daniel O'Connell, 1825

Lay the country under interdict, suggested one correspondent, then close all of the Catholic chapels, proclaim martial law, and turn the army loose. The Government did not adopt this modest proposal, but it did suspend habeas corpus and revive the Insurrection Act. In 1822–4 nearly 4,000 persons would be arrested under this statute and about 400 transported.[1] Southwestern Ireland in 1822 continued to be the scene of "the most horrid and sanguinary excesses": open warfare by Whiteboy armies sometimes numbering in the thousands, the nocturnal burning of barracks and surprise assaults on isolated parties of troops and Peelers, and "the most horrid and revolting of all the brutal Acts committed during the Insurrection," the rape of *seven* soldiers' wives.[2] Although it was said that "the Demon of mischief kept his sway" through 1823, in fact tranquility was returning to the disturbed districts. The causes of the new quiet discontent included a small upturn in agricultural prices, massive government repression and the "encreased boldness of [local] Gentlemen," Whiteboy exhaustion after more than two years of turbulence, and a new peasant interest in Daniel O'Connell's Catholic Association. No one in Ireland interpreted the tranquility as contentment. Lord Carbery noted that the peasantry "are quiet and endure ... with a Patience that is miraculous," and Bishop Jebb compared the cessation of outrages to "a silence like that of the grave."[3]

237

I. Beyond the Peelers

The forgotten founder of the Irish constabulary

The man who replaced Charles Grant as Chief Secretary was his political and personal opposite: a staunch Protestant and an able administrator. The thirty-seven-year-old Henry Goulburn – diligent and modest, "quiet, solid, and completely honest" – was very much in awe of his older Tory colleagues, Liverpool and Wellington, and of his close friend Peel, who was now Home Secretary. Such men, Goulburn would later write in his memoirs, "naturally threw me in the shade ... I was too sensible of my own inferiority." Nevertheless, he felt amply "repaid by unlimited confidence from men like Peel."[4]

The fortunes of the Goulburn family had since the seventeenth century been tied to landholdings in Jamaica. By 1822, after years of mismanagement, the West Indian estate was headed for "utter ruin." Despite straitened family circumstances, young Henry had attended public school (Sunbury) and Trinity College, Cambridge, and from 1807 on pursued a parliamentary career. In 1810 he was appointed an under-secretary at the Home Office. In 1812 Goulburn succeeded Peel as Under-Secretary for War and the Colonies; briefly in 1814, he served as one of His Majesty's Commissioners to conclude a peace treaty with the United States of America. In December 1821, after some hesitation, Goulburn accepted the offer of promotion to the post of Irish Chief Secretary, which he would hold until April 1827. Goulburn's success in that office would be due to his capacity for hard work, his ability to communicate with the Anglo-Irish gentry, and his warm relations with Home Secretary Peel, a man three years his junior.[5]

Goulburn's superior, the new Lord Lieutenant, was the first Marquess Wellesley. The elder brother of the Duke of Wellington, the sixty-one-year-old Wellesley emerged in 1822 from a retirement of "political obscurity and bankruptcy." Decades earlier he had enjoyed a brief, modest career in the Irish and British Parliaments and then reveled in the pomp of the Governor-Generalship of India (1797–1805). Ever since his return from the East, Wellesley had suffered from a sense of his own importance. A man of "very refined taste and ... literary attainments," Wellesley was a political liberal and supporter of Catholic Emancipation. In 1825 he shattered viceregal precedent by marrying a Catholic American heiress and permitting Mass to be held in his official residence in Phoenix Park! Perhaps most importantly, the aging Wellesley was a wretched man of business. He kept persons with scheduled appointments waiting for hours in his anteroom and delayed his replies to correspondents for months at a time. It was Wellesley's imperiousness and distaste for decision making, even more than his stance as a political "Catholic," that would prevent Chief Secretary Goulburn from working closely with him. For five years the amenable and long-suffering Goulburn, in constant touch with Castle Under-Secretary Gregory and Home Secretary Peel, would formulate Castle policy as Wellesley became an increasingly aloof, almost Oriental figurehead.[6]

"The first question," the new Chief Secretary recorded years later in his memoirs, "was how we should meet the spirit of outrage which had been for some time prevalent throughout the Country. The next was how, when the Spirit was subdued, we were to guard against its recurrence."[7] The local baronial police were certainly useless; they were in as wretched shape as Peel had found them in 1812. The county grand juries had been remiss in carrying out their duties of appointing constables by the police acts of 1787 and 1792. Policemen in County Limerick were "extremely difficult to procure"; in one area in Cork there was "not a constable within less than four miles," and "this evil exists in the other Baronies to a much greater extent." In Tipperary, one baronial force numbered five constables: One man was politically suspect, "another [was] old and drunken and the only one ... [of] any Dependence [was] charged with Murder." Throughout Meath the police were "wretched" and the magistracy "powerless." "All over the Kingdom," complained Colonel Thomas Cosby, the local constables "are only *old women*. They are not to be relied on in any Instance and unless some change shall be effected different from the *present* system (by a General Police or otherwise) it will be impossible to have the Laws properly enforced in Ireland."[8]

In framing his plan for a national police, Chief Secretary Goulburn confronted two existing institutions: the Yeomanry and the Peelers. Though a High Tory, Goulburn, like Peel, had little use for the Irish Yeomanry. The problems with the institution were not only its Orangeism but also its localism and expensiveness. The force was troublesome and costly: The 1,680 Yeomanry on permanent duty in Ulster in the spring of 1822 cost the Government £2,500 a month to maintain.[9] By nature they were a local force, and in the southwest there were insufficient numbers of Protestants to form effective Yeomanry corps; in the few places where the numbers were sufficient, strong anti-Catholic sentiments made use of the force worrisome. The local rule was occasionally broken. Northern corps had been shipped south at the height of the disturbances, but the thought of enthusiastic County Antrim Protestants on permanent service in Limerick was too wild to consider seriously. For all of these reasons, the Government resisted the incessant demands for Yeomanry placed in every hamlet of Ireland.[10]

The Peelers were even more expensive than the Yeomanry, and because local districts bore half of the costs, these forces were intensely unpopular. Irish local taxpayers had been billed £40,137 for 1,664 Peeler police in 1821. "The only fault of your bill," Goulburn wrote Peel, "is the expense which is certainly too heavy for a permanent system. Our police will be a cheap as well as an effective system." No questions about the constitutionality of the Peelers disturbed Castle authorities. Gregory and Goulburn both judged Peel's police to be "excellent" for dealing with extraordinary disturbances; indeed, they believed that discontinuance of the force "at this period" would have "very bad consequences."[11]

As early as 1817, many in Ireland had anticipated the creation of an effective police throughout the country. Peel in 1818 had toyed with the idea but never formulated a proposal. From November 1820 on, Grant was "trying to frame a bill regarding the police, 'ordinary police' or rather the constabulary of the country," but by May 1821 he had abandoned the idea. The London Government wanted a more powerful police than Grant was willing to support, and Grant feared that "the most clamorous" parties in Ireland would settle for nothing less than "a vigorous system of police by which they mean a Gendarmerie." Grant's chief secretaryship produced only an innocuous reform of the local magistracy. Now, in spring 1822, as the whirlwind of Whiteboyism began to abate, the new Chief Secretary turned his thoughts to a national police force.[12]

It is important to stress that the Constabulary Act of 1822 was Henry Goulburn's creation, not Peel's. On this point Goulburn was insistent. "Many have erroneously stated," he wrote years later, "that Sir R. Peel was the author of that which I believe to have been one of the greatest benefits to that Country, 'the Constabulary Act'. . . . That the measure originated with him or owed its preparation to any other than the Irish Government is an error." Goulburn accounted for this erroneous belief by noting that the term "Peelers" was "readily transferred to the new Constabulary"; that Peel had approved and supported the measure in Parliament; and that Peel was known to be the author of the 1814 Irish police and, later, the 1829 London police. Although Peel did express continuous interest in the constabulary, including even the smallest administrative details, it is significant that he never claimed authorship of the 1822 act.[13] It was Goulburn who, in the spring of 1822, pestered Gregory for information "in detail" about the persons, ranks, pay, and expenditures of the Peace Preservation Police, the civil aid rendered by military and revenue officers, and "your opinions" on the size of police forces needed for each county.[14]

The Irish Constabulary Act of 1822

Goulburn's bill, even in its early stages, never proposed to extend the principle of Peel's 1814 police throughout Ireland. The 1822 police was to be for regular, daily policing; the Peelers of 1814 would serve only in disturbed districts under circumstances of "extraordinary necessity."[15] What Goulburn sought was "the supersession of all the existing [local] Constables and Peace Officers of the Country," that is, the baronial forces of 1787 and 1792. He also wanted total government control. Realizing that the proposal would be controversial, Goulburn nevertheless judged it "most expedient to take into the hands of Government the appointment of Chief *and all other Constables* throughout Ireland." Further, the Castle should have the right to appoint special salaried "Police Magistrates . . . under the sole control of the Government whenever and wherever it might appear expedient to the Lord Lieutenant to do so." These magistrates "should not at once absolutely supersede all the Local Magistrates," but they should be sent into poorly administered districts. Finally, the Chief Secretary envisioned "Inspecting" Magistrates –

the future provincial Inspectors-General of Police – to superintend the entire force.[16] Goulburn's thoughts in April coalesced into the constabulary bill presented to Parliament on 24 May: In every county of Ireland there would be a centrally controlled force of subconstables, constables, chief constables, and police magistrates. Goulburn, in short, offered Ireland a French-style gendarmerie and was then surprised, as he later wrote, at the "prejudice, real or affected," that his scheme encountered.[17]

Only a fourth of the Members of the House of Commons attended the Second Reading of the constabulary bill on 7 June. The remarks of the proponents were brief. Chief Secretary Goulburn argued that "an effective police" in Ireland was more important than any "objection that it was against the principles of the constitution to vest such a power in the hands of the Government." The new Irish Attorney-General, William Plunket, saw nothing wrong with constables "nominated directly by the Crown.... What difference could it make whether the Crown appointed the [local] magistrates and the magistrate the constable, or whether the Crown appointed the constable directly?" To be sure, the projected costs for the constabulary (£218,000) would make it far more expensive than the old baronial police (£29,000) and the Peelers (£102,000), but the investment (an extra £87,000) would pay dividends in peace and good order.[18] In a short speech, Peel supported Goulburn's bill by arguing that it would permit reductions in the use of the military and the Peelers. A few Irish Members – Richard Martin, Vesey Fitzgerald, and Sir Nicholas Colthurst – added a few sentences in support of the bill.[19]

The Whig opposition startled the Government by its length, emotionalism, and vehemence. The greatest protests came from those most affected, the Anglo-Irish: Sir Henry Parnell, Thomas Spring-Rice, Sir John Newport. The proposed police was assailed as more costly than the Peelers. The patronage available to Dublin Castle for a force of 4,000 men was stupendous. What "pledge" could the Government give that the expensive Peelers would disappear and the army would be seldom employed in exchange for this "system of military police"? Finally, of course, Goulburn's bill was opposed on constitutional grounds. Critics ridiculed Plunket's argument for Crown appointments; Parnell professed to see no distinction between the Government's proposed police and the police of France.[20]

"So far from bringing public opinion to the side of the law," the bill was in fact "most calculated to awaken public indignation." A measure that bypassed justices of the peace, constables, and grand juries would destroy local government in Ireland. The bill "disgraced" the Anglo-Irish local authorities; if it were enacted, who could blame them for becoming hostile or indifferent to the laws? "If this bill passed," Newport stated that he "should no longer consider Ireland as his country." What was needed was not the abolition but the reform of Ireland's local institutions. It was alleged that this had been done in Longford, Kerry, and Mayo, and that those counties had escaped the brunt of the disorders. The creation of county Lords Lieutenant, such as England possessed, should be a part of the local reform.[21]

The most passionate critic of the bill was the former Irish Chief Secretary.[22] Charles Grant stated that the Government sought

to place the whole of Ireland under an armed police, to subject it to a species of gendarmerie.... [It] was at war with every principle of English policy ... it tended to disunite instead of to assimilate the legislation of England and Ireland.... [H]e objected in general to the system that the constitutional principles of government that were applicable to England were not also applicable to the sister kingdom.

The bill created a second army in Ireland, all of whose members "are bound to act just as the Lord Lieutenant should direct them." Grant informed Parliament that when he had served in Ireland, he had opposed a similar proposal that, after "considerable discussion," the Government had agreed to drop since it contravened "the great principle of constitutional freedom." His own subsequent bill reforming the Irish magistracy and baronial police had been "completely ready" by the 1820–1 session of Parliament. But because of the state of Ireland at that time, he had deferred to Sidmouth's wishes to postpone the bill's submission: "[I]t was not his fault that it was not brought in."

The Chief Secretary who had sent Peelers into thirteen counties now objected to the "habitual interference of the Government in all matters of internal police" in Ireland. Such practices led to "humiliation ... want of self-respect ... and supineness among the gentry." Why had the Government not completed the purification of the local magistracy begun during his chief secretaryship? Long-term peace in Ireland, argued Grant, would come only with the establishment of viable local institutions and the righting of economic and social wrongs. Artificial graftings like a government police were doomed to breed that resentment and hostility that were the already too familiar sentiments of Irishmen toward their rulers. Did the Government really believe that the people of Ireland would accept "unconstitutional measures ... to which [the Government] dared not resort for the administration of England"? In a desperate attempt to bolster the opposition, Grant argued finally that unconstitutional laws in Ireland might, by the passage of time, habit, and precedent, be the more easily "put in force in England."[23]

Henry Brougham, the next speaker, called the long speech of his close friend "able and unanswered." But Brougham's motion that consideration of the bill be postponed for six months was defeated. And, minutes later, the bill passed its Second Reading by a vote of 113–59. Among those voting against the police proposal were the Radical, Joseph Hume; the economist, David Ricardo; Christopher Hely-Hutchinson, brother of the Earl of Donoughmore; Henry Grattan's son, James; Sir Matthew Wood, a Radical City of London alderman; and Viscount Althorp, later Whig Speaker of the House of Commons.[24]

The fifty-nine Members who opposed the constabulary bill of 1822 were a handful of Radicals and a much larger number of English and Irish Whigs. Their views on police were part of a larger set of political beliefs. Analysis of contemporary voting lists reveals that the same men who opposed the police bill because, in their minds, it would establish a gendarmerie throughout Ireland were also strongly in favor of permitting Catholics to sit in Parliament and of broadening the suffrage in England. Many of these men also opposed the Government in the controversies growing out of the Peterloo and Queen Caroline affairs. They demanded a parliamentary inquiry into the Yeomanry violence that had occurred at Manchester in 1819; they favored the release of Henry Hunt from prison; and they wanted an investigation into Sir Robert Wilson's dismissal from the army. In sum, the views of the parliamentary opposition to the Irish police bill of 1822 were generally "liberal" on the other issues of the day. Their political behavior, in fact, was reminiscent of Henry Grattan's Irish Whigs of the 1780s.[25]

In the absence of a list of the 113 persons who supported Goulburn's police bill, it is not possible to make comparisons of the voting records of the police proponents on other issues. Yet if we assume that Tory MPs followed the political views of their leaders – Liverpool, Wellington, Peel, and Goulburn – we may surmise that those who wanted a powerful government police in Ireland also believed that Henry Hunt and Sir Robert Wilson had got what they deserved in 1819–21 and that Catholics and Reformers should be kept out of politics.

The debates on the Second Reading, which lasted for almost five hours and ended after midnight, deeply affected Goulburn. There is "the greatest opposition to it in all quarters," he reported to Wellesley. "I fear I must submit to many modifications." Yet he remained determined to "lay the foundation of a good police if ... not actually [to] establish it," even as Wellesley warned that defeat of the police bill would force him to demand an army augmentation for 1823.[26] Therefore, after "repeated discussion" with Members, certain sacrifices in patronage, control, and financing were made in the Government's bill. Despite the concessions, the Chief Secretary believed that "it will still be an efficient measure.... [I]t is a great improvement on the existing system and if found defective in practice will be with much less difficulty restored to the state in which we first presented it to Parliament than if it had been withdrawn." The amended bill passed in the Commons on 18 July and in the Lords on the 30th, and received the royal assent on 5 August.[27]

The Constabulary Act for the first time placed an efficient police in every county in Ireland. The Lord Lieutenant retained numerous powers. He was to appoint a Chief Constable to superintend the force in every one of the island's 250 baronies and "a General Superintendant ... [or] Inspector" of police for each of the four provinces. Though, as one of the concessions, the local county magistrates were to appoint the constables and subconstables, the Lord Lieutenant alone had the power to discharge them; or, if the magistrates were negligent, he might appoint the men. The rules and regulations of the provincial forces were to be drawn up by the Inspectors and approved by the local magistrates. Each Chief Constable was to reside in his barony, conduct monthly inspections of his men, and report in writing every three months to the Lord Lieutenant. Dublin Castle had the further power of sending up to two-thirds of the constables from any one barony to another, or indeed into a different county. Upon the written request of seven county magistrates (another of the concessions in place of Castle fiat), the Lord Lieutenant might create a "Stipendiary Magistrate" who would make monthly reports to Dublin.[28]

The constables and subconstables were to number no more than sixteen to a barony, for a total of about 4,000 nationwide; upon a request from local magistrates, the number might be increased in any barony. All of the locally appointed constables were to be

of a sound Constitution, able-bodied, and under the Age of Forty Years, able to read and write, of a good Character for Honesty, fidelity, and Activity; and ... no ... Constable ... shall be a Gamekeeper, Wood Ranger, Tithe Proctor, Viewer of Tithes, Bailiff, Sheriff's Bailiff, or Parish Clerk, or ... hired Servant in the Employment of any Persons whomsover, or shall keep any House for the Sale of Beer, Wine, or Spirituous Liquors; and ... if any persons who shall be appointed to be a Constable under this act, shall at any Time after ... [their] Appointment be or become ... [so employed], such Persons shall be ... incapable of acting as a Constable, and shall cease to be such Constable....

A constable or officer was to receive a "yearly Allowance" for any disabling injury, and pensions would be granted to the men according to their age and length of service. All costs of the police were to be paid from the Consolidated Fund, half of the total expenses to be repaid by the counties by grand jury presentments. The old baronial police acts, principally the 32d of Geo. III, were repealed but Peel's police act of 1814 was retained.[29]

The Constabulary Act of 1822 contained some key flaws. First, the force would suffer from the absence of county police chiefs. Second, the constables and subconstables were responsible to the Chief Constables, who were to obey the local magistrates or the Stipendiary Magistrates where they existed. These two kinds of magistrates, one locally rooted, the other accountable only to Dublin, were responsible in a loose way to the provincial constabulary inspectors, who in turn had final administrative control over the Chief Constable and other constables. Third, the allegiance of this police force, whether to local magistrates or to Dublin, was not clearly spelled out. The act's concessions to the Anglo-Irish gentry gave them not only appointment of the rank and file but also control over the *use* of the force. Throughout the 1820s, this uncertainty over the lines of authority would constitute the chief flaw in Goulburn's constabulary.

The concessions to local rights were similar to those a generation earlier in Thomas Orde's act of 1787. Constables' appointments and direction of the force resided with local magistrates. But the 1822 act would affect all counties, whereas Orde's act had applied only to certain disturbed districts. Moreover, Goulburn's act gave Dublin Castle extensive powers and, as the Chief Secretary himself had remarked, threatened future inroads on local government. In February 1822, the *Dublin Evening Post*, in a rare banner headline, had warned of the introduction of "A NEW PRINCIPLE INTO OUR CONSTITUTIONAL CODE ... A GENERAL POLICE." Despite the concessions, this paper continued to oppose an institution that it described as unconstitutional and dangerous.[30]

The mood of many Anglo-Irish was captured by John Swift Emerson who, in a pamphlet published in 1823, argued that England had chosen to police Ireland by a "French *gendarmerie*." Emerson's chief contribution to the arguments already developed in Parliament was his discussion of the long-range effects of the Government's decision. More to be feared even than unconstitutionality or the promotion of absenteeism was the permanence of the police measure. "Once firmly planted in a country," he warned, "it is more than doubtful that it will ever again be possible to expel them and restore the people to their rights." And even if the gendarmerie were in future removed, the damage would have been done. For, asked Emerson, will not the imposition of this new police

unfit the country gentlemen forever for the performance of duties to which it is proposed they should hereafter be recalled? to give them a distaste for the exercise of an irksome occupation? to diminish their interest in public affairs? . . . . Upon any future attempt to return from the French to the British system of Police, it will be discovered that French laws have made a French nation. . . . [Irishmen] will then appear like any continental people amongst whom it should be attempted to introduce the British system; unfitted for, because unpractised in, their duties.[31]

Emerson's prediction for late-nineteenth-century Ireland – a land stripped of its respectable gentry, bereft of public spirit and enterprise, and ruled by an armed standing force accountable only to central headquarters – was not far off the mark. Indeed, it may be argued that the diminishing independence of Protestant Ireland would contribute to the development of an exclusivist Catholic political and cultural revolution at the end of the century. The implantation of a centralized, English-controlled police, with a heavily Anglo-Irish officer corps dependent on Dublin Castle, would in the long run help to prepare the soil for the growth of Catholic republicanism and separatism.[32]

The magistracy and tithes

Such changed conditions of society lay, of course, decades in the future. In late 1822, as the new constabulary was being implemented, the Government turned to major related reforms. Because the effectiveness of the amended police act relied heavily on the local magistrates, the Castle determined upon "a thorough purgation of the Commission of the Peace in every County in Ireland." All existing commissions were canceled and new ones issued. Like the founding of that radically new institution, a constabulary, this wholesale reformation of a traditional institution, the magistracy, would have been unthinkable in England. The revised list weeded out many types of JPs. Gone were the old, the enfeebled, and the unfit (at least two were described as "Lunatics"). Also removed were absentee landlords, army officers and police constables given temporary commissions during the recent disturbances, and JPs of dubious activity, ethics, or loyalty. (The proposed cancellations in Clare – he retained his commission in Kerry – included one Daniel O'Connell, "a very corrupt man and of very disaffected principles.") As a result of the revision, the new constabulary would be directed, if not by Castle magistrates, at least by local magistrates judged acceptable in the recent revision of the rolls.[33]

It is impossible to say to what extent diligence and merit rather than party loyalty were rewarded. We do know that by the end of 1821 the Lord Chancellor, Thomas Manners-Sutton, had already completed revisions for all but three counties.[34] But it is not clear whether any Whiggish favoritism that might have crept into Chief Secretary Grant's list was reversed or counteracted in the final list assembled by the Tory Goulburn in early 1823. Certainly the revision was substantial. Perhaps 600, or about one-sixth of the commissioned JPs, were removed from the rolls.[35] Quiet as well as disturbed counties were purged. Antrim lost twenty-nine JPs; Armagh, thirty-two (two dozen being absentees); and Limerick, thirty-four. Hardly a county lost fewer than a dozen, and most lost at least two dozen. In Cork, 81 of 300 JPs were removed, being mainly "a large portion of the clergy, all the Military, and such Gentlemen as are connected with the Revenue." Willcocks and even O'Connell thought the purgation was thorough and salutary, and Lord Lieutenant Wellesley believed that "throughout Ireland, the mere knowledge of ... Revision" has increased the "diligence, accuracy, and careful conduct of the Magistrates."[36]

Related to the reform of the magistracy was the Castle's encouragement of a "practice [that] has gradually been creeping in, of neighbouring Magistrates meeting on a given day in each week at Petty Sessions." Legal disputes had hitherto been head-on confrontations between the plaintiff, the defendant, and a lone magistrate – "hall-door justice," as the Marquess of Westmeath termed it. Irregularity, corruption, negligence, and injustice had often been the result. By September 1823 Goulburn described the system of Petty Sessions as "generally established." These public judicial proceedings before a group of two or more sitting justices "work[ed] better than could have been expected"; the improvised courtrooms were soon thronged with the people and won the praise of military officers and even most magistrates. Rarely had a reform in Ireland been such an immediate success. The Petty Sessions Act of 1827 – which provided for a clerk, fixed fees, records, and prescribed times – merely formalized this growing practice.[37]

Another popular government reform concerned the matter of tithe. From time immemorial, individual landholders had paid their tithes in money or, in times of distress, in kind to individual clergymen. Protests arising from arbitrary valuations had often resulted in violent reprisals against tithe owners, viewers, and proctors. In 1823 the Government attempted to rationalize and reform tithe assessment and payment. The Tithe Composition Act of 1823 permitted, but did not require, a clergyman and his parishioners to arrive by negotiation at a fixed sum owed for tithes by the entire parish; each parishioner then had to pay his assigned share of the parochial total. The reform, which reduced the tithe burden on tillage generally, also filtered out much of the arbitrariness, uncertainty, and corruption involved in the old system of payment. The act was gradually adopted: By 1832 it was in effect in half of the Irish parishes. But it was probably the rise in tillage prices, not tithe composition, that helped keep the countryside relatively tranquil in the late 1820s.[38]

II. Planting the new county police

Even the implementation of the Constabulary Act went "remarkably well." The absence of hostility may be explained by the fact that in disturbed areas the new police displaced the unpopular Peelers and by the Government's decision to install the forces gradually over two years. A delighted Goulburn informed Peel, whose police had met a less cordial reception, that the constabulary "has even been called for in places where I thought there would have been a firm determination to resist it."[39] In late 1822 the southern and western counties with histories of disturbance were the first to be converted to the new police establishments. Throughout 1823 constabularies were established in Leinster and northern Connaught. Sligo did not receive the police until September 1823 because, as one correspondent complained, the gentry were practiced in "suppressing or making light of important truths and facts ... lest [they] should be saddled with the expense of an efficient police." But in Roscommon and Galway, where large Peeler establishments continued to penalize the residents, constabulary units were set up only in the summer of 1824, long after county residents had requested the Government to remove the more expensive Peelers. The last counties to receive the police were mostly in Ulster. Armagh assented in November and Antrim and County Dublin in December 1824; the next year, Down and Louth came in. The national system of police was finally complete (Map 7.1).[40]

Naming the rank and file: the Government's prerogative

By law, the appointment of constables and subconstables was the responsibility of local county magistrates. These men exercised their rights in Ulster and in some of the tranquil areas of Leinster.[41] But in many districts local appointments were rare enough that Daniel O'Connell could describe the practice in Kerry as an "experiment." At a meeting in that county in November 1822, seventy JPs endorsed overwhelmingly a motion that any selection not made by the magistrates was "most unconstitutional and humbling and degrading." The results in Kerry, according to one anonymous Castle correspondent, were unfortunate. "Some [appointed] in every barony" were unfit men, "some is [sic] over 40 years of Age," and some were Roman Catholics. Some were even "the very unsorgens [sic] that Disturbed the peace of the county. Mr. Willcocks," he added, "was not aware of their General Conduct."[42] Dublin Castle probably permitted the Kerry magistrates to make their own selections as a reward for the local diligence that had kept the Peelers out of the county; in any case, there was no Peeler establishment to serve as a recruiting pool.

CHRONOLOGY OF IMPLEMENTATION
OF THE CONSTABULARY ACT OF 1822

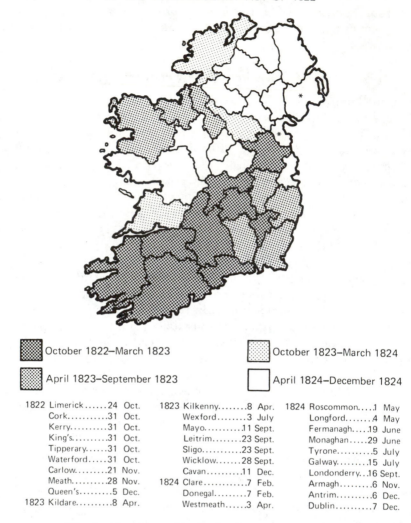

| ▨ | October 1822–March 1823 | ▨ | October 1823–March 1824 |
| ▨ | April 1823–September 1823 | ☐ | April 1824–December 1824 |

1822	Limerick	24 Oct.	1823	Kilkenny	8 Apr.	1824	Roscommon	1 May
	Cork	31 Oct.		Wexford	3 July		Longford	4 May
	Kerry	31 Oct.		Mayo	11 Sept.		Fermanagh	19 June
	King's	31 Oct.		Leitrim	23 Sept.		Monaghan	29 June
	Tipperary	31 Oct.		Sligo	23 Sept.		Tyrone	5 July
	Waterford	31 Oct.		Wicklow	28 Sept.		Galway	15 July
	Carlow	21 Nov.		Cavan	11 Dec.		Londonderry	16 Sept.
	Meath	28 Nov.	1824	Clare	7 Feb.		Armagh	6 Nov.
	Queen's	5 Dec.		Donegal	7 Feb.		Antrim	6 Dec.
1823	Kildare	8 Apr.		Westmeath	3 Apr.		Dublin	7 Dec.

* No returns from Down and Louth, where forces were not yet established

Map 7.1

Elsewhere local magistrates handed over appointments to the Government. In King's County, thirty-eight JPs voted unanimously to entrust all appointments to Major Thomas Powell, who made the selections from among his ex-Peelers. In Limerick City the magistrates voted, by 56–2, to give all appointments to Richard Willcocks, and indeed to retain the force as a Peeler police. In County Limerick, which also retained a Peeler force, the local magistrates agreed to hand over to Willcocks all appointments to the

Limerick constabulary. In Tipperary, a meeting of sixty-three magistrates decided, "with almost perfect unanimity" and Lord Donoughmore's approval, to follow "the recent precedent" in Limerick. Willcocks announced that he would transfer 176 of his Peelers to the constabulary, with the remaining 174 Peelers to continue as "a floating force" for especially disturbed baronies; and he gave assurances that the Peace Preservation force "would be left to die off" gradually. Only in County Cork, where the Peeler presence dated only from November 1821, was there resistance to government appointments. Dublin Castle, warned that local magistrates were bidding to make appointments from "favour and partiality," used its influence to turn out a large meeting. When the vote was taken on Colonel Longfield's motion that Willcocks be given the selection of all the constables, the result was 63 in favor and 63 opposed. The meeting's chairman, Lord Doneraile, gave his tie-breaking vote in favor of the motion on the understanding that Willcocks would consider the local magistrates' recommendations for one of every four constables for each barony. In Clare, in February 1824, Major George Warburton appointed "without exception" 144 former Peelers to the county constabulary. That April in Westmeath, county JPs asked the Government "to turn over the Peelers to be Constables." Three months later, when a county police force was established in Galway, a meeting of thirty-eight magistrates resolved unanimously that the 272 constables be appointed by Warburton from the existing Peeler force. In spring 1824 two witnesses before a parliamentary committee reported that it was the practice in many counties to give all appointments of the rank and file to the constabulary "chief constables" and other agents of the Government. Some years later, in March 1828, Major Powell indicated that the 1,152 men then in the constabulary in Kildare, Kilkenny, King's County, Meath, Queen's County, Wexford, and Wicklow "for the most part had been [first appointed] under the peace preservation [police] act." In sum, in many counties the local magistrates were willing to hand over to the Castle a power that was theirs by law; this practice was most widespread where the Peeler experiment predated the new one of a county constabulary.[43]

Distribution, uniforms, arms

By the end of 1824, the new police contained 214 Chief Constables, 1,113 constables, and 3,465 subconstables – a total of 4,792 men. The Peace Preservation Police, at its height in 1822, had numbered 2,326, only half as many. The size of the county forces ranged from 75 men in tiny Carlow and 85 in Leitrim and Londonderry to 385 in Galway and 421 in Cork.[44] The size depended in great measure not on a county's population or state of disturbance but on the number of baronies in each county. The 1822 act stated that sixteen constables and subconstables were to be appointed "for each Barony, or Half-Barony, or other Division of a Barony within each County."[45] Force strength thus depended on a largely irrelevant geopolitical unit, the product of Tudor constitutionalism: Large or small, congested or empty, each political division was to contain sixteen policemen. Naturally, exceptions were soon made to this artificial measure, but the standard of the barony remained until 1828.

In light of a given county's population or history of disturbance, the distribution of police sometimes assumed strange configurations. Tipperary's eleven baronies had 54 policemen per 100,000 population, while tranquil Antrim, with fifteen baronies, had 82. Sprawling, disorderly Cork had half as many police (69 per 100,000) as smaller and less disturbed Kilkenny (124). Galway possessed 124 police per 100,000 population only because magistrates there petitioned for an increase in the number of constables allotted to its fifteen baronies; in the nine baronies of neighboring, populous Mayo, the police (60) were only half as numerous. Medium-sized counties having numerous baronies, like Westmeath with thirteen, had very high police–population ratios (169 per 100,000). Ironically, Kildare – the county of Lord Cloncurry and the Duke of Leinster – contained in its fourteen baronies the highest number (230) of police per population in the whole island.[46] (For a map of the police district of the province of Leinster, see Map 7.2.)

By and large, the most heavily policed areas were in central and western Ireland. The northeast continued to feel the police presence only lightly. In the southwest, the apparent low density of constables was somewhat deceiving, for here Dublin Castle continued to rely for a few years on the Peelers. The City of Limerick was policed by fifty Peeler constables led by Magistrate George Drought, whereas the County Limerick Peelers, reduced to seventy-four men, continued to patrol under Magistrate Thomas P. Vokes. Larger establishments were maintained in Cork and Tipperary. Four northern Cork baronies, adjacent to Limerick and Tipperary, continued to pay £4,150 a year for 112 dismounted and 40 mounted Peelers led by Magistrate Samson Carter. The biggest Peeler force was in "untameable Tipperary" – 205 foot constables in ten of the county's eleven baronies at a local cost of £4,500 a year. Heading the force was Edward Wilson, one of the first and now one of the few remaining Peeler Chief Magistrates.[47]

If the Peelers continued to function across wide districts of the southwest, they did so at the expense of severe reductions. In 1822, there had been 2,300 men at a total cost of £102,000; in 1825 there were 480 costing £24,000. Nevertheless, the link between the Peelers, reduced to activity in three counties, and the new county police was strong because the constabulary Inspectors, or "Inspectors-General" as they came to be called, were appointed from among the leading Peeler magistrates. The Inspector-General for Munster was the highly deserving Richard Willcocks; the Connaught post went to George Warburton; Thomas D'Arcy had earned the command of Ulster; and Thomas Powell was rewarded with Leinster. With Wilson

Map 7.2 Police district of the province of Leinster, c. 1825. Colored map by J. Lyons, lithographed at the Quarter Master General's Office and presented to Insp.-Gen. T. Powell. Shown are the stations of Chief Constables and subconstables as well as the sites of garrisons, military posts, and petty sessions. (By permission of the 7th Marquess of Anglesey and the Public Record Office of Northern Ireland)

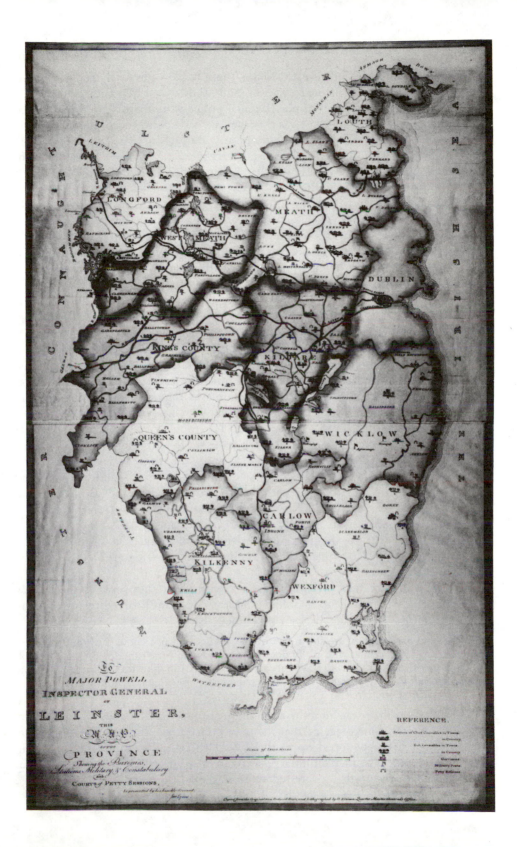

TO
MAJOR POWELL
INSPECTOR GENERAL
OF
LEINSTER,
THIS
MAP
OF THE
PROVINCE
Shewing the Baronies,
Stations, Military & Constabulary
AND
COURTS of PETTY SESSIONS,

REFERENCE.

remaining a Peeler magistrate, Major John Wills – the final member of the Tipperary trio of Willcocks, Wilson, and Wills – was allowed to retire.[48]

"The reason why the former Baronial police were inefficient," one correspondent wrote Goulburn, "was that they were dispersed thro' the Country at the mercy of the ill-disposed without any Barrack or Place of Protection." From its inception, the Irish constabulary was a barracked force. Detachments typically numbered fewer than 6 constables; in five baronies in King's County, 126 police were stationed in twenty-two barracks. Inspector-General Powell recalled in 1828 that the renting of barracks, empty and usually dilapidated buildings, was "an object of the greatest anxiety to the Government," for only barracks would "prevent the men [from] promiscuously mixing with the country people." Bedding, furniture, and cooking utensils were requisitioned from the army commissariat. Preferred were stone buildings with slate roofs, structures "as nearly fireproof as possible ... [for] the disaffected look[ed] upon the Arms and Ammunition of the Police as their own."[49]

In its first few years, the constabulary wore motley uniforms. A year after the police was established in Kildare, Lord Cloncurry called for uniformity of dress. He reported that some constables affected Orange decorations, others green, and still others black. Cloncurry called for a uniform, dark, and inoffensive color not easily discernible at night. In other counties and provinces, uniform dress appears to have been the rule as early as 1823.[50] Certainly by 1828, dress was standard. The men wore green trousers and a short jacket, with Russian white duck trousers for summer work. In cold or wet weather, the infantry wore greatcoats; and the cavalry, cloaks. The infantry donned soft cloth caps with a dress "tuft"; and the cavalry, "shakos," stiff military hats with a high crown and plume. Both foot and horse policemen carried "haversacks," knapsacks worn over one shoulder.[51]

The constables were heavily armed. Each man had to carry a saber, a pistol, and, over the shoulder not burdened with a haversack, a short carbine with an attached bayonet. Sixty rounds of ball cartridge was the standard issue of ammunition to each man.[52]

Many of the men were not pleased with what they saw as their fancy appearance, "dressed up in soldiers' clothes ... [and] forced to go about in full uniform." One ex-Peeler complained that

the new constabulary are too much of the soldier and not enough of the Peeler for me.... A policeman who really does his duty has but little time for dressing himself up. The "rough and ready boys" are the boys I like, though I fear the time will come when military appearance will supersede acute intelligence, and a well-dressed constable be preferred to a sharp Thieftaker.

In Westmeath, seven months after the institution of the constabulary there, Lord Castlemaine objected that the new police fired shots at "the Insurgents ..., but being wrapped up in their Watch Coats they could not come up with them." The men's military hardware also impeded them. Going about "armed to the teeth," protested one constable, "a weight of ball cartridge dangling before me ... with a long sword-bayonet dangling behind my leg," did not make for easy performance of police duties. Another policeman summed up the general feeling: "I believe we look well," he said, "but I shouldn't say we are of much use."[53]

The Castle's officer class: Chief Constables and Subinspectors

Control of all officers in this colorful force was vested in Dublin Castle. Lord Cloncurry's predictions about patronage were quickly fulfilled. A month before the introduction of the 1822 police bill, the Castle had already received 130 applications for the 250 posts; by early July, there were 500.[54] Four months later, that figure had doubled. In December 1822, staggering under the paperwork, Goulburn moaned to Peel: "What with Colonels of Militia remonstrating against reduction, and Magistrates remonstrating against having been excluded from the Commission, the furnace of the [Dublin Castle] office is at least seven times hotter than it used to be."[55] Already, in November, applicants were drawing terse Castle replies of "all filled up" or "nil." Still the letters poured in: By April 1823 there were "upwards of 1400" and by August "upwards of 1500 names on the List." This was patronage gone wild. Even after the completed establishment of the constabulary in 1825, Goulburn continued to be "persecuted to death with demands for [appointment as] Chief Constables." For job seekers numbering almost 2,000, the grim reality, reported the Lord Lieutenant the Marquess of Anglesey in 1828, was that in the last two years there had been only two vacant chief constableships.[56]

Despite the inundation of applications, the Government's appointments were made only after "strict inquiry" into the men's qualifications. A preference was given to army and militia officers – majors, captains, and lieutenants – who had been reduced on half-pay since the retrenchment of 1816. Special consideration was shown to veterans of Wellington's Peninsular campaign (1807–12) because of skills the soldiers had developed there in irregular guerrilla fighting. Inspector-General Willcocks stated in 1825 that "almost all" of his Chief Constables were military veterans, and his successor, Inspector-General William Miller, stated three years later that "a majority" had been in the service.[57] Extant incomplete quantitative data indicate that more than half of the Chief Constables in the 1820s were military men. An Ulster return shows that as late as 1829, twenty-seven of fifty-two Chief Constables, or 52 percent, had been in the military. In Munster "some" of Major Miller's Chief Constables were also "policemen of extensive experience"; in Limerick "a majority" had prior service as Peelers.[58] The preponderance of reduced, half-pay military officers meant that the Chief Constables of the constabulary were generally "persons most respectably connected." Indeed, those who made the "greatest exertions" for employment in the police officer class were "the younger Branches of highly respectable families"; these Chief Constables tended to be men "such as some years ago would not accept of such situations." The postwar slump in agriculture and fiscal retrenchment, which reduced or eliminated military officer status, had combined to make many gentlemen now compete fiercely to become Chief Constables of Police.[59]

The military emphasis in hiring, like the Castle's policy against a man serving in his native county, was not universally popular. One job seeker from County Waterford wanted to know

why [should] not a man who often ventured his life at home get it [a chief constable-ship]? Those [military] officers were remunerated for every hour they spent in the Service and most of them [are] still totally ignorant of country affairs. There is nothing more necessary than to know the people that you are to rule or govern.

To the rule against local connections was added one, in theory at least, that a man's religion should be no bar to his being an officer. Less controversial were requirements that no one who had been dismissed from the army, or had been an insolvent debtor, or was known as a "difficult character" could become a Chief Constable.[60]

The social background of the officers sometimes led to problems, not so much with their own constables, who were on the whole disciplined and deferential, but with the local magistrates, who were in contact with the constabulary in countless ways. The Chief Constables were instructed to execute magistrates' warrants, attend all court sessions, and obey county sheriffs and coroners. With a magistrate, they were to supervise all fairs and public meetings and to suppress disorders. In these situations of daily intimacy, the problem was that many Chief Constables, being "men of good family and connexions, [were] not likely to yield a ready obedience to the magistrates who in many instances are their inferiors in income, education, family, and rank in society." Some Chief Constables evinced an arrogant disdain for the local JPs; others, who had acquired a certain *noblesse oblige*, felt that some of the magistrates pressed too hard on the peasantry. In either case, the officers were sometimes reluctant to obey magistrates' directives. (Conversely, some magistrates were socially uncomfortable giving orders to their perceived superiors, the Chief Constables; a few even "did not like to ask them to go on duty to patrol after dinner"!) One knowledgeable observer in 1825 reported that some Chief Constables had a sufficiently elevated view of themselves that they chose to reside on nearby country estates rather than endure the "privation" of lodging with their men in barracks. By 1829, however, this problem had been solved, for a government study revealed that only 4 of 155 Chief Constables were not living at their police stations.[61]

The constabulary officers in the mid-1820s were likewise accused of being "too well paid" at £200 a year, of assuming "a style and appearance unnecessary to their situations." They "seldom" went anywhere except on horseback, attended by a mounted constable, even when neither their duty nor their security required it. By "the same motives of Vanity, [they] ... often throw off the Uniform and go about as private Gentlemen in coloured Clothes when there is no occasion for concealment or disguise." This government investigator in 1825 recommended nothing less than halving the officers' salaries and filling up any vacant chief constableships, especially in Cork and Tipperary, with "efficient Men from the Constables." Such a policy of promotion, he noted, "would furnish a great excitement to good conduct among the Constables." Many of the problems with the Chief Constables appear to have been curbed, in Munster at least, by the fall of 1828, for after a two-month tour of his district, Inspector-General William Miller found the great majority of his Chief Constables well qualified and active. Of fifty-five officers, only a handful drew his criticism. Those in Cork and Limerick he judged to be generally the best; only in Kerry did he detect a certain "want of exertion." In Waterford only one man was "less steady than I would like"; and in Tipperary he noted that Chief Constable Morgan suffered from being "unwieldy in person, and without Education, and therefore quite unfit for the Service." The Government remedied the pay problem in 1828 by cutting a Chief Constable's salary to £100.[62]

The single most important problem within the officer class in the 1820s was the absence of a county chief of police. The baronial Chief Constables had no sense of the larger needs of the county; the overworked Inspectors-General could not keep up with current developments in each county. Observers, including Richard Willcocks as early as February 1823, frequently referred to this administrative oversight in the 1822 Constabulary Act.[63] In 1830 the Irish Chief Secretary, Lord Francis Leveson Gower, would sponsor a bill to remedy this defect in police organization. Ultimately he abandoned his proposal, but unknown to many Members of Parliament in London, county police officers had for some time been in existence in Ireland.[64]

Bits of evidence indicate that these officers may in places have dated from 1824.[65] They were certainly in existence from January 1828. At first termed "Local Superintendents" or "Local Inspectors," by early 1828 they were known as "Subinspectors" (ranked immediately below the Inspectors-General) and established in all four provinces. In April of that year twenty-three Chief Constables were eliminated and thirty-three Sub-inspectors created (Cork, the largest county, receiving two). In each county, a meritorious Chief Constable was promoted to the new rank and his salary increased by half to £150 p.a. This greater administrative efficiency was accomplished at a saving of £1,505! An essential part of the reform was the reorganization of the constabulary from baronies into police districts; in Leinster, for example, 107 police baronies became 61 police districts. This reform, needless to say, entailed the elimination of traditional political divisions and local jurisdictions.[66]

Each county Subinspector functioned as "the Representative of the Inspector General within his County" and was "the medium" for all communications and reports from the Inspector-General and the Lord Lieutenant. He acted as the pay clerk for his force. He was responsible for all paper work – "Periodical Returns & Reports, the accurate Registry of all Casualties, and the record of all correspondence." He was to maintain the discipline, efficiency, "the Appearance [and] the Comfort" of his police. He was responsible for all clothing, arms, ammunition, "or other Stores." He was "required frequently to visit the several Districts" and to report any remissness to his Inspector-General. Finally, in addition to all of his administrative duties, he had "to keep up the best understanding with the [local] Magistracy." For all of these reasons, one Inspector-General in late 1829 could describe the Subinspectors as "the very mainspring of the [police] machine."[67]

Molding a professional force

The rank and file of the constabulary, the constables and subconstables, were by law appointed by the local magistrates. We have seen how in the formative years the Government, often with the approval of the JPs, had taken control of the appointments in many counties. "A large proportion" of these policemen had been Peelers or members of the militia staff – corporals, sergeants, and lieutenants reduced on half-pay. In the period 1824–8, when local magistrates asserted their legal rights, they appointed a more mixed group of constables: "men of the class of the peasantry, soldiers discharged, and in some instances, a better description of people, the lower farmers."[68] The influence of the Inspectors-General diminished; indeed, in Leinster, Major Powell's role verged on negligence. Increasingly, constables were selected from among local inhabitants and served in their home districts. By the late 1820s, the Lord Lieutenant could "suspect [that] a good many of the Constables are worthless fellows who have been jobbed in" by county magistrates. A Limerick Chief Constable, indulging rhetorical license, went so far as to describe his men as the magistrates'

illegitimate children, the connection of their concubines – persons known to be common Whiteboys – persons belonging to factions of no character whatever – the most ill-adapted persons that can be had. . . . [He] serves in that county wherein all his family and connections reside . . . [and is of] that class of persons the lowest in Ireland.[69]

It was difficult for the Castle to reverse this trend because the law gave all lower appointments to the magistrates. But a reversal appears to have begun in early 1828. Two new Inspectors-General – Colonel Sir John Harvey, Powell's successor in Leinster, and Major William Miller, who succeeded the retiring Willcocks in Munster – were especially active in reasserting Castle influence. Harvey established a solid, regular relationship with his JPs, and Miller instituted a serious overhaul of the Munster constabulary. A brother-in-law of Under-Secretary Gregory, Major Miller was a career military man before he became Inspector-General in November 1827. His detailed and highly literate reports, composed in a fine, trained handwriting, reflected a commitment to professionalism in the police that was almost obsessive. In 1836, he would be named a Deputy Inspector-General in the constabulary.[70] Miller worked in 1828 with local magistrates to weed out the inefficient men. Service in the police, he reported in October, was "daily becoming more popular, and respectable young men press forward for Appointments." Nine months later, Miller spoke of the continuing and "decided Improvement" in recruiting; police duties "which heretofore were looked upon as almost of an odious Nature are readily undertaken by the Sons of Opulent and respectable Farmers."[71]

Table 7.1. *Percentage of Catholics in the Irish constabulary, March 1824*

Connaught		Leinster		Munster	
Leitrim	41%	Carlow	35%	Cork	37%
Mayo	15	Kildare	29	Kerry	69
Sligo	29	Kilkenny	15	Limerick	20
		King's County	30	Tipperary	28
		Meath	36	Waterford	63
		Queen's County	26		
		Wexford	31		
		Wicklow	12		
Total	*25*	*Total*	*26*	*Total*	*39*

Note: Return includes subconstables, constables, and Chief Constables.
Protestants are identified as Anglicans, Presbyterians, and Methodists. No returns from sixteen as yet unpoliced counties, including all of those in Ulster.

The constabulary was slowly becoming not only more professional but also increasingly Catholic in the rank and file. Daniel O'Connell, who spent the decade working for political emancipation, had no objections to Catholics finding regular employment in the police. Where some might see a sell-out to the historic enemy, O'Connell saw not only jobs but also an end to discrimination and Ascendancy rule. Inspector-General Willcocks, who personally recruited 800 men to the force, said he "never asked a man what was his religious profession." Many Catholic recruits, eager for employment, kept their mouths shut or else lied about their religion. In Meath in 1823, a group of twenty-eight men drawn from a supposedly Protestant militia staff was later discovered to contain twenty Catholics. No doubt, until it became clear that Catholicism was no bar to public service, many men were less than honest about their religious beliefs. Already by 1825, Catholic policemen were becoming so numerous that the Attorney-General had to issue a ruling that, just as Protestant constables could not join Orange Lodges, so Catholic policemen could not subscribe to O'Connell's Catholic Association. Each group was prohibited since it was a "political association," loyalty to which would interfere with the performance of police duties.[72]

The findings of a Castle-authorized investigation of March 1824 into the religious composition of the new police presumably undercounted the number of Catholics (Table 7.1). The return, which excluded Ulster, showed a still-forming force of 2,670 men to be 68 percent Protestant and 32 percent Catholic. Because the return included the overwhelmingly Protestant officer class, and because of some "prevarication" among the constables, in actuality probably two of every five men in the rank and file were Catholics. In this light, Willcocks's remark that more than half of his men in Munster were Catholics can be interpreted not as mistaken, but as understandable, when compared with the official police return for his province as 39 percent

Catholic. Willcocks volunteered his opinion that "some of the best men in my establishment at this moment are Catholics" and stated that eight of his fifty-four Chief Constables (15 percent) were of that religion. The high percentage (39) for Munster largely reflects the enlightened policies of local magistrates in Kerry and Waterford, counties that since 1814 had received no Peace Preservation Police. The low figures for King's County, Limerick, and Tipperary are due to the massive infusion of Peelers, government-appointed and largely Protestants, into the constabulary. The low figure for Wicklow may reflect the greater availability of Protestant recruits in that anglicized county, but the surprising Mayo figure may indicate either rampant discrimination in that heavily Catholic county or a reluctance of Roman Catholics to serve. The omission from the return of police records for half of the counties in Ireland, including all of Ulster, signifies only that in March 1824 forces were not yet established in these counties.[73]

Finally, the 1824 return is useful because with it we can test the accuracy of a police Constables Register. Government statistics listed as Catholics 32 percent of the police in 1824 and 35 percent in 1832. Sampling of the register, apparently a pension register, indicates that 39 percent of the constables *joining* in 1823–8 were Catholics. This register percentage for Catholic recruits seems valid, for we know that over the years both more Catholics entered the force and fewer felt the necessity to lie discreetly about their religion. The officers' pension register reveals that of those men joining as officers in 1823–8 only 15 percent were Catholic, a figure that is identical to the percentage of Catholic chief constables in Willcocks's Tipperary force in 1824.[74]

The constabulary, still largely Protestant in composition and recently stocked with men named by the local magistrates, contained a number of older men, including some over the age limit of forty. Of the recruits in 1823–8 on the Constables Register, 28 percent were twenty-eight or older; this represented an increase from 19 percent for the Peelers of this same age group appointed in 1816–22. Correspondingly, the share of recruits aged nineteen to twenty-four dropped from 62 to 51 percent of the respective forces. Indeed, Major Miller reported in 1828 that the average age of the men in the Munster constabulary was thirty-one, with the lowest average being in Tipperary (twenty-eight) and the highest in Waterford (thirty-four). In Cork and Limerick, the average age of the men was thirty-three. The reassertion in 1828 of the Inspector-General's influence over the force of men produced dramatic changes, particularly in Munster. Major Miller reported that older men were not being hired and were being weeded out of the force. Discharging the old and infirm in the Kerry police lowered the average age to twenty-nine; the average age of the sixty-eight appointees authorized by Miller in Munster in the first ten months of 1828 was only twenty-three. This change in the age policy is reflected in the Constables Register, for the share of recruits twenty-eight years or older fell from 28 percent in 1823–8 to 9 percent in 1829–32 and to 3 percent in 1833–6. Correspondingly, the number of recruits aged nineteen to twenty-one nearly doubled from 27 percent in 1823–8 to 46 percent in 1829–32 (rising to 53 percent in 1833–6). Slowly and steadily, from 1828 on, the constabulary was filling up with young men.[75]

New standards of height and, to a lesser extent, of physique were tentatively introduced in 1828. Height statistics indicate no substantial changes over the period 1816–28, with a quarter of the recruits being less than 5 feet 8 inches tall. But we find Major Miller complaining in October 1828 that a June 1827 augmentation in the Tipperary police had let in too many men "of a puny bodily frame," whom he was now trying to discharge. He reported that in the first ten months of 1828 the average height of his sixty-eight appointees was 5 feet 9.5 inches. The results of the new policy against short men were soon evident. The share of recruits less than 5 feet 8 inches tall fell from 25 percent in 1823–8 to 11 percent in 1829–32 and to 4 percent in 1833–6. The percentage of very tall men did not increase (for 1823–36 the share of men 6 feet and above remained at 10–11 percent), so the constabulary was not becoming a race of giants. But it was, from 1828 on, increasingly becoming a younger force of men predominantly 5 feet 8 inches to 5 feet 11 inches in height.[76]

Developing a professional force with a strong esprit de corps entailed the Government's intrusion into the men's private lives. Indeed, in time, service in the constabulary would eliminate a policeman's private life. "The grand clog upon the Establishment," noted Miller in 1828, was marriage. The constabulary barracks, "inundated" with women and children, quickly became "untidy and filthy." A Munster return of 1828 showed that 68 percent of the constables were married, ranging from 60 percent in Kerry and Tipperary to 80 percent in Limerick. And each married constable had, on average, three children. Though Miller in October 1828 was "using my best endeavours to discourage Marriage," he still complained a year later of too many "needy and beggarly" married constables and of "barracks … crowded with a wretched Population." The problem was solved by a regulation of December 1829 that was of crucial significance for the future of the constabulary. Henceforth, on penalty of dismissal, no man could marry without permission of his Inspector-General.[77] For the moment, the force remained one largely of married men; in August 1830, Miller was still lamenting the "great inconvenience … from the large proportion of Married Men." In the future, it would become a race of young, tall bachelors. From 1829 on, married men were rarely appointed to the force. A twenty-five-year-old Protestant applicant from Roscommon discovered in January 1830 that his recent marriage to a young woman, "at the Request of his Clergyman," had disqualified him from an appointment in the constabulary. Despite his pleas "to admit Him on the Establishment to free him from Poverty and Want to that of Earning A comfortable Livelyhood," the young man was automatically rejected.[78]

On paper, standards for admission to and behavior in the constabulary were strict. The ability to read and write, it was felt, would eliminate the rougher characters and be an "encouragement … to education in the lower class of society." The Inspectors-General also required young, fit constables to abstain from drink. Sobriety would not only "ensure their safety" in critical situations but would also "prevent many acts of oppression." Regulations barred the men from entering public houses and shebeens except on business; drunkenness resulted in a fine for the first offense and dismissal for the second. With sobriety went a due respect for religion: Protestant and Catholic constables were required to attend their separate Sunday services.[79]

Such standards were meant both to tame the policemen and to offer, by example, a code of morality for the lower orders. The constable was expected to provide a role model of behavior: He was to be an orderly, impartial, and self-restrained member of society. Police work, the regulations made clear, was public service. Working for the Crown, a man was to be trammeled by no personal ties. Any constable who went into debt, who was caught gambling, or who accepted any fees or gratuities was to be dismissed. A policeman was required at all times to display

firm, orderly, peaceable, and Moral conduct.... It is of importance to the Public service that the demeanour of the Police should be such as not to excite any angry feeling or animosity, but insure the good opinion of the people of the Country.... The several Peace Officers ... whether Chief Constables, Constables or Sub-Constables, are required ... to maintain the mildest and most conciliatory spirit in their intercourse with all classes of the community, in order that the people may perceive it to be in their interest to look up to the Laws with respect & confidence, and may feel that individual happiness, as well as public safety, can only be secured by an equal, and undeviating, administration of Justice.[80]

The regulations enjoined the men "never to use more force, or violence, than is absolutely necessary." Even the handcuffing of prisoners was to be done so as to be "as little distressing to the feelings of individuals as possible." The thorny question of using force against armed parties encountered on nightly patrols was never entirely resolved legally, but Castle legal opinions emphasized restraint. If the police were attacked or met resistance to arrest, they could "repel force by force," but if the parties "merely fly and do not resist," the police were instructed not to shoot, "even tho' without firing they would not be taken."[81]

Of course, regulations and reality frequently differed. Indeed, the regulations recognized the dangers of policing in Ireland. "The first care" of a policeman coming off duty was to place his arms and ammunition in a safe place. At bedtime a constable should make sure that his uniform was close by "and so disposed of as to enable him to dress in the dark, if required, and in the shortest period of time." His weapons were also to be "arranged close to his place of rest," so that he might have "immediate recourse to them."[82]

Despite the best intentions of the Inspectors-General, their men, of course, sometimes misbehaved. In the early years of the constabulary, one in every ten men in the force was dismissed; by 1830 the rate was down to one in every twenty. Displays of Orangeism could result in instant dismissal. But drunkenness accounted for the great majority of the dismissals. One Tipperary constable who got drunk with his prisoner was fined one month's pay. In another case, a drunken Monaghan subconstable killed an old man before being restrained by his colleagues, and then, unrepentant, announced that "there is not a popish Dog in the street I will not give the same sauce to." He was dismissed from the force and convicted of manslaughter. The use of undue force was a recurring problem. At Bantry, County Cork, the constables, "ignorant of their Duties," left prisoners to languish in jail. A Kildare subconstable convicted of assaulting a soldier was removed from the force. The Lord Lieutenant in 1823 reprimanded the entire force at Nenagh, Tipperary, for "unnecessary vigour" in making arrests. The Limerick police likewise developed a reputation for violence and sauciness. Overall, in the constabulary in 1822–4, a total of twenty constables and subconstables were indicted for assaults and five convicted; and thirteen policemen were charged with murder, eight resulting in verdicts of manslaughter. The most sensational case involved six Queen's County constables, who were convicted and sentenced to transportation for life; in another case in the county, a Chief Constable received nine months' imprisonment for shooting two persons who allegedly attacked him.[83]

Dublin Castle was not always pleased with these grand jury judgments against policemen. Gregory in 1824 was irked by the conviction of a Constable Talbot for murder. "When contrasted with the acquittal of the murderer of the Kennedys," he found the conviction shocking. "Talbot, according to popish impartiality, deserved death being not only a Policeman, but a Protestant." Yet Catholic constables apparently handled the peasantry just as roughly. As Goulburn once noted wryly, "They get too roughly handled by the Mob to be very friendly to them."[84]

Along with drink and excessive force, financial corruption was a recurring problem. In 1826 a Sligo Chief Constable absconded with a £300 payroll. Inspector-General D'Arcy was suspected in 1825 of dubious financing of police horses. The worst financial shenanigans were in Leinster and involved Inspector-General Powell and a Wexford Chief Constable. Unauthorized stoppages from constables' pay, pay lists that included nonexistent policemen, excessive charges for stationery and uniforms, and forged accounts for foraging and stabling of horses headed the list of illegal activities. "Every day brings fresh Proof of the corruptions that have been practiced," moaned the Lord Lieutenant. Chief Constable Laurence Dundas and three other "participators in the plunder" were dismissed. Inspector-General Powell, who had destroyed his central accounting book, admitted his "culpable neglect" and "gross [financial] irregularities" and was allowed quietly to resign. He was replaced as Inspector-General in March 1828 by an army colonel, Sir John Harvey, an Englishman whose previous experience included service in 1813–17 as Assistant Adjutant-General in "one of the most disturbed districts in Ireland."[85]

The troubles of 1828 led not only to stricter requirements for the appointment of policemen but to new guidelines arising from the problem of "frequent" and "sudden" resignations of constables. An act of Parliament now required the men to give one month's notice or be fined £5. To handle disciplinary problems and break local connections, the act legalized the policy of circulating subconstables, constables, and Chief Constables from county to county. The 1822 act had authorized removal of up to two-thirds of a county force, and the Inspectors-General in 1827 had gone so far as to recommend a one-year limit to any policeman's length of service in a county. The act of 1828 set no time limits but did permit the Lord Lieutenant to move an entire force from one county to another. Thus began the standard practice of rotating policemen, even those with good service records, every few years from county to county.[86]

The reforms of 1828 also tightened up records of bookkeeping. Instructions and forms were issued for everything from clothing to foraging, traveling expenses to barracks costs, correspondence to casualty counts. The Irish police quickly developed the largest bureaucracy of printed forms, reports, and orders of any force in the British Isles. So voluminous became the correspondence – 1,095 letters in 1828 from police officers to the Castle – that in 1829 a new post, secretary for the constabulary, was created.[87] But for all of the administrative changes, one major problem remained unresolved. The local magistrates of Ireland still retained the direction of the constabulary. The mountain of paperwork did nothing to stop the growing rift between local magistrates and Dublin Castle.

III. Uses and effectiveness of the constabulary

Myriad duties, uncertain allegiances

The story of the everyday duties of the constabulary in the 1820s is one of a tug-of-war between local magistrates and Dublin Castle. The men caught in the middle were the constables, especially the Chief Constables. Time and again, local magistrates commanded a police officer to do one thing while directives from the Castle or his Inspector-General instructed him to refrain or do something else.

Police duties may be divided into four general categories: (a) chase and apprehension, (b) assistance in prosecution, (c) prevention of crime, and (d) interference in civil processes. In all four areas, tension developed between local and Dublin perceptions of correct police behavior. For pursuit and arrest, in cases where a crime or breach of the peace was in the act of being committed, the law clearly authorized police interposition. For the arrest of persons suspected of having committed past offenses, the Castle insisted that policemen have written warrants issued at petty sessions, whereas many local magistrates believed that a verbal command was sufficient. Similarly, in the heat of pursuit, the police frequently found it difficult to follow regulations urging restraint and mildness in dealing with prisoners. The conduct of the men, recalled a Limerick Chief Constable, is sometimes "barbarous in the extreme ..., beating [the prisoners] with their carbines and sabres."[88]

In the prosecution of criminals, policemen frequently had to act as witnesses in court. In King's County and in Kildare in the early 1820s, virtually every serious case that resulted in conviction and transportation was based on evidence given by constables. Yet the police often also performed duties of which the Castle disapproved. In Connaught as late as 1828 they served as clerks at petty sessions, despite the repeated objections of law advisers in Dublin. In Tipperary policemen assisted at the hanging of criminals and then actually helped to dig graves for the bodies, despite loud Castle protests that it was "the duty of the Sheriff to employ Persons to perform [such duties] – the Constables merely attend for the Preservation of the Peace." Too often local authorities, for their own convenience, prostituted the police to the most petty uses even as Dublin officials remonstrated against these practices.[89]

To Castle authorities, the principal purpose of the constabulary was the prevention of crime and violence. The police therefore saw duty at elections and also, more frequently, at fairs to prevent the traditional faction fights. A Chief Constable on the spot received little help from long, general legal opinions from the Castle, or from orders (like one in 1825) from his Inspector-General requiring him to do nothing unless a JP was present. It was hard to follow advice to "abstain from every act of unnecessary harshness" when, as frequently happened, both factions united and began pelting the police with stones.[90] In one incident in Tipperary, where violence at fairs was common, Chief Constable William Percy reported that his men "behaved very steadily and with forbearance for some time" before at length firing on the crowd, killing one person. In other cases, to be sure, the constabulary might be "the aggressors in an affray."[91] Over a six-year period (1824–9), fifteen rioters but only one policeman were killed in such incidents. On occasion, police officers tried preventive tactics to minimize the violence. In Tipperary in 1827, at Toomevara, the police arrested forty-one "notorious disturbers of the Peace" before the fair began; at Thurles, the leaders of each faction were seized as they entered the town. It was difficult enough for the police to develop a sensible riot policy at fairs, but local magistrates and owners of tolls associated with the fairs complicated the situation by demanding aid in the collection of these customs. No matter that the Castle declared that this toll collecting was "wholly out of their province"; the police were nevertheless badgered by local interests to perform these tasks.[92]

The most obnoxious and most frequent police duty was the execution of civil processes. The Castle had established the constabulary as a peacekeeping force, and the local magistrates turned it into a collecting and distraining civil claims unit. "The policeman's time," a Limerick Chief Constable complained,

is continually employed in looking after those petty matters, whereby his principal duty is in a great measure overlooked.... [His time is used in] executing petty warrants; looking after a branch of a tree cut on a gentleman's hedge; seeing that the peasant's dog is logged; that their pigs have got a patent ring in their nose, &c. &c.

The problem arose because Section 32 of the 1822 Constabulary Act had abolished the remnants of the old baronial police of 1792, and nowhere in the new act was there any mention of the prohibition of police serving as a collection force. The position of the Chief Constables was made especially difficult, for Section 9 of the 1822 act enjoined them to "obey and execute all the Warrants, Orders, and Commands" of magistrates "at their Sessions or elsewhere", on pain of a fine of up to £5 for each refusal. At first Dublin Castle seems to have allowed the constabulary to aid in the collection of rents, tithes, and debts and in distraint for nonpayment. But as early as 1824, Crown legal authorities were opposing such uses except in cases of "a breach of the peace." Employment of the police "in the first instance" in civil process cases, Goulburn explained in 1825, would "defeat the great object of their institution ... the purpose for which they were established": peace-keeping and the prevention of crime.[93]

A pattern soon developed of local magistrates, through written, legal warrants at sessions, ordering parties of police to go on civil claims expeditions. The local Chief Constable would balk and write either his Inspector-General or, from 1828 on, his Subinspector; this man would then write Under-Secretary Gregory in Dublin for instructions; Gregory would then consult the Castle's legal advisers for a ruling. A few days later, if he was lucky, the Chief Constable would receive a reply, usually to the effect that he should refuse the services of his police. Depending on the persistence of the local magistrates and the tenacity of the Chief Constable, police aid might or might not be provided in a particular instance. The Castle, in its letters to local magistrates, urged them to appoint constables or other persons for the special purposes of civil collection. Dublin argued in effect for a two-tier system: the constabulary to deal with crime and violence, and a system of old-style constables, bailiffs, and subsheriffs for civil claims.[94]

Not surprisingly, the magistrates resisted this argument to create "another class of Constables." To do so would make these constables dependent for their fees on those they served with civil warrants. Such constables would be from "the lowest class of society ... [and] open to corruption and every species of Malversation in their duties, and will return the County to the state from which it emerged in the undertaking of these duties by the new Constabulary." The Castle nevertheless persisted in exhorting local magistrates "to resort to Parish Constables" or any other kinds of local collectors, since use of the constabulary would only "lead to confusion & embarrassment."[95] And so the struggle went on throughout the 1820s, with the magistrates having the advantage of being not only on the spot but also, by law, in charge of the direction of the constabulary.

Against the protests of Dublin authorities, the local magistrates sought, sometimes successfully, to use the constabulary for a great variety of routine civil matters. Magistrates wanted the new police to enforce the fish and game laws and to distrain the goods of convicted poachers. When the police refused, the justices inquired "how we are to act and how these fines are to be levied as we have no other Constables in this County since the Police were appointed." The Government's reply that they should "appoint some for the purpose of executing these ordinary warrants" was hardly practical or helpful. Likewise, on the question of police assistance in the collection of Crown revenues, "the Magistrates are at a loss to know how to proceed" without police protection. The Attorney-General was nevertheless intransigent, even impatient, in stating the official "Opinion which we have *so repeatedly* explained." Excise commissioners also clamored for protection, and Chief Constables, fearing a £20 fine *from them*, gave in on more than one occasion.[96]

Police were wanted to protect bakers' carts in Westmeath; even though "lawless banditti" had previously waylaid the wagons, the Castle ruled against providing protection. The constables were likewise barred from enforcing local Sabbath shop-closing laws, from collecting the county cess, and from clearing "nuisances" from village streets and cattle from the roads. Typical was the complaint that "it is a great hardship to be deprived" of police aid; typical, the response: "I can see no reason for making this an exception to the general order given so repeatedly."[97]

The police assistance most frequently sought was for collection of arrears of rent and tithe and distraint of goods for nonpayment. Here, too, the Castle and the county magistrates clashed. As early as 1823, the law advisers in Dublin opposed loans of police unless physical resistance occurred. The High Sheriff of Limerick, who was "sorry to be so troublesome," informed Gregory that his "Situation has become truly alarming by reason of the opinion Conveyed in your letters.... If acted upon, I can with perfect safety state that the [Sub-] Sheriff's life and property are endangered." In Galway, the sheriff reported that it was "a matter of general Notoriety" that whenever his subsheriff, Andrew Mullery, distrained the goods of the peasantry without an armed guard, he was lucky to escape with his life. To Dublin's policy of police assistance only after resistance, the Sheriff replied: "In other words, that his [Mullery's] *Successor* in the office be supported upon *his Demise*, for that his own death would result ... [is] of little Doubt." The physical consequences of Castle policy were seen in an incident in Clare in 1825. Seventy men armed with "pitchforks, sticks, stones, &c." set upon a half-dozen distrainers, cutting two of them "so dreadfully ... about their heads from repeated blows of a pitchfork" that one was killed and the other not expected to live.[98]

Collection and distraint for tithe arrears was the second major subject of controversy between the Castle and the magistrates. The law stated that only in cases of "forcible resistance actually made," or where proven by legal testimony of a previous breach of the peace, could the police assist in tithe-collecting expeditions. A Limerick Chief Constable has given us a vivid picture of heavily armed policemen distraining a pig, a woman's old clothes, and other property for nonpayment of rent and tithe. But his memoirs, published in 1831, do not indicate whether these scenes occurred before or during the Tithe War of 1830–3. In the early years, magistrates appear to have employed police protection. In Cork in 1823 the magistrates were "in the Habit of" using police, since "in no Parish in the County ... is there any Constable except those under last year's act." As one man asked, "What is the Tythe-owner to do when he has obtained the Magistrates' decree?" In west Cork one wealthy tithe owner, Rev. Robert Morritt, rector and vicar of Castlehaven, had since 1820 been able to collect most of his annual tithe income of £900. In July 1823, in what became a celebrated incident at Castlehaven, Morritt employed eleven police on a tithe-collecting expedition. The venture led to an affray culminating in four deaths, including that of one policeman, no collection, and a government investigation and reprimand. In Clare later that year, a tithe owner resident in Tipperary revived a tithe claim that had lain dormant for twenty years; a collecting party, with ten policemen along, triggered a brawl that ended in one peasant's death.[99]

The evidence for 1824–8 indicates Castle intransigence on police loans and recurrent problems in tithe collection. From west Cork in November 1824, a tithe farmer's widow with eight children reported her frustrations in trying to collect even a portion of the £1,000 owed her in tithe arrears. Bailiffs and their assistants were repeatedly and "severely beaten ... and the Decrees taken forceably from them." No one could now be found to execute the legal decrees. Everyone was "in terror of their lives, ... and the police will not interfere, nor will the Magistrates direct that they may accompany the Bailiffs, or take any part therein." In a single barony in Cavan in 1825, a total of 150 decrees for tithe arrears were reported to be uncollectable, for the "Baronial Constables have been superseded by the Constabulary Police," and the constabulary refused to act. Churchwardens and other local collectors were "so frequently beaten that no persons can now be procured." The result, concluded the petitioners, was that their tithe income was "likely to become wholly unproductive." In Carlow in 1828, when twenty policemen provided a rare escort to a tithe-viewing expedition, the peasants mounted a tumultuous opposition and the party was forced to retreat. The Irish Chief Secretary admonished the Chief Constable and added, "The People have just cause of Complaint." In many other cases, the Castle warned its officers of the illegality of accompanying tithe expeditions.[100]

The effect of Dublin Castle's policy on police assistance is hard to gauge. Much depended on the willingness of the magistrates to abide by the law as laid down by the Castle; much depended on the sympathies of the Chief Constable, or even his Subinspector, over whom the provincial Inspector-General and Castle authorities kept a close eye. In some places, Castle policy, when enforced, meant an easing of the peasants' lot; in many others, the frequency of admonishing letters from Dublin Castle no doubt reflected a local disregard for policy and the illegal employment of police. It is clear, however, that in 1824–8 the Castle tried to make it difficult for the local magistrates to convert the peacekeeping constabulary into a force for the collection of civil claims.

But the demands on the constabulary were incessant. Already in 1829 we find a hint of the weakening of the Castle's position. In response to a familiar query from Major Miller in Munster, Crown Law Adviser Richard Greene replied:

The Execution of Warrants of this Nature are [sic] not properly part of the Constables' duties. If however he [sic] does act in obedience to them, he should distrain 1.

Between sun rise and sun set; 2. Only the goods of the debt; 3. Not a second time under the same warrant; 4. Not to sell but to deliver up to the Magistrates [the goods]; 5. Not to break open an outer door, even in case of penalties payable to the Crown.[101]

This opinion represented the beginning of a major shift in policy. In 1830–3 the Irish Government would reverse many of its directives of the 1820s. The "Tithe War" would be the product not only of a massive peasant boycott of payment but also of the Government's greatly intensified support for collection.

Decline of the Yeomanry and Peelers

One measure of the effectiveness of the constabulary was its growth. The constabulary expanded from a force of 4,792 men by the end of 1824 to 5,541 four years later and 5,940 by 1830. The force included 226 Chief Constables and, from 1828 on, 33 Subinspectors. These officers were mounted and each attended by one or two horse constables. All the rest of the men were dismounted or foot constables and subconstables. In 1830, the constabulary was working out of a total of 1,143 police stations scattered every few miles across the countryside with a half-dozen men at each post.[102]

The development of a police force of this size made it possible for the Government to abandon any reliance on the two older peacekeeping forces, the Yeomanry and the Peace Preservation Police. The Yeomanry, which was judged both "useless" and "a very perilous force against domestic tumult," came to be totally neglected. Whereas the Government had placed fifty-seven corps on duty in 1819–22, only four Wexford corps were used in 1823, and for the remainder of the decade not a single corps was ever called out.[103]

The Government's policy in 1822–4 was to replace the Peelers with the new constables. With the establishment of county police forces, most Peelers, as we have seen, simply became constables under Goulburn's Constabulary Act. From its zenith of 2,326 men in sixteen counties in late 1822, the Peace Preservation Police shrank in only two and a half years to 481 men in three counties. By the spring of 1828, there were only 330 Peelers; and by the end of 1829, 107.

The last big transformation came in 1824 when in Galway, Clare, Westmeath, Roscommon, and Donegal the Peelers were replaced with constabulary. In 1825 the Peelers existed only in Tipperary, Cork, and the County and City of Limerick. At the end of that year, the Government disbanded the force of 152 Peelers in four northeastern baronies in Cork. Fourteen years after their introduction, the Tipperary force, already reduced to 205 men in ten baronies, was disbanded in November 1828. Chief Magistrate Edward Wilson, after forty years of service beginning with the Dublin police in 1788, retired on a well-deserved pension. This left the Peace Preservation Police only in the County and City of Limerick. George Drought continued to lead the Limerick City police, which in May 1828 had been reduced from fifty to forty men; and T. P. Vokes remained in charge of the seventy-four Peelers, cut to sixty-seven in December 1829, who were assigned to assist the constabulary in the County of Limerick. These 107 men kept alive the police tradition established by Peel in 1814, but Goulburn's constabulary of 5,500 men now clearly bore the brunt of peacekeeping duties.[104]

For some Peelers, the end of police service portended a bleak future. In the Tipperary demobilization of November 1828, Major Miller transferred to the Munster constabulary "all who could possibly be admitted ... and even stretched a point" for some deserving veteran constables. But those who could not qualify for the constabulary – men who were less than literate or who were in poor health or far over the age ceiling of forty – now faced unemployment, and many realized their own unemployability. Records that have survived from the Tipperary disbanding not only reveal the men's desperation but provide a rare glimpse into the backgrounds of the policemen.

Subconstable Francis McGuire soon found work as a parish schoolmaster, but his Peeler background earned him the "deadly hatred" of the local people and he was forced to resign. The Government then tried to place him in a teaching post with the Society for the Education of the Poor of Ireland.

Subconstable Bernard Develin, a native of County Tyrone, had served in the militia and from 1814 in the 16th Regiment (infantry). He had joined Magistrate Wilson's Peelers in 1823. Unable to read or write and "worn out" from long service, Develin asked upon his release that "so old a Servant of the Government ... [not be] thrown begging on the World with a large Family."

Subconstable Lewis Gunning had joined the 3rd Regiment (infantry) in 1795, served in the West Indies, Canada, and Wellesley's Peninsular campaign, and "arrived at Waterloo a few days too late." Discharged in England in 1816, he had joined Willcocks's Middlethird force in 1821. Gunning wrote in 1828 that he had "suffered heardships and fatagues ... these last 7 Years ... from the sevear colds and heats"; he was now fifty years old, with a wife and four children, "bred to no trade," and too infirm "to work at Daily labour."

Subconstable John Lennon served the longest of any Tipperary Peeler. A native of Armagh and an eleven-year army veteran, Lennon had signed on with Willcocks in Middlethird in January 1815. In 1828 he was over fifty years old, "worn out" by injuries, rheumatism, and "the hardships of the Insurrection Act," and was now "incapable of any further exertion ... [and] thrown begging on the world in his old age."

In January 1829 local magistrates in Tipperary, meeting in Clonmel, voted an undetermined amount of "remuneration" (whether a gratuity or a pension is unspecified) to veteran Peelers, but whether McGuire, Develin, Gunning, and Lennon received any compensation is not known. An 1832 parliamentary return of 174 "superannuated" constables does include the name of John Lennon, pensioned by the Government at £15, 4s., 2d., for disability "by severe chronic rheumatism."[105]

As the Yeomanry was becoming irrelevant, the Peace Preservation Police disappearing, and the constabulary growing ("it may be indefinitely augmented," Goulburn exulted in 1824), it is significant that the force levels of the British army in Ireland were not being reduced. In the period 1822–9 the cavalry stabilized at about 2,000 men and the infantry at about 18,000;

total army levels never dropped below 19,600 or rose above 21,400. In November 1823, in the aftermath of a slave revolt in the British West Indies, Home Secretary Peel queried Goulburn about "the probabilities" that the presence of the new constabulary would allow Ireland to get by with "a smaller military force." The Chief Secretary's reply was unambiguous:

I do not think that Ireland could for some time to come be left with less than from twenty to twenty-one thousand men which is about the number we have at present.... I do not consider that the Police force is likely to relieve you for some time to come from the necessity of keeping up a considerable military force.[106]

The constabulary was judged to be "a substitute for the old civil force" and "for the Peelers, ... not for the Military." Nevertheless, a civil force of more than 5,000 armed policemen stationed at more than 1,000 barracks did permit, in a time of relative tranquility, the withdrawal of troop detachments from many outposts. A military officer reported that "since the establishment of the Police, the Troops are certainly much less liable to be called upon than formerly." The new reliance on a sizable police even enabled the Irish Government to meet Peel's request in 1826 for two infantry regiments to help repress strikes and disturbances in the North of England.[107]

Assessing the constabulary's impact on crime

Although the constabulary did replace the Yeomanry and the Peelers for peacekeeping purposes, its effectiveness in reducing crime in Ireland is more difficult to measure. Goulburn, Wellesley, and Peel believed that the new police played a large role in restoring peace after 1824; Inspector-General Willcocks cited the effects of not only the constabulary but also the Insurrection Act (which expired in 1825), the revised magistracy and the new system of petty sessions, tithe composition, and Daniel O'Connell's Catholic Association, which discouraged agrarian violence. The presence of the new police at least served notice of the Government's intention to enforce the law. "Almost in every section of a few thousand acres in the Province," Inspector-General Powell wrote of Leinster, "we have posts occupied by the Constabulary.... I look upon the Establishment in the posts they hold as forming the skeleton of an occupying army upon which the well disposed ... rally and communicate with."[108]

The official Irish criminal statistics give some support to the statements of Dublin Castle officials. From 1822 we have for the first time returns to Parliament of *national* totals of committals that differentiate (some five dozen) types of offenses. The number of persons charged with criminal offenses in Ireland in 1822 was nearly four times greater than in 1812, and the conviction rate was up from one-third to one-half of those committed. From 1822 to 1828, a period when the constabulary spread across the island and grew in size, the national committal totals stayed relatively constant (15,000–18,000), but conviction rates for all crimes continued to show a fairly steady increase (Table 7.2). The figures indicate that the new constables were quite effective in apprehending offenders for ordinary crimes such as common assault and

Table 7.2. *Crime in Ireland, 1822–8*

	All offenses		Murder/ manslaughter		Riotous assembly armed by night and attacking dwelling houses	
	I	II	I	II	I	II
1805	3,600	16.9%	...		...	
...						
1812	4,386	33.2	...		...	
Ave/yr.						
1805–12	*3,820*	*22.0*				
...						
1822	15,251	49.6	458	32.3	325	22.2
1823	14,632	49.8	384	30.2	149	18.8
1824	15,258	50.7	504	28.2	127	22.0
1825	15,515	55.2	422	28.2	84	17.9
1826	16,318	53.4	530	27.2	81	24.7
1827	18,031	55.6	522	30.8	134	26.9
1828	14,683	63.1	423	33.6	72	45.8
Ave./Yr.						
1822–8	*15,669*	*53.9*	*463*	*30.0*	*139*	*23.7*

Note: No published national totals for specific offenses are available for the years before 1822.
Key: I Number of persons charged with criminal offenses and committed to jail for trial.
    II Percentage conviction rate.

simple riot. Committals for "assault" rose steadily from an annual average of 3,503 in 1822–3 to 4,961 in 1827–8; for "riotous assembly" the average leaps from 303 a year in 1822–3 to 610 in 1825–6 and 929 in 1827–8. For these minor offenses, convictions came in three of every four cases.

Compared to 1813–22, the period of the middle and late 1820s was quiet in terms of agrarian crime. Annual committals for typical "Whiteboy" offenses – riotous assembly armed by night and attacking dwelling houses (972 *total* cases, 1822–8), administering and taking illegal oaths (370), shooting at persons (283), writing or sending "threatening letters" (121), and houghing and maiming cattle (76) – followed a generally downward trend, in some cases sharply so. It is tempting to credit the constabulary, seemingly ubiquitous and increasingly numerous, with an initial burst of preventive policing that deterred crime (though, by this reasoning, the police certainly did not deter assault and simple riot). More likely it was other factors, social and economic, that held down the number of major protest offenses because, after 1830, these would swell *despite* the presence of an ever-larger police force.

On one part of the criminal justice system, one largely beyond their control, the constabulary continued to have little impact. The Whiteboy system of terror against juries "is not yet removed," Inspector-General Powell reported in 1825, "where a conviction against the Rockite system is attempted." Those few persons who did testify had to be protected by the Government and "consequently never can again return to their own Country."[109] Although the incidence of serious agrarian crime abated in 1824–8, the rate of convictions stayed low, indeed showed no improvement over the decade. In the period 1822–8, when the conviction rate for non-agrarian crimes was rising (the average rate for *all* crimes was 54 percent), the average rate for agrarian offenses remained substantially lower: riotous assembly armed by night and attacking dwelling houses (24 percent), oath taking (21 percent), shooting at persons (14 percent), threatening letters (7 percent), and houghing and maiming cattle (16 percent). Over this same period some 1,497 persons were charged with rape – a crime in Ireland not infrequently associated with protest – but only 71 were convicted (5 percent).

The new county police also found themselves unable to do anything about the homicide rate, which actually increased slightly (an annual average of 442 committals in 1822–5 and 474 in 1825–8). A total of 2,590 persons were charged with *murder* (as distinct from manslaughter) from 1822 to 1828. Only 429 were found guilty – a 17 percent conviction rate. The subject was a frustrating one for the constabulary, for premeditated homicide, a crime notoriously difficult to deter in any society, was also particularly hard to prosecute to conviction in early-nineteenth-century Ireland. "If this behaviour on the part of juries spreads," noted an innocent Chief Secretary only recently arrived in Ireland, then "there is an end of justice in the country." The difficulty lay in the prevalence of agrarian-related homicides. In a case in Limerick in 1824 involving "the murder of a husband by a wife and her paramour," remarked Crown Counsel Matthew Barrington, "there was no great difficulty in getting witnesses to come forward; but in the murder of Major Going, *or any case of that nature*, there has been a great difficulty." Overall, the murder rate in Ireland continued to be alarmingly high and the contrast to England stark. In 1826–8, 1,143 persons in Ireland were charged with murder compared to 205 in England: Relative to population, the incidence of murder in England (based on committals) was only one-tenth that in Ireland. Over these same three years, in London, a city of 1.5 million inhabitants, only 40 persons were charged with murder: a per capita rate one-sixth that of Ireland.[110]

In one year, 1828, crime across Ireland did fall dramatically. Compared to the previous year, committals for all offenses declined by one-fifth. The number of persons charged with homicide also fell by a fifth, and the number of those charged with armed assembly by night and attacks on houses dropped by half. In traditionally disturbed Tipperary and Limerick, total committals in 1828 declined by 31 and 37 percent, respectively. In that year, nationwide, there were impressive jumps in conviction rates for total offenses and even for some Whiteboy crimes. This one-year drop in crime was not the result of the constabulary's sudden effectiveness but rather, in large part, an impressive demonstration of the force of public opinion. Throughout

1828 Daniel O'Connell, in his pursuit of Catholic Emancipation, asked the people for peace and good order. The committal statistics suggest that many persons, not least the Whiteboys, heeded the Liberator's call.

IV. Catholic Emancipation and the constabulary

Against the single dominating issue of Irish politics in the last half of the 1820s the constabulary was of little use. Until about 1825 the threat to order in Ireland had been agrarian turbulence: This was the setting in which first the Peelers and then the constabulary had been established. But the rise of Daniel O'Connell's Catholic Association, with its tactics of nonviolence and moral suasion, presented an entirely new kind of challenge. Not since the orderly intimidation of the Irish Volunteers of 1778–82 had English ministers had to grapple with such a gossamer adversary. "I never knew more tranquillity than exists [now]," observed one landlord in 1825.

At the same time ... there is a sort of violent agitation of mind that I never saw equalled ... [and is] I think a great deal more dangerous than any night walking, or any of that folly and nonsense that went under the name of ribbonmen and whiteboys, &c.... The whole body of the population are joined heart and hand with this Catholic Association.[111]

The story of this remarkable Association has been frequently told. In order to extract William Pitt's promise, vetoed in 1800 by George III, of Catholic representation in the Imperial Parliament in London, the Catholic lawyer Daniel O'Connell organized Ireland's priests and peasantry in a nationwide campaign to win "Emancipation." Funded by penny-a-month contributions to a "Catholic rent" (£52,300 were raised by 1829), and employing the nonviolent pressures of frequent meetings, burgeoning committees in the "little country towns and country villages," and a blitz of handbills and pamphlets "read by one individual to a great many," the Association grew rapidly and advanced dangerous new doctrines of Catholic self-worth, independence, and assertiveness. A Protestant nobleman gloomily reported: "The People say they have only just learned their Rights."[112]

The movement's specific goal was to change British law so that Catholic voters, enfranchised in 1793, could elect Catholic Members of Parliament. No peasant subsisting on a few acres of potatoes could, of course, in his wildest fantasies imagine himself in the House of Commons. But he resented the exclusion of his higher-class coreligionists; moreover, as O'Connell remarked, the peasant wanted his children to enjoy the rights denied to him. A Catholic bishop explained the lower orders' perception of Emancipation: "They perhaps would not be able to define it, but they have a feeling that they are belonging to an excluded cast[e].... They are anxious to be relieved from this kind of slavery, which they are not able to explain."[113]

Unlike in England where the lower orders were widely disenfranchised, in Ireland more than 100,000 40-shilling freeholders had the vote. Should these men rebel and cast their ballots not as their landlords told them but as they wanted, the results for Ascendancy Ireland would be disastrous. There had been occasional defections before 1826, but it was in the County Waterford election of that year that the new power of an aroused Catholic Ireland was first demonstrated. Weeks of planning paid off with the Association's defeat of the Ascendancy candidate by a voting margin of almost three to one. Inspector-General Willcocks, in reports to Under-Secretary Gregory, commented on the highly unusual orderliness and sobriety of the electors as they marched in military array to the polls. Even more impressively, in Louth, Monaghan, Westmeath, Armagh, Cork City, and County Dublin, pro-Emancipation candidates were elected with little propaganda or preparation by the Association. Home Secretary Peel realized in July that "a darker cloud than ever seems to me to impend over Ireland."[114]

Throughout 1827, the year before the final push by O'Connell's Catholic Association, the British Government was in disarray. Following Lord Liverpool's forced resignation due to a paralytic stroke in February, George Canning and Viscount Goderich each tussled for four months with the Prime Minister's post. In April Goulburn and Peel went out of office; Wellesley, though eager to leave Ireland, agreed to stay on through December. The Irish chief secretaryship fell to William Lamb (afterward Viscount Melbourne), who served for only fifteen months, and then, in June 1828, to Lord Francis Leveson Gower, who would serve through July 1830. Ministerial stability in England returned in January 1828 with the prime ministry of "the Iron Duke," Arthur Wellesley, Duke of Wellington, who named Goulburn his Chancellor of the Exchequer and restored Peel to the Home Office.[115]

To the lord lieutenancy of Ireland the Duke appointed his former cavalry commander, the sixty-three-year-old 1st Marquess of Anglesey, who had won honors and lost a leg at Waterloo. A pro-Emancipationist, Anglesey soon became the darling of the Catholics and conducted his administration with beneficence. Wellington, however, was increasingly upset by what he saw as the drift toward rebellion; in December 1828, on the eve of Emancipation, he would recall his old friend from Ireland. Lord Lieutenant Anglesey was at first not pleased with Leveson Gower's appointment as Chief Secretary, for the twenty-eight-year-old son of the Marquess of Stafford had only a mediocre literary and political reputation; nevertheless, their shared leaning to the Catholic cause and the young Chief Secretary's capacity for hard work and guidance from Peel soon made the Irish Administration less awkward than the old general had feared.[116]

In 1828 O'Connell brought the Irish crisis to a head when, in July, he offered himself to the electors of County Clare and was returned with two-thirds of the vote. The people had legally elected a Catholic, who, by law, could not take his seat in the House of Commons. At the polls in Ennis, the county town that 40,000 peasants (a number "beyond calculation," in Anglesey's words) had peaceably occupied, all was "Order – Obedience to the Laws – perfect sobriety." Throughout the south and west, on a dozen occasions in 1828, tens of thousands marched silently and impressively for

Emancipation. The Catholic Association kept the Whiteboys inactive, stopped the traditional faction fights at fairs, and avoided any show of physical force that would invite repression. "The Country is quiet," noted Anglesey. "But alas! for how long & for what good, if emancipation is not soon granted?"[117]

The unnatural tranquility only perplexed an Irish Government long used to agrarian turmoil. Leveson Gower recorded his frustration with "the novelty of meetings unattended with violence and not enlivened with intoxication." Goulburn had perceptively observed in 1826 that O'Connell sought to "keep up irritation and hostility to the highest possible pitch short of actual violence and to hope by intimidation to carry every thing he looks for." Two years later, on the eve of the Clare election, Anglesey asked in desperation: "Where is the Man who can tell me how to suppress it? They will carry their cause by increasing Agitation and by intimidation, without coming to blows. I believe their success inevitable, that no power under Heaven can arrest its progress."[118]

Puzzled and helpless before this new kind of challenge to its authority, and sympathetic to the Emancipationists' aims if not their methods, the Irish Government kept the constabulary from any collision with the people. Police stayed in their barracks to avoid provocation; other parties in uniform were kept nearby, but out of sight of the monster meetings. Still others moved incognito "in coloured Clothes mixed with the Crowd." But their reports were always the same: no plots, no crime, "no breach of the peace . . . in this immense multitude." A contemporary noted that the authorities "feel their weakness [and] know the slippery ground they stand on."[119]

By the late summer of 1828 the long-delayed Protestant reaction began. Hard-line Protestants, the Orangemen, were "almost in a state of frenzy," reported Anglesey. "They feel their cause is going down" and are "anxious for any mischief" rather than let the Catholic question be "quietly settled."[120] They formed Brunswick Clubs complete with subscriptions for a "Protestant rent"; by the end of the year, clubs existed in 148 towns and 26 counties.[121] The greatest threat of violence came not from the Catholic Association but from the confrontation between aroused Catholics and the now defensive Protestants. Had the Government wished to push Ireland over the edge – from agitation to rebellion and thus military repression – it would have permitted the two groups to fight it out. But the correspondence of Anglesey and Leveson Gower, and even of Wellington and Peel, reveals just the opposite. A government proclamation of 2 October, to which O'Connell gave his assent, banned all political meetings and processions. In Ulster, the constabulary intervened time and again to prevent affrays between Protestants and Catholics. A day-long brawl did devastate the town of Augher in County Tyrone, but the military and police were able to prevent a battle at Ballybay, Monaghan. Elsewhere in the disturbed North, the actions of the Government were similarly restrained and impartial.[122]

From the time of the Clare election, in July 1828, the army in Ireland was in the hands of the ablest military man in the British Isles. General Sir John

Byng had previously "conducted himself . . . with great prudence, firmness, and moderation" as commander of the Northern District in England (1816–28). But Byng's brilliance, and the restrained policies of military officers like (Londonderry-born) Maj.-Gen. Sir William Thornton, who prevented bloodletting at Ballybay, were overshadowed by a larger question: the reliability of the forces of order in Ireland. The basic problem was that two of every five men in the constabulary and at least half of the soldiers were Catholics. The Inspector-General of Connaught, Major Warburton, had in July informed his old friend and now Home Secretary, Robert Peel, that "the split in Irish society was . . . visibly affecting even the police . . ., and that implicit reliance could not permanently be placed on their continued loyalty and discipline."[123] Months later, in April 1829, after the crisis had passed, Peel would reflect that the constabulary and military, assigned to "watching the movements of tens of thousands of disciplined fanatics, . . . [would] no doubt do their duty, but is it consistent with common prudence and common sense to . . . incur such risk of contagion?" Anglesey, Byng, and Wellington were all troubled by "the large proportion" of Irish Catholics not only in the Irish but in English regiments. From July 1828 on, the Lord Lieutenant requested that only Scottish regiments be sent to Ireland, for these were composed entirely of Scotsmen.[124]

The fear of rebellion in Ireland led the Government to mobilize the necessary army of repression. In the autumn of 1828, in addition to drilling the regular army in Ireland, all disposable troops in Britain – six regiments of infantry and two of cavalry – were massed along the west coast at Liverpool, Bristol, and Glasgow, ready for immediate embarkation to Ireland. Two regiments were brought over in October. The rest were never used.[125]

The leading English ministers, Wellington and Peel, chose to conciliate, not coerce. Both were essentially practical men; since at least early 1828, they had recognized the inevitable in Ireland. In August, Wellington had sent the King a private memorandum on the absolute necessity of granting Emancipation. Indeed, by the end of the year, the only remaining obstacle was George IV: He was finally won over in February and on 13 April, 1829 the great bill became law.[126]

In retrospect, it may be said that the Irish masses, organized in an unprecedented movement of national solidarity, had pushed the British Government to the edge of the cliff: concession or a resort to force. Had the latter course been chosen, remarked Leveson Gower, "civil war would have been inevitable and interminable." Peel knew that the choice was "between different kinds and . . . degrees of evil": compromise on principle or "incessant agitation in Ireland." He was painfully aware that "the Roman Catholics have discovered their strength," that the crisis of 1825–9 had ended with a victory for the Irish masses.[127]

Peel also realized that the Government's obligation now was to reassert its diminished authority: "Can we forget what happened in 1782, what happened in 1793? . . . Let us beware that we do not teach them how easy it will be to paralyze the Government and the Law." The Home Secretary further feared the consequences of Emancipation in England and worried about the capacity of the overworked military to keep the lid on protests in both countries. For the last six months, he noted in February 1829, "five-sixths" of the foot soldiers in the United Kingdom had been committed to Ireland, being either in that country or poised on the west coast of Britain. For how long, wondered Peel, could the English Government be expected to commit this proportion of troops to Ireland? "I consider . . . such an application of military force much worse than open rebellion. . . . If this be the state of things at present, let me implore you to consider what would be the fate of England in the event of war?"[128]

War would come, though in the form of a "Tithe War" in Ireland and a crisis in England over the extension of suffrage. Catholic Emancipation, two scholars have noted, had three principal results: It rescued British rule in Ireland; it provided Englishmen with "an object-lesson in the effectiveness of mass action from below"; and it led to the collapse of Wellington's Government. Tory rule, with the party split apart on the question of Catholic rights, gave way to Earl Grey's Whig Government in November 1830, "and the country knew that Parliamentary Reform would be pressed forward at last."[129]

But before he left office, Robert Peel gave his country an important legacy. The former Irish Chief Secretary pressed ahead in 1829 with his proposal for the establishment of a powerful police in London. Peel introduced his metropolitan police bill in April, the same month that the Catholic Emancipation Act passed. Five months later, the new police were patrolling the streets of London. In at least one important part of England in 1830–2, the disorders swirling around suffrage reform would be controlled by means other than military force.

CHAPTER 8

Anglicizing the Peelers:
the London police of 1829

I believe we are improving here, at least I hope so; I shall be so
familiarized to murder and robbery, if I remain here much longer, that I
shall never be reconciled to an uninteresting state of tranquillity....
  – Robert Peel, Chief Secretary, Dublin, February 1814

... What a difference between Great Britain and Ireland. It frequently
happens that a day passes without a single letter to the Secretary of State.
  – Robert Peel, Home Secretary, London, December 1822

During the summer months of 1829, Peel was closeted almost daily with
the Commissioners, planning and drafting the detail of the new
organization. There is no doubt that Peel brought to the conferences ideas
which were the product of his experience in reforming the police of
Ireland when he was Chief Secretary.... Records of their deliberations
are almost non-existent, but the idea that the New Police Force was to be
as unmilitary and as wholly civilian ... as it was possible to make it
seems to have been suggested during the course of the discussions and not
before they began.
  – Charles Reith, *British Police and the Democratic Ideal* (1943)

The Metropolitan Police ... are very much a law to themselves, with
their own large bureaucracy at New Scotland Yard.... Ever since Peel
set them up, they have been directly under the home secretary, who
appoints the commissioner.... The commissioner himself is in a position
of almost unique personal power. He is difficult to control, almost
impossible to sack, and subject to inspection by no one....
  – Anthony Sampson, *The New Anatomy of Britain* (1971)

In the course of the 1820s the Englishman's image of Paddy had been
substantially modified: Whiteboy assassin was now orderly demonstrator.
That Irish papists could conduct nonviolent mass meetings was remarkable
enough. More importantly, the Irish Emancipation campaign served to
legitimate English workers' use of the same tactic back in 1816–19. Surely, if
Paddy engaged in mass moral force, free-born Englishmen had the same
right. After the crackdown at Peterloo, popular radicalism in England ebbed
temporarily, but it did not disappear. Economic depression in the North in
1825–6 stimulated a rash of strikes and, subsequently, revival of the demand

277

for universal suffrage. Paddy's fight for Emancipation in 1826–9 only egged on English workingmen to demand redress of their own grievances.

If Ireland, surprisingly, offered a model of nonviolent protest, it also now furnished a model for the means of repression. But for Englishmen of all ranks, the very idea of a government-controlled national constabulary remained political anathema. It was in part because of this *fear* of the Irish example that English policing in town and country would remain rudimentary and unreformed. Faced with disorders in the extensive northern manufacturing districts, local authorities responded with a laxness that verged on negligence. The Home Office would continue, reluctantly, to resort to military intervention and military officers, irritably, to complain about having to do the work of the civil power.

Frustrated in his hopes for establishing any sort of effective provincial police, the new Home Secretary, Robert Peel, would be successful in planting a new police in London. There the vastness of the metropolis and the multiplicity of its local jurisdictions seemed to *require* a basic change in the methods of policing. Peel's years at Dublin Castle had taught him the virtues of centralization. A single overarching police authority had been necessary for Ireland; he was convinced it was equally necessary for "the infernal wen." The nature of crime and of protest was, of course, different in the English capital. Peel realized that he would have to anglicize his gendarmerie: To issue firearms would be unnecessary and provocative. Nevertheless, Peel's police would in its early years prove to be as controversial among Londoners, especially the working classes, as his Peelers had been among Irishmen, especially the lower peasantry, a decade and a half earlier.

I. Continuing turmoil in the Northern District

If the centers of disturbance in Ireland were in the south and west, in England they lay among the teeming new industrial towns and villages in the northern counties, especially Lancashire and western Yorkshire. If in agrarian Ireland a trigger to that country's disorders was the high and steady unemployment, in provincial England in the 1820s it was the periodic unemployment characteristic of the new industrial districts. "The great cause of apprehension is not in the disaffection," Home Secretary Peel wrote to Irish Chief Secretary Goulburn during the depression of 1825–7, "but in the real distress of the manufacturing Districts. There is as much forbearance as it is possible to expect from so much suffering."[1]

The suffering was intensified by the doubling of the population in only two decades in Manchester (1821 pop.: 126,000) and in the new industrial towns – Bolton (32,000), Bradford (26,000), Blackburn (22,000), Macclesfield (21,000), Rochdale (13,000), and Burnley (8,000). In 1826, waves of rioting, attacks on factories, and machine breaking swept through these towns and others as far away as Norwich and Carlisle. The crowds blamed the distress on the new power looms for textile weaving; in one week in the spring, rioters destroyed 1,000 looms around Manchester. At Bolton and

Bradford several rioters were killed in clashes with the troops. To the north, at Newcastle and Sunderland, striking seamen contributed to the unrest. "Their great hope now," reported the general in charge of the disturbed districts, "is a disturbance in Ireland, which could cause the Troops to be withdrawn from Lancashire."[2] But Ireland was quiet; indeed, two regiments were shipped to England. Home Secretary Peel responded to the crisis by sending in the traditional military reinforcements, permitting the importation of agricultural staples at lowered duties, and contributing £60,000 in Treasury funds to supplement local relief efforts. Finally, the English poor, unlike the Irish, enjoyed the meager comfort of tapping the Poor Laws.[3]

The Government was fortunate in the 1820s to have a general like Sir John Byng in command of the restive Northern District. In his shrewdness and impartiality, his firmness combined with sympathy for the springs of the discontent, Byng was the counterpart of his Irish contemporary, Richard Willcocks, Inspector-General of Constabulary for Munster. Son of Major George Byng, MP for County Middlesex, and the great grandson of Adm. Sir George Byng, John Byng had entered the army as an ensign in 1793 and served in several continental campaigns under Col. Arthur Wellesley. In 1797 Captain Byng was sent to Ireland, where he was caught up in (and wounded during) the suppression of the Rebellion. From 1805 on, Byng was back on the Continent; promoted to colonel in 1810 and then to major-general in 1813, he served under Wellington in the Peninsula and at Waterloo. After the war, General Byng directed part of the Allied army of occupation in France. In 1816 Byng was recalled to command the Eastern District, where he performed so effectively in suppressing the "East Anglia Rising" that he was promoted to the command of the Northern District. In 1819, as senior military officer at Manchester, Byng watched with horror the outrage of Peterloo. Promoted to lieutenant-general in 1825, he would retain the Northern command until 1828, when he was named commander-in-chief of the army in Ireland.[4]

Troops! more troops!

The Northern District embraced eleven counties from the Scottish border to the Midland counties of Leicestershire and Nottinghamshire. By the summer of 1826 almost 8,000 soldiers, one-quarter of the army in England, were stationed in the district, mostly in Lancashire and Yorkshire (see Table 8.1). This was five times the number there in 1822–3 and approximated the size of the army of occupation in 1819–20. In the crisis of 1812 the army of the North had reached the then unheard-of level of 2,500 men; in the years *after* the crisis of 1826, troop levels would remain at double that number.

This influx in 1826 of thousands of troops created great logistical difficulties. In the absence of inland permanent barracks, the choice was either quartering the men among the inhabitants or renting temporary barracks. Often accommodations were not suitable, or too expensive, or not available at a moment's notice.[5] But in the 1820s there were other more important

Table 8.1. *Army force levels in the Northern District and in England and Wales, 1822–9*

Year	Northern District	England and Wales	Percent in North
1822	1,730	18,200	9%
1823	1,490	18,100	8
1824	2,160	18,900	11
1825	2,400	25,900	9
1826			
Apr.–June	4,340	30,200	14
July–Sept.	7,950	30,100	26
Oct.–Dec.	7,340[a]	29,800	25
1827	5,620	26,200	22
1828	4,690	25,700	18
1829	5,590	22,000	25

Note: For 1826, three-month averages of force levels on the first of each month; for all other years, average of force levels in April, August, and December.
[a] Peaks at 8,630 in October 1826; 29 percent of the army was in the Northern District.

reasons against billeting. Popular radicalism posed a threat to the integrity of the military. General Sir Herbert Taylor in London talked of "the danger of [soldiers] . . ., many of them Recruits, being tampered with by designing and mischievous Persons, . . . [I]t is not reasonable to expose young Soldiers removed from the immediate Superintendence of their officers." Byng himself was "glad that it is decided to have Temporary Barracks as without them – from exposure to constant drunkenness and perhaps seduction – I had fears for the Discipline of the Troops in the coming Winter." Barracks living ensured that the soldiers could "exercise together and not become too intimate in the Towns." Whenever quartering took the place of barracking, the Home Office was not pleased. Under-Secretary Henry Hobhouse in February 1827 reprimanded Colonel Ellison at Brigg for "this Evil . . ., the contamination of the Troops," and ordered the men at once to be "removed from the temptations to which at present they are subject." Hobhouse could not refrain from pointing out the absurdity of the situation: The soldiers were "constantly associating with the very Individuals whose Conduct in the first Instance induced the Magistrates to request the presence of the Military."[6]

Unlike in Ireland, the cost of this policing was paid by the Treasury. The Home Office judged it "inexpedient under the existing circumstances to squabble with the residents or local authorities as to the Expense of Rent. . . . It is desireable to keep the rate payers in good humour." There was to be no tax on disturbed districts. Again, unlike the situation in Ireland, the policing was only temporary. By the spring of 1828 soldiers had been withdrawn on a staggered schedule from temporary barracks at Oldham, Bury, Clitheroe, Accrington, Haslingden, Bradford, and Halifax; the troops were now concentrated in barracks at Bolton and Blackburn, "which are the best and can accommodate the greatest numbers."[7] But General Byng and other military officers realized that the industrial distress, being periodic, would return; indeed, they believed that in future it would recur at more frequent intervals. Permanent barracks were therefore contemplated. These were expensive, however, as well as unconstitutional, so by 1828 there were only two in all of Lancashire. A new one at Blackburn complemented the older one in Manchester, which had been built only in the aftermath of Peterloo. In 1830 new cavalry barracks would be added in Stockport and Manchester.[8]

In England the policing of disturbances continued to be by the military alone; in Ireland, by a 5,000-man constabulary as well as by the military. Despite this English reliance on troops, and despite the building of permanent barracks since the onset of the French wars, the number and size of the military barracks in England remained below the levels in Ireland. In 1828 England, with roughly double the population of Ireland, had 86 permanent barracks compared to 103 in Ireland. Sixteen of the forty English counties had no permanent barracks; only two of thirty-two Irish counties had none. Ten, or one-third, of the Irish counties contained government barracks with a capacity of 50 or more soldiers per 10,000 county population. In England, only five, or one-eighth, of the counties had barracks capable of accommodating this relative number of troops. Large concentrations in Kent (338 soldiers per 10,000 pop.) bordered on the Thames estuary and in Sussex (65) along the Channel coast, whereas in Hampshire (253) and Devonshire (68) the per capita capacity figures reflected large coastal military establishments at Portsmouth and Plymouth. Only in Berkshire, because of the royal castle at Windsor, was there a sizable inland concentration. Clearly, the purpose of *permanent* barracks in England was for war and defense, not domestic disturbances. Many interior counties, unlike those so situated in Ireland, were without barracks. The former Luddite areas (e.g., Nottinghamshire: nine soldiers per 10,000 pop.) and disturbed Lancashire and Yorkshire (eleven each) had alarmingly low relative capacities in their few permanent barracks. Even the two capitals, London and Dublin, grotesquely reflected the national differences, the Irish capital (160) having room for five times as many troops per capita as the English (34). It is evident that although the English Government adhered to the traditional military response against disorders, ministers were loathe to affront the constitutional sensibilities or the pocketbooks of Englishmen by erecting permanent barracks even in the disturbed parts of the country.[9]

It was not that requests for troops, or even for permanent garrisons, were lacking. Local magistrates were continually harassing London with troop requests; in 1826 alone, the Government granted military aid to at least twenty-nine towns.[10] This aid was temporary and circumstantial, however, as a typical reply (to the Mayor of Macclesfield) makes clear:

Both Mr. Peel and the Commander-in-Chief are most desirous to make the Military Force of the kingdom subservient to the greatest possible degree to the preservation of the Public Peace, but in its present reduced state it is impossible for Mr. Peel to hold out an Expectation that any given Force will be permanently stationed at any one Place during the Period of two Years which your Letter contemplates. All he can say is that as Circumstances arise the utmost endeavours will be used to place the Military Force where it can be most useful and that every practicable attention will be paid to the Representations of the Magistrates of Macclesfield.

The Government was in fact harried by requests from so many places (Table 8.2) that for tactical, even apart from constitutional or financial, reasons, permanent troop stations did not seem a wise policy. Major Eckersley had to tell the Macclesfield magistrates that their request for a permanent barrack was "without the most distant hope of being acceded to."[11]

General Byng exercised great restraint and parsimony in his loan of troops. "I must yet follow my commanding officer's policy," one lieutenant-colonel, probably happily, informed a group of magistrates, "of no troops sent 'unless Disturbances actually exist.'" Time and again, requests met refusals. The Government constantly railed against local laxities and cited "the impossibility of affording Military Aid to every detached Manufactory." The Home Office instructed Byng once again to "impress upon them the Impossibility for the Government to afford them an adequate defence, if they are not true to themselves."[12] The similarity to the Irish experiences is called to mind not only by the constant requests for troops but also by the Government's warnings of "the inconvenience likely to arise" from having great numbers of small, detached units. Perhaps the most basic guiding principle of the central authorities was the avoidance, unless absolutely necessary, of military usurpation of duties properly resting with the civil authorities. "If the Military are so often called for," Byng wrote confidentially to the Home Office, "the Civil Power will lose its consideration, and soon the Troops will be called on to assist in the Execution of Warrants.... I shall resist such application! as far as I am able – as I am certain it is Mr. Peel's wish that I should do so."[13]

In principle, the Government stated that troop loans should be determined by the degree to which the local civil forces had really tried to keep the peace themselves. Local failure to develop an adequate civil power supposedly entailed the forfeit of all military aid. The reality, dating to the Luddite period, was quite different: Everywhere the civil power remained inadequate, but troops were nevertheless despatched. With the exception of Leeds and Leicester, local authorities proved to be inept or even indifferent. Had Lancashire been Ireland, the disturbed districts would have been either threatened with or invaded by parties of the punitive Peace Preservation Police or county police forces.

But in England the recurring scenario was that the Government and the military commanders became first irritated, then furious, and finally in despair sent in the soldiers. "Sorry to find the civil power in your District so weak," the Home Office informed the magistrates at Brigg, who were advised to strengthen their local police but who were nevertheless permitted to keep a detachment of troops for twelve months. The Government was angry, too, with the authorities in Carlisle, who were exhorted to improve

Table 8.2. *Policing the North on the eve of the Reform Bill crisis*

Temporary Garrisons in 35 Towns in the Northern District, May 1829

Royal Horse Artillery	1 troop	Sheffield
	1 troop	Manchester
Royal Artillery	1/2 brigade	Burnley
	1/2 brigade	Newcastle
4th Dragoon Guards	3 troops and headquarters	York
	2 troops	Newcastle
	1 troop	Beverley
6th Dragoons	4 troops and headquarters	Manchester
	2 troops	Blackburn
	detachment of 15 rank and file	Haslingden
9th Lancers	2 troops and headquarters	Leeds
	2 troops	Nottingham
	1 troop	Sheffield
	1 troop	Rochdale and Bury
Coldstream Guards	8 companies	Manchester
7th Fusiliers Depot	4 companies	Hull
50th Regiment	4 companies and headquarters	Bolton
	2 companies	Preston
	3 companies	Blackburn
	1 company	Accrington
	detachment of 30 rank and file	Haslingden
67th Regiment	6 companies and headquarters	Stockport
	2 companies	Macclesfield
	2 companies	Ashton-under-Lyne
68th Depot	4 companies and headquarters	Barnsley
	detachment of 26 men	Clitheroe
74th Depot	3 companies and headquarters	Carlisle
	1 company	Isle of Man
80th Depot	3 companies and headquarters	Sunderland
	1 company	Tynemouth
87th Regiment	5 companies and headquarters	Chester
	2 companies	Rochdale
	2 companies	Oldham
	1 company	Bury

Note: Total of eighteen troops (cavalry) and fifty-four companies (infantry). The size varied, but a company was usually about sixty men and a troop about thirty.

their police; if the force "is not adequate for its purpose," asked the Home Office, "what are the impediments to its being rendered so?" Conditions in Barnsley were so bad that it was "found necessary almost daily to call upon the military to assist the civil power in dispersing the rioters." The Mayor of Liverpool answered government queries about the city's constables by saying, "It takes some time to collect them," even though the day police of

Table 8.3. *The English Yeomanry in aid of the civil power, 1822–7*

Year	No. of corps	No. of times called out	No. of counties in which employed	On authority of	
				Lord Lieutenant	Magistrates
1822	12	19	9	3	16
1823	7	13	7	1	12
1824	2	2	2	1	1
1825	3	3	3	0	3
1826	13	16	8	0	16
1827	4	6	4	1[a]	4[a]

[a] In one case, Yeomanry called out on another authority.

this city of 170,000 consisted of only twenty-one constables and thirty-one dock policemen. At Stockport the civil power was so poor that General Byng balked at stationing any soldiers there, since no one seemed to know what was going on in town.[14]

The situation was little different at the military headquarters of Lancashire. General Byng reported that "I experience much personal civility" from the Manchester authorities, "but no assistance." He told the Home Office that the large meetings and frequent disturbances in this city of 160,000 resulted from the "great inertness" of the police. "If the Magistrates and Police will only do their duty – the latter keeping a proper look-out – no movement of any numbers could then take place unknown to them." In July 1826 Byng was so angry with the dawdling local authorities that he ordered the cavalry, which had been posted daily throughout the city, to be withdrawn to their barracks; but because the police continued to be "idle," he was soon forced to rescind his order. By the end of the month, Byng threatened to remove the entire regiment "unless ... [the local authorities] are become more alert and attentive." This never happened in Manchester, and Byng remained irritable and impatient. "My temper is tried," he wrote London, "but as it is an imperative duty to set the example of acting with friendship and conciliation with the Civil Authorities, I will ride myself with *a sharp Bridle*, tho' I cannot entirely shut my eyes to great neglect."[15]

In the absence of effective police forces and faced with niggardly army officers, local authorities continued to rely on the Yeomanry. A typical feeling was that of the Macclesfield magistrates, who, lamenting "the diffi- culty ... in obtaining the aid of regular troops," affirmed "the value and importance ... of the Yeomanry in cases of sudden commotion and riot." Thus, at a time when the Yeomanry was decaying from disuse in Ireland, the same institution in England continued (despite the outrage at Peterloo) to function as a force for crowd control. In the period 1822–7 an average of seven corps were called out on duty ten times a year (Table 8.3). Whereas in Ireland only Dublin Castle could activate a corps, in England local initiative was sufficient. The Home Office continued to commend the Yeomanry whenever their services were used.[16] The Government also relied on other traditional techniques: the use of spies and even military officers "in coloured Cloaths" and, infrequently, a Bow Street officer or two. On one occasion, General Byng sent a military officer in mufti to Leicester to investigate, among other things, "what increase there has been made to the Civil Power."[17]

The crisis in provincial police

"What must I do with the Police?" Home Secretary Peel wondered in 1828. "I fear throughout the whole country it is most defective." In the midst of the Lancashire crisis of 1826, he had toyed with the idea of establishing "some kind of local force ... something less cumbrous and expensive than Yeomanry, but of a more permanent and efficient character than special constables." General Byng's response to Peel's idea was that "such a description of Force ... could not but be highly desirable and serviceable." Byng was not, however, optimistic. Manchester, he recalled, had tried something of the kind in 1818 but, with "the momentary panic subsiding, many of those withdrew." In 1826 Byng believed that if economic conditions did not soon improve, "some additional means" would be necessary to keep the peace in England. But he was not sanguine that local authorities would take the initiative, for "they look to Government to remedy every evil – to give every assistance."[18]

Robert Peel knew the remedy for his country's "defective" state of police. In April 1829, as Irish Catholic Emancipation was being enacted, the Home Secretary informed the House of Commons that he was considering some sort of general police for the English counties. In May 1830, as the Reform crisis raged in England, Peel urged the provincial towns to establish effective police forces. Even after he went out of office in November, he continued to press his ideas in public. He told the Commons in December 1831, in the aftermath of the Bristol Riots, that "unless a stipendiary police was established in the large towns, there could be no security for good order." In March and again in June 1832, Peel pressed the Whigs to establish effective police forces in the boroughs and counties of England.[19]

The problem, of course, for both Whigs and Tories, was that the concept of police in England continued to be that of an unconstitutional gendarmerie, that the belief in "Government to remedy every evil" was not license to establish a government-controlled police. England, however disturbed, should not be subjected to this foreign innovation. The military and centralized nature of the police recently established in Ireland, and Peel's central role in shaping the forces there, made it doubly difficult for him to sell this unpalatable idea in England. And yet, before the Tory Home Secretary left office in 1830, he was able to persuade Parliament to establish for London a numerous and effective police controlled by the Government. "The time is come," Peel had said in acceding to Catholic Emancipation in January 1829. He had used these very words earlier, in February 1828, in describing the necessity for a thorough reform of the police in London. "The time is come, when ... we may fairly pronounce that the country has outgrown her police institutions, and that the cheapest and safest course will be found to be the introduction of a new mode of protection."[20]

II. Radical reform of the London police

The year 1829 is traditionally cited as the date of origin of modern police institutions in the British Isles. In fact, as we have seen, the new police first appeared in Ireland as an experiment in the late eighteenth century and then as a more permanent innovation after the Napoleonic wars. The police of Dublin was modernized decades before the more well-known force appeared in the English capital in 1829. In England, it was neither from want of crime (whose nature was different from the Irish variety) nor from any absence of disturbances (though these, too, were less physically threatening) that serious consideration of police reform had lain dormant since the Gordon Riots. It was, rather, the great fear that the remedy – a powerful force of policemen – would necessarily involve the destruction of the historic rights and liberties of Englishmen. This had been the conclusion of a Select Committee on Police in 1822, the year of the founding of the Irish constabulary. *The Times*, in a discussion of crime in London in 1823, reasserted this conventional English wisdom by continuing to oppose the idea of "one supreme and resistless tribunal, such as is denominated in other countries the 'High Police' – an engine superfluous to the honest protection of life and property, invented by despotism for purposes inconsistent with the full and free enjoyment of those blessings." This was neither rhetoric nor veiled protection of corruption and privilege, but a heartfelt statement of political first principles. As recently as 1827 and 1828, select committees on crime in England could issue reports that purposely neglected any suggestion of a strong police as a solution to the problem.[21]

Why 1829?

How are we to explain the sudden reversal, the abrupt acceptance of an idea that for generations had been unthinkable? Two answers have traditionally been offered: a Home Secretary (Peel) who pushed the new concept, and the unchecked growth of crime in a metropolis of 1.7 million inhabitants.[22] The statistics that Peel presented to Parliament for crime in London from 1811 to 1827 clearly demonstrated a rise in the number of persons committed to jail. A modern authority, Leon Radzinowicz, has demonstrated, by measuring the average number of committals per 100,000 population, that committals from 1811–13 to 1825–7 rose in the provinces by 124 percent and in London and Middlesex by 53 percent. In either case, committal figures thus grew far ahead of population growth.[23]

But do these statistics reflect an increase in crime or more effective enforcement of the law? Thanks to Peel's criminal law reforms of the early 1820s, enforcement did improve; simplification of the law codes and the reduction in the number of capital offenses and severe punishments facilitated prosecution and encouraged witnesses to come forward and juries to indict and convict. Edwin Chadwick went so far as to state that "more crime is prosecuted and exposed to public view; not more committed." Set against these trends, however, were powerful countervailing factors. Changing attitudes toward the law, two recent scholars believe, probably affected the conviction rate more than the rate of committals.[24] Second, committals increased in the absence of large and effective forces of professional apprehenders: Virtually no police existed in the provinces, and the Nine Police Offices in London were essentially magistrates' courts. Third, the postwar (1815–19) surge in committals, "the most rapid of the whole century," occurred before Peel's legal reforms or any changes in existing police arrangements. Postwar economic dislocations, unemployment, and poverty undoubtedly produced a real increase in crime, both detected and undetected. Using the statistics for committals, we can conclude with some safety that the crime rate made "a cliff-face ascent" in 1815–19, leveled off in 1820–3, and then rose again, though not so steeply, after 1824.[25]

In the long view, ironically, it was England's economic success that produced this rising tide of crime. "Our offenses are *mercantile*, like our pursuits," observed one contemporary. The 1828 select committee on crime noted that our "crowded towns and flourishing manufactures tend to increase depredations on property, and to diminish acts of violence against the person."[26] In England throughout the first half of the nineteenth century, 80 percent of all crime was against property. Whereas statistics recently published in France showed that one-tenth of all crimes there were against the person, in England in the 1820s the proportion was only one-thirtieth. In both countries property crimes, not surprisingly, were concentrated in the urban and industrial areas; personal violence was greatest in poor and economically backward regions like Ireland and Corsica, the Ireland of France.[27] In England "protest" crimes, like violent crimes, were comparatively rare (5 percent of all offenses). Whereas collective protest and offenses against persons formed a large share of crime in Ireland, in England it was the preponderance of and increase in individual, self-aggrandizing property crimes that would lead many persons to consider the idea of a stronger police. Crimes growing at the fastest rates were all forms of theft – robbery, burglary, housebreaking, and above all, larceny.[28]

Two recent scholars have shown that rates of property crime followed trends in the economy. Crime "increased in times of depression and diminished in times of prosperity: more people stole in hard times than in good." These findings establish a relationship between crime and the economy that W. W. Rostow had earlier propounded in his "social tension chart" linking protest to the trade cycle. V. A. C. Gattrell and T. B. Hadden not only argue for "a positive correlation between poverty and property crime" in the first half of the nineteenth century but also see a coincidence in varying degrees throughout the century, but particularly in the first half, of increases in property offences and waves of popular agitation and dis-content.... [This] coincidence of depression, a high rate of property crime, and of working-class political unrest, was of more than incidental importance.... [The evidence] suggests indeed, that political protests were merely the surface manifesta-tions of social tension and frustration which can be quantitatively assessed in terms of the incidence of certain kinds of criminal activity.[29]

This recent finding becomes the more alarming when it is recalled, as Peel knew, that four-fifths of all English crime was property oriented. Gattrell and Hadden have demonstrated what General Byng knew to be true of the Northern District in the 1820s: Crime, protest, and public order were linked to the trade cycle. Indeed, it will be recalled that Byng urged the establish-ment of police forces not only from his belief that economic depressions would recur but his fear that they would become progressively more intense.[30]

But if crime was rising, why had there not been the proper response – a police – before 1829? Why were the prejudices against this foreign institution not overcome until 1829? Why the delay of half a century since Pitt's abortive police proposal in 1785? In part, it was the lingering fear of a gendarmerie. In part, too, the explanation was a delayed realization of the inadequacy of traditional institutions. Since 1793 Englishmen had been living in a protracted crisis: first the long wars on the Continent and then the severe postwar depression at home. When it was found that Peel's amelioration of the criminal statutes (1822–5) did not stem the rise in crime, resistance to the idea of a preventive police began to soften. In the "normalcy" of the peace-time 1820s, public opinion was finally being forced to choose between liberty and order, constitutional principles and daily realities.[31]

It is impossible to speculate how long substantial police reform would have been delayed in England had Peel not been in office in the 1820s. Certainly, a man of traditional views and average abilities, another Home Secretary like Sidmouth, would not have taken the bold step in 1829. But Peel's experi-ences as Chief Secretary in Ireland had hardened and sharpened him: The young man had become an effective administrator indifferent to popular prejudices. The challenge of Irish crime he had met with an altogether new institution for public order; now he would teach Englishmen that crime had made a mockery of their conventional wisdom against a strong police, that "liberty does not consist in having your house robbed by ... thieves."[32] Peel's colleague, the Prime Minister, had also served as Chief Secretary for Ireland. Indeed, two decades earlier, in 1808, the Duke of Wellington had reformed the police of Dublin. And, like Peel, he continued to be fascinated with the idea of a new civil power in the state. At the time of the Queen Caroline Riots, Wellington had urged to Sidmouth that the "Government ought, without the loss of a moment's time, ... to form either a police in London or a military corps, which should be of a different description from the regular military force." In November 1823, this idea reappeared in a private memorandum. The regular army, noted Wellington, was over-worked and untrained in the repression of "domestic insurrection and disturbance." Such duties, he argued, were "more properly the business of the civil government and of the police."[33]

But even apart from the growth of English crime, the force of Peel's personality, and the laboratory of Ireland, there was a final factor that has been curiously neglected by most historians: the growth of popular radicalism in England. The Tory Government had no doubt hoped that the disorders in London and the provinces after the Napoleonic wars would prove to be temporary. When, after Peterloo, the disturbances, the movement for suffrage reform, and workingmen's demands for unions continued to bedevil the authorities, the Government was pressed to reconsider its traditional definitions of liberty and order.[34] Pervasive, seemingly open-ended discontent – compounded by the perplexing challenge of Emancipation in Ireland – confronted the ruling orders. Their response was to begin to see not the disadvantages, but the advantages, of formerly unthinkable means of social control. The military demands of the French wars and the massive resort to troops in the suppression of disorders had accustomed Englishmen to the use of force in the form of uniformed redcoats; it was not unnatural that traditional prejudices against that civil standing army, a police force, should likewise be eroded.

It was this continuing popular radicalism, allied with the recognition of ever-rising crime, that was probably the decisive factor in the Government's new resolve to create a strong police for London. Wellington's views and Peel's first statement (in 1822) of his intention to establish "a vigorous, preventive police" for London were both direct products of the tumultuous radicalism of 1819–21. Of course, Peel's Metropolitan Police Act was not passed until 1829. With the building crisis of Catholic Emancipation in Ireland and the more hidden pressures in England for suffrage reform, it is arguable, as Wilbur Miller claims, that this was "the calmer end of the decade"; Elie Halévy even goes so far as to state that insurrection never "seemed more remote than at the time when the New Police Bill was carried."[35] The relevant point, however, is that from the early 1820s on, Home Secretary Peel gave serious attention to the London police. He realized that the postwar radicalism was deep-seated and abiding, that "1819 [Peterloo] was a rehearsal for 1832." It was Peel's prescience, not mere coincidence, that when his police "took to the streets," it was "amid England's constitutional crisis over parliamentary representation for disenfranchised middle-class citizens, whose protests were backed by a reserve of more militant working-class anger." Wilbur Miller has rightly perceived the origins of the police to be "fundamentally political amid challenges to the political order's legitimacy." Indeed, one of the basic questions at the outset was, "Would the police be identified as the cutting edge of the ruling minority's oppression?"[36]

The Metropolitan Police Act of 1829

From the first, Home Secretary Peel (Figure 8.1) immersed himself in the problems of the police of London. He would later remark: "*It has always appeared to me that the country has entirely outgrown its police institutions.*"

Figure 8.1 Home Secretary Peel, age thirty-seven, in 1825. (Painting by Sir Thomas Lawrence, P.R.A., by permission of the 3d Earl Peel)

Peel replaced Sidmouth in January 1822, five months after the Queen Caroline Riots; that spring he formed a select committee on the police of the metropolis, and by the summer had established a small foot patrol for Westminster and added a "Chief Constable" to each of the Nine Police Offices. In the early 1820s Peel toyed with plans to amalgamate the Bow Street Horse and Foot Patrols and to rebuild the central police office. He exerted pressure on the police magistrates to reside within their districts and to exercise their power of dismissal of watchmen given by an act of 1821. He maintained regular correspondence with the new Chief Constables and kept abreast of the smallest details regarding the appointment, behavior, and discipline of the constables. He applied a rule in force in the Irish police: The London constables, he insisted, were to have no business ties or other conflicts with their police work.[37]

By 1826 Peel was convinced, in Norman Gash's words, that "administrative probity ... could not compensate for fundamental defects in organisation." Policing in London remained a hodgepodge. The one-square-mile City of London had several forces for its twenty-six wards. Westminster, with a population larger than Dublin, and Southwark, greater than Bristol, were policed by sixty-four constables at the Seven Police Offices. The Thames Police Office boasted ninety-three men whose duties, except in emergencies, were mostly marine. The Bow Street Office still had only eight officers, and the combined Horse, Foot, and dismounted patrols totaled only 290 men – hardly an effective force for a metropolis with a huge population spread over an area of 400 square miles. And everywhere were the 3,500 decrepit, untrained night watchmen, beadles, and constables responsible to myriad uncoordinated local authorities.[38]

In December 1826 – as General Byng was trying to control the crisis in the North – the Home Office conducted a quiet inquiry into the state of the London police that, in Peel's words, resulted in "a thorough exposure of the defects of the present system." Peel now offered his first specific plan for a new police: Its outlines were strikingly similar to those of the Dublin police of 1786 and 1808. He proposed to form the city into a single police district ten miles in radius, to divide the district into six police divisions, and to place in charge of all of the constables and watchmen an officer to be known as a "divisional magistrate." A metropolitan police tax would replace existing local rates for the parochial constables and watchmen. Peel's plan came to naught because two months later Lord Liverpool, felled by a stroke, was forced to resign, and with him went Peel.[39]

In January 1828 Peel returned to the Home Office in Wellington's Government. A month later he asked Parliament to investigate, once again, the state of crime and police in the metropolis. Peel's speech was brilliant, perfectly tuned for his audience. As Gash aptly notes, it was "factual and unexciting," replete with "dampening statistics" of crime, and delivered in a fashion "deliberately intended to be dull." It would not do to scare Englishmen with colorful stories, as he had fourteen years earlier in pressing for his Irish police. He would have to be cautious: London, after all, was not Dublin. "I despair," he told the Commons in a performance of lachrymose hand wringing, "of being able to place our police upon a general footing of uniformity; I cannot hope to take St. Paul's as a centre, and have a radius of ten miles, in which our police could be able to act in unison."[40]

Parliament gave Peel his select committee, which met from March to May and presented its report in July 1828. To deal with the significant increase in crime in the metropolis over the last fifteen years, the committee made the following recommendations: The Government should establish a single metropolitan police district and a Police Office under the immediate control of the Home Secretary. The control of all existing police, including the night watchmen, would be awarded to this Police Office. Funding for the new system was to come partly from the Consolidated Fund and partly from a new locally assessed general police tax.[41] If we substitute "Lord Lieutenant" for "Home Secretary," the proposal becomes identical to that of the Dublin police established in 1808.

Two weeks after the report was issued, the parliamentary session ended. During the winter of 1828–9, as Wellington and Peel worked with King George IV to defuse the Catholic Emancipation crisis in Ireland, it was "remarkable"[42] that Peel had the time to work out the revolutionary principle that would enable the London police of 1829 to transcend the Dublin police model. Peel now proposed to do away with all of the night watch, to amalgamate all existing government-controlled day and night patrols, and to create a large single force of policemen who would work both day and night shifts. This grand conception was the signal original contribution of the new London police.

On 15 April 1829, Home Secretary Peel introduced in the Commons his revolutionary "Metropolis Police Improvement Bill."[43] His speech was unemotional and understated, filled with statistical recitations of the increase of crime in London. The metropolis, he argued, had simply outgrown its worthy local institutions; with the new civil force, moreover, "he was confident that they would be able to dispense with the necessity of a military force in London for the preservation of the tranquillity of the metropolis." Peel proposed to create "three magistrates" to comprise "a Board of Police" that would superintend one united police district stretching from Ealing to Poplar and Hampstead to Tooting – a ten-mile radius from Charing Cross. The new government-controlled force of day and night constables – he proposed to "abandon the term 'watchman'" – would replace all local authorities; all watch rates would be abolished and replaced by a metropolitan police rate. The new magistrates would control the police, and they would be answerable only to the Home Secretary. Peel was cautious, reassuring, in his description of the new force. He left unstated the number and distribution of these centrally controlled, salaried policemen. He would introduce the new system gradually, first in Westminster, then in other parts of the metropolis. The police would be implemented initially in those districts where the need was most apparent, and he hinted that local taxation would pay the costs of local application of the measure. In this respect, the plan was similar to that of Peel's Irish police of 1814. The most astounding feature of the London police proposal was its lack of specificity. Peel asked the permission of the House of Commons to return the bill to the select committee for revision and to trust the Home Secretary and the new police magistrates to flesh out the details of this radical proposal. The bill passed through the Commons without a division, was squired through the Lords by Wellington, and received the royal assent on 19 June.[44]

Considering the explosiveness of the whole subject of police since 1785, the opposition to Peel's bill on the floor of the Commons was "surprisingly feeble." Douglas Browne has written that "a revolution in British domestic history had been effected with such quietness and dispatch that it was only later that many ... were to realize fully what had happened." Jenifer Hart notes that "the Metropolitan Police Act of 1829 ... strangely enough passed

through parliament without opposition, indeed almost without debate."
T. A. Critchley calls it "one of the most remarkable facts about the history
of police in England that, after three-quarters of a century of wrangling,
suspicion, and hostility towards the whole idea of professional police, the
Metropolitan Police Act, 1829, was passed without opposition and with
scarcely any debate." Norman Gash points to the same absence of protest,
"or indeed of much public interest," and argues that Parliament's preoccupation with the final stages of the Catholic Emancipation crisis "diverted what
might otherwise have been vexatious opposition." It was the exhaustion of
the Irish crisis, rather than any parliamentary opposition to his police
measure, that probably explains Peel's remark to Wellington: "Pray pass the
[police] bill through this session, for you cannot think what trouble it has
given me."[45]

The revolutionary bill passed easily for a number of reasons. Peel's
familiarity with police and his parliamentary skills were crucial. Fearful of
repeating Pitt's mistake of 1785, Peel wisely decided to exclude the historic,
politically radical, constitutionally jealous, and geographically small City of
London from the jurisdiction of his new police.[46] Peel was insistent on
keeping local politics out of the police; in Dublin the city aldermen furnished
the majority of police magistrates, much to the objection of common
councilmen. Peel also decided not to insert irritating clauses regarding
vagrancy, licensing, and powers of search and arrest; he deliberately framed
his bill in as general a form as possible. Finally, the existence of government
magistrates and constables since 1792 served to defuse any controversy over
Crown interference or patronage.

But apart from Peel's political sagacity, the principal reason for the ease of
passage of the bill was the change in attitude among the ruling classes. The
Whig *Morning Chronicle*, now propolice, noted in 1828 that only "seven or
eight years ago" any respectable person who favored a strong police uttered
"a heresy deserving little less than the stake." The Tory *Quarterly Review*
pronounced that "police, in our view of the subject, when rightly understood, ... is the base on which men's liberties, properties, and social existence repose." It now condemned the "mis-called watchmen" of the metropolis, berated "the deteriorated and imbecile condition" of the existing civil
authorities, and demanded the creation of "a vigorous ... well-organized
... regular police force." A civil force of "despicable apparatus, which, in
cases of the slightest importance, can do nothing without the backing of red
coats and bayonets, ought to be struck to the ground." The journal
concluded by editorializing: "It should not be forgotten that the public good
... is entitled to some weight in the scale."[47]

The recognition of rising crime and the persistence of popular radicalism
led the English ruling classes in 1829 to consolidate their collective interests.
Parliament had reluctantly granted Catholic Emancipation in Ireland and,
three years later, would even accede to suffrage reform in England; the
acquiescence by both Whigs and Tories to the creation of a powerful police
for the English capital represented, in part, an attempt to brake the pace of

political and social change. Home Secretary Peel was aware that the ease of passage of his bill hardly guaranteed the success, or the popularity, of his new police. The real opposition would come from forces outside Parliament, not least from the supplanted local authorities, some of which were corrupt and almost all of which were inefficient, but also many of which were in 1829 spokesmen for a radicalized populace against an unreformed aristocratic government.

Shaw, Rowan, and Mayne

In implementing the Metropolitan Police Act, Peel's "first thoughts," as Norman Gash has noted, "not unnaturally turned to his Irish experiences." Police historian Charles Reith observed that "in this, *as in all other activities of his career*, he was strongly influenced by his earlier experiences as Chief Secretary for Ireland.... There is no doubt that Peel brought to the conferences ideas which were the product of his experience in reforming the police of Ireland."[48] Indeed, his restless mind was never entirely off Ireland, for, as we have seen, in 1829 Peel was in frequent correspondence with Irish Chief Secretary Leveson Gower regarding further reforms in the Irish constabulary.

The Irish connection is particularly evident in the early stages of forming the London police. In early May, Peel wrote General Sir George Murray, until 1828 the commander-in-chief of the army in Ireland, for names of possible candidates to head the London police. At the end of the month Peel wrote his old friend, William Gregory, Under-Secretary at Dublin Castle, asking in confidence – "Do not mention this matter to anyone" – for the names of suitable men to lead the new force. He confided that he planned to team a military man with "a sensible lawyer." "I require a man of great energy, great activity both of body and mind, accustomed to strict discipline and with the power of enforcing it, and taking an interest in the duty assigned to him. Then he must be a gentleman, and entirely trustworthy." The Irishmen whose names occurred to Peel – the ex-Dublin policemen and Irish police magistrates: the able Richard Willcocks (retired from the Munster constabulary two years earlier) and the experienced Wilson, Wills, and War-burton – were too old to make the switch to the altogether different duties in an unfamiliar city the size of London. And Under-Secretary Gregory was unable to recommend anyone he thought suitable. But in July, Castle authorities did grant a leave of absence to an Irish Chief Constable, a certain Captain Hunter, to visit London, where he advised Peel on the details of implementing the new police there.[49]

For most of June, Peel was still undecided on his appointments, now down from three men to two. His first offer, extended on 25 June, went to Col. James Shaw. A Scotsman and, at forty-one, the same age as Peel, Shaw had served in the army since 1805, distinguished himself under Maj.-Gen. Sir John Moore in the Peninsular campaign, fought at Waterloo, and super-intended the postwar occupation of France. In 1825 he was named Adjutant-

General for the Northern District (Belfast) in Ireland; the next year he was transferred to England, where, under General Byng, he served as the military commander at Manchester. His services there, especially in developing tactics to deal with disorders, attracted Peel's attention. Shaw found himself flattered by the Home Secretary's assessment that he was "the best qualified" military man to be a London police magistrate; "the experiment is a novel one," wrote Peel, "and the undertaking arduous ... [but there is] a great opportunity for distinction, and the office will become more important every day." For reasons that are not entirely clear (apparently he preferred army life), Shaw declined Peel's offer. Seven years later, he would accept the post of first Inspector-General of the reformed Irish constabulary. His two-year tenure in Ireland would be controversial and unappreciated. Moreover, Shaw's decision in 1829 to decline the London appointment assured his historical obscurity.[50]

Shaw's mistake was Col. Charles Rowan's opportunity. Home Secretary Peel now proceeded to appoint "two Irishmen who were almost unknown to the public at the time of their appointment, and of whom very little detailed knowledge has survived apart from the almost forgotten story of a task magnificently accomplished."[51] The forty-six-year-old Rowan came recommended to Peel by the excommander of the army in Ireland, General Sir George Murray, and by Wellington, under whom Rowan had served during the war. As Peninsular veterans had stocked the Irish constabulary, so now they received priority in the shaping of the London police. Charles Rowan was born in 1783, the fifth son of Robert Rowan, a distressed Ulster landowner and "profligate clergyman" of Scottish descent. The family from Mullans, County Antrim, produced several fine military men. Charles's brother, Sir William Rowan, would become a major-general and field marshal in the British army; another brother, Hill Wilson Rowan, would serve as an Irish police magistrate.[52] Charles in 1797 had joined the 52d Regiment (foot) as an ensign and was named a lieutenant at age fifteen. He served with distinction in the Peninsula (1809–12) and was second-in-command of the 52d foot at Waterloo, where he was wounded. After the war he served with the army of occupation in France, and then at home with the 52d regiment in the restive Midlands (1818–21) and afterward in Dublin. Rowan retired from the army in April 1822 and became a local magistrate in Ireland; there is no record of his ever serving in the constabulary.[53] Rowan was apparently attracted to the new London post, for he had approached Murray about the appointment in May, and he promptly accepted Peel's offer.

Because the London force was to be more civil than military, the other high-ranking appointment went to a young barrister. The story of Richard Mayne's selection is the stuff of novels. The fourth son of Edward Mayne, a judge of the Court of King's Bench in Ireland, Richard was born in Dublin in 1796. There he passed his youth and earned his B.A. from Trinity College, Dublin, in 1818; he was only twelve when Wellesley had reformed the Dublin police and eighteen when Peel created the Peace Preservation Police.

The year that Chief Secretary Peel left Ireland, Richard Mayne left, too, for studies at Trinity College, Cambridge, where he took a B.A. and an M.A. In 1822 he was called to the bar at Lincoln's Inn, and for the next seven years practiced on the northern circuit in England. Home Secretary Peel realized that the £800 salary for his police magistrates, "though attractive to a retired soldier, would not appeal at all to any successful lawyer." He would have to find a capable, and young, barrister. By coincidence, Peel had a young cousin, Lawrence Peel, a lawyer on the northern circuit, who wrote to recommend an able colleague, Richard Mayne. The thirty-three-year-old Mayne was modest enough never to have considered applying for such a high post. The recommendation could not have come at a better time. Recently, at the West Riding Sessions in Yorkshire, he had met and fallen in love with Miss Georgiana Carvick, but neither his own sense of duty nor her father would have permitted her marriage to a rising barrister in straitened circumstances. But £800 a year! Mayne could hardly believe the Home Secretary's letter that "of all the names mentioned . . ., yours was decidedly the best." Gratefully and immediately he accepted the offer of the London magistracy. Eighteen months later he and Georgiana were married.[54]

Mayne and Rowan, an unlikely pair, proved in fact to complement each other. Rowan, the elder by thirteen years, was the brusque military commander, used to ordering and disciplining men; serious, dignified, and tough, he had learned in the army the art of making seemingly quick decisions and of standing by them. Richard Mayne was entirely different. He was the cautious, cerebral lawyer, more at home with the paperwork and the planning necessary in a large bureaucracy. Mayne was also quicker verbally and more imaginative than Rowan. In the early years of the new police both types of personalities – authoritative and thoughtful, powerful and persuasive – were necessary to make the experiment a success.[55]

A civil force of men

After the Metropolitan Police Act was passed in June, the change in the titles of the two "superintending magistrates," one "civil," the other "military," demonstrated Peel's resolve to impose an entirely new system. Rowan and Mayne were to be "Commissioners of Police," a phrase jarring to English ears and recalling the *commissaires de police* of Paris.[56] By the end of July Commissioner Rowan, acting on Peel's instructions, had drafted a plan for a force organized along military lines with officers, noncommissioned officers, and men. The police district initially consisted of five divisions, eight sections to each division, and eight beats to each section. In the original plan each division was to consist of 165 men: 1 Superintendent (known for the first month as a "superviser"), 4 Inspectors, 16 sergeants, and 144 constables. Police headquarters was to be near the Home Office, at 4 Whitehall Place, in a spot known as Scotland Yard, so called because the Scottish Embassy had been there before the Union of 1707.[57] By the end of September 1829, when the new police began patrolling, the district had grown to eight divisions with an establishment of 8 Superintendents, 20 Inspectors, 88 sergeants, and 895 constables. By May 1830 the force would treble in size, reaching a level that held roughly constant until 1840. Thus, only eight months after its establishment, the London police numbered about 3,300 men: 17 Superintendents in as many divisions, 68 Inspectors, 318 sergeants, and 2,892 constables (Map 8.1). This was a force strength "considerably greater than that originally planned." Bow Street and the Police Offices established in 1792 were not abolished, as their functions were primarily judicial, but control passed to the Home Office in 1839. The Bow Street Horse Patrol continued until 1836. The Foot Patrol and the Thames Police were not absorbed into the Metropolitan Police until 1839. But wherever the extensive new police divisions spread throughout the metropolis in 1829–30, Peel's new policemen immediately supplanted all local watch forces.[58]

The Home Office, directed by Robert Peel until November 1830, maintained as complete a control over the new London police as the Castle did over the Dublin police and tried to maintain over the Irish constabulary. In the late summer of 1829, the Government made a series of crucial decisions about the character of the force. After what Rowan termed discussions "at great length," it was decided that the police should be uniformed. The absence of a uniform could lead to charges about an army of spies; the wearing of one, it was felt, would deter criminals, aid in the control of crowds, and reassure the public about the presence of a strong civil force. An initial suggestion that red and gold be the colors was rejected; perhaps the uniform of the Irish constabulary deterred Peel and the commissioners from outfitting the London police in anything remotely resembling military colors. At length, dark blue was chosen since the color seemed civilian, neutral, and (in Rowan's view) "quiet."[59] Blue trousers – with white ones (as in the Irish constabulary) optional for summer wear – were matched with a blue swallow-tail coat. A double-breasted greatcoat was worn with a detachable cape in wet or cold weather; boots and a leather (or "chimney-pot") top hat with ventilation holes and reinforced with cane and iron stays completed the outfit. The modern helmet was introduced only in 1864. A blue and white armlet, introduced in late 1829, was worn by the men when on duty; constables and sergeants were identified by their division letter and their own number. Although these men were issued uniforms, the Inspectors and Superintendents had to buy their own. The Commissioners did not wear a uniform until 1839.[60]

Another key early decision concerned arms. Whereas the police in Ireland carried pistols and bayoneted carbines, the London force from the outset was unarmed. Patrick Pringle has perceptively remarked that "the popular belief that the British police of to-day is of purely indigenous origin is absurd." The new police was, in fact, "a watered-down gendarmerie without the arms," though "it was the water and the absence of arms" that were its distinctive characteristics.[61] Certainly, the comparative rarity of violent crime in England made it easier for the Government to decide not to issue firearms

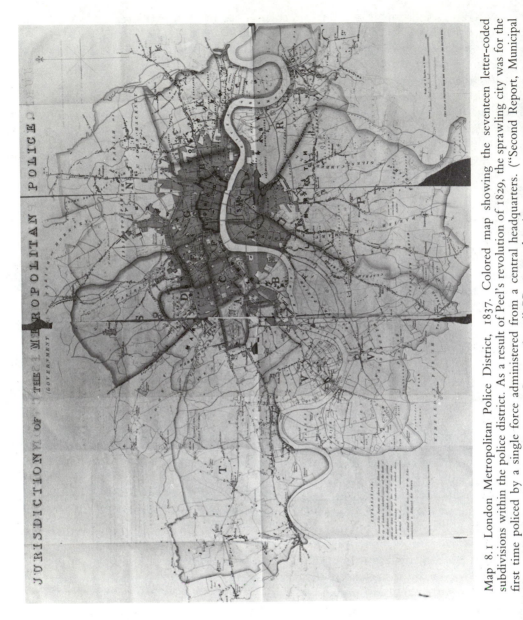

Map 8.1 London Metropolitan Police District, 1837. Colored map showing the seventeen letter-coded subdivisions within the police district. As a result of Peel's revolution of 1829, the sprawling city was for the first time policed by a single force administered from a central headquarters. ("Second Report, Municipal Corporations," PP 1837, vol. 26)

to the new police. But Peel's decision must be considered heroic. True, the constables at the old Police Offices were unarmed. But each man in the Bow Street Foot Patrol had a cutlass, and each captain sported pistols and a carbine as well; each man in the Horse Patrol carried a pistol.[62] Peel and the Commissioners, one of them a career military man, thus departed from the traditional weaponry of patrols in the metropolis. It was a bold step, and supremely wise, for this "watered-down gendarmerie" represented a vote of confidence in the English people. In the formative years of the force, this decision not to arm the 3,000 policemen would hasten public acceptance of the controversial new institution.

Each constable was given only a truncheon. A descendant of the symbolic staff of authority carried by the Bow Street thief takers and the parish constables, the hardwood (*lignum vitae*) baton was carried in the back pocket of the trousers, where it was covered – that is, *hidden* – by the long tail coat.[63] The truncheon remained concealed until 1863, when it made its appearance sheathed in a leather case and suspended from the constable's belt. Citizens' occasional requests that the police be given pistols, or even cutlasses, were invariably denied.[64] In one case in January 1832, the Home Secretary did permit a police party on the periphery of the metropolis to carry a "sabre" for night duty, but the commissioners were instructed to "carry it into effect carefully, both with respect to the place, and to the person to whom the weapon is entrusted."[65] This was a very rare exception to policy, and the men were never issued guns. Divisional inspectors were, however, allowed to carry a pocket pistol. For the constable on patrol the stick of wood, his moral authority, was his only protection. Although circumstances, of course, sometimes required that the baton be not only drawn but thoroughly employed, the ideal from the beginning was just the opposite. Charles Reith tells a story about a special constable and his truncheon that matches the instructions given Metropolitan policemen. "You put it out of sight," he was told. "You don't let anybody know you've got it. *And you forget you've got it!*" It is true that during the Chartist crises of 1842 and 1848 cutlasses were issued to selected constables, but these weapons were kept concealed and *never* employed; and during the Fenian scare of 1867–8 divisional headquarters were supplied with revolvers, but they were *never* issued to the constables on patrol. "Even 'the Wild Irish'," comments Wilbur Miller, "did not provoke that step."[66]

There was no shortage of men who sought positions in the new force. In October 1829, after the initial force of 895 constables had been put on the streets, there were a further 2,000 applicants. The recruiting standards were similar to those already in effect in the Irish constabulary: Each man had to be at least 5 feet 7 inches tall, under thirty-five years old, physically and mentally fit, and able to read and write. In the early years at least, the age requirement was waived in a few instances.[67] But the height requirement was "strictly and invariably observed"; one applicant in November 1831 was told that "the rule with respect to height has never yet been dispensed with."

Such requirements excluded virtually all of the watchmen from the pre-existing local forces; but from 1829 to 1833 some 170 men from the Bow Street patrols were transferred to the new police.[68]

There is hardly anything in the records that tells us about the backgrounds of the new policemen. Both Peel and Rowan valued discipline in the force and mocked those creatures who had comprised the old watch forces. In the initial recruitment of 1829–30 it appears that the Commissioners gave a preference to men with military backgrounds, well-recommended privates or sergeants with current or previous army service. But many of these men found it difficult to adjust to the civil and often solitary duties of a police-man. With great numbers of men being dismissed or resigning, the Commissioners were constantly adding replacements and from the early 1830s on, the emphasis in hiring seems to have shifted to men of civilian backgrounds. A return of June 1832, which lists the constables' previous occupations, indicates that a third of the men had been "laborers"; only a sixth, soldiers or sailors; and the remainder, a miscellany of artisans, servants, and petty tradesmen and shopkeepers (see Appendix IV).[69] From this return, it is not possible to say how many of these 3,200 men had had earlier military experience. Given the passage of time since the Napoleonic wars, it is certain that virtually none of the recruits (ages eighteen to thirty-five) had been part of the wartime mobilizations, since a thirty-five-year-old recruit in 1832 would have been eighteen years old at the time of Waterloo. In the event, the hiring of civilians did not stop the turnover in the force's rank and file. Mayne's disillusionment with recruiting was so great that the former barrister even suggested in 1835 that in future only men with experience in cavalry regiments should be hired. A subsequent police order of 1845 did state that "a certain number" of recruits must be military veterans. But most of the men who joined Peel's unarmed gendarmerie continued to come from civilian backgrounds.[70]

If in its basic recruiting standards the Metropolitan Police was similar to the Irish constabulary, the pay, even adjusting for the higher living costs in London, was considerably greater. An Irish constable earned £30 a year; a London constable, at 3 shillings a day, £50. Peel was clearly aiming for a better class of constables. This he probably got, but it was at the cost, in London terms, of a restive group of men who would leave the force in great numbers for even higher pay in other work.[71] In the English capital the bright lights and employment opportunities, as well as the force's pay and working conditions, would keep the rank and file of police in constant flux by comparison with the Irish constabulary.

The turnover in the early years of the Metropolitan Police was enormous. Of the first 2,800 constables enrolled, 2,238 were at some point dismissed; 1,790 of these dismissals were for drunkenness on duty. Of the 2,892 constables on the force in May 1830, only 562 were still policemen in April 1833. Dismissals and resignations in the first three years (October 1829–December 1832) totaled 4,629, a figure larger than the size of the force; by September 1834 the number totaled 7,493, and by the end of 1838 10,904 men. In these years, between one-third and two-fifths of the force was dismissed annually; and if resignations are included, well over half. With a seemingly endless list of applicants, there was a constant round of "dismissals, fresh enlistments, more dismissals, more enlistments, dismissals again, and so on, continually."[72] These departure rates compare with a dismissal rate in the Irish constabulary of 10 percent in 1822–4 and only 3 to 6 percent in 1830–36.

In both establishments the reasons were roughly the same – lack of punctuality and discipline and, above all, drunkenness. Commissioner Rowan testified in 1833 that in his force drink was the problem in "four out of five cases"; in Ireland it was the cause for three of every five dismissals.[73] In each case, the rank-and-file policemen were from the lower classes in societies given to enormous alcohol consumption by today's standards. But why the higher dismissal rate in London? In part, enforced standards of conduct were probably higher, and dismissals therefore more frequent, in the London force; moreover, temptations in the metropolis were more diverse and available than in the Irish countryside. Low pay, Rowan stated, was the chief reason cited by the men who resigned; Peel's calculation that an unmarried constable could save half of his weekly salary proved to be unrealistic.[74] The men also complained that their pay did not increase with length of service and that promotions to sergeant were so rarely available as to constitute no inducement to long service. The hours were long and the work continuous, seven days a week. Shift time was nine hours at night and ten during the day after 1832, and even longer before that date.[75] The men alternated between day and night duty; in the early 1830s, two-thirds of the force (2,340 men) patrolled at night and only one-third (968 men) during the day. Some constables could not or would not accept the discipline demanded in the force; others simply found police work tedious as well as exhausting. From the Commissioners' viewpoint, the biggest problem was to find young men, not already committed to other occupations, who had the necessary mix of "intelligence, education, and bodily power" required for police work.[76] The absence of a police training program only compounded all of these problems. High turnover would be a continuing problem in the Metropolitan Police. At the end of the century, two of every five recruits were still leaving within one year, three in every four within five years; only one in fifty stayed as long as twenty-five years.[77]

There were two principal ways in which the London police differed from the Irish constabulary. One was the absence of firearms; the other, an officer class based on promotion by merit. From the beginning, Home Secretary Peel insisted that social status and aristocratic patronage were to have no place in the London police. Appointments to officer rank would "depend exclusively upon character, qualifications, and services of the persons selected"; this was to be a "fixed and invariable rule, . . . [that] no person shall be qualified to fill a superior station, unless he shall have served a given time in a subordinate station."[78] In practice, this policy was strictly followed from the outset. The merit rule, so much heralded by historians, was revolutionary compared to the practices within the army officer class. But its adoption should hardly be thought surprising. In the City of London, police promotion was by merit.[79] It should also be remembered that Peel was a comparative parvenu in the English ruling class. His immediate ancestors were yeoman farmers and northern manufacturers; he himself was a disciple of the school of hard work, a man who had risen in politics entirely by his talents, not his connections. The Irish police of 1814–18 he had staffed with officers experienced in the Dublin police and in the army, militia, and Yeomanry. During his chief secretaryship he had ignored the protests of the Irish landed gentry, and since 1822 he was known to oppose the practice in the Irish constabulary of appointing "gentlemen" of no police experience to the post of Chief Constable. Thus, Peel's own nature, his administration of the Peace Preservation Police, and his reaction against recent policies in the Irish constabulary account for the decision in staffing the London force in 1829. On a more theoretical level, Peel may be said to have opted for promotion by merit for reasons of professional efficiency rather than from any liberal commitment to the ideal of equal opportunity. Nevertheless, Peel's advocacy of a policy of promotion of men of talent was widely perceived as democratic. This perception did much to allay popular fears of a gendarmerie directed by a closed officer caste and thus helped the new police to gain acceptance in circles where otherwise it was opposed.

The police promotion policy meant from the outset that active and half-pay army lieutenants and captains, men who in Ireland would move naturally into chief constableships, were in London passed over in favor of their social inferiors. Noncommissioned officers, principally sergeants and sergeants-major, discovered that the Government wanted them for police officer posts ranging from sergeant to Superintendent. Thirteen of the original seventeen Superintendents had been army sergeants-major who, in Mayne's words, had "raised [themselves] from the ranks entirely by [their own] merit." Beginning in September 1830, police constables were being promoted to sergeants, sergeants to Inspectors, and, infrequently, Inspectors to Superintendents. In the period 1839–41, twenty-four sergeants became Inspectors, but not a single Superintendent was appointed. Despite the Government's repeatedly stated policy, commissioned army officers, "reduced gentlemen," and aristocratic patrons continued to solicit posts in the police.[80] Even an occasional officer in the Irish constabulary requested a transfer to London; but Chief Constable John McClintock of County Meath learned to his dismay that "Mr. Peel has declined appointing persons of the Rank & Station of Gentlemen to these situations." The London policy indeed had ripple effects in Ireland, for in the early 1830s there was a brief emphasis on officer appointments based on prior, proven police experience.[81] In the Metropolitan Police, after the initial round of appointments and promotions, the attractions of the merit policy, even for promotion to sergeant, became less strong to the average constable because of the small number of vacancies. For although virtue was rewarded, so was seniority. The few constables who joined in the early years and stayed on would have a greater chance to move up than the new men hired in later years.

In a number of other ways, the London police of the 1830s differed from the constabulary in Ireland. London constables stayed in one district; removal or rotation was the exception, not the rule. Unlike the situation in Ireland, there was in London no rule barring local recruitment. Indeed, the Commissioners pursued a policy among the London constables of assigning the "good men" to their home divisions, since they would have the "advantage" of knowing the inhabitants. Unmarried constables lived together in police houses or "stations" (not barracks), and all of the men, married or not, had to live within their assigned division. One-third of the recruits in 1829 were married and, since there was in the London police no restraint on marriage, unlike in the army or in the Irish constabulary since 1828, the number grew, so that by 1833 two-thirds of the Metropolitan policemen were married. The Commissioners believed that married constables were steadier than bachelors; nevertheless, given the weekly pay of 19 shillings, the trend toward marriage probably contributed to the high turnover in personnel.[82] As with the men in the Irish police, the height and size of the average London constable were increasing. The Commissioners noted in 1833 "a great change in the size of the men since the first establishment of the police.... They are much larger than they were."[83] Still another social characteristic of the force that protected the English capital was that it was heavily seasoned with Irishmen. Commissioners Rowan and Mayne were both Irish, and so were 10 percent of the higher officers, 9 percent of the sergeants, and 17 percent of the constables. At the 1834 Select Committee on the Police, one witness, a hat manufacturer named Thomas Morris, found little good in those constables who were "of the lower order of Irish ..., red-hot Irishmen, just imported, who run out and strike every person they meet."[84]

III. Police and people

From controversy to confrontation

The Metropolitan Police Act had been passed with hardly a murmur from the aristocratic Parliament, but the new force was not quietly accepted by the people. Predictably, Londoners after 1829 behaved toward the new institution as Dubliners had after 1786. The force was "opposed and hated by all classes of the general public," Patrick Pringle has written. "There is not the slightest doubt that it was imposed on London against the will of the vast majority of the people." Almost everyone, notes Charles Reith, had a reason to dislike the police: criminals and the destitute; "vice-traffickers"; the hard-pressed working classes; skilled laborers and artisans "mostly Radical in outlook"; ratepayers resentful of a new tax; jealous parish officials; displaced watchmen and constables; traditionalists with old-fashioned constitutional beliefs; radicals and Whigs of advanced popular views; and soldiers and sailors who enjoyed street scuffles with the new constables. Even the City of London, exempt from the Commissioners' control, was scurrilous in its denunciations.[85]

That much of the opposition had a class basis is revealed in correspondence to the Government. Those who approved of the new police argued that the resistance came from such groups as injured local interests, "paupers," the propertyless, "a most violent Mob faction," the lower classes, "the rabble," and radicals.[86] "The more respectable part of the Parish," a gentleman in Shoreditch wrote Peel, "I say without fear of contradiction, ... are not adverse to the plan." A correspondent from Stepney wrote to the Commissioners: "Under the Metropolitan force the rabble are defeated ... and I hope and trust you will not be induced to change the present system. It is now in its Infancy but working well and will in a short time do wonders both for the State and the man of real Property." Local government units, the select vestries, especially those under radical control (principally Marylebone and St. Pancras), harbored the strongest feelings against the police. "A Loyal Subject" from the wealthy parish of St. James, Westminster, urged the Government to purge the vestries of the metropolis in order to prevent "an Insurrection in the Metropolis.... If not, you may probably find the Police force insufficient to withstand the Opposition of the lower Orders."[87]

Police investigations confirmed these claims that the opposition was concentrated not only in the local governing bodies in the eighty-eight metropolitan parishes but also among large radical sections of the city's population. The most coordinated resistance, reported Police Superintendent Washington Carden, came not from the rabble or the propertyless but from the vast body of lower-middle-class and working-class ratepayers.[88] Just as the rabble did not form the backbone of radicalism, as historians George Rudé and E. P. Thompson have shown, so they did not constitute the base of opposition to the new police. It was, above all, the small shopkeepers, artisans, and semiskilled laborers, political radicals on a variety of issues, who were also united in their resistance to "Peel's Bloody Gang." In short, it may be said that opposition to the police idea had, by 1829, become democratized. The antipolice principle, formerly the preserve of liberal aristocratic Whigs, had moved left as the Whigs retreated to consolidate their position among the ruling orders.

It was precisely because Peel's police was introduced in London on the eve of Reform – the rising agitation for an extension of the vote – that popular resistance to the new force was so intense. The recent concession of Catholic Emancipation only inflamed ordinary Englishmen who interpreted it as their Government's surrender to the papist masses of Ireland. Was it right to placate Catholics but ignore the demands of free-born Englishmen? The scenario was hauntingly familiar: In 1780 statutory concessions to Catholics had triggered disorders of volcanic proportions. Was the new police meant to guarantee the repression of the just grievances of Englishmen by preventing a repetition of the Gordon Riots?

Throughout London in 1830, popular protests gathered force as parish authorities, one by one, were superseded by the new police, which had grown from five to seventeen divisions. In Tottenham, St. Luke's, and St. Pancras, in St. George's, Marylebone, and innumerable other parishes, the city's inhabitants met to declare their opposition to the concept of one central authority having exclusive control over the policing of the metropolis, with the only retained local power being that of paying for the privilege. "Our great objection," argued *The Standard*,

is to the principle of taking away from the people all control over a force which is to control the Metropolis . . . and over which neither the courts of law nor the houses of parliament are to have any ordinary authority. . . . *The people for whose protection all this improvement is threatened are not the parties demanding it.* . . . The thing is not – never was English.

At meetings in Marylebone, speakers announced that they could never consent to a police under a minister or "suffer a Gendarmerie to be established throughout England." One thousand petitioners from that parish urged a return to the usages of "the common law." Residents of Covent Garden objected to this police "entirely independent of and unresponsible to the Householders" and warned the Government that "*in these times* any Measures are impolitic that bear even the semblance of encroachment on popular rights." One gentleman, who claimed to have "talked much with the working classes on the subject of the New Police," wrote the Home Office in late 1830 that the Government should expect great opposition, for the lower classes were united in believing that the Peelers had been created to crush popular reform.[89]

Numerous pamphlets, handbills, political satires and cartoons, and long, reasoned petitions criticized first the Tory, and then after November 1830 the Whig, Government for imposing its police on Londoners (for an example, see Figure 8.2). A typical handbill distributed throughout the metropolis was the following:

THE NEW POLICE

PARISHIONERS – Ask yourselves the following *Questions:*

Why is an Englishman, if he complains of an outrage or an insult, referred for redress to a Commissioner of Police?

Why is a Commissioner of Police delegated to administer Justice?

Why are the proceedings of this new POLICE COURT *unpublished* and *unknown?* and by what Law of the Land is it recognized?

Why is the British Magistrate stripped of his power? and why is Justice transferred from the Justice Bench?

Why is the Sword of Justice placed in the hands of a MILITARY Man?

Consider these constitutional questions . . . , then UNITE in removing such a powerful force from the hands of Government, and let us institute a Police System in the hands of THE PEOPLE under *parochial* appointments.

UNITY IS STRENGTH

At the bottom of this handbill, the printer, a Mr. Elliot in the Strand, advertised that "these Bills may be had at the Printer's, at 4d. per Dozen; 2s. per Hundred; or, 17s., 6d. per Thousand; and the enemies of oppression are requested to aid its circulation."[90]

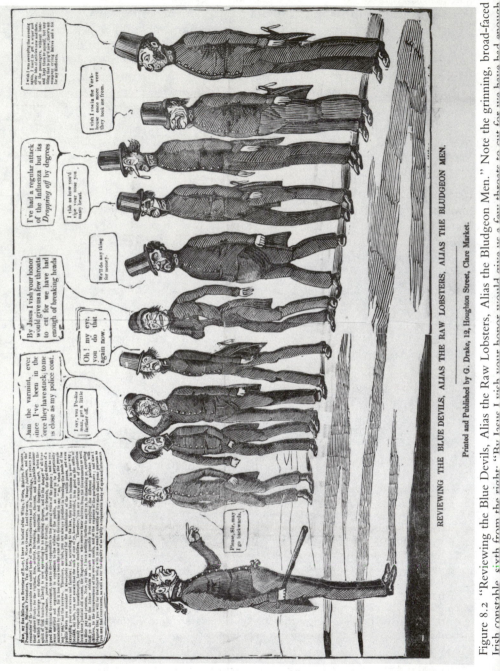

Figure 8.2 "Reviewing the Blue Devils, Alias the Raw Lobsters, Alias the Bludgeon Men." Note the grinning, broad-faced Irish constable, sixth from the right: "By Jasus I wish your honor would give us a few throats to cut for we have had enough

Of the many parish petitions, perhaps the most thoughtful, as well as the longest, was one from Marylebone in December 1832. It objected to the police on the grounds of "finances" and "general management" but, above all, "constitutionality." The petitioners called for some of the costs to be borne by the Consolidated Fund, for the abolition of the Commissioners, and for restoration of some local control. They admitted that the old watch was inefficient and that "a more uniform system may be required," but they now asked for some "alteration" in the police of 1829. The petitioners criticized the Government for having gone "from one extreme to another" and asked whether "there is not a medium course to be steered." In the long section addressing the question of "Constitutionality," the petitioners pointed out to the Whig Home Secretary, Viscount Melbourne, the long history of his party's opposition to a strong police and made clear their perception of the new force as an agent against not crime but popular protest.

> Your Memorialists respectfully beg leave now to approach that part of the subject the most delicate ..., viz., whether the Force, as at present constituted and governed, is, or is not, accordant with the spirit of the Constitution and the Freedom of the Subject; a Force which will most likely, 'ere long, pervade the whole Kingdom, formed upon a Military System, regulated and directed by persons appointed by the Government, and altogether uncontrolled by those who pay for it, and the protection of whose persons and property is the presumed object of its formation.
>
> It will require no power of argument or deduction of reason to satisfy a mind, constituted like your Lordship's, that a Force such as this must be incompatible with the Liberty of the Subject. It differs from a Military Force only in the name, and ... [with] all the attributes and powers of any army, it may, at any moment of public excitement, be called out, at the will of the then existing government, in array against the people, from whom its members derive their daily pay....
>
> Your Memorialists ... admit that so long as the Helm of the State is guided by those tried Friends of the People [the Whigs] who ... have for nearly half a century steadily pursued an undeviating course ... [toward] restoring to the People their long-usurped Rights, they have nothing to fear, but my Lord, ... it is not enough that the political integrity of the present Government is a guarantee to the people of the abuse of such a Force....
>
> Your Memorialists ... cannot forget that this Force was first organized by a power [the Tories], far from being the friends and uncompromising advocates of the People, nor can they forget the fears ... as to the use that *might* have been made of that Force ... [during a time] of the greatest popular excitement perhaps ever known in this Metropolis....[91]

The vestries and watch authorities may have been self-serving and many of them inefficient or corrupt, but they did reflect the sentiments of most Londoners. The resentment felt by the parishes was "extremely natural," a Middlesex JP told a parliamentary committee in 1834, since the new police was "altogether independent of their control." Even police historian Charles Reith, who is otherwise very sympathetic to the new force, notes that the "[o]bjection to central control of police by the Home Office was one of the few arguments against Peel's police idea which were [sic] reasonable in the circumstances of the time."[92]

There were also the financial objections. The new police was annually costing Londoners half again as much as the combined charges for the old watch. In 1830–2 the yearly expense was £207,000; the total annual cost for all of the pre-1829 parochial watch forces was £137,000. Many parishes that had expended little on watch establishments suddenly found themselves heavily assessed; a large parish like Marylebone, which had been spending £9,000 a year for its watch, watched its annual police costs rise to £24,000. With the purse their only remaining power, parochial authorities began systematically withholding police revenues from the Government. This "financial sabotage," which one historian has dubbed "the parish war," was orchestrated by the large parishes of Marylebone and St. Pancras. By October 1832, the metropolitan parishes owed the Government £56,000 in back police rates, and by the end of the year £70,000. Complaints against the new police, they asserted, "are far from being confined to such grounds" as taxes and expenses. "Every complaint against the Police ... is commonly urged in connection with the fact that the Commissioners are not responsible to – nor in any way connected with – the inhabitants who have in no sense any control or knowledge of the expenditure."[93]

By the end of 1832, the Government realized that local taxpayers could not or would not pay the full expense of the police. Indeed, ministers now grasped the logic that a government-controlled force should be at least in part government funded. This insight came the more quickly because some parishes, in order to cut police revenues, had submitted to County Middlesex authorities lowered valuations of house rentals – a stratagem "over which we have no control," lamented John Wray, treasurer of the new police. As early as 1830, correspondents, including an absentee Irish landowner, had suggested to Peel the use of the Consolidated Fund, a resort to which the former Irish Chief Secretary was, of course, familiar.[94] The Peace Preservation Police since 1817, and the Irish constabulary since 1822, had been partially subsidized by these central government revenues. But it was Home Secretary Melbourne and the Whig Party, those "Friends of the People," who basked in the glory of lowering the burden of taxation on Londoners. An act of 1833 stated that the Consolidated Fund would provide one-fourth of all police expenses up to £60,000, with the remaining three-fourths to be paid from parish rates that were reduced from 8 to 6 pence per £1 valuation.[95] The parochial authorities and London ratepayers had won a small victory, even though their share of police costs, at three-fourths of the total, was one-fourth higher than the local share levied in impoverished Ireland. For the Government, the lesson, learned earlier in Ireland, was that if it wanted innovations in police, it would have to pay at least part of the price.

The control of crowds

In the first half-dozen years of its existence, Leon Radzinowicz has noted, the Metropolitan Police found that its "most urgent challenge [was] the keeping of the peace, rather than the growth of crime." In Peter Laurie's judgment,

"The Metropolitan Police exists, historically, to control the London mob. It was created because the military had shown itself in several incidents unable to do the job. Crowd control is therefore the oldest police skill."[96]

From their first appearance on the streets on 29 September 1829, the blue-uniformed men were subject to almost constant taunts from the populace. "Blue Devils," "The Unboiled," and "Raw Lobsters" were cries inspired by the men's dress; more personal was the description "Peel's Bloody Gang." For those given to politics and patriotism, "The Gendarmerie" was the cry; literary types referred to "The English Janissaries" or "The Sanguinary Cerebruses." The popular press routinely reported police cases under headings marked by a familiar litany of nouns: "tyranny," "oppression," "brutality," "outrage," "ruffianism." Arrested criminals were described, with great rhetorical flourishes, as victims "in the merciless grip of an unboiled lobster's claw." "Inspector" was spelled "In-spectre."[97]

The abuse that the police received in the early 1830s was not merely verbal. In city streets, recurrent skirmishes between the police and individuals and organized groups were London's equivalent of the faction fights and "constabulary affrays" in Ireland. Apart from routine scuffles, fisticuffs, and stonings, there were the bizarre incidents: a constable lured into a public house and, to the crowd's amusement, savagely beaten by a prizefighter; other policemen heaved onto the iron spikes of fence railings; and a constable "held down in the road while a cab and horse were driven over him." Especially in the first two years, parties of soldiers – from the Grenadier Guards, the 10th Hussars, the Coldstream Guards, the Marines, and the Horse Guards – gleefully plunged into fracases with members of their rival, the civil standing army. Firemen throughout the metropolis and coachmen and servants of noblemen likewise vented their resentment of "the New Police" in physical assaults on "the Men [who] appear to be walking automata."[98]

By the summer of 1830, just when the London police had expanded to 3,000 men organized in seventeen divisions, the force was confronted with its greatest challenge. In the countryside of southeastern England raged widespread rioting by the agricultural laborers; on the Continent, the July Revolution in France placed the bourgeois King, Louis Philippe, on the throne, and in August the Belgians, by force of arms, won their independence from Holland. This rapid series of events, coming on the heels of Catholic Emancipation in Ireland, gave the popular enthusiasm for Reform in England a great stimulus and sense of historical inevitability. When the English Parliament assembled on 2 November, the failure of the new King, William IV, and of Prime Minister Wellington to consider reform triggered a week of rioting in the capital.

To handle the riots of 3–10 November, the uncompromising Tory Government deployed 7,000 troops in and around the metropolis, but never used them. Instead, full reliance was placed on Peel's new police, 2,000 of whom were now concentrated in Westminster. Mobs numbering in the hundreds roamed the city from Spitalfields, Whitechapel, and Bethnal Green to Charing Cross, Piccadilly, Hyde Park Corner, and the West End. Rioters targeted aristocrats' carriages and town houses, the clubs in Pall Mall, and selected shops including that of "the manufacturers of policemen's clothing." Policemen, as the symbol of Tory reactionism, were targeted for the crowds' wrath. Shouts of "Down with the New Police! . . . No Peel! . . . Down with the Raw Lobsters!" accompanied the mobs swirling through the streets. "The most hideous yells and execrations," reported the *Morning Chronicle*, "were directed against any member of the New Police who came in view." Printed handbills solemnly asserted that 6,000 cutlasses had been issued to "Peel's Bloody Gang. . . . These damned Police are now to be armed. Englishmen, will you put up with this?" Another handbill berated Londoners for being afraid of those

MERCENARY, DAMNABLE, VILE WRETCHES, PEEL'S BLOOD-THIRSTY GANG. From them we can expect no mercy, for their nature, like that of their founder, is base, blood-seeking, and villainous; but what is [sic] their numbers? Why, from 3 to 4,000! What is that compared even with one-hundredth part of the male population of London!

Remember what the French and the Belgians have done! and *what a pitiless [sic], helpless, and cowardly people we seem.* One hour of true liberty is worth ages of slavery! . . . . *You are not Englishmen* if you suffer your heads to be wantonly broken by that BLOODY GANG. . . .[99]

This tactic, the breaking of heads, was to be the greatest police legacy of the Reform riots. The "baton charge" was born. And ever since 9 November 1830, this nonlethal method of crowd control has been adopted by modern police forces around the world. It all began with an idea of Francis Place, the radical tailor of Charing Cross, who wanted Reform but feared revolution.[100] Place had seen policemen attacked and injured by the rioters; the standard police response was then to wade into the throng and take prisoners. Place suggested to Superintendent Joseph Thomas, C Division, that "when he saw a mob prepared to make an attack, to lead his men on and thrash those who composed the mob with their staves [truncheons] as long as any of them remained together, but to take none into custody; and that if this were done once or twice, there would be no more such mobs."[101] On 9 November, the seventh day of rioting, the idea was put into practice. A crowd of 400 gathered in the sanctuary of the City of London and rallied through Temple Bar to do battle with the Metropolitans. "My advice was followed," wrote Place. The police retreated, collected a group of sixty constables, and then attacked the surprised crowd, and, using their truncheons, drove it back into the City of London. "No one was killed, no limb was broken," commented Place. An alternative to Peterloo tactics had been invented. Although "many were bruised and many heads were broken, . . . there were no more mobs."[102] The next day the disturbances ended. A week's rioting in a city with a population nearing 2 million had for the first time in English history been suppressed without any resort to soldiers and by a large civil force armed only with pieces of wood.

Only days after the disorders subsided, Wellington's Government fell, Peel was out of office, and the Whigs came to power for the first time since

1806–7. But the rejection of a Reform bill in the Commons and the King's prorogation of Parliament on 22 April 1831 portended further trouble. It came on the evening of 27 April. Once again, troops were alerted but never used; peacekeeping was left to the New Police. Dispersed in groups of 15 to 60 men, a total of 1,100 police, including all of the central (A to F) divisions, were deployed across the metropolis. Constables in outlying districts were brought into the city center, and plainclothes police circulated to make arrests; the emphasis, however, was on baton charges to disperse the crowds in Charing Cross, Pall Mall, and Regent Street.[103] For the police, the night was long and the fighting intense; they made 168 arrests, and suffered and inflicted countless injuries.[104] No one was killed, but property damage was extensive. As before, the rioters' targets were carefully chosen: hundreds of windowpanes in the fancy shops along the Strand, gentlemen's clubs in St. James's Street, and dozens of Tory town houses. At Apsley House, the destruction ended when the Duke of Wellington's servants fired over the heads of the crowd and requested respect for the corpse of the Duchess lying on the premises. But the windows at Sir Robert Peel's residence were not spared. Nor was the house of Sir Robert Wilson, "who used to be an idol of the mob." His windows were broken, explained the *Annual Register*, by a crowd leavened with Irishmen "because while he supported the [Reform] Bill, he disapproved of that part of it which went to diminish the number of English Members."[105]

In June Parliament reconvened, and although the Commons passed a Reform bill by 136 votes, the Lords on 8 October rejected it by 51 votes. Once again, the capital was convulsed with window-breaking mobs. The scenario of 11 and 12 October was by now familiar: no soldiers, only baton-charging policemen trying to disperse rioters before they achieved much property damage. Tory town houses were again besieged, the worst damage being done at the Duke of Wellington's. By the time the police arrived, a mob had broken every windowpane in Apsley House. A furious Wellington afterward ordered iron shutters put across every window, prompting London radicals to dub him "the Iron Duke"; the shutters would remain in place until his death twenty years later. During the disturbances, the police, in Superintendent John May's words, "had to use their truncheons freely." The effectiveness of the hard-pressed police is best assessed when contrasted with the violence that rocked provincial England in October and November. Reform mobs burned Nottingham Castle, the seat of the Duke of Newcastle, and plundered large sections of Bristol; country gentlemen were barricading their estates and even Peel, at Drayton Manor near Birmingham, was "importing carbines" to protect his property. While the military struggled to keep order elsewhere in the country, in London Peel's Bloody Gang certainly bloodied some heads, but they killed no one in restoring order to the streets of the capital.[106]

In December 1831, the House of Commons passed a third Reform bill; the following April the House of Lords, under duress, finally gave its assent. Had the Lords not yielded, there is no telling what scenes would have ensued in the streets of London. In fact, however, the Reform violence was over.[107] The only trouble in the capital came in March 1832. The Government had called for a "fast day" in memory of the recent cholera victims in the metropolis; a group of radicals countered with a call for food distribution to the poor – a "feast day." A crowd estimated at 25,000 gathered in Finsbury Square and, after hissing was followed by stoning of the police, the Blue Devils, divided into two groups each three men deep, executed baton charges for thirty minutes before the square was finally cleared. In these Fast Day disturbances, eight men were arrested and an unspecified number injured. A year later, in May 1833, acting on Home Secretary Melbourne's orders, the police dispersed a meeting at Cold Bath Fields that had called for a "national convention" to press workingmen's demands including the right to vote. In only ten minutes, 180 police scattered the crowd of 4,000 and took 29 prisoners. But it was a bloody few minutes: Twenty demonstrators were injured and three policemen stabbed, one of them, Robert Culley, dying of his wounds.[108] The third mass meeting in as many years drew 30,000 persons to Copenhagen Fields in 1834. Having assembled to protest the recent transportation of six Dorsetshire laborers (the "Tolpuddle Martyrs") for their attempts to form a farm workers' union, the crowd peaceably marched to Parliament to petition for the men's release. This time there was no violence on either side: The police – backed by troops, artillery, and 5,000 special constables – watched the huge procession, which was allowed to disperse quietly.[109]

Two of these three mass meetings in 1832–4 had degenerated into violence. In each case the police, while pelted with stones and sometimes threatened by more lethal weapons, had initiated the disorders by carrying out their orders to disperse the meeting. Apart from the wisdom of this decision, it was undeniable that the level of resulting personal injuries was low: The incidents were hardly reenactments of the travesty at Peterloo. In the aftermath of Cold Bath Fields, the most controversial of the three cases, the popular outcry concerned busted heads and blocked escape routes. Significantly, the only killing was of Constable Culley; the policemen's batons took no lives. More serious was the revelation that a police sergeant named William Popay had for two years been a spy in the midst of radical meetings. This naturally awoke old fears that the purpose of the New Police was not only to prevent meetings of the people but also to act as the eyes and ears of government ministers. Significantly, however, the outcry, unlike the one in Sidmouth's day, produced two select committee inquiries into the people's grievances. The investigation into the violence at Cold Bath Fields found evidence of irregularities by individual constables, but not enough to condemn the force for brutality in dispersing the meeting; the Popay committee condemned the sergeant for activities that it judged to be more provocative than investigative and, although it recognized the Commissioners' right to use plainclothes police, reprimanded Popay's superiors for not keeping him under tighter rein. The Popay incident helped to delay for a decade the establishment of a detective department within the Metropolitan Police.[110]

From Peelers to Bobbies

By the mid-1830s, the unthinkable was slowly becoming the acceptable. It was clear that the new police force was not going to be abolished. Parliament, which had without controversy established it, pronounced in a committee report of 1834 that "the object ... long sought, viz. an efficient and systematic establishment of Police, has been practically attained." Not only was crime being brought under control, the committee found, but also "on no occasion since the establishment of the Metropolitan Police has the military authority been called upon to assist the civil power in repressing any disturbance." The 1834 report specifically rejected the famous finding of the committee of twelve years earlier that liberty and police were irreconcilable principles; whereas it described the old police as "a necessary evil," it found the new one to be a positive good, indeed "one of the most valuable of modern institutions."[111]

Even more remarkable was the slowly growing acceptance of the New Police outside Parliament. The Government's decision in 1833 to share the costs and reduce the local police rates proved to be a wise concession. This compromise removed "the principal grievance" of the mid-1830s: total local financing of a force totally beyond local control. Some parishes continued to lower or manipulate property ratings and to be delinquent in payments, but such practices were declining by the late 1830s. Opposition to the police for financial reasons was becoming separated from the political opposition concentrated among the more extreme political radicals.[112]

Many Londoners were coming to appreciate the positive role of the police in the prevention and detection of crime. The statistics revealed a decrease in house larcenies and burglaries, which the 1834 committee ascribed to police vigilance, and an increase in common assaults and street thefts, which was said to reflect higher police arrest rates. The new police's effectiveness against crime was used by the 1834 committee to dismiss the traditional counter-arguments based on cost and constitutionality: The government-controlled police simply worked better than the local parish forces. And most allegations of negligence, the committee found, came from the force's rivals, the city's fire companies and the supplanted magistrates at Bow Street and the other Police Offices.[113]

But the force had to be mild to win broad popular acceptance. The 1834 committee found the bulk of the charges brought by the parishes alleging police brutality to be unsupported. Peel's decision not to arm the police clearly helped to win the hearts of Londoners. Commissioner Rowan noted that for the control of crowds "the use of the baton" was not only "efficient against the mobs' weapons" but also that "contests solely of the baton, against the bludgeon, partake of 'fair fighting,' which is somewhat conciliatory to the feelings of English mobs."[114] Newspapers were increasingly treating their readers to stories of heroic constables grappling with criminals armed with knives and sometimes even guns; those in authority, the police, thus appeared in the role of the underdog against villains who did not abide by the rules of fair play. *The Times* summed up the changing mood towards the police by noting that

a military force supposes military weapons of some kind. The police have neither swords nor pistols to defend themselves; and recent circumstances suffice to prove that for the preservation of their own lives, to say nothing of the public, the bits of stick with which they are at present provided are anything but an adequate protection.[115]

By the mid-1830s, assaults against policemen *for being policemen* were diminishing. Grand juries were beginning to throw out bills alleging assaults by the police; the public even began to protest the Government's reluctance to pay constables' legal expenses. The parishes were now widely requesting assistance from the police, indeed protesting that there were not enough men to serve the public.[116]

What had begun in 1829 as an unpopular innovation was, a decade later, an everyday reality. In 1839 the Seven Police Offices became simply police courts, the Bow Street Foot Patrol and Thames Police were absorbed into the Metropolitan Police (the Horse Patrol having been incorporated three years earlier), and the City of London was pressured into reforming its police. The Metropolitan Police District was extended to 15 miles from Charing Cross, and the force level was raised by 590 men and costs by £44,000. Public acceptance was evident in smaller ways as well. In 1837 a large temporary augmentation was permitted for Queen Victoria's coronation; in 1838 small police stations were authorized for the first time in the House of Commons and Buckingham Palace; and in 1839 the Commissioners were granted their long-sought right to wear uniforms, which, to appear unmilitary, were "without epaulettes."[117]

Englishmen were beginning to understand the distinction between the individual's rights and liberties and society's claims to orderliness. Even working-class radicals who continued to object to a government-controlled police were finding it increasingly difficult to hate an unarmed gendarmerie with orders like these:

No constable is justified in depriving anyone of his liberty for words only, and language, however violent, towards the police constable himself, is not to be noticed; the constables are particularly cautioned not to answer angrily, or enter into altercation with any person while on duty. A constable who allows himself to be irritated by any language whatsoever shows that he has not a command of his temper, which is absolutely necessary in an officer vested with such extensive powers by law....

The constables are to recollect on all occasions that ... any instance of unnecessary violence by them ... will be severely punished. A constable must not use his staff because the party is violent *in behaviour* or language.... If he does his duty in a quiet and determined manner, such conduct will probably excite the well-disposed to assist him, if he requires them....

A constable will be civil to all people of *every* rank and class.

These instructions from Peel to his new London police would later evolve into what Charles Reith has called the "Principles of the British Police." Among them are the precepts that "the police are the public and that the public are the police," and that "the extent to which the co-operation of the public can be secured diminishes, proportionately, the necessity of the use of physical force and compulsion for achieving police objectives."[118]

There were many, many steps yet to be taken on the road to civilizing the Peelers. One of them can be seen in a letter of March 1838 from Charles Rowan to Joseph Hume. That Radical MP had asked the Commissioner for his opinion on the question of "free admission" of the working classes to Westminster Abbey and St. Paul's Cathedral. Rowan replied that "considerable improvement has taken place, within the last few years, in the conduct of the people on public occasions.... There has been comparatively little drunkenness or disorder, and every indication of good feeling evinced towards the police." Rowan hoped that his testimony to this "correct and orderly conduct of the people ... may be found in any degree useful" to opening "public places of enjoyment and recreation ... to every class of the community."[119] The extraordinary idea was beginning to take hold that the police were the public, the public the police. The Blue Devils were on their way to becoming Bobbies.

CHAPTER 9

Consolidation of the Irish constabulary

As to the Repeal question, it is merely a catchy word. Yesterday, the cry was "Emancipation"; to day, it is, "Tithes" and "Repeal"; tomorrow, it will be something else. And thus will the passions of the people be kept boiling over until, at some favourable opportunity, an effort will be made to throw off [the] English connection, and a free and undisguised licence be granted for the open indulgence of long cherished rancour and bitterness towards England.
– George Fitzgerald, Stipendiary Magistrate, Cashel, Tipperary,
December 1832

Do not believe all the malice and falsehoods propagated against the Government. Parsons and Policemen are like all humanity, and are not to be trusted – but they are well looked after. The latter are daily mending, but I believe a Parson of the old school is incorrigible. Considering the times and circumstances in which the two professions have been formed, it is a mercy that they are not worse.
– Lord Lieutenant Anglesey, in reply to a letter from Lord Cloncurry,
May 1833

"Historians have not ceased to ask how near the country was to revolution." Sir Llewellyn Woodward was referring to England in 1830–2. The growing impatience of the middle classes and the anger of the far more numerous working classes confronted the apparently obdurate Tories in the House of Lords. Such tinder was made the more combustible by the sparks of successful constitutional revolution in France, the revolt of the farm laborers across southern England, the destruction of Nottingham and the sack of Bristol by Reform Bill rioters, and the widespread hostility accorded the New Police in London. "The nation stood on the brink of mass violence, possibly revolution," T. A. Critchley has written. In a calmer assessment, two recent scholars have concluded that "in the ten days of greatest crisis" in May 1832 "there is ample testimony to the belief that revolution was a very serious possibility."[1] Because the Tory peers relented and the final crisis was in fact averted, we shall never know how near England came to upheaval.

But the crisis of 1830–2 was undeniably heightened by a new challenge from Albion's other island. In the aftermath of Catholic Emancipation, and chronologically precisely overlapping the crisis in England, the Irish peasantry launched a boycott of tithe payments to the Anglican church that was sufficiently widespread to be known as the "Tithe War."[2] These twin crises of English suffrage and Irish tithe reform placed an unprecedented strain on the authorities in both countries.

In early 1829, fully five-sixths of the troops in the United Kingdom were either in Ireland or poised for shipment on the west coast of Britain. But toward the end of that year the London Government began to tap its military reservoir: Army strength in Ireland dipped below 20,000 men in October, fell to 18,000 in April 1830, and sank to 15,000 by the winter of 1830. England's needs became Ireland's crisis. In December, the new Whig Home Secretary, Lord Melbourne, informed the Irish Lord Lieutenant, the Marquess of Anglesey, of a secret plan involving "vessels of war" that would help with the evacuation of Protestants from western Ireland "in case you should be compelled to abandon Connaught"; the Government was, however, prepared to fight to hold the country east of the River Shannon. Two months later, in February 1831, when Dublin Castle was pleading for more troops, Melbourne abruptly informed Anglesey that the regiments at Bristol, Liverpool, and Glasgow were needed against the Reform agitation in Britain. "Under these circumstances you will feel the prudence of not unnecessarily denuding us of troops at such a Moment." The Irish Government was thus left with no choice. The army, already reduced in size by one-fourth over the last seventeen months, would have to get by with thin detachments at its 145 posts across the island.[3]

As the pressures for Reform intensified in England, the Governments in Dublin and London continued to juggle the twin demands for troops. Lord Lieutenant Anglesey, a sensible man, feared that "the Insurrection" in Ireland would begin in January 1832; he begged London "in these times of danger on both sides of the Channel, ... to keep a large power of Steam Vessels available, so that we may be able to assist each other as wanted." In February 1831 he had called for a doubling of the army of 40,000 men; failing this, "an addition of 10,000 at this moment w^{ld} effectually prevent a rising." The crisis of 1831–2 did not blossom into political rebellion, but the Tithe War endured with unremitting intensity. "Some men," grumbled Lord Cloncurry, "think that a rebellion in Ireland would divert John Bull from the contemplation of his own grievances." These were settled in May 1832 when the House of Lords gave its grudging assent to suffrage reform.[4]

In July Anglesey again called for 10,000 more troops for Ireland. "The present state is worse than War," he wrote Prime Minister Earl Grey. "A vast number of generally well informed Persons believe that we are upon the very brink of Insurrection." The London Government responded by sending four regiments, "an immediate effective addition of 3500 Men." By the end of 1832 the army level in Ireland stood at 23,000. In March 1833 a buoyant Melbourne informed Anglesey that additional troops were available, since "both the North of England and Scotland are now tranquil, [and] troops might be safely spared from both."[5] Ironically, the Tithe War in Ireland was already slowly winding down.

I. A challenge to all constituted authority

After Emancipation: popular disillusionment and a new Castle toughness

The enactment of Catholic Emancipation in April 1829 left Irishmen in a surly mood. Hard-line Protestants resented this breach of their political privileges. To England's abolition of the Protestant state in 1800 and its erosion of traditional Anglo-Irish control of the magistracy, police, and Yeomanry was now added the heresy of parliamentary power for papists. Daniel O'Connell's peasant followers were little happier. The elixir of Emancipation had raised but not satisfied popular expectations. Although granting political representation to Catholics, the English Government of Wellington and "Orange" Peel had quintupled the franchise qualification to £10 in order to deprive O'Connell of a mass electorate. The number of freehold voters fell from 100,000 to 16,000. With freeholdings no longer politically valuable, landlords were discouraged from multiplying the number of holdings and encouraged to pursue a policy of eviction. To the peasant, Emancipation now seemed a bogus issue; he would never sit in Parliament, and to gain this right he had lost his vote. "I have often heard their conversations," reported a Catholic clergyman,

when they say, "What good did the emancipation do us? are we better clothed or fed ...? are we not as naked as we were, and eating dry potatoes when we can get them? ..." Then some of them that went to England, and saw the way the English labourers are fed and clothed, came back and told them, "If you saw the way that the English labourers lived, you would never live as you do."[6]

Emancipation had produced widespread political disenfranchisement and posed the seeming contradiction of a continued compulsory payment of tithe to the *Protestant* Church of Ireland. Not only did tithing in this period of poor harvests affect precisely those who had been recently disenfranchised (70 percent of tithe payers had holdings of less than fifteen acres), but, ironically, as a result of recent reforms, the tax now touched graziers and large farmers as well. In short, the tithe question, in Melbourne's words, was "most fearful and appalling" because it was "produced by real grievance and suffering."[7]

By contrast, after Emancipation, there was widespread agreement among the authorities in London and Dublin that the time for concession was past. Ever since 1826 the Government had been a largely passive observer of the challenges to public order in Ireland. To Peel in February 1829, the lesson of Emancipation was to "beware that we do not teach them how easy it will be to paralyze the Government and the Law." In July he urged the Irish Government to pursue a policy of "vigorous unsparing enforcement of the law, criminal and civil." In the Home Secretary's judgment, Dublin Castle authorities should "postpone ... extensive schemes for the employment, and education, and improvement of the people" in favor of "two measures ... indispensable to the success of all such schemes – the constitution of a thoroughly efficient police, and the punishment of crime." In the summer of

1829, while Peel labored over the details of the implementation of his police in London, he maintained a frequent and lengthy correspondence with the Irish Chief Secretary concerning reforms in the Irish constabulary. Only Leveson Gower's shortcomings as an administrator would dash Peel's hopes for a powerful and totally government-controlled police in Ireland.[8]

The fall from power of Wellington's Tory Government in November 1830 did not change the new policy of vigorous enforcement of the laws in Ireland. Earl Grey's Whigs, "the Friends of the People," would show a profound "respect for property in all its manifestations." The new London Government thoroughly overhauled the Irish Administration. The reappointment of the Marquess of Anglesey as Lord Lieutenant was well received in Ireland, for the sixty-six-year-old general was seen as a pro-Catholic and a reformer. Anglesey's popularity was, however, accompanied by his impatience with party politics and his inability to deal effectively with Grey's Government in London and his own colleagues in the Castle.[9]

The second change was a new Civil Under-Secretary. The sixty-three-year-old William Gregory was increasingly uncomfortable "in this age of *liberal* doctrine." The concession of Emancipation and the Whigs' subsequent electoral victory prompted him to resign after eighteen years' service. The new Under-Secretary, appointed in December 1830, was Col. Sir William Gosset. A veteran military officer who had seen "a good deal of service in bad climates," Gossett had been Anglesey's private secretary and, since January 1829, had filled the new Castle post of secretary for the constabulary. His appointment as Under-Secretary nullified the gains made in the administrative reform of 1829; Gossett would hold both offices until his replacement by Thomas Drummond in July 1835. Like Gregory, Gosset proved to be an able man of business who benefited in particular from his "intimate and detailed knowledge of the Constabulary system." But he was not possessed of Gregory's even temperament. Gossett was "a man of high and sensitive feelings," who, when questioned, believed "his honor [to be] attacked" and threatened frequently to resign. The Lord Lieutenant would find it increasingly difficult to work with him. In 1833, toward the end of Anglesey's term of office, he confessed to Lord Cloncurry that Gosset

is, indeed, much too sensitive, for he not unfrequently [sic] breaks out with me, and I have scenes by no means decorous or agreeable. Still, he is an honourable man, and I make allowances for temper. I have just this moment had one of these scenes.[10]

Anglesey's relations with his Chief Secretary, the third new man in the Castle, were equally stormy. The Irish Administration of 1830–3 fit the pattern of Talbot–Grant and Wellesley–Goulburn of 1818–27: One of the pair was "soft" on popular issues; the other, "hard." Anglesey's Chief Secretary, Edward George Geoffrey Smith Stanley (Figure 9.1), was the hard one. The eldest son of the 13th Earl of Derby, Stanley began his political career as a Whig and ended it as a three-time Tory Prime Minister (1852, 1858–9, 1866–8). After attending Eton and Christ Church, Oxford, the earl's son entered Parliament in 1822. Silent during the debates of that year

Figure 9.1 Edward Stanley, Baron Stanley (1844), 14th Earl of Derby (1851). A portrait of Lord Stanley, age forty-five, in 1844. (Painting by F. R. Say, by permission of the National Portrait Gallery)

on the Irish constabulary, Stanley spoke rarely in the 1820s, his only notable speech being an impassioned defense in 1824 of the Church of Ireland. In August 1830, at a Preston by-election, he was defeated by the Radical leader "Orator" Hunt of Peterloo fame; indeed, he was "mobbed and ran some risk of his life." After the Whig victory in November, Earl Grey found Stanley a safe seat at Windsor and named him Chief Secretary for Ireland.[11]

The thirty-one-year-old Stanley would fill this arduous post for the duration of the Tithe War, from the winter of 1830 to the spring of 1833. In English politics, he was a free trader and a moderate Reformer; in Irish affairs, he was both a constructive reformer and a stern upholder of public order and property rights. In his two and a half years in office he began a program of public works, established a national system of elementary education, reorganized the revenues, and reformed the grand juries. Stanley's Tithe

Act of 1832 established compulsory composition throughout the country and stimulated the trend toward commutation.[12]

But with his reformist streak went what R. B. McDowell has called "his latent toryism": a rigid insistence on obedience to the laws and enforcement of property rights. He had voted for Emancipation but adamantly supported a high property franchise. He supported tithe reform largely to improve the collection of Church revenues; in 1834 he would leave the Whig Party over the liberals' insistence on secularization of Anglican property holdings. To support property rights in Ireland, Stanley would stretch the police and military to their breaking points. Anglesey, who opposed using force to collect even a half-year's arrears of tithe, violently disagreed with Stanley's claim that two army battalions would be sufficient to collect all unpaid tithes in the most disturbed parts of the country. Stanley's proposed coercive legislation was so draconian that many of his colleagues – including Grey, Anglesey, and the English Attorney-General – were "appalled and disgusted."[13]

In great measure, Stanley's unpopularity in Ireland was the product of his personality. He was a man of great "driving power" and administrative competence. But he could also be haughty, overly frank, impatient, and brusque; many of his traits were a caricature of Robert Peel's harsher features without Peel's charm and affability. Long before he finished his term of office, Stanley had managed to antagonize not only O'Connell, who reviled him, but also many of his colleagues in the English Cabinet and in Dublin Castle. Anglesey, who never felt comfortable with him, described his Chief Secretary as a man of "strong *Church* prejudices – he has the *ton prononcé*." The people "do not like Stanley. He is too high and rough with them."[14]

Enforcing the law: the Tithe War of 1830–3

On many subjects, the Government's policy on police employment did not change. The Irish constabulary continued to keep the peace at elections. In 1832 two dozen constables from Kilkenny and Queen's County monitored the polls in County Carlow and 150 police stood guard in the Meath election. In a variety of matters, use of the police did continue to be restricted or prohibited. Constables might escort prisoners to jail but were not to act as jailers. Policemen were to avoid enforcing the fish and game laws and to decline conveying any offenders to prison. They could not serve as collectors of tolls. They might not assist in the collection of the county cess, and could distrain goods for nonpayment only with a warrant from magistrates at petty sessions documenting a case history of violent resistance or rescues. The police were prohibited from executing civil warrants to levy money from small farmers for the nonpayment of laborers' wages.[15] In the important matter of rents, the police were "not to be employed as bailiffs in distraining" for nonpayment; against local requests the Subinspector of Armagh "pleaded in excuse of his refusal his instructions from Government." But in cases of prior violent resistance, sworn upon oath, the police could legally interfere. They could not, however, help with landlords' ejectments of tenants. Adamant Subinspectors in Cavan and King's County were supported by their Inspectors-General and the Castle legal authorities. Thomas D'Arcy refused to have his men "degraded into Sheriffs' Bailiffs ... and placed in the most obnoxious as well as perilous Situations." Sir John Harvey objected that "the inevitable tendency ... if the police are employed in effecting compulsory Ejectments ... will be greatly to encrease the unpopularity of the Establishment." Crown Law Adviser Richard Greene ruled that only the subsheriff and his bailiffs might eject and went on to state his legal doubts that petty sessions could require police aid in such cases.[16]

The restraint in using police in these matters was overshadowed by the new policy of employing them in others. The Duke of Leinster objected to bayonet-toting constables managing crowds at the Curragh racetrack. The police were "frequently" employed in clearing road nuisances; Inspector-General William Miller complained that "no description of duty [was] more annoying to the feelings of the Police" and none "more rigorously enjoined by the Local Authorities." Apart from pigs, sheep, and carts, the nuisances now included beggars and vagabonds, who, by a new Castle ruling, might be seized and imprisoned for twenty-four hours. The police were also empowered to help army officers procure billets for the troops and impress carriages for conveying the army's baggage. Particularly irritating was the new policy that henceforth the police should not "suffer flagrant violations of the Lord's day [Sabbath] to be committed with impunity."[17] To the infringement on popular pastimes was added a tough attitude toward collection of the Church cess. Written commands from magistrates at petty sessions were now sufficient to require police aid; collection parties numbering sixty to seventy constables were typical in 1832. The ever-increasing use of police and the general relaxation of the Castle's attitudes toward the local magistrates may be seen in a general order from the Castle Under-Secretary to the constabulary. "In all Cases," noted Gosset, "where the interests of justice are likely to be defeated unless prompt Measures be taken ... it is the duty of the Constabulary to render full obedience and assistance to a Magistrate and to execute his Commands."[18]

The most dramatic change in Castle policy concerned police aid in the collection of tithes. This change coincided with the arrival of Edward Stanley as Chief Secretary and signaled the beginning of the Tithe War in Graigue, Kilkenny, in November 1830.[19] It all began when parishioners boycotted the purchase of livestock and property distrained by the Government for refusal to pay tithe to the Church of Ireland.[20] The Tithe War had many causes. There was, of course, the long-standing hostility to funding an alien church and the recent disillusionment over Emancipation. The composition of the tithe established a fixed rate, negotiable only every seven years, at a time when agricultural prices had declined by up to 50 percent in the last decade. Many landlords had lowered their rent charges; why not tithe owners? With grasslands now titheable, many large farmers found themselves allied with smallholders and conacre tenants, who formed three-quarters of all tithe payers. Parish priests, O'Connellites, and local factions at fairs composed the rest of this antitithe army, which adopted the techniques of passive resistance and the organization formerly employed by the Catholic Association.[21]

The Government's response was to get tough with tithe defaulters. The Inspector-General for Leinster, Sir John Harvey, later admitted that in November 1830 he had influenced the new Chief Secretary. "I did use the freedom of suggesting to the Government that this civil force assistance should be given, *though it is contrary to the regulations under which the constabulary force have hitherto acted.*" Most insistent, of course, were local tithe owners. As taxpayers who paid half of the costs of the constabulary, they vented their frustrations by insisting that, "with due submission, we have a claim upon their services."[22]

The police – totaling 120 constables – were used for the first time, at Graigue in December 1830, to protect the sale of goods seized in lieu of tithe payment. In early 1831 police aid was authorized for the collection of tithe and for distraining for nonpayment. The first application of the new policy came at Graigue in March and April 1831: 300 police and 300 soldiers were "indefatigable, out every day and frequently twice a day ... traversing a great extent of country."[23]

Graigue was the Government's test case, and the results were disappointing. Refusal to pay was widespread and distraining hampered, ironically, by the laws of the land. For example, it was illegal in distraint cases to break any lock or force open any outer door. A pattern soon developed of lookout parties signaling the arrival of the police; amid shouting and the trumpeting of hunting horns, the people would rush home and pen in their cattle, sheep, and pigs. The Kilkenny Subinspector reported that the people would even show their animals through the locked gate, "but we could not touch them. Every new padlock in the shops around Graigue was bought." The police were also legally prohibited from distraining between sunset and sunrise; in the evenings the people therefore released their animals to graze. A third law provided that, since tithe was a civil claim, defaulters could not be arrested and jailed.[24]

The 600 soldiers and police patrolling Graigue for two months collected only one-third of the parish tithe. Inspector-General Harvey believed that even if the men were kept on the march for a year, they would not be able to collect all the tithes. And, he noted, Graigue was only 1 of 150 parishes in Kilkenny. "If the law had been different," said Subinspector George Brown, "the whole parish would have been cleared in a week." But as it stood, said Brown, 50,000 police and troops would not have helped.[25]

In the spring of 1831 tithe resistance spread from Kilkenny to Queen's County and Carlow. That summer, opposition appeared in Kildare and Wexford. The boycott spread in the fall to Meath, Wicklow, Westmeath, King's County, and Tipperary. In 1832 the defiance spread to Cork, to counties in Connaught, and even into parts of Ulster. Large, peaceable meetings ranging in size from 30,000 to 100,000 persons protested the payment of tithe in the ever-widening circle of disaffected counties.[26]

Police aid was rendered "in almost every instance," reported the Crown Law Adviser. Typical was the 106-man police party wandering around two parishes in Galway, covering 642 miles in ten days in September 1832; in London the Secretary at War complained to Dublin about the excessive amounts of "Marching Money" charged by military regiments in Ireland. The troops, reported Anglesey, are "much harassed and are getting very savage." The police held up better, but Harvey noted in October 1832 that the patrolling for tithe, a duty in which the Kildare force had been "long engaged," was beginning "to try the steadiness and good conduct of the men." In Kilkenny the Subinspector complained of "being out several days with a whole party without bringing in anything." A massive final effort that involved thousands of police and soldiers in driving for tithe from August 1832 to May 1833 netted a national total of only £12,316. The Subinspector in Queen's County reported that the tithe would never be collected in his county; Inspector-General Harvey pronounced that "no force of military or police" could collect tithe in the province.[27]

As the years passed, the tithe obligation fell further in arrears. The past year's charge became uncollectable even as the new year's became due. And each year, more and more persons refused to pay. In 1831, in Kilkenny and Queen's County, half or more of the tithe went unpaid. In 1832 a similar proportion was unpaid in nine counties in Leinster and Munster; and, in 1833, in twenty-two counties in every province. The national total for default on the tithe in 1831 was £133,300; in 1832 it doubled to £266,800; in 1833 it reached £418,500 – a three-year total of £818,600. "The whole Country," moaned Anglesey, "is organized & acting upon one single subject.... This confounded system of Passive Resistance is perplexing to the last degree."[28]

The Government's handling of the Tithe War involved belated coercion, then conciliation. In July 1832 the crackdown began. Chief Secretary Stanley revived and extended Peel's Peace Preservation Police. He unearthed the Whiteboy Act of 1787, 27 Geo. 3 c. 15, which made it a felony to defraud a clergyman of his tithe and empowered the Government to arrest anyone attending antitithe meetings. The next several months saw scores of persons arrested, among them one Feargus O'Connor, the future English Chartist leader. A new act, 2 & 3 Will. 4 c. 51, defined tithe defaulters as Crown debtors, making them liable to imprisonment. Finally, in April 1833, Parliament passed a coercion act, 3 & 4 Will. 4 c. 3, which banned all meetings, imposed a night curfew, suspended habeas corpus, and established military law courts.[29]

Modest policies of conciliation dated from 1832. A tithe act of that year made composition compulsory but left unchanged the obligation to pay; another act assured tithe owners of government payment of their arrears for 1831. The Church Temporalities Act of 1833 reduced the number of pluralities, sinecures, and bishoprics and abolished an unpopular tax, the Church cess; but the act entirely avoided the tithe issue. In March 1833 Edward Stanley, in disgust and frustration, resigned his office. As it had begun with his arrival, so the Tithe War would end with Stanley's departure from Ireland.[30]

Substantive redress of grievances was achieved by the new Chief Secretary, "a modest and industrious [English] country gentleman," Sir Edward John Littleton (cr. Baron Hatherton, 1835). The forty-five-year-old liberal Whig had supported criminal law reform, Catholic Emancipation, and the suffrage extension of 1832. Before he left for Ireland, Littleton sponsored an act that created a "Million Fund" to pay off Irish tithe owners, using Treasury revenues. His chief secretaryship constituted a return to the Castle's policies of the later 1820s. "We shall restrain," he wrote Home Secretary Melbourne, "the too easy habit into which the Government had got of granting [police] aid and which of itself encreased the number of applications."[31] On a wide range of duties – the revenue, grand jury cess, protection of property, clearing of road nuisances, policing of fairs, distraining for nonpayment of rent – the employment of police was bridled.[32]

The most burning issue, of course, was tithe collection. Littleton was shocked to discover the widespread police interference. Citing the Constabulary Act, 3 Geo. 4 c. 103 s. 24 (1822), and the Petty Sessions Act, 7 & 8 Geo. 4 c. 67 s. 17 (1827), the Chief Secretary reprimanded Under-Secretary Gosset:

I must own they so clearly appear to me to prohibit the employment of Policemen in any manner, directly or indirectly, in any part of any process for the recovery of Tithe, that I am at a loss to comprehend the practice which seems to have obtained so generally of employing them for such purposes. Will you have the goodness to inform me how the Irish Government has hitherto construed these provisions in the statutes, and whether the complaint of their infraction be not well founded?

The use of police, he stressed, was not for "probable or apprehended resistance" but only for "forcible resistance, *previously made.*" Littleton stripped Gosset of his discretionary powers and demanded that all applications for police aid be forwarded to him; henceforth the Lord Lieutenant would approve all requests.[33] In June 1833 all police aid was suspended in the collection of tithe arrears. The Government's policy was "to force the clergy to apply for relief from the Million Fund." Littleton stated that "fiscal advantage" should not be "purchased at the cost of universal hostility to the Police force in Ireland." In February 1834 Littleton sponsored a bill, subsequently defeated in the Lords, that would have converted tithe payment into a land tax. In November the Whigs fell from office; Littleton returned to England; and in the summer of 1835, after the Whigs' return to power, Gosset would be pressured to resign. Littleton's tithe proposal served as the basis for the Irish Tithe Act of 1838, which reduced the assessment by one-fourth and converted it into a rent surcharge.[34]

The resurgence of agrarian crime

Coincident with the Tithe War of 1830–3 came a revival of Whiteboyism in western and central Ireland. The issues concerned wages and the letting of

Table 9.1. *Outrages reported by the constabulary: Connaught and County Clare, 1831–2*

	1831	1832
Administering oaths	952	133
Assaults connected with Ribbonism	566	119
Attacks on houses	1,684	209
Homicides	72	53
Houghing and maiming cattle	125	103
Illegal notices	875	268
Leveling	244	79
Robbery of arms	571	35
Demand of arms	135	24
SELECT TOTAL	5,224	1,023

Note: These figures represent the earliest police recording of agrarian outrages, which was first systematically done in the police district of Connaught (Clare, Galway, Leitrim, Mayo, Roscommon, Sligo). It is extremely misleading at this date to compare these figures with the other submitted provincial returns, or to calculate national totals, since in Under-Secretary Gosset's understatement, "The classification is not entirely uniform in each province." *PP 1833* (80), 29:429.

land; the criminals were the laborers, farmers' servant boys, and cottiers. Protests from this "least respectable Part of the Peasantry" complicated the situation of lawlessness in Ireland because the Whiteboy grievances were pressed against the farmers who protested tithe payment to the established church. In Clare, Galway, and Roscommon, and in Tipperary and Queen's County, a class war thus overlay the national campaign against the tithe.[35] The most intense disorders were in Clare, where "Terry Alts" and "Lady Clares" dug up farmers' grasslands, planted them with potatoes, and demanded lower conacre rents, higher wages, and "land more divided among the People" (see Table 9.1). The Government was forced to send in an extraordinary legal tribunal, a special commission, which sentenced nearly 100 offenders to be transported.[36]

Nationwide committals for Whiteboy offenses – stealing arms, attacking houses, assembling armed by night, and engaging in "seditious or treasonable practices" – trebled from 418 in 1828–30 to 1,288 in 1831–3. The worst personal violence was concentrated in Tipperary and Clare: In 1832 these counties accounted for 251 of the 620 committals for murder in Ireland. In 1831 and 1832 Clare, Galway, Roscommon, Tipperary, and Queen's County produced 579 committals for the crimes of riotously assembling armed by night and attacking dwelling houses. By contrast, counties that were in the forefront of the resistance to tithe payment registered low levels of criminal violence. In Wexford, Kilkenny, Carlow, and Kildare only thirty-five persons were charged with murder in 1832 and only sixty-three with the previously mentioned Whiteboy offenses in 1831 and 1832.[37]

Personal violence thus continued to be associated with traditional agrarian grievances. But as the tithe became a national question in 1832, violence in certain areas became directed against those persons – clergymen, proctors, and viewers – who opposed any tithe reform. In northern Kilkenny, and in Tipperary and Queen's County, Whiteboy groups, realizing that no tithe might mean higher wages, joined the antitithe movement. A recent scholar, Patrick O'Donoghue, has shown that where tithe opposition overlay pre-existing agrarian secret societies, the "opposition [to the tithe] was generally more violent." Southeast Leinster continued its passive resistance as distant, disturbed Clare began to discover the tithe question.[38]

II. Bolstering the forces of order

Enforcement of the law in Ireland in 1830–3 was seemingly impossible. Not even in 1821–4 had society come so close to "dissolving into its original elements." To manage the ungovernable island, the British Government resorted to a number of schemes. The army was greatly increased. The resolution of the Reform crisis in England permitted a 50 percent augmentation in the size of the army in Ireland: The effective rank and file grew from 16,800 in January 1831 to 19,400 a year later and to 24,100 by early 1833. The Government seriously considered reviving the militia in the two countries and interchanging them, as had been done in 1811–15. But the project would have been expensive and unpopular and the men deficient in training and physical condition. It was felt that English militiamen shipped to Ireland would "soon lose their Arms if not their Lives." By early 1832 the idea was abandoned.[39] A plan first proposed in 1828 to place army pensioners under the control of the Irish constabulary was activated in October 1830. Four months later, 2,100 veterans dressed as peasants were making reports to their assigned Chief Constable and 8,200 other pensioners were organized for garrison duty. The value of their services remains questionable, but Stanley believed that the arrangement at least "will keep them out of mischief." Anglesey was more concerned. If the men were not so organized, he believed, "they will inevitably be the most efficient men in the ranks of the *Rebels*. I make use of this word advisedly, being quite sure that rebellion is inevitable."[40]

Chief Secretary Stanley's pet project was the Yeomanry. Anglesey judged most of the men in the Yeomanry to be "most dangerous ... shallow – jealous – distrustful," but he knew that a role must be found for them. After Emancipation "it was necessary to reclaim and enlist the High Protestants" on the Government's side; moreover, Anglesey realized that the London Government in 1831 could not afford to send 10,000 troops to Ireland.[41] The Lord Lieutenant therefore assented to Stanley's revival of an institution numbering 19,000 effectives, nine-tenths of them in Ulster. No corps had been called out for eight years, and the men were not only "Protestant and Orange" but "ill clothed and worse armed." That spring 258 of the 340 corps were rearmed with pikes, muskets, flints, and ball cartridges. The reinvigorated institution soon brought on its own downfall. Magistrates used the corps over Castle protests, the men defied the Government by marching in ultra-Protestant processions, and in a number of cases of distraint for non-payment of tithe Yeomanry units displayed a reckless contempt for the Catholic peasantry. The most sensational incident came at Newtownbarry, County Wexford, on 18 June 1831. A party of Yeomanry insisted on rescuing some policemen against the wishes of their Chief Constable, who "begged [the Yeomanry] to withdraw from the scene; when the crowd continued to protest the seizure of three heifers for nonpayment of tithe, the Yeomanry opened fire, killing fourteen persons and wounding a greater number."[42]

By August even Stanley agreed that his plan had failed. Over the next few years, the Yeomanry was slowly dismantled. In April 1832 the brigade-majors were discontinued and the rank-and-file placed under the Sub-inspectors of the constabulary. Stanley's departure in March 1833 hastened the demise of an institution that Earl Grey and Anglesey, and his successor, the Marquess Wellesley (1833–4), now agreed to abolish. But the subject was delicate, for the London Government, composed of liberal Whigs consorting with the O'Connellites, was toying with a measure that would further alienate Irish Protestants still in shock over Catholic Emancipation. "It is a devilish awkward thing," observed Littleton, "to take the muskets from the men, or the sons of the men, who did good service with them in 1798." In March 1834 the Government abolished all Yeomanry staff positions and required officers to surrender their arms; from July on, the rank and file were encouraged to hand in theirs. By 1836, it was hoped, the force would be totally disarmed. "The Roman Catholics consider it a victory," reported the constabulary Subinspector for Westmeath; the Protestants thought it a betrayal and "an act of ingratitude."[43]

A return to the Peace Preservation Police

The pensioner plan was experimental, and the schemes involving the militia and Yeomanry had aborted, so the Government came to concentrate on the police as the force to assist the augmented regular troops. To meet the agrarian challenge in the west, Dublin Castle revived an old agent of repression: the Peace Preservation Police. Unlike the Irish constabulary, this force had the advantages of total Castle control and of trained, disciplined, and relatively impartial officers and men. By the end of 1831, Stanley had sent almost 500 Peelers into disturbed Clare and nearly 300 into Galway and Roscommon (see Table 9.2). Limerick, the only county to maintain an uninterrupted tradition of Peelers, continued to contain a small force of these men. In 1832 a force half as large as that in Clare was sent into Tipperary under the command of Richard Willcocks's son, John; the Peace Preservation Police were also introduced into three other counties. By 1833 Peelers were patrolling in ten counties; the revived force totaled 1,200 men, half as many as at its peak of strength in 1822.

Table 9.2. *Revival of the Peace Preservation Police, 1831–5*

	1831	1832	1833	1835
Kilkenny	—	52	249	135
Louth	—	—	155	92
Queen's Co.	—	83	49	20
Wicklow	—	62	61	45
LEINSTER	—	197	514	292
Clare	484	393	135	104
Cork	—	—	167	—
Limerick	74	74	74	124
Tipperary	—	227	117	22
MUNSTER	558	694	493	250
Galway	214	124	107	57
Roscommon	65	65	65	—
CONNAUGHT	279	189	172	57
IRELAND	837	1,080	1,179	599

Total number of Superintending Magistrates, Chief Constables, constables, and subconstables. No parliamentary return for 1834.

A decade earlier, Peel's force had served as a recruiting pool for Goulburn's constabulary. Now, in 1831–5, county police forces in tranquil Ulster exported men to serve as Peelers in the west. The vacancies in the North were filled by recruiting, and the attendant expenses were charged to the county receiving the Peelers. Peel's revived police was expensive: £200,000 over the period 1831–5. At £46 a year, each Peeler cost taxpayers 18 percent more than a county constable at £37. In Clare in 1831–2, 300 constables cost £8,000 and 484 Peelers £15,000. The higher cost of the Peelers, and the fact that they functioned in relatively poorer districts, prompted the Government to assess Irish county taxpayers only one-third of the total Peeler costs; by contrast, the constabulary was half locally funded. The difference in proportional assessments meant that overall the Peace Preservation force was less costly to local ratepayers than the Irish constabulary (£15.3 and £18.7 per policeman, respectively). But in heavily Peeler counties like Clare in 1831–2, taxpayers could find themselves paying more for Peelers (£5,000) than for the constabulary (£4,000). Moreover, the charge was often not proportional to force strength: Clare taxpayers paid their one-third share of £5,048 for 484 Peelers in 1831; £5,308 for 393 men in 1832; and £2,537 for 135 men in 1833. Total national costs for the Peace Preservation force were similarly disproportional: £53,055 for 1,179 men in 1833 and £31,108 for 599 Peelers (half as many men) in 1835. Indeed, the cost for 837 Peelers in 1831 (£31,078) was virtually the same as for a force one-fourth smaller four years later.[44]

Other grievances included the familiar protests that particular baronies in a county were "perfectly tranquil." In 1834 Major George Warburton admitted that this was a fair characterization of four baronies in Galway; "by some accident," however, the paper with this notation had been "lost in the Grand Jury room." Many taxpayers continued to feel that the Peeler tax was inherently unfair. Petitioners in Queen's County in 1832 objected that the act of 1814 "practically imposes upon those farmers, and upon the produce of their industry, heavy penalties, which they have neither deserved nor incurred, but which others beyond their control have both deserved and ought to have suffered." Finally, many opposed what they saw as a double tax: one for Peelers, another for the constabulary. In 1836 the Government would respond to these grievances by abolishing the Peace Preservation force and incorporating many of its members into the constabulary.[45]

Growth of the Irish constabulary

Short of the military, the most powerful weapon in the Castle's arsenal was the Irish constabulary. Stanley judged it "a very fine, efficient, and in general well conducted body of men." The force had grown from 4,792 in 1824 to 5,940 by 1830. The 1822 act had specified that, unless requested by local magistrates, no half-barony could contain more than sixteen constables. An amending act of 1828 authorized the Lord Lieutenant to make additional appointments as necessary. Pressured in 1830–2 by widespread tithe resistance and a resurgence of agrarian crime, Stanley recommended that the Government "step so far beyond the law as to augment indefinitely, though temporarily," without consulting local magistrates. By the end of 1832 the constabulary totaled 7,094 men, a 20 percent increase in only two years compared to the 24 percent increase over the previous eight. Four years later, after the important consolidating act of 1836, the force would contain only an additional 383 men.[46]

By the end of 1830 the police were posted at 1,143 stations, rising slightly to 1,182 two years later. Although the force covered the country like a sieve, with an average of five or six men at each station, its value consisted not so much in being a massive striking force in the event of insurrection as in being omnipresent. In 1832 the constabulary was most concentrated in Leinster, the cockpit of the Tithe War. In this province there were 155 police per 100,000 population; Connaught was next with 111; Munster had 80; and tranquil Ulster only 53. The most heavily policed counties were hotbeds of tithe resistance: Kildare, with 234 police per 100,000; and Kilkenny 230, Queen's County 226, and Westmeath 196. "Untameable" Tipperary now ranked no higher than eleventh in relative density of police; in Ulster the highest was Fermanagh, a volatile county of mixed religious composition, in fifteenth place.[47]

Since the time of the enabling act of 1828, the men in these county forces had been constantly circulating from one county to another. During the Tithe War, Ulster furnished great numbers of police to Leinster; and

Connaught contributed men as the Peelers were revived in the west.[48] Rotation served a variety of functions. It was a punishment for wayward or inefficient constables and officers. The Inspector-General for Ulster noted that rotation got the man away from "the *reproach of his Comrades* and probably of *the Public*" and also afforded the culprit "an opportunity of commencing a new character." Rotation served a second purpose of protecting policemen who had testified at county assizes; in March 1832 a total of twelve Kilkenny constables were reassigned for their own safety to forces in five different counties. Thirdly, as Lord Lieutenant Anglesey noted, regular rotation ensured that "both Officers and Men ... shall never stay long enough in any station to connect themselves with the [local] authorities of the neighbourhood." From November 1833 on, by the "imperative order" of Dublin Castle, it was standard policy to rotate the "senior third" in each county to different posts in the province. So frequent was the circulation of constables that Subinspectors complained of the "want of local knowledge" among their men and of confusion on the county rosters. Beginning in February 1834, each provincial Inspector-General logged in a Registry Book the permanent number, retained throughout his career, of every policeman ever recruited in Ireland.[49]

If the recent augmentations and gains in mobility were molding the Irish constabulary into a versatile, quasi-national force, the demands of the early 1830s were also reconfirming its military nature. Dublin Castle proceeded with a major rearmament of the county forces in 1832. Arms "in use since the year 1822" were replaced by new bayonets, flints, ammunition, cartridge pouches, and carbines. Record numbers of blank cartridges were "expended in drilling the recruits," and the standard issue was trebled to sixty rounds for each constable. Live ammunition was used up in shorter periods of time. Inspector-General Warburton reported from Connaught that "loading the arms of the Police during the disturbances has exhausted all their ammunition." The reissue to the 307-man Clare police comprised 6,000 rounds of blank and 18,000 carbine or pistol ball cartridges. In Kilkenny, where the police were "obliged to load their carbines in every instance of duty," the 402-man force in August was issued 16,000 rounds of live ammunition, having been granted 14,000 rounds of blanks six months earlier.[50]

Constabulary affrays

With the declining role of the army as the force of first resistance, the militia plan never implemented, the Yeomanry only briefly revived, and the small number of Peelers restricted to the most disturbed counties, the burden of policing fell on the constabulary. In Ireland in the early 1830s, this responsibility placed great strains on the men in the force. They were caught, on the one hand, between the Catholic masses disillusioned with Emancipation and adamant in resistance to tithe payment, and, on the other, the Protestant gentry and Castle officials who insisted on full enforcement of the laws.

The police, noted Peel, were resented precisely because they were in daily contact with the people and because they performed their duties. "The soldiery," said Leveson Gower, "meets with very little if any of the insult which is heaped upon the police." Despite the growing proportion of Catholics in its rank and file, the constabulary continued to be seen as representing English rule in Ireland, Ascendancy politics, and Orangeism. The widespread popular hostility made it inadvisable to place the constables in billets; out of barracks the men usually slept in Ordnance-supplied tents. And since few persons either wanted or dared to sell provisions to the Peelers, carts "escorted by Military" had to bring supplies to the scattered detachments of constables. The ill feeling between police and people was always close to the flashpoint of physical violence.[51]

In 1829 twenty-two peasants – more than in any prior year – were killed in affrays with the Irish constabulary. In the spring of the following year, the new Member for Clare, Daniel O'Connell, carried a motion in the still Tory-controlled House of Commons to "elicit facts" resulting from the employment of "an armed police" in Ireland.[52] By the end of 1831, records were produced for clashes dating to 1824. When added to later printed returns through 1844, these figures provide historians with a full record of the fatalities in these affrays. Over this twenty-one-year period, 1824–44, a total of 156 peasants and 44 police were killed. Two-fifths of all peasant deaths and half of all police deaths occurred in the four years after the granting of Catholic Emancipation in 1829.[53]

The violence, which increased steadily from 1824 on, climaxed in 1830–2, and thereafter fell to unprecedentedly low levels. Fewer peasants (thirty-eight) were killed in the next nine years 1833–41 than in the vicious triennium 1830–2. More policemen (twenty-three) were killed in 1830–2 than in all the other years combined (twenty-one in 1824–9 and 1833–44) (see Figure 9.2). In riots associated with fairs, elections, and tithe collection, and in attempted rescues of prisoners, the fatalities in 1830–2 were higher than in any other three-year period. Of the thirty-nine peasant deaths at fairs during 1824–44, only twelve came after 1832, only five after 1835. Only four of the eleven peasant fatalities at elections came after 1832. All fifteen of the peasant deaths produced by quarrels over tithe collection occurred in 1830–8, with nine coming in 1830–2 and four in 1833–5. Only two of the seventeen peasant deaths stemming from attempts to rescue prisoners occurred after 1832 (see Table 9.3).

The lethal violence was one-sided. Over the two decades 1824–44, four peasants were killed for every policeman killed. In riotous situations the ratio was 5:1; the proportion is far higher if we omit the tithe affray at Carrick-shock, where thirteen policemen were killed. If we exclude this incident, the total riot death figures would be ninety-one peasants and seven policemen killed. This ratio of 13:1 would be in line both with the 1824–44 kill ratios of 20:1 at fairs and 11:1 at elections and with the kill ratios for all riots at selected periods (16:1 in 1827–9, 16:0 in 1833–5). Nonriotous situations – rescues, criminal investigations, and other circumstances – lowered the dread ratio to 2:1 or 3:1 in favor of the police. The constabulary's superiority in

DEATHS IN CONSTABULARY AFFRAYS IN IRELAND, 1824-44

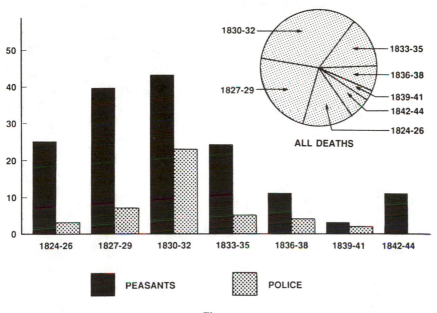

Figure 9.2

firepower prevailed against crowds, but in smaller confrontations often involving the element of surprise, the police could expect to receive relatively heavier casualties than from stone-throwing mobs.[54]

Of all the deaths in riotous situations in 1824–44, two-fifths, or thirty-nine of the ninety-three homicides, occurred at fairs. And three-fourths of these deaths were concentrated in 1827–35 and stemmed from ritualized confrontations between peasant factions and the police. A typical case was the affray at Borrisokane Fair, County Tipperary, on 26 June 1829, in which two peasants were killed and twenty-one injured. At the fair that day, for reasons that are not clear, a crowd of 600 began hurling volleys of stones at a 37-man police party. At length, following the reading of the Riot Act (1787), the Chief Constable, Captain Dobbin, ordered his men to fire; over a ten-minute period they expended seventy rounds of ball cartridge. In the aftermath, two police constables were indicted for murder and subsequently acquitted. The Government transferred Dobbin and all of his men to another county. Chief Secretary Leveson Gower observed that if the indicted constables had been found guilty, "The police may as well be broken up at once." He added: "I have little doubt that a conspiracy exists among the Peasantry directed against the Police.... The populace are taught to thirst for their blood." Curiously, the police in this engagement reported not a single injury.[55]

Two years later, on 23 May 1831, at Castlepollard Fair, County Westmeath, the constabulary again employed enormous firepower against the

Table 9.3. *Deaths in constabulary affrays in Ireland, 1824–44*

| | Riots | | | | | | | | | | Rescue | | Investigating a Crime | | Other | | Triennial total | | Triennial total as percentage of twenty-one-year total |
| | At fairs | | Tithe collection | | At elections | | Other | | Riots total | | | | | | | | | | |
	I	II	I	II	I	II	I	II	I	II	I	II	I	II	I	II	I	II	
1824–6	5	1	0	0	2	1	10	1	17	3	2	0	3	0	3	0	25	3	14.0%
1827–9	10	0	0	0	0	0	6	1	16	1	6	0	9	3	8	3	39	7	23.0
1830–2	12	1	9	14	5	0	3	0	29	15	7	5	0	0	7	3	43	23	33.0
1833–5	7	0	4	0	1	0	4	0	16	0	0	1	3	3	5	1	24	5	14.5
1836–8	1	0	2	0	2	0	0	0	5	0	2	1	3	1	1	2	11	4	7.5
1839–41	1	0	0	0	1	0	0	1	2	1	0	0	1	1	0	0	3	2	2.5
1842–4	3	0	0	0	0	0	5	0	8	0	0	0	2	0	1	0	11	0	5.5
1824–44	39	2	15	14	11	1	28	3	93	20	17	7	21	8	25	9	156	44	100.0
Percent distribution by type of incident									56.5%		12.0		14.5		17.0		100.0		

Key: I Peasantry.
    II Police.

peasantry. The incident began with two peasant factions battling each other until one, being badly beaten, invoked the help of a nearby twenty-four-man police detachment. Chief Constable Peter Blake at first appeared to succeed in restoring order. Suddenly, however, the factions revived their jeering and aimed their stone throwing at the police. According to Constable Crampton's later account, "3 or 4 of the policemen in the rere [sic] fired on the people and almost immediately the firing appeared to become general." In the next two minutes, the police sprayed fifty rounds of ball cartridge over an arc of 180 degrees. Nine peasants lay dead – two of them killed at a distance of 150 yards – and five were wounded. The police reported no casualties (see Map 9.1). The incident was especially serious because no order to fire had been given to the men. A county grand jury subsequently indicted eighteen constables and one officer, but the case was never prosecuted. Lord Lieutenant Anglesey noted the legal difficulty "to define at what instant armed men are justified in firing in self-defense" and suggested that the "massacre" of five policemen seven weeks earlier in Clare had "led perhaps prematurely to the catastrophe" by inducing an anxious overreaction among the constables at Castlepollard. The facts remained: nine Westmeath peasants dead, not one policeman reporting a scratch, and troops brought in from Mullingar to overawe the villagers.[56]

The incident at Carrickshock, County Kilkenny, on 14 December 1831 was by far the most lethal of all constabulary affrays. It was also "the most calamitous occurrence connected with the collection of tithes in which the constabulary were ever engaged." As Lord Lieutenant Anglesey noted at the time,

The Reports are this Moment arrived of a sad affray about Tithe, between the Police and Peasantry in Kilkenny. More will come in today.... A sad loss. A Chief Constable and 16 men killed and wounded. Only 4 of the People. The force was ample. There were 40 men!!!

The final count was even higher: thirteen policemen killed and fourteen wounded, and only two peasants killed.[57]

The tragedy began as a routine expedition to collect tithes. A party of police under Chief Constable James Gibbons, following a Castle directive of April 1831, was furnishing protection to Edmond Butler, process-server for Rev. Hans Hamilton, who in Anglesey's words was "a hard and imprudent man."[58] Gibbons, though a former army officer, betrayed a lack of judgment by escorting Butler without a magistrate or military support. The first two days passed without incident as the police party followed Butler around western Kilkenny near the Tipperary border. On the third day, near Kilnemagany, the police heard church bells ringing and were informed that it was for a funeral; only later, when they were fighting for their lives, did they realize that the bells had been tolling their deaths.

Outside the village, near a ravine called Carrickshock, the police first saw the crowd of 600 (or, as some said later, 2,000) peasants. Armed with turf spades, stable forks, scythes, bludgeons, and axes, and led by a man dressed

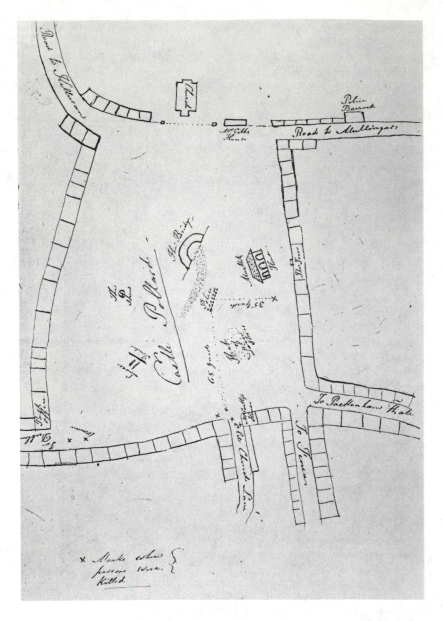

Map 9.1 Police sketch map of the affray at Castlepollard, County Westmeath, 23 May 1831. The map locates the "Police Barrack," line of "Police" at the moment of firing, site of "Heap of Loose Stones," and "X Marks where persons were Killed." There are seven such crosses (Xs); the official total later rose to nine dead. (By permission of the Public Record Office)

in a military cap and jaunty red sash – a man later identified as the school-master, Keane – the peasantry demanded that Gibbons surrender the process-server. To judge by the yells from the crowd, Butler was indeed an unpopular local figure: "Sheep stealer ... dirty butcher ... Blackguard ... you will not have the Police with you always." According to one survivor, Constable Peter Harvey, Butler was said to have replied several times, "I am better reared than any of you."

Toward the police the crowd appeared to show no hostility. The leader, Keane, who had for the past year led local resistance to tithe payment, told Gibbons, "There won't be one of your men injured, nor a hair of your head touched." From the crowd, shouts came: "If you give up the process-server, nothing will be done to you. ... Police, we don't want to hurt you, but the process-server we will kill." Many of the policemen and protesters knew each other; some constables even shook hands with persons in the crowd. Only Paddy Walsh, a local boy, was heard to be threatened; as Subconstable Walsh testified later, "They said I was a turn-coat."[59]

Chief Constable Gibbons refused the ransom, even though, in Inspector-General Harvey's words, he must have seen "that his life would be the forfeit." All the while, the party of police continued marching until it found itself at the base of a narrow ravine. At this point a man in the crowd, crying "this is the man we want," darted into the file of police and seized Butler. The assailant was immediately shot dead by Subconstable Andrew Sheane. Chaos ensued: Stones, "flying thick as hail," darkened the sky, and the police were able to fire only twenty shots before it was all over. "In a few minutes only," twenty-seven of the thirty-eight policemen were either killed or wounded. Butler, the process-server, died of his wounds the next day. The peasants lost two men, and government records listed only one man injured. Harvey, however, later estimated that "as many as 50 or 60" had probably been wounded but were dragged away by the crowd.[60]

The incident at Carrickshock left the authorities in a state of shock. In London, Home Secretary Melbourne reacted "with horror" to the news: "Gibbons was lured on to his destruction. It is like one reads both of the guile and the ferocity of the Hurons and the Iroquois." In Ireland a shaken Sir John Harvey moved to stem any spread of the violence. He withdrew police from all thatched barracks in Kilkenny and throughout Leinster concentrated his men in fewer, more heavily manned stations. For their own safety, the eleven survivors in Gibbons's force were exchanged for constables from the Westmeath police. Harvey wrote Stanley that "it would be the very best measure ... adopted with regard to the Constabulary force if it was made *interchangeable en masse* from one county to another." Finally, the Government announced that on all subsequent tithe expeditions the military would be required to accompany any party of police.[61] Carrickshock produced important changes in opinion as well as in policies. Harvey noted that after the incident "an idea very generally obtained" that Catholic policemen "were not to be depended upon." To this erroneous belief was added a feeling that Gibbons's men had been "crippled by the fear of incurring legal penalties" had they fired; the Archbishop of Dublin, testifying before a parliamentary committee in 1832, stated that the police were so fearful of legal wrangles that "they were deterred from firing till the rioters had actually seized the muskets and wrested them out of their hands."[62] The irony of Carrickshock, in short, was that the bloody incident stained the reputations of many loyal Catholics in the constabulary and, by triggering demands for unfettered police powers, contributed to the escalating violence in Ireland.

Crime and the constabulary, 1829–35

At its founding in 1822–4, and again in 1828, the Irish constabulary had been hard pressed to fulfill its charge to bring peace to Ireland. But no time was more difficult for the new institution than the early 1830s. The people's surliness after Emancipation worsened what were already poor relations with the police. For their part, the police during the Tithe War were increasingly frustrated by the peasants' passive withholding tactics and by the legal restrictions placed on police action against tithe defaulters. In the west there was also the resurgence of agrarian crime. The augmentation of the army to 24,000 and of the constabulary to 7,000 appeared to have little effect.[63] Attempts to enforce the laws in Ireland had produced only clashes between the police and the people.

The national criminal statistics, to be sure, argued for the growing effectiveness of the police. Comparison of the annual average figures for 1829–34 (a disturbed period) with those for 1822–8 (one of disturbance followed by comparative tranquility after 1824) indicates that, for all crimes, committals rose by 8 percent and the conviction rate by 9 percent. For the national totals the gains in prosecuting to conviction were remarkable: 22 percent in 1805–12, 54 percent in 1822–8, and 63 percent in 1829–34[64] (see Table 9.4).

Crimes against the person continued to constitute fully a third of all offenses.[65] Popular violence and police vigilance combined to produce record committals for homicide: 620 persons in 1832 and 687 in 1833. In the earlier Rockite period, murder/manslaughter (homicide) committals had peaked at 426 in 1824; now the annual average of 567 committals in 1831–3 was up 54 percent from 367 committals a year in 1822–4. For this offense in 1829–34, there were more committals in every year save one (1831) than in any year from 1822 to 1828. Serious Whiteboy crime – armed assembly at night and attacks on houses – was also up, by 118 percent, from 200 committals a year in 1822–4 to 435 in 1831–3. For these crimes, committals in 1832, 1833, and 1834 were greater than in any year from 1822 to 1828. The police made so many arrests that, for the want of jails, constabulary barracks were often overflowing with prisoners.[66]

But what of the disposition of the cases of those persons brought to trial? The gains in overall conviction rates in 1829–34 reflected the gains in the prosecution of nonagrarian crimes. For traditional Whiteboy offenses, convictions remained low; juries continued to be reluctant to convict. The 35

Table 9.4. *Crime in Ireland, 1829–34*

	All offenses		Murder/ manslaughter		Riotous assembly armed by night and attacking dwelling houses	
	I	II	I	II	I	II
1829	15,271	61.9%	539	36.5	126	31.0
1830	15,794	62.7	440	29.1	155	18.7
1831	16,192	59.3	393	33.8	301	23.3
1832	16,036	60.9	620	26.9	431	26.7
1833	17,819	64.2	687	39.7	574	24.4
1834	21,381	66.7	575	39.8	350	40.3
Ave./yr. 1829–34	*17,082*	*62.8*	*542*	*34.7*	*323*	*27.6*

Key: I   Number of persons charged with criminal offenses and committed to jail for trial.
II   Percentage conviction rate.

percent conviction rate for murder/manslaughter committals (up from 22 percent in 1822–8) was high only because it included the easier convictions for manslaughter; a mere 7 percent of the cases brought verdicts of guilty for murder. The Whiteboy offense of assembling in arms at night and attacking houses produced only marginal gains in convictions: 24 percent in 1822–8 and 28 percent in 1829–34. Disturbed districts were at times virtually out of control. In Queen's County and Kilkenny in 1831–2, sixty-three murder committals resulted in a lone conviction for manslaughter (a 2 percent rate). In Tipperary over a four-year period, 129 committals for armed assembly at night brought but twenty-one convictions (a 16 percent rate). The Crown Solicitor for Leinster told Parliament in 1839 that so far as he could recall, some 300 Whiteboy offenses in Kilkenny in 1832 had netted only five convictions.[67]

The disappointing courtroom results were largely beyond the control of the Irish constabulary. "Not guilty" verdicts were routine in cases where constables were often the Crown's only witnesses for the prosecution. The few persons who did agree to testify the Government had to protect and pay. In 1830–3 on one of the six judicial circuits, forty-eight persons received sums of up to £300 to serve as Crown witnesses. As a result of testifying thirty-eight of the witnesses were forced to flee their places of residence; twenty-nine left Ireland altogether, twelve sailing for America. Peeler Magistrate T. P. Vokes recounted the story of a witness to the Carrickshock police murders being escorted under heavy guard, using relays of horses, avoiding all villages, and not stopping to rest. When one of his constables questioned the need for this frantic dash to Kilkenny town, Vokes replied: "Harry, my boy, you're as green as any Englishman I ever met. Don't you see that if they could be caught, they'd soon be surrounded, and the approver dragged out and torn to pieces."[68]

Violent crime continued to be concentrated in those counties to which the first Peelers had been sent in the 1810s.[69] In the early 1830s, of all the committals in Ireland for murder/manslaughter and for riotous assembly, armed by night, and attacking dwelling houses, one-third occurred in Tipperary and Clare; if we add Galway and Queen's County, two-fifths of all homicide committals and three-fifths of those for armed assembly and house attacks occurred in these four counties (see Table 9.5). Here convictions even for manslaughter were difficult: The 25 percent rate was ten points below the national rate. For simple (daytime and unarmed) riot and riotous assembly, Tipperary was far in the lead, with 1,202 committals in 1831–2 and 1,574 in 1834–5. Queen's County and Clare were a distant second and third. Tipperary likewise led in "rescues," recording 444 committals in 1831–2 and 407 in 1834–5; Galway was second, with 260 and 275, respectively. In 1831–2 in the four most disturbed counties, conviction rates for riot/riotous assembly averaged 31 percent. By contrast, convictions for rescue were rare (9 percent in 1831–2 and 13 percent in 1834–5). At the height of the disturbances in Clare in 1831–2, 260 committals for rescue resulted in seven convictions, a 3 percent rate.

Counties prominent in the antitithe movement had low levels of violence (Table 9.5). In Kilkenny in 1831/5 the total committals (84) for homicide, armed assembly, and attacks on houses placed that county well behind neighboring Queen's County (197) and far behind Clare and Tipperary (542 and 583, respectively). Kilkenny emerges as a blend of the two extremes – antitithe nonviolence and Whiteboy violence – when it is compared to Carlow and Wexford. These two counties in the forefront of the antitithe agitation had combined homicide/Whiteboy committals in 1831/5 of thirty-one and thirteen, respectively. For simple riot/riotous assembly in 1831–2, at the height of the Tithe War, Carlow and Wexford together recorded only twenty committals.

Perhaps the major conclusion to be drawn from the criminal statistics (Table 9.5) is the dramatic decline in agrarian protest in the most disturbed counties. Simple riot/riotous assembly was up slightly, but so were convictions. But in 1834–5 major crimes, as measured by committals, had fallen by two-fifths from the 1831–2 levels. Nighttime armed assembly and attacks on houses were down 78 percent: "Whitefootism," reported Anglesey, "is quite out of fashion. The Country is tranquil."[70] These Whiteboy crimes had been halved in frequency in Tipperary and Queen's County; in Clare and Galway such crimes had virtually disappeared (declining from 225 to 22 and from 114 to 12 committals, respectively). It is arguable that the police were deterring this form of crime; it is certain that their presence did not improve the prosecution of cases. In these four counties in 1831–2, 505 committals produced a 37 percent conviction rate; 109 committals in 1834–5 brought only sixteen convictions, a 15 percent rate. Whiteboyism was much reduced

Table 9.5. *Violent crime in selected Irish counties: (A) agrarian disturbances and (B) the Tithe War*

	(1) Murder/manslaughter		(2) Riotous assembly, armed by night and attacking dwelling houses		Total of (1) and (2)		Riot and riotous assembly	
	I	II	I	II	I	II	I	II
				1831–2				
(A) Tipperary	183	23.0%	86	18.6	269	21.6	1,202	23.6
Clare	180	15.0	225	37.8	405	27.7	145	48.3
Galway	51	25.5	114	47.4	166	40.4	68	27.9
Queen's Co.	37	2.7	80	41.3	117	29.1	412	44.9
Total	*451*	*18.4*	*505*	*37.2*	*957*	*28.3*	*1,827*	*30.5*
(B) Kilkenny	26	0.0	19	47.4	45	20.0	114	7.9
Carlow	3	33.3	1	0.0	4	25.0	16	18.8
Wexford	5	40.0	0	0.0	5	40.0	4	100.0
Total	*34*	*8.8*	*20*	*45.0*	*54*	*22.2*	*134*	*11.9*
				1834–5				
(A) Tipperary	271	29.5	43	11.6	314	27.1	1,574	28.9
Clare	115	37.4	22	22.7	137	35.0	251	67.7
Galway	22	22.7	12	0.0	34	14.7	95	18.9
Queen's Co.	48	37.5	32	18.8	80	30.0	238	35.3
Total	*456*	*32.0*	*109*	*14.7*	*565*	*28.7*	*2,158*	*33.7*
(B) Kilkenny	12	33.0	27	25.9	39	28.2	172	36.6
Carlow	14	14.3	13	0.0	27	7.4	13	38.5
Wexford	6	16.7	2	0.0	8	12.5	117	51.3
Total	*32*	*21.9*	*42*	*16.7*	*74*	*18.9*	*302*	*42.4*

Key: I Number of persons charged with criminal offenses and committed to jail for trial.
II Percentage conviction rate.

in frequency, but the system of intimidation of juries was even more powerful

With the exception of Tipperary, murder/manslaughter committals also declined by the mid-1830s (Table 9.5). In Clare, Galway, and Queen's County, homicide committals were down by 31 percent in 1834–5 compared to 1831–2; and here the conviction rate, formerly 15 percent, had climbed to 36 percent. It was the murders in Tipperary that kept the four-county committal totals unchanged (451, 456) from 1831–2 to 1834–5, but the conviction rate did improve from 18 to 32 percent. Murder/manslaughter committals in Tipperary were up by 48 percent; convictions also rose, by a third, to a 30 percent rate in 1834–5. Tipperary in the mid-1830s was reassuming its role as the center of murder in Ireland. In 1831–2 Tipperary accounted for 41 percent of the homicide committals in the four most disturbed counties; and in 1834–5, for 59 percent of the four-county totals. Significantly, typical Whiteboy crimes were also becoming concentrated in Tipperary. In 1831–2 this county's share of the four-county Whiteboy committals (86 of 505) was 17 percent; in 1834–5 (43 of 109), it was 39 percent. Tipperary – to repeat Anglesey's description of 1828 – remained "untameable."[71]

Toward a professional police: forgotten reforms before Drummond

Given the pressures and hostilities confronting the Irish constabulary, the development of a highly disciplined and largely impartial force must stand as a remarkable accomplishment. In the half dozen years before the passage of the famous Constabulary Act of 1836, the constabulary changed far more than Thomas Drummond realized or subsequent historians have noted. Lord Lieutenant Anglesey was correct in his pithy assessment in the spring of 1833 that the police force was "daily mending."[72] Like the new London police, the older Irish force was developing professional standards of behavior and discipline. From its creation, the London force had had the advantage of total government control. For the Irish constabulary, the growth in professionalism involved hacking away at the remaining local ties and control. At the price of local liberties and traditional conceptions of constitutionality, both forces made advances in efficiency and impartiality.

The higher ranks in the Irish police were already firmly in the Government's hands. Since 1828, Subinspectors had been in charge of each county force in Ireland. In his county this officer acted as the principal representative of the central government; Leveson Gower in 1829 described the Subinspector as a surrogate Stipendiary Magistrate for each county. A number of witnesses told an 1832 parliamentary committee that salaried government magistrates should be placed in every county in Ireland. A return for 1833 disclosed that a total of twenty-two counties contained these Stipendiary Magistrates, who labored with both the county local magistrates and the constabulary officers.[73] Of the ten counties lacking Stipendiary Magistrates, four (Clare, Galway, Limerick, and Wicklow) had Peace Preservation Superintending Magistrates who performed similar functions. Increasingly, the Stipendiary Magistrates were recruited from the constabulary. Whereas only two of the ten Stipendiary Magistrates appointed before January 1831 were drawn from the police, ten of the fourteen appointed in the two years ending in February 1833 had served as Subinspectors in the constabulary. In May 1831 the six-month-old Whig Government named the first Catholic Stipendiary Magistrate. A second was appointed in February 1832. The other twenty-two Stipendiary Magistrates serving in 1833 were all Protestants.[74]

The Government was also making inroads into the control of the lower ranks of the constabulary. The appointment of constables and subconstables, given by the 1822 act to the local magistrates, had become a legal fiction ten years later. A constabulary circular of June 1833 boldly declared that all rank-and-file appointments lay with the Inspectors-General and the Lord Lieutenant. Where the JPs continued to contest their legal rights, constabulary officers, backed by the Castle, vetoed the local nominations or worked out compromises heavily favorable to the Government. From October 1833 on, a police regulation, citing past "inconvenience" and "embarrassment," barred private recommendations and stressed that persistent applicants would find their candidacy subject to the "marked disapprobation" of the Government.[75] Certainly by 1835, the separation of legality and reality was complete. In May of that year Inspector-General Miller, in reporting that he had filled all vacancies in Waterford, added, "I apprehend it will be necessary ... to insert the usual Proclamation in the *Dublin Gazette*, requiring the Magistrates to assemble in the Assize Town ... for the purpose of naming the additional Policemen, agreeably to the Provisions of ... the Constabulary Act 3d Geo. 4th c. 103." In August, in debates on the 1835 constabulary bill, a number of Irish Members, including O'Connell, acknowledged that the control of appointments "in almost every Instance" lay with the Government. "The inspectors had it already," noted the Marquess of Clanicarde, "and the present Bill went only to give [it to] them *de jure*."[76]

Government control of appointments permitted the application of strict recruiting standards. These had existed before the formation of the new London police in 1829, but the professionalization of the English force, especially during Peel's home secretaryship, did act as an impetus to the increasing standardization of the Irish police.[77] All applicants to the constabulary were asked five questions: age, height, marital status, military service, and medical history. The insistence on youthful recruits, pioneered in Major Miller's Munster in 1828, became widespread in 1829-36. Of the constables joining in 1829-32, 46 percent – increasing to 53 percent in 1833-6 – were of ages nineteen to twenty-one compared to 27 percent of the recruits in 1823-8 and 34 percent in 1816-22. Older constables were no longer being accepted. Nineteen percent of the men joining in 1816-22 and 28 percent in 1823-8 were at least twenty-eight years old. Only 9 percent of the recruits in 1829-32 were this old, and a mere 3 percent of those accepted in 1833-6.[78]

In these years the Government was fashioning a force of men not only

Figure 9.3 "The Constabulary Force of Ireland, Full and Undress," c. 1838. (Engraving from a drawing by P. Duffy, by permission of the National Library of Ireland)

younger but taller. The minimum height for constables was 5 feet 8 inches. Gone were the men, now dubbed "undersized," who had formed one-quarter of the recruits before 1829. The constabulary was hardly becoming a race of giants – only one-tenth were 6-footers – but rather a standardized collection of men above average, and only inches apart, in height (Figure 9.3). Words like "unobjectionable" were used to describe policemen who met the height criterion. One of the unfortunate ones was Thomas Scott, a Leinster constable, who was discharged in June 1832 as "inefficient," for, although of "excellent Character," he was "undersized." The decision was "a hard one," Anglesey told Lord Cloncurry.[79]

As the Irish constabulary was changing in outward appearance, so it was also in spirit. The tall, young recruit was unmarried and likely to remain so. Major Miller's spartan philosophy prevailed: service to the state unencumbered by personal obligations. Bachelors were given a preference among candidates; married men, whatever their character or abilities, were admitted only in a 1:5 ratio of all recruits. A Castle circular of April 1833 banned all marriages until the percentage of married men in the force fell to 20 percent. This policy did not go unprotested. Miller's most passionate opponent was Sir John Harvey. In a long letter of March 1835 the Inspector-General for Leinster lambasted "the Prohibition ... as at once impolitic & injurious, both as regards the Establishment and the Public." The policy corrupted "the Morals of Society"; it encouraged "Prostitution and Concubinage ... around Police Stations"; it sacrificed "domestic comfort and the consequent steadiness of the Police Man's Character"; it engendered among the men a cavalier and callous attitude toward women and, among local farmers, a universal "distrust" of policemen consorting with their daughters. In a society accustomed to early marriage and large families, the regulation imposed an exceptional hardship. Harvey spoke of "frequent resignations by men of excellent character for the sole purpose of *marrying*." Two months later, in May 1835, Dublin Castle made a minor alteration in the regulation. No marriage could occur until the number of married policemen in a county force equaled the number of bachelors; after that, upon the death, resignation, or dismissal of *two* married constables, *one* chosen bachelor constable might marry. With the inflow of single recruits, the new goal was a force in which 25 percent of the men were married. Harvey's victory amounted to 5 percentage points. Year by year the Irish constable would become more professional, the barracks tidier, and the force more divorced from the Irish people.[80]

Shaping the constabulary into a regimented, impartial civil authority required facing the problem of religion. In the era of Emancipation, the Tithe War, and Carrickshock, of Catholic rising expectations and Protestant defensiveness, the subject had to be handled discreetly. The official recruiting forms contained no questions about a man's religion. "Character, eligibility, & general qualifications alone are looked to," reported Major Miller. "I have never felt it to be any part of my duty," noted Sir John Harvey, "to question any Candidate as to his Religion." Of course, not asking the touchy question in fact favored the Catholics, who had traditionally been discriminated against and who formed the bulk of the population. But the Inspectors-General were not being entirely honest. At some point a policeman was asked his religion; official records showed that roughly two-thirds of the men – 68 percent in 1824, 64 percent in 1832 – were Protestants. The difference, in 1830–6, was that the question was now put because the Whig Government was actively searching for Catholic constables.[81] The Protestant share of recruits was decreasing: 84 percent in 1816–22, 61 in 1823–8, 58 in 1829–32, and 51 in 1833–6. Harvey reported in 1833 that the Government's new pro-Catholic bias in hiring had produced "the feeling which is assuredly very prevalent [among the constables] ... that they are sacrificed to every [popular] clamour." Typical was the case of the Kildare Subinspector who found the Government second-guessing his selection of six subconstables. The men were all from another county – a "good principle," noted Harvey – and were all "well educated, intelligent, fine looking Young Men," but, alas, they were all Protestants.[82]

In the age of Emancipation, the Government carefully monitored the religion of recruits to the Irish constabulary. Inspector-General Miller in 1834 huffily denied that his officers practiced any "bigotry or illiberality" in hiring; the force was sufficiently professional "that I hear nothing of jealousies or differences of a religious nature among our men." Sir John Harvey pointed out that in enforcing the law in Leinster, the Catholic constable was actually placed in a more difficult position than the Protestant policeman since many people, Catholic and Protestant, resented his position of authority. Harvey nevertheless "strenuously" believed that

the Roman Catholic Police man is, at all times and under all circumstances, as much to be depended upon as his Protestant fellow, and that at least one half of the Constables in every Southern County should be of the same religious persuasion with the great mass of the people, as the best means of reconciling the latter to an Establishment formed to coerce them, or at all events of rendering it less unpopular.

In Ulster, where the two religious factions were more evenly matched, the potential for strife was greater. Here police officers and men were preponderantly Protestant. In early 1834 the Government cracked down by replacing Thomas D'Arcy with Sir Frederic Stovin. Not only had Inspector-General D'Arcy been "a most nefarious peculator," he was also suspected of having encouraged "the spirit of Partizanship that prevails in the Northern Police." Such attitudes, Dublin Castle instructed Stovin, "cannot be too studiously checked."[83]

Religion was the code word in Ireland for issues not merely doctrinal. Throughout the British Isles in the early 1830s the dominant political issue was Reform. In England this took the form of demands for broader popular representation in lawmaking; in Ireland, of a Tithe War that contested the Government's right to tax for a church grossly unrepresentative of the people. Dublin Castle's response to the political challenge was to conduct in 1833–4 the first thorough "religious" census of the institutions of government in Ireland. The findings detailed an awesome, if unsurprising, Protestant hegemony:

	Total Protestants	Total Catholics	Percent Protestant
County lords lieutenant	30	2	94
Assistant barristers	29	3	91
Crown prosecutors	33	4	89
Justices of the peace	2,366	285	89
Stipendiary Magistrates	25	1	96
Constabulary	4,644	2,518	65
Peace Preservation Police	642	509	56

Chief Secretary Littleton, who had commissioned most of these returns, commented to his Catholic friend, More O'Ferrall: "I can judge by my own feelings what yours must be on all this class of subjects."[84] If the facts were long-standing, the official outrage was new.

The police totals, Littleton knew, were deceiving because the figures combined officers with men. The officer class was still overwhelmingly Protestant; in both the Peace Preservation force and the constabulary more than 90 percent of the officers were members of the English state church. By contrast, the rank and file was religiously mixed: 54 percent of the Peeler constables and 64 percent of the constabulary constables were Protestant (see Table 9.6). The Whigs found much fault with the Tories' pre-1830 record on hiring. All officer appointments since 1814 had rested exclusively with the Government; the Peeler rank and file had also always been named by the Castle. The nonofficer ranks in the constabulary had, however, in 1823–8 been intermittently under the control of the local magistrates, men supposedly prejudicial to Protestants. Yet, in 1834, all that the Government could show was a margin of 10 percent more Catholics in the Peeler force than in the constabulary. Provincial returns for the constabulary (Table 9.6) showed that only in Major Miller's Munster did Catholic constables predominate (53 percent); in heavily Catholic Connaught they formed 43 percent; in Leinster but 28 percent; and in Ulster, which had the most Protestant officer class in Ireland (98 percent), the rank and file was only 22 percent Catholic.[85] Though Catholics formed more than one-third of the total constabulary rank and file, they outnumbered Protestant constables in only five counties. In the Peace Preservation Police, they fared better, accounting for almost half of the total constables and predominating in four of the ten counties where the force was active in 1833. Of course, nowhere did Catholics have a majority in the officer ranks; their highest share was, in fact, in untameable Tipperary, where three of nine constabulary officers and three of seven Peeler officers were Catholics.[86]

"Roman Catholics do not appear, heretofore, to have been sufficiently brought forward in the Service." So wrote Littleton to Gosset in June 1834. Apart from prejudice, the basic obstacle was the absence of a merit policy of promotion from the ranks. Since 1822 it had been understood that a Chief Constable's post was "the only one with the exception of Inspector-General which a gentleman can fill in the Police."[87] The creation in 1828 of county Subinspectors, in reality simply promoted Chief Constables, only perpetuated the system: thirty-one of thirty-two subinspectors were Protestant. Believing it "a matter of the greatest importance" to break the old system, the Government in the early 1830s began to favor Catholics for vacant chief constableships and to initiate a policy of promotion from the ranks. The guidelines of merit and prior service for officer appointments in the new London police may have stimulated such thinking in Ireland; as early as December 1829, we find Chief Secretary Leveson Gower recommending similar standards for the constabulary. Certainly, the Emancipation and tithe questions challenged the Government to find ways to conciliate Catholic

Table 9.6. *The religious composition of the police in Ireland, 1833*

	Connaught		Leinster		Munster		Ulster		Ireland	
	No.	Percent	No.	Percent	No.	Percent	No.	Percent	No.	Percent
CONSTABULARY										
Subinspectors	5–0	100%	12–0	100%	5–1	83%	9–0	100%	31–1	97%
Chief Constables	39–4	91	66–8	89	40–9	82	49–1	98	194–22	90
Total Officers	44–4	92	78–8	91	45–10	82	58–1	98	225–23	91
Rank and file: constables and subconstables	835–617	58	1,871–718	72	791–902	47	922–258	78	4,419–2,495	64
PEACE PRESERVATION FORCE										
Superintending Magistrates	4–0	100	6–1	86	7–1	88	—	—	17–2	89
Chief Constables	6–0	100	9–0	100	7–2	78	—	—	22–2	92
Total Officers	10–0	100	15–1	94	14–3	82	—	—	39–4	91
Rank and file: constables and subconstables	116–44	73	301–184	62	186–277	40	—	—	603–505	54

Key: Number of Protestants – number of Catholics   Percentage Protestant

opinion in Ireland. In the event, Dublin Castle did establish two new merit ranks, Constable First Class and Chief Constable Second Class. A constabulary regulation of 1834 stated that two-thirds of all vacant chief constableships (now termed "second class") were to be filled by promotions of deserving constables.[88]

Some men continued to be appointed by the old rules. Mr. Henry West, a man who had no prior police experience but who was the son of Lieutenant-Colonel West, barrack master at Cork and a friend of Wellington's from the Peninsular campaign, was appointed Chief Constable Second Class in Donegal. The resignation of the Subinspector of Monaghan, Richard Free, on grounds of ill-health resulted in the appointment of his son, Edward, a young man with no prior service, as a Chief Constable in the county; Free was disappointed that no place could be found for his second son. On the other hand, many officer positions now did go to deserving policemen. Constable Richard Hadnett – twenty-six years old, unmarried, "of a highly respectable family, & has the necessary literate qualifications" – had served eight years in the constabulary and been "severely wounded in one of the many riots" in Tipperary; in January 1835 Hadnett was promoted to Chief Constable Second Class in the Cork City force. A vacant chief constableship in Meath led a dozen county subinspectors to submit names of meritorious constables. With all the applicants being "nearly of equal strength," the Government decided to appoint Meath Constable James Walker because none of that county's constables had yet been promoted and Walker, a twelve-year veteran, had compiled a brilliant record in curbing agrarian crime.[89]

With the new emphasis on merit and long service went a preference for Catholic officer appointments wherever possible. Take the case of Francis Bernard Haly. An army veteran, Haly had joined the constabulary in 1823 and served as a Chief Constable in County Dublin. Since 1829 Haly had sought a subinspectorship. He stated that Gosset told him in 1831 that "my being one of the few Roman Catholic officers in the Constabulary could in no way militate against my advancement." In June 1834 the subinspectorship of Cork City became vacant. Major Miller recommended his most senior officer in Munster, Chief Constable Francis Percy, who before the formation of the constabulary had served with the Peelers in Limerick. But the Government wanted to make a Catholic appointment. Gosset informed Miller that Percy was "deserving but he is a Protestant and there is only one Catholic holding the situation of Sub-Inspector." The Lord Lieutenant desired "to bestow favour upon a class which has not always had fair play." So the Government pressed the claims of Haly and Chief Constable John Burke in Kilkenny, while Miller grumbled that "my conscience tells me that the Catholics have had nothing but fair play from me." Haly was chosen but then forced to decline after the Government sheepishly discovered that he was a native of Cork City. Percy was then appointed and Burke was promised the next vacant subinspectorship. Haly, meanwhile, was offered in January and June 1835 the subinspectorships of first Fermanagh, then Monaghan. But he rejected both, since he now had his eye on the subinspectorship of County Dublin, where the incumbent was in "infirm health." In November, the Government appointed Haly to this post.[90]

In the half-dozen years before its statutory reform in 1836, the Irish constabulary was becoming more professional: It established guidelines for magistrates' use of the force, instituted strict internal regulations, and began to recruit Catholics and to promote by merit. But what, before 1836, was the quality of the men and the Government's tolerance for wrongdoing? "No doubt there are bad men in the Police, as ... in every other ... profession," Anglesey noted in 1833, "but not infrequently their misconduct has been visited with a good deal of severity." In 1833 a Louth subconstable who killed a man attempting to rescue a prisoner was transported for seven years. In Tipperary in 1835 a policeman who shot and wounded a man at a fair was convicted of aggravated assault, sentenced to nine months in prison, and dismissed from the constabulary; in the county in 1836 a subconstable was dismissed and jailed for three months for firing into a "Rockite" house and killing an occupant. In sum, as Gosset informed his concerned new Chief Secretary, Edward Littleton, "in a force of above 5,000 Men, there must be some indiscreet ones.... All that can be done is to get rid of them."[91]

Dismissal rates were low, averaging about 4 percent of the annual force strength. Resignations took a similar proportion of men, so that the overall annual turnover was less than 10 percent, far below the 30 percent annual rate in the London police.[92] The constabulary, however, employed a number of punitive tactics short of dismissal. In 1835–6 half as many men were reprimanded, fined, or reduced in rank as were dismissed.[93] The constabulary also sometimes used rotation as a punishment. The Irish dismissal rate is thus not strictly comparable to the London one. Nevertheless, the lower rate probably reflects the constabulary's greater military discipline and the relative absence of temptations to vice and indeed of co-mingling with the policed population. When infractions did occur, constabulary officials were more inclined to rotate than to dismiss due to the difficulties in recruiting not faced by the London Police Commissioners.[94] It would, in short, be misleading to argue that the low Irish dismissal rate necessarily indicates a wider tolerance for misbehavior than in the London police.

To some extent, however, dismissal rates before 1836 did reflect standards set by local petty sessions and the provincial Inspectors-General. In Connaught it was not so much that Warburton's men were extraordinarily well behaved as that the aging Inspector-General was reluctant to dismiss; in Munster, especially in the early 1830s, Miller acted as a tough disciplinarian; Harvey in Leinster in 1834–6 dismissed record numbers of men; and in Ulster Inspector-General Stovin was sterner than D'Arcy had been (see Table 9.7). Among Chief Constables the chief problems were irregular correspondence and indebtedness to "Trades people and others." Among the men, any of the following resulted in dismissal: stealing; chronic indebtedness; fraudulent expenses; slovenly appearance; using flagrant party expressions; being "of weak Mind & Intellect"; perjury; poor conduct as, or tampering with, a witness; and desertion, requesting a resignation, refusal to transfer to

Table 9.7. *Dismissals in the Irish constabulary, 1830–6*

	Connaught		Leinster		Munster		Ulster		Ireland: total dismissals	Constabulary force strength	Dismissal rate
	No.	Percent	No.	Percent	No.	Percent	No.	Percent			
1830	1	1%	50	31%	78	49%	30	19%	159	5,940	3%
1831	8	3	92	41	107	48	17	8	224	6,609	3
1832[a]	—	—	—	—	—	—	—	—	292	7,094	4
1833[a,b]	—	—	—	—	—	—	—	—	295	—	—
1834[b]	16	5	158	53	66	22	58	19	298	—	—
1835	39	13	151	52	56	19	45	15	291	7,365	4
1836	53	12	168	41	135	33	56	14	412	7,477	6
Percentage distribution of constabulary											
1832		21%		37		25		17			
1836		19		37		27		17			
Percentage distribution of population											
1831		18%		23		29		30			

Key: Number of dismissals   Percentage of annual national total of dismissals

[a] Source does not differentiate provincial totals.
[b] No parliamentary return for force strength in these years.

another county, and having a woman in barracks (or, in one case, "associating with a Prostitute in the Court House privy"). These last four offenses might be interpreted as individual protests against the constabulary's strict regulations. But none of these reasons accounted for more than 1 percent of dismissals a year.[95]

More frequent causes, taken from a sample year, 1836, were:

	Number	Percent of total
Drunkenness	222	53.8
Absence from duty or from barracks	55	13.3
Insubordination	26	6.3
Marrying without permission	26	6.3
Assault	17	4.1
Swearing	15	3.6
Permitting a prisoner to escape	10	2.4
Losing arms	6	1.4
Other	35	8.8
TOTAL	412	100.0

The incidence of offenses resulting in dismissal varied surprisingly little from province to province. Roughly one of every two dismissals was for drunkenness, ranging from 49 percent in Munster to 66 percent in Connaught. Absence from duty comprised from 11 to 17 percent of all dismissals, and insubordination and unauthorized marriages each from 2 to 9 percent. It is remarkable that only two types of offense accounted for two-thirds, and the four most frequent for four-fifths, of all dismissals.[96]

As in the London police, the biggest problem in the Irish constabulary was drink. It was a problem closely watched. Inspector-General Harvey reported that the records of 1,100 men in six counties over a six-week period in 1834 revealed not a single case of inebriety. For 2,590 men in eleven counties, again over six weeks, he found a total of only thirteen cases, six of them concentrated in Kilkenny, where the 392-man force contained "a considerable proportion of very young men."[97] Harvey suggested that since the constabulary was now stressing youthfulness in its recruits, drunkenness could be expected to be a problem. In the early 1830s, a constable usually had to be caught drunk a second time before he was dismissed. A regulation of August 1834 substituted suspension for a fine for the first offense of intoxication. But two cases from May 1835 indicate that the rules were not always enforced. In Leinster, Harvey dismissed Subconstable Matthew Coleman only after his third offense in twenty months. In Munster two subconstables, having escorted some prisoners to jail, proceeded to get drunk. Miller dismissed Michael Mulcahy but fined James Kelly one month's pay. The

Inspector-General explained the distinction by "the fact of one having been so drunk as to have been detained [in jail] all night at Rathkeale, while the other was not so overpowered with drink as not to be able to walk Home [to Newcastle barracks]."[98] The 1834 regulation, however widely enforced, was strengthened in the constabulary reform of 1836. Prospective police candidates were informed that two offenses would be punished with instant dismissal: marriage and intoxication.[99] Oddly, had the former been permitted, there might have been less of the latter.

III. The "new" constabulary

In the eight years before 1836, the Irish constabulary matured into a highly professional police under substantial government control. It was not the force's disorganization, as previous writers have argued, but its advanced development that urged the Government to inject the final doses of centralization.[100] The 1822 act (which no longer reflected police realities) had to be scrapped, the remaining 600 Peelers incorporated, and a single supraprovincial Inspector-General named to head the 7,000-man force.

It is, in fact, remarkable that this final centralization came only in 1836. Richard Willcocks had proposed a single Inspector-General as far back as 1823. William Lamb (later Lord Melbourne), when he was briefly Chief Secretary in 1827, had noted that the solution to the "inconveniences" of provincial forces was "to bring the whole Country as soon as possible under one uniform system of police." Major Miller in 1829 had called for "one system of management" for the constabulary. The need for centralization was clear not only in the matter of appointments but also in the direction of the force.[101] Local magistrates, citing the 1822 Constabulary Act, continued to believe that they had powers over the disposition of the police; Dublin Castle responded by quoting Section 24 of that same act and the Petty Sessions Act (1827), which prohibited the police from recovering tithes, levying rent distraints or fines, and collecting revenue. The disagreement persisted due to the niceties of legal interpretations and the absence, since 1822, of civil constables in virtually all of the counties' baronies. To resolve the problem, the Government had three options, as Crown Law Adviser Richard Greene explained to a parliamentary committee in 1832. The Government could (1) create a whole new set of baronial constables to act in civil cases; (2) repeal the prohibitions against the constabulary acting in civil cases; or (3) take all control of the police from local magistrates. Greene dismissed the first option as impractical and the second as inaugurating a land war in Ireland; he believed the third was inevitable in order to keep the peace, though it might entail some sacrifice in the satisfaction of civil claims.[102]

The antecedents of the 1836 Constabulary Act stretched as far back as 1829. In November of that year, Leveson Gower had prepared a bill that would legally transfer the appointment of constables to the Government, recognize the existence of county subinspectors, and establish provincial depots and reserve forces; there was no mention of an overarching Inspector-

General. The abortive bill reached the House of Commons in late March 1830, but the complaisant Chief Secretary failed to press it. Two months later Leveson Gower resigned his office, as he told Wellington, "on grounds of private affairs."[103] The following spring the Knight of Kerry and Lord Lieutenant Anglesey, working separately, composed plans for a new national police superintended by a single Inspector-General. By 1832 a bill, "prepared in the first instance under the Marquess of Anglesey and ... [which] had received the approbation of Lord Stanley," was ready for submission to Parliament. It provided for 1 Inspector-General, 4 provincial and 32 county inspectors, rank-and-file appointments resting exclusively with the Government, repeal of the 1814 and 1822 police acts, and absorption of the Peelers into the constabulary.[104] Anglesey and Stanley left office in the spring of 1833. In November, Littleton stated that the bill "prepared last year will require very little modification." But the new Chief Secretary was busy winding down the Tithe War; six months later, in May 1834, he complained to Gosset of "being fool enough to encumber myself to such an extent. ... I vow to Heaven, I hardly know on what day I could find time to bring on the Constabulary Bill."[105]

To be sure, the delay in the years before 1836 resulted in part from Castle officials' lingering doubts about the constitutionality of a national gendarmerie. Leveson Gower realized that the "obnoxious clauses" in his bill did represent "an attempt at dictation," that the "fractious resistance" by Irish local magistrates betrayed "a prevalent & as I thought a creditable feeling among the gentry." In the bill's brief transit through the Commons in 1830, six of the nine speakers opposed the measure. Dominick Trant even charged the Government with "a settled scheme ... to take under its control the police, not only of Ireland, but of England" at a time when "the people of Europe were generally struggling to get rid of the constraints of a police." Littleton, though he harbored no illusions about Irish magistrates, was affected by such arguments. He was hesitant to push for a police that many Irish Members "strenuously" opposed as being despotic.[106]

Thomas Drummond

The catalyst that finally transformed Anglesey's bill of 1832 into the Constabulary Act of 1836 was the arrival of a new Under-Secretary at Dublin Castle. During his five-year tenure, Sir William Gosset had proven himself "an excellent man of business," but with Whiggish liberalism now ascendant in government policy making, Gosset was increasingly uncomfortable with his superiors and "dreadfully unpopular" with Dubliners. He retired in July 1835. The new Castle triumvirate was the youngest in memory. The Lord Lieutenant, the 2d Earl of Mulgrave, was thirty-eight; Chief Secretary Viscount Morpeth was thirty-three.[107] The new Under-Secretary, also an outsider to Irish politics, was a thirty-seven-year-old Scotsman who by training was an army engineer. Thomas Drummond had worked on the Scottish (1819–24) and Irish (1824–31) Ordnance surveys, had headed the

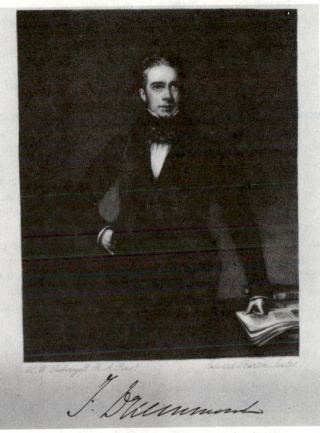

Figure 9.4 Thomas Drummond, Under-Secretary in Ireland, 1835–40 (McLennan, *Memoir of Drummond*)

English Boundary Commission (1831–3) that delineated the new political geography required by the Reform Bill, and since 1833 had been private secretary to the Chancellor of the Exchequer, Lord Althorp. But Drummond longed for a return to public service and to Ireland, and gladly accepted the important Castle post "with a head teeming with projects of reform and a heart overflowing with affection for the Irish people." When, only five years later, in 1840, he was dying of the painful skin disease erysipelas, Drummond is said to have asked to be buried "in Ireland, the land of my adoption."[108]

Thomas Drummond is undoubtedly the best known, and by the mass of the people was probably the most loved, Castle Under-Secretary in nineteenth-century Ireland (Figure 9.4). His career was eulogized and preserved for later generations by two Victorian biographers (1867, 1889).[109] But his role in the history of the Irish police has been overstated. William Lecky set the tone by writing in 1890: "The organisation by Drummond, in 1836, of that great constabulary force ... has proved, perhaps, the most valuable boon conferred by Imperial legislation upon Ireland." Subsequent historians have credited Drummond with the principal police reforms of the 1830s.[110] Drummond's role is probably so well known because of his long testimony before the 1839 Roden Committee, whose report became an important printed primary source for future scholars.[111] Moreover, Under-Secretary Drummond, unlike Gosset or Gregory, cultivated an activist style that placed him very much in the limelight. The late 1830s are remembered as the age of Drummond, not of Mulgrave or Morpeth.

Drummond's correspondence does reveal an insistence that the constabulary bill be pressed in Parliament. But he himself admitted that he "found in the Office in the Year 1835" the bill framed by Littleton and Gosset, which in fact was a revised version of the Anglesey-Stanley bill of 1832.[112] Drummond was certainly persistent, but he was also in the right spot at the right time: After a three-year gestation, birth was imminent. Another curiously neglected fact is that it was not Drummond, but Chief Secretary Morpeth, who steered the constabulary bill through the 1835 and 1836 sessions of Parliament. Drummond's correspondence also reveals a flawed perception of the state of the constabulary in 1835. The four Inspectors-General operated "different Systems." There was "a great want of proper" officers and "a bad description of Men from the Appointments being in the hands of the Magistrates." Drummond argued that the police was a "Partizan Force," seemingly unaware of recent policies of hiring Catholics and promoting by merit in a force already nearly two-fifths Catholic in the rank and file. Drummond himself admitted that any signs of "Party Spirit" brought "prompt dismissal" of the offenders; what he did not realize was that such political offenses were rare, that the great bulk of the dismissals were for nonsectarian lapses like drunkenness or absence from duty. The new Under-Secretary concluded that "nothing can be more unsatisfactory than [the] present state" of the constabulary.[113] In fact, the force was not as bad as he believed. Since 1828 the Government had been increasing its control of and making improvements in the police. Not all of the credit should be given to Drummond and Morpeth. We must also acknowledge the work of Leveson Gower, Gosset, Anglesey, Stanley, and Littleton, and of course of the Inspectors-General, Warburton, Stovin, Harvey, and especially Miller.

The Irish constabulary bill of 1835 and the act of 1836

In his first weeks in office in July 1835, Drummond concentrated on the police, for he believed that "no Improvement of any Consequence can be made in the Constabulary Force unless this Bill be passed." The following month, Morpeth introduced the bill in Parliament at the tail end of the session. The principal recommendations were to bring the entire force de jure under government control; establish a Constabulary Office in Dublin Castle; appoint an Inspector-General and a Deputy Inspector-General; divide the officers and rank and file into classes to encourage merit raises and stimulate rank promotions; create a new rank of Head Constable, which would serve as both the highest rank for enlisted men and a recruiting pool for a proportion of future Chief Constable appointments; increase the number of Stipendiary Magistrates; and abolish the Peace Preservation Police and absorb the men into the constabulary. Costs would increase by 50 percent, from £250,000 to £380,000 a year, with Irish taxpayers continuing to pay one-half. The 1835 bill called for a huge increase in the officer class: 32 County Inspectors; their assistants, 35 Subinspectors, 2 each in Cork, Galway, and Tipperary; and 576 Chief Constables, an average of 18 to a county. The proposal almost passed; it did clear the Commons but lost in the Lords by a vote of 51–39.[114] Reintroduced in February 1836, the amended bill contained reductions so as not to "frighten" Members; there would be 2 Deputy Inspectors-General, but the 32 County Inspectors were cut back to 4 Provincial Inspectors and the number of Chief Constables pared to 217. The bill passed in the Commons at the end of March and in the Lords in May, and received the royal assent on the 20th of that month.[115]

For the first time, in August 1835, it was the Whigs, historic foes of a centralized police, who were sponsoring strong police legislation for Ireland.[116] The irony of the event was not lost on the Earl of Roden, who noted that during the debates on "a bill introduced in the year 1822 by Mr. Goulburn," a bill that also proposed a government-controlled police, "it was objected to on this very ground by several individuals who were either members or supporters of the present Government." Roden reported from his researches in *Hansard* that "in the minority on the division on that occasion he found the names of Henry Brougham, Lord Althorp, Lord Duncannon, C. Grant (now Lord Glenelg), and several others, friends of the present Administration."[117]

There were a number of reasons for the volte-face. First, the Whig Government since 1830 had borne the responsibility for governing Ireland. Gone was the luxury of opposition based on high constitutional principles; Morpeth now talked of greater efficiency, of making the police "much more serviceable." Second, for those who believed in theory in local accountability, local magistrates' police appointments in 1823–8 and their use of the force in the Tithe War provided a harsh awakening to Irish realities. The third explanation was the changed state of Ireland since 1822. "The circumstances," said Brougham, "were different." Glenelg "defended his consistency . . . on the ground of the altered state of circumstances in Ireland."[118]

All depended, of course, on *who* controlled the government police. In 1822, power rested with a Tory and Protestant administration; in 1835–6, with a liberal Whig one predisposed to push Catholic claims in appointments and promotions. Morpeth's proposal for a fully centralized constabulary thus attracted curious support. Joining Brougham and Glenelg were the Irish Whigs, Henry Grattan and Lord Cloncurry, and even the Catholic chieftain, O'Connell himself. The parliamentary scenario was rich in historical symbolism. Robert Peel, the Tory police innovator, made a brief speech in favor of the Whig bill. Henry Grattan – second son of the Irish Patriot hero who had denounced the 1786 Dublin police bill – announced his reluctant support for the 1836 constabulary bill. The "recourse to the present measure," he explained, "and he admitted it to be a strong one, . . . was on account of the bad measures which had been adopted by the [Tory] party who had so long misgoverned Ireland." In the Lords, to which five years earlier he had been elevated, Peel's old foe, the sixty-two-year-old Cloncurry, also pledged his support. He admitted that Morpeth's bill institutionalized the principles of Peel's act of 1814, but the alternative of a police run by Protestant prejudice was worse; Cloncurry concluded, as Grattan had in the Commons, that "it was only the ill treatment which Ireland had received from successive Governments which rendered the present measure necessary." Finally, Daniel O'Connell, another earlier critic, now stated that the Government had acted "wisely" in giving total control to Dublin Castle. Would anyone contend that "the Grand Orange Lodge was the fittest body" to administer the force?[119]

The bill's opponents, political conservatives, used the familiar arguments of expense and erosion of local liberties. The Anglo-Irish Duke of Wellington, who had helped to establish a government police for Dublin and later London, objected principally to the costliness of the new constabulary. The proposed expenditures he calculated at £420,000, half of which would be assessed on Irish local taxpayers, who he doubted could afford the 25 percent increase in their share of the costs. Noting the legal restrictions on police aid in the recovery of rent and tithe, Wellington concluded that "at the same time, then, that they [the Government] increased the expense to the landed interest, they deprived that body of the aid of the only constabulary force in Ireland."[120] Constitutional objections were concentrated in the House of Lords. A parade of Ascendancy grandees – the Earl of Wicklow, the Earl of Winchelsea, the Marquess of Londonderry, Lord Gort, and the Earl of Roden – objected to Dublin Castle's monopoly of the powers of patronage. Roden's remarks were the most vituperative:

He found in this Bill the Lord-lieutenant of Ireland constituted into a very autocrat, little less powerful than the Emperor of all the Russias himself. . . . The whole of the measure seemed to him to be based upon patronage, injustice, and arbitrary power, inconsistent with the British Constitution, and uncalled for by the circumstances of the country. . . . All he could say was this, and he would leave it to the judgment of any unbiased man to decide, whether if it were possible to find a minister who would have the temerity and folly to propose such a law for England as a permanent measure, whether the cry throughout the land, from Land's End to John o'Groat's house, would not be – *Nolumus leges Angliae mutari.*

This line of argument, contrasting England to Ireland, had a long history but by the 1830s was wearing thin. The Whig Prime Minister rose to object to "the tone, manner, style, and tenour" of Roden's outburst. This "dangerous, unconstitutional, and oppressive novelty," observed Melbourne sarcastically, only "embodied the provisions" of Peel's 1814 Peace Preservation Act, to which Roden had given his approval.[121]

Behind the old arguments for local liberties lay new fears of the Catholic masses. O'Connell's alliance with the English Whigs gave Catholic Ireland a share of government power. Ascendancy Ireland was increasingly irritable and defensive. The great betrayal had begun, ironically, with "Orange" Peel persuading the English Tories to enact Catholic Emancipation. It had proceeded under the Whigs with the disestablishment of the Yeomanry, the suppression of Orange processions, and blatant favoritism toward Catholics in government appointments.[122]

During the constabulary debates, speakers at first merely alluded to these different circumstances in Ireland, then finally brought them out in the open. In August 1835 the Marquess of Londonderry remarked that, should the bill pass, "power ... would in effect come [in]to the hand of the individual [O'Connell] to whom the noble Viscount [Duncannon] and his friends [Melbourne and the English Whigs] were so much indebted for being in the Government." Toward the end of the debates in the Lords, in the spring of 1836, the charges became less veiled. Londonderry dismissed the bill as mere Catholic patronage; Wicklow had "no doubt that the real object ... was to introduce a great number of Roman Catholics into the police force ..., to throw power into the hands of the Catholics." The smoke screen of Ascendancy arguments over local liberties lifted; laid bare for all Englishmen to see were the Irish lords' prejudices and fears of loss of Protestant political power.[123]

Opposition in the Commons also concentrated on the issue of religion, which is to say, of democracy replacing oligarchy. Speakers alleged that the Government wanted to flood the Irish constabulary with Catholics, as it had earlier inundated the ranks of Crown Solicitors. One opponent of the bill charged that thirty of the last thirty-four solicitors appointed were Catholics; in fact, replied the Irish Attorney-General, *only* fifteen of twenty-four recent appointees were Catholic.[124] A Whig spokesman hardly calmed Irish Protestant fears by saying that, in light of Tory policies before 1830, "no apology would be due from the present Government, even if every one of the appointments ... were of Roman Catholics."[125] Opponents feared that the constabulary's new Inspector-General would be Sir Frederic Stovin, the recently named and reputedly pro–Catholic head of the Ulster police; Morpeth was sufficiently pressed that he agreed to submit a return of dismissals in Ulster in order to disprove "the charge ... of undue favour shown toward the Catholic portion of the police." The harassed Irish Chief Secretary was at length rescued by the Home Secretary, Lord John Russell, who announced that the new Inspector-General would be an outsider, a Scotsman of "the utmost impartiality ... connected with no party in Ireland," Col. James Shaw-Kennedy. Sir Robert Peel immediately rose to applaud the selection of this man, who had been his first choice for London Police Commissioner. Russell's timely intervention apparently silenced further protests. "The Orangemen had just shewn their teeth," Morpeth wrote Lord Lieutenant Mulgrave, "when Peel and even Shaw threw them quite over; the announcement of Col. S. Kennedy['s name] by John Russell did wonders, as they evidently had been afraid of Stovin."[126]

Two political lessons were learned from the Irish police debates of 1835–6. Both English parties now believed that the Government needed to mediate as a third party between Irish Protestants and Catholics. The Whigs, reported Russell, "wished ... to steer clear of all differences, whether of interest or passion, that might exist between Irish parties." The Tory leader, Peel, concurred: "The unfortunate state of religious animosities ... make[s] it better to trust the representative of the Crown than to allow the power to remain in the hands of the local authorities, however respectable." The corollary to this principle, and the second lesson, was that Irish factionalism had ensured that, in matters of policing, all Irishmen would be the losers. Ireland's police was now totally controlled by the English Government.[127]

The long journey, begun by Orde and Fitzgibbon in 1786, ended with Drummond and Morpeth in 1836. That it had taken fifty years is evidence that, although Westminster was willing to use Ireland as an experiment station for its harsher ideas of police, it was unwilling to impose by fiat any blueprints for despotism. Since 1787, with key benchmarks in 1814 and 1822, the Irish constabulary had grown fitfully by accretion and compromise. Such growth testified to the power of the old and cherished ideals of local control.

As late as 1822 these arguments still held much credibility; by 1836 they were hollow. The concessions to local authorities in Goulburn's Constabulary Act had resulted in inefficiencies, abuses, and institutionalized prejudice; the Government had responded by taking control of the police de facto from 1828 on and, finally, de jure in 1836. These constabulary reforms, and the success of Peel's police in London, had demonstrated that a police beyond local control need not be a monstrous force for despotism. Indeed, given the history of the police in the two countries, it was ironic that the establishment of a government police in the English capital seven years earlier gave legitimacy to the centralist concept and provided a prototype for the final reforms in Ireland in 1836. If in London police power descended through the Home Secretary and the Police Commissioners, why not in Ireland through the corresponding offices of the Lord Lieutenant and the Inspector-General of Constabulary?

Against this background, then, the English Whigs in 1835–6 joined forces with the O'Connellite Catholic faction and with enlightened Anglo-Irishmen like Cloncurry and the younger Gratten – and the three groups allied with the Peelite Tories – in seeing the advantages of a centralist, nonpartisan, professional police in Ireland. Such a political combination was overwhelming. Local liberties, once a matter of high principle, had become a cloak for prejudice and pettiness.

Rethinking 1836: a watershed in Irish police history?

The composition of the Irish constabulary of 1836 was not drastically changed. The great bulk – 94 percent – of the 7,400 constables and sub-constables continued to serve. After his inaugural tour of June 1836, Inspector-General James Shaw-Kennedy pronounced the police "an admirable Body of Men." The 250 new Head Constables, the highest rank of "the non-Commissioned Officers," were simply promoted constables from the old force. The Government filled 89 percent of the Chief Constable appointments with men of prior service in this rank, many with more than a dozen years' service. Of the thirty-five Subinspectors named in 1836, 80 percent had served as Chief Constables or Subinspectors, the average length of service being thirteen years.[128]

The greatest changes came at the top. At the time of the passing of the 1836 act, there were twenty-nine Stipendiary Magistrates, seventeen of whom had served in the constabulary; in its nineteen appointments for the year beginning July 1836 the Government appointed not a single man who had served in the constabulary. For the highest posts in the police, the Whig Administration selected veteran officers of congenial political beliefs. The Lord Lieutenant described the new Provincial Inspectors, one of whom was a Catholic, as men of *"very strong Liberal* opinions." Of the preexisting Inspectors-General, Stovin, judged "the best qualified" but "want[ing in] temper," was removed from his provincial command; Harvey retired; and Warburton, the old Peeler, and Miller, the administrative innovator, though both politically conservative, were promoted to be the Deputy Inspectors-General. The highest post went to Col. James Shaw-Kennedy, an apolitical military officer whose talents first Peel, and now the Whigs, found attractive.[129]

Just as the composition of the police remained largely unchanged, so did its size and distribution. Officers and men in January 1837 totalled 7,700; this figure was actually lower than the combined total of 8,200 men in the constabulary and the Peelers in 1832. As late as 1840 the constabulary numbered only 8,600 men – only 400 more than the police/Peeler totals of eight years earlier. Sizable growth would resume only in the mid-1840s. The distribution of the force was scarcely altered, with Leinster still containing one-third of the men, Munster one-fourth, Connaught more than one-fifth, and Ulster only one-sixth.[130] (See Appendix II.)

There were, however, important and noticeable changes. In June 1836 one wing of Dublin Castle was converted into the office for the Inspector-General of the Constabulary. Previously, the Under-Secretary had handled all police correspondence; now Gosset's successor, Drummond, was relieved of much of the work by the presence down the hall of Shaw-Kennedy, whom he met "at a fixed time" daily.[131] In the provinces were formally authorized depots where the recruits enrolled in four-month training sessions at Armagh (Ulster), Ballincollig (Munster), Ballinrobe (Connaught), and Philipstown (Leinster). In 1839 the Government would establish a fifth or central depot in Dublin housing a Reserve of 200 (and, by the mid-1840s, 400) men.[132] Other visible changes were standardized uniforms consisting of rifle green tunics with black facings, Oxford gray trousers, and black leather belts. Barracks, too, became more uniform in appearance. A traveler in 1840 described them as "exceedingly neat and clean looking houses ... in many cases built expressly" for the force. Above the door was a foot-high black iron badge with large, raised white letters, atop a shamrock and beneath a crown, spelling out "CONSTABULARY."[133]

Among the rank and file the Government stepped up its policy, begun in 1833, of seeking out Catholic recruits. Drummond talked of appointing them "in a proportionate Degree" to the local population. With retirements, dismissals, and resignations necessitating the hiring of nearly 1,000 recruits every year – a one-seventh annual turnover in manpower – the opportunities to bring in Catholics were great. The Inspector-General reported in 1839 that two-thirds of the recruits since 1836 were Catholics; the proportion of Catholic constables in the force rose from 36 percent in 1832 to 54 percent by 1842.[134]

Constables tended now to come from the laboring class and the small farmers; fewer recruits were farmers' sons "of the respectable class."[135] This trend was due in part to the hiring of Catholics but also to a reduction in salaries. Before the reform of 1836, all subconstables earned £27, 14 s. a year. In September 1835 Major Miller had proposed organizing three classes of subconstables salaried at £29, £27, 14 s., and £26 to "create a stimulus by a new management of the pay." In 1836 a two-class system was established, but at a pay of £27, 14 s. and £24 (a 13 percent decrease from existing pay). In 1839 the subconstables' salaries were again lowered to £25 and £23, and for the first time constables, previously all salaried at £32, 7 s., were divided into two classes at £32, 7 s. and £28. Most of the second-class subconstables and constables doubtless regarded this "new management" as a penalty, not a stimulus. To some, a policeman's regular pay, twice that of a fully employed laborer, remained attractive. To others, including "respectable" farmers' sons, it was becoming a burden; as one Monaghan subconstable explained in a letter of resignation to his Subinspector, "I could not support my Self upon it in a genteele manner as I would wish to do, Sir."[136]

Resignations and dismissals accounted for the loss of between 300 and 500 men every year. The annual rate of dismissals (200–300 men) remained in the pre-1836 range of 2 to 4 percent of force strength. Drunkenness continued to be the principal reason for dismissal. Also, reported the Inspector-General in 1839, "a great Number ... including some of our best Men" were dismissed for marrying in defiance of regulations. Deputy Inspector-General Miller continued to view marriage as "an indulgence."[137] Apart from dismissal, punishments could take the form of fines, extra duty, and disrating (now possible in the two-class ranks). The pre-1836 policy of rotation continued to be used as a punishment. Most celebrated was the contretemps in Carlow involving Stipendiary Magistrate Samuel Vignoles and Subinspector Thomas Gleeson in 1837; each was moved to another county and ordered never again to serve together in the same county.[138] Each year about half as many men resigned as were dismissed. Those leaving seem to have been either the adventurous or the more respectable, for a constabulary official reported in 1841 that emigration and farming were the "principal causes" of resignation. "Some" men enlisted in the army or got civil employment in their last county of service. "Some, but fewer than formerly," joined the Dublin or London police; "a few" went over to the newly forming "Rural Police in England"; and "some resign in order to *get married*."[139]

The officers in the constabulary after 1836 remained very much a class apart from the men. The great majority of appointments went to outsiders, not to men promoted from the ranks. Irish police officers thus resembled, not their counterparts in London's upwardly mobile Metropolitan Police, but rather the commissioned officers in the British army. This latter class served, in fact, as the principal recruitment pool for Irish police officers; and behind both lay the landed and socially prominent, who contributed their sons to these institutions. Inspector-General Shaw-Kennedy told Parliament in 1839 that not a single Chief Constable appointment in 1836–8 was the result of the promotion of a man from the ranks; his successor, Col. Duncan McGregor, reported that of forty-one officer promotions in 1838–9 only one was from the rank and file (Head Constable) into the officer class (Chief Constable). The officers' register confirms this trend: Men with prior police service accounted for 35 percent of all officer appointments in 1833–6 but only 12 percent in 1837–40. The system was equitable in the sense that officer recruits entered at the lowest officer rank and worked their way up; men were never brought in over the heads of *officers* already in the force.[140] In 1839 the officer ranks were reorganized: The Provincial Inspectors were reduced from four to two; the two-class Chief Constable rank was abolished and the men were appointed to the top two classes of the three-class rank of Subinspector; and the former Subinspectors were divided among the top two classes of a new three-class rank, County Inspector.[141] Government policies were institutionalized in 1842 with the creation of the "cadet" system. Each gentleman cadet, innocent of police experience, earned a constable's pay but wore a cadet's uniform during his course of studies at the recently established (1839) constabulary depot in Phoenix Park, Dublin. The cadet school was the first police academy in the British Isles. After passing examinations not only in police duties but also in arithmetic and geography, spelling, handwriting, and English composition, the cadet graduated into the officer class at the bottom rank of Subinspector Third Class.[142]

In its officer appointments, the Morpeth–Drummond Administration continued prereform constabulary policies; indeed, in 1836–9 it severely reduced merit promotions from the ranks. Whig liberalism did not envision an Irish officer class created by democratic vertical mobility, but rather by lateral insertions of men of merit. Officer appointments and promotions, noted Morpeth, were to be understood "not as a matter of right and condition of service.... They will continue to be made, as they have always been heretofore, at the discretion ... of the Lord Lieutenant." The Government would control appointments in the police, "just as [in] the Excise, Customs, [and] Post Office." Morpeth made it clear that he was unwilling to abandon traditional patronage powers. "I consider that it would be to depart from all previous practice to inflict a gross injustice on the friends of the present Government by introducing a regulation that would bear for the first time against them in contrast with the dealings of previous Administrations." Drummond believed that only by hiring officers from outside the police could the reactionary institution be improved. Looking down the list of officers in the summer of 1835, the Under-Secretary concluded, "All of them are so teinted [*sic*] with Toryism and so connected with the politics of the Castle in the worst times." If the Whigs' officer appointment policy permitted them to reward political friends, it also provided employment for and a share of governing responsibilities to the sons of the gentry. Gentlemen officers, liberal or conservative (a Louth Chief Constable was kept on though he was "a Conservative in disguise"), were expected to be more socially congenial with Irish local authorities than would a constable of humble background who found himself promoted into the officer class.[143]

There were exceptions. As before 1836, a few officer vacancies were reserved for sons of "old and deserving officers." Also, beginning in 1839, the Government instituted a policy that required *one of every three* officer appointments to constitute a promotion from the ranks of Head Constable First Class, the highest nonofficer rank. Drummond believed that he was introducing a new system; in fact, he was reinstating Littleton's merit policy of 1833. The constabulary regulation of 1839 was apparently enforced rather strictly: 27 percent of all officers appointed in 1841–50 had previously served in the rank and file.[144] The policy of hiring most officers from outside the constabulary did not impede the inflow of Catholics. Of twenty-five Chief Constable appointments in 1837, nine went to Catholics; of four Sub-inspectors, one was Catholic. In general, under the Whig Administration, one in every four officer appointments – 26 and 30 percent in 1833–6 and 1837–40 – went to a Catholic, compared to only one in ten before 1830. In the 1840s the Catholic share dropped slightly to about a fifth of all officer appointments. But the cadet system, which filled 60 percent of annual officer vacancies, did not discriminate against Catholics. The proportion of Catholics who joined as cadets was the same as for Protestants; indeed, the system boosted the Catholic share in the officer class, for more Protestants than Catholics (28 compared to 20 percent) became officers by promotion from the ranks. Those Catholics who did become officers fared slightly better than their Protestant colleagues in the number of promotions received throughout their careers.[145]

When Drummond and Morpeth stated that appointments and promotions rested with the Government, they meant with the Whig Lord Lieutenant. In 1836–8 the new Inspector-General watched with increasing impatience as his recommendations were ignored. Partisanship and political alliances seemed to dictate the selection of new Chief Constables and Subinspectors. For the Paymasters' posts the Inspector-General had submitted a list of ninety-six Chief Constables of eleven or more years' experience; the Lord Lieutenant appointed eighteen Paymasters in 1836–9, none of whom had served in the constabulary. The Inspector-General recommended deserving Subinspectors for positions as Stipendiary Magistrates; the Lord Lieutenant appointed nineteen men in 1836–7, none of whom had served in the constabulary. Significantly, Drummond was able to report to a parliamentary committee in 1839 that of twenty-five Stipendiary Magistrates appointed *since 1836*, none had prior service in the police. He later told the committee that he had been mistaken: Of thirty-four appointments in 1835–9, twelve, or one-third, had been constabulary veterans.[146]

As he worked in his new office in Dublin Castle, Inspector-General James Shaw-Kennedy, who seven years earlier had declined the London police commissionership from fear of involvement in politics, must have considered the irony of his Irish predicament. Independent, strong-minded, and non-partisan, this career military officer, a veteran of the Peninsular War and of Waterloo, had superintended the postwar occupation of France and the final withdrawal of British troops from the Continent.[147] After a year's service (1826–7) as adjutant-general in northern Ireland, Colonel Shaw (he became Shaw-Kennedy in 1834) had been transferred to England's tumultuous Northern District. For nine years in Manchester, he had kept aloof from local politics and had managed to keep the peace.[148] Now, in Dublin, he was able to do neither. His nominees for promotions were constantly rejected; he grumbled that his appointments were restricted to subconstables, constables, and Head Constables. The office of Stipendiary Magistrate he viewed as a rank promotion within the constabulary, an interpretation that Lord Lieutenant Mulgrave dismissed as "a very objectionable innovation." Even disciplinary matters (most recently, the Vignoles–Gleeson case) he found to be handled by the Castle's political authorities. Shaw-Kennedy's patience ran out after twenty-two months; he finally resigned, at age forty-nine, in March 1838.[149]

The old Peeler, sixty-one-year-old George Warburton, filled in for a few months as Inspector-General before retiring to England on a £1,000 pension. Indispensable William Miller, now a colonel, continued as Deputy Inspector-General, assisted by constabulary veteran and former Stipendiary Magistrate Lt.-Col. Stephen Holmes.[150] The new Inspector-General, fifty-one-year-old Col. Duncan McGregor, appointed in July 1838, was, like Shaw-Kennedy earlier, an outsider, a Scotsman. Called over from Canada, where he had assisted in putting down the rebellion the previous year, McGregor knew Ireland only from several months' duty in Dublin and Belfast in 1836.[151] Shaw-Kennedy's case had been a nasty affair. A year after his departure, as the first witness before a parliamentary committee on Irish crime, Shaw-Kennedy argued at length that he had been misled as to the extent of his powers in Ireland. Warburton thought that the former Inspector-General had been wronged; most of the men in the force agreed; and General William Napier stated bluntly that his friend had been "forced by intrigues to resign." Inspector-General McGregor profited by the Government's lessons from the affair. Dublin Castle retained its control of the Stipendiary Magistrates but granted to the head of the constabulary power over all appointments, promotions, and punishments in the force. Unfortunately for Shaw-Kennedy, the Irish Government implemented only in 1838 what had been the rule in the London police since 1829.[152] Like the Police Commissioners in the English capital, the Inspector-General of Constabulary knew best the needs of his force and should be entrusted with sufficient powers to develop a professional and nonpartisan organization.

Drummond, Morpeth, and Mulgrave believed that their reforms of the Irish constabulary were without precedent. Before their appointments, the Chief Secretary and Lord Lieutenant, like most who held those offices, were strangers to Ireland; the Under-Secretary was familiar with the land and its people but not with Dublin Castle. Whether from ignorance of the facts or unwillingness to share the credit for the reforms, all three men originated the myth that the Irish constabulary in 1836 was inefficient, corrupt, and partisan. Only once in his parliamentary testimony of 1839 did Drummond pay tribute to the man who had done the most to reshape the force. "Col. Miller," he admitted, "had his Force in great Order at the Time [1836]," and it was he "who has been mainly instrumental in introducing the admirable System as respects the interior Arrangement of the whole Establishment." Miller's daily labors over the past decade were recognized by his promotion to colonel in 1836 and a pay increase in 1839 from £800 to £1,200, a salary only £300 less than Inspector-General McGregor's.[153]

Like his changes in the force itself, Drummond's policies on the employment of the police were important but not novel. His circulars to the constabulary repeated the Castle's exhortations to caution and restraint that had characterized every chief secretaryship except Stanley's. The police were not to collect or protect the collectors of the parish cess. They were not to act except upon the authorization of magistrates assembled at petty sessions. They were not to execute distraint warrants for nonpayment of rent. They were not to protect tithe valuation, collection, or distraint for nonpayment. Of course (as in the past), in cases of previous "forcible resistance" attested to in sworn affidavits, resort to the police would be considered.[154] Although Drummond in his public statements gave the impression that these were new policies, private Castle correspondence shows an awareness of precedents for restraint. Crown Law Adviser J. Richards noted in 1836 that such policies were "in perfect conformity with the opinions of the different Law officers and advisers of the Crown from the time of the passing of the act [3 Geo. 4, c. 103] to this date." To argue anything else was "nothing less than absurd." On another occasion in 1836, Colonel Miller, enclosing copies of letters from Goulburn, Gregory, and Willcocks, informed Drummond that as far back as 1824 the Irish Government had instructed the constabulary not to intervene in tithe valuation and rent collection. Miller's history lesson brought no comment from the Whig Under-Secretary.[155]

In two areas – suppression of Orange processions and faction fights – Castle policies were new and controversial. Drummond was correct in asserting that "the first successful efforts" to deter Orangemen from marching in traditional displays of Protestant patriotism dated from 1835. Aided by the passage of an act that subjected marchers to prosecution and by the presence of large numbers of police and troops, the Government in 1836 made arrests in twenty-seven processions that resulted in 200 convictions and jail sentences of up to three months. Two years later, the number of processions declined to five.[156] The Whigs likewise punished Gaelic exuberance. Faction fights at fairs – traditional social and political gatherings for Catholic laborers and small farmers – were perceived by the English Whigs as merely mindless bloodlettings. One of Drummond's proudest claims was that he had suppressed "such disgraceful Outrages." He believed that the effect of this sporting violence on the Irish people was "to brutalize them a great deal"; Drummond's remedy, in the words of his mid–Victorian biographer, was that "nothing should be left undone to remove such copious springs of ruffianly feeling in the people."[157] Warburton noted that before 1835 it had been "the invariable practice" for police parties to attend fairs but not to intervene except in instances of the most serious violence. Drummond regarded this policy as patronizing and prejudiced, and ordered that all faction fights be prevented.[158] The three Inspectors-General in the south and west opposed the new policy in 1835–6 as tending to bring the constabulary into collision with the people; none was more vociferous than Sir John Harvey, and Drummond gladly accepted his retirement in May 1836.[159] Drummond's policies gathered force after the passage of the Spirit License Act, which authorized magistrates at dusk to clear drinking booths at fairs, thus removing the ritualistic pregame socializing and alcoholic stimulus to violence. By the late 1830s, the frequency of faction fighting appears to have declined significantly.[160]

The fundamental aims of Thomas Drummond and the Whigs may be described as an attempt to *civilize* Ireland. They pronounced Protestant local rule bankrupt but were unwilling to transfer power to the Catholic majority presumably predisposed toward breaking the connection with England.[161] Faced with these choices, the Whigs, like the Tories before them, concluded that civilization in factious Ireland would be best promoted by massive doses of Crown control. Drummond knew that conciliation had to accompany this centralization: He would kill local rule with kindness. "Civility and forbearance," he wrote Shaw-Kennedy, should constitute the foundations of all police behavior. The harried Inspector-General replied, "Every means that I can think of are in progress to accomplish that end." Unsatisfied, the Under-Secretary suggested that "perhaps a general order as to civility would not be amiss."[162]

Once again, Drummond's aims were not without precedent or irony. From the start (1822–4), the regulations for Goulburn's constabulary had contained similar exhortations to civil behavior. Ironically, it was the Whigs who, in the reform of 1836, had emphasized the military aspects of the constabulary. Drummond compared the rank gradations to those in the army.[163] Drill and discipline were more practiced than detective work. The force was headed by a single Inspector-General who was a career military officer; in Ireland, unlike London, there was no second Police Commissioner with a legal background. This oversight in 1836 would stamp the constabulary for future decades as mostly military in nature. Although the Whigs wanted a civil force, they required that its officers be men of military experience. They perpetuated the separate class structure for officers, and by opening only a third of the appointments to merit promotions bred uncivil resentments among the rank and file.

The Whigs remained uncomfortable with this hybrid Irish force. The Scottish Whig, J. R. McCulloch, noted disapprovingly that it possessed "more of a military than a civil character." Lord John Russell admitted in 1838 that "the force is a very peculiar one; it neither resembles the regular troops nor the militia nor the Metropolitan Police." As historic foes of a centralized police, the Whigs found themselves in the ironic situation of wanting to emulate that benign Tory creation, Peel's London police. "In England," a Clare correspondent chided Castle authorities in 1837, "the police ... are civil and courteous to the People and the Law thus mildly administered is obeyed dutifully by the People." To be effective, he concluded, the Irish police "must be made *a civil force civil to all.*" This lofty goal, the Whigs in Dublin Castle were coming to learn, was far more difficult to achieve in Ireland than in the streets of the English capital. It was one thing for Drummond to issue circulars requiring police "civility"; it was quite another to alter the foundations of Irish society, which encouraged incivility. In July 1836, two months after passage of the Constabulary Act, Lord Lieutenant Mulgrave rather testily summed up the situation to Morpeth:

As to the general military character of the appointments I hold as long as the force is armed that for the safety of the public as well as for its own character it must be disciplined.... If this was felt as a general objection, why was not some proposition for so entirely changing its character made during the progress of the Bill? How is it possible that they could, if unarmed and undisciplined, ... do their duty at fairs and amongst the great assemblages of the People? *The improvement in the tranquillity of the Country must have had some intervening time to assume a permanent character before such an alteration would be at all practicable.*[164]

IV. An "impenetrable mystery": agrarian crime and police frustrations

A man planted a vineyard, and let it out to tenants, and went into another country for a long while.... [W]hen the tenants saw [the man's son], they said to themselves, "This is the heir; let us kill him, that the inheritance may be ours." And they cast him out of the vineyard and killed him. What then will the owner of the vineyard do to them? He will come and destroy those tenants, and give the vineyard to others.
– Luke 20: 9, 14–16

One of the major post-1836 reforms was the standardization and centralization of record keeping. Since the early 1830s, the Irish constabulary had endeavored to compile returns of crime (outrages) known or reported to them. Such documents, explained Shaw-Kennedy, present "a much more ample View of the actual Crime committed than could be obtained from any Returns of Committals and Convictions." The old standard of measurement, committals, consisted only of figures for those arrested and charged, so that (in Warburton's words) they "would be at all Times fallacious as to [measuring] Crime." Beginning in 1832 "Outrage Returns" were compiled, rather incompletely, by the Chief Constables. They forwarded the returns to the county Subinspector, who "engrossed" them into a county schedule that he sent to the Under-Secretary's Office. In April 1837 Deputy Inspector-General Miller reformed the system. Each Chief Constable and Subinspector now provided only "a simple Statement of the Facts; he gives no Classification or Opinion about them." All analysis and classification was done in the Constabulary Office.[165]

By the old system, "the local officer became the classifier" and it "frequently occurred" that Chief Constables entered multiple offenses committed during one incident. From 1837 on, "the rule observed" was to make a judgment from "the several incidents of the case" and record each outrage as either "one offense" or "under the *Chief* Heads of the Crimes committed." Thus, if an armed party fired shots into and forcibly entered a house, and either beat the inmates or swore them to an unlawful oath, the offense would be listed only as a "house attack" or "unlawfully administering an oath." If, during a house attack, two major crimes were committed – say, an occupant killed and arms stolen – the outrage would be recorded as murder *and* robbery of arms. The new system was not perfect, but classifications were at least systematic and comparisons therefore possible.[166]

Committals for all crimes had changed little from 1822 to 1832. In all but one year, they were in the range of 14,000–16,000. The fastest gains came between 1832 and 1834, rising in the latter year to 21,400. From 1835 to 1842 they ranged from 21,000 to 26,000 (Table 9.8). The "new" constabulary of 1836 thus produced no startling increases in committals. The volume held fairly steady because, in "the absence of more serious disturbances," the police filled their time dealing with "comparatively minor offences."[167]

The Government was concerned more with the nature than the volume of crime. The Lord Lieutenant noted that Ulster recorded the highest number of committals, yet was the most tranquil province. Connaught was peaceful compared to the early 1830s, but assaults comprised two-thirds of all crime. In Leinster, the counties of Longford and Westmeath remained disturbed, though, in the opinion of the Crown Solicitor with twenty-one years on the circuit, they were not so disturbed as in the early 1820s. In Munster crime was now concentrated in Tipperary. Justice Arthur Moore, who had presided at special commissions in 1815, 1822, and 1831, believed that "the moral condition of the Country has been progressively though slowly improving." Another veteran observer, George Warburton, thought that crime was generally declining and that the "isolated Cases of Assassination and personal Attacks" were peculiar to a few counties. The outrage totals supported these arguments: Annual average returns for 1837–9 and 1839–42 were down 33 and 35 percent, respectively, from the levels in 1835–7[168] (see Table 9.9).

Traditional agrarian crimes in Ireland were on the wane. Over the period 1835–42 violent crimes against persons fell from 36 to 25 percent of all offenses. Both the most serious crimes of violence and "common assaults," which comprised four-fifths of all Class 1 offenses, were declining. Murder and manslaughter had averaged 370 annual committals in 1822–8, climbed to 542 in 1829–34, reached a peak of 712 in 1835, and stayed high at 524 in

Table 9.8. *Crime in Ireland, 1835–42*

	All offenses		Most serious offenses against persons with violence[a]		Murder/manslaughter		Assembling armed by night and attacking dwelling houses	
	I	II	I	II	I	II	I	II
1835	21,205	71.8%	922	44.4	712	43.4	157	35.0
1836	23,891	75.9	843	50.4	629	62.3	263	47.1
1837	14,804[b]	64.4	688	38.2	519	33.7	129	60.5
1838	15,723[b]	61.1	578	51.6	424	46.9	95	31.6
1839	26,392	45.7	891	32.8	659	32.5 (50.1, 11.2)[c]		200	20.0
1840	23,833	47.0	530	34.7	333	32.4 (52.2, 9.7)		192	49.0
1841	20,796	44.7	786	22.4	309	35.9 (49.2, 15.0)		165	19.4
1842	21,186	46.6	482	33.2	309	24.9 (55.0, 5.8)		207	32.9
Ave./yr.								
1835–42	*20,979*	*56.5*	*715*	*38.6*	*487*	*40.7 (51.2, 10.1)*	*176*	*36.9*

Key: I Number of persons charged with criminal offenses and committed to jail for trial.

II Percentage conviction rate.

[a] Comprising murder and manslaughter; shooting, stabbing, poisoning, &c., with intent to murder; assault with intent to murder; and conspiracy to murder.

[b] Published totals for committals in these years excluded all Petty Sessions cases, which *some* Clerks of the Crown and of the Peace had in previous years included. Adding these, totals in 1837–8 fall into a range of 22,000–24,000. *PP 1839* (486), 12:1097, Drummond's note. From 1839, totals are from "the assizes and [quarter] sessions."

[c] From 1839 on, the criminal statistics distinguish manslaughter committals from murder committals; separate conviction rates for manslaughter and murder, respectively, are provided in parentheses.

Table 9.9. *Outrages reported by the constabulary, 1835–42*

	1835	1836	1837	1838	1839	1840	1841	1842	Percent change 1839–42 compared to 1835–8
Homicide	250	229	230	247	189	125	105	106	−45%
Shooting a firearm at a person	81	78	91	48	56	43	66	74	−20
Aggravated assault[a]	1,260	1,184	975	863	832	605	803	691	−32
Demand or robbery of arms	184	196	246	179	180	177	111	158	−22
Appearing armed	208	164	110	46	57	41	66	55	−59
Administering unlawful oaths	103	73	69	53	65	49	60	51	−24
Attacking houses	708	431	606	330	280	229	295	337	−45
Shooting into dwellings	97	84	21	23	65	68	71	99	+26
SELECT TOTAL	2,891	2,439	2,348	1,789	1,724	1,337	1,577	1,571	−34
Select total as a Percent of total outrages	28%	31	35	36	34	29	29	24	
TOTAL OUTRAGES REPORTED	10,225	7,834[b]	6,775	4,945	5,039	4,626	5,361	6,535	−28

[a] Comprising aggravated assault, assault with intent to murder or to endanger life, and cutting or maiming the person.
[b] Beginning in June 1836, petty larcenies and common assaults were not reported as outrages.

1836–8. But by the early 1840s, the annual average committal rate (317) for homicide was about half that of a decade earlier (Table 9.8). The Outrage Returns for murder corroborate this trend: The murder rate, high until 1838, was halved from 1835–8 (239 cases) to 1839–42 (131) (Table 9.9). Traditional Whiteboy crimes also declined. Committals for riotous assembly, armed by night, and attacking dwelling houses dropped by *one-half* from 1829–34 (323) to 1835–8 (161). The Outrage Returns for seven major agrarian crimes (excluding murder) showed a decline by *one-third* from 1835–8 (2,128) to 1839–42 (1,421).[169] It is arguable, as Drummond told a parliamentary committee in 1839, that the constabulary was preventing outrages; Whiteboy offenses did drop steadily through 1840, but they rose again in 1841–2.[170] The increase in minor offenses – simple riot and breach of the peace, and common assaults – Drummond mistakenly explained by the more thorough enforcement of the law since 1836. By comparing the averages for 1826–8 with those for 1836–8, he gave the impression that the large increases had been achieved by his new constabulary. Drummond ignored the lesson from the annual statistics that the greatest increases in committals for riot and assault had come in 1830–6:[171]

Committals in Ireland (annual averages)

	1826–8	1828–30	1830–2	1832–4	1834–6	1836–8
Riot, breach of the peace, and pound breach	861	876	999	1,330	1,770	1,958
Assaults	4,763	4,788	4,223	5,317	6,459	6,533

One crime – homicide – resisted the downward trend. Even as the incidence of other Whiteboy outrages declined by one-fourth, the number of reported murders remained constant from 1835 to 1838 (see Table 9.9). But *committals* for homicide and for the most serious violent offenses against persons fell steadily, by two-fifths, from 1835 to 1838 (Table 9.8). These figures corroborate Warburton's statement in 1839 that the condition of the country was much improved, with the exception of "isolated Cases of Assassination and personal Attacks." Though the national homicide rate did begin to drop about 1840, it remained high in a few counties. Twenty of the island's thirty-two counties (63 percent) generated only 31 percent of the total prosecuted murder/manslaughter cases in 1836–8; by contrast, four counties – Tipperary, Limerick, Cork, and Mayo – produced fully 38 percent of all homicide cases in the country. No county was more lethal than Tipperary, which accounted for 46 percent of the totals in these four most murderous counties and fully 17 percent of all homicide cases in Ireland.[172] During the 1830s, murder in Ireland became increasingly concentrated in

Tipperary: The county's share of the national totals for homicide committals rose steadily from 18 to 28 percent from 1831–2 to 1837–8. Within Tipperary the violence was further concentrated: In 1839 an average of twenty murders a year were being committed in the four baronies around Thurles, the district to which Peelers had been sent as far back as 1815.[173] A recent scholar, M. R. Beames, has concluded that these assassinations, characteristic of the land war in Tipperary in the decade before the Famine, were efforts by the numerous small leaseholders to preserve "the norms of the local peasant community" threatened by demographic pressures and improving landlords.[174]

In convictions – an area largely beyond the control of the constabulary – the record in 1835–42 was disappointing to the authorities (see Table 9.8). The conviction rate for all offenses had been rising – an average of 54 percent in 1822–8 and 63 percent in 1829–34 – but in 1835–42 it fell to 57 percent.[175] Convictions for crimes against persons (all Class 1 offenses) followed the falling conviction rates for all crimes. Roughly three-quarters of those charged with common assaults – which comprised four of every five Class 1 offenses – were convicted, but for the most serious crimes – murder and manslaughter; shooting, stabbing, and assault with intent to kill; and conspiracy to murder – only about two-fifths of those charged were convicted. Although traditional Whiteboy offenses – assembling armed by night and attacking houses – were declining in frequency, they were also falling in rates of conviction. Annual average committals for these offenses were nearly halved: 161 in 1835–8 and 191 in 1839–42 compared to 323 in 1829–34. Whiteboy outrages reported to the constabulary also declined steadily in 1835–40 and rose only slightly in 1841–2. The steepest drop was in the number of reports of appearing armed by night and attacking dwelling houses, down 59 and 45 percent, respectively, in 1839–42 compared to 1835–8. But the declining frequency of Whiteboy crimes was unattended by improvements in the conviction rate. Convictions for riotous assembly armed by night and attacking houses had risen from 24 percent in 1822–8 to 28 percent in 1829–34 and 45 percent in 1835–8. But in 1839–42 the conviction rate dropped to 31 percent; if we exclude the high year 1840 (49 percent), the rate for the period 1838–9/1841–2 would be a dismal 25 percent. The criminal statistics for Whiteboy crime indicate that the constabulary was perhaps succeeding as a preventive police but, as in cases of homicide, could do little to see offenders prosecuted to conviction.

Dublin Castle and the highest police authorities believed that the declining frequency of crime, especially agrarian crime, was due, at least in part, to the efficiency of the constabulary. But despite the fall in the figures for committals and outrages, the network of agrarian crime was not broken. It appears rather to have been driven further underground. Crimes in the open – armed night riding, attacks on houses, robbery of arms – could be deterred by a patrolling paramilitary police. But against murder, the selective assassination by sudden fire from a pistol or musket, there was no defense. The resort to homicide as a major weapon in the land war is perhaps testimony to the success of the police in repressing other characteristic forms of Whiteboy activity.

In 1839, before a parliamentary committee of English and Anglo-Irish gentlemen, Thomas Drummond reported with satisfaction that crime in Ireland was declining.[176] What he did not stress in his testimony was that the *fons et origo* of Whiteboyism remained untouched. To some extent, the blame rested with the constabulary. The force, uniformed and drilled with military precision, did not engage in enough covert activities; many observers believed that the Peelers had been better at detective work. The Stipendiary Magistrates, who reported directly to the Chief Secretary's Office, did not work closely enough with the constabulary officers to be effective in crime detection. The rotation policy, which periodically moved one-third of the force into another county, led to a lack of local knowledge. Ordered by a Stipendiary Magistrate to arrest a certain man, one constable replied, "I have not been long enough in the Place to know him, Sir."[177]

To a far greater extent, however, the reasons lay beyond the control of the police. In 1839 a member of the parliamentary committee asked Joseph Tabuteau, a Stipendiary Magistrate with thirteen years' service in Tipperary, whether the reluctance of the people to prosecute resulted from "Intimidation or Sympathy." His answer was brief: "I think Sympathy."[178] A few months earlier, the crime of the decade had occurred in King's County near the Westmeath border. Shortly after evicting a tenant, the 2d Earl of Norbury had been shot and killed. Murders in that part of the country were not uncommon, but the prominence of the victim was almost unprecedented. The assassination was especially controversial because the earl was the son of John Toler, 1st Earl of Norbury (d. 1831), who a generation earlier as Irish Attorney General had obtained capital convictions against the Sheares brothers (1798) and as Lord Chief Justice had sentenced Robert Emmet to death (1803).[179] The execution of "old Norbury's" heir on New Year's Day, 1839, put great pressure on the constabulary. Inspector-General McGregor reported that "every possible Pains" was being taken to find the assassins. The police were "well aware" that every man who helped to crack the case could expect promotion and a share of the £6,000 offered in rewards. But thirteen years later, in 1852, Deputy Inspector-General H. J. Brownrigg informed another parliamentary committee that Norbury's murder had never been solved.[180]

Less dramatic but equally significant were popular attitudes in districts no longer considered seriously disturbed. Edward Hickman, Crown Solicitor for Connaught since 1815, noted that County Sligo had been quiet since 1833 but that "the People are as callous now as ever they were." In 1838 the county recorded 224 criminal committals, 155 cases leading to indictments and only 20 to convictions; this dismal record he deemed "the fault of the jurors." Police constables continued to serve as witnesses, sometimes as the only witnesses, in legal proceedings. In those cases proscribed by the Whiteboys, anyone who dared to prosecute or even to testify could expect punishment outside the courts. Such persons had to be paid as well as protected by the Crown, retired Inspector-General Warburton explained to the parliamentary committee. He added that these had been government practices for the past twenty years. Sir Matthew Barrington, Crown Solicitor for Munster since 1815, also felt compelled to educate the committee. The person who comes forward in Ireland "is obliged to be protected. It is not like England, where every Man aids in the Administration of Justice; in Ireland, almost every Peasant endeavours to avoid assisting."[181]

Thomas Drummond's constabulary found it as difficult to root out agrarian crime as had Goulburn's and Peel's forces. The police had succeeded in stopping faction fights and suppressing Orange processions. Police aid in rent and tithe collection was once again being bridled. The force itself – smartly attired, highly disciplined, ubiquitous – could boast of its growing professionalism and impartiality. But the Irish constabulary remained apart from and alien to the majority of the Irish peasantry. At a time when the London police were slowly gaining, even from the upper working class, the acceptance and trust necessary for successful policing, in Ireland the barriers between police and people remained in place. The Irish constabulary was thus handicapped by having to operate on the surface of Irish society. The ignorance in high places of the actual state of the country was staggering. What is clear from the evidence of numerous witnesses – police officers, Stipendiary Magistrates, local gentlemen – before the 1839 parliamentary committee is that for all of them the system of agrarian crime constituted a faceless threat that defied analysis.[182] Pressed for details on Ribbonmen, Thomas Drummond could only describe them as "an impenetrable Mystery; for we cannot even get a Surmise as to their Names or Residences." Another witness, John O'Ferrall, Commissioner of the Dublin Police, placed the Government's frustration in bleak historical perspective:

I have known Riband Societies to exist ever since 1822, and since that Period a most efficient Police has been organized throughout the Country; the most active Magistrates employed ..., and yet, notwithstanding their Exertions, and every Reward offered, we do not know more about the Objects of Ribandism at the present Moment than we did then.[183]

CHAPTER 10

Belated beginnings of police in England

I have seen, during my life, the Country twice mad – in a paroxysm of madness – and so have you – once with Anti-Jacobinism [in the 1790s], and now with something very like Jacobinism. I still, however, trust that we shall get through it.
> – Home Secretary Melbourne to Irish Lord Lieutenant Anglesey,
> 12 September 1832

Tyranny always comes by slow degrees; and nothing could tend more to illustrate that fact than the history of police in this country. When the establishment of a police force was first proposed, Englishmen were shocked at the idea. The name was completely new among us.... We continued for some time with a police office in Bow Street, a couple of police Magistrates, and a few police officers ... but at length the right hon. Baronet [Peel] came forward and said that "owing to the improvement of the age, we want something a little more regular in the form of our police" ... behold! We had now [in London] a police with numbered collars and embroidered cuffs – a body of men as regular as any in the King's service, as fit for domestic war as the red-coats were for foreign war.... The system was spreading. Formerly it was confined to London, but the ministers had been smuggling it into the great towns; before long there would be a regular police force established in every village.... He warned ... the people of England against the scourge which ... Government was preparing for them.... He believed the Government had the project in contemplation to govern England, as Ireland has been long governed.
> – William Cobbett, speech on the Irish Coercion Bill,
> House of Commons, 18 March 1833

Dear Chadwick,
It occurred to me ... that one means of getting over the humbug of danger to the liberties of the Country would be to give the power *absolutely*, of dismissal to the Magistrates. Thus if the Secretary of State should take it into his head to endeavour to enslave a whole County (which is not at all unlikely, after paying 20 Millions to enfranchise [*sic*] the *Niggars*) by sending six or seven additional Police Constables "armed with a bare bodkin," into that County, the Magistrates might, sensing the imminency of the danger, immediately dismiss the said six dangerous individuals and thus frustrate the base attempt. It is impossible to maintain gravity on the Subject.
> Yours very truly,
> C. Rowan

April 26/39   What a pity it is that all men who are not Rogues, should be fools. Present company excepted.

In the midst of continuing unrest – over the Reform Bill, the New Poor Law, and then Chartism – something would finally be done about the provincial police in England. Significantly, the response to the challenge would be less drastic than it had been in Ireland. No emergency "peace preservation" acts would be necessary, no suspension of civil liberties imposed. In England's incorporated towns, police reform would be accomplished not by any separate police legislation but rather as a part of general municipal reform. In three large northern towns in the process of incorporation, the Government would step in to manage the police until local authorities put their houses in order; but this intervention in Manchester, Birmingham, and Bolton would prove short-lived and controversial, an aberration in English police history. Finally, a "rural" or county police would at last be created to watch the sprawling unincorporated towns as well as the mining and agricultural districts; but, significantly, this force of 1839 was merely optional, not imposed on the counties.

These various provincial police forces, established in the years 1835–9, were pale imitations of the gendarmerie that had policed Ireland since the early 1820s. That the London Government could readily agree to watch committees and county magistrates being given full control over England's new borough and county police, respectively, was testimony to the importance and strength of existing local government institutions. Moreover, the differences in crime and protest in the two countries would enable the new English forces to operate without firearms. It is worthwhile to examine this point in some detail because, beginning in the mid-1830s, the first systematic efforts were made to collect and analyze the criminal statistics for England and Ireland.

I. Crime in England: its nature and extent

An Irish perspective

In the same year that Drummond's Irish constabulary bill passed through the English Parliament, a little-noticed book appeared in London under the imprint of B. Fellowes, a small publishing shop in Ludgate Street. *On Local Disturbances in Ireland; and on the Irish Church Question* was the fifth book from the pen of George Cornewall Lewis, who in 1836 was only thirty years old.[1] The young man's interest in Ireland stemmed from the career of his father, Thomas Frankland Lewis, who since 1821 had been a commissioner for Irish revenue and education and in 1828 had been considered for the post of Irish Chief Secretary, which was subsequently filled by Leveson Gower.[2] Lewis's elder son, George Cornewall, attended Eton and Christ Church, Oxford (B.A., 1829; M.A., 1831) and was called to the bar; in 1833–4 the Whig Government commissioned him to report on the condition of the poorer classes and the state of religious instruction in Ireland. Lewis's investigations were characteristically thorough, taking him through more than 3,100 pages of evidence in five parliamentary reports on "the state of Ireland" since 1824.

The Government published Lewis's findings in 1836–7; some of his re-commendations were embodied in the first Irish Poor Law of 1838. George Lewis also resolved to bring his ideas on the causes and nature of Irish disorders before the British reading public.[3]

On Local Disturbances in Ireland offered Englishmen the first scholarly analysis of Irish crime; recently reprinted (1977), the book remains an important pioneering work in social history.[4] In the 1830s the serious study of crime was grounded in statistical analysis of the criminal returns, which had been reorganized in 1834 into six categories or classes of indictable offenses. These revealed that Irish crime (as measured by committals) was per capita twice as frequent as English crime, and that crimes against persons and crimes against property with violence were four times as frequent. Criminality in the two countries was essentially different when (in 1835–7) 77 percent of all offenses in England, but only 33 percent in Ireland, were nonviolent crimes against property; when violent crimes against persons and property accounted for 35 percent of Irish but only 15 percent of English crime; and when public order offenses comprised some 20 percent of Irish but less than 5 percent of English crime (see Table 10.1). Such quantitative lessons were highly instructive.[5]

But to understand the basic distinction between crime in Ireland and England, Lewis argued, it was necessary to "consider all crimes as divided into two classes, not according to the ordinary distinction of crimes against the person, and crimes against property, but with reference to the motive with which they are committed, or the *effect* which they are intended to produce."[6] In Ireland most crime had an "exemplary" or "preventive" character: The object was either "to prevent, or to compel the performance of some future act," or "to punish a party for having done some act." Personal violence in the form of beatings, shootings, and murders, and violent or malicious property damage like the burning of houses, spading up of grasslands, or maiming of livestock, were "*physical* sanctions" employed by Whiteboys who acted as "administrators of a law of opinion, generally prevalent among the class to which they belong." Irish crime was thus preponderantly social and collective rather than individual and self-serving; "it usually happens that others profit more by his offence than he himself who committed it." Lewis noted that robberies and burglaries comprised but one-sixth of all crimes in Ireland. And in a disturbed province like Munster (1833), only fifty-nine thefts were recorded in a police Outrage Return that listed 968 total offenses. Lewis calculated that in Munster two-thirds of the criminal incidents were exemplary or preventive in nature, and his count did not include "homicides, firing at persons, rescues, illegal meetings, & c. ... [which] were doubtless committed with the same motive." The conclusion reached by Lewis was that the agrarian offenses peculiar to Ireland were not what an Englishman would call crime but rather were better described as the tactics of "a vast trades' union [operating] for the protection of the Irish peasantry."[7]

Table 10.1. *The nature of crime, 1835–41: class of crime as a percentile share of total indictable offenses*

| Ireland | | | | | | | | England | | | | | | |
Annual average committals, all crime	Class 1	2	3	4	5	6ᵃ	Years	Class 1	2	3	4	5	6	Annual average committals, all crime
19,967	32%	3	33	2	1	29	1835–7	9%	6	77	1	2	5	21,776
18,973	28	4	45	1	1	21	1837–9	8	6	79	1	2	4	23,716
23,674	26	5	42	1	1	25	1839–41	8	7	79	1	2	5	26,463

Class 1: Crimes against persons with violence
2: Crimes against property with violence
3: Crimes against property without violence
4: Malicious offenses against property
5: Forgeries and currency offenses
6: Miscellaneous offenses

ᵃOf all Class 6 Irish offenses, roughly one-half were "riot, breach of peace, and pound breach" and one-fourth were "rescue and refusing to aid peace officers."

Table 10.2. *Public order offenses in England and Ireland, 1835–41 (annual averages)*

	Riot		Assault	
	England	Ireland	England	Ireland
1835–7	619	1,870	711	5,308
1837–9	512	2,423	669	4,149
1839–41	521	3,156	662	4,979
1835–41	549	2,464	688	4,898

Committals for riot (riot, breach of the peace, and pound breach) and assault.

The second great class of crime, uncommon in Ireland but predominating in England, was the personal, individual, self-aggrandizing sort. In England, wrote Lewis, "a homicide is committed from motives of personal vengeance, or under ... momentary excitement; ... a house is broken open ... [or] a man is robbed on the highway ... simply to obtain property.... In these cases no general or prospective result is intended; the criminal merely seeks to gratify his own malice or avarice, or to satisfy his own personal and present want by the act." This attitude toward crime was pithily summed up by Edward Pierce, the mastermind of "the Great Train Robbery" in England in 1855; asked at his trial why he did it, Pierce replied, "I wanted the money." Lewis, who cited André Guerry's recent work on French criminal statistics, noted that these personal motivations characterized crime in "England, France, and indeed of almost every civilized country." The social or collective crime prevailing in Ireland "at ordinary times ... can scarcely be said to have any existence in England." Lewis stated that "the only crimes recently committed in England with the same general intentions" as Irish Whiteboyism were the rick burnings by the agricultural laborers, the anti-Poor Law riots, and the "crimes committed by members of trades' unions."[8]

Examination of the committal statistics supported George Lewis's general argument. Public order offenses, or "collective violence," formed a large part of Irish but a very small proportion of English crime. The high Irish figure for Class 6 offenses in Table 10.1 reflected the widespread incidence of riot, rescue, and refusals to aid police. In Ireland committals for "riot, breach of the peace, and pound breach" accounted for more than a tenth, and those for "assault" for about a fifth, of all Irish committals. Measured in terms of committals, riot and assault were, per capita, more than ten times more frequent in Ireland than in England (see Table 10.2). As for other protest offenses – arson (the classic protest crime in rural England), killing and maiming livestock, riotous destruction of buildings and machinery – the Irish figures, when adjusted for population differences, also outpaced the English ones. In addition, Ireland's judicial statistics recorded some kinds of protest – forcible possession of land, unlawful armed assembly (England's tamer version was armed poaching and assault on gamekeepers), and attacks on dwelling houses – that had no equivalents in English record keeping (see Appendix 1).

In recent studies of English crime and protest, a number of scholars have essentially restated George Lewis's findings of the 1830s. Scrutinizing national totals for riotous offenses in the disturbed Chartist period, 1836–48, John Stevenson (1979) discovered that they comprised an annual average of only 2.3 percent of all committals.[9] Cutting a wider swath, George Rudé (1973) tabulated "protest offenses," which he defined as arson (all types), riot (common and serious), machine breaking, destruction of manufactures, "being out armed taking game," high treason, sedition, and breaches of the peace (all types). These still accounted for only one in every twenty committals.[10] In their authoritative study of nineteenth-century criminal statistics, V. A. C. Gattrell and T. B. Hadden (1972) dismissed protest offenses in two paragraphs. The number of such offenses, they concluded, is "so small that they cannot meaningfully be reduced to a ratio of the population.... [W]hile explicitly political or semi-political responses of this kind may be the most dramatic, they are quantitatively the least important recorded indices of discontent."[11] To complement this contemporary statistical evidence, the historian should point out that although the English Parliament in the first half of the nineteenth century produced nearly a dozen reports on Irish crime, even apart from those on the state of Ireland, he is at a loss to find even a single committee report on riots and disturbances in England.[12]

English crime: coping with a statistical explosion

In England from 1805 to 1848, serious crime, as registered by committals to trial at assizes and quarter sessions, increased sixfold while the population doubled. These rates exclude the more numerous petty minor offenses – common assaults, minor riots and brawls, drunk and disorderly conduct, and vagrancy – that were adjudicated summarily at magistrates' courts (petty sessions). Begun in the 1820s, summary jurisdiction in minor criminal cases was extended to an increasing range of offenses by acts in 1848 and 1855; at midcentury, annual totals of summary offenses were about twice the number of committals for major crimes. Only from 1857 on, thanks to the police act of the previous year, do we have a national record of indictable offenses known to the police (similar figures had been kept in Ireland for the past twenty years). These series, the best indication of the extent of *major* crime, indicate that about three of every five known indictable offenses in England resulted in the filing of criminal charges (committals). If we extrapolate backward, using the ratio of known indictable offenses to committals in the 1850s, we may conclude that while the population of England doubled over

Table 10.3. *Committals for all crimes in London and the rest of England and Wales, 1814–49, per 100,000 population*

	London			Rest of England and Wales		
	I	II	III	I	II	III
1814–20	209	131		89	58	
1821–9	226	145 (64)	+8%	105	75 (70)	+18%
1830–9	218	156 (72)	−4%	136	98 (72)	+30%
1830–5	231	163	— —	131	93	— —
1836–9	198	146	— —	145	105	— —
1840–9	208	157 (75)	−5%	162	118 (73)	+19%

Key: I Committals.
    II Convictions (percent conviction rate).
   III Percent change in committals from previous period.
Source: Adapted from Hart, "Borough Police," pp. 413–14.

the first half of the nineteenth century, the incidence of major crime increased not six but ten times.[13]

Regional analyses are full of difficulties, but the evidence suggests that crime – four-fifths being property offenses – was on the increase not only in urban industrial counties like Lancashire but also in rural ones like Hereford or Somerset.[14] In the debate over the rising tide of larcenies, burglaries, and robberies, scholars have often overlooked the fact that the figures for committals for indictable offenses simply record the number of *apprehensions*. That is, the crime figures reflect, most clearly, the ability of the authorities to seize offenders and commit them to trial. Looked at in this way, the criminal statistics constitute not so much an approximation of the recorded levels of crime as of the efficiency of policing. Police historians have traditionally considered as an effective police only the New Police and the modern concept of deterrence.[15] In London after 1829 there is evidence, from the declining number of committals, that Peel's force was preventing the more serious offenses.[16] But in the counties and boroughs, both before *and* after the establishment of the New Police, deterrence was an inoperative concept (see Table 10.3). The new forces, note Gattrell and Hadden, were "scarcely effective on a national scale even by the 1850s"; the constable's vigilance (or lack of it) "scarcely influenced at all" local rates of committals for indictable offenses. And H. J. Perkin concludes that the growth in crime was "real and not the statistical effect of the activity of the new police."[17] Similarly, from 1831 on, the rapid erosion of the capital code – down from about 200 offenses at the turn of the century to 11 by 1841 (and only for murder or attempted murder among crimes of any frequency) – had little effect on the *rate* of committals, though it did push up the *conviction* rate. Leon Radzinowicz has even found that for certain property crimes, committals actually fell in the 1830s after abolition of the death penalty.[18] These findings, as far as they go, are true.

Real crime was undoubtedly rising rapidly, but in pointing to the short-comings of the small, scattered, and uncoordinated forces making up the new police after 1835, scholars have neglected the contributions of the old police. This has happened for four reasons. Police historians have had their eyes on *new* developments: the New Police and preventive policing. They have tended to focus on public disorders, not normal crime.[19] The variegated nature of the older forces – beadles, watchmen, parish constables, JPs – enormously complicates the task of research. Finally, the herculean challenge to cover not 40 English counties but 25,000 parishes has intimidated the most indefatigable of researchers.

The old institutions were certainly inept at preventive policing and woe-fully ineffective against organized criminal gang activities or serious public disorders.[20] But neither of these were statistically frequent crimes in England. Against normal crimes (offenses against property without violence) the old system could be remarkably effective. In his pioneering study of crime and policing in "the Black Country" in south Staffordshire and part of southwest Worcestershire, David Philips asks the obvious question:

The image of the ... parish constable, quite inadequate for the task he had to perform, is so firmly fixed in most historical accounts that they [historians] never seem to ask why, if that was the case, the system continued to work until the 1840s without any serious breakdown of law and order in those communities which relied on parish constables. The system had many flaws, but it coped with much of "normal" crime and small-scale disturbances.

Traditional institutions might not *prevent* crime or disperse mobs, but who else, before the later 1830s at the very earliest, was responsible for the rapidly increasing rate of criminal committals? Philips has found that his Black Country constables were farmers (in the rural parishes) and small tradesmen and artisans (in the towns). They were not an annual crop of n'er-do-wells or illiterates; in fact, they served for many years, were serious about law enforcement, and "regarded themselves as full-time policemen." Until the 1840s "the overwhelming majority" of persons committed to trial in the Black Country were apprehended by parish constables; and in Staffordshire men were appointed to this office until 1865.[21] Such men had the respect of the community, frequently knew the offender by name, and could call on neighbors for help; further, those apprehended by the constables "nearly always did as bidden."[22] This picture forms a strong contrast to Ireland, where crime was acceptable to a broad section of the population and appre-hension and conviction were difficult.

Other recent research is unearthing similarly strange truths about pre-modern policing in England. The absence (until 1879) of Public Prosecutors may reflect only the efficacy of private prosecutions. In Birmingham and Warwickshire in the 1830s and 1840s two-fifths – a surprisingly large propor-tion – of the prosecutions brought at Quarter Sessions by victims of crime were brought by unskilled and skilled manual workers. After midcentury this proportion declined steadily, evidence not only of the increasing role of the police in prosecutions but also perhaps of the workers' alienation from a force over which they had no control. The parish constable had visited pubs, had a "proper" occupation besides being a policeman, and did not patrol a beat or tell workers to "move on."[23] Assisting the local constables were the Associations for the Prosecution of Felons, some 450 of which were created throughout England between 1744 and 1856. Funded by private subscriptions, composed of a number of small property owners, and motivated by local initiative, the Associations sought to help the local authorities apprehend and prosecute persons for property crimes. The Associations were surprisingly effective in the era before police forces were acceptable institutions. In the 1840s when the new police were introduced, the Associations generally did not resist but rather aided them in law enforcement.[24] Finally, even in many of the medium-sized towns away from the turbulent North, both the old and the new police were capable of coping with normal crime. A recent study of Portsmouth has found little evidence of either political radicalism or uncontrolled crime; the personnel and policies of that borough's police were little changed after 1835.[25]

The state of policing *before* the advent of the new police of 1835–9 remains largely uncharted territory. But the old institutions, outside the North and the larger cities, were apparently coping surprisingly well with the rise in crime. At the time of the legislated reform of the borough police (1835), Jenifer Hart has noted, there was no talk of uncontrolled crime; "the statute," states T. A. Critchley, "was not exclusively, or even primarily, promoted for police purposes."[26] Borough police reform in fact came as a part of the Municipal Corporations Act, which sought to rationalize a variety of urban government functions, of which policing was but one. The only towns that did receive thoroughly overhauled, government-controlled police were those where, even more than crime, political radicalism was the issue: Manchester, Birmingham, and Bolton in 1839–42.[27] The rural police in 1839, the brainchild of Edwin Chadwick and Charles Rowan, were created not to deal with crime but to control Chartist disorders. In this sense, the numerous petitioners to the Constabulary Force Commission (1836–9) who protested that crime in their areas was under control missed the political point.[28] If most local authorities were dealing adequately, if also under increasing strain, with the war against normal crime, this would help to explain why the adoption of the borough and county forces was so piecemeal, so gradual after 1835–9. In this interpretation local resistance was not simply spiteful, self-interested, or hysterically constitutional. The fear of crime, whipped up by the lurid statements in Chadwick's Constabulary Commission report of 1839, has been accepted and overplayed by most police historians.[29] There was, however, one important duty for which, all can agree, the myriad local institutions *were* hopelessly inadequate: the control of large-scale or widespread public disorders.

II. Popular protest: challenge and response

The spur to police innovations in the 1830s was the threat of working-class protest. The criminal statistics certainly indicate the rarity of riotous offenses, by contrast to the large volume of property crime in England. To some degree, however, these statistics paint only a partial picture. In a country where rioting was an accepted national pastime, the great majority of rioters were not apprehended by the authorities. Because they went home rather than to jail, they do not appear in the criminal statistics; hence, the incidence of riot was far more widespread than the tables of committals would suggest. One has only to compare the size of crowds in the "Captain Swing" or Bristol riots with the number of rioters arrested to establish this point. Moreover, riot was one of the most visible offenses; newspapers were more inclined to report a riot than to carry stories of the numerous and comparatively humdrum property crimes. Because public disorders were dramatic, eye-catching events, they had a disproportionately large influence on official policymaking. Even a quick perusal of the Home Office's daily correspondence, or the private papers of Edwin Chadwick, reveals a concern not with petty daily crime but with public disorder.

After the tumultuous period from Waterloo to Peterloo, the 1820s had been comparatively peaceful. But the 1830s revived the alarms of the postwar years. Scarcely was one crisis ended than another began. In the last five months of 1830, the rural laborers rose in revolt across southern England. Contemporaneously, the recurrence of a cyclical economic slump in the North in 1829–31 produced such severe strikes and industrial violence that the Government considered a plan to revive and exchange the English and Irish militias; Home Secretary Melbourne anxiously wrote Lord Lieutenant Anglesey that "no one can foresee what would be the consequences, if anything serious should arise in Ireland."[30] To unrest from economic distress was added the political excitement of the Reform crisis in 1830–2 when the provincial cities erupted in protests. Trade union organizing intensified in 1833–4. Concentrated in the North and the Midlands, it flared briefly even in rural Dorset, where six Tolpuddle laborers, transported, became "martyrs"; the case triggered a protest march by 25,000 sympathizers in London.[31] Then, in 1835–8, disturbances erupted in both the South and the North against the New Poor Law (1834), a measure that restricted the poor's eligibility for relief and cut the assessments on ratepayers. Just as the anti–Poor Law Riots were subsiding, there arose the most serious challenge of all: Chartism, the workingman's demand for universal suffrage.

Captain Swing

Revenge for thee is on the Wing.
From thy determined
                Captain Swing

The decade's first disorders, the Swing riots, were spontaneous local protests by the numerous agricultural laborers in southern and eastern England. Originating in Kent, the disorders ultimately affected twenty counties from August to December 1830. The basic cause of the riots was the postwar fall in agricultural prices and the consequent immiseration of the rural proletariat; the protest triggers, which varied locally, were the poor harvest, low wages, the introduction of cheap Irish labor and threshing machines, strictly enforced tithes and game laws, and cuts in poor relief. "Captain Swing's" vengeful rioters were impressive in their numbers, organization, intervillage communications, stylized threatening letters, and extent and rapidity of movement.[32] In six months, they committed just under 500 indictable protest offenses, half of which were divided about equally between arson (rick and barn burnings) and destruction of threshing machines; in all, they inflicted about £120,000 in property damage. The Government's repression was swift and savage. A total of 1,976 persons were prosecuted and 1,176 convicted (a 60 percent rate). Some 644 rioters were imprisoned; for more serious crimes, a total of 505 persons were transported to Australia. The sentence of death was pronounced on 252 persons (nearly a fifth of all death sentences in England and Wales in 1830); of these, 19 were executed (two-fifths of all executions nationwide).[33]

There was no contemporary parallel for such savage repression in England: The Luddites in 1811–17 had had three dozen executed but fewer than fifty transported. The repression was almost Irish in its thoroughness. The Rebellion of 1798 had produced 80 persons officially executed, 400 transported, and another 400 otherwise deported; in the disorders of 1821–4, 2,100 had been sentenced to transportation and about 400 actually transported. In Britain one had to go back to 1745 and the brutal repression after the battle of Culloden (1,200 killed), when, of nearly 3,500 Scottish prisoners, 120 had been executed, a like number banished "outside our Dominions," and more than 900 transported to America. In England itself, one had to go even further back, to the aftermath of Monmouth's Rebellion in 1685, when 150 persons had been executed and 850 transported to the West Indies.[34]

The savagery against the Swing rioters contrasted sharply with the characteristics of the disorders. Most were brief localized flareups over in a matter of days; the unrest was sporadic, constantly moving, and persistent after 1830 only in Kent and Norfolk. There was nothing in the disturbances that can be described as chronic terrorism. As with the Luddites, national coordination was absent and the crimes were committed by locals over local grievances, which were economic and apolitical in nature; the country towns and London were unaffected. Like the Luddites, and unlike the Irish Whiteboys, Captain Swing and his men abstained from any serious physical violence against persons. Nor did the authorities resort to lethal force against the crowds. Property damage was widespread but selective. There was no plunder of country estates, no stockpiling of arms, no generalized terror.[35] These restrained, conservative disorders were a part of the tradition of collective bargaining by riot; genealogically, they were far closer to the eighteenth-century food riots than to Chartism. In short, Captain Swing's was, in E. P. Thompson's happy phrase, "a very English rising." In his review of Hobsbawm and Rudé's definitive work on Swing, Thompson notes:

> Even in the present account, with its insistence on "the General Rising," "the Last Labourers' Revolt," and so on, one is constantly amazed at the naturally deferential attitudes of most of the "Swing" men, when confronted with the authorities: magistrates, landowners, farmers, even the parson.... [T]hey accept the established order of village society and their expectations are fantastically minimal: a very slightly better wage, the destruction of the machines, the opportunity to work while preserving their dignity. They go about their task of riot politely, dressed according to many eyewitnesses' accounts in their best clothes, seldom using threatening language. *Nothing could be more unlike an Irish rising*; it is the revolt of the proud, conscious of their own rights.... It is a strange sort of rising that goes to the tune of "May it please you, Sir," and that strictly avoids any form of physical violence against persons (only one person was killed in the whole affair, and he a rioter, by the yeomanry).[36]

Why, then, the severity of official repression? Local justice had been remarkably flexible and socially bonded. The gentry's tenants and servants assisted a hodgepodge of peacekeeping bands with the apprehensions; in the subsequent prosecutions many local assizes and quarter sessions were so lenient that the Government felt compelled to send special commissions into five counties. These commissions conducted 992 of the cases; eighty-five other courts prosecuted a like number of offenders.[37] The repression reflected, in part, the severity of English law involving property crimes; the great bulk of the capital offenses remaining on the statute books in 1830 were for robbery and burglary, larceny, forgery, and malicious injury to property. In part, too, in the absence of preventive rural police and of troops, which were needed in the industrial North, the Government felt compelled to resort to the threat of legal terror. But in great measure, the Government's reactions stemmed from simple shock at the disorders. Large-scale rural turbulence was supposed to be an Irish phenomenon; since Waterloo, ministers in London had become inured to challenges to authority in the urban industrial North of England but not in the agrarian South.[38] The Government's worst nightmare was simultaneous violence in Lancashire and the Midlands, in Ireland, *and* in the southern half of England. The alarming aspect of the Swing disturbances was their wide swath and disciplined destruction of property. Thus, despite the limited aims and deference of the rioters, the Government felt it necessary to make examples, to inflict stern punishments as a warning that in the English countryside it was not prepared to accept ongoing collective extortion and serious violence to property.[39] The repression did crush the outbreak. But the long-term trends towards rural pauperization, demoralization, and (after midcentury) depopulation were the real factors in restoring the laborers in the southern counties to their "ox-like subservience."[40] The Government would have little reason to fear rural insurrectionism. The Swing Riots were the dying gasp of agrarian protest in England; the South would remain quiet for forty years until the appearance of altogether new tactics, union organizing, in the 1870s. Before midcentury the threat to public order remained unchanged: agrarian crime in Ireland and, in England, urban radicalism in London and the North.

Reform Bill crisis

By the time of the great agitation over national political reform, one in every three Englishmen was living in the large towns (20,000 or more population). In the early nineteenth century the rural counties were growing fast – the South swarmed with laborers – but the industrial North was growing faster. In 1830, Lancashire, having doubled in population since the turn of the century, was as heavily populated as Middlesex; and almost half of the people in Lancashire lived in nine towns having 10,000 or more inhabitants. Over the last thirty years, Manchester and Salford (1831 combined populations, 223,000) and the surrounding towns – Bolton (42,000), Preston (34,000), Oldham (32,000), Blackburn (27,000), Bury (19,000), and Rochdale (18,000) – had more than doubled in size. In the Midlands, Birmingham (144,000) had doubled over the same period; in the west, Bristol (104,000) and Nottingham (50,000) had grown almost as fast. By contrast, apart from London, the largest towns in the South were the old port towns of Plymouth (at 66,000, in ninth place) and Portsmouth (50,000) and the old textile center, Norwich (61,000).[41]

From urban England, especially the new industrializing North, came the Government's next challenge to public order. In 1829–30 Manchester, Bolton, and Preston were swept with a wave of strikes, assaults on factories, and destruction of machinery; at Rochdale troops killed several rioters. As General Byng had in the disorders of 1825–6, now Col. James Shaw, the military commander at Manchester (and future head of the Irish constabulary), witnessed the helplessness of the civil authorities. With the fall of Wellington's Government in November 1830, the disturbances assumed a more political character. Reform Bill riots occurred at numerous towns as far apart as Bristol and Norwich and Preston, where the Radical leader, Henry Hunt, defeated Edward Stanley (soon to be Irish Chief Secretary) at the polls. During the April 1831 elections, as the new police battled rioters in London, pro-Reform disturbances broke out in several Scottish and English towns, including normally tranquil places like Malmesbury, Rye, and Horsham.[42] The Lords' rejection of the Reform Bill in October unleashed a series of disorders. There was more street violence in London. A protest meeting in Birmingham drew a huge crowd estimated at anywhere from 15,000 to 150,000.[43] In Derby, whose mayor prohibited a public meeting, mobs attacked the city and county jails and freed prisoners, including some recently arrested Reform rioters; the military and Yeomanry killed three persons before order was restored. Nottingham produced four days (9–12 October) of riots. Mobs plundered a country house (Colwick Hall), destroyed a nearby silk factory (at Beeston), and burned down Nottingham Castle, the unoccupied seat of the Tory Duke of Newcastle. Riots also occurred at Leicester and Worcester and even swept through market towns in distant Dorset and Devon.[44]

The worst violence came in three days (29–31 October) of rioting at Bristol. In scenes of fiery chaos reminiscent of the Gordon Riots, angry mobs burned to the ground the Lord Mayor's Mansion House, the Bishop's Palace, the Custom House, three prisons, and a number of houses belonging to prominent anti-Reformers resident in Queen Square. Subsequent claims for property damage totaled £150,000, of which £56,000 was actually paid. Bristol's constables and nightwatch had proven useless. The Government handed the policing of the city to the military and specifically to a half-pay officer, Lt.-Col. Thomas Brereton. Irish-born (King's Co.) and with long military service in the West Indies, the 49-year-old Brereton proved to be an unfortunate choice. He rode into Bristol with ninety-three dragoons and shortly announced his sympathy with the crowds' demand; further, he refused to ride his troops over the people and indeed ordered them back to quarters. Only after the city was ablaze did reinforcements of military and Yeomanry arrive to suppress the outrages. The official estimate of casualties was put at 12 persons killed (although one contemporary suggested 500 as a realistic figure) and 94 wounded; 102 arrests were made, of whom 34 persons were transported and 4 executed. The mayor, Charles Pinney, was subsequently indicted for neglect of duty but acquitted, the jury staying out for twenty-three minutes. Brereton, arrested and facing a court martial, killed himself in January 1832.[45]

The provincial turbulence, culminating in the Bristol Riots, produced "a thrill of horror" and "introduced widespread apprehension into political life." The Home Secretary, Lord Melbourne, was "frightened to death" by the proceedings at Bristol; Peel ordered arms to be stockpiled at Drayton Manor, the family estate lying between Nottingham and Birmingham.[46] How great was the threat of revolution in 1831–2?[47] The actual violence peaked at Bristol in late October 1831; until the resolution of the crisis seven months later, there were no subsequent disorders of any magnitude. The physical terror did not have an Irish quality to it; like Swing in 1830, the urban violence of April and October 1831 was paroxysmal, not ongoing. There is evidence that radicals stockpiled arms in the northern towns, but the Birmingham Political Union and the National Union of the Working Classes both agreed, under government pressure, to abandon plans for military drillings and even mass protest meetings. Rumors and fear were rife, certainly, but the official correspondence indicates that Melbourne, like Sidmouth earlier, tended to read alarmist provincial reports with a measure of skepticism.[48]

It was, indeed, the *absence* of disturbances that made the situation in the spring of 1832 so ominous. "All *seemed* reserved," noted Sir Robert Heron, "for a tremendous explosion." But the seriousness of this very English crisis over Reform was due precisely to the employment of "subtler weapons" than arms. The Whigs and their temporary allies, the workers, used to great effect "the language of menace," a tactic developed by Daniel O'Connell during the Emancipation crisis of 1826–9. The threat of violence, it was hoped, would produce political concessions. The extreme Radicals, warned Francis Place, wanted reform only to start the revolution; moderate Radicals and liberal Whigs demanded it in order to prevent a bloodbath.[49] The second and even more effective tactic was economic sanctions. Again, the Irish experience was instructive: For the last eighteen months, Irish peasants had been practicing passive resistance and withholding payment in the Tithe War. Similarly, Reform-minded Englishmen now sought to disrupt the nation's economy in order to force an alteration in its political constitution. Rate-payers withheld taxes and shopkeepers refused to accept paper currency. The run on the banks (Place's ploy: "To Stop the Duke [of Wellington], Go for Gold") depleted almost half of the £4 million in gold reserves in ten days; William Cobbett judged this the most terrifying tactic used against the Government. Two recent scholars have argued that such weapons represented "not only a sophistication of technique beyond anything previously envisaged by tavern conspirators or workshop insurgents, but a real power being exercised.... A new power was clearly at work within the state."[50]

As a last resort, if Reform was denied, the possibility existed of popular rebellion. It is impossible to know how close the country came to staging this "non-event." Traditionally, historians have judged the period from Grey's resignation (9 May) to the acceptance of the terms of the Reform Bill (19 May) as the most critical juncture. Certainly, if temporarily, the lower and middle classes had never been so united of purpose. Unlike the postwar crisis of 1815–21, the unrest and expectations were now truly national, stretching from Devon to Norfolk, from London to the Scottish border and beyond.[51] Communications between Reform groups in myriad towns had never been so highly developed. Arms were doubtless available and were "something more than the sticks and the pikes that had created so much alarm in the years after 1815." Nevertheless, it must be stressed that proven military leadership was wanting, and the three names most frequently mentioned – two army colonels, one of them retired, and a Polish *emigré* aristocrat – not only furnished a touch of "comic opera" to but also revealed the unconscious deference behind the whole proceedings.[52] Perhaps most critically, in the deepening crisis the Government could bring little force to bear against a thoroughly aroused people. Outside London there were no police forces worthy of the name. The Yeomanry (19,000) was reduced in size, down by one-third since the aftermath of Peterloo; moreover, a surprising number of these men were now reformers. The army numbered 28,000, nearly two-thirds of whom were in the North and around London. Nagging and unanswered questions arose about the loyalty of the rank and file. The previous fall, the troops had been reluctant to shoot to kill in Bristol: Could they be counted on to shoot "low" against their fellow Englishmen? Even if the men obeyed orders, were there enough troops to keep the lid on risings in Birmingham, Manchester, Nottingham, and a host of other places?[53] In the event, Wellington and the Tories relented. Reform passed into law. Even obdurate Tory MPs were willing to apply the lessons learned in Ireland three years earlier: Concession and compromise were preferable to civil war.

The most revealing aspect of the crisis came after the concession of Reform. "To some extent," notes John Stevenson, "there was more danger of serious disturbances in the immediate aftermath of the crisis than there was before and during it." The obverse of giving the vote to the middle ranks of property holders was denying it to workingmen. At one stroke was severed the alliance of middle and lower classes against "Old Corruption"; the dashing of rising expectations would be traumatic.[54] In Ireland, where a similar disillusionment set in after Emancipation, the peasantry joined in constabulary affrays and launched the Tithe War. But in post-1832 England, when the workers' feelings of frustration and betrayal might have been expected to be most raw, there was no fresh wave of disturbances. The country did not disintegrate into angry mob violence; there were no more Bristols. In the spring of 1833, a protest meeting in Birmingham drew "an estimated 180,000 people" to hear denunciations of Whig "treachery." And in London 180 baton-wielding policemen broke up a crowd of 4,000 at Cold Bath Fields. "This was the last serious disturbance to arise from the reform movement of the early 1830s."[55] We may perhaps carry the argument one stage further and state that the absence of *political* disturbances in London and the provinces for several years after 1832 – until 1838 – is testimony to the weakness of the workers' threat of violent revolution in 1830–2. Perhaps, despite historians' traditional interpretations, workingmen had been political realists and had not expected to be given the vote.[56] In any case, they engaged in precious little violence after it was denied them. Instead, using "very English" nonviolent techniques, they fought for the ten-hours factory bill, decent wages, and the right to strike and form unions.[57]

The New Poor Law

The principal disturbances before the eruption of Chartism in 1838 were those against the New Poor Law (1834). The 1832 Reform Act had *continued* to deny workingmen the vote; but the amended poor relief act passed by the "treacherous" Whigs represented denial of a customary state obligation for the maintenance of the poor and the unemployed. The act of 1834 had a tangible effect that the political Reform Act did not. Perhaps no law did more to erode the tattered social compact of paternalism and its corollary, deference; it certainly prepared English soil for the planting of Chartism. The New Poor Law sought to tighten expenditures and increase government control by bringing relief "indoors" and restricting it to the desperately poor. It was the loss of freedom and the humiliation inherent in the workhouse requirement, as well as the ending (since Speenhamland in 1795) of relief as a form of unemployment insurance and wage supplement, that made the act outrageous to the lower classes.[58]

Beyond these practical considerations were two aspects of the new law that contributed to its unpopularity: its moralizing and its centralization. Poverty, now legally equated with immorality, was to be punished, the harshness to serve as a deterrent to the continuation of a state of penury; workhouses would "rehabilitate" by encouraging self-reliance and teaching a useful trade. In its imposition of middle-class values on working-class ones, the New Poor Law reflected the same civilizing intent of Whig humanitarianism as the suppression of popular faction fights in Ireland and the subsequent use of the new provincial police as "domestic missionaries" in the North of England.[59] The second controversial feature of the 1834 act was its centralization. The three London-based "commissioners" were to coordinate the uniform implementation of the new system. Here, too, poor relief was only one of several areas – police in London and Ireland, factories (1833), and prisons – that were subject to increasing government control in this decade.[60] Disregard for local circumstances, imposition of a class-biased ideology, and intended usurpation of existing Poor Law authorities all contributed to the protests against the New Poor Law.

Disturbances first appeared in the southern and eastern counties where implementation began. Crowds held protest meetings, attacked the new workhouses, and assaulted Poor Law guardians. The worst violence was in Suffolk; in December 1835 troops and London police were despatched to Ipswich to halt the rioting. In the South the disorders were sporadic and short-lived; there was little serious personal violence or even property destruction, and many parishes were unaffected. By early 1837 the brief spasms of protest had expended themselves. It was different in the North, where the act was put into effect in late 1836. By means of petitions, mass meetings, and a radical press, sophisticated tactics unknown in the rural southern counties, the northern workers unleashed storms of protest against "the poor man's 'Bastilles.'" The language of menace practiced by the Whigs in 1830–2 was now used against them. A series of disorders erupted in the numerous industrial towns of Lancashire. In Yorkshire a demonstration on Hartshead Moor in May 1837 drew a crowd of more than 100,000. In the general elections that summer, crowds numbering in the tens of thousands marched in protest, and anti–Poor Law riots at Huddersfield and Wakefield required the interposition of troops. The movement not only attracted old leaders like the Tory Radical Richard Oastler, fresh from the cause of factory reform, but also produced new ones like Feargus O'Connor, who had had a hand in the Irish antitithe agitation and would emerge shortly as chieftain of the English Chartists. The anti-Poor Law protests were fairly successful, delaying implementation in some places and forcing a return to "outdoor" relief in others. The unrest dissipated by the end of 1838 only because of the rise of a more general movement, Chartism, one of whose aims was the repeal of the New Poor Law.[61]

Historians' analyses of the severity of these public disturbances in the pre-Chartist years, 1830–8, often overlook the fact that during this period, which saw the consolidation of the Irish constabulary, the Government created neither a uniform and centrally controlled nor an armed police for the boroughs and counties of England. The failure to do so, and the absence even of serious proposals, suggest that for all of the turbulence the situation was largely under control. In London, the new police were managing to keep the lid on street disorders; in the provinces the disturbances in the southern rural districts and the northern towns did not verge on a breakdown requiring the imposition of a revolutionary new system of civil authority. Parliament, whether unreformed or reformed, did not rush to establish a gendarmerie.

Repressing Captain Swing

It is instructive to examine how the authorities controlled the rural and urban disorders that presented the greatest challenges. In the absence of a rural constabulary effective against mobs, the Government had at its disposal two military institutions, the Yeomanry and the army. During the Swing disorders the Yeomanry, reduced in size over the past decade, saw only scattered service. In places some corps were revived (the only crowd death was caused by one man in the Yeomanry), but army officers generally won their argument with the Government that widespread use of the Yeomanry would only tend "to create needless alarm."[62] The army itself was little used against Captain Swing. Most of the troops in England were stationed in and around London, at the ports, and in the northern towns. The only cavalry in the West of England was at Dorchester; the nearest troop concentrations were at Norwich, Leicester, and Bristol. The Government was reluctant both to remove soldiers from the North and to fritter away the army's strength by scattering small detachments throughout the rural South. It would be "harassing duty to both men and horses," noted Col. Ashe à Court, "and I still more regret it, from the terror which such a display of force creates throughout the Country and [the] hundreds of exaggerated reports that are immediately put into circulation." There was, in sum, no military buildup in the rural counties where the disorders occurred. "Outside a few strategic centres," note Hobsbawm and Rudé, "the justices were left largely to fend for themselves."[63]

The repression of Swing was accomplished by highly traditional and typically English means. Rewards were offered and subscriptions raised to combat arson. In the towns, special constables were at first difficult to enroll; in the small villages, the problem was not enough respectable inhabitants.[64] But the key to repression was the success of local policing in the countryside. Magistrates established nightly watches on farms and, assisted by military officers, coordinated 6,800 Ordnance out-pensioners who were distributed at 159 stations. Farmers formed ad hoc property associations and mutual protection societies. The resident English nobility stepped in with great gusto. In Norfolk Lord Suffield enrolled 100 men "actuated by a sort of feudal attachment." The Sheriff of Berkshire summoned "all Knights, Gentlemen, Yeomen, Husbandmen, Labourers, Tradesmen, Servants, and Apprentices." The Duke of Buckingham organized "something resembling a feudal levy"; one band of 100 tenants and laborers arrested forty machine breakers. The Duke of Wellington induced the Hampshire JPs to mobilize their own "servants, retainers, grooms, huntsmen, [and] gamekeepers, armed with horsewhips, pistols, fowling pieces, and what they could get." The repression, noted Wellington, was accomplished "in a spirited manner ... and it is astonishing how soon the country was tranquillised, and that in the best way, by the activity and spirit of the gentlemen." In west Sussex the Duke of Richmond – who on one occasion personally led fifty of his tenant farmers in routing a mob of 200 laborers – formed a special constabulary of shopkeepers, yeomen, and "respectable labourers," divided them into sections and districts under local commanders, and despatched them as mobile units to disaffected villages. The "Sussex Plan" was adopted by Lord Lennox in south Sussex, served as a model for other counties, and was strongly advocated by Melbourne at the Home Office.[65]

In the immediate aftermath of the disorders, in the winter of 1830–1, the only change in policing in the Swing counties was the Government's adoption of Lt.-Col. J. H. Mair's plan for town "special constabularies." Based on a successful experiment at Salisbury, the police, composed only of "respectable Householders" and with "no expense attending," was touted as "an active and zealous constitutional force under the orders of the Civil Authorities."[66] Each town, headed by a General Superintendent, was divided into districts, each district leader being responsible for twenty-five special constables. Patrols and points of rendezvous were arranged, and staves and arm bands were distributed to the men. The forces in each town numbered from about 100 to 500 men.[67] Lieutenant-Colonel Mair spent six weeks traveling "about 900 miles" to set up special constabularies in two dozen towns as far west as Bath, Bristol, and Exeter, as far north as Reading and Aylesbury, and as far east as Brighton and Lewes. Capt. Frederic Hovenden established forces at Dorchester and Weymouth before being sent north to Worcester and into South Wales; Lt.-Col. H. T. Custance was despatched to Norwich and the environs of Leicester.[68] It is impossible to say how effective these largely middle-class, part-time constabularies in some four dozen towns would have been in the event of renewed disturbances in the South.[69] It is significant that the Government was content to establish in the Swing counties police forces that were so tame and traditional.

Repressing the Bristol Riots

Suppression of the Reform Bill Riots at Bristol, like the Gordon Riots in London a half-century earlier, was the work of the military. Three troops of cavalry (ninety-three men), assisted toward the end by three Yeomanry troops, were sufficient to restore order. But for three days the mob had ruled. This was due in large part to the military's insistence on avoiding bloodshed. Colonel Brereton, the senior officer, took it upon himself to hold back the soldiers; on the second day he even sent the 14th Dragoons out of the city. When the troops did skirmish with the rioters, the fighting was inconclusive. Part of the problem, as in the London riots of 1780, was the military's confusion over its legal responsibilities for crowd control. Brereton later contended that city authorities had never authorized him to use force; Captain Warrington produced a printed order (of November 1830), issued during the Swing Riots, that barred military action without the presence of a magistrate.[70] Restrained by their own humaneness and their fear of breaking the law, the military in Bristol followed a course of indecisiveness that encouraged the mobs in their lawbreaking.[71]

The basic problem in Bristol was the lack of police. "The Magistrates, I may almost say, had *no* Civil Power," complained Brereton. Attempts by the anti-Reform, oligarchic borough Corporation to establish a civil force had produced opposition among the city's inhabitants, who favored an inexpensive police accountable to the ratepayers. The local police tax, kept low, was still difficult to collect; the Corporation's force of paid constables and night watchmen, once as high as 700 men, had shrunk to only 100 on the eve of the riots. The pay of even those men was in arrears, and their political sympathies made them suspect in any crisis.[72] To offset the decline in the city's police, in the aftermath of the Swing Riots the Government had created in December 1830 a large force of special constables. Composed of part-time respectable householders from the trades and professions, and to be used only in emergencies, the force numbered on paper 2,800 men organized in nine-teen districts. General and Parish Superintendents were named, stations pre-arranged, lists of streets and householders drawn up, constables' staves and even white hat bands distributed – all at no expense to the Government and, as it turned out, to no purpose.[73]

On the first day of the riots, when a large majority of the 2,800 specials refused to go to their posts, borough officials resorted to financial entice-ments to assemble a civil force. But of the 300 specials hired for pay the first day, only a third stayed on duty until nightfall, and the next day only 70 showed up to serve. These seventy were poorly organized and ill-informed, and nearly all refused to act without the help of the military, most of whom had been withdrawn. To those in the streets of Bristol who bore the actual responsibility for keeping the peace, the lessons of the riots were clear. "The Chief Real Faults," reported Maj. Digby Mackworth, were "a wretched Police; public indifference until private houses were fired; want of arrange-ment; and personal fear. Party politics, too." Only on the third day, after large sections of the city had been put to the torch, did the part-time police force of property owners finally appear. "*Then*," Mackworth noted with sarcasm, "we had 2 or 3,000 of the most active & zealous special Constables in the world; enough to have eaten the mob, if they would have come forward a day sooner."[74]

Recent historians have tended to place the violence in Bristol in the context of the Englishman's long-established "right to riot." The outburst, neither new nor revolutionary, was but "a reprise on an old theme": London, 1780; Birmingham, 1791. It revealed "the extremely thin line which lay between 'order' and 'disorder' in the era before the introduction of professional policing." The disorders, argues another scholar, were part of "the tradition of rioting" and simply got out of hand for the want of a strong civil power.[75] What should also be stressed, however, is that the days of this traditional tolerance for riot were running out. Reform mobs were ideologically more threatening to the state than No Popery or Church-and-King rioters. Still, if 1831 was in fact the year for "revolution," the authorities were remarkably slow to act. Four years would elapse before Parliament finally passed the act that reformed the police in all of the incorporated boroughs. In the interim, there was no recurrence of large-scale political turbulence in the provincial towns of England.

For five years after the Bristol Riots, the city authorities resorted to traditional forms of policing. A company of 100 army pensioners was organized. The Corporation doubled the number of its constables (to 114 men) and night watchmen (115). With the help of police officers sent from London, Mayor Pinney revised the system of special constables and reduced their number to 1,400 allegedly efficient men. The military officers stationed in Bristol were not impressed. General Sir Richard Jackson thought that perhaps 300 of the special constables could be relied upon. More to the point, the Corporation's tinkerings were ineffectual. What was needed, in Jackson's words, was "the establishment of some efficient Measure of Police. I cannot perceive or hear of any Measures with this object.... In Bristol at the present time without Soldiers there will be no Constables."[76] The reluctance of the Bristol Corporation to establish a police force was mirrored by popular pressures in the city opposing the creation of a powerful police accountable only to this closed Tory oligarchy. In 1835 the parliamentary commissioners on municipal corporations candidly reported that "at Bristol a notoriously ineffective police *cannot* be improved, *chiefly* in consequence of the jealousy with which the Corporation is regarded by the inhabitants." That politics was the stumbling block became clear after passage of the Municipal Corporations Act. With an elected Mayor and Borough Council, Bristol became the first major incorporated town to establish a police on the London model. In early 1836 Superintendent Joseph Bishop, of the V Division of the Metropolitan Police, took up his new job as head of a revamped Bristol force of 4 Inspectors, 24 sergeants, and 228 constables.[77]

III. The new borough police: extending and denying the people's "rights and liberties" in England and Ireland

The Reform Bill Riots and the anti-Poor Law disturbances dramatically exposed a fact of long standing: Urban, industrial England had grown enormously in wealth and population, but the local forces for civil order had remained unchanged from the days of the Luddites, or even earlier. Most of the new northern towns were unincorporated, that is, were governed without benefit of a chartered Corporation; in these towns, policing was conducted on an ad hoc basis by small courts leet and police commissioners. In all of these burgeoning towns and cities with a largely working-class population and few magistrates, the number of day policemen was (to use

Table 10.4. *Pre-reform police in northern towns in England, 1835–8*

Town	Constables	Nightwatch	1841 Population
Liverpool[a]	44	130	286,500
Manchester[b]	30	150	235,000
Birmingham[b]	30	170	182,900
Bradford	4	—	66,700
Salford	5	22	53,000
Bolton[b]	10	—	51,000
Preston[a]	5	—	50,900
Oldham	2	5	43,000
Blackburn	3	—	36,600
Halifax	4	—	27,500
Wigan[a]	—	14	25,500
Rochdale	3	13	24,300
Ashton-under-Lyne	4	—	22,700
Stalybridge	6	—	20,000
Wakefield	3	11	18,800
Burnley	1	9	14,200

[a] Incorporated towns in 1835.
[b] Incorporated in 1838, but charter legally contested.
Note: All other (unannotated) towns are unincorporated.

F. C. Mather's word) "ludicrous." The tiny forces were totally useless against crowds and riots (see Table 10.4). Moreover, given the people's "much greater indisposition to be sworn in as special constables" and the ineffectuality of those who did serve, the Government had had to resort to another traditional institution, the army "in aid of the civil power." What would happen, finally, in the 1830s was that the Government and Parliament would for the first time seek to strengthen the provincial police and lessen the age-old reliance on the military. We must now turn to the key question: Why in this decade did the towns and counties of England at long last seek to establish stronger police forces?[78]

The English corporate towns: a mild revolution

Reform of the borough police (1835) has rightly been interpreted as logically succeeding parliamentary reform in 1832. Police reform was but a part of a wide-ranging statute whose purpose was to improve local government by making it elective and thus accountable to a broad range of respectable ratepayers. Transforming the borough police was a product of Whig reformist politics, not of any settled blueprints for police reform.[79] But if the act took power from closed oligarchies in places like Bristol, Derby, and

Nottingham, it also represented an attempt by Whigs, no less than Tories, to consolidate the power of the new political order by obstructing the forces for change unleashed by the concession of 1832. Having extended political rights, Parliament sought to apply the brake to further demands. In Ireland after Emancipation (1829), the Government had insisted on a rigorous enforcement of the laws; so now, in England, men like Peel could "see nothing left, now that the House of Lords has approved the principle of the Reform Bill, but a strenuous concerted effort to mitigate the evil of it."[80]

The first indication of the Whigs' intentions came in the King's speech (6 December 1831) opening the parliamentary session. Alluding to "the violence and outrage" at Bristol and other provincial towns, William IV asked Members "to direct your attention to the best means of improving the Municipal Police of the Kingdom, for the more effectual protection of the public peace against the occurrence of similar commotions." In his remarks the King dwelled on Reform, the current Dom Miguel controversy (Portugal),[81] and the Tithe War in Ireland, but he did plant the seed of the idea of English police reform; significantly, few Members in their replies to the King's speech picked up on the idea.[82] The absence of political disorders after 1831 may explain the Whigs' slowness to act on their own suggestion. It was the Tories, and Peel in particular, who pressed the Government in 1832 to present its bill for a strengthened municipal police. The founder of the Irish and London police repeatedly argued that no matter in the King's speech was more important. Peel announced that "from the situation he had held, he felt much interest" in the subject; he insisted that the success of the Metropolitan Police should dictate that the provincial forces be "under the authority of the executive power, ... free from all party and electioneering influence." Peel's radical proposal, conditioned by his administrative experience since 1812, stood no chance of acceptance in an English Parliament inclined to reform, not abolish, the powers of local government.[83] But Peel's pestering did help lead to the creation, in July 1832, of a select committee on municipal corporations. Again there were more delays. The report recommended the establishment of an investigating commission, which was duly formed in July 1833 and reported only in March 1835.[84]

Acting on the report's unsurprising discovery of widespread, closed, and in places corrupt rule among the 246 town Corporations, Prime Minister Melbourne introduced in June a hastily prepared bill to revolutionize borough government by making all officeholders directly and indirectly accountable to local taxpayers. The measure passed in the Commons in July and, after protracted debates, in the Lords in September. The Municipal Corporations Act called for all male household ratepayers of three years' residence to elect borough councillors, who would then elect the town's aldermen; together these two bodies would elect the mayor. The act established a ratepayers' democracy. The new municipal electorate was broader than the three-year-old parliamentary electorate (which had enfranchised a fifth of the adult male population), but only by about 25 percent, and it still excluded from power the majority of small householders and the working classes whose dwellings were not rated. The Municipal Corporations Act did not inaugurate local democracy: For many working-men, it was more Whig treachery. But it was a victory for "a limited section of the local community," the new property owners over the old. For the business and professional men – merchants and manufacturers, shopkeepers and tradesmen – who filled the new town councils, the 1835 act was a far more tangible triumph than the Reform Act of 1832.[85]

Only one section of the detailed act dealt with police. Clause 76 required each borough council to establish a Watch Committee, which was to appoint paid constables and watchmen. The police aspects of the 1835 act were revealing for their very lack of controversy. Clause 76 was one of the few never debated or amended. In the hundreds of hours of speeches on the bill, one searches in vain for any discussion of the police. Only toward the end did Melbourne raise the subject. His remarks made *no* mention of crime as a problem in the boroughs. Instead, the Whig Prime Minister alluded to the success of Peel's new London police. Melbourne noted that the "great recommendation" of the Metropolitan Police was that since 1829 the Government had not once found it necessary to employ the troops against rioters in the streets of the capital.[86] In the provincial towns where the inhabitants had had "no confidence in the Corporation," ratepayers had refused to pay for adequate civil forces, and thus the military had had to police any disturbances. But the new town councils, Melbourne hoped, "will be able to organise an efficient police equal, perhaps, to that of the metropolis." The Prime Minister's remarks on the police were brief, consuming only five minutes of his hour-long speech on the Corporation bill. No subsequent speakers returned to the subject.[87]

Significantly, the parliamentary debates on the bill that (by Clause 76) established the English borough police record virtually *no* concern with crime, riot, or police. One scholar has noted "the lack of urgent popular interest" in the Corporation bill itself.[88] Clearly, the lack of Members' interest in the lone police clause attests to the absence of any perceived crisis of crime or disorder. An interpretation that sees borough police reform as the product of "a fit of absence of mind" goes far to explain the lagging and indifferent development of urban police forces *after* 1835.

From another perspective, the Borough Police Act, which enshrined the rights and liberties of ratepayers, was also a total victory for local control. The Home Office directed the police force in London, but from the numerous separate borough forces it was only the passive recipient of quarterly reports about pay, appointments, and regulations. The act made no provision for central inspection, for the number of policemen deemed sufficient, or for the manner or amount of payment or the qualifications of the constables. Even the precise local jurisdictional powers of the Corporation, Watch Committee, and magistrates in each borough were left unstated.[89] The act was a testament to the Government's confidence in the ability of local authorities to repress crime and disorders in their own neighborhoods. The contrast to police legislation for Ireland was startling.

What the Government did not foresee was that municipal ratepayers would often be more committed to fiscal economy than to paying the costs of preserving public order; in any crisis the military could always be called in. Englishmen might grudgingly admire the success of Peel's police in the capital, with its huge population and sprawling geographical area, but the London force was seen as an anomaly, not a model for provincial imitation. In the largest cities, where the challenges of disorder were most critical, a London-style police had the greatest appeal. Liverpool (1841 pop., 286,000), with its unruly population of Irish immigrants and shore-leave sailors, established the largest police force outside London: 590 men in 1839, growing to 822 by 1848. Manchester (pop. 235,000), incorporated only in 1838, had 343 policemen, rising to 447 by 1848, and in its ratio of police to population was second only to Liverpool. Bristol (pop. 124,000; 228 to 248 policemen, 1839–48) occupied third place. In these cities policing was a full-time, regularly paid job, and the organization and discipline of the police were highly professional. But these cities were the exceptions. In 1839 Birmingham (pop. 183,000; incorporated 1838) was content with a force of 30 day constables; in 1836 Leeds (pop. 152,000), an old borough, formed an initial force of 20 policemen, increased to 112 in 1839; Sheffield (pop. 111,000) did not establish a borough force (122 men) until 1848. Such was the state of the new police in the later 1830s in English cities of more than 100,000 population.[90]

In the medium-size towns of 15,000–100,000 population, the Borough Police Act of 1835 produced few noticeable changes in policing. Chester and Newcastle-on-Tyne, with twenty-nine and eighty-five police for populations of 24,000 and 70,000, respectively, were relatively well policed in 1840, with one policeman for every 790 inhabitants. The worst (in 1839) were Stockport, with thirteen policemen, for a police-to-population ratio of 1:3,806; Wigan, six (1:4,097); Bolton, ten (1:4,837); and Walsall, three (1:6,299). Most of the towns fell unsatisfactorily between these two extremes. In the small boroughs, sleepy country towns and villages, the act of 1835 established "forces" of fewer than half a dozen policemen. The greatest extreme was reached in places like Chipping Norton, Helston, and Tenby, which not only had ratios of 1:2,500 or 1:3,000 but in fact had only a single constable for the town.[91]

Because the Government had no power of enforcement, the legally compulsory establishment of borough police forces was slow and fitful. By 1837, only more than half of the boroughs (93 of 178) claimed to have formed a police force. Two years later, 29 percent of the boroughs had still not complied; and as late as 1842, 20 percent still had not. The nineteen new boroughs, mostly larger towns, which were incorporated between 1835 and 1853, were more conscientious: All set up a police force within two years of incorporation. The absence of government control also kept the size of police forces small and insufficient. The lowest acceptable police-to-population ratio was judged to be 1:1,000, but few boroughs reached this minimum requirement even by 1848.[92] The Government was hard put even to compel the

Table 10.5. *Police per inhabitants in the English boroughs, 1839–48:*
percentage distribution over four ranges of ratios

Year	1:<600	1:600–900	1:900–1,100	1:>1,100
1839	10%	19	17	54
1842	7	18	15	60
1848	6	12	17	65

Source: Adapted from Mather, *Public Order*, p. 114.

boroughs to submit their required quarterly reports or to send any infor-mation to London. A parliamentary return of 1854, purporting to list "the number of police ... in the several Cities and Boroughs ... in each year from their establishment," did not print, because it could not obtain, figures for 79 of 182 boroughs (43 percent) in 1839 and for 58 of 191 (30 percent) as late as 1848. In 1839, of the boroughs *returning figures*, only 29 percent had police forces with desirable ratios lower than 1:900 (by "lower," I mean one policeman for 900 or fewer inhabitants); more than half of the towns had ratios greater than 1:1,100 (see Table 10.5). In the 1840s, at the height of Chartism, widespread ratepayers' rebellions against the costs of police produced a continuing decline in the effective level of policing. By 1848 nearly two-thirds of the boroughs were deficient in manpower requirements. If we can assume that the boroughs *not returning statistics* to Parliament either had no police or were embarrassingly below standard – and as late as 1848, nearly a third of the boroughs submitted no returns – then the actual state of the English municipal police was far more wretched than can be shown in Table 10.5.[93]

The deficiencies and, in some cases, glaring inadequacies in numbers of policemen reflected the indifference, and often the hostility, of the new borough Watch Committees to modern notions of the police as a *force of men*, young, vigorous, and unconnected to local politics. The lessons of London and Ireland fell on deaf ears. In only a few (Liverpool, Bristol) of the largest boroughs was there a clean sweep in hiring new men. It appears that in the great majority of the 178 boroughs, the "new" borough policemen were simply reappointed constables, beadles, and watchmen who had served the old Corporation or the town's Improvement Commissioners.[94] In many cases, the new forces did not function as policemen but as a continuation of the nightwatch; in others, there were separate day and night forces. Because they were not prohibited by the 1835 act, certain features of the old system – such as part-time employment and fee taking – continued in many borough forces. Even as late as 1852 in Bath and Liverpool, where the police were numerous and relatively modern, the men were allowed to have second jobs.[95] In sum, Jenifer Hart concluded in a famous passage,

The impression gained from looking at the evidence is often that in the boroughs one is much nearer to the old world of early nineteenth-century watchmen earning a few shillings by casual police work than to the new world of professional, full-time, carefully recruited and supervised Metropolitan police officers.[96]

Why was the development of the new police in England's boroughs so slow? Local control was in part to blame: Impressive immediate change, as in London or Ireland, was not possible. In many instances, preexisting vested local interests, rivals for the functions of the new forces, obstructed any substantial changes. Ratepayers' concerns with costs also helped to restrict the size of the forces whose value was not self-evident. To some extent, our question is a modern one. The new police became in time the basis for the present forces, but we should resist the temptation to read history backward and assume that mid-nineteenth-century Englishmen should have seen the light and rushed to establish modern police. In many boroughs the old systems of civil order probably worked well enough, or were sufficiently comfortable, so that there were few inducements to swap them for the new; certainly this was the situation in a majority of the boroughs now controlled by all ratepayers. Experience had taught that in any temporary crisis, troops could be sent for. Perhaps the basic explanation for the lagging development of the police was the continuing suspicion of the institution. "Police" was still a foreign concept, a word associated with France or Ireland; at Newcastle-on-Tyne the new force was described as "these Austrian-looking gentlemen." Jenifer Hart aptly notes that

in spite of the successful example of London, there was opposition in the country to having professional policemen at all. Many people still felt that organized, permanent, uniformed police forces were not reconcilable with traditional English liberties; and in spite of the fact that the borough police were independent of the central government, the fear that they would be turned into "a new kind of standing army," "a gendarmerie," or "a centralized force of a servile character" was often voiced.[97]

It should be stressed that borough ratepayers, proud of their municipal rights and liberties granted in 1835, nurtured them by keeping the local police weak and constitutional. Working-class antipolice sentiment intersected with ratepayers' traditional fears of a powerful police. But the pressures from below were not so intense that the local authorities felt any urgency to establish strange, strong new civil forces of order. Most significantly, given the police developments in Ireland, neither the town councils nor the Government in London ever felt pressed to suggest a centralized police for the English boroughs.

The Irish exception: final English reform of the Dublin police

The city in the United Kingdom with the longest tradition of centralized police was Dublin. The experiment of 1786–95 belonged to the previous generation, and Wellington's reform of 1808 was likewise forgotten as the former capital sank into a peaceful decrepitude and, with it, its police. Since the Union, as the major industrial towns in the North of England more than doubled in population, Dublin grew only negligibly in numbers and declined in spirit. Once in truth "the second city" in the kingdom, Dublin by the

1830s was just another large British provincial town.[98] Dublin's civil forces –
peace officers, constables, the horse and foot patrol, and the nightwatch –
were numerous (750 men) in comparison to those in English towns of the

	Population (in thousands)		
City	1801	1831	1851
Dublin	175	204	258
Liverpool	82	202	376
Glasgow	77	202	345
Manchester	75	182	303
Birmingham	71	144	233

same size, and they had long been under a single governing authority. But
the 550-man watch force was now filled with "decrepid [sic], worn out old
men," and since Peel's London reforms in 1829, the very variety of the forces
in Dublin gave the city's police a marked quaintness.[99]

The stimulus to Drummond and Morpeth's police bill was no wave of
crime or disturbances in Dublin but rather, as with the Irish constabulary
bill, an administrative tidying up that completed a long history of centralization.[100] The bill passed in the English Commons but was lost in the Lords
late in the 1835 session; it carried in both Houses with no debate in 1836.
Whereas by the Borough Police Act (1835) the Whigs had confirmed the
"rights and liberties of Englishmen" by granting control of the police to all
municipal ratepayers, by the Dublin Police Act (1836) the Government took
the remaining powers from the Protestant, Tory Corporation of Dublin and
concentrated all control in Dublin Castle.[101] Unlike the situation in the
English incorporated towns, police reform in Dublin was not, and could not
be, a part of local government reform. To make Dublin's police responsible
to a reformed, representative town council, Wellington wrote Peel in 1837,
would place the police "in the hands of Priests and demagogues . . . [and] the
lowest Rabble of the Town."[102] In short, whereas in England all borough
ratepayers could be trusted with the local government ballot and control of
the police, in Ireland only the most respectable property holders were enfranchised and police powers rested exclusively with the Government.[103]

The London police, whose centralist concept had first been tested as an
experiment in Dublin in 1786, now became the model for reform of the
Dublin police. Just as the Home Secretary ultimately controlled the London
force, so the Irish Chief Secretary controlled the "Dublin Metropolitan
Police." Like the London force, the Dublin one was headed by two Police
Commissioners, a "civil" and a "military magistrate." Mayne's opposite
number in Dublin was Commissioner John O'Ferrall, an Irish Catholic
barrister; Rowan's counterpart was Commissioner George Brown, an
English Protestant army major and former constabulary officer and Stipendiary Magistrate. These appointments meant that three of the four Police

Commissioners in London and Dublin were Irishmen, and the lone English-man, who worked in Dublin, had by his own account lived mostly in Wales.[104]

Under the guidance of Superintendent James Johnston, on loan from the London police in February 1837, the old Dublin police was replaced by a new force that followed "as much as possible" the London system. The rank structure – constables, sergeants, Inspectors, and Superintendents – was a direct copy of the London organization. With the watch abolished, the new constables were divided about equally into day and night patrols, "exactly the same as it is in London." Because of the rarity of homicides and serious personal violence in Dublin compared to the countryside, the police were issued only truncheons; this policy would survive unchanged until, and beyond, the end of British rule in southern Ireland.[105] The London imprint was visible in the men themselves. Three of the original four Superintendents and ten of the seventeen Inspectors were officers brought over from London; other appointments went to army and constabulary officers. For the rank and file, the Government "obtained at first as many as possible from the London police"; the majority were Irishmen from the K Division of the Metropolitan Police. A critic charged that many were of "dissipated habits," men whom both the Commissioners and Londoners "might be happy to be rid of"; some of the repatriated Irishmen were said to have been originally informers who, as a reward and for their protection, had been given jobs in the London police. Of the men in the Dublin police in 1839, only one in seven had served in the Irish constabulary. Dubliners were ineligible to serve; and once past the original stocking with Londoners, the preference in recruits, who came "from every county in Ireland," was for laborers and small farmers. Put less favorably, in the words of our critic: "The sons and relations of [Dublin] Police Tax-payers, which in the English cities [excluding London] would be in itself a recommendation, were thrust aside to make room for the pauper tenantry of needy landlords."[106]

The constables were, in fact, physically impressive specimens, large men as well as tall; the height requirement (5 feet 9 inches) was two inches above the minimum in the London police, and one of every five Dublin policemen (in 1844) was a 6-footer. The police were barred from holding another job; the act specifically excluded those occupations (servant, brewer, and publican) that were not uncommonly found among the English borough constables. There were a number of attractions to police work in Dublin. The duty was less hazardous and the pay (at £32 p.a.) superior to that in the constabulary (though "much inferior" to the pay in London). The absence of a regulation barring marriages was attractive; half of the policemen (in 1839) were married. Finally, the promotion policy, as in London, was from the ranks by merit and seniority.[107]

As in the Irish constabulary, also controlled by the (Whig) Government, the highest officer posts in the Dublin police were filled overwhelmingly with Protestants. So, too, was the rank above constable: seventy of the ninety sergeants in 1839 were Protestant. Over time, however, by promotions through the ranks, the Catholic share would and did increase. Roughly two-thirds of the constables were Catholic. There were apparently few sectarian animosities among the rank and file. "Roman Catholic policemen in Dublin," reported Police Commissioner Brown, "get their Heads broken as fast as the Protestants.... A Policeman gets well beaten without reference to Religion." He judged it "a noble corps" with a sufficiently impartial sense of duty that "any Man of the Force would arrest the Pope or the Archbishop of Canterbury if directed." On one occasion, 250 mostly Catholic policemen monitored without incident a meeting of 500 Orangemen. In its misbehavior, the Dublin force was little different from the parent one in London. In the first year, one-third of the men resigned or were dismissed, three-fifths of the discharges being for drunkenness.[108] In sum, the Dublin Metropolitan Police, as its name suggested, was in many ways a double of the London Metropolitan Police. It was a force essentially different from the Irish constabulary.

Despite its similarities to the London police, the Dublin force retained definite Irish characteristics. The city continued to be the only provincial town in the British Isles whose police was controlled by the Government.[109] And in terms of cost and size, Dubliners had, relatively speaking, the most expensive and largest police force of any city in England and Ireland. The Dublin police tax of 8 d. per pound was higher than the sixpence in London and roughly double the rates in the large English boroughs. The high rate was necessary to fund the large police in a city smaller and poorer than London and poorer than provincial English towns of the same size.[110] In 1838, its first year of operation (funding problems having delayed implementation by one year), the Dublin police numbered 921 men in all ranks; by 1841 there were 1,115. Thereafter the size held fairly stable.[111] In Dublin the

City	Date	Police per inhabitant[a]
Dublin	1841	1:210
London	1840	1:440
Liverpool	1842	1:480
Bristol	1842	1:540
Manchester	1848	1:630
Birmingham	1848	1:690

[a] Figures have been rounded to the nearest ten.

ratio of police to population had long been high (see Table 4.2); in the 1840s, it was twice as great as the ratio in London and three times as large as that in the big English provincial towns.[112]

For all of these reasons – Castle control and the force's expense and size – the Dublin police continued its tradition of unpopularity with many Dubliners. John Flint, an ex-Inspector and the secretary of the "Police Grievance Association," produced a vituperative tract exposing *The Dublin*

Police and the Police System (1847). In 1840 a Dublin physician, James Henry, published a savage but more subtle satiric work of fiction that attacked the new police in the city of "Canton." This force, protested Henry, was accountable not to the people but to "the Imperial Government in Pekin." One scene from the book summarizes Dubliners' feelings about their police since 1786. The Mayor of Canton led a procession into the city's Great Hall, where he presented the people's petitions against the police force that had been created by the legislature in Pekin. But the President in Pekin "took his telescope and looked through it, and said, 'I see a man faroff but I cannot hear what he is saying.' 'I am from Canton,' the Mayor yelled. And the President said, 'What City of Canton? Is it in China?'"[113]

As in London after 1829, the new police patrols in Dublin produced a decrease in the number of committals for serious crimes (prevention) and an increase in the arrests for minor offenses (apprehensions). In Dublin there was little of the crime that characterized the Irish countryside; as in English cities, the great majority of the offenses were not social or collective in nature. "Ribbonism" in Dublin referred to trade union offenses aimed against young men ("colts") who had not served an artisanal apprenticeship, or against employers who either hired such workers or employed too many apprentices (payment being by the piece); the ritualized punishment often involved "slating" or knocking down and beating the offender with bludgeons. In 1836 there had been forty-four such "combination assaults" in the streets of Dublin; in 1837, ninety-seven; and in 1838, the first year of the new police, eight.[114]

This type of crime was, however, dwarfed by the thousands of cases of drunkenness, disorderly conduct, common assaults, and petty larcenies. "Crimes in Dublin," noted the Leinster Crown Solicitor in 1839, "are numerous but trifling"; in the previous year the police had recorded 5 homicides and 19,470 cases of "tippling." Significantly, the apprehensions for drunkenness were four times more numerous than in the last year of the old police. It appears that the new police performed the same role of "domestic missionaries" in Dublin that historian Robert Storch has described for the police in England's industrial towns in 1850–80.[115] In part, this new policing represented a return to the control of traffic, after-hours drinking, vagrancy, and disreputable market practices characteristic of the 1786–95 period. But an important act of 1842 carried the social control and *mission civilisatrice* much further. The police were instructed to arrest without a warrant vagrants, idlers, and park loiterers. They were to enforce the ban on sale of liquor to minors (under age sixteen) and to close down all drinking and gaming shops other than licensed public houses. They were to stop bear baiting and cock fighting; enforce a variety of sabbatarian restrictions; and regulate a battery of "street nuisances" that included animals and prostitutes, bill posting by salesmen, and even kite flying and snow sledding by children "to the annoyance and danger" of passersby. The assault on traditional liberties even went so far as to involve the police in the erection and control of "public Urinaries."[116]

IV. A police for the untamed North of England

"I do not know what to do or propose about the North – the expense must be defrayed by the disturbed district." So wrote Home Secretary Melbourne to Earl Grey in August 1832 concerning a police not for Ireland, but rather for the swarming proletarian towns of northern England.[117] The Municipal Corporations Act (1835) required police only in the incorporated towns. Older cities like Liverpool and Bristol received forces, but most of the new industrial towns did not. Manchester and Birmingham, without charters of incorporation in 1835, were exempt; so, too, were numerous turbulent towns of 25,000–50,000 population – Bradford, Bolton, Oldham, Stockport, Blackburn, Bury, and Rochdale. Here (see Table 10.4) police forces were nonexistent or grossly deficient due to the inhabitants' opposition for reasons of constitutionality and expense.

The situation in darkest Oldham (1831 pop., 32,000) has recently been illuminated, thanks to John Foster's brilliant sociological study. Foster has shown that for thirty years after Waterloo, the town's tiny employing class and the large new industrial working class battled at parish vestry meetings for control of the appointments and funding of the police commission that directed the few constables and half-dozen watchmen. The workers established outright control in 1812–20, lost it after Peterloo, and won it again in 1831 when they abolished the small nightwatch. Later that year, the property owners prevailed and reappointed a watch of five men, who, of course, continued to be hopelessly ineffective. The battle was largely over the trappings, not the substance, of police power, but the confrontation was bitter because of the intersection of class ideologies and practical politics. Foster goes so far as to state that "pretty well the whole purpose of Oldham working-class politics was control of the police." Real power resided with the two companies of soldiers, 120 men outnumbered and psychologically intimidated, who occupied the town under Maj.-Gen. Sir Henry Bouverie's command from 1820 until their withdrawal in 1834. In the later year, a Manchester newspaper correspondent described Oldham as "sadly deficient in its police force; they had no military at hand in case of disturbance; and the town was completely in the hands of the destructives." The workers defeated a middle-class bid in 1834 to petition Parliament to get the town incorporated and thus compelled to establish a ratepayers' police force. Working-class pressure would delay Oldham's incorporation until 1849.[118]

Doubts and delays

If the workers' obstructionist stance against effective policing in Oldham was typical of the many Lancashire towns of middling size (a subject on which we still know surprisingly little), then the Home Secretary had good reason to worry about "what to do or propose about the North." But Melbourne's concern was characterized more by puzzlement than desperation. He worried more about "the charge upon ... the County rate" than about imminent revolution. He judged that Parliament would not pass any compulsory police act "which burdened the parishes with the expense" and felt "certain it would be petitioned against from all quarters." A resort to national funding for Stipendiary Magistrates would be "quite contrary to every precedent," and, more practically, "once done ..., we should never obtain a local rate for any similar purpose again." Melbourne and Grey's correspondence reveals them to be, at the least, as worried about any schemes that would sap local self-reliance as with the threat of revolution.[119]

The deliberateness with which the Whig Government pursued the idea of a police for the North reflected the advice received from their most senior military officers. The Commander of the Northern District, Major-General Bouverie, composed for the Home Office in August 1833 a long and carefully reasoned memorandum that stressed the *disadvantages* of a powerful Northern police.

If a Police Force be formed in the Manufacturing districts with a view to the suppression of Riots, without military aid, it must [be] so numerous as to be highly expensive, and such expence would not be borne with Patience; but supposing the means were provided to meet such an expence, would any Police Force be able to meet the Mobs of those great Populations, armed as I am convinced they would be, to a considerable extent with weapons of all descriptions? I conceive, *certainly* not; even were a Police Force to be successful for a time, the Mob seeing themselves so much on an Equality with them in point of Weapons, and so much superior in point of Numbers, would soon turn upon and defeat them; it may be said that it would then be time enough to employ the Military Force were it at hand, but such a course of proceeding would be in the highest degree injudicious; as any previous success would only have tended to excite the Mob to such rashness of Action, as could be put down only by active Military measures and the employment of Arms; whereas the timely employment of the Military in sufficient Force, to render successful opposition to it vain, has constantly been successful and without unfortunate Results.

When Mobs are now met in the most populous parts of this district, it is by the very trifling regular Police, augmented by regular special constables, and wherever it can be done, by Pensioners sworn in as special constables, headed by the Magistrates, and supported *within Sight*, by the Troops. This mode of acting I consider to possess advantages which give it a decided superiority over a large regular Police Force; the special constables have not arrayed against them that Feeling which is so hostile to a regularly organized Police, and [they] carry with them more of the Public Voice and opinion, and their Conduct would find favour with Juries.

In the actual presence of Troops that Force [the special constables] is found to act well and vigorously, tho' easily paralyzed if not so supported; and it is not found that either they or the Troops get into popular disfavour by acting against Mobs.

Although I admit the Question to be one of considerable difficulty, yet I take the liberty of expressing my opinion that the employment of a large regular Police in the manufacturing district, such as might reasonably be expected to be effective, would be found to be liable to difficulties almost insuperable, and that even if established it would be found to act much less advantageously than the present System.[120]

Bouverie's impassioned fifteen-page letter is a valuable reminder of the persistence of Englishmen's doubts about the utility, or desirability, of police for purposes of crowd control. A major-general trained for war, not domestic peacekeeping, *should* have preferred that the unpleasant duty be transferred to a strengthened civil power. Instead, Bouverie judged that the arguments of expense, unpopularity, and (in his view) ineffectiveness – even apart from those of unconstitutionality – outweighed any benefits that "might reasonably be expected" from the establishment of new police forces.

Bouverie, not Peel, represented the views of the great majority of Englishmen. The police act that Parliament passed in 1833 was traditional and uncontroversial. The Lighting and Watching Act, "the first statute to deal with the establishment of paid police forces in the country generally," permitted (but did not require) local ratepayers meeting in vestry to levy a parish police tax and appoint a small force of paid inspectors, watchmen, and patrols. This act of 1833 was democratic in its intrusion on the cherished police powers of local magistrates and in its attempt to strengthen local government, but, being based on the parish, it was too small in scale to be effective.[121] The act's chief virtue had little to do with crime or disorder: The tiny forces – inexpensive, locally accountable, and not unpopular – did not inflame the public mind on the bristly subject of police.

A resort to Peelers

With the idea of a separate police in the North politically impractical, and the optional parish police of 1833 insufficient, the Government came to rely on a powerful force that it already controlled. Why not export Metropolitan policemen to the provinces? Modern policing concepts spread outward from London to the rest of England in the 1830s in much the same way that actual forces of men, the Peace Preservation Police, had on the orders of Dublin been sent throughout the Irish countryside in 1814–22. In England the process was physically facilitated because it paralleled the origin and growth of the railways. The first line of track, connecting Liverpool and Manchester, was opened in September 1830, exactly one year after the creation of the London police. By 1834 the country boasted 300 miles of track linking the principal cities; by 1838, on the eve of Chartism, almost 1,000 miles; by 1844, 2,200 miles; and by 1848, 4,900 miles (see Map 12.2). The railways gave the Government a penetrating power not previously available, and with each passing year the penetration was deeper, into ever smaller towns. Police or troops sent by railway from London could arrive, refreshed, in Manchester nine hours later; the same journey, before the advent of the railways, had required a forced march of seventeen days. In the early twentieth century, the radio and patrol car would effect a revolution in policing; in the nineteenth, it was the railroad that gave a decisive edge to the authorities. "Without that conveyance," reported a military officer in 1844, "you could not have done one tenth part of the work that it was required of the troops to do, and necessarily to do, in the year 1842."[122]

The differences between the Peelers in Ireland and England were instructive. Whereas the armed Irish Peace Preservation Police had always served as a collective force against disturbances, the milder and smaller English version performed a variety of functions. One, involving the detachment of Metropolitan policemen singly or in twos, was to stimulate local initiatives in policing. Official returns show that from June 1830 to January

1838 the London Commissioners dispatched 221 men of all ranks to 136 places in twenty-five English counties for the purpose of establishing local police forces. The places to which these London policemen were sent included rural districts, docks, and railway lines, as well as towns; the kinds of forces they helped establish ranged from special constabularies and Improvement Act police to rehabilitated parish watch or borough forces (under the acts of 1833 and 1835), and also included some more modern systems. A total of thirty-four incorporated boroughs received the London emissaries; four London Superintendents eventually became Chiefs of Police at Liverpool, Manchester, Bristol, and Hull. A few policemen traveled even farther afield to Barbados and New Brunswick, Wales and Dublin.[123]

In far greater numbers, Metropolitan policemen were sent – in groups of two to ten, but sometimes as many as fifty – across all of England for the general purpose of keeping the peace. By the end of 1836, nearly 2,000 constables had served outside London. And the demand was rising: 444 policemen in 1837 and 764 in 1838 were dispatched to between fifty and sixty places each year. Altogether, from June 1830 to November 1838, a total of 3,010 London constables were "sent to the Country for a Temporary Purpose." It is important to stress that the great majority of these London loans were *not* (as in Ireland) for suppressing disturbances but for less stressful purposes. Mostly the duty of keeping the peace meant watching crowds at racetracks, fairs, festivals, and elections or, less frequently, investigating especially serious crimes. On occasion the duty did involve the control of actual disturbances, and by the later 1830s, increasingly so. In 1837 some 37 London policemen were sent to Yorkshire, the West Country, and Essex to deal with anti–Poor Law rioters; in the first ten months of 1838, 114 constables (18 percent of all men sent outside London) were employed to suppress provincial disturbances;[124] and in July 1839, 90 Metropolitan policemen would be sent to Birmingham to control a single Chartist incident.[125]

So widespread were the provincial demands for London policemen that the Government in 1835 passed legislation authorizing local magistrates to swear in Metropolitan constables as "special constables."[126] Also, in June of that year, Police Commissioner Richard Mayne drew up for the Home Secretary, Lord John Russell, a secret memorandum outlining the provisions of a bill for "Providing Peelers 'occasional' to distant places." The proposal bears startling resemblances to Robert Peel's Irish Peace Preservation Police Act of 1814. A special unit, either separate from the other London divisions or attached to the A Division, would be created for exclusive use outside London. Initially to consist of four Inspectors, twelve sergeants, and fifty constables, the force would be available in whole or in part for use in disturbed areas upon the written request of a county Lord Lieutenant, a Mayor, or only two local magistrates, subject, of course, to Home Office approval. The disturbed district would pay up to two-thirds of the costs, the balance to come from the Consolidated Fund. Mayne clearly warmed to his idea of a special detachable riot police, for toward the end of his memorandum, he began referring to a force of 500 men costing £10,000 a year.

Russell, however, was not keen on such a controversial measure. Mayne's proposal was "put aside [for] the present"; it never reached the stage of a parliamentary bill, and indeed was never heard of again.[127]

It is tempting to speculate about the fate of Mayne's bill if that champion of police innovations and hardened veteran of Irish politics, Robert Peel, had stayed on as Prime Minister (December 1834–April 1835) instead of being replaced by Melbourne and the Whigs. Would Peel have pressed the bold proposal for an English version of his Peelers? Probably not: Peel's correspondence reveals his awareness that Englishmen generally assented to a species of police for Ireland that, if transplanted, "would excite much alarm in England."[128] Meanwhile, outside London, the demands for London policemen grew. By November 1838, Mayne, hard pressed by the demands of anti–Poor Law and now Chartist disorders, was complaining "how various and general the occasions have become upon which the services of the Police are now required.... [They are] much beyond what was originally contemplated." He warned the Home Office of the ill effects of these exports of constables on police service within the metropolis and stated the manpower "difficulties ... in continuing to meet these demands." Lord John Russell, who three years earlier had shelved Mayne's provocative proposal, now acknowledged the burden that had been placed on the Metropolitan Police by adding to the force 100 men designated for duty outside London.[129]

Chartism

The spur to the creation of effective police forces in the North, and indeed in many of the English counties, was Chartism.[130] This movement represented the height of the democratic threat in England in the first half of the nineteenth century. Chartism was the culmination of the radical political tradition of 1815–21 and 1830–2; it was the product of disillusionment with Reform, despair over the New Poor Law, anger over a new municipal franchise predicated on property, disgust at the failure of the national trade union movement, and hunger from the economic depression beginning in 1837. Chartism's appeal embraced most workingmen: Its adherents included West Country cottage cloth workers and Yorkshire handloom weavers, Lancashire factory hands, London artisans, and miners in Wales and northeastern England. The movement's goals were as broad as its popular base; beyond the call for one man, one vote, the workers' demands varied with their particular interests: repeal of the New Poor Law and the Corn Laws, regulation of machinery and labor in factories and mines, higher wages and the right to unionize and to strike. Chartism, to a Wiltshire laborer, meant "plenty of roast beef, plum pudding, and strong beer "; more bitterly, another workman explained that he was for universal suffrage because that was the system in which *everybody* suffers.[131]

The man at the head of this first truly national English working-class movement was an Irishman. It is remarkable that historians have not been more intrigued by this paradox. Feargus O'Connor was full of "Irish braggadocio about arming and fighting," or so objected the "moral force" London Chartist, William Lovett. But to English workingmen, especially those in the gray industrial towns of the North, where he was most popular, it was perhaps O'Connor's very swagger and defiance – his color and verve – that they found so appealing. Because he was Irish, he was not burdened with English traditions of paternalism and deference; moreover, as an Irishman, "the Lion of Freedom" could speak from the heart about oppression.[132]

Feargus O'Connor's radical credentials were strong.* His family, Protestants in County Cork, had been active United Irishmen, arrested in 1798. Young Feargus had associated with Cork Whiteboys in the early 1820s; indeed, he boasted of once being wounded in an affray. Although indifferent to Catholic Emancipation (a plus for many English workers), O'Connor was active in the subsequent antitithe movement, in the course of which he was elected MP for County Cork. But a series of events in the mid-1830s – the deaths of the English radicals Hunt and Cobbett, creating room at the top for new leadership; O'Connor's loss of his seat in Parliament; and, above all, his break with Daniel O'Connell – led O'Connor to shift his political interests from Ireland to England. He threw himself into the campaign against the New Poor Law, and from late 1837 on, with the appearance of his newspaper, *The Northern Star* (named for his uncle's United Irish Belfast paper,

*Feargus O'Connor (1796–1855) was the youngest son of Wilhelmina Bowen and Roger O'Connor (1763–1834). For his treasonable activities, Feargus's father, a friend of Sir Francis Burdett, was jailed in 1798–1801 and not allowed to return to Ireland until 1803; Feargus's uncle, Arthur O'Connor, the prominent United Irishman, was kept in prison from 1798 to 1803 and then set free in France. The youthful Feargus had an indifferent schooling in London, Clonmel (Tipperary), and Dublin. In 1820 he inherited a family estate near Bandon, Cork. Hereabouts he consorted with Whiteboys and by his own account had to flee to London. In 1822 he published a pamphlet, *A State of Ireland*, dedicated "to the People of England." Back in Ireland, he became involved in the Tithe War; his speeches and *Letter ... to the Marquis of Anglesea* led to his arrest in September 1832, but prosecution was subsequently dropped. As a reform candidate endorsed by Daniel O'Connell, O'Connor was elected MP for County Cork (1832–5) on a platform of no tithes, universal suffrage, and Repeal of the Union. In June 1835 he was stripped of his seat because he fell short of meeting the £600 freehold qualification. Next year came his break with O'Connell, largely because of O'Connell's alliance with the Whigs, authors of the New Poor Law and erstwhile "friends of the people." Following O'Connor's publication of a scathing *Series of Letters ... to Daniel O'Connell* (1837), the Irish leader disowned O'Connor, saying, "Let him stick to the Radicals of England."

After a period of prominence as the English Chartist chieftain, 1838–42, O'Connor became preoccupied with his "Land Plan," a scheme for worker-owned small farms that he had experimented with on his Cork estate twenty years earlier. Reelected to Parliament as MP for Nottingham (1847–52), O'Connor spoke mostly on Irish matters. In 1848 he returned to the national spotlight as the leader of English workingmen and the principal speaker at Kennington Common. From 1850 on, O'Connor was a broken man, victim of a progressive physical and mental breakdown. He died, helpless and insane, in London in August 1855. The body of the English radical leader from County Cork was buried in Kensal Green Cemetery; the funeral drew a crowd estimated by *The Times* at 30,000. A few years later, memorials, paid for by public subscription, were erected at the London gravesite and in Nottingham. No statue, so far as I know, honors "the Lion of Freedom" in his own country.

Figure 10.1 Two Irish leaders: Feargus O'Connor, English Chartist chieftain (*left*), and Daniel O'Connell, "uncrowned king" of Ireland. (Detail from full-length engraving of O'Connor, by permission of the British Museum; engraving in D. O'Connell, *Life and Speeches*, New York, publ. by J. A. McGee, 1872)

1792–7), O'Connor emerged as the Chartist leader in the North of England.[133] His rift with O'Connell in 1836 had cost him any influence he might have developed over the Irish masses. But his Irish loss proved an English gain: It enabled O'Connor to vie for, and by 1838 win, the leadership of the democratic movement among English workingmen (Figure 10.1).

Old historical works credited the strain of violence in Chartism. Recent studies, abandoning discussion of the contrast of Lovett's moral force to O'Connor's physical force, talk about the Chartists' "war of nerves." In this interpretation the workers' chief weapons, following the Whig–Radical tradition of 1830–2, were the "language of menace," the "rhetoric of violence," and the "tactic of bluff." There were certainly plenty of inflammatory speeches, pamphlets, and newspapers (led by O'Connor's *Northern Star*; 1838 circ., 50,000); and the ascendancy of the Irishman O'Connor as the Chartist chieftain in the North did contribute to the verbal fireworks.[134] But the Irish or the French historian looks in vain for violence. Disorders there were in abundance, but with a few exceptions, no serious damage was done. Riotous offenses (national totals) were up by a third in 1839–41 (annual average: 674) compared to 1836–38 (492). Reports and rumors of arming, arson, and military drilling flooded the Home Office. Troops filled the Northern District and London policemen were despatched as far afield as Wales, Dorset, and Durham.[135] But all the plots and skirmishes yielded few serious casualties. For all the talk of "universal suffrage or death," the only Chartists killed in action in 1839–40 were slain during the Newport Rising (in Wales) on 3 November 1839: Twenty-eight soldiers in the Westgate Hotel fired on an approaching crowd of Monmouthshire miners, killing twenty. Subsequent revolutionary "plots" in Yorkshire, the Midlands, and the northeast came to naught.[136] The Newport affair, little more than an ambush by jittery troops, acquired its revolutionary aura largely because none of the Chartist "risings" over the next decade produced nearly as many victims.

The real threat of Chartism was not physical revolution, which never came, but rather the conversion of many, many working-class minds to a revolutionary idea: England should be transformed into a political democracy.[137] "Chartism had two characteristics that neither reformers nor revolutionaries of the 1790s had ever been able to bring together in one movement, political consciousness and popular support." In a word, Chartism was an idea, not a gun. The movement's aims, set out in the "People's Charter" (May 1838), were certainly radical. Enactment of the famous Six Points – universal male suffrage, a secret ballot, annual Parliaments, equal electoral districts, and abolition of the income requirement for, and the substituted payment of, Members of Parliament – would have undermined the very foundations not only of the English state but of society. But the Chartist emphasis on political reform of the existing system, to the neglect of substantive economic or even social change, betrayed the movement's lack of a revolutionary ideology. Its techniques, too, were essentially constitutionalist: a political Convention; popular petitions; marches, demonstrations, and meetings. The national Chartist Convention (its motto: "Peace, Law, and Order"), which met in London from February to September 1839, and briefly in July in Birmingham, was at most times a model of parliamentary behavior. A monster petition, initiated at Birmingham in August 1838, was diligently circulated throughout the country, and by July 1839, when the House of Commons rejected it (by a vote of 235–46), the weighty document had collected 1,280,000 signatures. Perhaps most impressive were the numerous outdoor mass meetings. Under the Chartists this tactic, practiced in England for twenty years and in Ireland for ten, wedded justice to physical numbers. At Kersal Moor, outside Manchester, in September 1838, Feargus O'Connor could look out over a crowd conservatively estimated at 50,000 and declare, "Here is moral power with a vengeance." Since Peterloo, no meeting in Lancashire had attracted so many people; indeed, the old banners from 1819 were unfurled on the moor in 1838. Hoping "to extort concession by inducing fear," Chartist leaders urged the crowds at such meetings to avoid riot and bloodshed *but* to resist oppression, to maintain order *but* "better to die freemen than to live slaves" (O'Connor) – in short, in Oastler's pithy phrase, "Arm for peace."[138]

The geographical spread of Chartism was impressive. The strength of the movement was from the Midlands north – Birmingham to Manchester to Newcastle-on-Tyne – but Chartism also thrived in surprising places. The "agitation was as pronounced in rural Wales" as it was in the Welsh industrial and mining districts; it attracted artisans and journeymen in Suffolk, and appealed to workers in the declining cloth-manufacturing towns in Somerset and Wiltshire and to hard-hit framework knitters in Leicester. But Chartism was especially robust in those parts of the country on the leading edge of industrial change. It was in the woolen districts of Yorkshire and the cotton belt in Lancashire – Manchester and surrounding textile towns like Oldham, Bolton, and Blackburn – that Chartism was most deeply entrenched. Around Manchester, Chartist meetings dated to March 1837 and by early 1838 were being held frequently. The huge demonstration at Kersal Moor was only the largest of a number of similar assemblages, many of them held at night, eerily conducted by torchlight, and "noisily impressive." Continuation of the meetings in the autumn and winter of 1838 and the spring of 1839 induced alarm among the property-owning classes; crowds of up to 4,000 paraded in Stockport, Blackburn, and Bolton, and a second great meeting at Kersal Moor in May 1839 drew 30,000 people.[139]

To police these northern cities, the Government had had to rely on judicious admixtures of troops, Yeomanry, and special constables. There were no regular police forces. The civil power in Bolton, a cotton-spinning town of 51,000 (1841 pop.), was in total disarray. The town was incorporated in 1838, but the older authorities legally contested the charter, so that the establishment of a borough police force and a police rate was problematic. The new borough authorities were able to recruit only ten constables; these, however, coexisted with thirteen constables from the old court leet and some forty to sixty "perpetual" constables appointed under various earlier local police acts. There were also supposedly 1,000 available special constables, but many of them were suspected of being Chartists and the rest were cowed by the heavily Chartist town population. A goodly number, in fact, of these diverse policemen were believed to be Chartists; the Mayor of Bolton himself had been seen at the head of Chartist processions.[140]

In Manchester, a city five times more populous, the civil power had long been deficient. In 1829 the "force" of two constables and seventy-four watchmen was of no use against industrial strikes and riots; "the Police and Special Constables," reported General Bouverie, "appear to have little or no authority without the Aid of the Military." An attempt in 1830 to establish a mounted patrol failed due to the opposition of the court leet that controlled the policing of the town. Two years later, town authorities petitioned Home Secretary Melbourne with the request that a local "Police somewhat resembling the Metropolitan be adopted for Manchester and the adjoining Townships." Col. James Shaw, the Government's "Military-Political Agent at Manchester" (and future head of the Irish constabulary), urged the Home Office not to let "such an opportunity to slip [by]. . . . I promised at the Meeting to get all necessary information from Rowan and had before written to him." The opportunity did slip by. A city report in 1836 noted that recent disorders "easily might have been suppressed . . . had there been a sufficiently numerous and properly organized police force."[141] Shaw's successor, Col. Thomas Wemyss, reported in 1837 that the police consisted of 30 constables, 150 watchmen, and "some Hundreds" of special constables "not easily induced to come forward." After the city's incorporation in 1838, the new Manchester borough council managed to create a police of 48 officers and 295 constables. But the problems continued. The force had been funded by the council's loan of £20,000, and attempts to levy a police tax encountered great opposition, so in 1839 the future of the borough police appeared bleak. The pre-1838 authorities, the court leet and the police commission, refused to cooperate with the new borough police; so intransigent were the old police commissioners that they created a rival day and night police force of 240 men. In sum, an effective local police force in Manchester was blocked by local politics. Maj.-Gen. Sir Charles James Napier, Commander of the Northern District, warned the Home Office in May 1839 that Manchester's Tory Boroughreeve and Whig Mayor

are more hostile than I can describe, and between them there is no concert. . . . They would not unite though Manchester were in flames. . . . The civil force here is quite inadequate. What are 500 Constables and Specials in a town which would turn out 50,000 people to see a dogfight! Manchester should, as you no doubt know better than I do, have a strong well-organized police of, at least, 1,000 Men.[142]

In 1838–9, the provincial headquarters of Chartism was Birmingham. The revised (May 1837) and hitherto largely middle-class Birmingham Political Union announced its conversion to universal suffrage in November 1837. The previous June, a crowd of 50,000 had assembled outside the city, at Newhall Hill, in support of the Charter. During the general election in 1837, magistrates dealt with the boisterous crowds by reading the Riot Act on two successive days and calling out dragoons and Yeomanry. In August 1838, a monster meeting at Holloway Head, outside Birmingham, attracted 100,000 persons to hear Feargus O'Connor launch the Chartists' northern campaign; within a few days, their petition had acquired 95,000 signatures. More worrisome, by spring 1839, were the increasingly frequent meetings in a central part of Birmingham called the "Bull Ring." In May city magistrates banned all public meetings; but despite some arrests and prosecutions, the crowds continued to assemble almost nightly. By the end of June, radical orators were routinely urging arming and drilling, a general strike, and a run on the banks. On 1 July the national Chartist Convention, having moved north from London, reconvened in Birmingham.[143]

In this city of 180,000, the civil power still consisted of 30 day street keepers, 170 night watchmen, and, in emergencies, some 2,300 special constables. Birmingham had received its charter of incorporation in 1838, but because of legal challenges brought by Tory magistrates against the new Whig borough council, neither a Watch Committee nor a police rate could be established.[144] It was in this condition of impotence that the Mayor asked the Home Office for a sizable loan of Metropolitan Police. One group totaling fifty constables arrived by rail on the evening of 4 July; local magistrates waiting at the train station enrolled the Londoners as special constables and ordered them at once to the Bull Ring, where 2,000 Chartists were meeting. The appearance of the blue-uniformed strangers – "blue bottles," "Bourbon police" – triggered a riot that lasted for forty-five minutes and ended only with the arrival of a cavalry troop. Ten rioters were arrested, but the police had been humiliated. The next day, as forty more Metropolitan policemen arrived by train, the Chartist Convention, itself a recent arrival, passed a unanimous resolution deploring the

wanton, flagrant, and unjust outrage ... made upon the people of Birmingham by a blood-thirsty and unconstitutional force from London acting under the authority of men [the Whigs] who, when out of office, sanctioned and took part in the Meetings of the People, and now when they share in the public plunder, seek to keep the people in social and political degradation.

On 8 July the police, now ninety strong, dispersed a crowd in the Bull Ring without the aid of troops. On the 12th, Parliament in London over-whelmingly rejected the Chartists' national petition. Intermittent disorders flared in Birmingham, but by way of conciliation city magistrates held back the police and army. This policy ultimately produced serious consequences on the evening of 15 July when rioting, and then fire, destroyed scores of buildings and property. During this wild hour and a half, the Mayor and magistrates "effected a strange and mysterious disappearance"; only near 10 P.M. did the London police, followed by the military, restore order. The Birmingham Riots, which had begun twelve days earlier, were finally over. No one had been killed, but property losses conservatively totaled £20,000.[145]

A government police for Birmingham, Manchester, and Bolton

The collapse of authority in Birmingham was not restricted to the Bull Ring disorders. In the aftermath, the Mayor asked for a government loan of £10,000 to establish a borough police force. But the Birmingham Tories were adamant in opposing such a force, since it would confirm the recent city charter and Whig local control. To break the impasse the Tory leader, Sir Robert Peel, persuaded the Whig Home Secretary, Lord John Russell, to scrap the whole idea of a local police and substitute a government-controlled force on the London model.[146] As they had united a decade earlier to establish a police for the capital, Whigs and Tories in 1839 joined forces to stifle protest at the expense of local liberties.

The controversy over the Birmingham police bill came over two separate issues: first, from 23 July on, the Government's proposal to grant a loan from the Consolidated Fund to the city of Birmingham for the purpose of estab-lishing a Corporation-controlled police force; and second, from 29 July on, withdrawal of the original plan and substitution of a government-controlled police for Birmingham.[147] The local police proposal met virtually no opposi-tion in the Commons; Radical John Fielden's call for a "sense of the House" resulted in a lopsided vote of 144—3.[148] One Member, Radical Joseph Hume, did remark that Melbourne had supported the rights of the people at Peterloo and opposed the Six Acts, but now as Prime Minister favored "a gagging Act similar to that of 1819"; another Member, the Chartist T. S. Duncombe, observed that the £10,000 would be money wasted, "like that loan of a million ... given to the Irish parsons."[149]

Six days later, on 29 July, after private consultations with Russell, Peel threw the Commons into an uproar by proposing that Birmingham – and Manchester and Bolton – be given for a temporary two-year period a government-controlled police modeled on the Metropolitan London force. Birmingham, Peel charged, was paralyzed, on the one hand, by "inflammatory harangues ..., political unions, and meetings and marchings and large demonstrations of physical force," and, on the other, by intractable disagreements among the various old and new city authorities. To the objection that the Government could not interfere with the rights of corporate towns, Peel boldly put forward the precedent of Dublin, a chartered borough where the police was under the Government's control and had produced "universal satisfaction."[150] Following impassioned protests by the Mayor of Birmingham and Thomas Attwood, the rich radical banker who headed the Birmingham Political Union, Daniel O'Connell jumped into the parliamentary fray. In earlier remarks (23 July) on the use of the London police in the Birmingham riots, O'Connell had patiently asked his fellow MPs to compare the situation in Ireland, where the police were "armed with deadly weapons."[151] Now, temporarily overcome with nationalist pride, O'Connell appeared to give his support to the proposal for a government police in Birmingham.

He was not one of them who had joined in the cry against them [police] as being gend'armerie [sic]; but he knew that in Ireland, and in Dublin particularly, the system had worked well. In Dublin, all party feelings on the part of the police had ceased, since Major Miller had put an end to the plan of selecting political partisans to form that body. Take them for all in all, there could not be a better constabulary force than that which now existed in Ireland, and he had no doubt that a constabulary force would ultimately become popular in England.

Such an endorsement from the king of the Irish Catholics, of course, only stirred up the controversy. One speaker, the Chartist MP Thomas Wakley, already upset with the Government for abandoning the original "constitutional" bill, professed himself aghast that the Whigs' ally, O'Connell, "appeared to advocate something like the introduction of the Irish constabulary force" into England.[152]

Four days later, on 2 August, Home Secretary Russell made a motion to replace the Birmingham local police bill with Peel's proposal, now the Government's bill, for an unprecedented Crown-controlled police in the city of Birmingham. There was an immediate outcry against this introduction of "the French system of police." Peel was ready. Addressing the speaker, Charles Buller, a Whig liberal,[153] Peel coldly stated that

he did not know how the hon. Member could reconcile his opinion with the vote that he had given for placing the police force in Ireland under the control of the authorities in Dublin. The hon. Gentleman said that the institutions should be similar in the two countries, and yet he allowed the control of the 8,000 police in Ireland to be taken from the local authorities and placed under the government. If this was a barbarous system, and if Irish institutions should be like English institutions, why did not the hon. Gentleman urge this opinion when the subject of the Irish police was before the House?

Peel's brilliant, if startling, argument blocked any further protests. But the invocation of the Irish constabulary did worry Viscount Clements, Irish Whig MP for County Leitrim.[154] Clements mistakenly equated the proposed Birmingham police with the "armed police in Ireland.... [H]e had no wish to see the same system adopted in this country." At the call for a vote, one Member objected to "setting aside so great a principle ... in so thin a House"; the Commons then approved the withdrawal of the original local police bill by 80–14. Joining the minority of English Radicals was Daniel O'Connell, who apparently had decided (despite his encomium on the Irish police) to vote in favor of English local liberties.[155]

Russell immediately asked leave to bring in the bill for a government police in Birmingham. The House gave its approval by 77–3, with Attwood and O'Connell in the tiny minority. The bill passed its Second Reading on 7 August by 74–20, the "noes" constituting a mixed bag of Radicals, Whig and Tory back benchers uncomfortable with "centralisation," and O'Connell.[156] At the committee stage on the 9th, opposition speeches sounded themes heard in Dublin in 1786 and London in 1829. "The gendarmerie system was un-English; the word 'police' was not in our language; we only had 'peace officers' and constables." The Birmingham borough council petitioned against the bill, which it judged "insulting and despotic ..., unworthy of them, as men and as Englishmen.... [It] was the first step towards driving in the wedge for the French *gens d'armerie*." Buller's motion that the borough authorities, not London, should appoint the new Police Commissioner was defeated by 63–20. In the minority, joining the Radicals, were "B. D'Israeli" and O'Connell.[157] On 13 August the bill passed its Third Reading in the Commons, 38–8, and on the 19th it sailed through the Lords, where Melbourne and Wellington supported it and only Brougham opposed it. The bill received the royal assent on 26 August, three weeks after it had been introduced.[158]

In the meantime, faced with similar Chartist threats, legal wrangles involving the new borough police, uncollectable police rates, and impending civil chaos, the Government had on 7 August introduced bills for Crown-controlled police in Manchester and Bolton. The Manchester bill received the royal assent on the 26th, the same day as the Birmingham bill, and the Bolton police bill became law the next day.[159] These measures establishing government police forces in two more major English towns were almost anticlimactic. The furor had spent itself in the debates on the Birmingham bill. Russell announced that there would be no further attempts to "neutralize" squabbles in other cities. Older corporate towns (he cited Newcastle-on-Tyne and Stockport), however disturbed, would not be interfered with; he assured Members, and Mr. Buller in particular, that he did not seek to introduce universally what Buller had characterized as "the hideous feature of centralisation ..., the same system now in full operation in France," but rather only to bring London-imposed order on a temporary basis to those three recently incorporated towns.[160] Opponents did point out that Manchester, unlike Birmingham, already had a large borough police, and that in Manchester there had been no recent riots and no resort, recently, to troops or the Metropolitan Police. Against the protests of the Manchester town council, local ratepayers, 7,000 petitioners "professing all shades of politics," the older police authorities, and the Chartists, the Manchester police bill – like the one for Bolton – passed easily and quickly through both Houses of Parliament.[161]

In summary, a number of points stand out from the debates on these three important police measures. All were enacted in haste and at the eleventh hour of the session (Parliament was prorogued on 27 August). All passed with large majorities in sparsely attended Houses. And, perhaps most significantly, during all of the debates, the subject of ordinary daily crime was *never* mentioned. The parliamentary scenario in London in 1839 was virtually identical to the one in Ireland a half-century earlier on the occasion of the Dublin police bill of 1786.

In a strictly constitutional sense, the English police acts treated the inhabitants of Bolton, and Manchester and Birmingham, the third and fourth largest cities in the kingdom, little differently from rebellious Irishmen. Three years earlier the London Government, in imposing total central control over both the Dublin police and the Irish constabulary, had stepped in between Irish Catholic and Protestant factions; in Birmingham, Manchester, and Bolton in 1839, the Government interposed its authority over Chartist demonstrators, seemingly ineffectual borough councils, and obstructionist older local governing authorities. The new government police outside London seemed to many to represent the cancellation of the erstwhile Whig principle of ratepayer-controlled police embodied in the Municipal Corporations Act of 1835. As Englishmen in the summer of 1839 contemplated the reduction of a major city like Birmingham to the servile status of Dublin, they had to be worried about the future. Five months earlier, in March, a government commission had made the unprecedented recommendation that the old parish constables in the counties of England should be replaced by a large, efficient, and standardized "constabulary" controlled entirely by the Government in London.

V. A police for the "rural" districts

On 24 July 1839, the day after he introduced the subject of the Birmingham police, Lord John Russell asked leave to bring in a bill establishing a county police in England. Because of "the meetings, which had lately taken place, and the riots and alarm consequent upon them," he urged Members "not to lose any time" in approving the Government's proposal for "a civil force of constabulary."[162] Why the hurry in 1839? Reform of the county, like the borough, police had certainly been slow in coming. For nearly a decade after the Captain Swing disorders, rural policing had changed scarcely at all. By a local act of 1829, Home Secretary Peel had established in Cheshire tiny forces totaling seventy-five paid police, a handful of men scattered across each hundred (subdivision) in the county. Controlled by local magistrates but uncoordinated among the hundreds, the Cheshire police experiment proved to be a failure; by 1838, only twenty-seven constables remained. On a national scale, the parish Lighting and Watching Acts of 1830 and 1833 (initiated by Peel and amended by Melbourne) had also been ineffective.[163]

Passage of the New Poor Law awakened the Whigs to the need for a civil force to enforce the implementation of the act. "Rural Police, and increased taxation," complained one radical writer in 1841, "are the [Poor] Act's necessary assistants on the Government's side." Another commentator claimed to detect as early as 1834 the Whigs' aim to "cover the country with a well-organized police – an Irish constabulary force, or a French gens d'armerie – [in order to] reduce the English labourer to as orderly and submissive a state as such means can reduce him to."[164] Men as different as Edwin Chadwick, the political theorist; the 5th Duke of Richmond, the genial aristocrat who had personally waged war against the Swing rioters in 1830; and General Sir Richard Jackson, Commander of the Northern District, all pressed the Government to superimpose a county police on the geographical configurations of the Poor Law Unions.[165]

Despite such fears and demands, Whig ministers moved slowly. Home Secretary Melbourne ignored General Bouverie's recommendation in 1832 for a police force in the mining districts. Home Secretary Russell reported to Parliament in May 1836 that a rural police bill was "in preparation" and would be introduced in the current session "if he found that time allowed for it." He worried, however, that any proposal for a *uniformed* force would "meet many obstacles." The bill was not introduced in 1836. Instead, the Government appointed a commission "to inquire as to the Best Means of Establishing an efficient Constabulary Force in the Counties of England and Wales." Two and a half years would pass before this commission issued its 200-page report; during this time the Whigs, though besieged by anti–Poor Law disturbances, did not feel it necessary to press in Parliament any proposals for a nationwide county police. As late as December 1838, the Government was content to answer a Yorkshire query about the best means "for establishing a Police Force" with the suggestion that local magistrates should swear in special constables, or form a Voluntary Association, or ask the Metropolitan Police for an officer to assist them.[166]

The Constabulary Report of 1839

The Government's commission on the county police, appointed in October 1836, at the height of the Poor Law riots, issued its report in late March 1839, as Chartism was gathering force.[167] The commission shared two characteristics with Peel's 1828 select committee on the London police: Its conclusion was foregone, and its goal was to prepare the public mind for subsequent substantive police reform. Of the three commissioners, one was a somewhat obscure Whig MP;[168] the second, Charles Rowan, was the London Police Commissioner; and the third, and most important, was Edwin Chadwick, the Benthamite political philosopher who had for the past decade been ideologically committed to the Metropolitan Police model and who had served, most recently, as Secretary to the Poor Law Commissioners. The *Constabulary Report* was essentially Chadwick's creation. In the form of a long essay, using carefully selected statistics, facts, and quotations from witnesses, it was "systematically doctored" by Chadwick to paint a lurid picture of rampant criminality unchecked by bumbling, illiterate parish constables. The *Report*'s central argument, now disproven by Jenifer Hart (1955), was that criminals, from fear of the efficient new police in London and the corporate towns, had migrated to the rural districts to commit their crimes.[169] The obvious solution was to establish in the countryside equally effective police forces. The *Report*, which concentrated on daily crime and the deficiencies in existing arrangements for policing, did point out "the defective protection against riotous assemblages in the rural districts" and lauded "the advantages of Police over Military in suppressing Riots."[170]

The *Constabulary Report*'s recommendations landed like a bombshell. This three-man commission – the only parliamentary investigation in the first half of the nineteenth century into the state of the English police outside London – called for the creation in the counties of an 8,000-man uniformed national police appointed and controlled by the Metropolitan Police Commissioners and the Home Office. Three-quarters of the total costs (estimated at about £500,000) would be locally defrayed from the county rates; the remainder would be paid from the Consolidated Fund. The only local powers would be the right of local magistrates at quarter sessions to petition for the establishment of the force and to recommend constables' dismissals. Otherwise, Chadwick's prescription was for an unarmed, English-style gendarmerie. As a model, the commissioners specifically rejected "the Irish constabulary force," since it was "in its organization and action essentially inapplicable to England and Wales"; it had too much "the character of a military and repressive force." Nevertheless, as an adjunct to the proposed English constabulary, Chadwick did favor creation of a Peeler-styled, mobile force of 300–400 policemen to be deployed against "popular commotions." Overall, the model favored by Chadwick and Rowan throughout the *Report* was that of the London Metropolitan Police, which they proposed to re-create in all fifty-two counties in England and Wales. The breadth of Chadwick's private vision may be seen in his hope that even the borough forces might be abolished or subsumed under the new national constabulary.[171]

The revolutionary recommendations in the *Constabulary Report* of 1839 were seriously at odds with the thinking of the local magistrates throughout the country. To a questionnaire sent to them by the constabulary commissioners, half of the 400 magistrates who replied were opposed to any change and only one-quarter favored establishing a rural police force of any kind. In April 1839, after the appearance of the *Constabulary Report*, the magistrates at Shropshire Quarter Sessions, with the approval of the Home

Office, circulated to the JPs in the other counties – and sought their opinion on – a proposal for a county police appointed and controlled by county magistrates. Seventeen of the fifty-two counties did not reply. Of the thirty-five counties responding, twenty-five agreed to the idea *only* if the police were kept under total county control; ten counties were adamantly opposed even to this kind of police. Overall, the county JPs who bothered to answer these two questionnaires showed themselves (in Radzinowicz's words) to be "largely content with things as they were."[172] So, too, presumably, were those who thought the questions not worth a reply. Chadwick's ideas on police were about as popular with "roast beef" Englishmen as Colquhoun's had been a generation earlier.

The County Police Act of 1839

The Whig Government shrewdly perceived the political dangers in attempting to implement Chadwick's personal vision. The *Constabulary Report* was unpopular among all classes of Englishmen. Not only Tories and Chartists, but even Whig gentlemen and Whig organs like the *Morning Chronicle*, were loud in denouncing the "gigantic tyranny" proposed by the francophile Benthamite and the London Police Commissioner.[173] But as a scare tactic, the *Constabulary Report* of 1839 played an important role in the passage of the Whigs' County Police Act in August. For months fearing the worst, Englishmen of all classes were relieved by the constitutional mildness of Russell's proposal in late summer. Unwittingly, Chadwick had helped to assure enactment of the Government's bill, which, in the absence of the Constabulary Commission's *Report*, would probably have faced far tougher going in Parliament.

In introducing the bill on 24 July, Russell dismissed Chadwick's embarrassing recommendations as too extreme. Nor did he develop any argument about the migration of criminals to the rural districts. Instead, the Home Secretary devoted his remarks to the threat of Chartism. Russell's concerns reflected those of the Crown's military officers. On the 20th, Maj.-Gen. Sir Charles James Napier, Commander of the Northern District, had written him that "concession must be made to the people's feelings, or the establishment of a strong rural police hurried on. I would do both, thinking them absolutely necessary; if the police force be not quickly increased, we shall require troops from Ireland." In his speech in the Commons on the 24th, Russell recounted the historic problems in maintaining public order by traditional means. He cited the ineffectiveness of the special constables; the excessive reliance of JPs on the Yeomanry and the military; the consequent harm (quoting General Sir Richard Jackson) to the morale and discipline of the troops; the need to keep the soldiers concentrated; the dangers of billeting the soldiers; and the uselessness of the military for capturing and arresting rioters. It was time, Russell concluded, to move beyond special constables and the army; the time had come to establish a police force in the counties. He proposed to make the law permissive because "a paid and regular police in many districts ... was not wanted." He then explained that his "County and District Constabulary Bill" was not meant to establish police in those rural areas where crime and riot posed few problems. But "many districts in the counties had in the present time come to be thickly peopled with a manufacturing or mining population, which partook of the character of a town population, while at the same time it was impossible to confer upon them municipal institutions."[174] Thus, either of the names that the Government's bill would come to acquire, the "county" or "rural" police bill, was in some sense a misnomer. Among its targets, the measure was aimed directly at the tumultuous unincorporated northern conurbations. Melbourne in 1832 had not known what to do about "the North"; Russell in 1839 thought he had the answer.

The county police bill was a large concession to English local interests. It signified an acquiescence to public opinion and a reliance on the available and effective local authorities; neither of these had been possible in Ireland. Each county Quarter Sessions was left to decide whether or not to adopt the new police. The magistrates were given the sole power to decide the size of the force (indeed, the police-to-population ratio was *not* to exceed 1:1,000), to frame all rules and regulations, and to appoint the County Chief Constable (who, unlike his borough counterpart, was given exclusive control over the appointment of the constables). Incorporated towns within counties were excluded from the bill. The entire cost of the county police would be paid by the county rate. The only power given the Home Secretary was a general right to grant or refuse approval of all of the arrangements made by the magistrates.[175]

A few amendments were made to the bill in its transit through the Commons. Local control was kept intact, but to promote uniformity among the counties, the power of making rules and regulations for the forces was transferred from Quarter Sessions to the Home Office. Magistrates were granted greater flexibility in concentrating forces in particular divisions of a county. A proposal by the MP for Wigan (a Lancashire industrial borough with six policemen for its 26,000 inhabitants) to limit the duration of the bill to two years was defeated by 77–21.[176] Another proposal that would have permitted preexisting constables to continue alongside the new police was narrowly defeated by a vote of 32–30; this applied to watchmen and constables appointed under Improvement acts but did not affect parish constables, who would continue a statutory existence until 1872.[177]

Standing in contrast to the muted opposition in Parliament were the remarks of a thirty-five-year-old London Jew, a Tory MP for less than two years, Benjamin Disraeli. T. A. Critchley has characterized Disraeli's opposition as "a vicious attack on party political grounds"; Radzinowicz also makes sport of his splenetic outbursts in August 1839. But if Disraeli's remarks were shaped by his "Oriental imagination and satirical intellect," they were also founded on principle. A Tory paternalist and Chartist sympathizer, Disraeli was intensely interested in the "social question," the answer to which he believed should be a repudiation of sham Whig politics and the creation instead of a new governing philosophy combining Toryism with Radicalism. In the early 1840s he would emerge as a leader of the Young England party and a social critic (*Coningsby*, 1844; *Sybil, or The Two Nations*, 1845).[178]

Disraeli's criticisms of the county police bill of 1839 were founded on his contempt for Whig policies. Lord John Russell had declared that "civil war had commenced in the country," but what, asked Disraeli, were the *causes* of this civil war? Was it not that the Whigs, having stirred up the passions of the people in 1830–2, had by various means denied any further extension of popular rights since 1832? Implementation of the New Poor Law had been followed by indifference to the People's Charter by these erstwhile "Friends of the People." In the present session the Whigs had augmented the army by 5,000, had transformed "in a very few days" a police bill for Birmingham based on "a popular principle" into one founded on "the principle of centralisation," and had saddled similar government forces on Manchester and Bolton. Now Members in Commons were being asked in a "hurried and unsatisfactory manner ... [to] revolutionize the rural police of the country." Would the Government deny that this bill was "founded on a report which recommended centralisation," and that throughout the entire debate this report had been "studiously kept out of sight"? Disraeli objected that the proposed rural "constabulary" – a term he dismissed as "Gallomaniac jargon" – was in fact not needed in the rural districts where, he noted sarcastically, "the old constabulary" worked well enough. "Almost all the facts they [the Whigs] had in evidence on the subject related to the manu-facturing districts."[179]

No Tory leaders spoke in support of Disraeli, their colorful maverick MP. Peel was judiciously silent, and not voting, throughout the debates.[180] Sir James Graham, the future Home Secretary (1841–5), spoke against Disraeli. Graham argued that the county police bill was "intended to meet an emergency which had unhappily arisen"; he did not know whether or not the Whigs were to blame. But a measure was "imperatively called for" to break the "insurrectionary spirit" in the country. Graham favored the bill because it was not compulsory and because control rested with county JPs, not the Government; he would have opposed any bill founded on the principles of the Metropolitan Police Act of 1829.[181]

Two modern historians, T. A. Critchley and Leon Radzinowicz, have drawn the lines of debate in terms of local control versus centralization, of county magistrates versus the Home Office. But no speaker – Russell, Disraeli, or Graham – favored a centrally controlled police. The real question was: local control *by whom*? To pass their bill, the Whigs were prepared to establish a police largely controlled by Tory magistrates in the counties. The Whigs in 1839 proposed to leave untouched Tory bastions of power – the rural JPs – just as Peel in 1829 had wisely left untouched that Whig–Radical bastion, the City of London. In this sense, the Whig proposal was cannily conservative, not revolutionary. The measure was one of central control in the sense that the JPs were commissioned officers of the Crown accountable only to the Home Office.[182] Although they were men of local interests and prejudices, the county JPs did differ markedly from ratepayers who, had they been given control of the county police, would not be accountable directly to the Crown. John Foster, the historian of Oldham, one of the towns targeted for this "rural" police, has perceptively observed that what the Government was seeking to do in the county police bill was to "abandon attempts at a 'safe' but still rate-payer controlled police, and build up local police forces under direct crown control."[183] Foster continues:

The radicals [in Oldham in January 1840] knew what this would mean. A public meeting was held to appoint a liaison committee to act with other towns. "The evil arising from the said act is the placing of such police under the immediate control of justices.... [T]he whole power of appointing police was taken away from leypayers and they were left to the tender mercies of a set of men [Tories] from whom they knew what to expect when they had power [pre-1830].... [I]t was their duty to foil the magistrates in putting this Act into force."[184]

In the 1839 debates on the county police bill, a handful of radical MPs did demand a ratepayer-controlled police. Joseph Hume, who three years earlier had proposed a bill establishing this kind of police,[185] noted that the control of a police for the manufacturing and mining districts should not be given to "an irresponsible power," the county JPs, who would have "the right of taxing the whole community." Thomas Attwood, the Radical banker representing Birmingham, said that this was the "centralisation" to which he objected. Joseph Brotherton, Radical MP for Finsbury, argued that the consent of the ratepayers and Poor Law guardians should be obtained. John Fielden, Radical manufacturer from Todmorden and MP for Oldham, opposed the bill, which he saw as a *mésalliance* of Whigs and Tories, because it was wrong for control of these quasi-urban police forces to rest exclusively in rural hands. Fielden proposed that ratepayers in the unincorporated towns *share* power with the county JPs. All of these demands by a tiny number of Radical MPs were swept aside.[186] But to the majority of the inhabitants in the towns soon to be affected by the County Police Act, if not to Critchley and Radzinowicz, the key issue in the debate over local rights versus centralization was not whether local magistrates or the Home Office should control the new police (they equated the two), but rather, at the local level, whether control should lie with the elected representatives in the towns or with the nonelected gentlemen of property, social standing, and conservative politics in the countryside.

In a reformed Parliament still overwhelmingly dominated by gentlemen of property, the outcome of the debate was hardly in question. The county police bill passed the committee stage on 7 August by a vote of 85–14 (the minority consisting of Radicals, including the Birmingham MPs, and Daniel O'Connell), and passed the Third Reading in a virtually empty Commons on 15 August by a vote of 45–13 (O'Connell was either not present or not voting).[187] The bill sailed through the Lords, which gave its approval on 23 August, and received the royal assent on the 27th, the last day of the parliamentary session and the same day that the Bolton police bill became law. The previous day, the Manchester and Birmingham police bills had received the royal assent.[188]

VI. Reflections

In the late summer of 1839, the Whig Government, now totally alienated from its working-class allies of 1830–2, resorted to police measures that by English standards must be described as desperate. In a matter of weeks, Melbourne and Russell, backed by Peel and the Tories, enacted bills establishing government-controlled police forces in three northern hotbeds of Chartism and magistrate-directed county police to coerce the working classes in the densely inhabited unincorporated towns. The difference in control resulted not only from the disputed charters in Birmingham, Manchester, and Bolton but also (as in Ireland) from the perceived absence of any sizable conservative power base in these towns; by contrast, the hated notion of centralization did not need to be directly applied to the county police, whose control could safely be entrusted to local hands, that is, the rural JPs. Nonetheless, whether control was centralized or local, all four police bills of 1839 were revolutionary simply by the fact of establishing, at long last, effective police forces. In each case, the parliamentary proceedings indicate that Members assented to the unprecedented legislation from "alarm at Chartist activities," and not from any long-delayed response to the secular increase in ordinary crime.[189] Taken together, these four police bills, prepared in haste and rushed through Parliament, suggest that the post-1832 governing classes, Whig and Tory, were frightened as never before by the threat from below. To the question of when English society seemed closest to the brink of revolution, the historian of police, faced with this spate of legislation, is tempted to answer: the summer of 1839.

But even in 1839, the fear of revolution was greater than the reality. The strength of the Chartist threat began to ebb in the late autumn; the Convention disbanded in September and the "Newport Rising" was snuffed out in early November as massive arrests and troop buildups took their toll on the Chartist leadership.[190] For all the talk of arming and drilling, the revolution never came. In retrospect, this is hardly surprising, for Chartism was characterized by bluff and verbal intimidation; it employed the rhetoric of violence, not actual violence. Thomas Carlyle's *Chartism* (1839) symbolized both the movement and the fear it induced: fierce, fulminating, primal emotions. But for all the sound and fury, themselves a part of the heated rhetoric of the Romantic Age,[191] *where* was the violence? It came down only to the twenty Welsh miners shot at Newport; almost as many policemen had been killed at Carrickshock in one incident in the Irish Tithe War. In actual fact, Chartism proved to be an orderly mass movement whose rational political aims were parliamentary enactment of the Six Points. In its want of personal violence, Chartism takes its place in the long English tradition of ritualistic food rioting, constitutionalist demonstrations (Peterloo), deferential Swing rioters, and even ordinary, nonviolent, property-oriented crime.

As a Birmingham magistrate, W. L. Sargant, pithily described his city's Chartists in 1839: "Our mechanics, rude as they are to the eye and the ear, are a very peaceable race, far indeed from being addicted to violence."[192]

For all the fears of the ruling classes in that year, it is significant that neither the government police set up in the northern cities nor the county police were ever issued firearms. Not a single MP in all of the debates in 1839 proposed that the new policemen should carry guns. London policemen sent to the provinces throughout the 1830s took with them only their truncheons and an occasional cutlass. A government in genuine fear of violent revolution might have been expected to arm its new force for civil order with something more intimidating than a billet of wood.

Looking back over the decade, one is struck not only by the panic among the authorities in 1839 but, even more forcibly, by the Government's dilatoriness in establishing effective police. In the corporate boroughs the forces had been established as a part of municipal, not police, reform. The borough forces were undersized and inefficient, and the Government was content to let them remain so; ministers sought no interventionist powers of inspection or enforcement. Mayne's proposal in 1835 and Chadwick's revived suggestion in 1839 for the creation of a special force of several hundred Peeler-style, riot police for use throughout England and directed by the London Commissioners and the Home Office were never implemented. Despite the outcry against them, the government police created for Birmingham, Manchester, and Bolton were exceptional cases, not repeated in other towns, and meant only as temporary expedients for a two-year period. In the rural districts a decade after Captain Swing, there were still no forces resembling a constabulary, and the County Police Act of 1839 did not propose to establish them there. The rural police, intended largely for the manufacturing districts, were relatively mild forces. Just as the first reform of the London police in 1792 had been "a copy in faint colours" of the Dublin police of 1786, the first significant reform of the English county police – which Disraeli correctly described as effecting "a considerable civil revolution in the country" – was in fact a pale imitation of the armed, centralist constabulary established in Ireland in 1822–36.[193] The Government's decade-long delay in bringing in a bill for a county police would be matched by the widespread refusal by county authorities in the 1840s to see the need for a constabulary.

Police reforms in Ireland in the 1830s proceeded by the routine and purely administrative demolition of local rights and the unchecked advance of centralization. The Government consolidated police forces in Ireland that had originated in Pitt's time and had been greatly strengthened after the Napoleonic wars. That same decade in England, which began with Reform and ended with the Chartist crisis, produced only embryonic police forces outside London. And with the exception of the three northern cities (1839–42), all of the new forces were locally controlled, either by borough ratepayers or county magistrates. The pattern of police development in England attests to both the power of property and the loyalty of a broad section of the population; the Government could afford to delegate control of the police to local authorities because it felt it could rely on them and, at a deeper level, could trust English protesters to act within prescribed rules of collective behavior. Had societal conditions in England been less predisposed to order, the Government would have moved more quickly to impose police forces that more closely fitted the Irish model. But in England there was no need for the London Government to create a national police that kept order at the expense of all local liberties.

Chartism would not be suppressed by the creation of extensive police forces. The power of the state would instead come into play by employing a familiar, traditional tool: the army. Local authorities – magistrates, Yeomanry, special constables – would contribute to the preservation of law and order. In large measure, the new police, both borough and county, remained a negligible force for order because of the continuing national distrust of the institution. Almost all sections of the population had their particular reasons for opposing the police, and the result might be seen throughout the country in the absence or inefficiency of the new forces. In Ireland, by contrast, where no concession had been made to local feelings or interests, the idea of police thrived. Indeed, the advanced development of the police in the sister island was proof enough to many Englishmen of their good fortune in not enjoying the benefits of that modern institution outside London.

CHAPTER 11

English Chartism; Irish Repeal and Famine

The real question is, how we are to deal with what is called the disaffection of the Irish people.... [T]hat feeling of alienation is so strong, that nothing but simple fear keeps the great mass of the Irish people from breaking out into open violence. It is a frightful thing to believe that this terrible state of feeling exists among such a mass of our own people, to be constrained to believe that not less than one-fourth of the entire population of these two islands is as disaffected to our common government as Lombardy to that of Austria, or as Poland to that of Russia.... [O]ur Government retains its possession of Ireland solely by the means by which the Austrians and Russians hold Lombardy and Poland, namely, by the presence of an overwhelming military force.

The condition of Ireland is one which may justly inspire great anxiety and alarm.... How do you govern it? Not by love, but by fear; not as you govern Great Britain, but as you govern the recently-conquered Scinde [by General Sir Charles James Napier in the spring of 1843]; not by the confidence of the people in the laws and their attachment to the Constitution, but by means of armed men and entrenched camps.
– Charles Buller and Thomas Macaulay, respectively,
House of Commons, February 1844

In the aftermath of Parliament's rejection of the national petition in mid-July 1839 and the enactment of emergency police legislation in August, English and especially Welsh Chartism began a brief flirtation with the tactics of violence. In London in mid-September the proroguing of Parliament was followed by the dissolution, over Feargus O'Connor's objections, of the Chartist Convention; with neither body in session, the tactic of intimidation by rhetoric lost its force. By now the Government had begun to authorize local authorities to make arrests of local Chartist leaders. And some of these men, increasingly desperate, were attracted to "the physical force option," secret plots and harebrained schemes calling for a national rising.[1]

In early November came the "Newport Rising" on Britain's western, Celtic frontier. A crowd of 2,000 Monmouthshire ironworkers and miners marching on the South Wales town of Newport were routed by two dozen men of the 45th regiment holed up in the Westgate Hotel. The soldiers shot dead twenty "rebels." Local JPs were left with "a relatively simple job of rounding up prisoners" (cf. Ireland), and the leaders, including John Frost, were convicted of treason and their sentences commuted to life transportation.[2] Subsequent English "risings" in January 1840 involved 100 men at Dewsbury, Yorkshire, and 50 at Sheffield; both were easily suppressed.[3] These meek attempts at revolution, recalling fiascoes dating to the Luddite period, reflected the disdain felt by the bulk of the Chartists for the physical force option. In part, too, the whimper of revolt was a product of the Government's resolve "to pick off local leaders at the first sign of illegal activity."[4] In the seventeen months ending in May 1840, 480 persons in England and Wales were committed for political crimes. Four-fifths of these committals brought convictions, the great majority for minor offenses involving payment of a fine or imprisonment for six months or less. A total of twenty-two Chartists were tried for treason and sedition; half were convicted, eight for the Newport affair and three for their part in the Birmingham disorders. Most of them were transported. A reflection of both the mildness of the revolutionary threat and the reform of the criminal law since the Luddite era was the stark fact that not a single Chartist leader was put to death.[5]

I. Containing Chartism: the military response, 1839–40

Apart from the mostly unreliable contributions of spies, who were sometimes among the most active preachers of physical force,[6] and the supportive services of the still-forming constabularies in a few counties (see "Founding the county police, 1839–56"), the Chartist movement was contained by the traditional reliance on troops. Special constables were enrolled at Birmingham and Manchester. But in towns like Bolton, Oldham, Barnsley, Blackburn, and Colne, the class structure prohibited the creation of a middle-class special constabulary; here shopkeepers and merchants were in such isolated and fearful situations that they hesitated to enroll. Moreover, the institution was unpopular because the fees paid the specials became an extra charge on local rates, and the men usually proved useless unless under the guidance of an effective permanent police, which was often lacking.[7] Another little used group was the Chelsea Out-Pensioners, military veterans conscripted for service on pain of forfeiting their government pensions. In the spring of 1839, 200 fit pensioners were enrolled at Manchester and 500 at Birmingham. Their services included some patrolling, a bit of spying (i.e., drinking and talking in pubs), and even, on occasion, dispersing meetings. On balance, however, their age, local ties, and lack of discipline worked against the military pensioners' usefulness. General Napier, commander of the Northern District, noted of them: "Very likely half are Chartists, but that signifies nothing; they know the troops cannot be easily beaten, and will advise waiting until more resources are at hand, which will not happen. This will tend to quiet."[8] Finally, there was the Yeomanry. By now abolished in Ireland, the Yeomanry in England had been cut 25 percent in force strength in 1838. Still strong in the Midlands, the institution was weak in the North, with only 171 men in three troops in Lancashire. For a number of reasons, the Government did not use the Yeomanry extensively in 1839–40. Placing the men on duty was relatively costly; prolonged service interfered with their private business; and the Whigs and Napier shared an aversion to using men who were "overzealous for cutting and slashing."[9] By default, then, order had to be maintained by the regular army.

The Whigs' choice for military governor of the disturbed North in 1839–41 was a wise one. Maj.-Gen. Sir Charles James Napier* was a fifty-six-year-old Anglo-Irishman of radical political views. For Ireland, he favored land reform, a compassionate poor law, and a tax on absentee landowners; for England, he wrote, "I am an advocate for annual parliaments, universal suffrage, and vote by ballot."[10] He had as a young man witnessed violence in Ireland in 1798 and 1803, experiences that left him with "a deep abhorrence of civil strife."[11] It is highly significant that the Government named to the military command of the English North a man who believed that "Chartism cannot be stopped, God forbid that it should" (Figure 11.1). What are we to infer from this appointment of a man whom Police Commissioner Rowan could describe to Chadwick as "an old friend of mine ... a great Radical"?[12] It showed, first, that the Government could make the distinction between moral-force and physical-force Chartism, between the rhetoric of intimidation and actual violence. The appointment also revealed that the Whigs felt sufficiently comfortable with the crisis to appoint a radical general to control the radical working classes in the North. To the Chartists, it signaled that

---

*Charles James Napier (1782–1853) was the eldest son of Col. George Napier, a Scottish military officer, and Lady Sarah Lennox, fourth daughter of the 2d Duke of Richmond. Charles's maternal aunts were married to Thomas Conolly and James Fitzgerald, 1st Duke of Leinster; his cousins included Lord Edward Fitzgerald and Charles James Fox. The Napiers lived in Ireland from 1785 on, the family having moved from London to Celbridge, County Kildare, when Charles was three. Among the Napiers' close neighbors were the Cloncurrys, who resided at Lyons, Celbridge. At age eleven, Charles Napier was commissioned a lieutenant in the army; at sixteen he rode with his father and four brothers against the rebels of 1798; in 1803 his regiment in Dublin saw brief service in Emmet's Rising. Napier spent all of his formative years, to age twenty-one, in Ireland.

Military service took Napier to the Iberian Peninsula (under Wellington, 1808–11), America (1813), and the Mediterranean and Greece. From 1830 on, he lived mostly in London. Here he wrote two pamphlets on Irish agrarian problems, a book urging military reforms (specifically, the abolition of flogging), and another book advocating colonization as a remedy for the problems of "small farms and overpopulation." In 1835 Napier rejected the Government's offer to head an Australian colonization project, and later he was rejected in his bid for a military command in Ireland. By early 1839 Napier had decided to return to Ireland, which he had toured the previous summer, in order to become involved with agricultural education, which he judged "the best field for beneficent exertions in private life."

Instead, public service took Napier to the North of England (April 1839–September 1841) and then to India, where in 1843 he won his military reputation as "Conqueror of the Scinde" (today a province in southeast Pakistan). In 1850, following government charges of his mishandling a Sepoy rebellion, Napier, a tarnished hero, returned to England, where he spent his last years in quiet retirement. His funeral in Portsmouth is said to have drawn a crowd of 60,000. Shortly afterward, a statue, paid for by contributions from common soldiers, was erected in his honor in London. It still stands in Trafalgar Square.

Figure 11.1 General Sir Charles James Napier: a romantic portrait, 1848 (W. Napier, *Life of C. J. Napier*)

nonviolent and traditional modes of protest would likely be tolerated, that repression would not be immediate and heavyhanded. The selection of Napier appeared to lend to the Chartist cause a degree of political legitimacy and thus may have helped to keep the lid on disorders.

The Government's response to the social crisis in 1839–40 was largely unchanged from official actions in the 1810s and 1820s. Napier's complaint of "total dependence on the regular army"[13] would have been familiar to Generals Maitland and Byng. Lord John Russell promised Napier that he would have "about as many men as there were in 1832," when 7,500 troops filled the Northern District. Normal force levels were about 4,500 men; in late 1838 only 4,100 were on duty (see Table 11.1). But by June 1839 an influx of soldiers nearly doubled the level to 7,000, and by May 1840 the district contained 8,200 troops. (The decline would be equally swift: 6,300 by

433

Table 11.1. *The military in two crises: troop levels in the Northern District in the era of Reform and Chartism*

Year	Northern District			England and Wales	Percent in the North	
1829		5,590		22,000		25%
1830		5,490		20,200		27
1831		7,280		27,700		26
1832		4,790		24,900		19
1833		4,590		23,000		20
...						
1837		3,970		21,800		18
1838		4,150		21,300		19
1839	Jan.–Apr. [avg.]		5,170	23,400	22.1	
	May		5,447	24,209	22.5	
	June		6,920[a]	27,167	25.5	
	July–Sept. [avg.]		7,330	28,100	26.1	
	Oct.–Dec. [avg.]		7,590	27,800	27.3	
	(DEC.)	7,540		27,600		27
1840	January		7,636	28,503	26.8	
	February		7,715	29,172	26.5	
	March		7,790	30,138	25.8	
	April		7,905	30,936	25.6	
	May		8,185[b]	30,453	26.5	
	June		7,935	30,536	26.0	
	July		6,349[c]	29,929	21.2	
	July–Sept. [avg.]		6,040	29,700	20.3	
	Oct.–Dec. [avg.]		5,940	28,600	20.8	
	(DEC.)	5,620		28,500		20
1841		5,080		28,800		18

Army force strength on 1 December of each year; for 1839–40, force strength on the first of each month.

Notes pertaining to the Chartist crisis of 1839–40:

[a] Largest monthly increase.

[b] Peak force level.

[c] Largest monthly decrease.

July 1840, 5,750 by July 1841, and 4,750 by July 1842.)[14] One characteristic was, however, different from earlier military buildups. General Napier announced his preference for Irish soldiers – "Irish rather than Scotch, and Scotch rather than English." He requested not only that troops be sent from Ireland but that English regiments that contained "the greatest number of irishmen [sic] should if possible be selected" for northern duty. As Napier candidly noted, "The difference of religion and of country form additional barriers 'round the fidelity of the Soldiers."[15] Fortuitously, Ireland in 1839 was relatively quiet; moreover, the growth of the Irish constabulary to 8,000 men offset the decline in the number of troops (13,000) stationed there.

Dublin Castle thus was able uncomplainingly to give its approval to large troop loans to England. Between December 1838 and August 1839 six regiments – three infantry and three cavalry – were moved from Ireland to the Northern District. Disembarked at Liverpool, the troops traveled effortlessly by rail to Manchester.[16] The importation of these 3,600 men, nearly half of the total military presence in the North, meant that Ireland played a critical role in the suppression of English Chartism.

Like previous military governors of the North, Napier was hard pressed to find accommodation for his troops. Most of the permanent barracks were in the South, legacies of the war of 1792–1815; temporary quarters had to be rented and even less desirable billets found in public and private houses. Napier's correspondence is filled with criticisms of the overcrowded and filthy lodgings and with anxieties about the "corruption" and "seduction" to which his widely dispersed men were exposed. In January 1840, when Napier's troops were more concentrated than in the early months of his command, some 7,200 men were still scattered among thirty towns (see Table 11.2). Manchester and its surrounding towns contained 1,850 men and Newcastle 400, but eight of the towns lodged fewer than 100 soldiers. At Halifax forty-two cavalry were quartered in twenty-one houses.[17]

This dispersal of his men in quarters readily vulnerable to attack worried Napier, especially in the spring and summer of 1839. He warned of the possibility of "midnight massacre" in barracks that were "in the highest degree dangerous." "The Chartists," he fretted, "may place workmen at windows commanding egress from the barracks, and setting fire to the last shoot the soldiers as they attempt to form." He explained to Col. Thomas Wemyss, his commanding officer at Manchester: "In 1798 I saw poor [Captain] Swayne and his 100 Soldiers surprised at Prosperous in the County of Kildare by a suddenly assembled force of peasants who burned him and his *100 Men alive in their Barracks*."[18] For a time, Napier also feared Irish-style assassinations. The murder in Ireland of Lord Norbury, reported Napier in April, had resulted in the circulation in Lancashire of a grisly but "common joke" in which the teller took a bullet from his pocket and asked, "Do you want a Norbury pill?"[19] But Napier's worst Irish-based fears proved to be without foundation. Nocturnal attacks on barracks and selective assassination never became Chartist weapons in Lancashire. Indeed, Napier came to be impressed by the civility and timidity of English mobs. Open confrontations with the troops dissolved into exchanges of good-natured banter, or, on occasions when the demonstrators were more threatening, "the approach of a dragoon made them fly like sheep." Napier was struck by the theatrical quality of many of these confrontations. "In one instance," he noted, "the officer refused to fire, and everywhere the soldiers hung back from bloodshedding, the civilians crying out *slaughter!*"[20]

The Chartist crisis, in fact, produced little personal violence and no serious physical-force challenge to authority. The tumultuous Birmingham riots and the "Battle of the Forth," the so-called Peterloo of Newcastle (30 July 1839), produced no deaths among the police, military, and Chartists.[21] In Wales in

Table 11.2. *Distribution of troops in the Northern District, January 1840*

Town	Total number of effective rank and file	Regiment or part of regiment
Ashton	482	20th Regiment
	31	1st Royal Dragoons
Barnsley	26	1st Royal Dragoons
Blackburn	197	10th Regiment
Bolton	258	86th Regiment
Bradford	25	8th Hussars
	38	81st Regiment
Burnley	67	10th Regiment
Bury	34[a]	1st Royal Dragoons
	171	10th Regiment
Carlisle	78[a]	7th Dragoon Guards
	213	95th Regiment
	51	98th Regiment
	2	Royal Horse Artillery
Chester	212	14th Regiment
	70	Royal Irish Fusiliers
Dewsbury	26	7th Dragoon Guards
Halifax	104	79th Regiment
Haydock	183	86th Regiment
Hull	265	77th Regiment
	136	81st Regiment
	19	Royal Irish Fusiliers
Isle of Man	50	98th Regiment
Leeds	131	7th Dragoon Guards
	175	8th Hussars
	60	Royal Horse Artillery
Liverpool	186	86th Regiment
Loughborough	41	5th Dragoon Depot Guards
Manchester	458	79th Regiment
	74	Royal Irish Fusiliers
Mansfield	43	5th Dragoon Depot Guards
Newcastle-on-Tyne	398	98th Regiment
Newcastle-under-Lyme	68	7th Dragoon Guards
	100	79th Regiment
	61	Royal Horse Artillery
Nottingham	109	1st Battalion, Rifle Brigade
	199	5th Dragoon Depot Guards
	12[a]	5th Dragoon Depot Guards

Table 11.2. *(Continued)*

Town	Total number of effective rank and file	Regiment or part of regiment
Rochdale	101	79th Regiment
Salford	820	96th Regiment
Scarborough	62	81st Regiment
	16	Royal Irish Fusiliers
Sheffield	182	1st Royal Dragoons
	28[a]	1st Royal Dragoons
Stockport	309	20th Regiment
Sunderland	272	98th Regiment
Todmorden	34[a]	8th Hussars
	91	10th Regiment
Tynemouth	225	33rd Regiment
Wigan	159	86th Regiment

[a] Lodged in quarters, i.e. in public houses, public buildings, or private residences. All other troops were lodged in temporary or permanent barracks.

November it was the soldiers who killed twenty persons. "The Chartists," noted Napier, "must shew more pluck to make anything of it. They seem to have shewn none at Newport." In January 1840, "at Sheffield, not a man faced the dragoons."[22] The mildness of the revolutionary threat stemmed both from the reluctance of many Chartists to go beyond intimidation by rhetoric and from their realization that the Government held the preponderance of physical force. This contrast between rhetoric and reality may be seen in a letter Napier wrote to his brother William in May 1839. In it Napier quoted a long piece of Chartist verse whose conclusion urged:

> Let England's sons then prime her guns
>   And save each good man's daughter,
> In tyrants' blood baptize your sons
>   And every villain slaughter.
> By pike and sword, your freedom strive to gain,
>   Or make one bloody Moscow of old England's plain.

The reaction of Napier, the old soldier, to such flights of poesy was blunt and impatient. "This is a nice piece of advice! Well, I have just had out three regiments and two [artillery] guns, and they do not look as if they would be easily beaten!" Three months later Napier developed his thoughts even more explicitly in his journal:

Poor people! ... They will suffer. They have set all England against them and their physical force: fools! fools! We have the physical force, not they. They talk of their hundred thousands of men. Who is to move them when I am dancing round them with cavalry, and pelting them with cannon-shot? What would their 100,000 men do with my 100 rockets wriggling their fiery tails among them, roaring, scorching, tearing, smashing all that came near? And when in desperation and despair they broke to fly, how would they bear five regiments of cavalry careering through them? Poor men! How little they know of physical force![23]

Napier's concern was genuine – he had seen the Irish '98 – but his tone was patronizing. Most of the Chartists were able to see clearly that the military odds *were* against them. It was, in part, precisely because the protesters were aware of the balance of power that they rejected the physical force option.

If the Chartist crisis was contained by the Government's traditional resort to troops, the crisis had pushed the Government to pass the first legislation establishing optional county police. These forces were not in place or effective until the crisis of 1839–40 had passed. Certainly military men were heartened by the prospect of an alternative to the total dependence on the military, which, in Napier's view, only reflected "a want of self-reliance in society." Nevertheless, in the years after 1839, the introduction of modern police institutions outside London would continue to be blocked by a variety of groups, from Chartist workingmen to local ratepayers, from persons fearful of constitutional innovations to corporate bodies jealous of encroachments on their liberties. At Manchester, Colonel Wemyss could remark of the new police in May 1840: "It is well known that the feeling is now against them and that the Mass of the People would rather be kept in order by an Army in Red than by those clothed in Blue." In the 1840s the Government would continue to respect this widespread antipolice sentiment, not least among ratepayers, by moving cautiously to implant the new civil institution. The police were not forced on English counties, as they had been on Irish counties in the 1820s. Nonetheless, slowly if irregularly, the great task of establishing county police forces moved forward. In the meantime, noted Colonel Wemyss, "Until a well organized Civil Force is established, the only security for Life and Property in these populous districts is to have Troops *at hand*."[24]

II. The new police

The government police in Manchester, Birmingham, and Bolton

In consequence of the disturbances in Birmingham in 1839, and the inefficiency of the then existing Police, the Act of the 2 & 3 Vict. c. 88 was passed, by the 7th section of which the provisions of the 10th Geo. 4 c. 44 [the Metropolitan Police Act] were extended to Birmingham.
– Police Commissioner Burgess to Home Secretary Graham,
5 November 1841

Serving in aid of the military power in the critical years 1839–42 were the government police created for three of the most turbulent northern cities. The forces, totaling almost 800 men at their peak, had a mixed record of success and never did live up to their dreaded reputation among the Chartists and ratepayers. In fact, there were really only two forces, the one at Bolton (pop. 51,000) never having more than forty men; following the resignation in

October 1839 of its head, Lt.-Col. E. A. Angelo, the Bolton police became an administrative appendage of the Manchester force. As in Ireland and London, the leadership of the police in Manchester and Birmingham went to seasoned military officers. The Manchester command went to Sir Charles Shaw, a veteran of the Napoleonic wars and more recently (1832–6) the "liberal" British intervention in Portugal and Spain. The Birmingham police was headed by Capt. Francis Burgess, who had joined the army from the Leicestershire militia in 1812, had served under Wellington on the Continent, and after the war, retired on half-pay (1817), had become a Northampton-shire barrister.[25]

Burgess's police in Birmingham was recruited from "such materials as I could find on the spot."[26] The size of the force, which totaled 340 men (30 officers and 310 constables), held steady until 1842, when it was reduced to 300 men. At Manchester, manpower problems were greater. Shaw appointed 64 officers and 319 constables, the great majority of whom had served earlier as borough constables or watchmen. By September 1841, the 319 constables had shrunk to 200. Low pay, drunkenness, and grueling patrol work all took their toll. Shaw complained that his constables were "constantly leaving" and that his best officers were joining the newly formed Worcestershire county police, where salaries were nearly double those paid in Manchester.[27] Rate-payers expressed their feelings about the new police by keeping funding low.[28]

Considering the enormous initial hostility to the force from borough authorities, ratepayers, and Chartists, the accomplishments of the Manchester and Birmingham police were remarkable. Burgess and Shaw made inroads into the strong Chartist hostility by tactfully using the police to keep the peace but not to prevent meetings, processions, and speeches. In July 1840, the arrival of John Collins, a Birmingham shoemaker and Chartist leader just released from prison, drew a crowd of 30,000 to the Bull Ring; Burgess, who did not interfere, marveled that "so large a concourse of people got together by excitable means, disperse themselves so peaceably." More than a year later, in November 1841, he reported, "I have been now two years here, yet I have not had occasion to make *a single arrest for a political offence, nor has the Public Peace been once disturbed.*"[29]

At Manchester the situation was more difficult. Apart from the usual opposition, Police Commissioner Shaw, with a shrinking police force, had to face a refractory town Stipendiary Magistrate, a vocal Anti–Corn Law League, and a large Irish population. Shaw nevertheless became skillful in dispersing mobs and preventing riots. In May and June 1841 his police broke up skirmishes between O'Connor's Chartists and O'Connell's Irish followers; in July they dispersed a crowd of Irishmen turned out for an election fracas. In September, against Irish threats of violence, Shaw furnished protection to O'Connor and some 3,000 Chartists marching in procession.[30] In the Plug Plot Riots of August 1842, Shaw's civil force, reduced to 200 men, was less successful, being swept aside by mobs, numbering in the thousands, who spilled into his jurisdiction from the surrounding unpoliced industrial towns.[31] Overall, however, it seems clear that Shaw's task of peacekeeping was made easier in 1840–2 by the split between English and Irish radicals. They were less dangerous divided than united.

The new police earned the grudging respect of the towns' respectable inhabitants by their spying on the Chartists and the Irish. The Home Office authorities refused to grant money from the Secret Service Fund, for they believed that spying "generally ends in nothing but disappointment." Nevertheless, Shaw and Burgess, who could not afford such aloof idealism, operated their own small systems of spies. Burgess's appears to have been more highly developed; one of the Birmingham police inspectors was even placed in charge of detective work. Historian F. C. Mather has identified at least three constables who acted as undercover men at Chartist gatherings; to his own and Burgess's great embarrassment, Constable James Barnett was exposed as a spy at a Chartist meeting in November 1840. The police received help from Chartists who compromised themselves; the private spy list was headed by Birmingham's physical-force leader Joseph Fussell, who for his services wanted £2 a week. Burgess described him as "a bad one, but in these times the end must justify the means."[32]

More important to Birmingham ratepayers was the success of the new police against crime. In February 1840, Burgess claimed that committals for trial had increased "threefold" since the police were established. A parliamentary return indicates that although the conviction rate stayed the same, the number arrested in Birmingham in 1839–40 (6,000) was more than twice as high as in 1838–9. The great majority of the arrests were for the social offenses of drunkenness, breach of the peace, and vagrancy.[33] In Manchester, the police were instructed to keep the streets clear of layabouts on Sunday and to refrain from the former constables' custom of "knocking up" (awakening) working-class families in the morning.[34] This new brand of law enforcement, though it won plaudits from the middle classes, only irritated the lower orders.

In spite of all their exertions, the government police in Birmingham and Manchester continued to be merely tolerated by these two cities' 400,000 inhabitants as an unpleasant temporary expedient. The Chartists objected to police spying, the workers to "missionary" efforts to reform them. Ratepayers were grateful for police services against crime and Chartism, but they objected to the force's annual expense, which amounted to £24,500 in Birmingham.[35] All parties harbored constitutional objections to a police controlled from London. In July 1840, Birmingham's inhabitants voiced fears about another "intended irruption of London police, of emissaries being employed to create confusion & riot" in their city. The three urban police acts of 1839 were, by law, to lapse in 1841; instead, they were renewed for one year. But in October 1842, with Chartism in decline and the boroughs' charters now legally confirmed, the government police in Birmingham, Bolton, and Manchester were placed in the hands of local Watch Committees pursuant to the Municipal Corporations Act of 1835.[36]

Founding the county police, 1839–56

At the same time that these three northern cities were experimenting with a police controlled from London. the English counties, beginning in the fall of 1839, were considering adoption of the new rural police. The forces, though directed by county magistrates, were defined by regulations emanating from London. The first guidelines were issued in 1840 by the new Home Secretary, the Marquess of Normanby (formerly the Earl of Mulgrave), who had recently served as Lord Lieutenant of Ireland (1835–9).[37] Normanby and the London Government were careful to avoid any hint of comparison between the English county and Irish police. The rank structure of the London, not the paramilitary Irish, force provided the model: constable, sergeant, Inspector, and Superintendent. The Government chose, however, to avoid the foreign word "Commissioner," used in the London police, and adopted instead the ancient term "(Chief) Constable" for the highest county police rank. The force was to be uniformed, which was a departure from the system of parish constables, but apart from requirements that included a greatcoat, cape, and badge, the uniform design was left to the county. Firearms were prohibited; constables were issued only a "staff" (baton).[38] With the approval of two county JPs, the Chief Constable might issue a "small Cutlass," but this weapon was "to be worn at Night only, or at Times when rioting or serious public disturbance has actually taken place or is apprehended." In cases of "any sudden Emergency" the Chief Constable could so arm "One or more of the Constables," but he was required to notify two JPs of this arming "as soon afterwards as is practicable"; they, in turn, were required "immediately" to report the arming to the Home Office.[39]

The Government set certain minimal requirements in hiring. The Chief Constable, at his appointment, could not be more than forty-five years old. Recruits had to be under age forty, 5 feet 7 inches tall, "of a strong Constitution," literate,[40] and "generally intelligent." These qualifications were nearly the identical twin of those of the Irish police. The list of specific occupations (gamekeeper, wood ranger, etc.) that disqualified a man from police service, excepting those associated with the tithe, was a virtual copy of the Irish regulations dating to 1823. As in the London and Irish police, fee taking[41] and a second occupation were prohibited. The Government set the range of salaries at each rank, ranging from 15 to 21 shillings per week for constables through £250 to £500 p.a. for Chief Constables.[42]

Apart from these basic requirements, the Home Office's instructions to the county magistrates were kept general and brief; discretionary use of the force clearly resided with them.[43] The Chief Constable was required to report any serious crime or disturbance to two JPs; he was also required to submit quarterly reports to the county Quarter Sessions and to the Home Office. But he was under no legal compulsion to communicate with boroughs within his county or with other counties.[44] The intent was to establish an optional county police, not a national constabulary.

Table 11.3. *Establishing the county police in England, 1839–56*

Year	For entire county	Size of force		For part of county	Size of force	
		At founding	In 1856		At founding	In 1856
1839	Durham	81	132			
	Gloucestershire	250	250			
	Hampshire	106	247			
	Lancashire	502	593			
	Leicestershire	25	71			
	Shropshire	56	58			
	Wiltshire	201	201			
	Worcestershire	65	116			
1840	Bedfordshire	47	61	Cumberland	4	46
	Essex	136	199	Staffordshire	21	279[a]
	Norfolk	143	197	Suffolk (East)	68	88
	Northamptonshire	51	52	Sussex (East)	33	53
	Nottinghamshire	42	89	Warwickshire	45	74
1841	Hertfordshire	71	71	Cambridgeshire (Isle of Ely)	37	51[b]
				Herefordshire	5	—[c]
1842	Staffordshire	210	279			
1844	[Suffolk, East/West]	[109]	[162]	Suffolk (West)	41	74
1846				Westmorland	1	8
1849				Dorsetshire	12	12
				Rutland	1	1
				Yorkshire (East Riding)	9	9
1851	Cambridgeshire	70	70			
	Surrey	85	111			
1856 (Jan.)	Berkshire	111	111			

Size: Total of rank & file and officers, from second-class constable through Superintendent and Chief Constable.

1856: Force level in the spring of 1856, on the eve of the compulsory County Police Act of that year.

Note: As a result of the localized and sometimes haphazard record keeping, force levels vary slightly in the returns from a few English counties; generally, I have adopted the figure in the earliest return. Dates of founding also vary for some of the forces established in 1839–40; I have adopted the date that magistrates at sessions created the police, not its actual implementation a few weeks or months later.

Five of the ten *Welsh* counties set up police forces. In 1840, Denbigh, 28 men at founding, 33 in 1856; and Montgomery (15; 19). In 1841, Glamorgan (39; 69); in 1843, Carmarthen (57; 38); and in 1844, Cardigan (18; 26). By 1856, these forces totaled 185 men.

[a] Countywide force level; see year 1842.

[b] Separate from Cambridgeshire force; see year 1851.

[c] Disbanded c. 1850.

**ESTABLISHMENT OF ENGLISH
COUNTY POLICE, 1839-1856**

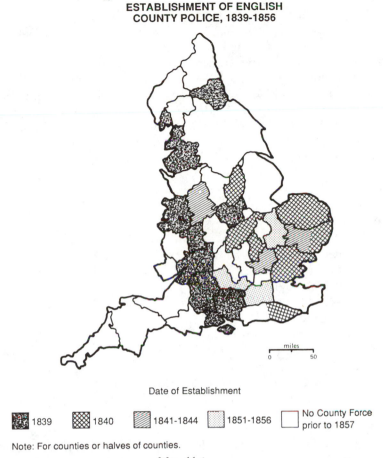

Date of Establishment

1839	1840	1841-1844	1851-1856	No County Force prior to 1857

Note: For counties or halves of counties.

Map 11.1

In the late fall and winter of 1839, magistrates at quarter sessions established the police in eight English counties; another five counties, plus two in
Wales, set up forces in 1840. By June 1840, the new forces were at work in a
third of England's forty counties (see Table 11.3 and Map. 11.1). The police
were concentrated in the industrial Midlands and North (Durham, Lancashire, Leicestershire, Shropshire, and Worcestershire in 1839; Northampton-
shire and Nottinghamshire in 1840). Lancashire, with 502 men, had by far
the largest force; that county's constables comprised about one-third of the
total number of constables recruited in the thirteen counties in 1839–40.
Outside the North, police were established in areas where Chartism had also
been strong. Wales adopted only token forces (157 police in five counties,
1840–4), but Hampshire, Wiltshire, and Gloucestershire, counties deeply
affected by Chartism and by Swing a decade earlier, established in late 1839
forces of 106, 201, and 250 men, respectively. (Hampshire and Wiltshire,
each with a total of 208 Swing incidents in 1830, had been the two most

disturbed of the Swing counties.[45]) In 1840, Norfolk, an old textile center, and Essex, to the east of London, also set up fairly large forces, 143 and 136 men, respectively.

But most of the southern agricultural counties chose not to introduce the new "rural" police.[46] And in many northern counties, establishment of the forces was also widely opposed. Magistrates in Westmorland, Cumberland, and Northumberland were virtually unanimous in seeing no necessity for the new police. In Cheshire and Derbyshire, the JPs also resisted the innovation. In Lincolnshire, a large northeastern county, there was widespread feeling against the police as "a system which tends to break the link of society, and to destroy that chain of good NEIGHBOURHOOD upon which our glorious Constitution was founded, and by which it was carried into effect by King Alfred." In Yorkshire, the largest county in England, the magistrates in the West Riding were united against the new police "inasmuch as for common times and purposes they conceive the present force sufficient, and that upon occasion of outbreak or riot ... no addition to the Police Force which can be contemplated would be sufficient for their protection."[47] The basis for resistance was as much financial as constitutional. Like Irish ratepayers in 1814–21, respectable English property owners in 1839–42 objected to a county-wide tax for the sins of the riotous districts. In Yorkshire, for example, ratepayers in the agricultural eastern part of the West Riding objected to a police tax to establish small forces at Dewsbury, Bradford, Halifax, and Sheffield, industrial towns in the southern and western parts of the Riding. The Government's solution was to pass an act, 3 & 4 Vict., c. 88 (1840), that allowed magistrates to tax parts of a county at rates based on a district's level of crime and disturbance. This amending act, which provided a national forum for county spokesmen to assail the constabulary,[48] did erode some of the hostility to the new institution. The differentiated-rate principle was adopted in Lancashire and Shropshire, and was instrumental in the establishment in 1842 of a countywide force in Staffordshire.[49] But elsewhere the 1840 amending act did little to hasten the spread of the new police. Lincolnshire was only one of many counties to resist implementation until it was made compulsory in 1856. In spacious Yorkshire at that late date, the lone police force consisted of nine constables established in a part of the rural East Riding in 1849.

No clearer evidence exists for the Chartist origins of the English county police than the chronology of implementation. Fully fifteen of the eighteen English counties that adopted the police on a countywide basis over the period 1839–56 did so in the first four years, 1839–42; indeed, thirteen of those fifteen counties acted at the height of the crisis, from October 1839 to May 1840. The late addition of Staffordshire to the county police rolls, in December 1842, was directly attributable to Chartist disorders. (See Map 11.1.) In Wales, after Home Office pressure, Carmarthenshire and Cardiganshire were forced to accept police forces in 1842–4 in the wake of the "Rebecca" Riots, just as earlier, in 1839–40, three other Welsh counties had established forces to counter Chartism. East Suffolk in England established a police force in 1840, and West Suffolk followed in 1844 after enduring a wave of rural protest and incendiarism.[50] Even in those counties where the police were set up only in particular districts, often small ones, the pattern was the same. Most of the police forces established under these circumstances were implanted in the early years. Of eleven counties creating such limited forces in the period 1839–56, seven did so in 1840–4. And the number of constables in these forces was far higher: 309 men in the seven partially policed counties in 1840–4 compared to 30 men in parts of four counties in 1846–9. The clear lesson is that the police were created for and largely implemented during the years of Chartist crisis, 1839–42; with the decline of Chartism after 1842, the stimulus to create police forces also disappeared. Indeed, in Lancashire in July 1842, with the apparent ebbing of the Chartist threat, the county magistrates reduced the number of county policemen by one-third, from 502 to 355.[51]

Antipolice riots, 1839–44

The establishment of the county police, particularly in the North of England, was itself a stimulus to disorders. In May 1840, a magistrate at Todmorden, John Fielden's home town, warned the Home Office: "The very circumstances of their introduction being odious to the greater portion of our inhabitants, renders it more than probable some serious disturbance will be attempted." At Todmorden and elsewhere, the forecast proved to be accurate. A recent scholar, Robert Storch, has identified a number of riots whose principal aim was to "drive the police out of the community." The hostility to the police derived from the workers' perceptions that the "blue devils" came not as crime fighters but as government bludgeon men to break trade unions and mobs and, stresses Storch, as "domestic missionaries" to impose new norms of working-class social behavior.[52]

Without denying the intensity of the feelings of the English protesters, it is important to point out that the English disturbances pale by comparison to the constabulary affrays in Ireland. Storch has discovered seven "anti-police riots" in 1839–44; the fighting was fierce by English standards but only one man, a special constable, was killed.[53] By contrast, in Ireland in 1839–44, sixty-one affrays between the peasantry and the armed and omnipresent constabulary produced sixteen deaths (fourteen peasants, two policemen). The contrast is the more alarming because these years in Ireland were relatively quiet ones after the mayhem of ten years earlier; in the nine years 1827–35, a total of 106 Irish peasants had been killed in constabulary affrays.[54] The relative absence of lethal violence in police affrays in England resulted from differing traditions of personal violence and police activity in the two countries. It must also be observed that in England the Government's lukewarm commitment to the development of a powerful police, indeed its respect for the people's hostility to the institution, kept the forces small. Their size, in turn, weakened the effectiveness of police against mobs. Most importantly, in England, neither the constables nor the crowds carried firearms. Pitched battles there might be, but the injuries on both sides were rarely fatal.

The new county police did record a handful of victories against crowds. In May 1840 at Bradford in Lancashire, a group of county police succeeded in dispersing Chartist rioters. But the key, reported Colonel Wemyss, was "the actual presence of the Troops; tho' not engaged, they gave that confidence to the Constables which caused them to act with Vigour and the Chartists, hearing they were at hand, retired – there can be little doubt of a different result, had the Troops been at a distance of even a few miles." In another incident, at the Lancaster racecourse in July 1840, thirty-four of the "Bloody Rurals," twenty of them being reinforcements sent by railway, managed without military aid to take three prisoners in a riot that was precipitated entirely by the arrival of the police. At Blackburn, in April 1842, a small party was able to curtail a riot without the help of the troops.[55] Such instances, however, were rare.

General Napier had hoped that by establishing "advanced posts of a constabulary force" he could "keep the enemy off" while reducing the age-old reliance on troops. But as a first line of defense, the new police were singular failures. On their introduction in Oldham in the autumn of 1840, a contingent of rural police was mobbed by the townspeople. In Colne a series of riots drove the Lancashire rurals out of the town. At Middleton in May 1840, the police, "strangers" planted there only two weeks earlier, attempted to serve a warrant and in the ensuing riot had to flee to the safety of Manchester. In August, at Bilston, Staffordshire, twelve of the new police were beaten by a mob that attacked a Tory political meeting.[56] In June 1841 at Ashton-under-Lyne, a party of sixty-four Lancashire police was routed by a mob at a local election; the constables, driven back into a police station, were subsequently withdrawn from the town. In November, the police were similarly ineffectual at Bolton, where Colonel Wemyss again reported them to be helpless unless troops were present. In 1842–4, the new police continued to demonstrate their impotence against mobs. In and around Manchester in August 1842 the police were overpowered by assemblages of "Plug Plot" rioters (see "The 'Plug Plot' disturbances, 1842"). Two incidents revealed the antipolice feelings among soldiers who, paid 13d. a day compared to the 3s., 6d. for county policemen, resented their duties of protecting the civil power. At Manchester in May 1843, a policeman's attempt to arrest a rowdy off-duty soldier triggered a riot that eventually involved nearly 1,000 soldiers; it had to be repressed by the military. At Leeds in June 1844, another minor incident involving a soldier and a policeman at a public house produced a three-day riot that was ended only by military intervention.[57]

The most protracted clashes came at Colne, where for five months "the lower classes of an old weaving community and a modern uniformed police" engaged in "a bitter war of attrition." The introduction of sixteen rural constables to the town in April 1840 triggered riots that routed the police; twenty constables dispatched from Burnley were likewise cleared from the streets. The arrival of the military brought cheers from the crowds and an end to the disturbances. But, noted Lt.-Col. H. T. Custance, "they will attack the police when we go away."[58] In May the police force was tripled to about fifty men. A reduction in July to the original level of sixteen constables led to more riots. On the night of 4 August the police were again driven from the town, and troops arrived, as in April, too late. In riots on 10 August the restored constabulary was again cleared out of Colne and one of the seventy special constables, mill owner Joseph Halstead, was killed. There were no further antipolice disorders because General Napier persuaded the Government to lodge a military force and build a barracks in Colne.[59]

III. Explaining the hostility to the new police

Any explanation for the unpopularity of the new police must go beyond the resentment of a constitutional innovation or of an added tax on county ratepayers. One objection was the military nature of the police. Directed for the most part by ex-army officers, the uniformed constables were governed by strict lines of command and operated on regularized beat patrols. Police regulation books of the 1840s emphasized routine military drill as the core of the men's training. As late as 1857, the newly established constables in Dorset were advised to use their own common sense to remedy "the unavoidable deficiency of general instruction."[60] It was this deficiency in the skills of preventive policing and crime detection that only confirmed the popular belief that this gendarmerie without firearms was intended for use against workingmen, rioters, and Chartists. To be sure, the English county forces were less military than their Irish counterparts. English constables were stationed in towns, not scattered across the countryside, and the bulk of the men lived in rented private lodgings, not barracks. But by English standards, the uniform and the command structure, the drilling and the beat patrolling, gave the appearance of an army in all but name. Even the constables were unsure of their new role. The Home Office, for example, had to instruct Norfolk magistrates in December 1840 that policemen were *not* to salute military officers.[61]

Local policing: the Parish Constables Act of 1842

Much of the ordinary policing in the parishes continued to be done by parish constables. David Philips has shown that in Staffordshire the older constables, who resented the intrusive uniformed police, continued to make arrests for larceny, robbery, assault, and breach of the peace, offenses that made up the bulk of normal crime.[62] That they knew the local people and were more popular than the new county policemen only enhanced the parish constables' ability, traditionally maligned by historians, to deal with the numerous petty offenses. Home Office directives explicitly recognized the limits of the new police's jurisdiction: They "may of course be employed in all cases of Assaults, in the Apprehension of Vagrants..., or in any criminal charge whatever," but they were not to act in taking bail, in "summoning Putative Fathers of Bastard Children," in executing distress warrants for nonpayment of poor or church rates, or in "serving Summons in any other *Parish business.*" Police interference in such cases would "greatly interfere with the regular routine of duty."[63] Nor were the police active in prosecutions, which continued to be initiated by private individuals or prosecution societies. Evidence from Warwickshire corroborates Philips's finding that in Staffordshire and Worcestershire the police were involved in a slowly rising percentage, but which by 1860 was still less than half of all prosecutions. Overall, recent studies of Lancashire, Staffordshire, and Bedfordshire have concluded that by midcentury the new police were not dramatically successful in preventing crime. But their presence constituted one reason why, "if crime was not fast disappearing, neither was it growing alarmingly."[64]

Clear evidence that the Government did not expect the new police to shoulder the entire burden of crime fighting in the counties may be seen in the passage of the Parish Constables Act of 1842. Based on reforms suggested two years earlier, the bill was introduced in April 1842 and became law four months later.[65] This mild traditional measure passed without debate because it was an attractive alternative to the county police. Parish vestry meetings were to nominate *ratepayers* aged twenty-five to fifty-five (gentlemen being generally excluded, and alehouse proprietors and gamekeepers disqualified) to serve as parish constables; from the lists supplied by the overseers of the poor, the county magistrates would make the appointments. As in the past, substitutes were permitted, but they had to be approved by the magistrates. In counties that had adopted the County Police Act, the constables would be subject to the commands of the Chief Constable. The act did not require that parish constables be paid, but vestries might authorize salaries drawn from the poor rates and county magistrates were given the option to appoint a salaried Superintending Constable to coordinate all parish constables. All dismissals, of the county officer and his men, rested with the justices.

The Parish Constables Act (1842) has customarily been seen as a belated effort to instill life into a dying institution. Frederic Maitland, writing in the comfort of the 1880s when the parish constable system was long since dead, termed the act "as obsolete as the laws of Ethelbert." Certainly, the Government's intention was to strengthen one of the oldest institutions of local government, but if the parish constables were as alive and active in other counties in the 1840s as they were in David Philips's Staffordshire, then the statute admits of another interpretation. Leon Radzinowicz, who debunks the importance of the act, has written that "the intention was merely to regularise the annual appointment of parish constables by the magistrates." But if we adopt John Foster's argument that the magistrates' control of the 1839 county police was itself an important extension of Crown influence, then the transfer of control of parish constables from the vestries, many of them centers of working-class radicalism, to the county magistrates gives the 1842 act an importance not previously recognized.[66]

Historians have generally described the Parish Constables Act as "a failure from the start." They have pointed to both the smallness of the jurisdictional unit and the great number of parishes (thirty-two in Kent in 1853) for which the Superintending Constable was responsible. We know that by 1846 only 368, a mere handful, of the country's parishes or parish unions had appointed 420 *paid* constables, who were scattered across twenty-one counties.[67] But these statistics tell us nothing about the performance of the numerous officially unpaid parish constables, many of them appointed by lighting, watching, and improvement acts of long usage. In part, historians' bemused criticism of the 1842 act results from the fact that, in retrospect, the statute represents an evolutionary dead end. The 1839 police in time did replace the older system of constables; by the 1860s, parish constables were certainly an anachronism. But in the interim, although they continued to be useless against major disturbances or serious crimes, the parish constables filled their allotted time span by discharging their daily duties against normal minor criminal and civil offenses. Finally, the 1842 act was important because for more than a decade it represented a popular alternative to the generally unpopular county police. In 1846, fifteen of the twenty-three counties in England and Wales that had refused to adopt the rural police had introduced the system of paid parish constables; in Staffordshire, which had both the 1839 and 1842 police, the parish constables were judged "quite adequate" for "any immergency [*sic*] in the Rural Districts."[68] Perhaps the chief virtue of the Parish Constables Act was to offer Englishmen a local police that, by comparison to the county forces, was politically safe. This alternative of adopting a police that was popular, traditional, constitutional, inexpensive, and of unquestioned Anglo-Saxon origins had the effect of diverting some of the heated opposition from the "bloody rurals." Whatever its impact on crime, the 1842 act was a shrewd political move.

"Domestic Missionaries"

The hostility to the new county police stemmed not only from its military organization and deployment against crowds and Chartists but also from its mission to "civilize" the working class. Prevention of crime and apprehensions for larceny, by far the most frequent indictable offense, formed only a part of police duties. The great bulk of arrests were for minor public order offenses like drunkenness and vagrancy, misdemeanors tried summarily by magistrates; many of these small-scale confrontations did not result in arrests. The coming of the new police represented, above all, the introduction of a new social policy regarding traditionally sanctioned working-class behavior. Under the old system, before the 1840s, parish constables and JPs had turned a blind eye to a wide range of working-class customs and pleasures. But the new police came as "unwelcome spectators" and "domestic missionaries" into working-class neighborhoods. Charged "to monitor all phases of working-class life," the police engineered a revolution in social relations by their constant "interference in neighborhood and recreational life." They routinely picked up vagrants, idlers, tipplers, and even patrons standing outside the doors of beer houses. Minor breaches of the peace, rowdyism, and even loud talking were now proscribed.[69] Especially resented was the "move-on system," which remains a central feature of present-day preventive policing. Constables would insist, and sometimes not merely verbally, that workingmen gathered in a small group in the street should "break it up" and "go about their business."[70]

Such policies, as the latter phrase suggests and as recent scholars have emphasized, were part of larger social trends transforming workingmen into time-oriented, sober, diligent *workers*.[71] The police presence at races, fairs, and wakes, and police suppression of gambling and prizefighting and the popular blood sports, dog and cock fighting and bull baiting, were visible signs of Evangelical and Radical sentiment that sought to "improve" English workingmen. In terms of police enforcement, the irony was that constables, men of working-class background, donned a uniform to impose the new middle-class standards of behavior. The workers' resentment grew in part from their perception of policemen as *ex*-workingmen: The constables were seen not to labor at a task but only to walk and watch, ceaselessly. The police seemed to do little for their wages, which at 18 shillings per week were higher than those of laborers or most factory workers; a policeman's job security, barring his proven misbehavior, was likewise resented by a laboring population inured to the cyclical wage cuts and work layoffs of the new industrial system. The crowds' taunts of "blue idlers" and "blue drones"[72] were, in turn, resented by police constables who had to learn to walk up to 20 miles a day in all weather and to work continuous eight-hour shifts with no day off except once every five weeks. Employed factory hands, they knew, had the luxury of a Saturday half-day and a Sunday.

Police recruitment and behavior

To sum up, popular hostility stemmed from the military nature of the new police; from a perception that the force was used more against crowds and Chartists than against criminals; and from its monitoring and missionary functions of watching workingmen and breaking them of their disorderly and dissipated ways. A final factor has to do with the men themselves. From time immemorial, English policing had been rooted firmly and locally in the parish. The revolution brought about in those counties adopting the 1839 County Police Act involved the introduction of strangers to the parish. Recruits were not legally required, as in Ireland, to be natives of another county, but many English constables were strangers to their county of service, and many more whose counties of birth and police service were the same were strangers to the parishes where they worked. Like the New Poor Law, the civil army of uniformed strangers was visible evidence of the new intrusiveness of the state into the parish, the most intimate unit of local government.

In filling the original appointments of Chief Constable in the forces established in 1839–40, county magistrates encountered great difficulties in finding men of professional police experience. The London Commissioners, whose officer staff was a magnet for county recruiting, resisted the drain of their best men; so, too, did the heads of the government police at Manchester and Birmingham and in Ireland. The Home Office warned in particular against imposing too heavily on the London force.[73] Two of the earliest appointments, in December 1839, went to a London police inspector (Richard Harris, Worcestershire Chief Constable) and an officer in the Irish constabulary (Anthony Lefroy, Gloucestershire Chief Constable), but the other county appointments by June 1840 went to five army officers, three navy officers, and two civilians.[74] Subsequent appointments in the 1850s continued the emphasis on men of a military background. A large number of the magistrates' choices proved to be wise ones. The Lancashire Chief Constable, Capt. John Woodford, a native of Preston and a veteran of the Rifle Brigade and the local militia, would become one of H. M. Inspectors of Constabulary in 1856; Chief Constable Capt. J. B. B. McHardy would form a model force in Essex and be a persuasive advocate at the 1853 select committee on police.[75] A few appointments were less happy. Samuel Eve, an ex-London inspector who left to police the small Derwent division in Cumberland, proved to be unpopular and incompetent. Another disappointment was the Norfolk Chief Constable, Lt.-Col. Richard Montagu Oakes. Twenty years earlier, in the Queen Caroline Riots, Oakes, then a captain in the 1st Life Guards, had been responsible for the shootings at Cumberland Gate. Controversy dogged him in the early 1840s as his force earned a reputation for negligence and brutality.[76]

Since repression of popular disorders was a principal reason for the creation of the English county police, the Irish constabulary would seem to have been a logical recruiting ground. But the force's extreme military nature, the differences in society and crime in rural Ireland, and the Irish Inspector-General's reluctance to recommend all reduced the contributions of the Irish constabulary. Only two of the fifteen county forces set up in 1839–42 were headed by Irish police veterans. The 250-man Gloucestershire police, established in November 1839 and judged by some at the Home Office to be too large, was organized by Chief Constable Lefroy, who had been "20 Years in the Irish Constabulary." He laid out his force on the Irish model, with small parties of men posted to different stations, rather than scattered on the English model, singly or by twos in each parish.[77]

Staffordshire was the other county to be headed by an Irish constabulary veteran. Prior to his being named head of the sixty-four-man East Suffolk constabulary (1840–2), Capt. John Hatton had served for seventeen years in the Irish constabulary. His record against Ribbonmen in Louth and tithe resisters in Wicklow clearly impressed the Staffordshire magistrates, who in November 1842 voted to establish a county police force as a means to block any recurrence of the "Plug Plot" disorders of the preceding August. To assist Hatton, the magistrates chose as Deputy Chief Constable (1842–8) Col. Gilbert Hogg, also an Irishman. An army veteran who had served with Sir Charles Shaw in Spain and in the Manchester police (1839–42), Hogg subsequently became Chief Constable at Wolverhampton (1848) and succeeded Hatton as head of the Staffordshire police in 1857.[78]

The peripatetic Hatton and Hogg were typical of the early Victorian police officers and even of their men. The geographical mobility of policemen was remarkable; rotation was a man's own choice, not a service requirement, as in the Irish constabulary, but the effect of introducing strangers to a locality was the same. The rank and file of the county police were drawn largely from the police in London and the half-dozen well-policed large boroughs (including Manchester and Birmingham, 1839–42), from the army (active men and veterans), and in time from the rural laboring class and other county forces.[79] Most recruits were, of course, Englishmen. In the border counties, Scots and Welshmen joined the English police. The Irish did make a small contribution. Irish constabulary officials in the 1840s complained of the drain of men to "the newly forming Rural Police in England."

In Lancashire, because of the tense, sometimes hostile relations between English Chartists and Irish O'Connellites, the Irish appear at first to have been kept out of the county police. But W. J. Lowe has shown that the share of *Irish-born* recruits to the force increased dramatically from 5 percent in 1845–55 to 18 percent by 1866–70. In the early 1840s, there appears to have been a disproportionate share of Scotsmen, the result of drawing on Manchester's disbanded government police, whose Commissioner, Shaw, was a Scot. Thereafter, Chief Constable Woodford, a native of Preston, tended to recruit local lads: Four of five recruits in the mid-Victorian force were from Lancashire, Cheshire, and contiguous counties. But they were not necessarily home-grown, for the Irish share was steadily rising.[80]

The early Staffordshire force (1842–3) has been closely studied. David Philips has discovered that although Chief Constable Hatton hardly drained the Irish constabulary – only one of his officers had served in that force – he did favor his fellow countrymen in hiring. Five of his original thirteen officers (for whom information exists) were born in Ireland. Of the original 210 constables, 82 were natives of Staffordshire and a surprising 56, or 27 percent, were Irish-born. Although Staffordshire men and those (twenty) from adjacent counties accounted for half of the constable recruits, the Irish-born recruits outnumbered the forty-one men who were from the other more distant English counties. The Irish-born (fifty-six men) in the early Staffordshire force greatly outnumbered those who had actually served in the Dublin police (thirteen) or the Irish constabulary (thirteen). The total (twenty-six) who had served in the two Irish police forces was dwarfed by the fifty-five men who were drawn from the recently disbanded government police in Manchester and Birmingham, but it was greater than the total number of men from the English borough forces (twenty-five men) or the Metropolitan Police (nine).[81] Whether a man was Irish-born or had served in the Irish police, the mere presence of Irishmen in the early Staffordshire police was inflammatory to the resident English population of that county.

The Staffordshire police was, of course, in no way representative of the English county police as a whole. We still have no history of the English county police, in part because there were so many separate forces (more than four dozen after 1856). Each force, being locally controlled, reflected local circumstances and needs and the personality of its Chief Constable. Any conclusive findings to match those for the centralized Irish constabulary must await laborious research on each of the county forces.[82] The contribution of the Irish police to the staffing of English county forces was, on balance, probably small, most important in the early 1840s, and greatest in northern England, where the Irish immigrants were concentrated and where the need for Irish constabulary veterans experienced in containing disorders was most acute. By the 1850s, with the growth of English borough and county forces, both the London and the Irish police were losing their uniqueness as recruiting pools. And in the aftermath of Chartism, the police were becoming more valued for fighting crime, not crowds; in the realm of police science, the influence of London, not Ireland, could be expected to increase. Nevertheless, the links between Ireland and England in matters of policing would continue well past midcentury.[83]

Popular reluctance to accept the new police can be explained, in part, by the conduct of the constables. "Lancashire's policemen were not so wonderful," writes Eric Midwinter. He details for the county force a sorry record of drunkenness and assaults on men and women. It is clear that the poorly trained, semiliterate policemen of the 1840s were, by and large, a rough bunch; even in the highly professional 622-man Liverpool force, a total of 2,674 disciplinary reports were filed against the men in 1842.[84] For his part, even the well-behaved constable had reason to grouse. The long, solitary beat patrol in all kinds of weather (the wet climate good for cotton, if not constables), no rest on the weekends, constant supervision by his officers, assigned duties that invariably made him personally unpopular – all of these made police work inherently stressful. Those who did pay him respect the constable seldom had to deal with professionally, and there were many even in the respectable classes who saw only his uniform and stamped him as just another paramilitary ruffian.

The arduous work, and the absence of licensing hours, made drink a strong attraction to men not unaccustomed to it before joining the force. A typical tableau, notes Midwinter, would portray "gloomy ... constables hunched for long hours over their lonely tankards." In the Lancashire and Staffordshire forces, as in the London and Irish police, drunkenness was "by far the commonest" reason for dismissal; other equally familiar causes were neglect of duty, breach of the regulations, insubordination, and assaults.[85] Constables' dismissals and resignations produced a high turnover in police personnel; this, in turn, meant that neighborhoods were policed by an ever-changing set of strangers.

Police records for the 1840s paint a bleakly uniform picture. In the first six months of the Lancashire constabulary (1840), 25 percent of the men were dismissed, the majority (60 percent) for intoxication. Two-fifths of the 892 recruits in 1845–50 left the force within a year. Of these 366 constables, half resigned and nearly two-fifths were dismissed.[86] In the Staffordshire police, half (104) of the original 210 recruits in 1842–3 left within a year and another 29 men left in 1844. By 1848, only one-fifth of the original recruits were still on the force.[87] Similar attrition characterized the Bedfordshire police: Of forty constables appointed in 1840, only twelve were still serving in 1845, and of the forty men serving in 1845, only eleven remained on the force a decade later. In the Cheshire force established in 1856, 30 percent of the original 214 constables were gone in less than a year, and only half were still serving in 1859.[88]

IV. Protest divided: English Chartism and Irish Repeal

To meet the renewed popular challenges in the early 1840s, the Government had in place in England and Ireland two quite different police systems.[89] Unlike the 8,000-man Irish constabulary, now twenty years old, armed, highly centralized, and professional, the new English police was, outside London, a jerry-built system. By 1842, seven years after the Municipal Corporations Act, only the very largest of the incorporated boroughs had efficient police forces. Manchester, Birmingham, and Bolton were about to end a short controversial experiment with London-directed police. The recent optional "rural" police, totaling fewer than 2,000 men in fourteen separate county forces, were equally controversial, so much so that magistrates in England's remaining twenty-six counties had declined the Government's suggestion to set up the new police establishments. The year 1842 even showed signs of a turning away from the experiment with the "Bloody Rurals." The Parish Constables Act attempted to pump life into the old system even as the largest of the new forces, the Lancashire constabulary, reduced its size by a third to some 350 men. In England's boroughs and counties, the halting, even grudging pace of innovations in police meant that protest would continue to be controlled by what, in Irish terms, were archaic means – troops and more troops.

There were other ironies as well. The recurrence of popular protest in the two islands would turn the national stereotypes on their head: widespread violence, mostly against property, in northern England and quiet, protracted moral force demonstrations across most of Ireland. Whereas in the spontaneous English Plug Plot disturbances of 1842 Feargus O'Connor's role was to be quite marginal, in his nonviolent campaign the following year for Repeal of the Union, Daniel O'Connell, now sixty-seven years old, would demonstrate that he was still the "uncrowned king of Ireland." In time and in followers, the two movements were to remain quite separate, the issues being unrelated and the participants even hostile to each other. Not until the end of the decade was there talk of uniting English and Irish radicalism. For Robert Peel, Prime Minister in 1841–6, the twin challenges held a particular interest. The Plug Plot disorders represented Peel's first brush with Chartism; the Repeal campaign, on the other hand, brought him again face to face with O'Connell. O'Connell: As long ago as 1815, the youthful Peel, then Irish

Chief Secretary, had challenged him to a duel;[90] as Home Secretary in 1828–9, Peel had had to grapple with "the Liberator" over Catholic Emancipation. Now England's chief minister would have his showdown with Ireland's ruler. In the twin crises, not the least of the ironies was that Peel, the great innovator of police in both countries, would watch the small new county forces be swept aside in northern England and his beloved Peelers be powerless against O'Connell's Repeal army in Ireland.

The "Plug Plot" disturbances, 1842

> The streets . . . were in an excited state, by the people being all up in arms. I mean by up in arms, that the people were coming out of their houses. I do not mean that the people had any arms in their hands. The people . . . were in expectation of something taking place.
> – Police Constable George Tandy, Birmingham, August 1842

The Chartist agitation in England came in three waves: 1839–40, 1842, and 1848. The second and most violent spasm of disturbances came in the summer of 1842, beginning in mid-July and ending by September. The disorders stemmed from widespread economic grievances and only in their later stages did they become politically motivated, when Chartist leaders attempted to convert local work stoppages into a General Strike.[91] The political situation was all the more inflammatory because now the Government was the traditional enemy: the Tories, led by Peel, now fifty-four, and his tough-minded Home Secretary, Sir James Graham. In early May, Parliament had rejected the second Chartist petition, bearing over 3 million signatures, by a vote of 287–49. The middle-class Anti–Corn Law League, centered in Manchester, was demanding repeal of the Corn Laws in place of the "sliding scale" passed by Peel in April 1842; and O'Connor's followers, in their desire for cheap bread, threatened a temporary alliance with the Lancashire cotton lords.[92] In 1842, one in every fourteen Englishmen was receiving poor relief; property offenses and jail committals hit a peak for the nineteenth century. Around Manchester the proportion on relief was one in five, and the city's comfortable inhabitants had raised a private relief fund totaling £70,000. Throughout the North, a record number of firms went bankrupt, mills and mines shut down due to the slackness of trade, great numbers of men were laid off, and wage reductions averaging 25 percent were demanded of hungry workingmen fortunate enough to have jobs.[93]

The Plug Plot disturbances began in early July 1842 when coal miners in north Staffordshire went out on strike and pulled the plugs from the boilers of the engines at the pitheads. A month later the "turnouts" spread to south Lancashire, where angry crowds had disabled the steam-driven machinery in the cotton mills.[94] In August the protests spread throughout Staffordshire, Lancashire, and Cheshire, and less seriously into western Yorkshire, the east Midlands, the Northeast, and South Wales.[95] The demands of the mobs, often ranging in size from 2,000 to 8,000 persons, and sometimes as high as 25,000, were pithily stated by one crowd at Burslem, Staffordshire: "Our rights and liberties, the Charter, and more to eat." Generally speaking, the crowds were more intimidating than destructive. The Crown Prosecutor, Attorney-General Sir Frederick Pollock, at the subsequent trials in Lancashire, bore "willing testimony" to the rioters' "respect for life and property" and "rejoiced that I live in a country where, if excesses ... occur, they are tempered by ... forbearance and moderation."[96] The worst property violence was born of hunger – assaults on bread shops and on Poor Law workhouses for provisions; mines and factories were stormed only when their owners resisted the call to shut down. The greatest violence occurred in the isolated rural Staffordshire coal districts; in Lancashire "the extremists were mainly Irishmen," minor Chartist leaders of strong "Irish nationalist" beliefs who rejected the moral force of both O'Connor and O'Connell. The Plug Plot rioters did not, like the Luddites, protest against the industrial machinery, but rather its want of regulation. "None but fools would object to its use," said the Irishman, Feargus O'Connor, "but it MUST BE REGULATED.... It is to the *abuse* that we object."[97]

The civil power played little role in the suppression of the Plug Plot disturbances. Special constables were usually nowhere to be found; when used, they were ineffective. The Government police, in their last months of service in Bolton and Manchester, proved to be of little help. The tiny force in Bolton was overpowered and the town occupied. At Manchester, with no cooperation from the city's Stipendiary Magistrate, Police Commissioner Shaw did his best to deploy his 200 men against a crowd of 5,000 marching from Ashton-under-Lyne, but they too were swept aside. In the ensuing disorders, one of Shaw's constables was killed, and the Government had to despatch a London police court magistrate to the city to help with the arrests of Plug Plot leaders.[98]

The county police fared no better. Staffordshire magistrates, content with the system of parish constables, had refused to adopt the new rural police for the entire county; in 1842 the only new police force, the twenty-one-man force established in 1840 for the mining district of Offlow South, was easily swept aside. The absence of the bloody rurals in Staffordshire undoubtedly contributed to the swift progress of the turnouts there, but the behavior of the county police in Lancashire suggests that their presence would not have stemmed the disorders. Lancashire Chief Constable Woodford faced the crisis with a reduced force; in an economy move at the July 1842 Quarter Sessions, magistrates had slashed the number of county policemen from 502 to 355. Woodford, following military policy, concentrated his remaining men at key points. Large areas were thus left exposed to the crowds' whims; the riots at Ashton-under-Lyne, Hindley, and Stalybridge occurred with no police present. But the presence of police made little difference. At Newton a mob of 5,000 destroyed the police station and killed two constables; a like number of Chartists turned aside a large body of police at Leigh; and another mob routed the seventeen policemen at Preston and seized the town. "The county," writes F. C. Mather, "was reduced to a dependence on military aid which could hardly have been exceeded had there been no rural police."[99]

The intensity and duration of the disturbances – continuing for nearly two months in north Staffordshire and for a month in Lancashire – were in part a product of what Queen Victoria unamusingly described as the "passiveness" of the troops and the laxity of local Whig magistrates. The initial reluctance of JPs to use the army led many contemporaries, including not only Peel and Graham but also the Chartist O'Connor, to view the disorders as a "plot" by the Whig–Radical Anti–Corn Law League to force the Tory Government to abandon its policy of agricultural protection.[100] This interpretation, now discredited, was plausible because of the numerous occasions when magistrates refused to employ troops against the rioters. The Manchester Stipendiary Magistrate refused to assemble the city's military force – 150 cavalry and 500 infantry – against the invasion of 5,000 east Lancashire mill hands.[101] At Bolton, Burnley, and Rochdale the authorities held back the troops. The Mayor and magistrates at Stockport, where the crowds took 700 seven-pound loaves from the workhouse, did not employ the forces at hand – three troops of Cheshire Yeomanry, a detachment of 72d Highlanders, and 2,000 special constables. In fact, magistrates' actions resulted from no plot but from a number of other reasons. Many viewed the disorders, originating in distress, as a kind of latter-day urban food riot and were willing to bargain with the rioters; others, seeing the troops outnumbered, gave in to prevent bloodshed. The Commander of the Northern District, Maj.-Gen. Sir William Warre, pursued extremely conciliatory policies. He refused to split up his troops and regularly denied requests for small detachments; he would not grant troop loans until proper barracks were prearranged; he preferred to keep the troops in barracks until riots broke out.[102] The perception in London of growing chaos in the north Midlands and Lancashire, thanks to a lack of firmness by magistrates and troops, led to direct government intervention. (See Figure 11.2.)

The Duke of Wellington assumed the command of the army on 10 August. Peel's Cabinet, after meeting with Queen Victoria on the 12th, issued the next day a Royal Proclamation prohibiting all public meetings and offering £50 rewards for prosecution of rioters.[103] That evening, to the groans of a crowd at Charing Cross Station, 700 Grenadier Guards and 36 artillerymen with two cannon left London by train; nine hours later, they arrived in Manchester at 5 A.M. on the 14th. That afternoon the Guardsmen were reinforced by 700 men of the 58th Regiment arriving by train from Liverpool; more troops and artillery arrived by train from Leeds and London on the 15th. The railway system thus enabled the Government to place 2,000 soldiers in Manchester in less than forty-eight hours. Momentarily, Wellington regretted his haste, for a London sympathy demonstration was announced for 22 August; but it went off uneventfully, watched by thousands of London police and troops rushed in by rail from Taunton and Plymouth in the quiet Southwest.[104] Five days after Sir Charles Shaw had watched helplessly the invasion of Manchester (9 August), the city was reclaimed by the Government. By the evening of the 14th, 500 placards and 5,000 handbills announced the Queen's Proclamation; the next day, in the

Figure 11.2 The English Plug Plot Riots, 1842. (*Illus. London News*) "Attack" on the Stockport workhouse (*above*), and the departure of troops by rail from London.

Town Hall, the army set up its command post, 2,000 special constables were quickly mobilized, thirteen police stations were given military support, and the turnpike gatehouses on every road out of the city were provided a complement of soldiers and special constables. Finally, on 17 August,

General Warre was replaced by Lt.-Gen. Sir Thomas Arbuthnot, who headed a new military district combining the Northern and Midland commands.[105]

The threat to order in 1842 was more psychological and political than physical. Whole districts appeared to be out of the control of established authorities; it was for this reason, and not because of any widespread personal violence from either protesters or police and troops, that the Government mobilized its forces of repression. Crowd deaths before 13 August had been few and scattered. At Newton on 6 August, two policemen were killed by a mob attacking the station; on the 8th, troops at Salford opened fire, killing no one but seriously wounding seven persons; on the 9th, at Stalybridge, defenders at a cotton mill owned by H. H. Birley, Tory Yeomanry captain of Peterloo fame, refused to shut down and had thrown paving stones from the roof onto rioters below, killing a little girl.[106]

The bulk of the lethal violence in the Plug Plot Riots came *after* the government crackdown (see Map 11.2). At Burslem, in north Staffordshire, troops killed a rioter on 16 August; to the south, in the Black Country, "most of the serious clashes," David Philips tells us, "came in the last week of August and first week of September." In Lancashire, at Preston on 13 August, a party composed of the 72nd Regiment (Highlanders), the Rifle Brigade, and the Wigan troop of Lancashire Yeomanry commanded by Lord Francis Egerton (the same man who, then named Leveson Gower, had been Irish Chief Secretary, 1828–30) opened fire on a mob, killing four persons. Three days later, at Salter Hebble, near Halifax, in the West Riding of Yorkshire, a crowd of several thousand stoned ten soldiers of the 11th Hussars who had just escorted seventeen prisoners to the railway station at Elland. In a short fierce fight, one soldier was killed; arriving cavalry reinforcements shot and killed two rioters.[107]

Historians, rightly emphasizing the scope, duration, and intensity of the Plug Plot disorders, have, however, not remarked on the relatively small amount of bloodshed. By my count, a total of twelve persons – eight "rioters" and four on the side of the authorities (one soldier, three policemen) – were slain in July and August 1842.[108] The Chartist disorders of 1839–40 had claimed twenty lives, all of them in the single incident at Newport; the Reform disturbances, sixteen (twelve at Bristol); and Swing, only one. Once again, in retrospect it seems that a "rising" in England had been suppressed rather easily. The "rebels" took few lives and lost twice as many as did the official forces. In the event, the Government used no more lethal violence against the protesters than was brought to bear against the peasantry in a constabulary affray in Ireland.

The country's rulers were genuinely alarmed by the Plug Plot disturbances. Former Prime Minister Melbourne judged the outbreak "certainly very near, if not actually, a rebellion"; Home Secretary Graham thought the situation was "more serious" than the Chartist crisis of 1839–40. There were a number of reasons for this fear. One was the Tories' alarm at a possible alliance between middle-class Anti–Corn Law Leaguers and working-class Chartists and union organizers; and had this eventuated, the Government

'PLUG PLOT' DISTURBANCES, 1842

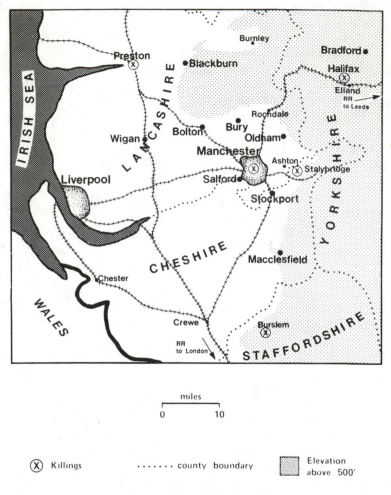

Map 11.2

would have been justifiably alarmed. As it was, the disturbances "broke with more concentrated force" than the earlier Chartist crisis; geographically the Plug Plotters cut a wider swath than had the Luddites, and property destruction may have surpassed the work of Swing's followers.[109] The lower orders controlled large areas of Staffordshire for two months and much of Lancashire and western Yorkshire for nearly a month. It was this successful intimidation, as well as the damage to property, that made the movement so alarming. The Government responded by making twice as many arrests in 1842 as in 1839–40. Special commissions were sent into Staffordshire and Lancashire to supplement the processing of rioters at county Assizes.[110] More than 1,100 persons were arrested; roughly three-fourths (749) received prison sentences, the great majority for one year or less.[111] In 1839–40, nineteen Chartists, fifteen of them Welsh, had been sentenced to transportation; in 1842, nearly eighty were, fifteen of them for life. Two-thirds (fifty-four persons) of those sentenced to be transported, and half (seven) of those receiving transportation for life, were colliers and potters from Staffordshire, where property destruction had been the fiercest.[112]

How serious was the revolutionary threat of the Plug Plot riots? Why did they fail? The massive and quick repression, once the Government entered the fray in mid-August, certainly helped to break the back of the movement. The Home Secretary's nature was critical here: Graham, unlike Russell in 1839, was highly intolerant of disorders and prone to see in them the darkest motives. As a result, in Mather's happy phrase, "he was a little disposed to wield a sledgehammer for the purpose of cracking a nut."[113] In discussing why the Plug Plots failed, we must ask what it was the rioters sought. Here the ground becomes treacherous because, more than in any other major disturbance in the early nineteenth century, the rioters of 1842 were not united in purpose. Most seem to have wanted simply a return to the wages of 1840; some also pressed for the Charter; many feared that they were the pawns of an Anti–Corn Law League plot.[114]

The debate over tactics – to restrict action to a local turnout or to call a General Strike; to destroy property in the mines or mills or to abstain from violence – similarly paralyzed the movement. Generally, it was the major Chartist spokesmen, including O'Connor, and the trade union leaders who preached nonviolence and the hungry, hard-pressed workingmen who ignored their leaders' pleas for restraint. Property destruction, although extensive, was also selective. The riots of 1842 produced no collective violence pitting one *class* against another; as in earlier food riots and the Luddite and Swing disorders, the property of obnoxious individuals or hated firms was targeted for damage. Aggravated violence against persons, and the fear of assassination that had surfaced in 1839–40, were noticeably missing in 1842.[115]

In sum, the disturbances were more in the nature of hunger riots than signs of imminent revolution. Begun as a protest against further major wage reductions, the disorders never achieved a commonality of political purpose. That they did not is hardly surprising. The Chartist call for a thirty-day General Strike, the "Sacred Month," came at a time when the workers were least able to afford a protracted work stoppage as the means of obtaining the vote. By the end of August, noted Home Secretary Graham, most of the workers were back at work.[116]

The aftermath of the Plug Plot Riots produced few innovations in public order. Despite Graham's threat of a widespread recall of soldiers who "cannot be allowed to supply the place of constables," only one county, Staffordshire, acted in November 1842 to establish a police force. This was accomplished by using the amending act of 1840, which permitted districts to be taxed for police proportional to the level of disturbance; the rate in "the Potteries," at 5d. per pound, was five times higher than in the Rural

District. Outside Staffordshire, in other disturbed counties, the opposition prevailed as JPs in Cheshire and Yorkshire refused to establish a civil institution they judged to be ineffectual, costly, and controversial.[117] Not until 1851, a full decade later, would the next English county elect to adopt the optional rural police.

Graham's proposal for paid government magistrates was even more controversial. A Home Office inquiry into the conduct of local magistrates in the disturbed districts had persuaded him of their partiality and unreliability. Graham therefore suggested, in November 1842, that Stipendiary Assistant Barristers attend sessions and assizes to assist county JPs. Edwin Chadwick, the centralist police reformer, favored this plan for "a resident, paid, and responsible Magistrate" and noted "the great service rendered by the appointment of Assistant Barristers in Ireland" since 1787.[118]

But Graham's Tory colleagues, including two former Irish Chief Secretaries, were less enthusiastic. Henry Goulburn, now Chancellor of the Exchequer, and Prime Minister Peel both opposed the scheme with arguments reminiscent of those of Lord Carysfort, a half-century earlier, on the occasion of the Irish county police bill of 1787. Chancellor Goulburn warned against

the growing tendency to withdraw the administration of business, judicial, financial, or administrative, from the hands of the upper classes of society, and to vest it in officers of the Government. . . . The man who now feels compelled to act in public as a magistrate . . . would otherwise degenerate into an idle and useless member of society, living either in London or by the seaside according to the season of the year, and failing, on the one hand, to perform his proper duty to his dependents, and, on the other, to receive the respect which is now justly paid to him.

Peel's comments, in light of his own contributions to Irish police history, were especially ironic. The Prime Minister disapproved of the measure as at once despotic and "democratic, . . . first, as an innovation on that which is established; secondly, as a material transfer of just and legitimate influence. . . . It will strike a blow against the useful influence of the best part of the local and provincial aristocracy of the country." Both men concluded that the English magistracy should be left well enough alone; otherwise it might follow the Irish example and be stripped of its legitimate power and influence.[119]

By mid-December, Home Secretary Graham, a Scotsman, acceded to their arguments and abandoned his proposal, which, in any event, would have stood no chance of passage in an English Parliament. The concept of Assistant Barristers, imposed on Irish gentlemen two generations earlier, continued to be viewed in England in 1842 as not only Crown tyranny but judicial superfluity. English JPs, for all of their occasional failings, were still sufficiently numerous, loyal, and capable that they could continue to be entrusted with the administration of the Queen's Justice.

Similarly conventional, in the aftermath of the Plug Plot Riots, was the Government's decision to make do with the military, not the police, solution. The Yeomanry, which saw more service in 1842 than in any

Table 11.4. *Military mobilization in the Plug Plot disorders and aftermath*

| | | Army force levels | | | Yeomanry called out in aid of the civil power | | | |
		Northern District	England and Wales	Percent in North	Officers and men	No. of troops	Total days on duty	No. of counties
1841		5,080	28,800	18%	c. 100[a]	2	6	3[b]
1842	Jan.–June [avg.]	4,990	29,400	17.0	c. 3,800[a]	71	208	12[c]
	July	4,391	27,403	16.0				
	August	4,463	27,943	16.0				
	September	6,933	28,488	24.3				
	October	6,601	27,937	23.6				
	November	6,980	29,392	23.7				
	(DEC.)	6,700	30,000	22				
1843		6,290	31,300	20		—		
1844		5,760	31,500	18		—		
1845		5,640	28,500	20	242	4	27	3[d]
1846		4,690	29,200	16		—		
1847		5,390	33,500	16	1,059	22	56	2[e]
1848		8,540	35,000	24	3,007	54	66	12[f]

Note: For Yeomanry, the *year* is the year ending 31 March; thus 1841 is 1 Apr. 1841 to 31 Mar. 1842. Figures *exclude* any Yeomanry called out in Scotland and Wales. No Yeomanry were called out in England in 1843, 1844, and 1846. Army force strength on 1 December of each year; for 1842, figures are for the first of each month.

[a] No data on numbers of men in source, *PP 1844.* Estimates for 1841–2, based on data for 1845, 1847–8, assume a range of 45 to 60 men per troop.

[b] Cheshire, Nottingham, Stafford.

[c] Cheshire, Derby, Gloucester, Lancashire, Leicester, Shropshire, Somerset, Stafford, Warwick, Westmorland, Worcester, York.

[d] Devon, Oxford, Westmorland.

[e] Devon, Somerset.

[f] Bucks, Cheshire, Derby, Essex, Lancashire (1 troop, 35 men, out one day only), Leicester (greatest usage in 1848: 8 troops, 490 men, out 40 days), Middlesex, Nottingham, Somerset, Warwick, Worcester, York.

previous year, was increased by 1,000 men. The expansion came in the Midlands and the North as Yeomanry troops in southern and eastern England were reduced or disbanded. Following a plan proposed by the Duke of Wellington, the army pensioners, little used in 1842, were reorganized into an auxiliary military force. One of the four military officers placed in charge of the new body was Lt.-Col. Angelo, the former Bolton Police Commissioner. An act of 1843 added the Greenwich naval out-pensioners to this army reserve force.[120] In 1844, 400 Enrolled Pensioners in Manchester, 300 in Liverpool, and 240 in Birmingham were available for emergency duty. By 1848 the national muster rolls totaled 8,700 pensioners; more than 1,000 of these men would be called out in that year for guard duty throughout London.[121]

The 1842 riots had caught the Government by surprise. Army strength in the Northern District in 1841 had fluctuated between 5,000 and 5,400 men; it declined in the spring of 1842 so that by early July, on the eve of the disorders, only 4,400 soldiers remained in the district. (See Table 11.4.) Rail shipments during the crisis in August swelled the troop level by the end of that month to 6,900, a 57 percent increase. After the Plug Plot Riots, the Tory Government maintained high force levels in the North; more than 6,000 soldiers were kept there until early 1844, and troop strength did not drop below 5,000 until late 1846. By an act of 1842, passed prior to the disturbances, and another of 1844, the Government clarified its contractual arrangements with railway companies for the transport of troops. The railway network itself, which had been crucial to the repression of the Plug Plot disorders, doubled in miles of track from 1842 to 1848 (see Map 12.2). The Tories also instituted a modest boom in barrack building. Expenditures for permanent barracks in the Northern District doubled in two years to £45,000 by 1843; in 1844, £117,000 alone was earmarked for the construction of a cavalry barrack at Manchester. Permanent barracks were also constructed at Bury and at Ashton-under-Lyne with a view to overawing Rochdale, Bolton, and Wigan, and Oldham, Hyde, and Stalybridge, respectively.[122] As the nineteenth century neared its midpoint, the Government continued to avoid innovations in police, choosing rather, as it had since the Luddite period, to rely on the less controversial military response to popular disturbances.

Irish agitation for Repeal of the Union, 1843

[I]n Ireland there exists, apart from, and hostile to, the regular government, a machinery of government wielding a more commanding influence over the people than is possessed by any regular government in the world. Mr. O'Connell ... wields six millions as if they had but one body and one soul.... To any thinking man this uniform obedience, and the perfect quiet consequent on it, are the most formidable signs of the feeling and purpose of the Irish people. They break out into no partial riots; they evince no disposition to resort to arms; ... they seem ... to know the exact measure of their strength, and to be determined not to

waste it, but to preserve it until they can strike with effect. This is the plain state of things in Ireland.
          – Charles Buller, House of Commons, February 1844

Only six months after the Chartist crisis in England, Peel's Government was faced with an even more formidable challenge. Daniel O'Connell's campaign in 1843 for Repeal of the Union had a number of causes. The Liberator's six-year alliance (1835–40) with the English Whigs and Radicals had won gains for middle-class Catholics in voting and officeholding but offered precious little to the mass of the people. Both the Irish Reform Act (1832), which left the county franchise at the level set by Emancipation in 1829, and the Irish Municipal Corporations Act (1840), which enfranchised only £10 householders, were far less liberal than their English counterparts.[123] Equally, the Whigs, in refusing to increase the Irish representation at Westminster, had made no concessions to Irish nationalism. Their economic policies were equally limp. The Whigs ignored the agrarian problems of Irish landlordism and small, unproductive tenant holdings. The tithe question they settled (1838) only by coverting the reduced tithe obligation to a tithe rent charge and transferring responsibility for payment from tenant occupiers to landlords. Finally, the Whigs' response to the challenge of Irish poverty only triggered protests, which in impoverished Ireland were widespread.[124]

In the Irish Poor Law Act of 1838 the Whig Government sought to replicate in Ireland the English New Poor Law passed four years earlier. Against the recommendations of their own Irish Poor Law Commission, which favored private relief and state-sponsored schemes of public works, emigration, and agricultural education, Melbourne and Russell insisted on indoor relief in workhouses administered by commissioners in Dublin and funded by local ratepayers.[125] For a country with a poor tax base and perhaps a quarter of its population immiserated, the Whigs' proposal was grossly unrealistic. Implemented in the summer of 1842, coincident with the English Plug Plot unrest, the Irish Poor Law produced immediate resistance and little revenue. In Waterford the poor rioted and the ratepayers withheld in a rebellion that spread to Cork, Tipperary, Limerick, and Wexford, thence throughout the three Catholic provinces and even into Ulster. On numerous occasions 100 police and military out all day would return with less than a shilling collected; in parts of the west in 1843, a total of 8,000 men on duty were able to collect only £1,600. Scenes from the Tithe War were re-enacted: The constabulary and then the army were sent in to protect rate collectors and to distrain livestock, whose sales at public auctions were widely boycotted.[126]

Just as Feargus O'Connor had channeled the anti–Poor Law agitation in England to the broader cause of Chartism, so his fellow Irishman, Daniel O'Connell, turned the protests against the Irish Poor Law to the grander cause of Repeal of the Union with England. Two years earlier, in 1840, O'Connell's bid to promote the Repeal cause had aroused little public interest. But in 1841–2 a series of events, in addition to the Poor Law crisis,

MONSTER MEETINGS FOR IRISH 'REPEAL', 1843

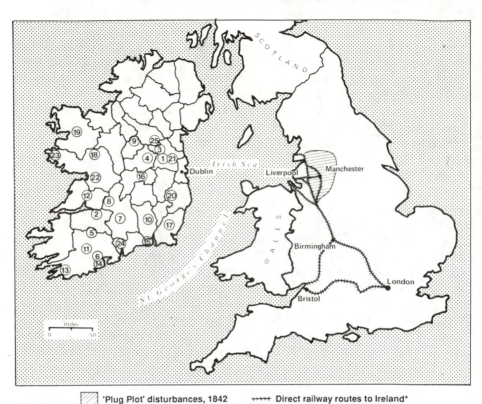

| | | 'Plug Plot' disturbances, 1842 | ┼┼┼┼ Direct railway routes to Ireland* |

Crowds of 100,000 and Over

1 Trim	7 Cashel	13 Skibbereen	19 Castlebar
2 Limerick	8 Nenagh	14 Donnybrook	20 Baltinglass
3 Kells	9 Longford	15 Waterford	21 Tara
4 Mullingar	10 Kilkenny	16 Tullamore	22 Loughrea
5 Charleville	11 Mallow	17 Enniscorthy	23 Clifden
6 Cork	12 Ennis	18 Tuam	24 Lismore
			25 Mullaghmast

1-9: March-May   10-19: June-July   20-25: August-October

*Virtually no railways in Ireland: only 65 miles of track by 1845.

Map 11.3

favored the reemergence of an Irish mass movement. The traditional enemy, the Tories, returned to power under "Orange" (or, as O'Connell now dubbed him, "crafty spinning jenny") Peel. O'Connell was elected Lord Mayor of Dublin, the first Catholic since 1688. The national journal, *The Nation*, began weekly publication in October 1842. And the temperance campaigns of a Capuchin friar prepared the way for O'Connell: Father Theobold Mathew drew huge outdoor crowds who took the pledge to sobriety and seriousness. Against this background, in January 1843, Daniel O'Connell launched the Repeal movement with his manifesto *To the Irish People*. In March the campaign gathered force as the Dublin Corporation, followed by other town authorities, endorsed Repeal. O'Connell's program was specific: abolition of the Poor Law and the rent tithe, universal suffrage by secret ballot, security of tenure for peasant occupiers, and protection for Irish industry.[127]

The Repeal campaign was the third and final great popular movement in Ireland before midcentury. O'Connell believed that the earlier struggles for Emancipation and against tithe had demonstrated that "every change of political institutions should be effected by exclusively moral and peaceful means." The preponderance of physical force – 9,000 police and 15,000 troops – lay with the Government.[128] History had demonstrated that in Ireland blood was spilled too easily, too copiously; the disastrous Rebellion had produced the Union whose repeal was now sought. "Multitudinous public sentiment ... could alone obtain success." Physical numbers and orderly behavior were to be the peasantry's most effective weapons; they guaranteed "both strength and safety."[129] O'Connell's tactics in 1843 thus bore many similarities not only to his own Emancipation campaign of 1826–9 but also to O'Connor's strategy in the Chartist meetings and processions of 1838–9.

For seven months, from March to October 1843, O'Connell roused millions of Irishmen in a grand moral crusade (see Map 11.3). In the late 1820s tens of thousands had turned out; in the "Repeal Year," hundreds of thousands assembled. The Chartist demonstrations paled before what *The Times* termed the Irish "Monster Meetings." O'Connell later claimed to have addressed forty such assemblages. Even allowing for the exaggerations of Repealers and newspapers, the estimates of crowd size are awesome:[130]

Monster meetings: date, location, and crowd size					
19 March	Trim	100,000	3 July	Donnybrook	200,000
19 April	Limerick	120,000	9 July	Waterford	500,000
23 April	Kells	150,000	16 July	Tullamore	150,000
9 May	Mullingar	100,000	20 July	Enniscorthy	400,000
19 May	Charleville	200,000	23 July	Tuam	200,000
21 May	Cork	500,000	30 July	Castlebar	400,000
23 May	Cashel	300,000	6 August	Baltinglass	150,000
24 May	Nenagh	500,000	15 August	Tara	500,000
28 May	Longford	100,000	10 September	Loughrea	150,000
8 June	Kilkenny	300,000	17 September	Clifden	150,000
11 June	Mallow	300,000	24 September	Lismore	150,000
15 June	Ennis	500,000	1 October	Mullaghmast	250,000
22 June	Skibbereen	500,000			

At every meeting, O'Connell exhorted the people to "abstain from crime" and alcohol, and millions temporarily took the temperance pledge. He counseled them to ignore Orangemen, landlords, the constabulary, and the army; to "join no Chartists, no physical-force men, no secret societies." The countryside became strangely quiet as agrarian crime subsided (see Tables 9.9 and 11.5). O'Connell told the multitudes at Kilkenny: "We will grind their faces by behaving well." The immense crowds, controlled by "O'Connell's police," were quiet and good-humored, filled with "decently dressed, respectable" men, women, and children (see Figure 11.3). Preceded by evening torchlight processions up to 5 miles long, the meetings, often held on Sundays, were marked by a festival atmosphere as temperance bands provided music and priests conducted dawn religious services.[131] O'Connell's belief in moral force was made clear in his choice of meeting places; almost all were near large military barracks.[132]

During the agitation, the bulk of the police and military were kept in the background, in barracks. Nothing was done to prevent the meetings. But army officers were widely employed to estimate crowd sizes and report on speeches, and police constables were "disguised in plain clothes" in order "to make observations." O'Connell was aware of the surveillance and good-naturedly asked the men to join the Repeal ranks; to the crowds' delight, he would sometimes lapse into Gaelic to confuse the note takers. At a meeting in early September, O'Connell exposed a London police officer who had been sent over as a "journalist"; the disguised English policeman, to his surprise, was well treated and only feared for his safety six weeks later after O'Connell's arrest. Constabulary reports established that the Repealers had few ties to the agrarian secret societies, that agrarian violence was on the decline, and that no insurrection was imminent.[133]

Until late spring, Prime Minister Peel was more concerned with Ireland's anti–Poor Law disturbances than with Repeal.[134] But from May on, Irish Tories and Orangemen led by the Earl of Roden and the alarmist Lord Lieutenant De Grey urged Peel to act to prevent a rebellion in Ireland. Graham and Wellington adopted this fear of insurrection, but Peel, supported by Chief Secretary Lord Eliot, refused to be panicked. The Prime Minister was convinced that a waiting game would be most effective. O'Connell, he reasoned, would lose credibility as the months passed and Repeal continued to be withheld; if others in frustration resorted to violence, the Government would have its excuse for a massive crackdown.[135] O'Connell, remembering the Tithe War, feared "the maniac disposition of Stanley," now Colonial Secretary in Peel's Cabinet, but in fact Stanley was one of the few ministers who opposed a coercion bill for Ireland.[136] Peel vetoed Wellington's suggestion to resurrect and deploy the northern Protestant Yeomanry.[137] Peel's refusal to ban the peaceable meetings stemmed in part from his fear that coercion in Ireland might exacerbate the current tithe resistance in Wales and the anti–Corn Law agitation in northern England.[138]

The London Government was not altogether inactive. First, in May, two dozen Irish magistrates who had announced their conversion to Repeal were

KING O'CONNELL AT TARA.

Figure 11.3 Two English views of Irish Repeal: the meeting at Tara, 1843. The *Illustrated London News* reports orderly multitudes demanding repeal of the Union. But *Punch's* satire shows "King O'Connell" fawned over by the Irish peasantry as he does the work of the devil, in the process trampling on the British Constitution. Note the "Paddy" policemen in light background left.

stripped of their commissions.[139] Second, Peel, though with private mis-givings, persisted with an arms bill he had prepared before the Repeal crisis. Essentially a police measure to bar the import of firearms and to require their registry and licensing with the constabulary, the bill proposed to give the police broad powers of search and seizure in the war against agrarian crime. The arms bill drew the opposition of English Whigs and Radicals, and Irish Repealers, and after interminable debates it passed in a much weakened form.[140] Third, Peel authorized the shipment of extra troops to Ireland. As early as April, four regiments were transferred from England. In June, more arrived from as far away as Gibraltar, Canada, and India, and still more were disembarked in October.[141] But the Government did not unleash the military in Ireland. Wellington and Home Secretary Graham, who had used troops to crush the Plug Plot disorders the previous year, were inclined to a military solution. But the unflappable Peel, drawing on his long Irish experience, prevailed and won the waiting game.

As early as June, O'Connell realized he had lost: Repeal would never be granted. By August the Repeal rent was declining weekly. The police reported that the people were concentrating on gathering the plentiful harvest. O'Connell's following was splitting apart as men like William Conner (a relative of Feargus O'Connor), frustrated with the failure of moral force, pressed ahead with demands for a boycott of rent, tithe, and poor rate payments.[142] O'Connell's great movement ended, abruptly and anticlimactically, in early October. In advertising the meeting outside Dublin, at Clontarf, where nearly a million people including Irishmen from Manchester and Liverpool were expected to attend, the Dublin Repeal Committee, without consulting O'Connell, rashly issued a proclamation laden with military language. Peel, after six months of waiting, finally had his mouse trapped: The Government issued its own proclamation banning the Clontarf meeting. Fearing bloodshed, O'Connell quickly agreed to honor the cancellation. On 8 October, 500 police patrolled the streets of Dublin and 400 armed constables and 2,500 soldiers plus four artillery pieces occupied Conquer Hill at Clontarf; at three o'clock in the afternoon, Lt.-Gen. Edward Blakeney, commander of the army in Ireland, and Col. Duncan McGregor, Inspector-General of constabulary, appeared at the meeting site and stayed for an hour. Even in defeat, O'Connell demonstrated his hold over his disciplined followers: No one showed up to challenge the forces of the Crown that day.[143]

To the end, the Liberator remained convinced that "no amelioration . . . in the laws or government, . . . is worth the purchase by the loss of one single life."[144] O'Connell's rejection of physical force demonstrated his great dilemma. He had counted on the power of a great moral argument witnessed by hundreds of thousands of Irishmen to sway the British Parliament to legislate Repeal. But if moral force carried Emancipation, by comparison a minor issue, it could not achieve Repeal. In 1829 many Englishmen and even some Protestant Irishmen had favored Emancipation as a reasonable and just measure; these same people were unalterably opposed to the destruction of the Union. Little had changed since 1834, when O'Connell's first motion in Parliament for repeal of the Union had drawn the support of *one* British Member. In the Repeal Year, Peel had announced as early as 9 May that his Government was prepared to go to war to prevent "the dismemberment of the Empire."[145] Nothing could change the fact that the Union of 1801 had been forged in the dreadful furnace of the 1798 Rebellion: No moral or intellectual reasoning could "repeal" such a dearly purchased political reality. Repeal required violence, but for O'Connell, violence was unthinkable.

The Repeal movement did bring some unintended results. The failed Irish cause produced great parliamentary debates in the British Commons and Lords; in unprecedented fashion, for nine successive nights in February 1844,

English Members gave their unbroken attention to the problems of Ireland past and present.[146] More substantially, after Clontarf, Peel's Government embarked on a program of Irish reform. In November 1843 a commission chaired by the Earl of Devon, an absentee landowner, was appointed to investigate ways to improve the agrarian condition of Ireland. Graham aptly noted to Peel that the commission would expose "the causes of discontent ...; but alas! I fear, that the remedies are beyond the reach of legislative power."[147] Peel's Government discussed halving the county franchise to a £5 freehold, but ultimately abandoned the idea. In 1845, in a bid to wean the priests from the people, Peel trebled the Maynooth grant (1795), and to reduce clerical influence he pressed legislation establishing secularized university-level "Queen's Colleges" at Cork, Galway, and Belfast. Also in 1845, the "maniac" Lord Stanley introduced a bill, based on the *Devon Report*, that would promote tenants' rights by compensating occupiers for improvements to landlords' properties. But opposition from Whig and Tory lords killed the proposal.[148]

V. Irish Famine, 1846–51

As it had been for the Tories, so, predicted Sir James Graham, Ireland would be the Whigs' "principal domestic difficulty." After Repeal the difficulty came in three forms: a surge in agrarian crime in 1844–9; a fungus blight, beginning in September 1845, that damaged the potato crop and in succeeding years brought on the Great Famine; and an attempted "rising" in 1848. The renewed agrarian violence was concentrated in Tipperary, Limerick, Clare, Roscommon, and Leitrim. Comprising only one-sixth of the island's population, these five counties produced in 1845 one-third of all homicides in Ireland, two-thirds of all shootings at persons, two-fifths of the cattle maimings, and one-half of the threatening letters. In 1846–7 70 percent of the national totals of major Whiteboy outrages – homicides, arms robberies, and shootings at persons and into dwellings – occurred in only the first three counties previously listed. The Irish disturbances, which altogether affected a dozen counties, produced much debate in Parliament. Members spoke of the "frightful" extent of the murderous "executions" that rendered parts of Ireland "uninhabitable." In some districts the police heard so many gunshots that they no longer took notice, lest "they be running about all day." In Tipperary, tales of murder were so commonplace as to be "heard without much emotion"; Peel spoke of that county's "inveterate ..., hereditary ... disposition to murder ... [in existence] so long since as the year 1814."[149]

Although the "broad-day murders and midnight assassinations" included that of a Resident Magistrate (Capt. John McLeod, in Leitrim, January 1845), a Tipperary JP (a Mr. Roe, October 1847), and an improving landlord (Maj. Denis Mahon, Roscommon, November 1847), the great majority of victims were not gentlemen, or even land agents or stewards, but rather laborers, cottiers, and petty farmers as well as wood rangers and cattle and sheep herders.[150] The desperate competition for land and food – which led to the brutal punishment of those who "grabbed" a man's smallholding or kept the soil out of cultivation – drove the lower peasantry to a war more often internecine than interclass.[151] As Tables 11.5 and 11.6 show, the rise in agrarian crime began in 1844–5, before the Famine, and continued through 1847–9. Comparison of the pre-Famine and Famine figures reveals that the increase in agrarian offenses was not so much in homicide and other serious crimes against persons as it was in other traditional Whiteboy outrages. From 1844 to 1847, attacks on houses doubled, shootings at persons increased threefold, and demands or robberies of arms increased sixfold. Under the circumstances, it is remarkable that conviction rates held up. For all crimes, agrarian and nonagrarian, the rates over the three periods 1843–5, 1846–51 (Famine), and 1852–6 increased from 42 to 60 percent; conviction rates for violent crimes against persons, traditionally lower than those for all offenses, actually increased in these years from 35 to 40 percent; and rates for two Whiteboy offenses – armed assembly and house attacks – rose from 31 to 44 percent before dropping to 34 percent after 1851.

The surge in agrarian crime, which "proved an overmatch for the constabulary, the magistrates, and the law," led Prime Minister Peel in early 1846 to bring in his "Protection of Life (Ireland) Bill." This coercive measure sought to permit drafting of additional police into disturbed districts (at local expense); to compensate victims of outrages by a fine on the district; and, most controversially, to institute a night curfew, with convicted violators legally subject to fifteen years' transportation.[152] Peel's Irish proposal, which coincided with his bill to repeal the Corn Laws, became enmeshed in party politics. The Irish coercion measure triggered an unprecedented volume of debate in Parliament; indeed, the session was largely devoted to just two topics, Corn Law repeal and Irish coercion.[153] At length, on 25 June 1846, the House of Lords gave its approval to Peel's bill repealing all duties on imported grain. Only hours later, in the Commons, an anti-Peel revolt created by the unlikely alliance of irate Whig landowners, English Radicals, O'Connell's Irish Repealers, and Tory mavericks led by Disraeli overturned the Government by voting, 292–219, against the Second Reading of Peel's Irish coercion bill.[154] Sir Robert Peel had no choice but to resign the prime ministership. Peel's second and last ministry thus ended, as his career had begun, on the subject of Ireland. Indeed, little did they know it, but for the two great protagonists, time was running out. Less than a year later, in May 1847, Daniel O'Connell, seventy-one, would die in self-exile in Genoa. In June 1850, four years out of power but still in Parliament, Peel himself would be gone, dead at age sixty-two from injuries sustained in a freak fall from his horse.[155]

In August 1846 the new Whig Government, headed by Lord John Russell, rewarded Irish MPs for their support by passing with little debate an act, 9 & 10 Vict., c. 97, that committed the British government to full funding of the Irish constabulary from the Consolidated Fund. The act was "a boon promised to the Irish counties," since landowners were expected to be hurt

Table 11.5. *Outrages reported by the constabulary, 1843–56*

	1843	1844	1845	1846	1847	1848	1849	1850	1851	1852	1853	1854	1855	1856
Homicide	122	146	139	170	212	171	203	139	157	100	110	106	101	126
Shooting a firearm at a person	58	93	138	158	266	97	93	69	65	54	37	37	42	22
Aggravated assault[a]	700	800	829	895	576	674	826	780	841	931	797	736	686	770
Demand or robbery of arms	119	159	551	621	1,053	237	113	89	82	68	28	17	29	19
Appearing armed	75	79	89	138	206	55	13	17	23	20	3	4	6	6
Administering unlawful oaths	51	59	223	232	24	30	48	59	49	56	7	17	14	18
Attacking houses	215	254	483	536	281	173	82	58	54	69	53	40	44	22
Shooting into dwellings	87	77	138	167	257	95	90	53	58	51	34	25	21	25
SELECT TOTAL	1,427	1,667	2,590	2,917	2,875	1,532	1,468	1,264	1,329	1,349	1,069	982	943	1,008
Select total as percent of total outrages	24%	26	32	24	14	10	10	12	15	17	20	21	22	24
Total outrages reported	5,875	6,327	8,095	12,380	20,986	14,980	14,908	10,639	9,144	7,824	5,452	4,658	4,204	4,125

[a] Comprising aggravated assault, assault with intent to murder or to endanger life, and cutting or maiming the person.

Table 11.6. *Crime in Ireland, 1843–56*

	All offenses		Most serious offenses against persons with violence[a]		Murder/manslaughter		Assembling armed unlaw... and attacking dwelling houses	
	I	II	I	II	I	II	I	II
1843	20,126	42.8%	447	35.1	265	37.4 (52.4, 12.9)[b]	109	30.3
1844	19,448	41.4	502	32.9	292	38.4 (56.4, 15.5)	167	35.3
1845	16,696	42.5	483	36.2	338	37.0 (45.5, 14.1)	236	25.8
1846	18,492	46.7	522	45.4	332	47.6 (62.4, 12.2)	184	28.8
1847	31,209	49.1	463	39.1	276	33.7 (42.8, 21.4)	328	43.0
1848	38,522	47.2	576	35.1	361	34.6 (45.2, 25.6)	377	41.9
1849	41,989	50.5	476	31.5	343	32.1 (45.1, 18.8)	385	54.0
1850	31,326	54.6	393	37.4	263	35.0 (50.7, 14.2)	294	53.7
1851	24,684	58.2	364	34.3	253	31.6 (45.9, 15.3)	225	39.9
1852	17,678	59.1	266	38.7	196	35.7 (42.5, 23.2)	96	32.3
1853	15,144	64.1	264	37.5	201	37.3 (45.3, 23.3)	57	14.0
1854	11,782	59.8	243	39.9	155	36.1 (49.0, 11.3)	18	16.7
1855	9,012	57.9	251	34.3	144	28.5 (41.6, 7.3)	10	30.0
1856	7,099	56.7	209	47.4	119	52.1 (61.8, 23.3)	60	80.0
Ave./yr.								
1843–5	*18,757*	*42.2*	*477*	*34.7*	*298*	*37.6 (51.4, 14.2)*	*171*	*30.5*
1846–51	*31,037*	*51.1*	*466*	*37.1*	*305*	*35.8 (48.7, 17.9)*	*299*	*43.6*
1852–6	*12,143*	*59.5*	*247*	*39.6*	*163*	*37.9 (48.0, 17.7)*	*48*	*34.6*

Key: I Number of persons charged with criminal offenses and committed to jail for trial.
   II Percentage conviction rate.

[a] Comprising murder and manslaughter; shooting, stabbing, poisoning, &c., with intent to murder; assault with intent to murder; and conspiracy to murder.
[b] Distinguishing conviction rates for manslaughter and murder, respectively.

by Corn Law repeal and were already being pressed by the onset of the Potato Famine. There were few objections to the removal of this last local feature of the Irish police. But in the Lords, the Anglo-Irish peer Thomas Spring-Rice, Baron Monteagle, did protest that "the repeal of this local charge must, in justice to Great Britain, lead to a much wider application of the same principle."[156] (Ten years later, by an act of Parliament, the English county and borough police would receive partial funding from British Treasury grants.)

In 1847 the Whigs offered their own Irish coercion measure. The "Crime and Outrage (Ireland) Bill," introduced in November by Home Secretary Sir George Grey, essentially restated the principles of Peel's 1846 bill but imposed no curfew. From a reserve force of constabulary now raised to 600 men (it had been increased from 200 to 400 only the previous year),[157] police might be dispatched to proclaimed baronies and half-baronies; there was to be no limit on the number of men sent in, and all of these *extra* police costs would be assessed on the disturbed district. Grey's bill passed its Second Reading in the Commons by a vote of 296−19, with Irish MPs favoring it by a margin of 91−14. Among the measure's myriad supporters were Peel and Henry Grattan, Jr., who stated that he "would have no parley with assassins." Among the handful of opponents were two Irishmen, Feargus O'Connor and William Smith O'Brien, from whom more would be heard in 1848.[158] Grey's punitive police act was immediately imposed on all of Tipperary and Limerick and on parts of Clare, Roscommon, Leitrim, and seven other counties. The following July, at the time of the "1848 Rising," the act would be applied to another dozen counties.[159]

"Let the truth go forth," declaimed the MP for Nottingham, Feargus O'Connor, "that, when the people of Ireland were dying for want of food, the Government of England gave them coercion." At the time of the Chartist chieftain's remarks, in November 1847, the Irish Famine was still short of its midpoint. But already hundreds of thousands of persons had died; the ghastly total for 1846−51 would surpass 1 million dead.[160] To the simple want of food from potatoes rotted by the fungus *Phytophthora infestans* was added the plague of diseases: typhus and relapsing ("yellow") fever, "famine dropsy," dysentery, and scurvy. In spite of the reigning laissez-faire economics, the Government in London did mount for a time a herculean relief effort. By March 1847, 730,000 persons were employed at public works projects; by late summer, at the peak of the soup kitchens' relief, 3 million persons daily consumed the free rations. But from late 1847 on, wearied by two years of unprecedented state welfare intervention, the British Government pulled back from giving further help and threw the burden of Irish immiseration on Irish local poor relief. Lodging capacity in the wretched Irish Poor Law houses expanded, trebling to 310,000 by 1851; at one time or another in 1849, 930,000 poor souls found refuge in the workhouses.[161]

But the resort to the bankrupt Irish poor rates was unconscionably inadequate since, by law, only the poorest of the poor qualified for relief. The Irish Poor Law Amendment Act (1847), sponsored by William Gregory, MP for Dublin City and grandson of the former Castle Under-Secretary, granted relief only to persons on holdings of a quarter-acre or less. This gradgrind provision, coupled with the fact that landlords were personally liable for poor rates on all holdings of less than £4 valuation, hastened the process of eviction and assisted emigration. Uprooting of the smallholders and encouragement of massive flight – more than 1 million left the island during 1846–51 – came to be accepted as the final solution to the problem of Irish penury. Some landlords – like Major Mahon in Roscommon, who evicted 3,000 persons and paid £14,000 for assisted emigration – were assassinated for their efforts. Others at a distance escaped harm. One of the biggest landlords to press emigration was Henry John Temple, 3d Viscount Palmerston, Foreign Secretary (1846–51) in Russell's Government. From Palmerston's County Sligo estates in late 1847, some 2,000 tenants were loaded onto nine ships bound for Canada; Palmerston's clearances were so thorough that only 2 percent of his tenants on poor relief in 1847 were still receiving relief in 1849. The mass evictions in Ireland and the subsequent consolidation of holdings – from 1841 to 1851 the number of those under five acres fell from 442,000 to 126,000 and the share of those above fifteen acres increased from roughly a third to a half of all holdings – drove many in the lower peasantry to commit crimes or to emigrate. No doubt, many persons did both.[162]

As the countryside degenerated into the horrors of famine and social chaos, the basic nature of crime in Ireland underwent a change (Figure 11.4). More remarkable than the final surge of Whiteboyism was the enormous rise in nonagrarian crime. Nonviolent property crime surged: Class 3 committals, as the criminal returns dryly classified them, rose from 6,603 in 1845 to 17,484 in 1847 and peaked at 23,173 in 1849; 12,260 of the 17,484 Class 3 committals in 1847 were for simple larceny. Rural distress of unprecedented severity was turning Ireland into a nation of common thieves. The 1848 constabulary report on crime noted that the committal statistics represented "an imperfect record of the actual amount of crime," since many offenders were not "arrested and made amenable to justice." The outrage statistics (see Table 11.7) kept by the constabulary also show that "the general dearth ... and the severest privations" produced far more crimes of hunger than of protest. Roughly half of all outrages in 1847–50 were incidents of cattle and sheep stealing, crimes that were committed "with apparent impunity." Robberies and burglaries also rose to new highs as great stretches of the country sank into "a state of social prostration but faintly shown even by criminal statistics."[163]

The transformation that occurred in Irish crime during the Famine is clearly seen if we compare the incidence of various types of crime in Ireland and England (see Table 11.8). Whereas the nature of English crime in the 1840s continued to be remarkably stable, Irish crime changed quickly and dramatically. The shift brought on by the Famine was characterized by a sharp drop in crimes against persons (Class 1 offenses) and of public order (Class 6) offenses, and by a sharp rise in a third category, nonviolent property (Class 3) offenses. As a proportion of total crime, property crime

Figure 11.4 Two English views of the Irish crisis: agrarian outrage as portrayed in *Punch* (1846), and the Famine as reported in the *Illustrated London News* (1847).

was still far less prevalent in Ireland than it was in England, and violent crimes against persons and public order offenses remained far more frequent in Ireland than in England. But the shift in the very nature of Irish crime was nevertheless dramatic and, indeed, long-lasting.

The military and the constabulary were worked hard in the Famine years. Assigned to deal with the upsurge in crime, they also played prominent roles in the administration of relief. The heads of the army commissariat and the constabulary served on the national relief boards and commissions. Commissary General Sir Randolph Routh administered the public works program, and Maj.-Gen. Sir John Burgoyne supervised the soup kitchens. Local relief committees were heavily staffed, until 1847 exclusively so, with "officials" – JPs, clergymen, Poor Law authorities, and army and police

Table 11.7. *Hunger and theft: outrages reported by the constabulary, 1844–53*

	1844	1845	1846	1847	1848	1849	1850	1851	1852	1853
Cattle and sheep stealing	821	652	3,025	10,944	6,738	8,157	4,780	3,683	2,295	1,909
Plundering provisions	—	—	116[a]	1,191	234	94	10	1	1	4
Robbery, highway robbery, burglary & housebreaking	583	672	1,605	3,081	2,260	1,700	1,238	1,232	1,041	828
TOTAL OUTRAGES	6,327	8,095	12,380	20,986	14,980	14,908	10,639	9,144	7,824	5,452

[a]A new statistical category; mostly attacks on ships and Poor Law workhouses.

Table 11.8. *The nature of crime, 1841–53: class of crime as a percentile share of total indictable offenses*

| | Ireland | | | | | | | England | | | | | | |
Annual average committals, all offenses	Class 1	2	3	4	5	6	Years	Class 1	2	3	4	5	6	Annual average committals, all offenses
20,703	26%	6	37	1	1	30	1841–3	8%	7	77	1	2	5	29,553
18,757	28	6	32	1	1	32	1843–5	8	7	77	1	2	4	26,812
22,132	22	7	45	1	1	25	1845–7	8	6	81	1	2	3	26,081
37,240	14	7	54	2	1	23	1847–9	7	7	80	1	2	3	29,016
32,666	13	7	55	2	1	23	1849–51	7	8	79	1	3	3	27,530
19,169	14	9	56	1	1	19	1851–3	8	7	79	1	3	3	27,509

Class 1: Crimes against persons with violence
2: Crimes against property with violence
3: Crimes against property without violence
4: Malicious offenses against property
5: Forgeries and currency offenses
6: Miscellaneous offenses

officers. To govern the deteriorating society, the Government divided the island into nine military districts, each under an inspecting officer. Commissariat depots in the west were transformed into central food depots; seventy-six subdepots on the south and west coasts and twenty-nine inland ones in Munster and Connaught were administered by the coast guard and constabulary, respectively.[164]

The constabulary swelled in size from 9,100 men in 1844 to 12,400 by 1848. Never had the policemen been asked to perform so many duties. In each district they reported weekly on the condition of the season's crops. They aided in food distribution at the depots. They guarded supply stores, escorted wagons loaded with provisions, and watched over the loading of emigrant ships. They were stationed at public works and soup kitchens and at poorhouse doors to keep applicants out. They were overwhelmed by swarms of vagrants and beggars searching for food; they attended funerals where paupers were buried without coffins or even shrouds. They had to cope with the proliferation of petty thefts; both police and military were "harrassed off their legs by daily calls" from property owners for protection. Not least among the police duties was assistance in the collection of rents that landlords persisted in demanding and that were paid often only after clashes with the constabulary. Police and military support was necessary to secure the eviction of smallholders and the destruction of their huts and cabins. Less successful were police efforts to collect poor rates or distrain for nonpayment.[165]

The Famine took a heavy toll on the morale of the constabulary, men and officers, Catholics and Protestants. Policemen had been the principal census takers in 1841; now they watched and reported as the people died. Day after day, for six years, they recorded the unspeakable horrors. Subinspector George Pinchin reported: "A stranger would wonder how these wretched beings find food.... They sleep in their rags and have pawned their bedding." A Cork Subinspector, reporting that 400 starving, spade-carrying laborers had besieged his office to beg for work, appended a terse postscript: "Employment is very much needed." A police report from Roscommon in 1846 noted that 7,500 people were surviving on boiled cabbage leaves eaten every forty-eight hours. From Swineford, County Mayo, in January 1847, Subinspector Edward Hunt wrote Inspector-General McGregor: "You would be horrified to see the multitude of starving men, women, and children, who daily swarm the town soliciting with prayers just one meal of food."[166]

The military, too, were affected by the bedlam around them. Soldiers, like policemen, came across bodies dead or dying in roads, fields, and cabins. Commissariat officers time and again reported scenes of "women and children sobbing with grief at the insufficient food"; hardest to bear, wrote the officers, was "the ceaseless misery of the children." "Mobs of men and women imploring employment assail you on the road," wrote Captain Glascock, a public works inspector. The remarks of Colonel Douglas, relief inspector in Tipperary, were echoed in other military reports. *"Nobody,"* he wrote General Routh, "who has not personally seen the state of matters in this country can form to himself any idea" of the horrors. At the Clonmel soup kitchen, Douglas reported crowds waiting all night, then wild brawls breaking out when distribution began; he ended his report in an unfinished scrawl: "*I have witnessed such scenes. . . .*"[167]

The officers protested policies that they were obliged to enforce. Food rations were "screwed down" to the lowest possible level, reported a commissariat officer who demanded an increase. Others objected to the Government's delays in opening food depots in the west. Relief officers, told to reduce aid, replied that they would continue to sell provisions until explicit counterorders came from the Treasury. Major-General Burgoyne, placed in charge of the soup kitchens, protested techniques of mass feeding that treated the people like "wild animals." Two points bear emphasizing. Burgoyne, Routh, and the other relief officers who lived with the Famine (and some died with it: police and soldiers were among the fever deaths in 1847), and who worked fourteen-hour days in the rural districts, were among the heroes in this national tragedy.[168] Blame for the failure of the plans they executed rests not with them but with government policy makers. Secondly, one has to acknowledge the great impact that the Irish Famine had on the minds of the men in the army (and constabulary). Historians have long noted the demoralization of the troops produced by the Crimean War campaigns of 1854–5. But those soldiers who had been in Ireland during the Famine years had already seen mass deaths and known disillusionment with politicians.

CHAPTER 12

1848 and aftermath

Saxon institutions have been tried and found not to harmonize with the Celtic mind. It cannot comprehend them, it does not appreciate them. . . . It wants that moral sense . . . which has been the soul and the strength of Anglo-Saxon jurisprudence. This it must be taught by a strong, an irresistible, and if need be, a coercive authority.
– *Blackwood's Magazine*, October 1848

In 1848, a year of deep and widespread economic depression, Europe was swept by a wave of revolutions from which only a few countries escaped. England, economically modern and constitutionally liberal, absorbed the assault with no real damage to its political system. English workingmen entered 1848 with no history of personal violence, no revolutionary tradition, and, most recently, in the aftermath of suffrage reform (1832) and Corn Law repeal (1846), no alliance with the middle classes. The absence of revolt in Ireland in 1848 was due not to any lack of a tradition of violence or rebellion, nor contrariwise to the lingering legacy of moral force of the now deceased O'Connell, but rather to the enervating effects of the Famine. In England and Ireland the "revolution of 1848" cannot be said to have failed because, in each country for very different reasons, it never got started. The Government's repression matched the level of the challenge. The army stayed in the background, and the police were massively deployed but kept in check.

The absence of fighting and the virtually bloodless repression in the British Isles stand in sharp contrast to 1848 on the Continent. In Italy, the nationalist revolution was highlighted by the "Five Days" of successful street fighting in Milan; by bloody patriot risings at Palermo, Naples, and Venice; by the Pope's flight from Rome; and even by open-field battles against the Austrian army at Custozza and Novara. In central Europe, rebellious Budapest and Prague had to be retaken by Austrian military bombardment and invasion. Vienna itself, lost to the rebels in March, was retaken in October by General Windischgrätz and 70,000 troops at the cost of the lives of 3,000 Viennese and 1,300 troops. In Prussia, the fighting in the "March Days" in Berlin produced 300 deaths and the promise of a new constitution. In France, the mother of revolutions, thousands of lives were lost in 1848. On 23 February troops in Paris fired into a large crowd, killing forty persons in the boulevard des Capucines. Parisians responded with violence of their own – tearing up 1 million paving stones, cutting down 4,000 trees, and erecting 1,500 barricades. The February fighting produced nearly 400 deaths, 80 on the government side and 290 among the people. But the violence that ushered in the Second Republic was mild by contrast to that of the "June Days." The Insurrection of 23–6 June in eastern Paris was undisguised class warfare: 15,000 of the city's unemployed and propertyless pitted against the victors of February. In crushing the revolt, police and troops under General Cavaignac, an Algerian veteran, killed 500 rebels in street fighting, absorbed heavy losses of 1,000 of their own men, and in the savage aftermath hunted down and killed 3,000 persons behind the barricades.[1]

I. English complacency, Irish desperation

In a far milder fashion in 1848, England was pricked by a threatened "revolution" and Ireland by an aborted one.[2] In both countries, the revival of protest movements was strongly influenced by events on the Continent, particularly in France. And in both, the protests assumed a somewhat forlorn air, in England from the past futility of Chartist petitions and demonstrations and in Ireland from the nightmarish effects of the Potato Famine. Mass starvation did not ravage John Bull's industrial island, but high bread prices and a deep trade slump did increase hunger and unemployment. Thus, economic depression in the one island and famine in the other provided the dreary backdrop to 1848 in the British Isles.[3]

In both countries the protests resulted in abject failure, but significantly, the repression differed markedly. In both England and Ireland, the latter only half as populous as the former, the army numbered about 30,000 men. In addition, in Ireland the countryside was saturated with a 12,000-man, armed, government-controlled constabulary; Dublin, the most heavily policed city in the United Kingdom, was protected by 1,100 government-controlled, if unarmed, constables. In England, the 4,000 unarmed, government-controlled police of London had won a reputation for preserving public order. The largest cities – Liverpool, Manchester, Bristol – had developed fairly efficient if locally controlled police. But throughout the rest of England, the new police were thin on the ground. A third of the 191 boroughs were still without police and several northern towns, as yet unincorporated, had only paltry civil forces. Two-thirds of the counties had refused to set up county-wide police. Parish constables continued to serve in many rural areas, and numerous small private police units guarded the canals, rivers, railways, and docks of England.[4] In sum, in Ireland in 1848, a powerful police machine was in operation; in England, with the exception of London and the very largest provincial cities, important parts of the machine were missing.

Whereas in Ireland the constabulary would play the leading role in the repression of protest, in England provincial unrest was to be contained by traditional means: Yeomanry, army pensioners, troops, and, most noticeably, special constables. Even in London, the center of protest in 1848, it was the awesome turnout of special constables rather than the routine efficiency of the Metropolitan Police that impressed contemporaries. To a large extent, the threat of revolution in England in 1848 was contained by the efforts of private citizens, not professional policemen.

1848 in England

Noblemen, tradesmen, and workmen thoroughly intermingled. No class stood apart. Grey-haired men and slim youths went side by side; coal-whippers and young dandies; literary men and those to whom books were unknown.... There was more grumbling ... regarding the defective arrangements for making special constables, from those who were impatient to be sworn in, than there was from the Chartists themselves against the Government.
    – Anon., *A Letter from One of the Special Constables in London* (1848)

It is a proud thing for England to reflect on the exalted post she has occupied during this marvelous and trying time. While other nations, possessed of far greater military forces, were reeling under the shock, ... she alone has repressed the danger by the constable's baton.... She has conquered the revolutionary spirit, by which so many of the military monarchies of Europe had been prostrated, by moral strength alone; scarce a shot was fired in anger by her troops, and not a drop of blood was shed on the scaffold.
    – *Blackwood's Magazine*, October 1848

The first disorders, in March 1848, took the form of food rioting at Glasgow, where five of the mostly Irish rioters were shot and killed by panicky military pensioners. Other hunger disturbances rumbled at Manchester and in the West Country. In London, on the nights of 6–8 March, skirmishes broke out around Trafalgar Square amid protests against Lord John Russell's proposal to double income tax rates. As in 1838–42, the Chartists now jumped on the issue of economic distress. In the winter of 1847–8 some 2 million signatures had been collected for the third petition. Using the tactics of a huge demonstration and a procession to Westminster, the Chartists would again demand the vote for workingmen. What David Large has called "a dress rehearsal" for the meeting of 10 April was held on Kennington Common in southwest London on 13 March. The meeting drew a crowd estimated at 15,000 but also brought out 2,000 Metropolitan Police and some 20,000 special constables. The only breach of the peace came after the meeting had adjourned; the police arrested two dozen laborers for smashing the windows of nearby shops. Three weeks later, on 3 April, the Chartist Convention reassembled and unanimously voted to call "an unarmed moral demonstration" a week hence to present the people's petition to Parliament.[5]

    There can be little doubt that the aim of the meeting on 10 April was simply the orderly petitioning of Parliament. All forty-nine Convention delegates had endorsed the tactic of moral force.[6] Many former Chartist firebrands – Taylor, Oastler, Stephens, Cooper, and O'Brien – were either dead, or inactive, or converts to moral force.[7] Feargus O'Connor himself, like Daniel O'Connell in 1843, consistently urged peace and good order. He counseled that if, as at Clontarf, police and troops occupied Kennington Common before the procession's arrival, the Chartists should disperse quietly and he would personally present the petition. At the meeting on 10 April, speeches were restrained and pikes and bludgeons noticeably absent. The Chartist George Jacob Holyoake, who was there, recalled that "there was absolutely nothing in the field against the Duke of Wellington in London but a waggon, on which a monster petition was piled." (See Figure 12.1.) There was no revolution in 1848, as Henry Weisser has cogently argued, because "the Chartists themselves saw revolution as a foreign, un-English phenomenon." Conditions were different in unfortunate countries like Poland or Italy, where the people did not enjoy representation by elective parliament or the freedoms of speech, press, assembly, and petition. "Foreigners needed revolutions to get these blessings." The upheavals on the Continent stimulated Chartist protest not to imitative revolution but rather to "a legal, English agitation aimed at a constitutional reform."[8] However serious the threat of revolution in 1848, the danger was in fact far greater in the distressed industrial North than in London, the heavily garrisoned capital, which boasted by far the most powerful police in Britain.

The Government's reaction to the scheduled meeting on 10 April was one of planned "massive overkill." The authorities had received reports from numerous informants, opened Chartists' correspondence, monitored the railways, and commandeered the electric telegraphs; Prime Minister Russell, Home Secretary Sir George Grey, and Police Commissioners Rowan and Mayne all were aware that the likelihood of a Chartist insurrection was remote. David Large has argued that the Government adopted its tough stance as a political ploy to bolster its image abroad and to reassure the English propertied classes anxious about the possibility of a Jacobin revolution in London.[9] As the 10th approached, the Home Office was inundated with suggestions and offers of help. A Mr. Curtis in Camberwell recommended his military invention, a portable wrought-iron mortar; Sir Henry Ellis demanded muskets and cutlasses for his 200 specials lest the British Museum be assaulted by 10,000 Chartists; the Duke of Buckingham volunteered a loan of 300 Yeomanry and two 6-pound field pieces; Lord Malmesbury announced that he was bringing his gamekeepers, suitably armed, to the capital. Most imaginative of all was a plan, subsequently implemented, that was submitted by the irrepressible Edwin Chadwick: the conscription of 300 sewer workers to form a subterranean army of special constables. "Should any barricade be formed across any main line of street," he wrote Rowan, "these constables might pass [under] it and emerge at any one of the man holes behind it with which they are acquainted, and of which they have keys, or they might lead a sapper [military underground tunneler or munitions expert] underneath it."[10]

The Whig Government proceeded with the most massive garrisoning in the history of the capital. A total of 8,148 troops, including two regiments

A GREAT DEMONSTRATION.

Mob-Orator. " TELL ME, MINION ! IS IT THE INTENTION OF YOUR PROUD MASTERS AT ALL HAZARDS TO PREVENT OUR DEMONSTRATION ? "

Magistrate (blandly). " YES, SIR."

Mob-Orator. " THEN KNOW, OH MYRMIDON OF THE BRUTAL WHIGS, THAT I SHALL GO HOME TO MY TEA, AND ADVISE MY COMRADES TO DO THE SAME ! "

Figure 12.1 The "Umbrella" Revolution: London, 1848. Informed that his meeting will not be permitted, a "mob-orator" (with umbrella) tells the "myrmidon of the brutal Whigs, that I shall go home to my tea, and advise my comrades to do the same!" (*Punch*)

from Dover and Chatham, were secreted at scattered locations; 1,231 military pensioners were deployed and six 6-pounders and nine howitzers rolled out. Virtually the entire Metropolitan Police, 4,012 men, was placed on riot duty: 1,650 constables were stationed at five key bridges leading into Westminster, and 1,000 were assigned to the Houses of Parliament and 700 to Trafalgar

Figure 12.2 The Chartists on Kennington Common, 10 April 1848. (*Illus. London News*)

Square. The Thames Police cruised the river in seven boats. The City of London police was out in force and kept in close contact with the Home Office. All across the metropolis special constables were enrolled in unprecedented numbers. The Chartist Holyoake offered his opinion that the Government's use of physical force was a "political imposture" whose aim was to bully the Chartists and, by "ostentatious provocation," to initiate violence against "an imaginary enemy."[11]

For the authorities, the actual meeting on 10 April was an anticlimax; for the Chartists, an embarrassment. From 9 A.M. on, processions from various parts of the metropolis converged on Kennington Common; two hours later, the crowd had reached its greatest size. Estimates vary enormously: from 12,000 to 20,000 (the police figures) up to as many as 250,000 (a Chartist claim); military observers guessed the size at from 23,000 to 33,000. David Large has calculated (erroneously, says David Goodway) that the Common, which was built up on all sides, could accommodate no more than 55,000 crushed spectators. Goodway argues for a crowd size of about 150,000. We shall never know for sure. Certainly Goodway's figure is believable if we include persons around the Common and marchers and spectators in nearby streets. In any event, the crowd on Kennington Common was large, though not monstrous the way the crowds a O'Connell's Irish Repeal meetings had been five years earlier[12] (Figure 12.2).

The Government had decided to let the Chartists meet but, invoking a statute of Charles II against "tumultuous petitioning," would not permit any procession across the Thames into Westminster. Subsequently, Police Commissioner Mayne even deprived the Chartists of the substance of an uninterrupted meeting on Kennington Common when, at 11:30 A.M., he summoned fellow Irishman Feargus O'Connor to a talk in a nearby tavern. All accounts describe the Chartist chieftain as in an agitated state. Mayne, the Dublin barrister, with a more diplomatic personality than the military Rowan, explained to O'Connor that there could be a meeting but no procession. (The Chartists thus got more than had the Irish Repealers at Clontarf.) O'Connor, apparently relieved, "thanked him effusively, begging to shake him by the hand." He told Mayne and, later that day, Home Secretary Grey that he agreed with their decision.[13] Some scholars have criticized O'Connor for cowardice and a surrender that was too quick, too easy.[14] But O'Connor's plan never had been to launch a rebellion. His alleged cowering may be explained by a fear of spontaneous or provoked fighting that would invite repression; like General Napier in 1839, O'Connor knew which side had the physical force.[15] And so, like O'Connell at Clontarf, O'Connor at Kennington surrendered when he saw the power of the state arrayed against the moral force of his followers.

After his meeting with Mayne, O'Connor returned to the Common and persuaded the crowd to give up the planned procession. The throng began to break up peacefully as speakers droned in the background. A short drenching spring shower – "the rain of terror," joked *Punch* – provided the final insult to the Chartist spectators, who fled for cover. The meeting dispersed, and the "Kennington Common Revolution" (*Punch*) was over. O'Connor and a few other leaders hired three cabs to carry the Chartist petition to Parliament. Three days later, in presenting the petition, O'Connor, MP for Nottingham, became embroiled in a heated debate with another Member, challenged him to a duel, and had to be restrained by the Serjeant-at-Arms.[16] O'Connor's only violence was thus a minor scuffle, on 13 April, on the floor of the Commons. The incident no doubt left many MPs shaking their heads at this display of Irish temper.

The most remarkable aspect of the affair at Kennington Common was not the meeting itself, or even the 12,000 police and military placed on alert, but rather the overwhelming turnout of special constables. Newspaper estimates of their numbers ranged from 120,000 to 250,000. The Chartists themselves were clearly impressed: The *Northern Star* reported 70,000 in the City of London alone, and Holyoake was so overwhelmed that he mused on "a million special constables ... out staff in hand." The most recent authoritative research deflates the total throughout the metropolis to about 85,000 enrolled specials, a figure that nevertheless remains huge and unprecedented.[17] Most of the specials belonged to the propertied classes, the clerks, shopkeepers, professionals, and businessmen so numerous in mid-Victorian England. Apart from their numbers, it was the diversity of social backgrounds of these specials in 1848 that struck contemporaries. One special noted, "Noblemen, tradesmen, and workmen thoroughly intermingled. No class stood apart." Lord Palmerston observed that "men of all classes and ranks blended together in defense of law and property." Joining Peel, Gladstone, and Louis Napoleon, and the stockbrokers and shopkeepers and representatives from corporate bodies ranging from the Admiralty to the Temple, the Bank of England to the Post Office, were some men from the working classes. Most of these were skilled craftsmen and artisans, but also present were tanners, wool sorters, and coal heavers, as well as workers from the railways, breweries, and building trades. These workingmen, some of whom were conscripted by their employers, appear to have sought the same ends as the moral-force Chartists, namely, the prevention of any unfortunate disturbances such as had occurred in Paris and Berlin. The achievement of what Palmerston called "the Waterloo of peace and order" was very much the work of all classes in London in April 1848.[18]

The celebrated affair at Kennington Common was not the end of the threat in England in 1848. As spring turned into summer, the joking complacency about "fearful Feargus, the cowardly lion at Kennington Common," gave way to alarm about increasing Irish influences on English radicalism. Outrage over the horrors of the Famine, the death in 1847 of the constitutionalist and anti-Chartist O'Connell, and the rise of Young Ireland produced in Ireland the potential for a revolutionary outbreak. In England, swarms of Famine emigrants – 300,000 pauper Irish arrived in Liverpool in only the first five months of 1847 – had quickly altered the character of large parts of many northern cities.[19] O'Connor was rejoicing in the union of the two national radical causes, even as the minority physical-force Chartists were eager to avenge the April humiliation at Kennington Common.[20]

In late May and early June, in the East End of London, crowds containing pike-wielding Irishmen battled parties of police armed with cutlasses. The police prevailed in a particularly furious fight at Bishop Bonner's Fields on the night of 4 June; at a meeting there on the 12th, the police made dozens of arrests, including that of Ernest Jones. This crackdown appeared to end the threat in the capital. In the North, there was a similar evolution from Chartist orderliness to crisis. A demonstration in Manchester on 9 April brought out 15,000 Chartists and also produced 11,000 special constables. In late April and May, large meetings took place at Liverpool, Halifax, Oldham, and Bradford and smaller ones at Manchester, Birmingham, and Nottingham. Processions in arms became more frequent and rhetoric adopting the Irish cause more strident. The Government kept an especially close watch on Liverpool, the gateway to Ireland; a group of citizens even demanded that the city be "proclaimed" under a recent *Irish* coercion act. At the end of May, at Bradford, riots by 3,000 pike-carrying Chartists were contained by a small party of Lancashire police, 300 troops, and 1,000 special constables.[21]

As in the past, the national rising never materialized. So-called crisis points on 12 June and 14 August passed without any serious attempts at insurrection. Around Manchester a series of skirmishes, largely against the police, involved no more than a few hundred desperate men. At Liverpool, the city's 800-man police force was supplemented by 2,000 troops, 800 Cheshire Yeomanry, 700 pensioners, 20,000 special constables, and 3 gunboats on the Mersey, all ready for the rising that never came.[22] Timely arrests, the massing of troops (see Table 11.4), and the decision by most English workingmen to stay away from Irish-influenced physical-force Chartism explain the absence of revolt in Lancashire in 1848.[23] The more serious threat to public order appeared to come, as always, from Ireland. Significantly, when that threat materialized in south Tipperary in late July, workers in the North of England did not join their Irish comrades in rising in rebellion.

1848 in Ireland

It is not in the language of the lawyer, or the police magistrate, that the wrongs and aspirations of an oppressed nation should be stated.
– Thomas Francis Meagher, speech to the Limerick Confederates,
May 1848

For my own part I cannot believe that 30,000 or 40,000 men could retain in servitude a nation of more than seven millions of persons, even though every soldier and policeman were faithful to the Paymaster rather than to his country. But remembering that all the police and more than one third of the soldiery are Irishmen, I feel convinced that if we had obtained . . . [a degree] of success . . . we should have been joined by no inconsiderable proportion of the police and of the Army.
– William Smith O'Brien, retrospect written in Kilmainham Gaol,
Dublin, August – September 1848

Catholic policemen ought to strip off their ignominious livery. . . . What they will do, for the present, is the reverse of . . . this.
– John Mitchel, journal, Newgate Prison, Dublin, 27 May 1848

In Ireland nationalist politics, dormant since Daniel O'Connell's bid for Repeal in 1843, reemerged following the news of France's February revolution. The Irish Confederates (est. January 1847), the political arm of the Young Ireland movement, proclaimed their alliance with the French republicans and, for the first time, with the English Chartists.[24] Like the Chartists, the Confederates employed the symbolic language of physical force; and like them, they made no real plans for an armed uprising and found little popular support for the idea. Unlike the Chartist leaders, the Confederate chieftains – Duffy, Meagher, O'Doherty, Dillon, O'Mahony, and O'Brien – were university-trained young men (most were in their twenties; O'Brien, at thirty-five, was the oldest) and had career aspirations in law, medicine, journalism, and politics. These who would lead the struggle for Irish separatism were, in short, well-educated, articulate, idealistic, and quite divorced from the mass of the people.[25] At a time when great numbers of men, women, and children were dying, emigrating, or stealing in order to eat (property crime quadrupled during the Famine years), the peasantry had more immediate concerns than coordinating an ill-timed, poorly planned rebellion.

The two men who would find themselves leading the rising of July 1848 were Thomas Francis Meagher and William Smith O'Brien. The twenty-five-year-old Meagher was the son of Thomas Meagher, prosperous merchant, Mayor of Waterford, and MP for Waterford City, 1847–57. Young Meagher, a handsome man and a powerful orator, had abandoned a career in law for one in Repeal politics; he gloried in the name "Meagher of the Sword," which in fact was a mocking phrase coined by Thackeray, the English novelist, after an especially rousing Meagher speech in 1846. O'Brien did not have Meagher's dash or eloquence, but his blood was aristocratic – son of a baronet and descendant of the noble O'Brien family – and since 1843 his dedication to Repeal was unquestioned. But O'Brien's background as a well-born Protestant nationalist landowner and his service, since 1828, as a Member of the Imperial Parliament – where he pressed for Poor Law and education reforms and, since 1843, for parliamentary inquiries into the causes of the Repeal agitation, the numbers killed in constabulary affrays (since 1831), and the death toll in the Famine – gave O'Brien's nationalism a constitutionalist tinge that he would find hard to remove in July 1848.[26]

Like other radical groups throughout the United Kingdom, the Irish Confederates combined an appeal to moral justice with the technique of the mass meeting. In mid-March a large crowd, estimated at 15,000, assembled in Dublin to laud the new government in France and to demand an independent one for Ireland. Subsequent meetings were held at Drogheda, Kilkenny, Roscrea, Cashel, and Clonmel. On 21 March the Government brought charges of sedition against Mitchel, Meagher, and O'Brien, but they were released after giving bail. O'Brien and Meagher then traveled to France to arrange a Confederate alliance with the new republic; but the intervention of Foreign Secretary Palmerston and Lord Normanby, now the English ambassador to Paris, caused Lamartine's government to rebuff the Irish delegation. This ended the French connection in 1848.[27] In Ireland, meanwhile, the constabulary reported arms buying and open drilling, but the Lord Lieutenant, the 4th Earl of Clarendon, noted that these threats did not constitute incipient rebellion. Indeed, fearing repression, the Confederates held back from any provocation of troops or police; and many in the peasantry thought that wild-talking John Mitchel was "nothing more than a vilifier of the name of the dead Liberator." At their trials in late May, Meagher and O'Brien were found not guilty of sedition; Mitchel's conviction and sentence to fourteen years' transportation produced little public outcry. Confederate clubs continued to arm and drill. By mid-June Clarendon was becoming increasingly concerned, and by early July even the London Government was coming to believe that an attempt at rebellion in Ireland was not unlikely[28] (see Figure 12.3).

Already in April, the Government had begun to react to the deepening crisis in both islands. The "Crown and Government Security Bill," introduced on 7 April, had its Second Reading on 10 April, the day of the great Chartist meeting on Kennington Common; among the opposition speakers in London that day was William Smith O'Brien, MP for County Limerick.

THE BRITISH LION AND THE IRISH MONKEY.
Monkey (Mr. Mitchell). "One of us MUST be 'Put Down.'"

Figure 12.3 The Irish Rising of 1848 (*Punch*). The Irish Sea separates two very different animal kingdoms. In Ireland, turbulent nonsense holds sway (note the torch and jester's cap on Mr. John Mitchel); in England, stately reason prevails (note the Crown). There is no question of who will be "put down": Monkeys may screech, but lions rule.

The coercion bill subsequently passed in the Commons by a vote of 295–40 and became law on 22 April.[29] The act made treason a felony punishable by transportation; its first victim, a month later, was the Irishman Mitchel. As the revolutionary threat receded in England, it appeared to become more intense in Ireland. From 9 to 13 July the Irish police made a series of key arrests: in Dublin, Charles Gavan Duffy and the radical editors, John Martin (*Irish Felon*) and D'Alton Williams and Kevin O'Doherty (*Irish Tribune*); in Cashel, Michael Doheny; in Wicklow, Thomas D'Arcy McGee; and in Waterford, Thomas Meagher. The first four were imprisoned in Newgate, the rest freed on bail. Meagher had thus now been twice arrested, twice released. The Government pressed ahead to prevent any rising, or, as O'Brien later charged, to hasten it on. On 21 July a Dublin Castle proclamation placed the cities and counties of Dublin, Cork, Drogheda, and Waterford under the 1847 Coercion Act and required all inhabitants in proclaimed districts to surrender their arms and ammunition.[30] The next day, in London, Lord John Russell, assisted by Home Secretary Sir George Grey, introduced a bill to suspend habeas corpus in Ireland for a period of seven months; the measure would permit the police to arrest and detain suspects without trial. The proposal, which met little opposition, became law on 25 July. A copy of

492

the act arrived in Dublin the next day: arrest warrants were issued for O'Brien, Meagher, and a dozen other Confederate leaders, and another proclamation legally dissolved the Confederate clubs.[31] Meanwhile, troops and police were massed and "a fleet of armed steamers" despatched to Waterford and Cork. The army in Ireland swelled from 20,000 men in 1846 to 29,000 by the end of 1848. The Government was behaving as if rebellion were imminent. The panic even affected *The Times*, the august London daily, which on 27 July reported that "the whole of the south of Ireland is in rebellion." *The Times*'s account – complete with reports of military disaffection and mob successes at Thurles, Clonmel, Carrick, and Kilkenny – was entirely erroneous.[32]

The rebellion, such as it was, was marked by high hopes and grand designs, and wretched planning and coordination. Fundamentally, the rebels' urge to action, as in 1916, was romantic, to commit a symbolic act. A few men, wrote Doheny afterward, determined "to throw themselves on the courage of the country." Mitchel recalled: "A kind of sacred wrath took possession of a few Irishmen at this period. They ... resolved to cross the path of the British car of Conquest, though it should crush them to atoms." In Meagher's sober retrospect, the rising was one "for which the country was very far from being sufficiently prepared."[33]

Dublin, with its 11,000 troops and 1,100 policemen, was wisely rejected as the place to begin the rebellion.[34] The choice of southeast Tipperary and western Kilkenny – a triangle 25 miles on each side bounded by Cashel, Kilkenny, and Carrick-on-Suir – was a good one. This region, not as Famine-ravaged as the western counties, had been heavily involved in the Rebellion of 1798, had given birth to the Tithe War, and had a long history of faction fighting and agrarian secret societies. Another consideration was the absence of rail communication. The recently completed railway from Limerick to Dublin had a branch line that stopped at Bagenalstown, a village fourteen miles north of Kilkenny town. Moreover, the hilly area, protected to the west and south by mountains, was one of thickly hedged fields and twisting, walled roads. Here was excellent guerrilla territory: "[W]hole regiments ...," Meagher would later write, "might have been surprised and cut to pieces, had the country been up."[35]

The favorable locale was to be wasted by the rebel leaders' almost total lack of planning. Provisions and sufficient arms were wanting, the numbers of Confederates exaggerated and communication between clubs inadequate, and links to the local agrarian secret societies undeveloped. Vague hopes and bizarre projects substituted for serious planning. Once Tipperary was "up," other risings were supposed to begin in Limerick and Meath.[36] Thomas D'Arcy McGee, a Young Ireland journalist, sailed from Belfast to Glasgow intending to seize a steamship and return with 400 Irish Confederates to Sligo in an attempt to "draw off some of the [government] forces from Munster." McGee did appear in Sligo, without any men, and the plan eventually aborted because the South had failed to rise.[37] From Liverpool, Terence Bellew McManus, a penurious shipping agent in that city, would join the

Tipperary rebels in time to fight at Ballingarry, but he too brought no force of men. From his residence in England, McManus was in fact unprepared for the shock of seeing people who "seemed to have had much of their physical courage starved out of them."[38]

The Rising of 1848 was actually a cat-and-mouse game between the confused Confederates and the military and police, who, by withdrawing detached parties into the towns, gave the rebels great freedom of movement. For a week, from 22 to 29 July, O'Brien, Meagher, and Dillon wandered from village to village. They addressed sympathetic crowds but found few armed supporters. Again and again, the leaders delayed the start of the rising. The land was "covered with detectives"; constables, sometimes "in coloured Clothes," were seen in the crowds taking notes on speakers' remarks. The Confederates treated the police and soldiers with remarkable courtesy and good humor; at each of the half-dozen places where the rebels encountered troops or constables, each side held back from fighting. O'Brien, Meagher, and Dillon later stated that they had seriously believed that government forces, mostly Irish and heavily Catholic, could be won over to the nationalist cause.[39]

The starting gun in the race to rebellion was the London Government's introduction of its bill to suspend habeas corpus, news of which arrived in Dublin by telegraphic dispatch on 22 July.[40] The Confederate executive council was now certain to be rounded up and held without bail or charge. O'Brien left Dublin for Wexford, where he was shortly joined by Dillon and Meagher.[41] From Enniscorthy, in the center of the county, the rebel leaders began their wanderings, heading westward toward Kilkenny (see Map 12.1). The band of 200 Confederates was preceded by a small advance party, lest the group be surprised by a body of constabulary. At Graigue, the birthplace of the Tithe War seventeen years earlier, the group received what would become a characteristic response: a rousing welcome but little ready armed support. The leaders pushed on to Kilkenny, the seventeenth-century capital and projected seat of the 1848 rising. There, on 23 July, they found 500 eager Confederates, only about 100 of whom were armed; O'Brien decided to postpone the rising at Kilkenny, whose military garrison contained 1,000 soldiers, until more men and arms could be secured.[42] O'Brien, Dillon, and Meagher headed south, to Callan, where they were impressed by the excited crowds, a bonfire in the main street, and houses decorated with laurel sprigs and green ribbons and flags. Here, unexpectedly, they encountered a troop of 8th Hussars on the march from Cork to Kildare. Neither side sought a confrontation; indeed, Meagher recorded that the flight of a terrified young English soldier produced raucous laughter from the Irish troopers. The rebel leaders fashioned their speeches to appeal to the soldiers and, on Meagher's prompting, the crowd raised three cheers for "the 8th Royal Irish Hussars." Police constables, who were also present, were likewise urged to come over to the people.[43]

The rebel party, unimpeded, continued south. At Nine Mile House, a stop to change horses, they conversed with a small party of police constables.

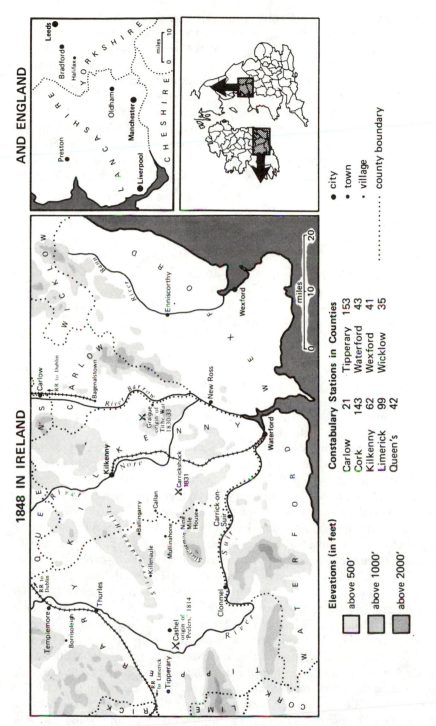

Map 12.1

1848 IN IRELAND

AND ENGLAND

WICKLOW

River Slaney

Enniscorthy

Wexford

River Barrow

Carlow

RR to Dublin

Bagenalstown

Graigue
origin of
Tithe War
1830–33

New Ross

CARLOW

KILKENNY

Kilkenny

Nore River

Carrickshock
1831

Callan

Ballingarry

Mullinahone Nine
Mile
House

Killenaule

Slievenamon

Carrick-on-
Suir

Suir River

Waterford

WATERFORD

WEXFORD

Clonmel

Cashel
origin of
'Peelers,' 1814

RR to
Dublin

Thurles

Borrisoleigh

Templemore

RR to Limerick

Tipperary

TIPPERARY

QUEEN'S

Slieveardagh

LIMERICK

CORR...CK

miles
10   20

Constabulary Stations in Counties

Carlow	21	Tipperary	153
Cork	143	Waterford	43
Kilkenny	62	Wexford	41
Limerick	99	Wicklow	35
Queen's	42		

Elevations (in feet)

above 500'

above 1000'

above 2000'

LANCASHIRE

Preston

Liverpool

Manchester

Oldham

Halifax

Bradford

Leeds

YORKSHIRE

CHESHIRE

miles
0   10

● city
● town
· village
·········· county boundary

Nearing Carrick, the rebels met Confederate John O'Mahony, son of a comfortable farmer and the future Fenian leader, who announced that his men were ready to rise. The rebels' arrival at Carrick-on-Suir on the evening of 24 July touched off wild celebrations. Dillon announced that the moment had come; "it was the Revolution, if we had accepted it," Meagher wrote later. But O'Brien held back, influenced by Carrick Confederate leaders who insisted that the district was not ready to rise. The deflated national leaders made the decision to turn west, toward Cashel, where Michael Doheny was thought to be mobilizing hundreds of well-armed peasants.[44] Plans for a rising, first at Kilkenny and now at Carrick, had collapsed in disappointment; a series of events was about to occur that would make the rebels appear pathetic.

Shortly after O'Brien, Dillon, and Meagher had left Carrick, O'Mahony arrived in town at the head of a large body of Confederates, some 12,000 men, if Doheny is to be believed. But these men, on finding the national leadership gone, simply dispersed. Doheny, meanwhile, had left Cashel to join O'Brien, Dillon, and Meagher in Carrick. The result was that O'Brien, Dillon, and Meagher arrived in Cashel to find Doheny gone, and Doheny arrived in Carrick to find them gone. In retrospect, the confusion at Carrick may not have been a crucial error. The town had allegedly enrolled 3,000 Confederates, but in fact only a tenth of them had rifles or muskets. The surrounding district was thick with troops, including the presence in Carrick itself of three infantry companies, two cavalry troops, and a large body of constabulary. Further, warships could easily have brought in reinforcements or shelled the rebels from the safety of the River Suir. Denis Gwynn's judgment must stand: A rising at Carrick would have been "crushed ... quickly and with much bloodshed."[45]

The end was near, and the rebels' final indecisive movements were those of a cornered animal. At Cashel, O'Brien ordered the Confederates to tear up the railway track at five spots between Dublin and Cashel; he abandoned a plan to assault the town's constabulary barrack and proclaim "the formation of a provisional government ... of an Irish Republic." O'Brien continued to delude himself that the mostly Catholic police constables would be sympathetic to his cause; Meagher, as part of his eight-point program for "an Irish Republic," invited all Irishmen in the British-controlled police and military to join a new-styled "Republican National Guard." O'Brien and Dillon now left Cashel, intending to return to Callan, where Meagher, reconnoitering the district between Clonmel and Carrick, was to meet them. En route to Callan, O'Brien and Dillon stopped at Killenaule, where the constables from the village's barrack listened intently as the rebel leaders described their travel plans to the crowd. Farther on, at Mullinahone, O'Brien harangued and drilled until late at night an estimated 2,000 Confederates armed with guns, pitchforks, and pikes. The next morning, O'Brien, Patrick O'Donohoe, and twenty-three-year-old James Stephens – a Kilkenny-born civil engineer employed by the Limerick and Waterford Railway, a Confederate local leader, and the future Fenian chief – approached the village's small constabulary barrack and demanded that the four constables and one sergeant surrender. The men refused, stating their fears of official reproval while also professing sympathy with the rebels' cause. O'Brien granted the men thirty minutes to consider his offer. When he returned, he found that the police had fled, taking their firearms with them, out the back door of the barrack.[46]

On 26 July, O'Brien arrived at Ballingarry. With him were Dillon and Stephens, who were soon joined by Meagher and, on the eve of the show-down, by McManus, the Liverpool merchant. Reacting to reports that a large body of military and police was assembling at Callan, the rebel group retreated in confusion and despair toward the mountain fastnesses of Slievenamon. Desertions cut the rebels' ranks from about 600 to no more than several dozen by the time they reached Mullinahone; O'Brien, now totally shaken, ordered the remnant to disperse, and the handful of leaders turned west to Killenaule. Here, on the 28th, they recouped their spirits while parading a fresh group of several hundred Confederates. News of the approach of two troops of the 8th Hussars led to the excited barricading of the village streets. But once again, both sides shunned violence. The genteel negotiations revealed that the Hussars were not on orders to make any arrests, only on their way to assize duty at Nenagh; on these assurances the 100 soldiers were allowed to pass, singly, through three barricades to the cheers of the crowds.[47]

There was no climax, only denouement, to this odd Irish rebellion of 1848. After Killenaule, fearing an imminent military and police attack, the would-be rebel organizers retreated to the collieries at Ballingarry. Here, in a final meeting, the small band decided to concede defeat. There would be no revolution in south Tipperary. O'Brien ordered everyone to return to his own district; as to Dillon, Meagher, O'Mahony, and Doheny, he "com-manded them to leave him, and consult for their own safety, to which at last they reluctantly yielded." Thus, remaining at Ballingarry commons on 29 July 1848, were only O'Brien, McManus, and Stephens and about 100 colliers, half of whom had firearms.[48]

The Government now began to close the trap. The previous day, in Dublin, rewards had been announced for the arrest of O'Brien (£500) and Meagher, Dillon, and Doheny (£300 each). Constabulary parties at Thurles, Kilkenny, Cashel, Callan, and Killenaule were ordered to converge on Ballingarry.[49] The final scene – later known as "the Battle at the Widow McCormick's Farmhouse" – was about to unfold.[50] Subinspector Thomas Trant and forty-six constables from Callan arrived at Ballingarry ahead of the other police parties. Seeing the isolated policemen, the crowd, estimated by Robert Curtis at "about 3,000," mostly women and children, gave chase. Trant's men fled up the hill to sanctuary in a slate-covered farmhouse. They got there just ahead of the mob; Trant had no time even to wrest the pistols from his saddle holsters. Mrs. McCormick was out, but her five young children were in the house. Trant kept them as hostages. Negotiations for the release of the children were proceeding between Trant and O'Brien (and the

Figure 12.4 The affray at the Widow McCormick's farmhouse, Ballingarry, County Tipperary, 29 July 1848. Holed up inside, the constabulary fire on the rebels, who are armed with firearms, pikes, scythes, rocks, and spades. (*Illus. London News*)

returned widow McCormick) at the front of the house when one person, "some fool in the crowd," threw a rock against a back kitchen window. After a shower of stones, the police fired into the large crowd, killing two young men and wounding several other persons.[51] The crowd thinned as the fighting began, the police responding with pistol shots to the barrage of stones, pistol shot, and musket balls aimed at them. Trant would later report using 230 rounds, with 1,600 unexpended cartridges still in the men's pouches[52] (see Figure 12.4).

Negotiations resumed when O'Brien – joined by the parish priest, Father Fitzgerald, and a recent arrival, a plainclothes constable named Carrol from Kilkenny – again conferred with Trant at a front window. Trant refused to give up his arms in exchange for a guarantee that the police would be allowed to depart uninjured. Carrol himself, as an exposed spy, owed his life to the rebel leader, for it is clear that "he would have been shot on the moment were it not that Smith O'Brien himself ordered and guaranteed his safety."[53] These second negotiations having failed, Carrol fled and Fitzgerald retired from the scene. Attempts were now made to set the house on fire, with the children still inside. The efforts proved unsuccessful only because the piles of hay were still wet from the heavy rain the day before. McManus and Stephens were the chief would-be arsonists; many of the colliers, whether from concern for the children or fear of exposing themselves to the policemen's fire, refused to help. O'Brien's role in this episode remains unclear.[54]

Arson having failed, some men began bringing up sledge hammers and heavy timber for an assault to break down the door. "Just then the cry arose, ... 'here are the Cashel police.'" Up rode Subinspector Joseph Cox with thirty-six constables; their first volley of shots scattered the crowd, and Trant's besieged party was rescued.[55] The Rising of 1848 thus ended

William Smith O'Brien

ARREST OF SMITH O'BRIEN AT THE RAILWAY STATION AT THURLES.

Figure 12.5 The arrest of Smith O'Brien. Photograph of W. S. O'Brien (*left*) from Doheny, *The Felon's Track*; and the melodramatic rendering of the incident in the *Illustrated London News*.

symbolically with the arrival of police from the Tipperary town to which, back in 1814, Robert Peel had despatched the first Peelers.

Though they had conquered the farmhouse at Ballingarry, the police were less successful in making arrests on the spot: O'Brien, McManus, and Stephens all escaped. O'Brien was nabbed a week later, at Thurles Railway Station on 5 August, when a porter named Hulme recognized him as he was about to board the train for Limerick (Figure 12.5). Hulme, with £500 on his mind, presented the passive rebel chief to a nearby Head Constable, 14-year veteran John Hanniver, who remarked, "All right, Hulme, you are the lucky man."[56] On the evening of the 12th, Meagher was arrested on a railway bridge not far from the police barrack at Rathgannon, five miles from Thurles.[57] McManus was subsequently seized in Cork Harbor aboard a ship about to sail for America.[58] Stephens, the Kilkenny surveyor, was the luckiest: He managed to escape to France. The arrested leaders, O'Brien, Meagher, and McManus, were convicted under the Treason Felony Act and transported "for life" in July 1849. In fact, their imprisonment would be short-lived; by the mid-1850s all three had left Australia.[59] Most of the Irish Confederate leaders who escaped arrest joined the wave of emigration to North America, where several of them established successful professional careers.[60] O'Mahony, like Stephens, fled first to France before heading for America. These men carried on the revolutionary tradition and are most remembered for their founding of the Fenian Brotherhood, jointly in New York and Dublin, in 1858.[61]

The English magazine the *Annual Register* dismissed it as "a miserable affair." John Mitchel, in penal exile in Bermuda, eloquently characterized it as "a poor extemporised abortion of a rising in Tipperary."[62] Why was O'Brien's rising doomed to failure? Was it an attempt at rebellion, or something else? What *were* the rebel leaders' intentions? What, finally, does 1848 represent in Irish history?

For a number of reasons, the rising was an abject failure. First, the timing was all wrong. The Potato Famine had taken a heavy physical and psychological toll: Tipperary's population, though not as ravaged as the populations of the western seaboard counties, did fall by one-fourth from 1845 to 1851. Second, the Catholic priests, supporters of O'Connell in 1843, were nearly all lined up against the Confederates in 1848. Hostile to the secularist, cosmopolitan, literary nature of Young Ireland, they also opposed any indulgence in violence. In every village the clergy counseled caution to their parishioners.[63] Third, the remnant of the O'Connellites, after their leader's death in 1847, refused to stray from constitutional reform. Fourth, many Confederates also opposed a policy of armed resistance; as recently as January 1848, by a vote of 317 to 188, the Irish Confederation had defeated Mitchel's call for rebellion.[64] Fifth, O'Brien and Meagher never built an alliance with key groups inured to violence – the peasant secret societies. The Confederates' emphasis on political nationalism to the exclusion of economic revolution – the refusal to promise a small farm, security of tenure, food – left many people uninterested. O'Brien's exhortation to the men assembled at Ballingarry on 26 July to return with four days' supplies of "oatmeal bread and hard eggs" brought groans from the crowd, many of whom had come "solely in the hope of being fed"; O'Brien's refusal to permit his followers to confiscate any livestock or private property only compounded the problem of provisioning.[65] In sum, in following the wanderings of O'Brien and his band through Tipperary in July 1848, one has the feeling of observing men who were out of place, detached from the local people. The "revolution" was a romantic set piece whose dramatic characters included too many leaders and never enough followers.

Moreover, the Confederates' behavior in south Tipperary suggests that there were no real plans or intentions for an uprising. In the course of the group's wanderings, such plans as there were, were not secretly hatched but publicly proclaimed, often in the presence of police. Dates for the rising were constantly postponed; a series of potential flashpoints passed without violence. Including Ballingarry, every rebel encounter with the Government's forces resulted in discussion and negotiation, often of a surprisingly good-natured kind. Time and again, the rebels demonstrated a pronounced unwillingness to fight.[66] The only incident in the 1848 Rising that involved bloodshed was the "battle" at Mrs. McCormick's farmhouse. This unplanned incident, triggered by the advance arrival of Trant's police party, was just another in a long line of constabulary affrays in early-nineteenth-century Ireland.[67] But contemporaries in the year of European revolutions, like some subsequent scholars, elevated it to the status of a rebellion.

O'Brien, Meagher, and the other leaders were comfortable with words, not guns. Angered beyond words by the Famine holocaust, desperate because of the premature British crackdown, including warrants for their own arrest, the Confederate leaders sought not to inaugurate a bloody revolt but to make a gesture, a symbol of protest. O'Brien on 21 July had stated that "armed resistance to the British Government had become a solemn duty." Afterward, in prison, he would explain, in rather vague terms, that his intent had been "not to throw the country into a state of actual insurrection" but to arouse "the moral energy ... and courage" of the Irish people.[68]

An interpretation of "the Irish '48" as a symbolic protest places the rising much closer to the 1916 Easter Rising than to the bloody wars for independence in 1798 and 1919–21. O'Brien's ideas of moral arming and defiance as "a solemn duty" represent a stage of protest somewhere between the constitutionalist agitation of O'Connell and the subsequent Sinn Fein ideology of Arthur Griffith. Also, in retrospect, it must be said that many features of the Irish '48 were remarkably similar to the English Chartist agitation in 1848. O'Brien and O'Connor believed in moral force; physical force was an exercise in rhetoric, a weapon to be used only as an implied threat.[69] Both men were romantic rebels who placed great value on symbolic, not bloody, deeds. Each man had considerable respect for the massive physical force of soldiers and policemen at the Government's disposal. Neither man chose physical confrontation or initiated a revolution in 1848. In Ireland in July, as in London in April, the Government waited for the protesters to make a false step. In London that step was never taken; in Ireland, after police and troops had waited ten days, it was finally taken at the widow McCormick's farmhouse.[70] The affray and its aftermath, in turn, helped to create the myth of the Irish rebellion of 1848 and to keep alive, for future generations, the idea of recurring revolution in modern Irish history. The year 1848 would be remembered as an inevitable revolutionary midpoint between 1798 and 1916.

II. After "the storm": the quiet reform of the English police, 1854–6

[T]he time would shortly arrive when they would reflect with surprise and astonishment that it had been seriously debated whether they should have throughout the country a uniform system of police, subject entirely to local management; or whether they should continue the present isolated, disjointed, and absurdly anomalous system, which was useless to the country at large.
– E. R. Rice, MP and chairman of the 1853 select committee on police, in a speech on the English county and borough police bill, March 1856

The completion of the modern system of police in England came in the aftermath of the age of "romanticism and revolt," 1815–48. In the 1850s –

Figure 12.6 Home Secretary Palmerston (*left*) and a pensive Edwin Chadwick. (Engraving in Palmerston, *Opinions and Policy*, 1852; Chadwick, as drawn in the *Illustrated London News*, 1848)

the dawn of a new era of "realism and nationalism,"[71] of railroads, working-men's unions, and state building – Englishmen would give their assent to a measure of centralizing police reform that only a decade earlier would have unleashed storms of protest. The final tidying up in England in 1856 was akin to the post–Tithe War consolidation of the Irish constabulary twenty years earlier. In 1856, as in 1836, the old antipolice attitudes based on fear of the loss of civil liberties were muted; when raised, they seemed hackneyed and old-fashioned. The contrast between the controversy over the 1839 county police bill and the placid reception accorded the English bill of 1856 was analogous to the earlier contrasting reactions to the Irish constabulary bills of 1822 and 1836.

   Yet, for all the similarities of 1856 to 1836, the differences remained critical. First, whereas the Irish Constabulary Act represented the capstone to administrative reforms in 1830–6, the English statute of 1856 merely required the establishment of forces in counties still without police and the improvement of policing in the smaller boroughs. Second, whereas the Irish reform of 1836 brought total centralization of police and the final triumph of English rule over Irish Protestant and Catholic factions, the English reform of 1856 represented a popular compromise that preserved local rights while adding a dose of central supervision. In Ireland, final police reform meant the end of any local control; in England, its reaffirmation. The 1836 constabulary bill had passed relatively quietly, apart from outbursts from Irish ultra-Protestants, because enlightened observers and former opponents, men like Cloncurry and Grattan, had come to recognize the necessity for an outside (i.e., English) third party to administer the police. Twenty years later, the English bill of 1856 passed equally easily because the consolidating measure simply confirmed past practices of local control; it inaugurated no revolutionary changes in the nation's policing.

The men behind the police reforms of the 1850s were Viscount Palmerston, Sir George Grey, and, in their shadow, Edwin Chadwick (Figure 12.6). The interests of Palmerston, an Englishman whose family had for five generations been absentee Irish landowners, had long been in foreign affairs.[72] Foreign Secretary for some fifteen years under four Whig Administrations, Palmerston had most recently, in 1851, been forced from office over his high-handed personal diplomacy with Greece and France. In December 1852, the sixty-eight-year-old Palmerston accepted the post of Home Secretary with an eye on the prime ministership, which he would attain in 1855. Nothing in Palmerston's papers suggests any strong interest in home affairs; specifically, there is no mention of the Government's police proposals in 1853–6. Palmerston's Home Secretary, Sir George Grey (1855–8), was no stranger to the office, having served in it for six years in Russell's Administration. Unfortunately, Grey's role in the police reform of 1856 will never be properly known, for his private papers as Home Secretary were destroyed in a fire at the family estate in 1917.[73] The extant records indicate that the driving force behind the revision of the English provincial police in the 1850s was Chadwick.

Both Palmerston and Chadwick believed that the most efficient police was one organized along the lines of the Irish and London models. Chadwick, who believed that public sentiment had turned toward a national police, now hoped for more than an amalgamation of borough forces with county ones. The borough police he judged generally inferior, and the county JPs were "generally entirely at sea upon the whole subject of the police organization." Chadwick thus counseled Palmerston to reorganize all existing forces into a new "General Police" governed from London. A new "Police Department" within the Home Office would relieve the overworked Home Secretary, supervise the separate London and General Police, and oversee the collection of national criminal statistics. For Chadwick, who repeatedly referred to the Irish and London examples, the key was "central initiative and government."[74]

But Chadwick's secret recommendations to Palmerston in 1853–4 – like his public ones to Lord Russell in the *Constabulary Report* of 1839 – were too radical to win acceptance. In April 1853, three months after he became Home Secretary, Palmerston promoted the appointment of a select committee on police. Its fifteen members, all gentlemen connected with the counties, did not include Chadwick, who appeared only briefly as one of the fifty-seven persons to give evidence.[75] The great majority of the witnesses in May and June were county police officers and county magistrates favorable to the new police; the boroughs, large and small, were virtually unrepresented among either the committee members or the witnesses.[76] The proceedings of the 1853 select committee were as well orchestrated as had been Chadwick's 1839 commission and Peel's 1828 committee. The evidence introduced in 1853 painted a vivid picture of unchecked crime in the smaller boroughs and in those counties without the new police. The committee report made three main recommendations. First, police should be made compulsory in all counties; committee members glossed over the fact that over the past decade, JPs in only seventeen counties had been sufficiently convinced of the advantages of the new police to adopt a countywide force. Second, the report recommended that small boroughs abolish their own separate forces and be "consolidated" for policing purposes with the surrounding county force; again, the committee disregarded the fact that since 1840 only thirteen boroughs (with a combined population of 62,000) had seen fit to exercise their legal option to consolidate. Large boroughs were to be encouraged to share manpower and information with the county force. Third, the central government should help to pay the costs of "an improved and extended system of Police."[77] Such, then, were the principal recommendations of the 1853 committee, "two-thirds" of whose members, a critic later charged, "had begun the inquiry with their minds made up."[78]

The "General Police" Bill of 1854

Buoyed by the committee report of July 1853, Chadwick's tutelage, and his own commitment to a powerful police, Palmerston drafted in December 1853 the "suggested heads of a bill ... for establishing a General Police in England and Wales." Although the proposal fell far short of recommending the establishment of a London-controlled national constabulary, it did serve as the basis for the strongest provincial police bill ever placed before Parliament. The bill's basic principles were preservation of local control and management but the addition of central supervision over, and improved coordination between, the various police forces. The principal clauses would do the following:

Require all counties to establish police forces

Abolish separate police forces for boroughs and counties with small populations and consolidate them with forces in the surrounding or adjacent county

Give the Home Office the power to set rules regarding pay, allowances, and clothing; establish general regulations; direct the police in the performance of their duties; and require regular reports from county and borough Chief Constables

Establish four government "Inspectors" to supervise all borough and county forces

What Palmerston's bill proposed was not merely the restructuring of the borough and county police. The recommendation of government inspection and the intended erosion of municipal autonomy were unprecedented in the history of the English provincial police. The bill's greatest impact would be on the boroughs, which, unlike the counties, had hitherto escaped any sort of accountability to London. It was from the boroughs that intense resistance quickly emerged.[79]

Municipal authorities, already angered by the 1853 committee's charges of lax and inefficient borough policing, began to unite against what they saw as "the proposed measure for consolidating the police of counties and boroughs." At York, on 2 February 1854, four months before the bill's introduction in Parliament, a meeting attended by 26 MPs (including Joseph Hume, Richard Cobden, and John Bright) and by mayors and aldermen from York, Leeds, Birmingham, Nottingham, and twenty smaller towns resolved "to resist by every legitimate means ... this most unjustifiable attack upon the rights and liberties of Municipal Corporations." The next day, after traveling by rail to London, a deputation of borough officials and twenty-one MPs met with Palmerston at the Home Office. As he listened, stunned but apparently unruffled, the deputation berated the findings of the 1853 select committee; remonstrated that the boroughs "possessed sufficient intelligence to manage their own affairs, and were quite capable of self-government"; and even argued that "the facilities afforded by the electric telegraph" and other modern forms of communication rendered unnecessary any consolidation or centralization of police. In reply, Palmerston promised that their arguments would receive his "fullest consideration" and "most careful attention." To be sure, the borough officials' talk of "unconstitutional interference with their privileges and independence" was not empty rhetoric, since any borough consolidated under the terms of the bill would forfeit municipal independence in police matters and exchange local elective control for rule by distant and electorally unaccountable county magistrates.[80]

Palmerston and Chadwick were conscious of the mounting opposition from the boroughs as they labored over the police bill. From December 1853 to June 1854 the bill went through several drafts; four are preserved in Chadwick's papers. Some of the changes strengthened the bill. The number of *counties* proposed for consolidation, all under 60,000 population, was increased from two to four (to Radnor and Rutland were added Merioneth and Westmorland). Control of the county police would shift from magistrates at quarter sessions to a smaller "County Police Board" elected by and composed of no more than twenty magistrates. In the boroughs, the appointment of constables was to be transferred from the Watch Committee to the Chief Constable, an officer who might be made more directly accountable to the Government

But some of the original proposals were seriously weakened. The population below which *boroughs* would be faced with compulsory consolidation with the county police was lowered from 60,000 to 20,000. By this change, not 20 but 50 boroughs would be saved from consolidation; nevertheless, 149 of the country's 199 boroughs, or 75 percent, still stood to lose their separate police forces. A second weakened provision concerned the power of establishing police districts within counties and determining the number of district constables; this power was to be transferred from the Home Office to each County Police Board. A third change was the elimination of the original requirement for a minimum (if unspecified) ratio of police to population in both counties and boroughs; in its place, the Home Office was to be given the right to appoint additional constables as it deemed necessary.

A few of the original proposals were simply abandoned. Missing in the bill presented to Parliament was a clause that would have empowered the Government to consolidate any "inefficient" borough with its adjacent county. A note in the draft bill of December 1853 explained that this provision was aimed at "a more populous class of boroughs" than the smallest ones; the point appears to have been covered in the draft bill dated March 1854, which specified compulsory consolidation for all boroughs of less than 60,000 population, but three months later it was effectively lost when, in the bill presented to Parliament, the population figure was cut to 20,000. Also absent from the final bill was the original proposal that the Government pay from the Consolidated Fund one-fourth of all police costs of the consolidated boroughs.[81] It is unclear why this inducement to consolidation was scratched as early as January 1854. The issue of government funding would resurface in another form in the 1856 police bill.

On 2 June 1854, after six months of revision, Palmerston introduced his watered-down bill in the Commons. What had begun as a draft measure to establish "a General Police," was now rather tamely titled "A Bill to render more effectual the Police in Counties and Boroughs in England and Wales." Only a handful of MPs (six) spoke, all in opposition, but Palmerston was surprised that they included county as well as borough Members. Municipal opposition was not far behind. On 21 June, sixty mayors who had traveled to the capital met with Palmerston to protest the liquidation of their historic liberties. Even large cities like Birmingham and Manchester, which would be unaffected by the plan to consolidate borough with county police, joined ranks with their smaller sister institutions. The *Birmingham Journal*, which professed "no crotchety notions on the subject of centralisation," objected to the bill's infringement of civil liberties and its potential for "espionage and coercion." The *Manchester Guardian* even claimed to discern an attempt by the Government to reimpose on the city the London-directed police of 1839–42, which had been "most unpopular amongst all classes."[82]

On 27 June, John Bright, the prominent Liberal MP for Manchester, asked in the Commons if the bill was to be withdrawn; three days later, Palmerston conceded, announcing that he had no intention of pressing a police measure against such opposition. The controversial bill was abandoned. The boroughs had won the first battle. In a parting shot, the Manchester Corporation sent Palmerston a formal protest against the dead bill, which, they alleged, had endeavored to "engraft on this country that system so objectionable in France, Germany, and Italy." The city councillors announced their outrage "that a bill of so ... indefensible a character should ever have been introduced in the House of Commons."[83]

On 3 July, in an attempt to salvage something from his months of preparation, Palmerston again tested the parliamentary waters by announcing his desire to bring in a bill that would only require every county to have a police force. This proposal, too, was hooted down and Palmerston was forced to withdraw it the very same day. A year later, he recalled that "he had no more chance of passing the Bill in that House than a parish constable in Somersetshire had of apprehending a thief."[84]

The 1854 bill was a stunning failure. One reason was that in its centralizing tendencies and its almost brutal disregard for historic municipal autonomy – three-fourths of all boroughs would lose their police – the proposal was far too radical a break with English traditions of local policing. In part, too, the bill's failure was due to the atmosphere of intransigence created by both parties, Palmerston and the borough authorities. Stunned by the opposition, Palmerston appeared, on the one hand, either frightened or else curiously unprepared to back his bill and, on the other, disinclined to amend it until it was acceptable. After months of preparation, the bill was discussed only briefly on the floor of the Commons; it vanished almost immediately after seeing the light of day. Palmerston probably made the mistake of inferring from the boroughs' hostility, and from the opposition of MPs who spoke against the bill, that Parliament was opposed to any major reform of the police.

Yet, only two years later, in the spring of 1856, Sir George Grey, Home Secretary in Palmerston's Administration, would achieve a dramatic success with the Government's second try at reforming England's provincial police. The keys then would be Grey's persistence and his willingness to compromise with local authorities; the impact of certain key events in 1854–6; and the emergence of a new public opinion on the police, which had perhaps existed but been untapped in 1854.

Failure in 1854, success in 1856: exploring the reasons

What were the conditions in England that prompted the 1853 select committee investigation and that kept alive the police issue in 1854–6? Perhaps the chief long-term inducement to police reform was the growth of the railways. Since the Chartist crisis of 1839, the iron highways had multiplied sevenfold to a length of more than 7,000 miles; the steam engine now carried modernity into even the smallest towns (see Map 12.2). As early as 1841, Manchester Police Commissioner Sir Charles Shaw had noted, "Since the establishment of the Railways, a complete revolution in Police affairs has occurred." Lancashire's industrial towns were less than a half hour's travel by rail, yet, Shaw complained, in them he had no jurisdiction and was, in fact, "totally excluded from knowing what was occurring in places at a distance of 15 Minutes" from the center of his city. In 1853, Chadwick, who remarked on "the extraordinary development of railway communication," recalled how in the anti–Poor Law Riots of the 1830s it had taken the military two days to move 28 miles; now, from London "we may send 1,000 Policemen in 4 hours into Lancashire after a telegraphic despatch." The railroads, which made both criminals and troops more mobile, had raised the police issue to more than a local question.[85]

Changes in another kind of transportation stimulated rethinking about the English police. Demands for self-government by the free settlers in the

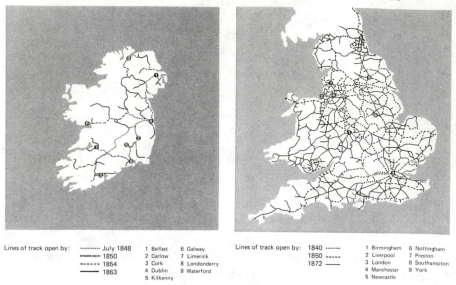

IRISH RAILWAYS   1848–1863   ENGLISH RAILWAYS   1840–1872

Lines of track open by:	········ July 1848		1 Belfast	6 Galway
	▬▬▬ 1850		2 Carlow	7 Limerick
	----- 1854		3 Cork	8 Londonderry
	▬▬ 1863		4 Dublin	9 Waterford
			5 Kilkenny	

Lines of track open by:	1840 ········		1 Birmingham	6 Nottingham
	1850 -----		2 Liverpool	7 Preston
	1872 ▬▬		3 London	8 Southampton
			4 Manchester	9 York
			5 Newcastle	

Map 12.2 The spread of railways in England and Ireland.

growing Australian colonies forced the English Government in 1853 to end transportation as a criminal punishment. The achievement, by 1856, of representative local government in Australia impinged directly on the police question in England. Denied its export outlet, and rejecting the solution of erecting a costly system of prisons, the Government devised a domestic scheme known as "penal servitude." The plan provided for early release, by a "ticket of leave," for convicts on good behavior. The new system, which prompted a select committee inquiry in 1856, led to fears that the country would be swarming with discharged prisoners.[86] Chadwick warned of 30,000 miscreants let loose, "greater than the British force . . . at Waterloo." Government leaders Palmerston and Grey cited the potential threat. Even opponents of the proposed new police could not ignore "the ticket-of-leave system which seemed to have frightened everybody so much"; a strengthened police force, it was conceded, was now "a matter of necessity." Newspapers opposed in 1856 to the Government's police proposals also acknowledged the crisis produced by the ending of transportation.[87]

Although the railroads had knit the nation together and the new system of criminal punishment appeared to require a nationwide supervisory police, other factors urged on police reform. One was the Crimean War. War on Russia was declared in March 1854; the fighting began six months later; Sebastopol fell in September 1855; the Paris peace conference assembled in February 1856 and the war ended officially in April. The Government had presented its first, abortive police bill in June 1854; debates on the second and final bill ran from February through June 1856.[88] The war impinged on the police question in a number of ways. First, military detachments, concentrated especially in northern England, had to be withdrawn as troops were shipped to the East. Second, the war took a heavy toll on both the men and the reputation of the British army. Aristocratic officers' incompetence and the Government's bureaucratic bungling played a large part in the deaths of 33,000 British and Irish soldiers, most of whom were victims of disease or untreated wounds. Third, for the 60,000 men coming home, the idea of returning to their traditional and, for them, long unpopular role as the bulwark against popular protest was unpalatable. In 1815–48, the over-reliance on the military in policing protest had harassed and tried the patience of officers and men alike. But it was, finally, the gruesome events in the Crimea that spurred the Government, in March 1856, to announce that its postwar domestic policy would be the concentration of troops in military camps.[89] The soldiers were no longer to be available for detached police duties; the proposed national police system would have to take up the slack in suppressing any domestic disorders.

There was, after 1848, a marked decline in riot and political protest. "The transition to order" was not sudden, but it was steady; by the 1860s, social commentators were "far more concerned with the general problems of crime than the specific question of disorder." It is clear from the extensive police debates in 1856 that social problems were seen to be sheep stealing and housebreaking, not political unrest; indeed, some speakers cited the absence of popular crisis as a reason for their opposition to police reform.[90]

A few lingering disorders did prompt some observers to argue for a strengthened police. In the "well remembered" No-Popery, anti-Irish riots at Stockport in 1852, fifteen constables proved helpless in a town of 54,000. The disorders required military intervention and left 1 dead and 100 injured. A strike at Preston in 1853–4 led to violence when the employers imported Irish "blackleg" labor.[91] In London in the summer of 1855, a Sabbatarian shop-closing bill sparked a series of protests. The largest meeting, in Hyde Park on 1 July, drew a crowd estimated at 150,000; police baton charges produced seventy-two prisoners and charges of police brutality. Effective police repression of the "Sunday Trading Riots" served to remind Englishmen of the utility of a civil force against crowds. In the police debates of 1856, when one speaker questioned the behavior of the Metropolitan Police in the recent riots, another asked the House to consider the condition of the capital in the summer of 1780.[92]

On the whole, however, in the 1850s popular disorders were viewed not as a pressing present problem but with the comfortable detachment of retrospect. It was not so much that 1848 had revealed the weaknesses in the English police system, as one scholar has argued,[93] but rather that after 1848 many Englishmen were at last coming to terms with the idea that a strong police might have been desirable earlier. The experience of provincial policing since 1839 had assuaged the fears of police tyranny; from the safe haven after the storms of 1815–48 came the belated realization that the police could suppress disorders without extinguishing civil liberties.

With this recognition came a sense of lost opportunities, of police reform long overdue. In his memorandum prepared for the 1853 police committee, Chadwick took a long look at the turmoil of the previous decade. He recalled how in 1842 the police in the northern boroughs acted "from jealousy" and "in practical isolation" from each other; how the Lancashire constabulary was "totally isolated from each of the Boroughs & acting separately"; and how, in general, "entire reliance had to be placed in the military." Had there been an effective coordinated police, stated Chadwick, "the rioting might have been stopped at once." The Benthamite utilitarian was not alone in his musings. The *Bath Herald* in March 1856 argued that the existence of a capable "purely civil force" in Newport in 1839 would have prevented the shedding of blood by the military. Indeed, the newspaper asked its readers to "look back to the SWING burnings of 1829 [*sic*]" when the military, Yeomanry, and makeshift vigilante bands had restored order. "How much more useful would have been a body of well-trained rural police."[94]

It was, then, in this changed climate of the mid-1850s – in a nation unified by the railways but challenged by the end to its overseas export of criminals; a nation quiet on the domestic front but embarrassed by military blunders abroad – that Englishmen were beginning to admit that some central supervision and control were essential to effective policing. Centralization, argued the *Brighton Examiner* in 1856, was accepted as necessary to administer the army and navy, collect excise and customs, and supervise poor relief and factory labor; why not for the police? Indeed, would not some central control "root out local abuses, and petty, ... mischievous local influences"? The newspaper recalled the fears when Peel had established the London police, noting that "after a few years, everbody wondered how the country had existed in safety under the 'Charleys' [the night watchmen]." The London *Morning Post* concisely pronounced Peel's creation of the Metropolitan Police "the most unquestionably useful act of his life." Even the Irish example drew praise. A correspondent to the *Brighton Examiner* stated that "the constabulary in Ireland has the reputation of being the best in the United Kingdom." The *Examiner*, which judged an effective police "as necessary to the proper management of a town as gas-lighting," argued that a centrally supervised police presented "no danger to general freedom," since the forces were required to report annually to Parliament. The old fears, concluded the *Norfolk Chronicle*, were

anachronisms, mere hypothesis and exaggeration – mere figures of speech got up to alarm timid Councillors and to make a "telling" speech.... With our free institutions who has any fear of Austrian despotism or a military police finding favour here, except, indeed, it be a few political lecturing firebrands ...?[95]

A second try: the Police Act of 1856

Palmerston and Chadwick did not concede defeat in 1854. The Home Secretary continued to be concerned about the inadequacies of the provincial police. In June of that year, even as his bill was being ignominiously rejected,

Table 12.1. *Police forces in English towns of "the secondary class," March 1856*

	Population	No. of police	Police-population ratio
Portsmouth	80,000	42	1:1905
Preston	70,000	37	1:1892
Bolton	61,000	27	1:2259
Stockport	54,000	24	1:2250
Oldham	53,000	32	1:1656
Blackburn	47,000	26	1:1808
York	36,000	29	1:1241
Ashton–under–Lyne	31,000	17	1:1824

Palmerston acidly penned a note to a police return from Aberdeenshire, Scotland: "The *number* of Police appears extremely scanty." In August he chastised the Mayor of Northampton that seventeen constables in a town of 27,000 could not be expected to contain the recent disorders there; the town authorities should "lose no time in organizing a Sufficient & Effective Police," since the Government in the future would not supply "Military assistance." In January 1855, in denying the request of a Berkshire JP for a shipment of Metropolitan Police, Palmerston noted that if the counties did not establish a police force, "they must abide by the Consequences of their choice." The following January the county established a police force.[96]

In February 1855, Lord Aberdeen's Government fell as a result of its mishandling of the ongoing war in the Crimea. Palmerston was elevated to Prime Minister and, under the circumstances, was diverted from domestic concerns. But in March, Palmerston's Home Secretary, Sir George Grey, issued a circular to thirty-eight boroughs of "the secondary class" – those above 20,000 but below 100,000 population. The circular urged these boroughs to increase the number of their policemen to at least 1 per 1,000 inhabitants and warned them that, because of military exigencies in the Crimea, the detachment of troops at home would no longer be available "as a substitute for police in cases of emergency." Only fourteen – well under half – of the boroughs bothered to acknowledge receipt of the circular; a year later, in the spring of 1856, the levels of policing in towns of the secondary class remained virtually unchanged[97] (see Table 12.1). A final sign of the Government's resolve to confront the police question came in May 1855 when, in a lackluster debate on a private Member's bill to reform the old parish constable system, Palmerston persuaded the bill's sponsor to withdraw his measure because of promised imminent changes in the system of borough and county police.[98]

The Government's second police bill in as many years was introduced on 5 February 1856. It was far less controversial than the 1854 bill. That measure had proposed compulsory police consolidation for boroughs under 20,000 population; the 1856 bill made it optional for any borough regardless of size.

The 1854 proposal to consolidate four small counties with adjacent larger ones was missing in the 1856 bill. Whereas two years earlier the appointment of borough constables was to have been transferred from the Watch Committee to the Chief Constable, now the appointment remained with the Watch Committee. The innovative concept of a County Police Board was scratched; justices at quarter sessions would continue to control the county police.

But some controversial proposals from 1854 were retained. For the borough as well as the county police, the Home Office would be empowered to frame "general regulations" and to set rules regarding pay, allowances, clothing, and accoutrements. County and borough constables were to perform such police duties as directed by county JPs, borough Watch Committees, or the Home Secretary. The heads of the police forces in the counties and boroughs were to report to the Home Secretary when and as he should direct. And by a new requirement, the four salaried Government Inspectors of Constabulary were to authorize reimbursement, by means of a Treasury grant, for one-fourth of all expenses for pay and clothing to boroughs and counties that were certified "efficient" in policing. No minimal police-to-population ratios were required, but as an inducement to the smallest towns to abolish their separate police forces, there was to be *no* Treasury payment to any unconsolidated borough, however efficient, of under 5,000 population.

In presenting the bill in Commons, Home Secretary Sir George Grey, MP for Stockport, explained that he hoped to "provide as efficient a police force, both for counties and boroughs, as is possible under the existing system of local management." Although, suggested Grey, "one uniform system of police under one central head, similar to that recommended by the Commission of 1839, ... might theoretically be the best system, [it] would not, I am afraid, meet with much support in the country." The 1856 bill would not establish a centralized government police, such as Ireland had, nor was it as revolutionary as Palmerston's 1854 bill. It did require that the twenty counties without a constabulary establish one. It did seek to improve crime prevention and police coordination by inducing the sixty-four boroughs of under 5,000 population to merge their tiny police with the neighboring county force. In short, the bill sought not to usurp local rights, but only to make the police system relatively uniform and efficient by means of government inspection and the Treasury grant. The reaction to the bill's introduction in Commons was deceptively congenial: All ten speakers gave their approval. Grey thanked Members for "the very favourable reception" to his bill.[99]

But opposition soon appeared, and from a familiar quarter. At a meeting in London on 20 February, mayors and councilmen representing Birmingham, York, Leeds, Portsmouth, and two dozen towns of the secondary class, denounced the bill precisely as a usurpation of local rights. The measure would put an end to Englishmen's "characteristic and time-hallowed municipal government"; it proposed "a virtual repeal" of the Municipal

Corporations Act of 1835. Borough police would become "mere fiscal agents of a Minister of the Crown." The next day, a deputation demanded from Grey nothing less than withdrawal of the police bill; Grey, intransigent, refused.[100] The bill's opponents began to circulate petitions, and within a month 150 boroughs had submitted protests to the Commons. The largest, with 18,000 signatures, was from Birmingham; only ten petitions favored the Government's bill.[101] Borough newspapers launched a brief, vigorous campaign. The *Portsmouth Times* objected to the proposed "continental police in free England." The *Birmingham Journal, York Herald,* and *Wigan Examiner* opposed the bill; the *Oldham Chronicle* reported its borough council's objection to this "nationalisation of the police force into a little army of truncheon bearers, with the Home Secretary for Commander-in-Chief, ... and the transition [sic] of town corporations into mere Commissariat Boards."[102]

Although most borough authorities and some newspapers were opposed, many provincial papers favored the bill. It was "wholly removed from ... party politics," proclaimed the *Bath Herald*, which noted that a series of recent events – the end of transportation, the army's experiences in the Crimea, the unpoliced Stockport Riots (1852), and the police-repressed Sunday Trading Riots (1855) – all argued for the bill's passage. The *Brighton Examiner* saw in the measure "nothing ... to be frightened at." The Conservative *Norfolk Chronicle* and the Liberal *Manchester Guardian* gave their approval.[103] Even newspapers, like the *Portsmouth Times*, that were against the bill conceded that the English police was "anomalous and inefficient ... a remedy is really required."[104]

At the bill's Second Reading, on 10 March, Home Secretary Grey went on the offensive, delivering a masterful, fact-studded, two-hour speech on the need for reform. The subsequent debate lasted for three hours. Only seven of the twenty-one Members speaking gave their support. The bill's proponents reiterated Grey's points that in an age of railways and telegraphs, of government control of prisons and the Post Office, it should be acceptable to have a complete system of police under government supervision. As Robert Palmer, MP for Berkshire, observed, "It was quite as much the duty of the Government to prevent crime as to punish it." The coming of age of this basic idea was the result of a number of recent pressures – the end of transportation and of the Crimean War and, to a lesser extent, the riots and strikes of recent years.[105]

The general tone of the speeches against the Government's police bill revealed the shift in basic attitudes. Few Members were now *antipolice*; most worried about the degree of centralization in the bill. But if the heated rhetoric and protests over the institution of police were now spent, a few speakers did keep the old fears alive. Frederic Knight, MP for Worcestershire (1841–85), was alarmed that the Government sought to add to Poor Law and public health inspectors "the curse" of a "Police Minister." George T. ("Captain") Scobell, MP for Bath, excoriated the bill as "the most un-English measure he had ever read ... more fitted for Naples than for England." His alarmist mind envisioned the country "overrun by 20,000 armed policemen – perhaps Irishmen or foreigners – upon whom a bad Government could rely for the perpetuation of acts of oppression." Significantly, the next speaker, Sir Henry Stracey, noted that "the history of Police Bills" in England was that the measures were at first unpopular, that the new police became progressively more popular, and that, unlike on the Continent, ministers had refrained from acts of oppression.[106]

By and large, the bill's opponents kept their arguments within rational bounds. When Members objected to the Government's interference in local borough government, they pointed out that corporate boroughs were elective, self-governing units, whereas county government, through JPs, was electorally unaccountable. The two entities were "essentially different."[107] Another objection, essentially unanswered, was, why the need now for police reform? The optional county police had been instituted in a time of serious domestic crisis. Now, in tranquil 1856, the constabulary was to be made compulsory even though, in the seventeen years since 1839, half of the counties in England and Wales, in whole or in part, had seen no need to establish police forces. "The only argument," noted one speaker, was the "convenience" of consolidation.[108] A third objection, also unrefuted, was that the criminal statistics gave no clear edge to the new police in deterring crime or increasing the apprehension of criminals. Joseph Henley, MP for Oxfordshire (1841–78) and an advocate of the parish constables system, presented detailed figures for 1840–54 that demonstrated that the number of committals in counties without rural police (Buckinghamshire, Kent, Lincolnshire, Oxfordshire) was "nearly the same" as in counties that had rural police (Cambridgeshire, Essex, Norfolk, Suffolk).[109]

All of these arguments fell on deaf ears in the Commons. After five hours, the House was weary of the debate. Members impatiently cried, "Divide! Divide!" When the vote was taken, the bill passed by 259–106.[110]

The seven speeches that had been made for and the fourteen against the bill had hardly reflected the sentiment of the House. Those Members who had spoken against the measure generally represented counties without the new police and boroughs of the secondary class.[111] Yet, in the voting, county MPs gave the bill strong support, and the borough MPs – who in the composition of the Commons outnumbered county representatives by more than two to one – actually voted 83–69 in favor of the bill. The vote also revealed that, as in 1829, 1835, and 1839, police was not a divisive issue between the major parties. The Liberals (by 99–42, or 70 percent in favor) and the Whigs (14–2, 88 percent) endorsed the bill sponsored by Palmerston's Liberal Government. But it was the support of the Conservatives and Liberal Conservatives (Peelite Tories) that gave the Government its victory; in these two groups, the vote was 119–50, or 64 percent in favor. Most significant was the Radical vote, of 15–12, or 56 percent, approving the police bill. Indeed, *none* of the parliamentary groups withheld its approval.[112]

The vote on the Second Reading – one of the largest votes in the parliamentary session – was a great victory for Palmerston's year-old Government.

One newspaper predicted that "the signal success of the Police Bill" would ward off a general election. At a time when Englishmen were restive over government ineptitude in winning the war in the Crimea, a defeat on its second police bill in two years might have been very damaging to Palmerston's Government.[113]

How to explain the easy passage of the 1856 bill? Most basically, the police had become accepted: Where earlier the very idea had been dismissed as a risky, unconstitutional innovation, now it had become a routine institution. Experience was also a great teacher: Since 1829 and 1839, the English police, whether under government or local control, had neither organized permanent, nationwide networks of spies nor institutionalized acts of oppression. Those Members voting for Grey's bill accepted his arguments for police reform and gave little credence to the scaremongering rhetoric of some opponents or, indeed, to the calmer argumentation of others. The uproar by local borough authorities was dismissed by MPs as unjustified by the bill's provisions and representative only of their own vested interests.

The Government also contributed substantially to the bill's passage. The 1856 bill was less frightening than the 1854 one, and Grey and a now wiser Palmerston accepted a series of amendments in the spring of 1856 that watered down the original bill until it was acceptable to a large majority in the Commons. Clause 6, "the backbone of the bill," was excised. The Government forfeited its power to establish rules over pay and clothing or to frame a set of general regulations; all that remained was a prohibition of constables' fee taking. Clause 5, giving the Home Office the right to direct police in the performance of their duties, was also stricken. The original requirement that the heads of the county and borough forces report at the will of the Home Secretary (Clause 8) was diluted to the requirement that they present him with an annual statement of crime (Clause 14). The Home Secretary's right to require counties to be divided into police districts (Clause 2) was softened by requiring affected county ratepayers to petition for this districting. By May, as these amendments altered the complexion of the bill, initial arch-opponents like Captain Scobell and Mr. Henley were congratulating Grey on his "prudence" in making concessions.[114]

The concessions to local control were matched by the attractions of tax relief. Borough and county police were, until 1856, funded entirely from local rates. Grey's bill proposed, however, that one-fourth of the expenses for pay and clothing be paid from the Consolidated Fund. A similar proportion of the costs of the Metropolitan Police were paid from this fund of national tax monies. In Ireland, half of the costs of the Dublin police and the constabulary had long been subsidized by United Kingdom taxpayers; indeed, since 1846, no Irish local taxes had paid for the constabulary. Grey's proposed Treasury grant to the English borough and county police was simply the last in a series of government police subsidies. After the settling of issues of principle, MPs in May 1856 concentrated on matters of principal. Several speakers sought to increase the Government's contribution to one-half amid cries of "justice" for local "real estate" owners. When the

Chancellor of the Exchequer, Sir George Cornewall Lewis, replied that this would "abolish the entire system of local taxation," MPs responded with groans of "No!, No!" So numerous were the demands in the final debates that the Radical John Roebuck, MP for Sheffield, charged Members with selling their constitutional principles in exchange for tax relief. The Government prevailed, however, and managed to hold its contribution to one-fourth.[115] The amended bill had its Third Reading in the Commons on 23 May, sailed easily through the Lords (Third Reading, 27 June), and received the royal assent on 21 July.[116]

III. A legacy of permanence

In the British archipelago, unlike on the Continent, the events of 1848 produced no overhaul of the system of police. In part, this was because of the tameness of the protests in 1848; in part, because of the effectiveness of the existing systems of social control. In Ireland, a nation prostrated by the Famine, the constabulary had easily suppressed the Confederates' symbolic rising; in England, where the Chartists attempted no rising, it was the police in London and the large cities, the military, and, seemingly everywhere, the special constables – the people in arms – who overwhelmed the protesters. The year 1848 in Ireland had demonstrated no need to reform the constabulary; in England it was not 1848 but, as we have seen, a number of other causes that led to the consolidation of the provincial police.

If in Ireland, two decades earlier, the act of 1836 had confirmed the trend to centralization in the constabulary, in England the act of 1856 essentially legitimated the status of the borough and county police of 1835 and 1839. A compromise measure assented to by members of all political parties and opposed only by some borough authorities but *not* to any noticeable extent by members of the working classes, the County and Borough Police Act represented the acceptance, at last, of the police as a legitimate institution in modern English society. This acceptance was based on a consensus, shared by ministers, Parliament, and people, that the police (outside London) were a part of existing local government institutions. What the 1856 act did was to make the county police complete, chastise financially the smallest boroughs for maintaining their scanty forces, and inject only those doses of central supervision that did not encroach on existing borough and county control.

The County and Borough Police Act laid the foundations of the country's provincial police system, but it represented only the beginning of the establishment of an efficient police. More than half of England's counties were now required to set up police forces, which many ratepayers and local authorities insisted on keeping small (see Table 12.2). A third of the county forces established in 1857, and a like proportion of the total county forces (twelve of thirty-seven), had fewer than 100 men. Police in the towns were far smaller: Two-fifths of the 178 borough police in 1857 consisted of "forces" of five or fewer men.[117] In validating the police system that had evolved since 1835, the act of 1856 left a legacy of permanence. Parliament

Table 12.2. *English counties newly establishing countywide police forces, 1856–7*

County	1857 force strength	County	1857 force strength
1. Buckinghamshire	102	11. Lincolnshire	212
2. Cheshire	173	12. Northumberland	61
3. Cornwall	179	13. Oxfordshire	89
4. *Cumberland/Westmorland	108	14. *Rutland	5
5. Derbyshire	n/a	15. Somersetshire	277
6. Devonshire	300	16. *Suffolk	195
7. *Dorsetshire	121	17. *Sussex	164
8. *Herefordshire	45	18. *Warwickshire	138
9. Huntingdonshire	48	*Westmorland	Merged with Cumberland force
10. Kent	222	19. *Yorkshire	660

Note: Prior to the 1856 act, a total of eighteen counties had adopted countywide police forces; in nine counties (*), police had been established only in certain districts. See Table 11.3.

sealed its approval of the English system of more than 200 police forces, ranging from the powerful Metropolitan to the one-man forces in thirteen boroughs. With the exception of some of the smallest boroughs that accepted consolidation after 1856, the police in the counties and boroughs were to remain basically separate and the force in London different from all the rest.

The triumph of local control and the consensus that central supervision should be mild would perpetuate the enormous disparity among the forces. The absence of uniformity was evident in the variety of uniforms, the different pay scales, and the existence or nonexistence of pension plans; in the boroughs the differences also extended to an array of titles for the chief police officer (Superintendent, Chief Constable, and, most often, Head Constable) and the varying definitions of police duties. The act of 1856, the capstone to the English police system outside London, legitimated the idea of police but did so, in a manner directly opposite to the Irish experience, by grounding it in the local communities. If in England the idea of police had at last come of age, the triumph was also one for local rights and local control, issues that had been at the heart of the controversy since 1780.

CHAPTER 13

Conclusion

It may seem to us a matter of course that there is a large body of policemen, highly organized on a military plan.... But all this is very new; it has come into existence during the last sixty years; indeed, down to 1856 there was no law for the whole of England requiring that there should be paid policemen.... We have been living very fast.

A full history of the new police would probably lay its first scene in Ireland, and begin with the Dublin Police Act passed by the Irish Parliament in 1786.

        – F. W. Maitland, *Justice and Police,* 1885

When eras die, their legacies
Are left to strange police ...
        – Clarence Day, *Thoughts Without Words,* 1928

By 1860, the modern police system in England and Ireland was in place. Its principal architects – Peel (d. 1850), and also Drummond (1840), Wellington (1852), and Goulburn (1856) – were gone, as were the two peoples' leaders, O'Connell (1847) and O'Connor (1855), who had confronted the new police.[1] A new generation would be in charge of managing the 33,000 men who comprised an institution that was unknown barely more than a generation earlier. The phenomenal growth of the police, in Ireland since Waterloo and in England since the Reform Bill era, would have astounded its earliest proponents, Thomas Orde (d. 1807) and Patrick Colquhoun (1820). By 1860, the London police had more than doubled its original size to 7,000 men; most recently, only since 1851, the English borough and county police had grown from 7,400 to 12,600 men. The Irish constabulary since 1830 had doubled in size. Sir Francis Head, after a trip to Ireland in 1852, explained to his readers how to make their own map of the 12,000-man constabulary distributed at 1,590 stations. "Buy a six-penny map of Ireland, nail it to a tree, and then, standing twenty-five yards from it, ... fire ... [at your target] a gun loaded with snipe shot"[2] (see Map 13.1).

England and Ireland had taken different paths in establishing their modern police. Both began in 1780 with a common hostility to systems of police on the Continent. In the initial period, 1780–1830, Ireland experimented with and then (from 1808) established the new police, while England held back. In

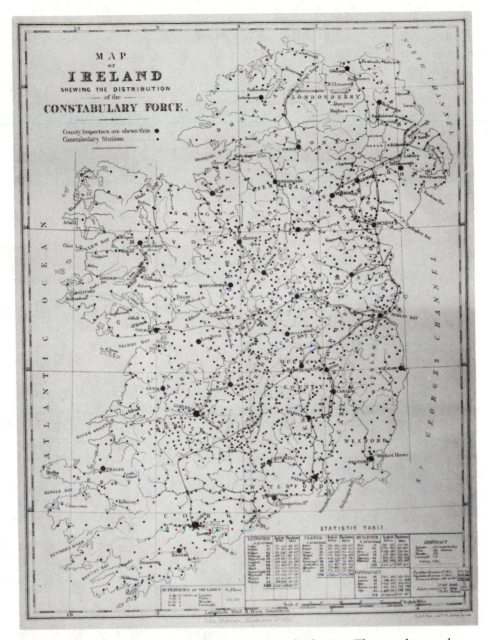

Map 13.1 Distribution of constabulary stations in Ireland, 1852. The map locates the county headquarters and attempts to plot the constabulary stations, a nearly impossible task since there were about 1,600 throughout the island (ranging from a low of 16 in County Londonderry to a high of 153 in County Tipperary). (Sir F. Head, *Fortnight in Ireland*)

the second phase, 1830–60, Ireland consolidated while England began its own innovations in police. The foreign, "un-English" nature of the police idea is demonstrated by the fact that for half a century the testing of this idea occurred in a country ruled by England yet alien to it.

Ireland was the pioneer, and England the laggard, in the new policing for several important reasons. Of the two, Ireland was by far the more disorderly and disordered society. There crime was never clearly separated from protest; crime itself tended to be collective, not individual as in England. Irish crime (recorded as "outrages") was chronic, community-supported, and personally violent. English crime was clearly distinguishable from protest, and both were characterized by low levels of personal violence. Ordinary crime brought community disapproval, prosecution, and conviction; protest ("disturbances") operated within understood and practiced guidelines. Unlike Irish crime/protest that offered a pervasive, virtually daily challenge to the authorities, English protest was sporadic and separated into distinct movements (Luddism, Swing, Chartism). Finally, it should be pointed out that Irish protest escalated to rebellion on one major occasion, 1798, and two minor ones, 1803 and 1848. By contrast, English protest never passed beyond the (rhetorical) stage of posing a *threat* of revolution.[3]

It was not only the nature of crime and protest but also the relative strength of traditional institutions of control that led the two countries down different paths of police development. The criminal justice system worked well enough in England, but due to intimidation and a popular feeling of its illegitimacy it failed in Ireland. The army was surprisingly popular with English crowds, but much less so with Irish ones. The English Yeomanry generally behaved itself, with the glaring exception of Peterloo; the sectarian Irish Yeomanry treated most occasions as Peterloos. Most significantly, as evidence of the contrasting degrees of community support, the system of special constables flourished in England but was impossible to implant in Ireland.

In Ireland the nature of collective violence and the weakness of existing forces for social control led successive Governments, from the 1780s on, to press ahead with the establishment of centrally controlled, armed police forces. By 1840 the burden of peacekeeping had been transferred to two new forces, the constabulary and the Dublin police. When the police idea was belatedly brought to England, it was stripped of its harsh Irish features. Throughout England, the new police were unarmed because they did not have to be. Only in London did the Government directly control the police. Outside the capital local control prevailed. London Commissioner Mayne's 1835 proposal to institutionalize the "occasional" dispatch of his "Peelers" into the provinces was never acted on, and the intrusion of government police into three northern cities was only a temporary expedient in 1839–42.

The Government in London could afford to let local control prevail because of not only the nature of English crime and protest but also the strength of preexisting local authorities. Whereas the Irish police *replaced* local civil authorities, the English police *strengthened* them. Police came to the boroughs as part of local government reform and to the counties as an enforcing body for the JPs. The police idea remained controversial, not least among laboring men and Chartists, who rightly saw the new army in blue as an institution meant to control them. But the belated arrival of the new police was softened by Watch Committees' decisions to keep the forces small and unthreatening and by county JPs' slowness to set up a nationwide police system. Over the long formative period, 1835–56, community consent came to replace the long-standing hostility to the new institution precisely because the provincial police were locally based, were slow to spread or grow in size, and were used in conjunction with traditional institutions – the army, Yeomanry, military pensioners, special constables, and even, for a time, parish constables. Ireland required a new police scattered across the country at 1,600 posts. Social control in post-Waterloo England also came to require the new police, but the forces were milder versions of the Irish model and supplemented existing institutions.

To sum up: A centralized, armed, military-style police was not established in England because, first, such a force would have provoked widespread public outcry and, second, no one, in or out of government, MP or minister, ever called for one. The need for such a force simply did not exist. I do not deny that 1815–48 in England was an age of popular protest and disturbance; but by studying the contemporaneous Irish case, we are able to bring into focus the tamer, more restrained nature of English protest. Even O'Connell's nonviolent modern collective action was more threatening than O'Connor's Chartism because it organized the moral outrage of the great mass of the disaffected Irish Catholic population. Nor do I argue that early-nine-teenth-century England was an Eden of harmonious class relations, aristocratic paternalism, and working-class deference. Indeed, I have tried to show that it was the decline of this pattern of social relations that led to the introduction of the new police.[4] Yet despite the post-Waterloo formation of class thinking and class rights, English protest, built on a belief in "the rights of Englishmen," was never marked by the hostility, bitterness, and violence peculiar to the protest by Ireland's subject population. Finally, the nature of the new police (the authorities' response to the challenge from below) has much to tell us about existing institutions of control, interclass relations, and crime and protest in the two countries. Had it been necessary for the English ruling classes to maintain their political hegemony by creating a centralized armed gendarmerie, I imagine that they would have swallowed the notion of constitutionalism and subjected the lower orders to military policing. But circumstances simply did not warrant such drastic measures of social control.[5]

In Ireland past rebellions, ongoing rural outrages, and deficient Protestant local authorities provided ample reasons for introducing an armed centralized police. English assumptions of cultural superiority, the belief that Paddy was often feckless and sometimes savage, united to the reality of Protestant political dominance within the British archipelago, ensured that the police would be kept out of the hands of the papist peasantry. Police centralization

from the 1780s to the 1830s usurped *Irish* Protestant local rights of governance and, more broadly, reflected *England's* need for control of public order
in the western island. The Irish settler minority, harassed on the one hand by
the native majority and on the other by an intrusive Dublin Castle, fought
this loss of their historic rights until many came to realize that Crown
interference in the form of police centralization represented their best protection against both traditional threats (rural Whiteboyism) and the new
demands of O'Connell's Catholic democracy. It was an acquiescence on both
sides, for Paddy, knowing England would not grant *him* control of the
police, was glad to have power wrested from the Protestant Ascendancy.
The postrebellion Union Act of 1800, "the most important single factor" in
the shaping of modern Ireland,[6] gave England a free hand in the governance
of the country. The resulting centralization of the police had the effect of
making local Protestant authorities feel useless and Catholics obstructed if
also protected. Both became wards of the English state: The Protestants were
given the sop of officering a native police, with the officers' allegiance going
to England (not, as in the late eighteenth century, to "their" Ireland), whereas the men in the increasingly Catholic rank and file were torn between
loyalty to class, country, and Crown.

Just as in England the idea was never seriously considered of establishing
an armed national police, so in British-ruled Ireland before the Famine a
locally controlled police was never really a possibility. Too many factors –
the nature and incidence of the unrest, low Protestant density, England's
strategic needs – argued the case for centralization in police as in other
departments of the English administrative state in Ireland. Even at the end of
the century, when a series of English liberal reforms culminated in the
granting of Catholic political democracy, local control of that key institution,
the police, was never proposed.[7] In the formative pre-Famine police era, it is
not clear that Irish taxpayers could or would pay from local rates the costs of
an effective and therefore controversial police, wherever control rested.
Ireland's locally assessed Poor Law (1838) collapsed in the 1840s as a result of
the country's weak tax base. Peel's 1814 police was initially locally rated, but
as early as 1817 the Government had to step in to pay a rising share of the
costs of its police. From the time of its creation in 1822 the constabulary was
half funded by British taxpayers, and from 1846 on it was entirely
subsidized by them.

I. Post-Famine Ireland, post-Chartist England

At midcentury, the Siamese twins emerged from the years of crisis with two
still separate personalities. Leaving behind the "Hungry Forties" and three
decades of political agitation, England entered an era of "prosperity, stability,
and complacency" that rested on the urban, industrial foundations laid down
over the previous half-century.[8] As Englishmen celebrated their socio-
economic superiority at the Crystal Palace Exhibition, Irishmen were
adjusting to and forging a new social order. The late 1840s and early 1850s

Table 13.1. *Outrages in Ireland: pre-Famine and post-Famine, 1838–81 (annual averages)*

Years	Homicide	Shooting at the person	Incendiary fires	Appearing armed	Attacks on houses	Demand or robbery of arms
1838–40	187	49	431	48	280	179
1841–3	111	66	459	65	282	129
1844–5	143	116	502	84	369	355
. . .						
1854–60	103	32	266	7	35	20
1861–8	71	29	230	5	23	27
1871–5	88	27	165	2	17	11
1876–8	81	22	200	0.0	6	9
1879–81[a]	77	72	478	0.3	43	112

Note: Because of a different system of recording for 1869–70, figures for those years have been excluded.
[a] No figures in parliamentary returns for 1882, the last year of the Land War, for *total* outrages distinguishing the type of outrage.

saw a massive reorganization of the Irish countryside as tens of thousands of small farmers were evicted and sheep and cattle grazed over the graves of the Famine dead. Pasturage advanced, absorbing four-fifths of the land by 1880; farming became businesslike and until the late 1870s, profitable. The tenuous prosperity of the new Ireland came at the cost of continuing high emigration (4 million fled, 1851–1901) and a drastic decline in the number of laborers and of overall population.[9] In the second half of the century the country seemed to be becoming a miniaturized, rural petit bourgeois West Britain. But the new orderliness occurred amid a sense of decay and depletion – the emptied, ruined villages; the strangely quiet countryside; the yearly flight of young people; and withal a lowered density and vitality of human life. In mood and spirit the new Ireland was "a diminished reality" where per capita prosperity required "the drying of the marrow from the bone."[10]

Crime and protest

With Ireland's modernization came a decline in the lawlessness that had marked the first half of the century. Total outrages reported by the constabulary fell by two-thirds from the mid-1840s to the late 1870s. Even if we compare the post-Famine figures with the outrage totals for 1838–43, a fairly quiet pre-Famine period, we note a steady drop in rural crime. The fall was steepest in the 1850s but continuous over the next two decades. Homicides fell to and then held steady at half their frequency in the pre-Famine years. Characteristic pre-Famine Whiteboy offenses – unlawful armed assembly, shooting at persons, and attacks on houses and demand of arms – virtually disappeared[11] (see Table 13.1).

Table 13.2. *Total outrages and agrarian outrages in Ireland, 1838–94*
(annual averages)

Years	Total outrages	Agrarian outrages	Agrarian outrages as percent of total outrages
1838–40	4,870	—	—
1841–3	5,911	—	—
1844–5	7,208	1,462	20.3%
1846–51 (Famine)	13,839	1,008	7.3
1852–60	4,571	349	7.6
1861–8	3,016	224[a]	7.4
1871–5	2,521	246	9.8
1876–8	2,292	250	10.9
1879–82 (Land War)	5,808	2,831[b]	48.7
1883–6	2,731	908	33.2
1887–90	2,070	649	31.4
1891–4	—	384	—

[a]Lowest annual figure in 1844–94 was eighty-seven in 1866.
[b]Highest annual figure in 1844–94 was 4,439 in 1881.

From 1844 on, constabulary reports distinguished "agrarian" from other outrages. Although the distinction is somewhat artificial, the series does permit us to track the post-Famine decline in land-based protest as recorded by the police (see Table 13.2). Compared to their rate in the mid-1840s, agrarian outrages were halved in frequency per 100,000 population immediately after the Famine and stayed low over the next quarter-century. These offenses skyrocketed during the Land War of 1879–82 but fell off steadily thereafter. Thus, unlike pre-Famine violence, which was high and more or less continuous, the Land War stands out as a statistical freak in the second half of the century. The Land War did produce protest at unprecedented levels: 11,325 agrarian outrages in four years at a time when the island's population was only three-fifths of what it had been in 1841. The entire quarter-century 1852–78 had produced a *total* of 6,915 agrarian outrages, an average of 256 a year. But for all of its virulence, the Land War represented the modernization of protest in post-Famine Ireland. The "war" began with the withholding of rents and later escalated to attacks on persons. But it was dominated by offenses against property and, above all, by intimidation (53 percent of the outrages were threatening letters and notices). In the years after 1882, agrarian outrages shrank in volume and changed in character. In 1852–78 offenses against persons had accounted for 14 percent of the unprecedentedly low total volume of agrarian outrage (in 1844–5 and 1846–51 these types of crimes had accounted for 9 and 13 percent. respectively). But beginning with the Land War itself (6 percent of the total) and continuing afterward in the era of substantive statutory land reforms, this hard core of violent protest declined. From 1882 to the mid 1890s, as the volume of agrarian outrage plummeted, offenses against persons stayed low (5–8 percent of the outrages) and the share of property crimes rose steadily from 23 percent in 1883–6 to 30 percent by 1891–4 compared to 14 percent in the immediate pre-Famine period (1844–5).[12]

Apart from agrarian outrages, a number of indicators point to a post-Famine decline in crime. From 1850 to 1900 the number of offenders committed to trial and the number of persons convicted and jailed for serious crimes dropped by more than 80 percent. The number of those in jail for lesser offenses also declined, by 33 percent, from 1855 to 1900.[13] The biggest decline in crime came in the decade after the Famine and a smaller but steady decline after the early 1880s. A statistical series existing only from 1863, the number of indictable offenses known to the police, indicates that the volume of serious crime held fairly steady from the early 1860s to the late 1870s (c. 9,000 offenses a year), rose in the Land War years (to 10,000–12,000), and then fell fairly steadily to about 7,000 offenses by 1895.[14] In the period after the Famine and before the Land War, Irish crime, as measured by indictable offenses known to the police, was sufficiently low that commentators remarked that its rate relative to the population was lower than the rate of serious crime in England.[15]

In Ireland the secular decline in the volume of crime was braked by two phenomena: a rise in the absolute figures during the Land War and the large, steady decline in the island's population (down 32 percent from 1851 to 1901), which in relative terms produced a small rise in crime in the period 1863–82 and flattened its fall after 1882. By contrast, in England (and Wales) the downward trend in crime was dramatic in both absolute and relative terms. There, in a largely unbroken pattern, the total number of indictable offenses known to the police decreased by one-third from 1857 (the start of the series) to 1890, although the population increased by one-half to 29 million. In England, offenses against the person held steady at 10 percent of the total and property crimes inched up toward 90 percent of all offenses.[16] In Ireland, the change in the character of crime, exclusive of agrarian outrages, came during the Famine and its immediate aftermath. By the last quarter of the century, property crimes annually accounted for about four-fifths of all indictable offenses known to the police; and roughly half of the property crime was concentrated in two places, Dublin and Belfast. Offenses against the person declined to about a tenth of all offenses. The incidence of murder and manslaughter was far below midcentury levels.[17]

Post-Famine Irish society, increasingly capitalist, was producing the kind of crime long familiar in England: urban, property-oriented, nonviolent. One sign of the convergence in criminality was that the commonest offenses in both countries were drunkenness and petty larceny.[18] Despite the improvement in or modernization of Irish crime, certain legacies from the pre-1850 era persisted. In comparatively minor offenses like riot and breach

Table 13.3. *Committals for murder and for riot, breach of the peace, and pound breach, 1850–1912 (annual averages)*

Murder							Riot			
England		Ireland			Population		England		Ireland	
No.	Per 100,000	No.	Per 100,000	Years	Eng.	Ire.	No.	Per 100,000	No.	Per 100,000
69	0.38	100[a]	1.54	1850–2	18.0 m	6.5 m	297	1.65	2,038	31.35
63	0.31	36	0.62	1860–2	20.1	5.8	129	0.64	531	9.16
55	0.24	32	0.59	1870–2	22.8	5.4	72	0.32	339	6.28
60	0.23	43[b]	0.84	1880–2	26.0	5.1	121	0.47	739[c]	14.49
58	0.20	32	0.68	1890–2	29.1	4.7	58	0.20	45	0.96
65	0.20	15	0.34	1900–2	32.6	4.4	18	0.06	49	1.11
71	0.20	14	0.32	1910–12	36.1	4.4	63[d]	0.17	129[d]	2.93

Note: Population in millions. Offense rate calculated from the decennial census.
[a] Compared with 161 in 1847–9. Over the period 1850–1914 the highest number of committals for murder in any one year was 118 in 1851; the lowest, 9, in 1906 and 1913.
[b] Figure skewed by the Land War, 1879–82. In both 1876–8 and 1883–5 the annual average was thirty.
[c] More representative of the general downward trend are the figures of 212 in 1876–8 and 111 in 1883–5.
[d] Labor unrest in Dublin and in Britain.

of the peace, and in the serious one of murder, Ireland remained, in relative terms, a rougher place than England. Per capita figures for indictable committals to trial show that Ireland in 1900 remained roughly twenty times more riotous than England. And despite a drastic drop in the murder rate since the Famine, Ireland was still marginally more murderous[19] (see Table 13.3).

Just as crime was on the decline, so protest after 1850 assumed new forms. Riot in England and agrarian outrage in Ireland became less important as means of demanding redress. In England the growth and legitimation of union activity, including strikes and picketing (1871, 1875); the provision for universal elementary education (1870, compulsory from 1880); the advent of urban (1867) and then rural (1884) ballot-box democracy; and the beginnings of a Labour Party (1893) – all offered workingmen new outlets within the reformed political system.[20] In Ireland, thanks to the restructuring of society and modernizing of the economy, "local and communal collective action" came to be replaced by political action organizations. Tenant associations supplanted the pre-Famine Whiteboy groups as protest was channeled within formalized institutions. The trend away from social violence was one away from local issues as well. The Land and National Leagues and the Home Rule movement represented the coming of age of "O'Connellism," of nationally coordinated protest tactics pioneered in the Emancipation, Tithe War, and Repeal campaigns of the pre-Famine era. As in England, the changing face of protest had much to do with a new attitude on the part of the authorities. To coercion was added conciliation. The last third of the nineteenth century saw a number of gains for the Irish people – the disestablishment and disendowment of the Protestant state church (1869); land reforms from 1870 on, including, after 1881, the establishment of state-supervised land courts and Exchequer loans for land purchase; and finally, the advent of popular politics at both the local (poor law boards; elective county councils, 1898) and national levels (the 1884 household suffrage act).[21] In both England and Ireland, all of these changes in the second half of the century took place in the midst of a sharp, continuous rise in literacy of the lower classes.[22]

With the emergence of alternative means of protest, collective violence declined in frequency and importance.[23] In England the "transition to order," to borrow John Stevenson's phrase, saw riot evolve into "demonstration," a development that represented the legitimation of the pre-1848 radical tactic of the orderly protest meeting. In London huge Reform demonstrations in 1866–7 and 1884 preceded the passage of suffrage extension acts; in a series of incidents from 1855 on, crowds contested their *right* to demonstrate in Hyde Park, a right conceded in 1867 and confirmed by statute in 1872. Trafalgar Square also became a standard gathering spot for protesters: At least twenty-one meetings were held there between 1867 and 1886.[24] If institutionalization of the popular demonstration was one characteristic of post-Chartist English protest, another was the continuation of the pre-1850 legacy of nonviolence. In mid- and late-Victorian England, riot as protest (quite separate from the perceived "social problem" of public house brawls) occurred most frequently at election times; one historian has counted seventy-one election riots in 1865–85. Yet these "unabated mob disturbances," to use Donald Richter's words, did not produce a single fatality. English rioting continued to be boisterous but good-natured business; windowpanes, not heads, were broken.[25] Just as Peterloo was notorious for its exceptional level of violence, so late-Victorian incidents are well known precisely because only a few rioters actually got killed. Two persons died at Trafalgar Square's "Bloody Sunday" (1887); the same number lost their lives in the incident at Featherstone colliery in Yorkshire (1893); at another celebrated affray, one involving miners and police at Tonypandy, Wales (1910), *no one* was killed.[26]

If collective violence was receding in England and across rural Ireland, it was on the rise in the North of Ireland. Fast-growing industrial Belfast was swept by periodic waves of riots. Between 1857 and 1898 ten major disturbances rocked the young, red-brick city, which by the end of the century surpassed Dublin in population. Belfast's prolonged, gun-shooting, sectarian, and often senseless disorders were bloody, mean-spirited affairs; eleven persons were killed in the 1864 riots and thirty-one perished in four months of mayhem in 1886. In 1865 the Crown-controlled constabulary replaced Belfast's Protestant local police, and in times of disturbance it became usual for the Government to move a minimum of 1,000 police and 1,000 troops into the city.[27]

One of the most important post-Famine developments was the exportation of Irish violence to the British mainland. Paddy brought his rough and ready ways into England's towns; the immigrant Irish contributed disproportionately to the statistics for common assaults and affrays, especially against the police.[28] The Fenians (1865–7) did something unprecedented, and most "un-English," by bringing protest by terror into English cities. In London the bombing of Clerkenwell Prison killed 12 persons and injured 120; plans for a raid on an army munitions store at Chester aborted only at the last minute; a rescue of Fenian prisoners at Manchester resulted in the killing of an unarmed policeman. The Government responded to the terror by suspending habeas corpus in England (February 1866) for the first time since 1818.[29] The Fenian crisis passed, but years later, when a wave of Irish bombings returned, the Government reacted by creating within the Metropolitan Police a special antiterrorist squad, the "Special Irish Branch" (1884).[30] The post-Famine "Irish problem" in England also triggered an upsurge of anti-Catholic feeling and nativist rioting. "By far the most destructive [disturbances] of the 1850s" were the bitter anti-Irish riots at Stockport in 1852 (1 killed, 100 injured). Anti-Catholic disturbances involving attacks on Irishmen took place in London, Liverpool, and Yorkshire in the early 1860s.[31] Perhaps the nastiest and certainly the most widespread were the anti-Catholic Murphy Riots of 1867–71, England's comparatively tame imitation of Belfast's sectarian disorders. Rioting between Englishmen and Irishmen invariably accompanied William Murphy, an ex-Catholic Protestant evangelical, on his extended lecture tours of the Midlands and the North. Disorders erupted in dozens of towns, the most severe occurring around Manchester and in Birmingham, where a crowd of 50,000 turned out. Overall, there were few deaths but much head bashing, property destruction, and ill-feeling. Murphy himself died in 1872 of injuries received a year earlier when, as he was spewing his hate in a speech in Cumberland, a group of Irish miners broke through and got to him, kicking him senseless. Ironically, Murphy's martyrdom only confirmed Englishmen's beliefs about the predictable behavior of the Irish.[32]

Police: England assumes the lead

The English Police always ridicule everything we tell them. So I have lately left them alone.
– Lord Mayo, Irish Chief Secretary, to Home Secretary Gathorne Hardy, during the Fenian crisis in England, 1867

[A]s you know, Sir, our companions, English policemen, are not cheap at any price ... but of course a Dublin officer is only an officer from Dublin, and London leads the day – of that more anon.
– Dublin detective Edward Entwissell to the Dublin Police Commissioner, 1867

After 1850 the roles were reversed. The western island that had pioneered police developments in the British archipelago was overtaken by the eastern, the British mainland that had long dragged its feet, indeed kicked against, implementing the new police. At midcentury both Ireland and England had the same number of modern police, the former thus being three times more densely policed than the latter. But whereas these 13,000 police represented the peak of growth of the Irish police, in England that figure marked only a beginning. That the Irish police did not *decline* in size is testimony to its importance in society, for Ireland's population fell by a third from 1851 to 1901. In England by the end of the century, the number of police sky-rocketed, trebling to 42,000 for a population that had nearly doubled to 33 million. Despite the dramatic growth of police in urban, industrial England, the ratio of police to population remained greater – in 1901 two times greater – in the smaller western island. Only in recent decades has England approached parity with Ireland in relative density of policemen, an advance that has statistically been set back by the growth in police in Northern Ireland and the Irish Republic since 1970 (see Table 13.4).

From the middle of the nineteenth century on, the stagnation of the Irish police and the growth of the English forces led many to forget or ignore Ireland's importance as a police laboratory in the years 1780–1840. The belief took root that the origins of the new institution were English and that its genesis, specifically, was Peel's London police of 1829. That force grew in stature and size, from its 3,000 men in the early 1830s to 20,000 by the time of the Great War. Scotland Yard became a model for cities around the world to emulate. By contrast, in "dear, dirty Dublin" decay set in. Whereas by 1900 London's population was more than 4 million, Dublin's, at about 250,000, was little changed from the time of the Famine or even of the Union. In Dublin, the most densely policed city in the United Kingdom, the number of policemen also held steady at 1,100. The London and Dublin police were similar in their central control, blue uniform, and absence of firearms, in their merit promotion and freedom to marry. But the two forces were far apart in morale. In a city that, more than any other in the British archipelago, was plagued with poverty, petty crime, and drunkenness, Dublin Castle's police felt underpaid, unappreciated, and ill-treated.[33] Nevertheless, to be a policeman was to have a job in the economically stagnant city. The force was five-sixths Catholic; few constables resigned, and fewer still after a belated pay increase in the mid-1870s. Some of those who did leave joined the Liverpool, London, or other English forces, just as some men in the Royal Irish Constabulary (RIC) went over to the burgeoning English county police. Significantly, there was virtually no reverse migration of England's constables looking for work in the Irish police.[34]

In the police throughout the archipelago, the essential principles of control established in Peel's lifetime remained intact after 1850. The Irish forces were centralized, run from Dublin Castle. In England only the London police was government controlled. By the terms of the 1856 act, the Home Office intervened in the affairs of borough and county forces only in regard to

Table 13.4. *Number of police and police forces, 1851 to the present*

Ireland				England & Wales		
Pop.	No. of forces	Police	Year	Police	No. of forces	Pop.
6.5 m	2	13,400	1851	13,000	253[f]	18.0 m
			1857	19,000	239	
5.1	2	12,700	1881	32,000	224	26.0
4.4	2	12,100	1901	42,000	187	32.6
	2	11,600	1921	57,000	183	37.9
	3/2	9,300[a]	1925			
			1939	64,000	179	41.5
			1945	59,000	157	42.6
			1955	68,000	124	44.4
4.3	2	9,600[b]	1965	84,000	120	47.8
	2	13,800[c]	1975			
	2	14,500[d]	1977	108,000	43	
5.1	2	17,300[e]	1982	120,000	43	49.0

Note: The larger English and Welsh totals have been rounded to the nearest thousand. The pattern of official record keeping has dictated inclusion of the small figures for forces in Welsh counties and boroughs. For 1856–1965, the totals for England and Wales are comprised of London and City of London, 47 English and 12 Welsh counties, and the remainder being boroughs, the number generally declining over time, e.g., 208 boroughs in 1851, 178 boroughs in 1857, etc. The totals for Ireland are for the Irish constabulary (RIC) and Dublin Metropolitan Police (DMP) to 1921; for 1922–5, the DMP, *Gárda Síochána*, and Royal Ulster Constabulary (RUC); and 1925 to the present, the *Gárda* (which absorbed the DMP), and the RUC.
[a] 1925: *Gárda*, 6,300; RUC, 3,000.
[b] 1965: *Gárda*, 6,600; RUC, 3,000.
[c] 1975: *Gárda*, 7,800; RUC, 6,000.
[d] 1977: *Gárda*, 8,800; RUC, 5,700.
[e] 1982: *Gárda*, 10,300; RUC, 7,000.
[f] Includes forces in parts of counties (eight) as well as whole counties (twenty-three).

minimal requirements of age, height, literacy, and fitness of the policemen. The three Inspectors of Constabulary, cut to two in 1907, were left alone by the Home Office; the independent Inspectors, when pressing for reforms, were careful to work with local authorities.[35] Consolidation of the police in boroughs of under 5,000 population with the county police forces proceeded slowly if steadily. Thirty of these tiny borough forces were consolidated in 1857; and by 1876 a total of eighty – accounting for one-third of the country's 245 incorporated boroughs – had been consolidated with county police forces. An act of 1877 barred the establishment of borough police in newly incorporated towns of under 20,000 population; legislation in 1888 abolished forces in *all* towns of less than 10,000 population. Nevertheless, by contrast to Ireland, England continued to maintain a huge number of separate police forces; there were about 200 in 1889 and 179 forces as late as 1939.[36]

SIZE OF COUNTY POLICE, IRELAND AND ENGLAND, 1870

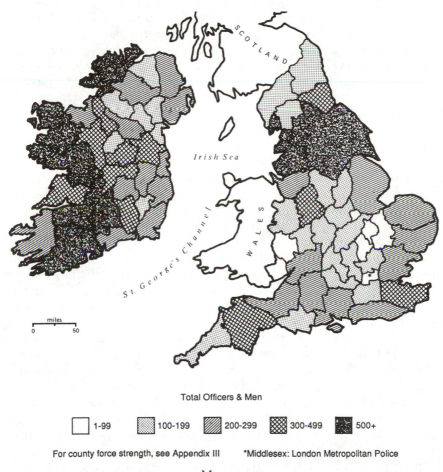

Total Officers & Men

☐ 1-99   ▦ 100-199   ▨ 200-299   ▩ 300-499   ▪ 500+

For county force strength, see Appendix III   *Middlesex: London Metropolitan Police

Map 13.2

By contrast to the Irish, the English police forces stayed small in size. No Irish county had fewer than 100 policemen: In 1870 and again in 1890, the smallest force was the one in Carlow, with 134 and 111 men, respectively. A few English counties maintained sizable forces – in 1870 Lancashire and Yorkshire each had over 900 men and Staffordshire nearly 500 – but three-fifths of the thirty-eight counties had forces with fewer than 200 men and six counties had fewer than 100 (see Map 13.2). It was local control and the great number of boroughs that kept the size of the English police small. In 1857, 69 of the 239 forces had five or fewer men; by 1875, only 29 of 227 were of this size but 138 forces, over half of the total, still had under fifty men. As late as 1945, two-fifths of the 157 forces had fewer than 100 men. In the late-Victorian period, Home Secretaries, men who had had extensive local government experience, were loath to impose a "fanciful cast-iron rule of so many men per 1,000 inhabitants." "If local government means anything at all," said Sir Vernon Harcourt in 1880, "it means that Local Authority and not the Government Inspector is the proper judge of the number of police required." London likewise refused to intervene in internal disputes in borough or county forces or to frame a countrywide code of police regulations. Until the eve of World War II, it was largely through the efforts of the Inspectors of Constabulary and of certain police chiefs, borough and above all county, that the English police evolved into a federated system of nearly 200 separate forces.[37]

Apart from the very largest forces, the English borough police were anomalous among police forces in the British archipelago in terms of professionalism. The centralized London and Irish forces were run by professional policemen. So, too, the English Chief Constable in each of the forty-seven county forces was completely in charge of his force; his powers, on a county basis, were equivalent to the national powers of the Irish Inspector-General of Constabulary. The borough Head Constable, on the other hand, was tied to elective local politics; he served his middle-class employers, the borough Watch Committee, which hired, fired, and directed his men. From the time of their origin in 1835, the borough police were a part of the local government system. The Head Constable, a career policeman promoted through the ranks, was the mirror image of the self-made town councillors to whom he answered on a daily basis.[38]

After midcentury the police in the archipelago grew together in other ways as well. In Ireland, the long-term decline in the volume and violence of crime enabled the police to become a more civil force; successive Governments sought "to assimilate the Constabulary of Ireland ... to that of England." As technology advanced – in the late 1860s the revolver, rifle, and short sword replaced the pistol, carbine, and long sword – the Irish policeman on duty came to carry fewer arms. On patrol (usually two men), one man carried a rifle, the other the sword-bayonet only, thus increasing pursuit ability. Truncheons, supplied to half of the force, became the usual weapon for town and village duty. The Dublin police remained without firearms, as it had since 1838. By the early twentieth century, RIC men "maintained familiarity" with guns by once-a-year target practice. "The military character of the Force is passing away," noted a select committee study in 1914. "The men do not, as a rule, carry arms, except for drill and for ceremonial occasions." On the eve of 1916–22, England's police in Ireland seemed, at least in terms of weapons, to be something of a paper tiger.[39]

All of the police forces in England and Ireland did maintain their military organization and nature. No matter that much of police work was civil and administrative, or that patrolling, singly in England or in pairs or small groups in Ireland, was highly discretionary duty. The unimaginative emphasis on drill, marching, and military formations continued. "We make them soldiers as far as we can," noted the Irish Inspector-General; "the drilling I believe to be nearly the same." In the English county forces, the military training in the 1860s and 1870s, and the trend to appointment of military officers as Chief and Deputy Chief Constables, raised cries of "militarism" from both the police and the public.[40] In part because of its military nature, the Irish constabulary after 1856 proved to be fertile training ground for Chief Constables in the English county police.

With the military drilling and the "incessant walking" that characterized mid-Victorian preventive police work went little emphasis on the detection or solution of crime. RIC District Inspector Garrow Green spoke for most policemen in and out of Ireland: "I could form the hollow square but of the necessary steps to be taken in a murder case my head was about equally empty." In Ireland, detective work suffered from lack of broad community support for the police; in England, from lingering fears of Fouché, Vidocq, and continental espionage.[41] In great measure, though, a policeman's rudimentary training simply reflected the primitive state of forensic science. Before 1850 it was not possible to identify a mark as a blood stain; not until 1895 could human blood be distinguished from animal blood. Suspect identification by photography was a new and tentative development, as also, from the 1880s on, was police adoption of the French-originated Bertillon system of measurement of a person's body parts. Police use of fingerprinting began only in the first decade of the twentieth century. Not until the 1930s did the English police systematically implement scientific investigative techniques, including the establishment of forensic science laboratories.[42]

The de-emphasis on detection in Victorian times is seen in the late creation (1842) of a detective branch at Scotland Yard: 8 men out of 4,400 on the force. By 1860 there were 15 detectives at headquarters plus 200 plainclothes policemen. In the Fenian crisis of the late 1860s, the Prime Minister, Edward Stanley, 14th Earl of Derby, found it "really lamentable" that the London force, "as detectives, are manifestly incompetent." Despairing of finding a man in the London police able to penetrate Fenian circles, the Home Office in 1867 brought over an army intelligence officer from Ireland. Subsequent reforms (1869) added 200 men to the detective branch but substantive changes in London did not come until a decade later, when a series of unsolved murders and detectives' complicity in the Turf Fraud scandal led to the creation of the Criminal Investigation Department (CID) in 1878. Modeled in part on the Paris system and staffed with 260 detectives, the CID was increased by the mid-1880s to 800 men out of a force of 13,000. Nevertheless, official bumbling continued, and contributed to the public's use of private detectives and the popularity of detective fiction. Sherlock Holmes was forever outwitting Inspector Lestrade of Scotland Yard.[43]

With the decline in major crimes, the diminished threat of riot and public disorder, and the de-emphasis on detection, ratepayers came to expect police, when not on patrol, to busy themselves with a number of administrative tasks. The police, increasingly thick on the ground after midcentury, justified their expense by acting as servants of the public. In both countries they inspected weights and measures, enforced vagrancy laws, assisted Poor Law guardians, registered dogs and supervised animals' diseases, enforced fishery and game laws, and carried out the decennial census. In England, they also watched juveniles and controlled prostitutes. In Ireland, the constabulary acted as a state civil service with a variety of duties, ranging from collecting annual agricultural statistics to tabulating the number of noninstitutionalized "harmless Idiots and Simpletons" to executing loan fund warrants. To this day, Irish *gardaí* are involved in a broader range of service activities than their English counterparts.[44] Police work changes with society's needs. Just as after 1850 preservation of public order represented a declining share of police work, so in our own time patrolling, in cars and on foot, has constituted a falling percentage of police time. A 1965 study indicates that traffic duty and work on criminal cases now make up a majority of the police work load. "Public order" duty accounts for a scant percentage, a fact that, Martin and Wilson argue, "might be cited as evidence of the long-term success of the service, *founded as it was largely to ensure the maintenance of public order.*"[45]

If in an age of modernizing protest public order was less of a concern, it is significant that on occasions of public disorder in the mid- and late-Victorian period it was the police that was resorted to for control of crowds. In Ireland the police was credited with "saving" the country during the Fenian rising; the force was rewarded in 1867 with the Queen's christening it the *Royal Irish Constabulary*. Belfast's periodic sectarian riots were contained by the constabulary, which after 1865 constituted the police in the city; by 1900 the force of 900 men was almost as large as Dublin's police. In the Land War the RIC served as the government's front-line force, and in the War of Independence (1919–21) it was the RIC, not the military, that bore the brunt of the fighting.[46] In London the Metropolitan Police polished its reputation for crowd control: 2,000 police repressed the Hyde Park Reform Riots in 1866, and a like number put down rioting at Trafalgar Square on "Bloody Sunday" in 1887.[47] The half-dozen largest boroughs with 250 or more men also demonstrated their mastery over crowds.[48] The only police to demonstrate inefficiency against mobs – as, for example, in the Murphy Riots and at election times – were those small forces in the great majority of the English boroughs.[49] Because the county police were larger in size and controlled by JPs, many boroughs developed the practice – legalized by a police act of 1890 – of "borrowing" county constables for use against crowds. Even larger boroughs did this: To deal with the Murphy rioters in 1867, Birmingham borrowed 180 county police to assist the town's 400 constables. This policy was not without problems. In 1893, when 260 Yorkshire county constables were on loan to the Doncaster races, striking miners in one police-depleted district triggered the Featherstone colliery disturbances. In sum, after mid-century the English county police operated in town and country as a crowd-control force used ahead of the Yeomanry and the army, both of which were seldom called out and even more rarely used. This practice of importing strangers to put down disturbances was a faint echo of Irish police policies dating to 1814.[50]

With the establishment of police as crowd-control agents, there continued in England the pre-1850 custom of calling out special constables. In Ireland the RIC acted alone. The police, said a Longford Head Constable in 1883, "are more or less Ishmaelites; every man's hand is against them." As to recruiting specials, "In my town you would not get half-a-dozen tomorrow."[51] But in urban industrial England, the police continued to be assisted by members of the great and growing shopkeeping and professional classes and even of the skilled lower classes. In the Reform disorders of 1866, the London trades organized 10,000 "Keepers of the Peace," workers' special constables. Some 12,000 specials turned out for the 1867 Reform demonstration. During the Fenian scare of 1867–8 it is estimated that 115,000 specials served throughout England; after the Clerkenwell explosion some 50,000 Londoners took up the special's staff and armband. In London in 1887, 7,000 specials enrolled on the eve of Bloody Sunday, and in the aftermath 30,000 volunteered. In the General Strike of 1926, 140,000 specials were sworn in.[52] This continuing pattern of authorized community assistance in England never proved workable in Ireland. In Ulster in this century, Stormont's experiments with special constables proved so controversial and the specials' behavior so prejudicial and bloody that London finally intervened to disband the "B-Specials" in late 1969.[53]

II. Emergence and convergence: trends in the English and Irish police, 1857 to the present

In its formative period, 1780–1840, police in the British archipelago was an innovative, controversial, foreign idea. Police were imposed on Ireland and, after experimentation and appropriate modification, they were grudgingly adopted in England. After 1850 the police story is less dramatic. In both countries the police, just another agency of government, became a conservative bureaucracy. The institution that had come into being to control workers and peasants was staffed by them. Like most of their fellows in the lower classes, policemen were "incorporated" by society so that their goals became the same as other workers' – job security, decent pay, opportunities for promotion.

Police work was a magnet to the unskilled and low paid. Above all, it was rural poverty – whether on Ireland's small farms or England's large estates – that drove into the police barely literate laborers endowed with stamina and good health, a barrel chest, and sufficient height. (See Appendix IV.) In post-Famine Ireland the trend to pasturage and in England, from the 1870s on, the reliance on imports of foreign grain only hastened the rural laborers' exodus. For the new policemen the work offered a steady wage, but the "incessant walking" was taxing. In England, the exhaustion, the loneliness, and the weather won out: For most constables, wearing the uniform proved to be a way station – or a useful elementary school – between jobs. One-half to two-thirds of the recruits left within two years; about a fifth served longer than five years. For fewer than one in ten was it a life's work.[54] It was different in Ireland. There the comparative scarcity of alternative employment and the historic importance of security of subsistence led to much lower turnover in police personnel. An RIC sergeant's son remembered that his father, a small farmer's son, "had almost an obsession about security; for him the first test of a career was that it should be permanent and pension-able." Far more so than in England, police work was a career. The recruit spent several months at the Phoenix Park training depot even before entering national service. In the RIC in the late nineteenth century, two-fifths of the recruits stayed for twenty years or more; in the Lancashire constabulary, perhaps the most professional of the English county forces, only a fifth of the recruits stayed for ten years or more.[55]

The resignation rate in Ireland was low. After a long "crisis" from the 1850s to 1870s when resignations amounted to about 5 percent of force strength (Lancashire's rate was 13 percent in 1866–70, down from 17 percent in 1856–60), the Irish rate plummeted to an average of 1 percent of force strength in 1883–1913.[56] Of those few who left, some (like many of their countrymen) went to "America or to the colonies," and others sought the somewhat better-paid police work in England, for "of course they compare their own service with the English service." Significantly, unlike constables in England, few in Ireland resigned to search for better-paying nonpolice employment. Although a high retention rate enabled the RIC to become a professional police with a strong esprit de corps, it also made for a closed service. Low turnover meant little hiring.[57] If England's police was a revolving door, Ireland's by the early twentieth century was a somewhat complacent, self-contained bureaucracy.

In many ways, the English and Irish police seemed to be converging after midcentury. The RIC still had a more military look than the English forces, but the men went about less heavily armed than in O'Connell's day. In both countries, the police in a given neighborhood were a set of rotating strangers. The lads hired in the English forces were preponderantly from the home county or an adjacent one. But it was general policy to keep the men out of their neighborhoods of birth or residence. This English practice was a com-pressed version of the founding principle in the Irish constabulary that men never serve in their home *county*. In both countries rotation of men from station to station, first practiced in Ireland, could function as a form of punishment.[58] In Ireland's national service, because of the idea that the men should develop no local ties, regular rotation was also a police regulation; in England the fresh faces occurred naturally, since so many men quit after short service.

In important respects, however, the police in the two islands remained apart. The Irish constabulary remained, as it had been since the late 1820s, a force of bachelors, only a fifth of the constables being permitted to marry. By contrast, although English recruits were usually single, they were later allowed to marry; roughly three-fourths of the English county constables were married.[59] Whereas the RIC men lived in military-style barracks, less than a third of the English police, mostly the single constables, lived in station accommodation.[60] A third legacy that persisted in distinguishing the two forces was that of the patrol: a single constable in England but no fewer than two in Ireland. A 1902 select committee found much good in the Irish system. Whereas the English constable had to endure loneliness and on occasion "very great risks" from his solitary patrol, the RIC constable not only had help at hand but, perhaps even more importantly, had "always a Companion."[61]

There were fundamental differences in the promotion systems. In the police of London, Dublin, the English boroughs, and the English counties (excepting the very highest ranks, Chief Constable and Deputy Chief Constable), all positions were open to merit promotion through the ranks. But in the RIC the bulk of the commissioned or "gazetted" officer ranks – County Inspector and District Inspector (formerly, Subinspector) – were appointive, entry-level positions. In a practical sense, however, to the vast majority of men in the forces, this theoretical distinction mattered little. The Irish officer class comprised only 2 percent of force strength and the analogous English ranks of Inspector and Superintendent an even smaller percentage. Very few posts opened each year. For constables, their only realistic hope was for a sergeant's position. In the English service there were, proportional to force strength, only half as many sergeant slots as in the RIC; the rank structure acted as a clog on the system and contributed to the high turnover in police personnel. By contrast, in the RIC the 225 Head Constable, 430 Acting Sergeant, and 1,800 Sergeant posts[62] – a fifth of all nonofficer positions – offered constables better prospects for promotion. Beyond the increase in pay and status, a further inducement for the Irish constable to stay in the force and await promotion was that with it went the right to marry. In 1881 less than a fourth of the constables were married, but two-thirds of the Sergeants and three-fourths of the Head Constables enjoyed conjugal ties. Finally, at this level of promotion, religion was not a factor: A large majority of Sergeants were Catholic (58 percent in 1860, 70 percent in 1880), as were a growing number of Head Constables (45 percent in 1860, 60 percent in 1880.)[63]

But for recruits, promotion opportunities in the RIC effectively stopped here. By regulation, three of every four of the elite officer posts, those of County and District Inspector, went to the "cadets," graduates of the Phoenix Park officers' training school. Appointment of these young gentlemen officers effectively blocked further promotion for ambitious Catholic Sergeants and Head Constables of twenty years' service. In the RIC the top leadership ranks – some 304 officers in 1860, cut to 279 in 1870 and to 266 in 1909 – continued to be the preserve of the landed Protestant Ascendancy.[64] This appointive Irish officer corps was drawn from the same social class as the county Chief Constable ranks in England. Both represented a tiny share of force strength, the English (and Welsh) Chief and Deputy Chief Constables numbering just over 100 men out of a total of 9,400 county policemen in 1870. The similarity in social background led to connections between the officer classes in the two countries, especially after 1856. Of the forty-seven English Chief Constables active in 1856–80, fourteen had Irish experience: Only three of twenty-three appointed before 1856 had served in the RIC, but eleven of the twenty-four appointed after 1856 had been RIC officers. Only four of the forty-seven had served in the London or English borough police.[65] In Ireland a lively debate persisted among the men and officers on the question of officer selection. Opinions tended to divide along lines of class. A fourteen-year Cork subconstable said that "the bulk of the service complain that the officers have no right to be appointed except by promotion from the ranks." The existence of such a system in all of the English forces and in the Dublin police only served to sharpen the grievances of the RIC rank and file. When Tipperary County Inspector De Courcy Ireland offered his view that the men like to take orders from gentlemen, a member of the 1873 select committee interjected that every nonofficer interviewed gave "an opposite opinion." Ireland replied, "I suppose every man holds by his order."[66]

The promotion controversy was the more heated because it was tied to religion. From 1860 to 1880, the proportion of Catholics in the rank and file increased from 69 to 76 percent, but that of Catholics in the officer corps declined from 22 to 20 percent. The RIC officer class was part of the old system of Protestant supremacy. In the age of ballot-box democracy (1884), land reform, and Home Rule proposals, that system came under increasing assault. For late-nineteenth-century Irish constables, the RIC officer issue was the Catholic Emancipation issue all over again. It was a matter of symbolism: Scarcely any of the 6,500 Catholic constables and few of the 1,200 Catholic Sergeants and Head Constables believed that they had a chance for a district inspectorship. But neither did a Birmingham or Devonshire constable delude himself; yet a constable in England had the satisfaction of knowing that one of *them* would one day be borough Head Constable or County Superintendent. In the simple words of James O'Connell, a Londonderry Head Constable, it would give the "three-fourths of the constabulary" who were Catholics "greater confidence" if more Catholics were "superior officers." Under pressure, the system did change. By 1895, "about half" of the RIC officer ranks were filled with men from the ranks; in 1920, in a force nearly four-fifths Catholic, two-fifths of the officers were Catholics. Indeed, the RIC's last Inspector-General, Sir Joseph Byrnes, was a Catholic.[67] Despite these changes in the last decades of the RIC's existence, the cadet system established in 1842 continued to provide a steady stream of officers, mostly Anglo-Irish. Toward the end, the fault line that in the nineteenth century had separated officers and men was fracturing the officer class itself.

In the twentieth century, as in their origins, major changes in police in the British archipelago occurred in Ireland a half-century before they did in England. But in Ireland this time, unlike in the 1780s, it was to create not a government but a people's police. The watershed was 1919–21, years of strife when a shrunken RIC, softened by decades of peace, lost men, morale, and credibility in the savage fighting with the Irish Republican Army (IRA) during the South's war for independence. This period gave birth to the modern state of Northern Ireland and to that RIC remnant, the Royal Ulster

Constabulary. In the South, independence spelled the end of nearly a century and a half of British policing. "Dublin Castle has fallen," said Michael Collins, "and with it will [sic] have gone all [the] bureaucratic regulations and tyrannies which the people of Ireland have suffered under the British regime."[68]

Among the first actions of the Irish Free State was the reform of the police. On 4 April 1922, exactly a century after its creation, the RIC staged its final parade before disbanding in Phoenix Park. That spring and summer, around the new country, groups of the old police, sometimes under IRA escort, made their way to the nearest military camp or railway station, thence to England, America, the colonial police forces, or Belfast, where the Royal Ulster Constabulary (RUC) was recruiting. Meanwhile, the new Irish government began "the novel and ambitious undertaking of creating an unarmed native civil police." This first *Irish* police was called the "Civic Guard" (recalling Henry Grattan's term for the 1795 Dublin police) or, more formally, the "Guardian of the People's Peace." It operated "unarmed in a community from which it drew its only weapon – the moral support of the citizen." In 1923 the force was given its present Gaelic name, *Gárda Síochána* ("Guardians of the Peace"), and two years later it absorbed the old, unarmed Dublin Metropolitan Police to form a single national police. The former RIC ranks were replaced with a mixture of native and English terms: "*gárda*," "sergeant," "inspector," "superintendent," "commissioner." The force, issued British blue uniforms, was cut to 6,300 men, a fifth of whom served in Dublin. After much discussion on the merits of county councils and town Watch Committees, it was decided to retain central control under the Minister of Justice.[69] Despite the violence in the post–Treaty Civil War years, the government armed its new police only with 15-inch truncheons; but a "Special Branch" (1925), an antiterrorist unit akin to Scotland Yard's, was established. The public and even the IRA were impressed by the Free State's decision against arming (only one *gárda* was killed in 1922–3). The force quickly gained a degree of popular support that, even in the best of times, had been denied to the RIC. For the men in the force, the new police service offered three things – "security, the chance of promotion, and a degree of esteem in the public eye" – only one of which had been available in the RIC. For forty years the *Gárda* stayed virtually unchanged in size. But nowadays the force is nearly twice as large (11,400 men in 1983) as it was in 1965 as the police struggle with the twin challenges of a surge in crime and the spillover of collective violence from the North.[70]

The British colonial police has continued in Northern Ireland. For half a century, Ulster was policed by the Stormont-controlled paramilitary RUC, a force limited to 3,000 men until 1969. In the Orange North, Catholic gains in the old RIC were wiped out; Roman Catholics, forming a third of the population, never comprised more than a tenth of the police. The RUC was relatively open in its hiring and promotion policies, but it suffered in Catholic eyes from being the enforcing instrument for its master, a frankly sectarian state. After the beginning of the current Ulster unrest, a number of

English-induced reforms attempted to "civilianize" the RUC. Labor Home Secretary James Callaghan persuaded City of London Police Commissioner Sir Arthur Young to come over to head the RUC (1969–70). Confirmed by the 1970 Northern Ireland Police Act, the reforms included a change of uniform; adoption of the English rank structure (including replacing "inspector-general," b. 1822–d. 1970, with "chief constable"); and accountability, at least in part, to a locally elective Police Authority. More basically, in late 1969 the RUC was *disarmed* – an unprecedented development that lasted for less than a year. Longer lasting were new police guidelines and political and social reforms that sought to end the RUC's role as servant to a sectarian government.[71]

The immediate result of this overhaul of the RUC was that the army and the locally recruited Ulster Defense Regiment (UDR), itself a replacement for the hated B-Specials, had to assume the burden of street duty through the mid-1970s. Over the past decade, however, largely because of an ebb in the violence, the RUC has won back from the military its role of patrol work. But in its volatile political environment, the men in the reformed, "professional, not overtly sectarian" RUC have become more than ever "targets for the IRA."[72] In recent years the total number of killings in the Ulster strife has declined, but the police now absorb an increasing proportion of the deaths.[73] Over the period 1972–7, more than half of the men on the force sustained injuries on duty.[74] So long as the politically related violence continues, it will be hard for the RUC, now grown to 7,000 men and backed by 8,000 UDR forces and 12,000 English soldiers, to shed its military origins and become a civil police. Nervous constables will continue to carry guns, resort to steel-shielded land rovers on patrol, and train with M-1 carbines.[75]

In England in 1919–21, crucial years in the transformation of the Irish police, some comparatively minor changes were made in the provincial police. The Home Office increased its Exchequer grant to pay half of *all* police costs, and set nationwide standards for pay and conditions of service. Institutions were established for communication between forces. But the county and borough police remained autonomous and locally controlled. The period through the 1930s was a slumbering one: The forces stayed small in size and great in number. World War II proved to be a catalyst as local authorities acquiesced to Home Office demands for amalgamation. In 1932 the Government had been defeated on a proposal to abolish separate police forces in towns of under 30,000 population; a 1946 act eliminated them in towns of under 100,000 population. The number of forces in the country shrank from 179 in 1939 to 131 in 1947. There was increasing cooperation among forces, as seen in the establishment of regional police laboratories and, in 1949, of the National Police College, the nation's first officers' training school.[76]

The modern trend has been to increasing central supervision. But the roots of the English police, planted in 1829–56, have held firm. Peel's Metropolitan Police remains the only force under direct government control. The 1962 Royal Commission on the Police rejected one member's proposal for the creation of a single national force. This latter-day Chadwick, Dr. A. L. Goodhart, had told the commission that "there is no need to apologize" for recommending the establishment of a "Royal English and Welsh Police, ... although it has been suggested that such a system would be unconstitutional and un-English." The commission quashed Goodhart's proposal by a vote of 13–1.[77] The subsequent Police Act of 1964 instituted many important changes, but it neither tore out the roots of local control nor cut the number of forces (120 in 1965). The landmark act did standardize for every police force, borough and county, the nature of local control by creating a new "Police Authority," two-thirds of whose members are elected local politicians and one-third local magistrates. And the act professionalized the borough forces by giving urban Chief Constables for the first time full control over hiring, firing, and directing their men. The Home Office maintained its historic position of not telling the Chief Constable or Police Authority "how to operate," but it retained the weapon of the Exchequer grant and did state for the first time its power to order a local Police Authority to sack its Chief Constable. Eight years later came the final important change. The Local Government Act of 1972 reduced, at one cut, the number of police forces in the country from more than 100 to 43, including the historic 2 in London.[78]

The English police today, as they have in the past, represent "a peculiar British compromise." The forty-three forces act independently but are accountable to local politicians and to Home Office standards of professionalism. The system is a delicate balance of intermeshed obligations and sometimes unclear lines of authority; at a time when police work is increasingly scientific and professional, the police feel more than ever "beleaguered by bodies exerting pressure upon them." And although the system "is supposed to be locally based," the tilt over the last few decades has been undeniably toward the center.[79] For a century and a half, Ireland has had a centralized police; by contrast, England is slowly, by increments, building a national police system.

What lies ahead for the police in the two islands is not reassuring. IRA violence in Ulster spills over into the Irish Republic and into England. In all three states, the incidence of crime has skyrocketed. In England, criminals use firearms to an extent unheard-of just twenty years ago. Complaints against the police and assaults on constables are at record levels. The wave of rioting, marred by ethnic conflict, that swept England in 1981 was the greatest in a century and a half. The police today seem engulfed by a rising tide of crime and violence: There are now twice as many policemen in England as in 1940, yet criminal offenses have increased tenfold, most rapidly since the mid-1960s.[80] Present circumstances in the British archipelago seem to portend a fresh round of major police reforms before the end of the century. Whether these will alter the foundations laid down in the period 1786–1856 remains to be seen.

III. Epilogue: beyond the archipelago

After the middle of the nineteenth century, the drama of police innovation and early development moved beyond the British Isles, out into those territories that together formed the British Empire. Given Ireland's status as England's first colony, it would be tempting but mistaken to argue that England developed one police for domestic use (the English) and another (the Irish) for export. Both were in fact exported: the London Metropolitan Police serving as the model for urban police, the Irish constabulary as the model for a rural or district police. More broadly, it may be said that just as the Irish police pioneered the concept of policing within the British archipelago and was then tamed or "civil(ian)ized" when imported into England (1830–60), so in the vast territories of the British Empire police went through a first, or "Irish," stage of military-style armed force controlled by British colonial governors, and then a second, or "English," stage in the early/mid-twentieth century characterized by de-militarization and increasing use of native peoples in leadership roles.[81] The Irish constabulary itself passed through this second stage from the end of the nineteenth century, just as the overseas colonial police would subsequently in the transition from colonialism to political independence.

Although the London police served as a role model for urban forces, Ireland's constabulary was the more valuable because, by using it as their enforcing agent, British civil authorities could mold large, loosely governed areas into centrally administered colonies.[82] Historians have variously interpreted the politics of the imperial police. Sir Charles Jeffries, the English historian of Britain's colonial police, asserted that in those areas "with indigenous populations which the British have been called upon to administer and govern," the Irish model was necessary until the people "developed to the point of being able to legislate for themselves and manage their own affairs." A predictably different perspective is offered by Conor Brady, the Irish historian of the *Gárda Síochána*. The Irish model was applied because it fit "other troublesome subject races of the Empire who could not be left to look after themselves and who could not be left under the permanent care of the army."[83] Whatever the motivations of the government in London, the RIC model was the one chosen to maintain public order, political control, and administrative efficiency in the colonies.

Without doubt, the London police was the model looked to by cities throughout the world. This was true not only for Sydney and Calcutta but also for New York, Boston, Paris, Berlin, Vienna, and Stockholm.[84] In southern Africa, in response to a request from the Governor of the Cape Colony, Sir George Napier (brother of Charles James Napier), London Police Commissioner Rowan sent out Inspector John King, son of a Norwich miller, to found a forty-man police at Cape Town (1840). King took with him a handful of the blank criminal returns used by the London police.[85] Four years later, a London policeman, Sergeant John Colepeper, arrived in Ceylon to form Colombo's first modern police. The city's force was uniformed in exact copies of the Metropolitan Police uniform.[86] London-style police were soon established in Bombay, Madras, and Calcutta, and subsequently in other Asian cities. Tourists today are startled to see blue-shirted "bobbies" patrolling the streets of Hong Kong, Singapore, and Kuala Lumpur.[87]

Nevertheless, it must be stressed that throughout the Empire "the really effective influence upon the development of Colonial police forces during the nineteenth century was not that of the police of Great Britain but that of the Royal Irish Constabulary." In foreign lands where the population was overwhelmingly rural, communications poor, society "largely primitive," and violence against the government not unexpected, it was "natural" for the RIC to serve as the model, since it provided "a more practical prototype."[88] Policing the Empire took one of two paths: either the outright adoption of the Irish model or a resort to it after the civilian British model failed. Various Caribbean colonies – Barbados, British Guiana, the Bahamas – established London-style police in 1835–40, only later to go over to the Irish constabulary system.[89] Jamaica's police (est. 1856) was armed and reorganized along military lines following the Morant Bay rebellion of 1867.[90] In west Africa, in Sierra Leone, a retired Irish army sergeant established in 1836 a sixty-man police officered by three "subinspectors"; the force was reorganized following the London model in 1861, but only two years later, after a bout of native unrest, it reverted to the Irish model.[91] So pervasive was the Irish influence that the historian of the British colonial police could write that "so far as I know the only Colonial force which has not passed through the phase of being a semi-military, armed constabulary" was the island force (est. 1838) in tiny, tranquil Bermuda.[92]

More frequent was the practice of establishing at the outset a military police along the lines of the Irish model. The pioneer here was none other than General Sir Charles James Napier, the Anglo-Irish ex-commander of England's Northern District (1839–41). Following his conquest of the Scinde (in present-day Pakistan), Napier established in 1843 a 2,400-man native police force "well armed and well drilled" under English officers.[93] The success of Napier's constabulary led him to propose its adoption in other Indian provinces. In a letter of 1849 proposing an 8,000-man police for the Punjab, Napier spilled out his thoughts:

Rendering the civil power dependent on the military for protection in ordinary cases, is of all evils the greatest. I speak from nearly fifty years' experience. I saw it in Ireland in 1798, and again in 1803. I saw it in the Ionian Islands. I saw it in the Northern District. I saw it in Scinde.[94]

Napier's proposal was adopted not only in the Punjab but also in Bombay and Madras provinces. And in 1861 the Irish-modeled system, headed by an "Inspector General," was centralized throughout the subcontinent.[95] A few years after Napier's Scinde experiment, the British government established modern police on the offshore island of Ceylon. In 1845–8 two constabulary officers were sent directly from Ireland to start up a rural force, and in 1866 this police was consolidated by an officer sent over from the Indian Police Service.[96]

From Ireland and India, its offspring, the constabulary example spread far and wide. In New Zealand an armed police was created (1867) for frontier duty against the Maoris; when the frontier closed, the force was disarmed in 1886. For Sydney and Melbourne the London police was the model, but after midcentury in the various states of Australia, a land with a large Irish settler population, the emerging provincial police in its organization, ranks, and functions bore strong RIC influences, not least because of those RIC officers and men who emigrated there. In the Canadian west, in an effort to control conflict between Indians and white settlers, the dominion government established (1873) a 300-man Northwest Mounted Police "after the models existing in Ireland and India"; like the Scinde police, the Northwest force evolved into a national police, the Royal Canadian Mounted Police (1920).[97] On Cyprus, two years after acquiring the island, Britain planted a semi-military police (1880).[98] British rule in Africa in the last quarter of the nineteenth century was extended in great part through the establishment of armed police forces – in Gambia, the Gold Coast (Ghana), Zanzibar, Nigeria, Kenya, Northern and Southern Rhodesia, and Uganda.[99] In South Africa the British had used the Irish model in appointing Stipendiary Magistrates in the Cape Colony as early as the 1820s and, from midcentury, in setting up constabularies in the Cape and Natal and frontier police in the Transkei and Zululand.[100] By the end of the century, Britain had established a virtually worldwide imperial police system. Paperwork and officers flowed from one colony to another. Kenya's police, later expanded into the British East Africa Police, dates from 1887, when a cadre of Indian officers and men were brought in to set up a force at Mombasa. The officers' register of the Gold Coast Constabulary (est. 1872) reads like an exotic travel brochure: one man with a record of service in London, Malaya, and Hampshire; another in Ireland and India; a third in Northamptonshire and Jamaica.[101]

London and Dublin formed the administrative center of the system. If policy was decided at the Colonial Office, police training in the home islands had to be in the country that had both a national police and an officers' training facility. The RIC depot in Dublin provided a six-month course that, from 1907 on, was compulsory for imperial police service. Tekena Tamuno, historian of the Nigerian police (est. 1879), has noted that there were other cogent reasons for Ireland's central role.

That the RIC, which had developed from Peel's Peace Preservation Act of 1814, inspired for a century or so the British police forces overseas was understandable. The RIC programme provided at that time the best training for the conditions expected in the British dependencies overseas. The RIC training had been adapted to the conditions in Ireland with its heritage of rebellion and opposition to British rule for many centuries. The British government expected similar opposition from the territories for whose police forces it recommended the RIC course.[102]

So "Irish" was the training at Phoenix Park that some Nigerian officials grumbled that *African* conditions were overlooked; if not a course in Lagos, one at least in Johannesburg would be more useful. In 1911 the Inspector General of the Uganda and East Africa Police, Capt. W. F. S. Edwards (a Devonshire-born veteran of the Sierra Leone and South African police), complained that he had to spend too much time with "the unteaching of what has been learnt in Dublin."[103]

The Irish connection remained even after Southern Ireland's political independence in 1922. Many men in the disbanded RIC joined the "quasi-military gendarmerie" established (1919) in British-mandated Palestine; indeed, it was they who "gave the force its backbone."[104] Within the British Isles the training center for the Empire's police officers stayed in Ireland, being moved to the RUC depot at Newtownards, Northern Ireland, where it remained for nine years. Only in the 1930s was the schooling of Imperial policemen brought to the British mainland, first at the newly opened Metropolitan Police College and subsequently at the national police college.[105] Just as the British RIC had matured into the Irish *Gárda Síochána*, so the police of the Empire, in finally receiving civilian-style training in England, reflected the de-colonizing needs of lands in the process of becoming countries in a new British commonwealth of nations. Today, as in their formative era, the police are tied to politics and society.

In the history of the modern world, it is well known that the British Isles have exercised an influence entirely disproportionate to their size. In the history of modern police, Ireland's contributions are little known. The time is long overdue to recognize the importance of this small island in the development of police in the British archipelago and beyond.

Appendixes

I. COMMITTALS FOR PROTEST OFFENSES IN ENGLAND AND IRELAND, 1835–56

In approaching the figures set out in Appendix I the reader must bear in mind that throughout the period 1835–56 the population of Ireland was *about half* that of England (1841 census: Ireland, 8.2 million; England and Wales, 15.9 million).

The conclusions from the sets of figures are, in general, that (1) Irish protest offenses were quantitatively much more frequent than were the English offenses; (2) Irish, unlike English, protest reached a decided peak in the years 1847–51; (3) English protest offenses tended to be spread somewhat more evenly over the period; and (4) both English and Irish protest offenses tailed off after 1851, more dramatically in the Irish case because of the peaks attained (or the nadir reached) during the Famine period.

Tables I.1 and I.2 record the number of indictable offenses (number of persons committed to jail or bailed for trial at assizes and quarter sessions) yearly from 1835 to 1856. The offenses selected are those commonly assumed to have had, more often than not, a protest dimension. There are, of course, problems in making national comparisons. I therefore simply present the raw figures, avoiding any further statistical manipulations. Table 1.3 presents annual averages for five representative time periods from 1835 to 1856.

In England, it must be stressed, certain offenses listed here might or might not be protest offenses. Take the English offenses of *arson* (Table I.1). Although it could, and on occasion certainly did, have overtones of collective protest, it was also frequently an individual, nonprotest offense. Secondly, in Ireland some types of crime had a protest dimension that was lacking in the "same" crime in England. For example, *homicide* in Ireland was often a protest crime; in England, rarely. For this reason, Tables I.1 and I.2 do not present comparative figures for homicide. The figures for *arming* (Table I.1) compare quite different phenomena but are presented here since, in the English records, the *only* category of arming is that of poaching, that is, being out armed, to take game by night, and perhaps in the process assaulting gamekeepers. Once again, the reader can surmise that poaching may or may not, depending on the case, constitute a protest offense. By contrast, the Irish category of assembling armed unlawfully is clearly collective protest involving a band of men.

The same caveats apply to other offenses. Traditionally, among scholars of English protest, *cattle killing and maiming* and *cattle, sheep, and horse stealing* (Table I.1) have been cited as protest offenses. I offer them here, with reservations, largely for the sake of the Irish comparison. Committals do not begin to measure the incidence of a particular crime. Nowhere can this be seen more dramatically than in the figures for sending *threatening letters* (Table I.2). In each county, few of these surreptitious letter writers were ever committed at assizes and sessions; the departure from reality is especially noteworthy in the Irish case, for in constabulary outrage reports several hundred, and sometimes more than 1,000, threatening letters or notices were listed annually. Committal figures are also given for two offenses that had absolutely no equivalent in England and thus form no criminal category. Nevertheless, as distinctive protest offenses, I have included in Table I.2 annual Irish committals for *attacking and injuring dwelling houses and lands* and *taking and holding forcible possession of land*.

Perhaps the most directly comparable types of offenses are those that I have arranged under "Riotous Offenses" and "Antipolice Offenses" (Table I.2). These two sets of figures are graphed in Figures I.1 and I.2. In both countries, records were kept under the five specific offense headings that comprise my categories of riotous and antipolice offenses. Here, too, a few words of warning are in order. Note that in Ireland no one was committed and tried for riot and sedition until 1863 (see Table I.2, note *g*). Also, anyone with a knowledge of the period is surprised by the comparatively low Irish committal figures for "assaults on peace officers in execution of their duty." The explanation *may* lie in the fact that some of the assaults on police were recorded as "rescue and refusing to aid peace officers" or else listed under general "assaults" (see Table I.1). The Irish figures for rescue and assaults are extremely high compared with the English figures for the same offenses. Conversely, it may be true to some extent that the English figures for assaults on peace officers are comparatively high because they were scrupulously recorded as such and not listed as common assault cases. Certainly the English figures for rescue and refusal to aid peace officers are almost too low to be believed: Perhaps not a few of these cases were simply recorded as "assaults on peace officers." The purest valid national comparison, where no caveats come to mind, appears to be that involving the figures for "riot, breach of the peace, and pound breach" and "riotously and feloniously demolishing machinery, buildings, etc."

On the subject of riot statistics, I feel obligated to point out an error that has crept into John Stevenson's *Popular Disturbances in England 1700–1870* (London: Longman, 1979), a book that has deservedly become the standard work on the subject. In Table 12.1, on p. 254, Stevenson presents erroneous statistics for committals and convictions for English riot and rescue, 1835–45; these are in fact figures for *Irish* riot and rescue [Stevenson's source cited: G. R. Porter, *Progress of the Nation* (London: J. Murray, 1847), p. 675; see also Porter, *Progress*, 1st ed., 3 vols. (London: C. Knight, 1836–43), 3:228, for the years 1835–41]. The data in Stevenson's other tables, on pp. 295, 352, and 356, are perfectly reliable, that is, consistent with the figures I know.

Table I.1. *Committals for protest offenses in England and Ireland, 1835–56*

Year	Arming		Arson			Assaults		Cattle killing and maiming		Cattle, sheep, and horse stealing[c]	
	Being out armed, to take game by night, and assaulting gamekeepers	Assembling armed unlawfully	Arson of cornstack, warehouse, crops, and plantations	Arson of dwelling house, or shop, with person therein	Capital Arson						
	England	Ireland	England	England	Ireland	England	Ireland	England	Ireland	England	Ireland
1835	184	15	76	0	53	844	6,175	34	25	424	528
1836	151	16	62	0	38	700	6,401	35	23	481	591
1837	143	20	49	0	41	590	3,013[b]	42	11	556	592
1838	79	25	39	5	18	695	3,254	24	5	531	550
1839	90	63	37	6	80	723	5,886	25	21	477	626
1840	91	128	67	1	40	604	4,777	34	14	634	806
1841	116	62	25	2	58	660	4,273	28	18	559	490
1842	101	207	48	12	91	727	4,105	37	25	654	512
1843	236	47[a]	94	8	85	742	4,457	34	9	644	330

Year											
1844	111	121	232	8	73	788	4,475	43	24	493	364
1845	95	144	90	3	52	797	3,851	28	9	357	254
1846	128	93	114	13	27	786	4,101	40	11	365	357
1847	75	240	115	1	46	672	3,774	25	103[d]	473	3,065[d]
1848	157	189	120	8	134	804	4,990	27	515	438	3,008
1849	201	208	206	7	189	567	4,476	42	193	538	4,707
1850	137	186	167	5	355	607	3,526	32	47	411	1,932
1851	141	159	208	2	160	768	2,259	31	44	399	1,341
1852	119	32	202	6	105	755	2,081	18	21	321	606
1853	122	47	144	5	50	740	1,857	22	14	281	375
1854	81	10	146	6	30	629	1,506	18	23	384	193
1855	56	1	142	2	25	495	1,607	31	4	327	157
1856	86	55	121	3	19	790	1,563	17	4	359	105

[a] The Repeal year.
[b] Many assault cases now handled by magistrates in petty sessions.
[c] In England, mostly sheep; in Ireland, mostly cattle and sheep.
[d] Onset of the Irish Famine.

Table I.2. *Committals for protest offenses in England and Ireland, 1835–56 (continued)*

| | Riotous offenses | | | | | | | | | | | | Anti-police offenses | | | | | |
| | Threatening letters | | Attacking and injuring dwelling houses and lands | Taking and holding forcible possession of land | Riot, breach of peace, and pound breach | | Riotously and feloniously demolishing machinery, buildings, etc. | | Riot and sedition[g] | Totals | | Rescue and refusing to aid peace officers | | Assaults on peace officers in execution of their duty | | Totals | |
Year	England	Ireland	Ireland	Ireland	England	Ireland	England	Ireland	England	England	Ireland	England	Ireland	England	Ireland	England	Ireland
1835	15	23	—	—	811	1,905	18	—	0	829	[1,905]	28	—	421	—	449	—
1836	7	17	—	—	524	2,013	8	—	0	532	[2,013]	28	—	477	—	505	—
1837	3	5	—	—	523	1,693	0	—	0	523	[1,693]	21	—	394	—	415	—
1838	3	6	—	—	420	2,168	1	—	0	421	[2,168]	14	—	339	—	353	—
1839	4	8	137	811	592	3,409	9	39	231	832	3,448	23	1,321	433	212	456	1,533
1840	2	9	64	707	413	3,203	0	41	212	625	3,244	22	1,555	485	92	507	1,647
1841	1	5	135	841	553	2,855	7	76	5	565	2,931	39	1,498	549	60	588	1,558
1842	6	9	73	815	595	2,890	71	28	962	1,628	2,918	12	1,594	467	237	479	1,831
1843	15	9	62	815	543	3,343	60	0	60	663	3,343	18	2,330[h]	464	93	482	2,423
1844	14	25	46	786	567	3,018	2	4	2	571	3,022	13	1,994	338	91	351	2,085
1845	6	33	92	853	363	2,574	0	5	0	363	2,579	14	1,119	329	98	343	1,217
1846	4	24	91	904	302	3,471	5	5	0	307	3,476	11	983	372	121	383	1,104
1847	7	26	88	657	373	2,437	13	14	0	386	2,451	2	2,251[i]	314	67	316	2,318
1848	4	19	188[e]	1,273[e]	387	3,222	4	28	253	644	3,250	9	4,131	348	166	357	4,297
1849	4	20	177	1,198	274	3,501	2	50	3	279	3,551	6	4,688	239	80	245	4,768
1850	4	18	108	915	304	2,951	14	15	0	318	2,966	8	3,077	218	66	226	3,143
1851	6	13	66	688	216	1,827	4	16	0	220	1,843	10	1,915	277	61	287	1,976
1852	2	14	64	429	370	1,335	0	5	0	370	1,340	1	869	330	73	331	942

1853	3	9	10	385	217	1,341	0	2	0	217	1,343	3	457	241	66	244	523
1854	3	3	8	290	230	1,033	0	52	0	230	1,085	11	325	207	78	218	403
1855	1	5	9	208	129	685	3	3	0	132	688	4	202	190	108	194	310
1856	1	4	5	223	155	661[f]	0	20	0	155	681	1[i]	276[k]	214	93	215	369

Note on criminal statistics: The Criminal Justice Act (England), 18 & 19 Vict., c. 126 (1855), led to a considerable decrease in the total number of persons committed for trial. The act, however, principally affected committals for larceny by extending to JPs summary jurisdiction in such cases; earlier acts of 1847 and 1850 had given JPs summary jurisdiction in larceny cases involving juvenile offenders below age sixteen. None of these acts appears to have affected the offense categories (statistics) presented here.

From 1857 on, statistics exist in England for *indictable offenses known to the police;* these figures represent only a very rough counterpart to the Irish outrage statistics (crimes reported by the constabulary) that date from the 1830s.

It should be noted that beginning in the mid-1830s, the governments of England and Ireland arranged the national totals of criminal statistics (committals) into six general categories of crime. The annual data for these six category totals have formed the basis for my calculations in two text tables, *Table 10.1* and *Table 11.8.* I have chosen not to reprint here the yearly six-category totals for the period 1835–53. The figures may be found in the annual and summary returns in the *Parliamentary Papers* [e.g., annual committals totals, for 1840–44, Eng. & Ire., are in *PP 1847* (807, 822), 47:64, 98–9]. The figures are also readily available in tabular summary form in G. R. Porter, *Progress of the Nation* (London: J. Murray, 1851), p. 646 (England, 1834–49) and p. 668 (Ireland, 1835–49).

[e] Depths of the Irish Famine.

[f] Rises to c. 1,000 in 1857, then a steady decline to a range of 250–400 in 1858–75.

[g] In Ireland the first prosecution for riot and sedition was in 1863 (two persons); 1865 (three); 1866 (nine); 1867 (sixty-one); 1868 (twenty-three); 1869 (two),

[h] The Repeal year.

[i] Onset of the Irish Famine.

[j] After 1856, even with the compulsory county police, the figures down to 1874 reach only an annual high of seven in 1864.

[k] Figures continue to fall until 1860, rise in 1861–4 (maximum of 554 in 1863), then steadily decline until 1874 (range, 100–150).

Sources: "Returns of the Number of Persons Committed or Bailed for Trial at the Assizes and [Quarter] Sessions." The *Parliamentary Papers* provide tabular summaries for each offense for the previous ten years. For my purposes, the years consulted in each source were as follows. *England:* For 1835–44, *PP 1845* (651), 37:76; for 1845–9, *PP 1850* (1227), 45:527; for 1850–6, *PP 1857* (2246), 35:106–7. *Ireland:* For 1835–8, "Report by the Lords' Select Committee ... to inquire into the state of Ireland, ... in respect of Crime and Outrage," *PP 1839* (486), 12:1092–3, ev. of T. Drummond; for 1839–45, *PP 1846* (696), 35:178–9; for 1846–8, *PP 1850* (1271), 45:624–5; for 1849–53, *PP 1854–5* (1930), 43:89–90; and for 1854–6, *PP 1861* (2863), 52:227–8.

Table I.3. *Protest offenses, England and Ireland, 1835–56: annual averages*

	Arming		Arson		Assaults		Cattle killing and maiming/cattle, sheep, horse stealing		Rescue and refusing aid, and assaults on, police		Riotous offenses	
	England	Ireland	England	Ireland	England	Ireland	England	Ireland	England	Ireland	England	Ireland
1835–8	139	19	58	38	707	4,711	532	581	—	—	576	1,945
1839–42	100	115	50	72	679	4,760	612	628	508	1,642	913	3,135
1843–6	143	101	141	59	778	4,221	501	340	390	1,707	476	3,105
1847–51	142	196	168	177	844	3,805	483	2,991	279	3,300	369	2,812
1852–6	93	29	155	46	682	1,723	356	300	240	509	221	1,027
1835–9 to 1856	123	94	119	81	740	3,746	490	1,030	346	1,803	491	2,361

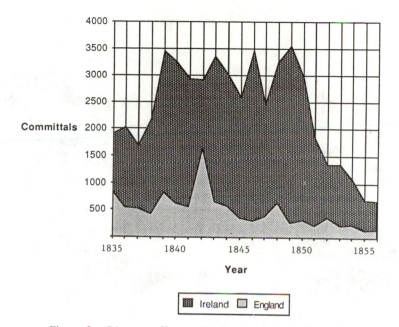

Figure I.1 Riotous offenses, England and Ireland, 1835–56.

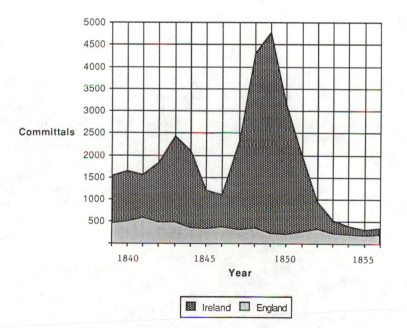

Figure I.2 Antipolice offenses, England and Ireland, 1839–56.

SIZE OF IRISH CONSTABULARY FORCE, BY COUNTY

1830 1848

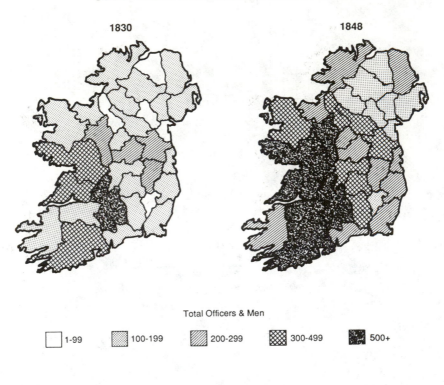

Total Officers & Men

☐ 1-99   ▦ 100-199   ▨ 200-299   ▧ 300-499   ▨ 500+

II. GROWTH OF THE IRISH CONSTABULARY, 1824–52

Table II.1 traces the increase in force strength of the Irish constabulary, county by county, during the first thirty years of its existence. Leinster's lead in percentage distribution of policemen by province was finally overtaken by Munster in the late 1840s, not least because of the growth of the forces in Tipperary, Cork, and Limerick. Historically the most policed county, Tipperary mustered a remarkable concentration of police (nearly 1,300 men) to put down the Rising of 1848. The table also reveals the relative paucity of police in Ulster and the generally stable distribution of police in Connaught throughout the period 1824–52.

   Map II.1 makes clear (1) the continued concentration of constabulary in the south and west from 1830 to 1848, and (2) the growth in size of all county forces between these two dates. In 1830, four counties had forces of more than 300 men; by 1848, thirteen counties had forces of this size.

Table II.1. *Growth of the Irish constabulary, 1824–52*

	1824	1830	1832	1837	1842	1848	1852
Carlow	75	75	99	128	178	163	152
Dublin	150	150	150	227	237	231	228
Kildare	229	229	253	233	257	247	249
Kilkenny	198	197	402	395	399	452	440
King's Co.	173	195	224	272	323	324	351
Longford	90	106	144	143	166	225	197
Louth	[b]	84	134	236	185	182	273
Meath	225	295	331	324	308	402	415
Queen's Co.	138	182	337	332	307	347	354
Westmeath	218	250	278	273	278	293	295
Wexford	144	147	154	238	301	246	239
Wicklow	126	134	134	171	204	217	222
LEINSTER	1,766	2,044	2,640	2,972	3,143	3,329	3,415
Clare	207	307	307	382	310	597	399
Cork[a]	421	428	424	522	622	917	916
Kerry	136	134	134	156	182	252	226
Limerick	184	182	181	293	384	837	631
Tipperary[a]	186	576	576	733	928	1,295	1,107
Waterford	105	116	116	150	155	294	257
MUNSTER	1,239	1,743	1,738	2,236	2,581	4,192	3,536
Antrim	178	176	174	190	206	207	237
Armagh	101	101	100	125	151	159	259
Cavan	136	150	151	189	193	402	394
Donegal	102	132	132	160	243	219	338
Down	[b]	136	136	161	179	176	285
Fermanagh	86	132	132	121	123	184	184
Londonderry	85	85	96	97	93	107	105
Monaghan	85	84	84	133	158	194	274
Tyrone	110	140	205	154	159	176	184
ULSTER	883	1,136	1,210	1,330	1,505	1,824	2,260
Galway[a]	385	384	698	595	489	699	720
Leitrim	85	97	112	134	169	307	321
Mayo	177	181	208	272	291	420	318
Roscommon	156	226	345	245	247	594	488
Sligo	101	129	143	186	181	223	228
CONNAUGHT	904	1,017	1,506	1,432	1,377	2,243	2,075
IRELAND	4,792	5,940	7,094	7,970	8,606	11,588	11,286

Table II.1. (*Continued*)

	1824	1830	1832	1837	1842	1848	1852
	Percentage distribution of police, by province						
LEINSTER	36.9	34.4	37.2	37.3	36.5	28.7	30.3
MUNSTER	25.9	29.3	24.5	28.1	30.0	36.2	31.3
ULSTER	18.4	19.1	17.1	16.7	17.5	15.7	20.0
CONNAUGHT	18.9	17.1	21.2	18.0	16.0	19.4	18.4

Years: Figures are for force levels at the end of each year. For 1824 and 1852, force level in December; for all other years, force level on the first day of the *next* year (hence, e.g., 1830 refers to force strength on 1 Jan. 1831).

Force strength: This is defined as all rank and file and all officers (including paymasters) active in counties. Not included in the table are police stationed in towns (by 1848, 340 men in seven towns), maintained at Dublin's Phoenix Park depot, and enrolled in the Reserve Force (est. 1839; about 400 men by 1848).

[a] From the early 1830s on, the three largest counties were subdivided: Cork and Galway each into an East and West Riding, and Tipperary into a North and South Riding. Figures here are county totals.

[b] No return; county force in process of being established.

Sources: For 1824, constabulary return, in Official Papers, Series 2, 615/2, ISPO, DC. For 1830 and 1832, "Return of the Police of Ireland, showing Number and Distribution thereof ...," *PP 1833*(518), 32:453–61. For 1837, HO 184/54, appendix, and "Amount of Constabulary Force employed in Ireland ...," *PP 1837–8* (383), 46: 333–5. For 1842, Official Papers Miscellaneous and Assorted 1A/72/4/78/2, ISPO, DC; and "Amount of Constabulary Force ...," *PP 1843* (183), 50:89–90. For 1848, HO 184/54, appendix, and "Amount of Constabulary Force ...," *PP 1849* (316), 49:201. For 1852, "Amount of Constabulary Force ...," *PP 1852–3* (995), 94:171–3.

III. STATISTICAL RETURNS FOR THE ENGLISH AND IRISH POLICE

The tables in Appendix III let the reader see how the story of police continues in the decades after the 1850s. The statistics are important because it is from them, in part, that the myth of English pioneering or primacy in police development gets fashioned.

Table III.1 shows the force strength of the four largest English city police and of the two Irish forces, urban and rural, as well as the totals for the English county and borough forces. The tale of the table is the great relative importance of the Irish forces in the first half of the century and their decline thereafter. In 1839, sprawling London had a police only three times larger than Dublin's, but by mid-century London's police was five times larger and, by 1880, ten times greater. Dublin's predominance over the major English provincial cities in the early Victorian period is likewise lost in the second half of the century. In 1839, Dublin's police force was two or three times larger than the forces in Manchester, Liverpool, or Birmingham. But from 1842 to 1880, while Dublin's police stayed virtually constant, the English forces spurted ahead: Manchester's police tripled in size, Liverpool's large force doubled, and even Birmingham's lagging police nearly doubled its size.

Even more dramatic is the comparison of the Irish constabulary with the police in the English boroughs and counties. As late as 1848 the force strength of the Irish constabulary was five times larger than the total for the (optional) English county police; even in 1860 it was nearly twice as large as the total for the English county forces. Indeed, in 1860, the Irish constabulary contained twice as many policemen as did all the borough forces in England and Wales. But, as Table III.1 also reveals, the growth trend in the second half of the century was exclusively in England. As the Irish constabulary held stable or even declined slightly in size, the English county police from 1848 to 1880 quadrupled in numbers and the borough forces doubled.

Table III.2 offers a comparison of the force strength of the county police in the two countries. This table shows that of the twenty largest forces in 1871, twelve were Irish and eight were English. More revealingly, the Irish county forces represented a high density of policemen relative to county populations (see the column, "Rank by Police to Population"). By contrast, the English forces that were large in size were also low in density of police to population.

Table III.3 shows in greater detail that the early-nineteenth-century pattern of heavy density of police in Ireland continued to characterize county policing in the British archipelago in the late Victorian period. Every Irish county but one (Protestant-dominated County Down) had a higher density of police than did *any* English county. At the top of the list were Tipperary and Westmeath, with a police-to-population ratio of 1:194. It is somehow fitting that Tipperary – the county to which Robert Peel had sent the first of his new police back in 1814 – was still crawling with Peelers as late as 1871. By contrast, the most lightly policed county in 1871 was Shropshire, with 1 policeman for every 1,752 inhabitants. Even restless Lancashire (Rank 54) had a ratio of only 1:1378.

Note: Returns by the English Inspectors of Constabulary specify the population of county police districts beginning in 1861, a census year. But two English counties, Derbyshire and Nottinghamshire, did not furnish police returns until 1868. For this reason, I chose for this table the next census year, 1871, when English county police returns were complete. The population of each *county police district* differs from (being always less than) the total *county population* as recorded by the census commissioners. The population of the boroughs (with their own separate police) added to the population of the county police district produces the total county population.

Table III.4 presents the trends in size in the county forces in the two countries. By 1890, the English county police were finally more numerous than the Irish constabulary. The English side of the ledger is a record of sometimes slow but nevertheless sustained growth; the Irish, one of fixity overall, a slight gain in one county offset by a decline in another. The English record is a contrasting one of a handful of very large forces – in Lancashire, Yorkshire, Staffordshire, Durham – counterbalanced by numerous small county forces. As late as 1890, seventeen of thirty-eight county forces had fewer than 200 men.

It was different in Ireland. Not only were there, from an early date, large county forces – in Tipperary, Cork, Galway, Limerick – but even more significantly there were few small ones. Despite the sustained post-Famine decline in population, the policy in Ireland was to maintain sizable county police forces. In 1870, and also in 1890, only seven counties had forces of fewer than 200 men. The large size of forces and indeed the relative uniformity in force sizes in Ireland are signs of the central control of police that remained largely lacking in England.

Table III.1. *Strength levels of urban and rural police, select forces and totals, in England and Ireland at seven dates, 1832–80*

	London	Dublin	Manchester	Liverpool	Birmingham	English and Welsh totals		Irish constabulary
						Counties	Boroughs	
1832	3,185	—	—	—	—	—	—	7,154
1839	3,499	966	383[b]	590	340[b]	—	—	8,647
1842	4,394	1,109	264[b]	622	300[b]	2,260	—	9,101
1848	4,910	c. 1,100[a]	447	822	314	2,434	c. 4,000[e]	12,828
1856	5,817	1,092	554	886	316	3,521[c]	4,831	12,039
1864	7,113	1,079	671	1,030	377	7,761[d]	6,082[d]	12,460[d]
1880	10,952	1,101	802	1,200	526	10,751	8,955	11,199

Note: Liverpool returns include the river (harbor) police.
Strength level: Total number of officers and men.
[a] No parliamentary return for this year.
[b] Government, not borough, force.
[c] The next year, 1857, when all counties established forces, the total rises to 6,567 men.
[d] Total size in 1860.
[e] The total in 1853 was 4,375 men.
Sources: "Return of the Number of the Metropolitan Police Force in . . . 1829 to 1844," *PP 1844* (189), 39:691–3; "Accounts . . . of the Metropolitan Police," *PP 1847–8* (67), 52:791. "Return of the Police of Ireland, showing the Number and Distribution thereof . . .," 1830 to 1832, *PP 1833* (518), 32:453–61. Annual returns of "Amount of Constabulary Force employed in Ireland . . .," *PP 1840* (290), 48:159–61; *PP 1843* (183), 50:89–90; *PP 1849* (316), 49:201; and also for 1842–8, Official Papers Miscellaneous and Assorted, 1A/72/4/78/2, ISPO, DC. "Return of the Police Force of the United Kingdom," *PP 1864* (409), 35:599–629. "Reports of Inspectors of Constabulary . . . in England & Wales," *PP 1881* (23), 51:86, 130, 164–5. John Flint, *The Dublin Police and the Police System* (Dublin, 1847), p. 16. F. C. Mather, *Public Order in the Age of the Chartists* (Manchester: Manchester University Press, 1959), pp. 134, 239–42. T. A. Critchley, *A History of Police in England and Wales*, 2d ed. (Montclair, N.J.: Patterson Smith, 1972), p. 146. Chris Cook and Brendan Keith, *British Historical Facts, 1830–1900* (New York: St. Martin's Press, 1975), p. 159. Tom Bowden, *The Breakdown of Public Security: The Case of Ireland 1916–21 and Palestine 1936–39* (Beverly Hills, Calif.: Sage, 1977), p. 31.

Table III.2. *The legacy: top twenty county police, by total force strength, in Ireland and England, 1871*

Rank order	County	Size of force	Rank by police to population[a]
1	Tipperary	1,112	1/2
2	Yorkshire	979	51
3	Lancashire	942	54
4	Cork	771	25
5	Galway	666	12
6	Donegal	578	17
7	Limerick	540	6
8	Mayo	536	20
9	Staffordshire	483	56
10	Meath	432	3
11	Roscommon	412	11
12	Westmeath	405	1/2
13	Clare	398	16
14	Kilkenny	353	5
15	Devonshire	348	36
16	Durham	328	59
17	Kent	300	42
18	Cavan	295	21
19	Gloucestershire	288	47
20	Somerset	286	43

Size of force: Total reported force strength, officers and men, in the counties of England, 29 Sept. 1871, and of Ireland, 1 Jan. 1871.
[a] See Table III.3.
Sources: See Table III.3.

Table III.3. *The legacy: relative density of police, from most to least, in Irish and English counties, 1871*

Rank	County	Ratio of police to population	County population	Rank	County	Ratio of police to population	County population
1/2	Tipperary	1:194	216,210	37	Dorsetshire	1213	163,730
1/2	Westmeath	194	78,416	38	Wiltshire	1215	244,274
3	Meath	219	94,480	39	Huntingdonshire	1226	63,771
4	King's Co.	241	75,781	40	Sussex	1238	268,671
5	Kilkenny	274	96,633	41	Warwickshire	1250	223,673
6	Limerick	281	151,485	42	Kent	1272	381,653
7	Leitrim	305	95,324	43	Somerset	1288	368,280
8	Queen's Co.	307	77,071	44	Cambridgeshire	1293	90,495
9	Dublin[a]	314	74,803	45	Hampshire	1303	336,218
10	Longford	339	64,408	46	Lincolnshire	1312	352,849
11	Roscommon	343	141,246	47	Gloucestershire	1320	380,275
12	Galway	353	235,073	48	Bedfordshire	1328	124,786
13	Kildare	358	84,198	49	Norfolk	1330	307,329
14	Wicklow	362	78,509	50	Buckinghamshire	1350	167,365
15	Louth	369	69,809	51	Yorkshire	1356	1,327,536
16	Clare	372	147,994	52	Cheshire	1362	374,478
17	Donegal	377	217,992	53	Hertfordshire	1365	159,658
18/19	Carlow	384	51,472	54	Lancashire	1378	1,298,108
18/19	Waterford	384	99,488	55	Worcestershire	1410	270,666
20	Mayo	459	245,855	56	Staffordshire	1413	682,564

No.	County	Ratio	Population
21	Cavan	476	140,555
22	Wexford	494	132,506
23	Fermanagh	518	92,688
24	Sligo	539	115,311
25	Cork	568	437,664
26	Monaghan	590	112,785
27	Kerry	745	196,014
28	Antrim	871	235,936
29	Tyrone	880	215,668
30	Armagh	943	179,221
31	Londonderry	1062	148,690
32	Essex	1073	305,825
33	Down	1077	277,775
34	Surrey	1115	137,152
35	Berkshire	1154	133,808
36	Devonshire	1183	411,814
57/58	Oxfordshire	1416	143,013
57/58	Suffolk	1416	290,189
59	Durham	1420	465,826
60	Northamptonshire	1486	172,339
61	Nottinghamshire	1515	221,130
62	Leicestershire	1597	174,091
63	Cumberland/Westmorland	1605	240,734
64	Northumberland	1614	206,608
65	Derbyshire	1619	301,111
66	Cornwall	1624	313,510
67	Herefordshire	1632	101,160
68	Monmouthshire	1641	162,500
69	Rutland	1698	22,073
70	Shropshire	1752	213,742

Note: Calculations based on total reported number of police (officers and men) in the counties of England, 29 Sept. 1871, and of Ireland, 1 Jan. 1871.

Ratio of police to population: One policeman per x number of policed county inhabitants.

County population: The population of the county police district, exclusive of towns or boroughs that had separate police forces (in 1871, 9 towns in Ireland and 171 in England, as itemized in sources).

Sources: England: PP 1890–1 (23), 42:254–7, 272–3, 288–9; Ireland: PP 1871 (443), 64:103. For the full titles, see Sources, Table III.4.

a Source note in PP 1871: "Population for 1861 [sic] for Dublin outside the Metropolitan Police District."

Table III.4. *Force strength of the English and Irish county police in 1842, 1857, 1870, and 1890*

County	1839–42[a]	1857	1870	1890	County	1842	1857	1870	1890
Bedfordshire	47	71	92	96	Antrim	206	325	271	260
Berkshire		114	116	162	Armagh	151	198	192	271
Buckinghamshire		102	124	145	Carlow	178	146	134	111
Cambridgeshire	(37)	70	70	70	Cavan	193	298	295	232
Cheshire		173	277	389	Clare	310	415	398	498
Cornwall		179	193	219	Cork	622	781	771	1,012
Cumberland/Westmorland	(4)	108	146	219	Donegal	243	582	578	332
Derbyshire		[b]	178	270	Down	179	260	258	265
Devonshire		300	345	414	Dublin	237	236	238	225
Dorsetshire		121	133	148	Fermanagh	123	180	179	166
Durham	81	199	357	499	Galway	489	690	666	704
Essex	136	241	251	316	Kerry	182	279	263	281
Gloucestershire	250	254	288	357	Kildare	257	359	235	206
Hampshire	106	243	258	290	Kilkenny	399	355	353	277
Herefordshire	(5)	45	62	77	King's Co.	323	338	314	247
Hertfordshire	71	92	117	161	Leitrim	169	309	313	237
Huntingdonshire		48	52	52	Limerick	384	550	540	556
Kent		222	300	382	Londonderry	93	145	140	144
Lancashire	502	657	931	1,377	Longford	166	205	190	176
Leicestershire	25	96	109	160	Louth	185	197	189	141
Lincolnshire		212	269	299	Mayo	291	419	536	503
Monmouthshire		49	99	134	Meath	308	377	432	309

This appendix table (continued) lists police force strength. The left portion lists English counties; the right portion lists Irish counties. Columns correspond to the years indicated in the Sources note (England: founding 1839–42, 1857, 1870, 1890; Ireland: 1842, 1857, 1870, 1890).

England (continued)

County	At founding[a]	1857	1870	1890
Norfolk	143	221	231	240
Northamptonshire	51	94	115	147
Northumberland		61	145	185
Nottinghamshire	42[b]		140	182
Oxfordshire		89	101	107
Rutland		5	13	14
Shropshire	56	58	122	149
Somerset		277	286	326
Staffordshire	210	367	483	603
Suffolk	(68)	195	205	237
Surrey		113	123	183
Sussex	(33)	164	216	322
Warwickshire	(45)	138	179	274
Wiltshire	201	201	201	216
Worcestershire	65	143	189	277
Yorkshire		660	998	1,338
TOTAL	2,178	6,382	8,514	11,036

Ireland (continued)

County	1842	1857	1870	1890
Monaghan	158	191	191	164
Queen's Co.	307	250	251	202
Roscommon	247	434	412	344
Sligo	181	201	214	251
Tipperary	928	866	1,112	776
Tyrone	159	255	245	252
Waterford	155	256	259	253
Westmeath	278	357	405	296
Wexford	301	276	268	272
Wicklow	204	216	217	194
TOTAL	8,606	10,946	11,059	10,157

Force strength: Total number of officers and men.

[a] Size of force at founding.

[b] No returns submitted until 1868.

( ) Police in one or more districts; no countywide force.

Sources:

England. For 1839–42, "Return of the Police ... in each County ...," *PP 1842* (345), 32:649–74. For subsequent years, "Reports of the Inspectors of Constabulary," for 1857, *PP 1871* (12), 28:125, 198–9; for 1870, *PP 1881* (23), 51:108–11; and for 1890, *PP 1890–1* (23), 42:254–7, 272–3, 288–9. *Ireland.* For 1842 and 1857, returns of "Amount of Constabulary Force employed ... in Ireland," *PP 1843* (183), 50:89–90 and *PP 1857–8* (463), 47:799; and for 1870 and 1890, "Judicial Statistics, Ireland, Part 1, Police," *PP 1871* (443), 64:103 and *PP 1890–1* (6511), 93:57.

IV. OCCUPATIONS OF POLICE RECRUITS

Table IV.1 shows clearly that in both Ireland and England, low-paid police work attracted unskilled and semiskilled laboring men. When a recruit was asked, "Previous occupation?", the usual reply was, "Laborer." Laborers comprised roughly two-fifths of English police recruits. In the Irish force the percentage of laborers (54.8 percent), the highest in the table, is probably in fact a low estimate, since in Ireland many "farmers" were small tenants who also worked seasonally as laborers.

The occupation of soldier is a bit misleading. It appears in the early London force (12.6 percent) but in none of the others. It is likely, however, that some police recruits had done military service but simply did not mention it as a previous occupation. Certain semiskilled and skilled trades, although of decidedly lower incidence than the job of unskilled laborer, do show up in more than one force. Appearing in three of the four columns in the following table are boot/shoemakers, carpenters, clerks, farmers, servants, and tailors; and, in two columns, blacksmiths, butchers, gardeners, miners, and weavers. Some of these (predominantly English) trades – blacksmith, carpenter, miner, shoemaker, weaver – are those that historians have associated with working-class radicalism; others, like clerk, gardener, and servant, are deferential occupations with requirements of authority and hierarchy not unsuited to police work.

Table IV.1 also provides dramatic testimony to the differences between English and Irish society. Of the listed Irish occupations, almost all are rural; of the English ones, most are town-centered. Also, the paucity of Irish and numerousness and diversity of English occupations stand out. In my computer sample of the Irish Constables Register, four-fifths of the 482 recruits listing a previous form of employment had worked in one of two occupations, laborer or farmer; moreover, the sampled register contains a total of only thirty-five different types of occupations. Although laborers also predominate in the English forces, there is a wealth of alternative employment not found in Ireland. The 4,300 recruits to the Lancashire constabulary in 1845–70 listed more than 250 distinct and separate occupations. Even in rural Buckinghamshire and the more mixed county of Staffordshire, the 700 police recruits in 1856–80 listed eighty-one different occupations, ranging from marble mason to draper, locksmith to silk twister.

The following table lists, in order of frequency, the total number of *known previous occupations* of police recruits in the Irish constabulary, the London Metropolitan Police, the Lancashire constabulary, and (conflated) the constabularies in Buckinghamshire and Staffordshire. The Irish figures are based on my computer sample of 709 recruits, 1816–40, as recorded on the Irish Constables Register, HO 184/1–2 (see Appendix V). Of the police forces listed, the Irish constabulary recruits had by far the highest percentage of men (32 percent) for whom the source lists *no* previous occupation. Figures for recruits with a known previous occupation and for *all* recruits are as follows: Irish constabulary, 482 out of 709; London police, 3,185 out of at least 3,263; Lancashire, 4,350 out of 4,357; Buckinghamshire and Staffordshire, 708 out of 730.

For the figures for the Lancashire recruits of 1845–70, I am grateful to my friend William J. Lowe, who loaned me prepublication copy and subsequently published his findings in an article, "The Lancashire Constabulary, 1845–1870: The Social and Occupational Function of a Victorian Police Force," *Criminal Justice History* 4 (1983): 41–62; for Buckinghamshire and Staffordshire, I have relied on Carolyn Steedman's book, *Policing the Victorian Community: The Formation of English Provincial Police Forces, 1856–80* (London: Routledge & Kegan Paul, 1984). The least reliable figures presented here are those for the London police; they are from a list (source uncited) printed in secondary accounts by George Dilnot (1927), Alwyn Solmes (1935), J. L. Thomas (1946), David Ascoli (1979), and Clive Emsley (1983). On the source problems, see my discussion in Chapter 8, n. 69. The London list cites eighteen occupations, with frequencies ranging from 8 stonemasons to 1,154 laborers. If we compare this London

Irish constabulary, 1816–40			London, 1832			Lancashire, 1845–70			Buckinghamshire and Staffordshire, at six dates, 1856–80		
Occupation	No.	Percent	Occupation	No.	Percent	Occupation	No.	Percent	Occupation	No.	Percent
Laborer	264	54.8%	Laborer	1,154	36.2	Laborer	1,642	37.7	Laborer	291	41.1
Farmer	123	25.5	Soldier	402	12.6	Skilled trade	608	14.0	Shoemaker	33	4.7
Bootmaker	19	3.9	Servant	205	6.4	Weaver	469	10.8	Groom	29	4.1
Clerk	15	3.1	Shoemaker	198	6.2	Cotton factory	298	6.9	Miner, collier	29	4.1
Silk weaver	12	2.5	Clerk	152	4.8	Other textile factory	194	4.5	Farmer	23	3.2
Carpenter	5	1.0	"Shopman"	141	4.4	Domestic servant	187	4.3	Servant	15	2.1
Gardener	4	0.8	Carpenter	141	4.4	Small business	149	3.4	Gardener	14	2.0
Clothier	3	0.6	"Superior mechanic"	141	4.4	Farmer	146	3.4	Butcher	10	1.4
Tailor	3	0.6	Butcher	135	4.2	General factory operative	142	3.3	Grocer	10	1.4
Yeoman	3	0.6	Baker	109	3.4	Nonfactory textiles	121	2.8	Blacksmith	9	1.3
			Sailor	101	3.2	Clerk, bookkeeper	82	1.9	Potter	7	1.0
			Bricklayer	75	2.4	Miner	70	1.6	Carpenter	6	0.8
			Blacksmith	55	1.7				Tailor	6	0.8
			Tailor	51	1.6						
			Weaver	51	1.6						
Other	31[a]	6.6	Other	74[b]	2.3	Other	242[c]	5.6	Other	226[d]	31.9
TOTAL	482	100.0	TOTAL	3,185	99.8	TOTAL	4,350	100.2	TOTAL	708	99.9

Note: Percentages calculated on the total number of known previous occupations.

[a] From twenty-five occupations.

[b] From three occupational groups: forty-six plumbers and painters, twenty turners, and eight stonemasons.

[c] From ten occupational categories.

[d] From sixty-eight occupations, finely differentiated (e.g., last maker, lathe cleaner, coppersmith).

Sources: Irish constabulary: Constables Register, HO 184/1–2, sampled by the author. London: David Ascoli, *The Queen's Peace: The Origins and Development of the Metropolitan Police 1829–1979* (London: Hamish Hamilton, 1979), p. 89. Lancashire: Occupational categories as given in Lowe, "Lancashire Constabulary," Table 1, p. 47, percentages (to exclude "unknown") recalculated by author. Buckinghamshire and Staffordshire: Figures for recruits in 1856, 1857, 1863, 1866, 1876, and 1880, in Steedman, *Policing,* pp. 73, 76, 86–90, her annual data totaled and percentages calculated by the author.

list (1832), which adds to a numerical total of 3,185 men, with an 1832 London force strength return [see *PP 1844* (189), 39:691] of 3,263 men – 2,930 constables and 333 sergeants – we arrive at a very conservative total of at least 78 *men on the force* who at recruitment had not stated a previous occupation. This figure must be a low estimate because of the high turnover in recruits in the early years of the London police. With these warnings, then, the London figures are presented solely for the purpose of rough comparison with the solid figures for the other forces.

V. THE CONSTABULARY AND THE COMPUTER: CALCULATING THE CHARACTERISTICS OF THE EARLY IRISH POLICE

> Quantification ... has greatly improved the general quality of historical discourse. . . . Historians can no longer get away with saying "more", "less", "growing", "declining", all of which logically imply numerical comparisons, without ever stating explicitly the statistical basis for their assertions. . . .
>   Despite its unquestionable achievements it cannot be denied that quantification has not fulfilled the high hopes of twenty years ago. . . . There are huge piles of greenish print-out gathering dust in scholars' offices; there are many turgid and excruciatingly dull tomes full of tables of figures, abstruse algebraic equations and percentages to two decimal places. . . . Quantification has told us a lot about the *what* questions ..., but relatively little so far about the *why*. . . .
> — Lawrence Stone, "The Revival of Narrative," 1979

Some years ago I discovered, tucked away on a shelf in the Rolls Room of the old Public Record Office in Chancery Lane, London, a thin light-blue folder, fingered and soiled, quite insignificant in appearance. Its contents were marked "ROYAL MARINES – ROYAL IRISH CONSTABULARY – DUKE OF YORK'S & ROYAL HIBERNIAN SCHOOLS –

REGIMENTAL RECORDS AT SOMERSET HOUSE." The RIC notation interested me, and after learning from Dr. C. J. Kiching, Assistant Keeper, that the folder was a calendar or index, I called out a sample volume. To my astonishment, the volume brought to me, HO 184/1, turned out to be part of a detailed general register of men who had served in the constabulary. For each man the following career information was listed: date of recruitment, age at joining, height, religion, native county, marital status, previous occupation, name(s) of recommender(s), counties of allocation (in order and length of service), record of promotions and punishments, date and mode of leaving, and (if awarded) size of pension. My mind reeled at the kinds of questions that could be asked, and answered, with the help of a machine beyond the comprehension of those hard-working nineteenth-century clerks who had recorded the information.

As I ruminated on my projected computer study, I was the more dumbfounded because in the small literature on the Irish police I had never seen any reference to the HO 184 series.[1] The first four dozen volumes in this series comprise the "RIC General Register," which covers the period 1816–1922 and lists almost 90,000 constables and officers. Volumes 1–42 are registers of constables (volumes 43–4, indexes); volumes 45–8, officers. Since my interest was in the origins of the police, I ordered microfilm copies of the early volumes, HO 184/1–2, which list constables joining up to 1840; and HO 184/45, which includes officers appointed up to 1850 and beyond.

Back in the United States, after receipt and analysis of my microfilm treasure, it soon became clear that, at least for the years before 1837, the "register" could not be a list of all the men who had ever served in the constabulary. The Constables Register, HO 184/1–2, contains exactly 4,000 names of men joining the police in 1816–35 and 1835–40; the Officers Register, HO 184/45, the names of nearly 1,000 men appointed 1817–84, of whom 485 were appointed in 1817–50. But I knew that as early as 1824, the force strength of the constabulary was about 5,000 men, and by 1840 it was double that number. I knew, too, that in the 1830s dismissals and resignations took anywhere from 2 to 6 percent of the men from the force every year; and that these few hundred men leaving annually were regularly replaced. In other words, the number of men who actually served in the Irish police in 1816–40 had to be far, far higher than the 4,000 constables listed on the register as joining in that same period. One veteran of the force later guesstimated that by the 1880s a total of 80,000 Irishmen had served in the constabulary since 1822.[2]

There was also telling internal evidence. Nearly two-thirds of the constables subsequently sampled on the HO 184/1–2 register received some rank promotion; no complete roster of the force would have such a high figure. Nearly 90 percent of the men on the Constables Register for 1816–40 received a pension (77 percent) or died in service (9 percent) before receipt of one; of those on the Officers Register for 1816–50, almost 80 percent received a pension (54 percent) or died in service (25 percent). Finally, over 90 percent of the constables and nearly 80 percent of the officers on the registers served for more than fifteen years.

What, then, are the two separate registers? The volumes themselves do not explain what they are. It appears that for the men joining in 1816–36 the registers are lists of constables and officers of sufficiently long service to qualify for a retirement pension.[3] Of the first 100 men on the Constables Register, HO 184/1, the length of service ranges from a minimum of twenty-one to a maximum of forty-three years. After 1836, certainly by the mid-1840s, the registers may well be actual force registers – that is, career records of all the men. For the period 1837–40, HO 184/2 lists 1,594 recruits, an average of 399 a year; this is a credible number of actual recruits in any one year. HO 184/3–7 lists 9,940 constables joining in 1841–50, an average of 994 per year.[4] The gap between register and reality thus exists principally for the pre-1837 period.

Both registers, for constables and officers, are clearly compilations from earlier registers. On each register the individual entries proceed annually by year of recruitment (Constable 0001, William Evans, Protestant, joined 1816; Officer 001, John Brown, Protestant, joined 1817). On the much shorter Officers Register, the entries run in correct chronological order by year *and* month of joining. But on the Constables Register, faced with a mass of names, the clerks did *not* arrange the individual entries chronologically by month and day *within each year*. Further, Constable Evans (who received his pension of £55 in December 1854 after thirty-eight years' service), although he is the first man on the register, is *not* the first constable on the register to receive a pension: This was Constable 0324, who was pensioned on 1 Jan. 1849. In sum, HO 184/1–2 and 45 are not registers of men pensioned in chronological order but, rather, seem to be lists of men of long service who could be expected to qualify for a retirement pension.

I

In the early years of the Constabulary retirement pay was hardly a pressing question. Understandably, given the temporary nature of its policemen, Peel's Peace Preservation Act of 1814 made no mention of superannuation funding. The Baronial Constables Act of 1815, amending 32 Geo. 3, c. 16 (1792), was the first statute to confront the issue. On the recommendation of the county grand jury, the Lord Lieutenant was authorized to grant superannuation pay to any local constable, the amount to be based on "a Man's Age, his Infirmities of Mind or Body, and the Length of Service."[5] This obscure act provided the model for all subsequent pension acts. The act's distinction between infirmity and old-age pensions, and its details regarding age and length of service, were reproduced in the Constabulary Act of 1822 and were not substantially altered in the subsequent well-known act of 1836 (see Table V.I).

Essentially, then, from 1822 on, the men in the Peace Preservation force and the constabulary were eligible for a pension on the basis of either infirmity or old age. To get an infirmity pension, by far the commonest, a man had to be so certified (usually described as "worn out") and to have served for ten years. In 1836 the length of service was raised to fifteen years, thus affecting the original constabulary recruits of 1822, but the gradation of superannuation pay proportional to length of service was changed somewhat in the men's favor.[6] It was much harder to get an old-age pension: A man had to reach the age of sixty with at least fifteen years' service. But nobody physically fit qualified after fifteen years' service because nobody joined the police at age forty-five. Realistically, a constable recruited at age twenty in, say, the year 1824 had to serve for forty years – and wait until 1864 – to get an old-age, length-of-service pension. If he stayed in until he was sixty-five, he could qualify for slightly higher retirement pay. For this reason, most men pensioned were pensioned by reason of infirmity. In addition, after 1824, any man in the Government's police, Peelers or constabulary, who received "any Maim, Wound, or Hurt, ... in the ... Performance of the Duty of his Office, whereby he shall be disabled from executing ... [his] Duty," might be eligible for "an annual Remuneration or Superannuation" not exceeding two-thirds of his salary.[7]

The system of funding also worked against the development of a strong pension program. Although after 1822 the ongoing costs of the constabulary were equally split between the counties and the government Consolidated Fund, *all* expenses of superannuation were paid by presentments of the county grand juries. Apparently the counties were not overly generous, for the act of 1836 transferred half of the burden of superannuation to the Consolidated Fund. A portion of the costs was also placed on the backs of the policemen themselves. The 1836 act established a mandatory 2 percent deduction from the salaries of all constables and officers, the proceeds to form a "Police Superannuation Fund."[8] Ten years later, by act of Parliament, all current *policing* costs of the constabulary were assumed by the central government.[9] By this time, the 2 percent police retirement tax was generating ample funds. The Police

Pension Act of 1847 freed the counties of any future obligations and restricted the Consols to a source of last resort.[10]

Because the constabulary was created in 1822, pension records for the 1830s and early 1840s list men "retired" only from infirmity or disabling injury. The earliest parliamentary return, printed in 1831, records superannuation payments totaling £2,718 disbursed to 174 veterans of the Peace Preservation force and the constabulary. All of the men had been judged "unfit for further duty" – ranging from Subconstable James Tormay, "disabled by severe beating" after twenty-eight months' service, to Subconstable John Shepherd, worn out after eighteen years' service. All of the superannuated had been discharged with medical certificates from the Army Medical Board. By 1843, 255 names were on the constabulary's pension list and by 1846, 450 names, all of the men having been medically certified as unfit for further service. Most of the men on the 1846 list were in their mid-forties, some in their fifties, and a few even older. The cost for such payments had risen to £10,800 in 1836 and £13,700 by 1846.[11]

The police acts of 1822 and 1836 had provided for pensions, to the point of listing often irrelevant categories involving sixty-year-old men. Relatively few men were pensioned. But by the late 1840s, the Government was forced to take seriously the subject of superannuation. The passage of time had caught up with the constabulary. A few men like Constable Evans (the first entry on the HO 184/1 register) were original Peeler recruits, men of thirty years' meritorious service. Those who had been the original constabulary recruits of 1822–4 were now twenty-five-year veterans. The list of older deserving men was lengthening, the men themselves growing restless and worried about their sunset years.

Against this background, in the summer of 1847 as the Potato Famine ravaged parts of Ireland, Parliament passed an act, 10 & 11 Vict., c. 100, that was the constabulary's first real pension act.[12] The act did nothing new to assist the worn-out fifty-year-old constable. But, as Table V.1 shows, it did improve old-age benefits. Whereas in the period 1822–46 a man had to be sixty-five years old with forty years' service to get a retirement pension of up to three-fourths of his salary, beginning in 1847 a man of age sixty with twenty years' experience could get up to the whole of his salary. The act also set up a "gratuity" system – a small lump-sum (not annual) payment – for deserving men of less than fifteen years' service.[13] In general, the act of 1847 rewarded the large cohort of older recruits from the 1820s who could be expected to clamor for pensions in the 1850s.[14] Faced with these imminent and increasing costs as the early generations of recruits came to retirement, the Government responded by enacting lower benefits for men joining the constabulary after 1847. These new recruits, both constables and officers, would have to put in longer service to get the same pension amounts as the pre-1847 recruits (see Table V.1). Settling the problems of the present came at the expense of creating new ones in the future.[15]

2

It appears, then, that the "RIC General Register," now catalogued as HO 184, was drawn up subsequent to the act of 1847 and used initially as a working list of long-service men likely to be pensioned. In the Constables Register, HO 184/1, the *earliest* year that is recorded for a man being pensioned, dying in service, or being dismissed is 1849 – respectively, Constable 0324, 1 January 1849; Constable 0019, 12 March 1849; and Constable 0640, 29 March 1849. The vast majority of the men in HO 184/1–2 (recruits in 1816–40) were pensioned in the 1850s and 1860s, only a few in the 1870s. For the recruits of 1817–50 in the Officers Register, HO 184/45, the earliest year recorded for a man's pension, death, or dismissal is 1839; there are a few entries for 1840–5, but almost all fall in the period 1849–70. Because they appear to have been working registers, it is impossible to date the separate registers precisely. They were almost certainly drawn up sometime after the Police Pension Act of 1847.

Table V.1. Constabulary pensions

	Infirmity: under age 60		Old age: age 60 and above		
1822[a]	*Service*	*Pension*	*Age*	*Service*	*Pension*
Constables and officers	10 yrs.	Sum not >1/3 of salary	60+	15 yrs.	Sum not >2/3 of salary
	10–20 yrs.	Sum not >1/2 of salary	65+	40 yrs.	Sum not >3/4 of salary
	20+ yrs.	Sum not >2/3 of salary	65+	50 yrs.	Sum not >100% of salary
1836[b]	*Service*	*Pension*	*Age*	*Service*	*Pension*
Constables and officers	15 yrs.	Not >1/2 of salary	60+	15 yrs.	Not >2/3 of salary
	15–20 yrs.	Not >2/3 of salary	65+	40 yrs.	Not >3/4 of salary
	20+ yrs.	Not >100% of salary	65+	50 yrs.	Not >100% of salary
1847[c]	*Service*	*Pension*	*Age*	*Service*	*Pension*
Constables and officers heretofore appointed	15–20 yrs.	Not >2/3 salary	60+	15–20 yrs.	Not > 2/3 salary
	20+ yrs.	Not >100% of salary	60+	20+ yrs.	Not >100% of salary

Summary: "15 yrs." eliminated; otherwise same as in 1836.

Summary: "15 yrs." eliminated; "old age" is set at 60; old-age service steps are lowered and *made identical* to infirmity steps set in 1836.

Infirmity and old age

	Constables		Officers	
	Service	*Pension*	*Service*	*Pension*
1847[c] (*cont'd.*)	15–20 yrs.	Not >1/2 of salary	15–20 yrs.	Not >1/2 of salary
Men hereafter appointed	20–5 yrs.	Not >2/3 of salary	20–30 yrs.	Not >2/3 of salary
	25–30 yrs.	Not >3/4 of salary	30–40 yrs.	Not >3/4 of salary
	30+ yrs.	Not >100% of salary	40+ yrs.	Not >100% of salary

Summary: "Old age" is set at 60; constables and officers are separated; service steps are identical for old-age and infirmity; and pension as a proportion of salary is *lowered*.

[a] Terms, service steps, and funding are identical to those in the Irish Baronial Constables Act, 55 Geo. 3, c. 158 s. 5. All funding to come from county grand jury presentments.

[b] Two percent deduction from salaries of all constables and officers to constitute a Police Superannuation Fund. Pensions hereafter to be paid half by county grand jury presentments and half by Consolidated Fund, unless moneys in Superannuation Fund are sufficient.

[c] Pensions hereafter to be paid entirely from Police Superannuation Fund.

They probably date from 1849 at the earliest, since it is unlikely that *no* constable or officer was pensioned in 1848. But it is impossible to say whether this register record keeping was done regularly from 1849 on or whether the volumes themselves are recompilations done in the 1850s or even 1860s.[16]

Given the nature of the documents HO 184/1–2 and 184/45, for the early recruiting period 1816–c. 1837, analysis of some of the data categories must be done with great caution or avoided altogether. For example, the length of service of the men on the register tells us nothing about the length of service for the vast majority of men *not on the register* who served for fewer than fifteen years and were never pensioned. Similarly, conclusions from the register data on number of punishments and rank reductions and promotions would paint a distorted picture of the constabulary, since the men on the registers had long and generally satisfactory careers. The register statistics no doubt deflate the true rates of punishment and rank reduction, and inflate the true rates of promotion and length of service, simply because the registers do not record the careers of the many, many men never or seldom promoted, men whose careers were mediocre or bad, men who left the force after a few months or even after several years.

Still, there is no apparent reason why certain characteristics of the men on the registers should be any different from those of the many other policemen missing from them. I am referring to a man's age at joining the force, his height, religion, native county, marital status, recommender, previous occupation, and counties of allocation. Though in the early period these registers are forced samples of the whole constabulary, careful analysis of HO 184/1–2 and 184/45 can answer some questions about the early Irish police that otherwise would remain a mystery.

Because there were 4,000 constables and 485 officers on the registers, it was decided to sample systematically 709 constables and 218 officers over several meaningful time periods.★ Because of the small number of register constables (sixty-eight) and officers (twenty-four) who joined the police in the original Peeler period, every case in the period 1816–22 has been used in the computer analysis. For the Officers Register for 1823–50 every other case was sampled; for the Constables Register for 1823–40 sampling was progressively less frequent, though still systematic within each time period (the lowest sample size was 142 men in 1833–6). For the specifics, see Tables V.2 and V.3. Each time period (date of joining) has a distinguishing characteristic. The period 1816–22 comprises the early years of Peel's Peace Preservation force; 1823–8 represents the infancy of the constabulary, a period of some local control; 1829–32 covers most of the Tithe War; 1833–6 constitutes the era of Whig reforms in the constabulary; and 1837–40 marks the consolidation of the police resulting from the act of 1836. For the officers, the data have also been interpreted for 1841–5, the years of Peel's Tory Administration, and for 1846–50, Russell's Whig Government and the years of the Irish Famine. Analysis within separate time periods of recruiting, as opposed to analysis of the whole period 1816–40, of course allows us to see changes in the characteristics of recruits over representative periods of time.

3

What follows are my findings, the computer-generated profile of the early Irish constabulary. Over the period 1816–40, the age of constable recruits steadily dropped. In the early years, in both the Peeler and early constabulary force, there was

★The computer project was made possible by the help of Professor David S. Landes, generous funding from the Harvard West European Studies Program and the James Fund of the Harvard Department of History (with special thanks to Professor Bernard Bailyn), and the expertise of a number of friends – Adolfo Garcia, Karen Heise, Randy Hudson, Katherine Porter, Stanley Yutkins, and above all Duncan Dwinell. Without the help of these six people in coding, transcribing, keypunching, and programming, the project could never have been finished.

Table V.2. *Sampling the Constables Register: HO 184/1–2*

Date of joining	No. of constables in register	Register: percent distribution	Method of sampling	No. of constables in sample	Sample percent distribution	Sample total as percentage of register total
1816–22	68	1.7%	Every case	68	9.6%	100.0%
1823–8	527	13.2	First five cases on every page	181	25.5	34.3
1829–32	879	22.0	First two cases on every page	156	22.0	17.7
1833–6	934	23.3	First three cases on every other page	142	20.0	15.2
1837–40	1,592	40.0	First case on every page	162	22.8	10.2
1816–40	4,000	100.2	—	709	99.9	17.7

Table V.3. *Sampling the Officers Register: HO 184/45*

Date of joining	No. of officers in register		Register: percent distribution	Method of sampling	No. of officers in sample	Sample: percent distribution
1816–22	[32]	24	5.9%	Every case	24	11.0%
1823–8	[102]	88	21.5	Every other case	44	20.2
1829–32	[33]	29	7.1	Every other case	15	6.9
1833–6	[92]	62	15.1	Every other case	31	14.2
1837–40	[69]	68	16.6	Every other case	34	15.6
1841–5	[54]	49	12.0	Every other case	25	11.5
1846–50	[103]	90	22.0	Every other case	45	20.6
1816–50	[485]	410	100.2	—	218	100.0

Note: A total of 485 men [the numbers in brackets] appear on the register for 1816–50. The listing of career information is complete for 410, or 85 percent, of these men. The seventy-five men with incomplete records were excluded from the sampling procedure.

a spread of ages from sixteen to twenty-eight and above. By 1840, lads of age sixteen to eighteen and men over twenty-seven were no longer taken. From the early 1830s on, as a result of the implementation of standardized hiring requirements, three-fourths and more of all recruits were age nineteen to twenty-four. (See Figure V.1.) The trend to youth was even more noticeable among officer recruits: Before 1830 the great majority were twenty-eight years of age and older; after 1836, most were

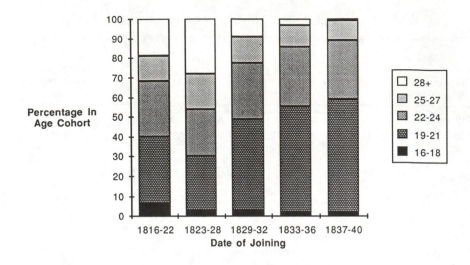

Percentage in Age Cohort

Legend:
- 28+
- 25-27
- 22-24
- 19-21
- 16-18

Date of Joining

Age summary 1816-40: 16-18, 3%; 19-21, 44%; 22-24, 28%; 25-27, 13%; 28+, 12%.

Figure V.1 Age at recruitment: constables.

considerably younger. By the 1840s, about a third of the officer recruits were younger than age twenty-two (see Figure V.2). As we shall see, the trend to youthful officers reflects the development of a cadet officer class after 1842.

If the age on joining became younger, the average height of recruits increased. The number of tall men (5 feet 10 inches and above) did not change over time, but short men were no longer taken. Before 1830 fully a quarter of the recruits were 5 feet 7 inches or less in height; this percentage then fell dramatically, and after 1836 short men virtually disappeared. The force thus became taller not because it recruited giants but rather from an increase in the number of men of middle height. The share of recruits who were 5 feet 8 inches or 5 feet 9 inches tall nearly doubled from 1820 to 1840. This trend reflects the imposition from the early 1830s of a minimum height requirement of 5 feet 8 inches (see Figure V.3). We have no height figures for officers.

As the men joining the constabulary became younger and taller, so increasingly they tended to be single men. This hiring of bachelor constables was intended, in part, to rid the force of "needy and beggarly" married constables.[17] It was intended, too, to cut the men's ties to the local population and to develop an esprit de corps by concentrating their loyalty on public service at the expense of a private life. From 1835 on, the constabulary's announced goal was a force in which only 25 percent of the men were married.[18] The constabulary's antimarriage policy, combined with the trend toward hiring nineteen- to twenty-four-year-olds, was a harsh one, for, of course, marriage (if not early marriage) was a common practice, and a common expectation, in pre-Famine Ireland.[19] It forced a man to choose between police work and connubial bliss, for, unlike the English constable, he could not have both.

The Constables Register provides telling evidence of the Government's policy on prohibiting marriages. In every time period, we find a rising percentage of constables and officers who remained single. The trend toward perpetual bachelorhood is sharp and steady, rising from a mere 14 percent of constable recruits in 1816–22 to 54 percent of the 1837–40 recruits (see Figure V.4). We see the same trend, but not quite

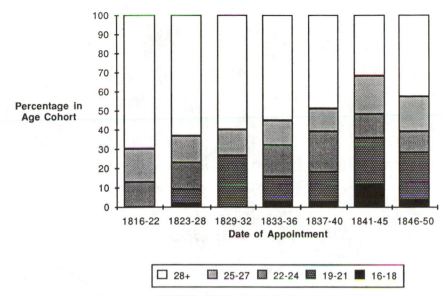

Percentage in Age Cohort

Date of Appointment

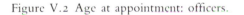

□ 28+   ▦ 25-27   ▨ 22-24   ▩ 19-21   ■ 16-18

Age summary 1816-50: 16-18, 4%; 19-21, 15%; 22-24, 13%;
25-27, 15%; 28+, 53%.

Figure V.2 Age at appointment: officers.

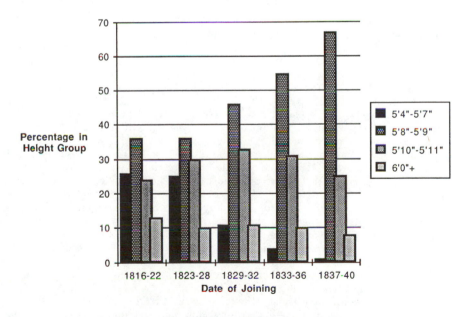

Percentage in Height Group

Date of Joining

■ 5'4"-5'7"
▦ 5'8"-5'9"
▩ 5'10"-5'11"
▨ 6'0"+

Height summary 1816-40: 5'4"-5'7", 12%; 5'8"-5'9", 49%;
5'10"-5'11", 29%; 6'0"+, 10%.

Figure V.3 Height of constables.

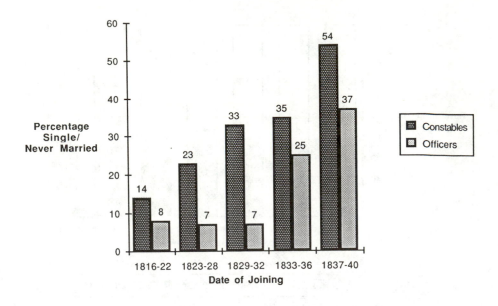

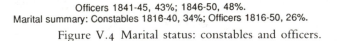

Officers 1841-45, 43%; 1846-50, 48%.
Marital summary: Constables 1816-40, 34%; Officers 1816-50, 26%.

Figure V.4 Marital status: constables and officers.

so sharp, for officers: 8 percent of those appointed in 1816–22 stayed single; 37 percent by 1837–40; and 48 percent in 1846–50 (Figure V.4). The register figures probably understate this trend to bachelorhood, for it was the long-service man who was eventually permitted to marry. The long-term results of this policy can be seen in the figures for the marital status of the men in the Irish constabulary and the London Metropolitan Police in 1864: In the former, 71 percent were bachelors; in the latter, only 30 percent.[20]

Who were these men who joined the constabulary – that is, what were their backgrounds or previous occupations? Here the registers are not very illuminating. For constables, the percentage whose occupation is "not given" varies from 23 to 36 percent in each time period. Where an occupation is listed, it is usually simply "farmer" or "laborer." Half to two-thirds of all recruits were designated as being farmers or laborers, with laborers preponderating. The distinction in many cases is not that helpful, for many Irish small farmers also worked as seasonal laborers; in any case, on the register there is no strong trend over time toward hiring more of one, less of another. In general, the Constables Register corroborates an Inspector-General's comment that the men were from the "class of the peasantry, soldiers discharged, and the lower farmers."[21] Apart from an apparent equilibrium in the hiring of farmers (17 percent of recruits in 1816–40) and laborers (37 percent), there was a steady trend away from hiring persons of other occupations – notably, bootmakers, clerks, silk weavers, gardeners, tailors, and so on (see Appendix IV). As the years passed, fewer and fewer recruits had a particular trade (26 percent of recruits in 1816–22; 18 percent in 1829–32; 10 percent in 1837–40). This trend in police recruiting may mirror larger social trends, namely, the progressive deindustrialization of pre-Famine Ireland.

The Officers Register gives virtually no occupational data (93 percent "not given") External evidence indicates that the officers were from "the most respectable class'

Table V.4. *Rank or title of recommenders of constables, 1816–40*

Date of joining	Gentlemen	Lords	Churchmen	Army officers	Police officers	Other	None listed
1816–22	17%	12	12	43	0	1	15
1823–8	27	14	10	20	3	1	25
1829–32	13	5	15	28	2	0	37
1833–6	11	7	9	17	8	1	47
1837–40	10	3	6	16	2	1	62
1816–40	16	8	10	23	3	1	39

Notes:
Gentlemen: Esquire, gentleman, knight.
Lords: Baron(et), lord, viscount, marquess, earl, duke.
Churchmen: Reverend, dean, deacon, archdeacon, bishop, archbishop.
Army officers: Lieutenant, captain, major, lieutenant-colonel, colonel, general.
Police officers: Chief constable, subinspector, county inspector, paymaster, inspector-general.
Other: Alderman, admiral, chief secretary, councillor, doctor, judge, lord lieutenant.

or, again, "the younger branches of highly respectable families."[22] Many had had army experience as lieutenants, captains, or majors (on the register, however, this service is recorded in only a small number of cases[23]). Perhaps the most telling point was made by the Irish Chief Secretary in 1829 on the eve of a shift to more officer appointments by promotion from the ranks. The office of Chief Constable, said Leveson Gower, is "the only one which a gentleman can fill in the Police."[24] It was not customary to inquire of a gentleman his occupation.

What do we know about *how* constables, of whatever background, were hired? The trend was away from personal recommendations toward a system of institutional, internal scrutiny of candidates. In 1816–22, only 15 percent of recruits had no private patrons or recommenders; after 1836, 62 percent had none. Before 1823, army officers vouched for most of the Peeler recruits. In the 1820s, local "gentlemen" recommended 27 percent of recruits, an all-time high. In 1829–32 (during the Tithe War), there was a surge in military and clerical recommenders, but from the mid-1830s on, the process became institutionalized as the share of private recommenders dropped.[25] By 1837 only one in five recruits listed a gentleman, lord, or churchman as a recommender. (See Table V.4.) On the Officers Register there is no column listing a man's recommenders.

Where did the constables and officers come from? Over the period 1816–40, Leinster produced far more constable recruits (32 percent) than one would expect from its share (25 percent) of the total population of Ireland, Connaught (17 percent of recruits, 17 percent of the population) the same, Munster a bit less (28 percent, 29 percent), and Ulster with its wider economic opportunities much less than its share of population (23 percent, 29 percent).[26] Over time Leinster's early predominance diminished as the shares of Munster and Connaught rose, but Leinster's lead was never overturned (see Table V.5). At the county level, populous counties like Tipperary, Cork, and Galway produced many policemen (see Table V.6). Seven counties supplied two-fifths of the constables; sixteen, or half of the counties, supplied altogether only a quarter of the men. The real surprise is King's County – No. 1 in supplying police, No. 25 in population; this was perhaps the influence of Inspector-General George Warburton, who was from King's County, and, more credibly, the

Table V.5. *Native province*

	Date of joining	Leinster	Munster	Ulster	Connaught
Constables	1816–22	49%	24	13	13
	1823–8	35	22	31	12
	1829–32	28	28	21	23
	1833–6	28	38	26	9
	1837–40	31	25	19	25
	1816–40	32	28	23	17
Officers	1816–22	53%	21	11	15
	1823–8	27	27	17	29
	1829–32	50	14	22	14
	1833–6	38	38	24	0
	1837–40	35	41	14	10
	1841–5	24	28	32	16
	1846–50	42	21	12	25
	1816–50	36	28	18	18

fact of the county's proximity to troublesome, heavily policed Tipperary and Galway. Among the other findings are that Fermanagh, Westmeath, and Queen's County greatly oversupplied the constabulary relative to each county's population; and that poor, heavily Catholic Mayo and prosperous, Protestant Antrim and Down under-supplied the constabulary. As Table V.5 shows, the native provinces of officers generally followed the trends among constables except that the predominance of Leinster (36 percent) and the unimportance of Ulster (18 percent) as recruiting sources for officers are even more marked than in the case of constable recruits.

From the beginning, policemen did not serve in their native counties. The men on the Constables Register routinely served in up to three counties (allocations). As Table V.7 shows, only 30 percent spent their whole careers in one county. Nine of every ten men served in one to three counties. It was rare (12 percent) for a constable to serve in four or more counties. Officers were rotated much more frequently: Only 11 percent served in one county, 62 percent in four or more counties, and as many as 48 percent in five or more (compared to 3 percent of the constables). It was more important for officers than men that they develop no local ties or succumb to such influences.

We can see from Table V.8 that constables with one or two punishments were not rotated more than the unpunished constables. About three-fifths in each group served in two or three counties. But the few constables (sixteen total cases, 5 percent of those punished) receiving the most punishments were rotated to four or more counties much more frequently than were constables with less spotted records. For officers, punishments were always more serious matters. Punished officers served in signifi-cantly more counties than did officers with unblemished records. Indeed, as Table V.9 reveals, there is a regular progression in the correlation of the number of punishments with the number of allocations: 26 percent of the officers with no punishments served in six or more counties compared to 86 percent of those with four punishments.

Table V.6. *Counties in rank order of frequency of supplying the rank and file of the constabulary, 1816–40*

No. of constables	County	Rank, police	Rank, 1831 population
51	King's Co.[a]	1	25
46	Cork	2/3	1
46	Tipperary	2/3	2
37	Galway	4	3
35	Fermanagh[a]	5	22
34	Kerry	6/7	9
34	Limerick	6/7	12
33	Cavan	8	13
28	Westmeath[a]	9	28
25	Clare	10	10
24	Queen's Co.[a]	11	24
23	Sligo	12	20
22	Wicklow[a]	13	29
21	Leitrim[a]	14	27
20	Kilkenny	15/16/17	21
20	Longford	15/16/17	26
20	Mayo[b]	15/16/17	4
19	Donegal[b]	18/19	7
19	Meath	18/19	18
18	Antrim[b]	20	8
15	Down[b]	21/22	5
15	Roscommon	21/22	11
12	Carlow	23	32
11	Armagh	24/25/26	15
11	Londonderry[b]	24/25/26	14
11	Monaghan	24/25/26	16
9	Dublin	27/28/29	19
9	Louth	27/28/29	31
9	Tyrone[b]	27/28/29	6
5	Waterford	30/31	23
5	Wexford[b]	30/31	17
4	Kildare	32	30

Total   691

Notes: The greatest discrepancies are indicated by choosing an entirely arbitrary rank difference of 12 points: [a]Oversupplied; [b]Undersupplied.
The remaining constables were born in: England 2; and the cities of Kilkenny 5, Cork 2, and Galway 1. None given: 8. Total: 709.

Table V.7. *Total career allocations: constables and officers*

	Number of county allocations					
	One	Two	Three	Four	Five	Six or more
Constables, 1816–40	30%	38	20	9	2	1
Officers, 1816–50	11	20	7	14	16	32

Table V.8. *Allocations and punishments: constables*

	Number of county allocations		
Number of punishments[a]	One	Two/three	Four or more
None	29%	58	13
One	26	63	11
Two	28	60	12
Three or more	31	31	38

[a] Of 709 constables, 136, or 19 percent, received one or more punishments.

Table V.9. *Allocations and punishments: officers*

	Number of county allocations			
Number of punishments[a]	One	Two/three	Four or more	Six or more
None	17%	30	53	26
One	14	28	58	26
Two	3	19	78	44
Three	0	13	87	74
Four	0	0	100	86
Five or more	5	11	84	42[b]

[a] Of 218 officers, 111, or 51 percent, received one or more punishments.
[b] This percentage represents eight men out of a total of nineteen men with five or more punishments.

The Irish constabulary came to be known for its separate classes of officers and rank and file. But it was not impossible for a meritorious constable to rise into the officer class. If 75 percent of the officers joined the force *as officers*, the remaining 25 percent did begin their careers as mere subconstables or constables. Indeed, in certain periods – 1829–36 and 1846–50, all coincident with Whig Governments in London[27] – there appears to have been a distinct emphasis on promotions from the rank and file. As Table V.10 shows, the most dramatic change came in the early 1830s. In 1823–8 only 7 percent of officer appointments (forty-four men in the sample) came from constables' ranks, but in 1829–32 fully 73 percent (only fifteen men in the sample) did so This shift, if shift it is, may reflect Home Secretary Peel's overseeing policies in

Table V.10. *Mode of joining the officer class*

| | Promotion from rank and file | | | Initial outside appointment[a] | | |
| | Original recruitment rank | | | | | |
	Subconstable	Constable	Total	Total	Subinspector	Cadet[b]
1816–22	0%	21	21	79	79	—
1823–8	0	7	7	93	93	—
1829–32	53	20	73	27	27	—
1833–6	29	7	36	64	64	—
1837–40	9	3	12	88	88	—
1841–5	16	0	16	84	24	60
1846–50	36	2	38	62	2	60
1816–50	19	6	25	75	56	19

[a] All initial outside officer appointments prior to 1842 are listed on the Officers Register at the rank of Subinspector. Actually, officers initially appointed in 1816–28 had the titles of Chief Magistrate (Peeler) and Chief Constable (Peeler and Constabulary). With these ranks no longer in existence, the register clerks instead recorded the initial rank as "Subinspector."
[b] The cadet officer rank was created in 1842.

1829–30, or the transition to a Whig Government beginning in November 1830, or both. Chief Secretary Littleton did note in 1834 that "two-thirds" of the rare vacancies in chief constableships were to "be filled up by promotions from the ranks."[28] But this trend was short-lived. Chief Secretary Morpeth in 1836 warned against rank promotions "as a matter of right and condition of service."[29] The long-standing practice of separate officer appointments was confirmed in 1842 with the establishment of the "cadet" officer rank. The cadets, young men with no prior police service, got constables' pay but wore officers' uniforms and trained at the Dublin depot (est. 1839), graduating at the rank of Third Subinspector. In 1841–50, 30 percent of officer appointments continued to be promotions from the ranks (thanks to a Whig infusion after 1845), but 86 percent of the direct officer appointments were now cadets. The cadet system was a refinement of the long-standing pattern of largely closed officer recruitment. It would characterize the force down to 1922.[30]

4

"Some of the best men in my establishment are Catholics" – so Inspector-General Richard Willcocks told a parliamentary committee in 1824.[31] In a country where four-fifths of the population was Catholic, it proved impossible to raise a large national police that did not include a number of Catholics. As time passed, experience showed that Catholic policemen could be as reliable and meritorious as Protestant ones. A constabulary return of 1824 indicates that 32 percent of all constables in the force were Catholic; by 1833, 36 percent; and by 1841, 53 percent.[32] As expected, the Constables Register records a steady decline in the proportion of Protestants recruited, falling from 84 percent in 1816–22 to 30 percent by 1837–40 (see Figure V.5). Although by the mid-1830s Catholics made up nearly two-fifths of the rank and file, their distribution around the country was uneven. More than half of the constables in Munster and slightly under half in Connaught were Catholic;

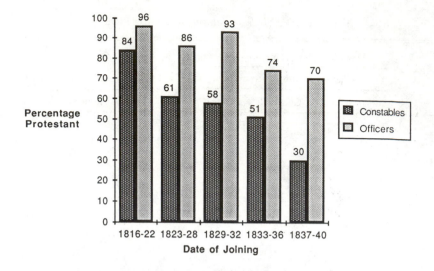

Officers 1841-45, 80%; 1846-50, 76%.
Religion summary: Constables 1816-40, 54%; Officers 1816-50, 81%.

Figure V.5 Religion: constables and officers.

in majority-Protestant Ulster, the constabulary was 22 percent Catholic. Most surprisingly, in largely Catholic Leinster, the police was only 28 percent Catholic.[33]

As the rank and file became filled with Catholics, the officer class changed little. Before 1830, more than 90 percent of the officers appointed were Protestant; by the 1840s, a figure of around 80 percent was common (see Figure V.5). The lowest figure came in 1837–40 when seven of every ten appointees were Protestant – at a time when a like proportion of constable recruits were Catholic. A constabulary force return of 1833 confirms these findings: At all officer ranks, the Protestants accounted for at least 90 percent, and often more than 95 percent, of all officers. Munster had the lowest proportion, 82 percent Protestant; and Ulster the highest, at 98 percent.[34] It was the Whigs who began what Chief Secretary Littleton called "a matter of the greatest importance": the appointment, where qualified, of Catholic officers.[35] Indeed, from 1833 on, the Officers Register does record a drop in the Protestant share of appointments from levels of 85–95 percent in 1816–32 to 70–80 percent in 1833–50.

Correlation of a man's religion with other variables in my computer study has led to findings of varying interest and importance. Among all of the Protestant recruits on the Constables Register for 1816–40, 52 percent joined before their twenty-second birthday, but only 41 percent of Catholics did so; more Catholics than Protestants, by 34 to 23 percent, joined at ages twenty-two to twenty-four; above age twenty-four, there were virtually no differences. The reasons behind the first finding are unclear, since with the twin trends toward hiring more young men (ages nineteen to twenty-one) and more Catholics, one would expect to find a higher proportion of Catholics in the nineteen- to twenty-one-year-old range at age of joining. On the Officers Register there are virtually no differences in age of appointment between the two religious groups.

Data on the Constables Register allow us to test one aspect of contemporary stereotyping of Irish Catholics. According to English popular prejudice, the "prognathous" native Irish were sometimes compared to monkeys, chimpanzees, and orangutans.[36] Were Catholic constables shorter than Protestant constables? (We have no height statistics for officers.) In point of fact, the register shows that a somewhat larger proportion of Protestants (14 percent of all Protestants) was short (5 feet 4 inches to 5 feet 7 inches) compared to Catholics (11 percent of all Catholics). This figure probably only reflects the disproportionate hiring of Protestants before the imposition, c. 1828, of the height rule in hiring (5 feet 8 inches minimum). If we define "short" as 5 feet 8 inches and below, neither religious group is noticeably shorter than the other.

Height	Percentage of all	
	Protestants	Catholics
5'4"–5'8"	38%	39%
5'9"–5'11"	50	55
6'0"–6'4"	12	6

Relatively more Catholics were men of middle height. Perhaps the most significant finding is that a greater proportion of Protestants was tall, 12 percent of them being 6-footers. We may conclude that Catholics in the constabulary were hardly a species of dwarfs. Any notion of Catholic shortness may have existed only because the Protestants included more tall men.

As we have seen, every year more constable recruits were single. Nevertheless, over the period 1816–40, two of every three men joining did marry at some time in their career. On the Constables Register 72 percent of Protestants married but only 59 percent of Catholics. Why the discrepancy? As men rose in the ranks (to constable and then Head Constable), they were increasingly permitted to marry; since Protestants predominated in the higher ranks, we would expect more of the register Protestants to be married.[37] Second, since the recruitment of Catholic constables increased coincident with the imposition of the antimarriage policy, we should find Catholics being harder hit than Protestants by the new strictures. Third, if married Catholics tended to have larger families, then Dublin Castle might be expected to prohibit a larger proportion of Catholic than Protestant constables from contracting "needy and beggarly" marriages. On the Officers Register three of every four officers were ever married: 75 percent of the Protestants, 68 percent of the Catholics. The difference in the proportion married is not as large as it is among the constables. Nevertheless, we do find for officers, as for constables, a higher proportion of bachelors among the Catholics. Here, too, Catholics were asked more often to make sacrifices to the no-marriage rule: More of them were hired single and more stayed single, without the responsibilities of wife and family.

It might be expected that Catholics would account for most of the laborers who became policemen. In fact, a like percentage of Protestants had been laborers (37 versus 38 percent of Catholics). And among those who had been farmers (17 and 18 percent, respectively) neither religious group predominated. These findings remind us that poor Protestant laborers did exist in Ireland and that the (small and very small) farmers included Protestants. Catholics recorded a higher percentage of "not givens" in the occupational category (35 percent versus 29 percent for Protestants). And Protestants had a percentage twice as high – 17 to 9 – of "other" occupations that were skilled or semiskilled.

Over the period 1816–40, which native provinces were the recruiting grounds for the two religious groups? Catholic constables came most often – 40% of all Catholics – from Munster, next most frequently from Leinster (30 percent), and lastly from Connaught (19 percent) and Ulster (11 percent). Two-thirds of all Protestant recruits were from Leinster (34 percent) and Ulster (34 percent), with predictably smaller proportions from the heavily Catholic provinces of Munster (17 percent) and Connaught (15 percent). From another angle of vision, that of province of birth, we find that 79 percent of constable recruits from Ulster were Protestant; also, 32 percent of all native Munster recruits were Protestants, as were a surprisingly high 57 percent of Leinster men. The greatest discrepancy between a policeman's natal province and the religious census of population was in Connaught: 48 percent of its police recruits were Protestant. For Connaught's scarce Protestants, police service appears to have been an especially attractive job opportunity.

In 1816–50, 81 percent of appointees on the Officers Register were Protestant. Two-thirds of these Protestants had been born in either Leinster (37 percent) or Munster (27 percent); only 20 percent of the overwhelmingly Protestant officer class were Ulstermen. The few Catholic officers on the force came about evenly from Leinster (32 percent), Munster (35 percent), and Connaught (25 percent); only Ulster lagged behind, furnishing but 8 percent of all Catholics. All four provinces, of course, produced a proportion of Catholic officers far below the Catholic share of each province's population. Looked at in this way – the officers' provinces of birth – Ulster sent to the constabulary officer class the lowest provincial percentage of Catholics (8 percent), followed by Leinster (18 percent), Munster (24 percent), and Connaught (29 percent). That is, nine of every ten officers (92 percent) born in Ulster were Protestant; seven of every ten (71 percent) born in overwhelmingly Catholic Connaught were, by religious background, Protestant.

Were there any differences between Protestants and Catholics in the kinds of recommenders – gentlemen, lords, churchmen, army and police officers – who endorsed a recruit's application for a constable appointment? For example, did churchmen recommend significantly more Protestants than Catholics? Did army officers tend to recommend Catholics? We find that, whatever the category, there is for each religious group of constables no significant departure from the proportional distribution for all constables; that is, Protestant and Catholic policemen listing recommenders used roughly the same *types* of recommenders (see Table V.11). But from another angle of vision, we see that some of the smaller *recommender groups* – notably, churchmen (62 percent), police officers (64 percent), and "others" (72 percent), who were mostly men in politics – did recommend proportions of Protestants well above the 54 percent share of Protestants on the register. Finally, note that over the period 1816–40 nearly two-fifths (39 percent) of all recruits listed no recommender. Since this category of "none listed" rose from 15 percent of all recruits in 1816–22 to 62 percent by 1837–40, and since the proportion of Catholics recruited in these two periods rose from 16 to 70 percent, we would expect a greater share of Catholic constables to have no recommender listed. And, in fact, 44 percent of Catholics had no recommender compared to 36 percent of Protestants.

Once the men were hired, what were the patterns of promotion among Protestants and Catholics? From the Constables Register for 1816–40, we can answer this question in several ways. What was the highest rank obtained by each man? Nearly three-fifths (58 percent) of all men, Protestant and Catholic, never rose above the rank of constable – subconstable, acting constable, constable (see Table V.12). Slightly more Catholics (61 percent) than Protestants (57 percent) stayed at this level; more significantly, 16 percent of Catholics but only 9 percent of Protestants remained at the lowest rank, subconstable. At the other extreme, one-fifth of the men ranked on the Constables Register rose to be Head Constables – 24 percent of the Protestants but only 16 percent of the Catholics. Five men (0.7 percent of all recruits) even became Subinspectors, only one of them Catholic. This comparative advantage enjoyed by the Protestants can be seen even more clearly in the proportion of Protestants in each

Table V.11. *Rank or title of recommenders of constables, 1816–40*

	Gentlemen	Lords	Churchmen	Army officers	Police officers	Other	None listed	Total
Constables, by religion, listing recommender type								
Protestant	16%	8	12	23	4	1	36	100
Catholic	17	7	8	20	2	2	44	100
Total	16	8	11	22	3	1	39	100
Recommender group recommending constables, by religion								
Protestant	53	57	62	57	64	72	48	54
Catholic	47	43	38	43	36	28	52	46

Note: For ranks and titles comprising each recommender group, see Table V.4.

Table V.12. *Highest rank obtained by constables, 1816–40*

	Subconstable	Acting Constable	Constable	2nd Head Constable	1st Head Constable	Subinspector	Rank not given	All ranks
Constables, by religion, at highest rank obtained								
Protestant	9%	2	46	16	8	1	18	100
Catholic	16	2	43	12	4	0[a]	23	100
Total	12	2	44	14	6	1	21	100
Highest rank, by religion								
Protestant	41	57	56	61	71	80	48	54
Catholic	59	43	44	39	29	20	52	46

[a] 0.306% (one of five men).

Table V.13. *Mode of joining the officer class: Protestants and Catholics*

	Promotion from rank and file			Initial outside appointment		
		Percentage of all		Percentage of all		
	Protestants	Catholics	Protestants and Catholics	Protestants and Catholics	Protestants	Catholics
1816–22	18%	*a*	21	79	82	0
1823–8	8	0	7	93	92	*b*
1829–32	71	*c*	73	27	28	0
1833–6	35	38	36	64	65	62
1837–40	17	0	12	88	83	100
1841–5	15	*d*	16	84	85 [20, 65]	*e*
1846–50	41	20	38	62	59 [3, 56]	80 [0, 80]
1816–50	27	19	25	75	73	81

Notes: Percentages for Catholics, a small minority of officer appointments, are for *eight* (1833–6) or more men appointed in each time period.

Prior to 1842, initial officer appointments were at the rank of subinspector; from 1842 on, they were generally at the rank of cadet. Figures in brackets represent the percentage of total officer appointments made at the rank of subinspector and cadet, respectively.

[a] One man (representing 100 percent of all Catholic officer appointments in this period and only 4 percent of all officer appointments).

[b] Six men (100 percent of all Catholics; 14 percent of all officer appointments).

[c] One man (100 percent; 7 percent).

[d] One man (20 percent of Catholics).

[e] Four men (80 percent [40, 40]).

rank. As Table V.12 shows, the Protestant share is a steadily rising one, from 41 percent of all subconstables on up to 80 percent of Subinspectors. As the ranks are ascended, the percentage of Catholics decreases.[38] One also finds from the Constables Register that more Catholics (40 percent of all Catholics) than Protestants (32 percent) had no *net* promotions, a measurement that adjusts for any rank reductions. For those men who did receive promotions, roughly equal shares of the two religious groups got two and three promotions; Protestants had a slight edge in the case of one promotion and a big advantage in the rare cases of four promotions (nine of twelve went to Protestants).

The Officers Register for 1816–50 distinguishes whether a man was promoted through the rank and file to officer status or was initially appointed as an officer (see Table V.10). Over this period, as Table V.13 reveals, a larger percentage of Protestant (27 percent) than Catholic (19 percent) officers were promoted from the ranks of the constabulary; this difference of eight percentage points happens to match the difference between the two groups of recruits for 1816–40 on the Constables Register, 54 percent Protestant, 46 percent Catholic. The higher share of Protestant officers who had served in the rank and file is in some sense understandable because in the first decade of the constabulary's existence they comprised a majority of all constable recruits. Nevertheless, in a force becoming increasingly Catholic in 1833–50, it is rather unsettling to find that so few Catholic officer appointments went to rank-promoted men of prior police service. Fully 81 percent of the Catholic officers (compared to 73 percent of the Protestants) entered the force at officer rank without prior service. Indeed, from its inception until 1850, more Catholics (67 percent) than Protestants (59 percent) began their officer careers at the cadet rank, established in 1842. This high Catholic share may point to the felt need to groom Catholics for the officer class. One hastens to note that a majority of Protestant officers after 1842 were also entering as cadets, and to recall that the great majority of officer appointments (76 percent as late as 1846–50) continued to go to Protestants.

Of the 218 men sampled in the Officers Register 1816–50, only 41 were Catholics. This small number vitiates any extended discussion of trends over seven time periods. We may state some brief conclusions. As Figure V.5 and Table V.13 show, hardly any of the pre-1833 officer appointments went to Catholics. In the 1820s, the constabulary's formative years, only 8 percent of Protestant officer appointments constituted promotions from the rank and file, and none of the half-dozen Catholic appointments represented promotions. In 1829–32 there appears to have been an uncharacteristic swing to a policy of rank promotion for both Protestants and Catholics. Beginning in 1833, the Government began to hire more Catholic officers: Thirty-three of the forty-one (80 percent) appointed in 1816–50 were appointed in 1833–50. At the same time, the Government reverted to a policy of outside appointments: From 1833 on, at least three-fifths of all officer appointments went to men who had not been in the rank and file and who in most cases had had no prior police experience. In the implementation of this policy, Protestants and Catholics fared about the same. Table V.13 reveals that of all officer appointments in 1833–6, 65 percent of the Protestants and 62 percent of the Catholics initially entered the force *as officers*; in 1837–40, 83 percent of the Protestants and all ten Catholics (100 percent) became officers by this same path.

Finally, it is worth observing that the promotion records in the Officers Register for 1816–50 suggest that the handful of Catholic officers contained some very fine policemen. Once appointed, the Catholic officer tended to rise through the officer ranks more readily than his Protestant counterpart. Fourteen per cent of all Protestant officers had no net promotions compared to only 7 percent of Catholic officers. For one to two promotions Protestants had a slight edge, 49 to 42 percent. But among the men with three or more promotions (ninety total cases) Catholics did significantly better: 51 percent of all Catholic officers compared to 39 percent of the Protestants.

Among the men on the Constables Register, was one religious group rotated to more counties of service than the other? For constables, it was not often that a man served in just one county – only 29 percent did so. Catholics (33 percent of all Catholic constables), more than Protestants (25 percent), tended to serve in a single county. But two-thirds of each group served in one to two counties, and neither religious group predominated among that one-third of all constables (34 percent of Protestants, 32 percent of Catholics) who served in three or more counties.

Four-fifths of the register constables never received any punishment (83 percent of Protestants, 78 percent of Catholics). Similarly, most men (65 percent) on the register had no rank reductions. And only a fraction (5 percent) were dismissed or resigned. For those men who were punished, if any strong correlation existed between punishments and number of career allocations, we should expect to see rather more than 32 percent of the Catholics having three or more allocations since Catholics tended to have more punishments. We should also expect to see relatively fewer Catholics than Protestants doing career service in a single county, when in fact the evidence points to just the opposite.

What is clear from Table V.14 is that, as a group, Catholics, comprising nearly half (46 percent) of all the sampled constables on the register, had a more spotted record than did the Protestants. In each category for delinquent Protestants and Catholics, the differences are not especially large but they are consistent in the areas of punishments (cautioned, admonished, severely admonished, reprimanded, fined, or reduced in pay), rank reductions, dismissals and resignations, length of service, and pensions. This finding is, of course, tentative and cautionary, and may be conservative, since

Table V.14. *Delinquency among constables, 1816–40*

	Percentage of all Protestants	Catholics	Catholic deficit[a]	Percentage of all constables
One or more punishments	17%	22%	−5%	19%
One or more rank reductions	33	37	−4	35
Dismissed	3	6	−3	4
Resigned	1	2	−1	1
Total dismissed/resigned	4	8	−4	5
No pension granted	20	26	−6	23
Of those pensioned, amount of pension:				
Below £25	21	26	−5	23
£50 or more	16	11	−5	14
Length of service				
0–15 years	5	12	−7	8
30+ years	38	31	−7	35

[a] A value-neutral term showing the degree to which one religious group had a worse record than the other. Low pension and short service are taken here to mean worse.

recruits on the register before c. 1837 represent a very small number of the men who actually served, and they are the men with the longest and best service records.

A much lower proportion, roughly half (49 percent), of the men on the Officers Register were never punished – 50 percent of the Protestants, 46 percent of the Catholics. Among those officers punished, the difference between the religious groups is thus marginal. But, as we see in Table V.15, a significantly larger share of Catholics (37 percent of all Catholics) than of Protestants (30 percent) received two or more punishments. Also, Catholics had relatively more dismissals, and virtually none of these were voluntary (resignations). Among the officers, unlike the constables, we find some correlation between punishments and allocations. Compared to Protestants, Catholics were more frequently punished and more often dismissed, and proportionally more Catholics (71 percent) served in four or more counties than did Protestants (64 percent).

One corollary of this finding regarding delinquency rates among Catholics is that relatively fewer Catholics than Protestants received pensions. But if Catholics tended to be more frequently reprimanded, cautioned, or fined, they also, as a group (even counting the men dismissed), tended to serve longer. Relatively more Protestants (23 percent) left the force within fifteen years, and Protestants also fell a bit short (39 percent) of the long-service (thirty or more years) mark set by the small number of Catholic officers on the force. Pension figures at various ranges correlate with these findings on length of service: A larger share of Protestants received small pensions, whereas relatively more Catholics were awarded big pensions.

In short, for promotions and punishments among officers, the Catholic record is quite mixed, if not wildly fluctuating. On the one hand, some Catholics were rewarded with a frequency of promotions that outdid the rate among the more numerous Protestant officers. But other Catholic officers chalked up demerits more frequently than the Protestants. The story of the Catholics in the officer class is reminiscent of that of the little girl who, when she was good, was very good, and when she was bad, she was horrid.

Table V.15. *Delinquency among officers, 1816–50*

	Percentage of all Protestants	Percentage of all Catholics	Catholic deficit[a]	Percentage of all officers
Two or more punishments	30%	37%	−7%	31%
Discharged	6	15	−9	8
Resigned	3	0	+3	3
Total discharged/resigned	9	15	−6	10
Left to become resident magistrate	5	2	−3	4
No pension granted	45	49	−4	46
Of those pensioned, amount of pension:				
Below £150	53	41	+12	50
£300 or more	12	23	+11	14
Length of service				
0–15 years	23	19	+4	22
15+ years	77	81	+4	78
30+ years	39	41	+2	39

[a] See the explanation of this concept in Table V.14.

5

Some summary devoid of detail or percentages may be welcome at this point. The rank and file of the constabulary was becoming younger and taller and increasingly filled with bachelors and Catholics. Most of the recruits had been farmers or laborers. The gentlemanly officer class also contained ever more unmarried men, and it remained overwhelmingly Protestant even as a few Catholics were admitted from the mid-1830s on (see Figure V.6). The force, at first dependent on personal recommendations, came to evaluate its own recruits. The native provinces of the officers and men, in order of frequency, were Leinster, Munster, Ulster, and Connaught. Three Munster counties – King's County, Tipperary, and Cork – furnished the most constables. Policemen never served in their native counties; during their careers, most officers and men served in more than one county, and officers served in many more than did the rank and file. Officers stood a much better chance than constables of being moved to another county as punishment for misconduct.

Between Protestants and Catholics there were no substantial differences in age on joining or in height, though the few very young and very tall recruits tended to be Protestant. More Catholic officers and substantially more Catholic constables were single. Among the farmers and laborers who became constables, neither religious group predominated, but those recruits who had worked in skilled or semiskilled trades tended to be Protestants. Munster contributed the highest share of Catholic constables and Ulster the lowest; Leinster and heavily Catholic Connaught were disappointing in their production of Catholic rank and file. The few Catholic officers on the force came about evenly from all provinces except Ulster.

More Catholic than Protestant constables filled the subconstable rank, fewer had rank promotions, and as the ranks were ascended the share of Catholics declined. Among the officers, a higher proportion of Protestants were men promoted from the increasingly Catholic rank and file. Catholic officers were more frequently appointed

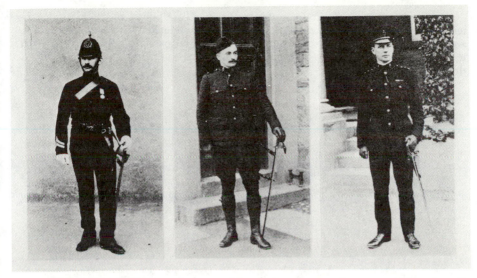

Figure V.6 Royal Irish Constabulary uniforms, late nineteenth century. Note that all wear swords as part of formal dress. The uniform of the Head Constable (*center*), who occupies the highest rank among the rank and file, is a step below the officer dress of the gentlemanly County Inspector (*right*). The sergeant with the hard helmet retains the mid-nineteenth-century uniform. (Brady, *Guardians of the Peace*, by permission of Gill and Macmillan, Publ.)

from outside the force, and proportionally more served as cadets. Out of the handful of Catholic officers, many did well in terms of promotions: Fewer Catholics than Protestants had no promotions, and more Catholics had multiple promotions.

Half of the officers but only a fifth of the constables on the registers had any kind of official blemish on their record. This could include a caution, admonition, or fine, rank reduction, dismissal or resignation, even denial of pension. Our conclusions here must be highly tentative, since the registers of appointments before c. 1837 include only men of long service and good careers. Given this fact, it is especially alarming to find that within this punished minority Catholic officers and men did consistently worse in each category, so much so that we can talk of a Catholic "deficit."

Statistics record performance but tell us nothing about men's motivations and grievances. No doubt in at least some cases this Catholic deficit is explainable because of Catholic frustrations in such areas as constable promotions that favored Protestants and Catholic officer appointments at a rate far below the percentage of Catholics in either the constabulary or the general population. Was this why, in some cases, disgruntled Catholic constables served shorter terms and left or were asked to leave the force more frequently than their Protestant fellows? The few Catholic officers compiled a record that is skewed at both ends. Faced with what must have seemed a policy of discrimination, some of the Catholic officers probably reacted by becoming troublesome, whereas others tried to prove themselves by becoming "good" officers. Unlike the Protestants, both Catholic groups, constables and especially officers, had to contend with prejudice from some of their Protestant fellow policemen, and also with a strong and widespread feeling in the general population that, by serving the Crown, they were traitors to their own people.

The purpose of this computer study has been to provide a quantitative dimension to our understanding of the early Irish constabulary. Numbers can be a useful corrective to opinions and preconceptions; they should certainly discourage us from making too easy generalizations about the force. Identifying the bare bones, the fleshless characteristics, of the pre–Famine constabulary informs us about the nature of the creature and perhaps its creators as well. But such a statistical exercise is incomplete, even misleading, without the analysis of opinions, attitudes, and political and social context that I have attempted in this book.

Abbreviations

A.H.R.	*American Historical Review*
BL (Add. MS)	British Library (Additional Manuscript), London
CHA	Castle Howard Archives, Yorkshire
CLB	Country Letter Books, ISPO, DC
CMC	*Cork Mercantile Chronicle*
CPD	*Cobbett's Parliamentary Debates*, 41 vols., 1803–20
CSORP	Chief Secretary's Office Registered Papers, ISPO, DC
Curtis, *RIC*	Robert Curtis, *History of the Royal Irish Constabulary*
DC	Dublin Castle, Dublin
DEP	*Dublin Evening Post*
DMP	*Dublin Morning Post*
DNB	*Dictionary of National Biography*
E.H.R.	*English Historical Review*
Econ. H.R.	*Economic History Review*
FDJ	*Faulkner's Dublin Journal*
FJ	*Freeman's Journal* (Dublin)
GPC	General Private Correspondence, ISPO, DC
Hansard	*Hansard's Parliamentary Debates*, 3d Series, 356 vols., 1830–91
HCJ	*House of Commons Journals*
Hist. Jour.	*Historical Journal*
HJ	*Hibernian Journal*
HO	Home Office records, PRO, London
I.H.S.	*Irish Historical Studies*
Intl. Rev. Soc. Hist.	*International Review of Social History*
ISPO	Irish State Paper Office, Dublin Castle
J. Br. Studies	*Journal of British Studies*
J. Econ. Hist.	*Journal of Economic History*
J. Mod. Hist.	*Journal of Modern History*

J. Soc. Army Hist. Research	*Journal of the Society for Army Historical Research*
J. Soc. Hist.	*Journal of Social History*
Lecky, *Eng.*	W. E. H. Lecky, *A History of England in the Eighteenth Century*, 8 vols.
Lecky, *Ire.*	——, *A History of Ireland in the Eighteenth Century*, 5 vols.
LGLB	Leveson Gower Letter Books, Public Record Office, Four Courts, Dublin
Mepol	Metropolitan Police records, PRO, London
NLI	National Library of Ireland, Dublin
O.E.D.	*Oxford English Dictionary*
OPMA	Official Papers Miscellaneous and Assorted ISPO, DC
OP 2	Official Papers, Series 2, ISPO, DC
Parl. Reg.	*The Parliamentary Register, or the History of the Proceedings and Debates of the House of Commons in Ireland*, 15 vols.
PD	*The Parliamentary Debates* (New [2d] Series), 25 vols., 1820–30
PH	*The Parliamentary History of England, from the Earliest Period to the Year 1803*, 36 vols.
PP [1816]	British *Parliamentary Papers* [Year: 1816]
PRO	Public Record Office, London
PRONI	Public Record Office of Northern Ireland, Belfast
Proc. R.I.A.	*Proceedings of the Royal Irish Academy*
Radzinowicz, *ECL*	Leon Radzinowicz, *A History of English Criminal Law and its Administration from 1750*, 4 vols.
SNL	*Saunders's News-letter* (Dublin)
SOCP 1	State of the Country Papers, Series 1, ISPO, DC
SP	State Papers, Domestic, George III, PRO, London
Studia Hib.	*Studia Hibernica*
TS	Treasury Solicitor Papers, PRO, London
VEP	*Volunteer Evening Post*
WO	War Office records, PRO, London
Y & C	Yeomanry & Constabulary (in CSORP), ISPO, DC

Notes

PREFACE

1 Lawrence Stone has pointed to historians' "belated recognition of the importance of power.... Future historians will undoubtedly severely criticize the 'new historians' of the 1950s and 1960s for their failure to take sufficient account of power: of political organization and decision-making, ... political and military power, [and] the use of brute force." L. Stone, "The Revival of Narrative: Reflections on a New Old History," *Past & Present* 85 (Nov. 1979):10.

2 *Economic Arithmetic: A Guide to the Statistical Sources of English Commerce, Industry, and Finance 1700–1850* (New York: Garland Publ., 1977).

3 Frederic W. Maitland, *Justice and Police* (London: Macmillan, 1885), p. 108.

4 William Craig, in the early 1970s, quoted in Geoffrey Bell, *The Protestants of Ulster* (London: Pluto Press, 1976), p. 12.

5 David Bayley, "The Police and Political Development in Europe," in Charles Tilly, ed., *The Formation of National States in Western Europe* (Princeton, N.J.: Princeton University Press, 1975), p. 360.

6 E. P. Thompson, *The Making of the English Working Class* (New York: Pantheon Books, 1964), p. 444, emphasis in the original. See also James Henretta, "Social History as Lived and Written," *A.H.R.* 84 (Dec. 1979):1293–1322.

7 A Citizen, *A Brief Treatise on the Police of the City of New York* (New York, 1812), quoted in Leon Radzinowicz, *A History of English Criminal Law and its Administration from 1750*, 4 vols. (London: Stevens & Sons, 1948–68), 3:344 n. 14. Patrick Pringle, *Hue and Cry: The Birth of the British Police* (London: Museum Press, 1955), p. 13.

8 Jenifer Hart, *The British Police* (London: Allen & Unwin, 1951), p. 27, my emphasis; Pringle, *Hue and Cry*, p. 209.

9 See Eric Monkkonen, "From Cop History to Social History: The Significance of the Police in American History," *J. Soc. Hist.* 15 (Summer 1982):575–91.

10 See Bayley, "Police and Political Development," pp. 328–79; Clive Emsley, *Policing and Its Context, 1750–1870* (New York: Schocken Books, 1984).

11 Charles Tilly, "Collective Violence in European Perspective," in Hugh D. Graham and Ted R. Gurr, *Violence in America: Historical and Comparative Perspectives* (New York: New American Library, 1969), pp. 4–5.

12 Wilbur R. Miller, "Police Authority in London and New York City, 1830–1870," *J. Soc. Hist.* 8 (Winter 1975):81.

13 A. P. Donajgrodski, ed., *Social Control in 19th-Century Britain* (Totowa, N.J.: Rowman and Littlefield, 1977), editor's introduction, p. 24.

14 Stone, "Revival," p. 21.

15 Ibid., p. 3.

CHAPTER I. INTRODUCTION

1 Geoffrey Bell, *The Protestants of Ulster* (London: Pluto Press, 1976), p. 1.
2 *Military* includes 366 army personnel killed and 125 members of the Ulster Defence Regiment (UDR), a locally recruited unit of the British army, composed of part-time and full-time members, and formed in 1970 as a replacement for the disbanded "B-Specials." *Police* includes 115 men in the Royal Ulster Constabulary (RUC), 58 RUC reservists, and 14 prison officers. Figures are for January 1969 through December 1982. Sources: John Darby, *Conflict in Northern Ireland: The Development of a Polarised Community* (Dublin: Gill and Macmillan, 1976), p. xix; Jack Holland, *Too Long a Sacrifice: Life and Death in Northern Ireland since 1969* (New York: Penguin Books, 1982), p. 196; Ruth Dudley Edwards, *An Atlas of Irish History*, 2d ed. (London: Methuen, 1981), p. 260; W. D. Flackes, *Northern Ireland: A Political Directory* (New York: St. Martin's Press, 1980), pp. 210–12, and Flackes, *Northern Ireland: A Political Directory*, 2d ed. (London: Ariel Books, British Broadcasting Corp., 1983), pp. 320–3. My thanks to Prof. David Miller, Carnegie-Mellon University, for referring me to the second edition of Flackes's book. A good recent study of the policing and violence is John Darby, ed., *Northern Ireland: The Background to the Conflict* (Belfast: Appletree Press, and Syracuse, N.Y.: Syracuse University Press, 1983).
3 Chronological abstracts of the violence are in Darby, *Conflict*, pp. xi–xix (to 1975), and in Flackes, *Directory*, 1st ed., pp. 3–13 (to 1979). Pseudonyms like "Captain Black" and the use of humiliating, hideous tortures (Holland, *Sacrifice*, pp. 92–3) indicate the persistence of Whiteboy names (e.g., "Captain Rock") and techniques from the first half of the nineteenth century.
4 Since the mid 1970s the security forces have had moderate success in charging persons for murder. The figures are as follows:

	No. of murders	No. of persons charged with murder	Percent charge rate
July–Dec. 1972	284	13	4.6%
1973–4	466	146	31.3
1975–8	737	449	60.9
1979–82	387	207	53.5

Calculated from data in Holland, *Sacrifice*, pp. 160–2; Flackes, *Directory*, 1st ed., pp. 211–12, and *Directory*, 2d ed., pp. 320–1, 323.
5 These figures (1980) do *not* include 4,500 men in the RUC Reserve and 8,000 in the UDR.
6 Victor Meally, ed., *Encyclopaedia of Ireland* (Dublin: Allen Figgis, 1968), p. 180. For a short "official" history, see Capt. Denis J. O'Kelly, *Salute to the Gardaí, 1922–1958: A Story of Struggle and Achievement* (Dublin: Parkside Press, 1958).
7 Conversely, in Ulster outside of the major cities, much of the violence occurs near the Border, across which the perpetrators can flee out of reach of the RUC and the British army. In South Armagh, five Catholics and ten Protestants were killed in January 1976 at Whitecross and Kingsmills and four RUC men were killed in April 1979 at Bessbrook.
8 Darby, *Conflict*, p. xv; Flackes, *Directory*, 1st ed., p. 4; *New York Times*, 19 July 1981. Deaths in the hunger strike (begun by the now famous Bobby Sands, who died on the sixty-sixth day of his fast) occurred from 5 May through 20 August 1981. The strike was called off in early October.

9 Statistics cited in *New York Times*, 15, 19 July 1981. See also T. A. Critchley, *A History of Police in England and Wales*, 2d ed. (Montclair, N.J.: Patterson Smith, 1972), p. vii; and Ben Whitaker, *The Police in Society* (London: Eyre Methuen, 1979), pp. 50, 81, 115. In the United States, 132 on-duty policemen were killed in 1974 alone. In 1979 about 100 murders were recorded in all of England and Wales (pop., 49 million); in the same year in New York City (pop., 8 million), there were 1,800 murders. The homicide rate in the United States is forty-nine times the rate in Britain, West Germany, and Japan put together.

10 Some recent studies are Ben Whitaker, *The Police* (London: Eyre & Spottis-woode, 1964) and *The Police in Society* (1979); and Tony Bunyan, *The Political Police in Britain* (New York: St. Martin's Press, 1976). Changing perceptions of the police may be traced in Anthony Sampson, *New Anatomy of Britain* (New York: Stein & Day, 1972), pp. 361-8, and *The Changing Anatomy of Britain* (New York: Random House, 1982), pp. 206-12. The 1962 and 1965 editions of the *Anatomy* did not include sections on the police.

11 Whitaker, *Police in Society*, p. 198. Total indictable offenses increased fourfold from 1955 to 1979; offenses involving personal violence, sixteenfold, from 1954 to 1979. *Ibid.*, pp. 19-22, 73-85. *The Wall Street Journal*, 7 Jan. 1985; *Dallas Times Herald*, 31 May 1985.

12 (London) *Economist*, 11 July, pp. 27-30; 18 July 1981, pp. 11, 26-8. *New York Times*, 15, 19 July 1981. *Time Magazine*, 20 July, pp. 30-2; 27 July 1981, pp. 32-3.

13 The lone fatality occurred after the height of the disorders, 3-12 July, when a police vehicle in Liverpool jumped the pavement and hit a bystander. *Economist*, 1 Aug. 1981. By contrast, urban riots in the United States are bloody gun-shooting affairs. A total of thirty-four persons were killed in the Watts riots in Los Angeles in 1965; forty-three were killed in the Detroit riots in 1967. Overall, race riots in twenty-five cities in 1964-7 produced a toll of 130 civilians killed (but only 12 policemen and soldiers), 4,700 persons injured, and 20,000 arrested. In the Watts riots alone, property losses were estimated at $200 million. The American disorders spawned two official studies: *The Report of the National Advisory Commission on Civil Disorders*, issued 1 March 1968 (Washington, D.C.: U.S. Government Printing Office), being the *Kerner Report*, named for the commission's chairman, Gov. Otto Kerner of Illinois; and *Violence in America: Historical and Comparative Perspectives*, a Report to the National Commission on the Causes and Prevention of Violence, June 1969, a scholarly study prepared and edited for the commission by Professors Hugh Davis Graham and Ted Robert Gurr and published by the New American Library (New York, 1969; rev. ed., Beverly Hills, Calif., Sage, 1979). For the 1960s riots, see also Robert M. Fogelson, *Violence as Protest: A Study of Riots and Ghettoes* (Garden City, N.Y.: Doubleday, 1971; repr., Westport, Conn.: Greenwood Press, 1980); and as a companion volume to Graham and Gurr's historical study, see the massive bibliography compiled by Dirk Hoerder, *Protest, Direct Action, Repression: Dissent in American Society from Colonial Times to Present* (Munich: Verlag Dokumentation, 1977), in English, 434 pp.

14 Newspaper headline cited in *Economist*, 18 July 1981, p. 26; William Borders, in *New York Times*, 19 July 1981, p. A-3.

15 *New York Times*, 15 July 1981.

16 *Dallas Times Herald*, 7, 8, 11 Oct. 1985. "After Ugly Riots, Britons Wonder if Police Are Misusing Weapons," *The Wall Street Journal*, 8 Oct. 1985. Manchester: *Economist*, 9 Apr. 1983, pp. 49-50; *Fort Worth (Texas) Star-Telegram*, 10 Apr. 1983. Newman: quoted in *Dallas Times Herald*, 8 Oct. 1985; Sampson, *Changing Anatomy*, p. 208.

17 Quoted in Borders's article, *New York Times*, 19 July 1981.

18 Flackes, *Directory*, 1st ed., p. 6; and see n. 9, above. *Dallas Times Herald*, 22, 24

July 1982 and 25 Dec. 1983 (bombing of Harrods department store). In its editorial of 22 July 1982, this Texas newspaper described the killings as "an outrage." It is worth noting that, since the early nineteenth century, Englishmen have used this term in its plural form to describe Irish homicides and indeed Irish crime in general.

19 Borders, in *New York Times*, 19 July 1981.
20 Lawrence M. Friedman, "The Long Arm of the Law," *Reviews in American History* 6 (June 1978):227.
21 F. W. Maitland, *Justice and Police* (London: Macmillan, 1885; repr., New York: Russell and Russell, 1972, and New York: AMS Press, 1974), pp. 105, 107.
22 Wilbur R. Miller, "Police Authority in London and New York City, 1830−1870," *J. Soc. Hist.* 8 (Winter 1975):81. For the context, see William L. O'Neill, *Coming Apart: An Informal History of America in the 1960s* (New York: Times Books, 1971).
23 F. C. Mather, *Public Order in the Age of the Chartists* (Manchester: Manchester University Press, 1959; repr., New York: Augustus M. Kelley, 1967), p. v.
24 See Percy Fitzgerald, *Chronicles of Bow Street Police-Office*, 2 vols. (London: Chapman & Hall, 1888; reprinted in one volume with an introduction by Anthony Babington, Montclair, N.J.: Patterson Smith, 1972); George Dilnot, *The Story of Scotland Yard* (Boston: Houghton Mifflin, 1927); Gilbert Armitage, *The History of the Bow Street Runners 1729−1829* (London: Wishart & Co., 1932); E. H. Glover, *The English Police, Its Origin and Development* (London: Police Chronicle, 1934), suggestive but too short; Alwyn Solmes, *The English Policeman 871−1935* (London: Allen & Unwin, 1935), in which see, for example, ch. 11, "Our Friend the 'Bobby'"; Sir Basil Thomson, *The Story of Scotland Yard* (Garden City, N.Y.: Doubleday & Co., 1936); George Howard [Frederick George Kay], *Guardians of the Queen's Peace: The Development and Work of Britain's Police* (London: Odhams Press, 1953); G. A. Minto, *The Thin Blue Line* (London: Hodder and Stoughton, 1965); James P. Wood, *Scotland Yard* (New York: Hawthorn Books, 1970), a barely literate work; and David Ascoli, *The Queen's Peace: The Origins and Development of the Metropolitan Police 1829−1979* (London: Hamish Hamilton, 1979). There are also books for child readers, e.g., G. A. Campbell, *Our Police Force* (London: Oxford University Press, 1943).
25 See W. L. Melville Lee, *A History of Police in England* (London: Methuen, 1901; repr., Montclair, N.J.: Patterson Smith, 1970); Sir John Moylan, *Scotland Yard and the Metropolitan Police* (London and New York: Putnam & Co., 1929, 2d ed. 1934); J. M. Hart, *The British Police* (London: Allen & Unwin, 1951), esp. ch. 2. Douglas G. Browne, *The Rise of Scotland Yard: A History of the Metropolitan Police* (London: Harrap & Co., 1956), a quite good but little-known study. In his preface, Browne notes that the first third of the book, covering roughly the period to 1850, was the work of his deceased friend, Ralph Straus, whose manuscript Browne revised "to achieve unity" in the book's text. The best modern study is T. A. Critchley, *A History of Police in England and Wales* (London: Constable, 1967; 2d ed., Montclair, N.J.: Patterson Smith, 1972).

Charles Reith (1886−1957), by far the most prolific of English police historians, was fifty-two when he published his first book on the police. The son of a Scottish doctor, Reith by 1938 had been a planter in Ceylon, an army officer (1914−18), a London businessman, and a novelist, journalist, and magazine editor. His colorful life was matched by his feisty and unacademic prose. Reith's pioneering if unannotated books are *The Police Idea: Its History and Evolution in England in the Eighteenth Century and After* (London: Oxford University Press, 1938), a study of London's pre-1829 police institutions; *British Police and the Democratic Ideal* (London: Oxford University Press, 1943), the story of the new London police in the 1830s; *A Short History of the British Police* (London: Oxford University Press, 1948), 117 pp.; *The Blind Eye of History: A Study of the Origins of the Present Police Era* (London: Faber and Faber, 1952; repr. Montclair, N.J.: Patterson Smith, 1975, with an introduction by P. J. Stead), which sees the modern American police system as essentially an unreformed version of the English police, and also distinguishes English "kin-police" from continental "ruler-appointed" police; and *A New Study of Police History* (Edinburgh: Oliver & Boyd, 1956), a biographical study of Col. Sir Charles Rowan, one of the two original London Police Commissioners. (Charles Reith should not be confused with another Scotsman, Sir John C. W. Reith, founder of the British Broadcasting Corporation, 1926.)

26 Victor Bailey, ed., *Policing and Punishment in 19th-Century Britain* (New Brunswick, N.J.: Rutgers University Press, 1981), pp. 12–14. In addition to the works cited in n. 25, see Sir Leon Radzinowicz, *A History of English Criminal Law and Its Administration from 1750* [hereafter, *ECL*], 4 vols. (London: Stevens & Co., 1948–68), vols. 3, 4; J. J. Tobias, *Crime and Police in England 1700–1900* (New York: St. Martin's Press, 1979), pp. 74–102; Wilbur R. Miller, *Cops and Bobbies: Police Authority in New York and London 1830–1870* (Chicago: University of Chicago Press, 1977), ch. 1, and Miller's essay on police origins, "London's Police Tradition in a Changing Society," in Simon Holdaway, ed., *The British Police* (London: Edward Arnold, 1979), ch. 2.

For the "conflict" interpretation, see Jenifer Hart, "Reform of the Borough Police, 1835–1856," *E.H.R.* 70 (1955):411–27; Mather, *Public Order* (1959); Allan Silver, "The Demand for Order in Civil Society: A Review of Some Themes in the History of Urban Crime, Police, and Riot," in David J. Bordua, ed., *The Police: Six Sociological Essays* (New York: Wiley, 1967), pp. 1–24; John Foster, *Class Struggle and the Industrial Revolution: Early Industrial Capitalism in Three English Towns* (London: Weidenfeld and Nicolson, 1974, and New York: St. Martin's Press, 1975); David Philips, "Riots and Public Order in the Black Country, 1835–1860," in J. Stevenson and R. Quinault, eds., *Popular Protest and Public Order: Six Studies in British History, 1790–1920* (New York: St. Martin's Press, 1974), pp. 141–80, and Philips's book, *Crime and Authority in Victorian England* (London: Croom Helm, 1977).

27 This point is sometimes acknowledged by conflict historians. Jenifer Hart argued that social unrest spurred the creation of borough and rural police in the 1830s (*E.H.R.* 70:411–27) but elsewhere admitted that "the slow development of the British police service is one of the most interesting aspects of the subject, illustrating as it does certain dominant political ideas" (*British Police*, p. v.).

28 Robert D. Storch, "The Plague of the Blue Locusts: Police Reform and Popular Resistance in Northern England, 1840–1857," *Intl Rev. Soc. Hist.* 20 (1975):61–90, and "The Policeman as Domestic Missionary: Urban Discipline and Popular Culture in Northern England, 1850–1880," *J. Soc. Hist.* 9 (1976):481–509. See also E. P. Thompson, "Time, Work-Discipline, and Industrial Capitalism," *Past & Present* 38 (Dec. 1967):56–97. A similar explanation for the *expansion* of urban police forces in the American Middle West is in Sidney Harring, *Policing a Class Society: The Experience of American Cities, 1865–1915* (New Brunswick, N.J.: Rutgers University Press, 1983). Harring argues that the police were active in four major areas: repressing strikes, controlling tramping, supervising leisure activities like drinking, and spreading the fear of crime to legitimize a repressive police force.

29 J. J. Tobias, *Crime and Industrial Society in the 19th Century* (London: B. T. Batsford, 1967), pp. 37–42, 170–1, 236–8, 244–5; and *Crime and Police*, ch. 3. David Jones, *Crime, Protest, Community, and Police in Nineteenth-Century Britain* (London: Routledge & Kegan Paul, 1982), chs. 1, 4–6. E. C. Midwinter, *Social Administration in Lancashire, 1830–1860: Poor Law, Public Health, and Police* (Manchester: Manchester University Press, 1969), pp. 165–72. Miller, *Cops and Bobbies*, chs. 1, 5.

30 Raymond B. Fosdick, *European Police Systems* (New York: The Century Co., 1915; repr., Montclair, N.J.: Patterson Smith, 1969), pp. 224, 298–9, 307–14; Critchley, *Police*, pp. 160–2, 209–15; Whitaker, *Police in Society*, pp. 106–11; and J. P. Martin and Gail Wilson, *The Police: A Study in Manpower. The Evolution of the Service in England and Wales 1829–1965*, foreword by Sir Leon Radzinowicz (London: Heinemann, 1969), pp. 24–5. Martin and Wilson go so far as to state that "the great emphasis in police work throughout the nineteenth century was on the preservation of public order; prevention and detection of crime were secondary and did not assume prominence until much later in police history" (p. 7).

31 Tobias argues that it was "the level of crime and not the fear of revolt" that induced Parliament to pass the (London) Metropolitan Police Act in 1829. But suppression of protest and fear of revolution are two quite different things. J. J. Tobias, "Police and Public in the United Kingdom," in George L. Mosse, ed., *Police Forces in History* (Beverly Hills, Calif.: Sage, 1975), p. 99. See also Tobias, *Crime and Industrial Society*, ch. 12, and *Crime and Police*, ch. 4; and Kellow Chesney, *The Anti-Society: An Account of the Victorian Underworld* (Boston: Gambit, 1970), pp. 31–2.

Jones notes that "significantly, one of the main reasons for the acceptance of Peel's Police Act of 1829 was the growing fear of political disaffection and mob rule." *Crime, Protest*, p. 123. Of his seven chapters, two treat the semiprotest crimes of arson and poaching; two others, vagrancy and working-class culture in Merthyr, Wales.

Miller points out that Wellington and Peel first proposed London police reform in 1822 in the aftermath of the Queen Caroline Riots, although the act did not pass until 1829, at "the calmer end of the decade." Shortly after their founding, Peel's police "took to the streets amid England's constitutional crisis over parliamentary representation for disenfranchised middle-class citizens, whose protests were backed by a reserve of more militant working-class anger." The original controversy over the police was "fundamentally political amid challenges to the political order's legitimacy," and the new institution had to face criticism of being "the cutting edge of the ruling minority's oppression." *Cops and Bobbies*, pp. 8–10.

It is sometimes pointed out (see Tobias, *Crime and Police*, pp. 3, 76–7) that in the brief debates leading up to the London police bill of 1829 crime, not public disorder, was most discussed. Two recent scholars, Norman Gash and T. A. Critchley, have suggested that this was a deliberate ploy by the Government to ease the fears of those constitutionally opposed to the considerable revolution in government proposed for the metropolis. Peel's remarks, "deliberately dull and unemotional," were filled with "unexciting statistics about crime." Critchley, *Police*, p. 48, restating the point originally made by Gash, *Mr. Secretary Peel: The Life of Sir Robert Peel to 1830* (Cambridge, Mass.: Harvard University Press, 1961), p. 493.

32 Friedman, "Long Arm of the Law," p. 226.

33 His only discussion of the subject for the period before 1850 is on pp. 69–71, 74; the index to "crime" in his 328-page book cites only seven pages, all to crime after 1900.

34 Vol. 1 and Vol. 4, ch. 8, deal with the criminal law and its reform; Vol. 2, the pre-1829 police, mostly in London; Vol. 3, "The Reform of the Police," a discussion of reform efforts, 1750–1828; and Vol. 4, "Grappling for Control," the implementation of the new police, London and provincial, from 1829 on (wherein see ch. 4, "The Control of Crowds"). Crime itself Radzinowicz very seldom discusses.

35 Hart, "Reform of the Borough Police," pp. 415, 426–7. Tobias, using largely impressionistic evidence, restates Edwin Chadwick's argument for the migration

of criminals from London to the provincial towns in the 1830s, an argument that Hart and Critchley reject. Tobias, *Crime and Industrial Society*, pp. 232–8.

36 Rumbelow, in his history of the *City* of London police, provides a chapter on "Riot and Reform" preceding his discussion of statutory changes in policing from 1785 to 1829. *I Spy Blue: Police and Crime in the City of London from Elizabeth I to Victoria* (London: Macmillan, 1971), pp. 77–94. Foster sees the police in northern England as an instrument of state authority against the radical political threat. *Class Struggle*, pp. 64–9. Philips demonstrates that the new police in Staffordshire was established in response to workers' unrest. "Riots and Public Order," pp. 141–2, and *Crime and Authority*, ch. 3. David Jones, a recent scholar of English and Welsh crime, notes of the new police in the industrial town of Merthyr Tydfil, Wales: "In the early days they were obliged to concentrate on public order crimes. Indeed this was the mandate given to the force when it was established." *Crime, Protest*, pp. 112, 222 n. 52. Note also John Field's finding that in one southern English city, unlike London and the northern towns, there was "no great sense of urgency" to implement the 1835 Borough Police Act precisely because of the absence of "political disturbances" and "mass crowd actions." Field, "Police, Power, and Community in a Provincial English Town: Portsmouth, 1815–1875," in Bailey, ed., *Policing*, pp. 46–7. See also John Stevenson, "Social Control and the Prevention of Riots in England, 1789–1829," in A. P. Donajgrodzki, ed., *Social Control in 19th-Century Britain* (Totowa, N.J.: Rowman & Littlefield, 1977), ch. 1; and Stevenson, *Popular Disturbances in England 1700–1870* (London: Longman, 1979), pp. 251–2, 321–2.

37 Rudé, *Protest and Punishment: The Story of the Social and Political Protesters Transported to Australia 1788–1868* (Oxford: Clarendon Press, 1978), p. 63.

38 Radzinowicz, *ECL*, 4:177.

39 Critchley, *Police*, p. 54.

40 Ibid., pp. 61–2.

41 Radzinowicz, *ECL*, 4:232. See also his article, "New Departures in Maintaining Public Order in the Face of Chartist Disturbances," *Cambridge Law Journal* (Apr. 1960), pp. 51–80.

42 David H. Bayley, "The Police and Political Development in Europe," in Charles Tilly, ed., *The Formation of National States in Western Europe* (Princeton, N.J.: Princeton University Press, 1975), pp. 328–79, quotation on p. 378.

43 Charles Tilly, "Reflections on the History of European Statemaking," in ibid., pp. 49–50; see also pp. 58–60.

44 Ted Robert Gurr, *Rogues, Rebels, and Reformers* (Beverly Hills, Calif.: Sage, 1976), pp. 122–3. This book is a shorter conceptual summary of Ted Robert Gurr, Peter N. Grabosky, and Richard C. Hula, *The Politics of Crime and Conflict: A Comparative History of Four Cities* (Beverly Hills, Calif.: Sage, 1977). See also the recent study by Clive Emsley, *Policing and Its Context, 1750–1870* (New York: Schocken Books, 1984), for a comparison of English with French police and, to a lesser extent, other European and American police forces.

45 Radzinowicz, *ECL*, 3:542–3; Alan Williams, *The Police of Paris 1718–1789* (Baton Rouge: Louisiana State University Press, 1979), pp. 86–9. See the excellent pioneering study of the *maréchaussée*, by Iain A. Cameron, *Crime and Repression in the Auvergne and the Guyenne, 1720–1790* (Cambridge: Cambridge University Press, 1981).

46 Sir William Mildmay, *The Police of France* (London: E. Owen and T. Harrison, 1763), pp. 26–42; Cameron, *Crime*, ch. 3.

47 Philip John Stead, *The Police of Paris* (London: Staples Press, 1957), p. 70; James Cramer, *The World's Police* (London: Cassell, 1964), pp. 294–5; Bayley, "Police and Political Development," p. 344; Cameron, *Crime*, pp. 242–60.

48 Howard C. Payne, *The Police State of Louis Napoleon Bonaparte* (Seattle: University of Washington Press, 1966), pp. 232–51; Cameron, *Crime*, p. 258; Whitaker,

Police in Society, pp. 175–6. See also L. Larrieu, *Histoire de la gendarmerie* (Paris, 1921).

49 On the early centuries, see Stead, *Police*, ch. 1; Williams, *Police*, pp. 17–25.

50 Stead, *Police*, pp. 21–2, 35, 46–7; Radzinowicz, *ECL* 3:539–41; Williams, *Police*, pp. 23–8, 67–84.

51 Stead, *Police*, pp. 22, 28, 36, 43–5; Williams, *Police*, pp. 68–9, 101, and chs. 5, 6.

52 Williams, *Police*, pp. 65, 68.

53 The popular term, some scholars claim, derives from a sixteenth-century spy, Antoine di Mouchi, a University of Paris theologian appointed by Francis I to persecute Protestants, many of whom died at the stake. To etymologically informed Englishmen, the word *mouchard* would thus convey a special horror. See Radzinowicz, *ECL* 3:544 n. 14; Bayley, "Police and Political Development," p. 363; and Williams, *Police*, p. 104 n. 56. However, it may be that the term simply derives from *mouche*, the French word for "fly."

54 Williams, *Police*, pp. 65, 68, 104–11. Williams finds that the police function of spying has been much exaggerated; he rejects traditional claims for 3,000 police spies in eighteenth-century Paris (ibid., p. 109 n. 63) and gives little space to spying in his book. Stead, *Police*, pp. 31, 36–41, 49–53, treats the subject in some detail; and Radzinowicz, *ECL* 3:543–52, gives it much emphasis. For Stead, the Lieutenant of Police, the Marquis d'Argenson (1697–1718), was "the pioneer of the large-scale employment of police spies." *Police*, p. 40.

55 Williams, *Police*, pp. 68, 212–21; and Stead, *Police*, pp. 53–6. Voltaire and Diderot served some time in prison; Rousseau escaped to Switzerland. Undesirable books from England and Holland were banned, shops searched, and booksellers and peddlers harassed. A contemporary objected to police measures "to shut out of the kingdom the truths which were coming to us from London or from Geneva." L. P. Manuel, *La Police de Paris dévoilée* (1791), quoted in Stead, *Police*, p. 55. On the effect of Paris police censorship, see Robert Darnton, *The Literary Underground of the Old Regime* (Cambridge, Mass.: Harvard University Press, 1982).

56 Stead, *Police*, ch. 4. On the brief flirtation with a local, civic-controlled police in 1789–95, see ibid., pp. 62–9. Manuel praised the "police" of London: "It has never recognized orders from the King, or spies.... It at least respects, even in its errors, the eternal principles of liberty." Quoted in ibid., p. 64. See also Antoinette Wills, *Crime and Punishment in Revolutionary Paris* (Westport, Conn.: Greenwood Press, 1981).

57 Stead, *Police*, pp. 73–4, 79–89, quotation on p. 75. See also Nils Forssell, *Fouché: The Man Napoleon Feared*, tr. from the Swedish by Anna Barwell (New York: AMS Press, 1970, reprint of the New York 1928 ed.).

58 Stead, *Police*, pp. 75–8, 94–6, 104–6; Whitaker, *Police in Society*, p. 39. See also P. J. Stead, *Vidocq: A Biography* (London: Staples Press, 1953); and Samuel Edwards, *The Vidocq Dossier: The Story of the World's First Detective* (Boston: Houghton Mifflin, 1977), pp. 170–82, which examines Vidocq's visit to London and meetings with the Metropolitan Police in the 1830s.

59 Stead, *Police*, pp. 97–101, 107–8.

60 Ibid., pp. 101ff., quotations on pp. 111, 115.

61 As state president, he engineered the *coup d'état* by ordering the city's forty-eight police *commissaires* to arrest eighty key opposition members in the Assembly; forty-seven obeyed, the other was himself arrested. Ibid., pp. 117–18.

62 Ibid., pp. 119–23, quotation on p. 123.

63 Quotations in ibid., pp. 121, 123.

64 Ibid., pp. 128–36.

65 Ibid., p. 182.

66 See Bayley's essay, "Police and Political Development," pp. 328–79; and Marc Raeff's broad legal study, *The Well-Ordered Police State: Social and Institutional*

Change through Law in the Germanies and Russia, 1600–1800 (New Haven, Conn.: Yale University Press, 1983).

67 Bayley, "Police and Political Development," pp. 346–7, 360 (quotation).

68 Reith, *Blind Eye*, pp. viii, 20–1, 25–33, 242–54; for a critique of Reith's interpretation, see Tobias, "Police and Public," pp. 96–101.

69 Frank J. Thomason, "The Prussian Police State in Berlin, 1848–1871" (Ph.D. dissertation, Johns Hopkins University, 1978), pp. 101–30, arming and "fighting" (*Wehrhaft*) on pp. 113–17, 126–7. See also Thomason's chapter, "Uniformed Police in the City of Berlin under the Empire," in E. C. Viano and J. H. Reimann, eds., *The Police in Society* (Lexington, Mass.: D.C. Heath, 1975), pp. 105–19. On the 1848 rising, see William L. Langer, "The Pattern of Urban Revolution in 1848," in Evelyn M. Acomb and Marvin L. Brown, Jr., eds., *French Society and Old Regime* (New York: Holt, Rinehart and Winston, 1966), pp. 105–9; and Priscilla Robertson, *Revolutions of 1848: A Social History* (Princeton, N.J.: Princeton University Press, 1952, Harper Torchbook ed., 1960), chs. 7–9.

70 Cramer, *World's Police*, pp. 326–34; Bayley, "Police and Political Development," pp. 347–8. On 1848 in Italy, see Robertson, *Revolutions*, chs. 15–19.

71 Cramer, *World's Police*, p. 250; Fosdick, *European Police Systems*, p. 120 n. 1. On 1848 in Vienna, see Langer, "Pattern of Urban Revolution," pp. 100–4; Robertson, *Revolutions*, chs. 10–12.

72 Cramer, *World's Police*, pp. 255–6, 348.

73 Ibid., p. 353. In 1813, after Napoleon's departure, an unsuccessful attempt was made to return to a decentralized system of policing; the next year, the jurisdiction of the gendarmerie was extended to the smaller towns. In the 1850s, owing to dissatisfaction with the military police, supplemental municipal and county constabularies were established.

74 Bayley, "Police and Political Development," pp. 346–7; Thomason, "Prussian Police State," p. 94; Fosdick, *European Police Systems*, p. 73 n. 1; Hans Rosenberg, *Bureaucracy, Aristocracy, and Autocracy: The Prussian Experience 1660–1815* (Boston: Beacon Press, 1958), ch. 9. In West Germany today, the provincial police are controlled by the eleven provincial parliaments (*Länder*). Whitaker, *Police in Society*, p. 175.

75 Fosdick, *European Police Systems*, p. 80 n. 2.

76 Cramer, *World's Police*, pp. 329–31; Bayley, "Police and Political Development," pp. 338–9, 347–8.

77 Cramer, *World's Police*, pp. 310, 377–9. Today's *Guardia Civil* numbers 65,000 men and is supplemented by a special riot police, the 40,000-strong *Policia Armada*. Whitaker, *Police in Society*, p. 176.

78 P. S. Squire, *The Third Department: The Establishment and Practices of the Political Police in the Russia of Nicholas I* (Cambridge: Cambridge University Press, 1968). This work is the best administrative history in English; see Squire's introduction for a summary of the historiography and also his useful bibliography (pp. 258–65). Another study that concentrates on police censorship of literature is Sidney Monas, *The Third Section: Police and Society in Russia under Nicholas I* (Cambridge, Mass.: Harvard University Press, 1961).

79 Squire, *Third Department*, pp. 13–47, quotation on pp. 41–2. The political nature of policing may be seen in the charge to the "Committee of Higher Police" (1805) to investigate the following: "incitement of the people by rumors of the liberation of the peasants," "suspected conspiracy against the csar," "insults to the csar and members of the Imperial Household," "treason to the state," "harmful books," "secret societies and proscribed meetings," "rumors concerning the restoration of Poland." Quoted in ibid., p. 26.

80 Count Alexander Benckendorff, head of the Third Department and Chief of Gendarmes (1826–44), had proposed to Alexander in an 1821 Memorandum on

Secret Societies the creation of a gendarmerie on the French model, but the czar declined the suggestion. Benckendorff, of Prussian, not Russian, background, apparently first formed the idea in Paris, 1806–8, while he was attached to the Russian embassy there. He may have met Fouché; he certainly knew the Austrian ambassador, Metternich, with whom he shared a mistress. Ibid., pp. 50, 107–10, 110 n. 3, and Benckendorff's proposal in the original French, reprinted as Appendix A, ibid., pp. 239–40. Note also General Kutuzov's statement in 1841 that "when the Corps of Gendarmes was instituted, an analogous organization in France was taken as an example." Ibid., pp. 236–7.

81 Ibid., pp. 40, 48–105, 177–224. C. F. Henningsen, *Revelations of Russia: or, the Emperor Nicholas and his Empire in 1844. By One Who Has Seen and Describes*, publ. anon., 2 vols. (London, 1844), 1:203, quoted in ibid., p. 214. Note that the word *surveillance* was still italicized in English in 1844, denoting its foreign origin.

82 A. T. Vassilyev, *The Ochrana, the Russian Secret Police*, edited and with an introduction by R. Fülöp-Miller (Philadelphia and London: J. B. Lippincott Co., 1930). Alexsiei Vasilev was the last chief of police under the czar.

83 For an introduction to postczarist policing, see John Barron, *KGB: The Secret Work of Soviet Secret Agents* (New York: Bantam Books, 1974), Appendix A, "History of the State Security Apparatus," pp. 457–62; Cramer, *World's Police*, pp. 400–6; Robert Conquest, *The Soviet Police System* (New York: Praeger, 1968). For the period 1917–22, see Lennard Gerson, *The Secret Police in Lenin's Russia* (Philadelphia: Temple University Press, 1976), and George Leggett, *The Cheka: Lenin's Political Police* (Oxford: Clarendon Press, 1981). For the 1920s, see the memoirs of a former division chief of the GPU: Georges Agabekov, *OGPU: The Russian Secret Terror*, tr. from the French by Henry Bunn (New York: Brentano's Inc., 1931; repr., Westport, Conn.: Hyperion Press, 1975). A highly readable overview of the czarist and Soviet police is Ronald Hingley, *The Russian Secret Police: Muscovite, Imperial Russian, and Soviet Political Security Operations 1565–1970* (London: Hutchinson, 1970).

84 See Reith, *Blind Eye*, chs. 6, 7; and Louis Hartz, *The Founding of New Societies* (New York: Harcourt, Brace & World, 1964), pp. 3–15, 33–40, 72–93. Among police historians, Reith is famous for his comment that had there been in Boston in the 1760s "a police force of the kind which was provided in London in 1829, ... there would have been no war in the American colonies." Reith reduces the revolution to a series of street riots. *Blind Eye*, p. 81.

85 The National Guard also originated in response to widespread labor unrest. From 1881 to 1892, all of the industrial states strengthened their militias and organized them as part of the National Guard, an institution established in 1879 and made a national one by a 1903 act of Congress. On the eve of World War I, the Guard, numbering 130,000 men, was four times the size of the army. Martha Derthick, *The National Guard in Politics* (Cambridge, Mass.: Harvard University Press, 1965), pp. 15–17; John K. Mahon, *History of the Militia and the National Guard* (New York: Macmillan, 1983), ch. 8.

86 This figure (for 1978) represents the total number of separate forces for 1,000 cities, 20,000 towns, and 15,000 villages, boroughs, and unincorporated towns; it *excludes* all state (50) and county (3,000) police agencies. In sum, there are about 40,000 autonomous police forces in the United States today. In 1978, of America's 420,000 full-time police officers, about 25,000 were in the Federal Bureau of Investigation. Whitaker, *Police in Society* (1979), pp. 38, 176; and cf. Cramer, *World's Police* (1964), pp. 425, 429, and Reith, *Blind Eye* (1952), p. 83. Patrick Murphy, former Police Commissioner of New York City, recently observed that America's police system "doesn't even deserve to be called a system – it is so grossly ineffective, antiquated, poorly managed and fragmented." Quoted in Whitaker, *Police in Society*, p. 177.

87 Stanley H. Palmer, "Cops and Guns: Arming the American Police," *History Today* 18 (June 1978):382–9, a brief account of the arming of the police in Boston, New York, and Chicago, 1850–80.

88 New York did not put its new police in uniform until 1856; Boston followed in 1859, Philadelphia in 1860, and Chicago in 1861. Raymond B. Fosdick, *American Police Systems* (New York: The Century Co., 1920; repr., Montclair, N.J.: Patterson Smith, 1969), p. 70 (quotations), and James F. Richardson, *Urban Police in the United States* (Port Washington, N.Y.: Kennikat Press, 1974), p. 28. A table listing the date at which each major city uniformed its police is in Eric Monkkonen, *Police in Urban America, 1860–1920* (New York: Cambridge University Press, 1981), App. A, pp. 162–8.

89 They became in 1874 a state investigative police and in 1935 were made a part of the Texas Department of Public Safety. In 1964 the force numbered sixty men. The Rangers wear no uniform. Cramer, *World's Police*, pp. 411–12.

90 Roger Lane, *Policing the City: Boston 1822–1885* (Cambridge, Mass.: Harvard University Press, 1967; repr., New York: Atheneum, 1971), pp. 136–41, 162–3.

91 Reith, *Blind Eye*, p. 100. See Pennsylvania State Federation of Labor, *American Cossack* (1915), and Katherine Mayo, *Justice to All: The Story of the Pennsylvania State Police* (1917), both reprinted, New York: Arno Press, 1971, in its Police in America Series.

92 Like the Pennsylvania force, the original New York force of 230 men was a cavalry unit, comprising four troops. The recent creation of state police may be seen in the fact that Raymond Fosdick, in his study of *American Police Systems* (1920), dealt solely with urban police; in his day, the concept of state police meant state control of city forces. As late as 1952, there were only 8,000 state police officers in the forty-eight states; by 1978, in the fifty states, the total had jumped to 45,000. Reith, *Blind Eye*, pp. 100–1; Cramer, *World's Police*, pp. 413–20; Whitaker, *Police in Society*, p. 176.

93 Cramer, *World's Police*, p. 414.

94 Richard Maxwell Brown, "Historical Patterns of Violence in America," in Hugh Davis Graham and Ted Robert Gurr, eds., *Violence in America: Historical and Comparative Perspectives* (New York: New American Library, 1969), pp. 50–1. For a later period, 1865–1915, Sidney Harring has recently argued (*Policing a Class Society*, 1983) that police forces expanded in response to industrial unrest, not crime.

95 For a detailed accounting, see Brown, "Violence in America," pp. 50, 73–4 nn. 45–54. See also Michael Feldberg, *The Turbulent Era: Riot and Disorder in Jacksonian America* (New York: Oxford University Press, 1980).

96 The 1844 Philadelphia riots have been well studied. See Sam Bass Warner, Jr., *The Private City: Philadelphia in Three Periods of Its Growth* (Philadelphia: University of Pennsylvania Press, 1968), pp. 125–57; Michael Feldberg, *The Philadelphia Riots of 1844: A Study of Ethnic Conflict* (Westport, Conn.: Greenwood Press, 1975). Elizabeth M. Geffen, "Violence in Philadelphia in the 1840s and 1850s," in Roger Lane and John J. Turner, Jr., eds., *Riot, Rout, and Tumult: Readings in American Social and Political Violence* (Westport, Conn.: Greenwood Press, 1978), pp. 112–32, on pp. 122 and 128, has counted sixty-nine riots among firemen in 1852 alone; a wave of arson in 1842 was attributed by at least one commentator to the "lower classes, Irish probably." See also, in this same volume, Michael Feldberg, "The Crowd in Philadelphia History: A Comparative Perspective," pp. 133–45. Feldberg notes that "it was the Irish [in the 1844 riot] who first broke the city's tradition of not using firearms in collective disorders"; nativist–Irish fighting "escalated to the use of weaponry on a permanent basis thereafter" (p. 140). David Montgomery, "The Shuttle and the Cross: Weavers and Artisans in the Kensington Riots of 1844," *J. Soc. Hist* 5 (1972):411–46, argues that the ethnic clash between nativist artisans and immigrant Irish weavers killed the

developing working-class consciousness in Philadelphia. On nativists' perceptions of the Irish in the mid-nineteenth century, see Dale T. Knobel, *Paddy and the Republic: Ethnicity and Nationality in Antebellum America* (Middletown, Conn.: Wesleyan University Press, 1986).

97 Fosdick, *American Police Systems*, pp. 63–6; and Richardson, *Urban Police*, pp. 25–6, quotation on p. 25. On the police, see Howard O. Sprogle, *The Philadelphia Police, Past and Present* (Philadelphia, 1887; several reprint editions, New York: AMS Press, n.d., New York: Arno Press, 1971, and Montclair, N.J.: Patterson Smith, forthcoming).

98 The same bar to hiring the foreign-born as policemen existed in Boston from 1838 and in Chicago from 1855, as well as in several other cities.

99 Lane, *Policing*, pp. 21, 27.

100 Volunteer firemen clashed with an Irish funeral procession; the Irish were beaten by mobs reaching a size of 15,000, one-sixth of the city's population. The militia was called out for the first time in Boston's history. A subsequent city council report condemned the nativists' actions but criticized the Irish for "retaining their national ways." Lane, *Policing*, p. 33.

101 Lane, *Policing*, pp. 34, 37–8. See ibid., ch. 3, "Riots and a New Police, 1829–1838"; and Fosdick, *American Police Systems*, pp. 65–7.

102 Cecil Woodham-Smith, *The Great Hunger* (New York: Harper & Row, 1962; repr., New York: E. P. Dutton, 1980), pp. 246–52, quotation on p. 247; Terry Coleman, *Going to America* (New York: Pantheon Books, 1972), pp. 128–32, 223–5 (Botany Bay), 226–34; and Oscar Handlin, *Boston's Immigrants* (Cambridge, Mass.: Harvard University Press, 1941, rev. ed. 1959), p. 244.

103 Lane, *Policing*, pp. 98–100. On the riots and the Irish problem, see ibid., pp. 72–81, 90–5; part of the latter was the controversial appointment in 1851 of the first Irish policeman, Barney McGinniskin, who proclaimed himself to be "fresh from the bogs of Ireland" (p. 77).

104 Ibid., pp. 103–5, 126, 173, 187–8, 203.

105 Ibid., pp. 141, 196–202, 213–19, 287 n. 1, quotation on p. 218. See also Fosdick, *American Police Systems*, pp. 5, 121–3; and John Bocock, "The Irish Conquest of our Cities," *Forum* 17 (1894): 186–95. By 1910, 36 percent of Boston's population was foreign-born, mostly Irish. Lane's police figures are for Irish *born in Ireland*: none on the force in 1860, 45 in 1870, and 100 in 1880 (15 percent of the force). Many American cities have had disproportionately high numbers of Irish policemen; see Richardson, *Urban Police*, pp. 53–4. The tradition of Irish police families is well known; we do not know how many of the immigrants, or their fathers, had ever served in, or been chased by, the Irish constabulary. What effect did the widespread antipolice sentiment in Ireland have on those Irish immigrants who became policemen in America?

106 James F. Richardson, *The New York Police: Colonial Times to 1901* (New York: Oxford University Press, 1970), pp. 9–20, quotation on p. 9.

107 Ibid., pp. 21 (pamphleteer), 25–36 (riots), 37 (city council report), 40.

108 Ibid., ch. 2, "The Movement for a London-style Police," pp. 46–8. An attempt by one nativist alderman, William Gale, to exclude Catholics and all foreign-born citizens from the police was not adopted by the Board of Aldermen.

109 Ibid., pp. 48 (quotation), 64–8, 78–9, 83–4; Fosdick, *American Police Systems*, pp. 70–1.

110 A vivid account is in Woodham-Smith, *The Great Hunger*, pp. 252–69; see also Coleman, *Going to America*, pp. 158–80, 218–23, 231–3, and appendix, pp. 297–8 (table of immigration by nationality). Three-fourths of New York City's relieved paupers in 1851 were listed as "foreigners," i.e., recent immigrants (ibid., p. 163). Under the supervision of Temple University's National Immigration Archives, co-editors Ira A. Glazier and Michael Tepper have compiled an important sourcebook, *The Famine Immigrants: Lists of Irish Immigrants Arriving*

at the Port of New York, 1846–1851, 7 vols. (Baltimore: Genealogical Publishing Co., 1983–6), an *individualized* listing of the Irish men, women, and children disembarked at New York, January 1846–December 1851.

111 Richardson, *New York Police*, pp. 70–3, 87–9, 92–5. Only a few of the foreign-born policemen were Germans. Of 1,149 men on the force in 1855, 305 had been born in Ireland. Fosdick, *American Police Systems*, p. 72 n. 2.

112 Richardson, *New York Police*, pp. 96–108, quotation on p. 105.

113 Ibid., pp. 162–3. As late as the early 1960s, when the city's population was 10 percent Irish-American, 40 percent of New York's policemen were of Irish descent. Arthur Niederhoffer, *Behind the Shield* (Garden City, N.Y.: Anchor Books, 1969), pp. 142–4, quoted in Richardson, *Urban Police*, p. 54.

114 Richardson, *New York Police*, pp. 129–46. Perhaps 300 persons were killed in the Draft Riots; see ibid., pp. 144–5.

115 Ibid., pp. 157–8, 166–7, 189–91. An English visitor in 1889, commenting on police tactics in pushing back onlookers at a parade, wrote: "The London police don't treat crowds in that way. Why do they push and club people in this way?" Quoted in ibid., p. 193. After the 1863 riots, the next most serious public disorders in the second half of the century were also Irish-based: Irish Catholics protesting parades by Irish Protestant Orangemen in 1870–1. In the July 1871 riot, repressed by militia and police, more than 100 persons were killed or seriously wounded. Joel T. Headley, *The Great Riots of New York, 1712 to 1873* (New York: E. B. Trent Co., 1873), ch. 21.

116 Richardson, *New York Police*, pp. 109–10, 113, 161–4, 196, 263, quotation on p. 164.

117 Mr. Podsnap is quoted in David Roberts, *Victorian Origins of the British Welfare State* (New Haven, Conn.: Yale University Press, 1960), p. 96; Elie Halévy, *England in 1815* (New York: Barnes & Noble, 1961), p. 36.

118 Roberts, *Welfare State*, pp. 101, 318.

119 The debate began eighty years ago with A. V. Dicey, who ascribed great influence to Jeremy Bentham. Dicey characterized the years 1825–67 as "the period of Benthamism or Individualism." J. B. Brebner, in 1948, countered that Bentham was in fact a "collectivist." Oliver MacDonagh (1958), David Roberts (1959, 1960), and Kitson Clark (1967), in interpretations with which I agree, downplayed Bentham's contributions and argued that social problems, not social philosophers, were responsible for generating the Government's collectivist solutions. Henry Parris (1960) and Jenifer Hart (1965) have argued for both: the urgency of social problems and the important contributions of the collectivist Bentham. For useful summaries of the debate and full bibliographic citations, see Geoffrey Finlayson, *Decade of Reform: England in the Eighteen Thirties* (New York: W. W. Norton, 1970), pp. 64–72; Harold Perkin, "Individualism Versus Collectivism in Nineteenth-Century Britain: A False Antithesis," *J. Br. Studies* 17 (Fall 1977):105–18, reprinted in Perkin, *The Structured Crowd* (Brighton, Sussex: Harvester Press, 1981), pp. 57–69; and P. W. J. Bartrip, "State Intervention in Mid-Nineteenth Century Britain: Fact or Fiction?", *J. Br. Studies* 23 (Fall 1983):63–83.

120 Perkin, "False Antithesis," pp. 107, 114.

121 Finlayson, *Decade*, p. 71.

122 On prisons, see Michael Ignatieff, *A Just Measure of Pain: The Penitentiary in the Industrial Revolution, 1750–1850* (New York: Pantheon Books, 1978).

123 For extended discussions of reforms in all of these areas, see Roberts, *Welfare State*, chs. 2–4, 6, 8; and the best recent study, Oliver MacDonagh, *Early Victorian Government 1830–1870* (New York: Holmes & Meier, 1977), chs. 3–6, 8.

124 W. L. Burn, "Free Trade in Land: An Aspect of the Irish Question," *Transactions of the Royal Historical Society*, 4th ser., vol. 31, p. 68, quoted in Oliver MacDonagh, *Ireland* (Englewood Cliffs, N.J.: Prentice-Hall, 1968), p. 23.

125 On the reforms discussed in this and the following paragraph, see MacDonagh, *Ireland*, pp. 22−32, and *Early Victorian Government*, ch. 10.

126 MacDonagh, *Early Victorian Government*, p. 193, and *Ireland*, p. 26, respectively. On Irish prison reform, see Oliver MacDonagh, *The Inspector-General: Sir Jeremiah Fitzpatrick and the Politics of Social Reform, 1783−1802* (London: Croom Helm, 1981).

127 Mark Finnane, *Insanity and the Insane in Post-Famine Ireland* (London: Croom Helm, 1981), pp. 14, 25−6. On England, see Andrew Scull, *Museums of Madness: The Social Organization of Insanity in Nineteenth-Century England* (London: Allen Lane, 1979).

128 MacDonagh, *Ireland*, p. 29.

129 MacDonagh, *Early Victorian Government*, pp. 182−5.

130 See Donald Akenson, *The Irish Education Experiment: The National System of Education in the Nineteenth Century* (Toronto: University of Toronto Press, 1970), esp. pp. 3−16; and W. H. G. Armytage, *Four Hundred Years of English Education*, 2d ed. (Cambridge: Cambridge University Press, 1970), pp. 112−16.

131 MacDonagh, *Ireland*, quotation on p. 31, and *Early Victorian Government*, pp. 193−6, quotation on p. 196.

132 See Donajgrodzki, ed., *Social Control* (1977); S. E. Finer, *The Life and Times of Sir Edwin Chadwick* (London: Methuen, 1952); Ian C. Bradley, *The Call to Seriousness: The Evangelical Impact on the Victorians* (New York: Macmillan, 1976); Foster, *Class Struggle* (1974), ch. 7; W. L. Burn, *The Age of Equipoise: A Study of the Mid-Victorian Generation* (New York: W. W. Norton, 1965), pp. 17, 55−87, 110−11, 270−85; and Francis Hearn, *Domination, Legitimation, and Resistance: The Incorporation of the Nineteenth-Century English Working Class* (Westport, Conn.: Greenwood Press, 1978), chs. 4−6.

133 Reith, *British Police*, p. 3 ("unique, not only in its organization, but more particularly, in the principles which it has adopted and evolved"). Browne, *Scotland Yard*, p. 5 ("a unique but typically British institution"). Patrick Pringle, *Hue and Cry: The Birth of the British Police* (London: Museum Press, 1955), pp. 13−15, 201−2.

134 W. Neilson Hancock, in judicial statistics, Ireland, 1863, *PP* 1864 (3418), 57:659. Maitland, *Justice and Police*, p. 108. Maitland sought to define legal history as the wedding of the study of law to social and political history. See Maitland's 1888 inaugural address as Downing Professor at Cambridge University, "Why the History of English Law Is Not Written," in H. A. L. Fisher, *The Collected Legal Papers of Frederic William Maitland*, 3 vols. (Cambridge: Cambridge University Press, 1911), 1:482−91. Over the years, Anglo-American law schools have ignored Maitland's plea: Internal logic, not the external force of historical circumstances, guides teaching in today's professional schools. On Maitland, see C. H. S. Fifoot, *Frederic William Maitland: A Life* (Cambridge, Mass.: Harvard University Press, 1971); and G. R. Elton, *F. W. Maitland* (New Haven, Conn.: Yale University Press, 1985). I am indebted to Professor Richard Cosgrove of the University of Arizona for a copy of his paper, "Frederic Maitland and the Dilemmas of Legal History," presented at the meeting of the Western Conference on British Studies, San Antonio, Texas, October 1985.

135 J. J. Tobias, "Police and Public in the United Kingdom," in George L. Mosse, ed., *Police Forces in History* (Beverly Hills, Calif.: Sage, 1975), pp. 95−113, esp. pp. 104−13.

136 Listed in order of publication. W. E. H. Lecky, *A History of Ireland in the Eighteenth Century*, 5 vols. (London: Longman, Green & Co., 1892; repr., New York: AMS Press, n.d., and St. Clair Shores, Mich.: Scholarly Press, 1972), 2:454. Moylan, *Scotland Yard and the Metropolitan Police* (1929), p. 19 n. 1. Browne, *Scotland Yard* (1956), p. 44, erroneously dates the *London* bill as 1786. Radzinowicz, *ECL*, 3 (1956):122 n. 4; in mistakenly saying that the 1786 act

"proved enduring" and that subsequent changes were "of detail rather than of principle," Radzinowicz misses the important developments of 1786–1808. Gash, *Peel* (1961), p. 181. Christopher Hibbert, *The Roots of Evil: A Social History of Crime and Punishment* (Harmondsworth: Penguin Books, 1966, orig. publ. 1963), p. 145. Critchley, *Police* (1967, 2d ed., 1972), p. 38. Anthony Babington, *A House in Bow Street: Crime and the Magistracy in London, 1740–1801* (London: McDonald, 1969), pp. 168–9. Gurr, *Rogues, Rebels* (1976), p. 119; and David Peirce, Peter N. Grabosky, and Ted Robert Gurr, "London: The Politics of Crime and Conflict, 1800 to the 1970s," in Gurr et al., *Politics of Crime and Conflict* (1977), p. 88. Rudé, *Protest and Punishment* (1978), p. 74, mistakenly dates the Dublin Police Act as 1796. Whitaker, *Police in Society* (1979), p. 38.

Douglas Grant has argued that it is not the London but the Glasgow police, established in 1800, that can be called "the oldest police force in Great Britain." *The Thin Blue Line: The Story of the City of Glasgow Police* (London: J. Long, 1973), p. 15. Perhaps so for Great Britain (England, Wales, and Scotland), but why exclude Ireland? The Dublin force was not only fourteen years older, it was also far larger than the force of seventy-eight officers and watchmen for Glasgow's population of 77,000.

137 Ascoli, *Queen's Peace*, p. 67 n. 2. Melville Lee, *History of Police*, p. 169. Two otherwise well-informed scholars, J. J. Tobias and Galen Broeker, make no mention of the 1786 Dublin police. Rather more understandably, the *Official Brief History of the Metropolitan Police* (Metropolitan Police Training School, n. d., 51 pp.), available at the Metropolitan Police Historical Museum, Bow Street, London, does not note these Irish precedents; tribute is, of course, paid to English medieval origins and to the Fieldings (pp. 1–5). On the early Irish connection, see Stanley H. Palmer, "The Irish Police Experiment: The Beginnings of Modern Police in the British Isles, 1785–1795," *Social Science Quarterly* 56 (Dec. 1975):410–24.

138 Fosdick, *European Police Systems*, p. 64 n. 4; see also Cramer, *World's Police*, p. 17. Melville Lee, *History of Police*, p. 169, wrongly states that the act applied to "the whole of Ireland"; this error is repeated in John J. Tobias, "The British Colonial Police," in Philip John Stead, ed., *Pioneers in Policing* (Montclair, N.J.: Patterson Smith, 1977), p. 244. A surprising number of eminent recent scholars – Broeker, Critchley, Gash, and Radzinowicz – do not mention the 1787 Irish police.

139 Sir Charles Jeffries, *The Colonial Police* (London: Max Parrish, 1952), p. 30; Minto, *The Thin Blue Line*, pp. 25–8; Glover, *The English Police*, p. 53. See also Moylan, *Scotland Yard and the Metropolitan Police*, pp. 25, 30; Ascoli, *Queen's Peace*, pp. 66–8; and Conor Brady, *Guardians of the Peace* (Dublin: Gill and Macmillan, 1974), p. 3. Critchley and Radzinowicz do not discuss Peel's 1814 police.

140 Gash, *Peel*, pp. 177–82, 311–12, 498. MacDonagh, *Early Victorian Government*, pp. 169–70. See also Peirce, Grabosky, and Gurr, "London: The Politics of Crime and Conflict," p. 92. In a one-sentence aside, an early writer, George Dilnot, sensed a connection to Ireland but got his facts scrambled. "The way [to founding the London police in 1829] had been partly paved by the success of the Royal [*sic*] Irish Constabulary, established as the Dublin Police of 1786, which, however, was modelled upon semi-military lines." *Story of Scotland Yard* (1927), p. 28. Charles Reith was equally confused. According to Reith, Home Secretary Peel, in his earlier role as Irish Chief Secretary, had had "some detailed experience of improving police organization in Ireland [he created the rural "Peelers," 1814–18] by extending a force which had been originally created by Wellington [the Dublin police, 1808] when he held the same post some years earlier." *Police Idea* (1938), p. 223.

141 Kevin Boyle, "Police in Ireland Before the Union," *The Irish Jurist*, new series, 7 (1972):115–37, and 8 (1973):90–116, 323–48; and Séamus Breathnach, *The Irish*

Police from Earliest Times to the Present Day (Dublin: Anvil Books, 1974), p. 26.

142 Eamon de Valera, speech in *Dáil Éireann*, 1919, quoted in Tom Bowden, *The Breakdown of Public Security: The Case of Ireland 1916–21 and Palestine 1936–39* (Beverly Hills, Calif.: Sage, 1977), p. 286; and Breathnach, *Irish Police*, pp. 26–7. See also Albert Memmi's study of the minds of *The Colonizer and the Colonized* (Boston: Beacon Press, 1967) in the context of French colonialism in North Africa.

143 The single study, John Flint's *The Dublin Police and the Police System* (Dublin, 1847), is a pamphlet treating only the period 1835–45. A copy is at the National Library in Dublin; the British Library copy, like many other contemporary works on police, was destroyed in German bombing during the Second World War.

144 The earliest is Thomas Doolan, *Munster: or, the Memoirs of a Chief Constable* (London: W. Davy, 1831), rare, available at the Royal Irish Academy, Dublin. Henry Robert Addison, *Recollections of an Irish Police Magistrate* (London: Parlour Library Edition [1862]; and London: J. and R. Maxwell, 1883), traces the career of Thomas P. Vokes; despite the date of publication, it pertains to our period. For the post-1850 period, see Frank Thorpe Porter, *Gleanings and Reminiscences* (Dublin: Hodges, Foster, & Co., 1875), and *Twenty Years' Recollections of an Irish Police Magistrate*, 8th ed. (Dublin: Hodges, Foster & Figgis, 1880); Michael Brophy, *Sketches of the Royal Irish Constabulary* (London: Burns & Oates, 1886) and *Tales of the Royal Irish Constabulary* (Dublin: B. Doyle, 1896); G. Garrow-Green, *In the Royal Irish Constabulary* (London: J. Blackwood, 1905); C. W. Leatham, *Sketches and Stories of the Royal Irish Constabulary* (Dublin: E. Ponsonby, 1909). The career of an Irish Resident Magistrate, Major Sinclair Yeates, is told in E. Somerville and Martin Ross, *The Irish R.M. Complete* (London: Faber and Faber, 1928, reprinted seven times, 1929–68). These works should not be confused with tendentious, fictionalized works like the anonymous *Tales of the R.I.C.* (Edinburgh and London: W. Blackwood & Sons, 1921), an apologia for the last days of British rule.

145 Robert Curtis, *The History of the Royal Irish Constabulary* (Dublin: Moffat & Co., 1869), pp. xiv, 195; 2d ed., Dublin: McGlashan & Gill, 1871, pagination unchanged from the 1869 edition. By a County Inspector of the RIC on the eve of his retirement.

146 Galen Broeker, "Robert Peel and the Peace Preservation Force," *J. Mod. Hist.* 33 (1961):363–73; and Tadhg O Ceallaigh, "Peel and Police Reform in Ireland, 1814–18," *Studia Hib.* 6 (1966):25–48.

147 Volume 8, Studies in Irish History, Second Series. London and Toronto: Routledge & Kegan Paul, 1970.

148 Breathnach devotes only sixteen pages to the years 1812–36 (*Irish Police*, pp. 23–39). See also Bowden, *Breakdown of Public Security*, pp. 20–6, a brief and in places unreliable account; R. B. McDowell, *The Irish Administration, 1801–1914* (London: Routledge & Kegan Paul, 1964), pp. 135–45; and Michael Beames, *Peasants and Power: The Whiteboy Movements and Their Control in Pre-Famine Ireland* (New York: St. Martin's Press, 1983), pp. 157–67.

149 Broeker mentions the subject only twice. *Police*, pp. 59, 197.

150 Melville Lee, *History of Police*, p. 169.

151 Brady, *Guardians of the Peace*, p. 3.

CHAPTER 2. TWO SOCIETIES

1 J. G. A. Pocock, "The Limits and Divisions of British History: In Search of the Unknown Subject," *A.H.R.* 87 (Apr. 1982):311–36, quotations on pp. 313, 317–18. See also Pocock, "British History: A Plea for a New Subject," *J. Mod. Hist.* 47 (Dec. 1975):601–28, with comments by A. J. P. Taylor, G. Donaldson,

and M. Hechter, and a reply by Pocock. On the islands' interrelationships, see Oliver MacDonagh, *Ireland* (Englewood Cliffs, N.J.: Prentice-Hall, 1968), chs. 1, 2; *Early Victorian Government 1830–1870* (New York: Holmes & Meier, 1977), ch. 10; and *States of Mind: A Study of the Anglo-Irish Conflict, 1780–1980* (London: Allen & Unwin, 1983). Patrick O'Farrell, *Ireland's English Question: Anglo-Irish Relations 1534–1970* (New York: Schocken Books, 1971), and *England and Ireland Since 1800* (London: Oxford University Press, 1975), esp. chs. 1–3. Michael Hechter, *Internal Colonialism: The Celtic Fringe in British National Development, 1536–1966* (Berkeley: University of California Press, 1974), esp. chs. 3, 4. L. M. Cullen, *The Emergence of Modern Ireland 1600–1900* (New York: Holmes & Meier, 1981), esp. ch. 1. What is striking on this list is the absence of English academics. Hechter, a sociologist at the University of Washington, is an American. Cullen is a professor at Trinity College, Dublin. Pocock and O'Farrell are New Zealanders, the former teaching in America (Johns Hopkins) and the latter in Australia (University of New South Wales). MacDonagh also is an Australian academic; since leaving St. Catherine's, Cambridge, twenty years ago, he has taught at Flinders and, most recently, at the Australian National University in Canberra. It appears that the concept of the "Atlantic archipelago" is beginning to make its way into the textbooks; see Richard S. Tompson, *The Atlantic Archipelago: A Political History of the British Isles*, Studies in British History, Vol. 1 (Lewiston, N.Y.: Edwin Mellen, 1986). Tompson, an American, is a professor of modern British history at the University of Utah.

2 Edward Brynn, *Crown and Castle: British Rule in Ireland 1800–1830* (Atlantic Highlands, N.J.: Humanities Press, 1978), pp. 12–18; Chris Cook and Brendan Keith, *British Historical Facts 1830–1900* (New York: St. Martin's Press, 1975), pp. 49–62. Henry Goulburn, Irish Chief Secretary (1821–7), was named Home Secretary by Prime Minister Peel (1834–5), a route Peel himself had taken. After 1850, Prime Ministers tended to have backgrounds in finance and foreign affairs. Arthur Balfour, Prime Minister from 1902 to 1905, was the first since Derby to have served as Irish Chief Secretary (1887–91). Of the seven men who served as Prime Minister between 1852 and 1902, only two – the Anglo-Irish Palmerston (1855–8, 1859–65) and Earl Russell (1865–6) – had been Home Secretaries, in 1852–5 and 1835–9, respectively.

3 "Siamese twins": MacDonagh, *Ireland*, p. 22. Trevelyan quoted in Max Beloff, *Public Order and Popular Disturbances 1660–1714* (London: Oxford University Press, 1938), p. 5. See W. A. Speck, *Stability and Strife: England 1714–1760* (Cambridge, Mass.: Harvard University Press, 1977), chs. 2, 3; Harold Perkin, *The Origins of Modern English Society 1780–1880* (London: Routledge & Kegan Paul, 1969), ch. 1; J. G. Simms, *The Williamite Confiscation in Ireland, 1690–1703* (London: Faber and Faber, 1956; repr., Westport, Conn.: Greenwood Press, 1976). On the penal laws, see W. E. H. Lecky, *A History of Ireland in the Eighteenth Century*, 5 vols. (London: Longmans, Green, 1892; repr., St. Clair Shores, Mich.: Scholarly Press, 1972), 1:142–70; "Memorandum on the Laws against Catholics," in the Papers of Henry Goulburn, Goulburn II/13, Surrey Record Office, Kingston-on-Thames; and Maureen Wall, *The Penal Laws, 1691–1760* (Dundalk: Dundalgan Press, 1961; 2d ed., 1967).

4 See Francis G. James, *Ireland in the Empire, 1688–1770* (Cambridge, Mass.: Harvard University Press, 1973); Edith Mary Johnston, *Ireland in the Eighteenth Century* (Dublin: Gill and Macmillan, 1974).

5 On population, see B. R. Mitchell and Phyllis Deane, *Abstract of British Historical Statistics* (Cambridge: Cambridge University Press, 1962), pp. 5–8; Phyllis Deane and W. A. Cole, *British Economic Growth 1688–1959*, 2d ed. (Cambridge: Cambridge University Press, 1967), pp. 6, 8; E. A. Wrigley and R. S. Schofield, *The Population History of England 1541–1871: A Reconstruction* (Cambridge, Mass.: Harvard University Press, 1981); Stuart Daultrey, David Dickson, and Cormac

Ó Gráda, "Eighteenth-Century Irish Population: New Perspectives from Old Sources," *J. Econ. Hist.* 41 (Sept. 1981):621−8; Joel Mokyr and Cormac Ó Gráda, "New Developments in Irish Population History, 1700−1850," *Econ. H.R.* 37 (Nov. 1984):473−88; and W. E. Vaughan and A. J. Fitzpatrick, eds., *Irish Historical Statistics: Population 1821−1971* (Dublin: Royal Irish Ireland, 1978; and New York: State Mutual Book & Periodical Service, Ltd., 1982). England's material expansion is traced in G. R. Porter, *The Progress of the Nation, in its various Social and Economic Relations, from the Beginning of the Nineteenth Century* (London: C. Knight & Co., 1836−43); 2d ed., 1846; 3d ed., one vol., 1851; hereafter, unless so noted, all references are to the 3d ed., London: J. Murray, 1851. See also J. R. McCulloch, *A Statistical Account of the British Empire: Exhibiting Its Extent, Physical Capacities, Population, Industry, and Civil and Religious Institutions*, 2 vols. (London: C. Knight & Co., 1837); four editions, 1837−54.

6 Significantly, in England "small farmers" referred to those working fewer than 100 acres. This class of farmers was numerous, accounting for almost two-thirds of all farmers in 1851. But, reflecting the English economies of scale, the remaining third of the farmers worked four-fifths of the land − indeed, less than a tenth of all farmers (17,000 of 215,000 in 1851) worked a third of the cultivated acreage, J. D. Chambers and G. E. Mingay, *The Agricultural Revolution 1750−1880* (London: B. T. Batsford, 1966), p. 93. Older estimates for Ireland had 81 percent of all holdings in a size range of 1−15 acres. Recent estimates have dropped this figure to 64 percent. Nevertheless, plots of 1−5 acres still accounted for 24 percent of all Irish holdings. P. M. A. Bourke, "The Agricultural Statistics of the 1841 Census of Ireland: A Critical Review," *Econ. H.R.* 18 (1965):376−92; F. S. L. Lyons, *Ireland since the Famine* (London: Weidenfeld and Nicolson, 1971), p. 39.

7 J. R. McCulloch, *A Dictionary, Practical, Theoretical and Historical, of Commerce and Commercial Navigation* ..., 8th ed., 2 vols. (London: Longman, Brown, Green and Longmans, 1854), 2:1030; Deane and Cole, *British Economic Growth*, pp. 7, 9; Gearóid Ó Tuathaigh, *Ireland Before the Famine, 1798−1848* (Dublin: Gill and Macmillan, 1972), p. 151.

8 Andrew Ure, *The Cotton Manufacture of Great Britain*, 2 vols. (London: C. Knight & Co., 1836), 1:353−6; Porter, *Progress* (1836), 1:196−7, 240; McCulloch, *Dictionary ... of Commerce*, 3d ed. (London: Longman, Rees, Orme, Brown, Green and Longman, 1837), p. 736; Deane and Cole, *British Economic Growth*, pp. 185, 187, 225; Conrad Gill, *The Rise of the Irish Linen Industry* (Oxford: Clarendon Press, 1925). For a recent controversial analysis of the Irish dilemma, see Joel Mokyr, *Why Ireland Starved: A Quantitative and Analytical History of the Irish Economy, 1800−1850* (London: Allen & Unwin, 1983); and Barbara L. Solow, "Why Ireland Starved," *J. Econ. Hist.* 44 (Sept. 1984):839−43.

9 Quotation: Liam Kennedy, "Studies in Irish Econometric History," *I.H.S.* 23 (May 1983):205. See Raymond O. Crotty, *Irish Agricultural Production: Its Volume and Structure* (Cork: Cork University Press, 1966), pp. 7−46; L. M. Cullen, *An Economic History of Ireland since 1660* (London: B. T. Batsford, 1972), chs. 4, 5; Lyons, *Ireland since the Famine*, pp. 34−42.

10 Quotation: Crotty, *Irish Agricultural Production*, p. 37. See Mokyr, *Why Ireland Starved*, passim; James S. Donnelly, Jr., *The Land and the People of Nineteenth-Century Cork: The Rural Economy and the Land Question* (London: Routledge & Kegan Paul, 1975), ch. 1; Samuel Clark and James S. Donnelly, Jr., eds., *Irish Peasants: Violence and Political Unrest, 1780−1914* (Madison: University of Wisconsin Press, 1983), editors' introduction, pp. 29−33; and the recent study of County Cavan, by Kevin O'Neill, *Family and Farm in Pre-Famine Ireland: The Parish of Killashandra* (Madison: University of Wisconsin Press, 1984).

11 Quotations, respectively, from Crotty, *Irish Agricultural Production*, pp. 37, 43, 45; Lyons, *Ireland Since the Famine*, p. 41.

12 Crotty, *Irish Agricultural Production*, p. 44; Lyons, *Ireland Since the Famine*, p. 38 note. In 1961, 24 percent of holdings were under 15 acres in size, and livestock generated 78 percent of the value of the agricultural sector. See David O'Mahony, *The Irish Economy*, 2d ed. (Cork: Cork University Press, 1967), pp. 24-9.

13 Elie Halévy, *England in 1815*, tr. from the French by E. I. Watkin and D. A. Barker (New York: Barnes & Noble, 1961, orig. publ. 1913), pp. 377, 379; Cobbett, quoted in Dorothy George, *England in Transition: Life and Work in the Eighteenth Century* (Harmondsworth: Penguin Books, 1965, orig. publ. 1931), p. 137. On England's innumerable private charities, see David Owen, *English Philanthropy 1660-1960* (Cambridge, Mass.: Harvard University Press, 1964).

14 Chambers and Mingay, *Agricultural Revolution*, pp. 119-21, 139-43; Mark Blaug, "The Myth of the Old Poor Law and the Making of the New," *J. Econ. Hist.* 23 (1963):151-78. For annual Poor Law expenditures, see Mitchell and Deane, *Abstract*, p. 410. On the Old English Poor Law's value in promoting economic development and labor mobility, see Peter Solar (University of York), "The Economic Effects of the Old Poor Law, 1600-1834: An Irish Perspective," paper presented at the Davis Center Seminar, Princeton University, December 1984.

15 See E. P. Thompson's excellent discussion in *The Making of the English Working Class* (New York: Pantheon Books, 1964), ch. 4, quotations on pp. 78-9, 87. See also Christopher Hill, "The Norman Yoke," orig. publ. in J. Saville, ed., *Democracy and the Labour Movement* (London: Lawrence and Wishart, 1954), reprinted in C. Hill, *Puritanism and Revolution: Studies in Interpretation of the English Revolution of the 17th Century* (London: Secker & Warburg, 1958; New York: Schocken Books, 1964), pp. 50-122; see pp. 94ff. for the post-1750 legacy. See also John Brewer, "The Wilkites and the Law, 1763-74: A Study of Radical Notions of Governance," in John Brewer and John Styles, eds., *An Ungovernable People: The English and their Law in the Seventeenth and Eighteenth Centuries* (New Brunswick, N.J.: Rutgers University Press, 1980), ch. 4. For a provocative discussion of class and class consciousness, see R. S. Neale, *Class in English History 1680-1850* (New York: Barnes & Noble, 1981). On the whole subject of national identities, I am indebted to Walter P. Metzger, "Generalizations about National Character: An Analytical Essay," in Louis Gottschalk, ed., *Generalization in the Writing of History* (Chicago: University of Chicago Press, 1963), pp. 77-102.

16 Shakespeare, *Richard II*, Act 2, Scene 1, ll. 48-9. See Alan Macfarlane, *The Origins of English Individualism* (New York: Cambridge University Press, 1979), esp. pp. 165-206. For an insightful look at a minority group's survival, see John Bossy, *The English Catholic Community 1570-1850* (London: Darton, Longman & Todd, 1975).

17 Scribbler: quoted in George Rudé, *Paris and London in the Eighteenth Century: Studies in Popular Protest* (New York: Viking, 1971), p. 215. J. R. Jones, *The Revolution of 1688 in England* (New York: W. W. Norton, 1972), ch. 4, "The Catholic Factor." For the political uses of antipopery in emerging English liberal thought, c. 1620-42, see Caroline Hibbard, *Charles I and the Popish Plot* (Chapel Hill: University of North Carolina Press, 1983). *Rule, Britannia!*: Thomas Arne's song, composed for a play, based on an ode by J. Thomson (1710-78). Cf. Christopher Hill's remark that "the political effect of surviving anti-papist sentiments on 18th-century Englishmen is one subject that, so far as I am aware, has never been properly investigated." *Reformation to Industrial Revolution: The Making of Modern English Society 1530-1780* (Harmondsworth: Penguin Books,

1969), p. 277. For our period, see G. F. A. Best, "Popular Protestantism in Victorian Britain," in R. Robson, ed., *Ideas and Institutions of Victorian Britain* (London: G. Bell & Sons, 1967), pp. 115–42; and Walter Arnstein, *Protestant versus Catholic in Mid-Victorian England: Mr. Newdegate and the Nuns* (Columbia: University of Missouri Press, 1982).

18 Thompson, *Making*, p. 86; Cobbett, quoted in Craig Calhoun, *The Question of Class Struggle: Social Foundations of Popular Radicalism during the Industrial Revolution* (Chicago: University of Chicago Press, 1982), pp. 95, 103; *Edinburgh Review* (Apr. 1807), 10:11, quoted in Halévy, *England in 1815*, p. 147.

19 "Slaves": William Cobbett, *Rural Rides* (London: W. Cobbett, 1830; repr., Harmondsworth: Penguin Books, 1967), p. 118, journal entry for 1 Aug. 1823. "Negroes": William Cobbett, *Selections from Cobbett's Political Works*, 6 vols. (London: A. Cobbett, 1835), 6 (1823–4):434–5. An 1830 handbill, signed "A True Englishman," in HO 50/2, PRO, London. E. J. Hobsbawm and George Rudé, *Captain Swing* (New York: Pantheon Books, 1968), p. 16. Thompson, *Making*, pp. 828–31, quotations on p. 831. See also David Goodway, *London Chartism 1838–1848* (Cambridge: Cambridge University Press, 1982), pp. 12–13, 240 n. 60.

20 Edward Gibbon Wakefield, *An Account of Ireland, Statistical and Political*, 2 vols. (London: Longman, Hurst, Rees, Orme, and Brown, 1812), 2:806. The same point was made by the American Benjamin Franklin to Lord Kames in 1767: "Every man in England seems to consider himself as a piece of a sovereign over America; seems to jostle himself into the throne with the King, and talks of *our subjects in the Colonies.*" Quoted in Sir Lewis Namier, *England in the Age of the American Revolution*, 2d ed. (New York: St. Martin's Press, 1966), p. 29.

21 Frederick Engels, *The Condition of the Working-Class in England in 1844*, orig. publ. in German in 1845, tr. by Florence K. Wischnewetzky, 1892 (London: Allen & Unwin, 1952), pp. 33, 93. Cf. the 1958 translation by British historians W. O. Henderson and W. H. Chaloner: "The national character of the Irish is partly responsible. The Irish ... on occasion actually seem to be happy in dirty surroundings"; *and* "[the Irishman's] coarseness, ... drags him down virtually to the level of a savage." Friedrich Engels, *The Condition of the Working Class in England*, ed. Henderson and Chaloner (Oxford: Blackwell, 1958; repr., Stanford, Calif.: Stanford University Press, 1968), pp. 40, 106. For a similar opinion by Karl Marx in 1870, see Robert Miles and Annie Phizacklea, eds., *Racism and Political Action in Britain* (London: Routledge & Kegan Paul, 1979), pp. 2–3.

22 See the numerous travelers' accounts, beginning with that of William of Malmesbury (1095), discussed in Edward Snyder's brilliant early study, "The Wild Irish: A Study of Some English Satires against the Irish, Scots, and Welsh," *Modern Philology* 17 (Apr. 1920):147–85. The quotation is from Edmund Spenser, *A View of the Present State of Ireland* ... (1596; first publ., 1633), in Snyder, "Wild Irish," p. 158. The term "wild Irish" dates from at least the fourteenth century; "meere [mere] irish," from the early seventeenth. Unaccountably, the negative image of Paddy has received far more attention from historians than has the Englishman's own positive self-image. The best recent studies are L. P. Curtis, Jr., *Anglo-Saxons and Celts* (Bridgeport, Conn.: Conference on British Studies, 1968), and *Apes and Angels: The Irishman in Victorian Caricature* (Newton Abbot: David & Charles, 1971); W. R. Jones, "England against the Celtic Fringe: A Study in Cultural Stereotypes," *Journal of World History* 13 (1971):151–71; three works by Richard Ned Lebow, "Cambrensis to Macaulay: British Historians and Irish History," *Eire-Ireland* 8, No. 4 (Winter 1973): 3–38, and *White Britain and Black Ireland: The Influence of Stereotypes on Colonial Policy* (Philadelphia: Institute for the Study of Human Issues, 1976), and "British Images of Poverty in Pre-Famine Ireland," in Daniel J. Casey and Robert E. Rhodes, eds., *Views of the*

Irish Peasantry 1800–1916 (Hamden, Conn.: Archon Books, 1977), pp. 57–85; and P. O'Farrell, *England and Ireland Since 1800* (1975), ch. 2, "Images." For a recent application, see John Kirkaldy, "English Cartoonists; Ulster Realities," *Eire-Ireland* 16, No. 3 (Fall 1981):27–42. Much work has also been done on linking English images of the Irish to English preconceptions about the "savages" in North America. See, e.g., Nicholas Canny, "The Ideology of English Colonization: From Ireland to America," *William and Mary Quarterly* 30 (1973): 575–98; James Muldoon, "The Indian as Irishman," *Essex Institute of Historical Collections* 3, No. 4 (Oct. 1975):267–89.

23 For a brilliant discussion of the "tidiness" of tillage versus the unkemptness of pasturage, see E. Estyvn Evans, "Peasant Beliefs in Nineteenth-Century Ireland," in Casey and Rhodes, eds., *Views*, p. 50. "Beings": Phillip Luckombe, *A Tour Through Ireland* (1783), p. 19, quoted in Lebow, "British Images," p. 68. Half of the occupied dwellings in Cork in 1841 were one-room windowless cabins; see Donnelly, *The Land and the People of Nineteenth-Century Cork*, pp. 24, 242–4.

24 Burke, quoted in Lecky, *Ire.*, 1:145. Yeomanry Brig.-Maj. D. Mahony to Dublin Castle Under-Secretary W. Gregory, 25 Apr. 1823, Killarney, State of the Country Papers, Series 1 [hereafter cited as SOCP 1], 2522/10, ISPO, DC.

25 "Niggers": Maurice O'Connell, berating a previous speaker, an unnamed English MP, for quoting this "vulgar proverb ... against the character of the Irish people." *Hansard* 95:897, 9 Dec. 1847, speech on the Irish coercion bill. On the post-1845 simianization of Paddy, see Curtis, *Apes and Angels*, pp. 29–48.

26 "Cunning": *Punch* 17 (1851):26, quoted in Lebow, "British Images," p. 67. "Outlaws ... robbers": Valentine Lawless, Lord Cloncurry, *Personal Recollections of the Life and Times, with Extracts from the Correspondence of Valentine, Lord Cloncurry* (Dublin: J. McGlashan, 1849), p. 212. Arthur Young, *A Tour of Ireland; with general observations on the present state of that Kingdom. Made in the years 1776, 1777, and 1778. And brought down to the end of 1779* (London: T. Cadell, 1780), Part 2, p. 75; Wakefield, quoted in Constantia Maxwell, *Country and Town in Ireland under the Georges* (London: G. G. Harrap & Co., 1940), p. 170. On Irish successes in the United States, see various witnesses' testimony in "Report from the Select Committee on Outrages (Ireland)," *PP 1852* (438), 14:QQ. 2081–2106, 2867, 3478–99, 4525–31.

27 Joseph Lee, "The Ribbonmen," in T. Desmond Williams, ed., *Secret Societies in Ireland* (Dublin: Gill and Macmillan, 1973), p. 33. On diet, see Cullen, *Emergence of Modern Ireland*, ch. 7, and his path-breaking article, "Irish History Without the Potato," *Past & Present* 40 (July 1968):72–83.

28 For national literacy rates, see Lawrence Stone, "Literacy and Education in England, 1640–1900," *Past & Present* 42 (Feb. 1969):109–11, 119–22; Donald Akenson, *The Irish Education Experiment: The National System of Education in the Nineteenth Century* (Toronto: University of Toronto Press, 1970), p. 376. For Irish protesters transported between 1826 and 1840, literacy rates were in the range of 40–45 percent; for those transported from 1840 to 1853, 45–55 percent. George Rudé, *Protest and Punishment: The Story of the Social and Political Protesters Transported to Australia, 1788–1868* (Oxford: Clarendon Press, 1978), appendix, pp. 249–52.

29 Rudé's figures reveal a big difference in literacy rates between, on the one hand, the Chartists transported in 1839 and 1848 (71 and 69 percent, respectively) and, on the other, the transported 1842 Plug Plot rioters (43 percent), many of whom were from rural or mining districts.

30 Lyons, *Ireland Since the Famine*, pp. 37–9, quotation on p. 39; Crotty, *Irish Agricultural Production*, pp. 39–41, 55–8. Decennial rates of population growth: 1781–1821, 17 percent; 1821–31, 15 percent; 1831–41, 5 percent. The standard

work on emigration is now Kerby A. Miller, *Emigrants and Exiles: Ireland and the Irish Exodus to North America* (New York: Oxford University Press, 1985); see chs. 5–7 for the period 1783–1855.

31 Leon Radzinowicz, *A History of English Criminal Law and its Administration from 1750,* [hereafter, *ECL*], 4 vols. (London: Stevens & Sons, 1948–68), 3:55 n. 5; *Saunders's News-letter*, 16 Nov. 1786; Brig.-Maj. D. Mahony to W. Gregory, 25 Apr. 1823, SOCP 1 2522/10. Statistics in Porter, *Progress*, p. 668. For England, see Terry L. Chapman, "Crime in Eighteenth-Century England: E. P. Thompson and the Conflict Theory of Crime," *Criminal Justice History* 1 (1980):139–55.

32 Radzinowicz, *ECL*, 1:148, 155–7, 708–9; Joel Samaha, *Law and Order in Historical Perspective: The Case of Elizabethan Essex* (New York: Academic Press, 1974), pp. 19–21, 115–16, 125–6; J. S. Cockburn, "The Nature and Incidence of Crime in England, 1559–1625: A Preliminary Survey," in J. S. Cockburn, ed., *Crime in England 1550–1800* (London; Methuen, 1977), pp. 52–60; Keith Wrightson, *English Society 1580–1680* (New Brunswick, N.J.: Rutgers University Press, 1982), pp. 160–1; Alan Macfarlane, *The Justice and the Mare's Ale: Law and Disorder in Seventeenth-Century England* (New York: Cambridge University Press, 1981), pp. 18–26, 185–6; and for medieval England, Ted Robert Gurr, "On the History of Violent Crime in Europe and America," in Hugh Davis Graham and Ted Robert Gurr, eds., *Violence in America: Historical and Comparative Perspectives*, rev. ed. (Beverly Hills, Calif.: Sage, 1979), pp. 354, 358. Spotty evidence suggests that in England homicide has been in long secular decline: In the thirteenth century the rate (per 100,000 population) was about seven times, and in the seventeenth century about three times, the homicide rate in late-twentieth-century England. In 1550–1800 roughly three of four indicted offenses were for property theft, a proportion similar to later figures.

33 Samuel Jacob to Attorney-General W. Saurin, 30 Nov. 1815, SOCP 1 1722/93. Compare the list of homicides committed in England, 1842–6, *PP 1846* (207), 34:773–84, with those in Ireland, 1842–5, *PP 1846* (220), 35:293–306.

34 Thomas Bartlett, "An End to Moral Economy: The Irish Militia Disturbances of 1793," *Past & Present* 99 (May 1983):41–64. William Fenge to W. Gregory, 4 July 1814, SOCP 1 1566/29; report of Chief Constable S. D. Martin, 8 Oct. 1824, SOCP 1 2610/19; *Annual Register*, 1820, Chronicle, p. 35, quoted in Michael Beames, *Peasants and Power: The Whiteboy Movements and Their Control in Pre-Famine Ireland* (New York: St. Martin's Press, 1983), p. 80.

35 *Ennis Chronicle*, 13 Feb. 1828, quoted in Beames, *Whiteboy*, p. 80. George Cornewall Lewis, *On Local Disturbances in Ireland, and on the Irish Church Question* (London: B. Fellowes, 1836), pp. 146–7, 226 ("vengeance"); reprinted Cork: Tower Books, 1977, as *Local Disturbances in Ireland*. Pagination in the reprint edition (pp. 119–20, 184) differs from that in the original 1836 edition. In notes hereafter, *all* page references are to the 1977 Tower reprint edition.

36 Lewis, *Disturbances*, p. 184; Chief Constable William Coffey to Insp.-Gen. G. Warburton, 11 June 1825, SOCP 1 2724/20.

37 For a revealing comparison of the differences in crime in the two countries, see the testimony of Sir William Somerville, MP for Drogheda and a County Meath JP and landowner, in "Report by the Lords' Select Committee appointed to inquire into the state of Ireland since the year 1835, in respect of Crime and Outrage," *PP 1839* (486), 12:QQ. 14570–14635. Somerville later served as Irish Chief Secretary, 1847–52.

38 "Assassin": clergyman quoted in Best, "Popular Protestantism in Victorian Britain," p. 115. "Select Committee on Outrages (Ireland)," *PP 1852* (438), 14:QQ. 863–5, ev. of E. Golding, JP, County Monaghan. For the English working-class prosecution of crime, see David Philips, *Crime and Authority in Victorian England: The Black Country 1835–1860* (London: Croom Helm, 1977),

pp. 123−9; Barbara Weinberger, "The Police and the Public in Mid-Nineteenth Century Warwickshire," in Victor Bailey, ed., *Policing and Punishment in Nineteenth Century Britain* (New Brunswick, N.J.: Rutgers University Press, 1981), pp. 71−4.

39 For England: arson, assaults on police, cattle maiming, conspiracy regarding wages, destruction of textile and threshing machines, poaching, riot, smuggling, threatening letters, and unlawful oaths. For Ireland: armed assembly, arson, assaults on revenue officers, attacks on houses and land, cattle maiming, combinations to raise wages, forcible possession of property (land), high treason (1848 only), oath taking, riot, robbery of arms, and threatening letters. From his list of Irish protest offenses, Rudé has unaccountably excluded several types of offenses against persons with violence, including homicide and attempted homicide. Rudé, *Protest*, pp. 15, 32.

40 Ibid., pp. 20, 36. Within these periods, English protest peaked statistically in 1842, in Lancashire, with protest offenses accounting for 13 percent of all county committals; Irish protest peaked in 1848, in Galway, at 40 percent of all county committals.

41 Porter, *Progress*, pp. 646, 668. See also Joseph Fletcher, "Progress of Crime in the United Kingdom," *Journal of the Statistical Society of London* 6 (Aug. 1843):218−39.

42 Charles Tilly, "Collective Violence in European Perspective," in Hugh Davis Graham and Ted Robert Gurr, eds., *Violence in America: Historical and Comparative Perspectives*, 1st ed. (New York: New American Library, 1969), pp. 13−27.

43 Rudé, *Protest*, pp. 52−8. See also his essay "The 'Pre-Industrial' Crowd," in Rudé, *Paris and London*, pp. 17−34.

44 Tilly, "Collective Violence," p. 13; and see Tilly's "Afterthoughts, from the Seventies" in *Violence in America*, revised 1979 Sage edition, pp. 111−15. George Rudé, *The Crowd in History: A Study of Popular Disturbances in France and England, 1730−1848* (New York: Wiley, 1964), pp. 3−15; and *Protest*, pp. 27−41, 56−8.

45 Lord Lismore to H. Goulburn, 4 Nov. 1822, SOCP 1 2356/74. See Dr. Crump's prize winning essay (1793) on the subject in Wakefield, *Account*, 2:813.

46 See James MacKillop, "Finn MacCool: The Hero and the Anti-Hero in Irish Folk Tradition," in Casey and Rhodes, eds., *Views*, pp. 86−106.

47 Wakefield, *Account*, 2:752, 795; and William Carleton, "The Battle of the Factions," in *The Works of William Carleton*, 2 vols. (New York: Collier, 1881; repr., Freeport, N.Y.: Books for Libraries Press, 1970), 2:722−40.

48 John Warburton, J. Whitelaw, and R. Walsh, *A History of the City of Dublin, from the Earliest Accounts to the Present Time* ... 2 vols. (London: W. Bulmer & Co., 1818), 2:1175−6; James Grant, *Impressions of Ireland and the Irish*, 2 vols. (London: H. Cunningham, 1844), 1:115−44. City authorities suppressed the fair in 1855.

49 Paul E. W. Roberts, "Caravats and Shanavests: Whiteboyism and Faction Fighting in East Munster, 1802−11," in Clark and Donnelly, eds., *Irish Peasants*, pp. 64−101.

50 William Carleton, "The Party Fight and Funeral," *Works*, 2:762−96; Maurice Harmon, "Cobwebs Before the Wind," in Casey and Rhodes, eds., *Views*, pp. 136−42. For new views on sectarianism in 1785−1800, see Marianne Elliott, "The Origin and Transformation of Early Irish Republicanism," *Intl. Rev. Soc. Hist.* 23 (1978):405−28, and her justly acclaimed book, *Partners in Revolution: The United Irishmen and France* (New Haven, Conn.: Yale University Press, 1982), pp. 15−20, 39−46; James S. Donnelly, Jr., "Propagating the Cause of the United Irishmen," *Studies: An Irish Quarterly Review* 69 (Spring 1980): 5−23; and David W. Miller, "The Armagh Troubles, 1784−95," in Clark and Donnelly, eds., *Irish Peasants*, pp. 155−91.

51 Rudé, *Protest*, p. 113.

52 For a listing of the various regional movements, see Beames, *Whiteboy*, Tables 3 and 4, pp. 25, 43. The long-neglected subject has recently − perhaps in part as a

result of the post-1970 wave of Ulster violence − attracted the attention of excellent scholars. See George Cornewall Lewis, *On Local Disturbances in Ireland, and on the Irish Church Question* (London: B. Fellowes, 1836; reprinted as *Local Disturbances in Ireland*, Cork: Tower Books, 1977); G. E. Christianson, "Secret Societies and Agrarian Violence in Ireland, 1790−1840," *Agricultural History* 46 (Oct. 1972):369−84; Maureen Wall, "The Whiteboys," and Joseph Lee, "The Ribbonmen," in Williams, ed., *Secret Societies in Ireland* (1973), pp. 13−25, 26−35; Michael Beames, *Peasants and Power: The Whiteboy Movements and Their Control in Pre-Famine Ireland* (New York: St. Martin's Press, 1983). And especially James S. Donnelly, Jr., "The Whiteboy Movement, 1761−5," *I.H.S.* 21 (Mar. 1978):20−54; "Hearts of Oak, Hearts of Steel," *Studia Hib.* 21 (1981):7−73; "Irish Agrarian Rebellion: The Whiteboys of 1769−76," *Proc. R.I.A.* 83, C, No. 12 (1983):293−331; "The Rightboy Movement, 1785−8," *Studia Hib.* 17 & 18 (1977−8):120−202; and the introduction in Clark and Donnelly, eds., *Irish Peasants* (1983), pp. 25−35. Prof. Donnelly is at work on a multivolume history of Irish agrarian secret societies, 1750−1845, forthcoming from Oxford University Press.

53 E.g., Lord Castlemaine to Henry Goulburn, 29 Nov. 1824: "30 Men well armed with *White Shirts* over their Cloathes" (SOCP 1 1824/2610/24). But the term was generic and the garb hardly universal.

54 Mr. Poulett Scrope, MP for Stroud, *Hansard* 95:945, 10 Dec. 1847.

55 Cullen, *Economic History of Ireland*, p. 113; Sergeant H. Joy's Memorandum on Project for Reform, Joy to Lord Lt. Anglesey, 11 May 1828, Anglesey Papers, T1068/20/23, PRONI, Belfast.

56 Donnelly, "Whiteboy," pp. 33−4, and Clark and Donnelly, *Irish Peasants*, pp. 27−8; Beames, *Whiteboy*, pp. 26−9, 47−50, 111−39.

57 On Tipperary, see G. Holmes, *Sketches of Some of the Southern Counties of Ireland, Collected during a Tour in the Autumn, 1797* (London: Longman and Rees, 1801), pp. 198−200; Wakefield, *Account*, 1:71−3; Samuel Lewis, *A Topographical Dictionary of Ireland*, 2 vols. (London: J. Lewis, 1837; repr., Baltimore: Genealogical Publishing Co., 1984), 2:628−34, quotation on p. 630; and Mr. and Mrs. S. C. Hall, *Ireland: Its Scenery, Character, & c.*, 3 vols. (London: J. How, 1846), 2:65−6, 79−89.

58 On fairs around London, see Hugh Cunningham, "The Metropolitan Fairs: A Case Study in the Social Control of Leisure," in A. P. Donajgrodzki, ed., *Social Control in 19th-Century Britain* (Totowa, N.J.: Rowman and Littlefield, 1977), pp. 163−84.

59 See Beloff, *Public Order and Popular Disturbances*, pp. 20−8; Rudé, *Crowd*, chs. 2−4; R. F. Wearmouth, *Methodism and the Common People of the Eighteenth Century* (London: The Epworth Press, 1945), pp. 32−6, 138−64. For earlier periods, see Barrett Beer, *Rebellion and Riot: Popular Disorder in England during the Reign of Edward VI* (Kent, Ohio: Kent State University Press, 1982); Buchanan Sharp, *In Contempt of All Authority: Rural Artisans and Riot in the West of England, 1586−1660* (Berkeley: University of California Press, 1980); and the important collection of nineteen essays, previously published in the journal *Past & Present*, 1968−82, and covering the period 1536−1800, in Paul Slack, ed., *Rebellion, Popular Protest and the Social Order in Early Modern England* (New York: Cambridge University Press, 1984).

60 J. R. Western, *The English Militia in the Eighteenth Century: The Story of a Political Issue, 1660−1802* (London: Routledge & Kegan Paul, 1965), pp. 290−302; Walter Shelton, *English Hunger and Industrial Disorders: A Study of Social Conflict During the First Decade of George III's Reign* (Toronto: University of Toronto Press, 1973), pp. 109−11; J. Stevenson, "The London 'Crimp' Riots of 1794," *Intl. Rev. Soc. Hist.* 16 (1971):40−58. In Ireland militia balloting in 1793 led to severe and bloody disturbances (see note 34, this chapter).

61 John Stevenson, *Popular Disturbances in England, 1700–1870* (London: Longman, 1979), pp. 30–4; John Walsh, "Methodism and the Mob," in G. J. Cuming and Derek Baker, eds., *Popular Belief and Practice* (Cambridge: Cambridge University Press, 1972), pp. 213–27.

62 M. Dorothy George, *London Life in the Eighteenth Century* (New York: Harper & Row, 1965, orig. publ. 1925), pp. 126, 132; Thomas W. Perry, *Public Opinion, Propaganda, and Politics in Eighteenth-Century England: A Study of the Jew Bill of 1753* (Cambridge, Mass.: Harvard University Press, 1962), an old-fashioned political history, but see ch. 6, "The Great Clamor of 1753."

63 George, *London Life*, pp. 117–18; George Rudé, "'Mother Gin' and the London Riots of 1736," *Guildhall Miscellany* 1, No. 10 (Sept. 1959):53–62, reprinted in Rudé, *Paris and London*, pp. 201–21. On the Gordon and Church-and-King riots, see pages 85–6, 140–1.

64 Chambers and Mingay have argued that enclosure increased employment among the laborers. J. D. Chambers, "Enclosure and Labour Supply in the Industrial Revolution," *Econ. H.R.* 5 (1952–3):319–42; and Chambers and Mingay, *Agricultural Revolution*, pp. 86–104.

65 Rudé, *Crowd*, pp. 35–6; John Stevenson, "Food Riots in England, 1792–1818," in J. Stevenson and R. Quinault, eds., *Popular Protest and Public Order: Six Studies in British History, 1790–1920* (New York: St. Martin's Press, 1975), pp. 35–6. See also Rudé, *Crowd*, pp. 33–46; R. B. Rose, "Eighteenth-Century Price Riots and Public Policy in England," *Intl. Rev. Soc. Hist.* 6 (Pt. 2, 1961):277–92; and especially John Bohstedt, *Riots and Community Politics in England and Wales, 1790–1810* (Cambridge, Mass.: Harvard University Press, 1983).

66 F. O. Darvall, *Popular Disturbances and Public Order in Regency England* (London: Oxford University Press, 1934, repr. 1969); Malcolm I. Thomis, *The Luddites: Machine-Breaking in Regency England* (New York: Schocken Books, 1972); E. J. Hobsbawm and George Rudé, *Captain Swing: A Social History of the Great English Agricultural Uprising of 1830* (New York: Pantheon Books, 1968).

67 See Francis Hearn, *Domination, Legitimation, and Resistance: The Incorporation of the Nineteenth-Century English Working Class* (Westport, Conn.: Greenwood Press, 1978), chs. 4, 6; J. P. D. Dunbabin, *Rural Discontent in Nineteenth-Century Britain* (New York: Holmes & Meier, 1974), chs. 3 (esp. pp. 30–6), 4, 5; and David Jones, *Crime, Protest, Community and Police in Nineteenth-Century Britain* (London: Routledge & Kegan Paul, 1982), chs. 2, 3.

68 Beames, *Whiteboy*, p. 28; John Brewer, "Law and Disorder in Stuart and Hanoverian England," *History Today* 30 (Jan. 1980):27.

69 Beames, *Whiteboy*, pp. 127–39; Lewis, *Disturbances*, pp. 77, 80.

70 Halévy, *England in 1815*, p. 148; R. K. Webb, *Modern England from the Eighteenth Century to the Present*, 2d ed. (New York: Harper & Row, 1980), p. 26.

71 Tilly, "Collective Violence," p. 16 (quotation); Perkin, *Origins of Modern English Society*, pp. 182–92; E. P. Thompson, "The Moral Economy of the English Crowd in the Eighteenth Century," *Past & Present* 50 (Feb. 1971):78–9, 107–15, 120–6; and David Roberts, *Paternalism in Early Victorian England* (New Brunswick, N.J.: Rutgers University Press, 1979).

72 J. E. Bicheno, *Ireland and its Economy* (London, 1830), quoted in Beames, *Whiteboy*, p. 91, my emphasis. Young, *Tour*, Pt. 2, p. 29. See also Lewis, *Disturbances*, pp. 41 n. 8, 42.

73 Rudé, *Protest*, p. 57.

74 SOCP 1 1819/2071/25 and 1824/2614/13. Quotations from 1787 and 1834, in Lewis, *Disturbances*, p. 81. Marquess of Clanricarde, *Hansard* 83:743, 12 Feb. 1846.

75 Rudé, *Crowd*, pp. 89–91; Hobsbawm and Rudé, *Swing*, pp. 296–9; Tilly, "Collective Violence," p. 19.

76 See Perkin, *Origins of Modern English Society*, chs. 2, 6.

77 Tilly, "Collective Violence," pp. 23–7; Hearn, *Domination*, chs. 4, 6. *The Oxford*

English Dictionary [hereafter, *O.E.D.*], 12 vols. (Oxford: Clarendon Press, 1933, repr. 1961), 11 (T–U): "Trade Union"; "Union," meaning 7(b). "Whig emissaries [were] to get up what, in their own conventional cant, they call a demonstration." Tory journal, *Britannia* (1839), quoted in *O.E.D.* 3 (D–E): "Demonstration," meaning 7. This modern meaning thus does not date from the 1860s, as Donald Richter claims (*Riotous Victorians*, Athens: Ohio University Press, 1981, p. 87).

78 See Stanley H. Palmer, "Rebellion, Emancipation, Starvation: The Dilemma of Peaceful Protest in Ireland, 1798–1848," in Bede K. Lackner and Kenneth Philp, eds., *Essays on Modern European Revolutionary History*, Walter Prescott Webb Memorial Lectures, No. 11 (Austin: University of Texas Press, 1977), pp. 3–38.

79 Rudé, *Paris and London*, p. 326. See George Rudé, *Wilkes and Liberty* (Oxford: Clarendon Press, 1962); a recent interpretation that stresses the traditional elements in Wilkes's movement is John Brewer, "The Wilkites and the Law," in Brewer and Styles, eds., *An Ungovernable People*, ch. 4. Walter Shelton, *English Hunger and Industrial Disorders* (Toronto: University of Toronto Press, 1973), argues for the dissemination of the new political ideas among agrarian and industrial rioters in the 1760s. For the pre-1760 seeds of modern collective protest, see Rudé, *Paris and London*, pp. 58, 201–21, 311–24; Gary S. De Krey, "Political Radicalism in London after the Glorious Revolution," *J. Mod. Hist.* 55 (Dec. 1983):585–617; Nicholas Rogers, "Popular Protest in Early Hanoverian London," *Past & Present* 79 (May 1978):70–100; and Linda Colley, "Eighteenth-Century English Radicalism Before Wilkes," *Transactions of the Royal Historical Society*, 5th ser., 31 (1981):1–19.

80 R. R. Palmer, *The Age of the Democratic Revolution*, 2 vols. (Princeton, N.J.: Princeton University Press, 1959–64), 1:294–302.

81 Malcolm I. Thomis and Peter Holt, *Threats of Revolution in Britain, 1789–1848* (Hamden, Conn: Archon Books, 1977), ch. 1; for an opposing view, see Thompson, *Making*, esp. chs. 5, 13. Marianne Elliott, in her *Partners in Revolution*, has recently argued for strong Irish influences in the wartime English republican movement.

82 Patrick Rogers, *The Irish Volunteers and Catholic Emancipation, 1778–1793* (London: Burns, Oates, & Washbourne, 1934); P. D. H. Smyth, "The Volunteers and Parliament, 1779–84," in Thomas Bartlett and D. W. Hayton, eds., *Penal Era and Golden Age: Essays in Irish History, 1690–1800* (Belfast: Ulster Historical Foundation, 1979), pp. 113–36.

83 Bartlett, "Irish Militia Disturbances"; Elliott, *Partners in Revolution*; and Thomas Pakenham, *The Year of Liberty: The Great Irish Rebellion of 1798* (London: Hodder and Stoughton, 1969). See also n. 50, this chapter.

84 The literature is vast. For a beginning, see Rudé, *Crowd*, chs. 12–16; Thompson, *Making*, chs. 15–16; Thomis and Holt, *Threats*, chs. 3–5. For a critique of Thompson that views the popular radicalism of 1815–32 as socially conservative and highly localized, see Calhoun, *The Question of Class Struggle*, chs. 2–3, 6–8. For 1832–48, see Dorothy Thompson, *The Chartists: Popular Politics in the Industrial Revolution* (New York: Pantheon Books, 1984).

85 "Driftless": quoted in Lewis, *Disturbances*, p. 128. By comparison, the Irish literature in thin indeed. But good studies are James Reynolds, *The Catholic Emancipation Crisis in Ireland, 1823–29* (New Haven, Conn.: Yale University Press, 1954; repr., Westport, Conn.: Greenwood Press, 1970). Three articles by Patrick O'Donoghue: "Causes of the Opposition to Tithes, 1830–38," *Studia Hib.* 5 (1965):7–28; "Opposition to Tithe Payment in 1830–31," *Studia Hib.* 6 (1966):69–98; and "Opposition to Tithe Payment in 1832–3," *Studia Hib.* 12 (1972):77–108. Kevin B. Nowlan, *The Politics of Repeal* (London: Routledge & Kegan Paul, 1965). Lawrence J. McCaffrey, *Daniel O'Connell and the Repeal Year* (Lexington: University of Kentucky Press, 1966). And Angus McIntyre's

excellent study, *The Liberator: Daniel O'Connell and the Irish Party, 1830–1847* (New York: Macmillan, 1965).

86 See A. G. L. Shaw, *Convicts and the Colonies* (London: Faber and Faber, 1966), pp. 363–8, for yearly arrivals in New South Wales and Van Diemen's Land, 1788–1853, distinguishing ships arriving from Great Britain and Ireland. According to Rudé, between 1810 and 1850 a total of sixty-six persons were hanged for *all* protest offenses; of these, forty-nine were Luddites and Captain Swing's men. Only twelve were hanged for political offenses: three men for the Pentridge rising, 1817; five for the Cato Street conspiracy, 1820; and four for the Bristol Riots, 1831. Rudé, *Protest*, p. 64. (But to these twelve we should add the seven executed in London for the Despard conspiracy in 1803. Thompson, *Making*, p. 483; Elliott, *Partners*, p. 295.)

87 Rudé, *Protest*, pp. 1, 8–10. Rudé's Irish protest total of 2,249 is conservative. Shaw asserts that about 5,000 "political and social" offenders were transported from Ireland between 1795 and 1853, some 1,200 in the period 1815–30. *Convicts*, pp. 182–3.

88 The British total is the sum of the 1790s radicals (21), Pentridge rebels (17), Cato Street conspirators (5), Bristol rioters (26), and Chartists (102) transported. One authority states that as a result of the Irish Rebellion, 418 persons were transported by military courts and, in addition, "great numbers" were so sentenced at assizes. Pakenham, *Year of Liberty*, p. 342.

89 Tony Hayter, *The Army and the Crowd in Mid-Georgian England* (London: Macmillan, and Totowa, N.J.: Rowman and Littlefield, 1978), p. 1.

90 See 1 Hawkins P. C. c. 65 s. 9; 13 Charles 2, c. 5 (1661); Henry Fielding, "The Case of Bosavern Penlez" (1749), in Henry Fielding, *The Complete Works of Henry Fielding*, ed. W. E. Henley, 16 vols. (London: W. Heinemann, 1902–3), 13:261–3; Richard Burn, *The Justice of the Peace, and Parish Officer*, 14th ed. (London: T. Cadell, 1780), pp. 79–81; Edward Wise, *The Law Relating to Riots and Unlawful Assemblies: Together with a view of the duties and powers of magistrates, police officers, special constables, the military, and private individuals, for their suppression; and a summary of the law as to actions against the Hundred*, 2d ed. (London: Shaw & Sons, 1848), pp. 17–62; W. F. Finlason, *A Review of the Authorities as to the Repression of Riot or Rebellion* (London: Stevens & Sons, 1868), pp. 1–47; and Wise, *The Law Relating to Riots and Unlawful Assemblies … The Treason Felony Act, 1848, the Conspiracy and Protection of Property Act, 1875, and the Riot (Damages) Act, 1886, with regulations thereunder*, 3d ed., revised by A. H. Bodkin (London: Shaw & Sons, 1889), pp. 1–61. See also *Halsbury's Laws of England*, ed. D. M. Hogg, Viscount Hailsham, 2d ed., 15 vols. (London: Butterworth & Co., 1931–3), 9:311, 314–15, 480; P. D. Fanner and C. T. Latham, eds., *Stone's Justices' Manual*, 101st ed., 2 vols. (London: Butterworth & Co., 1969), 2:2732–4.

91 1 Geo. 1 s. 2, c. 5 (1714). Charles Clode stated that the law was "little more than a re-enactment" of lapsed statutes against felonious riot, 3 & 4 Edw. 6, c. 5; 1 Mary s. 2, c. 12; and 1 Eliz., c. 16. Clode's Memorandum, 2 Feb. 1867, WO 33/18/12, PRO, London.

92 1 Geo. 1 s. 2, c. 5 (proclamation at sec. 2). In 1837, the death penalty was replaced by life transportation, which in 1857 was changed to penal servitude. 7 Will. 4 & 1 Vict., c. 91; 20 & 21 Vict., c. 3 s. 2. The 1714 Riot Act was repealed in 1967. T. A. Critchley, *The Conquest of Violence: Order and Liberty in Britain* (New York: Schocken Books, 1970), p. 73. See Ian Brownlie, *The Law Relating to Public Order* (London: Butterworth & Co., 1968).

93 Anon., "On the Suppression of Riots by Military Interference," *The Law Magazine; or, Quarterly Review of Jurisprudence* 9 (Feb. 1833):66–8; Wise, *Riots*, 2d ed., pp. 47–9, 51–9, and *Riots*, 3d ed., pp. 88–99; Charles M. Clode, *The Military Forces of the Crown*, 2 vols. (London: J. Murray, 1869): 2:126, 130–1.

94 Fielding, "Bosavern Penlez," p. 269. See also Anon., *Remarks on the Riot Act, With an Application to Certain Recent and Alarming Facts* ... (London: G. Kearsly, 1768), pp. 2–6.

95 Fielding, "Bosavern Penlez," p. 272; Wise, *Riots*, 2d ed., pp. 41–9, and *Riots*, 3d ed., pp. 83–91; *Halsbury's Laws*, 9:487–9.

96 Mansfield, quoted in Wise, *Riots*, 3d ed., p. 83; Critchley, *Conquest*, p. 73. A recent analysis is W. Nippel, "'Reading the Riot Act': The Discourse of Law-Enforcement in 18th Century England," *History & Anthropology* 1 (Pt. 2, 1985):401–26.

97 Lecky, *Ire.*, 1:413–15; 2:39–40, 456–8. Whiteboy statutes (Ire.): 29 Geo. 2, c. 12; 3 Geo. 3, c. 19; 7 Geo. 3, c. 20; 17 & 18 Geo. 3, c. 36; and, most importantly, 5 Geo. 3, c. 8 (1765) and 15 & 16 Geo. 3, c. 21 (1776). Irish Riot Act: 27 Geo. 3, c. 15 (1787).

98 F. W. Maitland, *Collected Papers*, ed. H. A. L. Fisher, 3 vols. (Cambridge: Cambridge University Press, 1911), 2:470, quoted in Esther Moir, *The Justice of the Peace* (Harmondsworth: Penguin Books, 1969), p. 9. Sidney and Beatrice Webb, *English Local Government from the Revolution to the Municipal Corporations Act: The Parish and the County* (London: Longmans, Green, 1906), pp. 294–364, 534, 550–1. On the distant origins, see Robert C. Palmer's magisterial study, *The County Courts of Medieval England, 1150–1350* (Princeton, N.J.: Princeton University Press, 1984).

99 The revisionist view may be said to begin with Eleanor Trotter, *Seventeenth Century Life in the Country Parish* (Cambridge: Cambridge University Press, 1919), pp. 202–15, a study of the North Riding of Yorkshire; it is continued in Moir, *Justice of the Peace*, pp. 82–8, and Moir's county study, *Local Government in Gloucestershire, 1775–1800: A Study of the Justices of the Peace* (Bristol: Bristol & Gloucester Archaeological Society, 1969); Philip Jenkins, *The Making of a Ruling Class: The Glamorgan Gentry 1640–1790* (New York: Cambridge University Press, 1983), esp. pp. 83–91; and Norma Landau, *Justices of the Peace 1679–1760* (Berkeley: University of California Press, 1984). See also David Heifetz, "The Justices of the Peace in Hampshire, 1625–1675," 1978 Ph.D. dissertation, University of California – Irvine; and James M. Rosenheim, "An Examination of Oligarchy: The Gentry of Restoration Norfolk, 1660–1720," 1981 Ph.D. dissertation, Princeton University, and his paper, "County Governance at the Restoration: The Case of Norfolk 1660–1720," presented at the 1982 meeting of the Western Conference on British Studies, Snowbird, Utah.

100 "Contemptible": Donnelly, "Rightboy," p. 187; Sir William Blackstone, *Commentaries on the Laws of England*, 3d ed., 4 vols. (Oxford: Clarendon Press, 1768–9), 1:354.

101 Norbury, quoted in Beames, *Whiteboy*, p. 140; see also ibid., p. 169. Donnelly, "Whiteboy," pp. 44–52; "Agrarian Rebellion," pp. 317–23; and "Rightboy," pp. 185–90.

102 Rosenheim (1981) has found that in early-eighteenth-century Norfolk, a tenth of the JPs were active. The Webbs (1906) "guesstimated" that one-fourth of eighteenth-century English JPs were habitually devoted to their work (*Parish and County*, pp. 320–1). My conservative estimate of one-fifth presumes a growing activity by JPs during the increasingly legalistic eighteenth century.

103 The late-eighteenth-century figure was probably higher. In its post-Union inquiry (1815), Dublin Castle unearthed these facts: 557 JPs deceased, 311 no longer serving, and as many as 1,355 no longer living in Ireland. Galen Broeker, *Rural Disorder and Police Reform in Ireland, 1812–36* (London: Routledge & Kegan Paul, 1970), p. 42. My highly conjectural figure of 400 is based on an estimate that one-fifth of about 2,000 resident JPs were active.

104 13 Henry 4, c. 7 s. 1; 2 Henry 5, c. 8 s. 2; 17 Richard 2, c. 8; 1 Hawkins P. C. c. 65 s. 22; Wise, *Riots*, 2d ed., p. 79. Hobsbawm and Rudé, *Swing*, pp. 255–6.

105 Donnelly, "Agrarian Rebellion," pp. 321–3, 329–31; and "Rightboy," pp. 187–90, 196–8.

106 Western, *English Militia*, pp. 290–302, quotation on p. 302; Shelton, *Hunger and Industrial Disorders*, pp. 109–11, 127–35; Clode, *Military Forces*, 2:134; Bartlett, "Irish Militia Disturbances," pp. 41–64; Anon., "Suppression of Riots," p. 80.

107 Blackstone, *Commentaries*, 3d ed., 1:407, 412–13; Clode, *Military Forces*, 2:125–8, quotation on p. 128, and his Memorandum, WO 33/18/3–10; and Beloff, *Public Order*, pp. 107–15.

108 Bill of Rights (1689), 1 William & Mary s. 2, c. 2 pt. 1 s. 5; Clode, *Military Forces*, 1:398–9. For foreign armies, see *The New Cambridge Modern History*, 14 vols. (Cambridge: Cambridge University Press, 1957–70), 7:179; Hayter, *Army*, p. 22. For France, the *NCMH* gives a peacetime establishment figure of 160,000; Hayter says 133,000. France in 1750 was three times as populous as England; Prussia ranked twelfth in population among European states.

109 "Queries" from Irish Chief Secretary Peel to Commander-in-Chief Gen. Sir George Beckwith, 22 Apr. 1817, No. 11 with reply, Official Papers, Series 2 [hereafter, OP 2], 568/482/11, ISPO, DC, citing statute 10 Henry 7, c. 19, reconfirmed by 14 & 15 Charles 2, c. 8. Donnelly, "Whiteboy," p. 45 (quotation); "Hearts of Oak," pp. 18–20, 62–6; "Agrarian Rebellion," pp. 323–4; and "Rightboy," pp. 190, 200–1. General Cunningham, in *The Parliamentary Register, or the History of the Proceedings and Debates of the House of Commons in Ireland*, 15 vols. (Dublin, 1784–95), 4:219; hereafter cited as *Parl. Reg.*

110 Clode, *Military Forces*, 1:398; Lecky, *Ire.*, 1:142. Irish Army Augmentation Act, 9 Geo. 3, c. 2 (1769). For Irish army levels at several dates from 1699 to 1818, see OP 2 1817/568/482/11 and 1819/574/26; and for the 1780s, Bolton MSS 15889 (3) and 15890 (3), Papers of Thomas Orde, 1st Baron Bolton, NLI, Dublin.

111 Blackstone, *Commentaries*, 3d ed., 1:413. Lord Bath and Mr. Mackay, quoted in Radzinowicz, *ECL*, 4:119.

112 *Dublin Evening Post*, 17 Apr. 1792.

113 Respectively, *Faulkner's Dublin Journal*, 21/23 Nov. 1786; *Saunders's News-letter*, 28 Jan. 1793.

114 "Return of all Permanent Barracks in the United Kingdom, including the Date of Erection of each," *PP* 1847 (169), 36:321–406. *Observations made by the Commissioners on their View of the Several Barracks throughout the Kingdom of Ireland* (Dublin, 1760); Young, *Tour*, Pt. 2, p. 141; Sir John W. Fortescue, *A History of the British Army*, 13 vols. (London: Macmillan, 1899–1930), 11:15.

115 Respectively, Young, *Tour*, Pt. 2, pp. 39–40; Wakefield, *Account*, 1:659.

116 Burn, *Justice of the Peace*, 14th ed., pp. 83–90; Anon., "Suppression of Riots," pp. 67–8; Wise, *Riots*, 2d ed., pp. 78–84. On Ireland, see n. 97, this chapter; and Insurrection Act: 36 Geo. 3, c. 20 (1796), and Lecky, *Ire.*, 3:451–4.

117 Donnelly, "Whiteboy," p. 44; "Agrarian Rebellion," pp. 323–4; and "Rightboy," pp. 185, 190. For military rules at a later period, see the printed *General Orders for the Guidance of the Troops, in Affording Aid to the Civil Power ... in Ireland* (Dublin, 1836), 63 pp., Chief Secretary's Office Registered Papers 1836/1222, ISPO, DC.

118 Donnelly, "Rightboy," p. 200. In County Kilkenny in 1764, in a narrow defile near Newmarket, an armed crowd of 300 attacked fourteen light dragoons escorting nine prisoners; the soldiers opened fire, killing at least twelve, and losing two of their own men. Donnelly, "Whiteboy," pp. 49–50. In the two most lethal Rightboy affrays (1786), four peasants were killed by thirty soldiers who were instructed to fire by a jittery JP, Rev. Patrick Hare, when they were surrounded by a throng of 2,000 near Cashel, in County Tipperary; three were killed in County Clare when a party of soldiers fired into a crowd of "over 1,000 persons who refused to disperse." Donnelly, "Rightboy," pp. 200–1. See also Donnelly, "Hearts of Oak," pp. 19, 63–4.

119 For 1785–8, Donnelly has found twenty-seven cases of torture and only six murders. "Rightboy," pp. 183–4.

120 Of the thirty-five Rightboy killings, ten came in rescue attempts and fifteen in *seven* confrontations with the military or armed private bodies. Donnelly, "Rightboy," p. 201. For the English food riots in 1766, Hayter, *Army*, p. 120, gives a total of thirteen rioters killed; Rudé, *Crowd*, p. 255, says nineteen.

121 Legal evolution: Clode, Memorandum, WO 33/18/17–23, and *Military Forces*, 2:131–4, 617–26; WO 34/103/1; WO 34/109/25–9. See also Hayter, *Army*, pp. 53 ("*ultra vires*"), 61–71; and Stanley H. Palmer, "Calling Out the Troops: The Military, the Law, and Public Order in England, 1650–1850," *J. Soc. Army Hist. Research* 56 (Winter 1978): 198–214.

122 Hayter, *Army*, pp. 94, 98, 105–7.

123 Ibid., pp. 115, 118 (Barrington), 120. Clode, Memorandum, WO 33/18/23, and *Military Forces*, 2:133–4. On the 1766 riots, see Rudé, *Crowd*, pp. 38–43; Shelton, *Hunger and Industrial Disorders*, chs. 1–4; Hayter, *Army*, pp. 114–27.

124 Hayter, *Army*, p. 120. Clode, Memorandum, WO 33/18/25–33, and *Military Forces*, 2:134–7.

125 Trial of Captain Porteous, in *A Complete Collection of State Trials*, ed. T. B. Howell, 33 vols. (London: Longman, Hurst, Rees, Orme, & Brown, 1816–26), 17:923–4; Clode, *Military Forces*, 2:34; Radzinowicz, *ECL*, 4:132–3; Critchley, *Conquest*, p. 76.

126 Clode, Memorandum, WO 33/18/27–33, and *Military Forces*, 2:135–7; Radzino-wicz, *ECL*, 4:132–4; Critchley, *Conquest*, pp. 77–81. An abstract of Gillam's trial is in the *Annual Register* 11 (1768): Chronicle, 227–33.

127 Anon., "Suppression of Riots," p. 74. Sir Charles James Napier, *Remarks on Military Law and the Punishment of Flogging* (London: T. and W. Boone, 1837), p. 23. Napier's passage is quoted in Clode, Memorandum, WO 33/18/193, and *Military Forces*, 2:152; Radzinowicz, *ECL*, 4:128; Critchley, *Conquest*, pp. 75–6. On the military's accountability before civil and military law, see Anon., "Suppression of Riots," pp. 68–74, 78–9; A. V. Dicey, *Introduction to the Study of the Law of the Constitution*, 8th ed. (London: Macmillan, 1915), pp. 297–302; Fanner and Latham, eds., *Stone's Justices' Manual*, 2:2739.

128 In the discussion that follows, I am much in debt to Hayter for his pioneering study, *The Army and the Crowd in Mid-Georgian England* (1978); see n. 89, this chapter.

129 Hayter, *Army*, pp. 176–7. Western, *English Militia*, p. 298, says that "after lengthy parleyings" the militia fired, resulting in "twenty dead at least and many wounded." Rudé's figures are extremely high. Not citing his source, he states that at Hexham forty-two were killed and forty-eight wounded by the Yorkshire militia (Rudé, *Crowd*, p. 35); elsewhere in the same book (p. 255) he says that "over 100" were killed or wounded at Hexham.

130 For the military policies, see Hayter, *Army*, pp. 139–44; for the events of March to May, Rudé, *Wilkes*, pp. 37–49, and Shelton, *Hunger and Industrial Disorders*, pp. 172–7.

131 My account relies principally on Hayter, *Army*, pp. 179–80 (quotations). See also Clode, Memorandum, WO 33/18/27–33, and *Military Forces*, 2:135–7; Finlason, *Review of the Authorities*, pp. 2–8; Critchley, *Conquest*, pp. 79–80; and Rudé, *Wilkes*, pp. 49–53. "There seems to be no agreement about the numbers killed," notes Hayter, *Army*, p. 218 n. 91. Most writers give a figure of six killed (the number reported in *The Annual Register*), but Rudé (*Wilkes*, p. 51 n. 3), citing Edmund Burke's "notes for a speech (of 8 March 1769?)," accepts a figure of eleven lives lost.

132 Hayter, *Army*, p. 180.

133 Ibid., pp. 24–5; Hew Strachan, "The Early Victorian Army and the Nine-teenth-Century Revolution in Government," *E.H.R.* 95 (Oct. 1980):784.

134 See Hayter's innovative analysis, in *Army*, pp. 167–86.

135 Strachan, "Early Victorian Army," p. 783. Two soldiers who got drunk, joined the mob on 10 May, and yelled "Wilkes and Liberty for ever" were each sentenced to forty-five lashes, administered "'three times, viz. every other day, and afterwards to drill for forty-five days.'" Shelton, *Hunger and Industrial Disorders*, p. 127.

136 Hayter, *Army*, pp. 168–71, 218 n. 89.

137 Ibid., pp. 172–4.

138 Ibid., pp. 174–5, 183–6.

139 Ibid., pp. 25, 48–51, 187. For the movement of troops in the disorders of 1756, 1757, and 1766, see Tables 7.1, 8.2, and 9.1 in ibid., pp. 88–92, 107–12, and 121–6.

140 Ibid., p. 29.

141 French visitor, 1720, and "Tom Tipsey," 1763, quoted in Radzinowicz, *ECL*, 3:1, 3. Chesterfield, in *O.E.D.* 7 (N–Poy): "Police," meaning 3. Jonas Hanway, *The Citizen's Monitor: Shewing the Necessity of a Salutary Police* (London: Dodsley, 1780), p. iii.

142 On eighteenth-century French notions of police, see Steven L. Kaplan, *Bread, Politics, and Political Economy in the Reign of Louis XV*, 2 vols. (The Hague: Martinus Nijhoff, 1976), 1:8–14. Adam Smith, *Lectures on Justice, Police, Revenue and Arms* ... (1763), ed. E. Cannan (Oxford: Clarendon Press, 1896), p. 154, my emphasis; Blackstone, *Commentaries*, 3d ed., 4:162–75; John Aikin, *A Description of Manchester* (London: J. Stockdale, 1795), p. 263; and *O.E.D.* 7 (N–Poy): "Police," meaning 3.

143 John Fielding, *An Account of the Origin and Effects of a Police Set on Foot by His Grace the Duke of Newcastle in the Year 1753, upon a Plan presented to His Grace by the late Henry Fielding, Esq.* (London: A. Millar, 1758). See also *O.E.D.* 7 (N–Poy): "Police," meaning 6, ex. "1758. Sir John Fielding." Anon., *Westminster Police Bill. Reasons why the Bill entitled 'A Bill for the more effectual Administration of the Office of a Justice of Peace ...,' should not pass into a Law* (London, 1774), p. 2, cited in Radzinowicz, *ECL*, 3:4 n. 19. See also Anon., *A Letter to Archibald Macdonald, Esq., on the Intended Plan for Reform in what is called the Police of Westminster*, second printing (London, 1784).

144 London: "A Bill for the Further Prevention of Crimes, and for the more speedy Detection and Punishment of Offenders against the Peace, in the Cities of *London* and *Westminster*, the Borough of *Southwark*, and certain Parts adjacent to them," *House of Commons Bills, 25 Geo. 3* (1785), pp. 477–507, British Library, State Paper Room. Dublin: "An Act for the better Execution of the Law within the City of Dublin, and certain Parts adjacent thereto; ... *Entitled*, An Act for improving the Police of the City of Dublin," 26 Geo. 3, c. 24 (1786), Irish Statutes. Irish constabulary: "Second Report by the Lords' Select Committee appointed to inquire into the Collection and Payment of Tithes in Ireland," *PP 1831–2* (663), 22:373, ev. of Rev. E. Stopford, Archdeacon of Armagh, 2 Mar. 1832.

145 Police Act: "An Act for the more effectual Prevention of Depredation on the River Thames, and in its Vicinity ...," 39 & 40 Geo. 3, c. 87, which succeeded the "Marine Police Establishment" organized in 1798 by West India Merchants; see *O.E.D.* 7 (N–Poy): "Police," meaning 5. London police, 1829: "An Act for improving the Police in and near the Metropolis," 10 Geo. 4, c. 44. Edwin Chadwick, "Police – Fundamental Principles, Early Notes on, 1830," in Chadwick MS 2, Papers of Edwin Chadwick, D. M. S. Watson Library, University College, University of London.

146 *O.E.D.* 2 (C): "Constable," meaning 5(d); interestingly, if incorrectly, the *O.E.D.* cites as the first usage of "constable" to mean "police constable" or member of a constabulary or police force, a passage from the *Penny Cyclopaedia*

(1836), vol. 13, p. 25, which lists the number of men in each rank in the recently reformed Irish constabulary.

147 "Constables (Ireland) Bill," *Hansard* 7:852−73, 7 June 1822; in the course of debate on the bill, speakers used the terms "police," "gendarmerie," "constables," and "stipendiary magistrates," but the first speaker to use the word "constabulary" was Charles Grant, at c. 872. Robert Peel to Henry Goulburn, 27 Nov. 1822, Peel Papers, BL Add. MS 40328 f. 256, British Library, London. *O.E.D.* 2 (C): "Constabulary," meaning 1, which cites the *Annual Register* (1824), p. 26 ("the [Irish] constabulary bill"), as the first modern usage.

148 On the disputed origins of the slang terms "cop" or "copper," see *O.E.D.* 2 (C): "Cop," "Copper," word entry 4. Theories range from "constable on patrol," to the police uniform's copper buttons, to word derivations from the corrupted Old English *cop, copp* (top, summit; hence, head or skull [-crusher]) and the unlikely *capare*, Latin, "to seize." The term may be a shortening from "escop," Victorian lower-class slang for policeman; "escop" may, in turn, derive from the Spanish word *escopeta*, a type of musket (*O.E.D.* 3 [D−E]: "Escopette"). "Pig," the word employed by many American youth to describe police in the 1960s, was applied to London policemen (Bow Street Runners) as early as 1812 (*O.E.D.* 7 [N−Poy]: "Pig," meaning 6, *slang*, citing J. H. Vaux, *Flash Dictionary*, 1812). Other colloquialisms for Peel's police included "crusher," "raw lobster" and "blue devil" (from the uniform's color), and "miltonian." The last term was a reference to the fact that the seventeenth-century poet John Milton had lived near the site of what from 1829 on was Metropolitan Police headquarters. Peel himself, when Under-Secretary for War and Colonies (1810−12), lived in a town house in Little Scotland Yard. See Kellow Chesney, *The Anti-Society: An Account of the Victorian Underworld* (Boston: Gambit, 1970), glossary, pp. 377−84; Douglas G. Browne, *The Rise of Scotland Yard: A History of the Metropolitan Police* (London: G. G. Harrap & Co., 1956), pp. 79−80; Norman Gash, *Mr. Secretary Peel: The Life of Sir Robert Peel to 1830* (Cambridge, Mass.: Harvard University Press, 1961), pp. 79, 116.

149 César de Saussure, *A Foreign View of England* ... (1725, tr. 1902), pp. 178−9, and J. W. von Archenholz, *A Picture of England* (1787, tr. 1790), pp. 206, 274−5, both quoted in Radzinowicz, *ECL*, 1:712, 714. Dijon: Stuart Andrews, *Eighteenth-Century Europe: The 1680s to 1815* (London: Longmans, 1965), p. 250.

150 Esther Moir, *Justice of the Peace*, pp. 10 (quotation), 120; David Roberts, *Victorian Origins of the British Welfare State* (New Haven, Conn.: Yale University Press, 1960), ch. 1; M. S. Anderson, *Europe in the Eighteenth Century 1713−1783* (New York: Holt, Rinehart and Winston, 1961), chs. 5, 6.

151 Samuel E. Finer, "State- and Nation-Building in Europe: The Role of the Military," in Charles Tilly, ed., *The Formation of National States in Western Europe* (Princeton, N.J.: Princeton University Press, 1975), p. 109.

152 Alan Williams, *The Police of Paris 1718−1789* (Baton Rouge: Louisiana State University Press, 1979), chs. 4−7. J. B. Le Blanc, *Letters on the English and French Nations*, 2 vols. (1737, tr. 1747), 2:297; P. M. Gaston, duc de Lévis, *L'angleterre au commencement du dix-neuvième siècle* (1814), p. 35; M. Rubichon, *De l'angleterre*, (1811), p. 350: "Tout ce que je puis observer est que la gloire de n'avoir point de police, paroit plus facile à acquérir, que la gloire d'en trouver une bonne." These French visitors are quoted in Radzinowicz, *ECL*, 1:725, 725 n. 56.

153 Sir William Mildmay, *The Police of France* (London: E. Owen and T. Harrison, 1763), pp. vi, 46, 52−5, 58, 61, 138.

154 W. L. Melville Lee, *A History of Police in England* (London: Methuen, 1901; repr., Montclair, N. J.: Patterson Smith, 1971), pp. 124−31; Browne, *Scotland Yard*, pp. 19−20; Critchley, *Conquest*, pp. 57−8; and David Rannie, "Cromwell's Major-Generals," *E.H.R.* 10 (July 1895): 471−506, quotation on p. 500. See also Lois G. Schwoerer, *"No Standing Armies!" The Anti-army Ideology in*

Seventeenth-Century England (Baltimore: Johns Hopkins University Press, 1974).

155 Rannie, "Cromwell's Major-Generals," pp. 478–93, 503–6. The vote in January 1657, even in Cromwell's stacked, shrunken Parliament, was 124–88 to abolish the force. "Memories": Browne, *Scotland Yard*, p. 20.

156 T. A. Critchley, *A History of Police in England and Wales*, 2d ed. (London: Constable, 1967; rev. 2d ed., Montclair, N.J.: Patterson Smith, 1972), p. 24 (quotation); 13 & 14 Charles 2, c. 12; Webb, *Parish and County*, pp. 291–2, 491–502.

157 Trotter, *Country Parish*, pp. 84–98, 106–8; Webb, *Parish and County*, pp. 466–71. Quotations are from Blackstone, *Commentaries*, 3d ed., 1:356–7.

158 *Much Ado about Nothing*, Act 3, Scene 3, ll. 22–81; Critchley, *Police*, p. 19 (quotation). See also Melville Lee, *History of Police*, pp. 181–6, 211–14; Webb, *Parish and County*, pp. 466, 471.

159 Samaha, *Law and Order*, p. 87. An early revisionist was Trotter, *Country Parish* (1919), pp. 115–17. Recent revisionist works are Joan Kent, "The English Village Constable, 1580–1642: The Nature and Dilemmas of the Office," *J. Br. Studies* 20, No. 2 (Spring 1981):26–49; Samaha, *Law and Order*, pp. 84–8; Macfarlane, *Justice and the Mare's Ale*, pp. 43–6; Keith Wrightson, "Two Concepts of Order: Justices, Constables, and Jurymen in Seventeenth-Century England," in Brewer and Styles, eds., *Ungovernable People*, pp. 27–31, and Wrightson, *English Society 1580–1680*, pp. 157–9, 165–6; J. A. Sharpe, "Crime and Delinquency in an Essex Parish, 1600–1640," in Cockburn, ed., *Crime in England*, pp. 93–6. Much work remains to be done on the post-1700 period; for a good beginning, see Brewer, "Law and Disorder," pp. 24–7, and Philips, *Crime and Authority*, pp. 59–64, 87. For an extensive bibliography on constables, 1500–1800, see Kent, "Village Constable," p. 27 n. 1.

160 Critchley, *Police*, pp. 25–7; George, *London Life*, pp. 99–103.

161 Quotations, respectively, are from Kent, "Village Constable," p. 46, and Wrightson, "Two Concepts of Order," pp. 45–6.

162 Critchley, *Police*, p. 27.

163 5 Edw. 4, c. 5 (1465); 10 Henry 7, c. 9 (1495).

164 See Boyle, "Police in Ireland Before the Union: I," *The Irish Jurist*, new series, 7 (1972):117–23; and Séamus Breathnach, *The Irish Police from Earliest Times to the Present Day* (Dublin: Anvil Books, 1974), pp. 11–18.

165 10 & 11 Charles 1, c. 13 (1634); 7 William 3, c. 21 (1695).

166 7 Geo. 2, c. 12 s. 3 (1733), amended by 23 Geo. 2, c. 14 s. 3 (1749) and continued by 13 & 14 Geo. 3, c. 32 s. 24 (1773–4).

167 2 Geo. 1, c. 10 (1715); 23 Geo. 2, c. 14 (1749). By 1 Geo. 2, c. 13 (1727), the number of constables was to be proportionate to the size of the parish.

168 6 Geo. 1, c. 10 (1719). Watchmen were appointed by the Protestant constables; Catholics might serve, though (by sec. 4) they were specially barred from service in times of tumult or danger.

169 The Act 13 & 14 Geo. 3, c. 32 s. 24 (1773–4) applied to all counties except Dublin; it was amended by 23 & 24 Geo. 3, c. 42 ss. 4, 23 (1783–4) and extended to County Dublin by 26 Geo. 3, c. 14 s. 37 (1786).

170 "S[ackville]. H[amilton].," Civil Under-Secretary, Dublin Castle, "Thoughts on the Police of Ireland," 13 Feb. 1786, Bolton MS 15928 ff. 13–16; and Bolton MSS 15933 (3), 15941 (8). "Useless": *Parl. Reg.* 7:470, speech of John Hely-Hutchinson, 5 Apr. 1787.

171 The 1787 police, which were established in only four counties, replaced the existing baronial subconstables. By the 1792 act, 32 Geo. 3, c. 16, baronial constables were appointed (not more than eight in each barony) in fifteen counties "in lieu of barony constables by former acts."

172 Francis Sheppard, *London 1808–1870: The Infernal Wen* (Berkeley and Los Angeles: University of California Press, 1971), pp. 23–9, quotations on pp.

28–9; George, *London Life*, pp. 8–10, 99–103; George Rudé, *Hanoverian London 1714–1808* (Berkeley and Los Angeles: University of California Press, 1971), pp. 130–8; Webbs, *Parish and County*, pp. 170–276.

173 Patrick Colquhoun, *A Treatise on the Police of the Metropolis*, 5th ed. (London: H. Fry, 1797), p. 213; Sir Walter Besant, *London in the Eighteenth Century* (London: A. & C. Black, 1902), pp. 515–18; Radzinowicz, *ECL*, 2:171, 176 n. 21, 181–6, 277–8, 500–3.

174 On constables, see 29 Geo. 2, c. 25 (1755) and 31 Geo. 2, c. 17 (1757); on the nightwatch, 8 Geo. 2, c. 15 (1735) and 14 Geo. 3, c. 90 (1774). Melville Lee, *History of Police*, pp. 159–64; Sidney and Beatrice Webb, *English Local Government from the Revolution to the Municipal Corporations Act: The Manor and the Borough* (London: Longmans, Green, 1908), pp. 212–31; George, *London Life*, pp. 99–100, 325 n. 17, 351–2; Radzinowicz, *ECL*, 2:80–2, 186–8, 305.

175 City population: George, *London Life*, p. 329; Radzinowicz, *ECL*, 2:174. Police: Webb, *Manor and Borough*, pp. 493, 579, 609–14, 688–9; Radzinowicz, *ECL*, 2:171, 179–81, 282–4, 492–9, 532–4. See also Donald Rumbelow, *I Spy Blue: Police and Crime in the City of London from Elizabeth I to Victoria* (London: Macmillan, 1971).

176 Webb, *Manor and Borough*, pp. 569–692, quotations on pp. 628, 656, 685; Sheppard, *Infernal Wen*, pp. 19–22. On the origins of City Radicalism, see De Krey, "Political Radicalism," pp. 585–617.

177 Radzinowicz, *ECL*, 4:171, 206; Critchley, *Police*, p. 56.

178 Patrick Pringle, *Hue and Cry: The Birth of the British Police* (London: Museum Press, 1955), pp. 59–76.

179 See, e.g., Percy Fitzgerald, *Chronicles of Bow Street Police-Office, with an Account of the Magistrates, 'Runners,' and Police . . .*, 2 vols. (London: Chapman and Hall, 1888; repr. in one volume, introduction by A. Babington, Montclair, N.J.: Patterson Smith, 1972); Melville Lee, *History of Police* (1901), ch. 8; Ronald Leslie-Melville, *The Life and Work of Sir John Fielding* (London: L. Williams, 1934); Radzinowicz, *ECL* (1948, 1956), 1:399–424, 3:31–68; F. H. Dudden, *Henry Fielding: His Life, Works, and Times*, 2 vols. (Oxford: Clarendon Press, 1952); Pringle, *Hue and Cry* (1955), pp. 77–113 and chs. 7–12, and *Henry and Sir John Fielding: The Thief-Catchers* (London: Dennis Dobson, 1968); Browne, *Scotland Yard* (1956), ch. 3; Critchley, *Police* (1967, 2d ed. 1972), pp. 20, 32–4; Anthony Babington, *A House in Bow Street: Crime and the Magistracy in London, 1740–1801* (London: McDonald, 1969); and Jonathan Rubinstein, "Henry and John Fielding," in Philip John Stead, ed., *Pioneers in Policing* (Montclair, N.J.: Patterson Smith, 1977), ch. 2.

180 Henry Fielding, *An Enquiry into the Causes of the Late Increase of Robbers* (1751), quoted in Critchley, *Conquest*, p. 69. On the Strand Riots, see H. Fielding, "Case of Bosavern Penlez," in Henley, ed., *Works*, 13:273–88. See also Pringle, *Hue and Cry*, pp. 81–7, 99, 105; and "Abstract of Sir John Fielding's Plan of Police," c. 1761–3, in Liverpool Papers, BL Add. MS 38334 ff. 75–9, British Library, London, and reprinted in Radzinowicz, *ECL*, 3:477–9.

181 J. Fielding, *Account of . . . a Police set on Foot by . . . the Duke of Newcastle in the Year 1753 . . .* (1758); Browne, *Scotland Yard*, pp. 27–8; Radzinowicz, *ECL*, 3:54–8; and Sheppard, *Infernal Wen*, p. 33 (quotation).

182 Pringle, *Hue and Cry*, pp. 165–8; Browne, *Scotland Yard*, p. 31; Radzinowicz, *ECL*, 3:58–62.

183 Pringle, *Hue and Cry*, pp. 163–4; and Radzinowicz, *ECL*, 2:423, 519 n. 40; 3:62 n. 16, 135–6. Browne, *Scotland Yard*, p. 31, gives no date, though from his context he implies c. 1760–70. J. J. Tobias, *Crime and Police in England 1700–1900* (New York: St. Martin's Press, 1979), p. 39, says "about 1782." Critchley, *Police*, does not mention the Foot Patrol. Melville Lee, the first modern police historian, gives no dates, but his panegyric on the reforms is typical of the older

historiography. Arguing, contrary to modern scholars, that the Foot Patrol predated the Horse Patrol, he states that the "great success" of that "valuable and far-reaching" reform, the creation of a Foot Patrol, led Fielding "a few years later" to establish a Horse Patrol, which, "though consisting only of eight men, . . . afforded a better state of security." Lee does not mention that this Horse Patrol was soon discontinued; on the contrary, the success of both patrols was "prompt and abiding." *History of Police*, pp. 156–7.

184 Pringle, *Hue and Cry*, p. 198; Browne, *Scotland Yard*, p. 43; Radzinowicz, *ECL*, 3:136. See "Twenty-Eighth Report from the Select Committee on Finance . . ., Police . . .," 1798, printed in *PP 1810* (348), 4:480–2.

185 Warburton, *History of Dublin*, 1:451, 454–7; Constantia Maxwell, *Dublin under the Georges, 1714–1830* (London: Faber and Faber, 1956), pp. 138–9, and visitors' impressions quoted on pp. 303 n. 2, 306 n. 1, 307–8.

186 The authors of a city history in 1818 noted the contrast to the London Corporation. The Dublin Lord Mayor's residence was "the most unsightly edifice in Dawson Street," and the City Assembly House, where the Corporation met, was "equally mean." Warburton, *History of Dublin*, 2:1064.

187 Besides these five, the guilds represented smiths, bakers, carpenters, saddlers, weavers, cutlers-painters-stationers, barbers, cooks, tanners, tallow-chandlers, glovers and skinners, sheermen and dyers, coopers, felt makers, bricklayers, hosiers, curriers, joiners, and apothecaries. Warburton, *History of Dublin*, 2:1064. Like the City Corporation, the guilds were housed in undistinguished physical surroundings. Only six of the twenty-five guilds had their own meeting halls; the rest rented various rooms in the city.

188 Warburton, *History of Dublin*, 1:214–16, 2:1063–7; John McGregor, *New Picture of Dublin* (Dublin: Johnston and Deas, 1821), pp. 159–61; Maxwell, *Dublin*, p. 72 (quotation).

189 Boyle, "Police in Ireland: I," pp. 121–2; Breathnach, *Irish Police*, pp. 20–1. The most important acts are 6 Geo. 1, c. 10 (1719); 8 Geo. 1, c. 10 (1721); 10 Geo. 1, c. 3 (1723); 3 Geo. 2, c. 13 (1729); 33 Geo. 2, c. 16 (1759); and 5 Geo. 3, c. 22 (1765).

190 17 & 18 Geo. 3, c. 43; "State of the Watch in Dublin, 1784," Bolton MSS 15926 (1, 3) and 15927 (1).

CHAPTER 3. A NEW IDEA: THE CONTROVERSY OVER POLICE

1 See Christopher Hibbert, *The Roots of Evil: A Social History of Crime and Punishment* (Harmondsworth: Penguin Books, 1966, orig. publ. 1963), pp. 58–66.

2 J. Steven Watson, *The Reign of George III, 1760–1815* (Oxford: Clarendon Press, 1960), pp. 143 ("hag-ridden"), 213–14, 232. On the links between Irish and English Reform movements, see the detailed memorandum, unsigned and undated (1831?), "Associations in England and Ireland from 1779 to 1783," Political Unions, No. 1, in Earl Grey Papers, Department of Palaeography & Diplomatic, University of Durham. Note John Adams's comment on the makeup of the crowd fired upon in the "Boston Massacre" of 1770: "A motley rabble of saucy boys, negroes and molattoes [sic], Irish teagues [Catholics], and out landish jack tarrs [British merchant seamen]," quoted in Jesse Lemisch, "Jack Tar in the Streets: Merchant Seamen in the Politics of Revolutionary America," *William and Mary Quarterly* 25 (1968):399.

3 See P. D. H. Smyth, "The Volunteers and Parliament, 1779–84," in Thomas Bartlett and D. W. Hayton, eds., *Penal Era and Golden Age: Essays in Irish History, 1690–1800* (Belfast: Ulster Historical Foundation, 1979), pp. 113–36; and John P. Reid, *In a Defiant Stance: The Conditions of Law in Massachusetts Bay, the Irish Comparison, and the Coming of the American Revolution* (University Park: Pennsylvania State University Press, 1977).

4 Steven Watson, *George III*, p. 210. The bill as a recruiting device is discussed in Christopher Hibbert, *King Mob: The Story of Lord George Gordon and the Riots of 1780* (London: Longmans, Green, 1958), pp. 17−19; and Robert Kent Donovan, "The Military Origins of the Roman Catholic Relief Programme of 1778," *Hist. Jour.* 28 (Mar. 1985):79−102. Recruits now took an oath to the Crown that was stripped of Protestant references. But Catholic education, office holding, arms possession, and the saying of mass remained illegal. During the riots, the Government would circulate handbills explaining the minor nature of the concessions; see SP 37/21/144, State Papers, Domestic, George III, PRO, London.

5 The characterization of Gordon is in T. A. Critchley, *A History of Police in England and Wales*, 2d ed. (Montclair, N.J.: Patterson Smith, 1972), p. 82; "petition": Dublin *Freeman's Journal* [hereafter, *FJ*], 6/8 June 1780.

6 George Rudé, "The Gordon Riots: A Study of the Rioters and their Victims," *Transactions of the Royal Historical Society*, 5th ser., 6 (1956):111; and Rudé, *The Crowd in History: A Study of Popular Disturbances in France and England, 1730−1848* (New York: Wiley, 1964), p. 62. His analysis is based on subsequent claims for property damage; Rudé himself states that shopkeepers, publicans, and "gentlemen" put in virtually all of the claims ("Gordon Riots," pp. 109−11). Was Langdell's distillery attacked because Langdell was Catholic, or rich, or because there were on the distillery's premises some 350 tons of spirits? "Pillage": M. Dorothy George, *London Life in the Eighteenth Century* (New York: Harper & Row, 1965, orig. publ. 1925), p. 119.

7 "Irish": evidence of Susannah Clark, 28 June 1780, quoted in George, *London*, p. 119; and "nine-tenths": Critchley, *Police*, p. 85. On the riots of 1780, see W. E. H. Lecky, *A History of England in the Eighteenth Century*, 8 vols. (London: Longmans, Green, 1901−3, orig. publ. 1878−90), 4:308−26; J. Paul De Castro, *The Gordon Riots* (London: H. Milford, 1926); Hibbert, *King Mob* (1958); and T. A. Critchley, *The Conquest of Violence: Order and Liberty in Britain* (New York: Schocken Books, 1970), pp. 81−90. See also Charles Dickens's novel *Barnaby Rudge* (1841) for a vivid re-creation of the antipopery riots.

8 Lord George Gordon was charged with high treason and acquitted. Figures are in Rudé, *Crowd*, p. 59, and "Gordon Riots," pp. 99−106; and Hibbert, *King Mob*, p. 131 n. 1. The death toll, still disputed, ranges from 285 (Rudé, "Gordon Riots," p. 99), the figure officially acknowledged by the Government, to "at least 700" and even as high as 850 (Hibbert, *Roots of Evil*, p. 108, and Hibbert, *King Mob*, p. 131 n. 1, respectively).

9 *Faulkner's Dublin Journal* [hereafter, *FDJ*], 15/17 June 1780 and *FJ*, **15/17 June** 1780, respectively. "Rabble": *The Parliamentary History of England, from the Earliest Period to the Year 1803* [hereafter, *PH*], 36 vols. (London: T. C. Hansard, Peterborough Court, Fleet Street, 1806−20), 21:700, speech of Edmund Burke, 19 June 1780; and "French": Allan Ramsay, *Observations upon the Riot Act, with an Attempt towards the Amendment of it* (London: T. Cadell, 1781), p. 1.

10 "English tradesman": *FJ*, 15/17 June 1780. The *Freeman's Journal*'s view has been restated by Rudé, who notes that of 110 persons arrested for whom occupations were known, 76 were wage earners and 22 were shopkeepers and craftsmen ("Gordon Riots," pp. 102−6). Recent research has challenged Rudé's sharp distinction between artisans and laborers; see Peter Linebaugh, "Eighteenth-Century Crime, Popular Movements, and Social Control," *Bulletin of the Society for the Study of Labour History* 25 (1972):11−15. "Poorer followers": G. D. H. Cole and Raymond Postgate, *The Common People 1746−1946*, 4th ed. (London: Methuen, 1964, orig. publ. 1938), pp. 107−8.

11 Rudé, *Crowd*, pp. 52−5, and his article, "'Mother Gin' and the London Riots of 1736," *Guildhall Miscellany* 1 (1959):53−62, reprinted in Rudé, *Paris and London in the Eighteenth Century: Studies in Popular Protest* (New York: Viking, 1971), pp. 201−21; George, *London Life*, pp. 118−19; and Nicholas Rogers, "Popular

Protest in Early Hanoverian London," *Past & Present* 79 (May 1978):74−9.

12 *FJ*, 15/17 June 1780.

13 WO 34/103/19, PRO, London; *PH* 21:671; Hibbert, *King Mob*, pp. 43, 49−50, 75.

14 Constable John Bradley, quoted in Rudé, "Riots," p. 96 n. 2. "Orderly": the Government's view in a memorandum of 13 June 1780, SP 37/20/262. The famous watchman story that appears in Lecky, *Eng.*, 4:320, is retold in Leon Radzinowicz, *A History of English Criminal Law and its Administration from 1750* [hereafter, *ECL*], 4 vols. (London: Stevens & Sons, 1948−68), 3:90; and in Critchley, *Conquest*, p. 86, and *Police*, pp. 35−6.

15 Quotation: Jenkinson to Stormont, 6 June 1780, WO 4/110/266−7. SP 37/20/91, 95; WO 34/103/14; Hibbert, *King Mob*, p. 79. Trial of *Rex v. Kennett*, 1781, 5 Car. & P. 282. For further details of troop movements, see De Castro, *Gordon Riots*, pp. 263−5; and Tony Hayter, *The Army and the Crowd in Mid-Georgian England* (Totowa, N.J.: Rowman and Littlefield, 1978), pp. 147−61.

16 The Government's tactics: in SP 37/21/44, 85, 88. "Moderate Men": SP 37/20/226. The associations are discussed in SP 37/20/238, 242 and SP 37/21/24, 137; WO 4/110/270; WO 34/234/37−8, 48, 62−7, 89, 94−6, 103; and *PH* 21:691−2, 727.

17 Drummond to Stormont, 12 June 1780, SP 37/20/226; Critchley, *Conquest*, p. 86; and Cole and Postgate, *Common People*, p. 108.

18 Privy Council, WO 34/234/36; and Hibbert, *King Mob*, pp. 91−2, 112, 116.

19 WO 34/234/111, 119; and SP 37/21/410. The "Guard House" at Buckingham House − known as Buckingham Palace after about 1825 − was "built at the period of the Riots of 1780." Duke of Wellington to Henry Goulburn, 14 Sept. 1828, in Goulburn II/12, Goulburn Papers, Surrey Record Office, Kingston-on-Thames. Nowadays London tourists are calmly informed by the *Blue Guide* that "since the Gordon Riots (1780) the Bank [of England] has been protected nightly by a picket mounted by the Brigade of Guards." *Blue Guide to London*, 9th ed., S. Rossiter, ed. (London: Benn, 1965), p. 140.

20 On the tradition of manipulation of mobs, see Lucy Sutherland, "The City of London in Eighteenth-Century Politics," in Richard Pares and A. J. P. Taylor, eds., *Essays Presented to Sir Lewis Namier* (London: Macmillan, 1956), pp. 49−74; George Rudé, "Collusion and Convergence in Eighteenth-Century English Political Action," *Government and Opposition* 1 (1966):511−28, reprinted in Rudé, *Paris and London*, pp. 319−40; James Fitts, "Newcastle's Mob," *Albion* 5 (1973): 41−4; Geoffrey Holmes, "The Sacheverell Riots: The Crowd and the Church in Early Eighteenth-Century London," *Past & Present* 72 (Aug. 1976):55−85; and Rogers, "Popular Protest in Early Hanoverian London," pp. 70−100.

21 Steven Watson, *George III*, pp. 246, 576, 578−80.

22 Quoted in Hibbert, *King Mob*, p. 121.

23 "Turkey," Burke, and Fox: quoted in Hibbert, *King Mob*, pp. 87, 113−14, 121. Mansfield and Richmond, in *PH* 21:698, 733, 19 and 21 June 1780.

24 Allan Ramsay, *Observations upon the Riot Act* (1781), written 10 July 1780. [B. Turner,] *A Plan for ... the Militia of London ...* (London, 1782). See also Anon. [attributed to G. Sharp], *Tracts concerning the Ancient and Only True Legal Means of National Defence, by a Free Militia* (London, 1781). "Dangerous": Granville Sharp, *Proposals and Remarks for the Improvement of the City-Militia, and for Watch and Ward* (London, 1782), pp. 2−3. On all of these proposals, see Radzinowicz, *ECL*, 3:96−100.

25 Associations: Jonas Hanway, *The Citizen's Monitor: Shewing the Necessity of a Salutary Police ... with Observations on the Late Tumults ...* (London: Dodsley, 1780), pp. iv, xxii−xxviii; Sir William Jones, *An Inquiry into the Legal Mode of Suppressing Riots* (London: C. Dilly, 1780), pp. 35−9, reprinted in 1819 (London: J. Fairburn) on the occasion of Peterloo; and Sir William Blizard

Desultory Reflections on Police (London: C. Dilly, 1785), pp. 81–2. On the Government's reaction, see *PH* 21:1317; and Radzinowicz, *ECL*, 3:92–3. On Hanway, a man of many interests, see John H. Hutchins, *Jonas Hanway, 1712–1786* (New York: Macmillan, 1940).

26 *PH* 21:1305–7, 25 Mar. 1781. Sir William Petty (1737–1805), 2d Earl of Shelburne, 1st Marquess of Lansdowne: Secretary of State, Southern Department, 1766–8; Secretary of State for Home and Colonial Affairs, 1782; Prime Minister, 1782–3. Shelburne was the great-grandson of Sir William Petty, the political economist and cartographer in charge of the Down Survey in Ireland at the time of the Cromwellian settlement. *Dictionary of National Biography* [hereafter, *DNB*], 15:1005–13. Shelburne spent part of his boyhood in Munster on the estates of his grandfather, the Earl of Kerry. The Shelburne estates were among the largest in Ireland; in 1780 the rental income to Lord and Lady Shelburne from their Irish lands was reported to be £33,000 a year. Arthur Young, *A Tour of Ireland* ... (London: T. Cadell, 1780), Pt. 2, p. 57. On Shelburne's Irish connection and his role in the Gordon Riots, see Lord Edmund Fitzmaurice, *The Life of William, Earl of Shelburne, afterwards First Marquess of Lansdowne*, 3 vols. (London: Macmillan, 1875–6), 2:81–117, 3:83–90, respectively.

27 *PH* 21:1305–7, 1317, 1322, 1325, 5 Mar. 1781. Sheridan would later oppose the Middlesex Justices Act of 1792, which established government-controlled, paid police magistrates in London. Radzinowicz, *ECL*, 3:128.

28 *PH* 25:888–9, 911, 23 and 29 June 1785; and Reeves to Sydney, 18 July 1786, in HO 42/9. "A Bill for the further Prevention of Crimes, and for the more speedy Detection and Punishment of Offenders against the Peace, in the Cities of *London* and *Westminster*, the Borough of *Southwark*, and certain Parts adjacent to them." Besides the MS draft in the Library of the House of Commons, there are printed copies in the British Library, one in the stacks (816.1.5 (43)) and another in the State Paper Room (see House of Commons Bills, 25 Geo. 3, pp. 477–507, quotations at sections 3–7, 58). The bill has also been recently reprinted in *House of Commons Sessional Papers of the Eighteenth Century*, ed. Sheila Lambert, 145 vols. (Wilmington, Del.: Scholarly Resources, Inc., 1975), 46:503–34.

29 "A Bill for the further Prevention of Crimes," 25 Geo. 3, sections 23–44; and Radzinowicz, *ECL*, 3:110–17.

30 *PH* 25:894–8 ("rashly," Lord Eden, c. 898), 899 (Johnstone), 23 June 1785. The bill was introduced with only forty Members present.

31 Reeves to Sydney, 29 June 1785, and Sydney to Lord Mayor, "July" 1785, in HO 42/7. Pitt: *PH* 25:906–7, 29 June 1785. Charles Reith, *The Police Idea: Its History and Evolution in the Eighteenth Century and After* (London: Oxford University Press, 1938), p. 97, blames Pitt for making no attempt to brook the opposition.

32 *Morning Chronicle*, 1 July 1785; *Daily Universal Register* [later *The Times*], 29 June 1785. Townsend is so described in Reeves to Sydney, 29 June 1785, in HO 42/7; and his speech in *PH* 25:900–6. On the Radical Townsend, textile merchant and former Lord Mayor, who broke with the flamboyant Wilkes in the early 1770s, see Rudé, *Paris and London*, pp. 258, 260 n. 174, 306, 337–8, and *Wilkes and Liberty* (Oxford: Clarendon Press, 1962), passim. Sydney to the Lord Mayor, "July" 1785, in HO 42/7. For an extended discussion of the 1785 bill, see Radzinowicz, *ECL*, 3:108–23.

33 For a discussion of the historiography on this transition from London in 1785 to Dublin the following year, see nn. 136 and 137, Chapter 1, this book.

34 *FJ*, 7/9 July 1785. *FDJ*, 28/30 June, and *Volunteer Evening Post* [hereafter, *VEP*], 28–30 June and 2–5 July 1785, which simply printed summaries of the parliamentary debates. The *Freeman's Journal* was at this time the subsidized organ of Dublin Castle. W. J. Fitzpatrick, *Secret Service under Pitt* (London: Longmans, Green, 1892), pp. 118–19, 242 n. 1, 246–9.

35 On the Volunteers, see Lecky, *Ire.*, 2:218–46, 268–72, 282–96; Patrick Rogers,

The Irish Volunteers and Catholic Emancipation (London: Burns, Oates, & Washbourne, 1934), pp. 113−33; and Smyth, "Volunteers and Parliament," pp. 119−32. On the peasant unrest, see James S. Donnelly, Jr., "The Rightboy Movement, 1785−8," *Studia Hib.* 17 & 18 (1977−8):120−202; and R. E. Burns, "Parsons, Priests and People: The Rise of Irish Anti-Clericalism, 1785−1789," *Church History* 31, No. 2 (June 1962):151−63.

36 Edward Gibbon Wakefield, *An Account of Ireland, Statistical and Political*, 2 vols. (London: Longman, Hurst, Rees, Orme and Brown, 1812), 2:805; Constantia Maxwell, *Dublin under the Georges* (London: Faber and Faber, 1956), p. 158.

37 *The Parliamentary Register, or the History of the Proceedings and Debates of the House of Commons in Ireland* [hereafter cited as *Parl. Reg.*], 15 vols. (Dublin, 1784−95), 9:407, 25 Apr. 1789; W. E. H. Lecky, *A History of Ireland in the Eighteenth Century*, 5 vols. (London: Longmans, Green, 1892; repr., St. Clair Shores, Mich.: Scholarly Press, 1972), 2:392−6; and James Anthony Froude, *The English in Ireland in the Eighteenth Century*, 3 vols. (London: Longmans, Green, 1872−4), 2:241−2, 395−6, 445. See also Henry Grattan, *Memoirs of the Life and Times of the Rt. Hon. Henry Grattan, by His Son, Henry Grattan, Esq., M.P.*, 5 vols. (London: H. Colburn, 1839−46), 3:116−50, 204−9; and Rogers, *Volunteers*, pp. 174−88. For a perceptive historical review of the Irish Volunteer crisis of 1778−83, see "Political Unions: Remarks in Answer to the Duke of Wellington's Memorandum," unsigned and undated [1831?], Political Unions, No. 15, in Earl Grey Papers.

38 On Irish tarring and feathering, see Irish Chief Secretary Thomas Orde to Prime Minister William Pitt, 16 Aug. 1784, PRO 30/8/329/100, the Papers of William Pitt, 2d Earl of Chatham, PRO, London; Froude, *English in Ireland*, 2:408−12; Kevin Boyle, "Police in Ireland Before the Union: II," *Irish Jurist*, new series, 8 (1973):98. On this practice, which originated in America, see Pauline Maier, *From Resistance to Revolution: Colonial Radicals and the Development of American Opposition to Britain, 1765−1776* (New York: Alfred A. Knopf, 1972), pp. 7−9, 273−5. Houghing was made a capital offense by 23 & 24 Geo. 3, c. 56 (Ire.); see also Froude, *English in Ireland*, 2:267, 395−7; Lecky, *Ire.*, 2:392; and *Parl. Reg.* 2:420, 8 Mar. 1784. On houghing in early-eighteenth-century Ireland, see Lecky, *Ire.*, 1:222−3, 361−7.

39 Maxwell, *Dublin under the Georges*, pp. 150−1; and PRO 30/8/329/99−103, 109−10.

40 Orde to Pitt, 2 Aug. 1784, PRO 30/8/329/86; and Rutland to Pitt, 15 Aug. 1784, in *Correspondence between the Right Hon. William Pitt and Charles, Duke of Rutland, Lord Lieutenant of Ireland, 1781−87* (London: A. Spottiswoode, 1842, repr. 1890), p. 37.

41 Orde to Pitt, 25, 28 Aug. 1784, PRO 30/8/329/109−10, 118. Censure: *Parl. Reg.* 3:86, 149−50. Volunteers: *Pitt−Rutland Correspondence*, p. 37; and Lecky, *Ire.* 2:396. For a colorful, if unannotated, account of the Castle's spies in Dublin in 1784−6, see Fitzpatrick, *Secret Service*, pp. 218−22, 231−45.

42 *DNB* 12:931−3, 14:1133−5; Fitzpatrick, *Secret Service*, p. 231. Sir Jonah Barrington, *Historic Memoirs of Ireland*, 2 vols. (London: H. Colburn, 1835), 2:219, and *Rise and Fall of the Irish Nation* (Dublin: J. Duffy, 1843), pp. 320−1. On Orde's health, see *Pitt−Rutland Correspondence*, pp. 163, 186−7; and Gt. Brit., Historical MSS Commission, *The Manuscripts of His Grace the Duke of Rutland ... preserved at Belvoir Castle* [hereafter, *Rutland MSS*], 4 vols. (London: Eyre & Spottiswoode, 1888−1905), 3:300, 320.

43 "Besotted," from a parliamentary speech, 15 Aug. 1785, quoted in Froude, *English in Ireland*, 2:444; "awful," the opinion of Thomas Moore, quoted in Alfred J. Webb, *A Compendium of Irish Biography* (Dublin: M. H. Gill & Son, 1878), pp. 195−8; and *DNB* 7:156−9.

44 Webb, *Compendium*, pp. 224−33; *DNB* 8:418−25. See Robert Dunlop, *Life of*

Henry Grattan (London: W. H. Allen, 1889); W. E. H. Lecky, *Leaders of Public Opinion in Ireland*, 2 vols. (London: Longmans, Green, 1912, orig. publ. 1861), Vol. 1, Pt. 2; Stephen Gwynn, *Henry Grattan and his Times* (London: G. G. Harrap & Co., 1939; repr., Freeport, N.Y.: Books for Libraries Press, 1971). A modern biography is much needed.

45 Grattan held government office for only three of his forty-five years in public life. Quotations are from a perceptive recent assessment, R. B. McDowell, *Ireland in the Age of Imperialism and Revolution 1760−1801* (Oxford: Clarendon Press, 1979), pp. 272−4.

46 Quotation, in Webb, *Compendium*, p. 229.

47 *Parl. Reg.* 4:225−38 (Fitzgibbon, 227; Grattan and vote, 238), 14 Feb. 1785; *Rutland MSS*, 3:262; Sir Henry McAnally, *The Irish Militia, 1793−1816: A Social and Military Study* (Dublin: Clonmore and Reynolds, 1949), pp. 5−8; Boyle, "Police in Ireland Before the Union: II," pp. 98−9; and Smyth, "Volunteers and Parliament," p. 135.

48 Lecky, *Ire.*, 2:432−53; and Paul Kelly, "British and Irish Politics in 1785," *E.H.R.* 90 (July 1975):536−63.

49 *Pitt−Rutland Correspondence*, pp. 126−32. Orde to Pitt, 15 Nov. 1785, PRO 30/8/329/250.

50 17 & 18 Geo. 3, c. 43 (1778); Bolton MSS 15926 (1−3), 15927 (1), in the Papers of Thomas Orde, 1st Baron Bolton, NLI, Dublin.

51 See, e.g., 21 & 22 Geo. 3, c. 17 and c. 60; 22 & 23 Geo. 3, c. 52; 26 Geo. 3, c. 61. *Saunders's News-letter* [hereafter, *SNL*], 25 May 1787, complained of "the sullenness or supineness" of the board of paving commissioners, "deaf to the requisition of the inhabitants."

52 Draft of letter to Rutland, "Most Secret & Confidential," 1 Jan. 1786, HO 100/18/5, PRO, London.

53 "Heads of a Plan of police as Executed in London by Sir John Fielding" (1777) and "An Account of the Plan and Establishment of the Public Office in Bow Street" (undated), Bolton MSS 15929 (3) and 15930 (1). The Edinburgh model was suggested by Viscount Ranelagh to Orde, 15 Dec. 1785, Bolton MS 15930 (2). On the heavily pensioned Ranelagh, see John Lodge, *The Peerage of Ireland*, orig. publ. 1754, rev. ed. by M. Archdall, 7 vols. (Dublin: J. Moore, 1789), 4:305; Edith Mary Johnston, *Great Britain and Ireland, 1760−1800: A Study in Political Administration* (Edinburgh: Oliver & Boyd, 1963), p. 267.

54 *SNL*, 7 Nov. 1787, noted of Hamilton that "the frequent indisposition of Mr. Orde left nearly the whole of that department for the last two years of the Rutland administration upon that gentleman."

55 Johnston, *Great Britain and Ireland*, pp. 59−60, 72.

56 "A Sketch of the Police of France," March 1786, Bolton MS 15929 (4). Hamilton concluded his paper with a direct but unacknowledged quotation from Sir William Mildmay, *The Police of France* (London: E. Owen and T. Harrison, 1763), p. 61.

57 "Invalid": Orde to Pitt, 15 Mar. 1786, PRO 30/8/329/273.

58 *Parl. Reg.* 6:327−8, 383, 20 and 25 Mar. 1786; Draft bill "for the better Execution of the Law," Bolton MS 15931 (3); 26 Geo. 3, c. 24 (Ire.), ss. 1−8, 13−17, 42, 61; Lecky, *Ire.*, 2:454.

59 London police bill, 25 Geo. 3 (1785), ss. 6, 9−10, 46−8; and Dublin Police Act, 26 Geo. 3, c. 24 (Ire.) ss. 3, 43.

60 London police bill, 25 Geo. 3, ss. 30−1, 53.

61 London police bill, 25 Geo. 3, ss. 6, 9, 31. Dublin Police Act, 26 Geo. 3, c. 24 (Ire.) ss. 3, 5; *Parl. Reg.* 6:350−1 (Grattan), 367−8 (J. Forbes), 22 and 25 Mar. 1786.

62 London police bill, 25 Geo. 3, ss. 21−2, 38−43, 52, 64−7; Dublin Police Act, 26 Geo. 3, c. 24 (Ire.) ss. 19, 33−41.

63 Police debates in *Parl. Reg.* 6:327−53, 365−86, 394−9, 20, 25, and 28 Mar. 1786.

Fitzgibbon: *Parl. Reg.* 6:341−2, 365; and supporting remarks by Godfrey Greene, John Warburton, Sir Boyle Roche, and John Hely-Hutchinson in ibid., 6:328, 343, 346 ("mischief").

64 *Parl. Reg.* 6:374, 377, 388. Orde to Pitt, 15 Mar. 1786, PRO 30/8/329/271. "Thin": James Stewart, Volunteer, MP for County Tyrone, *Parl. Reg.* 6:327. Also speaking in opposition were Thomas Conolly, MP for County London-derry; Travers Hartley and Grattan, the MPs for the City of Dublin; and Richard Griffith, J. Wolfe, and Sir H. Hartstonge, in ibid., 6:327−31, 347−53. Hour: Griffith and Hartley, ibid., 6:337−8. 20 and 22 March: ibid., 6:331, 353.

65 The arguments were similar, and linked, to those of the American patriots who criticized English "misrule" in North America. See Maier, *From Resistance to Revolution*, pp. 27−48, 162−3, 178−80, 255.

66 Respectively, Griffith and Thomas Burgh, in *Parl. Reg.* 6:338, 372.

67 Ibid., 6:327 ("counties," Sir Edward Newenham), and 330, 340, 349−52 (Grattan). Grattan's views paralleled Sir William Blackstone's doubts about the desirability of a powerful police, "considering what manner of men are for the most part put into these offices." *Commentaries on the Laws of England*, 3d ed., 4 vols. (Oxford: Clarendon Press, 1768), 1:355.

68 *Parl. Reg.* 6:348. The speaker, John Forbes, was best known for his attempts to restrict the pension list. In 1787 he unsuccessfully opposed a government grant of £987 to Sackville Hamilton for a town house in Dublin. Ibid., 7:89−90.

69 Ibid., 6:386, Mr. Francis Hardy; see also the speech of Thomas Conolly, in 6:344−5.

70 Ibid., 6:350, 370.

71 *Dublin Evening Post* [hereafter, *DEP*], 18 and 23 Mar. 1786. See also *DEP*, 30 Mar. and 1 and 13 Apr. 1786, and *SNL*, 23, 24, 30 Mar. 1786.

72 Meetings: *SNL*, 27, 28 Mar. 1786; and *Parl. Reg.* 6:372. Sir Edward Newenham, Volunteer, free trader, and MP for County Dublin, had been the first speaker in Parliament to oppose the bill (*Parl. Reg.* 6:327). At their meeting on 27 March, county freeholders thanked Newenham for his "upright conduct in the senate of the nation"; that evening in Parliament, Fitzgibbon berated Newenham and the petitioners. The Commons rejected the petition by a vote of 188−2. *SNL*, 28 Mar. 1786; *Parl. Reg.* 6:388−9.

73 *Parl. Reg.* 6:374, 377, 398−9.

74 Orde to Sir Evan Nepean, Under-Secretary, Home Office, 30 Mar. 1786, HO 100/18/158; and Orde to Nepean, 31 Mar. 1786, PRO 30/8/329/257−9. The Lords' proceedings are not recorded in the parliamentary debates; see *Faulkner's Dublin Journal*, 6/8 Apr., and *SNL*, 8 Apr. 1786. In London the *Public Advertiser*, 14 Apr., and *Morning Chronicle*, 15 Apr. 1786, printed the minority protest without comment. On the Duke of Leinster, see *DEP*, 13 Mar. 1788 and 18 Oct. 1792; *DNB* 7:151. His son would oppose Peel's police of 1814.

75 *DEP*, 6, 13 Apr. 1786; 26 Geo. 3, c. 24 (Ire.).

76 Five proponents represented counties and thirteen represented boroughs; eight opponents sat for counties and eleven for boroughs.

77 List of Whig Club members, in Grattan, *Memoirs*, 3:432−4. On the Whig Club, see Lecky, *Ire.*, 3:4−5, 20−2.

78 The following table, based wherever possible on a comparison of voting lists, represents the opinions of MPs on a number of issues.

	1786 police proponents		Opponents	
	For	Against	For	Against
Poynings' Law, 1780[a]	4	0	2	6
Parliamentary reform, 1783	5	9	11	6

Free trade, 1785	3	10	19	0
Militia, 1785[a]	6	2	2	6
Pension list reform, 1786[a]	0	6	8	1
Riot Act, 1787	7	0	0	11
Rural police, 1787	9	0	0	15
Tithe reform, 1788[a]	0	6	5	0

[a] In the absence of a voting list, a count has been made based on the content of a Member's speech(es).

Of course, not all police proponents or opponents spoke, voted, or were present at the debates on all of these issues. Analysis based on *Parl. Reg.*, vols. 4−8 (1785−8); *Hibernian Journal* [hereafter, *HJ*], 4 Apr. 1787; Grattan, *Memoirs*, 3:150−4, 316−30, 491−5; Webb, *Compendium*; George O. Sayles, ed., "Contemporary Sketches of Members of the Irish Parliament in 1782," *Proceedings of the Royal Irish Academy*, 56, C (1954):227−86; and Johnston, *Great Britain and Ireland*, pp. 362−8, 399.

79 Orde to Nepean, 30 Mar. 1786, HO 100/18/158−9.
80 See R. R. Palmer, *The Age of the Democratic Revolution: A Political History of Europe and America, 1760−1800*, 2 vols. (Princeton, N.J.: Princeton University Press, 1959−64), 1:45−8, 288−94, 302−6; Thomas Bartlett, "Opposition in Late Eighteenth-Century Ireland: The Case of the Townshend Viceroyalty" [1769−71], *I.H.S.* 22 (Sept. 1981):313−30; and J. C. Beckett, "Anglo-Irish Constitutional Relations in the Later Eighteenth Century," *I.H.S.* 14 (Mar. 1964):20−38.
81 See James S. Donnelly, Jr., "The Rightboy Movement, 1785−8," *Studia Hib.* 17 & 18 (1977−8):120−202.
82 HO 100/18/266−77, 326−9, 387−9; Donnelly, "Rightboy," pp. 152−4, 159−66, 179−85, 201, quotations on pp. 179, 182. Combing newspaper accounts from August 1785 to December 1788, Donnelly discovered only two dozen incidents of Rightboy maimings and three score of woundings, shootings, and firings at persons (p. 183).
83 Donnelly, "Rightboy," pp. 161, 185−91, 199; and *Pitt−Rutland Correspondence*, p. 157. "Torpidity": anonymous letter to *Cork Hibernian Chronicle*, 31 Aug. 1786, quoted in Donnelly, "Rightboy," p. 188. "Capacity": Donnelly, "Rightboy," p. 187.
84 Donnelly, "Rightboy," pp. 193−5. Cf. Froude's claim that in the autumn of 1786 insurgents "were sent in shiploads to Botany Bay" (*English in Ireland*, 2:473). "Insurrection ... plots": Orde to Pitt, 17 Feb. 1787, PRO 30/8/329/290; and two incisive memoranda, 24 Aug. and 21 Sept. 1786, HO 100/18/270−7, 326−9. "Grievance": Pitt to Rutland, 7 Nov. 1786, *Pitt−Rutland Correspondence*, pp. 174−5. Pitt favored some reform of the tithe, but Orde was skeptical. Commutation would "merely take the great pretence for complaint away from rioters." Orde to Pitt, 15 Mar. 1786, PRO 30/8/329/271.
85 Donnelly, "Rightboy," p. 192; Boyle, "Police in Ireland before the Union: II," p. 109 nn. 70−1; Lecky, *Ire.*, 2:456−61; Forfeited Recognizances Act, 27 Geo. 3, c. 32 (Ire.); and Orde to Pitt, 19 Feb. 1787, "secret," PRO 30/8/329/298.
86 English Riot Act: 1 Geo. 1 sess. 2, c. 5. Irish Riot Act: 27 Geo. 3, c. 15 (Ire.) ss. 1−5.
87 27 Geo. 3, c. 15 (Ire.) ss. 6−11.
88 On the chapel clause, see *Parl. Reg.* 7:181−4, 191; Grattan, *Memoirs*, 3:284−5; Lecky, *Ire.*, 2:457; Froude, *English in Ireland*, 2:476. Cf. English Riot Act, 1 Geo. 1 sess. 2, c. 5 s. 4.
89 Orde himself considered it a "long wished for" and "great accession to the

strength of executive Government." Orde to Pitt, 17 Feb. 1787, PRO 30/8/329/289.

90 *Parl. Reg.* 7:62, 184–6, 205–7, Fitzgibbon, 31 Jan., 19 and 20 Feb.; opposition, 7:181–201, 204–10, 214–16, 220–7, 232, 19 and 20 Feb. 1787. "Shudder": ibid., 7:191. The absence of anything resembling treason in Ireland in 1787 was a point frequently made; see ibid., 7:181, 186–9, 192–4, 204, 209–11.

91 Magistrates: ibid., 7:204. Local (the Rightboy counties of Cork, Kerry, Limerick, and Tipperary): ibid., 7:205, 214–16, 226–8, 232. Three of the five opponents represented Ulster constituencies; none represented Munster. Orde stated that the Northern Presbyterians were most vehement against universal application of the bill (PRO 30/8/329/298). Duration: *Parl. Reg.* 7:226–7. Chapel clause: ibid., 7:182; even Froude realized that this clause was inoperable (*English in Ireland*, 2:478).

92 *Parl. Reg.* 7:201, 232. Whig peers' dissent, in *FJ*, 10/13 Mar. 1787.

93 "An Act to prevent tumultuous Risings and Assemblies, and for the more effectual Punishment of Persons guilty of Outrage, Riot and illegal Combination, and of administering and taking unlawful Oaths," 27 Geo. 3, c. 15 (Ire.); and 40 Geo. 3, c. 96 (Ire.) For a discussion of the Riot Act (1787) in Irish law, and suggested ways of implementing it, see the circular from Under-Secretary William Gosset to magistrates at petty sessions, 23 Feb. 1831, Official Papers, Series 2, 588AA/825/4, ISPO, DC.

94 Orde to Pitt, 7 Jan. 1787, "private," PRO 30/8/329/285. *Parl. Reg.* 7:189, 19 Feb. 1787, Mr. Dunn, MP for Randalstown, County Antrim, a seat under the control of John O'Neill (Sayles, "Sketches," p. 234). For Pitt's views on a Union of Britain and Ireland as early as 1784, see *Pitt–Rutland Correspondence*, pp. 43, 52.

95 Orde to Nepean, 24 Feb. 1787, enclosing "A Sketch of a Plan for the reform of Magistracy in this Country," HO 100/20/125–8; Home Secretary Townshend sent a copy of this to John Reeves, author of the 1785 London police bill (HO 100/20/129–32). Bolton MSS 15934 (2) and (3), 15935 (1), and 15936 (2).

96 "Reform of the Magistracy, Lord Carysfort," Bolton MSS 15938 (2), a long and incisive analysis; and Orde to Pitt, 17 Feb. 1787, "secret," PRO 30/8/329/290. On John Joshua Proby, 2d Baron Carysfort, see Lodge, *Peerage of Ireland*, 7:70–1; Johnston, *Great Britain and Ireland*, pp. 402, 405; Sayles, "Sketches," p. 285; *Rutland MSS*, 3:361, 365–6; *DEP*, 8 Dec. 1792; and *Parl. Reg.* 7:466–7.

97 HO 100/18/36, 80; and *Parl. Reg.* 6:329, 337, 340, 343, 347.

98 Orde's abortive proposal, 4 Apr. 1786, in *Parl. Reg.* 6:440–2.

99 Earl of Charlemont to Mr. Halliday, 14 Nov. 1786, in James Caulfeild, 1st Earl of Charlemont, *The Manuscripts and Correspondence of James, First Earl of Charlemont*, [Gt. Brit.] Historical MSS Commission, 2 vols. (London: Eyre & Spottiswoode, 1891–4), 2:43–4. *DEP*, 6 Apr. and 30 Dec. 1786. See also *SNL*, 15 Sept., and *HJ*, 9 Oct. 1786.

100 John Fitzgibbon, *Parl. Reg.* 7:200.

101 *Cork Volunteer Journal*, 12 June 1786. Musgrave's "Hints on Police," in Bolton MS 15933 (3). On Musgrave, see HO 100/18/326–7; Grattan, *Memoirs*, 3:432; Froude, *English in Ireland*, 2:473; Sayles, "Sketches," p. 268; and Donnelly, "Rightboy," p. 198. Lord Hillsborough to Orde, 1 Mar. 1787, Bolton MS 15942 (1); on Hillsborough, see Lodge, *Peerage*, 2:332–4; Sayles, "Sketches," p. 276; and Froude, *English in Ireland*, 2:244, 289.

102 "Reform of Magistracy, Lord Carysfort," n.d. [31 Jan. 1787], Bolton MS 15938 (2); and cover letter, Carysfort to Orde, 1 Feb. 1787, Bolton MS 15938 (3). The county police of 1787 was restricted to Protestants, but Peel's police of 1814 would be open to Catholics.

103 Espinasse to John Lees, 15 Feb., in Lees to S. Hamilton, 23 Feb. 1787, Bolton MS 15939 (5). Blacquière's "Suggestions upon a Plan of General Police" were communicated to Orde, 30 Jan. 1787, Bolton MS 15938 (1). On Blacquière, see

Froude, *English in Ireland*, 2:479–82; Lecky, *Ire.*, 2:130–2; Sayles, "Sketches," p. 236; and Johnston, *Great Britain and Ireland*, pp. 137, 240, 243 n. 1. Blacquière later opposed Grattan's Dublin police bill of 1793, for it would give power to "the turbulent and seditious" (*Parl. Reg.* 13:462–3, 24 June 1793).

104 "A Sketch of the Police of France," by Castle Under-Secretary S. Hamilton, March 1786, Bolton MS 15929 (4).

105 A number of drafts and proposals, unsigned and undated but clearly prepared by Castle officials, are preserved in the Papers of Thomas Orde. See "1787. Hasty Idea of a Plan for Extending the Police upon a Principle similar to that Established in Dublin, throughout the Country of Ireland," Bolton MS 15934 (2); "Idea of a Plan of Proceeding upon the State of the Disturbances in the Southern Parts of this Country," Bolton MS 15934 (3); "Police," 29 Mar. 1787, Bolton MS 15940 (2); and "Mem$^{n.}$ of arrangements for execution of Police Act, Jany 1787," Bolton MS 15936 (3).

106 Ibid.; and 27 Geo. 3, c. 40 ss. 1–5. An early printed draft of the 1787 bill, with handwritten corrections, is in HO 100/20/323–7 and Bolton MS 15940 (3).

107 On plans for magistracy reform, see "Magistracy: Hints for an Act for the better execution of the Law," Bolton MS 15934 (1); "1787. Scheme for a Magistracy Act – Plans and Observations for better execution of Police Act," Bolton MS 15935 (1); "Heads of a Plan for the better execution of the Laws by means of an improved Magistracy and more frequent Sessions of the Peace," Bolton MS 15935 (2); and "Lord Chancellor. Scheme for a Magistracy Bill," Bolton MS 15936 (2). See also 27 Geo. 3, c. 40 ss. 1–2, 9–18.

108 *Parl. Reg.* 7:432, 30 Mar. 1787.

109 Quotation is Richard Griffith, Jr., ibid., 7:445. Motions to delay were lost by votes of 81–28 and 97–39 (ibid., 7:440, 451); petitions rejected, ibid., 7:506–7. The debates on the bill are in ibid., 7:431–40, 445–53, 461–76, 477, 480, 519, 30 Mar., 2, 5, 7, and 9 Apr., and 21 May 1787 (royal assent).

110 For Conolly's remarks, see ibid., 7:22, 438, 446–7, 452, 461, 474. Earlier, on 19 February, in answer to a question from Conolly, Fitzgibbon had denied knowledge of any "general police bill ... but through the medium of a newspaper" (see n. 100, this chapter); now, on 2 April, in reply to Conolly's fears about "an armed Maréchaussée," Fitzgibbon claimed that the Government's proposal "does not tend to establish one" (ibid., 7:447). On Conolly, see Sayles, "Sketches," p. 256; Johnston, *Great Britain and Ireland*, pp. 221–2; and *DNB* 4:954–5.

111 "Presbyterian": Orde to Pitt, 17 Feb. 1787, PRO 30/8/329/298. Calculation based on "An Alphabetical List of the Members, with their town and country residences," *Parl. Reg.* 4 (1785):ix–xiv.

112 *Parl. Reg.* 7:439 (Todd Jones), 447, 461 (Conolly). A barrister and writer, as well as an MP, Todd Jones pushed for parliamentary reform and Catholic concessions. After 1792, he lived in England for ten years. In 1802 he fought a duel with Sir Richard Musgrave. Shortly after his return to Ireland, on the day of Emmet's Rising, he was arrested on charges of high treason and not released until October 1805. R. B. McDowell gives little credence to Fitzpatrick's claim that Todd Jones was Emmet's co-conspirator in planning the abortive 1803 rebellion. On Todd Jones, see Johnston, *Great Britain and Ireland*, p. 186; Fitzpatrick, *Secret Service*, pp. 156–62, 205, 353; R. B. McDowell, *Public Opinion and Government Policy in Ireland, 1801–46* (London: Faber and Faber, 1952; repr., Westport, Conn.: Greenwood Press, 1975), pp. 50–1.

113 *Parl. Reg.* 7:435 (Hercules Rowley, County Antrim), 449 (James Stewart, County Tyrone).

114 Ibid., 7:461–9.

115 Ibid., 7:469, 477. Draft proposals: Bolton MS 15940 (2); see also Bolton MS 15936 (2). Lord Lieutenant's proclamation, 20 July 1787, in *SNL*, 2 Aug. 1787; and details of police districting in Bolton MS 15941 (3–8).

116 27 Geo. 3, c. 40 s. 4. County grand juries were to appoint in each district "sixteen proper persons, being protestants."

117 *Parl. Reg.* 7:470–1.

118 Ibid., 7:451, 472–4 (O'Neill), 474 (Conolly), 480, 519. "An Act for the better Execution of the Law, and Preservation of the Peace within Counties at large," 27 Geo. 3, c. 40 (Ire.). On O'Neill, see *DEP*, 24 June 1790; Lecky, *Ire.*, 3:142; Sayles, "Sketches," p. 234; and Johnston, *Great Britain and Ireland*, p. 185. O'Neill's speech is reprinted in Grattan, *Memoirs*, 3:310–12.

119 *FJ*, 21/24 Apr. and 28 Apr./1 May 1787; *VEP*, 29/31 Mar. and 10/12 Apr. 1787. The only London newspaper to note the Irish police developments was the *Public Advertizer*, 10 Apr. 1787, which printed abstracts of the parliamentary debate of 2 April.

120 *HJ*, 16 Apr. 1787.

121 Grattan quoted in J. C. Beckett, *The Making of Modern Ireland, 1603–1923* (London: Faber and Faber, 1966), p. 214. For a look at the dilemma of the Patriots' nationalism, see David W. Miller, *Queen's Rebels: Ulster Loyalism in Historical Perspective* (Dublin: Gill and Macmillan, 1978), pp. 24–42; and Smyth, "Volunteers and Parliament," pp. 130–6. Grattan would not have fared well amid the triumph of conservative Catholic nativism in the Irish Free State after 1922; see F. S. L. Lyons, *Culture and Anarchy in Ireland, 1890–1939* (Oxford: Clarendon Press, 1979), ch. 6.

CHAPTER 4. THE IRISH POLICE EXPERIMENT

1 In addition to the works by Radzinowicz and Stead (see ns. 3 and 6, this chapter), see W. L. Melville Lee, *A History of Police in England* (London: Methuen & Co., 1901; repr. Montclair, N.J.: Patterson Smith, 1971), who set the tone by calling Colquhoun "the architect who designed our modern police" and Peel "the builder who constructed its framework" (pp. 218–23; quotations on p. 219); and also Charles Reith, *The Blind Eye of History: A Study of the Origins of the Present Police Era* (London: Faber and Faber, 1952; repr. Montclair, N.J.: Patterson Smith, 1975), pp. 136–9, 146–9; Douglas G. Browne, *The Rise of Scotland Yard* (London: Harrap & Co., 1956), pp. 46–50; Christopher Hibbert, *The Roots of Evil: A Social History of Crime and Punishment* (Harmondsworth: Penguin Books, 1966), pp. 132–6; and T. A. Critchley, *A History of Police in England and Wales*, 2d ed. (Montclair, N.J.: Patterson Smith, 1972), pp. 38–42.

2 *Dublin Evening Post* [hereafter, *DEP*], 1 Apr. 1790; Major Doyle, Irish MP, *The Parliamentary Register, or the History of the Proceedings and Debates of the House of Commons in Ireland* [hereafter, *Parl. Reg.*], 15 vols. (Dublin, 1784–95), 11:271, 4 Mar. 1791; and (London) *Morning Chronicle*, 22 Apr. 1786.

3 Leon Radzinowicz, *A History of English Criminal Law and its Administrative from 1750* [hereafter, *ECL*], 4 vols. (London: Stevens & Sons, 1948–68), 3:62, 135–6.

4 *The Parliamentary History of England, from the Earliest Period to the Year 1803* [hereafter, *PH*], 36 vols. (London: T. C. Hansard, 1806–20), 29:1033–6, 1178–83, 1464–76 (Fox, Sheridan, and North on cols. 1464, 1474–5). A motion to defer the second reading was defeated, 50–37 (c. 1465). Among those who prepared the 1792 bill were Sir Archibald Macdonald, Pitt's Solicitor-General in 1785, and Sir John Scott, Solicitor-General in 1792, later Lord Eldon.

5 "An Act for the more effectual administration of the office of a Justice of the Peace ... in Middlesex ...," 32 Geo. 3, c. 53. *Public Advertizer*, 1 May 1792. Colquhoun quoted in Radzinowicz, *ECL*, 3:134. Norman Gash, *Mr. Secretary Peel: The Life of Sir Robert Peel to 1830* (Cambridge, Mass.: Harvard University Press, 1961), p. 311.

6 The science was slow to develop. The next, and far inferior, study was John Wade's *Treatise on the Police and Crimes of the Metropolis*, published in 1829.

Colquhoun's other writings on police were a pamphlet, *A General View of the National Police System* (1799); a 676-page *Treatise on the Commerce and Police of the River Thames* (1800); and the compendium, *A Treatise on the Functions and Duties of a Constable* (1803). An excellent summary of Colquhoun's life and work is in Radzinowicz, *ECL*, 3:211–312; less valuable is Philip John Stead, "Patrick Colquhoun," in Stead, ed., *Pioneers in Policing* (Montclair, N.J.: Patterson Smith, 1977), pp. 48–63.

7 Patrick Colquhoun, *A Treatise on the Police of the Metropolis*, 6th ed. (London: J. Mawman, 1800), pp. 406–9, 506, 509–10; and Radzinowicz, *ECL*, 3:284–94. Colquhoun showed little interest in the "hints" for a "Travelling Police" submitted to him by Edward Ashley, 8 Dec. 1796; reprinted in Radzinowicz, *ECL*, 3:521–2.

8 John Warburton, J. Whitelaw, and R. Walsh, *A History of the City of Dublin*, 2 vols. (London: W. Bulmer, 1818), 2:1038 n. 1; John McGregor, *New Picture of Dublin* (Dublin: Johnston and Deas, 1821), p. 162; Grattan, 24 June 1793, *Parl. Reg.* 13:459; Attorney-General, 4 Mar. 1791, *Parl. Reg.* 11:267.

9 *DEP*, 30 Sept. 1786; *Saunders's News-letter* [hereafter, *SNL*], 28, 29 Sept. 1786 and 8 Nov. 1787; *Freeman's Journal* [hereafter, *FJ*], 28/30 Sept. 1786; *Parl. Reg.* 11:272, 4 Mar. 1791. The radical press lampooned the original colors. "Drab was at length devised," intoned the *Hibernian Journal* [hereafter, *HJ*], 27 Sept. 1786; the *Dublin Evening Post*, 3 Oct. 1786, described "a kind of filthy brown jacket, with dirty white cape, which gave a *je ne scai* [*sic*] *quoi* to the corps."

10 *SNL*, 23 Sept. 1786; *FJ*, 28/30 Sept. 1786; and *HJ*, 4 Oct. 1786.

11 *HJ*, 29 Sept. 1786; *Parl. Reg.* 8:250. On the inutility of the horse police, see *HJ*, 6 Apr. 1787.

12 On watch strength 1786–8, see *DEP*, 14 Nov. 1786; *SNL*, 15 Nov. 1786; and Bolton MS 15940 (1), Papers of Thomas Orde, 1st Baron Bolton, NLI, Dublin. Quotations in 1788 in *Parl. Reg.* 8:250, 338, respectively. "Fatigue": N. Warren to Orde, 18 Feb. 1787, Bolton MS 15940 (1).

13 *DEP*, 2 Feb. 1788. Securities: *DEP*, 28 Sept. 1786. Salaries (exclusive of £2, 13 s., deducted each year for clothing): *Parl. Reg.* 6:383, 8:250; and 9:396, 421. The amending act, 28 Geo. 3, c. 45 s. 47, permitted the Lord Lieutenant to reduce the pay of petty and watch constables "so often as he ... shall think fit."

14 James S. Donnelly, Jr., "The Rightboy Movement, 1785–8," *Studia Hib.* 17 & 18 (1977–8):151; *DEP*, 28 Sept. 1786 ("respectable") and 14 Oct. 1790; *SNL*, 22 Sept. 1786.

15 *Parl. Reg.* 8:250, 9:421; 11:277; 12:296; 15:117. *DEP*, 4 Oct. 1788 and 14 Oct. 1790. 28 Geo. 3, c. 45 s. 27 (1788).

16 *SNL*, 11, 13, 16 Oct.; 13, 15, 29 Nov.; 4, 6 Dec. 1786; 11 Jan. ("bucks") and 23 July 1787 ("Riot"); and 2 May 1789.

17 26 Geo. 3, c. 24 ss. 34–5; and *SNL*, 14, 18, 29 Apr. 1789.

18 26 Geo. 3, c. 24 s. 38, 28 Geo. 3, c. 45 ss. 13, 18. *SNL*, 4 Oct. 1786; *FJ*, 15 Sept. 1786, 19 July 1787. *SNL*, 7 Oct. 1786, cited licensing laws in Bordeaux, France, as a model for Dublin.

19 *SNL*, 29 Nov. 1786, 16 Oct. 1789, respectively.

20 *SNL*, 26 Oct. 1786 ("called"); 18 Oct. 1787 ("incorrigible"); 4 Nov. 1789 ("Commissioners"); and 4 Nov. 1789. Petition in *Parl. Reg.* 8:386.

21 *SNL*, 16 Oct. 1786; *Faulkner's Dublin Journal* [hereafter, *FDJ*], 30 Sept.–3 Oct. 1786.

22 *DEP*, 24 Oct. 1786; *SNL*, 11, 13, 18, 20 Oct.; 13, 29 Nov.; and 9 Dec. 1786. Quotation in *SNL*, 4 Dec. 1786.

23 *HJ*, 23 Oct. 1786; *SNL*, 24 Oct. 1786; and Justice Graham to Orde, 21 Feb. 1787, Bolton MS 15939 (2).

24 *HJ*, 6 Apr. 1787. *SNL*, 2, 4, 6 ("duration") Apr.; 1 May ("dangerous"); 19 Sept.; 25 Oct.; 7, 10, 23 (murder) Nov.; and 5 Dec. 1787.

25 *SNL*, 9 Dec. 1786 (Baltinglass). Also *SNL*, 29 Nov. 1786; 23 Mar., 3 Apr., 16 Oct. 1789; 30 May and 4 Dec. 1793; and 13 Mar. 1795 (embezzler).

26 *SNL*, 12 Jan. 1787.

27 Printed assize records do not exist before 1796. R. B. McDowell, *The Irish Administration 1801–1914* (London: Routledge & Kegan Paul, 1964), pp. 140–50, and *Ireland in the Age of Imperialism and Revolution 1760–1801* (Oxford: Clarendon Press, 1979), pp. 75, 541–2. On newspapers, see n. 30, this chapter.

28 Fitzgibbon, 25 Apr. 1789, *Parl. Reg.* 9:399; and *FJ*, 22/24 May 1792 and 29 May 1796.

29 *Parl. Reg.* 9:399, 11:268. Grattan believed in 1789 that the numbers were on the rise (*Parl. Reg.* 9:422). Mr. Hardy attributed the decline in prosecutions to better enforcement of forfeited recognizances (*Parl. Reg.* 9:412).

30 *SNL*, 30 Oct., 15 Nov. 1786; 29 Mar., 2 and 4 Apr. 1787; 17 Mar. and 29 Apr. 1789. *FJ*, 22/24 May 1792. *SNL*, 30 May 1793; 13 Jan. and 2 Feb. 1795. A modern writer has stated that 2 to 7 percent of crimes are reported in today's newspapers. John Lofton, *Justice and the Press* (Boston: Beacon Press, 1966), p. 179.

31 *HJ*, 6 Apr. 1787; *DEP*, 25 Nov. 1790; Grattan, in *Parl. Reg.* 11:280–1; *SNL*, 13 Jan. 1795; and *FJ*, 22/24 May 1792.

32 *SNL*, 5 Jan. and 21 May 1787, 26 Dec. 1793; *DEP*, 14 June 1794. See also Grattan's remarks, 14 Mar. 1792, *Parl. Reg.* 12:296.

33 *FJ*, 26/29 Mar. 1787; *SNL*, 22 Dec. 1787, 13 Feb. and 2 May 1789; *DEP*, 11 and 13 May 1790; for January 1791, see *Parl. Reg.* 12:296; *SNL*, 7 June 1793.

34 "A Lover of Order" to *HJ*, 8 June 1787, 26 Geo. 3, c. 24 s. 27; and 28 Geo. 3, c. 45 s. 2. "Turncoating": *FDJ*, 30 Sept./3 Oct. 1786; *HJ*, 4 Oct. 1786; and *SNL*, 11 Oct. 1786. Other punishments: *SNL*, 18 Nov. 1786 and 6 Apr., 25 May 1787.

35 *FJ*, 31 Mar./3 Apr. 1787. Alderman N. Warren to Orde, 18 Feb. 1787, Bolton MS 15940 (1). 28 Geo. 3, c. 45 ss. 3–7.

36 "A Lover of Order" to *HJ*, 8 June 1787; and *DEP*, 13 Nov. 1790.

37 *Parl. Reg.* 8:306, 22 Feb. 1788; Godfrey was released upon paying £30 to Fleming whose costs for prosecution came to £40. *The Rights of Irishmen*, 7 Feb. 1792.

38 *Dublin Morning Post* [hereafter, *DMP*], 2 Feb., 25 Mar. 1788. *FJ*, 3/5 Oct. ("Cap") and 7/10 Oct. 1786, and 20/22 Nov. 1787.

39 Mr. Arthur Browne, opponent of the 1786 Dublin police bill, *Parl. Reg.* 7:477 and 10:310, 5 Apr. 1787 and 24 Feb. 1790.

40 *DMP*, 14 Feb. 1788; *Parl. Reg.* 8:306, 335, 22 and 25 Feb. 1788; *DEP*, 25 Sept. 1794.

41 *Parl Reg.* 8:334, 25 Feb. 1788. *FJ*, 20/22 Nov. 1787. In one case, two watchmen were fined and imprisoned for letting ladies of the night ply their trade (*SNL*, 25 May 1787).

42 *FJ*, 20/22 Nov. 1787. One watchman who quit his post for drinks while a house was being robbed received the maximum punishment, a 40 s. fine and one month in jail. Another who left his post, with no crime ensuing, received a week's detention and a 6 d. fine. *SNL*, 6 Apr. 1787. Assault: *SNL*, 27 Oct. 1789.

43 Respectively: *SNL*, 11 Oct. 1786 (the Commissioners discharged the two watchmen from the force); *DMP*, 29 Jan. 1788; *DEP*, 28 Feb. 1792; and *SNL*, 20 June 1789.

44 Annual costs reported in *Parl. Reg.* 8:305, 339, 342; 9:394, 400, 413, 417–18; 11:265; 13:455; and 15:117. Grattan quoted in *Parl. Reg.* 8:342, 25 Feb. 1788.

45 26 Geo. 3, c. 24 s. 19; 28 Geo. 3, c. 45 s. 12. *Parl. Reg.* 8:355; 9:267, 400. By 1794, the police tax accounted for three-quarters of the force's £17,000 income (*Parl. Reg.* 15:117).

46 Police expenditures reported in *Parl. Reg.* 8:336–9, 25 Feb. 1788; 9:106–7, 394–5, 414, 418–20, 17 Feb. and 25 Apr. 1789. The Dublin police were consuming, per capita, nearly twice as many coals and candles as the army in Ireland, which

expended £14,570 for its 15,000 men. "Expenditures of the Commissioners of the Barracks, 1786," Bolton MS 15900 (4).

47 *Parl. Reg.* 8:306, 344, 22 and 25 Feb. 1788; and 9:106–9, 394–424 (Curran's remarks on p. 415), 17 Feb. and 25 Apr. 1789.

48 *Parl. Reg.* 9:397, 25 Apr. 1789; and *DEP*, 20 Oct. 1789, respectively. On the Government's defense of the force, see *Parl. Reg.* 9:398–400, 407–9, 416–17.

49 *SNL*, 1 Oct. 1789 ("bidder"); *Parl. Reg.* 10:305–6, 24 Feb. 1790; and *DEP*, 26 Aug. 1790. Expenses: *Parl. Reg.* 10:306, 11:265, 278–80. The police accountant complained as late as 1800 that he had been dismissed in 1789 "without any explanation Whatever." T. Sankey to Ambrose Leet, Jr., 29 Sept. 1789, and Leet to E. Cooke, 17 Nov. 1800, both in Official Papers, Series 2, 1790–1831, "Magistrates and Police" [hereafter, OP 2], 1800/81/7, ISPO, DC.

50 The following were the basis of Doyle's calculations. For *Dublin* before and after 1786, he compared an average-sized parish, St. Michan's, having 56 watchmen in 1784 at a cost of £430, with St. Michan's 36 watchmen in 1791 at a higher cost of £1,128. For *Westminster* (London), he compared the largest parish, St. James's, with 70 men at £1,320, to Dublin's largest, St. Mary's, with 34 men at £1,456. For the *City of London*, he took a large ward, Aldersgate, with 26 men at £800, and a small ward, Bishopsgate, with 15 men at £500, and then added the costs (£1,300) and divided this figure by the total number of parishes in both wards; this calculation yielded an average parish cost of £119. For Dublin, he divided the police cost of £16,555 (excluding Commissioners' salaries) by the total number of parishes (19), and thus arrived at an average parish cost of £871. *Parl. Reg.* 11:270–1, 4 Mar. 1791.

51 *Parl. Reg.* 8:248–9, 305, 344; 9:362; 11:51, 262, and 12:294–8.

52 Chief Secretary Hobart to E. Nepean, 8 Mar. 1791, Private Official Correspondence 1789–93, p. 115, ISPO, DC; Attorney-General, *Parl. Reg.* 11:268, 5 Mar. 1791; Grattan, *Parl. Reg.* 12:295, 14 Mar. 1792. The "torpid indifference ... of the citizens insensible of their injuries," in Grattan's words, was the result of years of ineffective protests and a preoccupation with Catholic relief measures, the war with France, and news of the Terror in Paris. *Parl. Reg.* 13:459, 24 June 1793. 1795 petitions: *Parl. Reg.* 15:38–9, 70–1, 95–7, 126–7.

53 *DMP*, 9 Feb. 1788; and *SNL*, 13 Feb. 1789, respectively.

54 *DEP*, 24 Oct. 1789. For a summary of the Whig program, see *DEP*, 5 Aug. 1790.

55 *Parl. Reg.* 9:401 (Kearney), 420 (Grattan), 25 Apr. 1789; 10:311–12, 24 Feb. 1790 (Browne); 11:263 (Grattan), 272 (Doyle), 273 (Sheridan), 4 Mar. 1791.

56 *Parl. Reg.* 10:318 and 11:282. Grattan's outburst is in *Parl. Reg.* 11:262.

57 *Parl. Reg.* 10:304; *DEP*, 25 Mar., 17 and 20 Apr. ("death"), 29 May, 24 June 1790 ("instructed"), and 17 and 21 Apr. 1792; *SNL*, 3 Oct. 1794; Police Commissioners to T. Sedham, 13 Aug. 1795, OP 2 11/4. The council rejected James by successive votes of 65–61, 78–39, and 75–40, and Moncrieffe by 98–23. See also the brief account in McDowell, *Age*, pp. 345–6.

58 *DEP*, 8, 11, 13 May 1790; and McDowell, *Age*, pp. 347–8.

59 *DEP*, 16 Mar. 1790; and W. E. H. Lecky, *A History of Ireland in the Eighteenth Century*, 5 vols. (London: Longman, Green, 1892; repr., St. Clair Shores, Mich.: Scholarly Press, 1972), 3:67.

60 Lecky, *Ire.*, 3:67, and resolution quoted on p. 64. McDowell, *Age*, p. 418, and quotation on p. 419. On the rise of this popular Protestantism, see Jacqueline Hill, "National Festivals, the State, and 'Protestant Ascendancy' in Ireland, 1790–1829," *I.H.S.* 24 (May 1984): 30–51.

61 Lecky, *Ire.*, 3:4–5, 16 (Tone), 17–20 (Grattan), 21 ("secondary"), and 128.

62 *Parl. Reg.* 9:252–3, 423–4; and 11:262–82.

63 W. L. Langer, ed., *Encyclopedia of World History*, 4th ed. (Boston: Houghton Mifflin, 1968), pp. 631–2; *Parl. Reg.* 13:456; and Fitzgibbon quoted in J. C.

Beckett, *The Making of Modern Ireland 1603–1923* (London: Faber and Faber, 1966), p. 251.

64 Speeches of Dr. Duigenan, Mr. Marcus Beresford, Mr. Archdall, and Mr. Barrington, in *Parl. Reg.* 13:454−7, 465−6, 24 June 1793.

65 Ibid., 13:455−7, 459−60.

66 The charge had been made by Beresford, ibid., 13:457. On Tandy, see *DEP*, 25 Mar. 1790; W. J. Fitzpatrick, *Secret Service under Pitt* (London: Longmans, Green, 1892), pp. 70–93, 218–26. W. E. H. Lecky, *A History of Ireland in the Eighteenth Century*, abridged ed., L. P. Curtis, Jr., ed. (Chicago: University of Chicago Press, 1972), pp. 208, 230–2, 264–6, 267 ("indefatigable"); and McDowell, *Age*, pp. 315–17, 345–8, 418–19, 422–3, 431–2, 439–40, 650, 655. "Surliness": W. Drennan to Mrs. McTier, 3 May 1790, Papers of William Drennan, PRONI, quoted in McDowell, *Age*, p. 348. Tandy subsequently journeyed to France; returned to Ireland in 1798 as part of a belated invasion force; fled to Germany; was arrested, convicted, reprieved, and lived in self-exile on the Continent. A recent biography is Rupert J. Coughlan, *Napper Tandy* (Dublin: Anvil Books, 1976).

67 Vote, in *Parl. Reg.* 13:466; and Grattan's earlier remark, 15 Apr. 1789, *Parl. Reg.* 9:420. Lord Lt.: *Parl. Reg.* 13:458−9, 461. McDowell, *Age*, pp. 445–6. *DEP*, 20 Dec. 1794.

68 Lecky, *Ire.*, 3:299–317; McDowell, *Age*, pp. 445–61. The best life is E. A. Smith, *Whig Principles and Party Politics: Earl Fitzwilliam and the Whig Party, 1748–1833* (Manchester: Manchester University Press, 1975).

69 *HJ*, 18 Feb. 1795; *DMP*, 17 Feb. 1795.

70 *SNL*, 1−3 Apr. 1795; Lecky, *Ire.*, 3:325.

71 On police, see *SNL*, 8, 17, 28 Apr. and 5 May 1795. On the Catholic bill, see *Parl. Reg.*, 15:208–361, and Lecky, *Ire.*, 3:336–46.

72 Lecky, *Ire.*, 3:345−8, 4:67−75.

73 Camden and Home Secretary Portland, respectively, quoted in Kevin Boyle, "Police in Ireland Before the Union: III," *The Irish Jurist*, new series, 8 (1973):338. Petition: *SNL*, 14 Mar. 1795; and Grattan, quoted in Lecky, *Ire.*, 3:343.

74 See Lecky, *Ire.*, 3:449−64. Curiously, Lecky makes no mention of the 1795 Dublin Police Act.

75 35 Geo. 3, c. 36 ss. 1−5, 14, 60−1, 64, 84, 102.

76 35 Geo. 3, c. 36 ss. 21, 61; and *SNL*, 1 Oct. 1795. For the pay of the 1786 force, see 26 Geo. 3, c. 24 s. 61; for the pre-1786 watch, *Parl. Reg.* 9:421. The 1795 act provided that the previous Police Commissioners (one at £500, two at £300) and divisional justices (four at £200) "shall be paid their respective salaries which they now enjoy during their respective lives, or until they shall be elected to one of the said offices, or until they shall have obtained an office of equal value with the office by them now respectively held." 35 Geo. 3, c. 36 s. 58.

77 35 Geo. 3, c. 36 ss. 75−7, set the police tax at 1s. in the pound on houses valued at under £5; and at 1s., 3d., for those rated at £5 or more. The 1786 act had levied 1s. 6d. on all houses; the 1788 amending act, 1s., 6d. and 1s., for those above and below £5, respectively.

78 35 Geo. 3, c. 36 ss. 28−9, 42, 55, 81−3, 86−97.

79 *SNL*, 12, 29 Sept. 1795.

80 Ibid., 30 Sept., 1 Oct. 1795. See also Rules for the City of Dublin Watch, 26 Oct. 1795, OP 2 11/5.

81 35 Geo. 3, c. 36 ss. 7, 62−3, 72−3.

82 *SNL*, 5, 10, 16 (quotation) Oct. 1795.

83 *SNL*, 29 Sept. 1795. State of the Funds, 29 Sept. 1795; Memorial to Lord Lt., July 1796; Watch Demands, 2 Sept. 1796; and Watch Committee to E. Cooke, 8 Sept. 1796; all in OP 2 11/5. 36 Geo. 3, c. 30 s. 1.

84 35 Geo. 3, c. 36 ss. 59–64; 36 Geo. 3, c. 30 ss. 60, 64; and Rules, Orders, Bye-Laws of the Watch, 26 Oct. 1795, OP 2 11/5.

85 36 Geo. 3, c. 30 ss. 2–8, 15–19.

86 36 Geo. 3, c. 30 ss. 12–14.

87 The extensive plans may be seen in Bolton MSS 15941 (2, 4, 6–12) and 15943 (1). "Pecuniary distress" is in Sir John Parnell to Orde, 26 July 1787, Bolton MS 15946 (2). He wrote the Chief Secretary: "I am sure that you prefer governing the Country as nearly according to the practice of England ... as is possible."

88 Cork: Bolton MS 15947 (2, 4). Tipperary: Lord Earlsfort to Orde, 4 Aug. 1787, Bolton MS 15947 (4); in 1779 John Scott, then Attorney-General (and, from 1784 on, Baron Earlsfort), had seen his town house attacked by the Dublin mob [J. A. Froude, *The English in Ireland in the Eighteenth Century*, 3 vols. (London: Longmans, Green 1872–4), 2:242–3]. Kerry: John Sigerson to J. M. Harvey, 28 July 1787, Bolton MS 15946 (1). For the context of protests against a county police tax, see David Dickson, "Taxation and Disaffection in Late Eighteenth-Century Ireland," in Samuel Clark and James S. Donnelly, Jr., eds., *Irish Peasants: Violence and Political Unrest, 1780–1914* (Madison: University of Wisconsin Press, 1983), pp. 37–63.

89 Kevin Boyle, "Police in Ireland Before the Union: II," *The Irish Jurist*, new series, 8 (1973): 110. On the extent of the police districts, see *SNL*, 2 Aug. 1787, and OP 2 1828/830C/3.

90 Special sessions: proclamation of 13 Nov. 1787, signed by Sackville Hamilton, in *SNL*, 1 Jan. 1789. Uniform: *FJ*, 27/29 Sept. 1787. Effectiveness: *SNL*, 12, 25, 29, 30 Oct. and 1 Dec. 1787. Duration: Cork, 1793, Lords Kingsborough and Longueville to Lord Lt., 15 Jan. 1793, OP 2 11/7.

91 Opposition speeches in *Parl. Reg.* 10:298–304. MPs for Kerry, Kilkenny, and Tipperary quoted on pp. 299, 300, 303; vote, p. 349; "scourge," p. 299.

92 13 & 14 Geo. 3, c. 32 (1774); 32 Geo. 3, c. 16 (1792); Boyle, "Police in Ireland: II," p. 113. Donnelly calculates that day laborers in full employment could earn about £6 a year. "Rightboy," p. 151.

93 "Return of the Number of Constables in Ireland in 1792, 1822, and 1828," 10 and 17 Mar. 1828, OP 2 830C/3. *Parl. Reg.* 12:300–1, 16 Mar. 1792.

94 Opinions, respectively, of *DEP*, 19 July 1792; and of Mr. Ogle, MP for County Wexford, reported in *FDJ*, 17/20 Mar. 1792.

95 At Ballyboro, Meath, forty-seven Defenders were killed [Marianne Elliott, *Partners in Revolution: The United Irishmen and France* (New Haven, Conn.: Yale University Press, 1982), p. 43]. Near Bailieborough, Cavan, in January 1793, twenty were killed; in May 1794, at the Kilnaleck fair, near Cavan town, thirty-two were killed (*SNL*, 26 Jan. 1793; James S. Donnelly, Jr., "1798: The Agrarian and Sectarian Background," p. 9, draft of a conference paper kindly sent to the author). In unrelated violence, some 100 persons attempting a rescue of persons at Wexford were "massacred" after the military commanding officer was killed by a scythe. *Finn's Leinster Journal*, 13/17, 17/20 July 1793, cited in Donnelly, "Rightboy," p. 201. All of these disorders were separate from the great antimilitia riots of 1793.

96 Peace Preservation Act renewed again by 33 Geo. 3, c. 25 (1793); and extended in 1795, HO 100/58/171–4, 334–43 and *FJ*, 21 July 1795, Lord Lieutenant's proclamation of 13 July. Elliott, *Partners*, pp. 95–7. For a valuable recent analysis that includes published sources from HO 100/58, PRO, London, see Thomas Bartlett, "Select Documents XXXVIII: Defenders and Defenderism in 1795," *I.H.S.* 24 (May 1985): 373–94.

97 36 Geo. 3, c. 25 (1796). One applicant for a chief constableship described the post as "an office I hope of much emolument" (N. Sneyd to E. Cooke, 27 June 1796); for applications, July 1795–June 1796, see OP 2 1795–6/11/7.

98 *SNL*, 17 Apr. 1798; George Rudé, *Protest and Punishment: The Story of the Social*

and Political Protesters Transported to Australia 1788–1868 (Oxford: Clarendon Press, 1978), p. 72.

99 Lecky, *Ire.*, ed. Curtis, p. 258 (quotation); *Parl. Reg.* 13:384–91, 417–**18**, 426–7, 442–3. 33 Geo. 3, c. 22. See Sir Henry McAnally, *The Irish Militia, 1793–1816: A Social and Military Study* (Dublin: Clonmore and Reynolds, 1949).

100 Elliott, *Partners*, pp. 44–5; Thomas Bartlett, "An End to Moral Economy: The Irish Militia Disturbances of 1793," *Past & Present* 99 (May 1983):41–64.

101 See Marianne Elliott, "The Origins and Transformation of Early Irish Republicanism," *Intl. Rev. Soc. Hist.* 23 (1978):405–28, and *Partners*, chs. 2, 3; James S. Donnelly, Jr., "Propagating the Cause of the United Irishmen," *Studies: An Irish Quarterly Review* 69 (Spring 1980):5–23; McDowell, *Age*, pp. 462–75; and Nancy J. Curtin, "The Transformation of the Society of United Irishmen into a Mass-based Revolutionary Organisation, 1794–6," *I.H.S.* 24 (Nov. 1985):463–92.

102 Lord Edward Fitzgerald found that he could get no other MP to serve as teller for votes against the proposed bill; in 1797 a motion to repeal the act was overwhelmingly rejected, 127–15. Beckett, *Modern Ireland*, p. 258; McDowell, *Age*, p. 554.

103 Habeas corpus: Lecky, *Ire.*, 3:451–4, 459–60; McDowell, *Age*, pp. 552–8. Yeomanry: McDowell, *Age*, pp. 557–64; William Richardson, *History of the Origin of the Irish Yeomanry* (Dublin: R. E. Mercier, 1801); and R. G. Morton, "The Rise of the Yeomanry," *The Irish Sword* 8 (1967):58–64.

104 Elliott, *Partners*, ch. 4; Lecky, *Ire.*, 3:522–46, 4:19–20, 29–38, 42–62; McDowell, *Age*, pp. 507–12, 572–7.

105 An excellent discussion of the use of the military in aid of the civil power on the eve of 1798 is in McDowell, *Age*, pp. 575–93.

106 Newspapers carried only two brief notices. One was the case in May of a watch inspector who had arrested two men for treason; a constable's negligence enabled one of the prisoners to escape (*SNL*, 16 May 1798). The only other mention was of a former *County* Dublin "peace officer," Joseph Holt, who had been dismissed for "malpractices" and was now a United Irish leader in Wicklow (*SNL*, 27 June 1798). On Holt, see McDowell, *Age*, pp. 607–8; J. O. Baylen and N. J. Gossman, eds., *Biographical Dictionary of Modern British Radicals Since 1770*, 3 vols. (New York: Humanities Press, 1979), 1:236–9.

107 Major William Bellingham Swan, magistrate and senior revenue official. Assisted by plainclothes sergeants from the army, Swan arrested on 12 March the dozen principal United Irish leaders at Oliver Bond's house in Bridge Street (McDowell, *Age*, pp. 600–2); Major Sirr was probably also present, for Pakenham credits him with the arrests [Thomas Pakenham, *The Year of Liberty: The Great Irish Rebellion of 1798* (London: Hodder and Stoughton, 1969), pp. 43–6]. Lecky gives no names (*Ire.*, 4–262). On 19 May, Swan and Sirr, accompanied by Yeomanry Captain Daniel Ryan and seven soldiers, arrested Lord Edward Fitzgerald at a house in Thomas Street. *Dictionary of National Biography* [hereafter, *DNB*] 17:522–3, 18:317; Lecky, *Ire.*, 4:302–11; Pakenham, *Year of Liberty*, pp. 92–4; *SNL*, 21 May 1798.

    If Swan was the left arm of the Castle, the right was Major Henry Charles Sirr (1764–1841). A career army officer, Sirr in 1796 had been named "town major" of Dublin, a post controlled by the Castle. From the fall of 1797, Sirr was involved in searching houses, seizing arms, and chasing suspected rebels. On three occasions, he barely escaped with his life from the attacks of United Irishmen. *DNB* 18:316–18; Fitzpatrick, *Secret Service*, p. 122 n. 6; McDowell, *Age*, p. 672; *SNL*, 4, 25 Apr. 1798. Sirr's son donated his father's papers to Trinity College, Dublin; but the major apparently destroyed the papers on sedition and police, for the Sirr MSS (868–9) are disappointing on these subjects.

108 *SNL*, 7 Apr., 23 May 1798.

109 R. B. Rose, "The Priestley Riots of 1791," *Past & Present* 18 (Nov. 1960):68–88;

George Rudé, *The Crowd in History, 1730–1848* (New York: Wiley, 1963), ch. 9; and E. P. Thompson, *The Making of the English Working Class* (New York: Pantheon Books, 1964), pp. 112–15. The reported property destruction is based on claims paid out to victims. See *Birmingham Gazette*, 25 July 1791; John Langford, *A Century of Birmingham Life*, 2 vols. (Birmingham: E. C. Osborne, 1868), 1:486, 488, 498–9; *PH* 29:1445; and Rudé, *Crowd*, p. 145.

110 In Birmingham two magistrates "walked arm in arm with the crowd, enjoying their huzzaing, without attempting to disperse them"; on another occasion, JPs refused a military party's offer to break up the crowds. Langford, *Century*, 1:480; *PH* 29:1439, 1443. A motion in Parliament to prosecute the lax magistrates was lost, 189–46. *PH* 29:1464.

111 Langford, *Century*, 1:478, 496–7; and *PH* 29:1461.

112 John Stevenson, "Food Riots in England, 1792–1818," in J. Stevenson and R. Quinault, eds., *Popular Protest and Public Order: Six Studies in British History 1790–1920* (New York: St. Martin's Press, 1975), pp. 33–74; see also Alan Booth, "Food Riots in the North-West of England, 1790–1801," *Past & Present* 77 (Nov. 1977):84–107. "Crise": G. Williams, *Artisans and Sans-Culottes* (London, 1968), quoted in Stevenson, "Food Riots," p. 35.

113 Malcolm I. Thomis and Peter Holt, *Threats of Revolution in Britain 1789–1848* (Hamden, Conn.: Archon Books, Shoe String Press, 1977), pp. 24–6, quotation on p. 25. "Involvement" and "revolutionary": Stevenson, "Food Riots," p. 66.

114 See generally G. D. H. Cole and R. Postgate, *The Common People 1746–1946* (London: Methuen, 1964), pp. 150–78; Thompson, *Making*, ch. 5, esp. pp. 107–8, 140–50; Thomis and Holt, *Threats*, pp. 5–28. By contrast to Paine's work, Burke's *Reflections on the Revolution in France* sold 30,000 copies in its first two years (Thompson, *Making*, p. 108 n. 1). Clive Emsley has investigated a little-known example of the new tensions in "The London 'Insurrection' of December 1792: Fact, Fiction, or Fantasy?" *J. Br. Studies* 17, No. 2 (Spring 1978):66–86; he concludes that it was the latter two.

115 Thompson, *Making*, pp. 177–9; Thomis and Holt, *Threats*, pp. 127, 130. See Albert Goodwin, *The Friends of Liberty: The English Democratic Movement in the Age of the French Revolution* (Cambridge, Mass.: Harvard University Press, 1979).

116 Quotation is in Thomis and Holt, *Threats*, p. 17; Cole and Postgate, *Common People*, pp. 157–68. An excellent overview of this period, which stresses the importance of wartime demands, is Clive Emsley, *British Society and the French Wars, 1793–1815* (London: Macmillan, 1979). See also his article, "The Military and Popular Disorder in England, 1790–1801," *J. Soc. Army Hist. Research* 61, No. 245 (Spring 1983):10–21; continued in 61, No. 246 (Summer 1983):96–112.

117 The Reign of Terror claimed 17,000 lives. See Donald Greer, *The Incidence of the Terror during the French Revolution* (Cambridge Mass.: Harvard University Press, 1935); Richard Louie, "The Incidence of the Terror: A Critique of a Statistical Interpretation," *French Historical Studies* 3 (1964):379–89; and Gilbert Shapiro and John Markhoff, "The Incidence of the Terror: Some Lessons for Quantitative History," *J. Soc. Hist.* 9 (1975):193–218. In the entire Peninsular Campaign, 1809–13, Wellington's army lost 40,000 men from all causes.

118 More than 400 persons were transported to Australia; 318 were shipped to the royal salt mines in Prussia. In addition, seventy-six persons were sent to prisons in Scotland. Different authorities give slightly varying figures. See A. G. L. Shaw, *Convicts and the Colonies: A Study of Penal Transportation from Great Britain and Ireland to Australia and Other Parts of the British Empire* (London: Faber and Faber, 1966), p. 170; Lecky, *Ire.*, ed. Curtis, p. 423; Pakenham, *Year of Liberty*, pp. 342, 349–50, 401 nn. 40–1; Rudé, *Protest*, pp. 9, 73, 249. Rudé says that altogether perhaps 1,200–1,500 persons were sentenced to transportation.

119 Thompson, *Making*, p. 169; Elliott, *Partners*, pp. 185, 189 (quotations). See also Elliott, "Irish Republicanism in England: The First Phase, 1797–99," in Thomas

Bartlett and D. W. Hayton, eds., *Penal Era and Golden Age: Essays in Irish History, 1690–1800* (Belfast: Ulster Historical Foundation, 1979), pp. 204–21; and on English lower-class loyalism, H. J. Perkin, *The Origins of Modern English Society 1780–1880* (London: Routledge & Kegan Paul, 1969), pp. 192–5.

120 Elliott, *Partners*, p. 297. On Despard, see Thompson, *Making*, pp. 472–84; and Elliott, *Partners*, ch. 9, and her article, "The 'Despard Conspiracy' Reconsidered," *Past & Present* 75 (May 1977):46–62. On the provinces, see J. R. Dinwiddy, "The 'Black Lamp' in Yorkshire, 1801–1802," and J. L. Baxter and F. K. Donnelly, "The Revolutionary 'Underground' in the West Riding: Myth or Reality?" *Past & Present* 64 (Aug. 1974):113–23, 124–32, respectively. A recent study by Roger Wells, *Insurrection: The British Experience, 1795–1803* (Gloucester: Alan Sutton, 1983), overstresses the British threat of revolution and understates the Irish contribution.

121 *FDJ*, 26 July 1803. Most of the rebels were shopkeepers and artisans; for a list of occupations, see *DEP*, 22 Oct. 1803. For an excellent short account of the rising, see Elliott, *Partners*, pp. 297–322.

122 Colquhoun, *Treatise on Police*, 1805 ed., p. 290; Radzinowicz, *ECL*, 2:171–88 ("uncontrolled" on p. 187), 492–4, 499–500.

123 "Twenty-Eighth Report from the Select Committee on Finance, ... [and] Police, including Convict Establishments," 26 June 1798, plus appendixes (App. A, Central Board, pp. 37–42; App. D, Colquhoun's testimony, 4 May 1798, pp. 49–61); reprinted in *House of Commons Sessional Papers of the Eighteenth Century*, ed. Sheila Lambert, 145 vols. (Wilmington, Del.: Scholarly Resources, Inc., 1975), 112:3–61.

124 Radzinowicz, *ECL*, 3:298–312, quotation on p. 311; and Colquhoun quoted in report of the select committee on London police, *PP 1816* (510), 5:32, in idem. Critic: Anon., *Observations on a Late Publication intitled, "A Treatise on the Police of the Metropolis," by P. Colquhoun, Esq.*, by "A Citizen of London: but no Magistrate," quoted in Douglas G. Browne, *The Rise of Scotland Yard* (London: Harrap & Co., 1956), p. 48.

125 Colquhoun, *A Treatise on the Commerce and Police of the River Thames* (London: J. Mawman, 1800), pp. 200–1, 222, 230–1, 235; Radzinowicz, *ECL*, 2:358, 365, 373 n. 64, 368–72, 375, 380, 388 n. 32; Browne, *Scotland Yard*, p. 49.

126 Radzinowicz, *ECL*, 2:530–2. For the activities of the force down to 1840, see Tom Fallon, *The River Police: The Story of Scotland Yard's Little Ships* (London: F. Muller, 1956), pp. 15–108.

127 Radzinowicz, *ECL*, 2:190, 390–9, 529.

128 Ibid., 2:521; J. J. Tobias, *Crime and Police in England 1700–1900* (New York: St. Martin's Press, 1979), p. 50.

129 Radzinowicz, *ECL*, 2:512, 514 n. 36, 515–17; Tobias, *Crime and Police*, p. 52. On Ford, see Radzinowicz, *ECL*, 2:152 n. 68, 407 n. 13. A common mistake in the literature on police has been to confuse the "Robin Redbreasts" with Bow Street's thief takers (Runners) or with the Foot Patrol; see Browne, *Scotland Yard*, p. 52 n. 1.

130 Radzinowicz, *ECL*, 2:174, 195, 512.

131 Colquhoun did assemble a compendium, *Treatise on the Functions and Duties of a Constable*, published in 1803, but his growing interest in economic statistics can be seen in his *Treatise on Indigence* (1806) and, above all, his lengthy *Treatise on the Wealth, Power, and Resources of the British Empire* (1814; 2d ed., 1815). See Phyllis Deane and W. A. Cole, *British Economic Growth 1688–1959* (Cambridge: Cambridge University Press, 1967), pp. 3, 158ff. On Colquhoun's evidence before committees, see Radzinowicz, *ECL*, 3:224–5, 582–3. Biography: *DNB* 4:859–61; and the work by his son-in-law, Dr. Grant David Yeats [1773–1836], *A Biographical Sketch of the Life and Writings of Patrick Colquhoun, Esq., LL.D.*, by *Iatros* (London: G. Smeeton, 1818).

132 For an extended discussion of the alternatives to police reform, see the sections "The Persistence of Negation" and "The Search for Substitutes" in Radzinowicz, *ECL*, 3:348–74, 375–413, "talon" and tocsin on pp. 378–9. [Sir Richard Phillips,] *Modern London; Being the History and Present State of the British Metropolis* (1805), quoted in Radzinowicz, *ECL*, 3:312; emphases are mine.

133 Title of part 3 (chs. 6–8) in Radzinowicz, *ECL*, 3:141–207.

134 Quotations are, respectively, from Edmund Burke, "Thoughts and Details on Scarcity," November 1795, and *Observations on Indecent Sea-Bathing, &c.*, by Viator (1805), p. 11. Quoted in Radzinowicz, *ECL*, 3:141–2, 162.

135 Radzinowicz, *ECL*, 3:154, 166–70, 189, 498–506.

136 Ibid., 2:205, 207 n. 17, 464–6. See Adrian Shubert, "Private Initiative in Law Enforcement: Associations for the Prosecution of Felons, 1744–1856," in Victor Bailey, ed., *Policing and Punishment in Nineteenth Century Britain* (New Brunswick, N.J.: Rutgers University Press, 1981), pp. 25–41.

137 Radzinowicz, *ECL*, 2:215–16.

138 Statute 13 & 14 Charles 2, c. 12 s. 15 (1662); subsequent acts, 1 & 2 Will. 4, c. 41 (1831) and 5 & 6 Will. 4, c. 43 (1835). Radzinowicz, *ECL*, 2:217–29, 471; 3:351. On special constables, see also F. C. Mather, *Public Order in the Age of the Chartists* (Manchester: Manchester University Press, 1959), pp. 81–7. The only book-length study I know of is an amiable unannotated one: Ronald Seth, *The Specials: The Story of the Special Constabulary in England, Wales, and Scotland* (London: V. Gollancz, 1961), pp. 41–70 covering the eighteenth and nineteenth centuries. A scholarly monograph on the institution is much needed.

139 Valentine Lawless, Lord Cloncurry, *Personal Recollections* (Dublin: McGlashan, 1849), pp. 215, 218 ("hatred"); Warburton et al., *History of Dublin*, 1:235; 2:1101, 1103, 1107 n. 1, 1150–3, 1168 n. 1. On pre- and post-Union Dublin, see also Peter Somerville-Large, *Dublin* (London: Granada Publ., 1981), chs. 10, 11.

140 Castlereagh to Dr. Elliott, 20 Jan., and W. Wickham to Castlereagh, 28 Feb. 1799, HO 100/85/160, 281–2. E. Cooke to the Lord Lieutenant, 14 Mar., and Castlereagh to Wickham, 1 Apr. 1799, HO 100/86/142/241. In February, Major Swan nabbed his third gang that month (*SNL*, 27 Jan. 1799); see also *SNL*, 13 Mar., 19 Apr., 17 June, and 12 Oct. 1799.

141 Mayor Thomas Andrews to Castlereagh, and Memorial of the Watch to Lord Lt. Cornwallis, both dated 20 Oct. 1798, OP 2 45/2.

142 Ibid.; Watch Petition to Parliament, "1798," OP 2 45/3, and Cornwallis to Watch Directors, 5 Nov. 1798, OP 2 62/1.

143 HO 100/82/332; "interference": *SNL*, 1 May 1799. Statute 39 Geo. 3, c. 56 (1799), amended by 40 Geo. 3, c. 62 (1800), one of the last acts passed by the Irish Parliament. Castlereagh to Duke of Portland, 20 July 1799, HO 100/87/58; *SNL*, 2 May 1799; Number of Magistrates, Clerks, Constables, Peace Officers, Patroles, and Watch for the "old" and "new" police, OP 2 1808/260/8.

144 *SNL*, 8 July, 12 Oct. 1799; J. Atkinson to Col. William Alexander, 3 Aug. 1799, OP 2 62/5. "A Lover of Publick Justice" to Col. Alexander, 11 Feb. 1802, OP 2 127/1.

145 W. Logan to Under-Secretary Cooke, Alexander to Cooke, 24, 25 June 1799, OP 2 62/4; Alexander to Cooke, 14 Aug. 1799, OP 2 62/6. Memorial of the Watchmen of the Metropolis to Lord Lt. Cornwallis, 23 Jan. 1800, OP 2 81/1. Memorial of Joshua Smith, watchman, to Lord Lt. Cornwallis, 28 June, and Smith to Col. Littlehales, 4 July 1800, **OP** 2 81/7. On the quality of the force, see the speeches (quoted) by Giffard and Riddall, Dublin Corporation meeting, 7 April, in *DEP*, 9 Apr. 1808; and Sir Richard Hoare, *Journal of a Tour in Ireland, A.D. 1806* (London: W. Miller, 1807), p. 300.

146 Part of the problem was that from March 1805 to April 1807, three different men served as Irish Chief Secretary. On the 1805 police bill, see E. Lysaght to J. Lloyd, 6 July 1805, OP 2 197/1A; J. Grant to C. Long, 24 Dec. 1805, OP 2

197/4; "CAUTION" to Alderman J. Carleton, 16 July 1805, OP 2 260/6; and "The City Recorder's Thoughts on the 'Police Bill'," 1 Feb. 1806, OP 2 216/1.

147 Elizabeth Longford, *Wellington: The Years of the Sword* (London: Weidenfeld and Nicolson, 1969), pp. 97, 133-62, 169-74, 198-9. Wellesley to Malcolm, 15 Oct. 1807, quoted in Longford, *Wellington*, p. 140. Two days later he wrote Canning, "I shall be happy to aid the government in any manner they please, and am ready to set out for any part of the world at a moment's notice" (in Longford, *Wellington*, p. 137).

148 Longford, *Wellington*, pp. 136-7. Wellesley's police reform is virtually never cited by modern police historians, who have dwelled on Peel's more famous 1814 rural police. But a century ago, George J. Shaw-Lefevre (Baron Eversley), the prolific writer and English MP, commented that "the first idea of a police force seems to have originated with Sir Arthur Wellesley, who organized the Dublin police while he was Chief Secretary." *Peel and O'Connell* (London: K. Paul, Trench, 1887; repr., Port Washington, N.Y.: Kennikat, 1970), p. 45 n. Subsequent to his Irish service, Wellesley, while serving in the Iberian Peninsula, created a corps of military police, headed by provost marshals, to maintain discipline in the British army at home and abroad; see R. A. J. Tyler, *Bloody Provost: An Account of the Provost Service of the British Army, and the Early Years of the Corps of Royal Military Police* (Totowa, N.J.: Rowman and Littlefield, 1980).

149 Wellesley to Hawkesbury, 7 May 1807, in Duke of Wellington, *Supplementary Despatches, Correspondence, and Memoranda of Field Marshal Arthur, Duke of Wellington*, edited by his son the Duke of Wellington, 15 vols. (London: J. Murray, 1858-72), 5 (1860):32-3. Charles Long [Chief Secretary, September 1805 to March 1806; 1st Lord Farnborough, 1826] to Duke of Richmond, 8 Aug. 1807, Richmond MS 59 f. 190, Papers of the 4th Duke of Richmond, NLI, Dublin.

150 The preceding paragraphs are based on the bill, unamended, that became the Dublin Police Act of 1808, 48 Geo. 3, c. 140.

151 "Annual Charge of the Present Police Establishment of Dublin" and "Estimate of the Charge of the Proposed Establishment of Police in Dublin," OP 2 1808/260/10, 11. This "total annual charge of Police" provided for only fifty-two horses and sixty foot patrolmen, excluded compensation to supplanted police magistrates and officers, and overlooked the costs of purchasing, equipping, stabling, and foraging of the horses. When a Castle accountant later figured in these charges, the bill came to £53,000. Annual salaries, exclusive of secretaries and clerks: Chief Magistrate, £600; Divisional Justice, £500; Chief Constable, £100; office constable and peace officer, £40 each; watch constable, £30; watchman, 1s., 1d. per night [c. £20 p.a.]; Horse Patrol: officer £73, patrol £54; Foot Patrol: officer £36, patrol £27. The first-year charge of the new police is in "Return of Police Establishments in Dublin," *PP 1809* (280), 9:313-15. A man's pension (48 Geo. 3, c. 140 s. 26) could not exceed two-thirds of his salary.

152 The compilers of *Cobbett's Parliamentary Debates*, 41 vols. (London: T. C. Hansard, 1803-20), vols. 10-11 (1808), did not see fit to record the debates on the 1808 Dublin police bill, but Dublin newspapers printed them verbatim. Remarks of Wellesley, Shaw, and Grattan in *HJ*, 28 Mar., and *DEP*, 29 Mar. 1808; subsequent parliamentary speeches of 9 June in *FJ*, 14 June 1808.

153 *DEP*, 16 June 1808; *Correspondent*, 28 Mar. 1808; *HJ*, 9 Apr. 1808. See also the pro-police *FJ*, 28 Mar., 22 Apr. 1808; and, for the opposition, *HJ*, 7 Apr. 1808, and *Evening Herald*, 28 Mar., 1 Apr. 1808.

154 *FJ*, 9 Apr. 1808; see also accounts in *DEP* and *SNL* of this date. *SNL*, 20 Apr. 1808; *FJ*, 22 Apr. 1808.

155 *FJ*, 30 Apr.; *HJ*, 30 Apr. 1808.

156 *FJ*, 15 June ("usual"); *DEP*, 16 June 1808. Ten MPs, mostly Anglo-Irish Whigs, spoke in opposition; William Ponsonby and Henry Grattan raised the question of crime in London. Dublin crimes reported: one poisoning, one street robbery, and

an attack on the house of Supt. Magis. Col. Alexander. *SNL*, 13, 30 Jan.; 6 Feb. 1808. In 1807 the city recorded fifty-five committals for indictable offenses, up 22 percent from the previous year. "Return of Offenders committed to the different Gaols for Trial, in Ireland," *PP 1813–14* (264), 13:262–9. This low figure suggests that either the police were insufficiently challenged (low crime) or the force was ineffective and the magistrates lax (high crime but few committals). The evidence from newspapers and travelers' accounts (Hoare, *Tour*, p. 300) tends to support the view of little crime, at least within the existing police jurisdiction.

157 Browne, 1786: *Parl. Reg.* 4:337. *FJ* and *HJ*, 14 June 1808. In London, *The Times* (24, 31 Mar.; 1, 10 Apr.; 15 June 1808) printed the Commons' proceedings but not one word of editorial comment.

158 The amendments lost by votes of 40–17, 60–27, and 65–32, respectively. Note the small but growing attendance in the House. *FJ*, 14, 22 June 1808. 48 Geo. 3, c. 140.

159 *SNL*, 23 July, and *FJ*, 25 July 1808. Pemberton's role is clear from OP 2 1808/260/15, 17. "Total Strength of the Police Establishment," 8 Aug. 1808, OP 2 260/14. List of appointments: OP 2 1808/260/12. For compensation, see "Estimate of the Charge of the Proposed Establishment of Police in Dublin, 1808," OP 2 260/11; for pay, "Estimate of Expenditures of Patroles and Watch," 9 Sept. 1808, OP 2 260/17.

160 Foot Patrol: J. Pemberton to C. Saxton, 9 Sept. 1808, OP 2 260/17; Horse Patrol: "Plan of Patroles for Police," OP 2 1808/260/16.

161 Radius: For Dublin, see 48 Geo. 3, c. 140 s. 2; for London, Radzinowicz, *ECL*, 4:205.

162 The total of 2,937 constables in 1831 is very close to the average number for that decade; as late as 1837, there were only 3,071. At the founding of the Metropolitan Police in 1829 there were only 814 constables; in 1830, only 917. Thus, to make a fair comparison of the 1808 Dublin police with the 1829 London police, the 1831 strength figure has been selected. "Return of the Number . . . of the Metropolitan Police, in each year . . . ," 1829–44, *PP 1844* (189), 39:691.

163 For detailed expenditures, 1808–29, see "Report from the Select Committee appointed to inquire into the Irish Miscellaneous Estimates, respecting the Police of Dublin," *PP 1829* (342), 4:150, 419–20. The bulk of the local revenues – from a carriage tax, licensing fees, and the police tax on some 14,000 houses – paid for the watch. The Government was reluctant to assess the police tax at more than one shilling per pound; Londoners in 1829 squawked at paying an eightpence rate.

164 *DEP*, 18 Oct. 1808; *SNL*, 6 Oct., 2 Nov. 1808. See also *FJ*, 1, 5 Oct. 1808; and *SNL*, 3 Oct., 21 Dec. 1808.

165 Visitors: Maxwell, *Dublin*, p. 153; Warburton et al., *History of Dublin*, 2:1039–40; McGregor, *New Picture*, p. 164. Annual Report of the Police Magistrates, 29 Jan. 1823, Chief Secretary's Office Registered Papers [hereafter, CSORP] 5489, ISPO, DC; see also CSORP 1824/8205.

166 Calculated from criminal statistics in *PP 1813–14* (264), 13:213; *PP 1814–15* (331, 332), 11:313, 359; *PP 1829* (256), 22:427 (for 1822–8); and *PP 1830–1* (294), 12:631. Figures for assizes and quarter sessions, 1809–12, show an overall decline in committals; for the more minor crimes tried at sessions, the committal rate increased sharply and the conviction rate rose, though more slowly. The data suggest both preventive policing and better preparation of cases [*PP 1813–14* (264), 13:262–9]. Dublin's proportion of the total committals in Ireland stayed roughly constant at one in every six (700/4,000 to 3,000/18,000) from the early 1810s to the late 1820s.

167 Warburton et al., *History of Dublin*, 2:1039; McGregor, *New Picture*, p. 163.

168 OP 2 1810/302/5 and 1817/481/3; CSORP 1824/10390; McGregor, *New Picture*, p. 163; "Return of Police Force . . . of Dublin," *PP 1834* (310), 47:361.

169 5 Geo. 4, c. 28; *PP 1834* (310), 47:361.

170 OP 2 1810/302/5; CSORP 1823/5489. For police revenues, see "An Account of Fines, Fees, Forfeitures, Duties, and Taxes received by the Divisional Justices of the Police District of Dublin Metropolis, 1810 to 1830, ... pursuant to 48 Geo. 3, c. 140," *PP 1830–1* (66), 8:391–402. For amounts of local taxes and "aid sums" from the Treasury, 1819–36, some nineteen annual statements were consulted; they are listed in *General Index to Accounts and Papers, &c. [of Parliament], 1801–52*, under "Dublin City, 12. Prisons and Police, Estimate for the Police & Watch Establishments."

171 OP 2 1810/302/5; CSORP 1824/10372; City of Dublin Police Act, 5 Geo. 4, c. 102 ss. 1–3. The Castle, Liberty, Second Liberty, King's Inn, Mountjoy Square, and Merrion Square Divisions became the Castle, Barrack, Rotunda, and Stephen's Green Divisions, the names of the four *original* divisions of the city police of 1786–95. For the names of Dublin police magistrates, 1810–30, see "A Return of the ... Magistracy ... in Ireland," *PP 1830–1* (171), 8:320.

172 5 Geo. 4, c. 102 ss. 8–10; County Dublin Police Act, 5 Geo. 4, c. 28 ss. 3–5; and Irish county Constabulary Act, 3 Geo. 4, c. 103 ss. 1, 11. From 1824 on, this unique police "superintendent" for County Dublin worked with the four provincial Inspectors-General of Constabulary and the city police magistrates.

173 R. B. McDowell, *Public Opinion and Government Policy in Ireland 1801–1846* (London: Faber and Faber, 1952; repr., Westport, Conn.: Greenwood Press, 1975), pp. 52–3. In the mid-1820s the Government was becoming concerned with the influx of "Traitors, Felons, and other Offenders" (5 Geo. 4, c. 102 s. 9) – especially Ribbonmen – creeping *into* Dublin (CSORP 1823/5489, 1824/8205). See M. R. Beames, "The Ribbon Societies: Lower Class Nationalism in Pre-Famine Ireland," *Past & Present* 97 (Nov. 1982):128–43.

174 Army size: Charles M. Clode, *The Military Forces of the Crown*, 2 vols. (London: J. Murray. 1869), 1:398–9 (App. M); HO 100/176/429; Westmorland MSS 139, 146–8, 176, Correspondence of Lord Lieutenant, 10th Earl of Westmorland, ISPO, DC. Barracks: "Return of All Permanent Barracks in the United Kingdom, including the date of erection of each," *PP 1847* (169), 36:321–406.

175 See the debates in *PH* 30 (1793): 473–96; 32 (1796):929–44.

176 W. W. Pole to Earl of Harrington, 21 Oct. 1811, General Private Correspondence [hereafter, GPC] 1804–14, ISPO, DC. "The poorer Irish," commented an English visitor, "are perfectly acquainted with the nature of the barrack system, ... which is not intended so much for the defense of the country from a foreign enemy ... [but] which is maintained to awe them into subjection." Edward Wakefield, *An Account of Ireland, Statistical and Political*, 2 vols. (London: Longman, 1812), 2:822–3, 825. Barrack distribution calculated from the parliamentary return, *PP 1847* (169), 36:321–406.

177 English militia: Westmorland MSS 146, 172; *PP 1806* (51), 10:216–17; *PP 1808* (265), 7:233; Clode, *Military Forces*, 1:283–7, 292–7. Irish militia: Wakefield, *Account*, 2:820–9; HO 100/176/429. English Yeomanry: 34 Geo. 3, c. 31, amended by 44 Geo. 3, c. 54; for force levels, see *PP 1803–4* (10), 11:75; *PP 1808* (117, 184), 7:207, 224; *PP 1812* (100), 19:209. In wartime England, in addition to the Yeomanry, there was an important force of part-time, civilian foot soldiers, the Volunteers (abolished in 1816 by 56 Geo. 3, c. 3). See Clode, *Military Forces*, 1:313–32; and especially J. R. Western, "The Volunteer Movement as an Anti-Revolutionary Force, 1793–1801," *E.H.R.* 71 (1956):603–14. Irish Yeomanry: 36 Geo. 3, c. 2 (Ire.); *FJ*, 10 Sept., 26 Nov. 1803; McAnally, *Irish Militia*, p. 181; Pole to Harrington, 21 Oct. 1811, GPC 1804–14.

178 Quotation is in Clode, *Military Forces*, 1:292–3. Predictably, the Irish militia proved a barren recruiting ground for the regular army. Militia desertion rates were also far higher in Ireland than in England. Westmorland MS 176; *House of Commons Journals* [hereafter, HCJ] 62 (1807): app. p. 897; Wakefield, *Account*, 2:826 n. On this subject generally, see Thomas Bartlett, "Indiscipline and Dis-

affection in the Armed Forces in Ireland in the 1790s," in Patrick Corish, ed., *Radicals, Rebels, and Establishments* (Belfast: Appletree Press, 1985), pp. 115–34.

179 *HCJ* 62 (1807): app. p. 896. For the changing force levels, 1793–1801, see *HCJ* 61 (1806): app. p. 637; for 1804–13, *HCJ* 69 (1813): app. p. 638. On official concern, see Chief Secretary Wellesley to the Lord Lieutenant, 15 July 1807, Richmond MS 58 f. 27; on the people's "general joy" when troops were "withdrawn from the country," see Wakefield, *Account*, 2:825.

180 51 Geo. 3, c. 118; Clode, *Military Forces*, 1:300–2. On county regiment interchanges, 1811–15, see HO 100/186/211; WO 17/2793. Ireland, 1813: HO 100/176/431.

181 Mather, *Public Order*, pp. 141–50; Radzinowicz, *ECL*, 4:112–15. The only extended treatment is the now dated article by Maj. Oskar Teichman, "The Yeomanry as an Aid to the Civil Power, 1795–1867," *J. Soc. Army Hist. Research* 19 (1940): (Part I) 75–91, (II) 127–43. Historians have neglected the Yeomanry; a modern book-length assessment of the institution is needed. Such a study, I suggest, should be neither a regimental military account – see Maj. Patrick Mileham, *The Yeomanry Regiments: A Pictorial History* (Tunbridge Wells, Kent: Spellmount Ltd., 1984) – nor a sensationalist indictment that emphasizes the Peterloo incident.

182 Boyle, "Police in Ireland: III," pp. 345–8; the quotation, on p. 346, is by a County Tyrone JP named Knox.

183 Cloncurry, *Recollections*, pp. 211–12; Wakefield, *Account*, 2:373; Patrick Smyth, JP, to Sir Charles Saxton, 16 June 1812, Snugboro, Meath, State of the Country Papers, Series 1, 1409/60, ISPO, DC.

184 Post-1815 army levels: WO 17/1089–91, 2793. Figures for barrack building are calculated from the return of permanent barracks, *PP 1847* (169), 36:321–406. By the late 1840s, only two Irish counties, compared to eighteen English ones, were still without a permanent military barrack.

CHAPTER 5. ENGLAND UNDER SIDMOUTH: TRADITIONAL RESPONSES TO MODERN DISORDERS

1 *Dictionary of National Biography* [hereafter, *DNB*] 1:117–21, quotations on p. 119. See also George Pellew, *The Life and Correspondence of the Rt. Hon. Henry Addington, first Viscount Sidmouth*, 3 vols. (London: J. Murray, 1847), 1:201–3; R. J. White, *Waterloo to Peterloo* (Harmondsworth: Penguin Books, 1968, orig. publ. 1957), p. 94.

2 Quotation: Mr. Lovegrove to Home Secretary R. Ryder, 20 Dec. 1811, on the Ratcliffe murders, in HO 42/118, quoted in Leon Radzinowicz, *A History of English Criminal Law and its Administration from 1750* [hereafter, *ECL*], 4 vols. (London: Stevens & Sons, 1948–68), 3:317. On the popular reaction to Bellingham's deed, see E. P. Thompson, *The Making of the English Working Class* (New York: Pantheon Books, 1964), pp. 570–1; Malcolm Thomis, *The Luddites: Machine-Breaking in Regency England* (New York: Schocken Books, 1972), p. 90; and John Stevenson, *Popular Disturbances in England, 1700–1870* (London: Longman, 1979), pp. 160, 191. The Government decided against giving Perceval a public funeral. During the Corn Bill Riots of 1815, "chalked libels" appeared on streets and buildings all over London (N. Conant to Sidmouth, 5 Mar. 1815, in HO 42/143), e.g., "Don't Press the Poor too much. We have 200 Bellinghams and Supported They Shall Be" (J. Moser to Beckett, 8 Mar. 1815, in HO 42/143). The special constables had orders to erase all such inscriptions.

3 These murders assume a prominent place in all histories of the English police. See Christopher Hibbert, *The Roots of Evil* (Harmondsworth: Penguin Books, 1966, orig. publ. 1963), pp. 136–8; Douglas Browne, *The Rise of Scotland Yard*

(London: G. G. Harrap & Co., 1956), pp. 53–62; Radzinowicz, *ECL*, 3:315–23; T. A. Critchley, *A History of Police in England and Wales*, 2d ed. (Montclair, N.J.: Patterson Smith, 1972), pp. 40–1, and *The Conquest of Violence* (New York: Schocken Books, 1970), pp. 106–7.

4 Radzinowicz, *ECL*, 1:155–7.

5 R. B. Sheridan, who had spent part of his boyhood in Ireland, mocked the "vulgar prejudice" that assumed that the murders "could only have been done by Irishmen!" *Cobbett's Parliamentary Debates* [hereafter, *CPD*], 41 vols. (London: T. C. Hansard, 1803–20), 21:215–16, 18 Jan. 1812.

6 Proposed reforms: Radzinowicz, *ECL*, 3:323–32. Commons' debate: *CPD* 21 (1812):196–222. On the committee report and the bill to reform the nightly watch of the metropolis, see *PP 1812* (127), 2:95, and Radzinowicz, *ECL*, 3:333–47. A copy of the nightly watch bill is in *PP 1812* (242), 1:1041–76.

7 Petitions: *CPD* 23 (1812):950; copies of two petitions are in "Nightly Watch Bill," in 152M/1812, the Papers of Henry Addington, 1st Viscount Sidmouth, Devonshire Record Office, Exeter. Romilly, Brougham: *CPD* 23 (1812): 949–51. J. P. Smith, *An Account of a Successful Experiment for an Effectual Nightly Watch* (1812), pp. 16–17, 21; and J. W. Ward, letter dated 27 Dec. 1811; both quoted in Radzinowicz, *ECL*, 3:344, 347. Fouché, the French Minister of Police, was no longer in office; Napoleon had dismissed him in 1810 for exceeding his delegated powers.

8 54 Geo. 3, c. 37 s. 16; "State of the Police, with Observations by Mr. Read," in 152M/1813, Sidmouth Papers; and Radzinowicz, *ECL*, 2:192, 411–14.

9 51 Geo. 3, c. 119; and Radzinowicz, *ECL*, 2:426.

10 The occasions, complete with precise numerical allocations of police to different posts, are listed in HO 65/2. To Parliament: November 1812, July 1813, July and November 1814, July 1816, January 1817, June 1818, June 1819. Entrance of the Prince Regent into Westminster with the King of France: April 1814. Procession to Guildhall: June 1814. Procession to St. Paul's Cathedral: July 1814. Procession to Carlton House to receive the City Address: December 1816. Procession of the Persian Ambassador to Carlton House: May 1819.

11 John Beckett, Under-Secretary, Home Office, to Police Magistrates, Shadwell, 28 July 1815, in HO 65/2.

12 Circular from Beckett to Police Magistrates, 21 June 1814, in HO 65/2.

13 Petitions: Elie Halévy, *England in 1815* (New York: Barnes & Noble, 1961, orig. publ. 1913), pp. 158–9. Threatening letters: Anon. to Prince Regent, 6 Mar., and Anon. to G. Gwelf, Jr., 10 Mar. 1815, in HO 42/143. Member of Parliament reporting the crowd's remarks: *CPD* 30:33, 6 Mar. 1815. On the Irish landed interests, see the Papers of Robert Peel, BL Add. MS 40216 f. 281, British Library, London.

14 Beckett to Nine Police Offices, 5 Mar.; "Minutes of the Proceedings of the House of Commons on the Military Blocking the Approaches to Parliament," 6 Mar.; and Lord C. R. Hinrich to Sidmouth, 10 Mar. 1815, all in HO 42/143; and *CPD* 30 (1815):33–4.

15 J. Gifford and J. Moser to Beckett, 9 Mar., and Trenchfield to Rev. Gaskin, 6 Mar. 1815, in HO 42/143. But the High Constable of Hatton Garden was accused of not helping "in the slightest degree."

16 R. Baker (Marlborough St.), R. Birnie (Bow St.), R. Chambers (Mortimer St.), and P. Colquhoun (St. James Pl.) to Beckett, all dated 8 Mar.; Baker to Beckett, 9 Mar.; J. Fenton and T. Leach (Hatton Gdn.) to Sidmouth, 13 and 17 Mar.; and B. Sellon to Sidmouth ("skirmishing"), 8 Mar. 1815; all in HO 42/143.

17 Sidmouth to Col. Harris, 7 Mar., and Sidmouth's circular letter of 9 Mar. 1815, HO 41/25/1–8, 35–6. For patrols of special constables, see Fenton and Leach to Beckett, 9 Mar.; R. Jodrell to Sidmouth, 9 Mar.; and Clerk of St. Pancras to Sidmouth, 10 Mar. 1815; for pistols, J. Stow to Sidmouth, 10 Mar. 1815; all in

HO 42/143. Peel to Whitworth, 10 Mar. 1815, 40288 f. 97, Peel Papers. See also Radzinowicz, *ECL*, 2:220–1.

18 Peel to Whitworth, 11 Mar. 1815, 40288 f. 100. Memorandum, "Instructions to the Military," 10 Mar. 1815, HO 41/25/13, 27, 34; for patrols and houses guarded, see HO 50/461/16. See also Pellew, *Sidmouth*, 3:126–7.

19 Some writers have overemphasized the violence. Douglas Browne speaks of "scenes almost recalling the Gordon Riots" (*Scotland Yard*, p. 65), and the usually careful Radzinowicz describes the city as "dangerously near being exposed to a repetition of the events which took place in June, 1780" (*ECL*, 2:221).

20 Speeches in Parliament, 13 Mar. 1815, by Hammersley, Lockhart, Whitbread, and Wynn – all anti–corn bill Whigs. *CPD* 30:152–56.

21 "Regulations wanted for the Police of London": J. P. Hipkins to Sidmouth, 13 Mar. 1815, copies to Liverpool and Eldon, in HO 42/143.

22 J. T. Barber Beaumont, JP for Middlesex and late Major Commandant of the Duke of Cumberland's Sharp Shooters, to Sidmouth, 14 Mar. 1815, in HO 42/143. Six years later, Beaumont proposed a detailed plan for a police force; see his *Essay on Criminal Jurisprudence* (London: Ridgway, 1821), also printed as articles in *The Pamphleteer*, vols. 18 (1821), 19 (1822).

23 Home Secretary's notation on Beaumont's proposal of 14 Mar. 1815, in HO 42/143. Eighteen months later, on the eve of the Spa Fields Riots, the Government received suggestions for a police patterned after contemporary Paris and ancient Rome. See H. Lucas to Prince Regent, 29 Sept. 1816, in HO 42/153; and R. Sproule to Sidmouth, 25 Oct. 1816, in HO 42/154.

24 On Cobbett and Hunt, see Thompson, *Making*, pp. 607–30, and George Spater, *William Cobbett: The Poor Man's Friend*, 2 vols. (New York: Cambridge University Press, 1982).

25 Thompson, *Making*, p. 633.

26 See Thompson, *Making*, pp. 631–6; Arthur Calder-Marshall, "The Spa Fields Riots, 1816," *History Today* 21 (June 1971):407–15; White, *Waterloo to Peterloo*, pp. 151–2; Stevenson, *Disturbances*, pp. 193–6; and J. E. Cookson, *Lord Liverpool's Administration: The Crucial Years, 1815–1822* (Edinburgh: Scottish Academic Press, 1975), pp. 104–6.

27 Sidmouth to Charles Abbot, 8 Dec. 1816, in Pellew, *Sidmouth*, 3:159–61. Special constables: B. Sellon and R. Chambers to Home Office, 2 Dec. 1816, in HO 42/156. Military: HO 41/25/1, 98–104, 117. See letters and directives from Under-Secretary Beckett to numerous correspondents, 30 Nov. 1816, in HO 42/155. City: Mayor Wood to Sidmouth, 1 Dec. 1816, in HO 42/157.

28 "A Narrative of the Proceedings," HO 40/3/3/No. 14, ff. 875–99; and *Annual Register* 58 (1816): Chronicle, 191.

29 Calder-Marshall, "Spa Fields," p. 413, says mistakenly that no one was killed. Thompson, *Making*, p. 635, overstates the seriousness of the disorders: "in the Minories there was rioting for several hours, on a scale reminiscent of the Gordon Riots." Hunt himself had no truck with the violence; see Calder-Marshall, "Spa Fields," pp. 412, 414.

30 I have found no evidence for Calder-Marshall's claim that in the beginning troops and police were held back, for it was "Sidmouth's appraisal that it might develop a cohesion resembling planned conspiracy" ("Spa Fields," p. 414).

31 N. Conant to Beckett, 2 Dec. 1816, "past 12," in HO 42/157. Lord Mayor Wood to Sidmouth, 3 Dec. 1816, HO 40/3/3/No. 6, f. 881. Deposition of John Hall, JP for Essex, before the Lord Mayor, 28 Dec. 1816, in HO 42/157.

32 Thompson, *Making*, pp. 635 (quotation), 635 n. 1, 468 n. 2, 636, 640. Cobbett went into voluntary exile in America in March 1817.

33 HO 41/25/133; *CPD* 35:590–638, 837–58, 931–45, 1084–1102, 24 Feb., 3, 10, and 15 Mar. 1817; Pellew, *Sidmouth*, 3:168–9; and Cookson, *Liverpool's Adminis-*

tration, pp. 109−16. The acts suspending habeas corpus and prohibiting meetings were in effect until January 1818 and July 1818, respectively.

34 Col. Edward Despard's plot in 1802 had aborted. On Cato Street, see George T. Wilkinson, *An Authentic History of the Cato-Street Conspiracy ...* (London: T. Kelly, 1820); Percy Fitzgerald, *Chronicles of the Bow Street Police-Office*, 2 vols. (London: Chapman and Hall, 1888), 2:151−64; John Stanhope, *The Cato Street Conspiracy* (London: Jonathan Cape, 1962); Thompson, *Making*, pp. 700−9; and Stevenson, *Disturbances*, pp. 197−8.

35 Thompson, *Making*, p. 705 n. 1; Calder-Marshall, "Spa Fields," p. 415, gives a figure of seven hanged.

36 "Fantasies": Thompson, *Making*, p. 705. Thompson points out that among Cato Street's few supporters were some Irish veterans of the 1798 rebellion. Reports of "I.S.," 15 Nov. 1819, in HO 42/198, cited in Thompson, *Making*, p. 702.

37 Police select committee reports: *PP 1816* (510), 5:1−388; *PP 1817* (233, 484), 7:1−562; *PP 1818* (423), 8:1−296, quotations on pp. 32−3. Brief discussions are in *CPD* 34:1281−2, 1 July 1816; 36:1304−6, 7 July 1817; 37:740−1, 3 Mar. 1818; and 38:1264−6, 5 June 1818. Mr. Bennet, quoted in *CPD* 38:1265.

38 Sidmouth ignored at least two police proposals, one in 1817 for a 600-man military police and another, more civilian one in 1820 suggested by a police magistrate at the Whitechapel Police Office. Capt. J. South to Home Office, 18 Mar. 1817, in HO 42/162; and W. Williams to Sidmouth, 26 Dec. 1820, in HO 59/1.

39 Radzinowicz, *ECL*, 2:423, 512, 518−21.

40 Ibid., 2:193 ("professional"), 426−7, 427 n. 4. 513−14.

41 See J. B. Priestley, *The Prince of Pleasure and his Regency, 1811−20* (London: Heinemann, 1969); Cookson, *Liverpool's Administration*, pp. 200−300; and John Stevenson, "The Queen Caroline Affair," in J. Stevenson, ed., *London in the Age of Reform* (Oxford: Basil Blackwell, 1977), pp. 117−48. On the subsequent disorders themselves, see Fitzgerald, *Chronicles of Bow Street*, 2:165−85; Stevenson, *Disturbances*, pp. 199−204; and Stanley H. Palmer, "Before the Bobbies: The Caroline Riots of 1821," *History Today* 27 (Oct. 1977):637−44.

42 Maj. Lockyer to Lt.-Gen. Turner, 5 June, and Stow to Under-Secretary Henry Hobhouse, 6 June 1820, HO 44/2/26, 28. Sir Llewellyn Woodward, *The Age of Reform 1815−1870*, 2d ed. (Oxford: Clarendon Press, 1962), p. 66; and Pellew, *Sidmouth*, 3:327 n., 328 n., 330−1.

43 Mutiny: HO 44/2/88; Charles Abbot, Lord Colchester, *The Diary and Correspondence of Charles Abbot, Lord Colchester, Speaker of the House of Commons*, edited by his son, Charles, Lord Colchester, 3 vols. (London: J. Murray, 1861), 3:143. Anonymous letters: HO 40/13/629−31. Prostitute: "A Loyal Volunteer, J.N.," to Sidmouth, 17 June 1820, HO 44/2/91. Disorders: *Annual Register* 62 (1820): Chronicle, 228−9; and Pellew, *Sidmouth*, 3:330−1. It was at this period of uncertainty over the reliability of the military that Wellington proposed to Liverpool the establishment of a new institution, a military police for London. Hibbert, *Roots of Evil*, p. 144; Critchley, *Conquest*, p. 118; Radzinowicz, *ECL*, 4:156−7.

44 Woodward, *Age of Reform*, pp. 66−8. Special constables: Hobhouse to E. Robson, 8 Aug. 1820, in HO 43/29; and posts: HO 44/2/88.

45 For the arguments against moving the Queen's body by water, see the bulky folder marked "Caroline and the Queen's Funeral Procession" [hereafter cited as C & QF], n.d. [August 1821], in HO 44/9.

46 Government's proposed route, in Treasury Solicitor Papers [hereafter, TS] 11/662/1/2−5, PRO, London; City plans: HO 44/9/29.

47 Baker: Frank O. Darvall, *Popular Disturbances and Public Order in Regency England* (London: Oxford University Press, 1934, repr. 1969), pp. 65−7, 251. Pre-

parations: TS 11/662/1/6; Baker to Sidmouth, 16 Aug. 1821, in HO 44/9; and WO 17/2796 (army levels).

48 Weather: TS 11/663/3/12. "City": HO 44/9/164; and TS 11/663/3/3-4. Drinks: HO **44/9**/77, 86.

49 TS 11/663/3/2. Cf. Baker to Hobhouse, 18 Aug. 1821, in HO 44/9/C & QF; and Oakes to Maj.-Gen. Sir Herbert Taylor, 15 Aug. 1821, HO 44/9/45.

50 Baker's deposition, in TS 11/662/1/12; HO 44/9/45; and Baker to Hobhouse, 16, 17, 18 Aug. 1821, in HO 44/9/C & QF.

51 Sub.-Lt. Charles Gore to Maj.-Gen. Taylor, 18 Aug. 1821, in HO 50/440 ("staves"); TS 11/662/1/16, 18; TS 11/663/3/10 ("bloody ..."), 11, 15-16; Baker to Hobhouse, 16 Aug. 1821, in HO 44/9/C & QF; and Radzinowicz, *ECL*, 3:351.

52 TS 11/662/1/17, 19; "painted": TS 11/663/2/"Extracts"; TS 11/663/3/4, 25; memorandum of Sir Herbert Taylor, 15 Aug. 1821, HO 44/9/47; and "intimidate": Oakes to Taylor, 15 Aug. 1821, HO 44/9/45.

53 TS 11/662/1/23-5. At the inquest on the deaths of George Francis, bricklayer, and Richard Honey, cabinet maker, five of nine witnesses testified that the troops had fired straight ahead; William Spratt, shoemaker, said that one soldier "only laughed when he saw the man [he had shot] stagger." TS 11/663/2/"Extracts."

54 *DNB* 21:597-602. A good recent biography is Michael Glover, *A Very Slippery Fellow: The Life of Sir Robert Wilson, 1777-1849* (Oxford: Oxford University Press, 1978); see pp. 166-74 for Wilson's role in the Queen Caroline Riots.

55 Wilson's remarks and White's actions, in TS 11/663/3/8, 13, 18-21; Oakes to Taylor, 15 Aug. 1821, HO 44/9/45; and see Baker's account to Hobhouse, 22 Aug. 1821, in HO 44/9/C & QF.

56 TS 11/663/3/25; Baker to Sidmouth, 16 Aug., and to Hobhouse, 18 Aug., and White to Hobhouse, 20 Aug. 1821, all in HO 44/9/C & QF.

57 "Carol-loo": author's term for this people's victory; cf. "Peterloo," their defeat. Hobhouse to Sidmouth, 14 Aug. ("6 P.M.") 1821, in 152M/1820(ii)-1821(i), Sidmouth Papers. "I write ... amid 1,000 Interruptions.... I hope Sir R. B. will be able to vindicate himself. But it is an onerous task, for his directions were express, and thrice repeated." Added Hobhouse: "It strikes me that it is highly important to postpone all military Reductions, until the effect of this Day is seen." The underlining and exclamation point in the quotation in the text appear to have been added, and perhaps represent Sidmouth's agreement with Hobhouse's statement. See also Hobhouse to Sidmouth, 15 Aug., 3 P.M., and Liverpool's own outraged reaction in his letter to Sidmouth, 21 Aug. 1821, both in this same file of the Sidmouth Papers. On Baker's fate, see Browne, *Scotland Yard*, p. 72; and Radzinowicz, *ECL*, 3:30 n. 4. After 1821 Baker continued to serve as a magistrate in County Middlesex.

58 Oakes: *The Army List: A List of the General and Field Officers as they rank in the Army*, 1821, 1823, 1832 (resigned commission), PRO, London. Birnie: Letter to Hobhouse, 27 Aug. 1821, HO 44/9/97; *DNB* 2:548-9; Fitzgerald, *Chronicles of Bow Street*, 2:373-80. Douglas Browne's comment is apt: "A clever as well as a very ambitious man, Birnie never did anything for the police." *Scotland Yard*, p. 72 n. 1.

59 Sidmouth to Liverpool, 18 Aug. 1821, 152M/1820(ii)-1821(i), Sidmouth Papers. "Crisis": Sidmouth to Lord Bathurst, 7 Sept. 1821, in reply to Bathurst's letter of 5 Sept., marked "too private to be published," both in 152M/1821(ii)-1825. Captain Oakes and Magistrate White refused to discuss the matter with Wilson; see BL Add. MSS 30109 ff. 223-53, 313-18, and 30110 ff. 14, 17, the Papers of Sir Robert Wilson, British Library, London. Wilson was promoted to general in 1841, named Governor of Gibraltar in 1842, and died in that post in 1849. He is buried in Westminster Abbey. *DNB* 21:601; Glover, *Slippery Fellow*, pp. 175-96.

60 Cookson, *Liverpool's Administration*, pp. 330, 335-8, 382-3; Norman Gash, *Mr.*

Secretary Peel: The Life of Sir Robert Peel to 1830 (Cambridge, Mass.: Harvard University Press, 1961), pp. 294–9.

61 "Report from the Select Committee on the Police of the Metropolis," *PP 1822* (440), 4:91–103, quotation on p. 101. This passage is quoted in Hibbert, *Roots of Evil*, p. 144; Critchley, *Police*, p. 47, and *Conquest*, p. 118; and Radzinowicz, *ECL*, 3:362. It has also appeared in a newspaper article on the English riots of 1981; see page 6, this book.

62 Peel's speech of 4 June 1822, *The Parliamentary Debates*, New [2d] Series, 25 vols. (London: T. C. Hansard, 1820–30), 7:790–805, quotation on col. 803. On this force, see "Report from the Select Committee of Inquiry ... into the State of the Police of the Metropolis," *PP 1828* (533), 6:326–34; Radzinowicz, *ECL*, 2:424, 521–2; and Critchley, *Police*, p. 44.

63 On the Luddites, see George Rudé, *The Crowd in History, 1730–1848* (New York: Wiley, 1964), pp. 79–92; Darvall, *Disturbances*; Thomis, *Luddites*; Thompson, *Making*, pp. 547–602; and Stevenson, *Disturbances*, pp. 155–62.

64 Richard Ryder, in *CPD* 21:808, 14 Feb. 1812. For force levels, see WO 17/2793; HO 40/1/6/498; and Darvall, *Disturbances*, pp. 73, 83, 258–60.

65 The term is said to derive from one Ned Ludlam, a Leicestershire apprentice who years earlier had, "when ordered by his father, a framework-knitter, to square his needles, took a hammer and beat them into a heap." This etymological explanation "has satisfied most historians since that day" [Thomis, *Luddites*, p. 11, citing J. Blackner, *History of Nottingham* (1815), pp. 401–3]. But see Thompson, *Making*, p. 496.

66 Darvall and Thomis stress economic causes and interests; Thompson and, to a lesser extent, Rudé attribute to the Luddites a Radical political consciousness. See Darvall, *Disturbances*, ch. 8; Thomis, *Luddites*, ch. 3; Thompson, *Making*, pp. 543–52, 576, 601–2; and Rudé, *Crowd*, pp. 89–90. The most recent writer on Luddism scales down its incidence and violence; see Thomis, *Luddites*, pp. 87–8, 112–14, 142. On the increasingly political nature of traditional disturbances in at least one region, see Alan Booth, "Food Riots in the North-West of England, 1790–1801," *Past & Present* 77 (Nov. 1977):99–107.

67 Thomis, *Luddites*, pp. 96–7, 107–8, 110–28. Quotation: Malcolm I. Thomis and Peter Holt, *Threats of Revolution in Britain, 1789–1848* (Hamden, Conn.: Archon Books, 1977), p. 34.

68 Sir Francis Wood, Vice-Lieutenant, W. Riding, to Earl Fitzwilliam, 17 June 1812, HO 40/1/8/616. See also, on the Irish comparison, Thompson, *Making*, pp. 510, 594–9. The property figure is from Rudé, *Crowd*, p. 79; see also Darvall, *Disturbances*, pp. 209–10. The two murders: manufacturer William Horsfall, an "active pursuer of Luddites," 27 Apr. 1812, at Huddersfield, Yorkshire; and William Kirby, 14 Oct. 1814, in Nottinghamshire, allegedly for informing on Luddite leader James Towle. Three men were hanged at York, in January 1813, for Horsfall's murder; Kirby's killers were never discovered. Darvall, *Disturbances*, pp. 120, 126, 130–1, 146–8; Thomis, *Luddites*, pp. 80, 181–4. By contrast, defending mill owners and troops killed thirteen Luddites, eleven of them at the battle of Middleton, Lancashire, 20 and 21 Apr. 1812. Thomis, *Luddites*, appendix ("Diary of Events, 1811–17"), pp. 177–86; Darvall, *Disturbances*, passim; Thompson, *Making*, pp. 567–8.

69 Darvall, *Disturbances*, pp. 75–6; quotations and estimates, in Thomis, *Luddites*, pp. 82–9, 95.

70 Thomis, *Luddites*, pp. 80–97, 144; General Maitland's opinion, as paraphrased by Thomis, *Luddites*, p. 84. Maitland to H.O., 4 May 1812, HO 40/1/6/487.

71 Darvall, *Disturbances*, pp. 66, 70, 251–2. Population, in 1811: J. R. McCulloch, *A Dictionary of Commerce ...*, 2 vols. (London: Longman, Brown, Green and Longmans, 1854), 2:1030; and "greatest village": Philip Luckombe, *England's Gazetter ...* (London: Robinson and Baldwin, 1790), vol. 1, n. pag., "Manchester."

72 Darvall, *Disturbances*, pp. 252–3.

73 Conant was knighted in 1813 and named senior magistrate at Bow Street; Baker succeeded him in that post and was knighted in 1820. Browne, *Scotland Yard*, pp. 63 n. 1, 65, 70; and Radzinowicz, *ECL*, 3:30 n. 4. For the two magistrates' Luddite activities, see Darvall, *Disturbances*, pp. 65–7, 251; and for local requests, ibid., pp. 74, 109, 247–8, 272, 275, 291, 293.

74 Thomis, *Luddites*, pp. 129–30, 147–50, quotations on pp. 149–50; and Darvall, *Disturbances*, pp. 137, 241–2, 294–6.

75 It is impossible to be more precise because scholars' findings are divergent. Surely Thomis's statement of twenty-one executed and five sentenced to transportation is far under the mark (*Luddites*, pp. 180, 185–6). Darvall's figures add up to forty-seven actually executed and thirty-seven sentenced to transportation (*Disturbances*, pp. 86, 104, 130, 135, 154, 157, 159); Rudé's statistics are thirty hanged and thirty-seven sentenced to transportation (*Crowd*, pp. 86, 89, 91). Darvall's figures for 1811–17 total 89 Luddites convicted out of 185 indicted; Rudé's, for 1811–13, are 107 convicted of at least 164 indicted.

76 Clerk of the Peace at Wakefield to H.O., 23 Apr. 1812, in HO 40/1, quoted in Darvall, *Disturbances*, p. 257. See also Thomis, *Luddites*, pp. 152–3; Darvall, *Disturbances*, pp. 83 n. 4, 122, 256, 257 ("trustworthy").

77 Darvall, *Disturbances*, pp. 245, 274–303; and Thomis, *Luddites*, pp. 126–30. Quotations are, respectively, from Gen. Maitland to Lt.-Col. Nelthorpe, 24 June 1812, HO 40/2/1/23; and Raynes to Maj.-Gen. Acland, 28 June 1812, HO 40/2/2/148. On Raynes, see Thomis, *Luddites*, pp. 82, 93; Darvall, *Disturbances*, pp. 133, 262, 285–6, 295, 301. For Raynes's pressing and, finally, pathetic requests for a government position, see his correspondence with Sidmouth, 18 May, 10 and 26 Aug. 1815, and 28 Sept. and "Dec." 1816, all in 152M/1815(ii)– 1816(i), and 20 Apr. 1816, in 152M/1816(ii)–1817(i), Sidmouth Papers.

78 Darvall, *Disturbances*, pp. 247–9.

79 *The Times* [London], 1 Feb. 1812, quoted in Darvall, *Disturbances*, p. 83; and ibid., pp. 87, 258; WO 17/2793; HO 40/1/6/498.

80 Darvall, *Disturbances*, pp. 1, 259–60; Thomis, *Luddites*, pp. 144–5.

81 Darvall, *Disturbances*, pp. 263–5. General Maitland (1759?–1824), "King Tom" to his men, was described by Gen. C. J. Napier as a talented, "rough old despot." Prior to 1812 Maitland saw much service in India, and in 1798–1800 was in charge of secret English expeditions on the coast of France in aid of French royalists. After his Luddite service, Maitland was appointed Governor of Malta, a transfer much appreciated since he "suffer[ed] severely from Rheumatism"; here, among his other reforms, Maitland overhauled the island's police system. From 1815 to 1824 he was commander-in-chief of the British military forces in the Mediterranean. Maitland to Sidmouth, 28 Jan., 5 Dec. 1813, in 152M/1813/I, Sidmouth Papers; *DNB* 12:818–20.

82 Maitland to H.O., 4 May 1812, HO 40/1/6/487; Maitland to Hawkins, 21 May 1812, HO 40/2/2/120.

83 HO 40/2/2/132, 155. Huddersfield: *The Times*, 1 Sept. 1812, quoted in Darvall, *Disturbances*, p. 263; Thomis, *Luddites*, p. 145. Provisioning: HO 40/2/322. Magistrates: HO 40/1/6/511 and HO 40/2/2/212.

84 Maitland to Gen. Dyott, 16 June 1812, HO 40/1/6/517; see also Gen. Grey to H.O., 23 May 1812 ("the entire army would be insufficient"), in HO 42/13, quoted in Darvall, *Disturbances*, p. 262. Nelthorpe to Acland, 12 June 1812, HO 40/2/1/10.

85 These were followed in May by an Unlawful Oaths Act and in July by a Preservation of the Public Peace Act. The latter allowed magistrates in adjacent counties to act in a disturbed county and authorized the military to disperse crowds without a magistrate present or the Riot Act read. Darvall, *Disturbances*, pp. 221, 240.

86 "Abstract of an Act of the More Effectual Preservation of the Peace, by enforcing the Duties of WATCHING AND WARDING," HO 40/2/2/171-2; Darvall, *Disturbances*, pp. 83-4; Brig.-Maj. M. Chamberlin to Maj. Hawkins, 21 May 1812, HO 40/2/2/120; and Maitland to Mayor of Leicester, 16 June 1812, HO 40/1/6/517.

87 HO 40/2/1/1; HO 40/2/2/192; HO 40/2/3/297; Darvall, *Disturbances*, pp. 73, 81, 86, 118 (Darvall quoted), 135-6, 224.

88 Lt. A. Cooper to Gen. Acland, 8 and 11 Sept. 1812, HO 40/2/3/294, 307. Raynes's report, 15 Sept. 1812, HO 40/2/3/330-1; Sir Francis Wood, Vice-Lt., to Fitzwilliam, 17 June 1812, HO 40/1/8/616. General Thornton reported (to Acland, 5 Sept. 1812) that the Yorkshire magistrates "have never called out the Watch and Ward." HO 40/2/3/282.

89 Raynes to Acland, 1 Jan. 1813, HO 40/2/3/511. Darvall, *Disturbances*, pp. 122-3, 234-5, 254-5, 329-35; and Thomis, *Luddites*, pp. 154-6.

90 Darvall, *Disturbances*, pp. 135-44; Thomis, *Luddites*, pp. 159-61.

91 Darvall, *Disturbances*, pp. 88-9, 144-7, 209-10; Thomis, *Luddites*, pp. 181-2, 185.

92 See Thompson, *Making*, ch. 15; Thomis and Holt, *Threats*, pp. 41-70; Darvall, *Disturbances*, pp. 153-9; and White, *Waterloo*, passim. On the East Anglia riots, see A. J. Peacock, *Bread or Blood: A Study of the Agrarian Riots in East Anglia in 1816* (London: Gollancz, 1965).

93 Thompson, *Making*, pp. 631-9; Cookson, *Liverpool's Administration*, pp. 109-16.

94 Darvall, *Disturbances*, p. 162; Thompson, *Making*, p. 649; and Thomis and Holt, *Threats*, p. 42. See also the contemporary accounts in Samuel Bamford, *Passages in the Life of a Radical*, 2 vols. (Heywood: J. Heywood, printer, 1842-4), 1:44-5; and Archibald Prentice, *Historical Sketches and Personal Recollections of Manchester* (London: C. Gilpin, 1851), pp. 90-3.

95 Darvall, *Disturbances*, p. 164. Three years later, in March 1820, near Huddersfield, 300 men assembled to protest the five martyrs of Cato Street; half a dozen men were transported for this "rising" in Yorkshire. Thompson, *Making*, pp. 661-2, 706-8.

96 The Pentridge (Pentrich) conspiracy becomes full-blown insurrectionism in Thompson, *Making*, pp. 649-69. Less heated accounts are found in Darvall, *Disturbances*, pp. 163-4, and White, *Peterloo*, pp. 170-83. The recent revisionist view (Thomis and Holt, *Threats*, pp. 43-61, quotations on pp. 50-2), which downplays the threat of revolution, has been adopted by Stevenson (*Disturbances*, pp. 209-11).

97 See Peter Fraser, "Public Petitioning and Parliament before 1832," *History* 46 (1961):195-211; Leon Marshall, *The Development of Public Opinion in Manchester, 1780-1820* (Syracuse, N.Y.: Syracuse University Press, 1946). The quoted phrase is Thompson's, in *Making*, p. 679. See also Harold Perkin, *The Origins of Modern English Society, 1780-1880* (London: Routledge & Kegan Paul, 1969), pp. 208-17.

98 "Ragged": Thompson, *Making*, p. 679, paraphrasing Samuel Bamford. Crown Law Adviser quoted in the trial of Redford *v.* Birley, in *Reports of State Trials*, new series [1820-58], ed. Sir John Macdonell, 8 vols. (London: Eyre & Spottiswoode, 1888-98), 1:1144. General John Byng quoted in Thompson, *Making*, p. 681.

99 Donald Read, *Peterloo: The "Massacre" and its Background* (Manchester: Manchester University Press, 1958; repr., Clifton, N.J.: A. M. Kelley, 1973), pp. 111-12; Thompson, *Making*, pp. 677-9; and Redford *v.* Birley, in *State Trials* 1:1224-5.

100 Quotation is from Joseph Aston, *The Manchester Guide, a Brief Historical Description of the Towns of Manchester and Salford* (Manchester: J. Aston, 1804), pp. 50-1. On the "police" of Manchester, see Aston, *Manchester Guide*, pp. 50-4; J. T. Slugg, *Reminiscences of Manchester Fifty Years Ago* (Manchester: J. E. Cor-

nish, 1881), pp. 238–9; F. S. Stancliffe's history of a local Tory club, *John Shaw's 1738–1938* (Timperley, Cheshire: Sherratt and Hughes, 1938), pp. 80, 104–5, 109, 142–3, 397; Arthur Redford and I. S. Russell, *The History of Local Government in Manchester*, 2 vols. (London: Longmans, Green, 1939–40), 1:53–4, 82–6, 198, 203, 209, 247, 259, 338–41; and Read, *Peterloo*, p. 78. On Nadin, see Bamford, *Passages*, 1:82; Prentice, *Historical Sketches*, pp. 98–9; Redford and Russell, *Local Government*, 1:87–92, 223; Marshall, *Public Opinion*, pp. 92–4, 105; Read, *Peterloo*, p. 79; and Thompson, *Making*, pp. 488, 629, 646, 844.

101 "The State of the Magistracy of Manchester," in Boroughreeve and Constables of Manchester to H.O., 29 Oct. 1812, in 152M/1812, Sidmouth Papers; Redford and Russell, *Local Government*, 1:79.

102 53 Geo. 3, c. 72 (1813). E. H. Lushington to Sidmouth, 13 Mar. 1813, in 152M/1813(ii)–1814(i), Sidmouth Papers. The first Stipendiary Magistrate was Rev. William Hay. On Hay, see Read, *Peterloo*, pp.75–6; Thompson, *Making*, p. 684; and Robert Walmsley, *Peterloo: The Case Reopened* (Manchester: Manchester University Press, 1969), passim. After Peterloo, Hay would receive the £1,700 living of Rochdale. See Rev. Francis Raines, *The Vicars of Rochdale*, ed. H. H. Howorth, 2 vols. (Manchester: Chetham Society, 1883), 2:284–325.

103 Boroughreeve to Sidmouth, 22 Mar., and Hay to Sidmouth, 14 Sept. 1818, in 152M/1817(ii)–1818(i); and Read, *Peterloo*, p. 75.

104 Gen. Byng to Sidmouth, 4 and 6 May 1812, HO 40/1/6/492, 499. On the special constables, see Aston, *Manchester Guide*, p. 52; Slugg, *Reminiscences*, p. 235; and Stancliffe, *John Shaw's*, p. 106. On the 1812 riots, see Francis Philips, *An Exposure of the Calumnies Circulated by the Enemies of Social Order, and Reiterated by their Abettors against the Magistrates and the Yeomanry Cavalry of Manchester and Salford*, 2d ed. (London and Manchester: Longman, Hurst, Rees, Orme and Brown, 1819), pp. 4–5, 57–8 [hereafter, all references are to the 2d ed.]; Prentice, *Historical Sketches*, pp. 51–3, 76–82; and Read, *Peterloo*, p. 97.

105 Yeomanry force levels: *PP 1810* (182), 13:339; *PP 1812* (100), 9:209–21; and *PP 1817* (81), 13:225–8. Bolton corps and watch and ward: Sidmouth to E. Wilbraham, 1 Nov. 1816, and Sidmouth to Boroughreeve and Constables of Manchester, 13 Jan. 1817, in 152M/1816(ii)–1817(i). The founding of the Manchester corps is traced in F. A. Bruton, ed., *Three Accounts of Peterloo by Eyewitnesses: Bishop Stanley, Lord Hylton, John Benjamin Smith; with Bishop Stanley's Evidence at the Trial* (Manchester: Manchester University Press, 1921), p. 87; F. A. Bruton, "The Story of Peterloo," *Bulletin of the John Rylands Society* 5 (1919):282; and Read, *Peterloo*, p. 81.

106 This diversity of occupations must moderate Thompson's interpretation of Peterloo as "class war" (*Making*, p. 686). Thirty-nine different occupations are listed for 80 of the 101 men in the Yeomanry; the list is in *Wooler's British Gazette and Manchester Observer*, 10 Aug. 1822, which is quoted in Read, *Peterloo*, p. 81 n. 3. See also Bruton, ed., *Three Accounts*, p. 50; and Stancliffe, *John Shaw's*, p. 59.

107 On the meetings in 1816, see Nadin to E. Wilbraham, 14 Oct. 1816, in 152M/1816(ii)–1817(i), Sidmouth Papers; Prentice, *Historical Sketches*, pp. 90–2; and Marshall, *Public Opinion*, p. 147. 1817: see n. 94, this chapter. 1819: Read, *Peterloo*, pp. 98, 107–8. Others who pointed to the cool handling of meetings before Peterloo were Philips, *Calumnies*, pp. 3–7; Joseph Green, boroughreeve in 1816–17, in his evidence at Hunt's trial, in *State Trials* 1:251–2; and Stancliffe, *John Shaw's*, pp. 104–5.

108 Thompson's interpretation of a class-biased conspiracy to draw working-class blood (*Making*, pp. 683–9) is overdrawn. For criticisms of this view, see J. D. Chambers's review in *History* 51 (1966):183–8; and Thomis and Holt, *Threats*, pp. 63–5. Equally mistaken is Robert Walmsley's ponderous defense (*Peterloo: The Case Reopened*) of the Manchester magistrates and Yeomanry. For effective

demolitions of Walmsley's arguments, see the unsigned review, "Man Bites Yeoman," *Times Literary Supplement*, 11 Dec. 1969, pp. 1413–16; Donald Read's review in *History* 55 (1970):138–40; and F. M. Leventhal's review article, "Why a Massacre? The Responsibility for Peterloo," *J. of Interdisciplinary History* 2 (1971):109–18. Pro-Yeomanry accounts are in Philips, *Calumnies*, pp. 23, 26–33; Sir John W. Fortescue, *A History of the British Army*, 13 vols. (London: Macmillan, 1899–1930), 11:57; and Maj. Oskar Teichman, "The Yeomanry as an Aid to the Civil Power, 1795–1867," *J. Soc. Army Hist. Research* 19 (1940):82, 143, an account that is marred by errors of fact and interpretation. The fullest, most balanced account remains Donald Read, *Peterloo* (1958, repr. 1973).

109 Ev. of J. Norris in Redford *v.* Birley, in *State Trials* 1:1371–2. Committee: Read, *Peterloo*, p. 81. Gordon Riots: "Summary of Evidence and Informations," 16 Aug. 1819, in 152M/1819–1820(i), Sidmouth Papers; and evidence at Hunt's trial and Redford *v.* Birley, in *State Trials* 1:424–5 and 1180, 1207, 1210–19, 1240, respectively. Arms: *State Trials* 1:1151.

110 Byng to Under-Secretary Henry Hobhouse, 14 Aug. 1819, printed in Redford *v.* Birley, *State Trials* 1:1381. Robert Huish, *The History of the Private and Political Life of the Late Henry Hunt, Esq....*, 2 vols. (London: J. Saunders, 1836), 2:182; and *State Trials* 1:232–4, 1378. The correspondence between the Manchester authorities and the Home Office, from 1 March to 15 August, is printed in *State Trials* 1:1375–81. Emphasis in the quotation is mine.

111 The following accounts were used: *Annual Register* 61 (1819): Chronicle, 106–26; the trials of Henry Hunt and of Redford *v.* Birley, in *State Trials*, ed. J. Macdonnell, vol. 1; Prentice, *Historical Sketches*, pp. 161–3; Stanley's account, in Bruton, ed., *Three Accounts*, esp. pp. 14–18; Read, *Peterloo*, ch. 8; Thompson, *Making*, pp. 684–6; and Stevenson, *Disturbances*, pp. 213–15.

112 The estimate of "20,000 strangers" is from the testimony of J. Shuttleworth, cotton manufacturer, in Redford *v.* Birley, *State Trials* 1:1122. Corroborative accounts are in Bruton, ed., *Three Accounts*, pp. 65–6; *Annual Register* 61 (1819): Chronicle, 125; Huish, *Life of Hunt*, 2:194; *State Trials* 1:227; and Read, *Peterloo*, pp. 24, 128–32.

113 "Largest": statement of James Scarlett (later, 1st Baron Abinger), Crown counsel and prosecutor at Hunt's trial, *State Trials* 1:240; "hats": account of Lt. W. Jolliffe, 15th Hussars, in Bruton, ed., *Three Accounts*, pp. 51–2. The low estimate, 60,000, is in Prentice, *Historical Sketches*, p.159. The *Annual Register* 61 (1819): Chronicle, 106, and *Gentleman's Magazine* 89 (1819): Pt. 2, p. 172, reported the size as 80,000. At Hunt's trial, Roger Entwistle, a Manchester solicitor, volunteered a figure of 100,000 (*State Trials* 1:227). A radical and a conservative source both claimed that 150,000 were present; see, respectively, "An Observer" [attrib. to J. E. Taylor], *The Peterloo Massacre, containing a Faithful Narrative of the Events which preceded, accompanied, and followed the Fatal Sixteenth of August, 1819*, 2d ed. (Manchester: J. Wroe, 1819), p. 3 [hereafter, all references are to the 2d ed.], and Philips, *Calumnies*, p. 46.

114 *Gentleman's Magazine* 89 (1819): Pt. 2, pp. 173–4; and *State Trials* 1:205, 211, 214, 220, 260, 348, 425, 1089–90. Francis Philips, apologist for the Yeomanry, was frightened by the orderliness of the vast crowd (*Calumnies*, pp. 28–32).

115 *State Trials* 1:1150–1, 1190; Prentice, *Historical Sketches*, pp. 160–1.

116 Nadin's evidence in Redford *v.* Birley, in *State Trials* 1:1166; Joseph A. Dowling, ed., *The Whole Proceedings before the Coroner's Inquest at Oldham, &c., on the Body of John Lees* (London, 1820), pp. 165, 457–60.

117 Quotations are from Prentice, *Historical Sketches*, p. 161; and Thomas Brown [pseud.], *The Field of Peterloo: A Poem Written in Commemoration of the Manchester Massacre* (London: J. Fairburn, 1819), p. 23, lines 433–4.

118 Evidence presented in Dowling, ed., *Inquest*, p. 179.

119 Sidmouth's statement in *Annual Register* 61 (1819): Chronicle, 120. Huish, *Life of Hunt*, 2:198–9; Hunt believed that "peace officers probably suffered in at least an equal proportion with any other class." Accounts ranging from radical to conservative agree on the Yeomanry's culpability: *State Trials* 1:1103, 1190, 1382; Dowling, ed., *Inquest*, pp. 112, 180; "An Observer," *Peterloo Massacre*, pp. 11–12; Philips, *Calumnies*, p. 43.

120 The Chairman of the Salford Quarter Sessions, Rev. William Hay, who was present, declared that the figure of eleven killed was "overstated"; three years later, at the trial of Capt. H. H. Birley, Yeomanry commander, Justice Best first stated that no one, then admitted that two persons, had been killed (*State Trials* 1:1183, 1260–1). In Parliament, in May 1821, John Cam Hobhouse, Radical MP for Westminster, produced lists of injured persons "running to 25 to 30 sheets, and defied them to disprove it" (quoted in Bruton, ed., *Three Accounts*, App. B, p. 82). *DNB* 9:941–2.

   Prentice's figures, in *Historical Sketches*, pp. 167–71, are based on those of the Peterloo Relief Committee. Of the eleven killed, including two women and one child, most died from saber wounds. To 420 persons injured (of whom 113 were female and 140 had "severe sabre cuts") the Committee awarded money grants totaling £1,200 and declared further that 140 other persons had sustained injuries worthy of some compensation. Bruton, ed., *Three Accounts*, App. A, pp. 78–80; App. B, p. 83. See also the totals, prepared in 1888, in *State Trials* 1:1251 note a. A complete list, including the age and address, of "the killed, maimed, or wounded" is in "An Observer," *Peterloo Massacre*, pp. 199–216. Among historians, the most authoritative casualty counts (11 killed, 560 injured) are in G. M. Trevelyan, "The Number of Casualties at Peterloo," *History* 7 (1922–3):200–5; and Bruton, "Story of Peterloo," p. 291. Understated figures are in H. M. V. Temperley (1 killed, 40 wounded), Radzinowicz (11, 100), and Stevenson (11, 400). Temperley quoted in Trevelyan, "Number," p. 200; Radzinowicz, *ECL*, 4:114; Stevenson, *Disturbances*, p. 214. Thompson, *Making*, p. 687, accepts the maximum figure for casualties; Walmsley, in his apologia for the magistrates and Yeomanry (*Peterloo: The Case Reopened*), avoids entirely the unseemly issue of body counts.

121 The chief police officer in Manchester was *not* among the villains that day. Nadin only served the magistrates' warrant on Hunt; he had nothing to do with the Yeomanry's charge. Indeed, noted one pro-Radical, "Had it not been for the interference of Mr. Nadin, the Deputy Constable, whom these men have particularly calumniated, it is certain Mr. Hunt would not now be alive." Hunt himself was grateful to Nadin. "An Observer," *Peterloo Massacre*, pp. 26–7, and Huish, *Life of Hunt*, 2:221, respectively. After his arrest, on leaving the magistrates' house to cries of "bring him out ... let the rebel out" (note the comparison to Irish rebels), Hunt was escorted by Nadin, "who offered to take his arm." But Hunt "drew himself back, and in a sort of whisper said: 'No, no, that's rather too good a thing,' or words to that effect." Stanley's account (partially quoted in Thompson, *Making*, p. 688); see also Smith's account, both of which are in Bruton, ed., *Three Accounts*, pp. 20–1, 68–9, respectively.

122 Thompson, *Making*, p.689.

123 Sidmouth to Bathurst, 26 Oct. 1819, in 152M/1819–1820(i), Sidmouth Papers. Thompson, *Making*, p. 684. On the Six Acts (60 Geo. 3, c. 1, 2, 4, 6, 8, and 9), see Cookson, *Liverpool's Administration*, pp. 178–99. At his trial, Henry Hunt was found *not guilty* of conspiracy, riot, or military assembling; Justice Bayley's address to the jury was long and sympathetic to the Radicals. *State Trials* 1:449–81, 488, 494. The most recent study of Fitzwilliam's removal is in E. A. Smith, *Whig Principles and Party Politics: Earl Fitzwilliam and the Whig Party, 1748–1833* (Manchester: Manchester University Press, 1975), pp. 346–53.

124 Norris: Byng to Sidmouth, 10 Sept. 1819, in 152M/1819–1820(i), Sidmouth Papers; Read, *Peterloo*, p. 75. Norris was named chairman of Quarter Sessions in 1825. Nadin: Bamford, *Passages*, 1:82; and Marshall, *Public Opinion*, pp. 92–4, 105. Nadin retired in 1821 and bought a farm in Cheshire. Redford *v.* Birley, *State Trials* 1:1082–5, 1147 note a; the Government paid the defendants' costs, which totaled £3,309.

125 "Rebellious": Sidmouth to Bathurst, 26 Oct. 1819, in 152M/1819–1820(i), Sidmouth Papers. *Annual Register* 61 (1819): Chronicle, 132; army force levels: WO 17/2793–6. In the Lords, the Whigs, led by the 3d Marquess of Lansdowne (*DNB* 15:1013–17), objected to an army level "greater than had in former times been thought sufficient for internal defence and external operations"; their motion protesting the militarization of the North lost by a vote of 178–47. Another motion calling for an inquiry into the state of the manufacturing districts was also defeated. A generation earlier, Lansdowne's father, the first marquess and 2d Earl of Shelburne, had opposed the use of the military in the Gordon Riots and had advocated the reform of London's police.

126 Yeomanry force levels: *PP 1817* (81), 13:225–8; *PP 1821* (189), 15:131–40. Sidmouth to Canning, 12 Dec. 1819, in 152M/1819–1820(i), Sidmouth Papers.

127 For Yeomanry called out on duty, 1822–7, see *PP 1828* (273), 17:283–7. In the Reform decade the Whigs eschewed use of the Yeomanry. For the men called out in the 1840s, see *PP 1844* (128), 33:217–18 and *PP 1850* (121), 35:127–40. See Thompson, *Making*, pp. 709–10, for a brilliant analysis of the legacy of Peterloo.

128 Darvall, *Disturbances*, p. 341. "Hints of a Plan of Police," Dr. Samuel Meyrick to Sidmouth, 8 Sept. 1812, 152M/1812/12B, Sidmouth Papers. See also Sir John Sinclair's "Hints regarding the Measures to Crush the Spirit of Insurrection and Robbery of Arms, &c., in the disturbed districts," to Sidmouth, 28 June 1812, 152M/1812/K, Sidmouth Papers. Like Patrick Colquhoun, Sinclair (1754–1835), also a Scotsman, was a pioneering statistician. He is best known for his *History of the Public Revenue of the British Empire* (2 vols., 1784) and his magisterial *Statistical Account of Scotland* (21 vols., 1791–9). J. Hardy to Sidmouth, 29 Oct. 1814, answered with thanks, 9 Nov. 1814, in 152M/1814(ii)–1815(i), Sidmouth Papers. Allsopp to H.O., 16 Oct. 1816, in HO 42/153, quoted in Darvall, *Disturbances*, p. 250. Sidmouth to Lord Lt. Whitworth, 20 Dec. 1816, in 152M/1816(ii)–1817(i), Sidmouth Papers. Post-Peterloo: a magistrate's plan in Marquess of Bath to Sidmouth, 5 Sept., and Mr. Ravell, Secretary's Office, Royal Hospital, to Sidmouth, 10 Sept. 1819, both in HO 42/194, cited in Radzinowicz, *ECL*, 3:389. Wellington to Sidmouth, 23 Apr. 1820, in 152M/1820(ii)–1821(i), Sidmouth Papers; Pellew, *Sidmouth*, 3:326, comments that "it does not appear from the papers of Lord Sidmouth that any immediate steps were taken in furtherance of His Grace's valuable suggestion."

129 Darvall, *Disturbances*, pp. 215, 221, and quotation on p. 341; see also Thomis, *Luddites*, pp. 145–6. On London, see notes 6–8, 21–3, 37–8, and 43, this chapter.

130 Apparently, the use of this French word in English dates from the 1790s. *The Oxford English Dictionary* [*O.E.D.*], 12 vols. (Oxford: Clarendon Press, 1933, repr. 1961), 3 (D–E): "Espionage," first entry, word italicized, from Lord Auckland's *Correspondence* of 1793. The second entry in the *O.E.D.* is from Bentham's writings in 1825: "To the word espionage a stigma is attached."

131 The annual average of executions for murder in England and Wales in 1812–21 was eighteen, which was double the annual average in 1805–11. In terms of executions, the decade 1812–21 was the most lethal in the period 1805–50; London in 1812–21 was averaging one execution a year. G. R. Porter, *Progress of the Nation* (London: J. Murray, 1851), p. 635; Radzinowicz, *ECL*, 1:155.

132 Pellew, *Sidmouth*, 3:293–4; and Thompson, *Making*, p. 689.

CHAPTER 6. IRELAND UNDER PEEL AND GRANT:
INNOVATIONS IN POLICE

1 Norman Gash, *Mr. Secretary Peel: The Life of Sir Robert Peel to 1830* (Cambridge, Mass.: Harvard University Press, 1961), pp. 21, 32−7, 79, 91, 95. Peel's grandfather had his textile machinery destroyed in riots in 1779 at Altham, Lancashire, and moved the family to "a more peaceable district" in Staffordshire. His grandson Robert was born at Bury, northwest of Manchester, and at age ten moved with the family in 1798 to southeast Staffordshire. The Peel manor at Drayton Bassett was near Birmingham and about 25 miles southwest of Nottingham, in an area that formed the southwest quadrant of the Midlands district disturbed by Luddism in 1811−12. See maps in George Rudé, *The Crowd in History, 1730−1848* (New York: Wiley, 1964), p. 82; Malcolm I. Thomis, *The Luddites* (New York: Schocken Books, 1972), p. 34.

2 On Peel's boyhood and family background, see Gash, *Peel*, pp. 1−26 (quotation on p. 14), 33−40; at Harrow and Oxford, pp. 41−58; and his career from 1809 to 1812, pp. 59−82. Critic: Anon., *A Letter to the Right Hon. Charles Grant, on the Catholic Question, containing Remarks on the Speech of Mr. Peel on that Subject, on the Motion of the Right Hon. Henry Grattan, the 9th of May 1817*, 5th ed. (Dublin: R. Milliken, 1819), pp. iv−v.

3 Peel to Rev. C. L. Trench, 27 Apr. 1816, the Papers of Sir Robert Peel, 2d Bt., BL Add. MS 40290 folio 220, British Library, London, partially quoted in Sir Robert Peel, *Sir Robert Peel, from his Private Papers*, ed. Charles Stuart Parker, 3 vols. (London: J. Murray, 1891−9), 1:232−3. (Hereafter, the Peel Papers are cited by manuscript and folio number only.) See Peel's charge to police magistrates and their reports on the condition of Irish agriculture and society, April 1816, in State of the Country Papers, Series 1 [hereafter, SOCP 1], 1771/76, ISPO, DC; and SOCP 1 1818/1961/3. On tithe, unemployment: 40294 ff. 160, 199, 215.

4 Peel to Gregory, 9 Apr. 1816, 40290 ff. 206−7. Peel to Whitworth, 24 Jan. 1816, 40290 f. 473. Peel to Croker, 23 Sept. 1816, 40291 f. 173; for the context of this remark, see Gash's vivid account, in *Peel*, pp. 173−4. Peel to Gregory, 9 Feb. 1814, in Goulburn II/13, Papers of Henry Goulburn, Surrey Record Office, Kingston-on-Thames.

5 *Dictionary of National Biography* [hereafter, *DNB*] 21:163−6; Gash, *Peel*, pp. 130−4; and Edward Brynn, *Crown and Castle: British Rule in Ireland 1800−1830* (Dublin: O'Brien Press, 1978), pp. 32, 48, 52. Quotations in *DNB*; and Gash, *Peel*, p. 132.

6 On Gregory, see HO 100/180/186, PRO, London; 40193 f. 33; Gash, *Peel*, pp. 113−14; *DNB* 22 (Supplement):779−80. Quotations are in Gash, *Peel*, p. 114; and opinion of Lt.-Col. William Blacker, "Personal Recollections," vol. 6, p. 114, County Museum, Armagh, quoted in Gash, *Peel*, p. 114. Peel once apologized to Whitworth for so often sending his letters through Gregory: "I trust we [the Castle trio] are on such terms of perfect confidence that it is precisely the same thing [as sending a letter directly to you]" (15 June 1814, 40188 f. 234).

7 Duke of Wellington, *Supplementary Despatches, Correspondence and Memoranda of the Duke of Wellington*, edited by his son, the Duke of Wellington, 15 vols. (London: J. Murray, 1858−72), 5 (1860):34−6; 40280 ff. 108, 125 and 40281 ff. 119−20; and HO 100/178/19, 301−4, 356 and HO 122/11/106, 113, PRO, London. Quotation is in Whitworth to Peel, 25 Nov. 1813, 40187 f. 136; for force level, see 40220 f. 49 and HO 100/175/402.

8 Yeomanry Ordnance return, 1801−14, 18 Mar. 1816, Official Papers, Series 2 [hereafter, OP 2], 456/25, ISPO, DC. "Terror": Dunlevie to Excise Commissioners, 15 Mar. 1813, SOCP 1 1537/21.

9 SOCP 1 1812/1404/21 (Wicklow); SOCP 1 1813/1544/44 (Kilkenny); SOCP 1 1813/1537/55 (Down); SOCP 1 1813/1537/36, HO 100/176/505−6, and 40199 f.

37 (Londonderry, Armagh); SOCP 1 1813/1537/2, 7, 9 (Antrim). Shercock: *Annual Register* 56 (1814): Chronicle, 39; and Tadhg O Ceallaigh, "Peel and Police Reform in Ireland, 1814-18," *Studia Hib.* 6 (1966):28-9.

10 SOCP 1 1812/1404/18 (Cork); SOCP 1 1813/1537/18, 20-3 (Cavan), 41 (Donegal), and 57 (Monaghan); SOCP 1 1813/1539/2, 3 (King's County); and Beckwith to the Adjutant General, 11 Sept. 1813, SOCP 1 1539/7, Pt. 5.

11 "Militia": 40280 f. 129; 40282 ff. 98-9; 40285 f. 83; HO 100/176/389-90. "Court": SOCP 1 1813/1539/7, Pt. 1. Peel to Desart, 14 Oct. 1812, 40280 f. 60. Expenses: 40280 f. 34; 40286 f. 171; and OP 2 1814/412/6.

12 J. C. Curwen, *Observations on the State of Ireland*, 2 vols. (London: Baldwin, Cradock, & Joy, 1818), 1:225. General Sir George Hewett, *Private Record of the Life of the Rt. Honorable General Sir George Hewett* (Newport: W. W. Yelf, 1840), pp. 78-9. See also 40182 ff. 92-3, HO 100/176/547 and 178/363. English: SOCP 1 1813/1538/20; SOCP 1 1814/1554/1; and HO 100/178/166.

13 "Extracts of Correspondence to and from the Military Department relative to disturbances in Ireland and the Military Measures adopted thereupon," Jan.-Aug. 1813, SOCP 1 1541/2. Of fifty-two requests, twenty-one were granted. 40197 ff. 163-4; HO 100/176/547; SOCP 1 1813/1535/46 and 1537/18; and J. Hay to Lt.-Gen. Cuming, 21 Dec. 1813, in WO 35/25, PRO, London. Limerick JP: Rev. R. Smith to Dublin Castle, 24 May 1812, SOCP 1 1405/5.

14 40182 ff. 14-15; 40280 ff. 37-8, 55. Countermand: 40281 f. 146. Whitworth to Peel, 2 Dec. 1813, 40187 f. 162; request repeated, 4 Dec., 40187 f. 167. For monthly force levels, 1812-14, see WO 17/1084-6.

15 Returns from Assizes and Quarter Sessions in Ireland, 1805-12, *PP 1813-14* (264), 13:213-377; for 1813 and 1814, *PP 1814-15* (331, 332), 11:313-57, 358-404. See also G. R. Porter, *Progress of the Nation*, 1st ed., 3 vols. (London: C. Knight, 1836-43), 3:225; and the 1851 ed. (J. Murray), p. 635.

16 Rents: SOCP 1 1812/1406/2; 1813/1534/10, 29, 1535/12-14, 30, and 1540/39. Faction: SOCP 1 1813/1532/2, 15 and 1537/40; OP 2 1814/411/7; and Curwen, *Observations*, 1:434-5. Feuds: 40199 ff. 34, 37, 54, 103; 40287 ff. 34-6; SOCP 1 1812/1409/33 and 1813/1537/29. Mail: SOCP 1 1812/1402/7 and 1409/71; 1813/531/1 and 1540/1. Houses: SOCP 1 1812/1401/53, 1405/10, and 1406/20.

17 Fair: W. Hull to Gregory, 18 Oct. 1813, SOCP 1 1534/21. Four: Gash, *Peel*, p. 171. Two: Gregory to Peel, 4 May 1814, 40198 f. 156; see also Gash, *Peel*, pp. 172-3.

18 H. Cole to Gregory, 5 Nov. 1813, SOCP 1 1540/153. Westmeath: 40195 f. 105, and 40196 ff. 14-15. This incident so affected Peel that he discussed it at length in Parliament. *Cobbett's Parliamentary Debates* [hereafter, *CPD*], 41 vols. (London: T. C. Hansard, 1803-20), 26:369-72, 25 May 1813.

19 O Ceallaigh, "Peel," pp. 26-7. Lord Castlemaine to Gregory, 22 Nov. 1813, SOCP 1 1535/43; see also Gash, *Peel*, p. 172.

20 For Willcocks's activities, see SOCP 1 1810/1275/16 and 1277/46, 91. On Connaught, see George Cornewall Lewis, *Local Disturbances in Ireland* (London, 1836; repr., Cork: Tower Books, 1977), pp. 32-5 On Tipperary, see Paul E. W. Roberts, "Caravats and Shanavests: Whiteboyism and Faction Fighting in East Munster, 1802-11," in Samuel Clark and James S. Donnelly, Jr., eds., *Irish Peasants: Violence and Political Unrest, 1780-1914* (Madison: University of Wisconsin Press, 1983), pp. 64-101, quotation on p. 93. For a pioneering recent analysis of the complexities of the conflict in the midlands (Roscommon, Longford, Westmeath, and King's County) and in Waterford, Tipperary, and Clare, see James S. Donnelly, Jr., "The Social Composition of Agrarian Rebellions in Early Nineteenth-Century Ireland: The Case of the Carders and Caravats, 1813-16," in Patrick J. Corish, ed., *Radicals, Rebels, and Establishments* (Belfast: Appletree Press, 1985), pp. 151-69.

21 Peel to Sidmouth, 8 Jan. 1814, 40286 f. 60. SOCP 1 1813/1538/13 (Mayo);

40199 ff. 172–4 (Roscommon); SOCP 1 1813/1533/8 (Tipperary), 1532/11 (Kerry), 1534/18 (Cork), 1537/2, 6 (Antrim), 1536/18 (Kildare), and 1535/50 (Westmeath). See also W. J. Fitzpatrick, *The Secret Service Under Pitt* (London: Longmans, Green & Co., 1892), p. 224 n. 3.

22 Meath, Cork: O Ceallaigh, "Peel," pp. 30–1. On the inefficiency of police, see SOCP 1 1812/1401/2 and 1814/1553/8 (Cork); 1813/1538/21 (Roscommon), 1535/3, 15 (Westmeath), and 1541/3 (Longford); and HO 100/178/1 (Tyrone, Donegal). Meyrick to Military Secretary, Royal Hospital, Kilmainham, 16 June 1814, HO 100/178/265.

23 Mills: SOCP 1 1812/1408/40, 42. His zeal may be explained by the fact that "rebels" had burned down his house in 1795. Desart: 40216 ff. 102–3, 106–7, 115, 120, 162–3, 174–6, 187–8, 195, 198, 214–15, 219, 223. Peel to J. Bagwell, Clonmel, 8 Jan. 1814, HO 100/176/250–1. Gregory to Peel, 4 May 1814, 40198 f. 160.

24 F. Lloyd to Peel, Oct. 1812, in OP 2 1814/411/7. Edward Gibbon Wakefield, *An Account of Ireland, Statistical and Political*, 2 vols. (London: Longman, Hurst, Rees, Orme and Brown, 1812), 2:352. T. English, JP for Westmeath, to Peel, 26 May 1813, 40211 ff. 280–96. Peel to Gregory, 7 June 1813, 40283 f. 96.

25 "Pray procure them [firearms] by hook or by crook," Peel wrote Gregory in rare informality, 24 June 1813, 40283 f. 161. See also 40197 ff. 42, 104; and HO 100/176/133–4, 244.

26 Desart to Peel, 12 Sept. 1813, 40216 ff. 147–8; Peel to Desart, 15 Oct. 1813, 40285 f. 87. S. Tighe, JP for Westmeath, 10 and 30 Nov. 1813, 40197 ff. 207, 274–5. Peel to Desart, 24 Feb. 1814, and Peel to Sir Edward Crofton, 28 Feb. 1814, in Peel, *Private Papers*, 1:142–3. Only days later (1 Mar. 1814) "An Irish Farmer" suggested to Peel a virtually identical proposal; see OP 2 411/4.

27 "Horrors": Peel to Whitworth, 2 Apr. 1814, 40286 f. 69. Whitworth to Peel, 8 May 1814, 40188 ff. 80–1, and f. 260 (America). See also SOCP 1 1814/1563/7.

28 Kildare: 40199 ff. 25–6, 72, 97; HO 100/178/267–9, 295, and quotations on 360–2, 368–9. Military opinions: 40199 f. 25; HO 100/178/263, 279. Gregory to Peel, 17 June 1814, 40199 f. 87 ("false," "Emmett"). Contrast Galen Broeker, *Rural Disorder and Police Reform in Ireland, 1812–36* (London and Toronto: Routledge & Kegan Paul, 1970), p. 64, with Gash's more accurate analysis, *Peel*, p. 170.

29 40188, f. 207; 40199 ff. 71, 154–5; *CPD* 28:168–70, 23 June 1814.

30 Broeker, *Police*, pp. 58–9. Why Dublin should be a model Broeker does not explain. He supports his French reference only by the statement that "on several occasions the chief secretary assured his associates that he had no intention of creating a *gendarmerie*." Broeker, *Police*, p. 59 n. 16. But see Broeker's own later admission (p. 103) that this was precisely Peel's intention. The police of Paris and the *maréchaussée* had provided models for Castle officials in the Irish police experiment of 1786–7, but I have found no evidence that the Dublin or French police influenced Peel's thinking in 1812–14.

31 Broeker, *Police*, p. 59; O Ceallaigh, "Peel," p. 33. Broeker states that Castle magistrates had operated in Roscommon, Limerick, and Westmeath "since at least the fall of 1813"; O Ceallaigh places them in Kildare and Westmeath. In fact, since at least 1807, these magistrates had been active in Kerry, Tipperary, Cork, Waterford, Kilkenny, Meath, and Queen's County, as well as in the preceding four counties. See the Papers of Edward Littleton, Baron Hatherton, D260/M/OI/1086, Staffordshire Record Office, Stafford.

32 O Ceallaigh, "Peel," p. 32; Peel to Gregory, 3 June 1814, 40286 f. 224; and 54 Geo. 3, c. 131 (1814).

33 54 Geo. 3, c. 131. Costs might temporarily be paid out of the Consolidated Fund but had to be fully reimbursed by grand jury presentments. All police presentments were "to have Precedence" over any other kind.

34 Whitworth to Peel, 20 Apr. 1814, 40188 f. 18; Whitworth to Sidmouth, 21 Apr. 1814, HO 100/177/398–400, and 16 June 1814, HO 100/178/261–2. Gash, *Peel*, p. 180.

35 54 Geo. 3, c. 131, ss. 1, 14, 17–19. 40287 f. 27; Saurin to Peel, 14 June 1814, 40211 ff. 75–8, and Peel to Saurin, 18 June 1814, 40287 f. 41. On Saurin, see Gash, *Peel*, p. 99.

36 Whitworth to Peel, 15 June 1814, 40188 f. 235; Peel to Whitworth, 24 June 1814, in Peel, *Private Papers*, 1:146.

37 *CPD* 28:163–72. "Romantic," ibid., col. 168; "stipendiary," col. 172.

38 Ibid., 28:172–4. "That blockhead, Sir F. Flood, ... cannot say anything in opposition to a measure without in fact supporting it.... He is too ludicrous to be worth answering." Peel to Whitworth, 24 June 1814, in Peel, *Private Papers*, 1:144.

39 Peel to Whitworth and to Gregory, 24 June 1814, 40287 ff. 51–4.

40 "An Act to Provide for the better Execution of the Laws *In Ireland*, by appointing Superintending Magistrates and additional Constables in Counties, in certain Cases," 54 Geo. 3, c. 131; royal assent, 25 July 1814. A short statute, twenty sections filling seven printed pages.

41 *CPD* 28:646–9, 8 July 1814; Peel, *Private Papers*, 1:147–50; Peel to Whitworth, 14 July 1814, 40287 f. 83. 54 Geo. 3, c. 180. Heading the few opponents were the Anglo-Irishman Sir Henry Parnell; Samuel Romilly, the legal reformer; and J. P. Grant, later Chief Justice of Calcutta (*DNB* 8:398). "How would they feel," Grant asked, "if it were proposed to put any portion of England out of the pale of the constitution?" He thought that "the best cure" would be tithe reform. *CPD* 28:693.

42 *Faulkner's Dublin Journal* [hereafter, *FDJ*], 30 July 1814; *Patriot*, 28 June and 12, 18 July 1814; *Correspondent*, 1, 12 July 1814; and *Freeman's Journal* [hereafter, *FJ*], 28 June 1814.

43 *Dublin Evening Post* [hereafter, *DEP*], 28 June and 2, 12, and 23 July 1814. Inked, handwritten comment on *Cork Mercantile Chronicle* [hereafter, *CMC*], issue of 4 July 1814, National Library of Ireland.

44 *CMC*, 29 June, and 4, 20, 29 July 1814; "glory": *Cork Southern Reporter*, quoted in *DEP*, 6 Aug. 1814.

45 C. Langley [Kilkenny] to Peel, 1 Jan. 1814, SOCP 1 1559/1; see also 1557/18. *DEP*, 10 Sept. 1814. *CMC*, 4 July 1814, quoted in *DEP*, 7 July 1814. Robert Curtis, *The History of the Royal Irish Constabulary* [hereafter, *RIC*] (Dublin: Moffat & Co., 1869), p. 4, makes this same point. Note the early confusion of the title of the Insurrection Act with Peel's police act.

46 "Bills": *CMC*, 20 July 1814. "Uproar": Letter from "An Irishman," 11 July 1814, Liverpool, in *DEP*, 16 July 1814. "Luddites": *DEP*, 2 Aug. 1814.

47 Gregory to Peel, 29 June 1814, 40199 f. 129. *DEP* and *FJ*, 17 Sept. 1814. File of applications in OP 2 1814/411/7. Peel to Sir Edward Crofton, 3 July 1814, 40287 f. 65. On no local ties, see OP 2 1814/411/7 and 1815/433/6.

48 *CPD* 28:170, 173; 40188 ff. 162–3, 279–80; 40189 f. 43; 40287 ff. 59, 84; 40292 ff. 68, 100–1; Charles Abbot, Lord Colchester, *The Diary and Correspondence of Charles Abbot, Lord Colchester*, ed., Lord Colchester, 3 vols. (London: J. Murray, 1861), 2:516.

49 40192 f. 10; 40287 f. 58; magistrate quoted in Curtis, *RIC*, pp. 6–7.

50 *DEP*, 15 Sept. 1814; Broeker, *Police*, pp. 73–4. July: HO 100/179/52–3. Fawcett: SOCP 1 1814/1559/48; and *DEP*, 13 Oct. 1814.

51 Castle plans: HO 100/180/158; 40189 f. 77. Willcocks, Eccles: SOCP 1 1814/1559/49, 53. Meeting: *DEP*, 15 Sept. 1814 ("busy"); Eccles to Gregory, 7 Sept. 1814, SOCP 1 1772/51 ("Properties"); Colchester, *Diary*, 2:516–17; 40189 f. 79; and SOCP 1 1814/1559/52.

52 Dublin: SOCP 1 1814/1559/57; *DEP*, 8 and 29 Oct. ("flags") 1814. Cashel:

Colchester, *Diary*, 2:516; Gash, *Peel*, p. 183. The best source on Richard Willcocks's career is a short biography in the Hatherton Papers, D260/M/OI/1086. See also "Minutes of Evidence taken before the [Commons'] Select Committee [Session 1824] appointed to examine the nature and extent of the Disturbances ... in Ireland," *PP 1825* (20), 7:99; 40197 ff. 30, 160; HO 100/175/18, 373; HO 100/176/300−1; HO 100/180/49; and SOCP 1 1814/1564/24−5, 30, 34. "Commands": Willcocks to Gregory, 3 Aug. 1814, HO 100/179/50. "I never was in the North of Ireland but once," he said in spring 1824. *PP 1825* (20), 7:112.

53 Sensitive: SOCP 1 1814/1557/10 and 1816/1771/72. Whitworth to Peel, 24 June 1813, 40187 f. 12; Gregory to Peel, 20 Apr. 1816, 40202 f. 276; and Peel to Gregory, 9 Apr.1816, 40290 f. 207. Donoughmore to Willcocks, 13 Sept. 1814, 40238 f. 323. On Richard Hely-Hutchinson (1756−1825), 1st Earl of Donoughmore, a strong advocate of Catholic emancipation, see *DNB* 9:381; and Alfred Webb, *A Compendium of Irish Biography* (Dublin: M. H. Gill & Son, 1878), pp. 247−8. *DEP*, 11 Feb. 1815; see also *CMC*, 7, 24 Oct. 1814. On Willcocks's retirement in 1827 from his post of Inspector-General of Constabulary in Munster, his successor, Maj. William Miller, declared him "pre-eminent as a Police Magistrate." OP 2 1828/830C/4.

54 Willcocks to Peel, 19 Oct. 1814, SOCP 1 1559/65; weekly report, 23−9 Oct. 1814, SOCP 1 1721/126. Augmentation: SOCP 1 1815/1721/74.

55 "Support": Whitworth to Peel, 15 May 1815, 40188 f. 85. SOCP 1 1814/1559/57−80, and 1721/5, 41, 126; SOCP 1 1815/1721/4−23, 25, 45. *DEP*, 15 Oct., 8 Nov. 1814. "Disguised": Willcocks to Peel, 19 Oct. 1814, SOCP 1 1559/66.

56 Assizes: SOCP 1 1815/1721/115, 126. Cost: SOCP 1 1815/1721/26, 38, 126. Four-fifths of the expenses went for the men's salaries and the care of twenty-two horses. "Scattered": Willcocks to Saurin, 15 Apr. 1815, SOCP 1 1721/38. Peel believed that Middlethird was tranquil; see *CPD* 29:335−7, 24 Nov. 1814. Broeker's evidence of one burglary and a mail robbery will not support his claim of "a major crime wave"; indeed, he writes later of "few serious occurrences." Broeker, *Police*, pp. 76, 78.

57 *FJ*, 13 Sept. 1814; and *DEP*, 25 Oct. 1814; Walter Butler, Esq., letter to Peel, 25 Nov., printed in *DEP*, 26 Nov. 1814. Peel, in *CPD* 29:335, reprinted in *DEP*, 24 Nov. 1814.

58 The amending act, 55 Geo. 3, c. 13 (1 Dec. 1814), allowed a police magistrate to head forces in baronies situated in adjoining counties and required him and his constables to take an oath giving them the powers of JPs. See *CPD* 29:335−7, 501−4; and *DEP*, 24, 25, 29 ("Grattan") Nov. 1814. See also O Ceallaigh, "Peel," pp. 37−40. The opposition in the Commons was led by J. P. Grant, George Ponsonby, and Sir John Newport. Lord Lieutenant Whitworth dismissed Donoughmore as "a most pitiful figure" (HO 100/182/240).

59 *FJ*, 28 Sept., 7 Oct. 1814.

60 *DEP*, 17 Nov.−15 Dec. 1814. *DEP*, 29 Sept. ("scribbling"), 10 Nov. (Lancashire), 26 Nov. ("everlasting"), and 1 Dec. 1814 ("immense").

61 Saurin to Peel, 29 Apr. 1815, 40211 f. 107. May: SOCP 1 1815/1721/53, and 40201 f. 34. Roscrea: SOCP 1 1815/1559/19 and 1721/57−8. The Government's first choice, Major Hugh Eccles, Brigade-Major of Yeomanry in Wicklow, declined because he wanted to stay in southeast Leinster; Peel then vetoed Gregory's suggestion of Major Humphreys, Brigade-Major of Yeomanry in Tipperary, on the grounds of his local interests. 40193 ff. 130−2; 40201 f. 11; and 40289 f. 40. On Wilson, see Hatherton Papers, D260/M/01/1086; 40197 f. 164; SOCP 1 1814/1563/5, 1564/2, 11, 31, and 1566/79, 82; HO 100/175/36, 347, 367; and HO 100/176/131, 216. Wilson's Tipperary police: SOCP 1 1815/1721/74, 83, 107; and HO 100/185/175.

62 Whitworth to Peel, 1 Dec. 1814, 40189 f. 216. Peel to Gregory, 18 Apr. 1815,

40288 f. 185; and see Gregory to Peel, 25 Apr. 1815, 40200 f. 282. Westmeath magistrates to Lord Lieutenant, 9 Apr. 1815, 40200 ff. 205–6. On Wills, see Hatherton Papers, D260/M/01/1086; 40187 f. 65; HO 100/175/147; HO 100/176/296–7, 433, 454; HO 100/180/37, 109, 268; HO 100/185/105, 187–93, 292; and HO 100/187/119.

63 Gregory to Peel, 8 Oct. 1813, 40197 f. 160; and Gregory to Peel, 20 May 1815, 40291 f. 85. Cork, Longford: SOCP 1 1815/1718/30, 51, 68; 40200 ff. 226, 277; and 40289 f. 201.

64 Limerick, Clare: 40190 f. 130; 40201 ff. 66, 68; and HO 100/183/472. Gregory to Peel, 13 May 1815, 40201 f. 62. Broeker, *Police*, p. 82, says only that it was "possible" that these districts were part of a Peeler experiment, and indeed his cited evidence supports no stronger claim. Whitworth's letter of 19 April about "the experiment" is only anticipatory, for the decision was not taken until 25 April (40200 f. 282).

65 "Rebellion": R. Waller to Peel, 19 Sept. 1815, SOCP 1 1722/14. Proclamations: SOCP 1 1815/1722/25; 40201 ff. 234–42. Gash, *Peel*, pp. 163–7; Broeker, *Police*, pp. 91–2.

66 "Savage": Sjt. Arthur Moore to Saurin, 3 Dec. 1815, SOCP 1 1722/99–100. "Committees": Wills to Gregory, 16 Apr. 1816, 40202 ff. 256–7. On Baker, see *DEP*, 24 Nov. 1814; HO 100/185/123, 179, 245, 338; HO 100/186/147; and HO 100/187/39, 351.

67 Whitworth, Sidmouth: HO 100/187/429; and HO 100/188/66. Rewards: SOCP 1 1815/1722/99–100. Cashel: HO 100/188/104, 106, 118. "Unanimity" and "dragoons": Moore to Peel, 14 Dec. 1815, SOCP 1 1722/113.

68 Waterford: Willcocks to Peel, 29 Jan. 1816, SOCP 1 1771/31. Stack: SOCP 1 1816/1771/16. "Service": Memorial of Tipperary magistrates, 5 Jan. 1816, OP 2 455/1.

69 40290 f. 46; "active": Moore to Littlehales, 6 Oct. 1815, SOCP 1 1722/40; Gash, *Peel*, p. 175.

70 Saurin to Peel, 5 May 1815, 40211 f. 109; 40287 f. 84; 40288 ff. 96, 209–10, 222; and 40294 f. 162. Baronial Police Act: 55 Geo. 3, c. 158 (1815). No constable under age sixty could qualify for a pension unless incapacitated in the line of duty. The Consolidated Fund, established in 1787 on the same principle as the Consolidated Annuities (1751), was a composite fund made up of the produce of various taxes and revenues in Britain and Ireland, from which various expenditures including the Civil List, the interest on the national debt, and other charges not dependent on an annual vote in Parliament were paid. 25 Geo. 2, c. 27; 27 Geo. 3, c. 47.

71 Investigation: Report in HO 100/187, cited in Broeker, *Police*, p. 42; "1787": Saurin to Peel, 4 Apr. 1816, 40211 f. 176; and "wounding": Saurin to Peel, 4 Apr. 1816, 40211 f. 176. On County Sheriffs, see 40290 ff. 200, 204, 221; 40291 f. 189; 40292 f. 52; and 40293 f. 135, April 1816 to June 1817.

72 The recurring fears about the militia are seen in HO 100/184/236, 472; HO 100/185/31, 149; HO 100/186/111, 143, 165, 258; HO 122/12/39; and 40191 f. 84. In September 1815 the Lord Lieutenant urged Hewett's "retirement" to Sidmouth because, from "Prejudice & Indisposition," the military commander refused to use the Yeomanry (HO 100/185/55–6). Yeomanry establishment, 1814–17: OP 2 1817/482/12, 27. Funding: 40291 f. 110; and 40202 f. 68. Peel to Military Under-Secretary, Sir E. B. Littlehales, 16 Feb. 1816, 40290 f. 86, and printed in Peel, *Private Papers*, 1:209. Roscrea: SOCP 1 1816/1776/103; OP 2 1818/505/16; Peel to Littlehales, 9 Apr. 1816, 40290 f. 208, and printed in Peel, *Private Papers*, 1:223. On the government inquiry into the events at Roscrea, see SOCP 1 1816/1772/7.

73 France: "Memorandum on the Army Establishment," in 152M/1814(ii)–1815 (i), Papers of Henry Addington, 1st Viscount Sidmouth, Devonshire Record Office,

Exeter. Figures are for annual average force levels. For 1814, see HO 100/177/
260, HO 100/179/309, and Kilmainham MS 1035, National Library of Ireland;
for 1815, WO 17/1089–90, and Kilmainham MS 1035; for 1816–21, WO 17/
1091–8. Army expenditures: OP 2 1819/559/6. Castle reactions: 40290 ff. 66–72,
166–71. "I cannot yet stomach our Establishment of 25,000," fumed Whitworth
in 1816 (40191 ff. 72–3).

74 Government memorandum on constables, in reply to Desart to Peel, 10 Jan.
1817, OP 2 842/6; Peel to Maj.-Gen. Sir Henry Torrens, Horse Guards, 17 Jan.
1817, 40292 f. 113; and Peel to Talbot, 28 Feb. 1818, 40294 f. 171. See also SOCP
1 1817/1832/12; General Private Correspondence 1814–21, f. 267, ISPO, DC;
40290 f. 83, 40294 ff. 69, 81; and OP 2 1819/507/25.

75 "Cavan": Peel to Whitworth, 29 Feb. 1816, 40290 f. 111. On Wills, see 40193 f.
122; 40203 f. 3; and 40204 f. 159. Broeker, *Police*, p. 102, mistakenly first places
the police in Cavan in 1818. Louth: SOCP 1 1816/1763/13, 16, proclamation
dated 12 Mar. 1816. On D'Arcy, see HO 100/176/361–2, 511; HO 100/180/43,
87, 154; HO 100/187/339; HO 100/208/357; and Chief Secretary's Office
Registered Papers [hereafter, CSORP], 1832/6467, ISPO, DC.

76 On Pendleton, see OP 2 1816/455/2; 40202 ff. 175–6, and 40211 ff. 140–1. Peel
to Whitworth, 21 Apr. 1817, 40293 f. 30; Whitworth to Peel, 17 Apr. 1817,
40193 ff. 171–2 ("God," "choice"). Broeker, *Police*, p. 99, is unaware of Pendleton's appointment to Louth in 1816.

77 Removal: SOCP 1 1816/1763/24, 31A. Reaghstown: Gash, *Peel*, p. 173, and
Memorial of Louth magistrates, 17 Nov. 1816, SOCP 1 1763/36; and aftermath:
Foster to Peel, 10 and 17 Nov. 1816, SOCP 1 1763/36. Broeker, *Police*, p. 99,
mistakenly argues that throughout 1816 the Peelers were "highly successful" and
won "general approval"; in fact, only the murder of the Lynch family, of which
he makes no mention, made them in demand.

78 Memorials of 16 Mar. and 6 Apr. 1816, and E. O'Brien to J. Vandeleur, 15 Apr.
1816, SOCP 1 1768/12, 15, 17. May: SOCP 1 1816/1768/20 and 1776/36.

79 Stewart: 40192 ff. 57–8; and 40202 f. 338. In letters of 19 March and 16 May
1817, Warburton requested a posting to Wicklow. In 1806 he had married Anna
Acton of Westaston, Wicklow; his letters of 1817 stated that he wanted to move
in order to improve his six children's education (OP 2 1817/481/19). "Intelli-
gent": Peel to Hawthorne, 26 Sept. 1816, 40291 f. 176. King's County: *Hibernian
Journal*, 17 June 1808. Gaelic: *PP 1825* (20), 7:131; see also HO 100/176/304 and
HO 100/179/181. I have found no evidence for the later charge that Warburton
was "the mainstay of Orangeism in the King's County," T. Vokes to T.
Spring-Rice, 15 Aug. 1835, in CHA:J19/1/9, Papers of Viscount Morpeth, 7th
Earl of Carlisle, Castle Howard, Yorkshire. Warburton's sons, all of whom left
Ireland, would become more well known than their father. Bartholomew
Warburton (1810–51) was a peripatetic writer on historical and literary subjects;
Thomas (?–1894) entered the law and then religious orders; George Drought
(1816–57), the third son, named for his father's brother-in-law, Capt. George
Drought (a Wicklow JP who saw long service as a Peeler magistrate in the City
of Limerick, 1821–36), authored some works on Canada and killed himself by a
gunshot to the head in a temporary fit of insanity. On Warburton's sons, see
DNB 20:751–3; and Henry Boylan, *A Dictionary of Irish Biography* (New
York:Barnes & Noble, 1978), pp. 362–3.

80 Tax: F. Lysaght to Gregory, 5 June 1816, SOCP 1 1786/29. Informations: SOCP
1 1816/1768/34, 37–8. "Court House": Warburton to Peel, 4 Aug. 1816, SOCP
1 1768/34. Tranquil: Memorial of 18 Feb. 1817, SOCP 1 1834/35. In 1817 the
cost for the three baronies plus Bunratty rose to £7,573. "Proclamations Issued in
Disturbed Counties in Ireland, under 54 and 55 Geo. 3," *PP 1818* (75), 16:416.

81 40204 f. 326; 40293 f. 126; Gash, *Peel*, p. 184; and Broeker, *Police*, pp. 100–1.
57 Geo. 3, c. 22; royal assent, 29 Apr. 1817. The act also empowered the Lord

Lieutenant to appoint "an increased Number of Chief and Sub-Constables" under a Chief Magistrate, although in each barony the number remained restricted to one Chief Constable and fifty subconstables. On the Consolidated Fund, see n. 70, this chapter. For shares of local assessments, see Proclaimed Districts, 1815–19, SOCP 1 1819/2086/4; and Proclaimed Districts, 1814–22, dated Feb. 1822, 40328 ff. 27–9.

82 King's County: 40193 f. 123; 40203 f. 328; 40204 ff. 3, 159; and 40205 f. 196. Clare: SOCP 1 1817/1834/12–13, 16; and 40328 ff. 27–9. Donegal: SOCP 1 1817/1832/37, 42 and 1819/2085/2, 4, 8, 16, 22; and O Ceallaigh, "Peel," p. 45. Half of the illegal stills (257 of 590) that had been seized by the Government from August 1816 to March 1817 were in Donegal (40203 f. 278). Dublin: Gregory to Peel, 12 Feb. 1818, 40205 f. 34 ("lawless") and 40294 f. 157.

83 Meath: 40204 ff. 307–8. Feb. 1818: 40205 f. 33 and 40294 ff. 169–71. Peel to Gregory, 14 Apr. 1818, 40295 f. 49.

84 F. Trench to Gregory, 30 Apr. 1814, SOCP 1 1563/7. Whitworth to Peel, 20 Mar. 1817, 40193 f. 117; baronies proclaimed, 25 Mar. 1817, 40193 f. 128. Whitworth to Peel, 31 Mar. 1817, 40193 ff. 140–2.

85 Wills was sent in because Maj. Hugh Eccles had again declined the chief magistracy (40193 ff. 120, 130). 40193 ff. 120–3, 40203 f. 3; SOCP 1 1817/1826/39, 41–2. "Motive" and "hazardous": Wills to Gregory, 20 June 1817, SOCP 1 1826/70; see also SOCP 1 1817/1826/69. Similar attempts to enroll special constables in Clare in 1819 were also discouraged by Dublin Castle (SOCP 1 1819/2080/15).

86 Petitions: SOCP 1817/1826/40, 42, 45. "Ruin": Memorial of shopkeepers and landholders, Rathangan parish, 12 Apr. 1817, 450 signatures, and Under-Secretary's reply, SOCP 1 1826/40. October: SOCP 1 1817/1826/91; and meeting: SOCP 1 1817/1826/83. "Party": W. Evans to Gregory, 6 Sept. 1817, SOCP 1 1826/80. Wills to Gregory, 12 Sept. 1817, SOCP 1 1826/79. See also SOCP 1 1817/1826/81–2, 84.

87 Carbery: Memorial of 15 Sept. 1817, and Wills to Gregory, 17 Sept. 1817, SOCP 1 1826/85, 87. J. Aylmer to Wills, 28 May 1818, SOCP 1 1952/18; see also SOCP 1 1817/1826/82.

88 Memorials from Rathangan landholders, 9 and 21 July 1818, signed by forty-nine and twenty-five persons, respectively, SOCP 1 1952/18. W. Evans to Gregory, 6 Sept. 1817, SOCP 1 1826/80. Outrages: SOCP 1 1817/1826/53, 80, 87, 95 and 1818/1952/31, 42–3. For costs, 1 Apr. to 31 Dec. 1817, £4,697, see PP 1818 (75), 16:415. Withdraw: Proclaimed Districts 1815–19, SOCP 1 1819/2086/4.

89 For O'Donoghue's biography, see OP 2 1824/588C. He would later be "annoy'd at being the first put out of office of those who have long acted under the Peace Preservation Bill" (O'Donoghue to Goulburn, 23 Apr. 1824, OP 2 588C); see also OP 2 1817/481/29. But O'Donoghue's unemployment was brief. Named a Stipendiary Magistrate in 1825, he served in this position until his retirement in 1839. "An Account of the Number of Stipendiary Magistrates in Ireland...," PP 1833 (191), 32:466–7; and "Return of the [Irish] Police ... receiving Pensions and the Sums received ...," PP 1847 (571), 56:267. United baronies: SOCP 1 1817/1837/50. Patrols: Wills to Gregory, 31 Mar. 1816, SOCP 1771/62 and 1771/56. Weekly report for Kilnemanagh and Eliogarty, 27 Oct.–2 Nov. 1816, SOCP 1 1772/75.

90 On the Baker case, see Wills to Gregory, 16 Apr. 1816, Clonmel, SOCP 1 1771/71. A different account is in Gregory to Peel, 1 May 1816, 40202 f. 308. I have accepted Wills's account because it is firsthand, long, and detailed. See also SOCP 1 1816/1771/40, 62, 71 and 1772/35, 40–1, 73–8, and 1818/1960/23. Costs: SOCP 1 1816/1772/41; "Grand Jury Presentments (Ireland), Sums paid under the Peace Preservation, the Constables , and the Insurrection Acts," 1816–23, PP 1824 (351), 22:387–402; and O Ceallaigh, "Peel," pp. 45–6.

91 Peel to Earl of Farnham, 14 Jan. 1817, 40292 f. 97.

92 Desart to Peel, 17 Mar. 1817, 40216 f. 315. Rumors: Peel to J. Creighton, 25 Apr. 1817, and to J. Boileau, 3 June 1817, 40293 ff. 41, 102. Employment requests are in OP 2 1817/481/29, March to June 1817. Peel to Marquess Wellesley, 12 Apr. 1822, 40324 ff. 41–4, and quoted in Gash, *Peel*, pp. 184–5. On the idea of a national police, see also 40202 ff. 71–9; 40253 ff. 70–2; and 40290 f. 108.

93 Chief Secretary Walter Cary (1730–7) was the last to have served so long. Of eighty-one Chief Secretaries from 1566 to 1818, only ten served as long as six years, eight of them before 1680. Sir F. M. Powicke and E. B. Fryde, eds., *Handbook of British Chronology*, 2d ed. (London: Royal Historical Society, 1961), pp. 169–71.

94 40295 f. 118; Gash, *Peel*, pp. 230–8.

95 "Stout": opinion of Lt.-Col. William Blacker, quoted in Gash, *Peel*, p. 229. See 40191 f. 178; *DNB* 9:308–9; and Gash, *Peel*, pp. 228–30.

96 Choice: Goulburn "Memoirs," f. 13a, Goulburn Papers. On Charles Grant, Sr. (1746–1823), see *DNB* 8:378–80 and Henry Morris, *The Life of Charles Grant* (London: J. Murray, 1904). On Charles, Jr., see *DNB* 8:380–1; Morris, *Life*, pp. 68, 80, 194–5, 237–8, 270, 291, 374–8; and John Swift Emerson, *One Year of the Administration of His Excellency the Marquess Wellesley in Ireland* (London and Dublin: J. Hatchard, 1823), pp. 20–2, 31.

97 "Amiable": Emerson, *One Year*, p. 20. Memorandum: HO 100/199/351–88, May–June 1820. Sir George Cornewall Lewis, *On Local Disturbances in Ireland, and on the Irish Church Question* (London: B. Fellowes, 1836), reprinted Cork: Tower Books, 1977. Gregory to Talbot, 22 Feb. 1820, in 152M/1820(ii)–1821(i), Sidmouth Papers; an identical assessment is in Emerson, *One Year*, pp. 21–2.

98 Valentine Lawless, Lord Cloncurry, *A Letter, to the Duke of Leinster, on the Police and Present State of Ireland* (Dublin: J. J. Nolan, 1822), p. 13 n. 3. Gregory to Talbot, 22 Feb. 1820, and Talbot to Sidmouth, 26 Dec. 1820, in 152M/1820(ii)–1821(i), Sidmouth Papers. Peel to Gregory, 15 Mar. 1816, in Peel, *Private Papers*, 1:215. Grant's erratic behavior was also a problem when, as Baron Glenelg (cr. 1831), he served as Colonial Secretary (1835–9) in Melbourne's Government. Glenelg presided over the transition from slavery to freedom in the West Indies even as he had great numbers of Highland peasants cleared from his estates in Scotland (1824–37). Also as Colonial Secretary, Glenelg defended the native Kaffirs in the wars with the settlers in the Cape Colony in South Africa (1835), just as he had earlier sympathized with Irish peasants [see his long despatch to Sir Benjamin D'Urban in K. N. Bell and W. P. Morrell, eds., *Select Documents on British Colonial Policy 1830–1860* (Oxford: Clarendon Press, 1968), pp. 463–77]. Glenelg's Canadian policy managed to confuse and anger all parties in the struggle for national autonomy. William IV denounced him as "vacillating and procrastinating." Faced with open rebellion in 1837, successive Canadian Governors resigned due to the lack of any clear policy from London. At Westminster, Glenelg was finally removed from his post (1839) because of "the ambiguous, dilatory, and irresolute course" of his ministry. Glenelg's resignation speech "conveyed a sense of ill-usage and a mortified spirit." He never again held political office. Grant never married, and at his death at Cannes in 1866 his title became extinct. The National Register of Archives in London and in Edinburgh have no record of the location of Glenelg's papers, if in fact they exist. *DNB* 8:380–1; John Prebble, *The Highland Clearances* (Harmondsworth: Penguin Books, 1969), p. 243.

99 Grant to Sidmouth, 9 Dec. 1818, HO 100/195/290. For the battle from January to July 1819, see HO 100/195/240, 272–3, 289–93; HO 100/196/120–37, 159; and HO 100/198/248. Force levels: WO 17/1096–7.

100 Handbill: SOCP 1 1819/2083/22. Gregory to H. Hobhouse, 22 Aug. 1819, HO 100/197, quoted in Broeker, *Police*, p. 108; Grant to Sidmouth, 4 Nov. 1820, HO

100/199/251. On rumored links to England, see "Minutes of Evidence taken before the Lords' Select Committee appointed to examine the nature and extent of the Disturbances . . . in Ireland," *PP 1825* (200), 7:59, 84; and Broeker, *Police*, pp. 107–9. On Ribbonism, see SOCP 1 1819/2080/39 and *PP 1825* (200), 7:84–5. See also James S. Donnelly, Jr., "Pastorini and Captain Rock: Millenarianism and Sectarianism in the Rockite Movement of 1821–4," in Clark and Donnelly, eds., *Irish Peasants*, pp. 102–39.

101 40328 ff. 27–9; Broeker, *Police*, p. 113. Tipperary: Willcocks to Gregory, 14 Jan. 1820, SOCP 1 2186/2; see also SOCP 1 1819/2083/21–3, 46. "Tax": Rev. B. Bernard to Grant, 15 Dec. 1819, SOCP 1 2083/44; and "precarious": J. Cooke, JP, to Grant, 13 Oct. 1820, SOCP 1 2186/23.

102 Grant to W. Lawrence, 8 Feb. 1820, Private Official Correspondence, Vol. 7, p. 50, ISPO, DC; HO 100/198/77; and SOCP 1 1819/2071/32 and 1820/2171/10, 34. Loughrea: SOCP 1 1820/2171/12, 41–2; HO 100/198/77, 363–72; and HO 100/199/365–7. Number of police: 40328 ff. 27–9; HO 100/198/136.

103 "Lighten": Lord Gort to Grant, 6 Feb. 1820, SOCP 1 2171/42. The county grand jury in July 1820 tried to assess the police tax countywide, in order to include the unproclaimed western baronies, and was stopped only by the assize judge assisted by a letter from Gregory. D. Browne to Gregory, 11 July 1820, SOCP 1 2173/35.

104 Loughrea: Memorial to Lord Lieutenant, 3 Feb. 1820, HO 100/198/368. Cost: *PP 1824* (351), 22:387–402. Meetings: HO 100/198/370, 372; HO 100/199/367; and SOCP 1 1820/2171/61. Military: HO 100/198/136, 145, 364–6, 371–3; and HO 100/199/230–1.

105 Weekly report of Pendleton, 31 Jan.–6 Feb. 1820, SOCP 1 2171/34. Sheriff J. Blakeney to Grant, 5 Feb. 1820, SOCP 1 2171/41, 89, respectively. See also SOCP 1 1820/2171/41, 44, 61 and 2172/21; HO 100/198/372.

106 "Attitude": Talbot to Sidmouth, 23 Mar. 1820, HO 100/198/292. Quarter: Col. Brown to Gen. Beckwith, 4 Mar. 1820, HO 100/198/224. "Intimacy": Pendleton to Gregory, 3 Mar. 1820, SOCP 1 2172/5; see also SOCP 1 1820/2171/44 and 2172/21. "Hiss": Brown to Beckwith, 4 Mar. 1820, HO 100/198/224; "feared": Sjt. A. Moore to Pendleton, 27 Feb. 1820, SOCP 1 2171/84; and "contrasted": Pendleton to Gregory, 3 Mar. 1820, SOCP 1 2172/5.

107 "Miles": Weekly report of D'Arcy, 27 Mar.–2 Apr. 1820, SOCP 1 2172/55. "Sleeping": Pendleton to Gregory, 3 Mar. 1820, SOCP 1 2172/5; and "Fatigue": Pendleton to Gregory, 11 Mar. 1820, SOCP 1 2172/21. Barracks: Sgt. J. Tesham to Pendleton, 28 Feb. 1820, SOCP 1 2171/84. Patrolling party: SOCP 1 1820/2171/89 and 2172/5.

108 Pendleton boasted of "every man whom I brought to tryal [*sic*] having been convicted" (to Gregory, 28 Mar. 1820, SOCP 1 2172/44). For assize figures, see SOCP 1 1820/2172/41–4, 49–51. On Pendleton's resignation, see OP 2 1820/504/23.

109 Yeomanry: HO 100/198/218. Gregory to Hobhouse, 12 Apr. 1820, and Col. Sorell (for Gen. Baird) to Maj.-Gen. Sir Herbert Taylor, 3 June 1820, HO 100/198/340–1, 453–4.

110 For Castle officials' views on the Insurrection Act, see HO 100/198/292, 314–15, 327, 372 and HO 100/199/259. For local magistrates' opinions, see the Memorial to the Lord Lieutenant from the High Sheriff and twenty-three JPs in Clare, Mar. 1820, SOCP 1 1820/2183/34. Reenactment: Broeker, *Police*, pp. 134–5.

111 "Immense": Sheriff B. Blood to Warburton, 22 Nov. 1819, SOCP 1 2080/39. "Barony": Blood to Grant, 4 Nov. 1819, SOCP 1 2080/36. A meeting at Ennis on 4 November requested the Peelers, but two other meetings (23 November, 11 December) opposed their introduction. Grant asked for the names of those against the new police. See SOCP 1 1819/2080/36, 40, 43. For Warburton's activities in 1819, see SOCP 1 1819/2080/14, 19–20, 23–4. Entire county

proclaimed 1 March 1820; see 40328 ff. 27–9 and OP 2 1820/504/14. Constables' powers: SOCP 1 1820/2183/19.

112 Proclamation of Limerick, Cork: 40328 ff. 27–9. Going: SOCP 1 1815/1721/89, 116; and *PP 1825* (20), 7:107. Outposts: *PP 1825* (200), 7:117. On Limerick Peelers, see SOCP 1 1821/2296/18; HO 100/201/99, 218; and OP 2 1820/504/23.

113 Westmeath memorials are in SOCP 1 1820/2181/25–6, 28–9, 46–8. "Grief": Memorial, 15 Aug. 1820, fifty-six signatures, SOCP 1 2181/28; and "bear, distress": Memorial, 6 Aug. 1820, eighty-seven signatures, SOCP 1 2181/26. "Strangers": Memorial, 16 Dec. 1820, fifty-four signatures, SOCP 1 2181/47. Gregory's authorization in SOCP 1 1820/2181/29; 40328 ff. 27–9.

114 Twenty-eight petitioners: Memorial to Lord Justices, 11 June 1821, SOCP 1 2292/6; seventy-four petitioners: Memorial from barony of Ikeathy & Oughterany, June 1821, SOCP 1 2292/8. On Tandy's jurisdiction, see 40328 ff. 27–9 and a detail of his duties in Carlow, SOCP 1 1821/2292/1.

115 For petitions requesting police, see SOCP 1 1821/2292/16–17, 21; for duty report, 18 July–8 August, a period in which sixty-four arrests were made, see Powell to Gregory, 8 Aug. 1821, SOCP 1 2292/19. Talbot to Sidmouth, 15 Nov. 1821, HO 100/202/82; a copy in the Talbot Letter Books, D649/9/3/10, Papers of 2d Earl Talbot, Staffordshire Record Office, Stafford. On Powell's nationality and prior service, see *PP 1825* (20), 7:169, 178; and *PP 1825* (200), 7:95, 106.

116 Memorandum on Irish Disturbances, May–June 1820, filed in HO 100/199/351–88; folios 371–88 are "reflections" following the narration of historical facts. (See also the short précis in HO 100/198/426–32, undated but filed between 30 May and 2 June 1820.) Grant explained that houses were destroyed *when* used as barracks, and that murders occurred *when* victims raised rents, overvalued tithes, prosecuted Whiteboys, or acted as informers. Grant's memorandum became the basis for his celebrated parliamentary speech in April 1822 on the condition of Ireland. See *The Parliamentary Debates*, New [2d] Series, 25 vols. (London: T. C. Hansard, 1820–30), 6:1500–15; subsequently printed as a pamphlet, *Substance of the Speech of the Rt. Hon. Charles Grant deliver'd in the House of Commons on the 22d of April on Sir John Newport's Motion on the State of Ireland* (1822). For the unfavorable reaction to Grant's memorandum by Talbot, Gregory, and Saurin, see HO 100/198/418–22, 433–41. See also Grant to Talbot, 2 June 1820, HO 100/198/438; Grant to Sidmouth, 28 Sept. 1820, HO 100/199/230.

117 Warburton and Willcocks to Grant, 23 Oct. 1821, HO 100/202/26. Warburton to Grant, 7 Oct. 1821, "very private," HO 100/201/38; Warburton indicated that at present it would be "absolutely necessary" for the Government to pay two-thirds of the police costs. See also Maj.-Gen. J. Lambert to Col. Sorell, 9 Oct. 1821, SOCP 1 2296/18. Aylmer to Grant, 12 and 15 Nov. 1821, Ho 100/202/119, 125; responding to the military commander's views on police costs, Grant stated that "Ld Aylmer is somewhat bitten" by the Irish gentry (to Col. Sorell, 23 Nov. 1821, HO 100/202/215).

118 Warburton to Gregory, 15 Oct.; Willcocks to Gregory, 20 Oct.; and Sidmouth to Talbot, 23 Oct. 1821, HO 100/201/128, 138, 154. Broeker, *Police*, p. 122, incorrectly states that Going was a Chief Constable. The "List of Proclaimed Districts, 1814–21" (40328 ff. 27–9) lists Willcocks as Chief Magistrate, but this was only after Going's murder (HO 100/201/26). When Willcocks later informed a parliamentary committee of Orangeism in the Limerick police, he alluded to Magistrate Going: "I believe that Major Going's chief secretary and *a chief constable* were connected with it" (*PP 1825* (200), 7:57, my emphasis; see also ibid., p. 49). Correspondence quoted in "Papers relating to the Disturbed State of Ireland," *PP 1822* (2), 14:751, refers to the "late Chief Magistrate, Mr. Going," as does Thomas Doolan in his *Munster: Or, the Memoirs of a Chief Constable*

(London: J. Davy, 1831), p. i. In 1820–1 Doolan was a Chief Constable in Limerick under Chief Magistrate Going.

119 On Going's Orangeism, see SOCP 1 1821/2296/24; HO 100/202/26; and *PP 1825* (200), 7:57. On the burial incident, Willcocks later explained that "two medical gentlemen" in Rathkeale certified that the body was warm but had been "dead many hours." Nevertheless, the interment "had a very bad effect on the minds of the people." *PP 1825* (200), 7:50. "Tyrant": SOCP 1 1822/2356/8.

120 "Wretchedness": opinion of Richard Griffith, *PP 1825* (20), 7:237; "exultation": Warburton to Gregory, 14 Oct. 1821, HO 100/201/89. On the murder, see Warburton's report to Gregory, 16 Oct. 1821, SOCP 1 2296/21; HO 100/200/13–14; and OP 2 1820/504/23. John Going, a relative in Tipperary, later had his house attacked on ten different occasions; he eventually moved to Meath, where he became a subconstable in the 1822 constabulary (SOCP 1 1822/2356/78, 80).

121 Rewards: HO 100/200/15 and 201/99. Stewart: HO 100/201/26 and 202/44; and *PP 1825* (200), 7:49. Talbot's opinion in a letter to Sidmouth, 7 Nov. 1821, Talbot Letter Books, D649/9/3/8; Sidmouth thought that Willcocks's appointment was a "particularly reasonable and judicious" decision (to Talbot, 11 Nov. 1821, HO 100/202/65). "Inefficiency": Willcocks's report in Grant to Sidmouth, 18 Nov. 1821, HO 100/202/115. Cost: *PP 1824* (351), 22:387–402.

122 Insurrection Act: HO 100/202/33–4 and SOCP 1 1821/2296/24. Alert: Gen. Aylmer to Grant, 9 Nov. 1821, in WO 35/25. Pensioners: HO 100/202/214, 289, 316–17, 385. Yeomanry: OP 2 1821/559/20; HO 100/202/48, 55–6, 114–16, 128–9, 153, 169–70, 201–5, 236. The lengthy correspondence reflects Grant's reluctance and the growing anger of Talbot and Sidmouth. Depots: HO 100/201/186 and SOCP 1 1821/2296/49. "Risque": Sidmouth to Talbot, 23 Oct. 1821, HO 100/201/154. Embarkations: HO 100/201/158, 186, 216, 220; and HO 100/202/1, 37, 71–4, 91–3, 307.

123 "Sweep": Gash, *Peel*, p. 367. "Butler": Goulburn "Memoirs," f. 14c; these were Lord Lieutenant Talbot's words to the new Chief Secretary, Henry Goulburn, when the latter was shown into Talbot's office at Dublin Castle.

124 "Acting" and "delicate": Peel to Earl of Westmorland, 14 Apr. 1818, 40295 f. 51. Native: 40211 f. 112.

125 D'Arcy: OP 2 1818/573/15; militia staff: 40290 ff. 163–4.

126 Willcocks: *DEP*, 8, 29 Oct. 1814; Powell: SOCP 1 1821/2292/19.

127 Irish police register, HO 184/1. Willcocks: SOCP 1 1816/1771/31. Powell to Gregory, 8 Aug. 1821, SOCP 1 2292/19.

128 Quantitative analysis of police register, HO 184/1. See Appendix V, this book, Figures V.1, V.3, V.4, and V.5.

129 Uniforms, in "Proclamations ... in Disturbed Counties in Ireland," *PP 1818* (75), 16:407–18. Nicolson: Peel Papers, 40328 ff. 27–9; Curtis, *RIC*, pp. 3–7; and Séamus Breathnach, *The Irish Police from Earliest Times to the Present Day* (Dublin: Anvil Books, 1974), pp. 25–6. Warburton to Gregory, 19 Mar. 1817, SOCP 1 1834/27..

130 Pay: *PP 1818* (75), 16:407–18; and "An Account of All Proclamations Issued, and Expenses Incurred, in Disturbed Counties (Ireland)," *PP 1823* (546), 16:709–23. In 1824 it was further reduced to £30. The Limerick pay stoppages were for new uniforms (the county grand jury disliked the old ones) and for hair brushes. The constables complained that 2s., 8d. for each set of brushes was deducted from their pay when brushes of similar quality cost 1s., 6d. in town. Shoes, which the men needed, were not provided. Anonymous petition, "Co. of Limerick Police," to Grant, 11 Aug. 1820, OP 2 504/12. "Peculations": *"Ipso Facto"* to Goulburn, 13 July 1822, CSORP 2864. The police magistrate was not named; Thomas D'Arcy would later be suspected of and Thomas Powell forced to resign over financial irregularities.

131 Police register, HO 184/1. Chief Constable: Wilson to Grant, and reply, 19 Oct. 1818, OP 2 573/17. Wilson's son: Wilson to Grant, 23 Sept. 1818, OP 2 573/17. Drought: T. Barnard to Grant, 14 Dec. 1820, OP 2 504/23. John Willcocks: *PP 1823* (546), 16:709.

132 Warburton and Willcocks to Grant, 23 Oct. 1821, SOCP 1 2296/24. Abscond: SOCP 1 1816/1771/62. Weekly pay: SOCP 1 1819/2083/31. King's County: Powell to Gregory, 8 Aug. 1821, SOCP 1 2292/19.

133 Wills to Peel, 19 July 1816, SOCP 1 1772/31; the occasion was the anniversary of the Battle of Aughrim, 12 July 1691. Wilson to Peel, 2 Oct. 1817, SOCP 1 1837/56.

134 Ireland's population (6.8 million in 1821) comprised a third of the population of the two islands, but the Irish share of Crown revenues was pegged at two-seven-teenths of the annual total due in the United Kingdom. J. C. Beckett, *The Making of Modern Ireland, 1603–1923* (London: Faber and Faber, 1966), p. 281.

135 "Sedate": Anglesey to Wellington, 14 Nov. 1828, T1068/2/21–2, the Papers of Henry William Paget, 1st Marquess of Anglesey, PRONI, Belfast. On Sir Nicholas Lawless, 1st Baron Cloncurry, see Webb, *Compendium*, p. 284; for his role in the Dublin police controversy, see *The Parliamentary Register, or the History of the Proceedings and Debates of the House of Commons in Ireland*, 15 vols. (Dublin, 1784–95), 8:334. On Lawless's son, Valentine, see Valentine Lawless, 2d Baron Cloncurry. *Personal Recollections* (Dublin: McGlashan, 1849); W. J. Fitzpatrick, *The Life, Times, and Contemporaries of Lord Cloncurry* (Dublin: J. Duffy, 1855); *DNB* 11:686–8; Webb, *Compendium*, p. 284; and J. O. Baylen and N. Gossman, eds., *Biographical Dictionary of Modern British Radicals*, 3 vols. (Hassocks: Harvester Press, 1979), 1:280–2. On Cloncurry's role in 1798, see Fitzpatrick, *Secret Service under Pitt*, pp. 38–42, 195–7, and Marianne Elliott, *Partners in Revolution: The United Irishmen and France* (New Haven, Conn.: Yale University Press, 1982), pp. 175–6, 181, 253–4. For Cloncurry's suggestions on reform projects for Ireland, see Anglesey Papers, D619/9/1–49; and Cloncurry's pamphlets, *Suggestions on the Necessity, and on the Best Mode of Levying Assessments for Local Purposes in Ireland* (Dublin: R. Milliken, 1831) and *The Design of a Law, for Promoting the Pacification of Ireland and the Improvement of the Irish Territory and Population* (Dublin: R. Milliken, 1834). Though he was by then in his seventies, Cloncurry was a principal organizer of private relief efforts during the Great Famine of 1846–51.

136 Cloncurry, *Letter*, pp. 7, 11 n. 1, 13–14. For the full title, see n. 98, this chapter.

137 Ibid., p. 15 n. 1. The salary was actually £700. Peel to W. Irwin, 15 May 1815, 40289 f. 32.

138 These are expenses for the Peace Preservation Police in 1822, as distinguished from expenses for the constabulary set up under the Irish Constables Act of 1822. County grand jury presentments, Ireland, 1816–23, *PP 1824* (351), 22:387–402.

139 Cloncurry, *Letter*, pp. 4, 15 n. 1.

140 "Distress": Warburton to Grant, 7 Oct. 1821, HO 100/201/38. Col. Thomas Sorell to Maj.-Gen. Sir Herbert Taylor, 27 Oct. 1821, HO 100/201/184–5; Warburton and Willcocks (SOCP 1 1815/1721/123 and 1821/2296/24), and also General Aylmer (HO 100/200/326 and 202/119, 125, 215) agreed with Sorell's assessment.

141 "Soldiers": Maj. J. Smith to Col. Pearson, 24 Nov. 1821, SOCP 1 2298/9. The Churchtown massacre of 31 Jan. 1822 (the besieged police had surrendered) caused a sensation; see SOCP 1 1822/2344/2–3, 16, 26, 58, 67; 2345/22, 59; and 2346/38. The policemen were "so batter'd cut and bruised about the head body and limbs that it's beyond my capability to describe the horrid ... mangled spectacle" (Rev. M. Purcell to Goulburn, 1 Feb. 1822, SOCP 1 2344/2); it was "dreadful to see the dead Bodies ... so mutilated, cuts and scars – Horses & Men lying dead, and the Pigs tearing them" (H. Fortescue to Sir E. S. Lees, 2 Feb.

1822, HO 100/207/11). Peeler Magistrate Samson Carter noted that the White-boys were "only restrained by their Leader who evinced much humanity, otherwise not a man would have escaped" (to Goulburn, 1 Feb. 1822, SOCP 1 2344/3). A month later, three men were hanged for the murders, and in 1824 four more were hanged and seventeen transported (SOCP 1 1822/2344/67 and 1824/2615/7-8, 10, 13).

142 SOCP 1 1822/2344/15, 24, 33, and 2350/93; Gregory to Goulburn, 1 Mar. 1822, in Goulburn Box C, Goulburn Papers.

143 Porter, *Progress*, 1st ed., 3:225. For committals at assizes and quarter sessions in individual counties, 1816-22, see *PP 1823* (305, 306), 16:625-86. See also A. G. L. Shaw, *Convicts and the Colonies* (London: Faber and Faber, 1966), pp. 177-8.

144 Assize returns, 1813, 1814, *PP 1814-15* (331, 332), 11:313-57, 358-404; and for 1816-22, *PP 1823* (305), 16:625-38.

145 Quarter sessions returns, 1816-22, *PP 1823* (306), 16:639-86.

146 Cloncurry, *Letter*, pp. 7-10, 11 n. 1.

147 Ibid., pp. 11-12, 12 n. 1.

CHAPTER 7. THE MAKING OF THE IRISH CONSTABULARY

1 Capt. W. Girod, 101st regiment, to Lord Lieutenant, 26 Jan. 1822, Chief Secretary's Office Registered Papers [hereafter, CSORP) 3144, ISPO, DC. Insurrection Act: "Special Sessions . . . [under] the Insurrection Act, and Persons . . . tried at Assizes," *PP 1822* (552), 14:785; "Returns . . . of Persons tried under the Insurrection Act," *PP 1823* (311, 336), 16:687, 705; "Commitments and Convictions under the Insurrection Act," *PP 1824* (174, 478), 22:189, 259. George Rudé, *Protest and Punishment: The Story of the Social and Political Protesters Transported to Australia, 1788-1868* (Oxford: Clarendon Press, 1978), pp. 77, 249, says that 379 persons were actually transported; A. G. L. Shaw, *Convicts and the Colonies: A Study of Penal Transportation from Great Britain and Ireland to Australia and Other Parts of the British Empire* (London: Faber and Faber, 1966), p. 178, says "less than four hundred altogether." A penal establishment was opened in Bermuda in 1823. Nearly a third of the 332 persons executed in Ireland in 1822-8 were executed in 1822; two-thirds, in 1822-4. Of the thirty-six executions in 1822-8 for Whiteboy nighttime armed assembly and robbery of arms, twenty-one came in 1822. Committals, 1822-8: "Summary Statement of the Number of Persons charged with Criminal Offences committed to the different Gaols in Ireland for Trial at the Assizes and Sessions during the last Seven Years," *PP 1829* (256), 22:436.

2 Lord Lieutenant Wellesley to Peel, 1 May 1822, Papers of Richard Colley, 1st Marquess Wellesley, BL Add. MS 37299 ff. 104-5, British Library, London: and Under-Secretary W. Gregory to Irish Chief Secretary Henry Goulburn, 12 Mar. 1822, Goulburn Papers, Box C, Surrey Record Office, Kingston-on-Thames. See also State of the Country Papers, Series 1 [hereafter, SOCP 1], 1822/2344/15, 24 and 2350/93, ISPO, DC. On the rape, see Gregory to Goulburn, 23 Feb., 1 Mar. 1822, Goulburn Box C; and SOCP 1 1822/2345/54, 2346/7, 16, and 2350/69.

3 Major D. Mahony to Gregory, 25 Apr. 1823, SOCP 1 2522/10; and SOCP 1 1823/2510/46, 2516/13, 2521/12. Carbery to Gregory, 13 July 1823, SOCP 1 2514/17; Jebb to Inglis, 19 Nov. 1824, quoted in James A. Reynolds, *The Catholic Emancipation Crisis in Ireland, 1823-1829* (New Haven, Conn.: Yale University Press, 1954; repr. Westport, Conn.: Greenwood Press, 1970), p. 142.

4 Quotations, respectively: Norman Gash, *Mr. Secretary Peel: The Life of Sir Robert Peel to 1830* (Cambridge, Mass.: Harvard University Press, 1961), p. 80; Goulburn "Memoirs," f. 1a, Goulburn Papers. In his first administration (1834-5), Prime Minister Peel would make Goulburn his Home Secretary; the fastidious

Goulburn also served as Chancellor of the Exchequer under both Wellington (1828–30) and Peel (his second ministry, 1841–6).

5 On Goulburn, see *Dictionary of National Biography* [hereafter, *DNB*] 8:283–5; Gash, *Peel*, pp. 80, 368–9; Edward Brynn, *Crown and Castle: British Rule in Ireland 1800–1830* (Dublin: O'Brien Press, 1978), pp. 53–4; and the most revealing source, Goulburn's unpublished "Memoirs," in his papers at the Surrey Record Office.

6 On Wellesley, see *DNB* 20:1122–34; Goulburn "Memoirs," ff. 14e–14i, "taste" at f. 14e; Galen Broeker, *Rural Disorder and Police Reform in Ireland, 1812–36* (London and Toronto: Routledge & Kegan Paul, 1970), pp. 128–31; Gash, *Peel*, pp. 367–75; Brynn, *Crown and Castle*, pp. 33 ("obscurity"), 42–6, 143–6.

7 Goulburn "Memoirs," f. 15b.

8 Rev. J. Chester to Gregory, 26 Oct. 1821, and J. Harnett to Gregory, 5 Dec. 1821, SOCP 1 2299/11; M. Cox to Goulburn, 24 Dec. 1821, SOCP 1 2375/20; R. Ruxton to Goulburn, 18 Jan. 1822, SOCP 1 2367/5; and Col. T. Cosby to Military Secretary, Kilmainham, 13 Mar. 1822, SOCP 1 2371/24–5.

9 Exclusive of clothing and arming. Memorandum on the Yeomanry, 16 Mar. 1822, in Goulburn Box C.

10 SOCP 1 1822/2342/11, 14, 37, 39, 59; 2343/16, 24; 2344/59; 2348/35, 69; 2349/27, 36; 2351/45; 2355/43; 2358/20; 2362/18; 2374/4; and 2376/3, 5.

11 Police costs in "Grand Jury Presentments (Ireland) . . .," 1816–23, *PP 1824* (351), 22:387–402. Goulburn to Peel, 30 Jan. 1822, the Papers of Sir Robert Peel, 2d Bt., BL Add. MS 40328 f. 20, British Library, London; Gregory to Goulburn, 30 Mar. 1822, in Goulburn Box C.

12 Peel to Wellesley, 12 Apr. 1822, 37299 ff. 50–2. Grant to Sidmouth, 4 Nov. 1820, HO 100/199/360, PRO, London. Note also that Grant wrote Maj. Gen. W. Armstrong, 7 May 1821, that a bill "has been for some time under the consideration of the Government" (CSORP 28). On Grant's role, see also *The Parliamentary Debates* [hereafter, *PD*], New [2d] Series, 25 vols. (London: T. C. Hansard, 1820–30), 7:863 (police), 865–6 (magistracy), 872–3, 7 June 1822. The magistracy act, 59 Geo. 3, c. 92 (1819), permitted JPs to act "in certain cases" outside their home counties.

13 Goulburn "Memoirs," ff. 17c–d. Peel to Goulburn, 30 Sept. 1822, in Goulburn II/14. Galen Broeker states that Goulburn "yielded" to Peel and "accepted a proposal based on the county police plan worked out, but never used, by Peel between 1815 and 1818" (*Police*, pp. 142–3). I have not found any evidence that Peel drafted such a plan.

14 Goulburn to Gregory, 16 Mar. 1822; Gregory to Goulburn, 30 Mar., 16 Apr. 1822; all in Goulburn Box C. Goulburn may also have been influenced by "Observations on Police" (n.d.), a long, incisive proposal for a Castle-controlled constabulary, drawn up by Maj. Samson Carter, Peeler Chief Magistrate in Cork (CSORP 1822/2885).

15 Goulburn "Memoirs," f. 17c; Goulburn to Peel, 30 Jan. 1822, 40328 f. 20. Cf. Broeker's argument that Goulburn wanted "a modified Peace Preservation Force, established on a permanent basis, and expanded to include all Ireland" (*Police*, p. 142).

16 Goulburn "Memoirs," f. 17b; Goulburn to Wellesley, 11 Apr. 1822, 37299 ff. 56–7. See also "An Act to Establish a more effective System of General Police throughout Ireland," unsigned, undated (CSORP 1822/3164). This twenty-eight-page document appears to be an early draft of Goulburn's bill; it makes no mention of any powers for local magistrates. The later, actual statute was given a much less alarming title (see n. 28, this chapter). And see "Observations on the Police Bill," CSORP 1822/3163.

17 *House of Commons' Journals* [hereafter, *HCJ*] 77:298, 24 May 1822; Goulburn "Memoirs," f. 17d.

18 "Annual Expense of a County ... under the new act called the Constables Bill," unsigned, undated, CSORP 1822/3406. In 1829 the total cost of the 6,000-man constabulary was £270,000, half of which was paid from Irish local taxes. London's new 3,000-man police cost £207,000 in 1832. Lord Lt. Anglesey to Grey, 17 June 1831, Earl Grey Papers, Papers on Ireland No. 20, Dept. of Paleography and Diplomatic, University of Durham; London: Leon Radzinowicz, *A History of English Criminal Law and its Administration from 1750*, 4 vols. (London: Stevens & Sons, 1948-68), 4:167 n. 29.

19 *PD* 7:852-3 (Goulburn), 855-7 (Plunket), 860-1 (Peel), 869-70.

20 *PD* 7:853-73. Parnell on cols. 853-4 ("system"); Spring-Rice, 857-8 ("pledge"); Grant, 869.

21 Ibid., Parnell, 853-4; Spring-Rice, 857-9 ("calculated," 857); Newport, 859-60 ("disgraced" ... "his country"); J. Abercromby, 862; Grant, 866-8.

22 Ibid., 863-9, 872-3. See also Grant's earlier speech on the condition of Ireland (*PD* 6:1500-15), praised by the *Edinburgh Review* and subsequently printed as *Substance of the Speech of the Rt. Hon. Charles Grant delivered in the House of Commons on the 22nd of April on Sir John Newport's Motion on the State of Ireland* (1822). It was this speech, not his speech on the Second Reading of the Irish constabulary bill, as one authority states (*DNB* 8:380), that later appeared as a pamphlet.

23 *PD* 7:863, 866-9, 872-3.

24 Ibid., 870-1, 873. On Hely-Hutchinson, Hume, Ricardo, and John Charles Spencer, 1st Viscount Althorp, see, respectively, *DNB* 9:376, 10:230-1, 16:980-1, 18:769-70. Ricardo (1772-1823), the celebrated economist, was MP for the Irish borough of Portarlington, 1819-23; he never visited Ireland. On Hume, see the recent biography by Ronald Huch and Paul Ziegler, *Joseph Hume: The People's M.P.*, Memoirs of the American Philosophical Society, vol. 163 (Philadelphia: American Philosophical Society, 1985).

The fifth son of John Hely-Hutchinson (1724-94), who had been MP for the City of Cork, 1761-90, and Secretary of State during the Irish police controversy of the 1780s, Christopher Hely-Hutchinson (1767-1826) was MP for the City of Cork, 1800-12, 1819-26, and the younger brother of Richard Hely-Hutchinson (1756-1825), 1st Earl of Donoughmore (cr. 1800), who had been a leading critic of Peel's Irish police of 1814. Another of Christopher's older brothers, John Hely-Hutchinson (1757-1832; 2d Earl of Donoughmore, succ. 1825), had served as George IV's emissary to Queen Caroline, meeting her in France on 4 June 1820 to offer terms by which she was to relinquish all royal claims; she refused and left the next day for England. Subsequently, on George IV's visit to Ireland, John sought, in vain, to persuade the King to reverse Sir Robert Wilson's dismissal from the army as a result of his behavior in the Queen Caroline disturbances.

Grattan's speech is recorded in four lines (*PD* 7:870). The elder son of Henry Grattan, who had died in London in June 1820, James Grattan (1783-1854), a Peninsular and Waterloo veteran, served as MP for his native county, Wicklow, for twenty years. *DNB* 8:424; Alfred Webb, *A Compendium of Irish Biography* (Dublin: M. H. Gill & Son, 1878), p. 233.

Sir Matthew Wood, MP for the City of London, 1817-34, labored for more than twenty years to improve the City police. A champion of Queen Caroline, Wood had escorted her in her triumphal progress from Dover in June 1820; in London she stayed for a time at Alderman Wood's house. Donald Rumbelow, *I Spy Blue: Police and Crime in the City of London from Elizabeth I to Victoria* (London: Macmillan, 1971), pp. 109-13, 120-5; Francis Sheppard, *London 1808-1870: The Infernal Wen* (Berkeley: University of California Press, 1971), p. 305.

25 The preceding statements are based on a comparison of the minority voting list

of the fifty-nine MPs who voted against Goulburn's Irish constabulary bill (*PD* 7:873, 7 June 1822) with voting lists on other issues before Parliament.

1 On some issues we have majority as well as minority voting lists, that is, we have a complete picture of how the fifty-nine police opponents voted. On a motion for reform of Parliament (April 1822), of our fifty-nine police opponents, fifty-one voted for reform, eight did not vote, and not one voted against reform. On a motion for investigating "the Catholic claims," that is, that Catholics be entitled to serve as MPs (February 1825), of our fifty-nine police opponents, forty-six voted in favor of such an inquiry, ten did not vote, and only three voted against. In sum, of those *who voted* on these two issues, 100 percent favored parliamentary reform and 94 percent approved an inquiry into the Catholic claims.

2 On some issues we have only the *minority* voting lists. In these cases, we do not know how many of the fifty-nine police opponents voted with the majority *or* did not vote at all. From existing minority lists on different motions, we are able to say that 63 percent (thirty-seven of fifty-nine MPs) favored an inquiry into Peterloo (May 1821); 48 percent (twenty-eight MPs) voted for remission of Henry Hunt's prison term (April 1822); and 54 percent (thirty-two MPs) favored an investigation into Sir Robert Wilson's dismissal from the army (February 1822).

3 If on the preceding issues we knew how many of our fifty-nine MPs did *not* vote, the figures as percentages of *those voting* would be higher. On the aforementioned Reform and Catholic questions, for which we have majority as well as minority voting lists, we know that 13 and 17 percent, respectively, of our fifty-nine MPs did not vote. If we assume that on the other issues, for which we have only minority voting lists, an average of 15 percent (nine MPs) did not vote, we may conjecture that of our fifty-nine MPs who *actually voted*, perhaps about 74 percent favored an inquiry into Peterloo, 56 percent wanted Hunt released, and 64 percent thought Wilson's case should be looked into.

Sources. Minority voting list, 1822 Irish constables bill, *PD* 7:873; Peterloo inquiry, May 1821, 5:845–6; Wilson's dismissal, Feb. 1822, 6:344–5; Hunt's imprisonment and reform of Parliament, Apr. 1822, 7:49, 139–40, respectively; and Catholic claims, Feb. 1825, 12:840–4.

26 *HCJ* 77 (1822–3):327. Goulburn to Wellesley, 11, 15 June 1822, 37299 ff. 207, 213; Wellesley to Goulburn, 16 June 1822, in Goulburn II/22/ABCD.

27 Goulburn "Memoirs," f. 17d; Goulburn to Wellesley, 19 June, 7 July 1822, 37299 ff. 238, 277; *HCJ* 77:439, 474, 480.

28 "An Act for the Appointment of Constables, and to secure the effectual Performance of the Duties of their Office, and for the Appointment of Magistrates, in *Ireland*, in certain cases," 3 Geo. 4, c. 103 ss. 1, 9, 11–13, 15–19.

29 Ibid., ss. 1–2, 16, 23–9, 32–5.

30 *Dublin Evening Post* [hereafter, *DEP*], 2 Feb. (quotation), 16 Mar., 28 May, and 11 June 1822.

31 John Swift Emerson, *One Year of the Administration of His Excellency the Marquess Wellesley in Ireland* (London and Dublin: J. Hatchard, 1823), pp. 47–55, quotations on pp. 51–5. Emerson's other work, *Erin's Green Island* (1823), was printed for the "Irish Protestant Office." For a discussion of the argument that liberty withers from a history of government centralization, including the growth of "a military police," see Alexis de Tocqueville, *The Old Regime and the French Revolution* (written 1853–5, publ. 1856), tr. Stuart Gilbert (Garden City, N.Y.: Doubleday, 1955), pp. 67–76; and Richard Herr, *Tocqueville and the Old Regime* (Princeton, N.J.: Princeton University Press, 1962), pp. 33, 49–55, 82–7.

32 See Martin J. Waters, "Peasants and Emigrants: Considerations of the Gaelic League as a Social Movement," in Daniel J. Casey and Robert E. Rhodes, eds.,

Views of the Irish Peasantry 1800–1916 (Hamden, Conn.: Archon Books, Shoe String Press, 1977), pp. 160–77; more broadly, the Anglo-Irish dilemma is brilliantly explored in F. S. L. Lyons's Ford Lectures, given at Oxford in 1978 and published as *Culture and Anarchy in Ireland 1890–1939* (Oxford: Clarendon Press, 1979).

33 "Purgation": Goulburn "Memoirs," f. 17a; "corrupt": Warburton to Goulburn, 7 Dec. 1822, in revised list of magistracy, Official Papers, Series 2, 1790–1831 [hereafter, OP 2], 534/14, ISPO, DC. See also Wellesley to Peel, 27 Sept. 1822, 37299 ff. 338–40.

34 Charles Grant, in *PD* 7:872, 7 June 1822; cf. Broeker, *Police*, pp. 151–2.

35 This figure is conservative and conjectural, based on my identification of 259 persons removed from the rolls of *ten* of Ireland's thirty-two counties. Meath and Roscommon lost the fewest, four and ten persons, respectively. Broeker, citing only the case of Meath, concluded that the revisions were "not so far reaching as ... had [been] intended" (*Police*, p. 151). I have been unable to find actual totals for commissioned magistrates in 1823–4. We know that in 1815 there were 4,175 JPs on the rolls; of these, however, 557 were dead, 1,355 were not primarily resident in Ireland, and 311 were no longer acting as magistrates. There were thus about 1,900 resident commissioned JPs in 1815. But Peel in 1816 apparently steered clear of any substantive revision of the list, so, allowing for removal of the 557 deceased JPs (who presumably would not have objected had Peel removed their names), the rolls in 1816 might have contained about 3,600 names. In addition, in the period 1815–21, the Government issued new commissions, including many to military officers. Whatever the totals were immediately before and after the Castle's revision of 1822–3, we do know that ten years later, after another revision in 1832, the number of JPs on the rolls was down to a total of 2,651. See "A Return of the Number and Names of Magistracy in the Commission of the Peace in Ireland ...; Names and Number Superseded," *PP 1830–1* (171), 8:291–390.

36 *Dublin Morning Post* [hereafter, *DMP*], 11, 17 (Cork), 19 Dec. 1822; "Minutes of Evidence taken before the Lords' Select Committee appointed to examine the nature and extent of the Disturbances ... in Ireland," *PP 1825* (200), 7:55, 75 (hardly a county), ev. of Matthew Blacker; and magistracy lists in OP 2 1822/534/14, 15 and in Wellesley to Peel, 29 Jan. 1823, HO 100/208/31.

37 "Anonymous (a Magistrate)" to Goulburn, 10 July 1822, CSORP 2863; Westmeath quoted in *PP 1825* (200), 7:231; Goulburn to Peel, 16 Sept. 1823, 40329 f. 138; Maj. D. Mahony to Goulburn, 4 Aug. 1823, in Goulburn II/14; 7 & 8 Geo. 4, c. 67 (1827).

38 Gregory to Goulburn, 6 Mar. 1824, in Goulburn Box C; Peel Papers, 40329 ff. 11–16, 124–39; Wellesley Papers, 37299 ff. 49–50; Broeker, *Police*, p. 153; Angus Macintyre, *The Liberator: Daniel O'Connell and the Irish Party, 1830–1847* (New York: Macmillan, 1965), pp. 169–72. My thanks to James S. Donnelly, Jr., University of Wisconsin–Madison, for his remarks in correspondence on the subject of tithe composition.

39 Goulburn to Peel, 16 Sept. 1823, 40329 f. 138. Wellesley thought it "neither prudent, nor just, to precipitate the extension of *so considerable a change of system*, the beneficial progress of which might be frustrated ... by a premature effort to force its universal application" (letter to Peel, 29 Jan. 1823, HO 100/208/29).

40 Rev. James Burrowes to Gregory, 19 Sept. 1823, Ballina, Sligo, SOCP 1 2502/59; Roscommon: SOCP 1 1823/2502/34; constabulary return, Dec. 1824, OP 2 615/2.

41 3 Geo. 4, c. 103 s. 1; "Report of the Select Committee appointed to inquire into the state of Ireland, more particularly with reference to ... Disturbances in that part of the United Kingdom," *PP 1825* (129), 8:163, ev. of Lord Killeen.

42 *PP 1825* (129), 8:118, ev. of D. O'Connell. *DMP*, 25 Nov. 1822; on the meeting,

see also Gregory to Peel, 28 Nov. 1822, in Goulburn II/14, and Peel Papers, 40328 f. 258. Anonymous to Lord Lieutenant, 27 Nov. 1822, CSORP 3245; by contrast, the Knight of Kerry reported that one of the newly appointed constables had once "run down a Whiteboy after a chase of two miles, a man much larger than himself" (letter to Gregory, 30 Nov. 1822, SOCP 1 2349/72).

43 King's County: *DMP*, 14 Nov. 1822. Limerick City: *PP 1825* (200), 7:46. County Limerick: *DMP*, 9 Nov. 1822; SOCP 1 1822/2354/36. Tipperary: *DMP*, 19 Nov. 1822 ("floating"); Willcocks's report, 14 Nov. 1822, OP 2 534/12 ("unanimity"). Cork: *DMP*, 28 Nov. 1822; the quotation is in "A Friend to the Country & to the Public" to Goulburn, 11 Nov. 1822, CSORP 2985; see also M. Connell to Lord Lieutenant, 14 Sept. 1822, CSORP 1176, and "A Country Farmer" to Goulburn, 5 Oct. 1822, CSORP 1970, who closed by saying that he was "just on the eve of quitting Ireland, probably for ever." Clare: "Minutes of Evidence taken before the [Commons'] Select Committee appointed to examine the nature and extent of the Disturbances … in Ireland," *PP 1825* (20), 7:159. Westmeath: SOCP 1 1824/2610/9, 11. Galway: Warburton to Goulburn, 3 July 1824, and Lord Clancarty to Goulburn, 9 Aug. 1824, in SOCP 1 2624/21. Parliamentary committee: *PP 1825* (129), 8:9, 163, ev. of Lord Killeen and R. Sheil, Apr. 1824. Powell: "Minutes of Evidence taken before the Commissioners appointed to inquire into Charges of Malversation in the Police Establishment of the *Leinster* District, sitting during the last Winter in the Castle of Dublin," 19 Dec. 1827–12 Feb. 1828, printed 27 June 1828, *PP 1828* (486), 22:218 (App. 31, p. 39). My account conflicts with that of Broeker, who stated that "[e]vidently the magistrates in most of the counties resisted … the Castle and retained the right of appointment" (*Police*, pp. 155–6).

44 Constabulary return, Dec. 1824, OP 2 615/2. For force levels at other dates, see "4,335 subconstables, constables, and chief constables," in Goulburn to Peel, 26 Nov. 1824, 40330 ff. 240–3; and also "1,825 protestants and 845 catholics in the organization," Apr. 1824, in Peel Papers 40611, and "a force … totalling 4,500 men," Willcocks to Goulburn, 20 Sept. 1825, in HO 100/210, both cited in Broeker, *Police*, pp. 157, 158, respectively. Robert Curtis, *The History of the Royal Irish Constabulary* (Dublin: Moffat & Co., 1869), pp. 10–11, prints a return of 5,008 constables and 313 Chief Constables, apparently for the late 1820s, but unfortunately gives no date.

45 3 Geo. 4, c. 103 s. 1.

46 County police strength, Dec. 1824, OP 2 615/2; county population at the 1821 census. For Tipperary requests for police, see SOCP 1 1824/2621/50, and Tipperary applications, 1827–9, in Earl Grey Papers, Papers on Ireland, No. 23. In August 1824 Galway JPs requested a county force totaling 369 constables (SOCP 1 1824/2624/21).

47 City of Limerick: fifty men, cut to forty in May 1828, and County Limerick: seventy-four men, cut to sixty-seven in December 1829, both in "An Account of the Expenses incurred under the Peace Preservation Act during the last Three Years; Number of Men employed …," *PP 1830* (322), 26:427–32; see also CSORP 1827/333. Cork: "An Account of Proclamations Issued under the … Peace Preservation Act," *PP 1826* (210), 23:389–94; see also SOCP 1 1824/2615/61. Tipperary: "untameable," in Lord Lt. Anglesey to Lord Holland, 4 Aug. 1828, Papers of Henry William Paget, 1st Marquess of Anglesey, T1068/1/94, PRONI, Belfast; cost: *PP 1826* (210), 23:389–94 (only the barony of Iffa and Offa West was exempt).

48 Costs: *PP 1824* (351), 22:387–402; *PP 1826* (210), 23:388–94. Ex-Peeler Chief Magistrates Daniel O'Donoghue and Samuel Pendleton, who had had troublesome careers, were not appointed to the constabulary. But Peeler officers James Tandy and Joseph Nicolson were promoted to the high rank of county Stipendiary Magistrate. Gregory to Goulburn, 17 June 1822, in Goulburn Box C;

"Account of the Names of all Magistrates appointed under the 3d Geo. 4 c. 103 ...," *PP 1824* (301), 22:409-10.

49 J. Bryce to Goulburn, 23 Sept. 1822, CSORP 1155. SOCP 1 1822/2370/67; CSORP 1828/178. Powell: Inquiry into Leinster Police, *PP 1828* (486), 22:214 (App. 30, p. 35). "Fireproof": Quigley to Gregory, n.d., in Gregory to Goulburn, 10 July 1823, in Goulburn Box C.

50 Cloncurry to Peel, 3 Apr. 1824, in Goulburn II/15; see returns for 1823 in *PP 1828* (486), 22:217, 219-20 (App. 31, pp. 38, 40-1). "They provide their own shoes," noted the Inspector-General for Leinster (Powell to Goulburn, 9 Sept. 1823, CSORP 6571). One Dublin tailor solicited business as early as February 1822 (CSORP 1822/2735).

51 Curtis, *RIC*, p. 11; "Clothing and Necessaries for Use of the Constabulary – #H," June 1828, Mepol 2/20, PRO, London. H. Malcolm McKee, "Note on the First Uniform of the Irish Constabulary," *Irish Sword* 1 (1950):233.

52 Curtis, *RIC*, p. 11; "Return of Arms and Accoutrements for the Constabulary – #1," and "Inspection Report – #2," July 1828, Mepol 2/20.

53 Castlemaine to Goulburn, 29 Nov. 1824, SOCP 1 2610/24. All other quotations are in Henry R. Addison, *Recollections of an Irish Police Magistrate* (London: J. and R. Maxwell, 1883, orig. publ. 1862), pp. 76-9. Addison (1805-76), a former army lieutenant and ex-Peeler, joined the constabulary in the 1820s. His *Recollections* refer to a much earlier period than the date of publication would suggest. Frederic Boase, *Modern English Biography*, 6 vols. (Truro: Netherton and Worth, 1892-1921), 1:22.

54 See the notes by Gregory and Goulburn on C. Crawford to Gregory, 5 Feb.; T. Law to Gregory, 22 Mar.; W. Andrews to Lord Lennox, 2 Apr.; J. Nicholson to Lord Lieutenant, 28 Apr.; T. Hill to Lord Lieutenant, 1 July 1822; all in OP 2 544.

55 Gregory to Peel, 31 Oct., and Goulburn to Peel, 11 Dec. 1822, 40328 ff. 162, 291.

56 See applications of W. Fitzpatrick, 8 Nov.; H. French, 9 Nov.; and W. Henry, 12 Nov. 1822; in OP 2 544. Application of T. Ashe, 12 Apr. 1823, and of J. Smith, 5 Aug. 1823, in OP 2 558, 558IV, respectively. Goulburn to Gregory, 21 June 1825, in Goulburn Box C; Anglesey to Lieutenant General Murray, 12 Nov. 1828, Anglesey Papers, T1068/21/17.

57 See Castle comments on applications of Lt. G. Fitzgibbon, 26 Aug.; B. Holy, 4 Nov.; J. Hamilton, 30 Dec. 1822; all in OP 2 544. Peninsular veterans: application of J. Allen, 31 July 1822, OP 2 544; unsigned paper marked "Constabulary," 23 Feb. 1825, in Goulburn Box C. *PP 1825* (200), 7:52, ev. of R. Willcocks. Insp.-Gen. William Miller's report to Chief Secretary Leveson-Gover, State of the Munster Constabulary, Oct. 1828, OP 2 830C/4.

58 Report of Insp.-Gen. T. D'Arcy, 11 May 1829, CSORP 633; Miller's report, Oct. 1828, OP 2 830C/4. A less reliable source, the incomplete officers' pension register (HO 184/45), reveals that forty-one of the seventy-four officers (56 percent) joining in 1816-50 and listing a prior occupation had served in the army or militia; sixteen men, or 22 percent, had done previous police work. But these figures are of little value because two-thirds of the 218 men on this register had no previous occupation listed.

59 Unsigned paper, "Constabulary," 23 Feb. 1825, in Goulburn Box C; application file of Robert Atkin, Aug. 1822, in OP 2 544.

60 James Connery to Goulburn, 7 Dec. 1822, Ballyduff, Waterford, in OP 2 544. On the rule against a man's serving in his home county, see Goulburn to Earl of Kingston, 4 Nov., and Goulburn to Lord George Beresford, 12 Nov. 1822, in OP 2 544; and Goulburn's reply in Earl of Roden to Goulburn, 5 Sept. 1825, in OP 2 588D. Requirements: Anglesey Papers, T1068/20, 57, 107, May and August 1828.

61 Chief Constables' duties, Connaught, CSORP 1829/982. Report of Maxwell Blacker, King's Counsel, to Gregory, 10 June 1825, in OP 2 825/22. "Dinner": "Report of the Select Committee appointed to examine into the state of the Disturbed Counties in Ireland," *PP 1831−2* (677), 16:Q. 181, ev. of Matthew Barrington. Provincial police reports (except Leinster) to Leveson Gower, May 1829, CSORP 633.

62 Blacker's report to Gregory, 10 June 1825, in OP 2 825/22; Miller to Leveson Gower, October 1828, OP 2 830C/4. Pay cut: Memoranda on provincial police, April 1828, CSORP 262. One observer thought that the police had benefited recently from having "a rougher description of men" as Chief Constables. *PP 1831−2* (677), 16:Q. 952, ev. of Col. R. Johnson.

63 Willcocks to Gregory, 20 Feb., in Gregory to Goulburn, 3 Mar. 1823, in Goulburn Box C; "A Connaught Chief Constable" to Goulburn, 10 Nov. 1824, CSORP 10641; Blacker's report to Gregory, 10 June 1825, in OP 2 825/22.

64 A copy of the 1830 constabulary bill is in CSORP 1830/4073. PD 23:1110−15, 30 Mar. 1830. In his discussion of the bill, Broeker is unaware of the de facto existence of Subinspectors since at least 1828 (*Police*, p. 201).

65 The previous rank of D. J. Osborne, who was appointed a Stipendiary Magistrate in March 1826, was given as "Sub-Inspector of Police." Return of Stipendiary Magistrates, 14 Feb. 1833, Official Papers − Miscellaneous and Assorted, 1832−82, 101/3, ISPO, DC. One policeman wrote: "when in 1824 the present system of Sub-Inspectors was adopted ..." B. Nangle to Lord Killeen, 2 July 1834, CSORP 2706. I have found no other evidence that dates the creation of this post this early.

66 Major Miller refers to a Kerry Subinspector in January 1828. State of the Munster Constabulary, October 1828, OP 2 830C/4. See also Subinsp. S. Croker to Miller, 22 Feb. 1828, CSORP 262; and Memorandum on Subinspectors, April 1828, CSORP 540. On police districts, see Leinster police, 20 Aug. 1829, and memorandum, 26 Oct. 1829, both in CSORP 6099.

67 Insp.-Gen. Sir John Harvey to Leveson Gower, 12 Dec. 1829, CSORP 10085; and Harvey to Lord Lt. Anglesey, 12 Dec. 1829 ("mainspring"), in D619/1, Anglesey Papers, PRONI, Belfast. See also Leveson Gower's Letter Books [hereafter, LGLB] 736/276, 298 and 737/8−9, PRO, Four Courts, Dublin.

68 Castle memorandum to Inspectors-General of Constabulary, 23 June 1829, CSORP 790; *PP 1825* (20), 7:168, ev. of Insp.-Gen. T. Powell.

69 Inquiry into Leinster Police, *PP 1828* (486), 22:183, 190; Peel Papers, 40331 f. 120; CSORP 1829/790; Lord Lt. Anglesey to Chief Sec. William Lamb, 20 Mar. 1828, Anglesey Papers, T1068/15; Thomas Doolan, *Munster: or, the Memoirs of a Chief Constable* (London: W. Davy, Grosvenor Square, 1831), pp. 51−2 (rare; copy at the Royal Irish Academy, Dublin).

70 On Harvey, see CSORP 1829/790; Papers of Edward Littleton, Baron Hatherton, D260/M/OI/2, 2485, Staffordshire Record Office, Stafford; Mulgrave to Morpeth, 11 July 1835, in the Papers of Viscount Morpeth, 7th Earl of Carlisle [hereafter, 7 Carlisle], Castle Howard Archives [CHA] J19/1/9, Castle Howard, Yorkshire; Morpeth to Harvey, 23 Oct. 1835, 7 Carlisle, "Private Letter Book," CHA:J19/11/2. On Miller, see OP 2 1828/830C/4; SOCP 1 1822/2356/23; T. P. Vokes to T. Spring-Rice, 15 Aug. 1835, 7 Carlisle, CHA:J19/1/9. Upon his retirement, Willcocks was knighted and continued to serve as a JP in County Dublin. "Return of ... the Magistracy ... in Ireland," *PP 1830−1* (171), 8:319, 374.

71 Miller to Leveson Gower, October 1828, OP 2 830C/4; Miller to Gregory, 26 June 1829, CSORP 790.

72 *PP 1825* (129), 8:118, ev. of D. O'Connell; *PP 1825* (200), 7:51, ev. of R. Willcocks; Meath: Gregory to Goulburn, 7 Mar. 1824, in Goulburn Box C. Attorney-General's ruling, 1825, CSORP 10971; on Orange associations, see CSORP 1827/981, 2055.

73 "Return of the Total Number of all Magistrates, Constables, and Sub-Constables appointed under . . . the Constabulary Act," data assembled in March 1824 and printed for Parliament 15 Apr. 1824, *PP 1824* (257), 22:405–8. The return does not differentiate the men's religion within each rank (subconstable, constable, Chief Constable). The Chief Constables, overwhelmingly Protestant, formed only 4 percent of the total force. Willcocks quoted in *PP 1825* (200), 7:52; Kerry and Waterford: *PP 1831–2* (677), 16:QQ. 4063–70, ev. of Stip. Magis. M. Singleton.

74 Irish Constables [Pension] Register, HO 184/1; Officers Register, HO 184/45. (See Appendix V, this book.) For a religious census of subconstables and constables, 1832, 36 percent Catholic, see "A Return of the Number, &c., of Roman Catholics of each Rank, in each County, in the Constabulary," *PP 1833* (379), 32:446–50; for officers' religion, Chief Constables and Subinspectors, 1833, 9 percent Catholic, see Hatherton Papers, D260/M/OI/1022a, 1024–5, 1036. Overall, the constabulary in the early 1830s was 35 percent Catholic.

75 Inquiry into Leinster Police, *PP 1828* (486), 22:184, 192, 204; statistical analysis of recruits, 1816–36, Constables Register, HO 184/1; Miller's report to Leveson Gower, Oct. 1828, OP 2 830C/4.

76 HO 184/1; OP 2 1828/830C/4.

77 Miller's report, October 1828, OP 2 830C/4; Miller to Leveson Gower, 10 Oct. 1829, and Leveson Gower to Peel, 26 Oct. 1829, HO 100/229/200–9; see also HO 100/232/149. The regulation of 21 December 1829 is cited in Miller to John Rowan of Cork, 17 Mar. 1830, CSORP 608. According to Miller (HO 100/229/200), the rule in the army was no more than four women in every company of sixty men; hence, the incidence of married men in the constabulary was ten times greater than the standard, whether or not enforced, in the military.

78 Miller to Chief Sec. Sir Henry Hardinge, 31 Aug. 1830, CSORP 608. Memorial of Thomas Powell to Lord Lieutenant, 22 Jan. 1830, CSORP 116. The reply read: "Usual answer. Not in Ld. Lt.ˢ power to interfere with the Estabᵗ. regulation."

79 Quotations are in Maxwell Blacker to Gregory, 10 June 1825, OP 2 825/22. Regulations were first drawn up by Richard Willcocks for the Munster constabulary in February 1823 (CSORP 1823/5483) and later applied to the other provinces. "Regulations for the Leinster Constabulary, 1823" [see ss. 23, 24], CSORP 6571; see also CSORP 1824/8689.

80 Leinster constabulary regulations, ss. 11, 18, 23, 34 (CSORP 1823/6571). Gratuities were at first allowed in Kerry and Kilkenny, but sometime in 1823 the custom was suppressed. "Firm, orderly . . .": Leinster regulations, s. 13 and concluding paragraph of regulations.

81 Ibid., ss. 19–21. For legal opinions, see Crown Solicitors' ruling, 28 Dec. 1824, CSORP 10865 ("fly"); Warburton to Gregory, 2 Dec. 1825, and replies, CSORP 12686; *PP 1831–2* (677), 16:QQ. 1602–6, ev. of H. Stapleton, JP for Queen's County.

82 Leinster regulations, ss. 15–16, CSORP 1823/6571.

83 For the Queen's County case and dismissal rates in the early 1820s, see *PP 1825* (20), 7:168; on later dismissal rates, see Country Letter Book [hereafter, CLB] 1829–30, ff. 3–4, ISPO, DC; CLB 1830, ff. 3–4. Orangeism: *PP 1831–2* (677), 16:QQ. 6440–3, ev. of R. Cassidy concerning Leinster police, c. 1826. Tipperary: SOCP 1 1823/2518/54. Monaghan: SOCP 1 1828/2882/45. Cork: OP 2 1825/825/22. Kildare: CSORP 1824/9270. Nenagh: SOCP 1 1823/2518/45. Limerick: Doolan, *Munster*, pp. 51–4. Returns of the number of policemen brought to trial before sessions and assizes, 1822–4, for murder, robbery, and assault, listing whether found guilty or acquitted, in *PP 1824* (257), 22:405–8; no trial figures are listed for Connaught, and there are no returns at all from Ulster, where the constabulary was still forming.

84 Gregory to Goulburn, 22 Aug. 1824, in Goulburn Box C; Goulburn to Peel, 31 Oct. 1826, 40332 f. 176, and printed in Sir Robert Peel, *Sir Robert Peel, from his Private Papers*, ed. Charles Stuart Parker, 3 vols. (London: J. Murray, 1891–9), 1:420.

85 Sligo: Gregory to Goulburn, 4 Mar. 1826; and D'Arcy: Gregory to Goulburn, 6 May 1825; both in Goulburn Box C. On Leinster, see Inquiry into Leinster Police, December 1827–February 1828, *PP 1828* (486), 22:179–223. The charges were made by a Wexford Chief Constable, Capt. John Burke. "Every day": Anglesey to Lamb, 26 Apr. 1828, Anglesey Papers, T1068/15/45; other quotations are in Anglesey to Lamb, 17 Mar. 1828, T 1068/15/25–6. On Harvey's appointment, see T1068/1/2–4; "Lords' Select Committee to inquire into the Collection and Payment of Tithes in Ireland," *PP 1831–2* (271), 22:26–7, ev. of Sir J. Harvey, 20 Jan. 1832..

86 3 Geo. 4, c. 103 s. 13 (1822), amended by 9 Geo. 4, c. 63 ss. 1–3 (1828). Inspectors-General of Constabulary to Lamb, 14 Sept. 1827, HO 100/218/191; and Anglesey Papers, T1068/15/104. See also CSORP 1826/15047; Doolan, *Munster*, pp. 56, 66.

87 Irish constabulary regulation, 30 June 1828, recurrently cited in a large collection of detailed forms (April to December, but mostly July 1828) preserved, inexplicably, in the *London* police series, Mepol 2/20, PRO, London. One constabulary officer complained that "we are writing three or four hours a day" (Addison, *Recollections*, p. 78 n.). At Dublin Castle Gregory had a count taken of the number of letters received from police officers in 1828 and arrived at a total of "1,095," a figure that *excluded* letters from local magistrates (Gregory to Leveson Gower, 18 Feb. 1829, in Peel Papers, 40336 ff. 241–2). The police secretary was an army colonel, Sir William Gosset, who succeeded Gregory as Castle Under-Secretary in 1830, so the gains in the 1829 reform was nullified. On Gosset, see Hatherton Papers, D260/M/OI/3/293; Peel Papers, 40336 ff. 202–6.

88 Breach of the peace: Gregory to Insp.-Gen. William Miller, 29 Apr. 1828, CLB 1828 f. 74. Verbal command: Chief Constable Burton Lambert to Miller, 12 May 1829, CSORP 807. "Barbarous": Doolan, *Munster*, pp. 52, 54.

89 *PP 1825* (200), 7:28 ev. of G. Bennett. Insp.-Gen. George Warburton to Gregory, 1 May 1828, CSORP 625. Gregory to High Sheriff to Tipperary, copy to Inspector-General Miller, 20 Apr. 1828, CLB 1828 f. 81.

90 Elections: Goulburn to Gregory, 3 June 1826, in Goulburn Box C. Legal opinion, William Kemmis, for Gregory, 22 Dec. 1825, CSORP 12747. JP: G. Fennell to Goulburn, 20 Sept. 1825, SOCP 1 2729/17; Willcocks to Goulburn, 30 Sept. 1825, and Wilson to Goulburn, 3 Oct. 1825, both in CSORP 12747. "Abstain": Inspector-General Miller's regulations on riots at fairs, n.d. [1829], CSORP 1829/896.

91 Chief Constable William Percy to Willcocks, 13 Feb. 1823, SOCP 1 2518/6. Doolan, *Munster*, pp. 6–7, and see also pp. 52–3.

92 "Return of the Number of Persons who have lost their Lives, or been severely Wounded, in Affrays with the Constabulary in Ireland," *PP 1830–1* (67), 8:403–83. On Toomevara and Thurles, see Gen. Sir Colquhoun Grant to Sir Herbert Taylor, 5 Dec. 1825 and 4 Apr. 1826, in WO 80/6, Correspondence of Gen. Sir George Murray, commander-in-chief of the army in Ireland; and HO 100/219/96, 119, 127, 143. Tolls: R. Greene, Crown Law Adviser, opinion for Gregory, 23 July 1828 ("province"), and H. Pruitt to Gregory, 28 July 1828, both in CSORP 1089.

93 Doolan, *Munster*, pp. 50–1, 62; see also *PP 1831–2* (677), 16:Q. 3757, ev. of Rev. J. Burke. 3 Geo. 4, c. 103 ss. 9, 32 (1822). Legal opinion of J. Townsend, 14 June, favoring collection, in reply to letter from Col. J. Bagot to Gregory, 13 June 1823, CSORP 6134. Opinion of Attorney-General and Solicitor-General, 3 Oct.

1824, CSORP 8870. Goulburn to J. Blacker, J. Atkinson, and C. Woodward, 10 Oct. 1825, CSORP 12353.

94 See CSORP 1825/12353. The extreme in routing of letters may be seen in an inquiry of 8 May 1832 from Chief Constable N. Fitzhenry in Roscommon to his county Subinspector, who forwarded it to Inspector-General Warburton, who sent it to Under-Secretary Gosset, who sent it to the Chief Secretary, Castle legal advisers, and the Lord Lieutenant. Fitzhenry had to wait more than a week for a reply to reach him through this chain of correspondence. CSORP 1832/2172.

95 Memorial of thirty-one magistrates meeting at Roscommon, 24 Oct. 1826, to Lord Lieutenant, and Goulburn's reply for Wellesley, CSORP 15460. See also CSORP 1829/89.

96 "How": G. Atkinson et al. to Goulburn, and reply, 10 June 1825, CSORP 11709. "At a loss": S. Cassan to Goulburn, and reply, 2 Oct. 1826, CSORP 15193. Excise: Chief Constable William Nash to Miller, 21 Feb. 1828, CSORP 178. See also, for fish and game, CLB 1828 ff. 144, 234; and for revenue, CLB 1827–8 ff. 214, 234; CLB 1828 ff. 29, 98; and CLB 1828–9 f. 124.

97 Bakers: Harvey to Gregory, and reply, 9 Apr. 1829, CSORP 460. Sabbath: CLB 1828–9 f. 37. Cess: CSORP 1824/9742; Cloncurry to Peel, 3 Apr. 1824, in Goulburn II/15; and CLB 1828 f. 31. "Nuisances": CSORP 1826/15383. Cattle: Constabulary regulations, 1823, section on "roads," CSORP 6571. Complaint, response: T. Shearnuen, High Constable of Ida Barony, Kilkenny, to Goulburn, and reply, 19 June 1824, CSORP 9742.

98 G. Tuthill, Sheriff of County Limerick, to Gregory, 27 July 1823, CSORP 6296. Sir George Shea, Sheriff of County Galway, to Leveson Gower, 9 Sept. 1828; on this case, see also various correspondence, May–November 1828, involving Shea, Chief Constable Blake, Inspector-General Warburton, Gregory, Leveson Gower, and even Peel. Peel Papers, 40333 ff. 44–5; 40335 ff. 182–8, Shea, 9 Sept., at f. 183; 49336 ff. 51–2. Clare: Chief Constable H. Townsend to Warburton, 9 May 1825, SOCP 1 2724/13. See also SOCP 1 1824/2618/53.

99 Doolan, *Munster*, pp. 58–9. Cork: Lord Carbery to Gregory, 19 July 1823, SOCP 1 2514/1. The Castlehaven case is discussed at length in SOCP 1 1823/2514/1, 3, 57 and 2515/1; full inquest proceedings are in 2515/5; acknowledgments to James S. Donnelly, Jr., for information on Morritt's income. Clare: W. Casey to Goulburn, 12 Nov. 1823, SOCP 1 2510/74.

100 Cork: Memorial of Helena Cue to Lord Lieutenant, 9 Nov. 1824, CSORP 10490. Cavan: Memorial of Andrew, Thomas, and Henry Higginbotham to Lord Lieutenant, 18 Nov. 1825, CSORP 12544. Carlow: T. Cavanagh to Leveson Gower, 30 Oct. 1828, and reply, CSORP 1667. For other tithe cases and rulings, see HO 100/209/229; CLB 1827–8 ff. 146, 175–7, 183; CLB 1828 ff. 22, 41; and CLB 1828–9 ff. 41–2.

101 Chief Constable H. Brownrigg to Insp.-Gen. W. Miller, 2 Feb. 1829; Miller to Gregory, 5 Feb. 1829; and legal opinion of R. Greene to Miller, 13 Feb. 1829; all in CSORP 259.

102 For force levels in (December) 1824, see OP 2 1824/615/2; for 1828, OP 2 1828/830C/3; for 1830, including the number and sites of police stations, *PP 1833* (518), 32:453–61.

103 Wellesley to Goulburn, 5 July 1822, in Goulburn II/22/ABCD. "Return of the Dates, during 1818 to 1827, at which any . . . Yeomanry Corps in Great Britain and Ireland was called out for Actual Service," *PP 1828* (273), 17:283–7.

104 "Return of . . . Armed Constables in Ireland in 1792, 1822, and 1828," OP 2 1828/830C/3. "An Account of Proclamations Issued, and Expenses incurred, under . . . the Peace Preservation Act . . . ," *PP 1826* (210), 23:389–94; "An Account of Expenses incurred under the Peace Preservation Act, and the Number of Men employed, during the last Three Years," *PP 1830* (322), 26:427–32. Cork disbanding: *PP 1826* (210), 23:394, and "An Account of Proclamations Issued . . .

under ... the Peace Preservation Act ...," *PP 1826–7* (206), 20:113–18. Tipperary disbanding of 30 Nov. 1828 and Limerick police: *PP 1830* (322), 26:427–32. See also "Goulburn's Minute," undated, in C. W. Flint to Gregory, 13 Mar. 1824, Irish Office, London, CSORP 8424; Wellesley memorandum, 21 July 1825, in Goulburn II/22/EFGH; HO 184/45/171; CLB 1827–8 f. 214 and 1828–9 f. 200. Addison, *Recollections of an Irish Police Magistrate*, presents a somewhat fictionalized account of the colorful career of Peeler Chief Magistrate T. P. Vokes.

105 Inspector-General Miller to Gregory, 19 Jan. 1829, CSORP 60. In this file are memorials, all dated January 1829, from Tipperary subconstables to the Lord Lieutenant. "Return of all Superannuations Granted to Constables and Subconstables of Police in Ireland; stating the Periods of Service, and Cause of their Superannuations," 29 Mar. 1832, *PP 1831–2* (359), 26:465–7. Of the four men previously discussed, only John Lennon (constable 144) appears on this list.

106 Goulburn to Peel, 14 Dec. 1824, 40330 f. 273. Force levels: WO 17/1100–3; "A Return of ... the Effectives of the British Army, ... at Home and Abroad," *PP 1831–2* (317), 27:115–24. West Indies: Peel Papers, 40329 ff. 160–6; two regiments were shipped from Ireland to deal with "the Agitation amongst the Slaves" (f. 160). "Your West India friends," noted Peel, "are very much frightened, as well they may be, and very clamorous" (to Goulburn, 19 Nov. 1823, 40329 f. 224). Peel to Goulburn, 13 Nov., and Goulburn's reply, 15 Nov. 1823, 40329 ff. 215, 218–19.

107 "Civil": Wellesley to Peel, 15 Nov. 1823, 40324 f. 268; "Peelers": Goulburn to Peel, 30 Nov. 1822, 40328 f. 265. On withdrawal of troop detachments, see Peel Papers, 40324 f. 74 and 40330 f. 103. Military aid to northern England: Murray Papers, WO 80/6/49–50, 78–87 ("liable" on f. 87, June 1826); Peel Papers, 40332 ff. 195–203.

108 Goulburn to Peel, 16 Sept. 1823, 40329 f. 137, and 31 Aug. 1824, 40330 f. 102 ("our Police works very well and is generally admitted now to be most useful and effective"). Wellesley to Goulburn, 13 Sept. 1822, in Goulburn II/22/ABCD. Peel to Wellesley, 24 Feb. 1823, Peel Papers, 40324 f. 123. Willcocks to Wellesley, 29 Dec. 1824, HO 100/211/142–4. Kildare Stipendiary Magistrate Maj. James Tandy to Goulburn, 5 May 1824, in Goulburn Box C. "Report from the Select Committee appointed to examine into the nature and extent of the Disturbances ... in those districts of Ireland ... now subject to ... the Insurrection Act," *PP 1824* (372), 8:50, ev. of W. Becker, JP for Cork ("I think the Police has been one of the most useful measures that has been adopted within my recollection"). Insp.-Gen. T. Powell to Goulburn, 4 Dec. 1824, Peel Papers, 40330 f. 264.

109 For criminal statistics, see committals at assizes and quarter sessions, 1822–8, *PP 1829* (256), 22:427–36. Quotations are, respectively, in Powell to Goulburn, August 1825, Peel Papers, 40331 f. 119; Gregory to Goulburn, 15 June 1825, in Goulburn Box C.

110 Leveson Gower (appointed June 1828) to Peel, 15 Aug. 1828, 40335 f. 45. *PP 1825* (129), 8:575, ev. of M. Barrington. For the English figures, see *PP 1830–1* (105, 308), 12:461, 493; *PP 1831–2* (375), 33:1; *PP 1833* (135), 29:8.

111 *PP 1825* (129), 8:28, ev. of Denis Browne.

112 On the sum raised, see Thomas Wyse, *Historical Sketch of the Late Catholic Association of Ireland*, 2 vols. (London: H. Colburn, 1829), 2: appendix, pp. cclxx–cclxxiii. Quotations: D. Browne and Bishop Doyle, *PP 1825* (129), 8:34, 215. Earl of Sligo to Goulburn, 7 Sept. 1826, Peel Papers, 40332 f. 131. On the phenomenon, see Gash, *Peel*, pp. 384–99, 508–44; James A. Reynolds, *The Catholic Emancipation Crisis in Ireland, 1823–1829* (New Haven, Conn.: Yale University Press, 1954; repr., Westport, Conn.: Greenwood Press, 1970); G. I. T. Machin, *The Catholic Question in English Politics, 1820 to 1830* (Oxford: Clarendon

Press, 1964), an excellent if narrow political study that ignores events in Ireland; and the recent study by Fergus O'Ferrall, *Catholic Emancipation: Daniel O'Connell and the Birth of Irish Democracy* (Dublin: Gill and Macmillan, 1985). On O'Connell, see Raymond Moley, *Daniel O'Connell: Nationalism without Violence* (New York: Fordham University Press, 1974); and Kevin Nowlan and Maurice O'Connell, eds., *Daniel O'Connell: Portrait of a Radical* (New York: Fordham University Press, 1985). Broeker, *Police*, pp. 160−88, devotes his best chapter to the Catholic Emancipation movement, although, as he rightly shows, the role of the police was quite marginal.

113 *PP 1825* (129), 8:127−8, 215 (O'Connell), 270 (Bishop J. Magaurin).

114 Willcocks to Gregory, 23−6 June 1826, OP 2 915. Peel to Gen. Sir G. Hill, 16 July 1826, 40388 f. 66. See also Reynolds, *Crisis*, pp. 93−107. On the size of the electorate, see Reynolds's discussion in *Crisis*, p. 168 n. 30.

115 Brynn, *Crown and Castle*, pp. 14−15; Gash, *Peel*, pp. 423−53; Philip Ziegler, *Melbourne* (New York: Atheneum, 1982), pp. 88−99.

116 Anglesey Papers, T1068/1/62, 68; George Paget, 7th Marquess of Anglesey, *One-Leg: The Life and Letters of Henry William Paget, 1st Marquess of Anglesey* (London: Jonathan Cape, 1961); Brynn, *Crown and Castle*, pp. 29, 33−4, 147; Broeker, *Police*, pp. 173−4; and Gash, *Peel*, pp. 508−13, 516−29, 536−44. Leveson Gower was subsequently Lord Francis Egerton (1833) and 1st Earl of Ellesmere (1846) [*DNB* 6:571−2]; see also n. 107, chapter 11, this book.

117 Anglesey to Holland, 1 July and 19 Oct. 1828, Anglesey Papers, T1068/1/49 and 21/13, respectively. On Clare, see Reynolds, *Crisis*, pp. 156−60. On the meetings, see Peel Papers, 40335 ff. 109−10, 139−44, 218−19; Anglesey Papers, T1068/1/129−35; Reynolds, *Crisis*, pp. 149−55.

118 Leveson Gower to Peel, 19 Sept. 1828, 40335 f. 118; Goulburn to Peel, 25 July 1826, 40332 f. 69; and Anglesey to Leveson Gower, 2 July 1828, 40335 ff. 18−19.

119 J. Fitzgerald to Leveson Gower, 22 Sept., and Earl of Mountcashel to Anglesey, 29 Sept. 1828, 40335 ff. 144, 219. On the Government's bewilderment with the nonviolence, see 40335 ff. 20−1, 107−8, 118−19, 128−35, 156−7, 194−200.

120 Anglesey to Holland, 24 Aug. 1828, Anglesey Papers, T1068/1/102.

121 Named for Brunswick, one of the small duchies in northwest Germany that became a part of the Electorate and (after 1814) of the Kingdom of Hanover, from which had been drawn the first of the Protestant English monarchs of the Hanoverian line (1714−1837). On these clubs, see Reynolds, *Crisis*, p. 151; Gash, *Peel*, pp. 535−6; and Broeker, *Police*, pp. 184−6.

122 Gash, *Peel*, pp. 535−8; and Broeker, *Police*, pp. 186−7. On the police role, see Peel Papers, 40336 ff. 100, 128−9, and SOCP 1 1828/2882/63 and 2885/2, 9, 11; on that of the military, see 40335 ff. 149−50 and 40336 f. 13.

123 Byng: Peel to Anglesey, 29 May 1828, Anglesey Papers, D619/5/11. Warburton's opinion *as paraphrased by Gash*, in Gash, *Peel*, p. 524. On Catholics in the army, see Reynolds, *Crisis*, pp. 147−8; and Broeker, *Police*, pp. 176−7. On Catholic constables, see Broeker, *Police*, pp. 178−9; *PP 1824* (257), 22:405−8; and *PP 1833* (379), 32:446−50.

124 Peel to Sir Walter Scott, 3 Apr. 1829, in Peel Papers, 40399, quoted in Broeker, *Police*, p.179. Anglesey to Byng, 21 July ("large"), and to Peel, 26 July 1828, Anglesey Papers, T1068/1/80, 84. Wellington to Peel, 31 July 1828, 40307 f. 170. One Irish soldier commented: "There are two ways of firing, *at a man and over*; and if we were called out against O'Connell and our country, I think we should know the difference." Quoted in Reynolds, *Crisis*, p. 148.

125 Anglesey Papers, D619/5/44; and Peel Papers, 40336 f. 9. For troop movements into and out of Ireland, January−December 1828, see WO 17/1104. See also Reynolds, *Crisis*, pp. 148−9; Gash, *Peel*, pp. 537−8.

126 Machin, *Catholic Question*, pp. 157−8; Gash, *Peel*, pp. 545−85.

127 Leveson Gower to Peel, 22 July 1829, 40337 f. 59; Peel to Wellington, 11 Aug.

1828, 40307 ff. 195–6; and Peel to [? George IV], 8 Feb. 1829, 40326 f. 185 ("strength"). A good summary assessment is in J. C. Beckett, *The Making of Modern Ireland 1603–1923* (London: Faber and Faber, 1966), pp. 303–5.

128 Peel to [? George IV], 8 Feb. 1829, 40326 ff. 185–8.

129 G. D. H. Cole and Raymond Postgate, *The Common People 1746–1946*, 4th ed. (London: Methuen, 1956), p. 248. On the downfall of Wellington's Government, see Machin, *Catholic Question*, pp. 179–90.

CHAPTER 8. ANGLICIZING THE PEELERS: THE LONDON POLICE OF 1829

1 Peel to Goulburn, 22 July 1826, the Papers of Sir Robert Peel, 2d Bt., BL Add. MS 40332 f. 60, British Library, London.

2 *Annual Register* 68 (1826): Chronicle, 63–72, 109–11, 124–8; Archibald Prentice, *Historical Sketches and Personal Recollections of Manchester* (London: C. Gilpin, 1851), pp. 273–80; Norman Gash, *Mr. Secretary Peel: The Life of Sir Robert Peel to 1830* (Cambridge, Mass.: Harvard University Press, 1961), pp. 358–63; Gen. Sir John Byng to Peel, 12 Oct. 1826, Rotherham, HO 40/20/3/528, PRO, London.

3 Gen. Sir Herbert Taylor to Gen. Sir George Murray, commander-in-chief in Ireland, 28 Aug. 1828, Horse Guards, in Goulburn II/16, the Papers of Henry Goulburn, Surrey Record Office, Kingston-on-Thames; Henry Hobhouse, Under-Secretary (for Peel), to magistrates Fletcher, Hulton, and Ridgeway, 29 Apr. 1826, Whitehall, HO 41/7/147; Peel to Byng, 4 May 1826, HO 41/7/180–1.

4 *Dictionary of National Biography* [hereafter, *DNB*] 3:573–4. Sidmouth and Peel both thought highly of Byng. See Sidmouth to Byng, 12 Oct. 1819, in the Papers of Henry Addington, 1st Viscount Sidmouth, 152M/1819–20(i), Devonshire Record Office, Exeter; and Peel to Anglesey, 29 May 1828, the Papers of Henry William Paget, 1st Marquess of Anglesey, D619/5/11, PRONI, Belfast. Sir John Byng was the son of Anne Conolly Byng (m. Maj. George Byng), a sister of Thomas Conolly, the late-eighteenth-century Irish politician (*DNB* 4:954). In 1831 Byng was elected a Member of Parliament, and was one of the few generals to support the Reform Bill. Byng was created the Earl of Strafford in 1847, promoted to full general in 1841, and named Field Marshal at age eighty-three, five years before his death in London in 1860. Byng's grandson, Gen. Julian Byng (1862–1935), would serve a short successful stint as London Police Commissioner, 1928–31 (*DNB 1931–40*, pp. 132–6).

5 HO 40/18/78; HO 41/7/294, 393–4.

6 Gen. Sir Herbert Taylor to Hobhouse, 17 July 1826, Horse Guards, HO 40/20/2/190–1; Byng to Hobhouse, 1, 22 July 1826, Rotherham, HO 40/20/3/391, 454; Hobhouse to Colonel Ellison, 13 Feb. 1827, Whitehall, HO 41/7/385–7.

7 Hobhouse to Byng, 20 July 1826, HO 41/7/294. On local costs for barracks rentals, see HO 40/20/2/278 and HO 41/6/311, 372; on withdrawals, see HO 40/22/2, 186, 277, 279 (quotation) and HO 41/7/418–20.

8 HO 40/20/3/507–8; HO 40/22/2/278, 283; HO 41/7/514, 529; "Return of all Permanent Barracks in the United Kingdom, including the date of erection of each," *PP 1847* (169), 36:321–406.

9 The preceding paragraph is based on a return of permanent barracks in the United Kingdom, in "Select Committee Report on the Public Income and Expenditure of the United Kingdom," *PP 1828* (420), 5:364–9 (app. 25). The figures are for capacity, not occupancy, of barracks in each county. The capacity of permanent barracks in England (44,000) and Ireland (37,700) far exceeded the army levels of 25,000 and 20,000, respectively, maintained in the 1820s. County populations, 1831 census, in J. R. McCulloch, *Dictionary of Commerce*, 8th ed., 2 vols. (London: Longman, Brown, Green, 1854), 2:1028–9; B. R. Mitchell and P.

Deane, *Abstract of British Historical Statistics* (Cambridge: Cambridge University Press, 1962), pp. 20-1.

10 According to the index in HO 41/7, a volume containing Home Office "out-letters" to local authorities, seventy-five of ninety towns in 1822-30 requesting aid received a military party; in 1826 alone, twenty-nine of thirty-seven towns received one.

11 Hobhouse to Mayor of Macclesfield, 7 May 1824, in HO 41/7; Eckersley to Byng, 8 Apr. 1824, HO 40/18/196.

12 Lieutenant-Colonel Herries to Mayor and magistrates of Macclesfield, 5 Apr. 1824, HO 40/18/144. "Impossibility": Hobhouse to J. Thompson (Blackfriars), C. Swainson (Preston), and J. Crosley (Rochdale), all on 3 May 1826, HO 41/7/176-8. Hobhouse to Byng, 31 Jan. 1827, HO 41/7/381.

13 Under-Secretary S. M. Phillipps to Byng, 6 May 1828, HO 41/7/421-2. Phillipps repeated Peel's "positive order" against parties commanded by only a corporal or sergeant. Byng to Home Office, 17 June 1826, Rotherham, HO 40/20/3/346-7.

14 Leeds (May 1826), Leicester (August 1830): HO 41/7/189, 523. Brigg, in north Lincolnshire (June 1827): HO 41/7/409-10, 422-5. Carlisle (December 1826): HO 41/7/358, 384-7. Barnsley (October 1829): HO 41/7/493. Liverpool (April 1824): HO 40/18/217. Stockport (July 1826): HO 40/20/3/451.

15 Byng to Hobhouse, 15, 20, 27 July 1826, HO 40/20/3/438-9, 451, 465.

16 Mayor and magistrates of Macclesfield to the Earl of Stamford, 7 Apr. 1824, HO 40/18/188-9; for the Government's commendations, 1822-30, see HO 41/7/60, 69, 96, 201, 211-13, 451, 473, 527, and HO 51/13/51.

17 For July 1826-March 1827, see the activities of "Spy No. 1," HO 40/20/3/465, 495, 503, 507, 528, and HO 40/22/2/231-2; "Spy No. 2," HO 40/20/3/452 and HO 40/22/2/219, 226. And for June-July 1826, a spy named Bradbury, HO 40/20/3/356-9, 374, 392. Bow Street officers: HO 41/7/1, 399. Byng to Hobhouse, 11 June 1826, HO **40/20/3/**330.

18 Peel to Hobhouse, 9 July 1826, 4 Feb. 1828, quoted in Sir Robert Peel, *Sir Robert Peel, from his Private Papers*, ed. Charles Stuart Parker, 3 vols. (London: J. Murray, 1891-9), 1:405, 2:37. Byng to Home Office, 12 July 1826, Rotherham, "*confidential*," HO 40/20/3/428-9.

19 Gash, *Peel*, p. 505.

20 Peel to Leveson Gower, 17 Jan. 1829, Peel Papers, 40336 f. 221. For Peel's call for a new select committee inquiry into the state of London's crime and police, see *The Parliamentary Debates* [hereafter, *PD*], New [2d] Series, 25 vols. (London: T. C. Hansard, 1820-30), 18:795, 28 Feb. 1828.

21 *The Times*, 31 Jan. 1823, quoted in Leon Radzinowicz, *A History of English Criminal Law and its Administration from 1750* [hereafter, *ECL*], 4 vols. (London: Stevens & Sons, 1948-68), 3:363. "Select Committee on Criminal Commitments and Convictions," First Report, 22 June 1827, *PP 1826-7* (534), 6:7-74; Second Report, 17 July 1828, *PP 1828* (545), 6:419-83. In his book, *The Tocsin; or, a Review of the London Police Establishments, with Hints for their Improvement* (London: publ. by the author, 1828), Thomas Dudley devotes much space to the "police" of fire prevention and control.

22 See, e.g., Douglas G. Browne, *The Rise of Scotland Yard: A History of the Metropolitan Police* (London: Harrap & Co., 1956), pp. 75-6; Gash, *Peel*, pp. 493-4; T. A. Critchley, *A History of Police in England and Wales*, 2d ed. (Montclair, N.J.: Patterson Smith, 1972) pp. 47-8.

23 *PD* 18:786-91, 796-8, 28 Feb. 1828, and 21:869-71, 15 Apr. 1829; Radzinowicz, *ECL*, 4:70.

24 On law reform, see G. R. Porter, *The Progress of the Nation*, 3d ed. (London: J. Murray, 1851), pp. 636-45; Gash, *Peel*, pp. 308-43; Radzinowicz, *ECL*, 1:497-607, and 4:74-6, 303-26. Chadwick quoted in Radzinowicz, *ECL*, 4:75. V. A.

C. Gattrell and T. B. Hadden, "Criminal Statistics and their Interpretation," in E. A. Wrigley, ed., *Nineteenth-Century Society: Essays in the Use of Quantitative Methods for the Study of Social Data* (Cambridge: Cambridge University Press, 1972), p. 352.

25 Gattrell and Hadden, "Criminal Statistics," pp. 350–3, 368, 373–4, 387, quotations on pp. 352 ("rapid"), 374 ("ascent"). See also Radzinowicz, *ECL*, 3:236–8, 245, and 4:67–78. The work of Gattrell and Hadden demolishes J. J. Tobias's assertion that "the criminal statistics have little to tell us ... and can perhaps be disregarded without much anxiety" [*Crime and Industrial Society in the 19th Century* (London: B. T. Batsford, 1967), pp. 21, 235; see also pp. 265–7].

26 John Wade, *A Treatise on the Police and Crimes of the Metropolis* (London: Longman, Rees, 1829), p. 101; "Second Report from the Select Committee on Criminal Commitments and Convictions," *PP 1828* (545), 6:436–7, quoted in Radzinowicz, *ECL*, 4:77.

27 Eighty percent: Gattrell and Hadden, "Criminal Statistics," p. 367. On France and England, see Peel in *PD* 18:788–9, 28 Feb. 1828; George Cornewall Lewis, *On Local Disturbances in Ireland* (London: B. Fellowes, 1836; reprint ed., Cork: Tower Books, 1977), p. 78.

28 On "protest" and crime, see Gattrell and Hadden, "Criminal Statistics," pp. 367, 371–2; and George Rudé, "Protest and Punishment in Nineteenth-Century Britain," *Albion* 5 (Spring 1973): 1–23 (5 percent in Table 1, pp. 10–12).

29 Gattrell and Hadden, "Criminal Statistics," pp. 368, 378. W. W. Rostow, *British Economy of the Nineteenth Century* (Oxford: Clarendon Press, 1948), ch. 5, esp. pp. 123–5, had earlier played with a "social tension chart," 1790–1850, tracing positive correlations between times of economic hardship and popular protest. Gattrell and Hadden found that in six out of seven economic downturns in 1819–48 the committal rates rose; the only exception was 1826, when the crime rise was one year off (p. 379). Their general thesis is that until the 1870s crime was linked to economic hardship, and only after that date was it "professionalized" and, in the twentieth century, "prosperity-based" (see pp. 368–9, 376–9, 385–6). Studies of earlier periods have found a generally positive relationship between high bread prices (dearth) and property crime. See J. M. Beattie, "The Pattern of Crime in England 1660–1800," *Past & Present* 62 (1974):47–95; J. S. Cockburn, "The Nature and Incidence of Crime in England 1559–1625: A Preliminary Survey," in Cockburn, ed., *Crime in England 1550–1800* (London: Methuen, 1977), pp. 49–71; and J. A. Sharpe, *Crime in Early Modern England, 1550–1750* (London and New York: Longman, 1984), chs. 3, 6, 8.

30 Byng to Hobhouse, 22 Dec. 1827, HO 40/22/2/277–8; see also Major Eckersley to Byng, 4 July 1826, HO 40/20/3/402, and 8 Dec. 1827, HO 40/22/2/283.

31 Edwin Chadwick, the leading police publicist from the 1830s on, developed his interest in the subject only in 1828. He testified before Peel's select committee and a year later published his article, "Preventive Police," *London Review* 1 (1829):252–308. "Our present police," he wrote, "consists of disjoined bodies of men governed separately, under heterogeneous regulations.... A good police would be one well-organized body of men ... to prevent crimes and public calamities; to preserve public peace and order" ("Preventive Police," p. 252). In 1829 Jeremy Bentham persuaded Chadwick to write a section on "The Minister of Police" for his *Constitutional Code*. See Radzinowicz, *ECL*, 3:448–56; and Critchley, *Police*, pp. 45–7, 49.

32 "Liberty": Peel to Wellington, 5 Nov. 1829, in Peel, *Private Papers*, 2:115. Wilbur Miller shortchanges Peel's role by arguing that he merely "synthesized decades of thought" on the police. *Cops and Bobbies: Police Authority in New York and London, 1830–1870* (Chicago: University of Chicago Press, 1977), p. 2.

33 "Memorandum to the Earl of Liverpool respecting the State of the Guards," June 1820, and "Memorandum on the Insufficiency of our Military Establishments,

and Means of Augmenting them," 12 Nov. 1823, in Arthur Wellesley, Duke of Wellington, *Despatches, Correspondence, and Memoranda of Field Marshal Arthur, Duke of Wellington,* edited by his son, the Duke of Wellington, K. G., 8 vols. (London: J. Murray, 1867–80), 1:127–9, 2:173–7, respectively.

34 See Allan Silver, "Social and Ideological Bases of British Elite Reactions to Domestic Crisis in 1829–32," *Politics and Society* 2 (Feb. 1971):179–201. See also Silver, "The Demand for Order in Civil Society: A Review of Some Themes in the History of Urban Crime, Police, and Riot," in David J. Bordua, ed., *The Police: Six Sociological Essays* (New York: Wiley, 1967), pp. 1–24.

35 Miller, *Cops and Bobbies,* p. 8; and Elie Halévy, *A History of the English People in the 19th Century,* 4 vols. (New York, 1949), 2:288, quoted in Miller, *Cops and Bobbies,* p. 8 n.★.

36 "Rehearsal": J. O. Baylen and N. J. Gossman, eds., *Biographical Dictionary of Modern British Radicals since 1770,* 3 vols. (Hassocks: Harvester Press, 1979), 1:4. Miller, *Cops and Bobbies,* pp. 9–10.

37 2 Geo. 4, c. 118 (1821); HO 60/1/68–76, 87–99, 112, 134–7, 147–8, 165, 201–44; Gash, *Peel,* pp. 487–91, 493 (quotation, Peel to Hobhouse, 4 Feb. 1828).

38 Gash, *Peel,* pp. 488–9, 491 (quotation). HO 60/1/4; HO 61/1/175; Radzinowicz, *ECL,* 2:505–6, 533; Donald Rumbelow, *I Spy Blue: Police and Crime in the City of London from Elizabeth I to Victoria* (London: Macmillan, 1971), pp. 112–13. John Wade stated in 1829 that "the police has not materially improved since Colquhoun wrote" (*Treatise on the Police,* p. 65).

39 Gash, *Peel,* p. 492 (quotation, Peel to Hobhouse, 8 Dec. 1826).

40 *PD* 18:784–816, Peel at cols. 784–98, 815–16, quotation on col. 793, 28 Feb. 1828. Gash, *Peel,* p. 493; see also Browne, *Scotland Yard,* pp. 76–8.

41 "Report from the Select Committee . . . on the State of the Police of the Metropolis," 11 July 1828, *PP 1828* (533), 6:Report, pp. 3–32 (history of city's police since 1772, pp. 20–5: recommendations, pp. 30–2; no mention of Dublin); Minutes of Evidence, pp. 33–417.

42 Browne, *Scotland Yard,* p. 77.

43 For a rather perfunctory account, see J. L. Lyman, "The Metropolitan Police Act of 1829," *J. of Criminal Law, Criminology, and Police Science* 55 (Mar. 1964):141–54.

44 *PD* 21:867–84, quotations on cols. 876–7, 883 (Peel, 15 Apr.); 1487–8 (19 May); and 1750–3 (Lords, 5 June 1829). The idea of *three* Commissioners and a Board of Police was later dropped. Only two speakers in the Commons (including the Radical Joseph Hume) and two in the Lords (the Whigs, Holland and Durham) discussed the bill; all four gave their approval (cols. 881–2, 883–4, 1752–3). "An Act for improving the Police in and near the Metropolis," 10 Geo. 4, c. 44 (1829). It bears mention that nowhere in Peel's papers, the parliamentary debates, or the public press is there mention of the 100-man civil police, the *sergents de ville,* established in Paris in 1829. James Cramer, *The World's Police* (London: Cassell, 1964), p. 293; Philip John Stead, "The New Police," in David H. Bayley, ed., *Police and Society* (Beverly Hills, Calif., and London: Sage, 1977), pp. 78–9.

45 Browne, *Scotland Yard,* p. 78; J. M. Hart, *The British Police* (London: Allen & Unwin, 1951), p. 27; Critchley, *Police,* p. 50; and Gash, *Peel,* p. 496, where Gash quotes Peel's letter to Wellington.

46 Rumbelow, *I Spy Blue,* pp. 104–13, argues somewhat unconvincingly that Peel omitted the City because of improvements it had recently made in its police.

47 *Morning Chronicle,* 27 Mar. 1828, in the Francis Place Collection of Newspapers, vol. 31, f. 200, British Library, London; *Quarterly Review* 37 (Mar. 1828):495, 502–4.

48 Gash, *Peel,* p. 498; Charles Reith, *British Police and the Democratic Ideal* (London: Oxford University Press, 1943), pp. 33, 35, my emphasis.

49 Peel Papers, 40334 ff. 292–4, 302–20; Peel, *Private Papers,* 2:114; Gash, *Peel,*

p. 498; Peel to Gregory, 29 May 1829, quoted in Charles Reith, *A New Study of Police History* (Edinburgh: Oliver & Boyd, 1956), p. 126, and in Belton Cobb, *The First Detectives and the Early Career of Richard Mayne, Commissioner of Police* (London: Faber and Faber, 1957), p. 33.

50 Peel to Shaw, 25 June, and Shaw's short reply, 29 June 1829, declining the offer, quoted in Reith, *New Study*, pp. 127–8. On Shaw, see *DNB* 20:1311–13; Gash, *Peel*, p. 499; and Gregory Fulham, "James Shaw-Kennedy and the Reformation of the Irish Constabulary, 1836–38," *Eire-Ireland* 16, No. 2 (Summer 1981): 94–6. (In 1834 Shaw took the name Shaw-Kennedy after inheriting an estate through his wife's family.) On Shaw's service as "Military-Political Agent at Manchester," see Sir William Napier, *Life of General Sir William Napier*, ed. H. A. Bruce, 2 vols. (London: J. Murray, 1864), 1:321–9.

51 Reith, *British Police*, p. 33.

52 *DNB* 16:336–7; and "profligate": T. A. Critchley, "Peel, Rowan and Mayne," in Philip John Stead, ed., *Pioneers in Policing* (Montclair, N.J.: Patterson Smith, 1977), p. 83. Another of Charles's brothers, Robert, and an uncle, Charles, were military officers.

53 Only Reith, *British Police*, p. 33, notes Charles Rowan's service as an Irish magistrate. Sir John Moylan, *Scotland Yard and the Metropolitan Police*, 2d ed. (London and New York: Putnam & Co., 1934), p. 31 (source uncited), claims that Rowan was "a police magistrate in Ireland" after leaving the army, but no other writers mention this and I have found no evidence to support Moylan's statement. After the dismissal in 1828 of Thomas Powell, Inspector-General of Constabulary in Leinster, a man identified only as "Rowan" (perhaps Hill Wilson Rowan, who was Governor of the General Penitentiary, Dublin, before being named an Irish Stipendiary Magistrate in April 1830) was considered by Lord Lieutenant Anglesey as Powell's successor. Anglesey was a friend and former military colleague of Prime Minister Wellington. "I learn from the best authority [Sir George Murray? Wellington?]," Anglesey wrote Chief Secretary William Lamb, "that Rowan would be an excellent man for the situation, but if you hear of a better name him." Letter of 3 Mar. 1828, Anglesey Papers, T1068/15/10. Sir John Harvey was subsequently appointed. Rowan: "An Account of the Number of Stipendiary Magistrates in Ireland," *PP 1833* (191), 32:465–7.

54 Cobb, *Detectives*, pp. 34–8. Significantly, one of Mayne's recommenders was Henry Brougham, the liberal Whig who in 1822 had been a leading opponent of the Irish constabulary bill.

55 Rowan never married; he retired in 1850 and died in 1852. Mayne served as Commissioner (since 1850, the London police has been headed by a single Commissioner) until his death in 1868; Mayne's son, Richard Charles Mayne (1835–92), became an admiral (*DNB* 12:166). For their services the two Police Commissioners were knighted, Rowan in 1848 and Mayne in 1851.

On Mayne and Rowan, see *DNB* 12:165–6, 16:335–6; Browne, *Scotland Yard*, pp. 78–9; Gash, *Peel*, p. 499; Radzinowicz, *ECL*, 4:161; Critchley, "Peel, Rowan, and Mayne," pp. 82–95; Cobb, *Detectives*, passim; and Reith, *British Police*, pp. 33–5, and *New Study*, esp. pp. 5–6, 106–16, 132. Reith's *New Study* (1956), in large part a biography of Rowan, slights the roles of Peel and Mayne in shaping the new London police; a more balanced account is Cobb's *Detectives* (1957), a study of Mayne's career. No private papers of either Police Commissioner appear to have been preserved (Reith, *British Police*, p. 34 n. 1).

56 As late as 7 July 1829 Peel gave Rowan's title as "Military Magistrate" (Reith, *New Study*, p. 129). Reith, *British Police*, p. 44; Gash, *Peel*, pp. 497–8. The phrase "commissioners of police" had not been used since the days of the Dublin police of 1786–95.

57 Cobb, *Detectives*, p. 40; on the history of "Scotland Yard," see Browne, *Scotland Yard*, pp. 79–80.

58 "Return of the Number ... of the Metropolitan Police, in each year ...,"
1829–44, *PP 1844* (189), 39:691; HO 60/1/464, 478, 495; HO 65/12/298–9;
Browne, *Scotland Yard*, p. 92 (quotation); Cobb, *Detectives*, pp. 94–5; Critchley,
Police, pp. 52, 56–7; Reith, *British Police*, pp. 41, 62; and Radzinowicz, *ECL*,
4:193, 195, 203–4.

59 Rowan: "length" quoted in Reith, *British Police*, p. 35; and "quiet," in Browne,
Scotland Yard, p. 82. The marshals, or heads, of the City of London police wore a
red tunic with gold epaulettes. The City's small Day Police since 1801 sported a
dark blue uniform; wearing it was made compulsory in 1824. The late-eighteenth-century writer on police, Jonas Hanway, may have had a hand in selecting
sober blue as the color for the City uniforms. Donald Rumbelow, "Raw
Lobsters, Blue Devils," *British Heritage*, 1, No. 3 (Apr.–May 1980):14; and *I Spy
Blue*, pp. 104–7. The existing government-controlled Horse Patrol was outfitted
in scarlet waistcoats and blue trousers. In Paris the *sergents de ville*, the small civil
patrol established in 1829, wore blue uniforms, but I have seen nothing to
indicate that the French uniform was a model for the one in London.

60 Reith, *British Police*, pp. 35–6, 63, 196–7, 214; Browne, *Scotland Yard*, pp. 82–3;
Radzinowicz, *ECL*, 4:162–3; Gash, *Peel*, p. 503; Miller, *Cops and Bobbies*, p. 33.

61 Patrick Pringle, *Hue and Cry: The Birth of the British Police* (London: Museum
Press, 1955), p. 202.

62 On the arms of the pre-1829 forces, see HO 61/1/62; Wade, *Treatise on Police*, pp.
64–5; Reith, *British Police*, pp. 5, 10; Browne, *Scotland Yard*, pp. 51–2, 70–1, 83;
Cobb, *Detectives*, p. 17; Radzinowicz, *ECL*, 3:135–6, 4:159, 163; and Miller,
Cops and Bobbies, p. 49.

63 "Truncheon" is the correct term (at least since 1814), although in common and
even scholarly usage "baton" – as in "baton charge" – is often used interchange-
ably. According to one authority, the Home Office always used the term
"truncheon," never "baton." Since about 1820, "batons" were flourished by
musical conductors and, from early in our own century, carried by track relay
runners. For more on this topic, see Erland Fenn Clark, *Truncheons: Their
Romance and Reality* (London: Herbert Jenkins, 1935), pp. 229–30, an antiquarian
work that contains more than 100 plates illustrating some 500 truncheons and
also includes (pp. 216–21) a miscellaneous list of riots, 1729–1926.

64 Inhabitants of Tulse Hill, Brixton, to Home Office, 18 Nov. 1830, and M.
Whiting to Commissioners of Police, 10 Feb. 1831, both in Mepol 2/60, PRO,
London; Under-Secretary Phillipps to F. Vincent, High Wycombe, 3 Dec. 1830,
HO 41/8/311.

65 Home Office to Commissioners, 9 Jan. 1832, HO 65/11/387. Mayne testified in
1833 that *sergeants* in the "rural" horse patrol were allowed sabers. In a force of
3,400 men there were 46 mounted policemen. "Report from the Select
Committee on the Police of the Metropolis," *PP 1834* (600), 16:11–12. Cf.
"Return shewing the number of Horses ... in the Metropolitan Police Force,"
n.d., forty-eight horses, in HO 61/6.

66 Reith, *British Police*, p. 10 n. 1; Miller, *Cops and Bobbies*, pp. 48–50. See also
Browne, *Scotland Yard*, p. 83; Radzinowicz, *ECL*, 4:163.

67 Reith, *British Police*, pp. 38, 79; Browne, *Scotland Yard*, p. 84; Critchley, *Police*, p.
52. In 1829–33 a few soldiers in their later thirties were appointed; one recruit,
Thomas Kay, a private in the Scots Fusilier Guards, was forty-one. Mayne to
Phillipps, 27 Apr. 1833, HO 61/8; Kay (along with fourteen others aged thirty-
six to forty, appointed June–December 1832), in HO 61/7.

68 Home Office to G. Fishbourne, 10 Mar. 1830, and to Hugh Black, 5 Nov. 1831,
HO 65/11/79, 355. Bow Street: HO 60/1/495; Commissioners' memorandum on
transfers from Bow Street forces, 16 Jan. 1833, in HO 61/9 (86 of these 166 men
either resigned or were dismissed by the end of 1832).

69 Return, dated June 1832, printed in George Dilnot, *The Story of Scotland Yard*

(Boston: Houghton Mifflin, 1927), p. 36; and in Alwyn Solmes, *The English Policeman 1871—1935* (London: Allen & Unwin, 1935), p. 126. Subsequently printed in Inspector J. L. Thomas, "Recruits for the Police Service," *Police Journal* 19 (1946):293; Clive Emsley, *Policing and Its Context, 1750—1870* (New York: Schocken Books, 1984), p. 65. The identical return, this time dated June 1830, is also printed in David Ascoli, *The Queen's Peace: The Origins and Development of the Metropolitan Police 1829—1979* (London: Hamish Hamilton, 1979), p. 89. None of the authors identify the location of this document.

70 R. Mayne, "Memorandum relative to the Mode of Appointing Men in the Police," 1 Sept. 1835, printed in Reith, *British Police*, pp. 193—5; police order of 13 May 1845, WO 4/268/181.

71 HO 65/11/131, 263—5, 467; Gash, *Peel*, p. 502; Stead, "The New Police," pp. 80—1.

72 Resignations accounted for roughly two of every five departures. HO 65/12, appendix; HO 65/26, passim; *PP 1834* (600), 16:7, ev. of R. Mayne; "First Report from the Commissioners appointed to inquire as to the best Means of Establishing an efficient Constabulary Force in the Counties of England and Wales," *PP 1839* (169), 19:165; Reith, *British Police*, pp. 108, 194; and F. C. Mather, *Public Order in the Age of the Chartists* (Manchester: Manchester University Press, 1959), p. 97. The quotation is in Cobb, *Detectives*, p. 56.

73 *PP 1834* (600), 16:8, ev. of C. Rowan, 29 Apr. 1833; see also Mather, *Public Order*, p. 97, for dismissals, by offense, in the London police, 1834—8.

74 Rowan, in *PP 1834* (600), 16:8; John Wilson Croker, *The Croker Papers: The Correspondence and Diaries of the late Rt. Hon. John Wilson Croker*, ed. Louis J. Jennings, 3 vols. (London: J. Murray, 1884), 2:17—20; Reith, *New Study*, pp. 145—7; Rumbelow, *I Spy Blue*, pp. 148—9.

75 Browne, *Scotland Yard*, p. 90 n. 1; Critchley, *Police*, pp. 151, 168, 171. The men could not vote until 1885; there was no mandated "weekly rest-day" until 1910.

76 Day, night: *PP 1834* (600), 16:App. 9, pp. 443—4. Quotation: Mayne's memorandum of 1 Sept. 1835 (see n. 70, this chapter).

77 Critchley, *Police*, p. 153; Gash, *Peel*, p. 503; Browne, *Scotland Yard*, pp. 270—1. High annual "wastage," or turnover, continued until the founding, in 1907, of a recruit training center at Peel House, Regency Street, Westminster.

78 Peel to Commissioners of Police, 10 Dec. 1829, in Mepol 2/38, PRO, London. Only one man, Adolphus Bronckhurst, a friend of the Duke of Cambridge, was appointed by patronage (named Inspector, November 1830, HO 65/11/189, 229). In 1832 Bronckhurst's bid to be promoted to Superintendent was rejected (Reith, *British Police*, p. 106). For enforcement of the merit/service rule, see HO 61/2, HO 65/11, passim. Not till the 1930s did the Government rethink the policy of officer appointments by promotion from below; see Browne, *Scotland Yard*, pp. 347—9, and Critchley, *Police*, pp. 203—9.

79 Rumbelow, *I Spy Blue*, pp. 103—8.

80 *PP 1834* (600), 16:9, ev. of R. Mayne. On appointments and promotions, see HO 61/2, passim; unidentified paper, dated 26 Sept. 1830, Place Collection 31, f. 207; and for 1839—41, HO 65/13, app., p. 36. See also Reith, *British Police*, pp. 37, 54—5, 106, 128, 192.

81 Application of John McClintock, with recommendations by his county Sub-inspector and Inspector-General Harvey, July 1829, and reply, HO 100/228/101. My small sample of the Officers Register of the Irish constabulary (HO 184/45) suggests a dramatic shift: Of the officers appointed in 1823—8, only 7 percent had begun their careers in nonofficer ranks; of those appointed in 1829—32, 73 percent had joined as constables.

82 Reith, *British Police*, p. 62; *PP 1834* (600), 16:10. In the force in April 1833 there were 2,531 married constables and only 864 bachelors.

83 *PP 1834* (600), 16:49. See also the statement by a clothing contractor on alterations to uniforms for new recruits in Reith, *British Police*, p. 88.

84 *PP 1834* (600), 16:10 and 329-30 (Morris). The Commissioners' figures distinguished Englishmen, Scotsmen, and Irishmen. In 1833, Scotsmen comprised 9 percent of the higher ranks but only 3 percent of both the sergeants and the constables. The Irish share apparently declined over time. Dilnot cites figures – 370 Irishmen out of 4,931 men in 1855 – that would reduce the Irish share to 8 percent of the force. Mayne kept a close watch on where Irishmen were assigned; in particular, the inhabitants of Irish sections of London found it "objectionable" to be policed by Irish constables. Dilnot, *Story of Scotland Yard*, p. 328 n. 16 (source uncited).

85 Pringle, *Hue and Cry*, p. 206; Reith, *British Police*, pp. 50-1. See also Reith, *New Study*, pp. 149-53.

86 G. Smith to Peel, 23 Sept. 1830; "An Inhabitant" to H.O., 1 Nov. 1830; both in HO 61/2.

87 "An Old Man" to Peel, 2 Nov. 1830, Shoreditch; Daniel Stephens to the Police Commissioners, 18 Oct. 1830, Stepney; "A Loyal Subject" to the Police Commissioners, 9 Oct. 1830, St. James, Westminster; all in HO 61/2.

88 Report of Capt. W. Carden, Supt., S Division, 6 Oct. 1830, and "Return of Parish Meetings held within the Metropolitan Police District," 23 Sept.–5 Oct. 1830; both in HO 61/2.

89 *The Standard*, 16 Apr. ("protection"; my emphasis), 18 Apr. ("principle"), and 7 Dec. 1829, quoted in Reith, *British Police*, pp. 52-3. Marylebone: *Morning Chronicle*, 4 Dec. 1832, in Place Collection 31, f. 213. "Covent Garden Deputation – Representations made on the subject of the Met^n. Police," n.d., my emphasis; "Anonymous" (gentleman) to Home Office, 8 Nov. 1830; both in HO 61/2. The Home Office kept a close watch over these meetings. See the large tabular "Return of [10] Parish Meetings held within the Metropolitan Police District," 23 Sept.–5 Oct. 1830, which lists the names and occupations of speakers at and the "character" of each meeting ("400 Persons, Tradesmen and Mechanics ... 300 very respectable Parishioners ... 200 Persons of the lowest order"). A key to the table identifies speakers who were connected to the old watch establishments or whose "opinions were favourable to the Metropolitan Police" (return in HO 61/2).

90 Handbill, n.d., source uncited and quoted in Reith, *British Police*, p. 68. The (undated) original, in the Guildhall Library, is photographically reproduced in Rumbelow, "Raw Lobsters," p. 17.

91 "Memorial on Vellum," from Marylebone parish, Dec. 1832, in HO 61/7, based on resolutions adopted at vestry meeting, 17 Nov. 1832, printed (source uncited) in Reith, *British Police*, pp. 118, 120-2.

92 *PP 1834* (600), 16:279, ev. of C. B. Stutfield, JP; Reith, *British Police*, p. 52.

93 "Amount due from Parishes," 30 Sept. 1830, in HO 61/2; and expense of old watch establishments and new police, in *PP 1834* (600), 16:App. 5, pp. 434-8. "Sabotage": Radzinowicz, *ECL*, 4:168; "war": Reith, *British Police*, p. 116; other quotations are in "Covent Garden Deputation," n.d., in HO 61/2. One correspondent suggested that the higher costs would be more readily accepted if "a more intimate connexion between the Parishioners and the Police should be allowed, than exists under the present System." For instance, the Metropolitan Police Inspectors, now "Total Strangers," might, "having met certain qualifications," be elected by parish authorities. The men should "be always fixed and resident" in the parish. S. Palmer to Peel, 26 Oct. 1830, Walworth, Surrey, in HO 61/2. Cf. the petition from Paddington parish, June 1831, which called for the establishment of "a co-ordinate parochial authority ... should the Metropolis Police be continued" (in HO 61/4).

94 J. Wray, Metropolitan Police Receiver, to Under-Secretary Phillipps, 25 Mar. 1833, in HO 61/8. On this office, see R. M. Morris, "The Metropolitan Police Receiver in the 19th Century," *Police Journal* 47 (Jan. 1974):65–74. "Robert R. A." (Irish landowner, and applicant for the post of Stipendiary Magistrate in Ireland) to Peel, October 1830, Brompton; "Anonymous" to H.O., 8 Nov. 1830; both in HO 61/2.

95 3 & 4 Will. 4, c. 89 (1833). For 1834 the local assessment, £151,780, was only slightly above the combined parish expenses of £137,289 for all of the watch forces in 1828. The Consolidated Fund's contribution was £50,593. *PP 1834* (600), 16:App. 5, pp. 434–8, and App. 6, pp. 439–40.

96 Radzinowicz, *ECL*, 4:177; Peter Laurie, *Scotland Yard: A Study of the Metropolitan Police* (London: The Bodley Head, and New York: Holt, Rinehart, & Winston, 1970), p. 91.

97 Rumbelow, "Raw Lobsters," pp. 10–18; Reith, *British Police*, p. 134.

98 Rumbelow, "Raw Lobsters," p. 16; Reith, *British Police*, pp. 55–8, 61, 82–3, 143–5; "automata": J. E. Puddick to Peel, 12 Aug. 1830, in HO 61/2.

99 Edward Law, Earl of Ellenborough, *A Political Diary, 1828–1830, by Edward Law, Lord Ellenborough*, ed. Charles Abbot, Lord Colchester, 2 vols. (London: R. Bentley, 1881), 2:417–28. *Morning Chronicle*, 3 Nov. 1830, in Place Collection 31, f. 207. Cutlasses: handbill, in Reith, *British Police*, p. 70; "MERCENARY": handbill, "ENGLISHMEN! You have let a good opportunity escape you ...," my emphasis, in HO 59/2. See also Peel, *Private Papers*, 2:168–9; Reith, *British Police*, pp. 69–76 and *New Study*, pp. 154–7.

100 On Place, see *DNB* 15:1276–9; Graham Wallas, *The Life of Francis Place, 1771–1854* (London: Longmans, Green, 1898); Reith, *British Police*, pp. 112–13; and G. D. H. Cole and Raymond Postgate, *The Common People 1746–1946*, 4th ed. (London: Methuen, 1949, repr. 1964), pp. 231–4, 246–7.

101 Compare with J. T. Barber Beaumont's proposal in 1815 (see Chapter 5, "I. Challenges in London," "Riots and conspiracies: from the corn bill to Cato Street, 1815–20"). On Superintendent Thomas, see Reith, *British Police*, pp. 60, 91–3; Cobb, *Detectives*, pp. 59–71.

102 Wallas, *Place*, p. 248 n. 3; Browne, *Scotland Yard*, p. 98; Radzinowicz, *ECL*, 4:179; and Reith, *British Police*, pp. 72–4 (who mistakenly gives dates of 2 and 9 Sept. for 2 and 9 Nov. 1830). Some members of the crowd armed themselves with pieces of wood from the site of the Public Record Office, then under construction in Chancery Lane.

103 Orders to Superintendents, 27 Apr.; report of Supt. J. Thomas, 29 Apr.; report of Insp. J. E. Rogers, 7 May; Supt. R. May to Under-Secretary Phillipps, 10 May; and Commissioner Rowan to Phillipps, 12 May 1831; all in HO 59/2.

104 Of those arrested, most were eighteen to twenty-five years of age, mainly laborers, with a sprinkling of petty tradesmen, and only a few unemployed. "Apprehensions during the 27 April 1831 Disturbances," in HO 59/2. Note the large number of arrests despite orders to disperse the crowds "rather than to encumber themselves with a number of Prisoners," as Francis Place had suggested (report of Insp. J. Hornsby, 27 Apr., in HO 59/2).

105 *Annual Register* 73 (1831): Chronicle, 68. On the April disorders, see Reith, *British Police*, pp. 90–5; and Joseph Hamburger, *James Mill and the Art of Revolution* (New Haven, Conn.: Yale University Press, 1963; repr., Westport, Conn: Greenwood Press, 1977), pp. 139–42.

106 Browne, *Scotland Yard*, p. 102; Rumbelow, "Raw Lobsters," p. 18; Reith, *British Police*, pp. 95–9 (Superintendent May, Peel quoted on pp. 98, 99); Hamburger, *Revolution*, pp. 147–54. On provincial disturbances, see Chapter 10, "II. Popular protest: challenge and response," "Reform Bill crisis."

107 Wallas, *Place*, chs. 10, 11; Cole and Postgate, *The Common People*, pp. 254–7; Geoffrey Finlayson, *Decade of Reform: England in the Eighteen Thirties* (New York:

W. W. Norton, 1970), pp. 5–23; John Cannon, *Parliamentary Reform 1640–1832* (Cambridge: Cambridge University Press, 1973), ch. 10. For an interpretation that links the Tory leaders' obstinacy on Reform to their experiences in Ireland, see Silver, "Social and Ideological Bases," pp. 197–201.

108 Gavin Thurston, *The Clerkenwell Riot: The Killing of Constable Culley* (London: Allen & Unwin, 1967), pp. ix, 50–9. The only other constable killed in the line of duty in 1829–34 was John Long in August 1830. Browne, *Scotland Yard*, p. 95; *PP 1834* (600), 16:8.

109 On all of these disturbances, see Reith, *British Police*, pp. 139–55; and Radzinowicz, *ECL*, 4:180–4.

110 On Popay, see "Report from the Select Committee on the Petition of Frederick Young and Others," *PP 1833* (627), 13:407–588. The police continued to use private citizens as spies; see T. M. Parssinen and I. J. Prothero, "The London Tailors' Strike of 1834 and the Collapse of the Grand National Consolidated Trades Union: A Police Spy's Report," *Intl. Rev. Soc. Hist.* 22 (1977):65–107. On Cold Bath Fields, see "Report from the Select Committee on the Cold Bath Fields Meeting," *PP 1833* (718), 13:589–802; Thurston's book, *The Clerkenwell Riot*, is more prejudiced against the rioters than was the contemporary parliamentary inquiry into the incident. Reith, *British Police*, pp. 155–9; Browne, *Scotland Yard*, pp. 105–6; Radzinowicz, *ECL*, 4:185–9. The detective force consisted of eight men at its establishment in 1842, and as late as 1868, just prior to internal reforms, there were only fifteen full-time detectives.

111 "Report from the Select Committee on the Police of the Metropolis," 13 Aug. 1834, *PP 1834* (600), 16:Report, pp. 3–22, on pp. 4, 13, 21.

112 Reith, *British Police*, p. 138 ("principal"), 201–2; Radzinowicz, *ECL*, 4:169.

113 *PP 1834* (600), 16:Report, pp. 7–8. This view is accepted by Radzinowicz, *ECL*, 4:191–2; and by Jenifer Hart, "Reform of the Borough Police, 1835–1856," *E.H.R.* 70 (1955):414. Negligence: Reith, *British Police*, pp. 159–63, 188–9.

114 Brutality: Pringle, *Hue and Cry*, p. 208; and Wilbur R. Miller, "Police Authority in London and New York City, 1830–1870," *J. Soc. Hist.* 8, No. 2 (Winter 1975):84. Memorandum by Commissioner Rowan, n.d., "Metropolitan Police Draft Papers and Correspondence," in the Papers of Edwin Chadwick, Chadwick MS 16, f. 7, D. M. S. Watson Library, University College, University of London. "I believe," added Rowan, that "it is a mistake to confine the Irish Police [i.e., Constabulary] to the military weapons, & I am informed that the men believe so too." But he notes that in the Irish districts of London in the 1830s, if "ten police" were sent in, "a [war] whoop was raised and the Irish assembled by the hundreds." Chadwick MS 16, ff. 4–5.

115 Browne, *Scotland Yard*, pp. 95, 105; Reith, *British Police*, pp. 135–6. *The Times*, quoted in Browne, *Scotland Yard*, p. 96.

116 Reith, *British Police*, pp. 190–1, 199–200 and *New Study*, pp. 215–24; and Miller, "Police Authority," p. 91.

117 The City of London Police, reformed by 2 & 3 Vict., c. xciv, Local Acts (1839), stayed separate from the Metropolitan Police. The City Police Commissioner, appointed by the Common Council, had to be approved by the Home Secretary; he could be dismissed by the Crown or the Lord Mayor and aldermen. Each force had to get official approval before entering the other's jurisdiction. Memorandum by Edwin Chadwick, "City Police Reform," 1839, in Chadwick MS 3; Radzinowicz, *ECL*, 4:193–5, 203–7; Reith, *British Police*, pp. 214 ("epaulettes"), 220–1, 249.

118 Police instructions, 3 June, 21 Aug., and 1 Nov. 1830, quoted in Thurston, *Clerkenwell Riot*, pp. 36–7, and Reith, *British Police*, p. 48; my emphases. See also Miller, "Police Authority," pp. 86–8, 92–3; Reith, *New Study*, pp. 139–42; and Cobb, *Detectives*, pp. 55 n. 2, 84 n. 2. The "Nine Police Principles" are discussed in Reith, *British Police*, pp. 3–4; and T. A. Critchley, "The Idea of Policing in

Britain: Success or Failure?" in J. C. Alderson and Philip John Stead, eds., *The Police We Deserve* (London: Wolfe Publishing, 1973), pp. 25–38.

119 C. Rowan to J. Hume, 26 Mar. 1838, quoted in Reith, *British Police*, p. 218.

CHAPTER 9. CONSOLIDATION OF THE IRISH CONSTABULARY

1 Sir Llewellyn Woodward, *The Age of Reform, 1815–1870*, 2d ed. (Oxford: Clarendon Press, 1962), p. 86; T. A. Critchley, *The Conquest of Violence: Order and Liberty in Britain* (New York: Schocken Books, 1970), p. 121; Malcolm I. Thomis and Peter Holt, *Threats of Revolution in Britain, 1789–1848* (Hamden, Conn.: Archon Books, 1977), p. 97. See also Allan Silver, "Social and Ideological Bases of British Elite Reactions to Domestic Crisis in 1829–1832," *Politics and Society* 2 (Feb. 1971):179–201, esp. 197ff.

2 On the Tithe War, see R. B. O'Brien, *Fifty Years of Concessions to Ireland*, 2 vols. (London: Low, Marston, Searle, and Rivington, 1883–5), 1:372–87; J. C. Beckett, *The Making of Modern Ireland, 1603–1923* (London: Faber and Faber, 1966), pp. 294–5, 308–12; Gearóid Ó Tuathaigh, *Ireland Before the Famine, 1798–1848* (Dublin: Gill and Macmillan, 1972), pp. 165–8; and Galen Broeker, *Rural Disorder and Police Reform in Ireland, 1812–36* (London and Toronto: Routledge & Kegan Paul, 1970), pp. 204–6. The best recent studies are three articles by Patrick O'Donoghue in *Studia Hibernica* (see n. 19, this chapter).

3 Five-sixths: Home Secretary Robert Peel's memorandum on Catholic Emancipation, 12 Jan. 1829, quoted in Norman Gash, ed., *The Age of Peel* (London: Edward Arnold, 1968), p. 27; see also Peel to the Bishop of Limerick, 8 Feb. 1829, Papers of Sir Robert Peel, BL Add. MS 40326 f. 185, British Library, London [hereafter cited by file number only], and printed in Sir Robert Peel, *Sir Robert Peel, from his Private Papers*, ed. Charles Stuart Parker, 3 vols. (London: J. Murray, 1891–9), 1:360–2. Monthly force levels, 1828–34: WO 17/1104–10. Evacuation plan: Melbourne to Anglesey, 29 Dec. 1830, Papers of Henry William Paget, 1st Marquess of Anglesey, T1068/31/20, PRONI, Belfast [hereafter cited by file number only]. Melbourne to Anglesey, 28 Feb. 1831, Anglesey Papers, D619/6/31, PRONI, Belfast [hereafter cited by file number only]. Army posts: "Report from the Select Committee appointed to examine into the state of the Disturbed Counties in Ireland ...," *PP 1831–2* (677), 16:Q. 1448, ev. of Gen. Sir Hussey Vivian, commander-in-chief of the army in Ireland.

4 "Insurrection": Anglesey to Gen. Sir George Hill, 24 Dec. 1831, HO 100/242/279; and 40,000: Anglesey to Grey, 9 Feb. 1831, T1068/8/224. Cloncurry to Anglesey, "1832," in D619/1/"Cloncurry."

5 Anglesey to Grey, 5 and 6 July 1832, T1068/8/255–8. Grey to Anglesey, 8 July 1832, T1068/30/217. Melbourne to Anglesey, 26 Mar. 1833, T1068/31/155–6. 1832 force levels: WO 17/1108.

6 James A. Reynolds, *The Catholic Emancipation Crisis in Ireland, 1823–29* (New Haven, Conn.: Yale University Press, 1954; repr., Westport, Conn.: Greenwood Press, 1970), pp. 168–9; *PP 1831–2* (677), 16:Q. 3192, and quoted in George Cornewall Lewis, *Local Disturbances in Ireland* (London: B. Fellowes, 1836, reprint ed., Cork: Tower Books, 1977), p. 90. The Irish Reform Act of 1832 retained the £10 county franchise; the total electorate in 1841 was under 100,000. R. B. McDowell, *Public Opinion and Government Policy in Ireland, 1801–1846* (London: Faber and Faber, 1952; repr., Westport, Conn.: Greenwood Press, 1975), pp. 132–3. Witnesses before the 1832 select committee on the state of Ireland all pointed to disappointment over Catholic Emancipation; see *PP 1831–2* (677), 16:QQ. 2739, 5857–66, 5997–6000, 7446–9.

7 Patrick O'Donoghue, "Causes of Opposition to Tithes, 1830–38," *Studia Hib.* 5 (1965):10, 14–21. Melbourne to Anglesey, 4 Apr. 1831, T1068/31/58–9.

8 Peel to the Bishop of Limerick, 8 Feb. 1829, 40326 f. 185, printed in Peel, *Private*

Papers, 1:360–2, and cited in Reynolds, *Emancipation*, p. 165, and in Broeker, *Police*, p. 190. Peel to Leveson Gower, 30 July 1829, 40337 f. 74, printed in Peel, *Private Papers*, 2:120–2. Norman Gash notes that Leveson Gower "had in fact been virtually carried by Peel ever since his appointment [in June 1828]." Gash, *Mr. Secretary Peel: The Life of Sir Robert Peel to 1830* (Cambridge, Mass.: Harvard University Press, 1961), p. 604. On Peel's Irish police proposals, see HO 100/ 229/199; Edward Law, Earl of Ellenborough, *A Political Diary, 1828–1830, by Edward Law, Lord Ellenborough*, ed. Charles Abbot, Lord Colchester, 2 vols. (London: R. Bentley, 1881), 2:136, 160; Peel, *Private Papers*, 2:122–3; Gash, *Peel*, pp. 605–6, 624–5; and Broeker, *Police*, pp. 197–201.

9 "Respect": McDowell, *Public Opinion*, p. 132; on Anglesey, see ibid., pp. 147–52. See also Anglesey to Grey, 17 June 1831, Earl Grey Papers, Papers on Ireland, No. 20, Department of Paleography and Diplomatic, University of Durham; and Anglesey to Dr. Doyle, 19 June 1831, in T1068/23.

10 "Liberal": Peel–Gregory correspondence, c. 1825, document uncited, quoted in McDowell, *Public Opinion*, p. 103. Peel's conversion to Emancipation in February 1829 had shocked and embittered Gregory; see Gash, *Peel*, pp. 556, 584. For details of Gregory's retirement, see HO 100/235/231–4. On Gosset, see Leveson Gower to Peel, 6 Jan., and Peel to Leveson Gower, 12 Jan. 1829, 40336 ff. 202–3, 206. Anglesey to Cloncurry, 22 Feb. 1833, T1068/29/11–12. Chief Secretary Littleton (1833–4) said of Gosset that "a better man does not exist." Papers of Edward Littleton, 1st Baron Hatherton, D260/M/OI/3/293, Staffordshire Record Office, Stafford [hereafter cited by file number only].

11 *Dictionary of National Biography* [hereafter, *DNB*] 18:941–8, "mobbed" at p. 941; and Angus Macintyre, *The Liberator: Daniel O'Connell and the Irish Party, 1830– 1847* (New York: Macmillan, 1965), pp. 23–6.

12 *DNB* 18:941–3; McDowell, *Public Opinion*, pp. 143, 148; and Donald Akenson, *The Irish Education Experiment* (London: Routledge & Kegan Paul, 1970).

13 McDowell, *Public Opinion*, pp. 141 ("toryism"), 150 ("appalled"), 156; *DNB* 18:943; and Anglesey Papers, T1068/8/221–2. Stanley's suggestion to use the military came one month after the incident at Carrickshock (see this chapter, "II. Bolstering the forces of order," "Constabulary affrays").

14 McDowell, *Public Opinion*, pp. 141, 143 ("driving"). Edward Brynn, *Crown and Castle: British Rule in Ireland, 1800–1830* (Dublin: O'Brien Press, 1978), pp. 54–5, 156. *DNB* 18:947. Anglesey's comments in D260/M/OI/1/23, and Anglesey to Holland, 3 Sept. 1831, in T1068/5.

15 Elections: Chief Secretary's Office Registered Papers [hereafter, CSORP] 1832/ Yeomanry & Constabulary [hereafter, Y & C]/811, 814, ISPO, DC. Jail: Gosset to Miller, 23 Mar. 1831, General Private Correspondence [hereafter, GPC], 1830–1, f. 114, ISPO, DC; and CSORP 1831/2685. Fish and game: Gregory to G. Macartney, 13 Jan. 1830, GPC 1830–1 f. 13; and CSORP 1830/5. Tolls: CSORP 1832/4636 and 1833/194. County cess: CSORP 1831/2030. Wages: CSORP 1830/8035.

16 R. Greene's opinion, 23 Mar., in Chief Constable E. A. Douglass to Gosset, 21 Mar. 1833, CSORP 1381. Armagh: Greene's opinion, 13 July, citing 7 & 8 Geo. 4, c. 67 s. 17, in H. Caulfield to Gosset, 12 July 1832, CSORP 3389. Ejectments: D'Arcy to Gosset, 14 Apr., and Greene's ruling, 19 Apr. 1832, CSORP 1744; and Harvey to Gosset, 28 Mar., and Greene's ruling, 30 Mar. 1832, CSORP 1406.

17 Duke of Leinster to Sir J. Harvey, 4 June 1832, CSORP 2738. Miller to Gosset, 28 June 1832, CSORP 2997. Beggars: Gosset to W. Massey, 18 Feb. 1831, GPC 1830–1 f. 44, and CSORP 1832/53. Sabbath and army: Sir H. Hardinge to Miller, 14 Oct., and Gregory to Col. Hill, 29 Oct. 1830, Country Letter Books [hereafter, CLB], 1830–1, ff. 15 and 29, ISPO, DC.

18 Opinion of R. Greene, 9 Oct., in Harvey to Stanley, 6 Oct. 1832, CSORP 5161;

see also CSORP 1832/521, 1421. On the change in policy, compare Gregory's letter to Warburton, 30 June 1829, CLB 1829 f. 156, with that of Gosset to Rev. M. Corry, 3 Apr. 1832, CLB 1832 f. 200. On police parties, see CSORP 1832/Y & C/549, 590; and on the difficulty of collection, *PP 1831–2* (677), 16:QQ. 1625–8, 3337, 5031–4. General Order from Gosset, 10 Jan. 1832, CLB 1831–2 f. 178.

19 The best recent studies are three articles by Patrick O'Donoghue. See O'Donoghue, "Causes of the Opposition to Tithes, 1830–38," *Studia Hib.* 5 (1965):7–28; "Opposition to Tithe Payment in 1830–31," *Studia Hib.* 6 (1966):69–98; and "Opposition to Tithe Payment in 1832–3," *Studia Hib.* 12 (1972):77–108.

20 Valuation comprised not one-tenth but anywhere from one-twelfth to one-thirty-first of the rental. O'Donoghue, "Opposition . . . 1830–31," p. 78 n. 33.

21 O'Donoghue, "Causes," pp. 7–28; Macintyre, *Liberator*, pp. 172–6.

22 "First Report by the Lords' Select Committee appointed to inquire into the Collection and Payment of Tithes in Ireland," *PP 1831–2* (271), 22:10, ev. of Insp.-Gen. Sir J. Harvey; R. Fawcett to Lord Lieutenant, 10 Aug. 1831, CSORP 2106. CSORP 1830/208, 818. O'Donoghue, "Opposition . . . 1830–31," pp. 95–7.

23 O'Donoghue, "Opposition . . . 1830–31," pp. 69–70. *PP 1831–2* (271), 22:7–8 ("indefatigable"), 26, ev. of Harvey, and 135–6, ev. of Subinsp. G. Brown. The change in policy may be seen by comparing CSORP 1830/208 with 1831/3350, 3351.

24 O'Donoghue, "Opposition . . . 1830–31," pp. 71–2, and McDowell, *Public Opinion*, p. 144. *PP 1831–2* (271), 22:129–30 ("touch"), ev. of Subinspector Brown, and 171, 177, ev. of Law Adviser R. Greene. In June 1833 the Kildare Subinspector, Ephraim Flinter, was dismissed from the force for forcibly entering several houses at night and jailing twenty men for nonpayment of tithe valued at a total of £3. Flinter's case caused a stir; see CSORP 1833/2885, Hatherton Papers D260/M/OI/459–82, and "Report of Mr. P. O'Gorman on Charges against E. S. Flinter, Sub-Inspector of Kildare, with Minutes of Evidence," 8 July 1833, *PP 1833* (605), 32:477–88. Flinter was subsequently reinstated in the force and posted to Antrim, where he served for twenty-one years. His record in this county was marred by numerous admonishments for "inattention," "neglect," and "irregularities"; he sustained "an injury of the chest" while attending a "Political Meeting" at Belfast in June 1841. Irish Constabulary Officers Register, HO 184/45/26.

25 *PP 1831–2* (271), 22:27 (Harvey), and 129–30 (Brown). Macintyre, *Liberator*, 176–8.

26 O'Donoghue, "Opposition . . . 1830–31," pp. 75, 79–80, and "Opposition . . . 1832–3," pp. 79–84; Macintyre, *Liberator*, pp. 178–83.

27 *PP 1831–2* (271), 22:170 (Greene). Galway: Return dated 16 Sept. 1832, Ballinasloe, in Official Papers Miscellaneous and Assorted, 1832–82 [hereafter, OPMA], 641, ISPO, DC. Marching money: CSORP 1832/4294. Anglesey to Grey, 28 Nov. 1832, T1068/8/285. Harvey to Gosset, 19 Oct. 1832, CSORP/Y & C/676. Kilkenny: *PP 1831–2* (271), 22:129–30. Tithe driving, 1832–3: O'Donoghue, "Opposition . . . 1832–3," p. 87. *PP 1831–2* (677) 16:QQ. 2007 (Harvey) and 3907–8, 4158–68 (Queen's County Subinspector H. B. Wray).

28 Details are in O'Donoghue, "Opposition . . . 1830–31," p. 81; "Opposition . . . 1823–3," pp. 98, 104; and "Return of Applications for Tithe Relief, 1831 to 1833; Amount of Claims each year . . .," *PP 1834* (382), 43:321. Anglesey to Grey, 5 and 9 July 1832, T1068/8/256, 259.

29 CSORP 1832/2999; O'Donoghue, "Opposition . . . 1832–3," pp. 81–7, 101–2; Broeker, *Police*, pp. 213–15; and Macintyre, *Liberator*, pp. 44–50. The rare cases of police breaking open doors (May 1833) and of handcuffing prisoners who

were tithe defaulters (June 1833) produced great protests; see "Charges against E. S. Flinter, Sub-Inspector of Kildare," *PP 1833* (605), 32:477–8, and CSORP 1833/2907, respectively.

30 O'Donoghue, "Opposition ... 1832–3," pp. 102–4; McDowell, *Public Opinion*, pp. 146–9; and Macintyre, *Liberator*, pp. 186–8.

31 "Modest": McDowell, *Public Opinion*, pp. 159–60. Sir John Cam Hobhouse filled in for one month as Irish Chief Secretary; Littleton succeeded to the post only after James Abercromby and Thomas Spring-Rice had declined it. Anglesey Papers, T1068/29/29. On Littleton, see *DNB* 11:1248–51, and Macintyre, *Liberator*, pp. 129–34. "Restrain": Littleton to Melbourne, 9 Sept. 1834, D260/M/OI/4/13; on the Church Million Act, 3 & 4 Will. 4, c. 100 (1833), see Macintyre, *Liberator*, pp. 188–9.

32 For examples, see CSORP 1834/604, 1257, 1487, 2385, 2590, 2809, 2918, 3381, 3493. A typical comment by Littleton: "The policy of employing Policemen for the recovery of Crown debts was, no doubt, adopted after very mature reflection by Mr. Stanley. He knows that I dissent from his view of policy in this matter" (to Solicitor-General, 12 July 1833, D260/M/OI/49).

33 Littleton to Gosset, 27 June 1833, D260/M/OI/2, 20; "Tithes. Military and Police Aid in collecting Tithes. Copy of Paper Submitted to Cabinet," n.d., D260/M/OI/1786; and D260/M/OI/3/427, 454. Gosset, not surprisingly, did not surrender graciously; see Hatherton Papers, D260/M/OI/2/37 and 6/344–5.

34 Suspension: Lord Lieutenant's memorandum, 17 June 1833, and circular to Inspectors-General of Constabulary, CSORP 1833/3009 and D260/M/OI/161–2. Million Fund: Littleton to Lord Lt. Wellesley, 21 Aug. 1834, a retrospective analysis of the new policy, D260/M/OI/3/426. "Fiscal": Littleton to Solicitor-General, 12 July 1833, D260/M/OI/2/49–50. The 1834 tithe bill: Macintyre, *Liberator*, pp. 189–92; among the bill's supporters was Sir John Harvey (see OPMA 1834 IA/72/3/62/6). The 1838 act: O'Donoghue, "Opposition ... 1832–3," p. 108; McDowell, *Public Opinion*, p. 171; Macintyre, *Liberator*, pp. 192–200; and "Report from the Select Committee on Outrages (Ireland)," *PP 1852* (438), 14:Q. 4375.

35 "Report by the Lords' Select Committee appointed to inquire into the state of Ireland since the year 1835 in respect of Crime and Outrage," in four parts, 2 vols. (11, 12), *PP 1839* (486), 12:QQ. 14, 452 ("least respectable," ev. of Stip. Magis. R. Rathbone); and O'Donoghue, "Opposition ... 1830–31," pp. 90–2, and "Opposition ... 1832–3," pp. 81–2.

36 For Clare, see *PP 1839* (486), 11:QQ. 7452, 7512, 7627, and 9603 ("more divided," ev. of Stip. Magis. J. Tabuteau); 12:QQ. 14372–82 and 14444–56; and *PP 1852* (438), 14:QQ. 4800–7, 4874–92. The act 1 & 2 Will. 4, c. 44, changed many Whiteboy crimes from capital to transportable offenses. The Lady Clares dressed in women's clothes. The Terry Alts allegedly took their name from an unfortunate Protestant military pensioner whose name the agrarian protesters would utter ("Well done, Terryalt") as they committed an offense. The police on one occasion actually arrested Terryalt, only later to discover their error; the poor fellow was "discharged and put into the Police." *PP 1839* (486), 11:Q. 7446, ev. of M. Barrington. See also Flannan Enright, "The Terry Alts, c. 1827–35," M. A. thesis, University College, Dublin, 1980.

37 National figures for the number of persons committed for trial, from 1828 on, are in *PP 1835* (303), 45:343–4; and *PP 1839* (486), 12:1092–3. For returns of committals in individual counties, see for 1830, *PP 1830–1* (294), 12:631–96; for 1831, *PP 1831–2* (299), 33:19–92; for 1832, *PP 1833* (61), 29:89–162; and for 1834 *PP 1835* (295), 45:269–342. I have been unable to locate published returns of county committals for 1833. For police reports of incidents of homicide in Ireland, 1831 and 1832, see *PP 1833* (80), 29:411–30.

38 O'Donoghue, "Opposition ... 1830–31," pp. 74–5, 79–80, 91, 92 ("more

violent"), and "Opposition ... 1832–3," pp. 79–82, 98; and Macintyre, *Liberator*, pp. 178–80. Only one-fourth of the tithe in Clare was withheld in 1832.

39 "Elements": Stip. Magis. G. Fitzgerald to Gosset, 1 Feb. 1832, quoted in O'Donoghue, "Opposition ... 1832–3," p. 81. Army levels, 1828–39, in *PP 1839* (486), 12:1386. Militia: Anglesey Papers, T1068/3/59, 66–7; Duke of Richmond to Anglesey, 17 Jan. 1832, HO 100/241/74–5 ("Arms").

40 Gosset's recommendation to Sir H. Hardinge, 21 Sept. 1828, T1068/20/114–15. Implementation in 1831: WO 35/26/30–4, 39, 50, 66–7, 85–91. Stanley's memorandum, 25 Apr. 1831, in Earl Grey Papers, Papers on Ireland, No. 8. Stanley to Melbourne, 1 Jan. 1831, HO 100/236/9; and Anglesey to Melbourne, 26 Dec. 1830, T1068/3/51.

41 Anglesey to Sir Francis Burdett, 27 Aug. 1831, in T1068/24 ("shallow"); and Anglesey to Lord Holland, 4 July 1831, T1068/4/26. 10,000 troops: Anglesey to Holland, 23 Jan. 1831, in T1068/5; and T1068/4/27–8.

42 Stanley's memorandum, 25 Apr. 1831, Earl Grey Papers, Papers on Ireland, No. 8; Yeomanry memorandum, dated only 1831, Grey Papers, in Ireland II/6; and "Memorandum relative to the Yeomanry Arms," undated, Hatherton Papers, D260/M/OI/1303. Misconduct: HO 100/235/227–9 and 239/121. Newtownbarry: Anglesey Papers, T1068/4/26–8, and O'Donoghue, "Opposition ... 1830–31," p. 77. Robert Curtis, *The History of the Royal Irish Constabulary* (Dublin: Moffat & Co., 1869), pp. 29–30 ("begged"), gives a figure of seventeen killed and "a vast number wounded." R. B. O'Brien has the Yeomanry "killing twelve, and fatally wounding twenty" [*Thomas Drummond, Under-Secretary in Ireland, 1835–40* (London: K. Paul, Trench, 1889), p. 79]. In any event, more died at Newtownbarry than at Peterloo.

43 CSORP 1832/Y & C/231. Gosset's circular to Subinspectors, 26 Feb. 1833, OPMA 1A/72/2/50/5. Anglesey to Sir J. C. Hobhouse, 17 Mar. 1833, in T1068/28. Littleton to E. Ellice, 16 Oct. 1833, D260/M/OI/2/198. Wellesley's order, 7 Mar. 1834, HO 100/245/196. On disarming, see D260/M/OI/2/485–8 and 3/117, 368. Subinsp. N. Thompson to Harvey, 11 Apr. 1834, in questionnaire to the constabulary regarding the Yeomanry, D260/M/OI/245–58 on f. 250.

44 Gosset to D'Arcy, 5 Dec. 1832, CSORP 817A. Peeler costs in "A Return of the Peace Preservation Force in Ireland, ... the Number and Distribution thereof, Pay &c...," 1831 to 1833, *PP 1834* (201), 47:399–414; and "A Return of the Number of Peace Preservation Police, ... and Expense ..., in 1835," *PP 1836* (527), 12:145; see also HO 100/237/373–4. Constabulary expenditures for 5,516 men in 1827 totalled £206,228. Official Papers, Series 2, 1790–1831 [hereafter, OP 2], 1823–31/588AA/820/14, ISPO, DC.

45 Warburton to Gosset, 4 July 1834, CSORP 2747; *PP 1831–2* (677), 16:Q. 5762, ev. of M. O'Reilly, Queen's County landowner.

46 Stanley's memorandum, 25 Apr. 1831, Earl Grey Papers, Papers on Ireland, No. 8. 3 Geo. 4, c. 103 s. 1; 9 Geo. 4, c. 63 ss. 1–2. Force levels: OP 2 1824/615/2; "A Return of the Police of Ireland, showing the Number and Distribution ... 1830 to 1832," *PP 1833* (518), 32:453–61; and "A Return of the Constabulary Force employed ... in Ireland, 1 January 1837," *PP 1837* (391), 45:303.

47 A full list of stations is in *PP 1833* (518), 32:453–61. For a tabular list of tithe police parties in Kilkenny, September–October 1833, see D260/M/OI/1746. The 1831 Irish county population figures: J. R. McCulloch, *Dictionary of Commerce*, 2 vols. (London: Longmans, 1854), 2:1028. For county-by-county calculations of police density per population and acreage, see Stanley H. Palmer, "Police and Protest in England and Ireland, 1780–1850," Ph.D. dissertation, Harvard University, 1973, Table 22, p. 676.

48 In December 1832 alone, County Kilkenny received fifty policemen from Ulster, twenty-three from County Dublin, and fifty from County Galway (CSORP

1832/Y & C/756, 759, 761, 817A). For other rotations, see CSORP/Y & C/459, 528, 744, 784.

49 Punishment: Constables Register, HO 184/1, 2. Insp.-Gen. Sir F. Stovin to Drummond, 5 Oct. 1835, CSORP 3337; in Ulster, from March 1834 to October 1835, "upwards of 100 Men" were rotated from their posts for disciplinary reasons, "with the most beneficial effect." For the case of the slothful and ailing Chief Constable L. Kyffin, moved from Queen's County to pre–Tithe War, tranquil Wexford, see CSORP 1830/383, 673. Assizes: CSORP 1832/Y & C/521; see also ibid., 246, 262. Anglesey to Cloncurry, 28 Feb. 1833, T1068/29/15–16. "Order" and "want of knowledge": Insp.-Gen. William Miller to Littleton, 23 Nov. 1833, CSORP 6042. County rosters: Miller to Gosset, 1 Jan. 1833, CSORP 311. Registry Book: printed circular, Gosset to county Subinspectors, 1 Feb. 1834, and Miller to Gosset, 5 July 1834, CSORP 920, 2929, respectively.

50 CSORP 1832/Y & C/119 (drills), 336 (Warburton), 628 ("since ... 1822"), and 159, 625, 630 (Kilkenny). See also CSORP/Y & C/33, 119, 155–6, 160, 698, 749. The author has identified nineteen counties supplied with ammunition in 1832. The statistics for the rearmament contain enough pitfalls to invalidate extended analysis. Low numbers for reissue may only indicate already well-stocked arsenals; high numbers do not necessarily indicate centers of disturbance. But all of the evidence I have consulted suggests that the last armament on this scale occurred at the founding of the force in 1822–4.

51 Peel to Wellington, 27 July 1829, in Peel, *Private Papers*, 2:120. Leveson Gower to Peel, 9 July 1829, 40337 f. 21. Evidence in *PP 1831–2* (677), 16:QQ. 949, 964–8, 1442–4, 3756–8, 6435–9; and Anglesey Papers, T1068/29/15. Billeting and provisioning: Gosset to Stanley, 14 July 1831, HO 100/239/85.

52 *The Parliamentary Debates* [hereafter cited as *PD*], New [2d] Series, 25 vols. (London: T. C. Hansard, 1820–30), 24:390–4, 867–71, on 4, 19, 20 May 1830, quotation on col. 393.

53 "A Return of the Number of Persons who have lost their Lives, or have been Severely Wounded, in Affrays with the Constabulary; ... in each Year, since the formation of that Body," *PP 1830–1* (67), 8:403–83; and "A Return of the Number of Persons who have lost their Lives in Affrays with the Constabulary since 1830; specifying the Place where each Homicide occurred, Nature of Warrant which the Constabulary had to execute, Verdict of Coroner ...; also Number of Persons severely Wounded ...", *PP 1846* (280), 35:237–60.

54 The statistical discussion in this and the preceding paragraph is based on analysis of the data in the returns cited in n. 53, this chapter.

55 HO 100/228/78–84; CSORP 1829/312; Letter Books of Chief Secretary Leveson Gower [hereafter, LGLB], M737/37, 61, 152, PRO, Four Courts, Dublin; and Leveson Gower to Peel, 2, 22, 23 July 1829, 40337 ff. 6, 56, 58.

56 HO 100/238/229 (Crampton to Stanley, 27 May 1831), 231–5, and 239/87, 90, 154–5, 168–70; Anglesey to Grey, 4 June 1831, T1068/8/123; *PP 1831–2* (677), 16:Q. 3747, ev. of Rev. J. Burke. Curtis, *RIC*, pp. 28–9, reports thirteen persons killed.

57 Curtis, *RIC*, p. 30; Anglesey to Grey, 15 Dec. 1831, T1068/8/206. The incident is recounted in Curtis, *RIC*, pp. 30–2. A vivid account marred by numerous errors of detail is in Henry R. Addison, *Recollections of an Irish Police Magistrate* (London: J. and R. Maxwell, 1883), pp. 28–43. Broeker, *Police*, p. 212, dismisses Carrickshock in five lines. My account is based on HO 100/240/2–29, 98–104; CSORP 1832/Y & C/650; and, above all, the official eleven-page report, with sixty-five pages of evidence, submitted by T. Gould and R. Greene, 24 Dec. 1831, CSORP K25.

58 Anglesey to Grey, 26 Dec. 1831, T1068/8/210. For the background to the incident, see *PP 1831–2* (271), 22:81–8, ev. of Rev. H. Hamilton, 27 Jan. 1832.

59 CSORP 1831/K25.

60 Ibid; and Harvey's comments on casualties and Gibbons's bravery, HO 100/240/4, 26.
61 Melbourne to Anglesey, 9 Jan. 1832, T1068/31/74; Harvey to Gosset, 20 Dec. 1831, CSORP K25; CSORP 1832/50; HO 100/240/2–29 (Harvey, "interchangeable," 16 Dec., on f. 26), 98–104.
62 Harvey to Gosset, 20 Jan. 1833, CSORP 348; and *PP 1831–2* (271), 22:111–12, ev. of William Grace, Archbishop of Dublin.
63 On military force levels, see *PP 1839* (486), 12:1385–6.
64 See Tables 7.2 (1805/1812, 1822–8) and 9.4 (1829–34), this book.
65 Roughly four-fifths of these were common assaults; one-tenth, homicides; and most of the remainder, assaults with intent to kill. In 1832, 245 murders were reported to the police; see Report of 31 Dec. 1832, in Earl Grey Papers, Papers on Ireland, No. 1.
66 See the Castle's circular against this "great evil." CSORP 1833/2947.
67 *PP 1839* (486), 11:Q. 6735, ev. of William Kemmis.
68 Government funds advanced for prosecution "on one Circuit," 1830–3, Hatherton Papers, D260/M/OI/268; and Addison, *Recollections*, p. 31.
69 For his assistance in collating the criminal statistics from the printed county returns in Table 9.5, I wish to thank Mr. Dan Lewis, my student research assistant at the Woodrow Wilson International Center for Scholars.
70 Anglesey to Cloncurry, 27 Apr. 1833, T1068/29/29.
71 Anglesey to Holland, 4 Aug. 1828, T1068/1/94. "From what I read in the English newspapers and hear in conversation," Leveson Gower wrote Peel, "I am convinced that many very able and rational men fall into a common mistake of judging of the rest of Ireland from Tipperary." 13 July 1829, 40337 f. 30.
72 Anglesey to Cloncurry, 27 May 1833, T1068/29/35. For the historiography, see nn. 100, 109, and 110, this chapter.
73 See Leveson Gower to Peel, 5 Aug. 1829, LGLB M737/8–9. *PP 1831–2* (677), 16:QQ. 181–4, 219–21, 2671, 4236–8, 6383, 7229. The 1833 return: Hatherton Papers, D260/M/OI/984–5.
74 "A Return of the Peace Preservation Force in Ireland, during each of the last Three Years, containing the Number and Distribution thereof ... and distinguishing also the Number of Roman Catholics of each Rank ...," *PP 1834* (201), 47:399–414. A list of twenty-four Stipendiary Magistrates, dated 29 Mar. 1833, is in OPMA 1A/73/2/101/3 and printed in "An Account of the Number of Stipendiary Magistrates in Ireland ...," *PP 1833* (191), 32:465–7. On the Subinspectors as a recruiting pool, see also Anglesey Papers, T1068/22/136, and CSORP 1832/573, 862, 891.
75 Circular, 12 June 1833, CSORP 2952. CSORP 1829/1087 and 1834/996. Circular, 5 Oct. 1833, CSORP 6290.
76 Miller to Gosset, 7 May 1835, CSORP 1459. For Connaught, see Warburton's evidence, *PP 1839* (486), 11:Q. 591. *Hansard's Parliamentary Debates* [hereafter, *Hansard*], 3d Series, 356 vols. (London: T. C. Hansard, 1830–91), 30:1002–6, 26 Aug. 1835, quotations on cols. 1002 (Duncannon), 1004 (Clanicarde), respectively. See also *Hansard* 31:537, 539, 18 Feb. 1836. Analysis of the Constables Register, HO 184/1–2, reveals that the percentage of recruits listing a private recommender fell steadily from 85 percent in 1816–22 to 38 percent in 1837–40.
77 LGLB M736/276 and 737/8–9, 171, 174A, 222–5; Ellenborough, *Diary*, 2:136, 160; Peel, *Private Papers*, 2:120; Gash, *Peel*, p. 605.
78 Analysis of Constables Register, HO 184/1–2.
79 Ibid.; "Size Roll" of Kilkenny constables, CSORP 1832/Y & C/439; CSORP 1833/3951, 6290; Anglesey to Cloncurry, 16 June 1832, T 1068/22/163.
80 CSORP 1833/3951; and constabulary circular, 19 Apr. 1833, CSORP 1919. Harvey to Gosset, 13 Mar. 1835, and circular of 9 May 1835, both in CSORP 1593. On the execution of the new policy, see CSORP 1835/2027. The *first*

question asked the police candidate was his marital status; see printed questionnaire in CSORP 1835/3488.

81 Miller to Littleton, 25 July 1834, D260/M/OI/2567; D'Arcy to Gosset, 20 Jan.
1833, CSORP 348; "A Return of the Total Number of all Magistrates,
Constables, and Sub-Constables appointed under ... the Constabulary Act,
distinguishing those who profess the different Sects of Religion ...," *PP 1824*
(257), 22:405–8; "A Return of the Number, &c., of Roman Catholics of each
Rank, in each County, in the Constabulary," 1830–2, *PP 1833* (379), 32:446–50.
The share of Catholic constables in the Munster constabulary rose from 53 to 63
percent from 1832 to 1834. D260/M/OI/2567.

82 HO 184/1–2; Harvey to Gosset, 26 Aug. 1833, CSORP 4286; and appointments
by Subinspector E. S. Flinter, in Harvey to Gosset, 20 Jan. 1833, CSORP 348.

83 Miller to Littleton, 25 July 1834, D260/M/OI/2567; Harvey to Gosset, 20 Jan.
1833, CSORP 348. On Ulster, see *Hansard* 32:531, 23 Mar. 1836 (Morpeth);
Lord Mulgrave to Morpeth, 21 June 1835, in the Papers of Viscount Morpeth,
7th Earl of Carlisle [hereafter, 7 Carlisle], Castle Howard Archives [CHA]
J19/1/9 ("peculator"), Castle Howard, Yorkshire; Littleton to Stovin, 2 Oct.
1834, D260/M/OI/4/67 ("partizanship").

84 Littleton to More O'Ferrall, 1 Dec. 1833, D260/M/OI/2/281. For the constabulary, see D260/M/OI/984–5, 1022–5, 1036 and *PP 1833* (379), 32:446–50; for
the Peelers, *PP 1834* (201), 47:399–414. For the other offices, see D260/M/OI/
988–1020, 2058; and Reynolds, *Catholic Emancipation*, p. 65.

85 Religiously mixed counties like Fermanagh, Monaghan, and Armagh had forces
with Protestant:Catholic distributions (men) of 112:22, 68:12, and 73:23, respectively. In 1835, 1,700 persons complained in a petition to Dublin Castle that "no
impartial justice" could be had from the Armagh police. Mulgrave to Morpeth, 8
July 1835, in 7 Carlisle, CHA:J19/1/9.

86 *PP 1833* (379), 32:446–50.

87 Littleton to Gosset, 20 June 1834, CSORP 2495; and Leveson Gower to W. Peel,
10 June 1829, LGLB M736/161.

88 Littleton to More O'Ferrall, 15 Oct. 1834, D260/M/OI/4/118. For Leveson
Gower, see LGLB M737/94, 242. The 1834 regulation: in Littleton to Lord
Acheson, 2 Oct. 1834, D260/M/OI/4/66. "We are promoting from the ranks on
the occasions of most vacancies," Littleton told Lord Garvagh (17 Oct. 1834,
D260/M/OI/4/134.) Small sample data from the incomplete Officers Register,
HO 184/45, indicate that whereas 7 percent of officers appointed in 1823–8 had
begun their careers at nonofficer ranks, a spectacular 73 percent appointed in
1829–32 had entered the force as subconstables or constables.

89 West, Free: CSORP 1835/882, 1856, respectively. Hadnett: Miller to Sir H.
Hardinge, 29 Jan. 1835, CSORP 331. Walker: Sir J. Harvey to Gosset, 19 Feb.,
and Gosset to Harvey, 23 Feb. 1835, CSORP 628. For solicitations of lists of
other meritorious constables, see CSORP 1835/3720, 3815.

90 Quotations, in order, are Haly to Littleton, 19 Oct. 1833, CSORP 5779; Gosset
to Miller, 12 June, and Miller to Gosset, 14 June 1834, CSORP 2495; and Haly
to Hardinge, 9 Mar. 1835, CSORP 3085. Haly's efforts may also be traced in
CSORP 1834/500 and 1835/3755; and his career in HO 184/45/38. In 1836
Subinspector Haly was moved to Kildare. He later became a Stipendiary Magistrate and retired in 1843, at age forty-seven, on a pension of £320 p.a. "Return of
the [Irish] Police ... receiving Pensions, and the Sums received ...," *PP 1847*
(571), 56:250.

91 Anglesey to Rev. Dr. Murray, 24 Jan. 1833, T1068/29/5; Gosset to Littleton, 11
June 1833, D260/M/OI/6/181. Cases: *PP 1846* (280), 35:237–60.

92 I have found no resignation figures for the 1830s. For 1841–4 annual resignations
averaged 158, or 2 percent of force strength; for 1851–4, 621, or 5 percent.
Respectively, HO 184/54, appendix; and Gregory J. Fulham, "The Irish

Constabulary and Irish Police Policy, 1836–1867," pp. 90, 97–8. I would like to thank Mr. Fulham, a Ph.D. candidate at the University of Chicago, for the loan of his unpublished paper, written in March 1979. London figures, 1834–8, are in F. C. Mather, *Public Order in the Age of the Chartists* (Manchester: Manchester University Press, 1959), p. 97; see also Wilbur Miller, *Cops and Bobbies: Police Authority in New York and London, 1830–1870* (Chicago: University of Chicago Press, 1977), p. 41. Two-thirds of the annual removals from the London force were resignations.

93 In 1835, 291 policemen were dismissed and 146 otherwise punished; in 1836, 412 and 186, respectively. CSORP index volumes, 1835 and 1836, Letter "C," p. 45.

94 In 1835 6 percent, and in 1836 9 percent, of the dismissed constables were reinstated in the force. CSORP index volumes, 1835 and 1836, "C," p. 42.

95 Chief Constables: CSORP 1830/76 and 1834/2706, 3259. Constables: CSORP 1836/34, 49, 79, 213.

96 CSORP 1836/34/1–146 (Leinster), 49/1–49 (Connaught), 79/1–96 (Munster), and 213/1–49 (Ulster). Drunkenness accounted for roughly half of the dismissals in the London police in 1834–8; neglect of duty and insubordination, for about one fourth. Mather, *Public Order*, p. 97.

97 Harvey to Gosset, 8 Aug. 1834, CSORP 3211.

98 Castle circular to Inspectors-General, 6 Aug. 1834, CSORP 3211. Harvey to Gosset, 23 May 1835, CSORP 1740; and Miller to Gosset, 25 May 1835, CSORP 1767.

99 "Questions to be answered by Candidates for the Constabulary," n.d., filed with tithe circular, 26 Oct. 1835, CSORP 3488. Among those dismissed in 1836 for a first offense of drunkenness were a Longford subconstable of four years' service and a fifteen-year veteran in Westmeath. CSORP 1836/34/57, 146.

100 John F. McLennan, *Memoir of Thomas Drummond, Under-Secretary to the Lord Lieutenant of Ireland, 1835 to 1840* (Edinburgh: Edmonston & Douglas, 1867), pp. 266–70; Curtis, *RIC* (1869), pp. 13–14, 21–2, 42–3. Curtis, *RIC*, pp. 15–25, relies heavily on McLennan's work. Broeker, *Police*, pp. 218–27, also assumes that the constabulary was in considerable disorganization.

101 Insp.-Gen. R. Willcocks, memorandum on police, 20 Feb. 1823, in W. Gregory to H. Goulburn, 3 Mar. 1823, in Goulburn Box C, Papers of Henry Goulburn, Surrey Record Office, Kingston-on-Thames; W. Lamb to Lansdowne, 18 Oct. 1827, HO 100/219/58; Miller to Leveson Gower, 28 Aug. 1829, quoted in Miller's letter to Gosset, 8 Mar. 1834, CSORP 1834/1129.

102 3 Geo. 4, c. 103 s. 24; 7 & 8 Geo. 4, c. 67 s. 17; *PP 1831–2* (271), 22:177–9, ev. of R. Greene. The legal problems were also discussed by the Archdeacon of Armagh and the Archbishop of Dublin. "Second Report by the Lords' Select Committee appointed to inquire into the Collection and Payment of Tithes in Ireland," *PP 1831–2* (663), 22:313, ev. of Rev. E. Stopford; and "First Report . . . Tithes . . . ," *PP 1831–2* (271), 22:146, ev. of William Grace, respectively.

103 Provisions of the bill are in Leveson Gower to Peel, 22 Nov. 1829, LGLB M737/222–5, and CSORP 1830/4073. For the Cabinet's reaction, see Ellenborough, *Diary*, 2:136, 160. *Hansard* 23:1110–15, 30 Mar. 1830. On Leveson Gower's resignation, see Gash, *Peel*, p. 625. Broeker, *Police*, p. 201, surmises that the bill was "defeated or abandoned."

104 The Knight of Kerry's memorandum on police, 7 Jan. 1831, in "Ireland-I-Unlisted," Earl Grey Papers. Anglesey to Grey, 19 Mar. 1831, in T1068/4, and "New Plan of Constabulary, 1831," in D619/1, Anglesey Papers. The quotation is by Edward Littleton, Baron Hatherton, speaking in the Lords, 2 May 1836, *Hansard* 33:488.

105 Littleton to Melbourne, 16 Nov. 1833, and to Gosset, 13 May 1834, D260/M/OI/2/260 and 3/168–9, respectively. Many writers have traced Drummond's 1835 bill to Littleton's in 1833; in fact, it dated to Stanley's 1832 bill, which was based

on Anglesey's ideas in March 1831. McLennan, *Drummond* (1867), p. 268; O'Brien, *Drummond* (1889), p. 198 n. 4; Broeker, *Police* (1970), p. 219 n. 64.

106 Leveson Gower to Peel, 5 Aug. and 29 Oct. 1829, LGLB M737/8–9 and M737/174A (also in HO 100/229/199); and to Goulburn, 28 Oct. 1829, LGLB M737/171. *Hansard* 23:1113 (Trant); the most prominent opponent was Thomas Spring-Rice (subsequently, 1st Baron Monteagle, 1839), who had spoken against the 1822 bill. Littleton to Gosset, 13 Mar. 1834, D260/M/OI/3/14.

107 Mulgrave to Morpeth, 18 June 1835, in 7 Carlisle, CHA: J19/1/9.

Constantine Henry Phipps (1797–1863), 2d Earl of Mulgrave, had been Governor of Jamaica, 1830–5. Created the 1st Marquess of Normanby (1838), he left Ireland in February 1839 to replace Charles Grant, Lord Glenelg, as Secretary for War and Colonies; three months later he became Home Secretary, a post he held until 1841. Normanby drafted the first regulations for the English county police. *DNB* 15:1116–17.

George William Frederick Howard (1802–64), Viscount Morpeth, served as Irish Chief Secretary until 1839 and would later (as 7th Earl of Carlisle, 1848) return to Ireland as Lord Lieutenant, 1855–8 and 1859–64. More a gentle scholar than a powerful politician, Morpeth, who never married, produced a number of prose and verse works. He also wrote a preface to an English edition of Mrs. Harriet Stowe's *Uncle Tom's Cabin* (London, 1853). *DNB* 10:19–21. See the recent biography by Diana Davids Olien, *Morpeth: A Victorian Public Career* (Lanham, Md.: University Press of America, 1983).

108 Alfred Webb, *A Compendium of Irish Biography* (Dublin: M. H. Gill & Sons, 1878), pp. 158–9; *DNB* 6:41–5.

109 John F. McLennan, *Memoir of Thomas Drummond, Under-Secretary to the Lord Lieutenant of Ireland, 1835 to 1840* (Edinburgh: Edmonston & Douglas, 1867); and R. B. O'Brien, *Thomas Drummond, Under-Secretary in Ireland, 1835–40: His Life and Letters* (London: Kegan, Paul, Trench & Co., 1889).

110 W. E. H. Lecky, *A History of Ireland in the Eighteenth Century*, 5 vols. (London: Longman, Green, 1892; repr., St. Clair Shores, Mich.: Scholarly Press, 1972), 5:427; McLennan, *Drummond*, pp. 266–70; Curtis, *RIC*, pp. 17–22; O'Brien, *Drummond*, pp. 198–201; Broeker, *Police*, pp. 219–20, 229, 238; and Séamus Breathnach, *The Irish Police from Earliest Times to the Present Day* (Dublin: Anvil Books, 1974), pp. 35–9.

111 *PP 1839* (486), 12:QQ. 12178–478, 13091–135. Most of McLennan's infrequent footnotes (*Drummond*, pp. 264ff.) are to Drummond's evidence before Lord Roden's committee.

112 *PP 1839* (486), 12:Q. 12194.

113 Drummond to Morpeth, 6 Aug. 1835, in 7 Carlisle, CHA: J19/1/9.

114 Ibid.; *Hansard* 30:656–61 (18 Aug.), 1002–8 (26 Aug. 1835). Costs: 6 Will. 4, c. 13 ss. 35–42.

115 Mulgrave to Morpeth, 13 Feb. 1836, in 7 Carlisle, CHA: J19/1/10. Proceedings on the 1836 bill are in *Hansard* 31:532–51 (18 Feb.); 32:438–41, 521–33, 545–8, 873–93 (21, 23, 24 Mar., 12 Apr.); 33:1–4, 479–99, 613–15, 904–5, 1040–3, 1084–6 (21 Apr., 2, 6, 13, 17, 19, 20 May 1836). See also Curtis, *RIC*, pp. 34–8; O'Brien, *Drummond*, pp. 198–202; and Broeker, *Police*, pp. 219–23. It is unclear from Broeker's own evidence in what ways the 1836 bill was "somewhat stronger" than the 1835 bill (*Police*, p. 221).

116 The Tory leader Robert Peel had recently ended his short and unstable first administration (December 1834 to April 1835). Handicapped by a small majority and weakened by a series of defeats on floor votes, Peel's Government was in no position to pass major legislation. Woodward, *Age of Reform*, 2d ed., pp. 101–2.

117 *Hansard* 30:1004, 26 Aug. 1835.

118 *Hansard* 30:657 (Morpeth), 1004 (Brougham), 1007 (Glenelg), 18 and 26 Aug. 1835.

119 *Hansard* 31:538–9 (O'Connell), 542–5 (Peel), 545–6 (Grattan); and 33:490–1 (Cloncurry).

120 *Hansard* 32:883–5 (quotation on 884), 892–3; and 33:1–2, 486–7, 494–5. A subsequent act of 1836 freed county taxpayers from the charges for horses, arms, postage, stationery and printing, and salaries and expenses of the provincial inspectors. 6 & 7 Will. 4, c. 36 s. 2, amending 6 Will. 4, c. 13 s. 36. Wellington's projected figures were not far wrong. In 1835 the total cost of the constabulary was £314,000; in 1837, £380,000, a 21 percent increase. In 1838 the cost, at £423,000, did reach Wellington's projection of 1836. "A Return of the Amount of Constabulary Force employed in Ireland, 1 January 1839, ... and the Expense Thereof," *PP 1839* (302), 47:523–7.

121 *Hansard* 32:885–9 (Wicklow, Winchilsea, Londonderry); and 33:479–83 (Roden, quotation on 481–2), 483–4 (Melbourne), 490 (Gort). Robert Jocelyn, 3d Earl of Roden (1788–1870), a prominent Orangeman, served in 1839 as chairman of the select committee on crime in Ireland; in 1849 he was removed from the Irish magistracy for inciting an Orange riot. *DNB* 10:837–8; Macintyre, *Liberator*, p. 159; and John Mitchel, *Jail Journal, or Five Years in British Prisons* (Dublin, M. H. Gill & Son, n.d., originally written for and printed in Mitchel's newspaper, the New York *Citizen*, 1854), p. 208.

122 On the Whig alliance, see A. H. Graham, "The Lichfield House Compact," *I.H.S.* 12 (1961):209–25; and Macintyre, *Liberator*, chs. 2 and 4, esp. pp. 135–66. On the Irish Protestant reaction, see Hereward Senior, *Orangeism in Ireland and Britain, 1795–1836* (London: Routledge & Kegan Paul, 1966), pp. 254–73; and Ian D'Alton, "A Contrast in Crises: Southern Irish Protestantism, 1820–43 and 1885–1910," in A. C. Hepburn, ed., *Minorities in History* (New York: St. Martin's Press, 1979), pp. 70–83.

123 *Hansard* 30:1003, 26 Aug. 1835; and 32:886 (Wicklow), 888–9 (Londonderry), 12 Apr. 1836.

124 *Hansard* 31:538–50; and 32:531–2. See also Macintyre, *Liberator*, pp. 158–63.

125 Mr. H. W. Barron, MP for Waterford City, in *Hansard* 31:550. Three of six Irish judges appointed in 1835–41 were Catholics; the Irish Attorney-General, Michael O'Loghlen, was a Catholic.

126 *Hansard* 31:532–5 (Morpeth), 537–40, 540–2 (Russell), 542–5 and 551 (Peel); and 32:531–2 (Morpeth, including a return of Ulster police dismissals, by religion, February 1834–February 1836). Morpeth to Mulgrave, "Friday," n.d. (? 19 Feb. 1836, a Friday), Papers of the 2d Earl of Mulgrave, 1st Marquess of Normanby, Mulgrave Castle Archives M/513, Mulgrave Castle, Whitby, North Yorkshire.

127 *Hansard* 31:540 (Russell), 544 (Peel). See also David W. Miller, *Queen's Rebels: Ulster Loyalism in Historical Perspective* (Dublin: Gill and Macmillan, 1978), pp. 67–8.

128 Calculated from "A Return of the Names and Stations of all Persons appointed Stipendiary Magistrates, &c., under the Irish Constabulary Bill," 22 Mar. 1837, *PP 1837* (254), 46:335–9; *Hansard* 30:657, 18 Aug. 1835; *PP 1839* (486), 11:QQ. 124 (Shaw-Kennedy), 593 (Warburton), and 1428 (McGregor quoted); and *PP 1839* (486), 12:Q. 12183 (Drummond).

129 *PP 1839* (486), 12:QQ. 12363, 12421–3 (Drummond). Mulgrave to Morpeth, 8 June (and see also 3 July) 1836, in 7 Carlisle, CHA: J19/1/11. On Stovin, who lost a bid to become a Dublin Police Commissioner, see Drummond to Morpeth, 21 Aug. 1835 and 5 July 1836, CHA: J19/1/9, 11; and *Hansard* 31:542–3, 546–7; 32:531–3. For the political views of Warburton and Miller, see Stip. Magis. T. P. Vokes to T. Spring-Rice, 15 Aug. 1835, CHA: J19/1/9. For the names of the new provincial inspectors, see Curtis, *RIC*, p. 43.

130 "A Return of the Police of Ireland, showing the Number and Distribution thereof, 1830 to 1832 ...." *PP 1833* (518), 32:453–61; "A Return of the Peace

Preservation Force in Ireland, during each of the last Three Years ...," *PP 1834* (201), 47:399–414; "A Return of the Constabulary Force employed in each County or City in Ireland, 1 January 1837," *PP 1837* (391), 45:303; for growth after 1840, see the Irish Constabulary register, HO 184/54, appendix. Provincial distribution: Leinster, 34 percent of total; Munster, 26 percent; Connaught, 24 percent; and Ulster, 16 percent. *PP 1839* (486), 11:QQ. 1590–2 (McGregor).

131 *PP 1839* (486), 12:QQ. 12178, 12182, 13132.

132 *PP 1839* (486), 11:QQ. 378–9 (Shaw-Kennedy). Curtis, *RIC*, pp. 52–3, 56–8. In 1839 Drummond stated that a depot in Dublin was "almost the only thing wanting to make the Force nearly perfect." Such a depot had been provided for in Littleton's police bill of 1833; "that I am not aware of," replied Drummond to his questioner. *PP 1839* (486), 12:QQ. 12191, 12194.

133 Curtis, *RIC*, p. 42; Mr. and Mrs. Samuel Carter Hall, *Ireland: Its Scenery, Character, &c.,* 3 vols. (London, n.d. [1840?]), 1:418, quoted in Gregory J. Fulham, "James Shaw-Kennedy and the Reformation of the Irish Constabulary, 1836–38," *Eire-Ireland* 16, No. 2 (Summer 1981):93–106, on pp. 104–5.

134 *PP 1839* (486), 11:QQ. 1508–10 (McGregor), 12:Q. 13099 (Drummond). On Drummond's resolve to appoint Catholics, see ibid., 12:QQ, 13091–13102, 13115–22. Percentage of Catholics: "A Return of ... the Number of Roman Catholics ... in the Constabulary," 1830–2, *PP 1833* (379), 32:446–50; and Irish Constabulary register, HO 184/54, appendix. Inspector-General McGregor's statement that 67 percent of the recruits in 1836–9 were Catholics is close to the 70 percent figure yielded by computer analysis of my sample of the Constables Register for 1837–40 (HO 184/1–2). In 1841, 62 percent of the recruits attested at the four depots were Catholics. Under the Tory Administration (Peel's second ministry, 1841–6), the share of Catholics in the constabulary held constant at 53–54 percent. By 1848, after two years of Lord John Russell's Whig Administration, the Catholic share had risen to 62 percent. HO 184/54, appendix.

135 *PP 1839* (486), 11:QQ. 595 (Warburton), 3326 (McGregor quoted); and 12:QQ. 12358–9 (Drummond).

136 Miller to Drummond, 10 Sept. 1835, CSORP 3337; 6 Will. 4, c. 13 s. 29 (1836); *PP 1839* (486), 12:QQ. 12183, 12358–9 (Drummond); McLennan, *Drummond,* p.274; Fulham, "Shaw-Kennedy," p. 103; and Subconstable Hugh McVey to Subinsp. John Johnston, 17 July 1836, CSORP 213/28.

137 CLB 1829–30 ff. 3–4; CLB 1830 ff. 3–4; CLB 1830–1 ff. 1–3; CLB 1831 ff. 1–2; and CLB 1831–2 ff. 1–2. For 1832–5, see "'C'-Constables Dismissed," in the annual index volume to the Chief Secretary's Office Registered Papers (CSORP). For 1836, see CSORP 1836/34, 49, 79, 213. *PP 1839* (486), 11:QQ. 1511–12 (McGregor). Miller to Drummond, 9 July 1836, CSORP 1977. Now Deputy Inspector-General, and formerly the provincial Inspector-General for Munster, Miller bemoaned "the evil" of "License given to the Men to marry, when they pleased, by my Predecessor [Richard Willcocks]." The present regulations, stated Miller, should not be relaxed. Marriage should continue to be used "as a mode of rewarding men who have served long & faithfully." Miller noted in one case that a certain subconstable of seven years' service should be denied permission to marry, for he was "still a Young Man" of twenty-seven.

138 *PP 1839* (486), 11:Q. 1514 (McGregor). Neither man had served in the constabulary prior to his appointment, Vignoles in 1831 and Gleeson in 1836. In 1838 Gleeson was dismissed as a result of another altercation. See *PP 1839* (486), 12:1341–73, 1608.

139 *PP 1839* (486), 11:QQ. 1511–12 (McGregor); HO 184/54, appendix, "1841."

140 *PP 1839* (486), 11:QQ. 48 (Shaw-Kennedy) and 1414, 1421 (McGregor); statistical analysis of Officers Register, HO 184/45.

141 2 & 3 Vict., c. 75 (1839) ss. 5, 10–11. In 1848, by 9 & 10 Vict., c. 97 s. 6, the two

"Provincial Inspectors" were renamed "Assistant Inspectors General." In 1859, by 22 & 23 Vict., c. 22 ss. 2 and 3, a third assistant was appointed and the higher post of Deputy Inspector-General was reduced from two men to one.

142 Curtis, *RIC*, pp. 54–5; Fulham, "Shaw-Kennedy," p. 100. "Promotion from the ranks *versus* the cadet system" is discussed by an ex-Head Constable, Michael Brophy, *Sketches of the Royal Irish Constabulary* (London: Burns & Oates, 1886), pp. 13–14.

143 Morpeth to Shaw-Kennedy, 23 Sept. 1836, copy of letter, in Morpeth–Mulgrave correspondence, Normanby Papers, Mulgrave Castle Archives M/547a. Drummond to Morpeth, 2 Aug. 1835, in 7 Carlisle, CHA: J19/1/9. For Drummond's judgment on the Louth Chief Constable, among other officers, see his letter to Morpeth, 5 July 1836, CHA: J19/1/11; see also Morpeth to Drummond, 2 May 1836, in Morpeth's "Private Letter Book," CHA: J19/11/2. The names of 45 applicants for the post of Stipendiary Magistrate, 75 for Subinspector, and 389 for Chief Constable are in "MS List 1835," CHA: J19/11/4.

144 *PP 1839* (486), 11:QQ. 1423–31 (McGregor), and 12:Q. 12183 (Drummond); analysis of Officers Register, HO 184/45. By the 1860s, only one in every six officer appointments was from the ranks. Fulham, "Shaw-Kennedy," p. 100.

145 H. Brownrigg to G. S. Bell, 12 Jan., and official return, 6 Mar. 1837, OPMA 1A/72/3/70/8, 15. For officers originally appointed between 1833 and 1850, 81 percent of the Catholics and 76 percent of the Protestants had two or more promotions in their careers; 45 percent of the Catholics earned four or more promotions compared to 42 percent of the Protestants. Analysis of HO 184/45.

146 *PP 1839* (486), 11:QQ. 7–89 (Shaw-Kennedy); 12:QQ. 12421–6, 12434–5, 13123 (Drummond). For a list of 1836–7 appointments, see *PP 1837* (254), 46:335–9. Curtis, *RIC*, p. 55, states that one in every three appointments of Stipendiary Magistrates went to constabulary officers during McGregor's tenure (1839–58); the practice continued under Inspector-General Brownrigg until 1862, when, unaccountably, it stopped.

147 On Shaw-Kennedy, see *DNB* 10:1311–13; *Hansard* 31:542–3, speech of Sir Robert Peel, 18 Feb. 1836; H. A. Bruce, *Life of General Sir William Napier*, 2 vols. (London: J. Murray, 1864), 1:305–30; and Fulham, "Shaw-Kennedy," pp. 93–9. Gregory Fulham's useful article (see n. 133, this chapter) discusses the development of the force through the 1860s, but he credits Shaw-Kennedy with effecting many of the reforms that originated in the period 1828–36.

148 In Manchester, Shaw-Kennedy was a pioneer in the use of cavalry tactics against street rioters. See HO 40/32/3/187, 195; HO 40/53/367–70; and Bruce, *Life of Napier*, 1:322–9.

149 Mulgrave to Morpeth, 22 Mar. 1838, in 7 Carlisle, CHA: J19/1/17/36. The resignation is discussed briefly in Curtis, *RIC*, p. 46; and more fully in CSORP 1838/2101 and Drummond to Morpeth, 23 Mar. 1838, CHA: J19/1/17/38. Shaw-Kennedy retired to his small Scottish estate, reappeared briefly as military commander of Liverpool during the Chartist agitation in 1848, retired again, suffered increasing ill health, and died at Bath in 1865 at age seventy-six.

150 Warburton: *PP 1839* (486), 11:QQ. 566–70, 737; and "Return of the [Irish] Police ... receiving Pensions, and the Sums received ...," *PP 1847* (571), 56:269. Curtis, *RIC*, pp. 47–9; Breathnach, *Irish Police*, p. 38.

151 *PP 1839* (486), 11:QQ. 1441, 1633 (McGregor); Curtis, *RIC*, pp. 50–1; Frederic Boase, *Modern English Biography*, 6 vols. (Truro: Netherton and Worth, 1892–1921), 2:607.

152 *PP 1839* (486), 11:QQ. 7–89 (Shaw-Kennedy), 977–81 (Warburton). Bruce, *Life of Napier*, 1:323. On the changes in policy, see *PP 1839* (486), 11:QQ. 1413–37, 1491–3 (McGregor), and 12:Q. 12183 (Drummond). Curiously, the Shaw-Kennedy affair is not mentioned by Broeker, *Police* (1970), and is glossed over in

McLennan, *Drummond* (1867), p. 277, and in Fulham, "Shaw-Kennedy," p. 99 n. 25.

153 McLennan, *Drummond*, pp. 265–6, 449–53; *PP 1839* (486), 12:Q. 12259. Drummond also stated (12:Q. 12178) that the first police in Ireland began in 1814; he appears to have been unaware of developments dating to 1786–7. Miller's salary: Curtis, *RIC*, p. 54.

154 Cess: CSORP 1837/79/32 and 1837/1020. Petty sessions: CSORP 1835/4121. Rent and tithe: CSORP 1835/3488, 1836/633, and 1837/79/15, 28, 44, 65; *PP 1839* (486), 12:QQ. 14197–14203 (Drummond). See also the annual index volumes to CSORP, "Police Duties," beginning with the year 1835. O'Brien, *Drummond*, p. 202, and Broeker, *Police*, pp. 217–19, argue that Drummond initiated these policies of police restraint.

155 Legal opinion, 1 Mar. 1836, CSORP 633; Miller to Drummond, 4 Mar. 1836, enclosing correspondence from Goulburn to N. Taylor, 7 Aug. 1824, and from Gregory to Willcocks, 14 Mar. 1826, CSORP 1836/755.

156 *PP 1839* (486), 12:QQ. 12206 (quotation), 12295–12326; 2 & 3 Will. 4, c. 118 (1836); McLennan, *Drummond*, pp. 278–80.

157 Drummond's opinions in CSORP 1835/3358 and *PP 1839* (486), 12:Q. 12239, respectively. McLennan, *Drummond*, p. 265. The Whigs now enforced an act (1829) passed by the Tories that had changed the punishment for murder at a fair from twelve months' imprisonment to seven years' transportation. *PP 1839* (486), 11:QQ. 7465, 7491–7500.

158 Warburton to Drummond, 30 Sept. 1835, CSORP 3358. See William Carleton's essay, "The Battle of the Factions," in his *Traits and Stories of the Irish Peasantry* (1833), reprinted in *The Works of William Carleton*, 2 vols. (Freeport, N.Y.: Books for Libraries Press, 1970), 2:722–40, and cf. "The Party Fight and Funeral," in Carleton, *Works*, 2:762–96. See also Patrick O'Donnell, *The Irish Faction Fighters of the Nineteenth Century* (Dublin: Anvil Books, 1975).

   Drummond's attitude was part of the movement to civilize the lower classes by reforming their traditional social pleasures. In England this mission included the elimination of such blood sports as cock fights and bear or bull baitings; see Robert W. Malcolmson, *Popular Recreations in English Society, 1700–1850* (Cambridge: Cambridge University Press, 1973), chs. 6, 7. On the tamer English fairs, see Hugh Cunningham, "The Metropolitan Fairs: A Case Study in the Social Control of Leisure," in A. P. Donajgrodzki, ed., *Social Control in 19th-Century Britain* (Totowa, N.J.: Rowman and Littlefield, 1977), pp. 163–84.

159 *PP 1839* (486), 12:QQ. 12210–19 (Drummond). The Whigs judged Harvey "a weak man, the nominee of the Duke of Wellington." Harvey, who since 1833 had desired the Irish under-secretaryship, was disappointed when Melbourne chose Drummond. Harvey was on record as opposing the recent marriage rule and the military emphasis in the police. The Lord Lieutenant wrote Morpeth in July 1835: "You are quite right in thinking that I shall not much deplore the loss of *Granny* Harvey here." Mulgrave to Morpeth, 11 July 1835, in 7 Carlisle, CHA: J19/1/9. See also T. P. Vokes to T. Spring-Rice, 15 Aug. 1835, CHA: J19/1/9; Hatherton Papers, D260/M/OI/2485; and Morpeth to Harvey, 23 Oct. 1835, in Morpeth's "Private Letter Book," CHA: J19/11/2.

160 *PP 1839* (486), 11:QQ. 429–33 and 467–8 (Shaw-Kennedy), 683–4 (Warburton) and 9635, 9751–8 (Tabuteau); and 12:Q. 12242 (Drummond). See monthly statistical returns of "riots and faction fights," July 1834–May 1839, in *PP 1839* (486), 12:1088–91.

161 On the beginnings of Catholic local powers a half-century later, see William L. Feingold, "The Tenants' Movement to Capture the Irish Poor Law Boards, 1877–1886," *Albion* 7 (Fall 1975):216–31.

162 Drummond to Shaw-Kennedy, and reply same day, 3 May 1837, CSORP 102/21.

NOTES TO PAGES 367–73

163 *PP 1839* (486), 12:Q. 12183.

164 J. R. McCulloch, *A Statistical Account of the British Empire*, 2 vols. (London: C. Knight & Co., 1837), 1:556; Russell to Mulgrave, 8 Apr. 1838, Russell Papers 30/22/3, quoted in Broeker, *Police*, p. 223; Samuel Robinson to Morpeth, 7 Apr. 1837, CSORP 102/21; Mulgrave to Morpeth, 3 July 1836 [my emphasis in the quotation], in 7 Carlisle, CHA: J19/1/11.

165 *PP 1839* (486), 11:QQ. 413 (Shaw-Kennedy) and 915, 1298 (Warburton). Copies of Munster Outrage Returns for 1833 are in Lewis, *Disturbances*, Tower reprint ed., pp. 84–7, 281–5.

166 *PP 1839* (486), 11:QQ. 415–21 (Shaw-Kennedy), 915–21 (Warburton). See also Deputy Inspector-General Miller's explanation, cited in the speech of Irish Chief Secretary Lord Eliot, in *Hansard* 69:1005–6, 29 May 1843.

167 See Tables 7.2 and 9.4, this book; in 1827, 18,000 committals. Mulgrave to Russell, 16 Jan. 1836, in 7 Carlisle, CHA: J19/1/10.

168 Mulgrave to Russell, 16 Jan. 1836, in 7 Carlisle, CHA: J19/1/10. *PP 1839* (486), 11:QQ. 680 and 911 (Warburton), 8692–5 (Piers Geale, Crown Solicitor, Home Circuit); and 12:QQ. 14384–5 (Moore).

169 For the statistics for 1822–34, see Tables 7.2 and 9.4, this book.

170 Eager to make his case for a preventive police, Drummond glossed over the fact that his comparison of average committals in 1826–8 and 1836–8 revealed that *attacks on dwelling houses* and *forcible possession of land* rose 73 and 79 percent, respectively, even after his adjustments for the population increase. *PP 1839* (486), 12:1099.

171 Calculated from the annual statistics Drummond presented for 1826–38. *PP 1839* (486), 12:1092–3.

172 Warburton: see n. 168, this chapter. For crime statistics, see Tables 9.4, 9.5, and 9.8, this book; and my calculations from the table in "Return from Clerks of the Crown of 'Distinct Cases of Homicide,' 1836–38," submitted by Drummond, *PP 1839* (486), 12:1303. The Outrage Returns substantiate these proportions: 90 of 477 homicides (19 percent) reported by the police in 1837–8 occurred in Tipperary. *PP 1839* (486), 11:QQ. 9806–8 (Tabuteau).

173 Ibid.; "Return of Police Reports of Offences . . . in County Tipperary," 1832–5, *PP 1836* (226), 42:720–1; *PP 1839* (486), 11:QQ. 6743 (W. Kemmis, who lists the dozen most prominent murders in Tipperary since 1815), 9635–6 (Tabuteau). At this time, in another more distant part of the Empire, the British Government was having greater success in suppressing homicides in India. In 1830–5 a crackdown against *Thuggee* (Sanskrit, whence our word "thug") – the secret, ritualistic, quasi-religious group practice of murdering and robbing travelers – led to the arrest of 2,000 Thugs, of whom about 1,500 were convicted and sentenced to death, transportation, or imprisonment. W. H. Sleeman, *Report on the Depredations Committed by the Thug Gangs of Upper and Central India* (Calcutta: G. H. Huttmann, 1840). For this information I am indebted to Prof. Isaiah Azariah of Albany State College, Georgia, who presented a paper on "Organized Crime and Its Suppression in 19th Century British India" at the meeting of the Western Conference on British Studies, in San Antonio, Texas, October 1985.

174 M. R. Beames, "Rural Conflict in Pre-Famine Ireland: Peasant Assassinations in Tipperary, 1837–1847," *Past & Present* 81 (Nov. 1978):75–91, especially pp. 88–90 (quotation on p. 89). Beames's findings rest on twenty-eight case studies. By not using the committal statistics or Outrage Returns, he misses much of the criminal violence in Tipperary. For example, he lists 3 assassinations in 1837–8; in these years Tipperary recorded 132 distinct cases of and 281 committals for homicide [*PP 1839* (486), 12:1303]. Beames does not explain why evictions in other counties did not produce this level of homicide, nor why, in Tipperary and elsewhere, other Whiteboy crimes appear to have been on the decline.

175 See Tables 7.2, 9.4, and 9.8, this book; for England, see G. R. Porter, *Progress of*

the Nation (London: J. Murray, 1851), p. 635. The drop may be explained in part by the exclusion of petty sessions cases from the judicial statistics beginning in 1837. For committals including petty sessions cases, convictions in 1837–8 averaged 76 percent. But the discontinuity was not absolute; many counties before 1837 already excluded these cases from their returns. Convictions at petty sessions were for minor offenses and tended to be at a higher rate than at assizes and quarter sessions. The English figures are for assizes and quarter sessions. On these source problems, see *PP 1839* (186), 12:1097 (Drummond). The petty sessions question aside, the conviction rate from 1837 on was undeniably falling and rather fast.

176 *PP 1839* (486), 12:1076–99, 1303, 1335–6. Morpeth took the same view in the Commons; see the debate in *Hansard* 46:25–130, 7 Mar. 1839.

177 *PP 1839* (486), 11:QQ. 597–8 (Warburton), 4101 (Stip. Magis. G. Despard quoted), and 4335 (Stip. Magis. H. W. Rowan, brother of the London Police Commissioner).

178 *PP 1839* (486), 11:Q. 9625.

179 Emmet's speech in the dock (1803), published (in English) in Paris in 1835, was circulated in Norbury's neighborhood two months before his assassination. *Hansard* 46:42, 7 Mar. 1839.

180 *The Times*, 5, 7 Jan. 1839; *PP 1839* (486), 11:QQ. 1558–64 (McGregor); *PP 1852* (438), 14:Q. 1936 (H. J. Brownrigg). The murder produced debates in the Lords: *Hansard* 45:761–5, 946–50, 22 and 28 Feb. 1839; and in the Commons, *Hansard* 46:38–42, 74–6, 7 Mar. 1839. On John Toler, 1st Earl of Norbury (1745–1831), see Webb, *Compendium*, pp. 527–8, and *DNB* 19:922–4. In 1786–7, Toler had been a strong supporter of the Dublin and Irish county police bills [*The Parliamentary Register, or the History of the Proceedings and Debates of the House of Commons in Ireland*, 15 vols. (Dublin, 1784–95), 6:329, 7:451]. Toler's elder son was of unsound mind; the second, who inherited the title, was the murder victim. The latter's son became the 3d Earl.

181 *PP 1839* (486), 11:QQ. 1106–11 (Warburton), 7520–9 (Barrington, quotation on 7529), and 8373, 8507 (Hickman); and see QQ. 7965–9 (evidence of William Kemmis, Crown Solicitor for Leinster since 1801) on the use of policemen as witnesses.

182 *PP 1839* (486), 11:QQ. 2887, 3494–3511, 3569–71, and 3639–44. Drummond thought that Ribbonism was hydra-headed, having different aims in different counties (ibid., 12:QQ. 13316–28, 13368–73). Two Stipendiary Magistrates and a retired Chief Constable of twenty-two years' service believed that "some" or even "many" constables were Ribbonmen, "from the Class of Persons now introduced into the Police and from the Number of Individuals who are Riband-men throughout the Country." But Drummond reported that he knew of no such policemen other than the two Kilkenny subconstables who had been dismissed because passwords had been found on them. Ibid., 11:QQ. 2050–1, 3597; 12:QQ. 12348–9.

183 *PP 1839* (486), 11:Q. 4758 (O'Ferrall); 12:Q. 13356 (Drummond).

CHAPTER 10. BELATED BEGINNINGS OF POLICE IN ENGLAND

1 In his lifetime, Lewis would author twenty books and hold three Cabinet positions, including that of Home Secretary (1859–61). His prodigious scholarly output would include works on national finance, contemporary politics, ancient history, linguistics, crime and social questions, the Empire, and Ireland. See Stanley H. Palmer, "Sir George Cornewall Lewis, A Different Kind of Englishman," *Eire-Ireland* 16, No. 3 (Fall, 1981):118–33. Four of Lewis's books on government have been recently reprinted in the United States; see Palmer, "Lewis," p. 122 n. 17.

2 Thomas Lewis was awarded a baronetcy in 1846; George succeeded as second baronet in 1855. *Dictionary of National Biography* [hereafter, *DNB*] 11:1057–62, 1076–7.

3 The lengthy committee studies on Irish disturbances comprise *PP 1824* (372), vol. 8; *PP 1825* (20, 200), 7; *PP 1825* (129), 8; *PP 1825* (181, 521), 9; and *PP 1831–2* (677), 16. For reports on the condition of the poorer classes in Ireland, see *PP 1836* (43), vol. 30; *PP 1836* (369), 32; and *PP 1837* (68), 31. Lewis's remarks on the third report on the Irish poor are in *PP 1837* (91), 51:253–90; cf. Lewis's later anonymously published pamphlet, *The English Poor-Law . . . in 1847* (London: J. Murray, 1847). See also Angus Macintyre, *The Liberator: Daniel O'Connell and the Irish Party, 1830–1847* (New York: Macmillan, 1965), pp. 214, 225.

4 George Cornewall Lewis, *On Local Disturbances in Ireland; and on the Irish Church Question* (London: B. Fellowes, 1836), pp. xii, 458; reprinted as *Local Disturbances in Ireland* (Cork: Tower Books, 1977), pp. vii, 292. Hereafter, all references are to the Tower edition.

5 George Richardson Porter, *The Progress of the Nation*, 3 vols. (London: C. Knight & Co., 1836–43), 3:195–233; and the one-volume 1851 edition (London: J. Murray), pp. 633–72. Hereafter, all references are to the 1851 edition.

6 Lewis, *Disturbances*, p. 76.

7 Ibid., pp. 76–7, 80–7, 101–2, 172–3, 281–5.

8 Ibid., pp. 77–9, 244. Michael Crichton, *The Great Train Robbery* (New York: Bantam, 1975), pp. vii, 298; see also pp. xv–xvii, 293–8.

9 John Stevenson, *Popular Disturbances in England 1700–1870* (London: Longman, 1979), pp. 294–6; Stevenson's riot figures, 1836–70, are for riotously and feloniously demolishing buildings and machinery; riot, breach of the peace, and pound breach; and, from 1839 on, riot and sedition. For a statistical comparison of "riot" and "rescue" in England and Ireland, 1842–8, see Stevenson, *Disturbances*, pp. 323, 356 n. 40. In his study of the "Black Country" (South Staffordshire), David Philips found that "riot and public order offences" accounted for 2.7 percent of the total committals for indictable offenses. *Crime and Authority in Victorian England: The Black Country 1835–1860* (London: Croom Helm, 1977), Table 16, p. 142.

10 George Rudé, "Protest and Punishment in Nineteenth-Century Britain," *Albion* 5 (Spring 1973):10–12.

11 V. A. C. Gattrell and T. B. Hadden, "Criminal Statistics and their Interpretation," in E. A. Wrigley, ed., *Nineteenth-Century Society* (Cambridge: Cambridge University Press, 1972), pp. 371–2.

12 *General Index to the Reports of Select Committees, 1801–52*, printed by order of the House of Commons, 16 Aug. 1853, pp. 74, 86–7. From the Union of 1801 through 1833, Parliament appointed 114 commissions and 60 select committees to investigate all subjects relating to Ireland. *Hansard's Parliamentary Debates* [hereafter, *Hansard*], 3d Series, 356 vols. (London: T. C. Hansard, 1830–91), 22:1204–6, 23 Apr. 1834, list submitted by Thomas Spring-Rice in debate on O'Connell's motion for "Repeal of the Union."

13 Gordon Rose, *The Struggle for Penal Reform* (London: Stevens & Co., 1961), pp. 286–90; these data are condensed into a table in Chris Cook and Brendan Keith, *British Historical Facts 1830–1900* (New York: St. Martin's Press, 1975), p. 158. The statistics are discussed in Gattrell and Hadden, "Criminal Statistics," pp. 341–5, 356–7, 388–91; and in Philips, *Crime*, pp. 13–24, 298–300. See also Jenifer Hart, "Reform of the Borough Police, 1835–1856," *E.H.R.* 70 (1955):412 n. 2; and Harold Perkin, *The Origins of Modern English Society 1780–1880* (London: Routledge & Kegan Paul, 1969), p. 167–8.

14 Porter, *Progress*, pp. 646–8; Gattrell and Hadden, "Criminal Statistics," pp. 358–61, 430 n. 35.

15 F. C. Mather, *Public Order in the Age of the Chartists* (Manchester: Manchester

University Press, 1959), ch. 4; T. A. Critchley, *A History of Police in England and Wales*, 2d ed. (Montclair, N.J.: Patterson Smith, 1972), ch. 3; Leon Radzinowicz, *A History of English Criminal Law and its Administration from 1750* [hereafter, *ECL*], 4 vols. (London: Stevens & Sons, 1948–68), 4:ch. 6, esp. pp. 215–32; and J. J. Tobias, *Crime and Police in England 1700–1900* (New York: St. Martin's Press, 1979), ch. 5.

16 Hart, "Borough Police," pp. 413–14; Radzinowicz, *ECL*, 4:191–2.

17 Gattrell and Hadden, "Criminal Statistics," p. 353; Perkin, *Origins*, p. 168. See also Hart, "Borough Police," p. 421, and Stevenson, *Disturbances*, pp. 307–8, 321–3.

18 Gattrell and Hadden, "Criminal Statistics," p. 352; and Radzinowicz, *ECL* 4:317–18. On the remission of the capital code, see Porter, *Progress*, pp. 636–45; and Radzinowicz, *ECL* 1:ch. 5, esp. pp. 16–18, and 4:ch. 8. Useful summaries are in Chris Cook and John Stevenson, *British Historical Facts 1760–1830* (London: Macmillan, 1980), pp. 154–6, and Cook and Keith, *British Historical Facts 1830–1900*, pp. 151–3.

19 See T. A. Critchley, *The Conquest of Violence* (New York: Schocken Books, 1970), chs. 3, 4, and *Police*, chs. 2, 3; Radzinowicz, *ECL*, 4:chs. 4–6; and Victor Bailey, ed., *Policing and Punishment in Nineteenth-Century Britain* (New Brunswick, N.J.: Rutgers University Press, 1981), introduction, pp. 12–15.

20 See Philips, *Crime*, pp. 61, 77, 81, 90 nn. 38, 39.

21 Philips, *Crime*, pp. 59–63, 78–81, 87, quotations on pp. 60, 62.

22 William Derrincourt, *Old Convict Days* (1899), p. 10, referring to Darlaston in the 1830s, quoted in chapter epigraph in Philips, *Crime*, p. 53.

23 Barbara Weinberger, "The Police and the Public in Mid-Nineteenth-Century Warwickshire," in Bailey, ed., *Policing*, pp. 71–4. Her findings of working-class willingness to prosecute for ordinary property crimes confirm those of Philips, *Crime*, pp. 123–9. On "The System of Prosecution and the Prosecutors," see Philips, *Crime*, ch. 4.

24 Adrian Shubert, "Private Initiative in Law Enforcement: Associations for the Prosecution of Felons, 1744–1856," in Bailey, ed., *Policing*, pp. 27, 30, 34–9; and Philips, *Crime*, pp. 119–23.

25 John Field, "Police, Power, and Community in a Provincial English Town: Portsmouth 1815–1875," in Bailey, ed., *Policing*, pp. 44–9.

26 Hart, "Borough Police," p. 415; Critchley, *Police*, p. 62.

27 Field, "Portsmouth," pp. 47, 49; Radzinowicz, *ECL*, 4:252–9; Critchley, *Police*, pp. 80–8.

28 Bailey, ed., *Policing*, introduction, p. 13.

29 The report (for the full title, see n. 167, this chapter) is in *PP 1839* (169), 19:1–234. Among recent historians, see Critchley, *Police*, pp. 68–71; and Radzinowicz, *ECL*, 4:227–9.

30 Melbourne to Anglesey, 29 Dec. 1830, T1068/31/19, Papers of Henry William Paget, 1st Marquess of Anglesey, PRONI, Belfast. Anglesey's reply, 2 Jan. 1831, was unsettling (T1068/3/67).

31 Stevenson, *Disturbances*, p. 236.

32 The definitive study is E. J. Hobsbawm and George Rudé, *Captain Swing* (New York: Pantheon Books, 1968). See also George Rudé, *The Crowd in History: A Study of Popular Disturbances in France and England 1730–1848* (New York: Wiley, 1964), pp. 149–56; Stevenson, *Disturbances*, pp. 236–44. Among the sources listed by Hobsbawm and Rudé, *Swing*, p. 371, is a youthful work by the future biographer of Peel: Norman Gash, "The Rural Unrest in England in 1830 with particular reference to Berkshire," unpublished B. Litt. thesis, Oxford University, 1934.

33 Hobsbawm and Rudé, *Swing*, pp. 223–5, 262, 264 n. 25, 304–9. There were 1,404 capital convictions and 45 executions in England and Wales in 1830.

34 George Rudé, *Protest and Punishment: The Story of the Social and Political Protesters Transported to Australia, 1788−1868* (Oxford: Clarendon Press, 1978), pp. 72−8, 249−50. George H. Jones, *The Mainstream of Jacobitism* (Cambridge, Mass.: Harvard University Press, 1954), pp. 238−9; Bruce Lenman, *The Jacobite Risings in Britain, 1689−1746* (London: Methuen, 1980), pp. 271−5. Sir George Clark, *The Later Stuarts 1660−1714*, 2d ed. (Oxford: Clarendon Press, 1961), p. 120; Peter Earle, *Monmouth's Rebels: The Road to Sedgemoor 1685* (New York: St. Martin's Press, 1978), pp. 175, 178, 182.

35 Hobsbawm and Rudé, *Swing*, chs. 9−12; Stevenson, *Disturbances*, pp. 239−43; and Francis Hearn, *Domination, Legitimation, and Resistance: The Incorporation of the Nineteenth-Century English Working Class* (Westport, Conn.: Greenwood Press, 1978), pp. 115−21.

36 "A very English rising," *The Times Literary Supplement* [hereafter, *TLS*], 11 Sept. 1969, pp. 989−92, on p. 991, my emphasis. Stevenson, *Disturbances*, p. 350 n. 34, identifies Thompson as the reviewer. A contemporary historian reported that the Swing riots "presented a scene to be matched nowhere, save in Ireland"; the absence of murders and the rarity of serious personal violence he attributed to the existence of Poor Laws in England. Thomas Doubleday, *A Financial, Monetary, and Statistical History of England, from the Revolution of 1688 to the Present Time* (London: E. Wilson, 1847), pp. 297−8.

37 Hobsbawm and Rudé, *Swing*, pp. 253−63, 304−5; Stevenson, *Disturbances*, p. 241.

38 The exception proving the rule was East Anglia. See A. J. Peacock, *Bread or Blood: The Agrarian Riots in East Anglia, 1816* (London: Gollancz, 1965).

39 See Hobsbawm and Rudé, *Swing*, pp. 253−7, 284−8; Stevenson, *Disturbances*, pp. 243−4, 350 n. 40; and Perkin, *Origins*, pp. 181−2. A case in point was the bloody suppression of the brief, bizarre "rising" in 1838 in north Kent, between Canterbury and Faversham, by one J. N. Tom, alias "Sir William Courtenay," and some four dozen laborers. In a most un-English action, the demented Tom *killed* the constable sent to arrest him; in the ensuing battle, a military officer and thirteen rioters were killed, including Tom. See E. P. Thompson, *The Making of the English Working Class* (New York: Pantheon Books, 1964), pp. 800−2; and P. G. Rogers, *Battle in Bossenden Wood: The Strange Story of Sir William Courtenay* (London and New York: Oxford University Press, 1961).

40 Thompson's phrase in *TLS*, 11 Sept. 1969, p. 991; see also Hobsbawm and Rudé, *Swing*, pp. 281, 292−4.

41 J. R. McCulloch, *A Dictionary ... of Commerce*, 8th ed., 2 vols. (London: Longman, Brown, 1854), 2:1030; B. R. Mitchell and P. Deane, *Abstract of British Historical Statistics* (Cambridge: Cambridge University Press, 1962), pp. 24−6; Phyllis Deane and W. A. Cole, *British Economic Growth, 1688−1959*, 2d ed. (Cambridge: Cambridge University Press, 1967), pp. 7−9, 99−122.

42 Stevenson, *Disturbances*, pp. 218−20, 234−5.

43 Joseph Hamburger, *James Mill and the Art of Revolution* (New Haven, Conn.: Yale University Press, 1963; repr., Westport, Conn.: Greenwood Press, 1977), pp. 147−54. An anonymous observer wrote Wellington, 9 Oct. 1831, that "when the petition was read over to the meeting, as the petition of 100,000 people, there was a laugh throughout the crowd at the deception." Quoted in Hamburger, *Revolution*, p. 135. For an analysis of the often inflated reports of crowd sizes in 1831−2, see Hamburger, *Revolution*, pp. 122−4, 129−39, 147.

44 Hamburger, *Revolution*, pp. 154−61; Stevenson, *Disturbances*, pp. 220−1.

45 John Eagles, *The Bristol Riots, their Causes, Progress, and Consequences* (Bristol: Gutch & Martin, and London: Cadell, 1832). *Annual Register* 73 (1831): Chronicle, 171−6. Trials of Pinney and Brereton, in *Reports of State Trials*, ed. Sir John Macdonell, 8 vols. (London: Eyre & Spottiswoode, 1888−98), 3:30a, 42−3, 79−85, 112, 540−1. See also HO 40/28/1; TS 11/1263, PRO, London; Maj.

Oskar Teichman, "The Yeomanry as an Aid to the Civil Power, 1795–1867," *J. Soc. Army Hist. Research* 19 (1940):130–4; Hamburger, *Revolution*, pp. 161–81; Critchley, *Conquest*, pp. 123–5; and Stevenson, *Disturbances*, pp. 221–2.

46 Quotations: Malcolm I. Thomis and Peter Holt, *Threats of Revolution in Britain, 1789–1848* (Hamden, Conn.: Archon Books, 1977), p. 87. Greville's view of Melbourne, quoted in Stevenson, *Disturbances*, p. 223. Melbourne to Grey, 31 Oct., 1 Nov. 1831, Earl Grey Papers, Department of Paleography and Diplomatic, University of Durham. Sir Robert Peel, *Sir Robert Peel, from his Private Papers*, ed. Charles Stuart Parker, 3 vols. (London: J. Murray, 1891–9), 2:190–2.

47 An excellent summary of the historiography is in Hamburger, *Revolution*, pp. 112–14; a good if now somewhat dated introduction to the debate is William Maehl, Jr., ed., *The Reform Bill of 1832: Why Not Revolution?* (New York: Holt, Rinehart, and Winston, 1967). Accounts informed by more recent studies are in Thomis and Holt, *Threats*, ch. 4; and Stevenson, *Disturbances*, pp. 218–28.

48 Hamburger, *Revolution*, pp. 181–4, 195–9, 232–51; Stevenson, *Disturbances*, pp. 223–5; Thomis and Holt, *Threats*, p. 89.

49 Heron, quoted in Stevenson, *Disturbances*, p. 227, my emphasis. "Subtler": J. R. M. Butler, *The Passing of the Great Reform Bill* (London: Longmans, Green, 1914; repr., New York: A. M. Kelley, 1965), p. 377.

50 Butler, *Reform Bill*, pp. 377–85, 394–400, 417–26; Graham Wallas, *The Life of Francis Place, 1771–1854* (London: Longmans, Green, 1898), pp. 307–23; John Cannon, *Parliamentary Reform 1640–1832* (Cambridge: Cambridge University Press, 1973), pp. 238–9. Quotations: Thomis and Holt, *Threats*, pp. 89, 91–2.

51 Quotation: Thomis and Holt, *Threats*, p. 93. See Maehl, ed., *Reform Bill*, pp. 71–93; and Thompson, *Making*, pp. 807–19. There is now general agreement that the pressures at the center (London) were weaker than those from the provincial cities. See Hamburger, *Revolution*, pp. 139–42, 147–54, 195–9; and D. J. Rowe, "Class and Political Radicalism in London, 1831–32," *Hist. Jour.* 13 (1970):31–47, and his essay, "London Radicalism in the Era of the Great Reform Bill," in John Stevenson, ed., *London in the Age of Reform* (Oxford: Blackwell, 1977), pp. 149–76, esp. pp. 166–70.

52 The gentlemen were Col. William F. Napier (brother of Charles James Napier), who, though sympathetic, professed no desire to do battle "with a Birmingham attorney [Thomas Attwood] and a London tailor [Francis Place] against the Duke of Wellington"; a half-pay Colonel, William Johnson ("General Johnstone"); and Count Joseph Napoleon Czapski ("Count Chopski"). Cannon, *Reform*, p. 239. Note G. M. Young's comment: "In no age are Count Chopski and Colonel Macerone names to conjure with in English working [class] circles." *Victorian England: Portrait of an Age*, 2d ed. (New York: Oxford University Press, 1953; repr. 1964), p. 37.

53 Force levels: "A Return of the Establishment and Effectives of the British Army, Rank and File, at Home and Abroad," *PP 1831–2* (317), 27:118–21. Hamburger, *Revolution*, pp. 203–32; Thomis and Holt, *Threats*, pp. 98–9. Hamburger, discounting the claims of Place and a soldier named Alexander Somerville, argues for the reliability of the army; of the Yeomanry he is less sure. Thomis and Holt think that the military situation was combustible. Place, Thomis and Holt (p. 98), and Stevenson (p. 225) are mistaken in stating 11,000 to be the army strength; this was the number of men available at Windsor and in London, not throughout the country.

54 Stevenson, *Disturbances*, p. 227; and Thompson, *Making*, pp. 823–8.

55 Stevenson, *Disturbances*, p. 228.

56 Hamburger, *Revolution*, pp. 112–14, 184–95. Thompson notes that the letdown was less severe for Irish radicals in England, men like Bronterre O'Brien who had come to expect little from an English Government (*Making*, pp. 819–23).

Catholic "Emancipation" had, after all, disenfranchised a large section of the Irish electorate.

57 Hearn, *Domination*, pp. 104–5, 121–8.

58 Peter Dunkley discusses the attempted reassertion of paternalism and a new monitoring, by landed proprietors, of the behavior of the lower orders. See Dunkley, "Paternalism, the Magistracy, and Poor Relief in England, 1795–1834," *Intl. Rev. Soc. Hist.* 24 (1979):371–97, and his book, *The Crisis of the Old Poor Law in England, 1795–1834* (New York: Garland Publ., 1982). Anthony Brundage, *The Making of the New Poor Law: The Politics of Inquiry, Enactment, and Implementation, 1832–1839* (New Brunswick, N.J.: Rutgers University Press, 1978), explores government efforts to tie policy making to the traditional power elites in the counties. For a controversial restatement of the punitive immiseration wrought by the 1834 act, see Karel Williams, *From Pauperism to Poverty* (London: Routledge & Kegan Paul, 1981).

59 See Hearn, *Domination*, pp. 137–65; Robert Malcolmson, *Popular Recreations in English Society 1700–1850* (Cambridge: Cambridge University Press, 1973), pp. 104–10, 121–57; Robert D. Storch, "The Plague of the Blue Locusts," *Intl. Rev. Soc. Hist.* 20 (1975):61–90, and "The Policeman as Domestic Missionary," *J. Soc. Hist.* 9 (1976):481–509; and Thompson, *Making*, pp. 267–8, 343–5, and, for the broader context, his article, "Time, Work-Discipline, and Industrial Capitalism," *Past & Present* 38 (Dec. 1967):56–97.

60 David Roberts, *Victorian Origins of the British Welfare State* (New Haven, Conn.: Yale University Press, 1960), pp. 35–59; and Geoffrey Finlayson, *Decade of Reform: England in the Eighteen Thirties* (New York: W. W. Norton, 1970), ch. 2, esp. pp. 64–72.

61 See Cecil Driver, *Tory Radical: The Life of Richard Oastler* (New York: Oxford University Press, 1946), chs. 25, 26; Michael Rose, "The Anti–Poor Law Movement in the North of England," *Northern History* 1 (1966):70–91; Nicholas C. Edsall, *The Anti–Poor Law Movement, 1834–44* (Manchester: Manchester University Press, 1971), esp. chs. 2, 4–7; and John Knott, *Popular Opposition to the 1834 Poor Law* (New York: St. Martin's Press, 1986). A brief summary is in Stevenson, *Disturbances*, pp. 247–51. On the emergence of O'Connor, see Edsall, *Anti–Poor Law Movement*, ch. 8; and Donald Read and Eric Glasgow, *Feargus O'Connor, Irishman and Chartist* (London: Edward Arnold, 1961), pp. 50–3.

62 Lieutenant-Colonel Mair to Melbourne, 5 Dec. 1830, HO 40/27/5/408; Hobsbawm and Rudé, *Swing*, p. 253.

63 Col. Charles Ashe à Court to Mair, 29 Nov. 1830, HO 40/27/5/378; Hobsbawm and Rudé, *Swing*, p. 254.

64 HO 40/27/5/410, 465; HO 41/8/52, 87; and Hobsbawm and Rudé, *Swing*, pp. 255–6.

65 Norfolk, HO 52/10; Berkshire, HO 52/6; and Buckingham, Richmond, and Wellington, all quoted in Hobsbawm and Rudé, *Swing*, pp. 120, 255–6. See also Critchley, *Police*, p. 69 n.

66 Mair to Melbourne, 30 Nov. 1830, HO 40/27/5/374, and Melbourne's approval, HO 41/8/328–9.

67 HO 40/27/3/161; HO 40/27/5/366–71; HO 41/8/108, 170.

68 Mair: HO 40/27/5/388–496 passim, 512 (quotation). Hovenden: HO 40/27/1/3; HO 40/27/3/231–3; HO 40/27/5/380, 402, 421–3. Custance: HO 40/27/1/14–18, 26–8, 50–2.

69 Lieutenant-Colonel Mair was later sent to Newcastle-on-Tyne to organize a similar system, which "would be of great use in case of Riot." General Bouverie to Maj.-Gen. Fitzroy Somerset, 7 Apr. 1831, HO 40/29/1/38–9. The Swing and Reform disorders led the Government to pass "An Act for amending the Laws relative to the Appointment of Special Constables, and for the better Preservation

of the Peace," 1 & 2 Will. 4, c. 41, royal assent 15 Oct. 1831, repealing 1 Geo. 4, c. 37 (1820).

70 HO 40/28/1/38, 54−7, 60−1; *State Trials* 3:59, 102, 130, 154, 177, 261, 383, 404−9, 437. An incisive analysis is in Hamburger, *Revolution*, pp. 163−81, 207−8.

71 A recent study of the Trafalgar Square Riots of 1886−7 reveals that the Home Office and the London Police Commissioners were hampered by precisely the same concerns. See Victor Bailey, "The Metropolitan Police, the Home Office, and the Threat of Outcast London," in Bailey, ed., *Policing*, pp. 94−118.

72 Brereton to Somerset, 31 Oct. 1831, HO 40/28/1/32. Mayor Pinney was one of the very few Reformers in city government; the riots had begun on the return to Bristol of the City Recorder, Sir Charles Wetherell, who had made especially vituperative anti-Reform remarks in Parliament. Hamburger, *Revolution*, pp. 161, 173 n. 31, 174 n. 32, 178. See also *State Trials* 3:71, 78, 330, 507.

73 Mair to Melbourne, 7 Dec. 1830, Bristol, HO 40/27/5/417−19.

74 Mackworth to Somerset, 3 Nov. 1831, HO 40/28/1/81. *State Trials* 3:107, 156, 294, 298−300, 404, 418; Hamburger, *Revolution*, p. 169.

75 Respectively, Stevenson, *Disturbances*, p. 222; and Hamburger, *Revolution*, pp. 199−202, 209−11. A week after the Bristol Riots, King William IV, in opening the new parliamentary session, deplored the destruction but took care to affirm "our free Constitution" and the people's "legitimate exercise of those rights . . . and . . . making known their Grievances"; significantly, the King mentioned no such rights in his remarks on the tithe agitation in Ireland. *Hansard* 9:4−5, 6 Dec. 1831.

76 Pinney to Melbourne, 27 Dec. 1831 and 1 Jan. 1832, HO 40/28/1/150, 159. Jackson to Somerset, 3 Nov., 25 Dec. 1831, HO 40/28/1/87, 146; see also ff. 115, 127−8. Jackson later served as commander of the Northern District, 1836−9.

77 "First Report of the Commissioners appointed to inquire into the Municipal Corporations in England and Wales," *PP 1835* (116), 23:43; Tobias, *Crime and Police*, p. 94; and Critchley, *Police*, p. 64.

78 Mather, *Public Order*, p. 80. "Indisposition": Melbourne to Grey, 29 Oct. 1831, Earl Grey Papers. The commissioners on municipal corporations reported on a recent riot at Hull where, of 1,000 persons sworn as specials, only 7 showed up to serve. *PP 1835* (116), 23:43.

79 Municipal Corporations Act, 5 & 6 Will. 4, c. 76 s. 76. On borough police reform, see Critchley, *Police*, pp. 58, 61−2; and more broadly, Finlayson, *Decade*, pp. 85−8, and his article, "The Politics of Municipal Reform, 1835," *E.H.R.* 81 (1966):673−92. The reform of the police, borough and otherwise, is placed in the context of the Whigs' other reforms of the 1830s in John Roach, *Social Reform in England 1780−1880* (New York: St. Martin's Press, 1978), pp. 110−28.

80 Peel to J. W. Croker, 23 Apr. 1832, in Peel, *Private Papers*, 2:203. Identical sentiments are in correspondence to Croker, 12 May 1832, and to Henry Goulburn, 3 Jan. 1833, in ibid., 2:205, 212.

81 A dispute concerning succession of the Portuguese crown, in which Britain had become involved when Canning in 1827 had ordered 4,000 British troops to Lisbon to aid the constitutionalist supporters of Dom Pedro, rival and brother of the absolutist Dom Miguel. [Sir Llewellyn Woodward, *The Age of Reform 1815−1870*, 2d ed. (Oxford: Clarendon Press, 1962), pp. 211−12, 231−2.] Dom Pedro ultimately prevailed (1834), thanks in part to Capt. Charles Napier (*DNB* 14:38−44), Dom Pedro's fleet commander and first cousin of Charles James Napier, the Radical general who commanded England's Northern District during the Chartist era. Among those who served in the Portuguese adventure was Col. Sir Charles Shaw, who became Manchester's Police Commissioner in 1839−42 (see n. 25, Chapter 11, this book).

82 "King's Speech on Opening the Session," 6 Dec. 1831, *Hansard* 9:1−5, police on cols. 4−5. "Replies to the King's Speech," *Hansard* 9:5−97, police on cols. 71−2 (Melbourne), 78 (Peel).

83 *Hansard* 9:973−4 (Ellenborough), 27 Jan. 1832; and Peel, in *Hansard* 9:78 ("executive"), 143, 6 and 9 Dec. 1831; 10:1097, 1234, 1 Feb. and 7 Mar. 1832; 13:386 ("situation"), 4 June 1832; and 14:720, 25 July 1832. The annual indexes in *Hansard* list "Municipal Police" in 1832 but not thereafter, as the subject became subsumed under "Municipal Corporations."

84 "Report from the Select Committee on Municipal Corporations," 4 June 1833, *PP 1833* (344), 13:3−7 (Minutes of Evidence, pp. 8−352). "Report from the Commissioners on Municipal Corporations in England and Wales," 30 Mar. 1835, *PP 1835* (116), 23:1ff.; for the Report, see pp. 5−49, and for detailed studies of each Corporation, pp. 51−799. "Police" is discussed only in para. 102, p. 43, of the Summary Report, but for *each* of the boroughs (pp. 51ff.), the commissioners provided a useful paragraph of analysis of the town's "police." In the detailed tabular appendix (pp. 800−30), which includes all Corporations, the commissioners either did not think it important to list or were unable to obtain data on the number of constables and watchmen. See also Geoffrey Finlayson, "The Municipal Corporation Commission and Report, 1833−35," *Bulletin of the Institute of Historical Research* 36 (1963):36−52; and Finlayson, *Decade*, pp. 23−5.

85 Bryan Keith-Lucas, *The English Local Government Franchise* (Oxford: Blackwell, 1952), pp. 63, 67; Finlayson, *Decade*, pp. 26−31, quotation on pp. 30−1.

86 Four years earlier, an observer in Bristol during the Reform Bill Riots had written Melbourne: "Fifty of our London police could, I am confident, have dispersed any one of the assemblages I witnessed." P. Grenfell to Melbourne, 31 Oct. 1831, HO 40/28/64.

87 For the marathon debates, see *Hansard* 28:541−75, 820ff., and vol. 29, passim, 5 June−7 Sept. 1835. Melbourne, in Lords, 3 Aug. 1835, *Hansard* 29:1342−55, on cols. 1354−5.

88 Finlayson, *Decade*, p. 28.

89 5 & 6 Will. 4, c. 76 (1835) s. 76; Critchley, *Police*, pp. 63−5; Radzinowicz, *ECL* 4:213−14.

90 Mather, *Public Order*, pp. 115−16, 119−20, 239−42; Critchley, *Police*, pp. 64, 81, 105, 121; and Tobias, *Crime and Police*, p. 94.

91 Mather, *Public Order*, pp. 115−17, 239−42.

92 Hart, "Borough Police," pp. 415−16; Mather, *Public Order*, p. 112. Ratio of 1:1,000: opinion of W. C. Harris, Chief Constable for Hampshire, in "Report from the Select Committee appointed to consider the Expediency of adopting a more Uniform System of Police in England and Wales," *PP 1852−3* (603), 36:11. Chadwick favored a ratio of 1:700. "Extracts from Memoranda on . . . a General Police Measure," Chadwick MS 15 f. 7, Papers of Edwin Chadwick, D. M. S. Watson Library, University College, University of London.

93 "Return of the Several Cities and Boroughs of Great Britain, their Population . . . the Number of Police, and the Cost of the same in each Year, from their Establishment," 8 Feb. 1854, *PP 1854* (345), 53:509−80, analyzed by Mather, *Public Order*, pp. 114, 238. The returns are from England and Wales, the latter having only twelve boroughs. I have recalculated the percentages given by Mather in his table on page 114. Mather arrived at his percentages by *including* boroughs for which no data on force strength exist. For example, he states that in 1839 56 of 182 boroughs, or *31 percent*, had police:population ratios above 1:1100, that is, 1 policeman to 1,100 or more inhabitants. But he also states that only 103 of the 182 boroughs provided returns of force strength. We can only perform statistical comparisons where all the data are known, and in this instance police strength in seventy-nine towns is unknown. The only valid calculation we can make is from the pool of towns returning information. In this case, of the

103 towns providing returns, 56, or *54 percent*, had police:population ratios above 1:1100. The incompleteness and, in some cases, inaccuracies in the borough returns before 1856 are discussed in Hart, "Borough Police," pp. 417, 423.

94 This was the case in Leeds, Chester, and (in Wales) Newport and Swansea, cited in Critchley, *Police*, pp. 64–5; in Walsall, the only incorporated borough in the Black Country, in Philips, *Crime*, pp. 55, 57; and in Portsmouth, in Field, "Portsmouth," pp. 46–9. Similar findings are no doubt buried in the numerous histories of specific borough police forces; much local investigation remains to be done.

95 Hart, "Borough Police," pp. 419–20; Mather, *Public Order*, pp. 117–18; Critchley, *Police*, p. 65; Radzinowicz, *ECL*, 4:214; and Bailey, ed., *Policing*, introduction, p. 14.

96 Hart, "Borough Police," p. 421. Also quoted in Critchley, *Police*, p. 68, and Radzinowicz, *ECL*, 4:214; and paraphrased in Weinberger, "Police and Public," p. 67.

97 Hart, "Borough Police," p. 422.

98 Dublin population, 1801, projected from Whitelaw's Estimate of the Population of Dublin, 1798, in John Warburton, J. Whitelaw, and R. Walsh, *A History of the City of Dublin*, 2 vols. (London: W. Bulmer, 1818), vol. 2, table facing appendix p. vii. Dublin 1831, 1851: McCulloch, *Dictionary*, 8th ed. (1854), 2:1030. In the 1821 census, the first U.K. census to include Ireland, Dublin's population was listed as 186,000. British towns: Mitchell and Deane, *Abstract*, p. 24.

99 "A Return of the Police of every description in Dublin," 21 Feb. 1834, *PP 1834* (310), 47:361–2. Drummond's characterization, in "Report by the Lords' Select Committee appointed to inquire into the state of Ireland since the year 1835 in respect of Crime and Outrage," *PP 1839* (486), 12:Q. 12479.

100 In his remarks to the committee, Drummond's only reference to disorders was the statement that in August 1835 the Government had had no force at hand to monitor a public meeting at Coburg Gardens. *PP 1839* (486), 12:Q. 12484.

101 *Hansard* 30:1123–8, 1188–90, 1330–4, 31 Aug., 1 and 4 Sept. 1835; *Hansard* 32:244, 11 Mar. 1836; and *PP 1839* (486), 12:Q. 12485 (Drummond). Statute 6 & 7 Will. 4, c. 29, royal assent 4 July 1836; amended slightly by 1 Vict., c. 25 (1837). In the debate in the Lords in 1835, the Tories, led by Wellington and Roden, launched as spirited a defense of the unreformed City of Dublin Corporation as they had of the Municipal Corporations in England. One speaker, the Marquess of Londonderry, went so far as to say that the Dublin police bill handed over power to O'Connell! Whig peers, among them Hatherton and Brougham, spoke for the Government's bill. On the Dublin Corporation, see Macintyre, *Liberator*, pp. 234–5.

102 Wellington to Peel, 31 Mar. 1837, Peel Papers, BL Add. MS 40310 ff. 174–6, quoted in Macintyre, *Liberator*, p. 251.

103 The Irish Municipal Corporations Act (1840), which dissolved fifty-eight Corporations and reconstituted ten others, set the municipal franchise in the surviving Corporations at a high £10 valuation. The £10 householder meant "in effect a man with £150 [income] a year and upward." Young, *Portrait of an Age*, p. 28 n. 1.

104 On O'Ferrall and Brown, see *PP 1839* (486), 11:QQ. 4729–37, 4969–79, 5004–5, 5037, 5130, 5172.

105 Johnston: HO 65/12/286–7, 331. *PP 1839* (486), 11:QQ. 4741 (O'Ferrall), 5186 (Brown). For a printed copy of *Dublin Metropolitan Police: Instructions, Orders, & c.* (Dublin, 1837), see Chief Secretary's Office Registered Papers 1837/1719, ISPO, DC.

106 Officers: *PP 1839* (486), 11:QQ. 5187–9 (Brown). O'Ferrall gave slightly different figures: Two Superintendents and twelve Inspectors from London (QQ.

4738–9). On the rank and file, see QQ. 4738, 5173 (Brown). Critic: John Flint, *The Dublin Police and the Police System* (Dublin, 1847), pp. 7, 27. By the 1870s, at the latest, the old rule of not hiring Dubliners was broken; rural laborers were now preferred and men from the army and constabulary out of favor as recruits. "Report of the Commissioners appointed by the Treasury to inquire into the condition of the Civil Service in Ireland: The Dublin Metropolitan Police," *PP 1873* (788), 22:Q. 103.

107 Height statistics in Conor Brady, *Guardians of the Peace* (Dublin: Gill and Macmillan, 1974), p. 15; and *PP 1873* (788), 22:Q. 91. The *average* weight of the men in 1876 was 179 pounds; the celebrated Constable Wolfe weighed in at 286 pounds and was 6 feet 6.5 inches tall (Brady, *Guardians*, p. 15). Occupations: 6 & 7 Will. 4, c. 29 ss. 22–3. Constables' pay of 10–15 s. per week: *PP 1839* (486), 11:Q. 4743 (O'Ferrall). Marriage: *PP 1839* (486), 11:Q. 5185 (Brown). Promotion: *PP 1839* (486), 11:Q. 5178 (Brown); and *PP 1873* (788), 22:QQ. 115–23.

108 *PP 1839* (486), 11:QQ. 4741, 4745–6 (O'Ferrall), and 5175 (Brown). Quotations are in QQ. 5176 and 5196, respectively; and Orange meeting, Q. 5236. Discharges: Flint, *Dublin Police*, p. 20.

109 For the temporary expedient of government police in cities in the North of England in 1839–42, see Chapter 11, "II. The new police," "The government police in Manchester, Birmingham, and Bolton," this book.

110 The police district, when enlarged in 1840 to a radius of 8 miles around Dublin Castle, was equal to the scope of the old district in 1808–24. In the process, the jurisdiction of the County Dublin constabulary (established by 5 Geo. 4, c. 28) was reduced. 1 Vict., c. 25 s. 1; 3 & 4 Vict., c. 103. Difficulties in collection of the police tax (set by 1 Vict., c. 25 s. 4) resulted in a law authorizing distraint of goods for nonpayment (2 & 3 Vict., c. 78 s. 1). For the rest of the nineteenth century, Dublin was the most heavily taxed city for police services in the British Isles; see the comparative table listing Dublin and thirteen English and Scottish cities in 1906, in Séamus Breathnach, *The Irish Police from Earliest Times to the Present Day* (Dublin: Anvil Books, 1974), p. 67, who cites R. B. O'Brien, *Dublin Castle and the Irish People* (1909), n. pag.

111 *PP 1839* (486), 11:QQ. 4738, 4745 (O'Ferrall); 1838–42, Flint, *Dublin Police*, p. 16; 1844, Brady, *Guardians*, p. 15. In the long period from the Famine until World War I, force strength held steady at about 1,200 men. Breathnach, *Irish Police*, p. 67; Joseph V. O'Brien, *"Dear, Dirty Dublin": A City in Distress, 1899–1916* (Berkeley: University of California Press, 1982), pp. 179–80, 296.

112 Ratios for police in English cities in Mather, *Public Order*, pp. 113, 239–42.

113 Flint's pamphlet is exceedingly rare; so far as I know, the only copy in existence is at the National Library of Ireland (NLI), Dublin. James Henry, M.D. [Fellow, College of Physicians, Dublin], *An Account of the Proceedings of the Government Metropolitan Police in the City of Canton* (Dublin: Hardy & Walker, 1840), p. 79, quotation on pp. 74–5. This work is also rare: copies are at NLI, Dublin; U.S. Library of Congress, and listed as at three other American libraries (*Natl. Union Cat., Mansell*, vol. 241). The copy listed in The Catalogue of the British Library, London, was destroyed in the bombing during World War II. The Library of Congress copy is autographed, and was originally a gift from Dr. Henry in 1872 to "the *Smithsonian* Institution, Washington." By coincidence, more than a century later, during my term (1981) as a Fellow at the Wilson Center, which is housed in the old Smithsonian "Castle," I was able to reread Henry's delightful *Account*.

114 Table of committals, detailing sixteen offenses, 1837–8, in Drummond's evidence, *PP 1839* (486), 12:1100. On Dublin "ribbonism," see *PP 1839* (486), 11:QQ. 4748–50 (O'Ferrall); 5018, 5040 (Brown); 12492–4 (Drummond).

115 Evidence of William Kemmis, *PP 1839* (486), 11:Q. 6870; and statistics in *PP 1839*

(486), 12:1100. See also *Hansard* 30:1123–8, 1331–4, 31 Aug., 4 Sept. 1835. Storch, "Domestic Missionary," pp. 481–509.

116 1 Vict., c. 25 (1837) ss. 21–4; 5 Vict., sess. 2 c. 24 (1842) ss. 6–17, 26–7, 41–5. Section 1 of the 1842 act clarified these police powers by incorporating similar provisions in six previous acts dating to 1808: 48 Geo. 3, c. 140; 5 Geo. 4, c. 102; 6 & 7 Will. 4, c. 29; 1 Vict., c. 25; 2 & 3 Vict., c. 78; and 3 &4 Vict., c. 103.

117 Melbourne to Grey, 3 Aug. 1832, Earl Grey Papers.

118 John Foster, *Class Struggle and the Industrial Revolution: Early Industrial Capitalism in Three English Towns* (New York: St. Martin's Press, 1974), pp. 58–60, 65–8, 150, 159–60. Quotations: Foster, *Class Struggle*, pp. 59 (quoting *Manchester Guardian*, 17 May 1834), 61. On the state of the Oldham police, 1834, see HO 40/32/1/64–72, 101–19. For police as one of several working-class issues, see Foster's tables in *Class Struggle*, pp. 135, 137.

119 Melbourne to Grey, 3 Aug. 1832, and see Grey to Melbourne, 17 Sept. 1832, Grey Papers. In addition to Foster's book, we now have Robert Glen's *Urban Workers in the Early Industrial Revolution* (New York: St. Martin's Press, 1984), a study of Stockport, c. 1780–1830.

120 Bouverie to Under-Secretary S. M. Phillipps, 26 Aug. 1833, Bawtry, HO 40/31/1/44–6. On Bouverie (1783–1852), a veteran of the Egyptian and Peninsular campaigns, see *DNB* 2:944. He left the Northern District command to be Governor of Malta, 1836–43.

121 3 & 4 Will. 4, c. 90 (1833), repealing 11 Geo. 4, c. 27 (1830). On the 1833 act, see Sidney and Beatrice Webb, *English Local Government from the Revolution to the Municipal Corporations Act: The Parish and the County* (London: Longmans, Green, 1906), pp. 604–5; Mather, *Public Order*, p. 78; Critchley, *Police*, pp. 60–1 (quotation on p. 60); and Radzinowicz, *ECL*, 4:217. A recent writer has traced the activities, surprisingly successful, of the tiny police established by the act of 1833 in Horncastle, a Lincolnshire town of 4,000. See B. J. Davey, *Lawless and Immoral: Policing a Country Town, 1838–1857* (New York: St. Martin's Press, 1984), a short, unannotated work.

122 Trackage: Cook and Keith, *British Historical Facts 1830–1900*, p. 247; Mitchell and Deane, *Abstract*, p. 225. On the railways, see Mather, *Public Order*, pp. 161–3 (quotation from Select Committee on Railways, *PP 1844* [318], 11:144–5, on p. 161); and Mather's article, "The Railways, the Electric Telegraph, and Public Order during the Chartist Period," *History* 38 (1953):40–53.

123 "Return of Places where a Police has been Established by the Aid of the Metropolitan Police," 26 July 1837, in HO 61/19; another copy is in Mepol 2/21, PRO, London. Mayne to Under-Secretary Fox Maule, 15 Nov. 1838, in Mepol 2/21. The analysis in Charles Reith, *British Police and the Democratic Ideal* (London: Oxford University Press, 1943), p. 213, is criticized by Hart, "Borough Police," pp. 421–2; and both are discussed by Critchley, *Police*, p. 145 n. The figures are for the total number of policemen sent outside London, some of whom may have served on more than one occasion.

124 Reith suggests that on the document Russell's penciled notation, "Only 114 constables to suppress disturbances," was part of a Whig attempt to defend the party against charges that they were "making every possible political use of the Metropolitan Police." *British Police*, p. 213.

125 "Return of Police Constables sent to the Country for a Temporary Purpose," 1 Nov. 1838, in HO 61/21. Details of these journeys are in HO 65/11, 12, passim. See Reith, *British Police*, pp. 210–13, 232–8; Mather, *Public Order*, pp. 105–6; and Edsall, *Anti–Poor Law Movement*, pp. 97–8, 101–3, 110–11, 160.

126 5 & 6 Will. 4, c. 43 (1835), amending 1 & 2 Will. 4, c. 41 (1831), which had inadvertently restricted enrollment of specials to persons residing in the parish.

127 "Memo [*sic*] for Police Bill and Providing Peelers 'occasional' to distant places," 29 June 1835, in Mepol 2/29. This important plan is not mentioned by Mather,

Radzinowicz, and Critchley. The document bears this comment: "Put aside for [the] present, as Lord John Russell does not intend this year to bring forward any measure. R. M[ayne]. 29–6–35." Many years later, Edwin Chadwick would propose the creation of special squads, detached from the London police, to be sent anywhere in England to monitor trade union activities. "On the Consolidation of the Police Force and the Prevention of Crime," *Fraser's Magazine*, January 1868, pp. 11–18.

128 Peel to Henry Goulburn, 2 Jan. 1827, Goulburn Papers II/16, Surrey Record Office, Kingston-on-Thames. In 1839 Peel would speak strongly against the dangers and inconveniences of too frequent use of the Metropolitan Police outside London. *Hansard* 49:693–4, 701–2.

129 Mayne to Fox Maule, 15 Nov. 1838, in Mepol 2/21. Force augmentation: HO 65/13/37, 102.

130 The present author counts himself among those historians (listed in order by date of publication) who see Chartism, not daily crime, as the stimulus to police reform in 1839. Hart, "Borough Police" (1955), pp. 426–7. A. R. Schoyen, *The Chartist Challenge: A Portrait of George Julian Harney* (London: Heinemann, 1958), p. 82. Mather, *Public Order* (1959), ch. 4. Radzinowicz, "New Departures in Maintaining Public Order in the Face of Chartist Disturbances," *Cambridge Law Journal*, April 1960, pp. 51–80; and his book, *ECL* (1968), 4:232–3, 252–70. Critchley, *Police* (1967, 1972 ed.), pp. 61–2, 76–88. David Philips, "Riots and Public Order in the Black Country, 1835–1860," in J. Stevenson and R. Quinault, eds., *Popular Protest and Public Order: Six Studies in British History, 1790–1920* (New York: St. Martin's Press, 1974), pp. 141–2, 174 n. 4; and Philips, *Crime* (1977), ch. 3, esp. pp. 55–8, 76–81. Foster, *Class Struggle* (1974), pp. 60–9. Rudé, *Protest and Punishment* (1978), pp. 62–3. Bailey, introduction, in Bailey, ed., *Policing* (1981), pp. 12–15.

The writer most known for emphasizing crime, not public order, as the trigger to police reform is J. J. Tobias, in various works: *Crime and Industrial Society in the 19th Century* (London: Batsford, 1967), passim, esp. pp. 231–41; "Police and Public in the United Kingdom," in George L. Mosse, ed., *Police Forces in History* (Beverly Hills, Calif., and London: Sage, 1975), pp. 95–113; and *Crime and Police* (1979), esp. pp. 3, 95–7. See also E. C. Midwinter, "Law and Order in Early Victorian Lancashire," *Borthwick Papers No. 34* (July 1968), pp. 5, 11–12, 38, Borthwick Institute of Historical Research, University of York; and his book, *Social Administration in Lancashire 1830–1860: Poor Law, Public Health, and Police* (Manchester: Manchester University Press, 1969), pp. 138–40.

A variant explanation, which I find entirely compatible with the public order explanation, stresses the role of the new police as introducers and enforcers of middle-class values among the industrial working class. See three articles by Robert D. Storch: "Blue Locusts," pp. 61–90; "Domestic Missionary," p. 481; and "The Problem of Working Class Leisure: Some Roots of Middle-Class Moral Reform in the Industrial North, 1825–50," in A. P. Donajgrodzki, ed., *Social Control in 19th-Century Britain* (Totowa, N.J.: Rowman and Littlefield, 1977), pp. 138–62. In related work, Anthony Brundage has argued (like many contemporary working-class radicals) that the county police of 1839 was created, in large measure, to implement the New Poor Law and muzzle its critics. In my view, the broader challenge of Chartism in 1839 represented a maturation of the Anti–Poor Law movement. See Brundage, "Ministers, Magistrates, and Reformers: The Genesis of the Rural Constabulary Act of 1839," in *Parliamentary History: A Yearbook* 5(1986):55–64. I am grateful to Professor Brundage of California State Polytechnic University (Pomona) for a prepublication copy of his article.

131 Quotation is in Asa Briggs, "The Local Background of Chartism," in Briggs, ed., *Chartist Studies* (London: Macmillan, 1959), p. 10. Among the many works

on Chartism, the best are Briggs's edited volume, a collection of essays that remains a classic; G. D. H. Cole, *Chartist Portraits* (London: Macmillan, 1965); J. T. Ward, *Chartism* (London: Batsford, 1973), useful for detail but short on analysis; David Jones, *Chartism and the Chartists* (London: Allen Lane, 1975); David Goodway, *London Chartism 1838–1848* (Cambridge: Cambridge University Press, 1982); J. A. Epstein and Dorothy Thompson, eds., *The Chartist Experience: Studies in Working-Class Radicalism and Culture, 1830–1860* (London: Macmillan, 1982); and the recent study by Dorothy Thompson, *The Chartists: Popular Politics in the Industrial Revolution* (New York: Pantheon Books, 1984). A good short summary is in Stevenson, *Disturbances*, pp. 253–74. See also J. F. C. Harrison and Dorothy Thompson, *A Bibliography of the Chartist Movement* (Hassocks: Harvester Press, 1978).

132 Lovett, quoted in Briggs, "Local Background," p. 26. On O'Connor, see Read and Glasgow's still excellent biography, *O'Connor* (1961); and James Epstein, *The Lion of Freedom: Feargus O'Connor and the Chartist Movement, 1832–1842* (London: Croom Helm, 1982). Read and Glasgow pithily point out: "O'Connor *became* a Chartist: he was always an Irishman" (p. 5).

133 Read and Glasgow, *O'Connor*, pp. 12–29, 36–40, 50–7, 66–80; Edsall, *Anti–Poor Law Movement*, pp. 119–24, 168–76.

134 "Rhetoric": Stevenson, *Disturbances*, p. 255; "nerves … menace … bluff": Thomis and Holt, *Threats*, p. 103. On all of this, see Henry Weisser, *April 10: Challenge and Response in England in 1848* (Lanham, Md.: University Press of America, 1983), pp. 220–8. On moral and physical force, see F. C. Mather, *Chartism* (London: Historical Association, 1965), pp. 15–18; Rachel O'Higgins, "The Irish Influence in the Chartist Movement," *Past & Present* 20 (Nov. 1961):83–96; Read and Glasgow, *O'Connor*, chs. 8–10; Thomas Kemnitz, "Approaches to the Chartist Movement: Feargus O'Connor and Chartist Strategy," *Albion* 5 (Spring 1973):67–73; William Maehl, Jr., "The Dynamics of Violence in Chartism: A Case Study in Northeastern England," *Albion* 7 (Summer 1975):101–19. In addition to the demagogue O'Connor and the intellectual James Bronterre O'Brien, there were a number of local Chartist leaders who were Irish. See O'Higgins, "Irish," pp. 90, 92; and F. C. Mather, "The General Strike of 1842," in Stevenson and Quinault, eds., *Popular Protest*, pp. 133–4. Much work remains to be done on the Irish contributions to this language of menace.

135 Riot and rescue committals: see Appendix I, Table I.2, this book; and Stevenson, *Disturbances*, Table 13.1, p. 295. Thomis and Holt, *Threats*, ch. 5; Mather, *Public Order*, pp. 18–20, 105–6, 163–71.

136 David Williams, "Chartism in Wales," in Briggs, ed., *Studies*, pp. 234–43; and Ivor Wilks, *South Wales and the Rising of 1839: Class Struggle as Armed Struggle* (Urbana: University of Illinois Press, 1984). Mather, *Public Order*, pp. 23–4; Stevenson, *Disturbances*, pp. 260–1.

137 "Political democracy" requires some explanation, particularly for American readers. Most Chartists understood this to mean election of the House of Commons by enfranchisement of all adult males irrespective of property ownership. The monarchy, aristocracy, and House of Lords were to be retained unchanged. In this sense, all Chartists were democrats but few were republicans.

138 "1790s" and "extort concession": Thomis and Holt, *Threats*, pp. 100, 104. "Moral power," "slaves," and Oastler: quoted in Stevenson, *Disturbances*, p. 256. Peterloo: Donald Read, "Chartism in Manchester," in Briggs, ed., *Studies*, p. 44.

139 See Roy Church, *Economic and Social Change in a Midland Town: Victorian Notting-ham 1815–1900* (London: Frank Cass & Co., 1966), ch. 6, "Chartism in Notting-ham"; and Robert Sykes, "Physical-Force Chartism: The Cotton District and the Chartist Crisis of 1839," *Intl. Rev. Soc. Hist.* 30 (1985):207–36. And see the following essays in Briggs, ed., *Studies*: David Williams, "Chartism in Wales,"

pp. 220–48, quotation on p. 220; Hugh Fearn, "Chartism in Suffolk," pp. 147–73; R. B. Pugh, "Chartism in Somerset and Wiltshire," pp. 174–219; J. F. C. Harrison, "Chartism in Leeds" and "Chartism in Leicester," pp. 65–98, 99–146; and Donald Read, "Chartism in Manchester," pp. 29–64, especially pp. 42–8, quotation on p. 45. On geographical spread, see Dorothy Thompson's exhaustive place-name table, "Location and Timing of Chartist Activity," 1839–48, in *Chartists*, appendix, pp. 341–68, which may be usefully compared with F. C. Mather's table of "police" in England's towns and villages, also 1839–48, in *Public Order*, appendix, pp. 238–42.

140 Mather, *Public Order*, p. 120; Lt.-Gen. Sir William Napier, *The Life and Opinions of General Sir Charles James Napier* [hereafter, Napier, *Life*], 4 vols. (London: J. Murray, 1857), 2:74, journal entry, 19 Aug. 1839; and *Hansard* 50:427–34, 484–6, 20 and 22 Aug. 1839.

141 J. T. Slugg, *Reminiscences of Manchester Fifty Years Ago* (Manchester: J. E. Cornish, 1881), p. 239; Bouverie to Home Office, 6 May 1829, HO 40/23/239. The 1830 police and 1836 report: Arthur Redford and I. S. Russell, *A History of Local Government in Manchester*, 2 vols. (London: Longmans, Green, 1939–40), 1:370. The 1832 petition: HO 40/30/2/113–16; among the petitioners were the boroughreeve and constables of Manchester and Salford, local magistrates, constables of the adjoining townships, and the finance committee of the Manchester police commission. Col. James Shaw to J. K. Craufurd, 5 Feb. 1832, HO 40/30/2/116. On Shaw's service in Manchester, see H. A. Bruce, *The Life of General Sir William Napier* [hereafter, Bruce, *Napier*], 2 vols. (London: J. Murray, 1864), 1:322–9; and Napier, *Life*, 2:17–22.

142 Wemyss to Gen. Sir Richard Jackson, 18 Apr. 1837, HO 40/35/7. Redford and Russell, *Manchester*, 2:22–6, 42–3; Mather, *Public Order*, pp. 119–20; Radzinowicz, *ECL*, 4:257–8; Critchley, *Police*, p. 82 n. The figure of 240 police established in May 1839 is in *Hansard* 50:142, 9 Aug. 1839. Napier to S. M. Phillipps, 19 and 25 May 1839, HO 40/53/470, 485; also printed in Napier, *Life*, 2:36, 39.

143 John Langford, *A Century of Birmingham Life*, 2 vols. (Birmingham: E. C. Osborne, 1868), 2:633–4; Robert Dent, *Old and New Birmingham: A History of the Town and its People* (Birmingham: Houghton and Hammond, 1880), pp. 453–4; Conrad Gill, *A History of Birmingham: The Manor and Borough to 1865* (London: Oxford University Press, 1952), pp. 223–48; T. R. Tholfsen, "The Chartist Crisis in Birmingham," *Intl. Rev. Soc. Hist.* 3 (1958):461–80. A detailed examination of the Convention is in Thomas Kemnitz, "The Chartist Convention of 1839," *Albion* 10 (Summer 1978):152–70.

144 Gill, *Birmingham*, pp. 231–3, 319–20; Reith, *British Police*, p. 232; Mather, *Public Order*, p. 120; Critchley, *Police*, p. 81 n.; and Radzinowicz, *ECL*, 4:253. For the number of day and night police I have followed Critchley, who cites as his source the (modern-day) Chief Constable of Birmingham. For the nightwatch, Gill gives a figure of 115; Radzinowicz, 180. Reith talks of twenty street keepers and "a handful of local constables"; Mather mentions "a police force of thirty very inefficient men including constables, street keepers, and watchmen."

145 For the Chartist resolution, see HO 65/53/75; London police, HO 65/10, 13 and Mepol 2/61. The Birmingham riots sparked extensive discussions in Parliament (*Hansard* 49:85–8, 108–12, 370–85, 408–19, 437–70, 586–97, on 9, 10, 16–18, and 22 July 1839) and a government inquiry, 19–21 Sept. 1839 (HO 40/49). The riots are recorded in the *Annual Register* 81 (1839): Chronicle, 109–12. They are briefly discussed in Critchley, *Police*, p. 81; Radzinowicz, *ECL*, 4:253–4; and Stevenson, *Disturbances*, p. 258. Longer accounts are in Langford, *Century of Birmingham Life*, 2:638–48; Gill, *Birmingham*, pp. 248–52; and Reith, *British Police*, pp. 232–8, quotation ("disappearance") on p. 234.

146 Son of the 6th Duke of Bedford, Russell was a Whig liberal in the best oligarchic tradition. Headstrong, arrogant, and "so small as to be little more than a dwarf,"

Russell was not a well-liked or a particularly effective politician. Woodward, *Age of Reform*, 2d ed., p. 100; Cecil Woodham-Smith, *The Great Hunger* (New York: Harper & Row, 1962; repr., New York: E. P. Dutton, 1980), p. 103 (quotation).

147 The story of the Birmingham police bill is traced in John T. Bunce, *A History of the Corporation of Birmingham*, 5 vols. (Birmingham: Cornish Bros., 1878–1940), vol. 1, ch. 10; Gill, *Birmingham*, p. 257; Mather, *Public Order*, pp. 120–1; Critchley, *Police*, pp. 82–5; and Radzinowicz, *ECL*, 4:255–6. The parliamentary debates on the Birmingham police were lengthy. *Hansard* 49:691–707, 938–65, 1193–1200 (23, 29 July, 2 Aug.); 50:8–10, 149–55, 209–13, 247–8, 286–94, 368–9 (7, 9, 12–14, and 16 Aug. 1839).

Coincidentally, the Birmingham police controversy came hard on the heels of the reform of the City of London police (2 & 3 Vict., c. xciv, Local Acts, 1839). Home Secretary Russell, supported by Peel, had sought to bring the City under Metropolitan Police jurisdiction, but after meeting much resistance, the two men settled for a compromise that in fact represented a triumph for City interests. The City Corporation retained its control over the force, which was kept separate from the Metropolitan Police, but the Home Office did gain certain interventionist powers. *Hansard* 47:1064–5, 1290–1; 48:701–2; and 49:331–44 (3, 21 June and 15 July 1839). In the debates on the Birmingham police, the only speaker to mention the recent City police act was a City of London magistrate, Mr. W. Williams. *Hansard* 50:150.

148 *Hansard* 49:691–707, Fielden's motion on col. 694; among the three lonely dissenters was Benjamin Disraeli. Fielden had chaired the great Chartist meeting at Kersal Moor (September 1838); Read, "Chartism in Manchester," in Briggs, ed., *Studies*, p. 43. On Fielden, see n. 186, this chapter.

149 *Hansard* 49:692 (Duncombe), 699 (Hume). On Hume, see n. 24, Chapter 7, this book, and *DNB* 10:230–1; and on Duncombe, MP for Finsbury, London, see *DNB* 6:178–80 and Thomas H. Duncombe, *The Life and Correspondence of Thomas Slingsby Duncombe*, 2 vols. (London: Hurst & Blackett, 1868).

150 *Hansard* 49:703, 938–41. Peel's speeches guided the course of debate on the Birmingham bill; see *Hansard* 49:693–4, 700–4, 938–47 (29 July), 1196–7. "Thus for the second time in ten years Peel emerged as the sponsor of a centralized police" (Mather, *Public Order*, p. 121). But if one counts Ireland, 1814 and 1822, it was the fourth time in twenty-five years.

151 *Hansard* 49:947–8 (Mayor Scholefield), 948–51 (Attwood), and 951–6 (Russell endorsing Peel's proposal). O'Connell: *Hansard* 49:707. Compare General Napier's observation: "The London police should not have been sent down to Birmingham.... [O]ne thing strikes me as curious – if the people [in the Bull Ring] were armed, how came the police to escape." Napier believed that only three or four policemen were wounded in the riot on 4 July. C. J. Napier to W. Napier, "July" 1839, in Napier, *Life*, 2:53.

152 *Hansard* 49:959–62, quotations on cols. 960 (O'Connell), 964 (Wakley). MP for Finsbury and a Radical with wide-ranging interests, Wakley had been in the tiny minority of three MPs on Fielden's motion of 23 July. On Wakley, see *DNB* 20:461–5.

153 Buller (b. 1806), a middle-class reformer of Benthamite leanings, was described by Carlyle as "the genialist radical I have ever met." A friend of Mill, Roebuck, Molesworth, and George Cornewall Lewis, Buller served as MP for Liskeard, Cornwall, 1832–48; Chief Secretary to Governor-General Durham in Canada, 1838; and chief Poor Law commissioner, 1847. He died of erysipelas and typhus in 1848. *DNB* 3:246–8. In 1834, Buller was the parliamentary sponsor for the Australian colonization scheme that initially interested Sir Charles James Napier, who was Buller's first choice for governor (see footnote, p. 432, and n. 12, Chapter 11, this book). Napier, *Life*, 1:453.

154 On Lord Clements, "a dim figure in politics," see Macintyre, *Liberator*, p. 206.

Clements had recently written a treatise on the need for an Irish Poor Law. See Robert Bermingham, 1st Viscount Clements (1805−39), *The Present Poverty of Ireland convertible into the Means of her Improvement, under a well administered Poor Law* (London: C. Knight & Co., 1838).

155 *Hansard* 49:1193−5 (Russell), 1195 (Buller: "French"), 1196 (Peel).

156 *Hansard* 49:1200; 50:8−10.

157 *Hansard* 50:151 (Attwood), 154−5 (Buller). See also Bunce, *Birmingham*, 1:249; Mather, *Public Order*, p. 121; Critchley, *Police*, p. 84.

158 *Hansard* 50:247−8 (Commons); 286−94, 368−9, 373 (Lords); 588 (royal assent). 2 & 3 Vict., c. 88.

159 Manchester bill: *Hansard* 50:139−49, 248−59, 424−6 (9, 13, 20 Aug. 1839). Bolton bill: *Hansard* 50:427−34, 484−6, 493−6 (20, 22, 23 Aug. 1839).

160 *Hansard* 50:144 (Buller), 144−6 (Russell, "neutralize" on col. 145). See also Russell's remarks in *Hansard* 49:1197.

161 *Hansard* 50:248−50 (Lord George Somerset). Hume, apparently misinformed, argued that the Manchester borough council favored the bill (*Hansard* 50:257). See also Redford and Russell, *Manchester*, 2:44−5; Mather, *Public Order*, p. 121 n. 3. The only recorded vote was on the committal of the Manchester bill, which carried by 63−17 (*Hansard* 50:258−9). The Manchester act is 2 & 3 Vict., c. 87; Bolton: 2 & 3 Vict., c. 95.

162 *Hansard* 49:727−31 on col. 729.

163 10 Geo. 4, c. xcvii (Local Acts, 1829). See Radzinowicz, *ECL*, 4:216; and Critchley, *Police*, p. 60. On the acts of 1830 and 1833, see n. 121, this chapter.

164 G. R. Wythen Baxter, *The Book of the Bastilles; or the History of the Working of the New Poor-Law* (1841), p. iv, quoted in Radzinowicz, *ECL*, 4:261. Cf. Thomas Attwood: "The idea of a rural police was as odious as the New Poor-Law itself" (*Hansard* 49:707, 23 July 1839, speaking on the Birmingham police bill). Commentator: Thomas Hopkins, *Great Britain, for the Last Forty Years* (London: Simpkin and Marshall, 1834), p. 331. See also Edsall, *Anti−Poor Law Movement*, p. 62.

165 Chadwick: Mather, *Public Order*, p. 128; Radzinowicz, *ECL*, 4:67, 78; and Critchley, *Police*, p. 68. Richmond: *DNB* 11:927−9; Critchley, *Police*, p. 69. Richmond was the eldest son of the 4th Duke of Richmond, who was Lord Lieutenant when Wellesley overhauled the Dublin police (1808). Richmond's proposal to Russell specified that the police be controlled by local magistrates or Poor Law guardians. Jackson: Mather, *Public Order*, p. 129.

166 Bouverie to S. M. Phillipps, five letters from 12 Apr. to 30 July 1832, Bawtry, HO 40/30/2/139−42, 168, 190−2. Russell in 1836: *Hansard* 33:906, 13 May 1836, and quoted comment in *Dublin Evening Post*, 17 May 1836; and Hart, "Borough Police," p. 426. Russell to Chadwick, 1 Sept. 1836, in HO 43/51, quoted in Critchley, *Police*, pp. 68−9. Under-Secretary S. M. Phillipps to J. S. Crompton (Thirsk), 24 Dec. 1838, HO 43/56/306−7.

167 "First Report from the Commissioners appointed to inquire as to the best Means of Establishing an efficient Constabulary Force in the Counties of England and Wales," *PP 1839* (169), 19:1−234. Commission issued, 20 Oct. 1836; report presented, 27 Mar. 1839. Two modern historians, admirers of Chadwick's ideas on police, devote much space to this constabulary report. See Radzinowicz, *ECL*, 4:227−32; Critchley, *Police*, pp. 68−75.

168 Charles Shaw-Lefevre (1794−1888), Viscount Eversley (1857). He subsequently served as Speaker of the House of Commons, 1839−57, narrowly defeating Henry Goulburn for the post in May 1839. His nephew, George John Shaw-Lefevre (1832−1928), Baron Eversley, was the author of *Peel and O'Connell* (London: Kegan Paul, Trench, 1887). *DNB* 17:1388−9.

169 "Doctored": Victor Bailey, ed., *Policing*, introduction, p. 13, citing HO 73/6/1.

Hart, "Borough Police," pp. 411−15, 425−7. Hart's view is accepted by Mather, *Public Order*, p. 128 n. 4; and Critchley, *Police*, pp. 74−5. Dissenting views are in Tobias, *Crime and Industrial Society*, pp. 232−6; and Radzinowicz, *ECL*, 4:227−8. On Chadwick, see S. E. Finer, *The Life and Times of Sir Edwin Chadwick* (London: Methuen, 1952), pp. 164−80; and A. P. Donajgrodzki, "'Social Police' and the Bureaucratic Elite: A Vision of Order in the Age of Reform," in Donajgrodzki, ed., *Social Control*, ch. 2.

170 *PP 1839* (169), 19:para. 88, pp. 83−4; para. 130, pp. 106−7; and generally "State of Protection of Manufacturing Industry," para. 66−98, pp. 68−88.

171 Ibid., pp. 184−6; Irish constabulary in para. 244, pp. 160−1; "disposable" police against disorders, para. 245, p. 161. Chadwick, "Rough Draft of a Constabulary Force Report," n.d. [1839], Chadwick MS 5, Chadwick Papers.

172 Radzinowicz, *ECL*, 4:259−60. Questionnaire from Commissioners to Magistrates, in Report of the Constabulary Force Commissioners, *PP 1839* (169), 19:195−6; "Circular addressed by Lord John Russell to Chairmen of Quarter Sessions; Resolutions of Justices relative to Establishment of a Constabulary Force," *PP 1839* (259), 48:517−22. Anthony Brundage has recently shown how Lefevre and Rowan, too, assisted by Richmond and Russell, successfully pressured Chadwick to modify his centralist Benthamite vision, in part by granting police powers to the county JPs, not the Poor Law guardians favored by Chadwick. "Ministers, Magistrates, and Reformers: The Genesis of the Rural Constabulary Act of 1839," *Parliamentary History* 5(1986):56−61.

173 An excellent summary is in Radzinowicz, *ECL*, 4:260−3 ("tyranny," *The Times*, 15 Nov. 1836, one month after the appointment of the Commission, quoted in *ECL* 4:261). *The Times*'s opposition in 1839 was sustained and virulent; see issues for 25, 28 Mar.; 11, 13 Apr.; and almost daily from 24 July to 28 Aug. 1839.

174 Napier, *Life*, 2:57. *Hansard* 49:727−31.

175 County police bill debates: *Hansard* 49: (Commons) 727−40, 1385 (24 July, 6 Aug.); 50:6−8, 115−18, 263−4, 354−8 (7, 8, 14, 15 Aug.), and (Lords) 434−7 (20 Aug. 1839). See also Radzinowicz, *ECL*, 4:263−6, and Critchley, *Police*, pp. 78−80, 85−7.

176 For the motion by Mr. Ewart, MP for Wigan, see *Hansard* 50:115, 117−18. Wigan police: Mather, *Public Order*, pp. 238, 242.

177 *Hansard* 50:355−6. See also Mather, *Public Order*, pp. 78−9; Radzinowicz, *ECL*, 4:263−4. Philips, *Crime*, ch. 3, examines the reasons for the persistence of the old parish constables down to 1872. (An act of that year, 35 & 36 Vict., c. 92, abolished the requirement of parish constable appointments.) Given the lack of central control under the 1839 act and its patchy adoption until 1856, it is not surprising that in many counties old policing arrangements persisted past mid-century. Critchley, *Police*, pp. 79, 138−9, notes that the Parish Constables Act of 1842 was not repealed until 1964, and that "in a few areas for limited purposes" parish constables still functioned as late as the 1950s.

178 Critchley, *Police*, p. 79; Radzinowicz, *ECL*, 4:265. "Oriental": Hesketh Pearson, *Disraeli: His Life and Personality* (New York: Grosset & Dunlap, 1951), p. 76. See also W. F. Monypenny and G. E. Buckle, *The Life of Benjamin Disraeli, Earl of Beaconsfield*, 6 vols. (New York: Macmillan, 1910−20), vol. 2, chs. 3, 6.

179 *Hansard* 49:731−2, 740 (24 July); 50:117 (8 Aug.), 356−7 (15 Aug. 1839).

180 On learning on 23 July, at the time of the introduction of the Birmingham police bill, that the Whigs were also about to bring in a county police bill, Peel had angrily protested that there would be no time for "deliberate consideration" of "a measure of such immense importance." But Peel's concern, unlike Disraeli's, was that the force be intelligently conceived and effectively organized. *Hansard* 49:703−4.

181 *Hansard* 49:736−7.

182 In the Lords, Earl Stanhope's lone (printed) dissent was representative of the right-wing Tory view that the bill sought to transform JPs into government police inspectors and organizers of spies. *Hansard* 50:435–7, 19 Aug. 1839.

183 Foster, *Class Struggle*, p. 60.

184 Foster, *Class Struggle*, p. 60, quoting Alexander Taylor in Butterworth diary, 2 Jan. 1840.

185 *Hansard* 34:680–93, "County Boards," 21 June 1836.

186 *Hansard* 49:738 (Fielden, Brotherton); 50:6 (Hume, Attwood). "Honest John Fielden" (1784–1849) – MP for Oldham, 1832–47, and author of the pamphlet *The Curse of the Factory System* (Halifax: W. Milner and London: A. Cobbett, 1836; repr., London: Frank Cass & Co., 1969, and New York: A. M. Kelley, 1984) – was a leading advocate of the Ten Hours bill (passed 1847) to reduce the factory workday. Fielden Brothers, Todmorden, grew to be one of the largest cotton manufacturing firms in the United Kingdom. A statue of Fielden, paid for by subscriptions from factory workers, was erected in front of the Todmorden town hall in 1875. *DNB* 6:1279–80; Edsall, *Anti–Poor Law Movement*, p. 59.

187 *Hansard* 50:7–8, 357–8. Disraeli insisted on dividing the House on the Third Reading.

188 *Hansard* 50:369, 373, 434–7, 493, 601. Disraeli was now distracted by other interests: his marriage to Mrs. Anne Wyndham Lewis on 28 August and Young England's sublimely irrelevant medieval tournament at Eglinton Castle on 28–30 August.

189 Hart, "Borough Police," pp. 426–7.

190 Read, "Chartism in Manchester," and Harrison, "Chartism in Leeds," in Briggs, ed., *Studies*, pp. 49, 79; Thomis and Holt, *Threats*, pp. 109–11; Stevenson, *Disturbances*, pp. 259–61.

191 See G. S. R. Kitson Clark, "The Romantic Element, 1830–1850," in J. H. Plumb, ed., *Studies in Social History* (London: Longmans, Green, 1955), pp. 211–39; and W. L. Burn, *The Age of Equipoise* (New York: W. W. Norton, 1965), ch. 2, esp. pp. 62–8, 74–8. Kitson Clark has remarked on the "interesting affinity" between political speakers and dramatic recitations. "The oratory of some of the Chartists such as Harney, or of some of the Young Ireland group, such as Meagher 'of the sword,' is very close in its methods and its vocabulary to the tremendous speeches which were thundered out nightly at Covent Garden or at Drury Lane." *An Expanding Society: Britain 1830–1900* (Cambridge: Cambridge University Press, 1967), ch. 7 ("Romanticism"), on p. 121. Note also G. M. Young: "It is impossible to gauge the danger of a revolution which refused to happen. But in estimating the alarm we must allow for the melodramatic streak in the early Victorian temperament. When Wellington said on the morrow of the riots that no town sacked in war presented such a spectacle as Birmingham, he did not mean that he had gone to see it for himself." *Portrait of an Age*, p. 37. See also Raymond Williams, *Culture and Society, 1780–1950* (London: Chatto & Windus, 1958; Harper & Row Torchbook ed., 1966), Part 1; and his *The Long Revolution* (London: Chatto & Windus, 1961; Penguin ed., 1965), Part 1, ch. 2.

192 Quoted in Weinberger, "Police and Public," in Bailey, ed., *Policing*, p. 72.

193 F. W. Maitland, *Justice and Police* (London: Macmillan, 1885), p. 108; and Disraeli in *Hansard* 49:731.

CHAPTER 11. ENGLISH CHARTISM; IRISH REPEAL AND FAMINE

1 Thomas Kemnitz, "The Chartist Convention of 1839," *Albion* 10 (Summer 1978):155, 170.

2 Ivor Wilks, *South Wales and the Rising of 1839: Class Struggle as Armed Struggle* (Urbana and Chicago: University of Illinois Press, 1984), p. 253, who sees the conflict as, in part, Welsh versus Saxons ("foreigners"). See also David Williams,

John Frost: A Study in Chartism (Cardiff: University of Wales Press, 1939; repr., London: Evelyn, Adams & Mackay, 1969), pp. 225−30, 240−89, and his article, "Chartism in Wales," in Asa Briggs, ed., *Chartist Studies* (London: Macmillan, 1959), pp. 234−42; Malcolm I. Thomis and Peter Holt, *Threats of Revolution in Britain, 1789−1848* (Hamden, Conn.: Archon Books, 1977), pp. 109−11; John Stevenson, *Popular Disturbances in England 1700−1870* (London: Longman, 1979), p. 260 (quotation); Dorothy Thompson, *The Chartists: Popular Politics in the Industrial Revolution* (New York: Pantheon Books, 1984), ch. 4; and David J. V. Jones, *The Last Rising: The Newport Insurrection of 1839* (New York: Oxford University Press, 1985). Historians have cited a wide range of the numbers killed, from fifteen (in Stevenson) to twenty-four [in George Rudé, *The Crowd in History* (New York: Wiley, 1964), p. 255]. Most give a figure of twenty-two. I have accepted Wilks's figure.

3 F. C. Mather, *Public Order in the Age of the Chartists* (Manchester: Manchester University Press, 1959), pp. 23−4; J. T. Ward, *Chartism* (London: Batsford, 1973), pp. 136−7.

4 Stevenson, *Disturbances*, p. 261.

5 Leon Radzinowicz, *A History of English Criminal Law and its Administration from 1750* [hereafter, *ECL*], 4 vols. (London: Stevens & Sons, 1948−68), 4:249−51; Mather, "The Government and the Chartists," in Briggs, ed., *Studies*, pp. 383−5. "Half the land has been openly in arms," wrote Maj.-Gen. Sir Charles Napier, commander of the Northern District, "and not a drop spilt on the scaffold." Of the Whig Government, he added, "it is but just to say they have been patient and merciful." Sir William Napier, *The Life and Opinions of General Sir Charles James Napier*, 4 vols. (London: J. Murray, 1857), 2:135, Journal, 13 July 1840. For a detailed analysis of those who served prison terms, see Christopher Godfrey, "The Chartist Prisoners, 1839−41," *Intl. Rev. Soc. Hist.* 24 (1979):189−236.

6 Mather, *Public Order*, ch. 10, esp. pp. 182−217, demonstrates that spies were clearly widespread but coordinated by local authorities and the military commanders, not by the Home Office.

7 Ibid., pp. 81−7.

8 Ibid., pp. 87−9; Radzinowicz, *ECL*, 4:233. Napier, *Life*, 2:11, Journal, 18 Apr. 1839; see also *Life*, 2:100.

9 "Yeomanry Cavalry," *Hansard's Parliamentary Debates* [hereafter, *Hansard*], 3d Series, 356 vols. (London: T. C. Hansard, 1830−91), 42:647−54, 657−8, 660−4 (Russell, Fox Maule, Peel), 27 Apr. 1838; Mather, *Public Order*, pp. 143, 146−8; and Napier, *Life*, 2:73, Journal, 15 Aug. 1839 (quotation). But Napier would use them if necessary (*Life*, 2:30, 32, 34).

10 For Napier's views on Ireland, see the Papers of General Sir Charles James Napier, BL Add. MSS 49126, 49127, passim, British Library, London; and *Life*, 1:438−9, 442, 475. On his English politics, see Napier's *Remarks on Military Law and the Punishment of Flogging* (London: T. and W. Boone, 1837), p. 148 n.; and *Life*, 1:460, 467, and 2:63, 75, 153.

11 *Dictionary of National Biography* [hereafter, *DNB*] 14:45−7; Napier, *Life*, 1:6−11, 30−1 (quotation), 195−7.

12 Napier, *Life*, 2:109, Journal, 12 Jan. 1840; Rowan to Chadwick, 1 Apr. 1839, Chadwick MS 1722, Papers of Edwin Chadwick, D. M. S. Watson Library, University College, University of London. Napier was an inveterate writer. In addition to his daily journal, which forms the basis for the *Life* authored by brother William, and his *Remarks on Military Law* (wherein see pp. 23−49 for a brilliant discussion of the military's role and legal liabilities in civil disorders), Napier was the author of *Colonization, particularly in Southern Australia; with some Remarks on Small Farms and Overpopulation* (London: T. and W. Boone, 1835, repr., New York: A. M. Kelley, 1969); a short, anti-O'Connell *Dialogue on the*

Poor Laws (1838) proposed for Ireland; and an *Essay on the Present State of Ireland, showing the chief cause of, and the remedy for, the existing Distresses in that Country* (London: Ridgway, 1839). A full list is in *DNB* 14:53−4.

13 Napier, *Life*, 2:30, letter to Lord De Grey, 8 May 1839.

14 Gen. Sir R. Hill to Napier, 1 May 1839, HO 40/53/395; military returns, Northern District, WO 17/2801−2.

15 Napier to Under-Secretary S. M. Phillipps, 9 May and 29 July 1839, in Napier, *Life*, 2:32, 60−1; see also HO 40/53/465−6, 484, 578.

16 Mather, *Public Order*, p. 161. On troop shipments from Ireland, see HO 40/53/379−86, 409−13, 441, 458, and T. Drummond's evidence in "Report by the Lords' Select Committee appointed to inquire into the State of Ireland since the year 1835 in respect of Crime and Outrage," *PP 1839* (486), 12:Q. 14013, 24 June 1839.

17 "Return of all Permanent Barracks in the United Kingdom, including the date of erection of each," *PP 1847* (167), 36:321−75. On conditions in the barracks, see Napier Papers 54515, *passim*; on troop distribution, 54516 f. 13. See also Mather, *Public Order*, pp. 164−5, 168−9.

18 Napier, *Life*, 2:16, 47, letter to magistrates of West Riding of Yorkshire, 24 Apr., and Journal, 19 June 1839. Napier to Wemyss, 10 Apr., "confidential," and repeated to Under-Secretary Phillipps, 13 Apr. 1839, both in Napier Papers 49128.

19 Napier, *Life*, 2:9, letter to W. Napier, 15 Apr. 1839. Fears of assassination recur in Napier's journal and correspondence (*Life*, 2:8−10, 19, 96, 102, 111, 113, 148); see also his references to pikes, the weapons of 1798 (*Life*, 2:6−8, 15−16, 18, 21, 30−2, 54, 74, 97, 114, 135).

20 *Life*, 2:71−3, Journal, 12, 13, 17 Aug. 1839; HO 40/53/475, 480.

21 Stevenson, *Disturbances*, p. 259; G. M. Young, *Victorian England: Portrait of an Age*, 2d ed. (New York: Oxford University Press, 1953; repr., 1964), p. 37. On the Newcastle incident, see William Maehl, Jr., "The Dynamics of Violence in Chartism: A Case Study in Northeastern England," *Albion* 7 (Summer 1975):112−13.

22 Napier, *Life*, 2:90, 113, Journal, 9 Nov. 1839, and letter to W. Napier, 19 Jan. 1840.

23 Napier, *Life*, 2:30, 69, letter to W. Napier, 15 May, and Journal, 6 Aug. 1839. Similar sentiments are in *Life*, 2:14, 93. Napier wryly noted that, should he be killed, the Government had at its disposal 164 other major-generals. *Life*, 2:96, letter to Duke of Portland, 8 Dec. 1839.

24 Napier, *Life*, 2:30; and Wemyss to Napier, 20 Apr. 1839 and 15 May 1840, in HO 40/53/374−5 and Napier Papers, 54512 f. 51, respectively.

25 HO 65/10/25, 110. Shaw (*DNB* 17:1370−1) had served as a colonel in charge of British volunteers against Dom Miguel, 1832−5, and briefly in 1836 had been a brigadier-general. Police Commissioner Burgess pressed the Government for his military allowance. "Half-pay," he explained to the Home Office in January 1840, "is allowed to the Metropolitan and Dublin Police and Irish Constabulary, and I cannot imagine we were intended as an exception." HO 65/10/33.

26 Burgess to Under-Secretary Fox Maule, 8 Feb. 1841, HO 65/10/88.

27 Pay in Birmingham: constables, 17s. per week; twenty sergeants, 21s.; ten superior sergeants, 24s., 6d.; ten Subinspectors, 28s.; nine Inspectors, £100 p.a.; five Superintendents, £130; one Chief Superintendent, £200; Commissioner Burgess, £800. HO 65/10/70−1. In November 1841 Burgess complained of financial pressures on the force, including his claim of receiving only £700 of his salary. HO 65/10/111−12. Resignations: HO 65/10/29−31, 19 Dec. 1839, "7 of my best officers" have left for the Worcestershire force. "Constantly": HO 65/10/45, 25 Mar. 1840.

28 On the preceding, see HO 65/10/17–47; Conrad Gill, *A History of Birmingham: The Manor and Borough to 1865* (London: Oxford University Press, 1952), pp. 274–5; and Mather, *Public Order*, pp. 121–2. The Manchester police rate, initially 8d. per pound, was cut to 6d. by 1841.

29 HO 65/10/58–61, letters to Home Secretary Normanby, 27 and 28 July 1840; HO 65/10/112–13, letter to Home Secretary Graham, 5 Nov. 1841.

30 Mather, *Public Order*, pp. 123, 125–6; Donald Read, "Chartism in Manchester," in Briggs, ed., *Studies*, pp. 50–1; Sir Robert Peel, *Sir Robert Peel, from his Private Papers*, ed. Charles Stuart Parker, 3 vols. (London: J. Murray, 1891–9), 2:510; Shaw to Graham, 26 and 28 Sept. 1841, in Chadwick Papers, Chadwick MS 1794. See also John Werly, "The Irish in Manchester, 1832–1849," *I.H.S.* 18 (Mar. 1973):345–58; and J. H. Treble, "O'Connor, O'Connell, and the Attitudes of Irish Immigrants towards Chartism in the North of England, 1838–48," in J. Butt and I. F. Clarke, eds., *The Victorians and Social Protest: A Symposium* (Hamden, Conn.: Archon Books, 1973), pp. 33–70.

31 Read, "Chartism in Manchester," pp. 53–4; A. G. Rose, "The Plug Plots of 1842 in Lancashire and Cheshire," *Transactions of the Lancashire and Cheshire Antiquarian Society* 67 (1957):91–6.

32 HO 65/10/26 (20 Nov. 1839, Fussell), 28. Mather, *Public Order*, pp. 123, 194–6, 201 (Normanby), 204–5, 216–17.

33 HO 65/10/42 ("threefold"), 49. "Criminal and Statistical Returns of the Birmingham Police, 1840," *PP 1841* (312), 18:681–701. Radzinowicz, *ECL*, 4:256–7.

34 Arthur Redford and I. S. Russell, *A History of Local Government in Manchester*, 2 vols. (London: Longmans, Green, 1939–40), 2:139–40; Richard W. Procter, *Memorials of Manchester Streets* (Manchester: T. Sutcliffe, 1874), p. 100.

35 Schofield to H.O., 25 Nov. 1839, in HO 40/50, quoted in Mather, *Public Order*, p. 124. Cost: HO 65/10/71.

36 Burgess to Normanby, 23 July 1840, HO 65/10/57. On the Charters Confirmation Act, see *Hansard* 55:1145–6, 1297, 1301; 5 & 6 Vict., c. 111 (1842); and T. A. Critchley, *A History of Police in England and Wales*, 2d ed. (Montclair, N.J.: Patterson Smith, 1972), p. 83.

37 "RULES settled by the MARQUESS OF NORMANBY, one of Her Majesty's Principal Secretaries of State, for ESTABLISHING A UNIFORM SYSTEM for the GOVERNMENT, PAY, CLOTHING, ACCOUTREMENTS, and NECESSARIES of the CONSTABLES appointed under the Act 2 & 3 Vict., Cap. 93" [hereafter, "RULES"], four copies (the printed "RULES" filling less than a dozen small pages; one copy printed, three in manuscript), in Mepol 2/21, PRO, London. These copies contain numerous marginal comments by unidentified Whitehall authorities. Another copy of the "RULES," as well as a document marked "County Constabulary Force, Qualifications for Superintendent and Constables, 2 & 3 Vict., c. 93," is in Chadwick MS 3.

38 The Government took a hard line on the subject of guns. Normanby vetoed a proposal by the Shropshire magistrates to arm their county constables with pistols. Letter to Hon. T. Kenyon, 15 Feb. 1840, HO 65/4/64; see also HO 65/4/31, 106. In December 1843, Chief Constable Woodford reprimanded and disarmed two Lancashire constables who had begun carrying guns. Eric Midwinter, *Social Administration in Lancashire, 1830–1860: Poor Law, Public Health, and Police* (Manchester: Manchester University Press, 1969), p. 158.

39 "RULES," printed version, pp. 3–4, relating to the statute 2 & 3 Vict., c. 93 ss. 3, 20. The Government's painstaking on the subject of arming with cutlasses is revealed in a handwritten marginal comment by an unidentified Whitehall authority. "Are these Orders [from the Chief Constable instructing his men to wear cutlasses] necessary in all cases, as for instance, when actual rioting has commenced? Or, are the orders req$^{d.}$ only in sudden emergencies? The paper

[from the Chief Constable] at present is ambiguous.... If rioters are armed, Constables as well as any other Persons would be justified in arming themselves for self-defence."

40 The Government actually intervened to block the hiring in the Lancashire force of some men unable to read or write. Under-Secretary Phillipps to Chief Constable Woodford, 17 Mar. 1840, HO 65/4/72.

41 For enforcement, see HO 65/4/83, 89—90.

42 Sergeants were paid 19 to 25s. per week; Inspectors, £65–120 p.a.; and Super-intendents, £75–150 p.a.

43 Historian Eric Midwinter reports a total of only 118 letters sent from London to the Lancashire authorities from 1839 to 1856; the county was never visited by a Home Office official. *Social Administration*, p. 150.

44 "RULES," pp. 4–8; 2 & 3 Vict., c. 93 ss. 3, 6, 17.

45 E. J. Hobsbawm and George Rudé, *Captain Swing* (New York: Pantheon Books, 1968), pp. 304–5.

46 One of the few counties of this type to adopt the new police was Bedfordshire. Clive Emsley has argued that the county was relatively free of crime and disorder and that its magistrates adopted the Police Act largely from the fear that if they did not, criminals would "flee" to unpoliced Bedfordshire. The small force, which did not increase in size for fifteen years, led a relatively uneventful existence. Crimes remained petty and political radicalism rare in the county; the only major riot occurred at Luton in 1854. "The Bedfordshire Police, 1840–1856: A Case Study in the Working of the Rural Constabulary Act," *Midland History* 7 (1982):73–92. For another quiet rural county, Hertfordshire, which established a county force in 1841, see Neil Osborn, *The Story of Hertfordshire Police* (Letch-worth: Hertfordshire Countryside, 1969), pp. 24–30.

47 *History of the Lincolnshire Constabulary, 1857–1957* [no author or pag.], quoted in Critchley, *Police*, p. 91 n.; Wharncliffe to Home Office, 3 Oct. 1842, HO 45/264, quoted in Mather, *Public Order*, pp. 130–1.

48 *Hansard* 52:3, 387–92, 7 and 18 Feb.; 53:19–23, 250–5, 24 and 30 Mar.; 54:1268–82, 18 June; and 55:108, 762–5, 817, 26 June, 16 and 20 July 1840.

49 Divided into three districts: the Potteries, rated at 5d. per pound (2.1 percent tax rate); Mining, 3d.; and Rural, 1d. In 1840, pursuant to 2 & 3 Vict., c. 88, a twenty-one-man police force had been established in Offlow Hundred in the Mining District.

50 David Williams, *The Rebecca Riots: A Study in Agrarian Discontent* (Cardiff: University of Wales Press, 1955, repr. 1971), pp. 59–61, 213, 253, 265–72, 283–4; and David Jones, *Crime, Protest, Community and Police in Nine-teenth-Century Britain* (London: Routledge & Kegan Paul, 1982), pp. 35–61, esp. pp. 41–2, 50.

51 Under-Secretary Phillipps to Deputy Clerks of the Peace, Preston, 14 July 1842, HO 65/4/224–5; for reductions in the Nottinghamshire force, also in 1842, see HO 65/4/210, 236.

52 J. Crossley, Todmorden, to Normanby, 19 May 1840, HO 40/54/701. Robert D. Storch, "The Plague of the Blue Locusts: Police Reform and Popular Resistance in Northern England, 1840–1857," *Intl. Rev. Soc. Hist.* 20 (1975):61–90, quota-tion on p. 72; and "The Policeman as Domestic Missionary: Urban Discipline and Popular Culture in Northern England, 1850–1880," *J. Soc. Hist.* 9 (Summer 1976):481–509.

53 The victim was mill owner Joseph Halstead, killed when struck in the head by an iron bar at Colne on the evening of 20 August 1840. Richard Boothman, a twenty-year-old weaver, was later convicted for the murder and transported for life to Australia. Until his death there in 1877, Boothman professed his inno-cence. Storch, "Blue Locusts," p. 83 n. 2.

54 Returns of "the Number of Persons who have lost their lives ... in Affrays with

the Constabulary [in Ireland] ...": for 1824–30, see *PP 1830–1* (67), 8:403–83; and for 1830–45, *PP 1846* (280), 25:237–60. The most lethal affray since the early 1830s occurred at Ballinhassig, Cork, on 30 June 1845; seven peasants (and no police) were killed. Chief Secretary's Office Registered Papers 1845/6/15873, ISPO, DC.

55 Wemyss to Napier, 15 May 1840, Napier Papers, 54512 f. 51; Storch, "Blue Locusts," pp. 77–9; Mather, *Public Order*, p. 139.

56 Napier to Under-Secretary Phillipps, 24 July 1839, *Life*, 2:59; John Foster, *Class Struggle and the Industrial Revolution: Early Industrial Capitalism in Three English Towns* (New York: St. Martin's Press, 1974), p. 60; Storch, "Blue Locusts," p. 76; and David Philips, "Riots and Public Order in the Black Country, 1835–1860," in J. Stevenson and R. Quinault, eds., *Popular Protest and Public Order: Six Studies in British History 1790–1920* (New York: St. Martin's Press, 1974), pp. 152–3.

57 Mather, *Public Order*, pp. 137–8, 177–8; Storch, "Blue Locusts," pp. 73–4.

58 Custance to Napier, 26 and 28 Apr. 1840, Napier Papers, 54514 ff. 76–8, 81. At the time of the Swing Riots in 1830, Lieutenant-Colonel Custance had been instrumental in organizing householders into special constabularies in towns from Leicestershire eastward to Norfolk (HO 40/27/1/14–52).

59 HO 40/54/831; Napier Papers, 54514 ff. 64, 114, 120–3; Storch, "Blue Locusts," pp. 79–83.

60 Regulation book, Dorsetshire constabulary, quoted in Critchley, *Police*, p. 147.

61 Phillipps to Town Clerk, Norwich, 26 Dec. 1840, HO 65/4/145. W. J. Lowe, "The Lancashire Constabulary, 1845–1870: The Social and Occupational Function of a Victorian Police Force," *Criminal Justice History* 4 (1983):43, 52; David Philips, *Crime and Authority in Victorian England: The Black Country, 1835–1860* (London: Croom Helm, 1977), pp. 61, 76–7.

62 Philips, *Crime*, pp. 59–63, 78–81, 87.

63 Phillipps to J. Steel, Town Clerk, Cockermouth, 15 Apr. 1840; and to Chief Constable Goodyear, Leicester, 18 Apr. 1840, HO 65/4/90–1, 94.

64 Philips, *Crime*, pp. 83–7, 124–30, 283–9; Adrian Shubert, "Private Initiative in Law Enforcement: Associations for the Prosecution of Felons, 1744–1856," and Barbara Weinberger, "The Police and the Public in Mid-Nineteenth-Century Warwickshire", in Victor Bailey, ed., *Policing and Punishment in Nineteenth Century Britain* (New Brunswick, N.J.: Rutgers University Press, 1981), pp. 33–9, 71–2, respectively; and Midwinter, *Social Administration*, pp. 165–8, 171 (quotation). In the files of the Staffordshire Record Office are a number of antipolice petitions dated October 1846. These bear signatures of nearly 1,000 ratepayers, assessed for the police tax at from £2 to £400 a year, and come from dozens of towns, including tiny Croxden, where "every rate-payer" (all twenty-six) protested. The inhabitants' complaints, after four years' experience with the new police, were all much the same. "We do not find," wrote 153 Ashley ratepayers, "that our property or persons are any better protected with the present force than we were *before they were sent to us*" (my emphasis). Petitioners from the parishes of Abbott's Bromley and Hamstall Ridware "do not attribute any apparent diminution of crime to the efforts of the Rural Police, but to the general improvement of Trade & an increased demand for labour." Source: Q/ACp/3, Staffordshire Record Office, Stafford. In Bedfordshire in 1842, ninety-seven parishes, or two-thirds of the total number in the county, petitioned for the abolition of the new police. Emsley, "Bedfordshire Police," p. 87.

65 5 & 6 Vict., c. 109. *Hansard* 62:1177 (introduced, 26 Apr.); 65:671 (Third Reading, Commons, 27 July), 1061 (Third Reading, Lords, 5 Aug.), 1301 (royal assent, 12 Aug. 1842). Copies of an earlier bill are in Public Bills, *PP 1841* (59, 369), 1:271–8.

66 F. W. Maitland, *Justice and Police* (London: Macmillan, 1885), p. 108. Radzino-

wicz, *ECL*, 4:272; Foster, *Class Struggle*, p. 60. See also Critchley, *Police*, pp. 92−4.

67 For a list of parishes, unions, and districts establishing a system of paid constables under 5 & 6 Vict., c. 109 (1842), see *PP 1846* (715), 34:785−90. Critchley, *Police*, p. 94; Mather, *Public Order*, p. 78 nn. 3, 4.

68 Ashley petitioners, 19 Oct. 1846, Quarter Sessions, Q/ACp/3, Staffordshire R. O., Stafford.

69 Lowe, "Lancashire Constabulary," p. 45; Emsley, "Bedfordshire Police," pp. 82−5; Critchley, *Police*, pp. 158−9; Midwinter, *Social Administration*, pp. 158−60; and especially Storch, "Domestic Missionary," passim, and "Blue Locusts," pp. 66, 84 (quotations).

70 Philips, *Crime*, p. 85; and Storch, "Blue Locusts," p. 80. General Napier reported that in "moving on" a party of workingmen in Colne, Lancashire, one (Irish?) constable "prided himself on what he termed slating them: i.e. breaking their heads with his staff." Napier to Home Office, 15 Aug. 1840, in HO 40/58 and in Napier, *Life*, 2:138. "Slating" was a term used by Dublin Ribbonmen to describe the beatings given those who defied their wishes in the regulation of trade disputes.

71 E. P. Thompson, "Time, Work-Discipline, and Industrial Capitalism," *Past & Present* 38 (Dec. 1967):56−97; Robert W. Malcolmson, *Popular Recreations in English Society 1700−1850* (Cambridge: Cambridge University Press, 1973), ch. 7; Francis Hearn, *Domination, Legitimation, and Resistance: The Incorporation of the Nineteenth-Century English Working Class* (Westport, Conn.: Greenwood Press, 1978), esp. chs. 4, 6; Robert D. Storch, ed., *Popular Culture and Custom in Nineteenth-Century England* (New York: St. Martin's Press, 1982). For a revisionist interpretation that downplays the importance of repressive state intervention in the evolution of new working-class customs and time management, see Hugh Cunningham, *Leisure in the Industrial Revolution, c. 1780−1880* (New York: St. Martin's Press, 1980).

72 Storch, "Blue Locusts," p. 71.

73 Phillipps to J. S. Pakington, MP, 7 Nov. 1839, HO 65/4/7.

74 For names, previous occupations, and date and county of appointment, see HO 65/4/1−129, Lefroy at ff. 8−10 and Harris at ff. 24−6.

75 On Woodford, see HO 65/4/34 and "First Report of the Select Committee appointed to consider the Expediency of adopting a more Uniform System of Police in England and Wales . . .," *PP 1852−3* (603), 36:QQ. 1529−1720. On the better-known McHardy, see HO 65/4/63; "First Report," *PP 1852−3* (603), 36:QQ. 676−819; "Second Report," *PP 1852−3* (715), 36:QQ. 3389−96, 3809−14, and App. 1 at pp. 300−29; Radzinowicz, *ECL*, 4:284−6; and Emsley, "Bedfordshire Police," pp. 76−7.

76 On Eve, see HO 65/4/22, 108, 117. On Oakes, see HO 65/4/45;*Hansard* 61:1078−84 and 62:1171−5; "Rural Police (Norfolk)," *PP 1842* (159, 322), 32:675−90; Mather, *Public Order*, p. 136 n. 5; and Radzinowicz, *ECL*, 4:270.

77 Under-Secretary Fox Maule to Clerk of the Peace, County Gloucester, 18 Oct. 1839, HO 65/4/1; and *PP 1852−3* (603), 36:QQ. 2100−4, 2113.

78 For these biographical details I am indebted to David Philips, *Crime*, pp. 65, 76, 92 n. 54. "There is no mention," notes Philips, "in any of his [Hatton's] testimonials [from Irish landowners and magistrates] of commendation for more 'normal' police duties − the stress is on riot control and repression of disorders" (p. 76).

79 Critchley, *Police*, pp. 144−7.

80 Irish Constabulary register, HO 184/54, appendix, "1841"; Lowe, "Lancashire Constabulary," p. 46.

81 Philips, *Crime*, Tables 8 and 9, p. 73.

82 Critchley, *Police*, p. 343, lists thirty-six counties and thirty-five boroughs that

have compiled brief histories of their police; judging by his footnotes, he has used them sparingly. In his recent study of the early Bedfordshire police, Clive Emsley reports that "the origins and background of the men remain largely a mystery." "Bedfordshire Police," pp. 76-7.

83 One of the many men active in police forces in both islands was Sir William Nott-Bower. Chief Constable of Liverpool and later Police Commissioner of the City of London, Nott-Bower had early in his career served a short, unhappy stint in the Irish constabulary. See his autobiography, *Fifty-Two Years a Policeman* (London: Edward Arnold, 1926), pp. 86-8.

84 Midwinter, *Social Administration*, pp. 158-60, quotation on p. 160.

85 Ibid., p. 158; Philips, *Crime*, pp. 65-8, quotation on p. 68.

86 Lowe, "Lancashire Constabulary," Tables 3 and 4, pp. 55, 57. Turnover in the small government police force in Bolton was also great. In a force whose strength hovered at between thirty and forty men, a total of eighty-one constables were dismissed and fifty-seven resigned in 1839-42. Midwinter, *Social Administration*, p. 158.

87 Philips, *Crime*, pp. 65-7.

88 Emsley, "Bedfordshire Police," p. 77; Critchley, *Police*, p. 147. See also W. L. Burn, *The Age of Equipoise* (New York: W. W. Norton, 1965), pp. 172-3.

89 A good brief survey is I. Donnachie, *Britain and Ireland in the 1840s*, prepared for the Open University (Milton Keynes: Open University Press, 1976), pp. 84.

90 Peel showed up in Ostend, ready to redeem his honor, but O'Connell, on his way to the Continent, was arrested in London. Norman Gash, *Mr. Secretary Peel: The Life of Sir Robert Peel to 1830* (Cambridge, Mass.: Harvard University Press, 1961), pp. 162-7.

91 I subscribe to F. C. Mather's interpretation. On the Plug Plot disorders, see G. Kitson Clark, "Hunger and Politics in 1842," *J. Mod. Hist* 25 (1953):355-74; Rose, "Plug Plots," pp. 75-112 (for full title, see n. 31, this chapter); F. C. Mather, "The General Strike of 1842: A Study in Leadership, Organization and the Threat of Revolution during the Plug Plot Disturbances," in Stevenson and Quinault, eds., *Popular Protest* (1974), pp. 115-40; Stevenson, *Disturbances* (1979), pp. 262-6; and Mick Jenkins, *The General Strike of 1842* (London: Lawrence and Wishart, 1980). For a sociological analysis, see Brian R. Brown, "Industrial Capitalism, Conflict, and Working-Class Contention in Lancashire, 1842," in Louise and Charles Tilly, eds., *Class Conflict and Collective Action* (Beverly Hills, Calif.: Sage, 1981), pp. 111-41. I have also drawn on an ancient document, my 1967 Harvard graduate seminar paper for Prof. David Landes, "The Plug Plot Riots of 1842: A Study of Their Causes, Character, and Consequences."

92 Chartist petition, presented by T. Duncombe: *Hansard* 63:13-91, 3 May 1842 (Daniel O'Connell voting with the minority of forty-nine MPs). Peel's friend, John Wilson Croker, believed that the riots of the summer of 1842 were the result of a "plot" by Corn Law Repealers and Chartists; see n. 100, this chapter. On the Corn Law agitation, see the recent studies by Paul Adelman, *Victorian Radicalism: The Middle Class Experience* (London: Longman, 1984), ch. 1; and Norman Longmate, *The Breadstealers: The Fight Against the Corn Laws, 1838-1846* (New York: St. Martin's Press, 1984).

93 *The Times*, 8 Aug. 1842; R. C. O. Matthews, *A Study in Trade-Cycle History: Economic Fluctuations in Great Britain, 1833-1842* (Cambridge: Cambridge University Press, 1954), pp. 142-9; Kitson Clark, "Hunger and Politics," p. 356; B. R. Mitchell and P. Deane, *Abstract of British Historical Statistics* (Cambridge: Cambridge University Press, 1962), pp. 245-6, 410.

94 *Annual Register* 84 (1842):Chronicle, 133-4, 157-9; "Report of the Midland Mining Commission, South Staffordshire," *PP* 1843 (508), 13:22-6, 109-26; Rose, "Plug Plots," pp. 91-109; Rudé, *Crowd*, pp. 183-91; Mather, "General Strike," pp. 117-18; Philips, *Crime*, pp. 271-2, and his essay "Riots," in

Stevenson and Quinault, eds., *Popular Protest*, pp. 153—7; and Jenkins, *Strike*, ch. 3.

95 Mather, "General Strike," pp. 115—16, 135 n. 3, lists fifteen counties as affected but says that "in some ... the movement was not very serious."

96 Burslem, quoted in Stevenson, *Disturbances*, p. 264. Pollock, quoted in *The Trial of Feargus O'Connor, Esq., and 58 Others at Lancaster, on a Charge of Sedition, Conspiracy, Tumult, and Riot* [hereafter, *Trial*] (Manchester: A. Heywood, and London: J. Cleave, 1843), p. 12.

97 O'Connor on machinery: *Northern Star*, 5 Mar. 1842; see also the address of the Ashton-under-Lyne operatives, in *Trial*, p. 253. On the Irish role, see Mather, "General Strike," pp. 133—4, 139 n. 77; for background, see E. D. Steele, "The Irish Presence in the North of England," *Northern History* 12 (1976):220—41. Mather observes that "the role of Irish discontents in the Plug Plot is a subject which, so far as I am aware, has never been investigated, but, to judge by the names of men who played a leading role in fomenting it ... [is] one which would repay exploration" (p.134). On the list of those indicted at the Yorkshire Assizes, September 1842, Irish names are virtually absent, and at the great Lancaster state trial of March 1843, not a half dozen of the fifty-eight bore Irish names (*Northern Star*, 10 Sept. 1842; *Trial*, p. 2). The Irish appear to have been more active as agitators than as rioters.

98 Rose, "Plug Plots," pp. 91—6; Jenkins, *Strike*, pp. 72—90, 197—9; Radzinowicz, *ECL*, 4:278; Mather, *Public Order*, p. 74 n. 1. Police Commissioner Shaw later publicly berated Stipendiary Magistrate Maude for his laxity in responding to the mobs' takeover of Manchester on 9 August (Shaw's letter, 11 Oct., to *The Times*, quoted in *Manchester Guardian*, Supplement, 15 Oct. 1842). Earlier, the *Guardian* (24 Aug. 1842) had editorialized that Manchester's police "might just as well have been at Liverpool."

99 HO 65/4/224—5; Philips, *Crime*, pp. 55, 270—2; Mather, *Public Order*, p. 138.

100 Queen Victoria to Peel, 17 Aug. 1842, in Peel Papers, BL Add. MS 40434, quoted in Mather, *Public Order*, p. 33. *The Times* (12 Aug.) joined Feargus O'Connor (*Northern Star*, 20 Aug. 1842) in denouncing "the Anti—Corn Law League Riots." O'Connor charged that the cotton masters were using the workers as front-line troops to repeal the Corn Laws; for Graham, the "plot" consisted of a tentative alliance of Anti-Corn Law Leaguers, Chartists, and trade union leaders bent on unseating the protectionist Tory Government. (See also n. 114, this chapter.) J. W. Croker was the first to present this interpretation in print; see *Quarterly Review* 71 (1842):244—314. Croker noted that 147 of 172 JPs in key disturbed towns were Whig or Radical; of 45 JPs in Manchester (29—4) and Stockport (12—0), only 4 were Tories (*QR* 71:249). Historians Henderson and Chaloner state that Graham supplied Croker with material for the article and Peel read the proofs. Friedrich Engels, *The Condition of the Working Class in England* [hereafter, *Condition*], written 1844—5, publ. in German, 1845, new ed., tr. and annotated by W. O. Henderson and W. H. Chaloner (Oxford: Blackwell, 1958), p. 261, editors' n. 4. For contemporary assessments that exonerated the Anti—Corn Law League, see *Westminster Review* 38 (1842):391—413 and *Edinburgh Review* 77 (1843): 190—227. Historians have found little evidence to support Croker's claim that the League *initiated* the disorders. See Rose, "Plug Plots," pp. 75—83; Read, "Chartism in Manchester," pp. 54—5; and Mather, "General Strike," pp. 119—20.

101 *Northern Star*, 13 Aug. 1842; Rose, "Plug Plots," pp. 91—6, 106—9.

102 *Northern Star*, 20 Aug. 1842; Rose, "Plug Plots," pp. 100—1; Mather, *Public Order*, p. 157; Jenkins, *Strike*, pp. 247—8; T. W. Reid and Naomi Reid, "The 1842 'Plug Plot' in Stockport," *Intl. Rev. Soc. Hist.* 24 (1979):55—79. Mayor Nelstropp of Stockport told the crowd, "There was plenty in the store-rooms and mills, and if they would not give it [to] them, take it"; see also Figure 11.2,

this book. A mill owner, Mr. Howard, who had requested troops, was told "to be good-tempered with the people, and not to interfere with them." *Trial*, pp. 30, 48; *Quarterly Review* 71:282, 295. General Warre (*DNB* 19:407–8) advised JPs to "temporize with the people where they feel themselves quite unequal to enforce the law." Warre to Home Office, 11 Aug. 1842, HO 45/268, cited in Mather, *Public Order*, p. 155 n. 3.

103 Peel, *Private Papers*, 2:537; Sir Robert Peel, *The Private Letters of Sir Robert Peel*, ed. George Peel (London: J. Murray, 1920), pp. 201–2.

104 *Manchester Guardian*, 17 Aug. 1842; Read, "Chartism in Manchester," p. 55 n. 4; Jenkins, *Strike*, pp. 165–71; Mather, *Public Order*, pp. 98–9, 162–4, and his article "The Railways, the Electric Telegraph, and Public Order During the Chartist Period, 1837–1848," *History* 38 (1953):44. Crowds at Stockport and on the southern outskirts of Manchester attempted to tear up the railway tracks, and were prevented from doing so only by the timely arrival of troops (*John Bull*, 13 Aug. 1842). Note General Napier's remark in 1839 that he did not place much reliance upon "railways in case of disturbance, as they would be so easily destroyed." Letter to Phillipps, 27 June 1839, HO 40/53/527.

105 *Northern Star*, 20 Aug. 1842; *John Bull*, 13 Aug. 1842; Mather, *Public Order*, pp. 88–9, 155–6; Jenkins, *Strike*, pp. 191–7.

106 *Northern Star*, 13 Aug. 1842; Kitson Clark, "Hunger and Politics," p. 363; Jenkins, *Strike*, pp. 83–8.

107 *John Bull*, 20 Aug. 1842; Philips, "Riots," p. 157; Jenkins, *Strike*, map, p. 62, and pp. 96–104; Mather, *Public Order*, pp. 174–5, 230. Leveson Gower, MP for South Lancashire, 1835–46, and a prolific writer of history and literature, had assumed the name Egerton after the death of his father in 1833. *DNB* 6:571–2.

108 Rudé's account yields a total of five rioters and two policemen killed (*Crowd*, pp. 183–91); Stevenson's, seven rioters and two policemen (*Disturbances*, pp. 262–6); Jenkins's, six rioters (*Strike*, pp. 61–2, 98, 104).

109 Melbourne, quoted in Mather, *Public Order*, p. 2; Graham quoted, and also "force," in Mather, "General Strike," p. 115.

110 The motion by Thomas Duncombe, Chartist MP, for the censure of Lord Abinger, presiding justice at the Lancashire special commission, was defeated in the Commons by a vote of 228–73. *Hansard* 66:1038–1143, 21 Feb. 1843; *Northern Star*, 25 Feb. 1843.

111 Radzinowicz, *ECL*, 4:250, citing "Progress of Crime in the United Kingdom," *Journal of the Statistical Society* 6 (1843):226; cf. Jenkins, *Strike*, p. 222. *Northern Star*, 10 Sept. 1842. Significantly, it was Friedrich Engels who noted that "death or the galleys face the *French* worker who takes part in an armed rising." *Condition*, p. 255, my emphasis.

112 *Annual Register* 84 (1842): Chronicle, 163; Radzinowicz, *ECL*, 4:249. A. G. L. Shaw, *Convicts and the Colonies* (London: Faber and Faber, 1966), p. 153, says that seventy-two trade unionists and Chartists were *actually* transported between 1839 and 1842. Justice Rolfe, who had also been one of the judges on the Stafford Special Commission, remarked at O'Connor's trial at Lancaster, in March 1843, that violence in Staffordshire had been "infinitely more terrible than here." Yet even in Staffordshire, Rolfe noted, "there was ample evidence to satisfy my mind of the great moral advance in the least educated and most suffering parts of the population ...; because, even there, there was a steady absence [*sic*; abstention?] from personal violence, though not from violence as to property." *Trial*, p. 374.

113 Mather, *Public Order*, p. 43. See A. P. Donajgrodzki, "Sir James Graham at the Home Office," *Hist. Jour.* 20 (1977):97–120.

114 The variety of goals is explored in Mather, "General Strike," especially pp. 119–20, 132–5. The theme of Chartists as pawns of the Anti–Corn Law League runs through the editions of O'Connor's *Northern Star* from June 1842 on. Engels, too, blamed the League. "Masses of workers were turned loose on the

streets by their employers whether they liked it or not. They had no definite objective in view, and so could achieve nothing." *Condition*, p. 264. A recent writer, Mick Jenkins, sees the second half of the disorders, from mid−August on, as a workers' strike transformed into "class struggle" wherein "working−class consciousness asserts itself' (*Strike*, chs. 7, 11).

115 According to Engels, "the angry strikers showed very great self-control . . . [and] patient fortitude and determination. . . . [The] *unarmed* crowds . . . were easily held in check by *a handful* of dragoons and police." *Condition*, pp. 256−7, 264, my emphases. Engels was not an eyewitness to the riots (ibid., p. 261 n. 4).

116 Peel, *Private Papers*, 2:542.

117 Graham to JPs, Newcastle-under-Lyme, 23 Sept. 1842, HO 45/260. Philips, *Crime*, pp. 56−8; Critchley, *Police*, pp. 94−7.

118 Inquiry: HO 45/347, 350; Sir James Graham, *The Life and Letters of Sir James Graham, 2nd Baronet of Netherby*, ed. Charles Stuart Parker, 2 vols. (London: J. Murray, 1907), 1:333−6; Chadwick, "Cons. Force. First Draft of evidence on Rural Police," undated [?1836−7], in Chadwick MS 3.

119 Goulburn to Graham, n.d., and Peel to Graham, 18 Nov. 1842, in Graham, *Life and Letters*, 1:333−5.

120 6 & 7 Vict., c. 95, amended by 9 Vict., c. 9 (1846). For instructions to pensioners, with warnings about penalties for any misbehavior, see *PP 1844* (18, 625), 33:195−204.

121 Mather, *Public Order*, pp. 80, 89−90, 151.

122 7 & 8 Vict., c. 85, amending 5 & 6 Vict., c. 55. Mather, "Railways," p. 44, and *Public Order*, pp. 162, 170−2; Mitchell and Deane, *Abstract*, p. 225.

123 English suffrage reform in 1832 raised the proportion of voters in the total adult male population to 1:5; in Ireland after Emancipation, the ratio fell to 1:20 and did not rise to 1:6 until 1869. Chris Cook and Brendan Keith, *British Historical Facts 1830−1900* (New York: St. Martin's Press, 1975), pp. 115−19, 124−6. On Irish municipal reform, see Angus Macintyre, *The Liberator: Daniel O'Connell and the Irish Party, 1830−1847* (New York: Macmillan, 1965), ch. 7.

124 For the Irish−Whig alliance and its breakdown, see Macintyre, *Liberator*, ch. 2 and ch. 4, esp. pp. 163−6; for the background to Repeal, see Lawrence J. McCaffrey, *Daniel O'Connell and the Repeal Year* (Lexington: University of Kentucky Press, 1966), ch. 1.

125 On the Irish Poor Law, see R. B. McDowell, "Ireland on the Eve of the Famine," in R. Dudley Edwards and T. Desmond Williams, eds., *The Great Famine: Studies in Irish History, 1845−52* (New York: New York University Press, 1957; repr., New York: Russell & Russell, 1976), pp. 40−55; Macintyre, *Liberator*, ch. 6; and Gerard O'Brien, "The Establishment of Poor-Law Unions in Ireland, 1838−43," *I.H.S.* 23 (Nov. 1982):97−120.

126 *Hansard* 73:1527−8, 1616; 74:508−13. For details of the forces employed and the amounts collected and those remaining uncollected, see for 1843, *PP 1844* (186, 218), 40:785, 797; for 1845−7, *PP 1848* (766, 790, 863), 55:27, 141, 231; and for 1846−8, *PP 1849* (208, 1096), 47:735, 763. On the crisis in the collection of poor rates, see McDowell, "Eve of Famine," p. 54; Cecil Woodham-Smith, *The Great Hunger* (New York: Harper & Row, 1962; repr., New York: E. P. Dutton, 1980), pp. 174−5; and McCaffrey, *O'Connell*, pp. 17−20, 34−8.

127 McCaffrey, *O'Connell*, pp. 12−15, 21−34, 39−50, 54 ("crafty"). For background, see Thomas N. Brown, "Nationalism and the Irish Peasant, 1800−1848," *Review of Politics* 15 (Oct. 1953):403−45.

128 Troop levels in 1842−3 averaged 15,000, a figure well below the average of 17,000 for 1835−41 and 21,000 for 1830−4. The lowest point, under 13,000, was reached in May 1842 and represented, in Lord Stanley's words, "the least military force that has ever been maintained in Ireland since the Union." *Hansard* 72:1071, 16 Feb. 1844.

129 Quotations: Daniel O'Connell, *The Correspondence of Daniel O'Connell, The Liberator*, ed. W. J. Fitzpatrick, 2 vols. (London: J. Murray, 1888), 2:324, 433, 436. See also "The Queen against O'Connell," *Reports of State Trials*, ed. Sir John Macdonell, 8 vols. (London: Eyre & Spottiswoode, 1888–98), 5:394–5.

130 *State Trials* 5:110–38, 153–65, 195, 206, 266, 282, 627, 629, 632; O'Connell, *Correspondence*, 2:434. The *Times*'s term, "monster meeting," which O'Connell adopted, is discussed in McCaffrey, *O'Connell*, pp. 52–3.

131 *State Trials* 5:114–15, 126, 252, 268, 275, 296–7, 411, 613, 632; *Annual Register* 85 (1843):History, 224–40. See also McCaffrey, *O'Connell*, pp. 53–7, and Kevin Nowlan, *The Politics of Repeal: A Study in the Relations Between Great Britain and Ireland, 1841–50* (London: Routledge & Kegan Paul, 1965), pp. 41–7, 52–8. On the priests' roles, based on secret constabulary reports printed for Peel's cabinet, see Donal Kerr, *Peel, Priests and Politics: Sir Robert Peel's Administration and the Roman Catholic Church in Ireland, 1841–1846* (Oxford: Clarendon Press, 1982), pp. 81–7. The only instance of violence came in May, at Clones, Monaghan, when some Orangemen attacked and killed a Catholic cobbler on his way home from a small Repeal meeting. McCaffrey, *O'Connell*, p. 57.

132 *Holbrooke's Railway and Parliamentary Map of Ireland* (Dublin, Feb. 1846), Map Room, Pusey Library, Harvard University; and "Return of all Permanent Barracks in the United Kingdom," *PP 1847* (169), 36:376–405.

133 *State Trials* 5:252, 401 (quotations); Nowlan, *Repeal*, p. 55; McCaffrey, *O'Connell*, pp. 28, 71, 151 n. 38, 185–8, 208 n. 63.

134 Peel, *Private Papers*, 3:46–51; McCaffrey, *O'Connell*, p. 37 n. 36; Macintyre, *Liberator*, p. 268.

135 On the "Unionist Reactions to Repeal" and Peel's attitudes, see McCaffrey, *O'Connell*, chs. 3, 4, respectively; on Roden, see ibid., pp. 102, 113, 129–30.

136 Ibid., pp. 83 ("maniac"), 89, 141.

137 Ibid., pp. 146, 151; Nowlan, *Repeal*, p. 52.

138 Macintyre, *Liberator*, p. 265; Nowlan, *Repeal*, p. 49. As McCaffrey explains, Peel realized that "the Anti–Corn Law League was modelled on O'Connell's recipe for popular agitation, and any legislation designed to destroy the Repeal movement would automatically embrace the [English] free traders as well. Therefore any attack on the [Irish] Repeal Association would force Whigs, Chartists, Radicals, free traders, and all those 'who are in favor of democracy or of mischief and confusion' to rally around O'Connell." *O'Connell*, p. 147, quoting Peel to Irish Lord Lieutenant De Grey, 12 June 1843, Peel Papers, BL Add. MS 40478.

139 "Dismissal of Magistrates (Ireland)," *Hansard* 69:981–4, 1064–96, 1289–1300, 26 and 30 May, 9 June; and 70:1099–1189, 14 July 1843. See also Macintyre, *Liberator*, p. 270; Nowlan, *Repeal*, pp. 46–7; McCaffrey, *O'Connell*, pp. 60–2. Among the JPs who voluntarily resigned their commissions as a gesture of protest was William Smith O'Brien, MP, who a few years later would emerge as a leader of the 1848 Rising.

140 McCaffrey, *O'Connell*, pp. 113–34. For the Irish arms bill debates, see *Hansard* 69:(Commons) 996–1063, 1098–1221, 1578–1614, 29 May–15 June; 70:15–85, 101–45, 275–339, 453–70, 1092–9, 1191–1200, 1359–73, 16 June–27 July; and 71:426–71 (Third Reading, 9 Aug.), (Lords) 690–741, 897–906, 15 and 17 Aug. 1843. William Smith O'Brien interrupted the debates with his motion on 4 July for an inquiry into "the causes of the discontent prevailing in Ireland." O'Brien's motion was defeated, 243–164, but it triggered much debate on "the state of Ireland"; see *Hansard* 70:630–719, 746–823, 831–903, 910–1092, 4, 7, and 10–12 July 1843. The Irish Arms Act, 6 & 7 Vict., c. 74, was much weaker than Peel's original bill. The act was to be in effect for two, not five, years; and the punishment for possession of an unlicensed firearm was cut from seven years' transportation to imprisonment for one or three years for a first or second offense, respectively.

141 McCaffrey, *O'Connell*, pp. 138, 150−1, 205−6. On military investigations into what turned out to be unfounded rumors of disloyalty among the Queen's troops, see ibid., pp. 144, 146 n. 28.

142 Ibid., pp. 171, 176−80, 183−8.

143 Ibid., pp. 191−9; Graham, *Life and Letters*, 1:367−9, 397−400; Nowlan, *Repeal*, pp. 56−8. O'Connell was arrested on 14 October 1843, bailed, tried and convicted of sedition in February 1844, and sentenced to one year in prison (Richmond Gaol, Dublin), February to August 1844. In September the Law Lords, by a vote of 3−2, overturned his conviction. *State Trials* 5:91−3, 261−3, 306−7, 659−65, 724−7; McCaffrey, *O'Connell*, pp. 206−12.

144 O'Connell, *Correspondence*, 2:324.

145 McCaffrey, *O'Connell*, p. 9. Peel: *Hansard* 69:25, 9 May 1843; and also 69:331−2, 15 May, and 70:291−302, 23 June 1843.

146 The subject was raised in the House of Commons following a question about a street brawl involving drunken soldiers ("Military Outrage at Brighton") and debate on Sir Robert Peel's motion for "A Vote of Thanks to Sir Charles Napier and the Army in Scinde" (carried by 164−9). *Hansard* 72:514, 525−80, 12 Feb. 1844. The next evening, in the Lords, the Marquess of Normanby called for debate on the state of Ireland (*Hansard* 72:602−80, Normanby's speech on cols. 602−35). Concurrently, Lord John Russell in the Commons made a similar motion to discuss the present condition of Ireland (*Hansard* 72:683−787, Russell on cols. 683−726). The ensuing debates, in which Macaulay and Buller spoke (see the epigraph at the beginning of Chapter 11, this book) are in *Hansard* 72: 808−58 (Commons), 14 Feb.; 858−925 (Lords), 15 Feb.; 925−93 (C), 15 Feb.; 998−1000 (L), 16 Feb.; 1001−96 (C), 16 Feb.; 1106−1208 (C), 19 Feb.; 1209−1312 (C), 20 Feb.; 1331−64 (C), 21 Feb. 1844. And *Hansard* 73:23−73 (C), 22 Feb.; 135−271 (C), 23 Feb. 1844. Russell's motion was defeated on 23 February, the ninth night of debate, by a vote of 324−225.

147 Graham to Peel, 17 Oct. 1843, Peel Papers, BL Add. MS 40449 ff. 93−4, quoted in Nowlan, *Repeal*, p. 64.

148 The Devon Commission issued its massive report on the eve of the Famine. See "Report from Her Majesty's Commissioners of Enquiry on the State of the Law and Practice in respect to the Occupation of Land in Ireland," in 4 vols., *PP 1845* (605, 606), 19; (616), 20; (657), 21; and (672, 673), 22. On the Tory reforms in Ireland, see Macintyre, *Liberator*, pp. 280−4; Nowlan, *Repeal*, pp. 59−72; and McCaffrey, *O'Connell*, pp. 170−1, 214−37. On Maynooth and the "godless colleges," see Kerr, *Peel, Priests and Politics*, chs. 6, 7.

149 Graham to Peel, 28 Aug. 1847, Peel Papers, 40452 ff. 230−1, quoted in Nowlan, *Politics*, p. 161. Agrarian crime statistics cited in *Hansard* 83:1348−9 (23 Feb.), 85:337−40 (Sir J. Graham, 30 Mar.), and 87:646−7 (18 June 1846); and *Hansard* 95:277 (Sir G. Grey, 29 Nov. 1847). See also county committals in *PP 1846* (696), 35:176−7; *PP 1850* (1159), 54:140−1. Quotations: *Hansard* 83:1371 ("uninhabitable," Henry Brougham, 23 Feb.), and 85:1118 ("frightful," Peel, 27 Apr. 1846); and *Hansard* 95:298−9 ("running," Grey; and "emotion," S. Howley, Tipperary, quoted by Grey, 29 Nov.), 353 ("hereditary," Peel, 29 Nov.), and 983 ("not looked upon as murders, but rather as executions," John Bright, 13 Dec. 1847).

150 "Broad-day": *Hansard* 85:310 (Lord George Bentinck, 30 Mar. 1846). McLeod: *Hansard* 83:1356. Roe: listed in "Return of Counties ... proclaimed under the Crime and Outrage Act, 1847," *PP 1860* (195), 57:849. Mahon: *Hansard* 95:283−5, 1198−1202; Woodham-Smith, *Hunger*, pp. 324−5; *Annual Register* 90 (1848):Chronicle, 90. Sir James Graham stated that of 446 homicides in 1842−5, 261 were of laborers, servants, wood rangers, and "herds"; 91, farmers and their sons; 13, bailiffs and land stewards; and 10 "gentlemen." *Hansard* 87:853, 22 June 1846. Cf. the tabulations in Michael Beames, *Peasants and Power: The Whiteboy*

Movements and Their Control in Pre-Famine Ireland (New York: St. Martin's Press, 1983), App. 1, 2, pp. 220−32, for "assassination victims," 1806−47, and "assaults," January−May 1846.

151 The string of grisly *homicides*, recounted in great detail in Parliament, included the cases of Thomas Macnamara, Limerick, battered by spades, "the back of his head beaten in," for leasing land at a higher price than the previous tenant; a wood ranger in Cavan who was unpopular for prosecuting trespassers (his pregnant wife and their child were wounded by gunshots, the widow-to-be delivering a stillborn baby and the child sustaining brain damage); a "respectable farmer" in Clare, shot in the face, beaten with gun butts and clubs, his leg broken and "his head in a most frightful state"; and also in Clare a man, who had just leased a piece of land, shot in the face and stabbed in the back of his head with a sharp instrument. Those who *survived* murder attempts included an eighty-year-old woman, shot at for refusing to turn out two servants; and, over the issue of cottier rents, one Thomas Cowan, beaten "severely" by sixteen men who during the ordeal "compelled his wife to hold a candle for them." *Hansard* 83:1350−3, 1356−8; and 85:309, 343. For other incidents, see *Hansard* 83:1359−61, 1373−5; 84:687−91; 85:307−10, 333−60, 1097−1101, 1111−17; and 87:152−66, 177−80, 387−97, 425−8, 502−7, 645−50, 844−54. For extensive case-by-case descriptions, see also the reports and returns in "Homicides (Ireland)," *PP 1846* (179, 220, 363), 35:261−306.

152 *Hansard* 83:1248, 1348−89 (20 and 23 Feb., Lords); and 85:288−365 (30 Mar. 1846, Commons). "Overmatch": *Hansard* 83:1359 (Earl of St. Germans, 23 Feb. 1846).

153 For the Corn Law debates, see *Hansard* 86, passim. See also Betty Kemp, "Reflections on the Repeal of the Corn Laws," *Victorian Studies* 5 (Mar. 1962):189−204; and Norman Gash, *Sir Robert Peel: The Life of Sir Robert Peel after 1830* (Totowa, N.J.: Rowman and Littlefield, 1972), pp. 567−615. For the Irish coercion bill, debated on eighteen nights from February through June 1846, see *Hansard* 83: (Lords) 1348−89; and 84:684−716, 840−5, 976−7. And *Hansard* 85: (Commons) 288−365, 372−5, 492−569, 609−51, 703−86, 1022−47, 1084−1141, 1352−1409; and 87:129−96, 382−437, 482−539, 637−66, 818−68.

154 *Hansard* 87:939−63 (Corn Laws), 964−1032 (Ireland).

155 G. Shaw Lefevre, *Peel and O'Connell* (London: K. Paul, Trench, 1887; repr., Port Washington, N.Y.: Kennikat Press, 1970), pp. 292−5; Seán Ó Faolain, *King of the Beggars* (New York: Viking Press, 1938; repr., Westport, Conn.: Greenwood Press, 1975), pp. 321−9; Gash, *Peel ... after 1830*, pp. 697−701.

156 *Hansard* 88:876−9 ("boon," col. 877, Mr. Labouchere, Irish Chief Secretary); in the Commons, only Chartist MP T. Duncombe opposed the bill as "unconstitutional" (cols. 877−8). Monteagle, in Lords, *Hansard* 88:1021; royal assent, 28 Aug. 1846.

157 "An Act to provide for removing the Charge of the Constabulary Force in *Ireland* from the Counties; and for enlarging the Reserve Force ...," 9 & 10 Vict., c. 97 s. 4, which amended 2 & 3 Vict., c. 75. On Grey, see *DNB* 8:626−7.

158 *Hansard* 95: (Commons) 270−366 (29 Nov. 1847, Grey's speech on cols. 270−312, Peel's on cols. 347−55), 701−50 (Grattan on cols. 720−6, "parley" on col. 726), 860−923 (Second Reading), 936−62, 974−91 (Third Reading; W. S. O'Brien on cols. 976−9); 95: (Lords) 1123, 1182, 1230, 1341−2, 1404 (royal assent, 20 Dec. 1847). O'Connor's remarks, *Hansard* 95:317−21, 728−38, 889−93, 953. The other principal opponents were John and Maurice O'Connell (*Hansard* 95:312−17, 701−13, 867−76, 897−905, 974−6). Two Chartist MPs, T. Wakley (Finsbury) and J. Brotherton (Salford), cited the need for the bill (Mr. Wakley saying that "crimes in Ireland appeared to be of so horrible a character"), although only Brotherton voted for its introduction. *Hansard* 95:361−2.

159 "Return of Counties ... or Baronies ... proclaimed under the Crime and Outrage Act, 1847 ...," *PP 1860* (195), 57:849−54.

160 *Hansard* 95:318. Recent scholarship has increased traditional estimates of Famine mortality from c. 800,000 to c. 1.1 to 1.5 million persons. See Joek Mokyr, "The Deadly Fungus: An Econometric Investigation into the Short-Term Demographic Impact of the Irish Famine, 1846−51," in Julian L. Simon, ed., *Research in Population Economics, Vol. 2* (Greenwich, Conn.: Jai Press, 1980), pp. 237−77; and Liam Kennedy, "Studies in Irish Econometric History," *I.H.S.* 23 (May 1983):206−13. See also Kerby A. Miller, *Emigrants and Exiles: Ireland and the Irish Exodus to North America* (New York: Oxford University Press, 1985), ch. 7.

161 Woodham-Smith, *Hunger*, pp. 296−8, 302−3. Sir Charles James Napier wrote London that he could arrange shipment of 11,000 tons of wheat from India, but his offer was treated "with scorn" by Russell's Government. Letter to H. Napier, 11 May 1847, in Napier, *Life*, 4:63; for his concern with the Irish Famine, see also *Life*, 4:87−8, 104, 117−20.

162 Gearóid Ó Tuathaigh, *Ireland before the Famine, 1798−1848* (Dublin: Gill and Macmillan, 1972), pp. 207−18; Woodham-Smith, *Hunger*, pp. 228−30 (Palmerston), 324−5 (Mahon); Thomas P. O'Neill, "The Organization and Administration of Relief, 1845−52," in Edwards and Williams, eds., *Famine*, pp. 241, 249, 253−5. On Gregory, who in 1841 had defeated former Irish Chief Secretary Viscount Morpeth for the Dublin City seat, see *DNB* 22 (Supplement):780−2. Farm sizes: Raymond Crotty, *Irish Agricultural Production: Its Volume and Structure* (Cork: Cork University Press, 1966), p. 49; F. S. L. Lyons, *Ireland since the Famine* (London: Weidenfeld and Nicolson, 1971), p. 41.

163 Committals, 1846−50: see "Return of the Number of ... Offenders committed for Trial ... at the Assizes and Sessions," *PP 1851* (1386), 46:195−6. Annual report on crime, Chief Secretary's Office, Dublin, printed in "Return of ... Offenders committed for Trial ... in the year 1848," *PP 1849* (1067), 44:131−2.

164 O'Neill, "Relief," pp. 216, 226, 237; Woodham-Smith, *Hunger*, pp. 122−39, 152−68, 173−87.

165 Constabulary size: HO 184/54, appendix; and "Return of the Constabulary Force ... in Ireland," 1 Jan. 1844, *PP 1844* (193), 43:35, and "Return," 1 Jan. 1849, *PP 1849* (316), 49:201. Terry Coleman, *Going to America* (New York: Pantheon Books, 1972), pp. 129−30; Woodham-Smith, *Hunger*, pp. 41, 115 ("harassed"), 123, 125, 168; and constabulary reports in HO 45/1080/2.

166 Quoted in Woodham-Smith, *Hunger*, pp. 31, 92, 111, 137, 168.

167 Ibid., pp. 147, 179−80.

168 O'Neill, "Relief," pp. 237, 259; Woodham-Smith, *Hunger*, pp. 124, 133, 139 ("screwed"), 179 ("wild animals"), 181−2, 198−9.

CHAPTER 12. 1848 AND AFTERMATH

1 William Langer, *The Revolutions of 1848* (New York: Harper & Row, 1971; reprint of chs. 10−14 in Langer, *Political and Social Upheaval*, Harper & Row, 1969), pp. 11−12, 28−32; Peter N. Stearns, *1848: The Revolutionary Tide in Europe* (New York: W. W. Norton, 1974), pp. 73−4, 91−2; George Fasel, *Europe in Upheaval: The Revolutions of 1848* (Chicago: Rand McNally, 1970), pp. 51, 146; and Georges Duveau, *1848: The Making of a Revolution*, tr. Anne Carter (New York: Random House, 1967), pp. 29−30, 57−9, 133−56. For the number of lives lost, see Langer, *Revolutions*, pp. 51−2; Stearns, *1848*, pp. 116, 121, 147−8, 200−1; Fasel, *Upheaval*, p. 68.

2 On 1848 in England, see John Saville, "Chartism in the Year of Revolution, 1848," *Modern Quarterly* 8 (Winter 1952−3):23−34; David Large, "London in the Year of Revolutions, 1848," in John Stevenson, ed., *London in the Age of Reform* (Oxford: Basil Blackwell, 1977), pp. 177−211; John Stevenson, *Popular Distur-*

bances in England 1700-1870 (London: Longman, 1979), pp. 266-74; Henry Weisser, "Chartism in 1848: Reflections on a Non-Revolution," *Albion* 13 (Spring 1981):12-26, and his book, *April 10: Challenge and Response in England in 1848* (Lanham. Md.: University Press of America, 1983); David Goodway, *London Chartism, 1838-1848* (Cambridge: Cambridge University Press, 1982), pp. 68-96, 111-49; and Dorothy Thompson, *The Chartists: Popular Politics in the Industrial Revolution* (New York: Pantheon Books, 1984), ch. 13.

3 Sir William P. MacArthur, "Medical History of the Famine," in R. Dudley Edwards and T. Desmond Williams, eds., *The Great Famine: Studies in Irish History 1845-52* (New York: New York University Press, 1957; repr., New York: Russell & Russell, 1976), pp. 260-315; Cecil Woodham-Smith, *The Great Hunger* (New York: Harper & Row, 1962; repr., New York: E. P. Dutton, 1980), esp. pp. 411-13; Arthur D. Gayer, W. W. Rostow, and A. J. Schwartz, *The Growth and Fluctuation of the British Economy 1790-1850* (Oxford: Clarendon Press, 1953; repr., New York: Barnes & Noble, 1975), pp. 304-41.

4 On the "plethora" of private police, see Leon Radzinowicz, *A History of English Criminal Law and its Administration from 1750* [hereafter, *ECL*], 4 vols. (London: Stevens & Sons, 1948-68), 4:271-7.

5 Stevenson, *Disturbances*, pp. 266-8; Large, "London in 1848," pp. 182-3, 184 ("rehearsal"), 186 ("demonstration"); Goodway, *London Chartism*, pp. 71-2, 111-16.

6 Of the forty-nine delegates, eight were from London; ten, Lancashire; ten, Yorkshire; thirteen, Scotland; and eight, Ireland.

7 Henry Weisser, "Chartism in 1848," p. 22; Malcolm I. Thomis and Peter Holt, *Threats of Revolution in Britain, 1789-1848* (Hamden, Conn.: Archon Books, 1977), p. 109.

8 George J. Holyoake, *Bygones Worth Remembering*, 2 vols. (London: T. F. Unwin, 1905), 1:75; Weisser, "Chartism in 1848," pp. 13, 24, 26. On Holyoake, see Joseph McCabe, *The Life and Letters of George Jacob Holyoake* (London: Watts & Co., 1908).

9 Large, "London in 1848," pp. 187, 188 ("overkill"); Goodway, *London Chartism*, pp. 72-4. Among those who took the "revolution" less than seriously was the humor magazine *Punch*; see vol. 14 (January-June 1848):109, 112, 115-16, 120-2, 130, 192; 15 (July-December 1848):2-4, 102.

10 Large, "London in 1848," pp. 185-6; Chadwick to Rowan, 8 Apr. 1848, Chadwick MS 1722, Papers of Edwin Chadwick, D. M. S. Watson Library, University College, University of London.

11 Mepol 2/63, PRO, London; Large, "London in 1848," p. 189; Goodway, *London Chartism*, pp. 133-6; Holyoake, *Bygones*, pp. 77-9. Karl Marx judged 10 April 1848 the beginning of "the European counter-revolution" (quoted in Weisser, *April 10*, p. 294).

12 Crowd size is discussed in Large, "London in 1848," p. 192; Goodway, *London Chartism*, pp. 136-40; and Weisser, *April 10*, pp. 115-16.

13 *Northern Star*, 15 Apr. 1848; Donald Read and Eric Glasgow, *Feargus O'Connor: Irishman and Chartist* (London: Edward Arnold, 1961), pp. 133-4 ("effusively"); Large, "London in 1848," p. 191.

14 *Blackwood's Magazine* 63:652, and 64:35; *Annual Register* 90 (1848):Chronicle, 50-4; *Punch* 14:122, 130; Read and Glasgow, *O'Connor*, p. 133; William L. Langer, "The Pattern of Urban Revolution in 1848," in Evelyn Acomb and Marvin Brown, Jr., eds., *French Society and Culture since the Old Regime* (New York: Holt, Rinehart & Winston, 1966), p. 95.

15 Sir William Napier, *The Life and Opinions of General Sir Charles James Napier*, 4 vols. (London: J. Murray, 1857), 2:69, Journal, 6 Aug. 1839. Holyoake, *Bygones*, pp. 75-83; Large, "London in 1848," pp. 186-93; Weisser, "Chartism in 1848," pp. 24-5, and his unpublished paper, "A Rehabilitation of Fearful Feargus, the

Cowardly Lion at Kennington Common," presented at the Western Conference on British Studies, Snowbird, Utah, October 1982.

16 *Punch* 14:122; Large, "London in 1848," pp. 190–2; Read and Glasgow, *O'Connor*, p. 134; Goodway, *London Chartism*, pp. 76–7. For O'Connor's imbroglio with Mr. W. Cripps, MP for Circencester, over bogus signatures on the monster petition, see *Hansard* 98:284–301, 13 Apr. 1848.

17 Mepol 2/65; *Northern Star*, 15 Apr. 1848; Holyoake, *Bygones*, p. 73. Large, "London in 1848," p. 188; and Henry Weisser, "The People in Arms or the Bludgeon Men?: The Role of the Special Constables on April 10, 1848," pp. 3, 15 n. 1, 18 n. 11, a paper presented at the Western Conference on British Studies, Reno, Nevada, November 1981. I would like to thank Professor Weisser of Colorado State University for sending me a copy of his unpublished paper. Total of c. 85,000 specials: Goodway, *London Chartism*, pp. 74, 129–31.

18 See Large, "London in 1848," pp. 188–9; Harold Perkin, *The Origins of Modern English Society 1780–1880* (London: Routledge & Kegan Paul, 1969), pp. 317–18, 391; and Weisser, "Special Constables," pp. 5–12, and *April 10*, pp. 70–1, 130, 256–62. Goodway, *London Chartism*, pp. 131–3, states that "a substantial proportion of the 85,000 [specials] were workers," *but* "the great majority" of workers enrolled were coerced by their employers, and many others refused to be sworn.

19 See Woodham-Smith, *Hunger*, pp. 271–9. To police this Irish immigrant invasion, some 2,000 troops were encamped in the suburb of Everton. Two Liverpool police detectives were despatched to Ireland, where they traveled through seven counties in an effort to determine the causes of the invasion. Liverpool taxpayers petitioned Parliament for aid to relieve the pressure on their city's poor rates. The petitions were presented in the Lords by Henry Brougham. *Hansard's Parliamentary Debates* [hereafter, *Hansard*], 3d Series, 356 vols. (London: T. C. Hansard, 1830–91), 89:597–602, 612–14, 770–1, 1323–4, 29 Jan. and 1, 4, 15 Feb. 1847.

20 O'Connor: *Hansard* 95:752–65, 7 Dec. 1847; and 97:1354–5, 6 Apr.; 98:11–13, 83–5, 285–6, 7, 10, 13 Apr. 1848. Read and Glasgow, *O'Connor*, pp. 127–9. Louis R. Bisceglia, "The Threat of Violence: Irish Confederates and Chartists in Liverpool in 1848," *Irish Sword* 14 (Summer 1981):207–11; F. C. Mather, "The Government and the Chartists," in Asa Briggs, ed., *Chartist Studies* (London: Macmillan, 1959), pp. 394–8; and W. J. Lowe, "The Chartists and the Irish Confederates: Lancashire, 1848," *I.H.S.* 24 (Nov. 1984):178–80. I wish to thank Professor Lowe of Chicago State University for sending me a copy of the paper (a shorter version of the previously cited article) that he presented at the meeting of the American Historical Association, Washington, D.C., December 1982.

21 On London, see Mepol 2/59, 67; *Annual Register* 90 (1848): Chronicle, 72–4, 80; Large, "London in 1848," pp. 195–201; Goodway, *London Chartism*, pp. 79–88, 116–22, 142–3; and, generally, D. J. Rowe, "The Failure of London Chartism," *Hist. Jour.* 11 (1968):472–87. For the North, see Arthur Redford and I. S. Russell, *A History of Local Government in Manchester*, 2 vols. (London: Longmans, Green, 1939–40), 2:69; Stevenson, *Disturbances*, pp. 272–4; Bisceglia, "Threat of Violence," pp. 211–13; and Lowe, "Chartists and Confederates," pp. 185–7.

22 Goodway, *London Chartism*, pp. 89–96; Bisceglia, "Threat of Violence," pp. 213–15; Lowe, "Chartists and Confederates," pp. 187–91, who notes that "the most overt move to support a rising was at Oldham" (p. 190) on the night of 14/15 August, when some seventy persons set out at 1 A.M. to march to Manchester. The police made thirty-three arrests and confiscated nineteen pikes. At Manchester the police, who were issued and drilled with swords, contained the threat without resort to the military. "Second Report from the Select Committee appointed to consider the Expediency of adopting a more Uniform

System of Police in England and Wales ...," *PP 1852-3* (715), 36:QQ. 2919-25, ev. of Manchester Chief Constable E. Willis.

23 J. H. Treble, "O'Connor, O'Connell, and the Attitudes of Irish Immigrants towards Chartism in the North of England, 1838-48," in J. Butt and I. F. Clarke, eds., *The Victorians and Social Protest* (Hamden, Conn.: Archon Books, 1973), pp. 60-70; Thompson, *Chartists*, pp. 315-19, 326-9. On anti-Irish disturbances by workingmen in the North of England in the 1840s and 1850s, see Stevenson, *Disturbances*, pp. 276-82.

24 Kevin B. Nowlan, "The Political Background," in Edwards and Williams, eds., *Famine*, pp. 183-94; Denis Gwynn, *Young Ireland and 1848* (Cork: Cork University Press, and Oxford: B.H. Blackwell, 1949), pp. 163-70. On the French connection, see D. N. Petler, "Ireland and France in 1848," *I.H.S.* 24 (Nov. 1985): 493-505.

25 Gwynn, *1848*, pp. 4-8, 14-21, 65, 199, 246; see also Henry Boylan, *A Dictionary of Irish Biography* (New York: Barnes & Noble, 1978), pp. 91-2, 96, 226, 246, 258, 274.

26 On Meagher and O'Brien, see the *Dictionary of National Biography* [hereafter, *DNB*] 13:194-6; 14:777-82. Meagher wrote a narrative of 1848 while in Richmond Gaol, Dublin, in 1849. Subsequently published by Gavan Duffy in the *Nation*, the narrative was later printed in Thomas Francis Meagher, *Meagher of the Sword*, ed. Arthur Griffith (Dublin: M. H. Gill & Son, 1917), pp. 173-234, and in Gwynn, *1848*, pp. 275-98.

O'Brien was the son of Sir Edward O'Brien and the grandson of Sir Lucius O'Brien (*DNB* 14:763-4), an Irish Volunteer and contemporary of Grattan. For W. S. O'Brien's parliamentary efforts, see on Repeal, *Hansard* 70:630-77, 4 July 1843; on constabulary affrays, *PP 1846* (280), 35:237, return asked by Mr. W. S. O'Brien, MP for County Limerick, 13 Mar. 1846, and ordered to be printed by the House of Commons, 6 May 1846; and on Famine mortality, *Hansard* 89:1230-1, 12 Feb., and 90:1101-3, 9 Mar. 1847. O'Brien never published an account of 1848 (see n. 40, this chapter).

27 Kevin B. Nowlan, *The Politics of Repeal* (London: Routledge & Kegan Paul, 1965), pp. 184-91, and his essay, "Political Background," pp. 191-4; Gwynn, *1848*, pp. 163-70.

28 Nowlan, *Politics*, pp. 203-10, and "Political Background," pp. 196-203, quotation on p. 199; Gwynn, *1848*, chs. 16-18. Clarendon was the brother-in-law of George Cornewall Lewis.

29 *Hansard* 98:(Commons) 20-60, 73-135 (Second Reading, passed by a vote of 452-35, O'Brien's speech on cols. 73-80), 152-75, 223-59, 340-87, 417-31, 453-80 (Third Reading, Peel on cols. 463-70, vote on cols. 478-80), on 7, 10-12, 14, 17-18 Apr. 1848; and 98:(Lords) 485-507, 534-7, 19-20 Apr., and (royal assent) 537, 22 Apr. 1848. Also in opposition were the Liberator's son, John O'Connell, Feargus O'Connor, and the British radicals Hume, Muntz, Scholefield, and Wakley.

30 Gwynn, *1848*, pp. 215-16, 226; Nowlan, *Politics*, pp. 211-12.

31 *Hansard* 100:(Commons) 696-743, (Lords) 743-56, 22 and 24 July 1848. In the Commons the vote was 271-8 to approve the bill's introduction (22 July, col. 743). In the tiny minority was a lonely Feargus O'Connor, having been deserted by O'Connell and almost all of the British radicals. See also Nowlan, "Political Background," pp. 202-3; Gwynn, *1848*, p. 239.

32 *Annual Register* 90 (1848):Chronicle, 93-5, which quotes *The Times*'s account, itself based on an erroneous story received by the editor of the *Dublin Evening Post*. Army levels: WO 17/1116-17, PRO, London.

33 Michael Doheny, *The Felon's Track, or the History of the Attempted Outbreak in Ireland* (New York: W. H. Holbrooke, 1849; repr., Dublin: M. H. Gill & Son,

1914, ed. Arthur Griffith), p. 159. John Mitchel, *The Last Conquest of Ireland (Perhaps)* (1861), p. 201, quoted in P. S. O'Hegarty, *A History of Ireland under the Union, 1801–1922* (London: Methuen, 1952; repr., New York: Kraus Reprint Co., 1969), p. 331. Meagher, *Sword*, p. 182.

34 Doheny, *Felon's Track*, Griffith's preface, p. xv; and Meagher, *Sword*, pp. 185–7, 209 n. 1, who believed that a Dublin rising could result only in "squandered blood ... as that of the Rue St. Méry, in the Parisian insurrection of 1831" (p. 187). John Mitchel, by contrast, argued the case for Dublin; see his *Jail Journal, or Five Years in British Prisons* (New York: The Office of the "Citizen" [Mitchel's newspaper], 1854; repr., Dublin: M. H. Gill & Son, 1913), pp. xlvi, 73.

35 Meagher, *Sword*, pp. 178, 183, 198–9, 200 ("regiments"); Nowlan, *Politics*, pp. 213–14; Gwynn, *1848*, pp. 240–2. By the end of 1847, there were only 123 miles of railway track operating in Ireland (700 miles by 1852). The line from Dublin reached Thurles, County Tipperary, by mid-March 1848 and was completed to Limerick Junction on 3 July 1848. A projected southward feeder line to Carlow was open as far as Bagenalstown only as recently as 24 July 1848; the track into Kilkenny was not completed until November 1850. Ernest F. Carter, *An Historical Geography of the Railways of the British Isles* (London: Cassell, 1959), pp. 536, 541–5. For debate on Irish railways as public works projects during the Potato Famine, February to June 1847, see *Hansard* 89:1206–1317, 1358–1434, 90:37–126, 665–76; and 93:975–1048.

36 Meagher, *Sword*, p. 187; Nowlan, *Politics*, p. 214; Gwynn, *1848*, pp. 223–4, 232, 249.

37 Narrative by T. D'Arcy McGee, written in America in 1850 and printed in Doheny, *Felon's Track*, pp. 289–97; see also Gwynn, *1848*, pp. 240, 318–21 (reprint of McGee's narrative). In 1842 McGee had emigrated to America, where he became editor of the *Boston Pilot*; he returned to Ireland and became the London correspondent for the *Freeman's Journal* and, subsequently, for the *Nation*. McGee's intention in the summer of 1848 was "to land 400 or 500 staunch men in the north-west." Meagher, perhaps wishfully, inflated McGee's anticipated force to 2,000 men in three commandeered steamships (*Sword*, pp. 189–91).

38 Gwynn, *1848*, pp. 15, 65, 248, 254, 255 ("starved"), 311–15 (narrative of T. B. McManus, written August 1848 and sent to Gavan Duffy in Newgate Prison). In his accompanying letter (undated) to Duffy, McManus noted that "my business in Liverpool is ruined" (p. 311). McManus had been active in Repeal politics; and though he was active among Irish radicals in Liverpool, the police in that city had few files on him (correspondence with Prof. W. J. Lowe, November 1982).

39 "Detectives": Mitchel, *Jail Journal*, p. xli; Meagher, *Sword*, p. 202. In the Irish constabulary in 1848, 62 percent of the constables and subconstables were Catholic; in Tipperary's 1,300-man force, 74 percent were Catholic. Constabulary register, HO 184/54, appendix.

40 I have relied on the accounts by (1) Meagher, "A Personal Narrative of 1848," written in Richmond Gaol, Dublin, 1849, and subsequently published by Gavan Duffy in the *Nation*; later printed by Arthur Griffith in his edition of Meagher's *Sword*, pp. 173–234, and by Gwynn, in *1848*, App. 1, pp. 275–98. (2) Doheny, *Felon's Track*, pp. 159–86, covering the actual rising; reprinted in Gwynn, *1848*, App. 2, pp. 299–310. Doheny's book was written and published in New York in 1849. (3) Mitchel, *Jail Journal*, pp. xxxviii–xlvii, 72–6. His journal was begun in May 1848, continued on shipboard and in Australia, and finished in New York, where he first published it in his newspaper, the *Citizen*, January to August 1854. (4) O'Brien, though he lived until 1864, never published his version of the rising. While in Kilmainham Gaol in the fall of 1848, he did prepare a handwritten account of his motives and aims. I have consulted this useful "retrospect," which was not published until 1949 (in Gwynn, *1848*, pp. 227–38). The best secondary

accounts of the rising are Gwynn, *1848*, chs. 21, 22; and the recent study by Seán Cronin, *Protest in Arms: The Young Ireland Rebellion of July–August 1848* (Dublin: University Press of Ireland, 1984).

41 McGee's narrative, in Gwynn, *1848*, p. 318; Meagher, *Sword*, p. 182; Gwynn, *1848*, pp. 239–40.

42 I have accepted Meagher's figure of 500 Kilkenny Confederates, 100 of them armed (*Sword*, p. 211). Gavan Duffy (in a note in *Sword*, pp. 231–4) observed that the "17,000" Kilkenny Confederates reported in the *Freeman's Journal* and "copied by all the papers" was a misprint of the 1,700 reported by Kilkenny Club leaders. The 1,700, Duffy noted, included old men and boys; the effective force he believed, was 600, of whom 200 were armed and only half of these with guns. See also Gwynn, *1848*, pp. 242, 297–8.

43 Doheny, *Felon's Track*, pp. 163–9; Meagher, *Sword*, pp. 194–217 (three cheers, p. 214); Gwynn, *1848*, pp. 242–5.

44 Meagher, *Sword*, pp. 218–31; Gwynn, *1848*, pp. 245–8 (Meagher quoted, p. 246). Compare Meagher's account with Doheny's, in Gwynn, *1848*, pp. 291–7, 300–2, respectively. Meagher's detailed narrative ends with the episode at Carrick on 24 July.

45 Griffith's preface, in Doheny, *Felon's Track*, p. xviii; Gwynn, *1848*, pp. 246–8 ("bloodshed," p. 246), 302–3 (Doheny's narrative).

46 Doheny, *Felon's Track*, pp. 170–3; Gwynn, *1848*, pp. 249–51, 316–17 (Charles Kickham's "recollections" of the Mullinahone incident).

47 Doheny, *Felon's Track*, pp. 173–8; Gwynn, *1848*, pp. 255–61, 304–8 (Doheny's narrative), 311–12 (Terence McManus's narrative).

48 Doheny, *Felon's Track*, pp. 179–80; Rev. P. Fitzgerald, *Narrative of the Confederates of 1848*, p. 38, quoted in Gwynn, *1848*, p. 262.

49 *Annual Register* 90 (1848); Chronicle, 94; Robert Curtis, *The History of the Royal Irish Constabulary* [hereafter, *RIC*] (Dublin: Moffat & Co., 1869), pp. 67, 77; Gwynn, *1848*, p. 264.

50 My account of the Ballingarry incident is based on the following sources. Doheny, *Felon's Track*, pp. 181–3. Curtis, *RIC*, pp. 67–84. Gwynn, *1848*, pp. 264–7, who relies on Father Fitzgerald's *Narrative*; and also McManus's narrative (Gwynn, *1848*, pp. 313–15) and Subinspector Trant's *Reply to Father Fitzgerald*, published in 1868 (Gwynn, *1848*, p. 264 n. 23).

51 Curtis, *RIC*, pp. 78, 80. Gwynn accepts Fitzgerald's version that after *one* person, "probably under the influence of liquor," broke the kitchen window, the police "suddenly, as if only waiting for an opportunity," fired upon the "large and defenseless multitude." But Gwynn later informs us that Father Fitzgerald "did not arrive on the scene until the police had already opened fire" (*1848*, pp. 265–6). McManus, who was present, says that after "eight or ten" stones had shattered the windows, the police discharged into the crowd "a volley from about forty carabines" (Gwynn, *1848*, p. 314). Doheny, who was not present, writes that Trant ordered his men to fire only after the stonings had knocked down constables and injured an officer inside (*Felon's Track*, pp. 181–2). Writing two decades after the incident, but quoting "a messenger's" account to Mrs. McCormick, who had not yet returned to her house, RIC historian Robert Curtis describes the house early on as "riddled with bullets, for volley after volley of shots were firing into it and out of it!" According to Curtis, the window stonings were "a signal for a *fresh* volley from within," resulting in the two deaths. Curtis, *RIC*, pp. 79–80, my emphasis.

52 Trant, *Reply to Father Fitzgerald*, p. 13, quoted in Gwynn, *1848*, p. 264 n. 23. Fitzgerald had stated that the police used up all their ammunition.

53 Curtis, *RIC*, p. 81.

54 Gwynn, *1848*, p. 265, and McManus's account, in Gwynn, *1848*, p. 314; Curtis, *RIC*, p. 83.

55 Curtis, *RIC*, p. 83. McManus says that Subinspector Cox's large party numbered "about one hundred"; Doheny places the size at sixty. McManus's narrative, in Gwynn, *1848*, p. 315; Doheny, *Felon's Track*, p. 183.

56 Curtis, *RIC*, pp. 85–6. See also *Annual Register* 90 (1848): Chronicle, 95–6, quoting *The Times*, 7 Aug. 1848. Head Constable Hanniver, unmarried, resigned from the constabulary in 1853 in order to emigrate to America (HO 184/1).

57 Meagher, together with Maurice Leyne and Patrick O'Donohoe, was arrested by a police patrol. Seán Cronin, "'The Country Did Not Turn Out': The Young Ireland Rising of 1848," *Eire-Ireland* 11, No. 2 (Summer 1976):4; *Annual Register* 90 (1848): Chronicle, 96.

58 Cronin, "Rising of 1848," p. 5; Gwynn, *1848*, p. 271. The vessel, appropriately named, was the *N. D. Chase*.

59 A fourth leader, Patrick O'Donohoe (O'Donoghue), was convicted and transported. Two men not involved in the actual rising – the journalists John Martin and Kevin O'Doherty – were also transported. James Fintan Lalor, the philosopher of revolution, was released from prison by the end of 1848 because of his poor health. Gavan Duffy (1816–1903), editor of the *Nation*, was freed in April 1849 after five successive juries refused to find him guilty. Following a disillusioning return to politics (MP for New Ross, 1852–5), Duffy emigrated in 1855 to Australia, where he soon entered politics. He became Prime Minister of the State of Victoria in 1871 and two years later was knighted. In 1880 he left Australia and spent most of the rest of his life in southern Europe. See Sir Charles Gavan Duffy, *My Life in Two Hemispheres*, 2 vols. (London: T. Fisher Unwin, 1898; repr., Shannon: Irish University Press, 1969).

Meagher escaped from Australia in 1852 and settled in the United States. During the Civil War he rose to the rank of general in the Union army, fighting *against* the Confederates; he died in 1867 when, on his way to serve as Acting Governor of the Montana Territory, he drowned in the Missouri River. See Robert G. Athearn, *Thomas Francis Meagher: An Irish Revolutionary in America* (Boulder: University of Colorado Press, 1949; repr., Salem, N.H.: Ayer Co., 1976). McManus also escaped from Australia and went to America, where he died in poverty in San Francisco in 1860. O'Brien, not the type to escape, won a legal release from imprisonment in 1854, returned to Ireland to his Limerick estate in 1856, subsequently traveled extensively in Europe, and died in Wales in 1864. O'Donohoe, pardoned with O'Brien, emigrated to New York, where he died in obscurity. Martin later returned to Ireland, was elected a Member of Parliament, and helped to found the Home Rule movement. O'Doherty stayed in Australia, where he established a medical practice.

60 Thomas D'Arcy McGee, of the ill-fated Scottish steamship scheme, fled to the United States and in 1857 moved to Canada. Here he became a lawyer and subsequently an MP and Cabinet minister (Agriculture) in the Canadian government. McGee was assassinated in 1868, allegedly by Fenians. John Blake Dillon became a prosperous New York lawyer, returned to Ireland in 1855, was elected to Parliament in 1865, and died the next year of cholera. Richard O'Gorman practiced law with Dillon in New York City, chose to remain in his adopted country, rose to become a judge in New York State Superior Court, and died in 1895. Another veteran of the Irish '48, Michael Doheny, also became a successful New York lawyer. In sum, once past the trauma of exile, many of the Irish rebels went on to careers that an English radical might have envied.

61 After 1848, O'Mahony (d. 1877) and Stephens (d. 1901) lived in straitened economic circumstances in Ireland, America, and Europe. Sources for nn. 59–61: *DNB*; Boylan, *Dictionary*; Griffith's preface, in Meagher, *Sword*, p. xv, notes; Gwynn, *1848*, pp. 271–3; Cronin, "Rising of 1848," pp. 5–9; Nowlan, *Politics*, pp. 216–17; and Blanche Touhill, *William Smith O'Brien and his Irish Revolutionary Companions in Penal Exile* (Columbia: University of Missouri Press, 1981).

62 *Annual Register* 90 (1848):Chronicle, 96; Mitchell, *Jail Journal*, p. 72.

63 Meagher, *Sword*, pp. 216−17; Doheny, *Felon's Track*, pp. 167, 170, 175, 182; O'Brien's retrospect and McGee's narrative, in Gwynn, *1848*, pp. 234, 319, respectively; Cronin, "Rising of 1848," pp. 9, 11, 13, 16−17.

64 Griffith's preface, in Meagher, *Sword*, p. xi; Nowlan, *Politics*, p. 215; Gwynn, *1848*, pp. 152−3.

65 Fitzgerald, *Narrative*, quoted in Gwynn, *1848*, p. 253; O'Brien's retrospect, in Gwynn, *1848*, pp. 234−5; Griffith's preface, in Doheny, *Felon's Track*, p. xviii.

66 Doheny, *Felon's Track*, pp. 170−8; Meagher, *Sword*, p. 214; Gwynn, *1848*, pp. 242−5, 249−51, 255−61, 304−8 (Doheny's narrative), 311−12 (McManus's narrative), 316−17 (Charles Kickham's recollections).

67 After Ballingarry, a series of attacks on police barracks in Waterford and Tipperary peaked in September 1849. Doheny, *Felon's Track*, pp. 285−7; Nowlan, *Politics*, pp. 214, 217; Cronin, "Rising of 1848," p. 6.

68 O'Brien's retrospect, in Gwynn, *1848*, pp. 228−30.

69 An excellent discussion of the Chartist physical-force rhetoric is in Weisser, *April 10*, pp. 220−8.

70 Doheny (*Felon's Track*, p. 172) and O'Brien both commented on the withdrawal of detachments and the concentration of police and troops in the towns. O'Brien noted how the absence of police "afforded great facilities for preparation ... [since] we were enabled to move without interruption in armed bodies throughout the whole place lying between Thurles and Carrick and between Clonmel and Kilkenny" (O'Brien's retrospect, in Gwynn, *1848*, p. 233).

71 Robert Binkley, *Realism and Nationalism, 1852−1871*, Rise of Modern Europe Series (New York: Harper & Bros., 1935); Norman Rich, *The Age of Nationalism and Reform, 1850−1890*, 2d ed., Norton History of Modern Europe Series (New York: W. W. Norton, 1977). Cf., for the earlier period, J. L. Talmon, *Romanticism and Revolt: Europe 1815−1848*, History of European Civilization Series (New York: Harcourt, Brace, & World, 1967), and Charles Breunig, *The Age of Revolution and Reaction, 1789−1850*, 2d ed., Norton History of Modern Europe Series (New York: W. W. Norton, 1977).

72 His ancestor, Sir William Temple (1555−1627), a native of Warwickshire, had gone to Dublin in 1609 to be provost of Trinity College. Sir William came to be "possessed of much land" in Ireland. His son Sir John Temple (1600−77) served as speaker of the Irish House of Commons. Sir John's son Henry Temple (1673?−1757), created 1st Viscount Palmerston of County Dublin (1722), served from the 1720s in the English House of Commons and resided at the family estate in Hampshire. The first viscount's grandson, Henry Temple (1739−1802), 2d Viscount Palmerston, also lived in England while drawing the rentals from his Irish estates. His son Henry John Temple (1784−1865), the third viscount (1802) and prominent English statesman, traveled more in Italy than he ever did in Ireland. *DNB* 19:495−515, 520−2, quotation on p. 522.

73 No correspondence from Palmerston's home secretaryship is preserved in his Letter Books (173 vols., NRA 11930), the Papers of 3d Viscount Palmerston, National Register of Archives [hereafter, NRA], Quality Court, Chancery Lane, London. Neither Palmerston's Letter Books during his prime ministership nor the Broadlands MSS (NRA 12889) contain any references to police. But see David Roberts, "Lord Palmerston at the Home Office, 1853−1854," *The Historian* 21 (Nov. 1958):63−81. Grey: information of Sir Cecil Graves, July 1952, concerning the Papers of Sir George Grey (1799−1882), recorded in the Personal Indexes, NRA; and *DNB* 8:626−7. Grey's first post had been that of under-secretary to Charles Grant, Colonial Secretary in Melbourne's administration. A highly capable administrator, Grey would serve a third stint as Home Secretary, in 1859−66, under Palmerston and then Russell. See also n. 87, this chapter.

74 Palmerston: *Hansard* 133:1267–8, 2 June 1854; and Palmerston to J. B. Butler, Torquay, 15 Mar. 1854, HO 45/5800. Palmerston, whose family seat was near Romsey in Hampshire, had in 1852 unsuccessfully tried to get the mayor of that town to amalgamate the tiny borough force with the county police. "First Report from the Select Committee appointed to consider the Expediency of adopting a more Uniform System of Police in England and Wales ...," *PP 1852–3* (603), 36:QQ. 504–6, ev. of J. Beddome, former mayor, Romsey. See also Lord Fortescue's letter on police to Palmerston, 17 Jan. 1853, HO 45/4609, printed in full in T. A. Critchley, *A History of Police in England and Wales*, 2d ed. (Montclair, N.J.: Patterson Smith, 1972), pp. 102–4. Hugh Fortescue (1783–1861), 2d Earl (succ. 1839), was a long-time MP, 1804–39; served as Lord Lieutenant of Ireland, 1839–41, and of Devonshire, 1839–61; and was parliamentary secretary of the national Poor Law Board, 1847–51. He was instrumental in setting up the County Devon police in 1856. Frederic Boase, *Modern English Biography*, 6 vols. (Truro: Netherton and Worth, 1892–1921), 1:1087–8.

For Chadwick's views, see (1) his pungent remarks on the English police in a seven-page manuscript, "Rough Draft of a Constabulary Force Report," undated [1839], Chadwick Papers, in Chadwick MS 5. (2) "County Police, Heads of an Examination on, by E. C. submitted to the Chairman of the Committee of the House of Commons, 1853," thirty-five folios, ff. 25–31, in Chadwick MS 15; this document differs from his evidence before the 1853 select committee (see n. 75, this chapter). (3) Chadwick to Palmerston, 25 Mar. 1854, Chadwick MS 1947. (4) "Extracts from Memoranda on the proposed Draft Clauses for a General Police measure," 1854, twenty-one folios, in Chadwick MS 15. "The Irish Constabulary," noted Chadwick, "is a superior military force adapted to the suppression of riots & insurrections, ... and ready to aid the civil power in process serving and apprehensions; but it is not essentially a civil preventive police. The Metropolitan Police is a great advance upon the Irish Constabulary for the ordinary purposes of a Police." But he thought that even the London police was "too rigid" and too military. Its patrol beats were unchanging, "its action is too *routinier*," so that criminals could predict the arrival of "the shiny hats" of patrolling constables. "Extracts from Memoranda," ff. 17–18, in Chadwick MS 15.

75 *Hansard* 126:545–52, "National Police," 26 Apr. 1853. In his motion to appoint a select committee, Mr. E. R. Rice, MP for Dover, spoke much about "mob" violence, including "the late disgraceful riots" in Blackburn, and the advantages of police over soldiers for repression (cols. 545–6). On Rice, see also epigraph, this chapter, this book. "First Report from the Select Committee appointed to consider the Expediency of adopting a more Uniform System of Police in England and Wales ...; with Minutes of Evidence," *PP 1852–3* (603), 36:1–160; "Second Report," *PP 1852–3* (715) 36:161–344. Chadwick's testimony: *PP 1852–3* (715), 36:QQ. 3638–62, 17 June 1853. In January 1855, Chadwick declined Palmerston's request to serve on any new investigating commission, saying that he was tired of trying to educate Parliament on the subject of police. Chadwick to Palmerston, 16 Jan. 1855, in Chadwick MS 1947; another copy, dated 15 Jan. 1855, is in Chadwick MS 16.

76 Witnesses: twenty county magistrates; twelve county police officers; three Metropolitan Police officers; ten landowners, occupiers, or agents; seven men connected with boroughs – two borough magistrates, one town clerk, and four borough head constables (two of them previously in the rural police); and five others – two governors of county jails, one Poor Law district inspector, one county sheriff, and one commissioner from the 1839 county constabulary commission (Chadwick). London *Daily News*, 4 Feb. 1854, press clipping in Chadwick MS 15.

77 Borough/county consolidation: 3 & 4 Vict., c. 88 (1840); *Hansard* 140:232, 5 Feb. 1856 (Sir G. Grey). The idea of using the Consolidated Fund may be traced to the Earl of Ellenborough (who cited the Irish and London examples, in *Hansard* 119:1226, 18 Mar. 1852) and to Earl Fortescue (letter to Palmerston, 17 Jan. 1853, HO 45/4609, quoted in Critchley, *Police*, p. 104).

78 Capt. G. T. Scobell, MP for Bath, *Hansard* 140:2150, 10 Mar. 1856. Summaries of the committee report are in Critchley, *Police*, pp. 105–11, and Radzinowicz, *ECL*, 4:288–91.

79 "*Confidential*. Suggested Heads of a Bill. An Act for establishing a General Police in England and Wales," 20 Dec. 1853, printed at the Foreign Office, in Chadwick MS 15; Chadwick to Palmerston, 25 Mar. 1854, Chadwick MS 1947.

80 Mayor of York to Palmerston, 2 Feb. 1854, HO 45/5276; London *Daily News*, 4 Feb. 1854, "Police Centralisation: Deputation to the Home Office," press clipping in Chadwick MS 15.

81 The Government's contribution was suggested by Capt. J. B. B. McHardy, Chief Constable of the Essex Constabulary, to Palmerston, 20 Feb. 1854, HO 45/5276. On Chadwick's participation, see nn. 74, 79–80, this chapter, and "*Confidential* Draft of a Bill. An Act for establishing a General Police in England and Wales," 13 Jan. 1854, printed at the Foreign Office; and "Police Bill. Arrangement of Clauses. Draft of a Bill for Improving the Police throughout England," March 1854, both in Chadwick MS 15.

82 A copy of the bill is in Public Bills, *PP 1854* (127), 5:467–80; debate, in *Hansard* 133:1266–8. *Birmingham Journal*, 24 June 1854; *Manchester Guardian*, 17 June 1854. See also *The Times*, 9 June, 4 July 1854; *Brighton Examiner*, 13, 20, 27 June 1854; *Oldham Chronicle*, 1 July 1854.

83 *Hansard* 134:750–1, 957, 27 and 30 June 1854. *Manchester Guardian*, 1 July 1854.

84 *Hansard* 134:1073–5, 3 July 1854. "Thief": *Hansard* 138:709, 17 May 1855, debate on parish constables bill (see n. 98, this chapter).

85 Shaw to Home Secretary Graham, 26, 28 Sept. 1841, in Chadwick MS 1794; Chadwick, "County Police, Heads of an Examination on . . ., 1853," ff. 21–2, in Chadwick MS 15. See also *Hansard* 126:547, 26 Apr. 1853, and 140:2146, 2157, 10 Mar. 1856; and F. C. Mather, "The Railways, the Electric Telegraph, and Public Order during The Chartist Period," *History* 38 (1953):40–53.

86 Penal Servitude Act, 16 & 17 Vict., c. 99 (1853), amended by 20 & 21 Vict., c. 3 (1857). See A. G. L. Shaw, *Convicts and the Colonies* (London: Faber and Faber, 1966), ch. 15; select committee investigations into transportation and penal servitude, in *PP 1856* (244, 296, 355, 404), 17:1ff.; and M. Heather Tomlinson, "Penal Servitude 1846–1865: A System in Evolution," and Peter Bartrip, "Public Opinion and Law Enforcement: The Ticket-of-Leave Scares in Mid-Victorian Britain," in Victor Bailey, ed., *Policing and Punishment in Nineteenth-Century Britain* (New Brunswick, N.J.: Rutgers University Press, 1981), chs. 6, 7.

87 Chadwick: *PP 1852–3* (715), 36:Q. 3655. Palmerston: *Hansard* 138:707–8, 17 May 1855. Grey: *Hansard* 140:234–5, 5 Feb. 1856. Home Secretary Sir George Grey (see n. 73, this chapter) must not be confused with Sir George Grey (1812–98), colonial statesman and governor (1841–5) of South Australia, a colony that never admitted convicts. *DNB* 22 (Supplement):782–6. Opponents: *Hansard* 140:2146 ("necessity," C. Forster) and 2182 ("frightened," W. Deedes); see also *Hansard* 138:706 (Miles), and 140:2184 (Muntz). Newspapers: *Wigan Examiner*, 8 Feb.; *Birmingham Journal*, 13 Feb.; and *Portsmouth Times and Naval Gazette*, 15 Mar. 1856. The interest in police was further heightened by an "alien scare" that was prompted by the large number of Continental refugees from 1848 on taking up residence in England. Phillip Thurmond Smith has recently shown that the Metropolitan Police assisted with the paid emigration of 1,500 of these "republicans," French, Italian, and Polish, from England to New York City, 1852–8.

Policing Victorian London: Political Policing, Public Order, and the London Metropolitan Police (Westport, Conn.: Greenwood Press, 1985), pp. 79–87, 95–102, 107.

88 *Hansard* 140:(Commons) 229–45, 5 Feb.; 690–8, 14 Feb.; 2113–90, 10 March. *Hansard* 141:1564–85, 25 Apr.; 1928–44, 2 May. *Hansard* 142:293–309, 9 May; 606–14, 23 May; (Lords) 850, 2 June; 1398–1400, 13 June; 1673–6, 19 June; 1894–5, 24 June; 2048–50, 27 June. *Hansard* 143:(royal assent) 1064, 21 July 1856.

89 *Hansard* 140:243 (H. Stracey), 2129–30 (Grey).

90 Stevenson, *Disturbances*, pp. 275, 299. *Hansard* 140:694–5 (B. Denison), 2182 (W. Deedes).

91 "Well remembered": *Bath Herald*, 9 Feb. 1856. Stevenson, *Disturbances*, pp. 279–80, 284; Pauline Millward, "The Stockport Riots of 1852: A Study in Anti-Catholic and Anti-Irish Sentiment," in Roger Swift and Sheridan Gilley, eds., *The Irish in the Victorian City* (London: Croom Helm, 1985), ch. 10.

92 HO 45/6092; "Proceedings Taken before the Commissioners on the alleged Disturbances in Hyde Park [in July 1855]," *PP 1856* (2016), 23:1–509 (evidence), 509–46 (findings); Brian Harrison, "The Sunday Trading Riots of 1855," *Hist. Jour.* 8 (1965):219–45; Smith, *Policing Victorian London*, ch. 6; *Hansard* 140:2172–3, 2177 (J. W. Henley, answered by Sir William Heathcote).

93 Jenifer Hart, "The County and Borough Police Act, 1856," *Public Administration* 34 (1956):405; cf. Radzinwicz, *ECL*, 4:277, 286.

94 "County Police, Heads of an Examination on, ...," ff. 5–9, June 1853, in Chadwick, MS 15. *Bath Herald*, 9 Feb., 15 Mar. 1856.

95 *Brighton Examiner*, 19 Feb., 18 Mar. 1856. On the Irish constabulary, see the incisive letter from "Investigator," in *Brighton Examiner*, 27 June 1854. *London Morning Post*, 10 Mar. 1856. *Norfolk Chronicle and Norwich Gazette*, 1 Mar. 1856. "It will really seem incredible in after years," mused the *Brighton Examiner* (18 Mar. 1856), "that England, halfway through the nineteenth century, should have ... no system of national police, that it should have allowed the lazy and incompetent among its counties to foster crime at the expense of those who have more sense and vigour than themselves."

96 W. Anderson, Superintendent, Rural Constabulary, to Palmerston, 20 June 1854, and reply of 25 June, HO 45/5276; Palmerston to Mr. Williams, Mayor of Northampton, 22 Aug. 1854, HO 45/5244L; and Palmerston to Mr. Hopkins, 5 Jan. 1855, HO 45/6236.

97 Circular dated 28 Mar. 1855, discussed by Grey in *Hansard* 140:232, 2128–35, 5 Feb., 10 Mar. 1856, quotation on col. 2130. Grey said that a year after the circular had gone out, only Leeds and Wolverhampton had improved their police.

98 "A Bill to amend the Laws relating to the Appointment and Payment of Superintendents and Parish Constables," introduced on 26 Apr. 1855 by Mr. W. Deedes, MP for East Kent; a copy is in Public Bills, *PP 1854–5* (92), 5:13–42. In the debate on its Second Reading, the bill was criticized for, on the one hand, propping up an old, inefficient system and, on the other, *requiring* the appointment of superintending constables (*Hansard* 138:702–14, 17 May 1855). The bill drew very little support. For Home Secretary Grey's views on the parish constables, see *Hansard* 140:2121–4.

99 *Hansard* 140:229–45, Grey's speech on cols. 229–37, quotations on 230, 244. A copy of the "Bill to Render more effectual the Police in Counties and Boroughs in England and Wales," 5 Feb. 1856, is in Chadwick MS 15; another copy, "prepared and brought in by Sir George Grey, Viscount Palmerston, and [Home Office Under-Secretary, 1855–8] Mr. [W. N.] Massey," 5 Feb. 1856, is in Public Bills, *PP 1856* (18), 5:397–407.

100 *The Times*, 21 Feb., "time-hallowed" (Mayor of York), "virtual repeal" (Mr. Leeman, York alderman, and Mayor in 1854), "fiscal agents" (Mayor of Ports-

mouth); and 22 Feb. 1856. See also *The Times*, 3 and 18 Jan., 12 and 18 Mar., 14 June 1856.

101 *York Herald*, 15 Mar. 1856; *Hansard* 140:2151 (145 borough petitions against and 5 for), 2159 (150 against, 10 for), Captain Scobell and Sir J. Walmsley, MP for Leicester, 10 Mar. 1856. Of the 199 boroughs in England, 149 had populations under 20,000.

102 *Portsmouth Times and Naval Gazette*, 16 Feb., 15 Mar. 1856 (quotation); *Birmingham Journal*, 9 and 13 Feb., 12 Mar. 1856; *York Herald*, 9 Feb., 15 Mar. 1856; *Wigan Examiner*, 8 Feb. (correcting Grey: Wigan had not eleven, but twenty-three police for its 32,000 inhabitants!), 7 Mar. 1856; and *Oldham Chronicle*, 1 Mar. 1856.

103 *Bath Herald*, 9 Feb. (quotation), 15 Mar. 1856; *Brighton Examiner*, 19 Feb. (quotation), 26 Feb., 18 Mar. 1856; *Norfolk Chronicle and Norwich Gazette*, 16 Feb., 1 Mar. 1856; *Manchester Guardian*, 16 Feb., 21 and 22 Feb. 1856.

104 *Portsmouth Times and Naval Gazette*, 15 Mar. 1856. The *Wigan Examiner*, 14 Mar. 1856, came to accept the amendments to the bill and conceded that the Wigan colliers' riots of October 1853, with £3,000 in property destruction, had demonstrated the borough's need for a stronger police.

105 *Hansard* 140:2113-90, Grey's speech on cols. 2113-45. Palmer: *Hansard* 140:243, 5 Feb. 1856.

106 *Hansard* 140:2152 (G. T. Scobell), 2154 (H. Stracey), 2186 (F. W. Knight).

107 *Hansard* 140:2164 (W. Fox quoted), 2156 (C. W. Packe), 2180 (J. B. Smith). "Who gave municipal corporations to England? Earl Grey; and they formed one of the noblest monuments of his Administration. Who was now trying to take them away? Another of the same family" (Scobell, col. 2151).

108 *Hansard* 140:2181-3 (Deedes quoted); see also 140:694-5.

109 *Hansard* 140:2164-76, statistics on cols. 2167-70; and reply by Sir W. Heathcote, col. 2179. See also *Hansard* 141:1564-70, 1574-6.

110 *Hansard* 140:2188-90.

111 Many county MPs speaking for the bill were from counties with police (Berkshire, Worcestershire, Norfolk), while those speaking against the bill represented counties or parts of counties without the new forces (Oxfordshire, East Cornwall, East Kent, West Riding of Yorkshire). Borough MPs speaking for the bill tended to come from the larger cities (Liverpool, Leeds, Manchester and Salford, Newcastle, Huddersfield); those speaking against the bill represented boroughs of small or moderate size (Oldham, Walsall, Evesham, Droitwich; York, Portsmouth, Brighton, Bath, and Sheffield; but also one MP from Birmingham). Analysis of speeches in *Hansard* 140:229-45, 690-8, 2113-90.

112 For the vote analysis, I am indebted to Hart, "County and Borough Police Act, 1856," p. 407 n. 7. An "unclassified" group voted in favor by 14-2. Hart's figures add to 261-108; the vote, recorded in *Hansard*, was 259-106.

113 *Wigan Examiner*, 14 Mar. 1856 (quotation). See also *The Times*, 12 Mar. 1856; *York Herald*, 15 Mar. 1856.

114 "Backbone": *Birmingham Journal*, 12 Mar. 1856; "prudence": *Hansard* 142:613-14. From 25 April to 23 May, the bill was modified in the committee stage in Commons. See *Hansard* 140:2139-42; 141:1564-85, 1928-44; and 142:293-309, 606-14. Last-minute motions by two private Members, Mr. G. W. P. Bentinck and Lord Lovaine, respectively, to establish a minimum ratio of police to population and to increase borough Head Constables' powers over those of Watch Committees, were withdrawn for lack of support. *Hansard* 142:607-14, 23 May 1856.

115 *Hansard* 142:299-306, 9 May 1856. "Abolish": G. C. Lewis (col. 301); "Justice": Mr. E. Denison, MP for West Riding, Yorkshire (col. 303); Roebuck (cols. 304-5). The motion to keep the Government's contribution at one-quarter of

pay and clothing passed by a vote of 160–106. For earlier bids by three MPs to make the Government pay more than a fourth of the costs, see *Hansard* 140:239–42, 5 Feb. 1856. In 1855 total annual expenditures by the county police (in twenty-six counties, i.e., whole counties and parts of counties) was £216,000, Lancashire accounting for a fifth of the total. "Return of the Number of Rural Police in each County . . .; Salaries; Total Annual Cost to each County, 1853 to 1855 . . .," *PP 1856* (186), 50:665.

116 *Hansard* 142:(Commons) 606–14, Third Reading; (Lords) 850, 1398–1400, 1673–6, 1894–5, 2048–50 (Third Reading); and 143:1064 (royal assent). For the bill, as amended, see Public Bills, *PP 1856* (71, 145, 215), 5:407–44; statute 19 & 20 Vict., c. 69.

117 Critchley, *Police*, pp. 119–23; Hart, "County and Borough Police Act, 1856," pp. 407–8.

CHAPTER 13. CONCLUSION

1 Other principals would die within the decade: Normanby in 1863, Palmerston in 1865, and Derby in 1869. Only Sir Edwin Chadwick (1800–90) lived on well into the modern police era.

2 Sir Francis B. Head, *A Fortnight in Ireland* (London: J. Murray, 1852), pp. 45–56, and map facing title page. Douglas G. Browne, *The Rise of Scotland Yard: A History of the Metropolitan Police* (London: G. G. Harrap & Co., 1956), pp. 128, 133; T. A. Critchley, *A History of Police in England and Wales*, 2d ed. (Montclair, N.J.: Patterson Smith, 1972), p. 146.

3 Malcolm I. Thomis and Peter Holt, *Threats of Revolution in Britain 1798–1848* (Hamden, Conn.: Archon Books, 1977), passim; Henry Weisser, *April 10: Challenge and Response in England in 1848* (Lanham, Md.: University Press of America, 1983), pp. 220–8.

4 See Harold Perkin, *The Origins of Modern English Society 1780–1880* (London: Routledge & Kegan Paul, 1969), chs. 1, 2, 6, 7; and R. S. Neale, *Class in English History 1680–1850* (New York: Barnes & Noble, 1981), chs. 3, 4.

5 On the multiform nature of social control in England, see A. P. Donajgrodzki, ed., *Social Control in 19th-Century Britain* (Totowa, N.J.: Rowman and Littlefield, 1977).

6 Oliver MacDonagh, *Ireland* (Englewood Cliffs, N.J.: Prentice-Hall, 1968), p. vii.

7 T. W. Russell, "Irish Local Government," *Fortnightly Review* 50 (1891):657–62.

8 Walter Arnstein, *Britain Yesterday and Today: 1830 to the Present*, 4th ed. (Lexington, Mass.: D. C. Heath, 1983), p. 69. On the transition, see Geoffrey Best, *Mid-Victorian Britain 1851–1875* (New York: Schocken Books, 1972).

9 Evictions: David S. Jones, "The Cleavage between Graziers and Peasants in the Land Struggle, 1890–1910," in Samuel Clark and James S. Donnelly, Jr., eds., *Irish Peasants and Political Unrest 1780–1914* (Madison: University of Wisconsin Press, 1983), p. 393. Of the 69,000 families irrevocably evicted (not later readmitted) in 1849–80, fully three-fourths were turned out in the first eight years, 1849–56. Cattle and sheep statistics (cattle exports to Britain quadrupled, 1851–1901): Jones, "Cleavage," pp. 375–6. On pasturage and profitability, see Clark and Donnelly, *Irish Peasants*, editors' introduction, pp. 276–7; Jones, "Cleavage," pp. 374–413; Samuel Clark, *Social Origins of the Irish Land War* (Princeton, N.J.: Princeton University Press, 1979), pp. 107–22, 147–81, 225–45. Emigration statistics 1851–1921: B. R. Mitchell and Phyllis Deane, *Abstract of British Historical Statistics* (Cambridge: Cambridge University Press, 1962), p. 52; the greatest number that left in any one year was 190,000 people in 1852; the fewest, 32,000, in 1898. Laborers' and population decline: John W. Boyle, "A Marginal Figure: The Irish Rural Laborer," in Clark and Donnelly, eds., *Irish Peasants*, p.

312; see also David Fitzpatrick, "The Disappearance of the Irish Agricultural Labourer, 1841–1912," *Irish Economic and Social History* 7 (1980):66–92. The best overview is F. S. L. Lyons, *Ireland since the Famine* (London: Weidenfeld and Nicolson, 1971).

10 A perceptive analysis is Maurice Harmon, "Cobwebs before the Wind: Aspects of the Peasantry in Irish Literature from 1800 to 1916," in Daniel J. Casey and Robert E. Rhodes, eds., *Views of the Irish Peasantry 1800–1916* (Hamden, Conn.: Archon Books, 1977), pp. 129–59, quotations on pp. 147, 155. The sense of loss is also stingingly conveyed in Kerby A. Miller, *Emigrants and Exiles: Ireland and the Irish Exodus to North America* (New York: Oxford University Press, 1985), ch. 8.

11 Assaults on police also plummeted to low levels. See the table for the years 1870–90 in Charles Townshend, *Political Violence in Ireland: Government and Resistance since 1848* (Oxford: Clarendon Press, 1983), p. 152.

12 My calculations based on data in sources cited for Table 13.2. The importance of intimidation, as opposed to actual violence, has recently been stressed by Townshend, *Political Violence*, pp. 149–50. For the incidence of agrarian outrages by county, 1880–2, see the map in E. Rumpf and A. C. Hepburn, *Nationalism and Socialism in Twentieth-Century Ireland* (New York: Barnes & Noble, 1977), p. 52; for detailed outrage statistics, 1881–9, see the tables in Townshend, *Political Violence*, pp. 151, 177, 195.

13 Sources cited for Tables 13.2 and 13.3. Jail figures in Joseph V. O'Brien, *"Dear, Dirty Dublin": A City in Distress, 1899–1916* (Berkeley: University of California Press, 1982), p. 183. For comparative purposes the committals statistics must be treated with caution because, as in England, increasing numbers of cases after the middle of the century were dealt with summarily, not at assizes or quarter sessions.

14 "Criminal and Judicial Statistics, Ireland," *PP 1864* (3418), 57:667–8; *PP 1868–9* (4203), 58:749–50: *PP 1871* (443), 64:245; and a long series for 1876–95, in *PP 1897* (8616), 100:574–8, 618–19.

15 Indictable Offenses Known to the Police per 100,000 Population:

	1863	1870	1876	1879	1882	1887	1890	1892	1895
Eng. and Wales	253.1	231.0	202.4	206.7	198.1	152.3	134.4	132.6	—
Ireland Excl. agrarian crimes	—	—	169.8	219.7	206.5	185.2	171.3	174.0	157.9
Incl. agrarian crimes	161.1	175.6	173.8	236.1	273.8	203.3	182.3	182.7	163.8

Sources: For England, 1857–92, V. A. C. Gattrell and T. B. Hadden, "Criminal Statistics and their Interpretation," in E. A. Wrigley, ed., *Nineteenth-Century Society* (Cambridge: Cambridge University Press, 1972), Table IIIc, p. 394; for Ireland: sources cited in n. 14, this chapter. Author's calculations per 100,000 population based on demographic statistics in Mitchell and Deane, *Abstract*, p. 9.

16 Gattrell and Hadden, "Criminal Statistics," pp. 367, 369, 394.

17 See sources cited in n. 14, this chapter; and O'Brien, *Dublin*, pp. 182–7.

18 For England, see Gattrell and Hadden, "Criminal Statistics," pp. 365, 370–1, 391; and "Report of the Departmental Committee appointed to revise the Criminal Portion of the Judicial Statistics," *PP 1895* (7725), 108:107. For Ireland, *PP 1897* (8616), 100:582–3; and O'Brien, *Dublin*, pp. 183, 187–94.

19 For the long-term decline in homicide outrages and homicide agrarian outrages, see "Return of Outrages reported to the Royal Irish Constabulary from 1844 to 1880," *PP 1881* (2756), 77:887–913.

20 Among many other works, see Perkin, *Origins*, chs. 9, 10; Francis Hearn, *Domination, Legitimation, and Resistance: The Incorporation of the Nineteenth-Century English Working Class* (Westport, Conn.: Greenwood Press, 1978), ch. 6: Henry Pelling, *Popular Politics and Society in Late Victorian Britain* (New York: St. Martin's Press, 1968); David Kynaston, *King Labour: The British Working Class 1850–1914* (London: Allen & Unwin, 1976); Gareth Stedman Jones, "Working-Class Culture and Working-Class Politics in London, 1870–1900: Notes on the Remaking of a Working Class," *J. Soc. Hist.* 7 (Summer 1974):460–508; J. H. Porter, "Wage Bargaining under Conciliation Agreements, 1860–1914," *Econ. H. R.* 33 (Dec. 1970):460–75; and John S. Hurt, *Elementary Schooling and the Working Classes, 1860–1918* (London: Routledge & Kegan Paul, 1979). For the darker side, see Gareth Stedman Jones, *Outcast London: A Study in the Relationship Between Classes in Victorian Society* (Oxford: Clarendon Press, 1971); and Standish Meacham, *A Life Apart: The English Working Class, 1890–1914* (Cambridge, Mass.: Harvard University Press, 1977).

21 In addition to the works by Clark and Lyons (cited in n. 9, this chapter), see Clark and Donnelly, eds., *Irish Peasants*, pp. 10 (quotation), 271–83; L. P. Curtis, Jr., *Coercion and Conciliation in Ireland, 1880–92* (Princeton, N.J.: Princeton University Press, 1963); Barbara Solow, *The Land Question and the Irish Economy, 1870–1903* (Cambridge, Mass.: Harvard University Press, 1971); and William Feingold, "The Tenants' Movement to Capture the Irish Poor-Law Boards, 1877–1886," *Albion* 7 (Fall 1975):216–31.

22 Donald Akenson, *The Irish Education Experiment* (Toronto: University of Toronto Press, 1970), pp. 376–80; Richard Altick, *The English Common Reader: A Social History of the Mass Reading Public, 1800–1900* (Chicago: University of Chicago Press, 1957), pp. 169–71; Lawrence Stone, "Literacy and Education in England, 1640–1900," *Past & Present* 42 (Feb. 1969):118–23; and E. G. West, "Literacy and the Industrial Revolution," *Econ. H. R.* 31 (Aug. 1978):378–83.

23 Donald Richter has counted 452 "riotous disturbances" in the period 1865–1914. For a much shorter earlier period, 1790–1810, John Bohstedt has identified 740 "full-scale" riots, only 26 of which resulted in deaths. Richter, *Riotous Victorians* (Athens: Ohio University Press, 1981), p. 169 n. 15; Bohstedt cited in John Stevenson, *Popular Disturbances in England 1700–1870* (London: Longman, 1979), p. 306. But what is a riot? If we count "indictable riots known to the police," a set of statistics available from 1857 on, we can produce a total of 573 for 1865–70 alone. Calculated from the table in Stevenson, *Disturbances*, p. 295.

24 Stevenson, *Disturbances*, pp. 275 (quotation), 289–93; Richter, *Riotous Victorians*, pp. 51–61, 87–101. Return of the number of police supplied to meetings in Hyde Park (twenty-eight meetings, 1877–85) and Trafalgar Square, in "Report of the Committee on the Origin and Character of the Disturbances in the Metropolis on the 8th February 1886 ...." *PP 1886* (4665), 34:99.

25 Richter, *Riotous Victorians*, pp. 63–71, quotation on p. 68. In the 1886 Pall Mall Riots on "Bloody Monday," thousands of windowpanes were broken (£50,000 in damage claims). The riots produced the Riot Damages Act of 1886, compensating property owners for losses by a tax on the police district. Richter, *Riotous Victorians*, pp. 103–32; and T. A. Critchley, *The Conquest of Violence: Order and Liberty in Britain* (New York: Schocken Books, 1970), pp. 148–52.

26 Bloody Sunday, 13 Nov. 1887 (seventy-seven policemen injured; forty arrests made): Victor Bailey, "The Metropolitan Police, the Home Office and the Threat of Outcast London," in V. Bailey, ed., *Policing and Punishment in Nineteenth-Century Britain* (New Brunswick, N.J.: Rutgers University Press, 1981), p. 113; Richter, *Riotous Victorians*, pp. 147–52. On Featherstone, see "Report of the

Departmental Committee appointed to inquire into the Disturbances at Feather-stone, on the 7th September 1893," *PP 1893–4* (7234), 17:381–535. The report concluded that two persons were killed and eleven to fourteen wounded, and that in all ten shots were fired ("Report," p. 394). On Tonypandy, see Critchley, *Police*, pp. 176–81, and *Conquest*, pp. 166–9. In ? penetrating discussion Jose-phine Tey [Elizabeth MacKintosh], in *The Daughter of Time* (New York, 1951; Pocket Books ed., 1977), pp. 101–2, makes "Tonypandy" into an abstract noun that means the dominance of myth over the actual facts of history (i.e., bloody suppression of the workers versus the reality of "the whole affair was a bloody nose or two," p. 102).

27 The turmoil in Belfast produced lengthy investigations. See "Report of the Commission of Inquiry into the Origin and Character of the Riots in Belfast in July and September 1857," *PP 1857–8* (2309), 26:1–299; "Report of the Commission of Inquiry, 1864, respecting the Magisterial and Police Jurisdiction, Arrangements, and Establishment of the Borough of Belfast," *PP 1865* (3466), 28:1–397; and "Report of the Belfast Riots Commission," *PP 1887* (4925), 18:1–630. On the 1857 riots, see Constantine Fitzgibbon, *Red Hand: The Ulster Colony* (New York: Warner Books, 1973), pp. 208, 214–47; graphic if disjointed accounts of the Belfast riots of 1857, 1864, 1872, and 1886 are in Andrew Boyd, *Holy War in Belfast: A History of the Troubles in Northern Ireland* (New York: Grove Press, 1969).

28 In Manchester and Liverpool between 1846 and 1871, the Irish, a bit more than a tenth of the cities' populations, comprised one-third of all persons arrested for assaults on the police. In Birmingham in 1862–3 the Irish, only 4 percent of the city's population, accounted for 35 percent of all persons arrested for assaults on police (from 1867 to 1876, the Irish share fell to 11 to 20 percent of the total). Barbara Weinberger, "The Police and the Public in Mid-Nineteenth Century Warwickshire," in Bailey, ed., *Policing*, pp. 69–70, citing W. J. Lowe for the Lancashire figures. See also Roger Swift, "'Another Stafford Street Row': Law, Order, and the Irish Presence in Mid-Victorian Wolverhampton," in R. Swift and Sheridan Gilley, eds., *The Irish in the Victorian City* (London: Croom Helm, 1985), ch. 9. In Merthyr, Wales, in 1851, the Irish (9 percent of the population) committed half of the assaults on police. David Jones, *Crime, Protest, Community and Police in Nineteenth-Century Britain* (London: Routledge & Kegan Paul, 1982), pp. 86, 94, 105.

29 Richter, *Riotous Victorians*, pp. 19–33. Leon O Broin, *Fenian Fever* (New York: New York University Press, 1971), chs. 12–13; O Broin also explores the new Irish threat in North America. See the recent study by R. V. Comerford, *The Fenians in Context: Irish Politics and Society 1848–82* (Atlantic Highlands, N.J.: Humanities Press, 1985).

30 Browne, *Scotland Yard*, pp. 194–5; Kenneth Short, *The Dynamite War: Irish-American Bombers in Victorian Britain* (Atlantic Highlands, N.J.: Humanities Press, 1979); Rupert Allason, *The Branch: A History of the Metropolitan Police Special Branch* (London: Secker & Warburg, 1983). The Branch was initially staffed by RIC officers, and later by London detectives of Irish background.

31 Stevenson, *Disturbances*, pp. 279–81, quotation on p. 280; Pauline Millward, "The Stockport Riots of 1852: A Study in Anti-Catholic and Anti-Irish Senti-ment," in Swift and Gilley, eds., *The Irish in the Victorian City*, ch. 10; and Roger Swift, "Anti-Catholicism and Irish Disturbances: Public Order in Mid-Victorian Wolverhampton," *Midland History* 9 (1984):87–108.

32 Richter, *Riotous Victorians*, pp. 35–48; Walter L. Arnstein, "The Murphy Riots: A Victorian Dilemma," *Victorian Studies* 19 (Sept. 1975): 51–71. On popular anti-Catholicism, see Arnstein, *Protestant versus Catholic in Mid-Victorian England: Mr. Newdegate and the Nuns* (Columbia: University of Missouri Press, 1982); and G. F. A. Best, "Popular Protestantism in Victorian Britain," in R. Robson, ed.,

Ideas and Institutions of Victorian Britain (London: G. Bell & Sons, 1967), pp. 115–42.

33 A civil service inquiry commission of 1873 reported *inter alia* that the Dublin police was lacking in the libraries and billiard rooms, music bands, and educational and glee clubs that were available to London constables. "Report of the Commissioners ... into the condition of ... the Dublin Metropolitan Police," *PP 1873* (788), 22:App. 7, pp. 127–8. Conditions were not much changed a decade later; see "Report of the Committee of Inquiry into the Dublin Metropolitan Police," *PP 1883* (3576), 32:1–254.

34 Browne, *Scotland Yard*, chs. 14–18. O'Brien, *Dublin*, pp. 179–89; on Dublin's decline, see also Mary E. Daly, *Dublin: The Deposed Capital, A Social and Economic History 1860–1914* (Cork: Cork University Press, 1984).

35 Jenifer Hart, "The County and Borough Police Act, 1856," *Public Administration* 34 (1956):407–16; on the inspectors, see Henry Parris, "The Home Office and the Provincial Police in England and Wales, 1856–1870," *Public Law*, n. v. (1961):230–8.

36 40 & 41 Vict., c. 69 s. 8; 50 & 51 Vict., c. 41; Parris, "Home Office," pp. 242–55; Critchley, *Police*, pp. 120–2, 126–33. With the incorporation of new boroughs, the total number of forces oscillated in a range of 180–200.

37 On the size of forces, see, for Ireland, "Criminal and Judicial Statistics, Ireland, Part I, Police," *PP 1871* (443), 64:103 and *PP 1890–1* (6511), 93:57. And England: "Reports of Inspectors of Constabulary," *PP 1871* (12), 28:125, 198–9 and *PP 1881* (23), 51:108–10. J. P. Martin and Gail Wilson, *The Police: A Study in Manpower. The Evolution of the Service in England and Wales 1829–1965* (London: Heinemann, 1969), pp. 11, 48 (for 1857, 1945). Harcourt quoted in Hart, "County and Borough Police Act," p. 411. On Home Secretaries' local government experience, see Carolyn Steedman, *Policing the Victorian Community: The Formation of English Provincial Police Forces, 1856–80* (London: Routledge & Kegan Paul, 1984), pp. 27–30. A good local study is D. Foster, "The East Riding Constabulary in the Nineteenth Century," *Northern History* 21 (1985):193–211.

38 Steedman, *Policing*, pp. 41–7; Parris, "Home Office," pp. 249–51; Critchley, *Police*, pp. 143–4.

39 "Assimilate": Opinion of Insp.-Gen. Duncan McGregor, which was shared by London Commissioner Mayne, in "Report of the Commission ... to inquire into the State of the Constabulary ...," *PP 1866* (3658), 34:188. "Familiarity": Patrick Shea, *Voices and the Sound of Drums: An Irish Autobiography* (Belfast: Blackstaff Press, 1981), p. 29. The opinion of the 1914 select committee is quoted in Conor Brady, *Guardians of the Peace* (Dublin: Gill and Macmillan, 1974), p. 15. On arms, see *PP 1866* (3658), 34:186–8; "Instructions issued to the Royal Irish Constabulary in reference to carrying or using their Firearms," *PP 1868–9* (388), 51:523–6; Robert Curtis, *The History of the Royal Irish Constabulary* [hereafter, *RIC*] (Dublin: Moffat & Co., 1869), pp. 99–104; and Townshend, *Political Violence*, pp. 74–7.

The RIC solid-frame cartridge, .442 center-fire revolver, manufactured by the Birmingham firm of Philip Webley and adopted by the RIC in 1868, was "one of the most copied firearms of the last century, and look-alikes were turned out in Belgium, Germany, the United States, and Spain." Custer carried a pair at his famous "last stand" at the Little Big Horn. The RIC handgun was used throughout the British Empire – the Webley Mark IV.455 was "the British Army's workhorse during the Boer War" – because of the simplicity of its action and its cartridge ejection system. The RIC model led to the development of the short-barreled London Metropolitan Police revolver (1880), which because of its small size was easily concealable in a detective's jacket. Garry James, "Sixguns the Sun Never Set On," *1984 Guns & Ammo Annual* (Los Angeles, Petersen Publ. Co.,

1984), pp. 145–53, quotations on pp. 149, 152. I owe this reference to Mr. Steven Russell, a student in my undergraduate police history course.

For England, see Clive Emsley, "Arms and the Victorian Policeman," *History Today* 34 (Nov. 1984):37–42.

40 Inspector-General McGregor, 1853, quoted in Gregory Fulham, "James Shaw-Kennedy and the Reformation of the Irish Constabulary, 1836–38," *Eire-Ireland* 16, No. 2 (Summer 1981):100; Townshend, *Political Violence*, pp. 72–3, 76–8. Critchley, *Police*, pp. 147, 149, 157; Steedman, *Policing*, pp. 137–8. Steedman notes that fully twenty-two of twenty-four Chief Constables appointed in 1856–80 had been army or navy officers; in the formative period 1839–56, only seven of twenty-three Chief Constables appointed had had military officer experience (*Policing*, Table 1.2, p. 48).

41 Steedman, *Policing*, p. 116. Inspector Green, *In the Royal Irish Constabulary* (1905), quoted in Brady, *Guardians of the Peace*, p. 14. See also Townshend, *Political Violence*, pp. 79–84, 145–7, 176–7.

42 Christopher Hibbert, *The Roots of Evil: A Social History of Crime and Punishment* (Harmondsworth: Penguin Books, 1966), pp. 332–46; Critchley, *Police*, p. 162; Raymond B. Fosdick, *European Police Systems* (New York: The Century Co., 1915; repr., Montclair, N.J.: Patterson Smith, 1972), pp. 315–28, 344–8, 360–8; John J. Cronin, "The Fingerprinters: Identification as the Basic Police Science," in Philip John Stead, ed., *Pioneers in Policing* (Montclair, N.J.: Patterson Smith, 1977), pp. 159–77, esp. pp. 163, 173. As is well known, "English" work in fingerprinting was pioneered and practiced in British India – to keep track of the natives.

43 Fenianism: Derby to Disraeli, 17 Dec. 1867, and Senior Army Intelligence Officer in Ireland, Lt.-Col. W. H. A. Feilding, quoted and cited in Richter, *Riotous Victorians*, p. 30. On Feilding, see Phillip Thurmond Smith, *Policing Victorian London: Political Policing, Public Order, and the London Metropolitan Police* (Westport, Conn.: Greenwood Press, 1985), pp. 193–5. For the number of detectives and the creation of the CID, see Browne, *Scotland Yard*, pp. 149, 171–4, 182–96; Smith, *Policing Victorian London*, pp. 62, 67. In 1884 detectives formed 5 percent of London's police; a century later (1977) they accounted for 13 percent of all policemen in England [Ben Whitaker, *The Police in Society* (London: Eyre Methuen, 1979), p. 52].

"Sherlock Holmes," of course, dates from *The Strand Magazine* (1891). A recent writer has noted that the line drawings that accompanied the Holmes stories depict the great private detective as the *beau-ideal* Anglo-Saxon gentleman; Holmes's arch-enemy, the fiendish Professor Moriarty, was an Irishman. L. P. Curtis, Jr., *Apes and Angels: The Irishman in Victorian Caricature* (Newton Abbot: David & Charles, 1971), pp. 4, 52, 97.

44 Critchley, *Police*, pp. 157–9; Steedman, *Policing*, pp. 53–63; Curtis, *RIC*, p. 93; Mark Finnane, *Insanity and the Insane in Post-Famine Ireland* (London: Croom Helm, 1981), pp. 34–5; James Cramer, *The World's Police* (London: Cassell, 1964), pp. 84–5 (*Gardaí*). In 1871, the Constabulary Office in Dublin received "about 50,000" incoming letters, a number that exceeded the totals from any three other Castle offices put together; cf. n. 87, Chapter 7, this book. "Report . . . into the Civil Service in Ireland: Royal Irish Constabulary," *PP 1873* (831), 22:Q. 3350, ev. of Insp.-Gen. J. Stewart Wood.

45 Martin and Wilson, *Police: Study in Manpower*, pp. 78, 91–6, and 153–65, especially Tables VI.7–VI.9, quotation on p. 162, my emphasis. In 1965, 23 percent of police work-time was devoted to "traffic"; 29 percent to "crime," including investigative and court time and paperwork in the station; 39 percent to "civil order," 90 percent of this being patrolling; 9 percent to "internal organization"; and less than 1 percent to "public order." An army of civilians now

helps to push the paperwork around: 19,000 police civilians for the 84,000 police officers in England in 1965, compared to 5,000 civilians for 60,000 police in 1949.

46 Curtis, *RIC*, pp. 150–89. Belfast Police Act: 28 & 29 Vict., c. 70 (1865); Townshend, *Political Violence*, pp. 84–8, 189–90. Londonderry received a similar police in 1885. On police casualties in the 1872 riots, (one RIC man killed, seventy-three wounded), see Townshend, *Political Violence*, p. 87; in the 1886 riots (one Head Constable killed, 371 policemen injured), "Return of Officers and Men of the Military and Constabulary Forces Killed or Wounded in the Disturbances at Belfast during June, July, and August 1886," *PP 1886* (49), 53:371–80. Whereas in the Easter Rising of 1916 the military took the brunt of the killing (116 soldiers but only 16 policemen, of whom 3 were in the Dublin force), in the subsequent War for Independence the constabulary was targeted by the IRA, 176 RIC men being killed in 1920 alone. O'Brien, *Dublin*, p. 263; G. C. Duggan, "The Royal Irish Constabulary," in O. Dudley Edwards and Fergus Pyle, eds., *1916: The Easter Rising* (London: MacGibbon & Kee, 1968), p. 99.

47 Richter, *Riotous Victorians*, pp. 53, 143.

48 Force sizes in 1870: Liverpool, 1,097; Manchester, 753; Birmingham, 400; Bristol, 303; Leeds, 280; Sheffield, 270. Sources: see n. 37, this chapter, and Appendix III, Table III.1, this book.

49 Richter, *Riotous Victorians*, pp. 39–43, 67–9; Steedman, *Policing*, pp. 32–8; Stevenson, *Disturbances*, pp. 286–9.

50 Steedman, *Policing*, pp. 37, 67. "Report ... [on] Disturbances at Featherstone," *PP 1893–4* (7234), 17:381–93; and on the use of county police, see "Report of the Inter-departmental Committee on Riots," *PP 1895* (7650), 35:605–14. In 1910, at Tonypandy, Wales, 800 imported London police assisted county police and soldiers in suppressing riots by striking mine workers. Critchley, *Police*, pp. 179–81. (Cf. n. 26, this chapter.)

51 "Report of the Committee of Inquiry into the Royal Irish Constabulary," *PP 1883* (3577), 32:Q.3711, ev. of Head Constable Richard Allen; see also QQ.1132, 1332, 4413, 6822.

52 Richter, *Riotous Victorians*, pp. 9, 29, 57; Bailey, "Threat of Outcast London," p. 113; Critchley, *Conquest*, pp. 145, 191. On special constables today, see Cramer, *World's Police*, pp. 52–3.

53 Liam de Paor, *Divided Ulster*, 2d ed. (Harmondsworth: Penguin Books, 1971), pp. 98–9, 182–204; John Darby, *Conflict in Northern Ireland: The Development of a Polarised Community* (Dublin: Gill and Macmillan, 1976), pp. 60–1; Jack Holland, *Too Long a Sacrifice: Life and Death in Northern Ireland since 1969* (Harmondsworth: Penguin Books, 1982), p. 49. A highly critical account is in Fitzgibbon, *Red Hand*, pp. 355–7, 375–90. The longest and most impartial treatment is Sir Arthur Hezlet, *The "B" Specials: A History of the Ulster Special Constabulary* (London: Tom Stacey, Ltd., 1972).

54 Estimates based on figures in Critchley, *Police*, p. 153; W. J. Lowe, "The Lancashire Constabulary, 1845–1870: The Social and Occupational Function of a Victorian Police Force," *Criminal Justice History* 4 (1983): 55, for Lancashire, 1845–70; and Steedman, *Policing*, pp. 93–6, for Staffordshire and Buckinghamshire, 1856–80.

55 "Obsession": Shea, *Voices and the Sound of Drums*, p. 99. RIC retention figures: "Report of the Committee of Inquiry on the Royal Irish Constabulary," *PP 1902*, Command Paper [Cmd.] 1087, 42:279ff., "Report," p. 23, for men joining in 1877–9; Lancashire: Lowe, "Lancashire Constabulary," Table 3, p. 55, for men joining in 1866–70. For length of service in the RIC, see tables in *PP 1871* (443), 64:103; *PP 1883* (3577), 32:468.

56 RIC resignations: for 1850–9, see "Return of the Number of County Inspectors, Sub-Inspectors, Head and other Constables, by their respective ranks ...," *PP 1860* (509), 57:844; for 1865–72, "Report ... into the Civil Service in Ireland:

Royal Irish Constabulary," *PP 1873* (831), 22:116, 142; and for 1883–1913, "Report of the Committee of Inquiry on the Royal Irish Constabulary and the Dublin Metropolitan Police," *PP 1914*, Cmd. 7421, 44:247ff., "Report," p. 8. Dublin: O'Brien, *Dublin*, p. 179. The Lancashire rate I have calculated from figures in Lowe, "Lancashire Constabulary," pp. 42, 57, based on a force strength of 660 men in 1857 and 900 in 1868. In England, national turnover rates for *all* reasons (resignation, dismissal, death, pension) were high but falling – 13 percent of force strength in the 1860s, 7 percent by the 1880s. Resignations accounted for one-half to three-fourths of all turnovers. Steedman, *Policing*, pp. 92–3; Martin and Wilson, *Police: Study in Manpower*, p. 13.

57 *PP 1873* (831), 22:QQ. 976, 1375–7, 1397 ("compare"), 1554, 3148, 3195 ("America"). To recruit RIC men, the Staffordshire constabulary placed advertisements in Irish newspapers (ibid., Q. 3182). The number of Irish-born recruits in the Lancashire force rose from 5 percent in 1850 to 18 percent by 1870. Lowe, "Lancashire Constabulary," p. 46.

58 Steedman, *Policing*, pp. 75–84, 118–19; Lowe, "Lancashire Constabulary," pp. 44–6.

59 In the RIC in 1881, 76 percent of the subconstables were single; in the various English county forces in 1863, 15 to 37 percent of the men were single. In 1863, 68 percent of Dublin's policemen were single compared to 35 percent of the men in Manchester's force. "Return of the Police Force of the United Kingdom; giving ... Numbers of Married and Single Men," *PP 1864* (409), 35:599–629; Head, *Fortnight*, p. 51; *PP 1883* (3557), 32:470; Steedman, *Policing*, p. 81; Lowe, "Lancashire Constabulary," p. 46. The English attitude was summed up by the Liverpool Head Constable, who told his recruits that they might "marry (and I hope you *all* will, if she is a good washer, and can mend and darn)." "Address ... to Young Men," written 1852, revised 1879, in Critchley, *Police*, pp. 147–8, my emphasis.

60 Steedman, *Policing*, pp. 117–18; Lowe, "Lancashire Constabulary," p. 52.

61 *PP 1902*, Cmd. 1087, "Report," p. 24. The theme of the loneliness of the English constable pervades Steedman's book, *Policing*, esp. pp. 143–7, 161–3.

62 From the mid-1880s on, as part of the effort to have the RIC follow the English police, the "constable" rank was renamed "sergeant" and that of "subconstable" became "constable."

63 *PP 1902*, Cmd. 1087, "Report," p. 23, "Minutes of Evidence," QQ. 388–90, 2069–72, 2237–41, 3354–6. Married police, by rank: see n. 59, this chapter; religion, by rank: see Appendix V, n. 38, this book.

64 Head, *Fortnight*, p. 53; *PP 1860* (509), 57:843; *PP 1914*, Cmd. 7421, "Report," p. 25.

65 Steedman, *Policing*, Table 1.2, p. 48.

66 *PP 1873* (831), 22:QQ.267, 2557. The committee recommended (pp. 141–3) a higher proportion be promoted from the ranks. The arguments for merit promotion stressed the need for reward for service, improvement of rank-and-file morale, and an end to religious discrimination. Arguments for a gentlemen officer corps were varied and revealing. Merit promotion, it was objected, would have the force "officered and guided by a lower form of intelligence" (Subinsp. H. A. Blake, Q. 2374). Discipline would be harder to enforce, since a promoted man had over the years made too many friends and thus incurred too many obligations; but others argued that promoted career policemen would be *too* harsh on the rank-and-file men. It was also argued that older, merit-promoted men would be resistant to new ideas and would loaf in the twilight of their careers. By contrast, the present system of gentlemen officers was said to be advantageous because it included articulate men of "higher education" who were ambitious because they were young and who, because of their background, were able to get on socially with local gentry and magistrates. Ibid., QQ. 1232–6,

1349, 1450, 2555, 2918–23, 3258–61. An officer as high-ranking as Col. George Hillier, Deputy Inspector-General since 1867, thought the existing system a good one since "the Irishman has naturally a good deal of feudalism in his composition" (Q. 2918).

67 For 1860 and 1880, see Appendix V, n. 38, this book; *PP 1873* (831), 22:Q. 846, ev. of J. O'Connell; 1895: Brady, *Guardians of the Peace*, p. 13; 1920: Hezlet, *'B' Specials*, pp. 3, 25.

68 On the turmoil, see Patrick Shea's recollections, in *Voices and the Sound of Drums*, chs. 3–8. Collins quoted in Séamus Breathnach, *The Irish Police from Earliest Times to the Present Day* (Dublin: Anvil Books, 1974), p. 119.

69 Another feature retained from the British era was the regulation that no *gárda* could serve within 30 miles of his home.

70 Brady, *Guardians of the Peace*, pp. 1, 67–87, 132–41, 240–9, quotations on pp. 72–3, 87, 245; Breathnach, *Irish Police*, pp. 118–19; Cramer, *World's Police*, pp. 83–5; D. J. Hickey and J. E. Doherty, *A Dictionary of Irish History since 1800* (Dublin: Gill and Macmillan, 1980), p. 187.

71 Michael Farrell, *Arming the Protestants: The Formation of the Ulster Special Constabulary and the Royal Ulster Constabulary, 1920–27* (London: Pluto Press, 1983); Darby, *Conflict*, pp. 58–63; Holland, *Sacrifice*, pp. 158–71; John Magee, *Northern Ireland: Crisis and Conflict* (London: Routledge & Kegan Paul, 1974), pp. 70–1; W. D. Flackes, *Northern Ireland: A Political Directory*, 1st ed. (New York: St. Martin's Press, 1980), pp. 198–200; G. H. Boehringer, "Beyond Hunt: A Police Policy for Northern Ireland of the Future," *Social Studies* 2 (1973):399–414; and Paddy Hillyard, "Police and Penal Services," in John Darby and Arthur Williamson, eds., *Violence and the Social Services in Northern Ireland* (London: Heinemann, 1978), pp. 120–9. Liam de Paor, *Divided Ulster*, 2d ed., p. 204, notes that a general redistribution of arms, mainly Walther pistols, was made to RUC men from late 1970 on. On the rearming, see also Fitzgibbon, *Red Hand*, pp. 354–5; Hillyard, "Police and Penal Services," p. 123; and Richard Deutsch and Vivian Magowan, *Northern Ireland, 1968–73: A Chronology of Events*, 2 vols. (Belfast: Blackstaff Press, 1973), 1:47, 51, 73. I owe this last reference to Prof. David Miller, Carnegie-Mellon University.

72 Holland, *Sacrifice*, pp. 159, and 163, 171 (quotations). Flackes, *Directory*, 1st ed., p. 200.

73 Police as victims of the political violence have increased from roughly one in twenty killings in the early 1970s to one in five by the early 1980s. The worst single attack against police in sixteen years of bloodshed came in February 1985 when the IRA fired nine mortar shells into the police station at Newry, killing nine officers (seven men, two women) and injuring thirty-two (*Dallas Times Herald*, 1 Mar. 1985). The statistics for killings in 1971–83 are set out in the following table.

Security statistics for killings in Northern Ireland, 1971–83

		Police		Military			
Years	RUC	Prison Officers	RUC Reserve	British army	UDR[a]	Civilians	Total killings
1971–4	47	—	9	232	45	773	1,106
1975–8	32	8	26	57	41	573	737
1979–82	33	6	23	77	39	209	387
1983	9	0	9	5	10	42	75

Totals for three 4-year periods

Category totals and percentage distributions

	Police	Military	Civilians
1971-4	56 (5.1%)	277 (25.0%)	773 (69.9%)
1975-8	66 (9.0%)	98 (13.3%)	573 (77.7%)
1979-82	62 (16.0%)	116 (30.0%)	209 (54.0%)
1983	18 (24.0%)	15 (20.0%)	42 (56.0%)

*a*Replaces "B"-Specials, 1970. At one time 18 percent Catholic, by 1978 the UDR had fallen to 3 percent Catholic.

Sources: Annual data for 1969–78, in Flackes, *Directory*, 1st ed., p. 210; and for 1979–82, Flackes, *Northern Ireland: A Political Directory*, 2d ed. (London: Ariel Books, British Broadcasting Corp., 1983), pp. 320–1. For 1983, see *Dallas Times Herald*, 4 Jan. 1984. Figures for prison officers are available only from 1976 on. Flackes includes them in his civilian totals; I have included prison officers under police, not civilians.

74 Whitaker, *Police in Society*, p. 44.
75 Ibid., p. 86; Flackes, *Directory*, 1st ed., p. 200.
76 Jenifer Hart, *The British Police* (London: Allen & Unwin, 1951), pp. 45–68; Critchley, *Police*, pp. 190–236. A brief interwar development was the creation of Hendon Metropolitan Police College (1934–9), an innovative institute to train young direct-entry officers for the London police. The experiment, reminiscent of the RIC cadet program of 1842–1921, was highly controversial; amid charges of "class measures" and "militarism," it was abandoned on the outbreak of World War II. But since 1945, the English police forces have instituted programs, increasingly large, of cadet trainees for *constable* positions. Critchley, *Police*, pp. 203–9, 310–11.
77 "Royal Commission on the Police: Final Report," Cmd. 1728, Memorandum of Dissent, by Dr. A. L. Goodhart, pp. 157–79, quotation on p. 177. On the 1962 Commission, see Critchley, *Police*, pp. 267–92; Cramer, *World's Police*, pp. 101–8.
78 Statute 1964 c. 48 s. 64 (3), Sched. 10, Pt. 1, repealing 19 & 20 Vict., c. 69. Critchley, *Police*, pp. 293–5; John A. Rhind, "The Need for Accountability," in David Pope and Norman Weiner, eds., *Modern Policing* (London: Croom Helm, 1981), pp. 42–52.
79 Rhind, "Accountability," pp. 45, 51.
80 Whitaker, *Police in Society*, pp. 22, 74–84, 249–51, 307–11. Look at the figures for crimes of violence against the person in England and Wales:

1949	4,900
1969	37,400
1976	77,700

London, the center of crime, remains the area most seriously underpoliced. In 1977 the metropolis had the same number of police (21,000) that it had in 1921, even though over that half-century crime (known indictable offenses) had increased more than twentyfold. Ibid., pp. 79, 82, 116–17.
81 Sir Charles Jeffries, *The Colonial Police* (London: Max Parrish, 1952), pp. 30–3, 46, 219; John J. Tobias, "The British Colonial Police: An Alternative Police Style," in Stead, ed., *Pioneers*, pp. 249–59.
82 David H. Bayley, *The Police and Political Development in India* (Princeton, N.J.: Princeton University Press, 1969); and his essay, "The Police and Political Development in Europe," in Charles Tilly, ed., *The Formation of National States in Western Europe* (Princeton, N.J.: Princeton University Press, 1975), pp. 328–79.

83 Jeffries, *Colonial Police*, p. 25; Brady, *Guardians of the Peace*, p. 2.

84 See my discussion in Chapter 1, this book; and Ted Robert Gurr, *Rogues, Rebels, and Reformers* (London and Beverly Hills, Calif.: Sage, 1972), pp. 117−23.

85 Alan F. Hattersley, *The First South African Detectives* (Cape Town: Howard Timmins, 1960), ch. 3, esp. pp. 46, 51.

86 Jeffries, *Colonial Police*, p. 29; Cramer, *World's Police*, p. 123.

87 Stephen M. Edwardes, *The Bombay City Police: A Historical Sketch, 1672−1916* (London and Bombay: Oxford University Press, 1923), chs. 2−4; Jeffries, *Colonial Police*, p. 83; Bayley, *India*, p. 46.

88 Jeffries, *Colonial Police*, pp. 30−1, 219. In agreement with Jeffries is Tobias, "British Colonial Police," pp. 249−50. By contrast, Charles Reith, in his *British Police and the Democratic Ideal* (London: Oxford University Press, 1943), pp. 202−3, and *A New Study of Police History* (Edinburgh: Oliver & Boyd, 1956), p. 215 n. 1, argues for the London police as the model for colonial forces.

89 Jeffries, *Colonial Police*, pp. 30, 61−4, 126; Cramer, *World's Police*, pp. 182, 184, 188−90, 92−3.

90 Jeffries, *Colonial Police*, pp. 33, 35; Cramer, *World's Police*, pp. 150−1.

91 Cramer, *World's Police*, pp. 165−9.

92 Jeffries, *Colonial Police*, p. 126. See E. A. Burton, "The Policing of Bermuda from the Earliest Times," *Bermuda Historical Quarterly* 12 (1955):77−108.

93 H. T. Lambrick, *Sir Charles Napier and Sind* (Oxford: Clarendon Press, 1952); Lt.-Gen. Sir William Napier, *The Life and Opinions of General Sir Charles James Napier*, 4 vols. (London: J. Murray, 1857), 4:9−10, 79−80, 173−8; Bayley, *India*, pp. 43−4.

94 Napier, *Life*, 4:175−6, letter to Lord Dalhousie, 24 July 1849.

95 Jeffries, *Colonial Police*, pp. 31−2; Cramer, *World's Police*, pp. 136−48; Bayley, *India*, pp. 45−7; Tobias, "British Colonial Police," pp. 250−1; Sir Percival Griffiths, *To Guard My People: The History of the Indian Police* (London: Ernest Benn Ltd., 1971), chs. 7−9. See also J. C. Curry, *The Indian Police* (London: Faber and Faber, 1932); and Anandswarup Gupta, *The Police in British India, 1861−1947* (New York: Humanities Press, 1980). Today the unarmed Indian police, more than half a million men spread over 318 districts, is headed by an Inspector-General and has the same rank structure as the old RIC. In Pakistan, where Napier pioneered his Irish-style constabulary, the modern police remain organized along the lines of the 1861 Indian Police Act. Cramer, *World's Police*, pp. 148−9; Tobias, "British Colonial Police," pp. 258−9.

96 The Irish founders were Inspectors Thomas Thompson and William Macartney; the Indian police officer, Sir George Campbell, had also served in Ireland. Jeffries, *Colonial Police*, pp. 29−30, 36; Cramer, *World's Police*, p. 123; Tobias, "British Colonial Police," pp. 251−5; H. L. Dowbiggin, "The Ceylon Police and its Development," *Police Journal* 1 (1928):203−17; G. K. Pippet, *A History of the Ceylon Police, 1795−1870* (Colombo: The Times of Ceylon Co., 1938).

97 New Zealand: Cramer, *World's Police*, p. 160. Australia: Cramer, *World's Police*, p. 113; G. M. O'Brien, *The Australian Police Forces* (Melbourne: Oxford University Press, 1961), chs. 2−3, esp. pp. 40, 58, 62. Canada: Cramer, *World's Police*, pp. 115−22, quotation on p. 116. Among many excellent studies, the best on the formative period are Ronald Atkin, *Maintain the Right: The Early History of the Northwest Mounted Police, 1873−1900* (London: Macmillan, 1973); and R. C. MacLeod, *The North-West Mounted Police and Law Enforcement, 1873−1905* (Toronto: University of Toronto Press, 1976). Today eight of the ten Canadian provinces are policed by "the Mounties"; only thickly populated Ontario and Quebec have their own separate forces.

98 Cramer, *World's Police*, p. 125.

99 Countries listed in the order of their date of establishment of police, from 1866 to 1900. Cramer, *World's Police*, pp. 130, 153, 162−3, 175, 205, 222, 235, 241−2. See

also W. H. Gillespie, *The Gold Coast Police 1844–1938* (Accra: The Government Printer, 1955); Tekena N. Tamuno, *The Police in Modern Nigeria, 1861–1965* (Lagos: Ibadan University Press, 1970); W. Robert Foran, *The Kenya Police 1887–1960* (London: Robert Hale Ltd., 1962); Colin Harding, *Frontier Patrols: A History of the British South Africa Police and Other Rhodesian Forces* (London: G. Bell & Sons, 1937); and Cyril Marlow, *A History of the Malawi Police Force* (Zomba: The Government Printer, 1971), Malawi: formerly Nyasaland (Northern Rhodesia). The experience in Ghana (Gold Coast) was not atypical: Select native recruits were (from 1875 on) sent to Ireland for advanced instruction "of a military nature." The Gold Coast Constabulary was disarmed in 1896 but, after a wave of disturbances, rifles and sword-bayonets were reissued in 1898. Ghana's police remain armed today.

100 Cramer, *World's Police*, p. 374; Lennox Van Onselen, *A Rhapsody in Blue* (Cape Town: Howard Timmins, 1960), a history of the South African police.

101 Cramer, *World's Police*, p. 153. Gillespie, *Gold Coast Police*, chs. 1–2, esp. pp. 37–8, discusses the RIC influences; a useful appendix, pp. 74–82, lists some 200 officers in the Gold Coast Constabulary 1894–1938 by name, date of birth, and record of police service elsewhere.

102 Tamuno, *Police in Modern Nigeria*, p. 45. See his section, "RIC Influences on the Lagos Police, 1895–99," pp. 30–2; and also pp. 6, 29, 33–4, 43–8, 54, 60.

103 Quoted in Foran, *Kenya Police*, p. 39; on the RIC influence, see pp. 19, 25, 36–40.

104 Tom Bowden, *The Breakdown of Public Security: The Case of Ireland 1916–1921 and Palestine 1936–1939* (London and Beverly Hills, Calif.: Sage, 1977), ch. 4, quotations on pp. 163, 266; Jeffries, *Colonial Police*, pp. 152–62; Cramer, *World's Police*, pp. 321–2.

105 Jeffries, *Colonial Police*, pp. 172, 175; Critchley, *Police*, pp. 208, 246–8; Tobias, "British Colonial Police," pp. 255–6.

APPENDIX V

1 I have since seen it cited in Tom Bowden, *The Breakdown of Public Security: The Case of Ireland 1916–1921 and Palestine 1936–1939* (London and Beverly Hills, Calif.: Sage, 1977), p. 31; and in Charles Townshend, *Political Violence in Ireland: Government and Resistance since 1848* (Oxford: Clarendon Press, 1983), pp. 69–72, 78, 80.

2 Michael Brophy [ex-sergeant, RIC], *Sketches of the Royal Irish Constabulary* (London: Burns and Oates, 1886), p. 24. By contrast, the last recruit on the Constables Register, hired 31 Aug. 1922, is listed as Constable 83,743 (HO 184/42). But Brophy, writing in the 1880s, speaks of at least two "revisions" in the numbering of recruits.

3 In the early years of the English police (the 1860s), only 0.5 men per 100 *force strength* were pensioned in *all* of the forces in England and Wales and not many more, 2.0 per 100, in the London Metropolitan Police. J. P. Martin and Gail Wilson, *The Police: A Study in Manpower. The Evolution of the Service in England and Wales 1829–1965* (London: Heinemann, 1969), p. 73. On English police pensions, see T. A. Critchley, *A History of Police in England and Wales*, 2d ed. (Montclair, N.J.: Patterson Smith, 1972), pp. 168–71. London's policemen had the best pension system. This was established by an act of 1839, whose terms were similar to those set earlier for the Irish constabulary by the acts of 1822 and 1836.

4 These figures compare favorably with known actual recruiting figures for the later 1860s (an annual average of 1,185 men in 1866–71), a period of increasing personnel turnover. "Report of the Commissioners appointed by the Treasury to inquire into the Condition of the Civil Service in Ireland: The Royal Irish Constabulary," *PP 1873* (831), 22:149.

5 "An Act to enable Grand Juries to present additional Sums for Constables in

Ireland ...," 55 Geo. 3, c. 158 ss. 4–5, later amended by 5 Geo. 4, c. 28 s. 10. Government police: 3 Geo. 4, c. 103 ss. 34–5; 6 Will. 4, c. 13 ss. 46–8.

6 6 Will. 4, c. 13 s. 48.

7 5 Geo. 4, c. 28 s. 9, amending 3 Geo. 4, c. 103 s. 35, which had permitted a yearly payment of up to the whole of a man's salary. The 1824 act required the county to pay half of a man's disability payment.

8 3 Geo. 4, c. 103 s. 34; 6 Will. 4, c. 13 ss. 46–7.

9 9 & 10 Vict., c. 97 (1846).

10 10 & 11 Vict., c. 100 ss. 1–2, 7.

11 "Return of all Superannuations granted to Constables and Subconstables of Police in Ireland ...," PP 1831–2 (359), 26:465–8; "Return of the Names of all Persons receiving Pensions or Gratuities ... in the Irish Constabulary," PP 1843 (467), 50:95–8; and "Return of the ... Police Superannuation Funds ...," PP 1847 (571), 56:239–72. Costs: for 1836, see "Return of the Police Superannuation Fund ...," PP 1842 (427), 38:255; and for 1846, PP 1847 (571), 56:269.

12 The opinion is that stated in "Report of the Commission directed by the Treasury to inquire into the State of the Constabulary Force of Ireland, with reference to their Pay and Allowances, Strength and Organization, Classification, Conditions of Service, and System of Superannuation," PP 1866 (3658), 34:176–7.

13 "An Act to regulate the Superannuation Allowances of the Constabulary Force in Ireland, and the Dublin Metropolitan Police," 10 & 11 Vict., c. 100 ss. 1–10. A copy of the bill, dated 5 July 1847, is in PP 1847 (618), 1:189–95.

14 Analysis of HO 184/1 reveals that a very high proportion of the men joining in 1823–8 (28 percent) were age twenty-eight or older. A thirty-five-year-old recruit in 1822 would reach age sixty in 1847. By the early 1860s, about 140 men with twenty or more years' service were being superannuated out of the constabulary each year (total of 968 in 1860–6). "Return of the Number of Men who, since the 1st January 1860, have been superannuated from the Irish Constabulary," PP 1867 (262), 57:819.

15 See the investigations into the causes of high resignations and low force morale. "Report of the Commission ... to inquire into the State of the Constabulary," PP 1866 (3658), 34:167 ff.; "Report ... into the Civil Service in Ireland: Royal Irish Constabulary," PP 1873 (831), 22:131 ff.; "Report of the Committee of Inquiry into the Royal Irish Constabulary," PP 1883 (3577), 32:255ff.; Brophy, Sketches, pp. 40–3. The situation worsened: Pension rates were cut in 1866, and witnesses before the 1882 inquiry asked for a return to the rates set under the 1847 act. PP 1883 (3577), 32:266.

16 The documents give us only one cryptic clue. On the inside front cover of HO 184/45 a clerk has written in faint pencil, "Circular of 3d April [18]51. Sent out 17 Apr. 51." (There are no pencil notations on the front or back covers of the Constables Register.) Also in HO 184/45, on page 188, beginning with the appointment of Daniel O'Connell Fitzgerald, RC, Cork, "Appt. not Confirmed," and J. C. Nowlan, RC, Carlow, Cadet, appointed 16 May 1851, the records of these and all other officers appointed 1851–84 have been lined over as if they had been transposed to a later Register.

17 Insp.-Gen. William Miller to Chief Secretary Leveson Gower, 10 Oct. 1829, HO 100/229/200–1.

18 Police circular, 9 May 1835, Chief Secretary's Office Registered Papers [hereafter, CSORP] 1593, ISPO, DC.

19 See Joseph Lee, "Marriage and Population in Pre-Famine Ireland," Econ. H.R. 21 (Aug. 1968):283–95; Kevin O'Neill, Family and Farm in Pre-Famine Ireland: The Parish of Killashandra (Madison: University of Wisconsin Press, 1984), pp. 177–86. O'Neill finds for both laborers (c. age twenty-six) and farmers (c. age twenty-eight) a slightly rising age at marriage in the period 1815–40. By age thirty to

thirty-four, among males, 77 percent of farmers and 91 percent of laborers were married. By old age, nearly everyone in Killashandra (except perhaps clergymen and policemen) was or had been married.

20 "Return of the Police Force of the United Kingdom; giving Comparative Numbers of Married and Single Men . . .," *PP 1864* (409), 35:600, 629. By 1881, the percentage of single men in the force had dipped slightly to 67 percent. "Report of the Inquiry into the RIC ," *PP 1883* (3577), 32:468.

21 "Minutes of Evidence taken before the [Commons'] Select Committee appointed to examine the nature and extent of the Disturbances . . . in Ireland," *PP 1825* (20), 7:168, ev. of Insp.-Gen. T. Powell of Leinster.

22 "Minutes of Evidence taken before the Lords' Select Committee appointed to examine the nature and extent of the Disturbances . . . in Ireland," *PP 1825* (200), 7:52, ev. of R. Willcocks; unsigned paper, 23 Feb. 1825, in Box C, Papers of Henry Goulburn, Surrey Record Office, Kingston-on-Thames.

23 About one-fourth of the men on the register are listed as having had military service (army, navy, militia): 18 percent, immediately before their police appointment, and 5 percent, next-to-last to appointment.

24 Leveson Gower to W. Peel, 10 June 1829, Leveson Gower Letter Books, M736/161, PRO, Four Courts, Dublin.

25 A police circular of 5 Oct. 1833 barred private recommendations and warned recruits that persistence in this practice would hurt their candidacy (CSORP 6290).

26 Population shares are the percentage share of the total population of Ireland, by province, based on the average of the decennial censuses, 1821, 1831, 1841.

27 The drop in 1837–40 (see Table V.10), Melbourne's Administration, may represent a reaction to the shift to increasing promotion from the ranks in 1829–36.

28 Littleton to Lord Acheson, 2 Oct. 1834, Papers of Edward Littleton, Baron Hatherton, D260/M/OI/4/66, Staffordshire Record Office, Stafford.

29 Lord Morpeth to Insp.-Gen. James Shaw-Kennedy, 23 Sept. 1836, Morpeth Correspondence, Papers of 2d Earl of Mulgrave, 1st Marquess of Normanby, Mulgrave Castle, Yorkshire.

30 Robert Curtis, *The History of the Royal Irish Constabulary* (Dublin: Moffat & Co., 1869), pp. 54–5. On the cadets, see Brophy, *Sketches*, pp. 10–14. The ranks of County Inspector and Subinspector had been subdivided into three ranks by 2 & 3 Vict., c. 75 (1839). A generation later, one of every four officer appointments was still a promotion from the ranks. *PP 1873* (831), 22:140.

31 *PP 1825* (200), 7:51–2, testimony of 21 May 1824.

32 "Return of the Total Number of all Magistrates, Constables, and Sub-Constables appointed under . . . the Constabulary Act . . .; distinguishing those who profess the different sects of Religion . . .," *PP 1824* (257), 22:405–8; "A Return of the Number, &c., of Roman Catholics of each Rank, in each County, in the Constabulary," *PP 1833* (379), 32:446–50; and for 1841, HO 184/54, appendix.

33 *PP 1833* (379), 32:446–50.

34 Returns listing Chief Constables and Subinspectors, by religion, in each county, December 1833 and January 1834, in Hatherton Papers, D260/M/OI/1022a, 1024–5, 1036.

35 Littleton to More O'Ferrall, 15 Oct. 1834, Hatherton Papers, D260/M/OI/4/118.

36 See L. Perry Curtis, Jr., *Apes and Angels: The Irishman in Victorian Caricature* (Newton Abbot: David & Charles, 1971), ch. 4.

37 Many years later, in 1881, about a fourth of the lowest rank and file but three-fourths of Head Constables were married: subconstables (24 percent), acting constables (51 percent), constables (68 percent) and Head Constables (74 percent). Subconstables comprised 8,426 of the total of 10,846 men. *PP 1883* (3577), 32:470.

38 The percentages in Table V.12, which show the highest rank obtained by each religious group of constables recruited in 1816–40 (HO 184/1–2), may be

compared with the percentages of Catholics at each rank in the constabulary at two later dates.

	Percent of Catholics in the Irish constabulary	
	1860	1880
County Inspectors and Subinspectors	22.4%	19.9%
Head Constables*a*	44.5	60.4
Constables	58.0	70.0
Acting constables	66.9	63.7
Subconstables	72.3	74.3
TOTAL	69.2	71.8

*a*The highest of the nonofficer ranks.
Sources: "Return of the Number of County Inspectors, Sub-Inspectors, Head and other Constables, by their respective ranks; religious denominations ...," *PP 1860* (509), 57:843–8; "Return showing the Number of Officers, and Constables, in the Royal Irish Constabulary ... distinguishing Protestants and Roman Catholics ...," *PP 1880* (256), 59:505–6.

Sources

EPIGRAPHS

"First Report of the Select Committee appointed to inquire into the State of Ireland . . ." *PP 1825* (129), 8:118, ev. of Daniel O'Connell. 237

Robert Peel to Henry Goulburn, 9 Feb. 1814, in Goulburn II/13, Papers of Henry Goulburn, Surrey Record Office, Kingston-on-Thames. 277

Peel to Goulburn, 26 Dec. 1822, Papers of Sir Robert Peel, BL Add. MS 40328 f. 309, British Library, London. 277

Charles Reith, *British Police and the Democratic Ideal* (London: Oxford University Press, 1943), p. 35. 277

Anthony Sampson, *The New Anatomy of Britain* (New York: Stein & Day, 1971), p. 365. 277

G. Fitzgerald to William Gosset, 23 Dec. 1832, Cashel, Tipperary, HO 100/243/252, Public Record Office, London. 316

Anglesey to Cloncurry, 27 May 1833, T1068/29/35, Papers of Henry William Paget, 1st Marquess of Anglesey, Public Record Office of Northern Ireland, Belfast. 316

Melbourne to Anglesey, 12 Sept. 1832, Anglesey Papers, T1068/31/118. 376

William Cobbett, speech of 18 Mar. 1833, in *Hansard's Parliamentary Debates* [hereafter, *Hansard*], 3d Series, 356 vols. (London: T. C. Hansard, 1830–91), 16:731. 376

Charles Rowan to Edwin Chadwick, 26 Apr. 1839, Papers of Edwin Chadwick, MS 1722, D. M. S. Watson Library, University College, University of London. 376

"Revenge . . .": Threatening letter printed in E. J. Hobsbawm and George Rudé, *Captain Swing* (New York: Pantheon Books, 1968), p. 206. 385

Charles Buller and Thomas Macaulay, speeches of 16 and 19 Feb. 1844, respectively, *Hansard* 72:1056–7, 1170–1. Buller's speech brought an immediate and lengthy reply by Lord Stanley (cols. 1068–96). 430

Francis Burgess to Sir James Graham, 5 Nov. 1841, HO 65/10/109. 438

Constable George Tandy, evidence at the trial of Chartist George White, Birmingham, 15 Aug. 1842, in *Northern Star*, 3 Sept. 1842. 455

Charles Buller, speech of 16 Feb. 1844, *Hansard* 72:1058. 465

Blackwood's Magazine 64 (Oct. 1848):490. 482

[Sir Arthur Helps, pseud.,] *A Letter from One of the Special Constables in London . . . on the Late Occasion of their being Called Out to Keep the Peace* (London: W. Pickering, 1848), p. 5. 484

Blackwood's Magazine 64 (Oct. 1848): 477. 484

Thomas Francis Meagher, *Meagher of the Sword*, ed. Arthur Griffith (Dublin: M. H. Gill & Son, 1917), p. 158. 490

William Smith O'Brien, quoted in Denis Gwynn, *Young Ireland and 1848* (Cork: Cork University Press, 1949), p. 231. 490

John Mitchel, *Jail Journal, or Five Years in British Prisons* (New York, 1854; repr., Dublin: M. H. Gill & Son, 1913), p. 6. 490

E. R. Rice, speech of 10 Mar. 1856, *Hansard* 140:2181. 501

Maitland, *Justice and Police*, pp. 105, 107–8. 518

Clarence Day, *Thoughts Without Words* (1928), reprinted in *The Best of Clarence Day* (New York: Alfred A. Knopf, 1948), p. 451. The full quotation is: 518

> When eras die, their legacies
> Are left to strange police.
> Professors in New England guard
> The glory that was Greece.

Mayo to Hardy, and Entwissell to Dublin Police Commissioner, 1867, quoted in Phillip Thurmond Smith, *Policing Victorian London: Political*

TABLES

assizes, exclusive of quarter sessions; for the latter, see *PP 1823* (306), 16:639–86.   232

7.1   "Return of the Total Number of all Magistrates, Constables, and Sub-Constables, appointed . . . under the Act of the 3d of Geo. IV c. 103; distinguishing those who profess the different sects of Religion . . . ," *PP 1824* (257), 22:405–8.   257

7.2   For national totals, 1805–12 and 1822–8, see G. R. Porter, *Progress of the Nation*, 1st ed., 3 vols. (London: C. Knight, 1836–43), 3:225–6. For national totals differentiated by type of offense, 1822–8, see "Summary Statement of the Number of Persons charged with Criminal Offenses . . . during the last Seven Years," *PP 1829* (256), 22:427–36.   270

8.1   Monthly returns of military force levels, WO 17/2797–2800. Figures rounded by author to the nearest ten for the Northern District and to the nearest hundred for England and Wales.   280

8.2   Distribution return, by regiments, of the number of troops and companies in the Northern District, May 1829, HO 40/23/291.   283

8.3   "A Return of the Dates, during 1818 to 1827, at which any Volunteer or Yeomanry Corps in Great Britain and Ireland was called out for Actual Service," *PP 1828* (273), 17:283–7.   284

9.1   "Return of the Number and Nature of Offences committed in Ireland . . . in 1831 and 1832; as far as such have been reported to Government," 9 Mar. 1833, *PP 1833* (80), 29:422, 432.   326

9.2   For 1831–3, "A Return of the Peace Preservation Force in Ireland, . . . the Number and Distribution thereof . . . ," *PP 1834* (201), 47:399–414; for 1835, "A Return of the Number of Peace Preservation Police . . . ," *PP 1836* (527), 12:145.   329

9.3   "A Return of the Number of Persons who have lost their Lives . . . in Affrays with the Constabulary," *PP 1830–1* (67), 8:403–83; "A Return of the Number of Persons who have lost their Lives in Affrays with the Constabulary," *PP 1846* (280), 35:237–60.   334

9.4   For all offenses, "Return of the Comparative Number of Criminal Offenders committed in Ireland, and the Number convicted, 1828–1834," *PP 1835* (303), 45:343–4, and Porter, *Progress*, 1st ed., 3:226. Figures for murder/manslaughter and for riotous assembly armed by night and attacking dwelling houses are calculated from committal statistics in "Report by the Lords' Select Committee appointed to inquire into the state of Ireland since the year 1835 in respect of Crime and Outrage," *PP 1839* (486), 12:1092–3, ev. of T. Drummond.   339

9.5   Calculated from "Returns, from each County, of the Number of Persons Committed to the different Gaols for Trial in Ireland." For 1831, *PP 1831–2* (299), 33:19–92; for 1832, *PP 1833* (61), 29:89–162; for 1834, *PP 1835* (295), 45:269–342; and for 1835, *PP 1836* (97), 42:379–458.   341

9.6   Constabulary: Papers of Edward Littleton, Baron Hatherton, D260/ M/OI/1022a, 1024–5, 1036, Staffordshire Record Office, Stafford; "A Return of the Number, &c., of Roman Catholics of each Rank, in each County, in the Constabulary," *PP 1833* (379), 32:446–50. Peace Preservation Force: *PP 1834* (201), 47:399–414.   348

9.7   Dismissal statistics for 1830–1 are in Country Letter Books [hereafter, CLB] 1829–30 ff. 3–4, CLB 1830 ff. 3–4, CLB 1830–1 ff. 1–3, CLB 1831 ff. 1–2, CLB 1831–2 ff. 1–2; for 1832–5, "'C' – Constables Dismissed," annual index volume to Chief Secretary's Office Registered Papers [hereafter, CSORP]; and for 1836,

CSORP 1836/34, 49, 79, 213. All of the preceding sources are in ISPO, DC, Dublin. For constabulary distribution in 1832 and 1836, see "A Return of the Police of Ireland ...," *PP 1833* (518), 32:453; and "A Return of the Constabulary Force employed ... in Ireland ...," *PP 1837* (391), 45:303.   351

9.8   All offenses: G. R. Porter, *Progress of the Nation*, 3d ed. (London: J. Murray, 1851), p. 668. Specified offenses: *PP 1839* (486), 12:1096–7, ev. of Drummond; and "Return of the Number of Criminal Offenders committed for Trial ... in each County in Ireland," *PP 1846* (696), 34:178–9. See also *Hansard* 46:27–9, 84–5, 7 Mar. 1839, speeches of F. Shaw and Morpeth.   370

9.9   *PP 1839* (486), 12:1088–91, ev. of Drummond; "Return of Outrages reported to the Constabulary," 1838–42, *PP 1843* (460), 51:152; and *Hansard* 46:29–31, 86–7.   371

10.1   Calculated by author from statistics for each category in Porter, *Progress*, 3d ed., pp. 646, 668.   379

10.2   For England, 1835–41, see "Return of the Number of Criminal Offenders Committed for Trial ...," *PP 1845* (651), 37:76. For Ireland, 1835–8, *PP 1839* (486), 12:1093, ev. of Drummond; and for 1839–41, *PP 1846* (696), 35:178–9.   380

10.3   Committals per 100,000 population adapted from figures in Jenifer Hart, "Reform of the Borough Police, 1835–1856," *E.H.R.* 70 (1955):413–14.   382

10.4   For Birmingham, see T. A. Critchley, *A History of Police in England and Wales*, 2d ed. (Montclair, N.J.: Patterson Smith, 1972), p. 81 n.; for Oldham, John Foster, *Class Struggle and the Industrial Revolution: Early Industrial Capitalism in Three English Towns* (New York: St. Martin's Press, 1974), pp. 57–9. Other towns: F. C. Mather, *Public Order in the Age of the Chartists* (Manchester: Manchester University Press, 1959), pp. 79–80, 120; and Eric Midwinter, *Social Administration in Lancashire, 1830–1860: Poor Law, Public Health, and Police* (Manchester: Manchester University Press, 1969), pp. 136–7.   397

10.5   Adapted from Mather, *Public Order*, p. 114. See my explanation, n. 93, Chapter 10, this book.   401

11.1   Monthly returns of military force levels, WO 17/2799–2802. Annual figures and monthly averages rounded by author to the nearest ten for the Northern District and to the nearest hundred for England and Wales.   434

11.2   Distribution return of regiments and number of rank and file in the Northern District, January 1840, the Papers of Sir Charles James Napier, BL Add. MS 54516 f. 13, British Library, London.   436

11.3   "Return of the Police established in each County or Division of a County in England and Wales ... stating ... the Date when the Police was Established ...," *PP 1842* (345), 32:649–74; "Return of Police Constables in each County in England and Wales, in 1846," *PP 1847* (540), 47:631–41; "Return of the Number of Police in each County of England and Wales, ... 1840–1853," *PP 1854* (211), 53:617–30; and "Return of the Number of Rural Police in each County in England and Wales, ... 1853–55," *PP 1856* (186), 50:665.   442

11.4   Monthly returns of military force levels, WO 17/2802–5; annual figures and monthly averages rounded to the nearest ten for the Northern District and to the nearest hundred for England and Wales. "Return of the ... Yeomanry Cavalry called out in aid of the Civil Power in the Years 1840, 1841, and 1842, showing the

Number of Days each Corps was on Duty," *PP 1844* (128), 33:217–18; "Return of the Number of Yeomanry Corps, the Number of Officers and privates in each Regiment, and the Number of Times . . . called out in aid of the Civil Power," *PP 1850* (121), 35:127–40.   463

11.5   For 1843, "Return of Outrages specially reported to the Constabulary Office in Ireland . . .," 1842–5, *PP 1846* (217), 35:451; for 1844–56, "Return of Outrages reported to the Royal Irish Constabulary from 1844 to 1880," *PP 1881* (2756), 77:911.   473

11.6   "Returns of the Number of Criminal Offenders committed for Trial . . ., in Ireland." For 1843–5, *PP 1846* (696), 34:178–9; for 1846–9, *PP 1850* (1271), 45:624–5; and for 1850–6, *PP 1857* (2248), 42:268–9.   474

11.7   *PP 1881* (2756), 77:911.   478

11.8   Calculated by the author from statistics, for England and Ireland for each category of crime, in the following sources. For 1841–9, see Porter, *Progress*, 3d ed., pp. 646, 668. For 1850–3, see "Return of the Number of Persons Committed or Bailed for Trial at the Assizes and Sessions," for Ireland, *PP 1854–5* (1930), 43:88–9; and for England, *PP 1857* (2246), 35:106–7.   479

12.1   *Hansard* 140:232, 2128, 2132, speeches of Sir George Grey, 5 Feb. and 10 Mar. 1856.   511

12.2   "Reports of the Inspectors of Constabulary," *PP 1871* (12), 28:125, 198–9.   517

13.1   Outrage returns 1838–41, *PP 1843* (460), 51:152; 1842–5, *PP 1846* (217), 35:451; and 1854–81, "Numerical Returns of Outrages reported to the Constabulary Office in Ireland during 1881, with Summaries for Preceding Years," *PP 1882* (3119), 55:628–9.   523

13.2   In addition to the sources listed for Table 13.1, see returns of *agrarian* outrages and total outrages, 1844–80, *PP 1881* (2756), 77:887–906, 911–12; for 1880–1, "Return of Outrages reported to the Royal Irish Constabulary Office in each Month of 1880 and 1881, and in January 1882," *PP 1882* (7), 55:615; and for 1881–2, "Return of Outrages reported . . . in 1881, 1882, and January 1883," *PP 1883* (6), 57:1047–9. For agrarian outrages only, 1876–94, see "Criminal and Judicial Statistics, Ireland, 1895," *PP 1897* (8616), 100:590–1, 622–3. For returns of total outrages 1883–90, I have relied on Charles Townshend, *Political Violence in Ireland: Government and Resistance since 1848* (Oxford: Clarendon Press, 1983), Table 1, p. 151.   524

13.3   Committal statistics for riot and for murder were extracted from the following sources. *England*: "Return of the Number of Persons Committed or Bailed for Trial at Assizes and Sessions," 1851–60, *PP 1861* (2860), 60:566. "Criminal and Judicial Statistics, England," 1861–70, *PP 1871* (442), 64:52; 1871–80, *PP 1881* (3088), 95:52; 1881–90, *PP 1890–1* (6443), 93:52; 1876–95, *PP 1897* (8352), 100:39–40; and for 1894–1913, *PP 1914–16*, Command Paper (Cmd.) 7767, vol. 82, p. 13.
    Ireland: "Return of the Number of Persons Committed or Bailed for Trial at Assizes and Sessions," 1848–54, *PP 1854–5* (1930), 43:88–9; 1851–60, *PP 1861* (2863), 52:266–7. "Criminal and Judicial Statistics, Ireland," 1861–70, *PP 1871* (443), 64:387–8; 1871–5, *PP 1877* (1822), 86:414–17; 1876–95, *PP 1897* (8616), 100:614–15; and for 1895–1914, *PP 1914–16*, Cmd. 8077, vol. 82, pp. xxvi–xxvii.   526

13.4   Annual returns of force strength for nineteenth-century Irish and

English police are readily available in the *Parliamentary Papers*; and see Appendixes II and III, this book. In addition, for Ireland to 1921, see RIC Register, HO 184/35, 36, PRO, London; and Tom Bowden, *The Breakdown of Public Security: The Cases of Ireland 1916–1921 and Palestine 1936–1939* (London and Beverly Hills, Calif.: Sage, 1977), Table 2, p. 31. For the period 1921–70, see Conor Brady, *Guardians of the Peace* (Dublin: Gill and Macmillan, 1974), pp. 77, 87, 124; D. J. Hickey and J. E. Doherty, *A Dictionary of Irish History since 1800* (Dublin: Gill and Macmillan, 1980), p. 187; *Encyclopaedia of Ireland* (Dublin: Allen Figgis, 1968), p. 180; Liam de Paor, *Divided Ulster*, 2d ed. (Harmondsworth: Penguin Books, 1972), p. 100; John Darby, *Conflict in Northern Ireland* (New York: Barnes & Noble, 1976), p. 59; and Michael Farrell, *Arming the Protestants* (London: Pluto Press, 1983), pp. 169, 203, 267–8, 290. For 1970 to the present, see Paddy Hillyard, "Police and Penal Services," in John Darby and Arthur Williamson, eds., *Violence and the Social Services in Northern Ireland* (London: Heinemann, 1978), p. 124. And for information on the most recent *Gárda* and RUC force strength my grateful acknowledgments to Prof. Kevin Boyle, University College, Galway; Prof. David Miller, Carnegie-Mellon University, Pittsburgh; and Mr. D. O Luanaigh, Keeper of Printed Books, National Library of Ireland, Dublin, for their helpful correspondence.

For the total number of police and total number of forces in England, see Critchley, *Police*, pp. 146, 244 n.; J. P. Martin and Gail Wilson, *The Police: A Study in Manpower. The Evolution of the Service in England and Wales 1829–1965* (London: Heinemann, 1969), pp. 12, 32, 47–8, 61, 78, 82, 84; and for the most recent figures, Ben Whitaker, *The Police in Society* (London: Eyre Methuen, 1979), pp. 115, 120–1, 173, 223, and *New York Times*, 15 and 19 July 1981.

530

MAPS

Note: Maps not listed here, plus Maps 6.1, 11.3, 12.1, and 12.2, are original maps drawn by the University Media Services Center, the University of Texas, Arlington, on the instructions of the author.

For Maps 4.1, 5.1, 6.1–6.3, 7.1, 11.1–11.3, 12.1, 13.2, and II.1 (appendix), see the adjacent text and notes for sources.

ILLUSTRATIONS

Note: Figures not listed here are graphs. For Figure 9.2 and the figures in the
appendixes, Figs. I.1–I.2 and V.1–V.5, see the adjacent text and notes for sources.

Select bibliography

NOTE ON ARCHIVES

Just as the fires of civil war in Paris in 1871 destroyed most of the historical records of the Prefecture of Police, so in Dublin a half-century later during the Irish Civil War, the fires set at the Public Record Office, Four Courts, incinerated much of the history of the British-administered police in Ireland.* Comparison of pre–Civil War police and constabulary records in the Chief Secretary's Office [as calendared in Herbert Wood's *Guide to the Records Deposited in the Public Record Office of Ireland* (Dublin, 1919), pp. 206–7] with the records that remain and are housed at the Irish State Paper Office in Dublin Castle reveals just how extensive the destruction was in 1922. For years scholars believed that no history of the Irish police could ever be written.

But with the help and enthusiasm of the staff at the Irish State Paper Office, I was able to locate certainly incomplete but also perhaps sufficient, if scattered, documents that became the basis for this book. In the process I learned, as have many other scholars over the past two decades, that it is worth rummaging through the State Paper Office in Dublin. For the subject of public order and police, three long series at the Public Record Office, London – Home Office 100, 122, and 184 – comprise the principal supplements to the extant public records in Dublin.

It is worth noting that historical collective violence has destroyed some sources of English police history. Half a century ago, the wing of the British Library that housed printed primary source materials on police sustained heavy damage – appropriately enough, the result not of domestic strife but of German aerial bombardment during World War II. The book call slips returned to me with this notation were mute testimony to the Battle of Britain. I was fortunate in being able to locate some of the missing works at the National Library of Ireland, a curious benefit of the Free State's neutrality during the war.

By and large, however, the English records are intact and ample. At the Public Record Office, the voluminous Home Office 40–5 series ("domestic" and disturbances) contain abundant materials on public order and disorder in early-nineteenth-century England. In researching the subject of police in England, the biggest problem is that, like the forces themselves, the records for the English town and county police are decentralized. The historical materials are located in dozens of

---

*In April 1922 an anti-Treaty faction of the IRA had occupied the Four Courts. In June, Free State authorities used British artillery to shell the rebels. The IRA group surrendered, but before leaving they set fire to the building. The obliteration of the historical record affected countless subjects besides police and protest.

On Paris, see Alan Williams, *The Police of Paris, 1718–1789* (Baton Rouge: Louisiana State University Press, 1979), pp. 305–6.

municipal archives and county record offices. The time, travel, and labor required for this cross-country research have deterred scholars from producing even a single comprehensive, truly national history of the nineteenth-century English provincial police.

By contrast, writing the history of the London police has been a far easier task. In 1959 most of the Metropolitan Police records were transferred from New Scotland Yard Library to the Public Record Office. The addition of this "Mepol" series to the already deposited Home Office 59–65 series has meant that the vast bulk of the Metropolitan Police records are housed at a single location. A residue of historical police records remains at New Scotland Yard Library and at the Police Museum in Bow Street.* Unfortunately, I was informed that these records are closed to the general public and to scholars, though they are available to members of police departments. If I were an American *policeman*, I remember being told, then I might see them!

For both countries, England and Ireland, the private papers of public figures were consulted. The Papers of Sir Robert Peel, 2d Baronet, at the British Library, of course constitute essential reading. A number of other collections proved to be surprising mines of information: the Papers of Thomas Orde, 1st Baron Bolton (at the National Library of Ireland), the Papers of Henry Goulburn (Surrey Record Office), the Papers of Henry William Paget, 1st Marquess of Anglesey (Public Record Office of Northern Ireland), and the Papers of Edward Littleton, 1st Baron Hatherton (Staffordshire Record Office). In tracking down private papers, my only real disappointment came when I was informed that the Papers of Edward Stanley, 14th Earl of Derby, which were in the care of The Hon. Robert Blake, Provost of The Queen's College, Oxford, might be seen only when Lord Blake was in town. Alas, he was out when I could be in. I was fortunate, however, in finding much of Stanley's correspondence during his Irish chief secretaryship in the Earl Grey Papers at Durham and in the archives of the State Paper Office in Dublin.

Some investigations resulted in dead ends. Inquiries at the National Register of Archives, Chancery Lane, London, and at the National Library of Scotland, Edinburgh, brought replies that no papers exist for two important Scotsmen, Charles Grant (Baron Glenelg) and Thomas Drummond. Grant, Irish Chief Secretary in 1818–21, was a lifelong bachelor; his title became extinct at his death. Drummond, Irish Under-Secretary in 1835–40, married in 1835 but died five years later, at age forty-two, leaving three young daughters and his widow, who lived on until 1891. Much of the correspondence of Grant and Drummond can be found in the great public depositories in London and Dublin, and also in the private papers of their contemporary fellow office holders.

What follows is a *select* bibliography, a list of the principal primary and secondary sources used. Among the latter, the reader will find many recently published books and articles, which are recommended for further reading.

Parliamentary sources listed are the collections of debates and the select committee reports. Specific parliamentary accounts and papers are simply too numerous to list here; full citations are given in the book's extensive chapter notes.

For printed primary and secondary works, full citations including the publisher are given in the chapter notes. In this bibliography, only the place and date of publication are listed. The place of publication is understood to be London, unless otherwise stated. "Cambridge, Mass." is distinguished from "Cambridge [in England]." (Reprints: date of publication only.)

---

*See Leon Radzinowicz, *A History of English Criminal Law and its Administration from 1750,* 4 vols. (London: Stevens & Sons, 1948–68), 3:615–16, 4:425–6.

SELECT BIBLIOGRAPHY

I. MANUSCRIPT SOURCES

(a) PRIVATE PAPERS
  ENGLAND
    LONDON
      BRITISH LIBRARY ADDITIONAL MANUSCRIPTS
        30109–30110   Papers of Sir Robert Wilson
        37298–37305   Papers of Richard Colley, 1st Marquess Wellesley
        40181–40360   Papers of Sir Robert Peel, 2d Baronet
        49125–49130,   Papers of Sir Charles James Napier
        54512–54516
      PUBLIC RECORD OFFICE
        PRO 30/8/329   Papers of William Pitt the Younger:
                          Chatham Papers, 1784–7
        WO 80/1, 6   Papers of Gen. Sir George Murray, commander-in-chief
                          in Ireland, 1825–8
      UNIVERSITY OF LONDON. UNIVERSITY COLLEGE.
      D. M. S. WATSON LIBRARY
        Papers of Edwin Chadwick
          Memoranda, plans, proposals, etc. MSS 2, 3, 5, 15, 16
          Correspondence MSS 1382, 1722, 1733, 1794, 1874, 1947

    CASTLE HOWARD, YORKSHIRE
      Papers of George William Frederick Howard, Viscount Morpeth,
        7th Earl of Carlisle J 19/1/9–11
                              J 19/11

    DEVONSHIRE RECORD OFFICE, EXETER
      Papers of Henry Addington, 1st Viscount Sidmouth 152M, 1812–25

    UNIVERSITY OF DURHAM. DEPARTMENT OF PALEOGRAPHY
      AND DIPLOMATIC
        Papers of Charles Grey, 2d Earl Grey
          Correspondence with Melbourne and Anglesey, 1830–2
          Papers on Ireland

    MULGRAVE CASTLE, YORKSHIRE
      Papers of Constantine Henry Phipps, 2d Earl of Mulgrave, 1st Marquess of
        Normanby
          Morpeth Correspondence

    STAFFORDSHIRE RECORD OFFICE, STAFFORD
      Papers of Edward Littleton, 1st Baron Hatherton   D 260/M/OI/
        1   Anglesey Correspondence
        2–5   Letter Books
        6–15   In-Letters
        157–2617   Constabulary and Peace Preservation Police
      Letter Books of Sir Charles Chetwynd, 2d Earl Talbot
        Chetwynd Papers, D 649/9/1–3

    SURREY RECORD OFFICE, KINGSTON-ON-THAMES
      Papers of Henry Goulburn
        Box C [actually nine boxes]   Gregory Correspondence
        II/12   Wellington Correspondence
        II/13–16   Peel Correspondence

II/21–2   Wellesley Correspondence
Goulburn "Memoirs"

IRELAND
BELFAST
PUBLIC RECORD OFFICE OF NORTHERN IRELAND
Papers of Henry William Paget, 1st Marquess of Anglesey
D 619/1–6   T 1068/1–8, 15, 20–31

DUBLIN
NATIONAL LIBRARY OF IRELAND
Papers of Thomas Orde, 1st Baron Bolton
Bolton MSS 15889–909, 15926–48
Papers of Charles Gordon-Lennox, 4th Duke of Richmond
Richmond MSS 58–9, 65–74

PUBLIC RECORD OFFICE, FOUR COURTS
Letter Books of Lord Francis Egerton Leveson Gower,
1st Earl of Ellesmere M736–M738

STATE PAPER OFFICE, DUBLIN CASTLE
Correspondence of Lord Lt. 10th Earl of Westmorland
Westmorland MSS 139, 146–8, 172, 176

(b) PUBLIC DOCUMENTS
DUBLIN
NATIONAL LIBRARY OF IRELAND
Kilmainham Papers (the Army in Ireland)
Kilmainham MSS 1035, 1043–7 Military, 1814–15, 1821–9
Kilmainham MS 1218 Yeomanry, 1804–14

STATE PAPER OFFICE, DUBLIN CASTLE
Chief Secretary's Office Registered Papers, 1819–39
Country Letter Books, 1827–32
General Private Correspondence, 1804–14, 1814–21, 1821–30
Official Papers Miscellaneous and Assorted [1832–82], 1832–8
Official Papers, Series 2, 1790–1831
  Magistrates and Police
  Military
  Yeomanry
Private Official Correspondence, 1789–93, 1820
State of the Country Papers, Series 1 [1796–1831], 1810–31
  MS Calendar
  Correspondence

LONDON
PUBLIC RECORD OFFICE
Home Office Records
HO 40. Disturbances. In-Letters to Home Office, Civil and Military
Reports

1–3	Luddism	1812–17
6–7	Luddism and London	1817
11–13	Radicalism and Parliamentary Reform	1820
18–35	Radicalism in "distressed areas"	1823–37
	[Midlands and North] and in London	

39–40   Chartism   1838
49–54   Chartism   1839–40

HO 41. Disturbances. Entry Books [Out-Letters from Home Office]
  1   1816
  6–8   1820–30

HO 42. Domestic. George III. Letters and Papers
  6–9   1785–6
  143   1815
  153–7   1816

HO 43. Domestic. Entry Books
  23   1814–15
  29   1820
  56   1838–9

HO 44. Domestic. George IV and Later. [Continuation of HO 42]
   2   1820
   9   1821
  18   1828–9

HO 45. Registered Papers, 1841–1927
  260, 347, 350, 4609, 5244L, 5276, 5800, 6092, 6236
  Specific cases or incidents, police and public order, 1842–55

HO 50. Military. Correspondence
  431, 435, 440, 461   1815–21

HO 59. Police [London]. Courts & Magistrates. Correspondence
  1–2 1820–31

HO 60. Police [London]. Entry Books
  1   1821–30

HO 61. Police. Metropolitan. Correspondence
  1–9   1820–33
  19–21   1837–8

HO 65. Police. Entry Books
  2   London, 1811–20
  4   County police, 1839–54
  10   Manchester and Birmingham, 1839–42
  11–13   London, 1829–41

HO 100. Ireland. Correspondence. Letters and Papers
  11–21   1784–7
  47–59   1794–5
  82–7   1798–9
  175–256   1813–38

HO 122. Ireland. Letter Book (General)
  11–13   1813–27

HO 184. Irish Constabulary
  1–2   Constables Register, 1816–40
  45   Officers Register [1816–84], 1816–50
  54   Index

Records Other Than Home Office
  Mepol 2. Metropolitan Police Records [prior to 1959 at New Scotland
  Yard Library]

20   Irish constabulary, 1825–9
21   English county police, 1830–57
29, 38 London police
59–67 Chartism

PC 2. Pleas of the Crown
  196 1815

SP 37. State Papers. Domestic. George III. Letters and Papers
  20–1 1780

TS 11. Treasury Solicitor Papers
  662/1 Queen Caroline Riots, 1821
  663/3 Queen Caroline Riots, 1821
  1263   Colonel Brereton's trial, 1831

War Office Records. WO 4, 17, 33, 34, 35

WO 4/110	Letter Book of C. Jenkinson, Secretary at War, 1780
268	Recruits to London police, 1845
WO 17/1084–1117	Army in Ireland: Force Levels, 1812–48
2793–2804	Army in England and Wales: Force Levels, 1812–48
WO 33/18	Memorandum on use of troops to suppress riots, by C. Clode, 1867
21	Memorandum on military aid to the civil power in Ireland, 1870
WO 34/103	Correspondence relating to the Gordon Riots, 1780
109, 234	The Riot Act, the military, and crowds, 1715–35
WO 35/25–6	Army in Ireland, Out-Letters from Royal Military Hospital at Kilmainham, 1813–33

II. PRINTED SOURCES

(a) PARLIAMENTARY
DEBATES AND JOURNALS

The Parliamentary Register, or the History of the Proceedings and Debates of the House of Commons in Ireland, 15 vols., 1784–95.

The Parliamentary History of England from the Earliest Period to the Year 1803, 36 vols. Vols. 21–9, 1780–92.

Cobbett's Parliamentary Debates, 41 vols. 1803–20.

The Parliamentary Debates, New [2d] Series, 25 vols., 1820–30.

Hansard's Parliamentary Debates, 3d Series, 356 vols. [1830–91]. Vols. 1–142, 1830–56.

House of Commons Journals. Vols. 61–77, 1802–23.

REPORTS OF SELECT COMMITTEES

Year	Volume (Number)	Subject
1812	II (127)	Nightly Watch & Police of the Metropolis (i.e., London)
1816	V (510)	Police of the Metropolis
1817	VII (233, 484)	Police of the Metropolis

Year	Volume (Number)	Subject
1818	VIII (423)	Police of the Metropolis
1822	IV (440)	Police of the Metropolis
1824	VIII (372)	Disturbances in Ireland
1825	VII (20, 200)	Disturbances in Ireland
1825	VIII (129)	Disturbances in Ireland
1828	VI (533)	Police of the Metropolis
1829	IV (342)	Police of Dublin
1831–2	XVI (677)	Disturbed Counties in Ireland
1831–2	XXII (271, 663)	Payment of Tithes in Ireland
1833	XIII (344)	Municipal Corporations (England)
1834	XVI (600)	Police of the Metropolis
1835	XXIII (116)	Municipal Corporations (England)★
1839	XI, XII (486)	Crime and Outrage in Ireland
1839	XIX (169)	County Constabulary (England)★
1852	XIV (438)	Outrages in Ireland
1852–3	XXXVI (603, 715)	Police in England and Wales
1866	XXXIV (3658)	Irish Constabulary★
1873	XXII (788)	Dublin Metropolitan Police★
1873	XXII (831)	Royal Irish Constabulary★
1883	XXXII (3576)	Dublin Metropolitan Police
1883	XXXII (3577)	Royal Irish Constabulary

(b) NEWSPAPERS
ENGLAND
Bath Herald, 1856
Birmingham Gazette, 1856
Birmingham Journal, 1854, 1856
Brighton Examiner, 1854, 1856
Brighton Herald, 1856
Daily Universal Register (London), 1785 [later named The Times]
General Advertiser (London), 1785
John Bull, 1842
Liverpool Mercury, 1856
London Chronicle, 1785–6
Manchester Guardian, 1842, 1854, 1856
Morning Chronicle (London), 1785, 1814
Morning Herald (London), 1786
Morning Post (London), 1856
Norfolk Chronicle and Norwich Gazette, 1856
Northern Star, 1842
Oldham Chronicle, 1854, 1856
Portsmouth Times and Naval Gazette, 1856
Public Advertizer (London), 1786–7, 1792
The Times (London), 1808, 1814, 1822, 1829, 1835–7, 1839, 1854–6
Wigan Examiner, 1856
York Herald, 1856

Francis Place Collection of Newspapers, Vol. 31 (years 1827–9), Department of Printed Books, British Library

★Report of a commission, not a select committee.

IRELAND
>   *Cork Mercantile Chronicle*, 1814
>   *Cork Volunteer Journal*, 1786
>   *Correspondent* (Dublin), 1808, 1814, 1822
>   *Dublin Evening Mail*, 1836
>   *Dublin Evening Post*, 1785–94, 1803, 1808, 1814, 1822, 1835–8
>   *Dublin Morning Post*, 1788, 1795, 1822
>   *Evening Herald* (Dublin), 1808, 1822
>   *Faulkner's Dublin Journal*, 1780, 1785–6, 1792, 1795, 1803, 1814, 1822
>   *Freeman's Journal* (Dublin), 1780, 1785–92, 1803, 1808, 1814–16, 1822, 1836
>   *Hibernian Journal* (Dublin), 1786–96, 1808
>   *Patriot* (Dublin), 1814, 1822
>   *Rights of Irishmen*, 1792
>   *Saunders's News-letter* (Dublin), 1786–99, 1808, 1835
>   *Volunteer Evening Post* (Dublin), 1785–7

(*c*) PERIODICALS
>   *Annual Register*, 1768, 1780, 1792–1848
>   *Blackwood's Magazine*, 1848
>   *Gentleman's Magazine*, 1819
>   *Illustrated London News*, 1842–8
>   *Punch*, 1842–8
>   *Quarterly Review*, 1828, 1842

(*d*) MEMOIRS AND BIOGRAPHIES

Addison, H. R. *Recollections of an Irish Police Magistrate*. 1862, 1883.

Anglesey, 7th Marquess of, George Paget. *One-Leg: The Life and Letters of Henry William Paget, 1st Marquess of Anglesey*. 1961.

Bamford, Samuel. *Passages in the Life of a Radical*. 2 vols. Heywood, 1842–4.

Bruce, H. A. *Life of General Sir William Napier*. 2 vols. 1864. Vol. 1.

Cloncurry, 2d Baron, Valentine Lawless. *Personal Recollections*. Dublin, 1849.

Colchester, 1st Baron, Charles Abbot. *Diary and Correspondence of Charles Abbot, Lord Colchester, Speaker of the House of Commons*. Edited by his son, Lord Colchester. 3 vols. 1861.

Cookson, J. E. *Lord Liverpool's Administration: The Crucial Years, 1815–1822*. Edinburgh, 1975.

Correspondence between the Rt. Hon. William Pitt and Charles, Duke of Rutland, Lord Lieutenant of Ireland, 1781–87. 1842.

Croker, J. W. *The Croker Papers: Correspondence and Diaries of the late Rt. Hon. John Wilson Croker*. Ed., L. J. Jennings. 3 vols. 1884.

Doheny, M. *The Felon's Track, or the History of the Attempted Outbreak in Ireland*. New York, 1849. Repr., Dublin, 1914, ed. A. Griffith.

Doolan, T. *Munster: or, the Memoirs of a Chief Constable*. 1831.

Ellenborough, Earl of, Edward Law. *A Political Diary, 1828–1830*. Ed., Charles Abbot, Lord Colchester. 2 vols. 1881.

Epstein, J. *The Lion of Freedom: Feargus O'Connor and the Chartist Movement, 1832–1842*. 1982.

Finer, S. E. *Life and Times of Sir Edwin Chadwick*. 1952.

Fitzpatrick, W. J. *Life, Times, and Contemporaries of Lord Cloncurry*. Dublin, 1855.

Gash, N. *Mr. Secretary Peel: The Life of Sir Robert Peel to 1830*. Cambridge, Mass., 1961.

Glover, M. *A Very Slippery Fellow: The Life of Sir Robert Wilson, 1777–1849*. Oxford, 1978.

Graham, Sir J. *Life and Letters of Sir James Graham, 2d Baronet of Netherby.* Ed., C. S. Parker. 2 vols. 1907.

Grattan, H. *Memoirs of the Life and Times of the Rt. Hon. Henry Grattan, by His Son, Henry Grattan, Esq., M.P.* 5 vols. 1839–46.

Gt. Brit., Historical MSS Commission. *The Manuscripts of His Grace the Duke of Rutland . . . preserved at Belvoir Castle.* 4 vols. 1888–1905. Vol. 3.

Hewett, Sir G. *Private Record of the Life of the Rt. Hon. General Sir George Hewett.* Newport, 1840.

Holyoake, G. J. *Bygones Worth Remembering.* 2 vols. 1905. Vol. 1.

Huch, R., and P. Ziegler. *Joseph Hume: The People's M.P.* Philadelphia, 1985.

Huish, R. *History of the Private and Political Life of the Late Henry Hunt, Esq.* 2 vols. 1836.

Longford, E. *Wellington: The Years of the Sword.* 1969.

Macintyre, A. *The Liberator: Daniel O'Connell and the Irish Party, 1830–1847.* New York, 1965.

McLennan, J. *Memoir of Thomas Drummond.* Edinburgh, 1867.

Meagher, T. F. *Meagher of the Sword.* Ed., A. Griffith. Dublin, 1917.

Mitchel, J. *Jail Journal.* New York, 1854.

Monypenny, W. F., and G. E. Buckle. *Life of Benjamin Disraeli, Earl of Beaconsfield.* 6 vols. New York, 1910–20. Vol. 2.

Napier, W. *Life and Opinions of General Sir Charles James Napier.* 4 vols. 1857.

Nott-Bower, Sir W. *Fifty-two Years a Policeman.* 1926.

Nowlan, K., and M. O'Connell, eds. *Daniel O'Connell: Portrait of a Radical.* New York, 1985.

O'Brien, R. B. *Thomas Drummond, Under-Secretary in Ireland, 1835–40.* 1889.

O'Connell, D. *Correspondence of Daniel O'Connell, The Liberator.* Ed., W. J. Fitzpatrick. 2 vols. 1888.

O'Ferrall, F. *Catholic Emancipation: Daniel O'Connell and the Birth of Irish Democracy.* Dublin, 1985.

Olien, D. *Morpeth: A Victorian Public Career.* Lanham, Md., 1983.

Palmer, S. H. "Sir George Cornewall Lewis, A Different Kind of Englishman," *Eire-Ireland* 16, No. 3 (Fall 1981):118–33.

Peel, Sir R. *Private Letters of Sir Robert Peel.* Ed., G. Peel. 1920.

Sir Robert Peel, from his Private Papers. Ed., C. S. Parker. 3 vols. 1891–9.

Pellew, G. *Life and Correspondence of the Rt. Hon. Henry Addington, 1st Viscount Sidmouth.* 3 vols. 1847.

Read, D., and E. Glasgow. *Feargus O'Connor, Irishman and Chartist.* 1961.

Smith, E. A. *Whig Principles and Party Politics: Earl Fitzwilliam and the Whig Party, 1748–1833.* Manchester, 1975.

Wallas, G. *Life of Francis Place, 1771–1854.* 1898.

Wellington, Duke of, Arthur Wellesley. *Despatches, Correspondence, and Memoranda of Field Marshal Arthur, Duke of Wellington.* Edited by his son, the Duke of Wellington. 8 vols. 1867–80. Vols. 1, 2.

Supplementary Despatches, Correspondence, and Memoranda of Field Marshal Arthur, Duke of Wellington. Edited by his son, the Duke of Wellington. 15 vols. 1858–72. Vol. 5.

Yeats, G. D. *Biographical Sketch of the Life and Writings of Patrick Colquhoun, Esq., LL.D., by Iatros.* 1818.

(e) CONTEMPORARY AND LATE-NINETEENTH-CENTURY WORKS

Blackstone, Sir W. *Commentaries on the Laws of England.* 3d ed. 4 vols. Oxford, 1768–9.

Blizard, Sir W. *Desultory Reflections on Police.* 1785.

Brophy, M. *Sketches of the Royal Irish Constabulary.* 1886.

Bruton, F. A., ed. *Three Accounts of Peterloo, by Eyewitnesses.* Manchester, 1921.

Burn, R. *The Justice of the Peace and Parish Officer.* 14th ed. 4 vols. 1780.

Chadwick, E. "Preventive Police," *London Review* 1 (1829):252–308.

Clode, C. M. *Military Forces of the Crown.* 2 vols. 1869.

Cloncurry, 2d Baron, Valentine Lawless. *Letter, to the Duke of Leinster, on the Police and Present State of Ireland.* Dublin, 1822.

Colquhoun, P. *Treatise on the Police of the Metropolis.* 1796. 5th ed., 1797. 6th ed., 1800. 7th ed., 1806.

  Treatise on the Commerce and Police of the River Thames. 1800.

Curtis, R. *History of the Royal Irish Constabulary.* Dublin, 1869. 2d ed., 1871.

Curwen, J. C. *Observations on the State of Ireland.* 2 vols. 1818.

Dowling, J. A., ed. *The Whole Proceedings before the Coroner's Inquest at Oldham, &c., on the Body of John Lees.* 1820.

Dudley, T. *The Tocsin; or, a Review of the London Police Establishments, with Hints for their Improvement.* 1828.

Eagles, J. *The Bristol Riots.* Bristol, 1832.

Emerson, J. S. *One Year of the Administration of His Excellency the Marquess Wellesley in Ireland.* 1823.

Engels, F. *The Condition of the Working Class in England.* 1845. Eds., W. O. Henderson and W. H. Chaloner. Oxford, 1958.

Fielding, J. *An Account of the Origin and Effects of a Police Set on Foot by His Grace the Duke of Newcastle in the Year 1753.* 1758.

Finlason, W. F. *A Review of the Authorities as to the Repression of Riot or Rebellion.* 1868.

Fitzgerald, P. *Chronicles of the Bow Street Police-Office.* 2 vols. 1888.

Fitzpatrick, W. J. *Secret Service under Pitt.* 1892.

Flint, J. *The Dublin Police and the Police System.* Dublin, 1847.

Hanway, J. *The Citizen's Monitor: Shewing the Necessity of a Salutary Police . . . with Observations on the Late Tumults . . .* 1780.

Head, Sir F. *A Fortnight in Ireland.* 1852.

[Helps, Sir Arthur, pseud.] *A Letter from One of the Special Constables in London . . . on the Late Occasion of their being Called Out to Keep the Peace.* 1848.

Henry, J. *An Account of the Proceedings of the Government Metropolitan Police in the City of Canton.* Dublin, 1840.

Hoare, Sir R. *Journal of a Tour in Ireland, A.D. 1806.* 1807.

Jones, Sir W. *An Inquiry into the Legal Mode of Suppressing Riots.* 1780. Repr., 1819.

Langford, J. *A Century of Birmingham Life.* 2 vols. Birmingham, 1868.

Lecky, W. E. H. *A History of Ireland in the Eighteenth Century.* 5 vols. 1892. Repr., 1972.

Lewis, G. C. *On Local Disturbances in Ireland; and on the Irish Church Question.* 1836. Repr., 1977.

McGregor, J. *New Picture of Dublin.* Dublin, 1821.

Maitland, F. W. *Justice and Police.* 1885.

Mildmay, Sir W. *The Police of France.* 1763.

Napier, C. J. *Essay on the Present State of Ireland, showing the chief cause of, and the remedy for, the existing Distresses in that Country.* 1839.

  Remarks on Military Law and the Punishment of Flogging. 1837.

O'Brien, R. B. *Fifty Years of Concessions to Ireland.* 2 vols. 1883–5.

"Observer, An" [attrib. to J. E. Taylor]. *The Peterloo Massacre, containing a Faithful Narrative of the Events which preceded, accompanied, and followed the Fatal Sixteenth of August, 1819.* 2d ed., Manchester, 1819.

"On the Suppression of Riots by Military Interference," *The Law Magazine; or, Quarterly Review of Jurisprudence* 9 (Feb. 1833):66–82.

Philips, F. *An Exposure of the Calumnies Circulated by the Enemies of Social Order, and Reiterated by their Abettors against the Magistrates and the Yeomanry Cavalry of Manchester and Salford.* 2d ed., 1819.

Prentice, A. *Historical Sketches and Personal Recollections of Manchester*. 1851.

Ramsay, A. *Observations upon the Riot Act, with an Attempt towards the Amenament of it*. 1781.

Raynes, F. *An appeal to the Public, Containing an Account of the Services Rendered during the Disturbances in the North of England in the Year 1812 ... 1817*.

Remarks on the Riot Act, with an Application to Certain Recent and Alarming Facts ... 1768.

Ritson, J. *The Office of the Constable; being an entirely new Compendium of the Law concerning that ancient Minister for the Conservation of the Peace ... 1791*.

Slugg, J. T. *Reminiscences of Manchester Fifty Years Ago*. Manchester, 1881.

Smith, A. *Lectures on Justice, Police, Revenue and Arms*. 1763. Ed., E. Cannan. Oxford, 1896.

State Trials. *A Complete Collection of State Trials*. Ed., T. B. Howell. 33 vols. 1816–26. Vol. 17, trial of Capt. Porteous.

Reports of State Trials. Ed., Sir J. Macdonell. 8 vols. 1888–98. Vol. 1, trials of H. Hunt and Redford *v*. Birley; Vol. 3, Pinney and Brereton; Vol. 5, D. O'Connell.

Trial of Fergus O'Connor, Esq., and 58 Others at Lancaster, on a Charge of Sedition, Conspiracy, Tumult, and Riot. Manchester, 1843.

Wade, J. *Treatise on the Police and Crimes of the Metropolis*. 1829.

Wakefield, E. G. *An Account of Ireland, Statistical and Political*. 2 vols. 1812.

Warburton, J., and J. Whitelaw and R. Walsh. *History of the City of Dublin*. 2 vols. 1818.

Wise, E. *The Law Relating to Riots and Unlawful Assemblies*. 2d ed., 1848. 3d ed., rev. by A. H. Bodkin, 1889.

Wyse, T. *Historical Sketch of the Late Catholic Association of Ireland*. 2 vols. 1829.

Young, A. *A Tour of Ireland; with general observations on the present state of that Kingdom. Made in the years 1776, 1777, and 1778. And brought down to the end of 1779*. 1780.

(*f*) MODERN SECONDARY WORKS: BOOKS AND ARTICLES

Arnstein, W. L. "The Murphy Riots: A Victorian Dilemma," *Victorian Studies* 19 (Sept. 1975):51–71.

Bailey, V., ed. *Policing and Punishment in Nineteenth Century Britain*. New Brunswick, N.J., 1981.

Bartlett, T. "An End to Moral Economy: The Irish Militia Disturbances of 1793," *Past & present* 99 (May 1983):41–64.

and D. W. Hayton, eds. *Penal Era and Golden Age: Essays in Irish History, 1690–1800*. Belfast, 1979.

Baxter, J. L., and F. K. Donnelly. "The Revolutionary 'Underground' in the West Riding: Myth or Reality?", *Past & Present* 64 (Aug. 1974):124–32.

Bayley, D. "The Police and Political Development in Europe," in C. Tilly, ed., *The Formation of National States in Western Europe* (Princeton, N.J., 1975), pp. 328–79.

Beames, M. *Peasants and Power: The Whiteboy Movements and their Control in Pre-Famine Ireland*. New York, 1983.

"The Ribbon Societies: Lower-Class Nationalism in Pre-Famine Ireland," *Past & Present* 97 (Nov. 1982):128–43.

"Rural Conflict in Pre-Famine Ireland: Peasant Assassinations in Tipperary, 1837–1847," *Past & Present* 81 (Nov. 1978):75–91.

Bisceglia, L. "The Threat of Violence: Irish Confederates and Chartists in Liverpool in 1848," *Irish Sword* 14 (Summer 1981):207–15.

Bohstedt, J. *Riots and Community Politics in England and Wales, 1790–1810*. Cambridge, Mass., 1983.

Boyle, K. "Police in Ireland Before the Union: I," *Irish Jurist*, n.s., 7 (1972):115–37.

"Police in Ireland Before the Union: II," *Irish Jurist*, n.s., 8 (1973):90–116.

"Police in Ireland Before the Union: III," *Irish Jurist*, n.s., 8 (1973):323–48.

Brady, C. *Guardians of the Peace*. Dublin, 1974.

Breathnach, S. *The Irish Police from Earliest Times to the Present Day*. Dublin, 1974.

Brewer, J., and J. Styles, eds. *An Ungovernable People: The English and Their Law in the Seventeenth and Eighteenth Centuries*. New Brunswick, N.J., 1980.

Briggs, A., ed. *Chartist Studies*. 1959.

Broeker, G. "Robert Peel and the Peace Preservation Force," *J. Mod. Hist.* 33 (1961):363–73.

Rural Disorder and Police Reform in Ireland, 1812–36. 1970.

Brown, T. "Nationalism and the Irish Peasant, 1800–1848," *Review of Politics* 15 (Oct. 1953):403–45.

Browne, D. G. *The Rise of Scotland Yard: A History of the Metropolitan Police*. 1956.

Brundage, A. *The Making of the New Poor Law: The Politics of Inquiry, Enactment, and Implementation, 1832–1839*. New Brunswick, N.J., 1978.

"Ministers, Magistrates, and Reformers: The Genesis of the Rural Constabulary Act of 1839," *Parliamentary History: A Yearbook* 5(1986):55–64.

Brynn, E. *Crown and Castle: British Rule in Ireland, 1800–1830*. Dublin, 1978.

Butt, J., and I. F. Clarke, eds. *The Victorians and Social Protest: A Symposium*. Hamden, Conn., 1973.

Calder-Marshall, A. "The Spa Fields Riots, 1816," *History Today* 21 (June 1971):407–15.

Calhoun, C. *The Question of Class Struggle: Social Foundations of Popular Radicalism during the Industrial Revolution*. Chicago, 1982.

Clark, S., and J. S. Donnelly, Jr., eds. *Irish Peasants: Violence and Political Unrest, 1780–1914*. Madison, Wis., 1983.

Cobb, B. *The First Detectives and the Early Career of Richard Mayne, Commissioner of Police*. 1957.

Cole, G. D. H., and R. Postgate. *The Common People, 1746–1946*. 4th ed., 1949. Repr., 1964.

Corish, P., ed. *Radicals, Rebels, and Establishments*. Belfast, 1985.

Critchley, T. *The Conquest of Violence: Order and Liberty in Britain*. 1970.

A History of Police in England and Wales. 1967. 2d ed., Montclair, N.J., 1972.

Cronin, S. "'The Country Did Not Turn Out': The Young Ireland Rising of 1848," *Eire-Ireland* 11, No. 2 (Summer 1976):3–17.

Protest in Arms: The Young Ireland Rebellion of July–August 1848. Dublin, 1984.

Curtin, N.J. "The Transformation of the Society of United Irishmen into a Mass-based Revolutionary Organisation, 1794–6," *I.H.S.* 24 (Nov. 1985):463–92.

Curtis, L. P., Jr. *Apes and Angels: The Irishman in Victorian Caricature*. Newton Abbot, 1971.

Darvall, F. O. *Popular Disturbances and Public Order in Regency England*. 1934. Repr., 1969.

Davey, B. J. *Lawless and Immoral: Policing a Country Town, 1838–1857*. New York, 1984.

Donajgrodski, A. P. "Sir James Graham at the Home Office," *Hist. Jour.* 20 (1977):97–120.

, ed. *Social Control in 19th-Century Britain*. Totowa, N.J., 1977.

Donnelly, J. S., Jr. "Hearts of Oak, Hearts of Steel," *Studia Hib.* 21 (1981):7–73.

"Irish Agrarian Rebellion: The Whiteboys of 1769–76," *Proc. R.I.A.* 83, C, No. 12 (1983):293–331.

"Propagating the Cause of the United Irishmen," *Studies: An Irish Quarterly Review* 69 (Spring 1980):5–23.

"The Rightboy Movement, 1785–8," *Studia Hib.* 17 & 18 (1977–8):120–202.

"The Whiteboy Movement, 1761–5," *I.H.S.* 21 (Mar. 1978):20–54.

See also Clark, S., and J. S. Donnelly, Jr

Dunbabin, J. P. D. *Rural Discontent in Nineteenth-Century Britain*. New York, 1974.

Edsall, N. *The Anti–Poor Law Movement, 1834–44*. Manchester, 1971.

Edwards, R. D., and T. D. Williams, eds. *The Great Famine: Studies in Irish History, 1845–52.* New York, 1957. Repr., 1976.

Elliott, M. "The 'Despard Conspiracy' Reconsidered," *Past & Present* 75 (May 1977):46–62.

——— "The Origin and Transformation of Early Irish Republicanism," *Intl. Rev. Soc. Hist.* 23 (1978):405–28.

——— *Partners in Revolution: The United Irishmen and France.* New Haven, Conn., 1982.

Emsley, C. "Arms and the Victorian Policeman," *History Today* 34 (Nov. 1984):37–42.

——— "The Bedfordshire Police, 1840–1856: A Case Study in the Working of the Rural Constabulary Act," *Midland History* 7 (1982):73–92.

——— *British Society and the French Wars, 1793–1815.* 1979.

——— "The Military and Popular Disorder in England, 1790–1801," *J. Soc. Army Hist. Research* 61 (Spring 1983):10–21; and 61 (Summer 1983):96–112.

——— *Policing and Its Context, 1750–1870.* New York, 1984.

Farrell, M. *Arming the Protestants: The Formation of the Ulster Special Constabulary and the Royal Ulster Constabulary, 1920–27.* 1983.

Foster, D. "The East Riding Constabulary in the Nineteenth Century," *Northern History* 21 (1985):193–211.

Foster, J. *Class Struggle and the Industrial Revolution: Early Industrial Capitalism in Three English Towns.* 1974.

Fraser, P. "Public Petitioning and Parliament before 1832," *History* 46 (1961):195–211.

Fulham, G. "James Shaw-Kennedy and the Reformation of the Irish Constabulary, 1836–38," *Eire-Ireland* 16, No. 2 (Summer 1981):93–106.

Gattrell, V. A. C., and T. B. Hadden, "Criminal Statistics and their Interpretation," in E. A. Wrigley, ed., *Nineteenth-Century Society: Essays in the Use of Quantitative Methods for the Study of Social Data* (Cambridge, 1972), pp. 336–96.

Gill, C. *A History of Birmingham: The Manor and Borough to 1865.* 1952.

Goodway, D. *London Chartism 1838–1848.* Cambridge, 1982.

Gwynn, D. *Young Ireland and 1848.* Cork and Oxford, 1949.

Hamburger, J. *James Mill and the Art of Revolution.* New Haven, Conn., 1963. Repr., 1977.

Harrison, B. "The Sunday Trading Riots of 1855," *Hist. Jour.* 8 (1965):219–45.

Hart, J. M. *The British Police.* 1951.

——— "The County and Borough Police Act, 1856," *Public Administration* 34 (1956):405–17.

——— "Reform of the Borough Police, 1835–1856," *E.H.R.* 70 (1955):411–27.

Hayter, T. *The Army and the Crowd in Mid-Georgian England.* 1978.

Hearn, F. *Domination, Legitimation, and Resistance: The Incorporation of the Nineteenth-Century English Working Class.* Westport, Conn., 1978.

Hezlet, Sir A. *The 'B' Specials: A History of the Ulster Special Constabulary.* 1972.

Hibbert, C. *King Mob: The Story of Lord George Gordon and the Riots of 1780.* 1958.

——— *The Roots of Evil: A Social History of Crime and Punishment.* 1963. Repr., 1966.

Hobsbawm, E., and G. Rudé. *Captain Swing.* New York, 1968.

Jeffries, Sir C. *The Colonial Police.* 1952.

Jenkins, M. *The General Strike of 1842.* 1980.

Johnston, E. M. *Great Britain and Ireland, 1760–1800: A Study in Political Administration.* Edinburgh, 1963.

Jones, D. J. V. *Crime, Protest, Community and Police in Nineteenth-Century Britain.* 1982.

——— *The Last Rising: The Newport Insurrection of 1839.* New York, 1985.

Lee, W. L. Melville. *A History of Police in England.* 1901. Repr., 1971.

Lowe, W. J. "The Chartists and the Irish Confederates: Lancashire, 1848," *I.H.S.* 24 (Nov. 1984):172–96.

——— "The Lancashire Constabulary, 1845–1870: The Social and Occupational Function of a Victorian Police Force," *Criminal Justice History* 4 (1983):41–62.

McAnally, Sir H. *The Irish Militia, 1793–1816: A Social and Military Study*. Dublin, 1949.

McCaffrey, L. *Daniel O'Connell and the Repeal Year*. Lexington, Ky., 1966.

MacDonagh, O. *Early Victorian Government, 1830–1870*. New York, 1977.

Ireland. Englewood Cliffs, N.J., 1968.

McDowell, R. B. *Ireland in the Age of Imperialism and Revolution, 1760–1801*. Oxford, 1979.

The Irish Administration, 1801–1914. 1964.

Public Opinion and Government Policy in Ireland, 1801–1846. 1952. Repr., 1975.

Maehl, W., Jr. "The Dynamics of Violence in Chartism: A Case Study in North-eastern England," *Albion* 7 (Summer 1975):101–19.

Malcolmson, R. W. *Popular Recreations in English Society, 1700–1850*. Cambridge, 1973.

Martin, J. P., and G. Wilson. *The Police: A Study in Manpower. The Evolution of the Service in England and Wales 1829–1965*. 1969.

Mather, F. C. *Public Order in the Age of the Chartists*. Manchester, 1959.

"The Railways, the Electric Telegraph, and Public Order during the Chartist Period," *History* 38 (1953):40–53.

Midwinter, E. C. *Social Administration in Lancashire, 1830–1860: Poor Law, Public Health, and Police*. Manchester, 1969.

Miller, W. C. *Cops and Bobbies: Police Authority in New York and London, 1830–1870*. Chicago, 1977.

Moir, E. *The Justice of the Peace*. Harmondsworth, 1969.

Moylan, Sir J. *Scotland Yard and the Metropolitan Police*. 2d ed., 1934.

Nippel, W. "'Reading the Riot Act': The Discourse of Law-Enforcement in 18th Century England," *History & Anthropology* 1 (Pt. 2, 1985):401–26.

Nowlan, K. B. *The Politics of Repeal: A Study in the Relations between Great Britain and Ireland, 1841–50*. 1965.

O'Brien, G. "The Establishment of Poor-Law Unions in Ireland, 1838–43," *I.H.S.* 23 (Nov. 1982):97–120.

O'Brien, J. V. *"Dear, Dirty Dublin": A City in Distress, 1899–1916*. Berkeley, 1982.

O Ceallaigh, T. "Peel and Police Reform in Ireland, 1814–18," *Studia Hib.* 6 (1966):25–48.

O'Donoghue, P. "Causes of the Opposition to Tithes, 1830–38," *Studia Hib.* 5 (1965):7–28.

"Opposition to Tithe Payment in 1830–31," *Studia Hib.* 6 (1966):69–98.·

"Opposition to Tithe Payment in 1832–3," *Studia Hib.* 12 (1972):77–108.

O'Higgins, R. "The Irish Influence in the Chartist Movement," *Past & Present* 20 (Nov. 1961):83–96.

Palmer, S. H. "Before the Bobbies: The Caroline Riots of 1821," *History Today* 27 (Oct. 1977):637–44.

"Calling Out the Troops: The Military, the Law, and Public Order in England, 1650–1850," *J. Soc. Army Hist. Research* 56 (Winter 1978):198–214.

"The Irish Police Experiment: The Beginnings of Modern Police in the British Isles, 1785–1795," *Social Science Quarterly* 56 (Dec. 1975):410–24.

"Major-General Sir Charles James Napier: Irishman, Chartist, and Commander of the Northern District in England, 1839–41," *Irish Sword* 16 (Winter 1982):89–100.

"Rebellion, Emancipation, Starvation: The Dilemma of Peaceful Protest in Ireland, 1798–1848," in B. Lackner and K. Philp, eds., *Essays on Modern European Revolutionary History* (Austin, Tex., 1977), pp. 3–38.

Parris, H. "The Home Office and the Provincial Police in England and Wales, 1856–1870," *Public Law*, n. v. (1961), pp. 230–55.

Peacock, A. J. *Bread or Blood: A Study of the Agrarian Riots in East Anglia in 1816*. 1965.

Perkin, H. J. *The Origins of Modern English Society, 1780–1880*. 1969.

Petler, H. J. "Ireland and France in 1848," *I.H.S.* 24 (Nov. 1985):493–505.

Philips, D. *Crime and Authority in Victorian England: The Black Country, 1835–1860.* 1977.

Pringle, P. *Hue and Cry: The Birth of the British Police.* 1955.

Radzinowicz, Sir L. *A History of English Criminal Law and its Administration from 1750.* 4 vols. 1948–68.

Read, D. *Peterloo: The "Massacre" and its Background.* Manchester, 1958. Repr., 1973.

Redford, A., and I. S. Russell. *A History of Local Government in Manchester.* 2 vols. 1939–40.

Reid, T. W., and Naomi Reid. "The 1842 'Plug Plot' in Stockport," *Intl. Rev. Soc. Hist.* 24 (1979):55–79.

Reith, C. *British Police and the Democratic Ideal.* 1943.

A New Study of Police History. Edinburgh, 1956.

The Police Idea: Its History and Evolution in England in the Eighteenth Century and After. 1938.

Reynolds, J. A. *The Catholic Emancipation Crisis in Ireland, 1823–1829.* New Haven, Conn., 1954. Repr., 1970.

Richter, D. *Riotous Victorians.* Athens, Ohio, 1981.

Roberts, D. "Lord Palmerston at the Home Office, 1853–1854," *The Historian* 21 (Nov. 1958):63–81.

Paternalism in Early Victorian England. New Brunswick, N.J., 1979.

Victorian Origins of the British Welfare State. New Haven, Conn., 1960.

Rogers, N. "Popular Protest in Early Hanoverian London," *Past & Present* 29 (May 1978):70–100.

Rogers, P. *The Irish Volunteers and Catholic Emancipation, 1778–1793.* 1934.

Rose, A. G. "The Plug Plots of 1842 in Lancashire and Cheshire," *Transactions of the Lancashire and Cheshire Antiquarian Society* 67 (1957):75–112.

Rose, M. "The Anti–Poor Law Movement in the North of England," *Northern History* 1 (1966):70–91.

Rose, R. B. "Eighteenth-Century Price Riots and Public Policy in England," *Intl. Rev. Soc. Hist.* 6 (Pt. 2, 1961):277–92.

"The Priestley Riots of 1791," *Past & Present* 18 (Nov. 1960):68–88.

Rowe, D. J. "Class and Political Radicalism in London, 1831–32," *Hist. Jour.* 13 (1970):31–47.

"The Failure of London Chartism," *Hist. Jour.* 11 (1968):472–87.

Rudé, G. *The Crowd in History: A Study of Popular Disturbances in France and England, 1730–1848.* New York, 1964.

"Protest and Punishment in Nineteenth-Century Britain," *Albion* 5 (Spring 1973):1–23.

Protest and Punishment: The Story of the Social and Political Protesters Transported to Australia, 1788–1868. Oxford, 1978. *See also* Hobsbawm, E., and G. Rudé.

Rumbelow, D. *I Spy Blue: Police and Crime in the City of London from Elizabeth I to Victoria.* 1971.

"Raw Lobsters, Blue Devils . . . ," *British Heritage* 1, No. 3 (Apr.–May 1980):10–18.

Seth, R. *The Specials: The Story of the Special Constabulary in England, Wales, and Scotland.* 1961.

Shaw, A. G. L. *Convicts and the Colonies: A Study of Penal Transportation from Great Britain and Ireland to Australia and Other Parts of the British Empire.* 1966.

Silver, A. "The Demand for Order in Civil Society: A Review of Some Themes in the History of Urban Crime, Police, and Riot," in D. J. Bordua, *The Police: Six Sociological Essays* (New York, 1967), pp. 1–24.

"Social and Ideological Bases of British Elite Reactions to Domestic Crisis in 1829–1832," *Politics and Society* 2 (Feb. 1971):179–201.

Smith, P. T. *Policing Victorian London: Political Policing, Public Order, and the London Metropolitan Police.* Westport, Conn., 1985.

Steedman, C. *Policing the Victorian Community: The Formation of English Provincial Police Forces, 1856–80.* 1984.

Stevenson, J. *Popular Disturbances in England 1700–1870.* 1979.

———, ed. *London in the Age of Reform.* Oxford, 1977.

——— and R. Quinault, eds. *Popular Protest and Public Order: Six Studies in British History, 1790–1920.* New York, 1974.

Storch, R. D. "The Plague of the Blue Locusts: Police Reform and Popular Resistance in Northern England, 1840–1857," *Intl. Rev. Soc. Hist.* 20 (1975):61–90.

——— "The Policeman as Domestic Missionary: Urban Discipline and Popular Culture in Northern England, 1850–1880," *J. Soc. Hist.* 9 (Summer 1976):481–509.

———, ed. *Popular Culture and Custom in Nineteenth-Century England.* New York, 1982.

Swift, R. "Anti-Catholicism and Irish Disturbances: Public Order in Mid-Victorian Wolverhampton," *Midland History* 9 (1984):87–108.

——— and S. Gilley, eds. *The Irish in the Victorian City.* 1985.

Sykes, R. "Physical-Force Chartism: The Cotton District and the Chartist Crisis of 1839," *Intl. Rev. Soc. Hist.* 30 (1985):207–36.

Teichman, Maj. O. "The Yeomanry as an Aid to the Civil Power, 1795–1867," *J. Soc. Army Hist. Research* 19 (1940):75–91, 127–43.

Tholfsen, T. R. "The Chartist Crisis in Birmingham," *Intl. Rev. Soc. Hist.* 3 (1958):461–80.

Thomis, M. *The Luddites: Machine-Breaking in Regency England.* New York, 1972.

——— and P. Holt. *Threats of Revolution in Britain, 1789–1848.* Hamden, Conn., 1977.

Thompson, D. *The Chartists: Popular Politics in the Industrial Revolution.* New York, 1984.

Thompson, E. P. *The Making of the English Working Class.* New York, 1964.

——— "The Moral Economy of the English Crowd in the Eighteenth Century," *Past & Present* 50 (Feb. 1971):76–136.

——— "Time, Work-Discipline, and Industrial Capitalism," *Past & Present* 38 (Dec. 1967):56–97.

Thurston, G. *The Clerkenwell Riot: The Killing of Constable Culley.* 1967.

Tobias, J. J. *Crime and Police in England 1700–1900.* New York, 1979.

——— "Police and Public in the United Kingdom," in G. L. Mosse, ed., *Police Forces in History* (Beverly Hills, Calif., 1975), pp. 95–113.

Townshend, C. *Political Violence in Ireland: Government and Resistance since 1848.* Oxford, 1983.

Webb, S. and B. *English Local Government from the Revolution to the Municipal Corporations Act: The Manor and the Borough.* 1908.

——— *English Local Government from the Revolution to the Municipal Corporations Act: The Parish and the County.* 1906.

Weisser, H. "Chartism in 1848: Reflections on a Non-Revolution," *Albion* 13 (Spring 1981):12–26.

——— *April 10: Challenge and Response in England in 1848.* Lanham, Md., 1983.

Werly, J. "The Irish in Manchester, 1832–1849," *I.H.S.* 18 (Mar. 1973):345–58.

Western, J. R. *The English Militia in the Eighteenth Century.* 1965.

Whitaker, B. *The Police in Society.* 1979.

Wilks, I. *South Wales and the Rising of 1839: Class Struggle as Armed Struggle.* Urbana, Ill., 1984.

Williams, D. *John Frost: A Study in Chartism.* Cardiff, 1939. Repr., 1969.

——— *The Rebecca Riots: A Study in Agrarian Discontent.* Cardiff, 1955. Repr., 1971.

Williams, T. D., ed. *Secret Societies in Ireland.* Dublin, 1973. See also Edwards, R. D., and T. D. Williams.

Woodham-Smith, C. *The Great Hunger: Ireland 1845–1849.* New York, 1962. Repr., 1980.

(g) REFERENCE WORKS

Army List: A List of the General and Field Officers as they rank in the Army. 26 vols. 1815–40.

Baylen, J. O., and N. Gossman, eds. *Biographical Dictionary of Modern British Radicals.* 3 vols. Hassocks, 1979.

Boase, F. *Modern English Biography.* 6 vols. Truro, 1892–1921.

Boylan, H. *Dictionary of Irish Biography.* New York, 1978.

Carter, E. F. *An Historical Geography of the Railways of the British Isles.* 1959.

Cook, C., and B. Keith. *British Historical Facts 1830–1900.* New York, 1975.

Cook, C., and J. Stevenson. *British Historical Facts 1760–1830.* 1980.

Cramer, J. *The World's Police.* 1964.

Dictionary of National Biography. 22 vols. 1885–90. Repr., Oxford, 1921–2; 1964–5 printing.

Edwards, R. D. *Atlas of Irish History.* 2d ed., 1981.

Fanner, P. D., and C. T. Latham, eds. *Stone's Justice's Manual.* 101st ed. 2 vols. 1969.

Flackes, W. D. *Northern Ireland: A Political Directory.* New York, 1980. 2d ed., 1983.

Halsbury's Laws of England, being a complete statement of the whole law of England. 2d ed. 15 vols. 1933. Vol. 9.

Lodge, J. *The Peerage of Ireland.* Rev., M. Archdall. 7 vols. Dublin, 1789.

McCulloch, J. R. *Dictionary ... of Commerce.* 8th ed., 2 vols. 1854.

  Statistical Account of the British Empire. 2 vols. 1837.

Meally, V. *Encyclopaedia of Ireland.* Dublin, 1968.

Mitchell, B. R., and P. Deane. *Abstract of British Historical Statistics.* Cambridge, 1962.

Oxford English Dictionary. 12 vols. Oxford, 1933. Repr., 1961.

Powicke, Sir F. M., and E. B. Fryde, eds. *Handbook of British Chronology.* 2d ed., 1961.

Webb, A. *Compendium of Irish Biography.* Dublin, 1878.

Index